Edited by
David Knights
and Hugh Willmott

Introducing
Organizational
Behaviour
and Management

Third Edition

Written by
Joanna Brewis, Alessia Contu, Christopher Grey, Deborah Kerfoot,
David Knights, Pemela Ohih, Damian O'Doherty, Glenn Morgan,
Lara Pecis, John Roberts, Andrew Sturdy, Sheena Vachhani,
Theodore Vurdubakis, Hugh Willmott, Frank Worthington, Edward Wray-Bliss

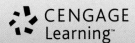

CENGAGE
Learning™

Australia • Brazil • Japan • Korea • Mexico • Singapore • Spain • United Kingdom • United States

Introducing Organization Behaviour and Management, 3rd Edition
David Knights and Hugh Willmott

Publisher: Annabel Ainscow

Commissioning Editor: Jenny Grene

Content Project Editor: Sue Povey

Manufacturing Manager: Eyvett Davis

Marketing Manager: Vicky Pavlicic

Typesetter: Cenveo Publisher Services

Cover design: Cyan Design

Text design: Design Deluxe Ltd

While the publisher has taken all reasonable care in the preparation of this book, the publisher makes no representation, express or implied, with regard to the accuracy of the information contained in this book and cannot accept any legal responsibility or liability for any errors or omissions from the book or the consequences thereof.

Products and services that are referred to in this book may be either trademarks and/or registered trademarks of their respective owners. The publishers and author/s make no claim to these trademarks. The publisher does not endorse, and accepts no responsibility or liability for, incorrect or defamatory content contained in hyperlinked material.

All the URLs in this book are correct at the time of going to press; however the Publisher accepts no responsibility for the content and continued availability of third party websites.

For product information and technology assistance, contact **emea.info@cengage.com**.

For permission to use material from this text or product, and for permission queries, email **clsuk.permissions@cengage.com**

British Library Cataloguing-in-Publication Data
A catalogue record for this book is available from the British Library.

ISBN: 978-1-4737-2664-2

Cengage Learning EMEA
Cheriton House, North Way, Andover, Hampshire, SP10 5BE
United Kingdom

Cengage Learning products are represented in Canada by Nelson Education Ltd.

For your lifelong learning solutions, visit **www.cengage. co.uk**

Purchase your next print book, e-book or e-chapter at **www.cengagebrain.com**

Printed in China by RR Donnelley
Print Number 01 Print Year 2017

To our students

Brief contents

1   Introduction 1

PART I   **The human dimension** 39

     2   Motivation and the self 40

     3   Individual differences, personality and self 78

     4   Groups and teams at work 113

     5   Managing people: Contexts of HRM, diversity and social inequality 158

     6   Knowledge and learning: Consuming management? 198

PART II   **The organizational dimension** 239

     7   Organization, structure and design 240

     8   Management and leadership 296

     9   Politics and decision-making in organizations 350

    10   Culture 377

    11   Change and innovation: New organizational forms 411

    12   Technology 447

PART III   **Emergent issues** 489

    13   Globalization and organizations 490

    14   Bureaucracy and post-bureaucracy 535

    15   Ethics at work 564

Contents

Preface xiii
Acknowledgements xvi
Contributors xvii
About the website xx

1 Introduction 1

Overview and key points 2

Introduction 3

Why study organizational behaviour? 4

Connecting ideas and experience 5

What is organizational behaviour? 7

Beyond mechanical prescription 8

Thinking about organizations 10

Organizational behaviour and everyday life: Going down the pub 11

Organizational behaviour as a contested terrain 14

Competing logics of organizing 14

'New managerialism' in the public sector 15

Back to the pub: The personal and the organizational 19

Organization and institutionalization 22

The significance of routines 22

The centrality of people 23

Views of organization: Entity, process and concept 24

Identifying organization 24

An entity view 25

A process view 26

A concept view 27

Distinctiveness of work organization: Instrumental rationality 28

Game-playing and resistance 30

Theory and practice 31

Distinctiveness of this text 32

Six key concepts 33

PART I
The human dimension 39

2 Motivation and the self 40

Overview and key points 40

Mainstream approaches to motivation and the self 41

Introduction 41

Key problems 42

Key ideas and contributions 42

Motivation: It is about fulfilling human needs (Abraham Maslow) 42

Motivation: It is managers' assumptions that matter (Douglas McGregor) 45

What motivates managers? (McClelland and Burnham) 46

Motivation: What satisfies is different from what causes dissatisfaction (Frederick Hertzberg) 48

Motivation: It is the design of jobs that can make a difference (Hackman) 49

Motivation: It is a person's expectations that count (Victor Vroom) 50

Motivation: A new competitive imperative 51

Self-motivation: It is the ideals we have for the self that motivate (Harry Levinson) 52

Self-motivation: It is the ideals we have for the self that motivate (Harry Levinson) 53

Self-motivation: It is the goals set for the self (Locke and Latham) 54

Self-motivation involves empowerment (Thomas and Velthouse) 54

Self-motivation: Selective recognition by managers helps (Luthans) 55

Limitations of mainstream approaches 55

Critical approaches to motivation and the self 57

Introduction 57

Marxist analyses 58

The profound creativity of human action 58

The process of production 59

The contradictions of capitalism and alienation 60

Core assumptions of the Marxist perspective 62
Rethinking motivation: Efficient and rational for whom? 63
Important studies 64

Power and the 'self' 66
The formation of the 'self' 66
Finding my self in the mirror of others' responses 66
The self as a synthesis of images 67
Learning what the self must be (to be loved) 67
Acquiring a (guilty) conscience 67
Securing the self at work 68
The power of being made visible and knowing it 69

Key studies 70
Reframing human resource management (Barbara
    Townley) 70
'Someone to watch over me' (Sewell and Wilkinson) 71
Happy families at Hephaestus (Catherine Casey) 71

Limitations of critical approaches to motivation 71
Conclusion 74

**3 Individual differences, personality
and self** 78

Overview and key points 79

**Mainstream approaches to individual differences,
    personality and self** 79

Introduction 79

**Central problems in the field: Mainstream and
    critical** 80

Personality, management and organization 82
The psychometric test 82

Introduction to personality 83
Nomothetic and idiographic approaches 84

The four temperaments 85

Jung and personality theory 86
The shadow world 87
Jung's theory of extroverts and introverts 88

**The Myers-Briggs type indicator test of
    personality** 89
The four preferences 90
The case of the messenger 91
Personality type and leadership style 92

The science of personality 93
Trait theory 94
Factor analysis 94

The 'personality' of science: Power and politics 95
Biological and sociological explanations 95
Applications in organization and recent case studies 96

Idiographic approaches to personality 97

Psychodynamic approaches 98

Maslow: Personality and the hierarchy of needs 98
Transcendence and self-actualization 99

The end of the individual? 102
The historical construction of 'the individual' 102
Group dynamics 102
Identity and existential anxiety 103
Ronald Laing: The schizophrenic self 103
Erich Fromm: The authoritarian and marketing
    personalities 104

**Existential anxiety and contemporary organization:
    Beyond personality?** 105
Synthetic cultures and cynical employees 105
ZTC Ryland: Managers in crisis 105
Critique 106

**Key contributions and major controversies in the
    field: Mainstream and critical** 106
Conclusion 108

4 Groups and teams at work 113

Overview and key points 113

Mainstream views on teams at work 114
Introduction to mainstream thinking on groups and
    teams 114

Key problem: What is a team? 114
'Real' teams at work 117
Case Study 4.1 AML 118

**Key ideas and contributions to thinking and
    empirical studies** 120
Teams for flexibility: Lean production 121
Teams for motivation: Participation, satisfaction and
    humane ways of working 123

Classical studies 125
The Hawthorne experiments: The importance of social
    needs and group norms at work (See Chapter 2) 125
Trist and Bamforth: Autonomous responsibility and
    socio-technical systems (See Chapter 2) 126
Kurt Lewin: The importance of participation and
    democratic style 126

Key problems and open questions 129
How do teams develop? 130
How should teams be designed? 130
How do you make teams work? 131
Addressing leadership 134
Working across different knowledge domains 136
Teamworking in the global era 136
Summary of key mainstream contributions and empirical
    studies 138

Contribution and limitation of mainstream 138
Conceptual and methodological contributions and
   limitations 138
Empowerment, control and power relations 140

Critical perspectives on teams at work 141
Introduction to critical approaches to teams at work 141

The other side of the coin 142
Working smarter *and* harder 142
Teamworking as control and consent over labour effort
   and cost 144

A murkier picture of teamwork 146
Self-discipline and surveillance 146
Resistance is futile (?) 148

**Summary of key contributions, empirical studies
   and limitations in the critical approach** 150
Conclusion 151

5 Managing people: Contexts of HRM, diversity and social inequality 158

Overview and key points 158

Mainstream approaches to HRM and diversity 160
HRM 161
Managing diversity 165

**Managing people and diversity: Integrating HRM
   and diversity** 169
Using the case study 171
Overview – about FinanceCo 171
Managing people: A case from the financial services
   industry 172

Key problems 173
How do we study the management of people? 174

Summary – what does it all mean? 176

Critical approaches to HRM and diversity 176

The changing nature of business 179

Critical HRM 179

Critical diversity perspectives 185

The case of disability at work 186

Intersectionality 189
Conclusion – managing people 193

6 Knowledge and learning: Consuming management? 198

Overview and key points 198

Chapter structure 199

**Mainstream approaches to knowledge and
   learning** 199

Introduction 199

Key problems 202

Key ideas and contributions 203
What is knowledge? 203
What is learning? 205
What is management knowledge? 208
How is management knowledge adopted and
   evaluated? 211

Continuing debates 213

Selected studies 214
Kolb's experiential learning cycle 214
Nonaka and Takeuchi: Learning as knowledge
   transformation 214
Abrahamson's 'fads and fashions' 215

Core concepts and the mainstream 215

**Critical approaches to knowledge and
   learning** 216

Introduction 216

Key problems 218
Beyond learning theories? 218
Four alternative views of management
   knowledge 219
Four alternative views of the adoption of management
   ideas 221

Psychodynamics 223
Integrating perspectives and the art of
   persuasion 225
Ideas, translation and practice 227
Translating the critical to the managerial 228

Important studies 229
Braverman and de-skilling 229
Guillen's models of management 230
Contu *et al.* (2003): Against learning 230

Contribution to thinking about the field 230
Conclusion 233

PART II
The organizational dimension 239

7 Organization, structure and design 240

Overview and key points 240

**Mainstream approach to structure
   and design** 243

Introducing structure and design 243

Key contributions of mainstream thinking 249
Classical thinking about organizational design 249

Modern thinking 252
Systems thinking 252

From structure to process: Informal understandings and practices 257

Working to rule 257
Summary 258

Other perspectives: Organizations as complex institutions 259
Institutional economics: Markets and hierarchies 259
Institutional theory 260
Resource dependency 262
Population ecology theory 263
Network theory 263
Virtual organization 264

Reinvention of 'one best way': Business process re-engineering and total quality management 266
Business process re-engineering 266
Total quality management 267

Organizations and technologies 269
The importance of 'tacit knowledge' and 'user involvement' 270

Contributions and limitations of the mainstream 271
Contributions 271
Limitations 271

Critical approach to structure and design 273
Introduction 273

A critical approach to organization and structure 274
The production of knowledge 276

Major issues and controversies 276

The structure of work organization 278
Subordination – formal and real 279
Exploitation at Bar Mar? 279
The factory system 280

***Braverman's* Labor and Monopoly Capital** 281
Manufacturing consent: Obscuring exploitation 285
Comment 287

Controversies and debates 287
Self-discipline and the panopticon 287
Designing today's prisons – Los Angeles twin towers jail 288
Conclusion 290

8 Management and leadership 296

Overview and key points 296
Mainstream approaches to management and leadership 297

Fuzzy boundaries: Management and leadership 299

The mainstream agenda 304
Management: Discipline, function, social group 304
Management as ever-present? 305
Classical thinking about management 306

Major issues/controversies in this field: Mainstream debates 309
The human dimension of work 309
What do managers do? Behavioural approach 317

Key ideas and contributions on leadership 319

Classical thinking about leadership 319
Leadership as a personality trait 319
Modern thinking about leadership 320
Leadership and contingency 323

Major issues/controversies in this field: Mainstream debates 324

Contribution and limitations of the mainstream approaches 326

Critical approach to management and leadership 327
Introduction: Overview of a critical approach to management and leadership 327

A critical perspective on leadership 331
Leadership and ethics 334
Feminist scholarship and leadership 335
Doing leadership differently 336
Leadership and management development 336
The prerogative and politics of management 338

Selection of important studies within the critical approach 339
Doing managerial work 339
Leadership processes in a financial services company 340
'Making out' 341

Contributions and limitations to thinking about the field 342
Contributions 342
Limitations 343
Conclusion 345

9 Politics and decision-making in organizations 350

Overview and key points 350

Mainstream approach to politics and decision-making 351

Introduction to the mainstream approach 351

Mainstream account of political activity in organizations 353

Central problems in the mainstream agenda 358
Constructing typologies 358
How rules are maintained 358
How conflict is contained 359
How legitimacy is sustained 360

Mainstream concepts 361
1. Micro-politics (freedom) 361
2. Decision process (knowledge) 361
3. Negotiated order (identity) 362
4. Plurality of power 362
5. Contingency 362
6. Mobilization of bias (knowledge) 362
7. Conflict (inequality) 362
8. Political rule systems (power and inequality) 363

Major controversies 364
Flexibility as an effective political response to emergent
    sectors? 364
Political activity as a rational process? 365

Key mainstream studies 366
Differentiating cliques and coalitions 366
Factors motivating group formation 366

**Contributions and limitations of mainstream
    approaches** 367

**Critical approach to politics and
    decision-making** 369

Broad overview of the critical approach 369
Rethinking the pluralist account of decision-making
    dynamics 369
A critical 'organizational politics' perspective 370
Considering limitations of the critical alternative 371
Conclusion 374

10 Culture 377

Overview and key points 377

Introduction 379

Mainstream perspective on organizational culture 381

**Introduction to the mainstream perspective, aka
    culture is something that an organization 'has'** 381

Key issues and controversies 382
One best culture vs horses for courses 384

Important empirical studies 390

Limitations and contributions 394

**The critical perspective on organizational
    culture** 395

**Introduction to the critical perspective, aka culture
    is something that an organization 'is'** 395

Key issues and controversies 399
Collinson's factory workers 405
Ackroyd and Crowdy's slaughtermen 406
Conclusion 408

**11 Change and innovation: New
    organizational forms** 411

Overview and key points 411

Mainstream approach to change and innovation 417

Introduction to the mainstream approach 417

**Key controversies surrounding the mainstream
    approach** 420
Re-engineering in the public sector 421

Benefits of new organizational forms 421
The flexible firm 421

**The shift from Fordism to post-Fordism in
    context** 424
The politics of scientific management 424
Non-Fordist organizational forms 428

**Strengths and limitations of the mainstream
    approach** 429

Critical approach to change and innovation 430

Introduction to the critical approach 430

Searching for excellence in the new workplace 431

Turning Japanese 431
But why let the facts get in the way of a good story? 433

Occupational identity 434

**Change and conflict at work in the UK National
    Health Service (NHS)** 434
From professional to responsible autonomy? 435

New organizational forms 436

Resistance in the new workplace 437

**Strengths and limitations of the critical
    approach** 440
Conclusions 442

12 Technology 447

Overview and key points 447

Introduction 448

Definitions: Making sense of 'technology' 448

Technology and organizational behaviour 452

**Mainstream perspectives: Technological
    determinism** 453

Key issues and controversies 454

Implications of technological determinism 458

Contributions and limitations of technological determinist approaches 460

Critical perspectives: Technological determinism 462

The social shaping of technology 463

Social shaping of technology: Review and implications 467

The social construction of technology 468

Social construction of technology: Review and implications 474

Actor-network theory 475

Actor-network theory: Review and implications 480

Conclusion 481

PART III
Emergent issues 489

13   Globalization and organizations 490

Overview and key points 490

Introduction 493

Structure of the chapter 497

Central problems in this field: The mainstream agenda 499

Approaches to internationalization 499

Selling: Export strategy 499

Licensing and franchising 500

Subcontracting 500

Overseas production 501

The big multinationals 502

The economic logic for the multinational firm 503

Extending the product life cycle 504

Internalization advantages 504

The eclectic theory 504

Strategy and structure in multinationals 505

Bartlett and Ghoshal's model 506

Harzing's control focus 508

National cultures and universalist solutions: The problems for MNCs 509

Leave alone 514

Train managers in cultural awareness 514

Create an international management cadre 514

Contribution and limitations of the mainstream approach 515

The critical approach to globalization and organizations 516

Introduction 516

Multinationals and power 519

Silences and absences in the mainstream approach 519

The economic power of the multinational 519

The political power of the multinational 521

Retheorizing the multinational 524

Managing the multinational across national and institutional divides 528

Conclusion 531

14   Bureaucracy and post-bureaucracy 535

Overview and key points 535

Mainstream approaches to bureaucracy and post-bureaucracy 536

Introduction 536

Key problems 540

Bureaucracy 540

Post-bureaucracy 541

Key ideas and contributions 543

Does size matter? 543

The dysfunctions of bureaucracy 544

Key issues and controversies 547

Important studies 549

Limitations of the mainstream approach to bureaucracy and post-bureaucracy 550

Critical approaches to bureaucracy and post-bureaucracy 551

Introduction 551

Key issues and controversies 554

Important studies 556

Limitations of critical approaches 558

Contributions 558

Limitations 559

Conclusion 561

15   Ethics at work 564

Overview and key points 564

Mainstream approaches to ethics at work 565

Introduction 565

Key problems 568

The problem of relevance 568

The problem of conscience 569
The problem of translation 570

Key ideas and contributions 570
Overcoming the problem of relevance 570
Overcoming the problem of conscience 572
Overcoming the problem of translation 572

Key issues and controversies 573

Important studies 575

**Limitations of mainstream approaches to ethics
    at work** 577

Critical approaches to ethics at work 578
Introduction 578
Questioning the ethics of organization 579
Questioning the ethics of obedience 580
Questioning the corporate takeover of ethics 581

Key issues and controversies 583
Questioning The Cooperative Bank as an ethical
    organization 583
Questioning the ethics of obedience 584
Questioning the corporate takeover of ethics 585

Important studies 585

**Contribution and limitations of the critical approach
    to thinking about the field** 591
Conclusion 593

Appendix 596
Glossary 598
Index 610
Credit Lines 617

Preface

About this book

Existing organizational behaviour textbooks generally harbour an ambition to be *exhaustive*. They try to cover everything in considerable detail, and in a way that students tend to find remote or removed from their own, everyday experiences. These books cram in a mass of information but rarely do they help their readers to appreciate recurrent themes or to read more deeply or critically into the subject. They also give the impression that the body of knowledge in the field of management and organization is cohesive, unified and incontestable. Yet, arguably, it is deeply divided across a range of issues and perspectives.

Packing mind-boggling and potentially mind-numbing detail into a textbook in a way that conveys an impression of unanimity is misleading and unhelpful, and not least because it is the divisions and associated debates that produce colour and interest. It is indeed ironic that so many textbooks claim to be comprehensive, yet they exclude or at best marginalize much critical and controversial material. We have sought, in our text, to be more selective in what we present, more accessible in how material is presented, and more attentive to differences of approach.

This text is written by scholars who are committed to thinking differently about the field. A specialist on the topic writes each chapter and therefore is in a position to identify and explore the key contributions in a more effective way than if we had written the whole text. All of the authors have over many years worked closely with us in teaching and/or research. This long-standing association gives the chapters thematic continuity.

Each chapter provides stand-alone treatment of its topic that is thematically linked to other chapters by a common approach. Each chapter:

- *Adopts a selective rather than exhaustive approach* to the established introductory organizational behaviour topics but remains with the principal topics that frame the more orthodox textbooks.
- *Covers both mainstream and critical literatures* – largely by exploring them in separate sections.
- *Links chapter content to everyday experience.* A basic assumption of the text is that students already know from their own day-to-day experience a good deal about work organizations (e.g., schools, retailers, service providers). The book asks students to draw on and reflect upon this knowledge to help understand the content of chapters.
- *Introduces and applies a conceptual framework* based upon six core concepts – power, identity, knowledge, freedom, inequality, insecurity – to discuss the issues presented in each chapter.
- *Seeks to engage the reader* by breaking up the text through the use of case studies, boxed issues, key point summaries, discussion questions and other ways of preventing the analysis becoming dense and turgid.

The last point is particularly important if readers are *to retain key ideas and examples* long after sitting examinations. These may be as valuable to students when taking up a job as they are in obtaining a degree qualification. It may therefore be helpful for readers to make a mental note of the above thematic points and perhaps return to them occasionally when using the text.

Approach and style

The aim of this text is to provide a fresh approach to addressing and rethinking core aspects of managing and organizing. Our intention has been to encourage students to reflect upon their experience rather than merely acquire information. Instead of equating relevance with exhaustiveness, our text is framed in terms of making the subject matter relevant to the experience of students. That is to say, we relate its contents to how our lives are organized and managed as we participate in organizations or institutions. The book treats the subject matter not just as something to learn in order to pass exams and gain qualifications, but also as a key to better understanding our experience of living in modern, highly managed societies.

Structure and format

Our text is different as it presents two distinct and highly contrasting perspectives on organizational behaviour. One perspective covers key elements of the subject matter found in mainstream texts, and so familiarizes readers with what is conventionally studied in this field. This orthodox approach to management and organization is generally treated as *the* only perspective and its study is presented as an end in itself. It is not engaged in that way here. Rather we treat the orthodox approach as a foil for introducing a critical or unorthodox perspective on organizational behaviour.

Each chapter introduces its focal topic and presents an overview of the key, orthodox contributions of it. But each chapter then also revisits and re-examines the issues by critically focusing on what the mainstream literature says, and what it fails to say, by considering issues of identity, (in)security, freedom, power, inequality and knowledge – the six central concepts around which the more critical content of this book is organized.

In seeking to make 'organizational behaviour' and 'management' more relevant and accessible, we stress how practices of 'organizing' and 'managing' are first and foremost similar, rather than alien to what we experience in everyday life. Instead of excluding the human detail of organizations in favour of a focus on functions and tasks, as do many textbooks, we reverse this emphasis. We do so because we believe that orthodox treatments of our subject matter are very glossy or rose-tinted (idealized, to use a bit of jargon) in comparison to the lived experience of organizing and managing. We also believe that most students find it easier to learn about organizations when they are able to appreciate how work relations and management activities are not so distant or different from their own everyday lives.

This textbook, therefore, moves away from a narrow view of the various stakeholders in organizations – managers and employees, shareholders and financiers, suppliers and customers, government personnel and interest or pressure groups – as rational and instrumental functionaries. The performance of these functions is not ignored but we show how managers and employees carry them out as gendered, sexually charged, ethnically located, emotionally embodied, human beings.

Third edition

Each chapter has been thoroughly revised and updated in the light of experience of using the text to teach and comments received from expert reviewers. In response to feedback, we have also included a new chapter on 'Managing People: Contexts of HRM, Diversity and Social Inequality'. The format of the book has also been updated, to reflect the academic and journalistic style of the textbook. This third edition also benefits from a streamlined pedagogical structure, including marginal key terms throughout and a consolidated conclusion for every chapter.

Key features

The book is packed with pedagogical features, which have been carefully designed to help you in studying and learning when using this text:

Learning objectives provide an overview of the key concepts that underpin the chapter, highlighting what you will learn and helping you monitor your progress.

Aims provide an outline of some of the key themes of the chapter and set the chapter in context.

Case studies explore the topics covered in each chapter and present concepts in the context of real life examples.

Thinkpoints throughout each chapter highlight important concepts and promote critical thinking, so you can discover as much as possible about the subject for yourself.

Key terms are highlighted in the text and definitions are provided in the margin throughout the book; they are intended to further your understanding of the topic and increase your academic vocabulary.

Boxed features throughout present a wide variety of examples and perspectives, designed to expand your knowledge of key topics.

Discussion questions can be used as the basis for discussing or debating issues, strengthening your understanding of the material covered.

Exercises help you further check your understanding of key concepts and ideas covered in the chapter.

Conclusion summarizes the chapter and facilitates reflection upon the significance of the chapter's contents.

Further reading at the end of each chapter allows you to explore the subject further and offers a starting point for projects and assignments.

Glossary at the end of the book includes thumbnail explanations of key terms in the book. For ease of reference the words included in the glossary are highlighted in **bold** blue in the text.

We hope you will find reading this text enjoyable and stimulating, as well as useful and informative.

David Knights and Hugh Willmott

Acknowledgements

We would like to thank the following people:

- Our students over several years at UMIST (now Manchester Business School), and for much shorter periods at Nottingham, Keele, Exeter, Cambridge and Cardiff Universities, whose comments and feedback have influenced the 'selective' content and attempted 'interactive' style of this text.
- Our colleagues, all of whom were involved with us in teaching and research at UMIST, and who have made this project possible by contributing chapters based upon their interests in the context of our requirements.
- For developing the first edition, Geraldine Lyons, our commissioning editor at Thomson Learning, now Cengage Learning, who provided unstinting advice, guidance, enthusiasm and support, and remained good-humoured throughout. This excellent support has been sustained in the preparation of the third edition, especially by Jenny Grene whose assistance has been invaluable, as well as by Sue Povey.
- Secretarial and administrative staff who have assisted us in preparing and revising the manuscript, including Valeen Calder, Annie Dempsey, Andrea Derrick, Julie Hargreaves, Carmen Neagoe, Jane Pope, Katherine Webster and Angela Cox.
- Sasha Willmott for commenting extensively on chapter drafts and Jamie Knights for a less extensive commentary about our tendency to use jargon. They are not to blame for our inability to respond to their comments as adequately as they might reasonably hope.
- And, above all, our long-suffering wives and families who encouraged us to prepare the text and have patiently endured our preoccupation with its completion and revision.

Reviewers

- Christina Volkmann, University of Essex
- Christine Parkin Hughes, Plymouth University
- Dorota Bourne, Queen Mary College, University of London
- Graham Baker, University of the West of England
- Iain Henderson, Edinburgh Business School
- Ismael Al-Amoudi, University of Reading
- Laurent Taskin, FUCaM
- Malcolm Lewis, University of Otago
- Mike Riley, University of Surrey
- Nancy Harding, Bradford University
- Stephen Benton, University of Westminster
- Samantha Lynch, University of Kent
- Torkild Thanem, Stockholm University

Contributors

DAVID KNIGHTS is Professor in the Department of Organisation, Work & Technology in Lancaster University Management School, UK. He has held previous professorships at Exeter, Keele, Nottingham and Manchester Universities and visiting chairs at Gothenburg, Stockholm, Melbourne, Macquarie and Sydney Universities. He is a founding and continuing editor of the journal *Gender, Work and Organisation*. He is also the founder and continuing director of the Financial Services Research Forum that funds academic research and engages in critical debate on this sector with practitioners from corporations, government departments, regulators, consumer interests and voluntary bodies. His most recent books are *Organizational Analysis* with H. Willmott (Cengage, 2010), and *Gender, Work and Organization* with E. Jeanes and P. Yancey-Martin (Blackwell/Wiley, 2010).

HUGH WILLMOTT is Professor of Management, Cass Business School, City University London, Research Professor, Cardiff Business School and is a visiting Professor at the University of Technology Sydney. He has previously held appointments at the Universities of Cambridge, Manchester and Aston, visiting appointments at the Universities of Copenhagen, Lund, Cranfield and the University of Technology, Sydney. His books include *Making Quality Critical, The Re-engineering Revolution, Managing Knowledge, Management Lives, Studying Management Critically, Organization Theory and Design* and *Fragmenting Work*. He has published widely in social science and management journals and currently is an Associate Editor of *Academy of Management Review* and a member of the editorial boards of the *Academy of Management Review, Organization Studies* and *Journal of Management Studies*.

JOANNA BREWIS is a Professor in Organization and Consumption at the University of Leicester School of Business. She has previously worked at UMIST and the Universities of Portsmouth and Essex. When not engaged in intellectual pursuits such as buying shoes, reading chick-lit and watching America's Next Top Model, Jo writes on the intersections between the body, sexuality, identity and processes of organizing, and teaches research methodology.

ALESSIA CONTU is a Lecturer in the Department of Management Learning and Leadership at Lancaster University Management School. Her work revolves around critical views of management and organization and the attempts to develop studies of concrete formations of capitalist relations of work to understand the significance of antagonism and its possibilities for politics and social change. The areas she is particularly interested in and has written about include: learning practices in organizations and the ideology of learning; hegemony, ethics and democracy in organizations and organizing practices; the role of Lacanian psychoanalysis in understanding the political; and organization of work, politics of production and resistance.

CHRISTOPHER GREY is Professor of Organization Studies, Royal Holloway, University of London, UK. Recent publications include *A Very Short, Fairly Interesting and Reasonably Cheap Book About Studying Organizations* (4th edn Sage, 2016), *Secrecy at Work* (Stanford University Press, 2016) and *Decoding Organization. Bletchley Park, Codebreaking and Organization Studies* (Cambridge University Press, 2012).

DEBORAH KERFOOT lectures in organizational analysis at Keele University Management School. Her research interests and publications are in the fields of sociology and critical studies in management, work and organization, empirical research on management and managing practices and gender and sexuality in organizations. She is joint

Editor in Chief of the journal *Gender, Work and Organization* (published by Wiley/Blackwell) and convenes the journal's international interdisciplinary conference series.

GLENN MORGAN is Professor of Management at the University of Bristol.

PAMELA ODIH (PhD University of Manchester Institute of Science and Technology UK), is a Senior Lecturer in Sociology at Goldsmiths University London. Gendered time and its bearing on consumption and wider gender relations is her specialist area. Recent publications include these books: *Adsensory Financialisation* (Cambridge Scholars Publishing, 2016), *Advertising and Cultural Politics in Global Times* (Routledge, 2016), *Watersheds in Marxist Ecofeminism* (Cambridge Scholars Publishing, 2014), *Gender and Work in Capitalist Economies* (Open University Press, 2007).

DAMIAN O'DOHERTY is Senior Lecturer in Organization Analysis at the Alliance Manchester Business School in the University of Manchester. Dr O'Doherty has published widely in areas of critical management studies, labour process analysis, ethnographic studies of organization, and the philosophy of organization. He is director of the Alliance Manchester Business School Ethnography Centre and is Associate Editor of Organization. He was an executive board member of the Standing Conference in Organization Symbolism and past editor of Culture and Organization and sits on the editorial committees of a number of scholarly journals.

LARA PECIS is a lecturer in Organisation Studies at Lancaster University Management School. Her work focuses on issues of gender in innovation, knowledge intensive organisations, and emotions in relation to innovation and ICT usage. Her work is informed by a number of theoretical perspectives, including sociomaterial and practice-based approaches, agential realism, and post-structural feminism. Her most recent research investigates the role of mobile technologies in organizations and their effects on employees' behaviour and well-being.

JOHN ROBERTS is a Professor at the University of Sydney Business School. He was formerly at the Cambridge Judge Business School. His current research is focused on corporate governance and in particular the dynamics of accountability in and around boards of directors. He has published widely on this topic as well as on the associated issues of ethics and corporate social responsibility.

ANDREW STURDY is Professor and Head of the Department of Management at the University of Bristol, UK. He has a particular interest in the production and use of management ideas, especially the role of management consultants and their clients. His most recent book (with Wylie and Wright) is *Management as Consultancy* (Cambridge University Press, 2015) and he has also done wok *McKinsey & Co. and power.*

SHEENA VACHHANI is a Senior Lecturer in Management at the School of Economics, Finance and Management, University of Bristol. Her research interests lie in understanding embodiment, difference, ethics and the feminine in organization as well as critiquing and investigating the relationships between language, bodies and subjectivities. At present she is engaged in projects on leadership and corporeality, cancer patient narratives, ethico-political feminist resistance, domesticity and the home.

THEODORE VURDUBAKIS is Professor of Organization and Technology at Lancaster University Management School. His research interests include the role of technologies in social organization and the handling of complexity in organizational settings.

FRANK WORTHINGTON is Director of Learning & Technology at Newcastle University Business School. His main teaching and research interests include the study of behaviour in organizations and the theory and practice of management and employee relations from a labour process perspective.

EDWARD WRAY-BLISS is Associate Professor of Management at Macquaire University, Sydney, Australia. His research focuses upon a range of ethical and political issues in organizations and has included writings on organizational evil, sex discrimination, workforce drug testing, telephone call centres, business ethics, the ethics of leadership, and the ethics of academic research.

Digital Support Resources

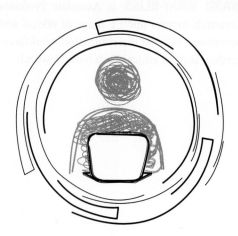

All of our Higher Education textbooks are accompanied by a range of digital support resources. Each title's resources are carefully tailored to the specific needs of the particular book's readers. Examples of the kind of resources provided include:

- A password protected area for instructors with, for example, a testbank, PowerPoint slides and an instructor's manual.

- An open-access area for students including, for example, useful weblinks and glossary terms.

Lecturers: to discover the dedicated lecturer digital support resources accompanying this textbook please register here for access: login.cengage.com.

Students: to discover the dedicated student digital support resources accompanying this textbook, please search for **Introducing Organizational Behaviour & Management** on: cengagebrain.co.uk

1 Introduction

DAVID KNIGHTS AND HUGH WILLMOTT

Key concepts and learning objectives

Our intention for this book is to introduce management and organizational behaviour (OB) in a way that:

- Values your *own knowledge* and its contribution to understanding management and organizing.

- Encourages you to scrutinize and develop what you know about management and organization.

- Appreciates how the study of management and organization draws from a number of academic disciplines (e.g., sociology, politics, psychology and economics). It is, in this sense, multidisciplinary.

- Develops an awareness of how knowledge of management and organizations reflects and reproduces the particular framework or *perspective(s)* of the author (e.g., 'mainstream' or 'critical').

- Recognizes how different perspectives conjure up and provide contrasting and competing ways of making sense of management and organizations.

- Understands how knowledge of organization(s) is significantly dependent upon people's preoccupations and priorities and, in this sense, is *politically charged*.

- Challenges the way organizations are conventionally understood in mainstream texts as 'things' consisting of parts (e.g., people, functions, goals).

This approach, we believe, is mechanical and removed from human experience.

- Appreciates how, fundamentally, 'management' and 'organization' are rendered meaningful. This encourages awareness of the diverse and multiple ways in which they are conceived. Each meaning associated with 'management' or 'organization' does not simply *describe* something 'out there' because it also contributes to the very *construction* of what it claims to describe.

- Considers how the interrelated key concepts of power, identity, knowledge, freedom, inequality and insecurity provide a framework for analyzing aspects of organizational behaviour.

- Shows how key concepts in the study of management and organization are as relevant for making sense of everyday life as they are for studying behaviour in organizations.

Aims of this book

- This book seeks to connect the study of management and organization to readers' everyday experience.

- As this connection is made, the study of managing and organizing becomes more engaging and less remote.

- Ideas and insights explored in the following chapters should become more personally meaningful and therefore easier to recall.

Overview and key points

Much of our waking life is spent in contexts where relationships are structured in comparatively formal and impersonal ways – that is, in 'organizations': as students, for example, in schools or universities; as consumers in shops, bars, sports centres, leisure clubs; or as producers in work organizations, such as factories or offices (which, of course, include shops, schools and clubs). By relating our everyday *experience* in such contexts to the study of management and organizations, we are likely to become more aware of how much we already know implicitly about them. Recognizing that we are already very familiar with organizations can increase our confidence when studying them. It can also encourage us to develop our understanding, question what we already know, and it may even result in us changing our habitual ways of thinking and acting. We illustrate this process in Figure 1.1.

Figure 1.1 Experience, reflection and knowledge of management and organization

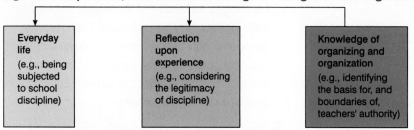

It would of course be possible to make further connections in this diagram – for example, by adding more boxes, by using double-headed arrows or by representing the elements as overlapping circles. How might additional elements and linkages offer other interesting ways of connecting our experiences, our reflections and our knowledge of organizations?

Before moving to the main part of the Introduction, please have a look at the two boxes (Box 1.1 and Box 1.2) below.

**Box 1.1
Learning as a challenging process**

Learning best takes place when we relate meaningfully to what is being learned. If we take this view to heart, then it can make little sense for us to *tell* you *exactly* what you will have learned from each chapter of this book as the circumstances of each reader will differ. Instead, we encourage you to appreciate and explore your own understandings of the relevance of the various ideas and issues that we examine.

A very good and often enjoyable way to do this is by engaging in discussions with other students on your course. Consider how others are interpreting this text, and how these interpretations can challenge or advance your own understanding. For example, what assessments do you and they make of the arguments about learning and organizations presented in this chapter? What kinds of concepts and language are being used to articulate these views? What differences are emerging and how would you characterize these differences? Do others share your interpretation of these differences? Do these mixed reactions illustrate our point about the creativity, wilfulness and unpredictability of people? Needless to say, an awareness of these issues is highly relevant for working in organizations, and not just for studying them.

Box 1.2
What you will find in this book

Instrumental rationality
Behaviour that is exclusively concerned with a self-interested end result such that the end always justifies the means. It seeks the most efficient (i.e., high output/effort ratio) means to achieve a given end. The two terms often (but need not) go together to emphasize how the behaviour is single-minded in its 'technical' and non-emotional pursuit of specific goals.

Each chapter of this book addresses a topic that is central to both the theory and practice of organization and management. Every chapter considers both mainstream and critical contributions to knowledge by exploring its subject matter using one or more of the six central concepts – *identity, (in)security, freedom, power, inequality* and *knowledge*. These are the key concepts around which the more critical content of this book is organized (see the final section of this chapter and also Appendix: The conceptual framework).

Throughout the book we endeavour to make the subject matter relevant and accessible. We do this by viewing organizational behaviour first and foremost as ordinary practices of organizing and sense-making. These involve thinking, feeling and acting, not unfamiliar to us in everyday life. This approach acknowledges, rather than ignores or denies, the politically and emotionally messy human detail of organizations.

By taking this approach, it is possible to appreciate and emphasize the continuities between the experiences of students and people working in organizations – managers as well as staff. We are all engaged in, and shaped by, a world in which organizations are as central as they are familiar. In this text, we have sought to make this understanding central as it is our belief that what is learnt 'sticks' when we can identify with, and participate in, the 'object' of our learning. This approach may sometimes demand a leap of imagination and a refusal to compartmentalize our everyday lives (e.g., going to clubs, pubs, bars or parties) from what we are studying. Of course we are not suggesting that the social world of the student is equivalent, let alone identical, to that of a manager or administrator. We do not deny the distinctiveness of organizations in which the working lives of employees are routinely conditioned by the demands and trappings of an **instrumental rationality** where people tend to be treated as means rather than ends in themselves. But, at the same time, we refuse to reduce the messy complexities of organizing simply to a series of abstractions and idealizations that are far removed from everyday life, as is the tendency within the mainstream, orthodox OB literature (e.g., Brooks, 2008; Buchanan and Huczynski, 2016; Robins, Judge and Cambell, 2010).

INTRODUCTION

This book explores how people are organized and managed at work. Managing people is repeatedly identified by managers as the most demanding as well as the most important aspect of their jobs. Managing people is often troublesome. Why might this be? To appreciate why 'organizational behaviour' is central to the study of management and business, it is necessary to provide a convincing answer to this question.

Unlike other factors of production (e.g., raw materials and technology), human beings are wilful and comparatively unpredictable. The creative power of human beings is crucial to production but it can also be deployed to frustrate, and not just facilitate, what they are paid to do. Organizational behaviour has emerged as a body of knowledge that identifies, explores and frequently suggests methods of controlling or 'empowering' the tricky 'people dimension' of managing and organizing.

To illustrate the relevance of key ideas that comprise our conceptual framework: employees may exercise their *freedom* in ways that are creative or obstructive by applying their *knowledge*. They may seek to defend or advance a sense of *identity* (e.g., as a 'professional' and/or as a 'manager') that increases or reduces *inequalities* of income and resources that facilitate or constrain exercises of *power*. Such endeavours may be fired by feelings of *insecurity*, and they may serve either to reduce or intensify such feelings. As a consequence, the scope for exercising freedom and creativity may be enhanced or diminished.

As a field of study, OB comprises a wide variety of topics – such as, decision-making, leadership, innovation and organizational design – that relate to different aspects of behaviour in organizations. The examination of these topics has involved the adoption of numerous perspectives, and has generated insights from various disciplines. (We elaborate this understanding later in this chapter in the 'What is organizational behaviour?' section.)

Something of the diversity of perspectives is apparent in the sometimes conflicting purposes and objectives embraced by, or attributed to, 'management' and 'organizations'. These purposes include: producing profits for share-holders, generating income for employees and their dependents, acquiring or building knowledge and skills, caring for others and so on. This diversity is not surprising if it is accepted that people – whether academics or organizational members – rarely have just one purpose, and the various purposes do not always fit together neatly or achieve consistency one with another (see Box 1.3). To further complicate matters, organizations are affected by the changing circumstances in which they operate, as well as the politics through which these are defined as self-evident.

Because of these complexities, it is difficult and potentially unhelpful to provide a single definition of 'organization'. Still, when approaching a new area of study, it can be helpful to have a provisional or working sense of what we are studying. So, provisionally, we will say that 'organization' is a term used both by practitioners (e.g., managers) and analysts (e.g., consultants, researchers) to describe the activities and interactions of people who are working collaboratively to create, develop and distribute products or services.

Notions of 'organization', 'management' or 'leadership' provide us with the possibility of thinking (or 'theorizing') about our experiences as employees, contractors or customers of a productive entity. They also speak to our experiences of practical, *collective* activity, such as the collaborative effort involved in making products or delivering services. (We explore the competing logics of organizing later in this chapter, in the 'Organizational behaviour as a contested terrain' section.)

In order to explain their behaviour to others, individuals or groups often claim a purpose. But these claims may be rationalizations or simply socially acceptable accounts. Expressed purposes, therefore, are not to be taken at face value, or as the causes of behaviour. They are often invoked to make behaviour seem rational and coherent. Purposes are not self-evident. Sometimes we are only dimly aware of purposes after the event of their achievement. They are then ascribed 'on the hoof' (ad hoc) or after the next event (post hoc). (See Chapter 2.)

**Box 1.3
What about
'purpose'?**

Why study organizational behaviour?

Given the demanding nature of organizing and managing people, it is not surprising that OB is widely regarded as the foundation of management studies. Nor, relatedly, is it surprising that there have been repeated efforts to reduce the troublesome, as well as expensive, human element through mechanization, automation and the use of robots. Within the notion of 'behaviour', we include thinking and feeling as well as acting. OB aspires to have relevance for understanding the behaviour of people working at all **hierarchical levels** – from the workers employed part-time or on a casual basis on the **shop floor** or in the office, to the

Hierarchy/Hierarchical levels Positions in an organization associated with different levels of status, power and economic reward.

most senior executive. Each is, to a degree, involved in processes of organizing and being organized, and managing and being managed. Whereas the management of lower hierarchy employees is well known, it is also the case that boards of directors (or their equivalent) are appointed to manage or oversee the broader picture within which senior executives work.

Shop floor Location in factories where industrial or manufacturing workers are employed.

As a student, you may well have experienced casual work, undertaking jobs that are classified as 'unskilled' (and therefore poorly paid because there is no market shortage of people able to undertake them). Such work nonetheless requires considerable concentration and effort, and can have damaging consequences if done badly. You may have found yourself in jobs where you have time on your hands and where your initiative and skills are underutilized or not used at all, except perhaps unofficially when your creativity becomes directed at elaborating the work or minimizing your involvement in 'boring' or unpleasant tasks.

In principle, studying OB should enable you to better understand how and why people are organized; identify and assess the likely consequences of making changes; and introduce changes in ways that anticipate and minimize counter-productive effects (see Box 1.4). We have emphasized how this understanding is facilitated by considering organization primarily as an idea or concept rather than an entity or description of it, and also by applying insights derived from our conceptual framework that link identity, insecurity, power, inequality, freedom and knowledge.

OB may be of most direct relevance for understanding general management but its importance extends to specialist areas, such as accounting, production and marketing where, inevitably, organizing and managing people are also central activities. For this reason, OB is a 'subject' taken by a growing number of students, either as core element of a single degree in management or business, or as a specialist element of degree programmes in engineering, modern languages and sports studies among others. OB has very wide relevance because the practices that comprise managing and organizing involve capabilities such as leadership, communication, decision-making and motivation. And, for this reason, everyday experiences, including work experience, have relevance for appreciating, assessing and challenging the body of knowledge of OB.

Box 1.4
The extensive relevance of organizational behaviour

Connecting ideas and experience

Consider your experience as a participant in a higher educational organization. With due consideration to what we have already said about how purposes are **invoked** and **ascribed** (see Box 1.3), one or more of your purposes in studying this course, which may change over time, might be identified from the following list:

1 Intellectual curiosity.
2 Understand the basics of business.
3 Enhance your management capabilities.

Invoked The drawing out, or encouraging, of some idea or action.

Ascribed Behaviour that is imposed upon people by virtue of their position or role. In earlier societies, roles were often ascribed at birth rather than achieved through demonstrating competence.

4 Avoid an alternative choice of degree that you view as impractical/boring/intellectually demanding.
5 Obtain a degree with the minimum of effort.

This selection is not exhaustive and we encourage you to add other purposes or question this list and then discuss with other students in your class. Such discussions in organized seminars can really help learning but they can also be done informally outside of class.

What about the purposes of your teachers, the university authorities (whoever you deem them to be) or the government? How would you identify those?

You might reflect upon how our 'attitudes' towards studying (and work more generally) are influenced by our interactions with others – parents and teachers as well as other students. Such considerations are often described in OB in terms of motivation, involvement or group dynamics. They are significant, practically and theoretically, in so far as they affect the quality and direction of collective forms of action– such as teamwork or where mutual adjustment is involved. In the context of higher education, there are implications for the extent to which students actively seek and encourage participation in class discussions, how much willingness there is to question the 'received wisdom' found in textbooks, and generally whether education is experienced as a process of passive or active learning.

Thinkpoint 1.1

Learning and relevance Think of some information that you find easy to remember – for example, popular singers, CD tracks, sports stars, soap opera characters and story lines, etc.

- What makes it easy for you to recall this information?
- Why is it often difficult to retain other kinds of information, such as the contents of some of the courses that you are studying?

Discuss with fellow students your conclusions. How might learning be organized differently to make it easier to retain what is otherwise soon forgotten?

The mixed and shifting motivations of students (as listed above, pp. 5–6) present teachers and textbook writers with a dilemma. Do we seek to 'manage' your learning by providing you with easily digestible 'nuggets of knowledge' that you can memorize and regurgitate with the minimum of effort or thought? This could be seen as the most '*efficient*' (i.e., low-effort) way to satisfy (4) and (5) in the list on pp. 5–6. But is it '*effective*' in enabling you to understand management, organization or business (see 2) as a lived, practical activity, let alone in enhancing your management and organizing capabilities (see 1)? Think about the design of modules and courses that you have taken in the past, or are currently attending. In their contents and delivery, do some courses approximate to the 'efficiency' model while others incorporate some concern with 'effectiveness'? Which approach do you find to be of more value or could it be a matter of both rather than either/or?

As with all forms of management, this text might encourage and enable you to 'play the game' by doing your best to appear interested in (1) or (2) while secretly you remain closer to (5) or (4) or vice versa. If you can relate OB to your experience of everyday life, you may find that it is 'less boring' (4) than some courses and/or at least a comparatively 'easy option' (5). For our part, we intend and hope that our approach is more capable of feeding and nurturing your intellectual curiosity (1), as well as your understanding of organization and business (2) and ultimately your management capability (3)! But, of course, you may exercise your freedom to question this intent. You may interpret our approach as 'patronizing' and our ambitions as grandiose. You may simply find our approach irksome as it invites more personal involvement and reflection than other elements of your studies that involve a more mechanical and 'spoon-fed' form of delivery. Your present preference may be for something more conventional that is perhaps 'boring' but 'safe', requiring only that you memorize and regurgitate its contents. Our challenge is to engage your interest by encouraging you to try something different.

On this issue, it is worth considering some similarities and continuities, as well as some differences, between organizing people at work and processes of teaching and learning. What might these be? Challenges and frustrations in the lives of teachers and students – for example, in relation to commitment and performance – are often paralleled in the experiences of managers and workers. *For this reason, when studying OB it is frequently helpful to reflect upon our own educational experiences in order to bring to life, and grasp the relevance of, key topics and concepts.* That might seem like an obvious, uncontroversial proposition. But it is not what most textbooks, which prioritize the 'spoon-feeding' of information, endeavour to do. This is not to say that we refuse to provide such easily digestible information. We do, and partly that is why each chapter is divided into a mainstream and a critical section. But we attempt to present everything in a manner that invites you to make connections with your own experience, and encourages you to think critically about its authority and significance. We now move on to identify some of the distinguishing features of OB.

WHAT IS ORGANIZATIONAL BEHAVIOUR?

OB draws upon elements from a wide range of social scientific disciplines. For example:

- *Sociology* examines human behaviour in relation to various social, political and economic conditions that affect it, but in turn are produced or reproduced by it. It connects most directly to our key concepts of 'freedom' and 'insecurity'.
- *Psychology* concentrates on how individuals think and behave. It connects most directly to our key concept of 'identity'.
- *Politics* focuses on competitive struggles for political power and influence in society. It connects most directly to our key concept of 'power'.
- *Economics* examines how wealth is produced and distributed. It connects most directly to our key concept 'inequality'.

Each of these disciplines generates a *distinctive* form of 'knowledge' (our final key concept) for conceiving of organization(s) and understanding the human behaviour that reflects and reproduces it. So, when considering the work undertaken by managers or other organizational members, we recognize the importance of (*psychological*) *orientations*, perceptions and motivations for understanding their behaviour. We also appreciate how these are formed and coloured by wider, historical and cultural (i.e., *sociological*) identifications and relations both at work and beyond the workplace. Seemingly 'psychological' factors and forces are conditioned by, and deeply embedded in, social relations that stretch beyond both organizational members and the boundaries attributed to organizations. Organizational behaviour is not just about perceptions and motivations; it is also, and perhaps more importantly, about the *economic* and *political* conditions and consequences of work. Furthermore, people at work are simultaneously family members with diverse social affiliations (of age, gender, class, ethnicity, etc.) that directly or indirectly reflect and reinforce their identities and their engagement with, or separation from, others (see Chapter 5). It is therefore highly relevant to pay attention to the historical and cultural formation of managers' and employees' material (e.g., pay) and symbolic (e.g., career) aspirations.

When placed in this wider context, awareness increases how the disciplines of economics and politics, as well as psychology and sociology, are directly relevant for understanding work organizations. People who work in organizations come from diverse social backgrounds. They have varied social responsibilities and affiliations outside, as well as within, their workplaces. Divergent motivations and interests are also forged and pursued as people develop and defend their individual and collective sense of security and identity. Given these differences, it cannot be presumed that, for example, employees or other stakeholders (e.g., customers, suppliers) fully support managerial decisions (e.g., layoffs, pay constraints, price rises, product range reductions) when, for example, in the private sector, these are intended primarily to benefit the interests of shareholders.

Beyond mechanical prescription

We can illustrate the distinctiveness and value of our approach by considering the 'skill profile' attributed to effective managers (see Box 1.5), amongst whom we would include head teachers or departmental heads in schools. What is your reaction to the contents of this skill profile? Do you consider that knowledge of this profile would make managers that you have come across, as a pupil/student, as a customer or as an employee, more effective? If not, what other elements might be relevant?

Common sense What is assumed to be self-evident, obvious and fundamentally correct. It is often used to silence all alternative understandings on the basis that common sense is clearly and universally authoritative and dependable.

The 'skill profile' identified in Box 1.5 is based upon extensive research, with much of the data drawn from responses obtained from managers' subordinates. Yet, in our view, it contains few surprises or insights that potentially may challenge or enrich our understanding. In our experience, small groups of school students or undergraduates are able to produce very similar lists within a matter of minutes. If this is the case, it places in doubt the value of such lists, as it seems that they do little more than recycle and reinforce **common sense** thinking (see Box 1.6).

- Clarifies goals and objectives for everyone involved.
- Encourages participation, upward communication and suggestions.
- Plans and organizes for an orderly workflow.
- Has technical and administrative expertise to answer organization-related questions.
- Facilitates work through teambuilding, training, coaching and support.
- Provides feedback honestly and constructively.

Source: From Kinicki and Kreitner (2009), p. 8, emphases omitted.

**Box 1.5
The effective
manager's skill
profile**

**Box 1.6
Isn't it all just
common sense?**

When knowledge about something is considered to be 'common sense', we tend to treat it as a self-evident or unquestionable 'truth'. How often have you been told, especially by parents or supervisors, to use your common sense, or to be sensible? The term is used to convey the view that there is no room for debate or discussion as to deviate from, let alone challenge, common sense is to appear stupid or, unreasonable or even deranged.

An everyday example of common sense is the notion that the sun rises and sets. Rising and setting is what the sun appears to do. Yet if we accept contemporary scientific authority, then we should talk about the earth rotating: what common sense tells us is misleading. Another example of common sense is the way that people describe the pursuit of economic self-interest as 'human nature'. If we consider this claim more carefully, we find that it is problematic. This is because economic self-interest is also often denigrated as greediness – as in 2008 – when, following the financial meltdown, bankers were castigated for their greediness. Their greed was condemned and they were urged to moderate their self-interest, suggesting that self-interest is not essential to human nature. If something is human nature, it is the equivalent of the dog barking when it senses that its territory is being invaded; and, as any dog owner knows, this is nigh impossible to prevent. In the example of economic self-interest, we can see that despite its claims to truth, common sense is self-contradictory and rather impervious to reflection. It can, for example, allow two mutually inconsistent or diametrically opposed views to be held at one and the same time.

We rarely think about organizations in a systematic way, we infrequently seek to understand precisely why or how they failed to meet our expectations. There is a tendency to account for failures by relying upon common sense – for example, by diagnosing failure as a 'lack of communication' as if, by labelling the problem in this way, we need pay it no further attention. The study of OB can provide us with the conceptual and analytical resources for thinking beyond common sense 'explanations'. We may then begin to open the **black box** of behaviour in organizations to discover what lurks inside.

Black box Metaphorical term for describing something that need not be or never is investigated. It is as if to uncover what is inside the black box would destroy its benefits, much like discovering the sleight of hand of magicians undermines their mystique.

Having signalled its dangers and limitations, from time to time most of us, including scientists, rely upon common sense thinking, or at least are prepared to suspend disbelief in it. We will rely on a common sense understanding of organization as an entity, even though we repeatedly question this common sense 'truth'. Everyday conversations and communications would simply collapse if every word or statement that relied on common sense was instantly challenged or questioned.

Box 1.7

Why are many organizational behaviour texts so wide of the mark?

When considering the skill profile attributed to effective managers (see Box 1.5) we claimed that texts based upon such thinking are of limited value and relevance. This view immediately begs the question: why, then, are they so popular and widely adopted? Our response is that their appeal resides in the highly positive image or 'spin' that they give to organizations and managers. Their reassuring and even slightly glamorous image is attractive as it portrays management as a respectable and responsible profession where the manager's role is 'simply' to enable others to achieve established, shared goals and objectives. Largely absent from the benign image presented in most OB texts is any recognition of how the practicalities of management are shaped – impeded as well as enabled – by conflicts, frustrations, insecurities and inequalities that are endemic but also routinely papered over in modern organizational life.

If this analysis is accepted, then what *is* of value to prospective managers? It is not, we believe, what is contained in the production and consumption of lists of effective skills or techniques. Rather, effective management involves drawing embodied insights into particular (context-contingent) work relations as a means of developing a better understanding of how to manage without following simple, universal (context indifferent) prescriptions.

Our skill profile example (see Box 1.5) is typical of an approach that introduces OB through the provision of abstract lists or idealistic prescriptions of management behaviour. Because they are removed from an understanding of the ever-shifting complexities of human behaviour at work, they are likely to be of limited and possibly counter-productive assistance in practical situations of managing.

Without an awareness of the messy, politically charged practicalities of organizing and managing, any amount of worthy prescription will be of limited value, and it may be damaging. It is dangerous to apply a set of principles or 'best practices' without first making an assessment of the particular circumstances and developing an evaluation of their relevance. While common features of the early 'classical studies' of management (e.g., Fayol's administrative principles, Taylor's Scientific Management (see Chapter 7), universal prescriptions cannot take account of the different contexts in which they are to be applied. It might also be argued that forms of management education and training based upon prescriptive thinking also tend to reinforce a passive learning experience in which students are invited to absorb and regurgitate information without reflecting upon its value to them, except perhaps as a means of passing exams and obtaining a qualification.

We do not question that there can be value in identifying skills that enable managers to be effective. However, profiles and checklists do not allow us to discern and diagnose why, and in what circumstances, these skills may be effective. In our view, the point of studying OB is to scrutinize and move beyond commonsensical, ultimately superficial and frequently misleading, ideas about working in, and managing organizations. We elaborate our views in a later section of this chapter where we directly address the question 'Why study organizational behaviour?'. For the moment, we focus upon organizations as the context for the study of human behaviour.

Thinking about organizations

When beginning to think about organizations we might consider, for example, a public sector organization (e.g., a hospital, a university or a school), a major retailer (e.g., Ikea), a manufacturer (e.g., Apple), your favourite football club, an office or a pub (see Box 1.8).

It is not difficult to reel off an extensive list of organizations. But what, if anything, do they have in common? It is easy to identify some shared features. Most organizations involve employment relations, a division of labour, hierarchy and a degree of permanence or continuity. Earlier, we ascribed comparative formality to (being in) organizations. What other common features would you add?

With the construction of this list, we appear to have identified a number of the distinctive characteristics of organizations. The difficulty is to find a single item on this list that is *exclusive* to organizations. Consider employment. We can think of examples of forms of employment that are not directly associated with organizations such as the single person self-employed. Also there is the 'black economy' where people work unofficially for cash in hand, thereby avoiding taxation. Many people work without being a member of an organization. Within organizations, a division of labour is present wherever members do not undertake identical tasks. But this is true of many other institutions, such as the family where certain jobs are frequently reserved by, or left to, particular members. A degree of permanence exists in families but we would not today readily identify families as organizations, even though, in small local enterprises, family members may run a business.

There is further discussion of 'organization' in a later section in this chapter (see 'Distinctiveness of work organization: Instrumental rationality'). For the moment, it is worth repeating our earlier emphasis on organization as an idea or concept that directs our attention and energies – theoretical and practical – in particular ways, rather than assuming it to be a distinctive kind of social institution. It is also worth re-emphasizing that our purpose throughout this text is to connect its content with your experience of studying, working or consuming in a variety of settings. Our intent is to make the contents of OB less remote – think of those prescriptive lists – and more personally relevant. In line with this approach, we now introduce an example from everyday life. We have deliberately chosen the 'pub' – or public house – as our example because it illustrates how it is often difficult to draw a hard-and-fast distinction between organizations – in this case, a small business but increasingly these days a large business in the sense of being part of a corporate chain – and other social institutions.

Box 1.8
What is a pub?
A sociologist's
answer

According to Clark (1983):

The 'typically English pub' has its particular place in 'English' culture for its symbolic role as an 'icon of the everyday'.... Historically, in Britain, public houses have served as the social focus for geographical and occupational communities. The public house has taken different forms over time and has its origins in the 'inns', 'taverns' and 'alehouses' of the pre-industrial era. In that period, alehouses were more numerous than any other type of public meeting-place and were the focus for a huge range of social and economic activity. Ordinary people went there to buy and sell goods, to borrow money, to obtain lodging and work, to find sexual partners, to play folk games and gamble in addition to the usual eating, dancing, smoking and carousing.

However, it was not until the early 1800s that the purpose-built public house as we know it today began to be built in large numbers and the 'alehouse' gave way to the 'public house'. By the beginning of the nineteenth century the term 'alehouse' had all but disappeared and by 1865, according to the *Oxford English Dictionary*, the word 'pub' had entered the language. (Watson, 2002, p. 18)

Organizational behaviour and everyday life: Going down the pub

In most cultures, there are institutions where people get together socially. Cafes or coffee bars are an obvious example. In the UK, the 'public house' (or 'pub') has been a central institution (see Box 1.8). In the following example of a pub – the Dog and Duck – we deliberately consider an organization that is ambivalent and shifting in its status as an organization. Alcohol is increasingly consumed in other places, including at home, and so most pubs have diversified to provide meals and/or entertainment (e.g., live televised football matches) or have been driven out of business. For readers who derive from other cultures, including those where alcohol is socially unacceptable and where women would not be found in the equivalent of the UK pub, we invite you to consider the differences and also the similarities to other examples of social gatherings or venues.

In exploring the case of the Dog and Duck, we begin to introduce some of our key concepts (in italics) to demonstrate their relevance for analyzing the pub as a work organization and a place of leisure where products (e.g., drinks and food) and services (such as live music and sports events) are consumed.

Pubs can be found in most large villages, towns and cities in the UK. In university towns, there is a degree of market segmentation, to deploy a bit of marketing jargon, which makes them attractive to different 'types' of clientele. Some pubs appeal to heavy drinkers ('boozers') and organize their space for 'vertical drinking'. Others are 'gastro' pubs where food and not just drink is the principal source of attraction and revenue. In university towns, apart from student union bars, some pubs become student venues for various reasons (e.g., price, music, proximity to student residences). However, there are some large chains of pubs (e.g., Wetherspoons, Yates) that appeal to a broader clientele principally on the basis of being 'cheap and cheerful'. In terms of material *inequality,* many students are (albeit usually temporarily) low down on the social scale, the exceptions being those whose parents provide them with plenty of money, obtain a large bank loan or are earning through a part-time job while at university. Even when not 'hard up', some students prefer drinking in student pubs rather than heading for more expensive bars and clubs to which they might more readily gravitate when they return home. Why is this? Take a moment to reflect upon what draws students to particular pubs. Do these work organizations have distinctive features that attract or repel potential staff and customers?

Generally, student pubs are friendly towards young people. Their staff are willing to put up with occasional boisterousness and noise. Student pubs also have facilities valued by a student clientele, like pool tables and music.

But, beyond this, how do such places make students feel 'at home', relaxed and comfortable? Does *identity* provide a key to understanding why we tend to gravitate to places where we expect to find people like ourselves? When we find ourselves in a room largely full of strangers, there is a strong inclination to seek out a person we know. Why? Case Study 1.1 provides a story or scenario about going down the pub.

Case study 1.1
Jackie at the pub (1)

Jackie finished her assessed work that was due to be submitted the next day and felt she needed a drink – a reward for a stressful day rushing to finish the assignment which had taken her a couple of hours longer than she had hoped. Her flatmates had gone out earlier that evening and she knew where she would find them – at the nearby pub, the Dog and Duck. Her mates usually congregated in the pub around 7.00pm most weeknights. That's because there were special deals on the drinks – two for the price of one. The landlady and landlord (the managers of the pub) were happy for their pub to be full of students and did not hassle them when they became a bit rowdy. The main reason for going to the D&D – or the 'B&Q' (the Bitch and Quackers) as her mates called it – was that you could virtually guarantee that some of your friends would be there.

On this occasion, Jackie arrived late because of the time it had taken to finish her essay. Her mates had all disappeared. She had some idea that they would have gone off to one of the student clubs in the town, but she was rather tired. So she decided to have a quick drink on her own before heading back for a long-promised early night. Most of the students had moved on, and the bar was filling up with 'locals'. This was the first time that Jackie had found herself in the pub on her own and she felt a little embarrassed just standing at the bar with a drink. So she sat down in a corner of the pub, hoping she would be left alone.

However, within a few minutes a group of young people, mainly lads, came towards her table. They seemed friendly enough and were talking in an animated way about the poor performance of the local football team. To her surprise, Jackie felt that she might fancy one of these lads. When he asked, on their behalf, if anyone else was sitting at her table, the absence of other glasses made it difficult for her to refuse, and anyway her desire for a quiet drink had now been overtaken by her interest in the lad.

Soon the conversation turned to the changing clientele in the pub. The previous landlord had not encouraged students. One of the lads started 'slagging off' the students, describing them as 'toffee-nosed' and 'cliquey'. It was clear to Jackie that they resented the 'takeover' of their local by the students. Jackie felt embarrassed that these locals were 'slagging off' students as she believed that they would know that she was a student, and so were deliberately winding her up. She wasn't at all sure how, or even whether, to respond.

Cartoon 1.1
'Do you accept my strategic recommendation now?!'

'Do you accept my strategic recommendation now?'

Like any other institution, the pub comprises a complex set of *power* relations – that is, relations of dependence (Case Study 1.1) that are reproduced or transformed through relations of power. As a regular customer, Jackie is dependent upon the staff of the pub who serve her, as they are for her custom. Jackie is also important to the landlord of the pub who, in this case, is seeking to attract the potentially profitable custom of students. It can be seen how power operates not just in one direction because while the landlord has the ultimate authority to accept or decline a customer, he or she is dependent on students like Jackie returning regularly to use the pub. Even though Jackie and her student friends occupy a comparatively low rung on the income scale, the existence of material *inequality* does not imply an absence of power as long as her custom, and that of other students, is valued. However, as our case study **vignette** shows, other 'established' customers, or even pub staff, may not share the positive value being ascribed by the landlord to students as clientele.

Vignettes Brief excerpts from a larger story that may help us to understand what happens to people in everyday life.

Having read this account of Jackie's visit to the pub, what do you think you would have done in her position? Consider first what you perceive her position to be. What features of this position do you regard as significant? Once you have clarified your understanding of Jackie's situation, consider some possible responses Jackie could make:

- Pretend not to be listening to what they are saying?
- Confront the locals and attempt to defend the students?
- Pretend not to be a student and find a way of joining in on the stereotyping of them, if only as a way of attracting the lad who had asked if the table was free?
- Ignore the attack on students but try to get into conversation with them?

Can you think of other ways that a student in Jackie's position might react?

We will return to develop our analysis of this case. For the moment, we note only that what happened to Jackie indicates in a practical way how, even in places of leisure, experiences are unpredictable because others – in this example, other customers – act in ways that may be experienced as intrusive and objectionable, and which can also be interpreted as friendly, wilful or mischievous. Traditionally, the pub has been associated not only with symbolic violence – as experienced by Jackie, who felt personally affronted by the lads' slagging off students – but also physical violence when, fuelled by alcohol, frayed tempers spill over into 'punch-ups'.

Outright physical violence involving an exchange of blows is exceptional but not wholly unknown in other work organizations. Symbolic violence, however, is much more widespread. It can be based on physical characteristics (e.g., sexual or racial harassment) or take the form of verbal bullying. Many critics of the workplace argue that the demand to perform repetitive, physical work tasks that require minimal manual involvement is itself a form of symbolic violence, in which case a majority of employees experience it at some point. We hope to show in this text how employees suffer a sense of frustration not just from the routine nature of their tasks *per se* but from the absence of power to decide how tasks are to be organized. In our case, Jackie's levels of stress and *insecurity* – in the form of anxiety, embarrassment and irritation – were increased by her sense of powerlessness and lack of control. She wanted to challenge the lads' stereotypical views about students, but she felt inhibited and intimidated. Whether their purpose was to insult Jackie, the lads' prejudices constituted a form of symbolic violence that 'wound her up', and she was finding it difficult to calm down and collect her thoughts.

Symbolic violence – in the form of aggressive or insulting verbal or gestural behaviour – might include, for example, the strong expression of differences of opinion among bar staff (and customers) about the desirability of students as clientele. In this process, there is a celebratory elevation of the *identity* of one group through a negation of the other. In its most extreme versions, there is a complete polarization so that members of the 'out-group' are demonized as unworthy of respect.

There are also disagreements among researchers, consultants, and indeed employees, about the usefulness and meaning of ideas deployed to analyze behaviour and pursue practices in organizations. These disagreements – such as our criticizing conventional texts – may not result in the trading of physical blows but they can, and do, involve passionate and sometimes unequivocally hostile exchanges of views and uneasy 'stand-offs'. Even when people recognize discussion and debate to be 'healthy' and a source of new ideas, they may still feel threatened, or *insecure*, when their own ideas are challenged. Take a moment to reflect on some of the ideas or beliefs that you are attached to, and would defend against a challenge. Often these are so deeply ingrained or taken for granted (e.g., your gender, class, nationality, race or religion) that it takes considerable reflective effort to bring them to mind.

ORGANIZATIONAL BEHAVIOUR AS A CONTESTED TERRAIN

In many textbooks, OB is presented as largely cut-and-dried and settled, lacking in any significant controversy, conflict or contest. Such tranquil appearances are deceptive. They gloss over fundamental differences of view – cultural, political and ethical – about how organizations are organized, how they should be organized and how they can be studied. Theories that articulate and feed our common sense preconceptions and prejudices are most appealing, as they are the easiest to grasp and make us feel secure (see Box 1.6). Conversely, when people are adversely affected by such prejudices (e.g., anti-student, sexism, racism), they will want to expose and resist them. Women, sexual and ethnic minorities are more likely than white men to appreciate how relations of gender, sexuality and ethnicity implicitly or explicitly, affect workplaces in terms of recruitment, selection and promotion. We invite you to discuss and reflect upon why this may be the case.

Many researchers and textbook authors favour and elaborate analysis that presents practices of organizing as largely *consensual* and *routine*. Others contend that organizing is precarious and conflict-ridden. Differences – within and between practitioners and researchers – can be confusing and frustrating. But these differences are also what make the field of OB dynamic and engaging. Glossing over these differences can make knowledge of OB easier to present and absorb, but this does students and practitioners a disservice. Challenging forms of thinking that skirt around, or skate over, complexity, difference and paradox, are necessary for developing both practice and theory. It is through conflict and debate – in practice as well as theory – that intellectual reflection and organizational innovation is stimulated. It is very difficult to imagine how reflection and innovation would otherwise occur.

Competing logics of organizing

We have repeatedly stressed that organizations are complex institutions. Their complexity does not arise directly from their scale or even from the diversity of their operations, but rather from the conflicting priorities and preferences of their members who, in turn, are caught up in webs of others' demands upon them (e.g., families, customers, shareholders, etc.). An expression of these conflicting priorities is found in the operation of competing logics for organizing material and human resources to provide diverse goods and services. We have seen, for example, how Jackie found herself in a situation complicated by the competing priorities and preferences of the pub manager and the local customers. The new manager wanted to maximize the use of the premises at all times. But this priority risked losing an established customer base of local regulars who resented 'their pub' being targeted at, and taken over by, students.

Exercise 1.1

Encountering organization Consider an organization where you have worked or have been a customer. List some differences of view, or grievances, among employees and/or customers that you encountered. How do these concerns connect to how activities were being organized and managed? Are there other issues that *you* would raise as an employee or as a customer? Reflect upon how your values and preoccupations led you to raise these issues.

A much broader example of competing logics of organizing concerns the issue of how 'public goods', such as health and education, should be provided. In recent years, questions have been asked with increasing frequency and urgency about the adequacy, and even the viability, of the provision of such goods by public sector organizations. Public sector organizations have been repeatedly criticized for being too bureaucratic, unresponsive and insufficiently alert to the (changing) preferences and expectations of those who are their patients, students, clients or customers. Their critics point to an ingrained inflexibility (i.e., of managers, professional staff and workers) as the greatest obstacle to delivering value-for-money public goods.

Since the 1980s, many people have been persuaded, or at least told, that the answer to problems identified in the public sector – such as waste, rigidity and inefficiency – is to run public utilities as private businesses. For those elements of the public sector that were not privatized, the 'modernization' plan was to staff public sector organizations with 'professional managers', and to introduce more entrepreneurial ideas from the private sector. This process has included setting targets linked to financial incentives. It has also involved competition and discipline associated with performance measurement and comparisons between different services (see Thinkpoint 1.2).

Thinkpoint 1.2

League tables Consider the pros and cons of introducing league tables to measure the performance of schools or university departments. Imagine that you are advising a government in a country that has no equivalent to these tables. Consider the probable effects of their use upon the organization – e.g., scope and delivery – of educational provision. What arguments would you make to recommend or resist the introduction of league tables? How would you illustrate your position by reference to your own experience and knowledge as a recipient of educational services?

In many countries, the substitution of private for public forms of financing and organizing has been widely welcomed, or at least tacitly supported. This is unsurprising as a reluctance to fund public services through taxation has resulted in underinvestment in the public sector, substantial elements of which have become run down and demoralized by neglect.[1] Almost everyone has a tale to tell of poor or worsening standards of public housing and health care. People suffering a bad experience with the public sector are already receptive to the suggestion that government should be run like a private business that is rendered efficient by market discipline, with professional managers being given the prerogative and discretion to manage resources.

'New managerialism' in the public sector

Reform of public services is advocated in order to ensure that they are run for the benefit of those who use them, and not primarily for 'the bureaucrats' who administer them. Paradoxically though, the result of such 'reforms' has been an increase of managerial and monitoring staff whose salaries are paid by cutting the numbers, and eroding the terms and conditions of the front-line employees, who are the target of private sector managerial techniques. These take the form of budgets, competitive targets, financial incentives, project management, performance league tables and procedures of audit and accountability that are more concerned with evidence of compliance with rules than any substantive content.

Managerialism refers to a view that assigns to managers the exclusive power to define the goals of the organization and their means of achievement. In extreme

Managerialism or managerialist Terms applied by critical academics to describe a type of thinking and kinds of social science output that serve the objectives of managers, as these critics see them, rather than offering an independent or alternative perspective. Managerialism usually entails the technocrat idea that effective management is the solution to an array of socio-economic problems.

form, it proposes that everything can be managed efficiently through the application of 'correct' techniques. In higher education, elements of this can be seen in the performative pressures imposed upon academics through competitive rankings and evaluations as well as the delivery of programmed education provided in modularized chunks, using standardized packages and student workbooks. Likened to the provision of (fast) food, this has been described as increasing the 'McDonaldization' of education. To cater for a mass education market, textbooks are produced to a standard formula just like burgers, and are probably not to be recommended as part of a 'healthy educational diet'.

The failure of many dot-com companies and e-commerce ventures in the 1990s and the meltdown of the banks in 2008 indicated that private sector methods and strategies are not guaranteed to be superior, and indeed may be economically disastrous compared to less fashionable (e.g., co-operative, democratic, bureaucratic) ways of running organizations. Indeed, the stock market has been likened to a giant global gambling casino (Strange, 1997) and the fiasco of bundling subprime mortgages into packaged securities which led to the global financial crisis was a clear demonstration that the market does not always produce the equilibrium adjustments to prevent, but can actually spawn, Armageddon (Knights and McCabe, 2015). Very few predicted the market crash but, as reported in the film 'The Big Short', the costs fell not on those who perpetrated it but on the less well-off who continue to suffer the austerity measures that have followed in its wake. What is being suggested here is that the faith in neo-liberal market or managerialist solutions to organizational problems should be considered circumspectly, especially when it comes to delivering public services.

The complaint about self-serving public sector bureaucrats deflects attention from the importance (backed up by corporate law) given to the focus on shareholder value in the organizing logic that distinguishes private sector service provision. Private sector companies are forced to compete not only because the market is ostensibly 'free' and open to new entrants but also because they are under pressure to operate profitably in order to raise returns on capital. Of course, they may fail to do this, in which case they are starved of capital, experience a cash flow crisis and eventually go to the wall unless they are bailed out by government (that is, taxpayers), as in the case of the over-leveraged US and UK banks in 2008. Or some companies may stay afloat by engaging in sharp (e.g., anti-competitive) practices that restrict consumer choice and raise prices. Alternatively they may engage in 'creative accounting' to inflate their earnings or conceal the extent of their liabilities and expenses – a practice that can, of course, backfire as in the case of Enron in 2001 (see Willmott, 2011b). Private sector companies frequently claim that their priority is to serve customers as a means of retaining or increasing market share. However, serving customers well is not the only way of controlling the market since monopoly, oligopoly and product differentiation all can have the same effect. Can you think of examples from your own experience?

It has become increasingly clear that the private sector does not have all the answers. In the worst case, customers experience increased prices, lower levels of service and safety (see Action for Rail report 'The Four Big Myths of UK Rail Privatisation', 2015) and may involuntarily incur a massive burden of debt in the case of the bail out of the banks. Services contracted to the private sector are repeatedly shown to be far from perfect. Through a bidding process, the paper cost may be lower, but the quality of the service (e.g., cleaning of hospital wards) is often poor and perhaps dangerous to the health of patients, resulting in substantial knock-on costs.[2] In order to make a highly competitive bid, a low-cost supplier is under pressure to 'cut corners' in order to maintain profit margins and the resulting fall in standards can have a serious impact, especially where health, safety and well-being are involved. (A comparison of the private and public sectors is set out in Table 1.1.)

In an effort to counteract this endemic problem of wholly market-based relations, increasing interest is being shown in private–public partnerships. In principle, the entrepreneurial features of private business are conceived to shake up and inspire improvements in public sector organizations without entirely abandoning an ethos of public service delivery. The assumption underlying this move is that market competition between private contractors can reduce cost while maintaining or even improving quality. However, this apparently rational assumption does not take significant account of the limited capacity/expertise of staff in the public sector to secure a good deal and hold the contractor to account.

Table 1.1 Comparing private and public sectors

Sector	Private	Public
Focus	Produce what is profitable for investors	Provide what is demanded by voters
Governance	Accountability to shareholders	Accountability to electorate
Logic of organization	Innovation to produce better returns on capital invested	Standardization to provide continuity of service and security of employment
Shortcomings	Lack of concern with anything (e.g., the environment, ethics, other stakeholders) that does not contribute to profits	Underinvestment, bureaucratic rigidity and ineffective use of resources

Figure 1.2 Public–private partnership: design, build, finance, operate (DBFO)

Source: Adapted from US dot, Federal Highway Administration. www.fhwa.dot.gov/ppp/dbfo.htm

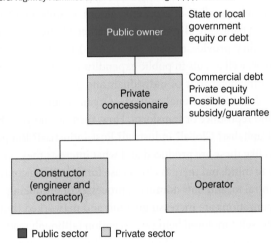

With the design-build-finance-operate (DBFO) approach, there is a bundling together of responsibilities for designing, building, financing and operating, which are transferred to private sector partners. A common feature of such schemes is their part or total financing by debt leveraging revenue streams. For example, direct user fees (tolls) on roads constructed by the DBFO approach can provide a revenue source. In such cases, future revenues are leveraged to issue bonds or other debt that provide funds for initial capital and project development costs (e.g., building roads, hospitals, etc.).

Supporters of private–public partnerships suggest that entrepreneurial flair can be transferred without damaging the ethos of public service delivery. In place of the lowest bidder, 'best value' is taken as the baseline for evaluating competing private sector bids for public service contracts. Best value ostensibly incorporates a concern with the ethos of the contractor, including their track record on collaborating in long-term partnerships, as a basis for arriving at mutually acceptable ways of securing cost-effective improvements in service delivery.

Whether or not faith in public–private partnerships is justified or sustained, there is no doubt that a defining feature of capitalist business is placed in question. Critics of the 'enterprise culture' ask: 'If you are ill do you want to be treated by an entrepreneur or a doctor following professional and regulated standards of good practice?' This question has become all the more relevant or significant since senior executives at major international companies (e.g., Enron, Freddy Mac, Parmalat, WorldCom and VW) have been exposed for engaging in fraudulent behaviour (e.g., massaging their balance sheets) to secure better stock market prices. As shareholders themselves, many of these executives were the direct beneficiaries of the increased valuations and offloaded their shares prior to the company's collapse.

Companies stay in business only as long as they can maintain the confidence of investors (e.g., shareholders and financiers), customers, suppliers and regulators, or as in the case of the banks, are crucial to a capitalist economy and are 'too big to fail'. When confidence is dented, investment is withdrawn as capital is transferred to less risky propositions. Depleted of capital, financially weak companies relying upon inflexible or 'unrealistic' business models then struggle to survive as an economic downturn favours those with sufficient reserves to reduce margins and/or weather the storm.

In the wake of major company scandals and bank collapses, the idea that 'government should be run like a business' is destined to lose some of its common sense appeal. Perhaps, after all, solutions for organizational problems are not so simple, and maybe despite the problems of rigidity characteristic of bureaucratic organizations, there is some merit in the checks and balances built into 'old' public sector management (Willmott, 2011a).

At the time of writing (early 2016), the impact of the financial crisis of 2007/8 continues as the public, world markets and debt-ridden governments seek to cope with the austerity and recessionary 'fallout' from the crisis. Part of the problem is global overproduction (i.e., too many goods/services chasing too few customers) and economic instability caused by fragile commodity markets and the West's dependence on China where growth rates are declining. Numerous other economic and political uncertainties are triggered by wars in the Middle East, the European refugee crisis, immigration pressures on more affluent countries, and global terrorism. Despite low interest rates that would normally fuel consumer spending, talk is of economic gloom, despite a ballooning of consumer credit, and a knock-on sovereign debt crisis that banks are ill-prepared to weather. Contexts such as this cannot be ignored when studying organizations because they provide reasons (or excuses) for decisions that, for example, lead to downsizing, mergers and acquisitions, as well as cuts in public expenditure in many economies.

Instead of focusing narrowly upon the behaviour of individuals and groups in organizations, we locate 'organizing' within wider historical, cultural and institutional contexts. Organizational behaviour is embedded in such contexts, which it cannot but reflect and reproduce or transform. How, then, would you characterize the contemporary context? Modern? Democratic? Capitalist? Global? Industrial? Post-industrial? But perhaps, more importantly, should we not reflect upon why labels like these are produced and what interests they serve?

These and other terms may spring to mind, but there is also a case for describing contemporary society as 'organized'. Organizations have become central to, and now dominate, processes of producing and consuming goods and services of all kinds even if these organizations are increasingly fluid and networked (but see Box 1.9). People find employment within organizations – the self-employed being an exception (although many of them are contracted to work for organizations on a casual or temporary basis). While we usually work in one organization, we spend most of our earnings in other organizations, notably in the retail outlets where we buy food, clothing, cars, mortgages and so on. Organizations provide us with most of our material, and a considerable number of our less material, demands for services including finance, travel, education, health and leisure. In the absence of organization, most of us would struggle to obtain an equivalent income, and there would be an acute shortage of goods and services. Organizations have become crucial to our material lives and perhaps survival.

The provision of goods and services through the creation of organizations is clearly not a 'natural' (i.e., a part of the human condition like food, water and oxygen) or necessary way of sustaining our lives. We need only think of how (even today, and more so in the past) a majority of people in the world produce and consume their everyday goods by depending much more on family and community than they do upon the activities and arrangements that we describe as organizations.

Box 1.9
The 'unnaturalness' of organizations

Back to the pub: The personal and the organizational

When thinking of organizations, there remains a tendency to think first of a service or manufacturing company or perhaps an established public sector organization, such as a school or hospital. We could easily have situated Jackie's experience of organization in a school, office or factory instead of a pub. The pub is, however, an interesting space as it combines processes of production, in the form of service delivery and sometimes micro-brewing, with processes of consumption that are partly commodified (e.g., through purchasing and branding of goods) but largely self-organized (e.g., through socializing, conversing, etc.).

In contemporary societies, leisure has become a distinctive sphere of (recreational) life. Historically the 'public house' has been a recreational space and of central significance in 'disposing' of leisure time (see Box 1.8). Increasingly, however, advanced industrial societies are becoming deindustrialized as manufacturing is more profitably undertaken in industrializing economies where access to labour and raw materials is cheaper, more plentiful and less regulated. As the proportion of income available to be disposed on non-essentials (e.g., accommodation, food, clothing) has grown, the leisure sector has enjoyed sustained growth by commodifying the means of entertainment. That is to say, forms of leisure are increasingly 'packaged' for sale in the marketplace rather than self-organized within families or communities.

Let us therefore go back to our narrative about Jackie in the Dog and Duck, a pub owned by the brewery which has not (yet) sought to give it a 'theme' or 'facelift'. Remember she was sitting in a corner of the pub, having to listen to locals openly engaging in what she experienced as a character assassination of students.

We invite you to reflect further upon Jackie's visit to the pub (see Case Study 1.2, p. 20), concentrating this time upon the landlord and landlady's approach to managing this organization. To assist in this process, we encourage you to consider, preferably with other students on your course, the following questions:

1 Jackie is taking a business studies degree. How do you think her experience of working in the pub might help with her studies and, how might her studies help her when at work?
2 How does the case illustrate the concepts of identity, insecurity, power and inequality, and illuminate the practicalities of management and organization? (See final section of this chapter and the Appendix for further discussion of these concepts.)
3 Are there any other questions relating to this case study that you feel are important?

To read mainstream textbooks, it might seem that organizations have relevance, value or significance only as instruments for producing and providing goods and services. Yet despite not being their primary purpose, organizations are also often of central importance in facilitating a sense of identity for owners, managers, employees and customers. For consumers, the proliferation of information technology, especially mobile phones, has intensified this to a point as great as, if not greater than, car or home ownership. It is through our participation in organizations (e.g., as producers or consumers) that we develop, confirm or manage our sense of identity – for example, as employable (in work organizations), as prosperous (in retail outlets), as sick or cured (in hospitals), as well-educated or ignorant (in schools) and as enjoying ourselves (in pubs and clubs). As we have seen in our case study of the Dog and Duck, organizations can also be contexts where our identities are threatened in ways that fuel our insecurities. We saw how Jackie experienced this when the local lads launched a verbal assault on students – an assault that was provoked, apparently, by insecurities aroused by the landlord's desire to attract students into 'their' local.

Inescapably, what happens in organizations has personal as well as instrumental significance. Our experiences in organizations reinforce (or threaten) our sense of who we are, and what is meaningful and valuable to us (and about us). In this process, relations of power operate to enable or obstruct how interactions and identities are accomplished. For example, Jackie's identity as a student is not just created by herself but also by the locals and the landlord and landlady. This identity degrades her value in the eyes of the locals but enhances it from the perspective of the landlady. The landlady regards Jackie as a potential employee who can assist in developing a student clientele. Formation, development and change in our identities occurs through social interactions – with ourselves as well as others – as we reflect upon our experiences and resolve, perhaps, to change our ways. Change is, of course, not easy

Case study 1.2
Jackie at the pub (2)

In the event, Jackie decided to make her excuses, leave the table and return to standing at the bar. After a short time she entered into conversation with the landlady and landlord as they served other customers. The conversation meandered through a number of topics, until Jackie felt sufficiently relaxed to bring up the experience of being criticized by the locals.

The landlady sympathized with Jackie, recognizing that there was some animosity between the locals and the students, especially since they had sought to attract students into the pub. Ordinarily there was little trouble as the students were inclined to move on to other bars before the locals came in. The landlord went on to explain his decision to attract students when he became the tenant of the pub 12 months earlier. He was hoping to make their tenancy a great success, as this was the way to obtain a much bigger pub from the brewery. Eventually they were hoping to buy their own pub in a nice coastal village in Cornwall where the tourist trade during the summer would provide financial security and allow them more time to pursue their hobbies – of astronomy and artwork – during the quieter winter months. As they were talking, some customers were becoming impatient at not getting immediate service, and the landlord responded by returning to serve some locals. The landlady then confided in Jackie that the growth in business in the pub had presented a staff problem for them.

As she left the pub Jackie felt a lot more at ease. The friendliness of the landlord and landlady had reassured her that students were genuinely welcome; and she knew that, in future, she could always talk to them. In fact Jackie had found herself saying that if ever they were short of staff, she would be happy to help out. On her next visit to the pub, the landlord asked her if she was still interested in helping out and, if so, could she do a few hours the following night when one of the staff had to visit her mother in hospital.

as is evidenced by the number of New Year resolutions that are broken as habitual patterns of action override our good intentions.

From Jackie's standpoint, her limited income as a student made the opportunity to do some part-time bar work more attractive than for someone in a healthier financial situation. But it was not simply material inequality that rendered Jackie receptive to this job opportunity. She also regarded it as a chance to enhance her status in the eyes of her parents who had been exerting pressures upon her to find part-time work. It is hardly surprising, then, that Jackie felt much better after having had a more pleasant interaction with the landlord and landlady, and being asked to help them out. A few months later, after demonstrating a flair for interacting with customers, she was asked by the landlord if she would be able to manage the pub for a weekend. We take up the story on her first night in this enhanced role (see Case Study 1.3).

Jackie had experienced a big boost to her self-esteem by being asked to manage the pub. In contrast, not being chosen to manage the pub was a terrible blow to Christine. We can hint at some of the complexities of this organizational and managerial situation. Christine was more experienced in pub work, older, and of even more importance, she had ambitions to run a pub of her own. These circumstances help us to understand Christine's reactions when Jackie sought to manage her resistance. Christine's defiance threatened Jackie's sense of identity, and especially her stand-in role as manager of the pub. Jackie felt that her position as a temporary manager had been undermined in the eyes of the clientele, and that her standing with the landlord and landlady would be damaged. Jackie was also concerned about how the landlord would react to the possible loss of Christine as a valued employee. While she had been embarrassed by Christine's walkout, Jackie's dignity and self-esteem remained intact by virtue of her not exploding in the same way as Christine. However, she felt some mild resentment towards the landlord who, she believed, must have had some inkling of how Christine might react. She felt that she had been placed in a difficult situation. It even crossed her mind that the landlord and landlady had perhaps seized, or even created, an opportunity to force Christine out so as to replace her with someone who they could trust to act as a reliable manager in their absence.

Case study 1.3
Jackie at the pub (3)

Jackie felt some trepidation about acting as 'pub manager' for a night and, in particular, the reactions of the two other bar staff. They were both slightly older and also locals. John was pretty relaxed and she didn't expect much of a problem with him, not least because he displayed a 'soft spot' for her and this gave her a sense of control. Christine, however, was a different kettle of fish. When Jackie had started working behind the bar, Christine had obviously felt threatened. Now, as the elder and more experienced bartender of the three, Christine was clearly angry that she had not been asked to manage the pub. This was particularly upsetting for Christine as she had ambitions to become a landlady.

Things were going all right until it became very busy. One of the customers was clearly expressing impatience at not getting served. Both Jackie and John were serving other customers but Christine was engaged in a lengthy chat with a friend who was sitting at the bar. Jackie asked Christine if she could serve the waiting customer. She appeared to accept the request but then continued to chat with her friend. A bit of a row then occurred as Jackie tried to get Christine to come into the back where they could discuss the problem. Christine simply blew her top, condemning Jackie for embarrassing her in front of the customers. Christine walked out, saying she was not going to be bossed about by a trumped-up student who knew nothing about bar work.

The pub was very busy and it was going to be extremely difficult to manage with just two bar staff. At the first opportunity, Jackie tried to ring the landlord but couldn't get an answer. So she rang one of her flatmates – Carol – to see if she would come and help out. Fortunately Carol agreed to come at once and, despite needing a lot of help, the evening went reasonably smoothly. Eventually the landlord rang back and Jackie was able to explain the situation. He was sympathetic but was also worried about how to replace Christine who, he feared, was gone for good. Maybe Carol, he suggested, would fill in for Christine, although Christine was working more hours than might be expected from a full-time student. Carol seemed quite keen. She had seen how Jackie had flourished since taking the job, plus the extra money was difficult to turn away.

Once again, we encourage you to reflect upon staff relations at the Dog and Duck as illustrative of different aspects of behaviour in organizations. Here are some questions:

1 If Jackie is right that the landlord had contrived a situation that would provoke Christine into walking out, what implications does this have for 'the effective manager's skill profile' presented and discussed earlier (see Box 1.5)?

2 How are the concepts of insecurity, identity, knowledge, power, freedom and inequality relevant for exploring and analyzing the dynamics of the relationship and interactions between Jackie, Christine and the landlord?

3 Can you draw some parallels between the actions of the landlord, Jackie and Christine and your own experiences of work or leisure relationships?

4 Can you think of media reports of disputes at work, past or present, whose content might be illuminated through a similar analysis to the one we have sketched to interpret aspects of organization and management at the Dog and Duck?

5 Our 'Dog and Duck' example is fictional rather than based upon research (see also Knights and Willmott, 1999/2004 for our use of novels for a similar purpose of understanding organization). Does this limit or enhance its usefulness for the purpose of illustrating the relevance and applicability of the elements of our conceptual framework?

Jackie's experience illustrates how organizations are not only important to our material existence but are also meaningful areas that have *symbolic* significance. Organizations involve not just our objectives and interests, but also our bodies, feelings, sentiments and identities. Organizations are among the core institutions – including the family and school – that foster and embellish our embodied existence as well as our aspirations and attachments to particular social identities.

ORGANIZATION AND INSTITUTIONALIZATION

When we highlight the personal and social significance of organizations, we are also acknowledging their status and importance as arenas within which people – employees and customers – become institutionalized. When sets of actions and relations are seen as fairly predictable, they are termed 'institutions'. Institutions involve common ways of doing things. So, for example, in schools and work organizations, processes of

Institutionalization Process whereby people are fully integrated into an institution (repeated and routine practices) so as to rarely think to challenge them.

institutionalization include the acquisition of habits, aspirations and discipline (e.g., time-keeping and deference to authority) that enable classes to run on time, students to attend, and a degree of order to be maintained. Of course, there are many 'institutions' that are not readily or plausibly identified as organizational. For example, a series of activities may become institutionalized around preparing for mealtimes, such as breakfast. The kind of breakfast that is prepared and the particular interactions with others during the process of preparing and consuming breakfast, assumes a pattern that becomes 'normal' and taken-for-granted. It is only when this pattern is disturbed, intentionally or otherwise (e.g., a valued ingredient runs out), that an awareness of the 'institution' as a routine is aroused (see Thinkpoint 1.3).

When we participate in an institution, we presume implicit as well as explicit knowledge of the conventions that we expect to find in such contexts. As a regular customer in a supermarket, for example, we learn how the store is arranged in terms of how the goods are grouped and where they can be found on the shelves. Again, this knowledge may be so taken-for-granted that it surfaces only when there is a 'reorganization'. Such change is usually justified by a managerial calculation that, in this case, will produce more traffic down the supermarket aisles and thereby increase revenues. It disrupts our shopping pattern, and perhaps makes us more aware that we had such a pattern, but it is effective from the viewpoint of the supermarket's managers and shareholders if it has the effect of us purchasing other goods that previously had been ignored by, or become 'invisible' to us.

What such disruptions risk, of course, is a negative reaction from customers who, in the absence of any marked loyalty, may respond by changing their routines entirely as they decide to shop elsewhere. A parallel analysis could be applied to the locals, as customers, at the Dog and Duck (see earlier) who were reacting negatively to what they were finding as the equivalent of a reorganizaton of 'the shelves' in the supermarket – that is, the influx of a student clientele.

Thinkpoint 1.3

It's just routine Consider some other routines (e.g., going to lectures) and how their presence and significance only comes to light when they are disrupted, or when we reflect critically upon them by imagining the possibilities of their disruption. An example of 'breaking with routine' is the inability to 'make' the 9.00am lecture because of a hangover or lack of sleep the night before (assuming, of course, that such a routine was ever established). Student life can result in late nights and leisure becoming the routine, and this might only be disrupted when realizing that the lifestyle could result in failing the degree. Can you think of other examples of how routines become established or disrupted? How are the concepts of identity, insecurity and power relevant for making sense of the condition and consequences of processes of institutionalization or their disruption?

The significance of routines

Actions and relations are institutionalized in the sense that there is regularity and routine – for example, in how pupils relate to teachers, how doctors treat patients and how ticket inspectors check passengers. As we noted earlier, over several decades, pubs have been expanding their services in an attempt to appeal to new customers or responding to changing patterns of consumptions due, for example, to more severe drink-drive laws. This has involved disrupting established identities and routines by, for example, creating play areas for children to attract young families, providing food, and, like the Dog and Duck, installing pool tables to attract a potentially profitable segment (e.g., students). In each case, the traditional clientele may feel, as we saw at the Dog and Duck, 'pushed out' or denied their institutionalized expectations.

As a consequence of such changes, employees as well as customers in many organizations are obliged to make sense of, and deal with, disruptions to established practices and routines. Think, for example, of the use of call-centres in low cost economies such as India to replace domestic services, the shift to self-service (e.g., bank ATMs, supermarket consumption) or the exploitation of brands to generate customer loyalty and a high pricing strategy.

The centrality of people

As we all know, our everyday relationships with parents, friends or lovers can be difficult. The more we try to organize them, the more difficult they often become. Work organizations exhibit these same difficulties, except we do not usually or necessarily share the same intensity of commitment and loyalty to relationships at work – something that we signalled earlier when commenting that organizations are comparatively formal and impersonal.

At work, we may be faced with pressures to increase productivity or improve levels of service. Managers may attempt to coerce staff into working harder (e.g., by incentives, bullying or imposing penalties for failure to meet arbitrary targets). Earlier, when considering the actions of the landlord at the Dog and Duck, we raised the possibility that he engineered the situation that resulted in a staff member (Christine) walking out. When detected or even suspected by staff, such methods reinforce the impersonality of the relationship, and make it more difficult to engineer more personal or involved forms of motivation and leadership. This tells us something significant about work organizations. Participation in them is usually based on an impersonal contract of employment in which a wage is paid for the application of skill and effort. In itself, this impersonal contract carries with it no moral obligation to work diligently or to be loyal to the employer.

Exercise 1.2

Organizing in everyday life Think about a tension or conflict you have had personally with someone close and reflect on the degree to which it can illuminate an aspect of organizing, being organized or relating to some organized activity (e.g., a place of education, work, consumption or leisure). If convenient, this could be done in pairs whereby one of you probes the other and vice versa so as to try and avoid the tendency that we all have of rationalizing (i.e., reinterpreting unpleasant experiences in a more favourable light in terms of our own part in them). Consider, for example, how a sense of 'fairness' is negotiated or imposed, or reflect upon how trust is established or undermined.

People in organizations vary in the degree to which they consent to organizational control. Ultimately, willing co-operation or grudging compliance depend upon a sense of the legitimacy (fairness) of the demands made upon us, and of course the capacity of managers to generate the conditions that make compliance the normal employee response. We saw earlier how compliance is not to be taken for granted when Christine was unwilling to be managed by a younger barmaid in the pub in which they both worked. People can be creative, responsible, dedicated and loyal, but, equally, they can act in ways that, from a managerial perspective, are destructive, subversive, irresponsible and disloyal.

VIEWS OF ORGANIZATION: ENTITY, PROCESS AND CONCEPT
Identifying organization

On the face of it, what 'organization' means is obvious or self-evident. Ask anyone to name six organizations, and they would have few problems providing a list. What would you name? Let's make the question a little more testing by asking you to identify six *educational* organizations. Which six would you choose from the list in Table 1.2?

Table 1.2 Types of educational organization

• School	• Workplace	• University	• Community centre
• Family	• Hockey	• Night class	• Beach party club
• Friendship group	• Garden centre	• Chat room	• Toddler group
• Bookshop	• Library	• Cinema	• Media

Once you have chosen the six that, in your view, are 'educational organizations', think back to what led you to pick them. If you now had to justify your selection, what would you say? What is it about your six selections that differentiate them as 'educational *organizations*'?

Perhaps the most obvious candidates are 'school' and 'university'. These, commonsensically, are bodies that provide educational goods or services. When we think of 'education' we tend to privilege *formal* methods of teaching – as found in classrooms. That is what education commonsensically means, even if there are alternatives which challenge that understanding, like 'the school of hard knocks' which celebrates learning through the 'university of life' – doing and making mistakes.

Parents are also involved in educating their children – by teaching them how to speak and to interact with others. Parents may also try to compensate for perceived shortcomings in their children's formal education by supplementing it with their own instruction or employing tutors. Governments may even build a view of 'responsible parenting' into educational policy by, for example, prosecuting (even gaoling) parents of truanting children for not instilling the values of education in their offspring. So, do we count the family as an educational *organization*?

In the workplace, various kinds of education abound, both in training and through learning from others who are colleagues, friends or mentors and the same could be said for many other forms of human association. In the process of meeting up with friends, going to discos, clubs, pubs and parties, playing sports and even watching TV, visiting retail stores, chat rooms, etc., we become educated about various aspects of the world in which we live. Many of these activities are 'organized' and/or take place in organizational contexts. Indeed, they can and do provide alternative forms of education, even to the point of placing in question the authority and value of formal education. Formal education, regulated by the state, can indeed be seen as a narrow indoctrination into certain 'respectable' patterns of belief and behaviours that restrict rather than expand intellectual and moral horizons. That is why, for some parents, home schooling is the preferred way to educate children. Critics of formal education are inclined to place some scare quotes around much of the 'education' provided by schools and universities. Purposely, we placed on our list a number of non-educational organizations/institutions that, nonetheless, may facilitate education. The last two – cinema and media – indicate that almost anything can be educational; it depends on their content but also, and critically, on how we relate to them.

When education is seen as a process, almost everything we do has educational significance and implications; it all depends on how we *relate* to what we do. Learning can be seen as synonymous with our everyday practices of talking and interacting with one another and the world around us. Take the case of organizations. Why assume that we know little or nothing about organizations or organizing just because we have never attended an OB course or read a textbook? Why, in the absence of such formal instruction do we jump to the conclusion that we are ignorant of the subject? In doing so, we effectively disempower ourselves as we cede authority to 'experts' who are deemed to possess a monopoly of knowledge in this field – a view that allows our direct experience and understanding of organizations and organizing to be ignored, devalued or marginalized. Instead, we might usefully recognize how frequently and continuously we participate in organizations and organizing processes, and how much we 'pick up' or learn in this process. In our view, it is unfortunate that so many textbooks do not recognize, and so fail to facilitate, the exploration of this knowledge as part of studying OB.

In the next three subsections, we consider some different ways in which 'organization' is defined, identified and analyzed.

An entity view

When considering the definitions set out in Box 1.10, you may well respond by thinking: 'Yes, that makes sense. It is a bit technical but it is along the lines I was expecting.' We acknowledge the contribution of such thinking, at least to the extent

Entity Something that exists as a solid or concrete thing. May refer to human institutions, such as organizations, as well as to objects.

that it highlights how, in work organizations, there is a great deal of emphasis on the means to achieve what are presumed to be shared objectives. In families or in friendship groups, in contrast, doing things in a formal and efficient, instrumental manner (see definitions in Box 1.10) is not ordinarily a priority. Instead, there is greater emphasis upon preserving the informal quality (e.g., closeness and intimacy) of our relationships. In this respect, there is logic in emphasizing how formality and instrumental reason is largely associated with the impersonal criteria of, for example, appointment and promotion based primarily upon qualifications and/or measurable length of service.[3]

- 'Organization refers to social arrangements such as factories, bureaucracies, armies, research and development teams and so on, created to achieve technical, productive ends.' (David Buchanan and Andrei Huczynski, 1997/2013, p. 552.)
- 'An organization is a consciously coordinated social unit, composed of two or more people, that functions on a relatively continuous basis to achieve a common goal or set of goals. It's characterized by formal roles that define and shape the behaviour of its members.' (Stephen P. Robins, 2003, p. 2.)

Box 1.10
Mainstream
entitative definitions
of 'organization'

In short, mainstream definitions are inclined to reflect and reinforce the common sense understanding of 'organizations' as *entities* consisting of a distinguishing set of characteristics including roles and positions that delineate the boundaries of responsibility and discretion (see Box 1.11).

Like the common sense idea of education as something that occurs within specific organizations, we are not convinced by the definitions provided in Box 1.10. That is not because we consider them to be wide of the mark but because we regard them as unhelpfully limiting and potentially misleading. They reflect a view of those occupying senior ranks of organizations favoured by their designers, and it is one that portrays organizations as malleable, instrumental tools for achieving their established objectives. Minimal attention is given to the conflicting priorities of other members of the organization, stakeholders (e.g., suppliers, local community) or the dangers in managing organizations as if such conflicts were of little consequence.

The notion of role is not unlike that used in the theatre but the script is unwritten and therefore, in principle, more open to interpretation, improvisation and inspiration than is the case for the actor. A role consists of a set of expectations and obligations. To the extent that people identify with these roles as a source of security and/or sense of power, they operate to constrain the individual almost as much as scripts constrain actors on stage.

Box 1.11
Roles, security and power

Definitions found in mainstream textbooks may appear to be uncontroversial and politically neutral, but this is far from the case. Their adequacy and credibility can be challenged on account of the exclusion of issues of power, domination and exploitation from their presentation and analysis of the staple topics of OB. Their contents operate to discipline how organizations are thought about and how we act within them. Mainstream texts invite us to accept their knowledge of organizations without presenting alternatives, and without actively encouraging us to reflect critically upon their analyses and prescriptions. To assume that organizations are created and/or maintained simply 'to achieve technical, productive ends' excludes consideration of many (mixed) 'motives' and 'preoccupations' that inspire and shape the design, development and everyday operation of the activities that comprise organizations. To believe (commonsensically) in the entity view is the equivalent of thinking of the sun rising, rather than the earth rotating.

A process view

To say that organization is a process rather than an entity is not to deny that there are activities occurring that are identifiable as 'organized', and that they are located, as it were, in organizations. By conceiving of organization as a process, however, the focus of analysis is not upon organizations as things or collections of elements, but upon processes of organizing wherever organized activities occur (see Box 1.12).

The concept of 'the organization' is extremely difficult to define and, additionally, depends upon what use is to be made of the definition. ... For this reason, *our focus is not on organization as a thing but on organization as process*: the activity of organizing and being organized. All particular organizations are examples of this process ...
Source: N. Jackson and P. Carter (2006), p. 7; emphasis added.

Box 1.12
A process view of 'organization'

The process view draws our attention to the ways in which organizing, in diverse settings, is accomplished through social interactions in which we seek to manage ourselves as well as others. It understands organizational behaviour as a process of skilful negotiation in accomplishing whatever is done. A process view might perhaps be seen as 'more theoretical', and yet it is arguably more focused on the practices that comprise organization than is the entity approach. An entity definition is strongly associated with abstracted prescriptions and models, such as the allocation of tasks, the grouping of activities, systems of measurement and reward and so on. In contrast, the process view considers the concrete activities and interactions that comprise organizing as a dynamic activity.

A concept view

The difficulty of single, universal definitions – whether 'entity' or 'process' – is that they do not take account of how definitions are framed and are changed in relation to how they are invoked in particular contexts. We see no problem, in principle, in engaging alternative definitions of organization – entity, process, etc., – for different purposes. But it would be devious not to declare our own preference for a third, 'concept' view of organizing and organization. In doing so, we acknowledge the meaning of organization(s) to be multiple and contested. Does this imply that differences over the meaning of organization can be settled? In our view, they cannot: each definition, or way of conceiving of organization, is partial and political as well as contextually meaningful. It is partial not in the sense that it reveals just one aspect of organization, but, rather, it is partial because each definition supports a *particular* view, and it necessarily excludes other ways of thinking about organization. It is political because each definition invites us to 'see' and *organize the world* in particular ways.

What makes the 'concept' view distinctive? It understands 'organization' as, first and foremost, a word that assumes a variety of meanings and exerts a number of (often powerful) effects. It is recognized that 'organization' *can* be conceived as an entity; and it *can* also be conceived as a process. At the same time, it insists that organization is not reducible to an entity or a process. Organization is, rather, a concept to which a variety of qualities and meanings may be attributed – including, of course, the view that it is a concept. The entity and process views render organizations identifiable as social units or as examples of organizing activities. The concept view draws attention to how all definitions are politically charged as they construe activity in *particular* ways, and anticipate or constitute the very behaviour they claim only to describe. In this sense, ideas of organization do not just describe but also implicity call for, and so tacitly or explicitly *prescribe* (i.e., outline what should happen); and these ideas can be highly powerful in directing and disciplining the behaviour of their members. That is what makes them partial and political.

The principal merit of identifying organization as a concept is that it disrupts the tendency to assume that language (e.g., organization) reflects or captures some element(s) of the world external to it – such as the features attributed to 'entities' and 'processes'. The concept view thereby reminds us of our involvement, as subjects or agents,

Thinkpoint 1.4

It's kind of hard to define ... Given our concern to make studying organizations more interesting and connected to everyday life, you might justifiably object that our attention to definitions of organization is rather contradictory. Surely, you might say, definitions are abstract and boring; and that is why, in everyday life, we prefer simply to 'point' to the object that we are talking about rather than rigorously define it. Our response is that definitions remain important for communication. Clarifying how terms are being defined can limit talking at cross-purposes. Even so, we prefer to regard definitions as 'views'. The term 'definition' tends to imply that words can capture the basic features or essence of what they aspire to describe, whereas 'view' better conveys our understanding that words operate to make us see, make sense of, and enact or perform the world around us in particular ways.

in helping to produce, sustain and change the organization(s) – as entity or process – that otherwise may appear(s) to exist independently of us. The concept view also serves to remind us that there is no one universal or authoritative way to define or study organizations. When we accept or adopt a particular view, we are engaging in a political, reality-defining act. This recalls how 'knowledge is power'. In that moment of decision, we act in a way that construes any 'object' (e.g., organization) as 'this' rather than 'that'. It follows that different definitions of 'organization' should *not* be evaluated according to their claimed correspondence to what they aspire to describe but, rather, in terms of their conditions – what makes them possible and plausible – and their consequences in relation to whatever values are prioritized.

When we examine different definitions of organizations, it is tempting, yet ultimately mistaken, to ask the question: 'How realistic is this view?' The difficulty with this question is that it assumes that we already know reality, and so are able to evaluate definitions according to their correspondence with it. On reflection, this seems unlikely. We have no direct access to social reality, and so we rely upon a set of interpretations, past experiences, prejudices and hunches to develop a view of it, and to evaluate our sense of it. In this process, we affirm, refine or discard our interpretations and (re)direct our actions. Consideration of diverse views can open up alternative lines of action and/or provide ways of challenging dominant thinking, but their summation does not produce a more comprehensive grasp or map of the terrain. Attention is more appropriately directed to scrutinizing the values, preferences and *effects* embedded in different conceptions of organization and organizing.

DISTINCTIVENESS OF WORK ORGANIZATION: INSTRUMENTAL RATIONALITY

> Bureaucratic work shapes people's consciousness in decisive ways. Among other things, it regularizes people's experience of time and indeed routinizes their lives by engaging them on a daily basis in rational, socially approved, purposive action. (Jackall, 1998, pp. 5–6)

Community and family are conserving institutions. In general, their members act to maintain stability and to prevent, or at least to slow down, change. But the modern organization is a destabilizer. It must be organized for innovation, and innovation, as the great Austro-American economist Joseph Schumpeter said, is 'creative destruction'. (Drucker, 1992, p. 96)

Earlier, when considering the entity view of organizations, we noted how organizations are conventionally and commonsensically associated with the use of instrumentally rational means to achieve explicit purposes or goals (see Box 1.13). This rationality is reflected in the definitions of organization provided by the entity view, where 'organization' is conceived largely in terms of the technical or functional means to achieve 'a common set of goals'. The entity view is a product of instrumental rationality that its adoption serves to advance. It has come to be regarded as commonsensical as soon as we use the word organization. We repeatedly draw upon the entity view of organization when we talk about organizations (as entities) pursuing objectives, or refer to managers in organizations engineering employee loyalty.

We have also suggested that processes of *organizing* occur within different kinds of institutions (e.g., the family or peer groups) and also not confined to organizations. We have differentiated (work) organizations from other institutions by their degree of formality and impersonality. While instrumental rationality may be present to some degree in many institutions, it is most dominant and legitimate within (work) organizations, although clearly highly visible in political institutions. This is why we describe them as organizations, rather than families or communities.

However, given the pervasiveness of instrumental rationality in modern societies, it would be surprising if it did not also extend to family life and friendship groups, which may indeed come to resemble organizations when planning, resourcing and implementing an event or set of tasks. Consider throwing a party. Someone proposes a party and individuals or groups respond by agreeing to take on particular tasks such as arranging an appropriate venue, doing the invitations, ordering or preparing the food and drink, etc. This way of 'making it happen' is

**Box 1.13
Instrumental
rationality**

An instrumentally rational organization or person is concerned primarily, if not exclusively, with the most efficient means to achieve specific ends or objectives. The *value* of those objectives is taken for granted and therefore is not open to debate or challenge. One might suggest, for example, that private companies are preoccupied with establishing the best means to increase profits; or that public corporations are, in principle, concerned with the most efficient means of providing a public service such as health or education. Each is geared to increasing labour productivity and reducing the costs of production even if, in practice, such efforts are thwarted so that there is always 'more to do'.

widely regarded or calculated to be the least time-consuming and individually onerous way to organize such an event. So, a leisure group can, for limited periods, look not dissimilar to a work organization. You might raise the objection that this group does not get paid, or seek to make a profit. These are relevant distinctions but ones that define an *economic* work organization as opposed to an organization *per se*. What makes holding a party similar to a work organization is a degree of reliance upon instrumental rationality that supports the logic of a division and co-ordination of the labour involved in making it happen.

Conversely, managers often try to secure loyalty, co-operation and commitment from employees by emphasizing family and community values, such as solidarity. Of course, their primary motivation is often an instrumental one: they calculate, perhaps correctly, that developing a more attentive and friendly attitude towards their staff will improve morale and employee retention. A popular device for securing both co-operation and commitment is teamworking, drawn from team sports (see Chapter 4). Identification and solidarity with an 'in-group' in opposition to an 'out-group' is used as a competitive device for raising productivity. Where co-operation and collaboration between groups or teams is important, this pursuit of competitiveness may prove elusive and counterproductive.

A family can be seen as an economic work organization when, for instance, some of its members run a small business, such as the corner shop or a small farm. In such cases, there is some effective blending (or uneasy combination)

**Box 1.14
Community,
organization and
Manchester United**

Fans of Manchester United have appealed to family and community notions when seeking to question or resist multinationals taking over the club. In 2000 the community of fans demonstrated their power when Rupert Murdoch and his media empire tried to take over the club, partly to strengthen its TV rights monopoly over the most attractive football matches. The official fan club mobilized Manchester United fans to persuade the directors not to pursue the offer, and this probably had some effect. Eventually the Competition Policy Committee outlawed the bid on monopolistic grounds, but it is likely that the community protest had some effect on the outcome. It had much less effect, though not for want of trying, when Malcolm Glazier bought the club through enormous borrowing in 2005 and saddled what was previously the most profitable soccer club in the world with huge debts. Amidst considerable anger from the fans and even the wider public, Manchester United became a private company owned solely by Glazier, whose interest would seem to be the purely financial one of exploiting the brand to maximum effect.

of instrumentally rational principles, such as a division of labour with respect to particular tasks (and associated responsibilities), and other, familial values that demand a degree of flexibility and commitment – qualities in a workforce that are more difficult to engender and mobilize in the absence of family and community ties. The significance and impact of instrumental rationality is well illustrated when, for example, a hobby or leisure activity, like playing football, is turned into a job that provides a source of income. What previously was pursued casually and in an ad hoc manner then becomes a target of more careful calculation, as time becomes money.

Game-playing and resistance

Colonized Process where usually a larger, richer or more powerful unit (organization, country) takes control of a weaker one – as when, for example, in the eighteenth and nineteenth centuries, European states appropriated the wealth and labour of Africa, Far East Asia, the Indian subcontinent, Latin America and the New World.

In practice, there can be considerable resistance to instrumental rationality in organizations. As we have repeatedly noted, other rationalities may be present that are resistant to being supplanted or **colonized** by instrumental rationality. People enter organizations with diverse values, objectives and senses of what is reasonable. They may also think, or be persuaded, that it is appropriate to leave behind or suspend their values and priorities when they are employed in the workplace. But they may also resent and resist punishments that are intended to secure their compliance. Or they may become more instrumentally rational – not by directly pursuing corporate objectives but by calculating how to set, protect and fulfil their own agendas, while managing an impression of dedication, loyalty and commitment.

Career systems allow some coincidence of personal and corporate agendas inasmuch as commitment can be acknowledged and rewarded with recognition, promotion and/or pay. But because of the complexities of organizations, where outcomes cannot easily be attributed directly to the efforts or skills of a single individual, there can be a lot of game-playing in which individuals claim responsibility for 'successful' outcomes and endeavour and shift the blame for 'unsuccessful' ones.

In schools and universities, students and staff engage in various forms of game-playing. Lectures, tutorials/seminars, and self-study or library work are regarded as the instrumentally rational way of enabling large numbers of students to gain degree-level education. This education is meant to involve a creative component that takes students beyond the comparatively programmed and packaged experience of pre-university education. In practice, many students (at least in management) discover that substantial elements of degree level work, especially during the first and second years, is less demanding and less creative than some of their pre-university courses.

There is often ambivalence about this. On the one hand, the lack of intellectual challenge can be frustrating and disappointing, with a possible sense of being cheated and this has become more intense as student fees have risen and there is a realization of the debt created through studying at university. On the other hand, it is a relief in that it leaves more time for leisure pursuits. What tends to emerge is a conspiracy of silence – a kind of grand game-playing – in which neither students nor staff are inclined to acknowledge this particular 'elephant in the room'. Staff say that some creative input into essays is required but then often penalize students when it appears. To do otherwise, would require considerable time in assessing the merit of eccentric approaches that deviate from model answers, which are often required to standardize assessment processes.

Less-privileged (i.e., lower-ranking) staff in organizations generally have fewer opportunities to play games that substantially improve their material (income) or symbolic (social status) wealth. Nonetheless, they may pretend to be committed while remaining psychologically distant from what they are doing. Staff may daydream or spend much of

Sabotage Conscious intention to disrupt 'normal service' or production. It is often considered a deviant activity.

their time chatting except when the supervisor appears, at which time they put their heads down and give the impression of being engaged on the task. Occasionally, resistance to the instrumentally rational pursuit of production goals will be more disruptive or subversive. Workers may purposely slow down the machine or even **sabotage** technologies by causing them to fail. In this way, staff clearly demonstrate the dependence of managers and shareholders upon their productive efforts. This dependence is even more dramatically exposed when there is a strike.

Theory and practice

An underlying assumption of educational provision, including the delivery of OB modules, is that exposure to academic or 'scientific' knowledge about behaviour in organizations will make workers, and especially managers, more efficient and effective. This view is seductive but also problematic. Let us imagine someone who possesses a first degree in business studies followed by an MBA, yet he or she is notoriously bad at organizing and managing people. Such a manager has sat through numerous courses, including OB modules, to gain these qualifications, and has also passed examinations that apparently demonstrate an expert knowledge of the field. So, why doesn't this expertise translate itself into effective ways of managing and organizing people?

We doubt that there is a simple or universal answer to this question. To assume that there is would be to fall into the trap of believing that the equivalent of a medical model is appropriate for 'treating' problems attributed to organizations: all that is required is to diagnose what is wrong, prescribe the medicine and await the recovery. The assumption that organizations can be likened to the human body has attracted many students, and particularly management consultants, who propose a whole range of prescriptions for diverse symptoms of 'organizational ill health!' We have yet to find the organizational equivalent of the aspirin, let alone antibiotics; and we argue that we never will because organizations are not the same as bodies. To put this another way, the theory – including its conception of the relationship between practice and theory – is poorly aligned with the practice.

Nor are organizations like machines even though this has been another popular metaphor for thinking about organizations, with the assumption that knowledge of engineering will yield effective solutions to perceived problems. Some of the most prominent classical, and contemporary theorists of organization (e.g., Fayol, Taylor, Crosby and Deming) were trained as engineers who have sought to treat organizations as machines in order to bridge the gap between theory and practice in one 'quick fix'. Our own view is that thinking drawn from the social sciences rather than biology or engineering is more relevant and instructive. Ideas of **contextual embeddedness**, for example, can help us to explore possible reasons for the gap between theory and practice.

Contextual embeddedness
Way in which any action on the part of, for example, managers or employees, is ascribed different meaning and significance depending on the context in which it occurs. Highlights the historical and cultural conditioning (and relativity) of what may appear to be normal and natural.

On the basis of what we have explored so far, we can sketch a number of reasons for the theory–practice gap, and we invite you to add others:

- Theory presented in textbooks provides an over-rosy or 'idealized' view of complex behaviour, leading to simplistic interventions. When textbook knowledge fails to appreciate particular, contextually embedded aspects of the situation, it offers seemingly universal (e.g., 'best practice') but locally inappropriate solutions to problems.
- Students often view knowledge of organizations and management instrumentally merely as a way to secure qualifications. In such learning, there is little thought for, or grasp of, the messy practice of managing and organizing. Knowledge is often inappropriately regarded as a reliable instrument of power and thereby applied mechanistically or naively to practice in ways that overlook the dependence of managers upon those they manage.
- Politics and power operate to frustrate consultants' and managers' efforts to reorganize activities by applying currently fashionable theories, even of the most sophisticated variety. Attempts to impose control frequently provoke resistance that is unanticipated, or is dismissed as 'irrational' or temporary, when it is assumed that those being managed will share managers' priorities.

- The practice of managing and organizing involves, above all else, interaction with people – colleagues and superiors as well as subordinates. There is little in management textbooks, or indeed in education and training, that directly addresses this critical issue.

What other possible factors behind the theory–practice divide can you think of?

We have cautioned against using common sense as a guide to the study of organization (see earlier examples). Yet we also recognized how it is adopted uncritically to guide management practice: Jackie was hardly consulting a textbook when running the pub for the weekend. She just drew on her everyday experience of organizing, and as we have said, this is extensive for us all. Every day of our lives we are involved in a great deal of organizing. Some of this, of course, we have learned consciously at school or at home. Knowing this, the managers of the pub could assume that Jackie would be able to add up the takings at the end of the day and communicate with the other bar staff. Yet, as we saw, in the case of Christine, not all such tasks are simple. What Jackie did not appreciate or anticipate was how Christine would interpret, and react to, the landlord's decision, and how this would result in an embarrassing and threatening display of defiance. Despite taking a business studies degree, what Jackie lacked was a knowledge of organizational behaviour that would have sensitized her to this possibility, and thereby enabled her to think through how she might deal with such an eventuality. Of course, even if she had used this text to study OB, we cannot guarantee that she would have coolly applied its insights rather than reacted spontaneously as she did!

DISTINCTIVENESS OF THIS TEXT

The curriculum and teaching of OB has given priority to ideas that are conservative and broadly pro-managerial. OB has been superficially pro-managerial in the sense of presuming that managers *alone* have a monopoly of knowledge of, and an almost divine right to determine how, work should be organized. As a consequence, the orthodox treatment of OB has taken the form of a technology of control, with each of its topics (e.g., motivation, leadership) being presented as an element of an (instrumentally rational) control toolkit. Ideas and perspectives that do not fit neatly into this toolkit have been either ignored or they have been treated as just one more dimension to consider. Efficiency, performance and/or profit are seen to inform everything that occurs in organizations, whereas social and moral responsibility are either seen as outside the sphere of OB or they are simply tagged on as an afterthought. Where ethical issues are included, the focus is on compliance with codes of conduct and regulations so as to avoid bad publicity or financial sanctions against the organization. In short, the concern with business ethics (see Chapter 15) is largely another instrumental means to the end of preserving the status quo by reducing the risk of reputational damage.

Our text attempts to be different primarily by presenting and contrasting alternative conceptions – mainstream and critical – of OB. In each of the following chapters, an account of how the subject matter is presented in mainstream texts serves to familiarize the reader with how the field is conventionally understood. However, the orthodox narrative is not presented here as an end in itself. Instead – as we have shown in relation to the entity and process concepts of organization – mainstream or orthodox thinking is engaged as a foil for introducing unorthodox thinking on OB (see Box 1.15).

Our approach leads us to recognize and stress how instrumental rationality, as embraced by mainstream thinking, is neither politically nor morally neutral. Notably, it presents and cultivates a particular, **impersonal and disembodied** way of thinking and living. It is, of course, ironic that this ethos is introduced, applied and celebrated by economically and politically interested managers and employees who are gendered and embodied, sexually charged, ethnically located, emotionally involved and more or less passionate human beings. Interests, emotions, bodies and identities are fundamental to our lived experience, whether at work or not (Knights and Willmott, 1999/2004). We challenge the very idea that life in organizations is separate from life outside them, and vice versa. To explore this connection, contributors to this text have been guided by a framework of six interrelated concepts.

Impersonal and disembodied Relates to the way that our relations with one another can lack any sense of personal intimacy and be so instrumental and calculative or cerebral and cognitive (i.e., linked to powers of the intellect and logic) as to deny any bodily and emotional content.

Box 1.15
Orthodox and critical wings of organizational behaviour

WHAT DO WE MEAN BY 'ORTHODOXY'?

The term orthodox is used to describe what most people *currently* recognize as a legitimate way of doing or thinking about things – it is conventional and conservative, or a continuation of the way things have traditionally been done. The orthodox, or mainstream, view regards managing primarily as a technical activity and work organization as a neutral instrument for achieving shared goals.

WHAT DO WE MEAN BY 'CRITICAL'?

The term 'critical' is used to signal an interest in interrogating and challenging received wisdom – both theory and practice – by drawing upon social science perspectives that are routinely ignored or excluded from OB. The critical view regards organization as a political instrument for achieving contested goals.

Of course, if widely accepted, a critical approach may become the orthodoxy. Examples that spring to mind include the challenge to religion made by science, the challenge to monarchy posed by republicanism, the discrediting of imperialism generated by anti-colonialists, and the challenge to anti-apartheid in South Africa represented by the (after the fact) heroic figure of Nelson Mandela. These examples also suggest that critical thinking fosters progressive change whereas orthodox thinking tends to favour the preservation, or glacial reform, of the status quo.

Six key concepts

The central concepts that provide the framework for all the chapters are explored in the Appendix to this text.

We have deployed the six concepts throughout this chapter but we now articulate them more systematically, specifically in relation to Jackie's experiences in the pub, in order to develop an appreciation of their dynamic interrelationship.

If you return to the case study, you will recall that when first standing at the bar Jackie had felt uncomfortable and perhaps a little *insecure*, as all the students had already left the pub to go on to one of the clubs. Our assumption is that uncertainties and associated insecurities are a widespread feature of everyday life, which of course includes working in organizations. They may range from a general feeling of uneasiness to more fundamental questioning of its purpose, accompanied by unvoiced doubts such as 'is this all there is?'

Box 1.16
Insecurity

Insecurity typically arises when people are unable to interpret a situation in a way that confirms their own sense of themselves – for example, as a 'bright student' or as a 'caring person'. Social situations are especially difficult in this respect since we can never be fully sure of, let alone control, how others view us. Yet, it is through our sense of how others view us that we develop and evaluate self-identity. 'Knowing' someone reduces the stress or tension of this uncertainty in social encounters. However, this uncertainty cannot be entirely eliminated as people are continually changing as a result of new circumstances, experiences and relationships.

When the local lads who sat at Jackie's table started criticizing students, Jackie felt that her own *identity* was being undermined and was under attack. People routinely attribute an identity to others, in part as a way of dealing with their own uncertainties and insecurities. We also, often subconsciously, take on identities and only realize the extent of our identifications when they are challenged. Much of the time we are unconsciously as well as consciously performing in well rehearsed ways that reproduce a sense of identity (or identities – student/non-student, brother/sister, son/daughter, man/woman, etc.) that we have largely taken for granted.

Identity refers to how people are identified or classified – as a man, brother, student, fighter, etc. Our sense of self-worth or significance is related to our social identity. But an identity is not only an image presented by oneself or attributed to us by others. It is also associated with expectations and obligations about how to behave. When how we behave is consistent with what others expect, there will tend to be a reassuring coherence between our sense of self-identity and the social identity ascribed to us.

Box 1.17
Identity

Returning to Jackie, on her own in the pub, she felt *powerless* to intervene when the locals were ridiculing students and, by implication she could not defend her own sense of identity. While partly realistic in that she was outnumbered, Jackie's sense of impotence also resulted from a commonsense belief in power as a possession – the lads had it, Jackie lacked it. But it is perhaps more illuminating and empowering to conceive of power relationally, as reflecting and reproducing who we are and what we do. Thinking of power in this way enables us to consider the extent to which the lads and Jackie were both objects and agents of power (e.g., the power that defined Jackie as a student and the power that sees strength in numbers) – power that placed them in a particular relation to each other.

Power has traditionally been associated with the coercive and repressive means through which, respectively, a class of capitalists exploits proletarian labour (Marx), political elites control the masses (Pareto) or management cadres dominate subordinate employees (Burnham). Such concepts of power see it as a wholly negative control of one class, group or person over another. More recently, an alternative has rejected this coercive conception of power. Instead, by allowing that there are no social relations that are 'free' of power, power is seen not just as constraining in its effects but also productive (Foucault, 1980, 1982). An individual or group can exercise power positively by transforming individuals into subjects who find meaning, purpose and identity in the practices that it demands or expects (Knights, 1992). The effect of power can be to make those over whom it is exercised more creative, productive and powerful, which, of course, does not imply that they always and everywhere accept or defer to the ostensibly powerful. Sometimes subjects will exercise power be transformed by power-infused practices to resist what is demanded or expected of them.

Box 1.18
Power

Why did Jackie feel powerless to resist the negative stereotypes of students that the local lads were constructing? Largely it was because of being outnumbered and marginalized, with this *inequality* making her feel insecure in a way not dissimilar to when she had stood alone at the bar. This situation of inequality would have been reversed had she come to the pub earlier when the students outnumbered the locals. However, were we to examine the future prospects of the students compared to those locals who had not attended university, we would probably conclude that many of the locals suffered more from inequality – in terms of housing, employment opportunities, life expectancy, pension provision, etc. – than the students.

Inequality describes differences in wealth, status and opportunity, such as the inequalities of income and privilege between managers and employees and between men and women, or those suffered by ethnic minorities. These inequalities may be seen as institutionalized insofar as they are embedded in, and reproduced by, work relations (e.g., hierarchy and job segregation by gender or ethnicity) and employment practices (e.g., recruitment and promotion). They are also reproduced by other social formations such as markets, where inequalities of wealth are reinforced because money makes more money, and inheritance reproduces intergenerational inequality.

Box 1.19
Inequality

It is this *knowledge* of how inequality works that can help explain the verbal abuse of the students. Arguably, the locals were feeling swamped by students who had begun to 'take over' a pub that they regarded as 'theirs'. This antagonism was, in all likelihood, prompted and fuelled by resentment of how students can trade on their knowledge, in the form of degrees, to secure comparatively well-paid jobs and a privileged social status in life.

Knowledge is sometimes referred to as power ('power is knowledge'), and this is probably because, when exercising power, knowledge is very frequently drawn upon. Knowledge – both everyday knowledge and more specialist knowledge – leads us to interpret and produce the world in particular, historically and culturally specific, ways. Just think of how disempowered we feel when, as we move out of our sphere of knowledge, we do not *know* the language or *know* the culture.

Knowledge and power are so intimately related that Foucault (1980) insisted on speaking about power/knowledge relations. Acquiring knowledge through education is something that, as a reader of the textbook, you may be doing not for its own sake but as a means of getting a 'good' job. But it is not just that knowledge is a resource for the exercise of power. Knowledge is also often an effect of, or produced by, the exercise of power. For example, the very exercise of power by a coaching team over a football club will generate knowledge of how to exercise that power, and this is why nothing is seen to substitute for experience.

Box 1.20
Knowledge

Perhaps the reason why the local lads were antagonistic to the students was because they resent the *freedom* that students appear to enjoy. Students do not have to get up at a certain time every day for work, enjoy long holidays, experience few controls, etc. The locals overhear them recounting exciting experiences of travelling to exotic locations during vacations and they always seem to be partying.

Box 1.21
Freedom

Freedom has often been defined as autonomy or an absence of constraints on the individual. We all may seek fewer constraints on our choices and behaviour. But a moment's reflection would suggest that an absence of all constraints would be chaotic. We are urged and disciplined to exercise our freedom (and power) responsibly so that it at least does not directly violate others' freedom; and, of course, failure to do so may provoke others to retaliate by restricting our freedom. We can see here that our very concept of freedom is based on a (humanistic) constraint of being respectful to the 'other', or upon an instrumental calculation that it will limit our options. With the development of the environmental movement, respect is extended from the world of human beings to that of nature. Human freedom or autonomy then, as Foucault (1982) reminds us, is both liberating and disciplining.

We apply this conceptual framework when interpreting the key elements of, and present an alternative to, the orthodox or mainstream treatment of OB topics. In addition to providing some insights into behaviour in organizations, the six concepts can readily be related to students' everyday experiences, thereby making the study of OB more meaningful and memorable. We are not of course claiming that these are the only relevant concepts for making sense of OB, or that the combination of these concepts is all that matters. Clearly we could think of other concepts (e.g., emotion, rationality) that are helpful for understanding behaviour in organizations, including Jackie's experiences and actions. However, when speaking about Jackie's emotions or rationality, it would, we believe, be difficult to ignore one or more of the six concepts. That is because her emotions revolve around feelings of insecurity and concerns about identity, and her rationality is dependent on (because it is exercised through) her freedom, knowledge and power. We view Jackie exhibiting rationality and emotion when maintaining her position within a system of social inequality – for example, by succeeding in education, and through her social skills and capacity to present a favourable impression to the landlord and landlady, thereby gaining a job as a barmaid.

Each concept in our framework is, we suggest, intuitively relevant for understanding people in organizations. We are all routinely ascribed an *identity* – as students, academics, employees, customers, suppliers and so on – that will have some effect upon how we understand, present (and manage) ourselves. We may invest in more than one identity, and sometimes these may be in conflict. You might, at this point, return to the case study of the pub to list the different identities that relate to Jackie and then consider whether there are conflicts between them. Or you might consider the issue of gender and sexual preference. These are important identity issues for most people. Misconceptions and misunderstandings in these areas can cause considerable offence, embarrassment and pain when they are not a source of humour and pleasure. When others (e.g., customers) identified Jackie as a barmaid, she was seen differently. Again, you might wish to reflect upon the possible explanations of such different reactions.

As employees, we may comply with certain expectations but we may also seek to challenge and change them. In dealing with others, including those who hope to persuade or coerce us to perform organizational tasks, we mobilize everyday *knowledge* of others as well as of ourselves. In doing so, we exercise both *power* and *freedom*. In this process, we encounter relations of *inequality* as we discover that others have more money/income or status than ourselves. This, combined with the difficulties of fulfilling or wanting to challenge other people's expectations, can make us *insecure* – as Jackie felt when, as a student, she felt personally subjected to a character assassination of students by the locals, although she might have just laughed it off as petty and a form of envy.

This way of thinking about behaviour in organizations, which we have illustrated by reference to the example of Jackie's experience, is intended to connect directly to students' experiences. Regardless of whether you are familiar with pub culture, the considerations and associated insights introduced in this chapter rarely surface in mainstream, orthodox OB texts. Why not? On the whole, orthodox texts are preoccupied with conveying an exhaustive and comprehensive list of theories and topics; and they are comparatively forgetful of their readership, except as containers into which to pour the prescribed knowledge. Such texts may cover the literature in exhaustive detail, but how much is retained beyond the examination?

In this text we are concerned to show how behaviour in organizations can be illuminated and made meaningful to readers. We do this principally through the style and format of the book that is underpinned by our conceptual framework. The framework provides a basic analytical *aide-memoire* that has wide applicability for interpreting and participating in the dynamics of OB. We hope that you will continue to find it useful when you have completed your studies and are facing the challenges of working with people in organizations.

References

Brooks, I. (2008) *Organizational Behaviour: Individuals, Groups and the Organization,* fourth edn, London: FT Pitman.

Buchanan, D. and Huczynski, A. (2016) *Organizational Behaviour: An Introductory Text,* ninth edn, London: Prentice Hall.

Clark, P. (1983) *The English Alehouse: A Social History 1200–1850,* London: Longman.

Drucker, P. (1992) 'The New Society of Organizations', *Harvard Business Review,* 70(5): 95–104.

Foucault, M. (1980) *Power/Knowledge,* edited by Colin Gordon, London: Tavistock.

Foucault, M. (1982) 'The Subject and Power', in H. Dreyfus and P. Rabinow (eds) *Michel Foucault: Beyond Structuralism and Hermeneutics,* Brighton: Harvester Press.

Hadley, Philip. (2015) 'The Four Big Myths of UK Rail Privatisation', available at actionforrail.org/the-four-big-myths-of-uk-rail-privatisation/ [Accessed 3rd November 2016].

Huczynski, A. and Buchanan, D. (2010/2013) *Organizational Behaviour: An Introductory Text,* seventh edn/eighth edn, London: Financial Times/ Prentice Hall.

Jackall, R. (1998) *Moral Mazes: The World Corporate Managers,* New York: Oxford University Press.

Jackson, N. and Carter, P. (2006) *Rethinking Organizational Behaviour,* 2nd edn, London: Financial Times/Prentice Hall.

Kinicki, A. and Kreitner, R. (2009) *Organizational Behaviour: Key Concepts, Skills and Best Practices,* New York: McGraw-Hill.

Knights, D (1992) 'Changing Spaces: The Disruptive Power of Epistemological Location for the Management and Organizational Sciences', *Academy of Management Review,* 17:3, 514–36.

Knights, D and McCabe, D. (2015) 'Masters of the Universe: Demystifying leadership in the context of the 2008 Financial Crisis', *British Journal of Management,* 26: 197–210.

Knights, D. and Willmott, H. C. (1999/2004) *Management Lives: Power and Identity in Work Organizations,* London: Sage.

Robins, S. P. *Essentials of Organizational Behaviour,* seventh edn, Upper Saddle River, NJ: Prentice Hall, 2003, p. 2.

Robins, S. P., Judge, T. A. and Cambell, T. (2010) *Organizational Behaviour,* London: Financial Times/ Prentice Hall.

Strange, S. (1997) *Casino Capitalism,* Manchester: Manchester University Press.

Watson, D. (2002) 'Home From Home: The Pub and Everyday Life', in T. Bennett and D. Watson (eds) *Understanding Everyday Life,* Oxford: Blackwell.

Willmott, H. C. (2011a) 'Back to the Future: What Does Studying Bureaucracy Tell Us?', in S. Clegg, M. Harris and H. Hopfl (eds) *Managing Modernity: Beyond Bureaucracy?,* Oxford University Press.

Willmott, H. C. (2011b) 'Enron Narrative', in M. Painter-Morland and R. Ten Bos (eds) *Continental Philosophy and Business Ethics,* Cambridge University Press.

Notes

1 In addition, substantial capital gains were made by those who bought shares in privatized industries at knock-down prices, provided that they sold their investments before the privatization bubble was burst by scandal and subsequent regulations.

2 We have direct experience of contract cleaners rarely doing more than emptying the waste bins in universities, but in hospitals cleanliness is more than a mere aesthetic.

3 These are the kinds of criteria used to justify the shortlisting of candidates. Thereafter, other less readily auditable and quantifiable criteria come into play, such as assessments of their character and ability to lead, or the anticipated – genuine or contrived – knock-on effects of appointing particular individuals.

The human dimension

2 **Motivation and the self**

3 **Individual differences, personality and self**

4 **Groups and teams at work**

5 **Managing people: Contexts of HRM, diversity and social inequality**

6 **Knowledge and learning: Consuming management?**

PART I

Part I examines a number of topics and themes that are closely interrelated in the mainstream literature. These chapters draw primarily on a psychological approach to understanding organizational behaviour in which the individual in the group is centre stage. They complement this orientation by drawing extensively on a wider social science literature and, in particular, on a critical literature that pays attention to their wider significance in relation to society and politics. These chapters consider the standard approaches to managing people at work through motivation, attitude and personality analysis, teamworking and learning strategies, but challenge their assumptions so as to provide alternative insights.

2 Motivation and the self

JOHN ROBERTS

Aims of the chapter

This chapter will:

- Explain why the study of motivation at work has received so much attention.

- Explore some of the key ideas that have marked the evolution of management's understanding of the different factors that shape motivation.

- Examine some of the key mainstream studies of motivation.

- Explore some of the important ideas that have marked the evolution of critical understandings of motivation theory.

- Examine some of the critical studies of motivation.

- Explore the linkages between insecurity, identity and the workings of power relationships in order to better understand motivation.

Key concepts and learning objectives

By the end of this chapter you should understand:

- The key mainstream approaches to motivation, as well as their limitations.

- Some of the shared and opposed interests that shape motivation at work.

- How our sense of self is socially constructed and maintained.

- How our so-called 'ego needs' mean that we are always vulnerable to the attitudes of others towards us, and how they serve as a key way in which our conduct can be controlled and influenced.

- How power comes to work largely through processes of self-discipline in which we appraise and judge ourselves against an internalized standard of how we should be.

Overview and key points

When we get a job there is typically an employment contract with the organization, which specifies what we will do, for whom and for how long, and what we will get in return by way of pay, holidays, etc. But the contract does not determine what then happens. There can be a huge difference in both the quantity and quality of our work depending on our experiences and attitudes, and the response of others to us. It is this difference that is the focus of 'motivation theory' and both manager and employee have an intense interest in the subject. As employees, given that work occupies such a large part of our lives, we have a very strong interest in the satisfaction to be drawn from work. As a manager, a highly motivated employee is likely to be both happier and also more productive. He or she will therefore be both easier to manage, though possibly more demanding, and will help realize the objectives by which the manager is judged and appraised. These dual interests in motivation have ensured that the search for the key to effective motivation has served as the 'holy grail' of management theory; a search for the key that will unlock the virtuous circle of productivity *and* satisfaction.

This chapter will first review some of the key mainstream ideas that emerged during the twentieth century as part of this quest for the secrets of what releases human energy and effort. We start with what are termed **content theories of motivation**; the ideas of Maslow on human needs and how these were developed by subsequent theorists of motivation such as McGregor, McClelland, Hertzberg and Hackman. We then look at **process theories of motivation**, Vroom's expectancy theory and contemporary theories of motivation and the emphasis they place on an employee's autonomy and self-motivation, supported by management empowerment.

In the second half of the chapter we will take a more critical look at what is involved in motivation. We look first at Marx's analysis of 'alienation' at work and his suggestion that in capitalism there is a fundamental conflict of interests between owners and their agents and employees. Second, we take a critical look at the current interest in promoting individual autonomy at work and suggest that motivation techniques now involve not just the use of economic insecurity but also the deliberate manipulation of a person's sense of self and self-worth.

Content theories of motivation These theories try to identify the specific factors – individual needs, task factors, management styles – that shape individual motivation.

Process theories of motivation These theories look at motivation as the outcome of a dynamic interaction between the person and their experiences of an organization and its management. Such processes depend critically on the sense individuals make of their experiences at work.

Thinkpoint 2.1

Think of two activities; one you really love doing and one that you really dislike. Compare the two different states of motivation associated with the two activities in terms of the effort you make, your focus and attention, the energy you have and your thoughts and emotions. If you think of yourself as a 'human resource' who would you wish to employ – the motivated or seriously unmotivated you?

MAINSTREAM APPROACHES TO MOTIVATION AND THE SELF
Introduction

Late in the nineteenth century Frederick Taylor developed one of the earliest conceptions of management and the management role – his 'principles of scientific management'. Here we merely want to touch on some of these principles as they reflect a set of assumptions about motivation against which many of the writers on whom we will later focus can be seen to be reacting and responding.

Taylor was the first person to attempt to provide a rationale for the emergent role of the manager in increasingly large American enterprises. The foreman or chargehand was no longer merely the stand-in for the absent owner, free to exercise power in a personalized and arbitrary fashion. Instead, Taylor drew upon the wider authority and methodology of science to offer a version of what the manager should do. The division of labour between worker and manager was seen in terms of a separation of the planning function from that of execution. It was the manager's job to make a 'scientific' study of tasks and on this basis to develop the most efficient form of work that could be taught to new employees. The division of labour could then be greatly extended, allowing relatively unskilled labour to be trained in the most efficient means for carrying out a particular part of a task. It was also part of the management task to then control this labour through close monitoring and through the use of piece rates to ensure that the economic rewards of work were tied to actual productivity. It is this attempt to relate reward to the efficiency of effort and output that has led many to insist that Taylor placed a primary motivational value upon money.

For Taylor there was no necessary conflict between the interests of workers and those of management. Instead, if managers were to exercise their responsibilities in the ways in which he described, then what was possible was a rational division of labour that made optimal use of the purely manual skills of labour through the mental skills associated with the study and optimization of work, planning and monitoring by managers. The laziness or 'systematic soldiering' that Taylor observed in employees could in this way be resolved in the service of both the organization and the employee. Both would gain economically from the application of this new managerial rationality.

The separation of mental and manual capabilities, the focus on the efficiency gains of an intense division of labour, coupled with management training and monitoring, offer us an early image of the beliefs and practices that shaped human motivation. One of the targets and exemplars for Taylor for these new management techniques was a pig-iron shoveller called Schmidt – a man who was seemingly deficient in all respects bar brute physical strength. Once his labour had been scientifically studied and analyzed, his capacity for shovelling increased enormously and seemed to offer clear evidence of the potential gains for all, including Schmidt, of this new scientific version of the manager's role in relation to labour.

In the 1920s and 1930s a set of American studies at the Western Electric Company, often referred to as the Hawthorne Experiments, began to unravel the assumptions of Taylor's early work. The experiments began with a scientific study of the impact of different levels of illumination on worker output. Much to the surprise of all those involved, output increased whatever adjustments were made to the level of lighting; a result that gradually led to the recognition of the importance of individuals' social needs. The economic atom that Schmidt symbolized is seen now as a person who craves the attention of the manager, and who, as a social being, is found to be highly responsive to the pressures brought to bear by his or her work group. While the Hawthorne studies are typically held to have founded the human relations movement, it was left to later theorists to draw out and develop the more complex view of human motivation that the studies began to uncover. In what follows we will briefly review some of the seminal studies and theories that then shaped something of a revolution in how managers were supposed to understand, and ideally practise, motivation.

Key problems

The major issues that mainstream motivation theory has sought to address are:

- What motivates a person? Should we look for the answer 'inside' the person in their 'needs' for money, status or power? Should we look outside at the work they do and how they are managed?
- Is there a universal truth to be discovered, or is motivation highly contingent and dependent on the specific character of a person and situation?
- How does motivation change over time? Is what motivates the same as what demotivates?
- Can my manager know more about what motivates me than I do, or does my motivation depend on the sense I make of my experiences?
- Can a manager motivate someone else or is motivation always something I do to myself?
- What allows or gets in the way of such self-motivation?

Hierarchy of needs Maslow suggested that individual needs were organized in a hierarchy from physiological needs, to safety needs, to needs for love, affection and belonging, to esteem needs and finally, at the top of the hierarchy, the need for self-actualization.

Key ideas and contributions

MOTIVATION: IT IS ABOUT FULFILLING HUMAN NEEDS (ABRAHAM MASLOW)

Although Maslow was writing over 60 years ago, his ideas about a **hierarchy of needs** have retained a peculiar currency. At the bottom of the hierarchy are what he called 'physiological' needs; the needs for food, sleep, drink, etc. Maslow suggests that while such needs are unsatisfied, then we are completely preoccupied by them and all our capacities are put to the service of meeting them. Other needs or concerns are in this way marginalized and become unimportant. But Maslow, writing in a US context, suggests that the dominance of such physiological needs is very rare; appetite should not be confused with hunger in this sense – men live by bread alone only when there is no bread.

So what happens when such physiological needs are routinely met? It is here that Maslow introduces his notion of a 'hierarchy of needs'. He suggests that as one level of need is met 'at once other (and "higher") needs emerge' and come to dominate. In this sense, the meeting of a need is important in allowing other, more social needs to emerge. At the same time, however, a need that is satisfied no longer motivates.

Case study 2.1
A problem (of motivation) at PYT plc (1)

Peter Drake has just been appointed as the Sales Manager of the UK Manchester office of PYT plc. He has been with PYT since leaving school nine years ago. At school he had done all right, and his teachers had told him that if he worked hard at his A levels he could get to college. Peter, however, was keen to get out and start earning some money as soon as possible, but he was clear that, unlike his dad who was a school caretaker, manual work was not for him; he wanted a job in an office. The job at PYT seemed ideal. He started as a telephone sales representative, and four years later became a section leader.

PYT had a contract with the national telephone company to publish a telephone directory of business services. Every business in the country had a free entry in the directory but PYT made its money from selling additional advertising space to individual businesses. Looking back, Peter thought that part of his success was simply a matter of good luck and timing. When he first joined PYT it had only been going for a year and he quickly discovered that there were rich pickings to be had. The product was new to the UK and the potential market for additional advertising was huge. The company did not put him straight on the phones but instead took him away for a two-week training course at a hotel in the south of England. Here he was taught all the benefits of the product and introduced to the skills of selling.

His mum and dad had always told Peter that he would go far because he had the 'gift of the gab' and telephone sales offered him the chance to make good use of this. For every bit of additional space he sold he was paid a commission that meant that, in a good month, he could add something like 50 per cent to his basic salary. Within a year he had bought himself a car and had moved into a shared flat in town. Compared to his friends who had gone to college, he had loads of money and the chance of getting on if he did well.

Peter had just got back from his first sales managers' meeting – a meeting of all the office, regional and national account managers, held in Birmingham with the sales director. The picture of the state of the company that Peter had gathered from this meeting was not very encouraging. Given the strength of PYT's sales training, new sales had always been good, but two problems had begun to emerge. The latest figures indicated that a growing number of their customers were not renewing their adverts from one year to the next. In the past this had not mattered much – there were plenty of new 'punters' to be caught – but the sales director had pointed out that, if current trends continued, in three years' time they would be losing more business than they were selling. Their licence for publishing the directory was also due for renewal in two years' time. Matters were possibly being made worse by the fact that staff turnover in the offices was approaching 100 per cent. Not only was this a big cost to PYT, given its initial training costs, but it also meant that there was no incentive for staff to be realistic in what they sold to customers. Staff would oversell one year and then leave rather than go back to the same customer a year later. At the meeting the sales director had announced a number of changes and initiatives that were to be introduced across the company to address the situation. There were to be immediate changes to the incentive system; in future staff would only be paid commission for any net gain in sales (new sales less dropout from the previous year). Managers were also encouraged to change the profile of the people they recruited; it was thought that older, more mature people would probably stay longer. Finally, there was the suggestion that part of the problem was poor management and Peter heard that he was to attend a one-week management development course next month.

QUESTION
Drawing on the above and your own experiences, what factors do you think might affect the motivation of a group of sales staff?

The second set of needs that Maslow identified in his hierarchy he termed 'safety' needs. Such a need for safety, Maslow suggests, is evidenced in our taste for routine and predictability. When safety is disturbed, panic or terror set in. Maslow suggests that, in developed societies, one must look to the neurotic or the 'economic or social' underdog to see where these needs dominate. According to Maslow (1989, p. 26): 'Their reaction is often to unknown, psychological dangers in a world that is perceived to be hostile, overwhelming and threatening. Such a person behaves as if a great catastrophe were almost always impending'.

As with physiological needs, once met safety needs no longer dominate attention and leave room for yet higher needs to emerge. The third set of needs to emerge is framed by Maslow in terms of needs for 'love, affection and belongingness'. While some of these needs may well be met through relationships outside work, in the context of work Maslow was thinking of a person's need to find their place within a group; a need to make contact and establish friendships with colleagues.

The fourth set of needs that emerge, once 'love' needs are met, Maslow termed 'esteem' needs. He describes these in the following terms: 'all people in our society (with a few pathological exceptions) have a need or desire for a stable, firmly based (usually) high evaluation of themselves, for self-respect, for self-esteem and for the esteem of others' (Maslow, 1989, p. 27). This, he suggests, should be based on real capacity, achievement and respect for others. He further divides these needs in terms of, first, 'the desire for strength, for achievement, for adequacy, for confidence in the face of the world, and for independence and freedom', and second, as the desire for 'reputation or prestige, recognition, attention, importance or appreciation'. If such needs are met, he suggests that they lead to feelings of 'self confidence, worth, strength, capability and adequacy, of being useful and necessary in the world'. If they are thwarted they lead to feelings of 'inferiority, of weakness and of helplessness'.

But even with the meeting of such 'esteem' needs, Maslow suggests that a 'new discontent and restlessness will soon develop', which arises from needs for what, at the top of the hierarchy, he terms the need for 'self-actualization' (see Chapter 3). He uses this term to refer to the desire for self-fulfilment; the desire to make actual all that is potential within the self.

Importantly, Maslow sees the thwarting of these basic needs as a source of sickness. For him a 'healthy man is primarily motivated by his needs to develop and actualize his fullest potentialities and capacities'. Such a notion of health is very demanding. Insofar as the pursuit of such self-actualizing needs characterizes only a few people in organizations, then the sad conclusion is that there is much sickness in our organizations.

Exercise 2.1

Consider the following questions:

1   From your own experience and what you know of the experiences of your parents, siblings or friends, what merits are there to Maslow's idea of a hierarchy of needs?
2   Think of occasions when each of the different needs – physiological, safety, love, esteem and self-actualization – have been dominant in your mind. What feelings arise with the satisfaction of each need? What feelings dominate when these needs are frustrated?
3   Can you see in others the dominance of different needs?
4   In terms of each set of needs, think about what might need to be done by colleagues, managers and those who design organizations to make the meeting of such needs possible.
5   Where in the hierarchy would you place money as a motivator?
6   What is your potential?
7   How 'sick' is our society in terms of the satisfactions it offers people in their work?

In what follows we will explore how Maslow's ideas have been taken up and developed in at least two different directions. The first looks at how behaviour at work, or the lack of motivation, may be the *unintended consequence* of how manager's think about employees – they simply do not understand their needs. The second takes these needs more seriously and then looks at the design of work to understand what motivates.

MOTIVATION: IT IS MANAGERS' ASSUMPTIONS THAT MATTER (DOUGLAS McGREGOR)

We turn to Douglas McGregor's work immediately after looking at Maslow because there is a clear and explicit link between Maslow's view of 'sickness' as the failure to be able to meet one's basic needs and McGregor's attempts to think this through in terms of the effects that *manager's own assumptions* have on how they then go about seeking to motivate others. While Maslow focused on defining a hierarchy of largely unconscious needs that shape conduct, McGregor is more interested in how managers' *beliefs* about what drives others (and themselves perhaps) feed through into their practice of motivation.

The story McGregor tells contrasts a conventional conception of management's task – **theory X** – with a new, theoretically informed theory Y. Theory X's propositions are as follows (McGregor, 1989, p. 315):

1 Management is responsible for organizing the elements of productive enterprise – money, materials, equipment, people – in the interest of economic ends.

2 With respect to people, this is a process of directing their efforts, motivating them, controlling their actions and modifying their behaviour to fit the needs of the organization.

3 Without this active intervention by management, people would be passive – even resistant – to organizational needs. They must therefore be persuaded, rewarded, punished and /or controlled – their activities must be directed.

Theory X McGregor used this term to characterize a set of negative assumptions by managers about the attitudes and capabilities of employees; people are passive and need to be persuaded, rewarded, punished and controlled if they are to align their efforts with the needs of the organization.

McGregor suggests that other, less conscious assumptions inform this conventional theory, including the belief that the average person is lazy, lacks ambition, prefers to be led and dislikes responsibility. These assumptions, he suggests, shape organizations in the way that they come to be embedded in structures, policies and practices.

It is not that these assumptions are wrong, but rather that they are *assumptions,* and, once embedded in management structures, policies and practices, they begin to have effects on how people behave. McGregor's innovation was to suggest that, while behaviour supporting the assumptions of theory X could easily be discovered in organizations, it was the result not of humans' inherent nature, but rather an unintended consequence of management philosophy, policies and practice. The problem of motivation lies not in the worker but in the mind and assumptions and resulting conduct of the manager.

It is at this point that McGregor draws on Maslow's work to offer a critique of current management practice. He suggests that arbitrary management action, uncertainty over continued employment, favouritism or discrimination, all serve to keep safety needs strong in the employment relationship. Similarly, he suggests that management can fear group resistance to the pursuit of its objectives and therefore leave what he calls employees' 'social' needs unsatisfied. In relation to the needs for self-esteem, status and respect, McGregor suggests that, at least at lower levels in the hierarchy, these needs are completely ignored, and thereby thwarted. This is even more so for the needs for self-actualization (McGregor, 1989, p. 320):

People, deprived of opportunities to satisfy at work the needs which are now important to them, behave exactly as we might predict – with indolence, passivity, resistance to change, lack of responsibility, unreasonable demands for economic benefits. It would seem that we are caught in a web of our own weaving.

McGregor then offers an alternative **theory Y** based on what he argues is a more adequate set of assumptions about human nature and motivation (McGregor, 1989, p. 321).

Theory Y McGregor used this term to characterize a set of positive assumptions by managers about employees; that people are co-operative, able to take responsibility and set their own goals if managers provide the conditions under which they can do this.

1 Management is responsible for organizing the elements of productive enterprise – money, materials, equipment, people – in the interest of economic ends.

2 People are *not* by nature passive or resistant to organizational needs – they have become so as a result of their experience in organizations.

3 The motivation, the potential for development, the capacity for assuming responsibility, the readiness to direct behaviour towards organizational goals, are all present in people. Management does not put them there. It is the responsibility of management to make it possible for people to recognize and develop these human characteristics for themselves.

4 The essential task of managers is to arrange organizational conditions and methods of operation so that people can achieve their own goals best by directing their efforts towards organizational objectives.

Change, McGregor suggests, will inevitably be slow, but in job enrichment and new forms of decentralization, delegation, participation and consultation he sees hope for the gradual implementation of theory Y. Management by objectives is to replace management by control. External control will be replaced by '*self-control and self-direction*'.

Thinkpoint 2.2

Think about the good and bad teachers, lecturers or managers that you have encountered. How do you think your own behaviour was influenced by the assumptions they seemed to have about your ability and motives?

WHAT MOTIVATES MANAGERS? (McCLELLAND AND BURNHAM)

A striking feature of studies of motivation is that they are typically addressed to those who would motivate others. As an exception to this, in the 1970s David McClelland and David Burnham published an article in *Harvard Business Review* called 'Power is the great motivator' that focused directly on managers' motivation. Drawing on studies of managers in the USA they contrasted three possible sets of motives – the need for achievement, the need for power and the need to be liked. They argued that the 'need for achievement' had typically been assumed to be the measure of business success, for example, with successful entrepreneurs. Their innovation was to question whether such a need for achievement was related to good management, particularly in large, complex organizations. They argued that, in practice, a high need for achievement may encourage an individual to focus on personal improvement, and encourage them to do things themselves. The need to achieve might typically also be associated with a need for concrete short-term feedback. Against this they argued that, in large complex organizations, the key requirement is to manage others to perform, and this will often mean a lack of immediate and personal feedback for the manager. Here they suggested that the 'need for power' might be more important and appropriate than the 'need for achievement'.

They decided that perhaps the best index of a manager's effectiveness would be the climate he or she creates around themselves and that this would be reflected in the morale of subordinates. It was this that they then measured. Their version of a good manager was as follows (McClelland, 2003, p. 109):

A good manager is one who, among other things, helps subordinates feel strong and responsible, rewards them properly for good performance and sees that things are organized so that subordinates feel they know what they should be doing. Above all, managers should foster among subordinates a strong sense of team-spirit, of pride in working as part of a team.

Through their surveys they found that some 70 per cent of managers had a higher than average need for power, suggesting that the need for power is important in managers. They also found a strong correlation between the strength of a manager's need for power and good team morale. But the results also contained a surprise, for the main driver of high morale turned out to be not whether a manager's need for power was higher than their need to achieve, but whether it was higher than their need to be liked. This latter group they termed 'affiliative managers', whose strongest need was to be liked. This, they argued, would result in a kind of weakness that would make exceptions out of sentiment or the desire to be thought well of by a particular subordinate. The result would be a team-wide perception of unfairness that led to low morale. This thought about the impact of perceived fairness on motivation has been further developed in Adams' **equity theory**, and more recently by Greenberg's work on **procedural justice**.

Equity theory These ideas focus on the importance people attach to perceptions of fairness in how managers deal with them relative to others.

Maslow's early ideas about a hierarchy of needs and the way in which these were then taken up by McGregor define at least two key axes along which motivation can be understood – the nature of human needs and, as importantly, a manager's assumptions about the needs of those they manage. McClelland and Burnham's studies were an interesting addition, for in Maslow's terms, they suggest that a manager's love and status needs may well get in the way of effectiveness. Managers should need power but in a mature and non-egocentric way if they are to manage well.

Procedural justice Like equity theory, procedural justice is interested in the effects, either positive or negative, that arise from how fairly and transparently managers implement decisions affecting their staff.

Exercise 2.2

Consider the following question: In your experience of teachers, lecturers and managers can you think of instances where it seemed as if their own needs to be liked, or for power or for achievement, helped or hindered their work?

Box 2.1
Perception is everything

In his 'equity theory' Adams argues that a major driver of motivation and demotivation, is perceptions of equity or fairness in work relations. Inequity is felt to exist if a person perceives that the balance of his or her outcomes to inputs is not equivalent to another person's balance of outcomes to inputs. The insight here is that we are all prone to be very alert to the treatment of ourself *relative to* others. Take a team project when you know that one person in the team did virtually no work on the project and yet ends up getting a mark that reflects the rest of the team's work. The mark may be a good one but still it has a bitter taste because it is perceived to be unfair. Importantly, when it comes to equity, perceptions are everything, and in the face of perceived unfairness you may decide to either put less into work or demand more out of it. The following is a quote from a book on the recent financial crisis by Karen Ho about how compensation is viewed in investment banks (Ho, 2009, p. 260).

> In the worst case scenario, it breeds an environment where you may be working on a team for one project, but when it comes to compensation, everybody is trying to shove each other out of the way, saying 'I did the most, I spent the most hours. I made the biggest contribution'. There is always the issue of this person made that much money, and I did just as much, so I should be making that much money, too. It is everybody wanting to be paid as much, if not more, than everyone else. That is a very big deal. Most people on Wall Street realize that they are already hugely over-compensated relative to the rest of the population, but when it comes to actually getting their bonus, what matters to them is the fact that somebody else has made this much money and whether you 'deserve' it or not, you want that much too.

Cartoon 2.1 'Motivation: What satisfies is different from what causes dissatisfaction'

In the next section we will explore another slightly different approach to motivation; one that gives primary importance to the work itself as a source of motivation. We will begin by looking at the very influential ideas of Frederick Hertzberg.

MOTIVATION: WHAT SATISFIES IS DIFFERENT FROM WHAT CAUSES DISSATISFACTION (FREDERICK HERTZBERG)

Hertzberg made the useful observation that it is often the manager rather than the employee who is motivated. Managers want to get people to do things – in this sense they are motivated – but the means they use, he suggests, often serve only to produce movement rather than motivation in employees. His own views on motivation emerged as a result of his asking this question to a wide variety of people in different jobs: 'What job events had occurred in their work that had led to extreme satisfaction or extreme dissatisfaction on their part?' Answers typically suggested that the factors that cause dissatisfaction are almost entirely different from those that cause satisfaction. His conclusion was that job satisfaction and dissatisfaction involve different feelings and are not polar opposites. As he puts it (Hertzberg, 2003, pp. 55–56): 'The opposite of job satisfaction is not job dissatisfaction but, rather, *no* job satisfaction: and similarly, the opposite of job dissatisfaction is not job satisfaction, but *no* job dissatisfaction.'

Hertzberg argued that two different needs of human beings are involved here. One set of needs can be thought about as stemming from human's animal nature – the built-in drive to avoid pain from the environment, plus all the learnt drives that become conditioned to the basic biological needs. The other set of needs relates to what he argued was a unique human characteristic – 'the ability to achieve and, through achievement, to experience psychological growth'.

The growth or 'motivator factors', he argued, were intrinsic to the job. They are: achievement, recognition, the work itself, responsibility and growth or advancement. The dissatisfaction-avoidance or what he termed 'hygiene factors' are extrinsic to the job and include company policy and administration, supervision, interpersonal relationships, working conditions, salary, status and security. 'Motivators are the primary cause of satisfaction, and hygiene factors the primary cause of unhappiness on the job.' (Hertzberg, 2003, p. 57)

On the basis of his studies Hertzberg was scornful of many of the personnel practices that were the outgrowth of the Hawthorne experiments and the human relations movement. Things like sensitivity training, employee participation and counselling. The primary implication of his work was that the focus of motivational effort should be on work itself and the way it could be 'enriched' to bring about the more effective utilization of personnel.

Rather than pursue Herzberg's ideas on job enrichment we will look at some slightly later work of Hackman, who, in collaboration with Oldham, tried to discover what creates what they called 'intrinsic' motivation, and what job characteristics are associated with such motivation.

MOTIVATION: IT IS THE DESIGN OF JOBS THAT CAN MAKE A DIFFERENCE (HACKMAN)

A lot of the problems of motivation fall away when someone is well matched to the job they are doing. In such circumstances, working hard and performing well happens simply because it is rewarding and satisfying. Hackman and Oldham (1980) talk about this happy congruence of person and job as 'internal motivation', and suggest that this depends upon three key conditions:

1 The work should be experienced as 'meaningful' – as something that matters to the person.
2 Work must involve the experience of 'responsibility' for the results.
3 A person must have 'knowledge of the results' of their work. Without this kind of feedback a person will have no basis upon which to feel good or bad about what they are doing.

Problems of motivation arise when one or more of these 'critical psychological states' is missing. While the three psychological states are internal to the person, Hackman and Oldham suggest that they are related to three key job characteristics.

In order to experience work as *meaningful*, three job characteristics are necessary:

1 *Skill variety.* A job needs to involve a variety of different activities drawing upon a variety of skills.
2 *Task identity.* A job needs to involve completion of a whole or complete piece of work with a visible outcome.
3 *Task significance.* A job and its output needs to make a difference to others either inside or beyond the organization.

In order to encourage feelings of *responsibility* for what one does, a job needs to involve substantial freedom, autonomy and discretion in how it is carried out. Only with this will there be a sense that outcomes are the result of one's own efforts and therefore something for which one has personal responsibility.

The ideas of Maslow, McGregor, McClelland, Hertzberg and Hackman that we have looked at so far, when taken together, sketch the three main dimensions around which motivation has and continues to be thought about: (a) the person and their needs, (b) the manager's needs and beliefs and (c) the characteristics of the job itself. Together they bring us a long way from Taylor's view of scientific management. The employee is not merely a body but a human with 'social' needs. Taylor's scientific view turns out to be a set of assumptions he was making about others, and these assumptions were part of the motivational problem. They assumed the need for close control and monitoring without seeing how this thwarted human needs. The fragmentation of jobs that he then promoted in the name of efficiency in effect robbed work of any 'intrinsic' motivation.

Box 2.2
Taylor's view

Finally, in order to have *knowledge of the results* of what one does, a person needs feedback. Such feedback they suggest needs to come directly from the work, rather than indirectly through one's boss.

In contrast to Maslow's focus on needs, Hackman and Oldham conclude that: 'motivation at work may actually have more to do with how tasks are designed and managed than with the personal dispositions of the people who do them'.

Thinkpoint 2.3

What is the most enjoyable task that you have ever done – at work, school or as a hobby? Analyze this task with Hackman and Oldham's categories to see if they were present and explain why you enjoyed the task so much.

The theories that we have looked at so far are often referred to as 'content' theories; they offer a concrete view of what motivates – needs, behaviour, and different aspects of work and the organization of work. Such theories are then contrasted with what are called 'process' theories that explore motivation as the outcome of experience and the sense made of experience. We will begin with the ideas of Vroom, who in the 1970s developed what he called an expectancy theory of motivation.

MOTIVATION: IT IS A PERSON'S EXPECTATIONS THAT COUNT (VICTOR VROOM)

One of the problems of Maslow's theory of needs is that motivation seems to be the product of needs that are largely given as part of 'human nature' and that for the most part are unconscious. This is a convenient myth for managers for it denies that what people do – the level of effort that they put into their work – is in part the *product of their experiences at work* and the sense that they have made of these. The employee is not just a need-driven entity but rather a self-conscious person making sense of their experiences and adjusting their effort in the light of earlier experience. It is here that Victor Vroom, writing in the early 1970s, made an important contribution to conventional theories of motivation with what became known as 'expectancy theory'.

In line with earlier behaviourist theories, Vroom assumes that humans are motivated to maximize pleasure and minimize pain, but humans are capable of choice, and such choices will depend upon their perceptions and the beliefs and attitudes that are formed from these. 'Valence', 'instrumentality' and 'expectancy' were the terms that Vroom selected to identify three sets of belief involved in deciding to commit effort to a course of action.

Valence refers to largely emotional orientations people have in relation to particular outcomes. These can be both positive (I want these) and negative (I'm keen to avoid these.) It is also possible to be indifferent to some outcomes. What was significant about Vroom's formulation was to suggest that in relation to work it is people's *expectations* rather than actual outcomes that matter. For example, the effort you make at any moment will be driven by what you expect to get out of your course, rather than its actual outcomes.

The second term – instrumentality – explores the factors that shape the expectations or valence for an employee. Something is instrumental if it is believed to lead to something else. So you may expect that reading this text will allow you to write a good essay and get a good degree, which in turn may mean that you can get the job you really want. However, the relation between effort and outcome is not certain, or rather we will have different expectations, born of experience, of the certainty or otherwise with which outcomes will follow from effort. For example, your past experience may lead you to believe that there is a strong positive relationship between your essay writing efforts and the feedback and results that you get. This will create a positive valence. On the other hand, your experience may have been negative or frustrating and leave you feeling that it was not worth the effort, or that those who make no effort are also rewarded by high marks. How have your own efforts on your course been changed by the sense you have made of your experiences so far?

The third belief involved in Vroom's model he termed expectancy, and he writes of this as the 'action-outcome' association in a person's mind. Several things might shape your expectations about the outcome of your essay writing. Do you think that you have the ability to do the course? Will your lecturers give you the help you need? Will the library have the right books?

It is the combination of beliefs about valence, instrumentalities and expectancies that results in a certain level and pattern of motivation. Motivation and the performance that flows from this are the products of *choice;* choice shaped by expectations born of past experiences.

One implication of Vroom's ideas is that, like it or not, managers and the jobs they design, and the decisions and systems that they put in place, are shaping employees' expectations and choices as to whether it is worth the effort, or at least how much effort to make for what. The second implication is that the employee is not a 'need'-driven entity but rather a self-conscious person capable of autonomous choice. Behaviour is shaped not just by needs but by 'cognitions'; by an active process of sensemaking.

MOTIVATION: A NEW COMPETITIVE IMPERATIVE

In the late 1970s and early 1980s a new urgency was given to the topic of employee motivation by the emergence of Japan as a major competitor in the world economy. Many of the subsequent studies of the Japanese employment system, often by Western academics or consultants, were used to hold up a less than flattering mirror to the West's own management and motivational practices. The contrast was perhaps sharpest at the level of production workers in Japan. Here a system of company unions and associated security for core employees apparently allowed for much greater flexibility and responsibility among employees and enabled the Japanese to achieve both high-quality and low-cost production. That other systems could be both more profitable and encourage greater employee motivation was alarming.

Case study 2.2
A problem (of motivation) at PYT plc (2)

Peter's management training course was a real eye-opener to him. He had never thought much about human needs or management styles. What he knew about managing came from what he'd learnt working for his old boss, Mr Thomas. But the course had made him think about this experience a bit differently. For some reason Peter had always got on well with Mr Thomas; he encouraged Peter even when things were not going so well and it was Mr Thomas who had encouraged Peter to put in for his first promotion. But with the rest of the staff Mr Thomas was often very strict; and some of his colleagues used to call Peter the 'teacher's pet' as a result. Mr Thomas regularly listened in to sales calls and told people where they were going wrong. You had to ask permission if you wanted to leave your desk, and apart from at breaks, talking to colleagues was discouraged. At the end of each day he would check on who had sold what to whom and, if people had failed to meet their targets, it was not unusual for him to shout at them in front of the whole office.

Thinking about this on the course, Peter began to wonder whether this was good management. He had been particularly impressed by the ideas about 'theory X' and 'theory Y', and that being a manager should really be about creating opportunities for people to grow. His own time at PYT had allowed him to grow a lot and become a supervisor and now office manager. It was clear enough that profits were important but he liked the idea that he was also able to help people develop and grow. That way there was no 'us' and 'them'.

QUESTIONS
1 Drawing on all the ideas presented above, what suggestions could you give Peter for improving staff motivation at PYT?
2 What might he need to do to implement theory Y in relation to both staff and managers?
3 What other factors would he need to consider to improve motivation?

The result in the West has been two decades in which human resource strategies have come to be seen as central to business recovery, and old motivational certainties have been augmented by a growing emphasis upon the team, on creating commitment and on encouraging high performance. The high-performance team it is argued is now a competitive necessity. While Walton announces an American corporate revolution, in practice there is a great deal

Box 2.3
'From control to commitment in the workplace'

Richard Walton's 1985 *Harvard Business Review* article announced a 'significant change' that was under way throughout US industry in approaches to organization and the management of work. Comparing two plants, Walton argued that the differences could be traced to two 'radically different strategies' for managing the workforce; a strategy based on 'imposing control' and a strategy based on 'eliciting commitment'. The traditional 'control' strategy involved a rigid division of labour and individual accountability that assumed low levels of staff skill and motivation. Managers in control mode were organized in a hierarchy of specialist roles with clear status demarcation. Labour was treated as no more than a variable cost, and assumed to have an inevitably adversarial relationship to controlling managers. Walton argued that at the heart of this traditional model was the 'wish to establish order, exercise control and achieve efficiency in the application of the workforce' (Walton, 1985, p. 78). However, this wish, Walton argued, was now threatened both by changing worker expectations and the inability of this strategy to meet the 'standards of excellence' set by world-class competitors. Market success, he suggested, required a superior level of performance that needed 'the deep commitment, not merely the obedience – if you could obtain it – of workers', and it is in the context of this need that the new strategies of eliciting commitment began to emerge. Unions and managers began talking of common interests and the need for mutual trust, layers of hierarchy were stripped out and overt status differentials reduced. Responsibility for integration and quality were being pushed back down to the shop floor. Jobs were being redesigned to be broader and more flexible and included responsibility for continuous improvement. Accountability was shifted from the 'individual' to the 'team' with an acknowledgement of the 'heightened importance of group achievement, the expanded scope of individual contribution, and the growing concern for such questions of "equity" as gain sharing, stock ownership and profit sharing'. To help elicit commitment from the workforce, companies were giving employees some assurance of security with retraining and consultation. Unlike the old control strategy with its exclusive focus on the rights of shareholders, management now acknowledged the 'legitimate claims' of a company's multiple stakeholders – owners, employees, customers and the public.

of continuity between current human resource management and the earlier theories of motivation that we have already looked at. In this way, current motivation theory both builds upon the past as well as adding new points of emphasis and focus. Some aspects of these – the focus on groups and teams, and on organizational culture – will be covered in other chapters. Here we will look at the emphasis that is now placed on autonomy and self-management and the ways that the manager can support these.

In one sense, Walton's recognition of the counterproductive consequences of control marks the triumph of motivation theory over management. What starts with a concern to find ways that managers can control employees' motivation, ends with the grudging recognition that people manage themselves, and that, at best, managers can seek to create the conditions under which employees will commit their energies to the organization. But in another way, recognizing and coming to understand the reality of 'self-management' has also opened up new avenues for management influence.

SELF-MOTIVATION: IT IS THE IDEALS WE HAVE FOR THE SELF THAT MOTIVATE (HARRY LEVINSON)

One clear statement of the reality of self-motivation came from a psychoanalyst and management writer, Harry Levinson, who in a *Harvard Business Review* article in the 1970s, 'Management by Whose Objectives', suggests that we need to begin with an understanding of a person's own objectives since managers' objectives will have no incentive effect if they are unrelated to a person's own dreams and wishes. These he talks about as an 'ego-ideal' (Levinson, 2003, p. 111):

> If a person's most powerful driving force is comprised of needs, wishes and personal aspirations, combined with the compelling wish to look good in her own eyes for meeting those deeply held personal goals, then management by objectives should begin with her objectives. ... Each of us has a built-in road map, a picture of his or her future best self. Psychologists speak of this as an ego-ideal, which is comprised of a person's values, the expectations parents and others have held out for competences and skills, and favourite ways of behaving. An ego-ideal is essentially the way an individual thinks he or she ought to be.

Some of the focus on leadership, on corporate vision and values, and on culture management (see Chapters 8 and 10) can be understood as attempts to shape such ideals.

SELF-MOTIVATION: IT IS THE IDEALS WE HAVE FOR THE SELF THAT MOTIVATE (HARRY LEVINSON)

Another aspect of the self that has become the object of attention is a person's belief about how effective they are. As part of his 'social cognitive theory', Albert Bandura suggests that a person's sense of their own efficacy is one of the most important and pervasive influences on how they act. Some people, he suggests, do not even try to do something because they simply doubt that they have what it takes to succeed. Conversely, others have a strong belief in their capacity to succeed even in the face of setbacks and obstacles.

Such beliefs about self-efficacy will have a pervasive effect on what a person aspires to do and how to approach almost any aspect of work in an organization, including a person's resilience to stress. Bandura suggests that we cannot influence our own motivation and actions very well if we do not keep track of our thought patterns and performance, what is happening around us and the effects we are having. Self-observation of behaviour is part of the solution, as are various forms of goal-setting and emotional 'self-regulation'. Although such beliefs will most probably have been shaped early in life, Bandura suggests a number of strategies that can be pursued to develop and strengthen a 'resilient' sense of self-efficacy. As regards perceptions of self-efficacy (Bandura, 2000, p. 121).

> People of high efficacy focus on the opportunities worth pursuing, and view obstacles as surmountable. Through ingenuity and perseverance they figure out ways of exercising some control even in environments of limited opportunities and many constraints. Those beset with self-doubts dwell on impediments which they view as obstacles over which they can exert little control, and easily convince themselves of the futility of effort. They achieve limited success even in environments that provide many opportunities.

Thinkpoint 2.4

Think about your own sense of self-efficacy. Is it high or low? How might this be shaping what you do, along with what you try to do? With these ideas, how might you try to strengthen your sense of how effective you can be? How might others help in this?

As a resource for thinking about motivation, Bandura's ideas focus not on an assumed set of needs that we possess by virtue of being human, but rather on the very ways in which we have come to think about ourselves. In terms of the development of motivation theory, this involves a step change – a new focus of knowledge on thought processes within the person.

SELF-MOTIVATION: IT IS THE GOALS SET FOR THE SELF (LOCKE AND LATHAM)

This theory, which the authors claim has been tested on over 40 000 people in many countries, suggests that the most simple and direct explanation of why some individuals perform much better than others lies in the fact that they have different performance goals. The theory builds on four broad propositions:

1 Difficult goals lead to higher performance than easy goals, or no goals, or abstract injunctions like 'do your best'.
2 The higher the goal the higher the performance.
3 Praise, feedback or participation in decision-making makes a difference to what people do only insofar as it increases commitment to a difficult goal.
4 In addition to affecting choice, effort and the persistence of effort, goal-setting can also increase the effort people make to discover ways of meeting a goal.

Latham and Locke argue that, in addition, a goal must be challenging and specific. Their idea is that as well as serving as *targets* to attain, goals are 'the standards by which one judges one's adequacy or success'. There is a competitive element here so that part of the pleasure of setting high goals is that they are higher than other people's goals. Moreover, high goals are accompanied by expectations that achievement will bring feelings of self-efficacy, as well as recognition by one's peers, along with the more tangible benefits of salary increases and promotion.

Latham (2000) argues that 'the management of oneself lies at the core of goal-setting theory' and that 'without commitment goal-setting is meaningless'. In other words, goal-setting is something that we should do in order to motivate ourselves. But managers can support this self-management. Feedback is important because measurement signals what is actually valued in an organization rather than what is claimed to be valued. Relatedly, coaching aimed at improving performance through increasing a person's sense of self-efficacy can be most effective. Managers should set 'SMART' *goals* – that is, goals should be specific, measurable, attainable, relevant and have a clear time frame. The manager's own expectations of employees can also be important in shaping the goals they set themselves.

SELF-MOTIVATION INVOLVES EMPOWERMENT (THOMAS AND VELTHOUSE)

While empowerment is often presented as a management initiative, Thomas and Velthouse (1990) argue that empowerment should be understood in terms of four different cognitions related to a person's sense of meaning, competence, choice and impact. Meaning is about my assessment of the value of a task in relation to my own ideals and standards. Competence relates to my beliefs about my own capability (self-efficacy), choice refers to my beliefs as to whether I can direct my own actions, and impact to my sense of being able to 'make a difference'. Conger (2000) later suggests that understanding empowerment requires understanding the psychology of power and control. Power must be understood as 'an intrinsic need for self-determination along with a belief in self-efficacy'. But if employees have such a need for self-determination, management can affect this in a variety of ways:

- *Factors that undermine empowerment cognitions.* A rigid and impersonal hierarchy may limit a person's sense of being able to exercise initiative, or exercise real responsibility. Authoritarian styles of management can deny any sense of self-determination. Rewards may be allocated in a way that is perceived as unfair or unresponsive to competence or creativity. Similarly, as we have seen, jobs that have little meaning or challenge, or where there is overload or conflict, readily produce a sense of powerlessness.
- *Factors that encourage empowerment cognitions.* Organizational policies and cultures that emphasize self-determination, collaboration over competition, and high performance standards and open communication systems, help create the conditions for empowerment. Leadership or supervision that sets high expectations while expressing confidence, allows autonomy and sets inspirational or at least meaningful goals, also contributes to empowerment. Jobs with high variety, relevance, autonomy and control as well as good advancement prospects empower, as does rewarding innovative and creative performance.

SELF-MOTIVATION: SELECTIVE RECOGNITION BY MANAGERS HELPS (LUTHANS)

Along with a focus on how management can create the conditions for empowerment cognitions, the other focus in the 1990s has been on the effect of recognition on performance. Some of this takes us back to our initial focus on the impact of pay on performance. The 1980s and 1990s saw a renewed interest in pay as a way to influence performance, and both attract and retain employees. Along with traditional practices, many advocated new forms of profit sharing and share ownership schemes for employees at all levels as an inducement for better performance. Interest in such traditional forms of recognition were accompanied by a new awareness of the power of 'social recognition'. Luthans and Stajkovic (2000), for example, argue (at p. 167) that: 'If social recognition is provided on a contingent basis in managing employee behaviour it can be a powerful motivator of employee behaviour'. Such a use of 'contingent recognition' by management, they suggest, both shapes expectations of future reward as well as offering a signal of belonging. It also has a direct regulatory effect (Luthans and Stajkovic, 2000, p. 170):

> Based on the recognition received and, thus, the perceived prediction of desired consequences to come, people will self-regulate their future behaviours by forethought. By using forethought, employees may plan courses of action for the near future, anticipate the likely consequences of their future actions, and set performance goals for themselves. Thus people first anticipate certain outcomes based on recognition received, and then through forethought, they initiate and guide their actions in an anticipatory fashion.

Thinkpoint 2.5

Think about your reaction to the marks that you receive for an essay or in an exam, and how that makes you feel. Marks are in this instance a sort of 'selective recognition' and the fear of failure or being seen to fail, or the hope of being seen to be the intelligent person that you are, then start to influence how you 'regulate' yourself to get the kind of marks/recognition that you want.

By using recognition selectively managers can influence how staff will manage themselves. Self-management, it seems, does not mark the end of managers' attempts to control staff after all. Rather, a clearer understanding of the self – the ideals and standards by which we judge ourselves, our beliefs about our own competence and the value, meaning and effects of what we do – offers both a new object for our own self-observation and self-management, and new opportunities for managers to influence the very ways in which we exercise our autonomy.

Limitations of mainstream approaches

We began this review of mainstream theories of motivation with the work of Frederick Taylor, his development of a 'scientific' view of management, and, within this, his assumption that money in the form of piece rates would be enough to motivate Schmidt, the pig-iron shoveller. In the subsequent century of work on motivation our understanding has come a long way.

We saw how the humanist views of Maslow challenged the patronizing views of Taylor, insisting that managers recognize a much broader range of needs, beyond money, in their employees. McGregor took this a step further by suggesting, with his distinction between theory X and Y managers, that the laziness Taylor imagined to be a part of Schmidt, may have been no more than a reflection of Taylor's own negative assumptions and the way that these informed his treatment of Schmidt. Hertzberg's and Hackman's work then challenged Taylor's views on the separation of mental from manual labour, and the efficiency of an intense division of labour, by insisting that it was the nature of jobs, rather than human needs, that was the key to motivation. Schmidt was neither stupid nor lazy, but bored out of his head by the mindless, fragmented work that he was asked to do. To be meaningful and motivating, jobs need to allow one to use a variety of skills, to deal with complete tasks rather than fragments, and allow one to feel that what one does is important to others and the success of the organization.

But these early attempts to uncover the universal truths, or 'content', of what motivates – individual needs, the task, the managers' assumptions and conduct – were themselves challenged by ideas that insisted that motivation is a dynamic 'process'. Schmidt had perhaps learnt through long experience to expect little beyond money from his work. He was not, as Taylor imagined, just a body to be trained, or even a bundle of needs, but a self-conscious person who acted on the basis of the sense he made of his experiences.

Now if the employee is a self-conscious, thinking being, just like the manager, then suddenly motivation theorists realized that motivation could never be what a manager *does* to an employee. People motivate themselves, and the most that managers can do is to create an enabling environment for this. Under the pressure of growing international competition since the 1970s this has led to an explosion of interest, and study, of all the different dimensions of self-motivation. In part this depends on the ideals we have of what we should seek to become, the beliefs we have acquired about how effective we can be, and the goals we set for ourselves. The role of managers in relation to self-motivation involves them thinking about whether the environment they create is empowering for staff, and whether they create opportunities for achievement, as well as offer staff recognition.

Many of the studies we have described were sincerely motivated by a concern to address what the writers felt was the waste of human potential at work, but the interest their work aroused was perhaps less noble in its intentions. Who was investing in developing our understanding of motivation, and why? On the one hand, managers like to think well of themselves and how they treat their staff. But, on the other hand, they know that their own success

Case study 2.3
A problem (of motivation) at PYT plc (3)

Val had worked as a sales representative at PYT for a couple of years when she was promoted to a vacant post on John's team of sales executives. She was a bit worried about this move; she wasn't sure she could handle the larger clients, and John had the reputation of being fiercely ambitious and felt much less approachable than her present boss, Mel. Her fears were quickly confirmed. She was having some problems with her partner outside work and she began to slip behind on her sales targets for her first campaign. John said he would give her some training and spent one Friday morning listening in to her calls. But the training in practice involved John telling her all the things she was doing wrong. She tried to explain to him that it was just a bad patch she was going through. She even hinted at the troubles she was having outside work but John ignored this. By the end of the morning she was feeling awful about herself and finally burst into tears and rushed out of the office. She went to the doctor and was off sick for the next week. When Mel, her old team leader, heard about what had happened she was furious with John for what she saw as the way he had undermined Val. He, however, insisted that she was simply 'no good' and 'not up to it' and would have to leave or take a demotion. When Val returned fearfully the next week, John took her into an office and told her that she had the choice either to leave the company or go back to her old job on Mel's team. Val was shattered. It was Mel who later came and found her in the toilets, took her out to lunch, and tried to persuade her to give it a go with her old job. 'Never mind what John said, I know that you're a great sales person and I want you on my team.' Val went back to work for Mel, but it was weeks before she began to regain her confidence.

QUESTIONS
1 How do theories of self-motivation in relation to ideals, self-efficacy, targets, empowerment and selective recognition help understand Val's contrasting experiences of being managed at PYT?
2 What does her experience suggest about the problems of these new forms of self-motivation?

Thinkpoint 2.6

After this century-long journey of 'discovery' about motivation have we reached the promised land of healthy, productive and satisfied employees? What does your own experience tell you? Is this the sense you have of your own experiences of working, or those of your friends or parents?

will depend on their ability to get as much as they can from staff. So although thinking about motivation seems to have moved way beyond Taylor, in another way it still shares his *instrumental* interest in efficiency. Other people are still seen as means to an end. Managers' interests lie in making full use – exploiting – other people; their jobs and future careers as managers depend on this. We might also ask why it has taken a century for theory to discover that employees are people like us. Do we really need social scientific studies to discover what should be obvious from our own experience of families and friendship? And why is it still so easy in the course of our work to find discontent and unacceptable conduct?

The unspoken story in all of these studies of motivation is about power. The desire to fully use others' power in the service of our careers and the organization, and all the resources – research and training – that are put into this. The power that allowed Taylor to treat Schmidt like a mindless machine, and kept Schmidt working despite this. The power that makes the use of motivation theory a sort of optional extra for managers; something that they can embrace but also ignore if they choose to do so.

Superficially, the recognition of the damaging impact of imposed control, and the apparent recognition of employee autonomy suggests that, in theory at least, motivating managers have given up using their power in this way – they merely empower and enable. But as we shall explore in what follows, the more recent attention to the autonomous self – its ideals, self-beliefs and aspirations – can be seen as an even more intense, intrusive and effective form of power in the service, not of the employee, but of corporate profit.

CRITICAL APPROACHES TO MOTIVATION AND THE SELF
Introduction

While many of the studies that we have looked at in the first part of this chapter were very critical of current management practice, what they all share is a hope or a belief that the 'problem' of motivation can be solved through the development and application of knowledge; i.e., a better understanding of human needs, the redesign of work and more appropriate management behaviour. Critical views of motivation theory challenge the adequacy of these mainstream approaches on two very different but related bases. In the first – views shaped by Marx's analysis of the structures of capitalism – we return to the role that economic interests have in shaping conduct at work. While mainstream theory emphasizes the unitary nature of interests in organizations, for Marx, capitalism involves an essential *conflict of interests* between ownership (and its agents) and those who must sell their labour in order to live. Acknowledging this fundamental conflict of interests arguably offers a more historically accurate account of how management has been able either simply to ignore employee interests, or alternatively has (selectively) recognized them only in order to maximize profits. Either way, it points to management's instrumental interests in motivation; its interest is not in making work more satisfying for employees but in getting more out of them. It also suggests that much motivation theory can be seen as an 'ideology' that justifies hierarchy and inequality and presents the sectional interests of owners and their agents as if they were universal and shared. A real change in motivational practice would require a different structure of ownership and the power relations that this creates.

The second critical account of motivation draws upon ideas about the 'social construction' of the 'self', as well as the work of Michel Foucault and those who have been influenced by his analysis of what he calls the operation of 'disciplinary power'. As we have seen, over time mainstream motivation theory has come to emphasize the motivational importance of individual autonomy and self-management and used this to suggest that the exercise of management control has often been counterproductive and should be replaced by strategies of empowerment that promote employee commitment. Here, power and individual autonomy are treated as opposites, as indeed they often are in classic Marxist accounts. But in this final section of the chapter we want to explore how power comes to shape the very ideals that we set for the exercise of individual autonomy. Our knowledge of the 'self' is socially produced, and as a result is never under my autonomous control. Motivation here is seen to be animated by the desire to fix and secure the very sense we have of ourselves as this is reflected in the attitudes of others towards us. Many of the new motivational strategies involved in contemporary 'human resource management' can be seen to rely upon and play with these aspects of the ego.

**Box 2.4
James Wolfensohn –
President of the
World Bank**

'I personally feel that the world is out of balance. The way the world is dealing with problems of poverty and peace seem to be disconnected. Military spending is now probably US$1000 billion and spending on subsidies or tariffs to protect the developed world farmers is about US$300 billion. Meanwhile the rich countries offer no more than US$50–60 billion in aid to developing countries while blocking most of their agricultural exports – one of the few ways these countries could pull themselves out of poverty.

'The three things are linked. There are five billion people in the developing world, three billion earning under US$2 a day, and 1.2 billion earning under US$1 a day. If you can't give them hope, which comes from getting a job or doing something productive, giving them their self respect, these people become the basis upon which terrorists or renegades or advocacy groups can flourish. It's an essentially unstable situation.

'If you cannot deal with the question of hope or economic security there is no way that with military expenditure you can have peace ... if you do nothing about poverty and development you're not going to have stability.'

Source: The Australian, 4 February 2004.

Marxist analyses

'Men make history, but not under conditions of their own choosing.'

(Karl Marx)

THE PROFOUND CREATIVITY OF HUMAN ACTION

Typically when we first join an organization it already exists – it has a history, buildings, rules that govern its operation, established procedures and systems. From this perspective it is as if our actions and thoughts and motives have nothing at all to do with the nature of the organization in which we work; the purposes of the organization and our purposes can be thought about in isolation from each other. Take university, for example. It is easy to see it simply as the context in which you can pursue your own individual goals of getting a degree, having a good time, etc. This sharp separation between subjective reality and the organization as an objective reality can encourage us to have a very limited view of work and the effects of what we do. It can lead us to ignore or deny the profoundly creative aspect of what we and others do.

For Marx, what distinguishes humans from other animals is that we do not have a biologically fixed or instinctually predetermined relationship either with ourselves or with the world. There is, therefore, neither a fixed human nature to which we might refer, or seek to discover, in order to understand human motivation; nor is there a fixed structure of external determinants of human responses. Instead, human nature is itself only shaped and reshaped through work and the consciousness that arises through such work. Work or labour then becomes a central explanatory concept – it is not to be understood as an aspect of a person's life alongside leisure, family, sport and so on, but rather as a historical process through which we humans create and recreate ourselves and our world. Moreover, work organizations cannot be understood in isolation from the social and political relationships in which they are embedded. Nor can the present social or organizational reality be treated as if it is somehow 'natural' and not itself the product of historical forces and thus subject to change and further development.

THE PROCESS OF PRODUCTION

Let's take a closer look at what is involved in action/work/labour. Work can be thought of as a relationship between us and the world, or as our way of relating to the world. It involves a moment of **conception** in which we draw upon all our existing tacit knowledge and understanding to conceive of what we will do. For the most part we act habitually, doing what we have always done through drawing upon the skills and knowledge that we have accumulated in the course of our lives. Look at an infant or a child and it is immediately obvious how much and how long it takes each of us to acquire even the most basic of skills.

The second moment involved in work is one of **externalization**. We combine our accumulated knowledge, skills and thought with materials to hand and produce something – this can be an idea, work, picture or other kind of object.

Finally, what has been created becomes part of the external world – **objectification** – and is available for both ourselves and others, and for future generations.

While all labour involves such processes of conception, externalization and objectification, there are two further potentials – **reification** and **alienation** – that are important for our understanding of human motivation (see Box 2.6).

Conception What characterizes human creativity is that it begins with a mental process of imagination or conception.

Externalization The process of creation through which what has been conceived in the mind comes to be embodied through work in an object.

Objectification The end point of the creative process at which point what has been produced comes to have an independent existence in the world.

Reification Describes the tendency to treat a human creation (say an organization or technology) as if it had an independent existence of its own rather than being the product of human thought and work.

Alienation Marx famously employed this concept to describe the experience of labour under capitalism; a condition in which individuals feel separated or estranged from some part of their existence (e.g., the product or process of their labour) because they are subjected to external controls.

Thinkpoint 2.7

When you go to the library to find books to write an essay what is your sense of your relationship to these? Are they oppressive, non-human 'truths' that you must wade through simply to get your essay written? Here, work and its means of production – books and articles – are felt to have no relationship to you and your own thoughts and experience. Instead these objects dominate and oppress you. Alternatively, are the books merely the objectification of other people's thoughts – thoughts that were shaped by their own history and interests and reflections – upon which you can then draw in shaping your own thoughts and opinions? Here, writing becomes a creative relationship between yourself and the objective world through which both you and the world are developed and changed.

Box 2.5
Tacit knowledge

Tacit knowledge is a set of skills and ways of understanding that is so familiar that we take it for granted as what we know of how things are, and can only with difficulty explain or describe it. A good example is riding a bicycle. Like so many of the skills upon which we depend, riding a bicycle is something that we learnt, possibly with some difficulty. It took time and effort to co-ordinate our legs working on the pedals with steering. We fell off a few times before we learnt the basic skill and then refined it. We also had to learn the rules of the road so that we stop and give way at the right places, and ride on the correct side of the road and are not a danger to ourselves and others. But today we just get on a bike and cycle and do not even have to think about what we are doing deliberately. Despite our obvious 'practical' skill, however, when we try to teach someone else to cycle we are hard pressed to find the words that explain it. It's obvious, taken for granted.

Box 2.6
Reification and alienation

Reification: to treat something as if it has an independent existence of its own, rather than as the product of human thought or work.
Alienation: a reversal of the relationship between the producer and their product such that what is humanly produced comes to dominate the producer.

THE CONTRADICTIONS OF CAPITALISM AND ALIENATION

The story that Marx tells of human history is a story about the relationship between an evolving 'means of production' – the accumulating knowledge, skills and artefacts through which we manage our relationship to nature – and the forms of social relationships or 'relations of production' that come into existence around any particular set of productive relations. Although he offered a broad historical sketch of these relationships, starting with tribal society, then the ancient societies of Greece and Rome, and then an agrarian-based 'feudal' society, Marx's key concern was with the emergence and dynamic of productive and social relationships under capitalism.

For Marx there is a contradiction at the very heart of capitalism. On the one hand the move from feudal to capitalist society involved a massive positive development in the means of production and, in this process, the emergent merchant class played a progressive role. In part this was achieved, as Adam Smith described, through an intensification of the division of labour, such that traditional craft skills were broken down into specialized tasks that could be carried out by a number of workers. But the success of the market also stimulated technological innovation and the huge increase in productive capability that industrialization allowed. In principle, such positive developments in the means of production should have been associated with the progressive liberation of humans from need. For Marx, however, the experience of work under capitalism turned into the exact opposite. Marx analyzed these paradoxical effects of capitalism in terms of four forms of 'alienation'; four ways in which under capitalism what is humanly produced comes to impoverish the human producer.

Alienation from the product

Under feudalism, although the worker would have had to give a proportion of what was produced to his lord, he was in other respects his own proprietor who was free to produce according to his own immediate needs and those of his family. Under capitalism this relationship to the land as a means of production is broken and, instead, increasing numbers of workers become entirely dependent upon the sale of their own labour on the market. Their labour becomes just like any other commodity, and what they produce is no longer determined by what they or others need but by monetary exchange driven by the search for profit and the accumulation of capital. For Marx, the key 'class' division emerges between those who must sell their labour in order to live and those who, by virtue of owning the means of production, are able to expropriate not only the surplus produced through their own efforts but also the surplus produced by others. This conflict of interest at the very heart of capitalism is expressed in the different meaning of wages; for the employee they are their only means of living, for the owner they are a cost to be minimized. The more the worker produces the cheaper labour becomes.

Alienation from the process of production

Work does not allow the worker 'to develop freely his mental and physical energies'. Work can no longer be experienced as an end in itself but rather is just a means to ends that are external to work. Marx took as evidence of this the fact that 'as soon as there is no physical or other compulsion, men flee from labour like the plague'.

Alienation from others

For Marx the 'individual' of economic theory was a peculiar invention of capitalist society. The person is fundamentally social and it is impossible to conceive of the person as somehow apart and distinct from the society and culture out of which he or she emerges. Yet under capitalism, relationships between people come to be dominated by the logic of the market. Colleagues become rivals for jobs and for wages, as means or obstacles to one's own success. Others are seen solely through the calculative lens of profit or advantage.

Alienation from the self

Finally, and in a sense as an accumulation of these effects, Marx talked of capitalism as involving the alienation of both the worker and owner from themselves, from their own social nature. While an individual is always the

'The 'isolated individual' is a fiction of utilitarian theory; no human being exists who has not been born into and thus shaped by an ongoing society. Each individual is thus the recipient of the accumulated culture of the generations which have preceded him, and in his own interaction with the natural and social world in which he lives, is a contributor to the further modification of that world as experienced by other.

"Individual life and species life are not different things", Marx asserts. "Though man is a unique individual he is equally the whole, the ideal whole, the subjective existence of society as thought and experienced."' (Giddens, 1971, p. 13)

Box 2.7
The 'isolated individual'

product of the society in which he or she is born, under capitalism awareness of this relationship is reversed and the social is subordinated to the pursuit of individual goals. We begin to treat the self and others like a market commodity.

It is important to point out that the alienation that is being talked of here is not from some ideal natural man; there is no such thing. Alienation arises instead from the contradiction between the socialized nature of production and the privatized ownership of the means of production under capitalism, which itself sets up a tension between the productive possibilities of capitalism and the experiences of those who produce within it. The solution, however, also lies within capitalism, for Marx believed that by bringing people together in large numbers – in cities and factories – there would be the potential for these contradictions themselves to be overthrown. To date, at least capitalism has proved remarkably adaptable.

Thinkpoint 2.8

Investigations into the recent global financial crisis have revealed just how much investment bankers, even quite junior investment bankers, were being paid. The same is true of senior executives more generally. There is something odd happening here. Why at the very highest levels of organizations, where people are doing the most interesting work, do they need such huge financial incentives? Whilst urging others to economic efficiency in order to deliver shareholder value, the bankers have set up a kind of co-operative profit sharing with their investors – staff take 50 per cent of profits and the shareholders get what is left over. The rationale economists offer for such 'incentives' is that they align the interests of managers with those of the owners. Critics suggest that the scandal of executive pay has seen the largest peaceful transfer of wealth from owners to managers in history. The global financial crisis, for which we are now all paying with increased taxes and reduced public services, was in part caused by the effects of these incentives. People were being rewarded immediately for the assumed profits that would come from taking longer term risk. When the risk proved greater than had been anticipated, the traders kept their bonuses and the employing organizations lost money or even failed. How does power get away with such abuse?

CORE ASSUMPTIONS OF THE MARXIST PERSPECTIVE

- Man is a social animal rather than a self-seeking 'individual'.
- Production for exchange rather than use is a feature of capitalism rather than a universal of economic activity.
- Under capitalism, production is motivated not by the meeting of human needs but by the pursuit of profit and the accumulation of capital.
- The self-seeking opportunism that is the grounding assumption about the nature of human beings in neoclassical economics is better understood as historically specific to capitalism.
- There are different interests for different groups in organizations that are shaped not by 'individual' needs but by class position – whether one is an owner, or must rather sell one's labour in order to live.

If the interests of labour and owners (and their agents, management) are fundamentally opposed, then this suggests two things as regards motivation. First, it suggests that the problem of motivation is built into capitalist organizations. This explains why motivation has become a 'holy grail' of management writers that has been pursued for over a century. Second, it suggests that the problem will never be solved within capitalism and so the managerial quest for performance and satisfaction will be endless, in part because it wants to solve the problem without addressing its root cause, which lies in the exploitation made possible by private ownership.

Case study 2.4
A problem (of motivation) at PYT plc (4)

Emily had worked at PYT for the past eight months. She'd worked in a shop before that, but had not liked the weekend working. At least here her weekends were her own. She had got married last year and she and her husband, Robin, spent most weekends doing up the house they'd bought.

She enjoyed the training course that PYT sent her on when she first arrived and she'd been amazed to discover that the techniques they had taught her really worked. The trick seemed to be to get people talking after you'd told them that you were just phoning to check their entry in the directory. The 'open' questions she'd been taught to use – Where exactly is your shop? Have you been there long? What sort of area is it? – really did seem to get people talking and then she'd change to closed questions – Would you like a quarter or half page? Shall I go ahead and book that for you? – to try and make the sale. She was surprised how many people went along with what she suggested.

Sometimes she felt a bit guilty with the small businesses – she wasn't sure they needed to spend that much – but then, as they'd taught her, advertising is important if you want to grow your business. She liked working on Ruth's team and when she'd made her first sales Ruth had shouted it out and everybody clapped. The thing she still felt most uncomfortable about was some of the other people in the office. They were a bit posh and were always talking about the designer clothes they'd bought, the restaurants they'd been to and the expensive holidays they were going on. She and Robin barely had enough to live on, what with the new house. Emily had started taking a Selfridge's bag with her when she went shopping. She couldn't afford to shop there but at least they wouldn't know that she had to buy her clothes at cheaper stores. But Emily saw PYT as a place where she might be able to make something of herself. If she worked hard and was successful then perhaps she could get to be a manager in a year or so.

QUESTION

Can you find examples of Marx's four versions of alienation in Emily's attitude to herself, her work and her co-workers?

RETHINKING MOTIVATION: EFFICIENT AND RATIONAL FOR WHOM?

Motivation theory as ideology

In whose interests are theories of motivation developed and whose interests do they serve? Marx argued that at any moment in history the dominant class would typically disseminate ideas that serve to legitimize its own position of dominance. He talked of this as 'ideology' – presenting the interests of a particular group as if they were universal interests. Take Maslow's ideas of a hierarchy of needs. How might the idea of a hierarchy of needs serve to justify and legitimize the current structures of hierarchy and power in an organization? Now it is clear that Maslow and McGregor were critical of the way organizations fail to meet human needs, but as their ideas have been popularized by management texts, these critical aspects of their ideas are typically edited out. Instead their ideas are read as if they offer a 'natural' justification for hierarchy. It is tempting to simply assume that those doing lower-level or menial work in an organization are somehow at a lower level of development, preoccupied with lower-level needs, while those at the top have 'grown' and are (rightly) rewarded with the opportunity for 'self-actualization'.

Motivation and economic inequality

While knowledge of motivation might be said to have developed over the years, it is still up to management, rather than the employee, particularly at lower levels of an organization, as to whether these ideas are taken seriously. Motivation is in this sense an optional extra for management – they can always fall back on the force implicit in the employment contract to get people to do what is required. The fear of unemployment is all the motivation that most people need. The theories have not led management to address or change the structures of power in which they work. It is for managers to introduce empowerment – employee power on managers' terms – rather than acknowledge a real dependence upon employees. All this means that a concern for motivation can be applied selectively and strategically. If you need a high level of commitment and loyalty, or if you fear the power of a union or a political shift of power towards the interests of labour, then perhaps we should invest in winning hearts and minds, or treat certain groups of employees very carefully. However, if unemployment is high and replacements easy to find, if the costs of motivation exceed the likely benefits, then there is no need to weigh employee needs against the interest in profit. The rhetoric changes but not the power structures.

Case study 2.5
A problem (of motivation) at PYT plc (5)

As Damian Rawls, the Sales Director, had feared, PYT was continuing to haemorrhage customers and Peter was becoming increasingly alarmed at the prospect of the office missing its half-year profit target. Damian was on the phone to him every week now to ask about how the office was doing and had just told Peter that he was going to visit the office next week to take a closer look at operations. Peter immediately called his section leaders, Mel, John and Ruth, into his office. Perhaps Peter did not know how thin his office walls were, but staff heard him shouting at them: 'I don't care if the staff are under huge pressure, we've just got to meet these targets'.

QUESTIONS
1   Are profits all that matter?
2   If we need a job in order to live then why should managers give another thought to our motivation?

The power of dividing

One final criticism of conventional theories emerges from a consideration of Marx's views on alienation. For Marx, the contradictions of capitalism were likely to be removed by its own internal dynamics. As an unintended consequence of capitalist production, the organization of work would bring large groups of employees together in factories and offices, and as citizens. Given the conflict of interest around production between wages and profits he believed that people would begin to see their true interests. While as an 'individual' I might be weak relative to my employer, as a member of a trade union or a political party I could be powerful. While conventional theories of motivation acknowledge the 'social' needs for belonging, affection and recognition, these do not extend to the collective needs for concerted resistance or political action. But they also point to the political significance of what has been termed 'individualized' attention. By focusing on the 'individual' employee, by emphasizing the hierarchical differences between individuals, by keeping them absorbed with their careers and promotion prospects, a whole set of forces are set up that avoid or preclude collective action.

IMPORTANT STUDIES

Labour and monopoly capital (Harry Braverman)

Braverman's reinterpretation of Taylor's scientific management in the 1970s draws its inspiration from Marx's analysis of the dynamics of capitalism. What Taylor suggested was the product of the application of scientific methods to the study and organization of work, is seen by Braverman in terms of the logic of capitalism that sets the pursuit of profit on a collision course with the human importance of meaningful work. What Taylor offered as a rational separation of mental and manual work is seen by Braverman as a process of deskilling, driven by concerns to reduce costs, intensify work effort and reduce the potential for worker resistance.

Braverman's starting point is the nineteenth-century craftsman; the coherence, knowledge and skill embodied in craft work, and the relatively autonomous organization of craft labour within craft unions. The scientific application of seemingly neutral rationality to such work by proponents of scientific management can be seen to be driven by the logic of profit rather than a universally beneficial efficiency. The separation of mental and manual labour is from this point of view an act of theft in which management captures the skills and knowledge of skilled labour and on this basis is able to deskill and fragment jobs, and in the process extract more output for less cost. Coherent jobs with their own intrinsic satisfactions are broken down into relatively meaningless fragments and these fragmented tasks can then be performed by unskilled labour that is both much cheaper and more easily replaced than the skilled craftsman.

Braverman's work was important because its focus on the labour process was an important antidote to the rather abstract and idealized images of employment coming from management writers. The early introduction of new computer-controlled technologies in the 1970s where skilled work was recorded on computer tape pointed to the continuing relevance of his critique of Taylor. Braverman's (1974) book inspired a host of critical studies of work but was itself criticized for its rather passive portrayal of the worker and the degradation of work under the relentlessly unfolding logic of capitalism. Workers are portrayed as the victims of strengthened management control.

Manufacturing consent (Burawoy)

One of the difficulties faced by Marxist accounts of work is to explain why, given the conflict of interest between profit and wages, there is so little resistance on the part of organized labour to its own exploitation. Explaining this seeming paradox was the task that Michael Burawoy set himself in his 1979 study, *Manufacturing Consent*. Where Braverman explains work intensification in terms of increased management control achieved through the separation of conception from execution, Burawoy suggests that work intensification has been achieved through a management strategy of worker 'self-organization'.

What his empirical study observed was workers' enthusiastic participation in worker-led games of 'making out'—attempts by a host of means to maximize bonus payments. Playing such games, Burawoy suggests, creates a sense of personal autonomy and choice, it relieves the boredom and drudgery of work and gives people a sense of accomplishment. While such games are played in the spirit of an assertion of autonomy against management, by playing the game people inadvertently come to accept the rules of the game; a logic of capital in which labour is systematically disadvantaged. The pleasures and apparent freedoms of the game ensure greater productivity. Importantly, Burawoy's study observes how the bonus system games, and the defence of wage differentials between different groups of workers, have the effect of separating people off from one another and encouraging workers to see work in the same instrumental terms as they themselves are viewed by management. The game gives us a sense of being in control, of being able to use the company rather than just being used, but the result is that we work ourselves hard.

Cartoon 2.2 'Rethinking motivation: Efficient and rational for whom?'

Power and the 'self'

Marxist analyses focus on how ownership gives some the power to exploit others through creating economic insecurity. The second set of ideas that we will explore suggests that modern motivation techniques play not just on economic insecurity but a person's insecurity about the value of the self. These ideas involve questioning the very notion of 'individual' autonomy and raise the possibility that power works not to constrain this autonomy from the outside but instead by shaping our very notion of what it is to be an individual. It is here that notions of economic power associated with the private ownership of property can be seen to be intimately linked with personal concerns with self-identity and security. To begin to introduce these ideas we will in what follows look a little more closely at how a person's sense of self is developed and maintained, and then see how this becomes a key lever for motivating both ourselves and others at work.

THE FORMATION OF THE 'SELF'

In everyday language we often talk about the self as if it were a something that we have. We treat the self as if it were the psychological equivalent of our bodies; something that is relatively fixed, stable and independent from the world. Although the self is unique to us, here it is being thought about as if it were indeed a 'something' – an object. Here we will look at some ideas about how such a sense of a solid self emerges.

Thinkpoint 2.9

How far back can you remember? Usually people have no memories that they can easily bring to mind much before the ages of three or four. Even then the memories are fragmented – a particular scene or taste or event – always laced with the doubt that it might be something that others have talked about rather than an actual memory. So why is there this critical gap in our memory and what does this mean for our understanding of what it is to be or have a 'self'? Does it mean that early experiences are simply unimportant? This seems unlikely and here we will pursue an alternative explanation; that we are not born with a developed sense of self but instead 'self-consciousness' is the product of early experiences and development.

One of the most influential early accounts of this process comes from an American pragmatist, George Herbert Mead. In his book, written in 1934, called *Mind, Self and Society,* he drew a distinction between three aspects of the self – the 'I', the 'me' and what he termed the 'generalized other'. Mead suggested that we are not born with a developed sense of self but merely the potential for such 'self-consciousness'.

FINDING MY SELF IN THE MIRROR OF OTHERS' RESPONSES

Mead argued that I come to my first sense of self, not through defining my own experience for myself but, instead, through 'taking over' the attitudes of 'significant' others towards me. So I can think of myself surrounded by parents, grandparents and siblings and finding my first sense of self as if in the mirror of how these people responded to me. But language can be deceptive here for this is the very foundation of these differentiations of the self as 'I', 'me', 'my', 'others'. Mead argues that I become aware of the self first as a 'me', as an object to/for others, and indeed as a child acquires language he or she typically refers to the self initially in the third person – as 'me'. My sense of self as an active agent, as an author or subject, as 'I', only comes after I have begun to organize a sense of 'me' as the 'object' I am for others. Mead talked about the relation between the 'me' and the 'I' in terms of *the "I" of this moment becoming the "me" of the next'*. As an 'I' the self has to be understood as a continuous, active but endless process of becoming.

As lived the self is in a 'constant transition from a now thus to a new now thus'. But I can also reflect on this active process of being and experiencing, and in doing so come to define the self as this or that, 'me' or 'not me'. What is important to note is that I cannot ever quite capture the self in reflection; I can never reduce the self to the status of a known object. Instead the mind is constantly moving very rapidly between engagement with the world, and reflection on this engagement.

THE SELF AS A SYNTHESIS OF IMAGES

Mead's account of the formation of the self allows us to differentiate between the active, engaged and reflexive moments of selfhood. But in his description of my first sense of self being acquired through 'taking over' the attitudes of others towards me, he also allows us to see the social nature of the self, and thereby come to understand some of the difficulties of achieving and maintaining a sense of autonomous 'self-identity'. My identity is a set of ideas as to what defines me uniquely as a human being, but Mead's analysis suggests that this definition of self is always socially constructed.

'Taking over' has a rather mechanical tone to it but, in practice, this involves my coming to understand who I am through making sense of others' responses to me. In reality this can mean that our initial sense of self is in many ways more about others around us than it is about the self. As a child it is too easy for us to ascribe the other's response as being to do with who we are rather than what is happening to them. For example, a mother who is depressed can leave a child feeling as if they do not quite exist and a parent who is angry can leave a child feeling that they are bad. Alternatively, the very different needs, aspirations and expectations of parents can simply make it difficult for the child to synthesize into a coherent unity all of the different experiences they have with their 'significant others'. Ideally, of course, the parents will have the psychological maturity and space to respond with love, to the child's own initiative and this then founds a strong positive sense of the goodness of the self as a resource for future life. What should be emphasized here, however, is that our initial sense of self as 'me', is made up of my *synthesis of others' responses to me* – it is this synthesis that actually constitutes or creates my founding sense of 'me'. These processes go hand in hand with the acquisition of language as a ready-made set of differentiations between self and other, past and present, me and not me.

LEARNING WHAT THE SELF MUST BE (TO BE LOVED)

Even in the most loving of environments, part of what the parents will be concerned to do is to introduce the child to the 'norms' or standards of behaviour of the wider society in which the child must eventually take his/her place. While initially some physical constraints may be placed upon the child, with the entry of the child into language and the formation of an early sense of self, then it becomes increasingly possible for the behaviour of the child to be influenced *symbolically* by the parents. The response of 'significant others' to the child is in part shaped by their sense not only of who the child is but of what the child must be. Here praise ('what a good girl, well done') as well as criticism ('don't do that, that's very naughty') as well as straight bribery ('if you do that then you can ...') are all used to try to direct the child's conduct towards desired ends. So the sense of self that we acquire from others contains not just a sense of who we are, but also a sense of what we must be in order to be liked, loved, recognized or belong. Such is our dependence that, again, our very existence seems to depend upon our being able to be what the other wishes us to be (or at least what we imagine we must be to win their recognition and love).

ACQUIRING A (GUILTY) CONSCIENCE

Psychologists talk of two related processes that together further differentiate the psychological structure of the early ego – the formation of an 'ego ideal' and a 'superego'. Part of what is involved in 'taking over' the attitudes of others is what Freud calls 'identification'; the internalization of some aspects of another as a part of the self. The ego ideal involves the internalization of some idealized aspect of the parent, which then serves as an internal standard against which the self is measured. It has a double aspect. On the one hand, it is an ideal of what we can be or should be like. It is akin to the borrowing of another's power – a sense of what one also might become. But any ideal is also necessarily a description of what we are not, and depending on the gap between the self and ideal self it can become an internalized voice that constantly berates and criticizes the self for being less than perfect – for our inadequacy, incompetence and insignificance. Freud referred to this 'critical agency' as a 'superego' that turns its frustration and anger not out towards others, but back upon the self for being bad, inadequate or not good enough.

What has happened then is that an external relationship with a very powerful other – a parental figure – has been internalized as a relationship between two aspects of the self; what we are and what we must be (to be loved). Such internalized ideals can be motivating. But it is important to remember that ideals can never be fulfilled. The self is always in the process of becoming and will never become a perfect 'something' whose value is established unambiguously once and for all. But the *pursuit* of such perfection is another thing, and perhaps precisely because the self is 'open' there is a strong desire to know, fix and secure the self.

Thinkpoint 2.10

Think of those inspiring figures – teachers, parents, heroes – who have become models of what you would like to be like. In our minds they can seem a bit like gods whose protection and admiration we long for – we idealize them. But then these ideal people become a model for what we aspire to become. How do you react to failure? Do you forgive yourself easily or instead is there a voice in you that endlessly criticizes yourself for not being good enough? (See also discussion of masculinity in Chapter 5 on Diversity and HRM.)

SECURING THE SELF AT WORK

How then do these ideas about the formation of our early sense of self-consciousness help us to understand adult human motivation more fully, and in particular how power, self-identity and insecurity become linked? Although the force of our early experiences with others makes these founding experiences of the self highly consequential for how we think about ourselves for the rest of our lives, it would be wrong to imagine that once formed, our self actually becomes independent of others. If we have a good start in life then this gives us a certain basic security or confidence that allows us to more easily withstand negative experiences, but because the idea we have of the self or 'self-concept' is a 'synthetic' object, our sense of who or what we are (of 'me' in Mead's terms) is always vulnerable to the responses of others. We are all typically prone to treat the responses of others as if they were a mirror in which we see ourselves.

When we talk about 'self-identity' we are talking about the creation and maintenance of a certain synthesis of experiences; a sense of the continuity over time of our experience of being a self and of the coherence of our own and others' 'objectifications' of the self. As a fundamental aspect of my knowledge of the world, my sense of self is obviously among my most precious possessions. But what if this knowledge is 'reified' – that is, treated not as an always partial and selective definition of me as 'this' or 'that', but rather as the 'whole' and 'objective' truth of who I am? This makes protecting my identity seem like a matter of life or death. I am therefore prone to be constantly comparing myself with others (am I better or worse than them?) and alert to how they see me (do they like, admire, respect me, are they insulting me?). It is this vulnerability of the 'self' that is central to modern motivation techniques. In the mirror of the other's response I look both for confirmation/recognition and feel myself to be exposed to possible rejection or attack.

That each of us is self-conscious, with a sense of our uniqueness and capacity for autonomous action, means that we are both aware and typically resistant to others' attempts to control us overtly. At least in the management literature, if not in practice, part of the history of ideas about motivation that we have traced is a grudging but

Thinkpoint 2.11

I once visited a factory in the north-west of England. It was a plastics factory and the operators each worked at the end of a large moulding machine, pressing and abstracting mouldings for car bumpers. The factory was staffed largely by Asian immigrants but managed by white English managers. I was shown round the factory by a white manager, and we had a conversation about the production process across an employee as if he was not there. Later I went to talk to this man who turned out to be a university-educated schoolteacher who had come abroad and found factory work only because he could find no work as a teacher at home in Bangladesh. What do you think it was like for him to be ignored in the way that he was by the manager? How do you think this may have fitted with his earlier experiences at university? Over time what effect do you think being ignored, overlooked and disregarded would have on his sense of himself?

dawning recognition that the exercise of control is often likely to have negative motivational consequences. Earlier, we saw Walton argues that controlling managers are likely to produce adversial employment relations as opposed to a disciplined environment. I am another person not an object to be used merely for management's purposes, and if I feel myself being manipulated in that way I am likely to resist. Management's seeming recognition in recent years of individual autonomy looks promising, as if enlightened managers have given up control and are now wise enough to simply try to encourage individual commitment.

Here management power and employee autonomy seem to be at odds. But in what follows I want to argue the exact opposite; that power works precisely, and much more efficiently, through shaping the exercise of individual autonomy. It does this in part through coming to shape the very ideals in terms of which I come to judge my own and others' actions. And as Luthans observed, selective recognition by managers is a very powerful way to influence this self-management. To develop this alternative view of power we will briefly look at some of the ideas of Michel Foucault, in particular his analysis of what he called 'disciplinary power'.

THE POWER OF BEING MADE VISIBLE AND KNOWING IT

In his book *Discipline and Punish,* Foucault (1979) notes a shift in the late eighteenth century from what he calls a 'sovereign' view of power to what he terms 'disciplinary' power. We often locate power elsewhere with the 'powerful' – the boss, chief executive, prime minister, Queen – but Foucault argues that this idea merely conceals how, in fact, we practise power upon the self and upon each other. He offers a prison design by Jeremy Bentham, the nineteenth-century utilitarian, as a model for this new form of the exercise of power. Cells in the prison were organized around a central tower, in which, behind blinds, a guard could watch over the prisoners. The key question to ask is: what is the effect of the blinds?

On a railway station in central London, a printed sign with a symbol of an eye tells pedestrians that they are being filmed by security cameras. Road signs tell drivers that there are speed cameras in operation as they drive home. Again the question is why, if they want to catch drivers speeding or pedestrians committing crimes, do they tell them in advance that they are being watched? Or closer to home perhaps, what is the effect of knowing that, at the end of the academic year, a student is going to have to sit an exam?

It is because knowing that one is being watched, that what we do is visible, but not being able to know at any moment in time quite who is watching, changes our behaviour. Foucault suggests that in effect we can do away with the guards, at least for some of the time, since each of us prisoners will over time come to internalize the power relationship and will effectively watch over our own conduct, and those of others. As he puts it, we will 'simultaneously play both roles'. Foucault argues that a whole host of contemporary social technologies have similar effects. These technologies work through making us knowable and visible in certain ways, and through classifying, comparing, homogenizing, hierarchizing and excluding have the effect of both 'individualizing' and 'normalizing' people.

Let's explore what such processes might mean in the context of work and motivation. When Maslow and others began writing of basic human needs for belonging, for love and status, and recognition, they were exhorting managers to recognize employees as other human selves rather than just anonymous labour. Their intentions were no doubt humane, but given the 'synthetic' nature of the self and its vulnerability to others' responses, such *recognition* then becomes a powerful lever on conduct.

- At its simplest the adult relationship between boss and employee can have echoes of earlier power relationships; the boss can become the ideal around which I model myself, a person whom I want to please, for whom I want to be special.
- The hierarchy itself can also serve as a mirror of the value of the self. I can feel a failure when I compare myself to others higher up the hierarchy, and more successful compared to those 'lower' down. I can see promotion as an opportunity to 'make something of myself' and see my colleagues as competitors for such promotion.
- Through performance figures and accounting information the 'results' of my work are made visible to me and others. Praise and criticism, and the occasional dismissal or promotion, advertise what kind of employee I must be if I want to keep my job, if I want to be a success.
- In anticipation of desired recognition and feared blame I supervise my own conduct. Company standards over time become the lens through which I judge and supervise myself. I set myself targets and goals, I criticize my own performance and identify the strengths I need to build on and the weaknesses I need to work on.
- I come to view my 'self' as a project – as my own bit of capital, to be developed, marketed, packaged and sold.
- As Foucault puts it, I become 'the principal of my own subjection'.

Key studies

REFRAMING HUMAN RESOURCE MANAGEMENT (BARBARA TOWNLEY)

Barbara Townley (1994) has drawn extensively on Foucault's writing to offer a very different view of human resource management. Her work picks up on a recurrent theme in this chapter – the indeterminacy or incompleteness of the employment contract – and offers a very different view of the history we have traced. One way to read this history is as a gradual and progressive 'uncovering' or 'discovering' of the truth of motivation – a cumulative knowledge of individuals and their responses to different kinds of job and management. We can see this knowledge as an objective, even scientific, fact that any 'rational' manager should be keen to use. But Townley questions this view of knowing; what if it is not so much an uncovering of some essential truths about the 'self' but rather a way of producing the 'individual' at a particular point in history?

Following Foucault she argues that ways of knowing are also always a form of power relationship. The progressive study of motivation is both stimulated by the desire to render the person controllable, and the knowledge that is produced then has important power effects in the way that it becomes embodied in techniques and practices of organizing the workforce. Part of human resource management involves what she calls 'dividing practices'; work is separated from home, and jobs are ranked in terms of skills, responsibility, experience, seniority and function. Similarly, the individual comes to be categorized in increasingly elaborate ways, as we have seen, in terms of needs, expectations, skills, attitudes, goals and ideals. This knowledge then becomes embedded in ways of *examining* the person in processes of selection, training and development, appraisal, feedback and surveys. It also becomes embedded in ways of talking and getting employees to talk about the self in mentoring and coaching, appraisal and development. The accumulation of knowledge about motivation in this way can be seen, over time, as providing a way of distinguishing 'myself' from others, as well as shaping the norms through which I will judge and appraise myself and others. In the context of work at least it becomes the very means through which we think about the self.

'SOMEONE TO WATCH OVER ME' (SEWELL AND WILKINSON)

Graham Sewell and Barry Wilkinson (1992) drew on Foucault's ideas in a study of shop floor work at a UK engineering firm they called Kays. They suggested that the new physical layout of the shop floor and use of electronic data associated with the introduction of total quality management and just-in-time stock control had greatly increased the visibility of shop floor work and greatly decreased the opportunity for workers to exercise discretion. The quality of what was produced could be traced to particular individuals, and was then reinforced by the public display of quality and productivity information that advertised both desired standards and individual deviations from this. All this was backed up with an emphasis on teams who were given responsibility for achieving targets and continuous improvement. Following Foucault, they suggested that workers were much more effectively controlled under the new production systems. Increased visibility, the knowledge that every aspect of work was being monitored and the likelihood that any failure would bring public humiliation to an individual were enough to ensure that individual employees managed themselves in line with management expectations.

HAPPY FAMILIES AT HEPHAESTUS (CATHERINE CASEY)

Casey's (1999) study of culture change in a transnational company she calls Hephaestus adds a psychological dimension to our understanding of quite how effective new forms of management control can be. Casey suggests that employees typically embraced the values of a happy family that management advertised; they believed the story that management told them. In this way the values of the organization came to act as an ideal that informed individual conduct and the way that they judged themselves and others.

Her argument is that modern management techniques work in part through encouraging such identification with ideals. Whereas in former times employee aggression would be channelled outwards towards management, now she suggests it is channelled back on the self for failing to live up to the ideal of a competent, caring and committed employee. The problem at Hephaestus was that the organization was not quite like the ideal it claimed to be. Repeatedly, members of the family were 'killed off', and the emphasis on being a good team member also involved team attacks on those who had let them down, and rivalry for the recognition of the team leader. The results for employees were considerable levels of individual stress caused by concerns about their own competence, and confused and ambivalent feelings about the official rhetoric of their being all part of one big happy family. For the most part, however, people went along with the official story, and challenged and criticized themselves and colleagues rather than management, for the hypocrisy of saying one thing and doing something different.

Limitations of critical approaches to motivation

The principal contribution of the approaches informed by Marx's analysis of the dynamics of capitalism is to draw attention yet again to the inequalities of power relations at work and how these inform management's selective interest in theories of motivation. While many of the mainstream writers were informed by concerns to improve the human condition, their ideas arguably gained currency because it was hoped that they could help managers to bridge the gap between employing labour and turning that into effective labour power. Capitalist organizations had managed quite well without theories of motivation, and, like John at PYT, managers can still rely on the fact that people need a job as a powerful force for motivation. Changing political, educational and economic conditions have altered the nature of work and employee expectations such that brute force and coercion are less possible, and their negative effects more obviously counterproductive, but employees' calculation of self-interest still goes a long way in ensuring that, as individuals, they will be compliant with what is asked of them. Particularly at lower levels of organizations it is still easy to find all the abuses of economic power: low wages, poor working conditions and coercive and arbitrary management practices.

But if economic exploitation is a reality then, as we have seen, this creates a puzzle as to quite why those who are disadvantaged by a system are so willing to co-operate in their own exploitation. Some of this, as Burawoy argued, can be seen as the unintended side-effects of their own attempts at 'making out', but it is here that ideas about the social construction of the self and in particular Foucault's ideas are particularly helpful. If theories of motivation in the end become the very means through which we come to understand, think and judge ourselves, and if motivation involves self-management, a preoccupation with making something of ourselves, a competitive orientation to others, and a tendency to view failure as a failure of the self rather than the product of economic forces over which we have no control, then the aggression that Marx hoped might be turned outwards against the institutions of private ownership is instead turned inwards against the self.

But these later views of power also disturb some of the reassurance that comes from a view of the world where the worker is cast as the victim of external forces and relatively powerless, at least as an individual, to make a difference. Foucault's analysis of the 'micro-physics of power' robs us of the illusion of being victims, or of the hope that if only we can rid ourselves of the 'bad' other – bosses, owners, lazy workers – then all will be well. We practise power upon ourselves and each other – manager and worker are in this sense both subjects – and it is much more difficult to even conceive of resistance if the effects of power are to be discovered in the very ways in which we think about ourselves.

This section began with a quote from James Wolfensohn, the president of the World Bank, talking about global poverty and inequality. What the motivational emphasis upon individual autonomy and self-discipline ensures, perhaps, is that we are simply too preoccupied with ourselves to notice or feel part of such global processes, let alone to figure out the role that our own conduct has in both reproducing the problem and creating the solution.

Thinkpoint 2.12

The PYT case study that runs throughout this chapter and is used to illustrate some of the different ideas about motivation was researched and written in the 1990s. By way of a final set of thoughts let's try to imagine what might have changed in the organization of work and staff at PYT had it survived as an organization.

Let's think about the work itself. There have, of course, been massive changes in technology in the last 20 years. One possibility is that the call monitoring technology that PYT used would by now have been greatly improved. Rather than simply having the ability to listen in to staff calls on the pretext of delivering training, it would now be possible for managers to monitor every second of staff activity whilst at work. Via a staff member's use of their computer and telephone it would be possible to automatically record everything and log how many calls they had done, how much time they spent on each call, and how much time processing information after a call. It would even be possible to log the length of toilet and lunch breaks. The incentive structures and target systems would still be in place but perhaps with some greater consideration of the importance of customer retention, and with much more information that could be used to set targets for average call length, call processing times, size of advertisement sold, etc. Information would be available in real time to team managers allowing them to observe even the smallest shifts in individual and group productivity. Whereas at the time of the study there was a certain glamour for at least some staff to working at PYT, call centre work is now much more common and arguably much more oppressive. One version of this describes call centres as 'electronic sweatshops'. The suggestion is that new digital technology allows much more intensive forms of electronic surveillance that then allows managers to seek to control every aspect of what an employee does at work. For the employee, the work of selling advertising space to customers will perhaps not have changed much, although online media are possibly now much more important. But it would likely have become a much more oppressive environment in terms of the routines of call centre work. Of course, PYT, had it survived, may have decided to simply move its call centres offshore to reduce costs.

In terms of motivation it is possible that PYT may have invested in training its managers in the most up-to-date methods. The shift that some have observed in the last 20 years can be seen as attempts to counter the increased direct control of work by creating a work environment that emphasizes employees' freedom and ability to 'be yourself' (Fleming and Sturdy, 2011). Rather than try to use the team to impose powerful group norms of expected behaviour on its members, now management would be selling the benefits of working at PYT in terms of the freedoms it offered staff to be whatever they wanted to be at work. The new 'liberation management' encourages staff to have fun at work and with each other; it celebrates the diversity of its staff and will perhaps introduce all sorts of charity or health initiatives of which they can be part. Its managers will no longer demand conformity from staff but rather celebrate diversity and difference. No longer will staff have to worry so much about where they shop or what they wear or even perhaps what they say to each other or their managers – as long, of course, as they are meeting their targets. The managerial injunction to staff to 'be yourself' can be seen perhaps as the triumph of motivation theory since there is, as it were, nowhere else for staff to go. How can such a demand to just 'be yourself' be anything other than good? For the organization, however, such new motivational techniques are just a further attempt to finally capture all the energies that a person would normally reserve for their life outside work, so that work becomes life itself.

Conclusion

This chapter began with the ideas of Frederick Taylor and his principles of scientific management. Motivation here was about money and the potential for the interests of management in profit, and workers in higher wages, to be reconciled through a division of mental and manual labour. Such ideas stand in sharp contrast to the earliest ideas that we have explored in this chapter; those of Marx, and his suggestion that there is a fundamental contradiction at the heart of capitalism. We produce together, but then some people, by virtue of being owners, can exploit those who have only their labour to sell. The owners' interest in maximizing profits is always at odds with the employees' interest in maximizing their earnings. Economic power gives owners and managers a powerful lever to dictate the terms on which others work – in this sense economic insecurity is all the motivation that many need. But then there is a huge difference between dull conformity under pressure of coercion and enthusiastic participation. The challenge for management has been to find ways in which they can turn labour into committed employees. It is not enough for employees just to turn up; what is wanted is their commitment and energy and the effort that goes with this.

Marx's ideas, and the associated fears of industrial conflict and political change, haunt the subsequent study of motivation. For the mainstream theories that we considered there was, and continues to be, a problem of motivation, but for these writers the problem is assumed to be solvable within capitalism if only they can understand the individual more thoroughly. The early content theories that we considered were those of Maslow, McGregor, McClelland, Hertzberg and Hackman. Each focuses on a different dimension as the explanation of motivation. For Maslow, motivation was to be achieved through a better understanding of human needs and the integration of this understanding into the organization of work. Maslow suggests a hierarchy of needs from physiological, through safety and belonging, to status and recognition and finally self-actualization. McGregor, drawing upon Maslow, suggests that the behaviour associated with theory X is easily discovered in work organizations but is to be explained not in terms of some truth about workers – they are lazy, will refuse responsibility, etc., – but rather in terms of the assumptions management make about workers and the effects of these assumptions on workers. The problem of motivation is in the manager not the employee. McClelland develops this thought further with his exploration of managers' motivation – their needs for achievement, power and to be liked. His finding was that the need for power is the best predictor of good management in terms of the climate such managers create among staff – as long as they have their own ego needs under control.

But then Hertzberg enters with a different story. The focus on management–employee relations misses the point. The key drivers of motivation are intrinsic to the job a person does; the work itself and the opportunities it offers for achievement, recognition and responsibility, all of which allow individuals to grow psychologically. These factors produce positive satisfaction, and should not be confused with the factors that cause dissatisfaction, which include supervision, salary and security. Removing sources of dissatisfaction will not produce satisfaction but rather an absence of dissatisfaction. Hackman and Lawler pursued this thought that it is the work itself that matters with their assertion that 'internal motivation' depends upon work being meaningful, involving the experience of responsibility, and where there is knowledge of the results. These motivations in turn imply the need for jobs to have skill variety, task identity and significance structured into them.

The second mainstream set of theories that we explored are often termed 'process theories'. In their earliest form – Vroom's expectancy theory – it was argued that motivation is the product of valence (what I want and do not want), instrumentality (my expectations of what leads to desired outcomes) and expectancy (my expectations about what I want, and how to achieve it, are related). Importantly, the employee is rediscovered here as an intelligent person, making sense of their experiences and then acting on the basis of the expectations that these experiences have created.

These process views were further developed in the 1980s and 1990s under the weight of renewed competitive pressure to solve the problem of motivation through a recognition of individuals' capacities for self-motivation.

Reluctantly, it seems that managers have finally learnt the lessons of earlier studies. Management cannot control staff, pull their strings like puppets or rely on coercion. This will, at best, only produce dull compliance if not outright opposition. People need to motivate themselves, and the manager's task is to create the conditions that support this. We looked at Levinson's argument that it is a person's own ego-ideal – what they aspire to achieve – that motivates. Locke and Latham relatedly argued for the importance of stretching goals for motivation; ideally these are goals that we set for ourselves and to which we are committed. Bandura, as a social psychologist, takes us further into the mysteries of self-motivation with his ideas about the importance of our own 'self-efficacy'. Past experience will have shaped a set of beliefs we have about what we can do and its likely success, and these will shape what we attempt and how strongly we pursue the goals we set for ourselves. Managers can support such self-motivation by creating empowering conditions that allow people to feel that they can make a difference. Luthans also suggests that ideals, goals and people's views of themselves can be influenced by the selective use of recognition by managers.

Now, taken at face value this history of motivation theory suggests a progressive movement towards enlightened management conduct. It begins with Taylor stripping out the mental content of work and insisting that thinking and planning is manager's work, along with close control and monitoring of mindless staff. Then gradually what he had taken away is rediscovered in employees – the range of different needs beyond money, the damaging results of certain management assumptions, the importance of whole and meaningful tasks. Then, with the process theories, the rediscovery of the thinking self-conscious employees, who are as capable of autonomous action as the manager, and who must therefore be encouraged to manage themselves, with management in a supporting and enabling role. The theory is seductive. We would all like to think of ourselves as in control – as able to make a difference. We have all been taught to work upon ourselves, to improve ourselves and make something of ourselves. What could possibly be wrong about that?

For Marx and those influenced by his thoughts, the problem of motivation needs to be understood on a wider canvas. Getting people motivated will always be a problem under capitalism because, although we depend upon each other to produce wealth, private ownership of the means of production allows owners to exploit those who must sell their labour in order to live. Though profits are only made through labour, the interests of owners diverge since labour is a cost to be minimized if profits are to be maximized. Either managers can rely on job insecurity to ensure compliance, or if it is cost-effective, they can invest in winning hearts and minds. But still the contradictions persist. While Marx looked at the power effects of ownership and focused on economic insecurity, more recent theories have explored how insecurity about the self, and management's power to create insecurity about the value of the self, is used to motivate. The seeming celebration of individual self-management in empowered organizations is here recast as a more subtle and effective form of domination. Power works not through constraining us from the outside but through shaping the way we think about ourselves, the goals we set ourselves and the judgements we make about ourselves. Managers and employees are no different from each other in this respect; both are shaped as subjects by the new forms of organizational control. But while we are encouraged to become and remain preoccupied with ourselves, then all sorts of collective and political opportunities for resistance and change are foreclosed. Inequality and injustice remain, but we are now prone to blame ourselves and our colleagues for failure. We are so busy making something of ourselves, so eager to compete with our colleagues for promotion, so keen to have the security of belonging to a happy family, that we cannot even think that things could or should be otherwise.

Motivation theorists set out to discover the secrets of human nature so that more could be got out of it. Others with more humane interests wanted managers to see the employee in more than economic terms but still believed that the interests of managers and workers could be reconciled within capitalism. Others have identified not with the organization and its goals but with those who suffer from being managed. Mainstream theory here reappears as an ideology that masks the conflicts of interest at the heart of capitalism, and in the recent recognition of employee autonomy has simply found a new object for more subtle forms of domination.

Case study 2.6
A PROBLEM (OF MOTIVATION) AT PYT PLC (6)

PYT ceased to operate as a company when its contract to manage the directory was not renewed. One of the factors involved in the decision not to renew the contract was the discovery of certain financial irregularities by PYT auditors in the previous year. The new incentive structure for sales people – under which they were to be paid commission only on net new business – had a fatal flaw. Staff in one office realized that if a single record card was removed from the office of the support staff all records of net customer losses attributable to an individual sales person were lost, and their commission earnings were thereby greatly inflated. The scam was only discovered after eight months, by which time it had spread to a number of offices and cost nearly US$1 million. In this case, then, the highly incentivized pursuit of self-interest had an unanticipated yet disastrous effect on the common interest in the future of the business.

QUESTIONS
1   Is there such a thing as a common interest in work organizations?
2   How could we arrive at a shared definition of such a common interest?

Discussion questions

1   How has our understanding of how to motivate ourselves and others developed since Frederick Taylor first introduced his ideas about scientific management more than a century ago?

2   Which of the ideas covered in this chapter did you find particularly helpful in thinking about your own motivation?

3   What are the key differences and similarities between content and process theories of motivation?

4   Can managers motivate or is motivation always self-motivation?

5   In what ways is it impossible to understand motivation without also thinking about how power works on the self and in relationships?

6   Is Marx's concept of alienation still useful in understanding the modern experience of working?

7   Why is personal autonomy so important to motivation? In what ways is the image of the autonomous self always something of an illusion?

8   What are the key lessons that managers should draw from the study of management over the last century and a half?

Further reading

Richard Sennett, *The Corrosion of Character: The Personal Consequences of Work in the New Capitalism,* Norton and Company, London, 1998.

This is a follow-up study to an earlier classic that Richard Sennett and Jonathon Cobb wrote called *The Hidden Injuries of Class.* It is based on interviews with the now grown-up child of first generation immigrants in the United States, and offers a compassionate view of how they make sense of their own experiences of failure and dislocation arising from the globalization of capitalism.

Peter Fusaro and Ross Miller, *What Went Wrong at Enron?,* Wiley and Sons, London, 2002.

This is a very readable account of the recent collapse of Enron. It offers a description of the fatal consequences of

economic incentives for senior executives, and the way in which the organizational culture – 'Rank and Yank' – helped to keep employees quiet as the company headed for collapse.

E. Locke (ed.), *'The Blackwell Handbook of Principles of Organizational Behaviour,* Blackwell, Oxford, 2000.

There are a number of good articles in this collection of current thinking about motivation. They are clear and easy to read but completely uncritical.

Tracy Kidder, *The Soul of a New Machine,* Allen Lane, 1982.

This is a great read and an exciting account of the development of a new computer. It is a story that illustrates both the frustrations of large organizations as well as the energies that can develop in a small group committed to a task they all believe in.

References

Bandura, A. (2000) 'Cultivate self-efficacy for personal and organizational effectiveness', in E. Locke (ed.) *The Blackwell Handbook of Principles of Organizational Behaviour*, Oxford: Blackwell.

Braverman, H. (1974) *Labor and Monopoly Capital*, New York: Monthly Review Press.

Burawoy, M. (1979) *Manufacturing Consent*, Chicago: Chicago University Press.

Casey, C. (1999) 'Come join our family: Discipline and integration in corporate organizational culture', *Human Relations*, 52(2): 155–178.

Conger, J. (2000) 'Motivate performance through empowerment', in E. Locke (ed.) *The Blackwell Handbook of Principles of Organizational Behaviour*, Oxford: Blackwell.

Fleming, P. and Sturdy, A. (2011) 'Being yourself' in the electronic sweatshop: New forms of normative control', *Human Relations*, 64(2) 177–208.

Foucault, M. (1979) *Discipline and Punish: The Birth of the Prison*, London: Allen Lane.

Giddens, A. (1971) *Capitalism and Modern Social Theory: An Analysis of the Writings of Marx, Durkheim and Weber*, Cambridge: Cambridge University Press.

Hackman, J. R. and Oldham, G. R. (1980) *Work Redesign*, Reading, MA: Addison-Wesley.

Hertzberg, F. (2003) 'One more time: How do you motivate employees?', *Harvard Business Review on Motivating People*, Boston, MA: Harvard Business School Press.

Ho, K. (2009) *Liquidated: An Ethnography of Wall Street*, Durham: Duke University Press.

Latham, G. (2000) 'Motivate employee performance through goal-setting', in E. Locke (ed.) *The Blackwell Handbook of Principles of Organizational Behaviour*, Oxford: Blackwell.

Levinson, H. (2003) 'Management by whose objectives?', in *Harvard Business Review on Motivating People*, Boston, MA: Harvard Business School Press.

Luthans, F. and Stajkovic, A. (2000) 'Provide recognition for performance improvement', in E. Locke (ed.) *The Blackwell Handbook of Principles of Organizational Behaviour*, Oxford: Blackwell.

Maslow, A. (1989) 'A theory of human motivation', in H. Leavitt, L. Pondy and D. Boje (eds) *Readings in Managerial Psychology*, fourth edn, pp. 20–35, Chicago: University of Chicago Press.

McClelland, D. (2003) 'Power is the great motivator', in *Harvard Business Review on Motivating People,* Boston, MA: Harvard Business School Press.

McGregor, D. (1989) 'The human side of enterprise', in H. Leavitt, L. Pondy and D. Boje (eds) *Readings in Managerial Psychology*, fourth edn, pp. 314–324, New York: McGraw-Hill.

Mead, G. H. (1934) *Mind, Self and Society*, Chicago: University of Chicago Press.

Sewell, G. and Wilkinson, B. (1992) 'Someone to watch over me: Surveillance, discipline and the just-in-time labour process', *Sociology*, 26(12): 271–289.

Thomas, K. and Velthouse, B. (1990) 'Cognitive elements of empowerment: An interpretative model of intrinsic task motivation', *Academy of Management Review*, 15(4): 666–681.

Townley, B. (1994) *Reframing Human Resource Management-Power, Ethics and the Subject at Work*, London: Sage.

Vroom, V. H. (1964) *Work and Motivation*, New York: Wiley.

Vroom, V. H. and Deci, E. (1992) *Management and Motivation*, Harmondsworth: Penguin.

Walton, R. (1985) 'From control to commitment in the workplace', *Harvard Business Review,* March–April: 77–84.

3 Individual differences, personality and self

DAMIAN O'DOHERTY AND SHEENA VACHHANI

Aims of the chapter

This chapter will:

- Explore why the study of personality at work has received considerable attention.

- Explore concepts and ideas that have been used to build up theories about individual differences, personality and self.

- Explore some of the **key ideas that have influenced** management's understanding of personality.

- Examine **the limits of mainstream approaches** to personality in management and organization as we begin to understand 'personality' in terms of subjectivity and identity.

- Examine some of the linkages between the study of personality and **identity** as they are presented by various writers.

Key concepts and learning objectives

By the end of this chapter you should understand:

- **Personality type** theories and how they differ from what are called **trait theories** of personality.

- The development of key personality type theories from the ancient Greeks through **Carl Jung** to the more recent experimental and laboratory-based work of the **Eysencks**. We will also look at the influential **Myers-Briggs** type indicator (MBTI) of personality.

- The central ideas that inform what many people believe to be the **biological basis** of personality.

- Some of the **criticisms of mainstream** approaches to the study of personality.

- The development of **theories of identity** that allow us to see how a wider set of social forces shape the development and emergence of unique selves.

- The contribution of writers who show how **self is a dynamic and open-ended process** – one that develops and changes over time.

- A more **existential interpretation of the individual** in which it makes more critical sense to think about people through the concept of identity rather than personality.

Overview and key points

We tend to think of ourselves as *having* a personality. Maybe we understand ourselves, for example, as an extrovert or an introvert, or perhaps we think we are 'easy going', depressive or melancholic personality types. We also attribute personality to our friends and colleagues. This is likely to mean that there will be differences between how others view us and how we view ourselves. Imagine that? You think of yourself one way, but others see you in a completely different way! It's that kind of thinking that can lead to paranoia! However, before the paranoid personality type rears its head, let's think some of this through a little more carefully because the issues it raises are central to the concerns of this chapter. Essentially, managers responsible for organizational behaviour want to know if different jobs require different personalities – or whether some kinds of personalities are better than others in terms of job performance.

Such knowledge would prove very useful to management because it would allow them to help work organizations decide on who is the 'right' individual to recruit or promote. However, as our opening remarks hint, whilst personality is complex and fascinating, it is also elusive and difficult to define – or in mainstream management terms, *operationalize* – for the purposes of work, effort and efficiency. The astute manager of a contemporary organization is one who is both attentive to the different personalities of people at work, but also suspicious about the value of 'personality' as a determining factor shaping work success, whilst able to see wider group and social influences, work effort and organizational behaviour. In addition, the up-to-date manager should also be aware that personality might not be something these days which is exclusively human. If we are entering a world populated by digital technologies and artificial intelligence then management is going to have to learn to deal with things like robot personalities, chatbots, androids, and various avatars that mix human and non-human qualities. This is likely to lead to the emergence of 'personality' types for which we have little experience or understanding.

This chapter begins with popular, mainstream ways of thinking about individual personality before introducing more critical and theoretically innovative understandings of subjectivity and identity. Note the difference in concepts: we move from personality to identity. And there are good reasons for this move. We also intend to take you *into* the texts and thinking of some of the most important writers and thinkers to help you work out how and why they thought as they did and how they arrived at their conclusions. This will help us to start analyzing and – moreover – in a way that is more critically advanced. In this way we will begin to see some of the implications of *adopting the terminology of personality* and of thinking of the management of work organization in terms of the supervision of personality. However, in order to make this move we need to tackle some quite difficult issues concerning methodology, namely the methodologies of the natural sciences and how they may apply to organizations. For there is a difference between natural and social sciences in this field which replays the perennial question in business and management: is management a science or an art?

MAINSTREAM APPROACHES TO INDIVIDUAL DIFFERENCES, PERSONALITY AND SELF

Introduction

The question of science and whether the methods of the natural sciences are appropriate in the study of personality remains one of the main debating issues in the field. The use of laboratories for testing and research alongside techniques of formal hypothesis testing, quantification, and modelling remain popular in studies of personality. A whole series of assumptions and implications for management and organization behaviour (OB) are bound up with these methods associated with the natural sciences. One needs to be clear about the influence of the natural sciences. This explains, for example, both the existence and the faith that people have in things like psychometric testing as a way of recruiting and managing human resources in an organization.

Nomothetic approach (to personality) Distinguished by the beliefs that there are underlying universals (e.g., of personality) against which everything and everyone can be measured and classified. Personality, for example, tends to be understood as an inherited phenomenon and one that is the product of biology, genetics and heredity. The nomothetic approach is based on large-scale quantitative and scientific study with the aim of discovering the mechanisms and 'laws' that explain human behaviour.

Idiographic approach to personality An approach that is suspicious of the value of generalized 'scientific' categories of classification and thereby understands personality in the terms used by individuals to describe themselves. It perceives individuals in terms of personal experience; their personality is learned through social and cultural interaction as opposed to biological or genetic determination.

Experiential Pertaining to direct experience rather than thought or imagination.

Social construction – social constructionists (Similar to the definition of social construction of technology or SCOT) focus on social interpretations that produce and define given situations. Social constructs are seen as the result of human choices rather than being essentialist (i.e., having an underlying essence) or preordained. Social constructionism stresses the importance of perspective and ideologies of individuals and social groups that affect our understanding of situations and are socially shaped. The purpose of social constructionism is to understand how social phenomena are created and reproduced as part of the ongoing accomplishment of reality.

Modern science inherits the ancient classification of personality, which identifies four basic temperaments (see discussion of these later). Later developments reclassified and organized these four temperaments in terms of two fundamental dimensions of personality – namely, changeability and emotion. These categories are central to the work of Katherine Briggs and Isabel Myers-Briggs who remain two of the most influential writers in the field of personality and management. Influenced by Carl Jung they developed a practical tool that many claim helps managers identify or 'measure' personality: the Myers-Briggs type indicator (MBTI) test of personality. According to Myers-Briggs there are four basic underlying tendencies or preferences evident in the way we think and act and which define the *type* of personality we have.

Such 'scientific' approaches are popular amongst many hard-pressed managers, in part because it seems to offer relatively straightforward and simple, practical solutions to problems of OB. The thinking and methods of the natural sciences have been used predominantly to develop what are called **nomothetic** theories of personality based on **traits** or personality **types**. The foundations of this approach to thinking about personality are associated with the studies of Hans and Michael Eysenck, who laid the groundwork for how most people today think about and study personality. **Idiographic** approaches to personality, on the other hand, emphasize the more living and variable nature of personality, in which hard and fast categories and classifications might not be appropriate.

Where 'types' and the influence of 'traits' can be identified and catalogued, management can more quickly and efficiently recruit and select individuals, build teams and develop leadership in organizations. Or, at least, that is the promise. The critical approach favours a more sensate or 'inner' and **experiential** study of personality, studying how it emerges *in situ* and how it is lived, where its complex and dynamic nature may be studied. In the second half of this chapter we build on this critical approach in ways that allow us to better look at the existential dilemmas confronting individuals where theories of identity are more helpful than those theories preoccupied with the scientific identification and classification of personality. This brings into focus the influence of society and the **social construction** of individuals in shaping and determining personal identity.

Central problems in the field: Mainstream and critical

The mainstream follows what is called a **positivist** approach to scientific method in its approach to studying personality; the more critical studies of management and organization behaviour reject positivist methods of science, but are perhaps more theoretically speculative and adventurous. However, both the mainstream and its critics have scientific and anti-positivist tendencies. We explore the idea that scientific methodology may be predisposed to seeking explanations for personality in simple and reductive terms. Rather than challenge common sense assumptions about traits such as 'anxiety', 'irrational behaviour', or being 'emotional', 'hopeful' etc., people influenced by the Eysencks would take these as a given and go out and try to 'test' or measure them. In so doing they ignore the changing social and historical construction of these categories – what counts as 'moody', for example, is never fixed culturally or historically.

Critical thinkers tend to think more in terms of *identity*, that allows one to explore the more political, spiritual and emotional make-up of individuals, dimensions of being human that may change over time. Critical thinkers sometimes go even further and question the very institution of science because of its dangerous tendencies. Science is, of course, disciplinary, part of which involves a training – or intellectual regimen – that encourages us to see and think in disciplined but inevitably partial and limited ways. It is disciplinary in another sense in that every way of *looking* is a way of **acting** or bringing about different kinds of worlds. Science has practical effects in the world – not just in terms of the effects its medicines or technologies have *in the world* but also world-making.

These preliminary thoughts should be suggestive that the individual as a species being-in-the-world might suffer a disservice or even be impoverished by restricting our focus to 'personality'. Critical thinkers want to go beyond the superficial, the mundane and the practical, which continues to drive the thinking and activity of most managers in work organizations. They want to think in terms of wider and deeper questions, such as the quest for meaning and purpose. This is why the

Positivism Term used especially by critical analysts to identify a method of social science research in which the differences between the 'natural' phenomena of the physical sciences and human phenomena are downplayed. Positivists are those who presume, and/or seek to emulate, the causal methods of the natural sciences. In doing so, they neglect the problems of meaning and interpretation, or how researchers are active agents (not merely passive recorders) in constructing the events and behaviour they may claim merely to report.

Case study 3.1
SenseCreatives

Veronica Marsh is the human resources director at the head office for SenseCreatives, a Chicago-based, medium-sized creative agency. SenseCreatives markets itself as a 'creative thinking' organization that will be attuned to an organization's needs and is able to offer the most innovative advertising solutions to its customers. In the coming weeks Veronica is looking to recruit ten university graduates into the organization to build on the increasing customer base. As part of their recruitment and selection exercise they run a psychometric test that, it is claimed, cuts through the presentation of self, those illusions and images projected by individuals, and even the deluded beliefs people often have about themselves. Only certain personalities have proven to be a success in working in the creative advertising industry. The psychometric test used by SenseCreatives is based on the latest scientific research and findings. It gets right to the heart of your personality so that Veronica Marsh and her colleagues can base their selection decision on the type of person you actually are and not the kind of person you might like to think you are. As she argues:

> *You need a strong, vibrant personality for this job ... Our success has been built upon individuals and their commitment to meeting customer needs creatively and enthusiastically. Are you tenacious? Ambitious? Bubbly? Outgoing? A problem-solver? A good communicator? We are seeking the best graduates for jobs at SenseCreatives.*

As you listen to Veronica you begin to think about something your Dad said one day. 'It's all about *who* you know, not *what* you know that gets you on in this world'. As a number of important studies have shown (Jackall, 1988; Grey, 1994; Watson, 1994; Casey, 1995) often what is important in career advancement is connections, making connections and political skills that determine success. Rather than a particular type of personality you might wonder whether it is more important to find ways of 'fitting in', being adaptable, even chameleon-like by cultivating, developing and presenting the right attributes – that it is, in essence, all about image and manipulation. Maybe in the creative industries personality is better thought of as something that is manufactured and packaged. One could argue that those careful to maintain a certain corporate reputation are careful in the kind of image they present to the world, continually self-monitoring their behaviour and 'impression management' (Goffman, 1959) for personal and political goals. Many people will go further and claim that they will leave their personality at home when they go to work – that their 'true self' is something far different from the kind of image they project and use to advance their careers.

central problem for critical thinkers is the question about identity, not personality. The challenge posed by this more critical agenda is that, unless we shift the terms of the debate into these more complex realms and challenge management thinking, we will continue to create negative and detrimental tendencies in work organization.

Personality, management and organization

We have a number of ways of classifying personality, from the relatively simple to the more complex. It is often said, for example, that someone has a 'nice' personality. On the other hand we might overhear a conversation in which it is remarked that Veronica Marsh of SenseCreatives is a good manager but that she oscillates unpredictably between what we will learn to call a 'type a' and a 'type b' personality. But which of these personalities is the one that is going to work most successfully in organizations today? You may well have your own personality but we need to remember that all of us have to work with a diverse range of other personalities in organizations, some of whom we are compatible with, and others who we find very difficult to work alongside. One thing that we do know about organization in the future is that nearly everyone will have to learn to manage other personalities as we learn to understand, shape and manage our own.

THE PSYCHOMETRIC TEST

The psychometric test is often our initial introduction to the world of work and our first experience of business organization by virtue of the fact that part of the recruitment and selection process will involve candidates completing a personality 'test'. In order to recruit and develop employees in organizations, management frequently use psychometric tests but it remains one of most controversial techniques deployed by managers. Associated with the practices of management forged out of what was referred to in Chapter 1 as the 'entity view of organization', psychometric testing is also used to help management assess candidates for promotion.

In this chapter you will discover a number of different ways in which it might be claimed that personality can be 'extracted' from an individual and defined in a neat and succinct way. Despite our best efforts it would seem we cannot permanently hide or disguise our 'true' personality. You may possibly have seen newspaper articles reporting, for example, that scientists have discovered how even the position and shape of your body during sleep reveals your type of personality!

In many areas of contemporary work organization, the significance of personality as a factor in determining success or failure is beginning to be realized by senior management. As Chapter 4 examines, working in teams has become an almost universal mode of organizing work today – but getting the right blend of personalities has proved to be a most confusing and complex task (Belbin, 1981; cf. Barker, 1999).

The most effective managers of future organizations may well be those who are able to tackle the problems associated with personality at work with a broader and critical understanding of the issues concerning personality. In order to begin to address this issue we will look in some depth at the kind of thinking that grounds two of the most popular and enduring theories of personality: the type indicator test, associated with the research team of mother and daughter Katherine Briggs and Isabel Myers; and trait theory, established and most exhaustively studied by the brothers Hans and Michael Eysenck.

Thinkpoint 3.1

Have you experienced psychometric testing? If so, do you think it provided the best way of determining the best candidate for the job?

Psychometrics are a way of measuring mental capacities and abilities. In psychology, psychometrics are concerned with designing and using psychological tests that interpret and measure individual constructs such as attitudes, knowledge or personality. Psychometrics provide a way of measuring psychological constructs where mathematical techniques are applied to understand the outcomes and scores of tests. These may then be matched to job profiles or ideal types of employees for an organization.

Box 3.1
Psychometrics

Introduction to personality

According to *Webster's Encyclopedic Dictionary*, personality is the 'visible aspect of one's character'. In other words, this is what other people see or perceive. It is not necessarily then, what you might think of yourself, but how you come across to other people. The English word 'personality' is derived from the Latin *persona*, which means 'mask', as in the face mask that was worn by actors on stage in the theatre. In Latin, *persona* also has associations with 'role', as in one's *role* in life, in a play or a tale that is being told. The dictionary goes on to further clarify personality by saying that the person is an embodiment of a collection of qualities and that personality is the 'essential character of a person' or the 'organized pattern of behavioural characteristics of the individual'. It is often used to define the sum total of the physical, mental, emotional and social characteristics of an individual. Further enquiry into definition finds that the word personality is often used in a disparaging or hostile sense, as in the phrase, 'the conversation deteriorated into personalities'. We might also think here of a personality clash or the disparaging judgement often intended in the phrase 'a cult of personality'.

Box 3.2
Definition of
personality

Our search for definition is getting confusing, complex and even a little contradictory. It seems to be at one and the same time, a mask or a disguise, something that is presented to others, or something that is presented to satisfy the demands of the situation or the environment, *and* the innermost authentic core of a person, which is what distinguishes people. As we go on to examine later in the chapter, personality occupies a strange, double space – both public and private, 'fluid' or malleable and objective or concrete.

Table 3.1 Examples of personality profiles

Name	Elements of personality as presented to others	Personality as you see it	Ideal job
Jackie Paper	Quiet, sensible, helpful, caring	Extravert, likes talking to people, quite 'deep', emotional	Bar Manager? The Caring Professions? Personnel Manager?
Christine Pharos	Loud, fun-loving, flirtatious, vivacious	Envious, insecure, quiet, suspicious	Band Manager? Marketing?

Exercise 3.1

Take a look around at your group of friends. Of all those people you know, who do you think is most likely to be a success working to sell and promote contemporary DJs and bands in the music industry? Some of your friends, for example, might be very popular. They are sociable, they seem to mix easily, and enjoy being with large groups of people. Others are likely to be quieter, reserved, or, as some people say, 'bookish'. Think carefully and try to make a list of all your friends or family and then next to their names list what you take to be a few of the most salient features of their personality. Indicate what you think might be their 'strengths' and 'weaknesses'. Are they impatient for example? Or, do they tend to talk too much and then not listen to others carefully enough? Then make a list of all the things you think SenseCreatives might be looking for in its ideal graduate account executive. It is important to be mindful of the fact that some elements of personality which *you* find disagreeable or unpleasant might in fact be deemed essential to the successful execution of a professional role with all its associated duties and responsibilities. Furthermore, remember that the company will be thinking about the future. They are likely to want people who are flexible and adaptable, and not so stuck in their ways that they appear to have an over-rigid personality. We will be referring back to this list as the chapter develops so spend some time thinking carefully about the people you know. Bear in mind that people are often very different from the way they come across in social company. Therefore you might want to compile your list so you can distinguish how your friends might define their own personalities and how you or others might interpret their personality. Table 3.1 provides one or two examples.

NOMOTHETIC AND IDIOGRAPHIC APPROACHES

One of the difficulties involved in drawing up a catalogue of personalities is the problem you have no doubt encountered in this relatively simple and schematic exercise – namely, what is to count as relevant? What is relevant or significant in one person's character and what elements of personality would serve to distinguish and identify that person? Is there a difference? Many people doing this exercise for the first time find that they have no common reference against which to measure people. We arrive at a jumbled list of characteristics from which it is very difficult to really say what it is that defines somebody's personality. Typically we end up with that all too banal conclusion that everybody is different, that we are all unique and you cannot hope to generalize. In some ways this is probably true, but it does not help our human resources director, Veronica Marsh, who is trying to identify which applicants are likely to be the most successful at SenseCreatives. This problem can be understood more formally as a reflection of different approaches or methodologies in the study of personality, namely a nomothetic approach as against an idiographic one (Eysenck and Eysenck, 1985, p. 3).

One way round this problem is to standardize the measurement of personality. That is, you extract two or three elements of personality that then form a template against which comparisons can be made. You might think, for example, that what is most important in somebody's personality is whether they are driven by emotion, or whether they are, instead, more logical and rational, using their intellect to guide their actions. Take a look at the table you have drawn and see if there are any commonalities that your friends and families share. Take the category emotion/intellect as a test case and try to assess your group against this scale. Do half your friends fall on the side of emotional and the other half you have categorized as rational? Can you quantify *how* emotional your friends are? Could you say that one of your friends is almost 100 per cent driven by their emotions, whereas another is only 80 per cent driven by emotion? What we need in order to be able to accurately measure people in this kind of way is some very accurate definitions of the category 'emotional'. We also need an outer limit, or an extremely emotional person, against whom we can then measure the rest of our population. Once we start constructing tools of measurement in this way, we are beginning to think of personality through a nomothetic approach.

Among some of the most important work that has been conducted in the nomothetic approach is the research and writings of Hans Jurgen Eysenck who studied personality from the 1940s through to the late 1980s. However, there is a long history of study and interest in this approach that takes us back to the pioneers of what is today's more formal research.

The four temperaments

Most people identify Hippocrates as 'the father of medicine' but it was he who first began to think about the classification and explanation of personality during the third and fourth centuries BC. Hippocrates tells us that from his observations and studies there are basically four temperaments – the melancholic, the choleric, the sanguine and the phlegmatic (Eysenck and Rachman, 1965). In a more modern light we might define the melancholic type as someone who seems to suffer from introspection and withdrawal, or heavy, downcast moods; somebody who is generally depressive in nature. The choleric person, by contrast, is quite cranky, fiery and irritable. We would experience someone who is sanguine as cheerful, hopeful and basically optimistic; and the phlegmatic person would appear sluggish or apathetic, listless or laid back.

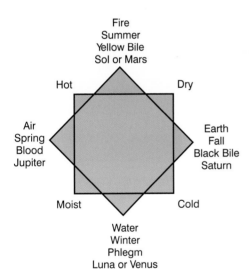

Figure 3.1
The humours or temperaments and reasons related to the qualities established in the Corpus Hippocrericum (fifth century BC)

For Hippocrates, people are born and 'made up' out of four basic material substances: black bile, yellow bile, blood and phlegm. In Hippocratic observation these four body substances equate to the four basic 'universal' elements – earth, fire, air and water, respectively. The exact composition, the mixture or 'temperament' of one's inheritance, is largely determined by spiritual and material forces in action at the time of one's birth – including the 'pull' exerted by the arrangement of the planets (see Short, 2000). Born under the influence of the remote and slow-moving planet Saturn, for example, an individual is likely to be subject to an excess of black bile which leaves the individual predisposed to melancholia. These ideas were taken up and developed by another Greek physician, Galen, who introduced a greater degree of order and classification to the exercise. He noted how people born with an excess of black bile tended to become melancholic, or, in our terms, depressive in character. Yellow bile equates to the choleric type; blood with a sanguine temperament; and phlegm with the phlegmatic person.

Wilhelm Max Wundt (1832–1920), a German physiologist and early psychologist, was the first to recognize that these categories should not be understood as sealed boxes but rather as continuums along common dimensions. In other words, where the influence of melancholia was fairly mild in one person they might begin to feel the effects of more choleric type factors. It is not simply a case of either/or, then, but of competing forces that find expression in a myriad of personality complexions. What explains the basic distribution of personality characteristics are the strength of feelings and the speed of change in a person's feelings. Somebody who is highly anxious would normally be considered to have a melancholic temperament where feelings are generally considered quite stable, but Wundt showed how anxiety could be observed in combination with people who are 'quickly roused'. He suggested that what explains the melancholic, the choleric, etc., and what underlies the four temperaments, are the fundamental dimensions of 'changeability' and 'emotion'. The Eysencks (1985, p. 45) developed a schematic diagram that helps us picture what Wundt was getting at, as shown in Figure 3.2.

Figure 3.2 Diagrammatic representation of the classical theory of the four temperaments

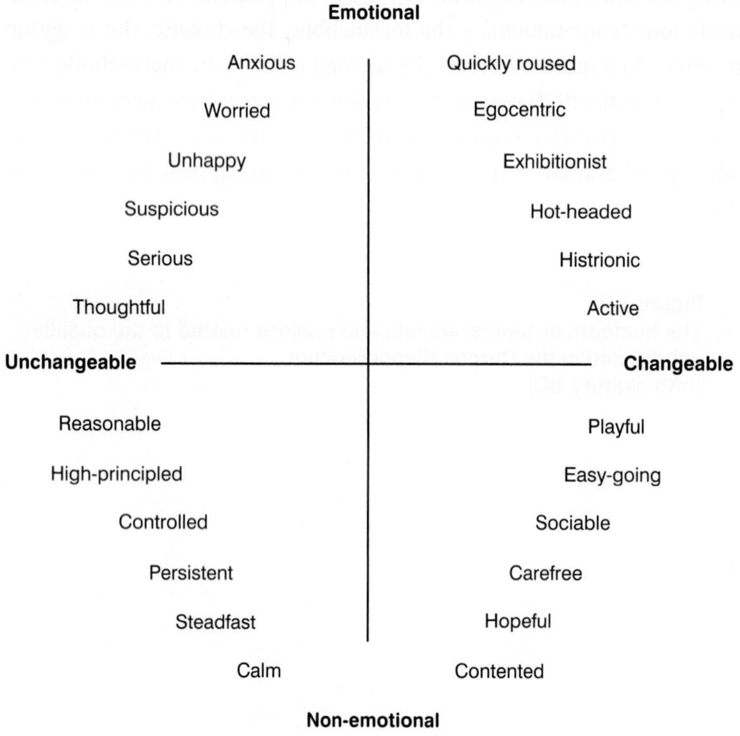

Emotional

Anxious	Quickly roused
Worried	Egocentric
Unhappy	Exhibitionist
Suspicious	Hot-headed
Serious	Histrionic
Thoughtful	Active

Unchangeable ——————————————— Changeable

Reasonable	Playful
High-principled	Easy-going
Controlled	Sociable
Persistent	Carefree
Steadfast	Hopeful
Calm	Contented

Non-emotional

Jung and personality theory

The work of Carl Jung (1875–1961) has become central for many working within personality theory and offers an alternative way of thinking. He identified a related but nonetheless different set of dimensions which he believed more accurately and more comprehensively explained distinctive personalities (Jung, 1923). After the break from his former teacher and colleague, Sigmund Freud, Jung developed what was to become known as 'analytical psychology'. This approach proved extremely influential in what was to become the orthodox and mainstream teaching in management and OB. Management research conducted in the 1950s and 1960s, particularly that developed in the USA, bore the influence of Jung's potentially quite radical methodology and ideas.

Management research tends only to take those sections from Jung's voluminous writings that can be systematized and organized in ways that make it possible to produce highly proceduralized and rational laboratory-based, scientific research. Extracting only elements of his writing inevitably leads to distortions and on occasion encourages research that entirely misses the point of Jung's intention and ambition. Those elements of Jung's work that do not permit simple formulaic prescription and application are quietly forgotten (see Mullins, 1993, pp. 107–109;

Huczynski and Buchanan, 2001, pp. 147–148; cf. Bowles, 1991; Case and Williamson, 2004). It is unlikely that Jung would have approved of what many have done with his work. This is particularly so where this has led to a belief in the possibility and legitimacy of cast-iron taxonomies of people.

THE SHADOW WORLD

Having said that, some simplification of his ideas is inevitable if we are to introduce the potential of his thinking. This will allow us to show at a later stage how his ideas have only been taken up and used to extend what we have been describing in this book as the 'entity view of organization'. For Jung, the individual is a participant in a 'collective unconscious'. As we can see from Figure 3.3 the collective unconscious and the personal unconscious form one part of a system called the 'inner world' out of which and through which the **persona** or personality is extracted to create a kind of surface between the inner and the outer world. At best we are only partly self-determining and autonomous agents and what we like to think of as 'the individual' is in fact partly driven by non-rational and unconscious forces. We are, in effect, actors on two stages, split between two worlds. The **rational everyday** that we most immediately relate to, the here-and-now of the conscious world. But we are also simultaneously resident in another world that we can partly gain access to during certain modes of consciousness, such as our dreams. Despite its relative obscurity, this other **shadow world** continues to exert its influence on us and determines some of the most profound things in our life, things such as destiny and fate (Jung, 1968).

According to Jung, some people are more in tune with the collective unconscious and find it easier to discover and navigate their way through it. You might recall that in our earlier discussion concerning the definition of personality we discovered that an important element in the term 'personality' is the idea of a role, as in our role in a play or a tale being told. We may be able to think, therefore, that in Jung's thinking, we have a role on another stage, or that – probably a more accurate reading of Jung – our role is yet to be found and shaped. It is essential that the two sides of one's personality are explored and cultivated; only out of the interaction of the two realms and the resolution of a series of dilemmas and contradictions thrown up out of this alternation is it possible for individuals to progress in ways that allow them to fulfil their potential and destiny. Hence, for Jung it is the *contradictions* that are significant for understanding personality rather than surface factors that might be termed a personality 'type'. Personality type remains a simplification that is simply an illusion or self-deception.

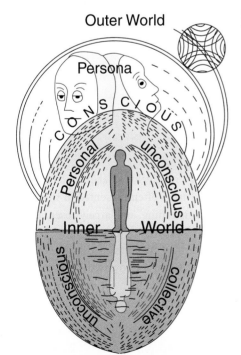

Figure 3.3
The inner world and outer world

Thinkpoint 3.2

Corporate heroes People often fantasize about their role in organizations. Many corporate executives tell stories of organizational recovery in which they cast themselves in arche-typal roles such as the hero, the saviour or the white knight (see Frye, 1957). Michael Edwardes' (1983) account of his time at the old British car manufacturers, British Leyland, is typical of this genre. Think of an organization where you have worked. This might even be your university. Are there people there who you might characterize or who see themselves in these roles? What role might you have played in this drama? Imagine a story that could be told of this organization in which the organization comes to assume a 'personality'. Is the organization friendly, perhaps, or is it maybe greedy?

JUNG'S THEORY OF EXTROVERTS AND INTROVERTS

According to Jung it is the introverts who are more receptive to the force and influence of the collective unconscious. Introverts have a much more expansive and more developed inner world. We tend to categorize introverts as those people who are characterized by the following traits:

- withdrawn
- unsociable
- prefers to be alone
- shy
- passive
- careful
- thoughtful

Extroverts, on the other hand, are people who we recognize as having more recognizably *social* skills. We think of them as outgoing and practical, those who are always on the go, for example, or getting practical things done. Typically we draw up a list of extroverts that includes the following characteristics:

- sociable
- outgoing
- talkative
- gregarious
- active
- optimistic
- impulsive

Before we continue, it is worth recalling that Jung would see the extrovert as a relatively unbalanced character, someone who is in flight from, or in denial of, their other needs. The dualism that is often presented in the text-books – an either/or, where one is *either* an extrovert or introvert – is, however, misleading, and largely absent from Jung's thinking. For Jung, each person has *both* introverted and extroverted characteristics, despite most people having tendencies towards one or the other. In other words, they find it easier, or they are compelled to one end of the introvert/extrovert continuum – that is, they may have a developed (or overdeveloped) extroverted character, but often at the expense of their more introverted traits. If these aspects of self are not attended to they can become quite problematic and unpredictable, in effect, forming a 'shadow personality' that dwells in the background, eclipsed by the primary-dominant self.

Exercise 3.2

Return to the list you made at the beginning of this chapter and see if you can identify people who you would describe as extrovert or introvert. What is it that makes
some of your friends extroverts and others introverts? Once you have redrafted your
character list look again at the two columns in which you have tried to think about those
elements of personality that are presented to others and those kinds of things that you
feel are more representative of the real personality of your friends and family. Can you
spot people who might have both extrovert and introvert dimensions in their personality? Are there some who you might describe as 'unbalanced', or who are excessively
extroverted or introverted? Then, how would you describe yourself?

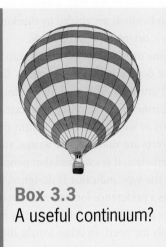

Box 3.3
A useful continuum?

You will now be familiar with the terms extrovert and introvert. Extroverts are usually
associated with outgoing behaviours such as the ones listed above and introverts
are more commonly associated with being withdrawn or shy. It is often assumed that
extroverts are more privileged than introverts, especially in organizations. Jung thought
that extroverts demonstrated more developed social skills but were also more prone to
being imbalanced. Introversion may be seen as something which needs to be overcome
in order to be more dynamic, vibrant and outgoing in the workplace. Jung emphasized
that, in fact, we should think about these terms as a continuum between extroversion
and introversion. The question is: how does this impact on our understanding of people
in organizations? Increasingly, organizations are in search of distinct individuals that
are flexible and may not conform to the characteristics of a complete extrovert as
these may be associated with narcissism or neuroticism, or a complete introvert (as
is discussed later in the section on psychodynamics). Individuals may have to behave
in introverted or extroverted ways depending on the situation. The question therefore
remains whether these dimensions are still appropriate for understanding the demands
of the modern workplace.

The Myers-Briggs type indicator test of personality

Isabel Myers-Briggs, in collaboration with her mother Katherine C. Briggs, developed what is widely considered to
be a robust practical tool that enables psychologists to classify and identify people in ways they claim are consistent
with the theory worked out by Jung in his 1923 publication, *Psychological Types*. According to the interpretation
made by Myers-Briggs, the gist of the theory developed by Jung 'is that much apparently random variation in human
behaviour is actually quite orderly and consistent' (Myers-Briggs, 1962, p. 1). Once the influence of certain key
determining factors is isolated and understood, the diversity of behaviour can be organized and classified in ways
that form distinct personality types.

The research produced in preparation for the writing of this type indicator test originated out of a series of studies
that began in 1942. The first period of research was focused on the writing of a number of preliminary questions, the
responses to which were used to refine and develop the test. Myers-Briggs and her research collaborators tested these
prototype questions on a group of 20 friends and relatives. Later, in the second stage of the research (1956–58), more
than 200 new questions were tested out on 120 men and women.[1]

People are the 'unique product of their particular heredity and environment', Myers-Briggs wrote (1962, p. 51).
At the same time there is a wide variation in the way people *accept* and *reject* different features of their environment.

What we are receptive to and that which we respond to is unique to our personality, and these responses tell us something about ourselves. How we act and react to situations are also multiple and diverse. This is not to say, however, that this diversity cannot be organized or classified. Myers-Briggs was also looking to discover the underlying principles that would explain this make-up of people and hence, personality. Despite this, the 1962 handbook is never clear whether people are *endowed* with a certain personality by birth and environment, or whether in fact people are compelled to make certain life choices in which the resulting decisions help form and shape personality. If this is the case, individuals remain, at least in part, autonomous, self-choosing agents, so that by implication personality remains more open and subject to change.

THE FOUR PREFERENCES

Myers-Briggs writes that the basic differences that explain individuals 'concern the way people *prefer* to use their minds', and as she goes on to specify and clarify, 'specifically the way they use perception and judgement' (1962, p. 51; emphasis in original). She took from Jung the idea that there are four preferences that structure the individual personality, namely: the degree to which people have a preference towards extroversion or introversion (EI), whether they prefer to use the senses or would rather rely on intuition (SN), the extent to which individuals are guided by thinking or feeling (TF) and, finally, their bias towards judgement or perception (JP) as a basic orientation in the world.

There are some quite subtle differences here in the way Myers-Briggs uses some of these terms, which stands in marked contrast to the way we have been using them up until now. What we do not get, for example, is the stereotypical list of features that normally accompany the category extrovert and introvert. This probably reflects the legacy of Jung's work and the efforts of Myers-Briggs to respect his more rigorous understanding that extroverts and introverts are products of a more complex combination of features, many of which take place within the group rather than the isolated psyche of an individual. Both extroverts and introverts are valuable, she writes, and no judgement is intended as to which is a more useful or 'better' personality. Nonetheless, it is assumed that people are *either* extrovert or introvert in **essence**, and the type indicator is designed to provide a way of identifying whether someone has a preference for extroversion or introversion. It is worth noting here that it is quite possible that somebody may be acting out as extrovert, but in essence they are truly introvert. In other words, they are going against their natural preference.

Essence That which is fundamental and unchanging in an 'object', situation or person and most commonly recognized in the phrase 'human nature' (see **determinism**). There is an assumption of some deep, inner essence that can be discovered and which defines the individual. Once an essence is attributed to an object, no further examination is seemingly required. That is why a phrase such as 'human nature' or 'common sense' gives the impression of providing the final and ultimate explanation of anything.

The SN index is designed to categorize people depending on their perceptual preferences. Do people tend to rely mainly on their five senses in their awareness of things – namely, sight, touch, hearing, smell and taste – and to generate facts about the world around them on this basis? Or, do we rely to a greater extent on our more indirect form of perception, namely intuition, which is more in touch with unconscious dimensions of reality. Some people, for example, talk about a masculine 'hunch' in their perception and awareness of events around them, and many will be familiar with the idea of 'feminine' intuition. We might think of this SN index as the way information about the world finds its way into the mind. Another basic difference arises in the way we use this information. There are individuals who predominantly use thinking, the logical and rational processes of the mind. Others tend to go with their feelings about situations and events.

Finally, the JP (judgement–perception) index is constructed to determine whether individuals tend to be driven by the desire to come to conclusions about the world, or instead whether they are more inclined towards coming to an awareness of things around them that shies clear of absolute definition and conclusion. It is found that people who have a bias towards perception are not so preoccupied with forming conclusive judgements but, rather, remain open to different possibilities.

Individuals who take the Myers-Briggs test produce 'scores' that indicate the strength of E–I, S–N, T–F, J–P. In taking the test one scores points for each of these categories and the results are produced by calculating a simple sum from these figures. A typical test result might be E12, S26, T35, J20 indicating that this person is a combination of extrovert, reliant on their senses and faculties of logical thought and driven by judgement. The figure 12 is reached by the sum of all the extrovert and introvert scores. In other words, there are more extrovert responses than introvert; in fact, in this case, extrovert responses exceed the introvert ones by 12. In total there are 16 different combinations: the popular ESTJ type is one kind of personality but there are also INFP types, ENTP personalities, ESFP and so on. In order to establish one's precise combination and strength of type factors one has to sit the test.

The final version of the test takes the form of a questionnaire with 166 questions (Myers-Briggs, 1962), divided into three parts. There is no time limit, but it is suggested that around 45 minutes is required on average. Parts 1 and 3 take the form of phrase questions in which you are asked to indicate a preferred response and Part 2 offers 51 word pair options where candidates are asked to express the one word that appeals to them the most. Let's take a look at some of these questions:

- **Part 1 Questions**
    41. In your crowd, are you
        (A) one of the last to hear what is going on
        (B) full of news about everybody

    48. Are such emotional 'ups and downs' as you may feel
        (A) very marked
        (B) rather moderate

    51. In your early childhood (at six or eight), did you
        (A) feel your parents were very wise people who should be obeyed
        (B) find their authority irksome and escape it when possible

- **Part 2 Word pair options**
    96. (A) affection tenderness
        (B) 103.(A) compassion foresight
        (B) 107.(A) make create (B)

Myers-Briggs tells us that these questions and options have been devised to *maximize* the chance of forcing option choices one way or another on the four type indicator scales. The assumption is clearly being made that people are either intuitive or sense orientated, which is evident in the very design of the test. Therefore, through trials and experiments those questions that proved most adept in separating people into this either/or categorization were the ones that were retained and used as models to refine and adjust the questionnaire.

In the original 1962 manual, Myers-Briggs suggests that the benefits of the questionnaire include: identifying likely career options for individuals; choosing the form of education through which different people would have the best chance of success – engineering as opposed to the arts, for example; recruitment and selection decisions; and even more complex manpower planning decisions where different combinations and the balance between the different types are required in order to maximize productivity and efficiency. To illustrate some of these benefits Myers-Briggs (1962) provides in Appendix E of the manual a summary of a study conducted at a large bank: The case of the messenger.

THE CASE OF THE MESSENGER

Messengers were required to transport 'cylinders' and finished work between different departments of the bank. During the intervals between deliveries they were asked to monitor and maintain supplies of materials for the typists. The previous two individuals in the post had both proved unsuitable and had not been particularly successful in their role. Type indicator tests were requested by the bank and then carried out on these two individuals. The first messenger was found to be an ESFJ, and as Myers-Briggs tells us one of the distinctive characteristics of the ESFJ type is over talkativeness. In fact, this particular employee had been periodically criticized for spending too much time talking with other employees. In effect she would turn every errand into a 'social occasion'. The second role holder was found to be an ISTJ, driven by her senses and just like the previous candidate, judgemental in disposition. By contrast she was introverted and thoughtful rather than extroverted and orientated by her feelings. Her problem had been judged to be one of inflexibility. Once engaged in a task she found it impossible to suspend current work that she was doing in order to run an errand.

On this evidence Myers-Briggs suggested the bank try an '– SFP type', the 'S for awareness of detail, F for desire to comply with expectation, and, above all, P for adaptability to the needs of the instant' (Myers-Briggs, 1962, E-3). The '–' indicates that the extrovert/introvert index was not significant in this case. The appointment of a candidate with this type indicator proved to be highly successful.

Thinkpoint 3.3

Have you ever gone for a job and tried to present yourself according to the characteristics of the job profile? What kind of characteristics did you choose to display? Reflecting on this, why did you choose to manufacture yourself in this way?

PERSONALITY TYPE AND LEADERSHIP STYLE

More recent studies of leadership profiles and leadership success have extended this work of Myers-Briggs. Kuhnert and Russell (1990) and Church and Waclawski (1998), for example, have been able to identify the ENTP types as 'motivators'. While 'motivators' may have an overinflated sense of their impact on others, they are nonetheless perceived as transformational in their leadership style (see also Chapter 8). What the studies define and identify as the 'innovators', on the other hand, tend to be orientated more towards the IN–P personality type. Recall that the '–' indicates that the TF (thinking–feeling) is not so relevant in forming this kind of approach to work; what is significant is the extrovert–introvert dimension. The IN–P types have a more accurate awareness of how they come across to other people and may remain equally transformative due to their capacity for innovation and creative problem solving. They may facilitate transformation rather than seeking to drive it through by enthusiasm and force of personality. Introverted, in comparison to the motivators, and driven as much by 'feeling' as by 'rational thinking',

Concepts of leadership have evolved over time and numerous definitions are used in the literature. Most broadly, leadership can be defined as an influence relationship among leaders and followers who intend real changes and outcomes that reflect their shared purposes. Thus, leadership involves people in a relationship, influence, change, a shared purpose and taking personal responsibility to make things happen (Daft, 2008, p. 27). Given this broad definition, leadership is expressed in school classrooms as much as it is in boardrooms in multinational organizations. Leadership style refers to the ways in which leaders choose to approach issues such as control, crisis and instability in a changing world.

Box 3.4
Leadership and leadership style

the innovators are 'likely to be interested in theoretical and abstract thinking with a penchant for problem solving' (Church and Waclawski, 1998, p. 112). They are more concerned, the authors write, 'with the world of concepts than the world of social interaction'. We might conclude from this that the Myers-Briggs test proves useful in identifying leadership potential, but more than this, it helps us to see that there might be different routes to effective leadership. Each leadership style brings with it a different set of consequences, which tells us something about the kind of organization that is being created as a result of leadership.

Exercise 3.3

Think again of your group of friends. Can you guess how they might be classified under the Myers-Briggs type indicator? Are some of these people more judgemental than others, for example? What about yourself? Which 'type' of person do you think Veronica Marsh from SenseCreatives is looking for?

Can you think of some of the problems that might occur if people learn to identify with the MBTI categories? You might be able to answer this question most effectively by considering whether you find it easy to make your choices from the example questions from the MBTI provided earlier in this section.

The science of personality

So far we have been looking at ways of identifying and classifying individual differences in terms of personality types and we have spent quite a bit of time exploring the influential Myers-Briggs personality type theory. While the Myers-Briggs type indicator is quite typical, there are, in fact, a whole series of alternative methods of identifying personality. In our references, you will come across Raymond Cattell's 16 personality factor inventory (Cattell, 1965), the Minnesota multiphasic personality inventory (see Mischel, 1993, pp. 181–185) and the California psychological

Cartoon 3.1
'You clearly know about his toxic personality.'

'You clearly know about his toxic personality.'

inventory (Gough, 1957). By closely exploring the Myers-Briggs type indicator we are in a position to explore some of the underlying methodological and theoretical assumptions that are being made here about the individual and individual differences. One such issue is self-reporting, which is notoriously problematic and has a number of obvious methodological weaknesses: people do not always judge themselves accurately, nor can they always be trusted to do so; there is also a tendency that people try to second-guess what the test is looking for. This is also a problem in all aspects of a hierarchical organization in that subordinates often feed information up the hierarchy in terms of what they think their managers wish to hear rather than what is happening at the 'grass roots' (see Chapter 9).

Throughout their distinguished careers, Hans J. Eysenck and Michael W. Eysenck developed a whole series of scientific tests and sophisticated statistical modelling to identify and explain personality. In their approach, personality is like any other scientific phenomenon, it can be explored and made observable through the application of laboratory techniques. The Eysencks' work is typical of the kind of scientific approach that leads to explanations of personality being biological or genetic. This might be appealing for hard-pressed managers seeking quick-fix solutions to organizational problems, but tends to be reductive and overly simplistic. The growing popularity of management techniques that assume the possibility of objectivity in identifying and measuring personality, and indeed that personality provides a reliable indicator of performance, is part of a trend in the management of organization that is seeking greater precision, prediction and reliability. For these reasons it is worth unpacking in some detail the Eysencks' work because of its influence on ways of understanding and studying personality and because it exemplifies in its most clear form the scientific approach to personality.

TRAIT THEORY

Unlike Myers-Briggs, the Eysencks begin from their observation of repeated actions that, according to them, gives evidence of the influence of 'personality traits'. Traits are not directly observable, but can only be inferred from behaviour. Quoting Allport (1937, p. 129), the Eysencks note that traits are not active all the time, 'but they are persistent even when latent, and are distinguished by low thresholds of arousal' (Eysenck and Eysenck, 1985, p. 12). Traits are defined as the '*dispositional* factors that regularly and persistently determine our conduct in many different types of situations' (p. 17) and they are identified by way of observing statistically significant correlations between behavioural acts or action tendencies among test subjects that form intercorrelated traits.

For most of their careers the Eysencks worked with the two major clusters of intercorrelated traits that formed around the types 'extroversion' (E) and 'neuroticism' (N). Extroversion we have already met, and once again it is here defined in opposition to introversion. Neuroticism is defined by things such as emotional volatility, inconsistency, and unpredictable mood swings, and it is measured against stability and predictability. The traits or 'primary factors' that relate to the neurotic type concept include anxiety, low self-esteem, feelings of guilt, tension, depression, displays of 'irrational' behaviour, being shy, moody or emotional.

Later in their careers the Eysencks introduced a third major type concept, namely 'psychoticism' (P), which they defined in opposition to 'impulse control'. Those who cannot control their 'impulses' tend towards the psychotic. Individuals are never identified as pure types – as extroverts or neurotics, for example. Rather, these are better thought of as 'mechanisms', the effects of which are 'normally distributed' (as in the bell curve used in statistical analysis) throughout the population. Extroversion, therefore, is 'felt' to varying degrees by *all* individuals. It tends to be exaggerated or overdeveloped in some people, but underdeveloped in others. The significance of these type concepts is that they allow us to define and make sense of regular, routine behaviour. We must remember that it is only behaviour that can be observed; extroversion for example, in itself, cannot be.

FACTOR ANALYSIS

In our everyday language we often think of people and describe their character as 'emotional'. Some might go so far as to claim that it is a personality type rather than simply a trait. Why do the Eysencks then privilege only these three mechanisms and what is it that defines a 'trait' as opposed to a personality 'type'? Furthermore, does this not reduce the subtle and variegated complexity of personality as it is typically experienced to two or three universal tendencies, which, as they admit, can never be observed in a pure state? The point is that the kind of research on personality conducted within that school of thought championed by the Eysencks is preoccupied with the question of statistical accuracy and prediction. So, while it is quite common to describe somebody's personality as 'shy', for the population as a whole – and as a statistical average – being shy tends to be associated or 'correlated' with a whole series of other traits that together form an aggregate or broader personality type made up of all these traits. According to the Eysencks, being shy is not significant in terms of explaining behaviour and would form only one component that makes up introversion. The point is that neuroticism or extroversion are more powerful concepts than being shy and, as such, provide greater statistical accuracy in explaining behavioural variation. Another way of explaining this is to say that the set of people defined as neurotic personality types *contains* the population of individuals who are shy. In other words, a subpopulation of people who are shy will be moody and emotional, while others might have low self-esteem and suffer from guilt feelings. What they all share in common, however, and what explains a greater degree of their behaviour, is that they all tend towards the neurotic dimension of personality. More formally, this technique of measurement is called 'factor analysis' (Eysenck, 1950; Eysenck and Eysenck, 1985, pp. 19–33).

The 'personality' of science: Power and politics

At various points in this book we have sought to question the diverse assumptions and consequences inherent to particular forms of knowledge and research. So far in this chapter we have been studying theoretical and empirical research in personality that has developed out of the natural sciences. Our intention here is to make some preliminary observations at this stage if we are to prepare the ground and explain the move we make into more critical and existential approaches to individuality and the self.

BIOLOGICAL AND SOCIOLOGICAL EXPLANATIONS

One of the first things we notice is the restricted frame of reference in the work of researchers like the Eysencks. Their commitment to study the physiological and biological basis of personality ignores a whole series of other influences that undoubtedly shape personality. In addition to genetic factors, there is surely a significant amount of social determination that explains personality. It seems common sense to argue that children brought up in parental homes where education and study have been valued and rewarded by parents who practise patience and tolerance will cultivate a personality undoubtedly different from a child who has been ignored, neglected or even abused. Likewise, we might say that different types of work organization cultivate distinctive personalities among their employees rather than the other way around. Personality is the product of organization and socialization. This means that personality might well change over time as it is drawn out in various ways by differing forms and types of organization. The problem with this form of critique is that science values precision, accuracy and prediction, and what we have said here would seem a little imprecise and generalized. Science also tends to deal with macro-scale explanations, with aggregates that hold for populations as a whole, rather than the isolated and exceptional or individual case.

Most scientists, even the Eysencks, do not completely ignore social and environmental conditioning. However, extending their ideas we will find that environmental and social conditions are, in fact, understood to be an effect of personality – or, more strictly by the degree of relative balance within and across the dimensions of psychoticism, extraversion and neuroticism (PEN). Antisocial behaviour and crime in the community is then a product or an outcome of certain types of personality (Eysenck, 1964; see also Gray, 1981). Extending this argument we would have to argue that it must also be certain types of personalities who find themselves unemployed, and so it is once again personality that is the cause of social deprivation. We are then left with the apparently simple solution, namely that to improve social conditions we need to more carefully select from the genetic pool. We can see here how close writers like the Eysencks come to eugenics. Indeed, throughout their research their work attracted a great deal of controversy and was, for many, fundamentally tainted by discriminatory and prejudiced overtones. This does not appear to have undermined the popularity of this kind of approach in mainstream business and management studies.

One of the main problems with the search for genetic causation is that research sets off to seek explanatory factors for things like behavioural acts, personality, or social problems, which are themselves not definitive or self-evident. The precise definition of 'psychotic' or 'neurotic' are historically relative and remain subject to a great deal of dispute and debate. By this we mean that what might count as extroverted in the year 2010 will be different from how extroversion might have been understood in 1910. Indeed, it is probably unlikely that extroversion was even a meaningful category of analysis in pre-modern times. Just recently in the UK we have seen how the question of drug use and its legal regulation is constantly changing. What might have been described as a criminal act 20 years ago is now no longer identified as illegal. The 'criminal' is in fact a category socially constructed out of political and historical struggle. Consider the category of sexual deviance. Some 20 or 30 years ago homosexuality was outlawed and suppressed in many Western countries, but it has now become not only acceptable but rightly celebrated as an expression of human diversity and freedom. If you look at any 'criminal' activity – even 'murder' and 'theft' – you will find that they are constantly being debated and negotiated. Not only historically, but also culturally and socially, even subculturally such phenomena are understood and defined in a variety of ways. For one person an act might be murder, for another manslaughter, yet for someone else a crime of passion or the result of 'diminished responsibility' in which the individual is not deemed capable of exercising reason or recognizable forms of consciousness.

Thinkpoint 3.4

A 'criminal' personality? Can you think of ways in which the very act of legislating, of inventing laws, is also an invention of criminality – or indeed represents an act carried out by criminals? In this respect it might be worth recalling the fact that the early founders of nation states acquired their land through the victory and conquests of war. Reflect on the foundation of the USA or Australia, and the treatment of their indigenous populations. Following this logic through, might we say that it is the rebels, the outlaws (Nelson Mandela?) – in one sense the criminal 'personalities' – who are absolutely essential for the birth of the modern nation state. How then might we distinguish 'the law' from 'outlaws', the criminals from the legislators? What are the implications of this for work organizations? Use the six key concepts as a way of approaching this question.

APPLICATIONS IN ORGANIZATION AND RECENT CASE STUDIES

Despite these methodological and theoretical problems, the promise of this kind of science for someone like Veronica Marsh at SenseCreatives is that things like job performance can be measured and determined by personality. Work on 'proactive personality' for example, sees proactivity as a predictor of career success, measured in terms of salary progression, promotion within two years and career satisfaction (Seibert *et al.*, 2001). Proactive personalities are those people who assume and exercise 'personal initiative' in work organizations, who affect environmental change, and who go beyond normal role expectations – that is they are driven to go the 'extra mile'. Studies testing the influence of what is called the 'Big Five' personality dimensions – extroversion, emotional stability, agreeableness, conscientiousness and culture (Barrick and Mount, 1991; see also Digman, 1989; 1990; Norman, 1963) – find that across a range of jobs the degree of conscientiousness is the most important factor in determining high job performance. If personality can be thought of as a phenomenon that remains an inner core defining feature of the individual *and* something that is stable and enduring over time *and*, moreover, something that can be accessed and measured through methods such as the psychometric test, *and* if the results of studies linking personality to job performance are robust and reliable, then we may have some confidence that personality type is a useful predictor of job success. However, there are a lot of 'ands' and 'ifs' here and we still might not be able to determine the direction of causality – i.e., whether personality is cause or effect of environment. Moreover, if someone has a personality that indicates high career potential, we may still not appoint them because we may fear their ambition might mean they are footloose or impatient for promotion such that we might easily lose them to competitor organizations. Once we make these acknowledgements we are beginning to recognize that appointment, progression and success in organizations might be driven by another agenda to that of personality: one of power and politics, and it would be reductive to explain all this by way of personality.

IDIOGRAPHIC APPROACHES TO PERSONALITY

The limitations associated with the hard sciences' approach to personality and the hidden political assumptions and consequences latent within its practice have motivated some writers to adopt the 'softer' and more idiographic methods. We have seen how the nomothetic orientation to the study of personality is motivated by the desire to uncover objective, law-like mechanisms that are deemed to explain personality and to locate individual personalities within relatively simple dimensions of classification and comparison. As we have seen, most of this research emerges out of a concern with biology and behaviour. In the idiographic approach, the emphasis is more on the detailed, richer texture of personality that stresses change, evolution and development, where differences are emphasized and understood to be much more subtle, shifting and complex. Critics of these approaches claim that we end up with a confusing disorder that says little more than everybody is different – but without any substantial scientific basis for being able to say this.

Within studies labelled 'idiographic', authors interpret and elaborate more speculatively on personality. Their writing relies more on the readers' intuition to determine whether the account is persuasive or correct. This is not to say that idiographic approaches lack rigour or consistency, only that the methods by which these standards are achieved are different. Idiographic writings are constructed with their own rigour and precision. Writers in the idiographic tradition tend to build from simple principles that, through synthesis and elaboration, provide grounds for more sophisticated diagnosis and speculation about personality. Idiographic approaches are not so much concerned with experimental testing or behavioural prediction and precision. Indeed, the idea that personality can be distilled and categorized into observable and measurable 'behavioural variables' is anathema.

When one considers that emotional and spiritual dimensions of human life form important elements in personality, we might see why laboratory testing and experimentation remain crude and inappropriate. One may consider the capacity for love and empathy, for example, to be the most important dimensions of personality, but most of us would still find it difficult to believe that it was possible for science to define love and persuasively demonstrate or convince us that there was a 'normal distribution' of love against which the normal and deviant could be measured. Indeed, one of the most important aspects of idiographic writing is that there is less emphasis on traditional notions of personality and a recontextualization of personality within a broader and more expansive realm of self and being that draws in aspects of our being that we do not normally attend to. This is particularly important when we seek to understand the theory and practice of management and, as we see in Chapters 2 and 4, the motivation and behaviour of individuals and collectives at work. Within the more idiographic approach there are a number of important theoretically distinctive schools of thought. One such approach is **psychodynamics** which we will now briefly explore.

Psychodynamic approaches Defined by a concern with internal processes and forces within the psyche that clash and conflict with varying degrees of intensity in each individual and in ways that take time to resolve. In this approach, individual behavioural routines, oddities or little peculiarities and idiosyncrasies are seen as surface acts of behaviour that are really 'symptoms' of more underlying, deep-seated and unconscious forces and desires. In the Freudian approach to analysis, psychodynamic forces are understood to reach eventual compromise or 'settlement' through the negotiation of a series of relatively well-defined stages – the anal, the oral and the oedipal, for example – the resolution of which help stabilize personality.

Neurosis Unhealthy compulsion and attachment to routines or behaviour patterns that, if taken away, stimulate feelings of nervousness and anxiety.

Psychosis Breakdown of our normal ways of thinking and perceiving in which objects in the world lose definition and precision, merging and collapsing into one another in a surreal and agitated, highly charged riot of images. Objects in the world and even the sound of words can come to take on a seemingly malevolent force. In Freudian terms, psychosis is associated with the collapse of the distinction between the conscious and the unconscious so that our waking world takes on dream-like qualities.

Narcissism Preoccupation with self-image, and with making the world enhance this image. In the ancient Greek myth, Narcissus became fixated with his mirror image as he saw it reflected in a pool of water.

Inhibition Inability to do or say something that one desires to say or do. There are numerous sources of inhibition from the fear of embarrassment of being wrong to the consequences of speaking your mind when in a position of subordination.

Anxiety Unlike fear, which has an identifiable source, anxiety has no specific object to which it responds. It is a *general* feeling of malaise or disease for no particular reason, and indeed cannot be understood. In extreme form, it may be associated with **neurosis** or **psychosis**.

Regression Compulsion to repeat or return to earlier patterns of behaviour and interaction as a way of avoiding the challenges associated with more adult or demanding situations and relations, such as returning to childish behaviour in adulthood.

Psychodynamic approaches

Here the emphasis is on the development of personality over time, in which the individual is conceived as a processual phenomenon that, during the course of life, is periodically challenged to resolve a series of unconscious internal conflicts. The writings of Sigmund Freud (1900; 1933) pioneered this approach to personality and encouraged researchers to begin to see how behavioural oddities or personality 'problems' were surface symptoms of more profound, underlying disorders in what Freud identified as an internal psychic structure. He discovered that there were three interacting components in an individual psyche – the ego, id and superego. In Freudian analysis **the ego** is understood to be the mechanism that resolves primal desires, those desires that seek satisfaction through the **id**, with the values and norms of society that demand their repression. The **superego** represents these social norms, and the ego is balanced in-between these two competing pressures. It is from Freud's early work that we trace the understanding of personality problems such as **neurosis, psychosis, narcissism, inhibition, anxiety** and **regression**. Post-Freudian schools of psychodynamic research have extended, advanced, adapted and amended elements of Freudian psychoanalysis. We might conveniently label these approaches Jungian, Kleinian, object relations and Lacanian, an exposition of which would take us beyond the scope of this chapter. However, their importance to the study of management and organization is growing. These approaches are now sufficiently established to have been organized and catalogued in a number of helpful textbooks, such as Gabriel (1999), with more focused studies on management found in Kets de Vries and Miller (1984), Hirschhorn (1988), Schwartz (1990) and Sievers (1994).

In the psychodynamic approach to personality there is a greater degree of allowance for the idea that personality changes over time and that it is partly learned through social interaction and self-development. It is much more consistent with our emerging **process view** of organization, although critics might point out that the ideas are more impressionistic and less verifiable through scientific experiment.

We are going to briefly focus on Abraham Maslow to detail and illustrate some of these ideas. In part because most of us will have heard something of Maslow – his work is extremely popular in management education – but also because he is still badly read in mainstream management textbooks, and to develop our critical evaluation skills it is useful to find ways of challenging these readings. His writings have a great deal to teach us about personality, particularly with respect to the organized and systemic inhibition and control of personality. What he has to say on personality is potentially far more interesting and radical than is commonly thought.

Maslow: Personality and the hierarchy of needs

Maslow explores the interactions between personality and motivation, but his work is usually referenced in discussions about motivating employees at work. Building on the discussion of Maslow and motivation in Chapter 2, in this chapter we are mainly concerned with his writings as they relate to an understanding of

Pioneered by Sigmund Freud, psychodynamics stress the importance of unconscious processes in determining behaviour. Psychodynamics refers to the conscious and unconscious processes at work in individual and group behaviour. Practitioners of psychodynamics may look at the internal 'conflicts' suffered by an individual (i.e., a desire for approval, and a desire for autonomy and independence) which allow us to understand his/her motivations. But beware, there is a sting in the tail: the very process of analysis can bring about the very same behaviours the analysis is trying to treat, including anxiety, neurosis and narcissism.

Box 3.5
Psychodynamics

Thinkpoint 3.5

A neurotic accountant? Try to think of the various ways in which it is possible to understand the 'neurotic'. What symptoms of neurosis might an accountant responsible for millions of pounds worth of money display in their daily work life? If you think the category 'neurotic' is useful in this case, what reasons could be found to explain their neurosis?

---

personality and change. Indeed, his reputation as a management theorist largely relates to Frederick Herzberg's development of the hierarchy of needs (see Chapter 2), since Maslow actually shows very little concern with the practical hands-on problem of managing and motivating employees in work organizations.

TRANSCENDENCE AND SELF-ACTUALIZATION

The individual is an 'integrated whole', Maslow writes (1970, p. 20). He is not so interested in finding ways of defining and cataloguing a whole series of personality types like 'neurotic', 'psychotic', the introvert or extrovert. Rather he is seeking to explain the dynamic basis of personality. Throughout his writings Maslow develops and employs a quite sophisticated understanding of the role of the human being in the world and, beyond that, to the position of the individual in the realms of a spiritual cosmos. He draws upon a diverse range of Western and Eastern philosophy, literature and esoteric mysticism to articulate his vision to readers. We might well wonder what could possibly be the managerial lessons of this understanding of personality. Practical examples of organizations that come closest to embodying his vision might be the Israeli kibbutz communities or local community self-development/spiritual groups. In the main these organizations tend not to be driven primarily by economics or the values of consumerism. On the other hand, there has been an upsurge of interest in alternative communities, ecology groups, collective forms of living, co-operative organizations, nomadic communities and groups of land reclamation activists that are suggestive of the possibility that there are more people dropping out of mainstream society in order to develop something more healthy and meaningful (Melucci, 1986; Crossley, 2002; Parker *et al.*, 2007).

The intention of Maslow's critique is radical and clear. Self-actualization might only be possible once we relinquish the control that the ego maintains over our experience and vision of the world. Maslow talks here in terms of 'peak-experiences' and self-actualized cults of people experimenting with ways of overcoming our routine confinement in isolated and individualized forms of being. It is only when we realize the scale and ambition of Maslow's work that we can really make sense of his exposition of a hierarchy of needs and its significance for understanding personality (see Chapter 2).

Thinkpoint 3.6

Self-actualization We might think of the ecstasy and spontaneity associated with self-actualization in terms of the kind of experience reported by gold-winning Olympic athletes, the artist realizing his/her vision or a collective musical experience. Consider the possibility of self-actualized experiences in the workplace. Is it possible that organizations can be developed in ways that might motivate individuals so that they can achieve self-actualization? What kind of workplaces might these be?

Literally this means to rise above or go beyond, to overpass or exceed all known limits. For some it means an achieved state of being that leaves behind all earthly and material worries or concerns, to be disconnected from all that is contingent and accidental in human experience. A transcendent personality would then be someone who is 'free'.

Box 3.6
Definition of transcendence

There are certainly many problems and objections to Maslow's understanding of personality. Self-actualized people are 'strongly ethical' with 'definite moral standards', we are told; they are democratic and will give their 'honest respect to a carpenter who is a good carpenter' (Maslow, 1970, p. 168). Yet, Maslow shows little awareness of how partial and limited a view of the world this actually is and that democracy, ethics and morals are all historically and culturally relative and far from the 'absolutes' he seems to assume. The dynamics that operate in his hierarchy of needs are also abstracted from any detailed treatment of social conditions and social forces. Individuals are assumed to be inherently driven by the quest for knowledge and self-actualization. There is no recognition of political economy, nor of the persistence of structured patterns of power and inequality in which it is only the relatively privileged who are able to think and aspire to this version of self-actualization. Moreover, many of the features of self-actualization might be better thought of as ideals and images that are fostered and cultivated through education, mass media and commercial advertising.

We also lose sight of some of the precision around personality. We might have raised objections earlier to the categorical taxonomy of personality, but might personality 'type' offer quite a useful way of approaching the question of the individual and individual differences? At the very least it might provide a starting point for analysis. Maslow implies that everything, from the introvert to the extrovert, the neurotic and psychotic, the narcissist to the obsessive compulsive, is subsumed into a universal dynamic where personality is explained away. There might be very good reasons why we might want to retain the category 'neurosis'. It helps understand and explain forms of human suffering as the product of issues with family, arising out of abuse or neglect, and interacting with wider forces of economic competition and political economy.

One reason for this neglect might be that Maslow is not really interested in personality; for Maslow what is more important is the question of the 'self' or the more generalized struggle of the human being. Perhaps one reason for this limitation is that Maslow tries to inscribe his more universal interests and concerns back into the rather more limited discussion of personality. In the next section we briefly question the value of the categories of the 'individual' and 'personality' before looking at the more existential tradition of writers such as Ronald Laing and Erich Fromm. These writers are able to avoid some of these problems because personality gets relocated within the wider dynamics that operate across what is understood to be an existential and political *context*. In part, these moves are made by shifting the focus of concern from personality to identity.

Thinkpoint 3.7
Robot personalities?

Food, clothes, books, holidays and other recreational and entertainment services are increasingly being bought online through dedicated mobile apps where customer support is provided by online chat facilities. In recent years there has been a marked increase in the use of avatars, chatbots, virtual assistants and other digitized service 'workers' that provide these customer support facilities. More and more sophisticated, these avatars and virtual workers now simulate or mimic human personalities through the use of artificial intelligence that has been designed or 'released' by the application of algorithms and other programming and coding techniques. Not only are avatars put to work for modern corporations, they are also increasingly being used for human counselling. Consider the use of avatars in online psychotherapy for example, and particularly the work of Dee Anne Merz Nagel (Nagel and Anthony, 2011), co-founder of the Online Therapy Institute www.onlinetherapyinstitute.com/. This might mean our own personalities at work are being shaped in relation to co-workers who have virtual or digital personalities. In addition, it is now more likely that where job performance might be deemed to be below standard – because of 'personality issues' – our line managers might recommend counselling or therapy with an occupational health team made up of avatar therapists. Are we all becoming robots?

Figure 3.4
Avatar personalities?

The end of the individual?

Today one feels responsible only for one's will and actions, and finds one's pride in oneself. All our teachers of law start from this sense of self and pleasure in the individual as if this had always been the fount of law. But during the longest period of the human past nothing was more terrible than to feel one stood by oneself. To be alone, to experience things by oneself, neither to obey nor rule, to be an individual – that was not a pleasure but a punishment; one was sentenced 'to individuality'. (Nietzsche, 1974, *The Gay Science*, p. 117.)

THE HISTORICAL CONSTRUCTION OF 'THE INDIVIDUAL'

We still live in times where it is almost impossible to think that 'the individual' might not exist or that it may be a recent social 'invention'. Society openly celebrates the individual: we believe ourselves to be individuals; we style our lives in *individual* ways; we have *individual* opinions; we believe at work the *individual* should be rewarded for their contribution; in sum, we sense that our self ends at our skin. There was a time, however, when we thought of ourselves not so much in terms of individuals but more as role holders in a wider collective, and today there are many parts of the world in which this is still thought. It is possible to understand many Eastern communities or societies, for example, in that way. Residues of this may be evident in the West, in ideas such as 'groupthink' and the behaviour of groups such as football crowds or rioting mobs, where there seems to be a collective personality at work and where the rational, autonomous individual seems to dissolve or disappear (see Le Bon, 1960).

GROUP DYNAMICS

We have looked at a number of theories and ideas in personality studies that might indicate that we are not simply individuals, but rather personality 'types'. In some versions of this theory the world might be made up of only 16 different types, or various combinations across three different personality dimensions. However, at the same time, many of us will think of personality as the most distinctive feature of our individuality. This is what Veronica Marsh at SenseCreatives tells us she is looking for. Remember, however, how we discovered earlier that the word 'personality' also embodies the sense of 'mask', a fabrication or an illusion – something that is invented and acted out. Is it possible that we only play out our personalities but that we have become so good at our performance we have forgotten we are acting? We then need to ask who or what is doing the inventing and what are its benefits and disadvantages. In another tradition of thinking, developed out of the work of Melanie Klein and Wilfred Bion – the group dynamics approach (Bion, 1961; see also Kreeger, 1975; Lawrence, 1979) – it is possible to understand personality as a (partly unconscious) 'negotiation' between the individual and the group where personalities are selected and developed for the needs of the group. We can also think of this at a more societal level. Consider what would happen if six extremely extrovert individuals formed a team to work for an extended period of time in a confined space. Over time 'individuals' are likely to begin shaping and developing different personalities – or roles.

Exercise 3.4

In your seminar group, organize a reading of Belbin's (1993) book *Team Roles at Work*. Share your ideas about what it is that makes a successful team. Then, reflect once more on your group of friends. Are there any 'personality clashes'? How does your group resolve these if and when they break out in the open? In what ways could the group be 'disciplining' all of you to 'give room' to each other while maintaining bonds of friendship. What is missing from Belbin's analysis?

IDENTITY AND EXISTENTIAL ANXIETY

One way of understanding the ambiguities around personality and individual differences is to recontextualize this problem in terms of identity. Ronald Laing (1965), drawing on his study of the French philosopher Jean Paul Sartre (1958), argued that what was significant in the dynamics of individuality and personality was the broader 'existential' questions confronting each of us, namely questions around 'meaning' and 'purpose'. The combination of certainty and uncertainty that we may not complete or fulfil our own objectives, means our life may still remain unfinished, without 'closure'. We may then wonder if our life can be given any overall 'shape' or 'purpose', whether each of our everyday activities – the moments or 'parts' of our everyday, the routine and humdrum, through to the painful and distressing – can be provided with some overall contextual meaning. If the 'parts' do not add up to serve some greater value or ideal, some purpose or meaning, they can become disconnected and fragmented. We are then in danger of losing motivation for the everyday.

For the existentialists this provokes what is called 'anxiety' – a vague, disturbing unease with the world and ourselves, but a feeling that cannot really find a reason or object for that which is the cause. In response to this anxiety there is a tendency to withdraw into ourselves. To not know who we are, or to face a future in which we might lose our sense of identity – the change from adolescence to adulthood for example – is to find ourselves in situations that are sometimes overwhelming. So overwhelming, in fact, that we retreat from those situations that are threatening; alternatively, we might regress or 'act out' a reassuring version of our self, but which might nonetheless be inappropriate, selfish or uncreative. Faced with the enormity of possibilities in a universe where we seem insignificant, it is perhaps understandable that many think that all there is to rely on is ourselves and our sense of selfhood. In these circumstances our identity becomes a treasured 'resource'. Responding to these difficulties in a way that avoids depression, neurosis or more extreme forms of 'personality disorder' requires that the individuals assume personal responsibility for their situation and seek out their true 'authentic' self.

In recent years the question of 'identity' has been of interest to numerous researchers of work and organization. In part, this turn has reflected the changing nature of work and the need to present one's 'self' as a valuable and often authentic member of an organization. Whereas there are no unequivocal definitions, we can say that 'identity' helps us to take into account wider factors, such as social factors, that have had an impact on our existence in this world and allows us to move away from the sometimes narrow focus on personality. 'Identity' can be thought of as the means by which we see ourselves in a more holistic way. Some would say that 'identity' makes us recognizable to ourselves. You may think 'identity' relates to who you are rather than what you do or it could be seen as a combination of the two. More broadly, 'organizational identity' is a term that has been used to describe the 'identity' of an organization, including its corporate culture and corporate objectives.

Box 3.7
Identity

RONALD LAING: THE SCHIZOPHRENIC SELF

Laing draws on this kind of existential thinking to chart a series of case studies that show the psychological dangers of remaining 'inauthentic' – that is, individuals who fail to stand up and choose, to discover and create their own identity, and instead act out that which has been 'given' to them or that has been 'demanded' of them by parents, family, community or religion. We might add that, in today's world, it is commercially developed role models – images in media and advertising, pop stars, movie actors, and maybe even characters in computer games – that may affect our quest for identity and self-meaning. Trying to maintain a public self, to be that person which is expected – to be 'happy', 'cheerful', 'good' or 'successful', for example – can lead to what Laing calls 'split personalities', through which we develop a person whom we display to society around us whilst knowing that this is only an act to disguise or cover up that person who we truly believe ourselves to be, the inner real self. Maybe the cover-up operation is maintained because of a sense that there might be nothing behind the costumes and masks, no real self that is struggling to get out. To sustain this act stokes up even greater levels of insecurity as we are forced to continually monitor and maintain our performance, to 'keep our guard up' and not let anyone see cracks in our performance. This causes us to spin around ever faster in self-reinforcing cycles of insecurity and identity, a 'snowballing' effect that motivates individuals to hold on to the identity of their inauthentic selves, but in ways that only serve to generate its equal and opposite reaction, the fear of its loss, or disconfirmation, or rejection. For Laing this doubling or 'divided self' is inevitably doomed to become entrenched and pathological and helps explain the dynamics and condition of schizophrenia. Laing recognizes that the source of this problem does not reside in the individual; rather the schizophrenia is social. The family, and more broadly, modern society, both *exaggerate* restlessness, desire and insecurity and offer images, ideals and models to (albeit temporarily) placate and relieve anxiety.

ERICH FROMM: THE AUTHORITARIAN AND MARKETING PERSONALITIES

Fromm (1942) works from a similar position to Laing, but what he emphasizes is that anxiety is provoked by the 'fear of freedom', a fear that he traces historically to show how modern secular society (note: his concerns are with the West) no longer provides enduring social structures within which individuals can find their role or place. Nor does modern society provide any unifying, religious answers to those existential questions concerned with purpose and meaning. Without a universal foundation of belief and truth, individuals are rendered far more vulnerable to anxiety. But, at the same time, we face a greater degree of choice and freedom in what to do and what to believe in.

Faced with such uncertainty individuals may have a tendency to look towards strong leaders to provide direction, guidance and reassurance. These leaders are themselves products of changing social and economic conditions. They seem to offer a role model of fortitude and identity in response to this distress and worry. Perhaps leaders are those who feel the threat of uncertainty and insecurity the most, or are those cynical enough to perceive these conditions as an opportunity to acquire status, power and leadership by capitalizing on collective fears. Writers routinely point to Hitler and his ascendancy in 1930s Germany as an example of this kind of charismatic leadership, but we see it all around us today, whether we think of Thatcher in Britain during the 1980s, Ronald Reagan in the USA during the same period, Milosevic in Serbia during the 1990s, and even George Bush Junior in more recent times.

Fromm argues that the modern political economy stimulates the emergence of an 'authoritarian personality', and when we look around the world of work organization we can find many examples of such authoritarianism. During the 1980s, for example, there was a debate about the rise of the 'macho manager' (Mackay, 1986). In more recent developments such as total quality management, downsizing and business process reengineering (BPR) (Hammer and Champy, 1993; see Grint, 1994; Willmott, 1995), with its language of obliterating the organization, of 'shooting' those resistant to BPR (see Strassman, 1994), and taking a hammer to rules and procedures, we can see how prevalent and pervasive is the spread of authoritarian personalities (see also Jackall, 1988).

In his later writings, Fromm (1976) was drawn to consider the effects of the rise of mass consumption, advertising, marketing and entertainment, and found that in response a new type of personality was ascendant, what he called the 'marketing personality'. This type of personality is preoccupied with image and the 'right' presentation of self to others. People are becoming increasingly superficial, Fromm argues, driven by an insatiable desire to purchase the latest fads and fashions, dominated by gossip and display. It is almost as if we might be able to posit a relationship between collectivism and individualism. Communities where people once knew each other as neighbours and extended families and with whom they were able to share their preoccupations and concerns have declined, to be replaced by evermore fragmentation and isolation characterized by more insular and privatized forms of living. One symptom of this is the increased investment in privatized forms of home security as people seek to protect their own possessions and encourage criminals to seek out those properties less well protected by intruder alarms. In these conditions the quality of social relations becomes evermore fragile and tenuous as individuals withdraw into the seclusion of personal and privatized spaces. As a more complex part of these social forces, vast resources are being invested into the development of 'lifestyle' marketing, to create images, ideals and ready-made identities within which individuals can find guidance and orientation.

Exercise 3.5

In your seminar group discuss the problem of access to books and other library resources at your university. Consider some of the books on the 'Further reading' list at the end of the chapter. Who among the group thinks that the way to achieving the highest marks in coursework and exams is one in which individuals chase and accumulate material on their own? If we *collectively* organized and shared the material in a way that raised the average mark but reduced the marks of those individuals who would have been top of the class, who would say there has been an improvement in educational standards? What do you think is of most benefit to society? Which of the two alternatives might raise the most anxiety? In your discussion can you identify certain personality 'types' from the different positions they take with respect to this debate?

Existential anxiety and contemporary organization: Beyond personality?

SYNTHETIC CULTURES AND CYNICAL EMPLOYEES

These existential themes have been important for many studies of contemporary organization where research has tried to understand some of the workplace dynamics that are mobilized and activated through its influence (Collinson, 1992; Jermier, Knights and Willmott, 1994; Watson, 1994; Casey, 1995). In these studies we discover that the uncertainty and anxiety of work in organizations today contributes to a whole series of workplace conflicts and tensions. Casey (1995) charts the various strategies used by individuals to escape anxiety in the world of work and shows how corporate management preys on these insecurities in the development of organizational culture. She explains that corporate culture is in part a 'postmodern' organizational response to the demise of 'modern' community forms of belonging. Work organization seeks to replace and compensate for the sense of isolation and anonymity by creating a sense of team and family, and by building up emotional ties between individuals and their workplace. The result is, however, the emergence of a synthetic culture that cultivates a pretence or artificial form of belonging and commitment. She writes (p. 154) that the 'most obvious and pervasive effect of the experience of working in the new culture is a condition of ambivalence', going on to propose that this ambivalence is a 'manifestation of an incomplete internalization of the new cultural values and behaviour'. In other words, employees remain guarded and suspicious in response to the efforts of senior management to develop a culture of trust and belonging. Various forms of accommodation are reached between the individuals and the organization. Some remain distant and cynical about the organization and others only 'play' at being committed and involved. They might play along with the game but they would not think twice about quitting their employment if something better comes along. They remain strategically and *instrumentally* attached to their organization, not emotionally involved. Others display what Casey calls a 'colluded self', distinctive because employees show a 'compulsive optimism in their beliefs about the company, its products and their future within it' (Casey, 1995, p. 169).

ZTC RYLAND: MANAGERS IN CRISIS

Watson's study of the organization ZTC Ryland is also helpful in showing how managers are routinely driven by questions of self and wider existential preoccupations with value, purpose and meaning. Typical of his study is the manager who reports that now he is a manager he feels less in control than ever and that he is now told what to do far more than he ever was before he attained management grade. 'I sometimes wonder if I'm even in control of myself', the manager goes on to tell the researcher. As Watson (1994, p. 44) argues on the basis of his study:

Managers are often 'searching for themselves' in the way they think about and do their managerial work. They are maintaining and developing their concept of who they are or 'what sort of person they are' in reflecting on their occupational activity.

In order to understand the nature of work organization, Watson argues that he needed to abandon the attempt to explore social relations in terms of personality (Watson, 1994, pp. 59–61). A focus on personality simply did not allow an appreciation of the processual and dynamic features that define the way people work and interact with each other in organizations. Whereas a focus on personality encourages us to see organization as a rational, scientific and technical administrative system of appointment, career development, work allocation and regulation, the type of theory and methodology deployed by Watson takes us into the unpredictability and flux of social relations at work.

CRITIQUE

However, the value of these studies, with their commitment to subjectivity and identity, and particularly the existential nature of this interest in subjectivity and identity, has been challenged by a number of writers (see Thompson, 1990; Ackroyd and Thompson, 1999). Although the position of these writers appears to shift in respect to the significance of subjectivity and identity, it seems that a focus on these aspects disregards the more important collective and 'material' dimensions that structure the workplace. For Thompson (1990), we are in danger of becoming preoccupied with the individual and his or her struggles for meaning and identity at the cost of understanding the more significant constituents of intensity and struggle in organization. What is far more immediate in people's working lives are their struggles over wages and terms and conditions of work. At the risk of oversimplifying the work of Thompson and his colleagues, we might characterize their approach as one that focuses on conflict and struggle in the workplace as a symptom of wider social and political conflict. Material struggle over wages and terms and conditions of employment acts as a convergent force, one that all workers share in common, and so mobilizes an underlying collective consciousness that ultimately pits workers as a mass against the owners of organizations and their agents (management).

Exercise 3.6

C onsider the following questions:

1   In what ways might the 'individual' be coming to an end? What are the implications of this for our understanding of personality?
2   What is distinctive about a focus on identity and what insights does it offer that make it different from the ideas of those who are more preoccupied with the study of personality?
3   How might organization and contemporary management practice exaggerate schizophrenic tendencies in individuals?

Key contributions and major controversies in the field: Mainstream and critical

Our chapter has introduced the key contributions and major controversies in the field of individual differences, personality and the self. We have found that the mainstream approaches, building on the foundations and nomothetic orientation of writers such as the Eysencks and Myers-Briggs, have developed increasingly refined and forensic techniques of observation, measurement and classification that 'explain' personality and its effects in work organization and wider society. Myers-Briggs has achieved some impressive results, showing that the successful selection and deployment of staff to posts in organizations depends upon the correct identification of personality. Leadership-style studies have shown that there is not one type of personality that can be considered 'successful' in terms of leadership; rather there are different types of leaders, with different types of personalities. According to Myers-Briggs we all have distinctive types of personalities based on the different ways we are predisposed to use our minds. Different personalities develop different leadership styles – some more motivational in style, while others are more innovative, but both styles can be successful modes of transformational leadership (Kuhnert and Russell, 1990; Church and Waclawski, 1998). It would all seem to depend on what we do with the type of personality we have, or how we can make it work for us, or what we do with our inherited dispositional traits. Belbin (1981) shows that successful teams need to seek a mix of different personality types. Recently, research examining the influence of the so-called 'Big Five' personality dimensions finds that differences in job performance can be explained most by conscientiousness. The correct identification of this personality dimension would seem then to be an essential task of management in the recruitment, selection and promotion of its human resources so that it can retain and enhance its productivity and competitiveness.

We have suggested that there is a need to think more critically about how we evaluate and study people at work and their organizational behaviour. The scientific abstraction of personality through the identification of discrete components that can be measured and statistically correlated with 'effects' such as job performance, transformational leadership or organizational success, is a technical orientation to the study of management and organization. It does not ask what are perhaps the more important questions. Why is high job performance a good thing, in itself? What kinds of work should be encouraged? Is personality the cause or consequence of wider social and historical conditions and influences? Can personality be thought of as a category or entity? What are the consequences of understanding the individual in terms of personality, rather than say, identity?

These are the type of questions that mark out what is distinctive about the critical study of OB. Its main contribution has been to shift the terms of the debate away from a rather narrow and pragmatic preoccupation with personality towards a more expansive reflection on the question of identity. For the critical scholar the restrictive methodology of the natural sciences is the most controversial aspect of the research and study into personality and the individual at work. They question the extent to which 'personality' can be identified with any degree of accuracy, particularly statistical accuracy, and doubt that it remains predictable and consistent over time. One of the major achievements of writers such as Maslow, Laing and Fromm is to return the study of the individual to a richer understanding. Critical studies have taken us out of some of the limitations associated with the preoccupation with personality. The study of identity invites a consideration of those deeper questions that seem to haunt us, namely questions concerning meaning or purpose – questions that act as a source of motivation and preoccupation for members of work organizations.

Critical scholars of identity have helped elucidate how there is a basic anxiety that arises from 'being in the world'. We constantly seek to flee this anxiety through the quest for an (egotistical) robust identity, which encourages efforts to acquire power and control over others, to crave identity confirmation through the allure of consumption, worldly goods and the marketing of 'idealized' identities. Contemporary organization is riddled with pathological forms of identity, schizophrenic tendencies and authoritarian personalities. This helps us to see and understand organization as fractious, disorderly and unstable – something that requires sensitive and sophisticated management. Critical studies of personality might risk being Utopian or impractical, but they invite a more imaginative relationship with our world, one that raises deeper questions and possibilities for organization and our future, collective being in the world.

At the same time the intellectual preoccupation with identity might be equally dangerous and inhibiting at a time when the humanist legacy in existential thinking might be reaching its end as new technologies and digital media challenge the human-centred view of personality. Must we now think of non-human personalities and objects with 'personality' employed in work organizations made up of various synthetic and artificial intelligences, avatars, cyborgs and virtual life? Towards what kind of personality clashes might this lead? Indeed, we might ask whether human personality is something consigned to history by this brave new world in which 'personality' becomes constituted by technological prostheses, and in part an amalgam or outcome of synthetic 'add-ons' and download apps, all promising to produce an attractive, high-performing personality.

Conclusion

We began our study of personality by tracing an explanation of personality back to Hippocrates and the ancient Greeks. We then saw how Carl Jung deepened the exploration of personality. He located personality within a much deeper, more complex cosmology that identified the influence of archetypes and the collective unconscious in the formation and distribution of personality types. Myers-Briggs attempted to standardize and proceduralize the work of Jung in ways that made it appear amenable to a more rigorous scientific method and application in mainstream management thinking and practice. The Eysencks extended this scientific approach through the exercise of sophisticated statistical measurement and laboratory experiments. Preoccupied with the biological basis of personality and behavioural manifestations of different personalities, we noted how the Eysencks are motivated by classification, order and control. Although often denied, this remains inherently political.

The idiographic orientation to personality offers a richer and more generous comprehension of personality, showing how it is more 'open', shifting and changing over time in response to our deeper struggles and questions about freedom and meaning. Formed out of learning and social interaction, personality appears to be more of a processual phenomenon, and as part of wider organization this helps us to understand the process view of organization. The legacy of idealism and assumptions evident in the work of Maslow conceal deeper *existential* struggles that make more sense when thought of in terms of identity. Shifting focus to the question of identity also helps restore a concern with wider structures of power and inequality. This brings into focus the interactions between the individual and political economy. When we combine the existential with political–economic dynamics we can begin to understand how identity seems to offer a retreat or defence against powerful forces of disorder and insecurity. But as a 'defence', identity can become unhealthy and pathological. Paradoxically, all of us could then be prey to the conservative appeal of the entity view of organization. We might be unable to question or engage with the predominant relations of power and politics that restrict the development of the process view of organization – development that relies upon imagination, risk, political 'voice' and (perhaps) digitally enhanced *personality*.

Case study 3.2
VERONICA MARSH
'LOSES HER RAG'

'Complete incompetence, I cannot believe it. Where do we get these people from?... What? .... Yes. Uh? What, No, you tell me: WHAT WENT WRONG? What can we .... [inaudible, incoherent transcription] .... DO about the situation? You need to answer that in the next 30 minutes? This is a real mess and I'm not covering your ass here, Mike. We need to sort this out ASAP.' [Holds receiver away from her ear and gesticulates to the ethnographer – eyes rolling, twirling her finger in small circles next to her temple]. *'I can't listen to you any longer Mike, you need to get the proofs back.... I DON'T CARE HOW. This is set to be a media disaster and it's your ass.'* Phone slams down. *'Asshole'*, she shouts.

Veronica Marsh, the director of Human Resources at SenseCreatives, is shouting down the phone to one of the senior marketing managers in the Chicago office. Veronica does her best for the agency, she tells people she drives the search for imaginative talent and has been complimented in the past on how she approaches recruitment for SenseCreatives in an effective manner. She gets things done! When she's not at work she competes in the Iron Girl sports events and claims to admire Jeremy Clarkson. She is ambitious to a fault and she sets agendas for the organization. SenseCreatives was not expecting such a *tour de force*. Indeed, she had revolutionized the way in which human resources were thought of in the organization. She had impressed the CEO Martin Garnish so much that they had regular chats outside the boardroom about the strategy of the company and where she thought it should be heading. She was powerful! Some said she was too powerful for her position. Some said that she had a direct line to the boss and this made others feel uncomfortable, anxious and sometimes unable to put their point across. They felt marginalized. Garnish seemed to like her, she was 'straight talking' as he put it. One could say that Garnish and Veronica shared similar sensibilities and characteristics. They would discuss the same TV programmes and sport, they liked the same music and were both career driven. Veronica would sometimes boast to colleagues in the break room about her long conversations with Martin. Perhaps others felt threatened, but they didn't want to confront Veronica.

Veronica is enthusiastic but has been accused in recent years of being increasingly aggressive and self-centred. Initially, Veronica was new to managing human resources at a creative organization, so she approached the task of recruitment with some trepidation. She has worked hard to build her reputation over the last seven years and is now tasked with impressive responsibilities given her age and experience. She was central in recruiting key talent for landing a multi-million dollar account for one of the major record labels in the industry, Evolve Inc. Everyone sits up and listens to her and the SenseCreatives CEO is increasingly impressed.

However, something has gone wrong. She is attempting to deal with an employee who has stolen the confidential proofs for a million-dollar advertising campaign about to be launched for Evolve Inc. She is seething. Some would say that she is acting somewhat out of character. Veronica is ordinarily composed and copes well under pressure, but this time the enormity of the issue has tested her skills in managing the human resource function. Veronica is far from her composed self today. Management in a time of crisis is what's needed here. Veronica always thought she was good in a crisis but others could see she was unravelling in the wake of what was unfolding (see O'Doherty, 2016). Others around her were starting to become wary and avoiding her in corridors and in the break room. Some had started to question whether she should even be in such a position of responsibility. Veronica was feeling the pressure. Was she meant to save the day? This was an account that could make or break the company. Who would tell Evolve Inc.? How would she deal with something so extraordinary for the first time in her career? She needed to think creatively, she was in the creative industries after all!

She remembered one of the quotes St Lukes, the famous creative agency, have on their website: '"Be yourself" is about the worst advice you can give to some people.' SenseCreatives needed to think and act quickly in order to manage their own reputation as well as that of Evolve Inc. They needed to be reflective and manage effectively. But how?

After the telephone call with Mike, Veronica called her two graduate account executive assistants into the room. Richard and Valerie had been recruited and nurtured since their arrival two years ago. Richard's psychometric test results had been 'weaker' than Valerie's but he showed some potential in the interview so Veronica decided to take a chance. It was clear Valerie was a hard worker and she would do anything to meet a deadline. Richard was more laid back and Veronica kept a close eye on him.

'What happened?' Veronica said. 'Did you not suspect anything? How do you think this makes me look? How do you think it makes all of us look? How about you, Richard, do you care?' Both account executives remained silent. They had been enthusiastic when they arrived but Richard in particular had become quiet and withdrawn. Valerie dealt differently with some of the latest developments at SenseCreatives; being put on a big account, rushing around meeting deadlines, having to work all hours, she was feeling the pressure too. Her home life had suffered to the point that her personal and work relationships were strained. 'Teamworking is hard sometimes,' she said. She tried to push forward and take a positive attitude and imagine the future rewards of working long hours and sometimes not getting credit for work she had done. 'It's part of a wider scheme of things, I reckon. You get rewarded at some point, it's just not exactly known quite when. Goodness knows what will happen now the account is down the drain.' Richard, in contrast, said, 'I'm alright where I am really, I suppose. I can't really think of where I want to go. Sometimes I don't even know what I'm doing here. Does any of this mean anything anyway? I'll probably be blamed for this too. What's the point?'

QUESTIONS

1 How do you think the Eysencks would understand these different characters? In what ways are they likely to explain these different personalities? Reading through the case study again, what might be being overlooked by the trait theory of personality?

2 Compare your impressions of Veronica Marsh here with the impression you formed from Case Study 3.1. What kind of personality is she?

3 What is the significance of personality in the organization and work that takes place at SenseCreatives and the advertising industry more broadly? Is there anything here that Ronald Laing's work might help us to see or understand?

4 Think now more in terms of identity. What are the possible struggles that all these characters might share? Consider the possibility that people might not simply be 'identities', but rather a multiplicity of different, half-formed identities, perhaps with one dominant at most times and in most situations.

5 Consider the influence of wider power relations and politics – where it might be a case of not *what* you know but *who* you know. How do you think power might be at work at SenseCreatives? What might be the factors holding the account executives back from career ambition, for example?

6 How might the various personalities be seen to be outcomes of each other? i.e., To what extent do you think Richard has been unfairly characterized? What other types of personality might Richard be capable of expressing?

Discussion questions

1 Which of the ideas covered in this chapter do you find helpful in thinking about your own personality and that of those around you?

2 What is the so-called 'shadow world' and what is its significance for understanding personality and its management?

3 Define the four 'preferences' that Myers-Briggs identifies as the key components that help explain personality. How might this assist management?

4 What is meant by psychoticism, extroversion and neuroticism?

5 What are the typical features we associate with a scientific approach to personality?

6 Do you think personality can change? If so, what would this tell you about some of the theory we have been considering so far?

7 Think about your behaviour at work and at home. Write down different behaviours you think you might display at work and how they differ from how you are at home. Do you see two different sets of behaviour emerging?

8 Visit chatbots.org and debate the possibility that these avatars or virtual agents enjoy something akin to 'personality'. If personality is something that can be enjoyed by objects and non-human avatars, how would you go about designing an attractive personality for an online travel consultant?

Further reading

Casey, C. (1995) *Work, Self and Society: After Industrialism*, London and New York: Routledge.

Casey explores how large-scale restructuring and workplace redesign affect individuals at work. Casey explores different discourses of the self in society as they relate to the changing nature of work, production and organizational culture. There are many interesting threads in the book that will help you to understand the relationship between the individual and the organization.

Collinson, D. (1992) *Managing the Shopfloor*, Berlin: De Gruyter.

Collinson's study looks at manual labour and focuses on subjectivity. The book explores various issues and workers' relationships to power, resistance, joking and masculinity.

du Gay, P. (1996) *Consumption and Identity at Work*, London: Sage.

Consumption is a central theme in the development of our understanding of identity and du Gay explores how consumer culture and other pervading discourses affect the way we conceptualize identity.

Mischel, W., Shoda, Y. and Smith, R. E. (2004) *Introduction to Personality*, Chichester: John Wiley.

In this introduction, Mischel and colleagues explore the different dimensions associated with the concept of personality and offer a broad perspective using different theoretical frameworks such as biological and evolutionary perspectives.

Watson, T. (1994) *In Search of Management: Culture, Chaos and Control in Managerial Work*, London: Routledge.

As we have discussed, Watson's influential study explores a company called ZTC Ryland. Watson's concern is the nature of management and managing and his study shows how managers act to shape their own lives and we can see this clearly at a time of organizational change.

Useful websites

www.humanmetrics.com/cgi-win/JTypes2.asp

Discover your personality by completing this online test based on the Myers-Briggs personality type indicator. Rather crude, but it is fun to do. Best taken with a large dose of salt!

www.colorquiz.com/

An even more simplistic modelling of personality based on the idea that colour preference can give clues to your personality. Again, quite amusing, albeit a little superficial; the principles upon which this is based remain rather unsound both theoretically and methodologically.

www.outofservice.com/bigfive/

This online test measures what many psychologists consider to be the five fundamental dimensions of personality.

www.ship.edu/cgboeree/perscontents.ritml

This website provides material on all the major theorists and writers we have been looking at in this chapter. You will find material here on Freud, Jung, Eysenck, Erikson and Fromm.

www.radpsynet.org/

A critical and radical organization committed to exposing and examining the politics and ideologies

that inform most mainstream psychology. Papers, essays, critical reviews and an online discussion forum provide a space for people to question and interrogate many aspects of psychology. Includes important essays relevant to the study of personality.

References

Ackroyd, S. and Thompson, P. (1999) *Organizational Misbehaviour,* London: Sage.

Allport, G. (1937) *Personality: A Psychological Interpretation,* New York: Holt, Rinehart & Winston.

Barker, J. (1999) *The Discipline of Teamwork: Participation and Concertive Control,* London: Sage.

Barrick, M. R. and Mount, M. (1991) 'The Big Five personality dimensions and job performance: A meta-analysis', *Personnel Psychology,* 44: 1–26.

Belbin, M. (1981) *Management Teams,* London: Heinemann.

Belbin, M. (1993) *Team Roles at Work,* London: Butterworth-Heinemann.

Bion, W. (1961) *Experiences in Groups,* London: Tavistock.

Bowles, M. (1991) 'The organizational shadow', *Organization Studies,* 12: 387–404.

Case, P. and Williamson, G. (2004) 'Alchemy, astrology and retro-organisation theory: An astro-genealogical critique of the Myers-Briggs type indicator', *Organization,* 11(4): 473–495.

Casey, C. (1995) *Work, Self and Society: After Industrialism,* London and New York: Routledge.

Cattell, R. B. (1965) *The Scientific Analysis of Personality,* Baltimore, MD: Penguin Books.

Church, A. H. and Waclawski, J. (1998) 'The relationship between individual and personality orientation and executive leadership behaviour', *Journal of Occupational and Organizational Psychology,* 71: 99–125.

Collinson, D. (1992) *Managing the Shopfloor,* Berlin: De Gruyter.

Crossley, N. (2002) *Making Sense of Social Movements,* Buckingham: Open University Press.

Daft, R.L. (2008) *Leadership,* fifth edn, London: Cengage Learning.

Digman, J. M. (1989) 'Five robust trait dimensions: Development, stability, utility', *Journal of Personality,* 57: 195–214.

Digman, J. M. (1990) 'Personality structure: Emergence of the five-factor model', *Annual Review of Psychology,* 41: 417–440.

Edwardes, M. (1983) *Back from the Brink,* London: Pan.

Eysenck, H. J. (1950) 'Criterion analysis: An application of the hypothetico-deductive method to factor analysis', *Psychological Review,* 37: 38–53.

Eysenck, H. J. (1964) 'The biological basis of criminal behaviour', *Nature,* 203: 952–953.

Eysenck, H. J. and Rachman, S. (1965) *The Causes and Cures of Neurosis,* San Diego, CA: R. R. Knapp.

Eysenck, H. J. and Eysenck, M. W. (1985) *Personality and Individual Differences: A Natural Sciences Approach,* New York and London: Plenum Press.

Freud, S. (1900) *The Interpretation of Dreams,* Harmondsworth: Penguin.

Freud, S. (1933) *New Introductory Lectures on Psychoanalysis,* Harmondsworth: Penguin.

Fromm, E. (1942) *Fear of Freedom,* London: Routledge and Kegan Paul.

Fromm, E. (1976) *To Have or To Be?,* London: Abacus.

Frye, N. (1957) *Anatomy of Criticism: Four Essays,* Princeton, NJ: Princeton University Press.

Gabriel, J. (1999) *Organizations in Depth: The Psychoanalysis of Organizations,* London: Sage.

Goffman, E. (1959) *The Presentation of Self in Everyday Life,* Harmondsworth: Penguin.

Gough, H. G. (1957) *Manual, California Psychological Inventory,* Palo Alto, CA: Consulting Psychologists Press.

Gray, J. A. (1981) 'A critique of Eysenck's theory of personality', in H. J. Eysenck (ed.) *A Model for Personality,* Berlin: Springer.

Grey, C. (1994) 'Career as a project of self and labour process discipline', *Sociology,* 28(2): 479–497.

Grint, K. (1994) 'Re-engineering History', *Organization,* 1(1): 179–202.

Hammer, M. and Champy, J. (1993) *Re-engineering the Corporation: A Manifesto for Business Revolution,* London: Nicholas Brealey.

Hirschhorn, L. (1988) *The Workplace Within: Psychodynamics of Organization Life,* Cambridge: MIT Press.

Huczynski, A. and Buchanan, D. (2001) *Organizational Behaviour: An Introductory Text,* fourth edn, London: Pitman.

Jackall, R. (1988) *Moral Mazes: The World of Corporate Managers,* New York: Oxford University Press.

Jermier, J., Knights, D. and Willmott, H. (eds.) (1994) *Resistance and Power in Organizations,* London: Routledge.

Jung, C. (1923) *Psychological Types,* London: Routledge and Kegan Paul.

Jung, C. (1968) *The Archetypes and the Collective Unconscious,* London: Routledge.

Kets de Vries, M. and Miller, D. (1984) *The Neurotic Organization: Diagnosing and Changing Counterproductive Styles of Management,* San Francisco, CA: Jossey-Bass.

Kreeger, L. (ed.) (1975) *The Large Group: Dynamics and Therapy,* London: Constable.

Kuhnert, K. W. and Russell, C. J. (1990) 'Using constructive developmental theory and biodata to bridge the gap between personnel selection and leadership', *Journal of Management,* 16(3): 595–607.

Laing, R. (1965) *The Divided Self,* Harmondsworth: Penguin.

Lawrence, W. G. (1979) *Exploring Individual and Organizational Boundaries: A Tavistock Open Systems Approach,* New York: Wiley and Sons.

Le Bon, G. (1960) *The Crowd,* New York: Viking.

Mackay, L. (1986) 'The macho manager: it's no myth', *Personnel Management,* 18(1): 25–28.

Maslow, A. H. (1970) *Motivation and Personality,* second edn, New York: Harper and Row.

Melucci, A. (1986) *Nomads of the Present,* London: Radius.

Mischel, W. (1993) *Introduction to Personality,* fifth edn. Orlando, FL: Harcourt Brace College Publishers.

Mullins, L. (1993) *Management and Organizational Behaviour,* third edn, London: Pitman.

Myers-Briggs, I. (1962) *The Myers-Briggs Type Indicator,* Princeton, NJ: Educational Testing Service.

Nagel, D. and Anthony, K. (2011) *Avatar Therapy.* The CAPA Quarterly, Counsellors and Psychotherapists Association of NSW Inc. Australia. 3: 6–9.

Nietzsche, F. (1974) *The Gay Science,* New York: Vintage.

Norman, W. T. (1963) 'Toward an adequate taxonomy of personality attributes: Replicated factor structure in peer nomination personality ratings', *Journal of Abnormal and Social Psychology,* 66: 574–583.

O'Doherty, D. (2016) *Reconstructing Organization: The Loungification of Society.* Houndmills, Basingstoke: Palgrave Macmillan.

Parker, M., Fournier, V. and Reedy, P. (2007) *The Dictionary of Alternatives: Utopianism and Organization.* London: Zed Books.

Sartre, J. P. (1958) *Being and Nothingness,* London: Routledge.

Schwartz, H. (1990) *Narcissistic Process and Corporate Decay: The Theory of the Organization Ideal,* New York: New York University Press.

Short, J. R. (2000) *Alternative Geographies,* London: Prentice Hall.

Seibert, S. C., Kraimer, M. L. and Crant, J. M. (2001) 'What do proactive people do? A longitudinal model linking proactive personality and career success', *Personnel Psychology,* 54: 845–874.

Sievers, B. (1994) *Work, Death and Life Itself,* Berlin: De Gruyter.

Strassman, P. A. (1994) 'The hocus-pocus of reengineering', *Across the Board,* 34(6): 35–38.

Thompson, P. (1990) 'Crawling from the wreckage: The labour process and the politics of production', in D. Knights and H. Willmott (eds) *Labour Process Theory,* London: Macmillan.

Watson, T. (1994) *In Search of Management: Culture, Chaos and Control in Managerial Work,* London: Routledge.

Willmott, H. (1995) 'The odd couple? Re-engineering business processes, managing human relations', *New Technology, Work and Employment,* 10(2): 89–98.

Note

1 Some of whom it transpires had prior knowledge and some familiarity with the emerging personality type indicator, which undermines the claims for rigour and objectivity made on behalf of the MBTI.

4 Groups and teams at work

ALESSIA CONTU AND LARA PECIS

Aims of the chapter

This chapter will:

- Explore the meaning of teamwork.

- Explain how and why teamwork is used in organizations.

- Highlight the problems, open questions and limitations of mainstream models of teamwork.

- Indicate the contribution of critical approaches to teamwork.

- Explain and illustrate the implications of power, insecurity, identity and knowledge for understanding teamwork.

Key concepts and learning objectives

By the end of this chapter you should understand:

- The traditional and mainstream views of teams at work and why they are important for work organization.

- The main contributions to the subject, and their differences, drawing upon various theoretical approaches and empirical studies.

- Critical perspectives on teamwork, the political issues they highlight in terms of inequalities, identity and resistance, and the opportunities they offer for understanding the difficulties and challenges of organizational life.

Overview and key points

The first part of this chapter introduces mainstream views of teams at work. Referring to a case study of a new media company, it elaborates the assumptions held and the importance attached to the idea that teamwork is good for organizational performance, and that teamwork favours flexibility, motivation and learning. The text makes connections to contemporary ideas about teamwork, as well as referring to past studies that have been significant for our understanding of the ways teams, and their members, behave.

In the second part of the chapter, problems of mainstream thinking are unravelled and addressed by drawing upon the work of radical and critical studies of teamwork to show that:

- The categories we create can become prescriptions and lose their relevance for understanding the challenges and difficulties of organized life.
- Organizational life is complex, ambiguous and embedded in relations of power.
- Teamwork is neither intrinsically good nor new.
- Radical and critical views can enhance democratic debate by questioning taken-for-granted assumptions about teamwork.

MAINSTREAM VIEWS ON TEAMS AT WORK

Introduction to mainstream thinking on groups and teams

There are many types of groups, including self-managing teams, task forces, 'hot groups', Japanese teams, etc. Most people assume the benefits of working in teams and many recognize the importance of belonging to a group, of whatever kind, to get a job done.

Thinkpoint 4.1

Have you ever worked as part of a team in a company or similar organization? What explanation or justification was offered by managers or team members for the organization of workers into teams?

Management gurus and academics give a consistent message which reinforces the belief in the importance of teamworking. The message is clear: 'if the organization is to perform it must be organized as a team' (Drucker, 1992). Others say that 'teams will be the primary building blocks of company performance in the organization of the future' (Katzenbach and Smith, 1993, p. 173). International surveys (see Cohen *et al.*, 1996; Waterson *et al.*, 1999) indicate that managers have acted upon this message. According to one estimate in 2000, 80 per cent of all Fortune 2000 companies had over half of their employees working in teams (Flores and Gray, 2000, cited in Thrift, 2001, p. 420). Recently an article featured in *Fortune* magazine (*Fortune*, 2015) suggested that teamwork in America's largest corporations plays a fundamental role in achieving success.

The reasons behind teams' popularity are diverse. Summarizing the arguments of both popular and academic mainstream literature, we can suggest that teamworking ranks highly on three dimensions that are central for today's organization: flexibility, motivation and learning (see Figure 4.2). We shall discuss these dimensions in turn, but first we need to understand what a team actually is.

Key problem: What is a team?

Work organizations seem to have discovered the importance of teams. At the same time teams, or groups or 'groupings' of various kinds, are everywhere. We support, or play, in sports teams and we have groups of friends. At university and in many courses you are assigned to teams and have to collaborate, working with others as a unit, rather than individually.

There is a certain confusion associated with groups and teams, given that we often use these words interchangeably and on different occasions and circumstances. What is the difference between 'teams' and 'groups'? In sociology, for example, a group is a social unit that stands between the individual and the collective/institution/organizational level. Psychologists suggest that a group is a socio-psychological dimension where each individual satisfies the need of affiliation, i.e., of being part of something bigger than him or herself, thereby enhancing the feeling of safety, security and well-being.

Perhaps you have a *group* of friends with which you go out regularly and whose company you enjoy very much. You probably would not call this group of friends a team. Yet, you would describe as a *team* the same group when it enters a quiz competition, let us say during a student union fund-raising event. We are calling a 'group' an ensemble of people sharing certain interests and passions, or perhaps simply enjoying each other's company. The 'quiz team'

Thinkpoint 4.2

In thinking of the social units you belong to, what would you describe as a group? What as a team? What do you think is the difference between a group and a team?

is still a group, because it is still an ensemble of people, but they now also have a specific purpose, or goal – namely compete in a quiz with the aim of winning it. Their task is clear: combine their knowledge to answer the most questions correctly. They must collaborate with each other to answer the questions correctly. The key point is that a 'team' implies collaboration between 'players' or members to undertake a task and achieve a goal.

Management writers also say it is very important to be precise and explicit on the difference between work groups and teams. For Katzenbach and Smith (1993) the orientation to the task and clarity of performance goals are the fundamental characteristics of the difference between **work groups** and **teams**.

Most often than not we are assigned to teams by default as we enter an organization. We do not choose the people, or the time/space of engagement, or the type of engagement. We, in other words, enter *formal* groups. As a student you might be assigned to a seminar group, or, for your course work, you might be required to complete a team-based project. Perhaps this last example is the one closer to what you might experience in your future working life. In the team-based project, the team is responsible for the delivery of an outcome (presentation, report), just like at work a team may be responsible for the management and delivery of a project, such as a new product or service. Knowledge about working in teams therefore becomes important in situations where you are not 'with your friends' but still have to get the job done, i.e., get the presentation prepared or report written. In other words, knowledge about teams can help you become more aware of what is happening in your team and why, for example, in your team some people are always out of the loop, or why you always seem to end up doing all the work!

Studies that have influenced the teaching, training and the implementation and management of teams at work have come from sociology, psychology and psychoanalysis. Understanding how teams work is also important for your future, as career advisers often emphasize in their presentations to students. Schools and universities are 'invited' by policymakers and governors to train students in teamworking skills (see Flores and Gray, 2000, p. 24), which is both cause and effect of the sheer number of companies employing teams at work in one form or another. So, when being assessed for a job as a trainee, the selectors might well try to discover whether you are a 'team player'. Does your behaviour enable others to contribute to defining and accomplishing a task, or do you either dominate or withdraw?

Teambuilding is constituted by a series of games and exercises through which the participants learn to become a cohesive team. These games are based on the understanding of the nature of groups, their processes and behaviours, which goes under the name of 'group dynamics'.

It was Kurt Lewin and his colleagues, mainly at the MIT Centre for Group Dynamics, who suggested (building on a series of experiments, an example of which is included on page 126) that a group is a particular psycho-social dimension distinct from the individual one. In other words, a group is more than the sum of the individuals comprising it, an aspect that is signalled by the sense of cohesion of the team. Lewin describes this as the 'we-feeling'

Work group A small number of people working in a collaborative style with individual input and accountability. An example can be your discussions in a small seminar group.

Team A small number of people with complementary skills who are committed to a common purpose, performance goals and approach for which they hold themselves mutually accountable. The team has a joint, specific 'collective work-products' such as experiments, reports, products, etc. An example can be a team report and presentation, often part of the coursework in many university modules.

or 'belongingness' exhibited by the members. Teambuilding aims to build a team out of what starts as a mere collection of three to eight individuals. Reynolds (1994, p. 45) proposes a list indicating the 'group processes' one should be aware of, and suggests some questions you can use to investigate and understand the processes of the groups you belong to:

- *Communication.* Who talks to whom, who supports whom? Who seems actively involved? Who does not?
- *Decision-making.* How are decisions and choices made? Who is involved in this and in what way?
- *Power and influence.* What seems to be the basis and pattern of power and influence in the group? Does it change over time?
- *Conflict.* How are conflicts of ideas, opinions or interests worked out within the group? Are they resolved and if so how?
- *Ethos.* What does it seem to be like to belong in this group? Are there accepted norms of behaviours? What roles or rules developed?

However, not everything that happens in groups is easily subjected to scrutiny. Psychoanalytic approaches have shown that group processes are not always conscious – i.e., they are not always intentional and guided by a known and linear rationality. In particular, the work of Wilfred Bion has identified the existence of specific 'group phenomena', which are unconscious reactions to the group situation characterized by high emotional responses, such as hate, love, fear or anxiety. For Bion (1961), every work group activity, hence also the ones you are involved in, can be obstructed, diverted, and on occasions assisted by these powerful emotional responses that cluster in what he calls the group's 'basic assumptions'. These are instantaneous, inevitable and instinctive ways in which individuals in a group combine and associate unconsciously in specific ways. There are three fundamental basic assumptions:

- *Dependency.* When the group is completely dependent on a leader who is invested with all the powers, just like a god, for providing answers to the anxieties of the group, hence providing security.
- *Expectancy or pairing.* When in the group there are two people (or sub-groups) that focus the attention of everyone. These are invested by the group with the hopes that something great will come – a Messiah – be it a person, idea or Utopia, which will solve all the problems/issues/anxieties of the group. It is the hope itself that provides security.
- *Flight/Fight.* When the group transforms the insecurity into a threat from a person or an object that needs to be fought or escaped. It is the action itself that keeps the insecurity at bay.

Non-psychoanalytic approaches, mainly in social psychology, have been the main sources for management theory and managerial practice regarding or involving groups and teams (for example, in training and development).

To illustrate some of the insights of social psychology for understanding team behaviour, let's return to the example of the team-based project. As is often the case in this situation, the project report is marked for the team as a whole. Each student is not assessed individually: the mark for each individual is the team mark. A complaint is often made that some people in the team do not 'pull their weight' and a few members end up doing most of the work. In this case the team might be affected by the 'free-riding tendency' (see Albanese and van Fleet, 1985) – that is, the tendency of some individuals to reduce effort and contribution in a team situation. This phenomenon in social psychology is called 'social loafing' and is mainly said to occur in situations, where, for example:

- The number of participants is very high, making it difficult to assess individual's contributions.
- The interest in the task is low and rewards are unclear or irrelevant.
- There are no systems in place for checking and improving individual's contributions.

This diagnosis also suggests that the free-riding tendency can be effectively managed by limiting the size of the group and by introducing rewards and control systems.

Team-based work (such as the project for your coursework) can be an anxiety-provoking and unfair experience. But it may also be exciting for the possibilities it offers – for example, of actually sharing the workload, of creating new interpersonal relationships and learning new things. This excitement, social psychology tells us, can also be frustrated or perhaps taken too far.

Groupthink (Janis, 1972, 1982) is a phenomenon whereby the team tends to search for, and reach, an immediate agreement. The explosion of the NASA Shuttle *Challenger,* 73 seconds after it launched in January 1986, is considered one of the clearest examples of groupthink. Even if the engineers working for NASA raised concerns on the readiness and safety of the shuttle's structure in the conditions expected at the launch, those concerns, and the information they were based on, were silenced. The NASA team gave the 'all go' clearance, initiating a tragedy that killed the seven astronauts of the *Challenger's* crew. Groupthink, it has been suggested, distorted the decision-making processes of the small groups of people involved in taking these delicate decisions. Reaching a premature consensus halted the detailed collection and open evaluation of information and the analysis of alternatives. Learning stopped as any further development was effectively frozen by a consensus that was more based upon insecurity than upon an open and considered assessment of diverse sources of information and possible options. Groupthink, therefore, may also be involved in a 'risk shift': an illusion of invulnerability and enthusiasm for a certain action or decision that polarizes the group towards higher risk. The risk that the group takes is higher than what people would risk individually.

When the group is affected by groupthink the issues at stake are poorly discussed and examined, leaving many possible solutions or routes unexplored. Dissenting voices are often stereotyped and marginalized, or 'invited' to reconsider their position, as happened in the case of the engineers working for NASA. This lack of dialogue, ultimately, may invalidate team performance (see page 118) and participate in creating disasters that, similar to the case of *Challenger,* could have been prevented.

While there is some controversy about this interpretation (Kramer, 1998), Janis argues that many important historical fiascos in US foreign policy (for example, the involvement of the USA in the Vietnam War or The Bay of Pigs operation) were at least partially due to groupthink. It has also been argued that the decision to start the war in Iraq by G.W. Bush's administration was affected by groupthink (see Levine, 2004). The decision to start the war, and the actual management of the war itself, is said to present all the characteristics that Janis considered important for identifying groupthink (check them to see if your team is suffering from groupthink):

- illusion of invulnerability
- belief in inherent morality of the group
- collective rationalization
- out of group stereotypes
- self-censorship
- illusion of unanimity
- direct pressure on dissenters
- self-appointed mindguards

'REAL' TEAMS AT WORK

Teams are not in themselves a panacea (Dunphy and Bryant, 1996) and are not infallible (Plunkett and Fournier, 1991, p. 32). Yet, mainstream management theory suggests that when teams are introduced in the right way and nurtured as part of a wider organizational philosophy and strategy, they outperform individuals and collaborative groupings.

In the management literature there is a wide utilization of the word 'team' and almost a blind acceptance of the value of teams for organizational success. Many authors have tried to identify the factors that intervene in heightening team performance (see Hackman, 1987; Campion *et al.,* 1993; Cohen *et al.,* 1996; Tannebaum *et al.,* 1992; West, 2004). These authors have ventured to explain exactly what teamwork is, and in what sense teams are important for organizational success.

For Katzenbach and Smith (1993), for example, the connection between teams and organizational success is performance. Teams, or what they call 'real' teams, should be understood as discrete units of performance and not, or not only, as examples of positive organizational values such as sharing, collaborating or listening to others.

Katzenbach and Smith (1993) propose that the importance and the impact of teams at work is dependent on how much they are *not* a simple new label attached by senior managers (or by your professors) to old ways of working; they are *not* to be equated with well-intentioned team-building events proposed by management consultants and they are *not* the same as recipes presented in the popular management books making the bestsellers lists.

Teams, rather, are identified as a distinctive form of organizational technology – i.e., a particular way of organizing work that is designed to achieve specific ends. As Katzenbach and Smith (1993) put it, there is a 'wisdom' related to teams at work (Figure 4.1). To create 'real teams' (i.e., teams that reach high performance) managers need to learn a proper *discipline* which requires application, time and commitment.

Features of team discipline are:

- adequate level of complementary skills
- truly meaningful purpose
- specific goals and performance objectives
- clear working approach
- mutual accountability.

The discipline needed to create a high-performance team is demanding for all those involved. It cannot be improvised or faked, and it is intrinsically connected to a clear strategic commitment to create a high-performing organization. So senior executives, warn Katzenbach and Smith (1993), need to be realistic and clear on what high performance means for their organization. Then, they need to implement it correctly. There can be resistance to real teams, but effective discipline reduces this resistance and prepares for the advent of 'real', high-performing teams. We shall now consider an example of a team at work in a SME, a digital media agency.

CASE STUDY 4.1 AML

AML is a digital marketing and communication agency. Among its services, the company designs and builds websites, and it develops marketing campaigns using multiple digital platforms – i.e., the Internet, mobile phones,

Figure 4.1 Team performance curve

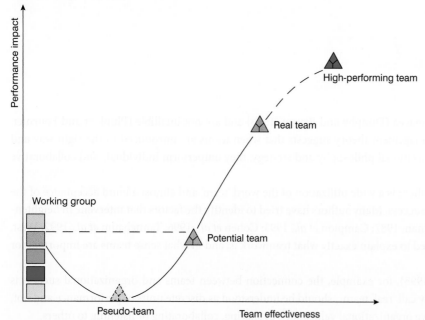

CDs, etc. The philosophy of work of AML is that better digital solutions can be obtained by working in teams made up of multiple, complementary skills. So, by putting together content, graphic and technical experts, it is possible to design and produce solutions that are neither over-designed nor too technical, but a 'perfect' balance. Case Study 4.1 provides an example of a real-life teamworking situation in a knowledge-intensive SME, involving a series of meetings for creating what they call 'the detailed content design' of the email system for a product at the interface between the Internet and mobile phones. In this vignette they are discussing specifically the design of the mailing system address book.

Case study 4.1
AML(1)

Present at a Monday morning meeting were: Laura, a junior content designer, Teresa, the account manager/producer, also an expert in content design and John, a technical developer. They are in a meeting discussing a document that Laura has produced over the weekend, supposed to express the ideas and solutions they came up with on the previous Friday. They had a series of email exchanges over the weekend and they are now going through the amendments to the document that Laura has written. Laura reads the document aloud. The discussion is rather careful and specific. John asks Laura if it is possible to explain in detail the diagrams in the document, and also if she can explain better the folder view. John is a developer in his late twenties. He is helpful in proposing changes, such as a dropdown folder, that are well received by Laura and Teresa. But John is also rather distant and annoyed. He leaves the meeting twice excusing himself but without explanation, leaving his fellow workers stunned and puzzled. Having made the corrections, Laura is left to make the further amendments on her own. Later, when Amber, the creative director, sees the revised document, her reaction is unequivocal: 'It is too complicated. This is the messiest document I have ever seen. It is too technical and there is no consideration of the user's point of view.' Laura points out that the specification produced by the client is very technical. She tries to explain the client's point of view. Amber just says 'Yeah, OK, but this is so not cool!' At that point John comes along. He sits next to Amber who repeats her verdict that the design is too technical. John explains that S4 (the client company) is telling them how to do the design. They have been provided with a functional specification that the client expects AML to beautify. But this is not what AML does. AML designs and builds 'perfect' solutions. It does not do cosmetic work.

Amber, the MD, is drawn into the project. In fact she suggests to Laura that she should do a bit more research on the subject and then they agree a meeting 'to sort things out'. Amber is unhappy as now she is the MD, and should not get involved in the details of design. But the client needs to be presented with something that is cool and right.

Later, Teresa, Laura, John and Amber are together in the meeting room. Laura starts describing the design and the problems. They are not starting from scratch because they have the S4 specification and Laura's document. In a way, the atmosphere is rather playful with jokes and laughter, but the joke also alludes to subtle tensions. John offers to prepare tea. When he comes back, Laura, who knows he knows how she likes her tea, finds he has put in sugar and exclaims 'Revenge!'.

The meeting is now very different from the one in the morning. Amber just asks 'OK, what are we trying to do? What do we need to achieve?' Everything that is needed becomes a specific feature, even if there is a long discussion on what the feature might look like. So, for example, they agree that in the address book there will be cartoon characters that can be associated with the names in the address book. They all participate in coming up with suggestions and ideas, and at the end of the meeting the room is wallpapered with sheets of drawings, sentences and navigation diagrams. Laura, as content designer, has to put everything together in a document that presents exactly what was agreed in this meeting: the detailed content design of the project. Laura returns to her workstation to start doing that, even though she thought she had already accomplished her task during the weekend. She is still smiling but it is already five o'clock and she still has a long way to go before going home. Teresa and John are staying too because they are catching up on the other work they had to do that was left aside because of this project. Moreover, Teresa is the direct contact to the client. If they are unhappy she has to deal with them, and John, as a developer, is also liaising with the client on the specificities of their software and the interface needed with it, so he wants to make sure that the explanation of the navigation is done properly. In order to avoid any mess he decides to help Laura in putting together the artefact that specifies the detailed content design, 'even if it is not my job!' he adds.

Here are a few questions that can help you to think about the case and the various issues involved in understanding teams at work:

- How would you describe AML's work organization?
- Is this a 'real team'? Can you identify and summarize the features listed in Katzenbach and Smith (1993)?
- Where do you think there are problems? What do you think they are due to?
- Do you think the team could improve their performance? How? What should the managers do in order to help the team?
- In what ways are the three dimensions we have signalled earlier of flexibility, motivation and learning, activated and affected?
- How do you explain the fact that the workers stay at work even if their working time is over?

Perhaps one of the reactions to the AML teamwork is that they seem to be very disorganized! Yet, many characteristics of AML are often associated with post-bureaucratic organizational forms (see Chapter 14). Their main organizing structure to get the work done is a team. This has all the characteristics indicated by Katzenbach and Smith (1993). The common purpose is to design the outline of the mailing system, which is the joint work-product. The members of the team need to collaborate in order to achieve this objective – they could not design it individually. They all have different, complementary skills (content designer, developer and graphic designer), and each of them is fundamental and necessary for realizing the design. Yet, everything is rather loose and unclear. There are no templates that specify what a detailed content design should look like, for example. They spend a lot of time discussing what should be in a detailed content design, and also how it should be presented, which does not seem an efficient utilization of time. As soon as they show the document/artefact they have produced to the creative director, she says that is not cool enough. This does not strike one as a useful, constructive comment, as it does not give any clear direction. Then, when Amber gets heavily involved in the second meeting, things seem to be different. She does not tell the others what to do but she facilitates their thinking, helping them to achieve a successful balance between the user point of view, creativity, usability and the constraints dictated by the client's specifications. You might have noted that there are no clear rules about how each person should participate, or what they should do. Everything seems to be left to personal interpretation and willingness. Yet they also seem highly committed. They work a great deal, including weekends via email exchanges, and well beyond 'normal' working hours. Accountability is also shared. They are accountable not only to Amber, the creative director, but also to each other. In the vignette we see how individuals' contributions, suggestions and ideas are not only expected but closely monitored and judged by the team members.

As indicated earlier, teams in the mainstream are said to activate/enhance three main organizational dimensions: flexibility, motivation and learning. We shall look at these dimensions and suggest why teams are considered to be involved in enhancing and activating these dimensions.

Key ideas and contributions to thinking and empirical studies

Many popular and academic authors include 'teams' as a central feature of their favoured prescriptions for improved organizational performance. Teams, for example, are identified as essential components of the implementation of the principles of total quality management (Oakland, 1996). They are the building blocks of 'excellent organizations' (Peters and Waterman, 1982), key elements of the 'learning organization' (Senge, 1990) and they are critical components of virtually all high-performance management systems that build profit by putting people first (Pfeffer, 1998).

Despite having different accents and connotations, they share a common theme. Responsible teams or self-managing teams or semi-autonomous teams are some of the names given to the building blocks of new 'post-bureaucratic' organizational forms, which are comparatively flat and agile because they have few hierarchical layers (Peters, 1988). Teams tend to enhance organizational flexibility and learning as they can explore and react quickly to any problem or new challenge. Decisions can be taken at the team level and do not need to go through a long chain of command. Motivation is also greatly enhanced as teams are 'empowered' by bestowing upon the members responsibility and autonomy in performing organizational tasks, in contrast to traditional organizations with their tight rules of command, short span of control and co-ordination (Jenkins, 1994, p. 852).

The three organizational dimensions that teams enhance are summarized below. The three dimensions are inter-related. The distinction between them is analytical because it enables us to distinguish theoretical resources and empirical studies for each of the dimensions that teams are said to activate and favour in organizations.

TEAMS FOR FLEXIBILITY: LEAN PRODUCTION

'Dynamic work teams are at the heart of the lean factory.' This is the way Womack *et al.*, (1990, p. 90) put it when introducing their influential book, based on five years and US$5 million of research on the status of the organization of work in the automobile industry around the world. Lean design defies traditional criteria of organization of production and management thinking. Its aim is to avoid waste, slack and redundancies. It is in this sense that production is 'lean'. The system must be fast and efficient, with few errors, and this is what lean design aspires to achieve.

The differences between mass and lean production (See Chapter 11)

In traditional mass production, the assembly line is the place and the time where all the thinking and design behind the product – for example, a car – comes together in a predetermined and closely specified manner. The entire process is designed by industrial engineers according to classical (e.g., Taylor's) principle of organization. This means that the engineers have conceived, at least in principle, the best way in which workers should assemble the thousands of parts necessary to make a complete car. There is a strict division of labour and allocation of specific roles. The production process is broken down into small operations, and each individual is required to perform a very narrow range of discrete tasks. Each action, down to the time and motion, is studied in minute detail and prescribed in clear order.

Lean production involves a very different approach to work organization. In lean production, work is organized around teams. We take the real example of NUMMI (New United Motor Manufacturing Inc.), a study that has become a classic, in order to describe what this means in practical terms. NUMMI was, in origin, an assembly plant

Figure 4.2 Organizational dimensions where teams intervene, according to mainstream literature

Flexibility: The organizational ability to change. The faster an organization can change the better it can perform in a competitive environment.

Motivation: The willingness to exert oneself. The higher the motivation, the better and higher the productivity.

Learning: The process and the ability to create and distribute knowledge. The more you learn the more you can innovate or improve how things are done.

owned by General Motors (GM) and one of its worst in terms of productivity levels, quality and absenteeism. Case Study 4.2 provides an account based on Adler (1993) and Womack *et al.*, (1990).

Here are a few questions that can help you to analyze the case of NUMMI and explore the various issues involved in understanding teams at work:

- Can you summarize and explain the main differences between mass and lean production?
- What is the position of the workers in each of them?
- If you were a worker can you envisage any problem with working under the conditions of lean production? And if you were a manager?
- Can you explain in what way teams are enhancing flexibility, learning and motivation at NUMMI?

The NUMMI case not only illustrates minutely the way teams enhance flexibility but also helps in questioning the simplistic connection that sees teamwork as exemplification of post-bureaucratic organizational forms. Teamwork can still be key to the organization when principles of bureaucracy are firmly maintained and teams work in what could be described as an advance Taylorism. For example, Adler (1993) and Adler and Borys (1996) point out that NUMMI has clear hierarchies; it has standards and formalized procedures designed to achieve the best way opera-

Kaizen This is the process of continuous improvement developed in the Japanese organization of work and then introduced as an important element in Western organizational designs, such as total quality management.

tions can be realized. It also has structured flows of information/communication and control, just as the 'traditional' bureaucracy. More importantly, these authors contend that NUMMI's organization of work cannot be considered in any way *beyond* Taylorism. Rather, they argue, NUMMI represents the perfecting of fundamental Tayloristic precepts of time and motion, and standardization, but these principles are inserted in a virtuous circle of continuous improvement, what we have said below is called **kaizen**. The system that makes this possible they call 'enabling' or 'learning bureaucracy' (See Box 4.1 Learning and bureaucracy):

…using learned analytical tools, their own experience and the expertise of leaders and engineers, workers create a consensual standard that they teach to the system by writing job descriptions. The system then teaches these standards back to the workers, who then by further analysis, standardization, reanalysis, refinement and re-standardization create an intensely structured system of continuous improvement. The salient characteristic of this bureaucracy is learning, not coercion (Adler, 1993, p. 104).

Case study 4.2 NUMMI

NUMMI, a joint venture between Toyota and GM in Fremont, California, was formally established in 1984. It has approximately 350 teams in production made up of five-to-seven people and a leader. Small teams are supposed to encourage participative decision-making and team bonding (Adler, 1993, p. 5). Each team is responsible for a different portion of the assembly line. Four teams form what is known as a group, with the first layer of management being the group leader. Each team has to co-ordinate its own work and the relations with other teams. Also, the cleanliness and tidiness of their workspace is the responsibility of the team. Team members are trained in all the tasks necessary to the team operation, and they can rotate when needed. Teams are responsible for quality checks and small repairs. Problems are solved when they occur. Any defective operation on the line is tackled immediately, rather than being pushed up to 'quality control' and being left to pile up for attention in a rectification section. In order to solve the problems when they appear, and even before they occur, workers must be able to do something that was unthinkable in the traditional production line, namely to stop the line.

Teams are also encouraged to utilize the 'Five Whys' – a questioning strategy designed to get to the bottom of the problem the team is facing. They are also asked to propose improvements to the system of production beyond immediate problem-solving, through a system of suggestions or, for example, by joining **quality circles**. These are teams made up of workers as well as specialist engineers, looking at implementing suggestions and ideas with the goal of improving the system of production continuously.

> **Quality circles** Meetings of group of workers committed to continuous improvement in the quality and productivity of a given line of production.

Management's role in NUMMI, as in Toyota, is that of providing expertise to help production teams with problem solving. In order to compete with the performance gains – in quality as well as price – achieved by Toyota, other auto makers have followed their lead in introducing lean manufacturing methods. And the basic ideas of lean production have been applied in many other industries, with mixed results. The system organized around production teams has often proved to be extremely efficient, much more than traditional plants. The fact that teams are constantly attentive to the work and detect errors immediately reduces the rework needed at the end of the line. In other words, the essence of the teamwork in NUMMI is its flexibility because workers can do all the different tasks and are collectively responsible for improving their ability to work productively as a team. Each new idea, new successful implementation and new process is not only adopted by the team but is spread to the whole organization in a continuous race to improvement. This is known by the Japanese word *kaizen*.

By the end of 1986 NUMMI's productivity was the highest in GM and was twice that of the old plant. More than 90 per cent of the workers declared themselves to be satisfied with their employment in NUMMI and absenteeism fell from 20–25 per cent to 3–4 per cent. Both in Toyota and NUMMI there are formal agreements in place that seal a true reciprocal obligation between workers and employers (Womack *et al.*, 1990, p. 102). For example, there are agreements on a certain level of job security and policies, which avoid job cuts as a way out of financial crisis. The teams are part of a system in which the workers, the managers, the suppliers and the distributors are integrated and are said to share a common destiny, 'a community of fate' (Berders and van Hootegem, 2000, p. 55). This is also obtained through the socialization of the employees into an organizational culture (see Chapter 10), that values their work and their knowledge, putting them at the centre of the production process. Emblems of traditional differences in status such as different dress codes, different food facilities, parking spaces, etc. are erased in order to inspire a spirit of communality and equality. The main idea is that the whole organization shares the same values and same destiny, so everyone has to do their best to make the company succeed.

TEAMS FOR MOTIVATION: PARTICIPATION, SATISFACTION AND HUMANE WAYS OF WORKING

When teams are empowered to solve problems, to offer innovative solutions, all the workers become active participants in their work. They can shape the specificities of their working practices, and they can improve them, rather than being mere executors of managers' orders. In other words, employees' importance and value is recognized; they are not considered as simple appendices of the machines or bureaucrats of impersonal organizations. The 'empowerment' of employees has become extremely significant in recent times. With the motto of 'people first', for example, Pfeffer (1998) proposes a seven-point list for organizational success where enlightened 'people management' is at the centre of a profit-making organization that invests and treats its employees with respect, building up relations of trust and co-operation rather than relying upon expensive direct control systems. When people are empowered to work in teams they can manage themselves and develop real commitment and ownership of what they do. The autonomy and discretion that people enjoy in teams translates into intrinsic rewards and job satisfaction (Pfeffer, 1998, p. 74). This in turn has an impact on employee morale and productivity.

> **Quality of working life movements** Denotes programmes of organizational design and development dedicated to improving productivity and workers' retention and commitment by bettering the relationship between employers and employees and the work environment.

The assumptions underlying this view are part of an extended legacy that stretches back to the socio-technical tradition, the human relations movement, and the **quality of working life movement** (see Procter and Mueller, 2000; Buchanan, 2000; Huczynski, 1996). Classical studies linked to these approaches are summarized at the end of this subsection. It is important to consider that this legacy emphasizes that:

Social system Refers to a specific pattern of relationship, maintained by a certain flow of interactions and a common goal.

- An organization is not only a technical system but also a **social system**; and both need to be managed.
- In social systems, groups are an important source of norms of conduct and informal rules.
- A democratic approach to a task, which favours participation and autonomy, enhances the quality and quantity of the output.

Scientific management (Chapter 8) considers material benefits primary for generating motivation in otherwise uninterested, idiosyncratic, recalcitrant workers who require constant control and supervision to be kept on the task. In contrast, 'modern management thinking' maintains that social, psychological and moral factors also intervene in regulating workers' motivation and satisfaction (Chapter 2). Many commentators suggest that successful organizations are those able to fulfil the psychological and social needs of the employees, where personal growth and organizational growth are not in conflict, but fulfil and reinforce each other. A humane, motivating and respectful working life is regarded as fundamental for successful organizations, both as a business solution, as well as the application of values of the democracies of the West to the workplace (Lammers and Szell, 1989; Heller *et al.*, 1998; Plunkett and Fournier, 1991).

Box 4.1
Learning and bureaucracy

For Adler there are three aspects involved in creating a 'learning and enabling bureaucracy':

1 The open, trustworthy and prompt relationship between management and workers' unions which 'on the basis of the recognition that job security is fundamental to an employee's well-being' agrees to a no-layoff policy and to a listening and prompt response on employees' demands.
2 Standardization of operation is a fundamental factor. This, in NUMMI, is extensive. NUMMI still uses the Tayloristic precepts of studying and defining procedures of time and motion. But these precepts, rather than being decided by some engineer detached from production and without any consultation with those on the shop floor, are actually devised by the workers themselves. In NUMMI, the workers 'hold the stopwatch'. The members of the team will observe and time each other, finding the most efficient and safest way to perform a certain operation. Then they break the work down into small parts and try to improve each of these parts. The team then compares the results with other teams on the same station during other shifts and the best one becomes the standard procedure for that particular operation in the plant. The workers themselves become work engineers. In this respect they are 'empowered' because, rather than being told what to do, they find out for themselves what is the best way of doing something. They are managers of their own activity. They are not alienated appendices of a machine or mere executors of someone else's design. Rather they execute their own design.
3 The other aspect, which is connected with standardization, is that it offers a basis for continuous improvement. The improvements of one team, in a particular shift, for example, become the benchmark to be improved upon by the other teams. This introduces the challenge that continues the virtuous circle of the learning bureaucracy.

These ideas might seem more applicable to professional and services companies or the so-called 'knowledge intensive firms' (Alvesson, 1993). These are companies, of which AML is an example, where the products and services are the knowledge itself. Yet, the studies regarding Volvo are a classic example of a company that has implemented the ideas of employees' participation and autonomy in car manufacturing (see Case Study 4.3).

Classical studies

THE HAWTHORNE EXPERIMENTS: THE IMPORTANCE OF SOCIAL NEEDS AND GROUP NORMS AT WORK (SEE CHAPTER 2)

In 1927 Elton Mayo was commissioned to study the factors that intervened in the productivity of the workforce of the Hawthorne Plant of the Western Electric Company in Chicago. During the research process, the researchers manipulated the lighting level on the shop floor. The result was that, at every level, productivity unexpectedly increased.

The researchers then asked for volunteers to work in a room separate from the rest of their colleagues (the relay assembly room). A group of women accepted and their work was observed by a researcher who stayed in the room and interacted with them. Variables were manipulated such as pauses, working time and lunch breaks. The results again showed an increase in productivity regardless of the modifications.

The researchers inferred from these results that it was not the *working* conditions but the actual *social* condition of being observed and studied that had brought about the changes in productivity. The 'Hawthorne effect' came to be known as the phenomenon whereby observation interferes with what is studied. But an equally significant aspect of this result was the insight that, by working together and sharing the experience, the workers had created a wider unit, a *group*, which the researchers started thinking had something to do with the increase in productivity. After a long process of interviewing, the final part of the study was an observation of 14 male bank wirers. By studying their interactions the researchers realized that informal groups had emerged that did not coincide with the formal groups based on the spatial and sequential organization of work. These informal groupings were shown to have a leader who emerged in the process of interaction. The researchers found that these groups had **informal** norms and their members were strongly conditioned by these norms, which regulated the workers' general behaviour and also the pace of production.

> **Informal or Informality** Behaviour that is not officially recognized or approved.

Case study 4.3
Self-managing teams at Volvo

In the 1960s Volvo started a series of experiments designed to improve on the repetitive, straining and alienating conditions of Tayloristic forms of work. These problems, as Bernstein (1992) suggests, were made more urgent by the lack of 'external labour' to cover for jobs that the Swedish workers did not want to do. Volvo experimented with a socio-technical work design (see Trist and Bamforth, 1951) and a participatory style of management. This resulted in a design of the Uddevalla plant that abandoned the assembly line altogether in favour of 'standstill' production stations. Multiskilled self-managing teams work in parallel stations, each member acting as teachers, assemblers, inventory managers and quality controllers, entirely responsible for building a complete car.

These experiments have, however, almost been completely terminated and traditional assembly systems have been reintroduced in Volvo. Lower productivity is often indicated as the main reason for this. But empirical evidence in this respect is dubious and contested (Jonsson et al., 2004), and more complex explanations seem to be involved (see Wallace, 2004; Berggren, 1992) including, for example, changes in the economic situation in the early 1990s, with unusual levels of unemployment in Sweden. It has also been suggested that the 'Swedish model for work life development' brought into question sedimented power relations – for example, the differences in availability and ownership of symbolic and material resources for employers and employees, which was threatening traditional and established interests. This also explains the reassertion of traditional management control in the system of production (Jonsson et al., 2004).

TRIST AND BAMFORTH: AUTONOMOUS RESPONSIBILITY AND SOCIO-TECHNICAL SYSTEMS (SEE CHAPTER 2)

In 1951 Trist and Bamforth published in *Human Relations,* the results of research on the working methods and conditions of miners in England in which the method of coal-getting had been changed from 'hand-got' to 'LongWall'. The LongWall is a method that reproduces the mass production engineering method with rigid sequence, functional interdependence and spatio-temporal extension of the factory regime. This replaced the 'hand-got' method based on small group work. In the 'hand-got' system each member was self-selected, and consisted of a workers' pair to which often one or two external individuals were associated. This group was the primary unit responsible for the whole cycle of operation for getting the coal. They had an embodied knowledge of themselves, of each other and of the conditions and situations in which they worked, also because often there were ties of kinship between the members who all came from the close-knit local community. This knowledge and the leeway in their action enabled the members to modulate their work as a whole, guaranteeing continuous coal-getting as well as safety for all in the harsh underground conditions. This situation of group leadership and self-supervision was called 'responsible autonomy'.

The LongWall system broke down the cycle, giving specific roles to each individual, effectively segregating the workers into the seven categories of skills, as well as pay, in which it was constituted. At the technological level a new integration was achieved by the introduction of a new task sequence. But this new method disturbed the existing social order and equilibrium and this was neither recognized nor addressed by management. Hence, new problems and issues emerged. For example, new informal groups substituted the ones based on the 'hand-got' system. But these were solely private arrangements without any institutional and mutual obligation that offered support to its members and were also open to antisocial behaviour, coalitions, etc.

KURT LEWIN: THE IMPORTANCE OF PARTICIPATION AND DEMOCRATIC STYLE

In 1948 Lewin recounts the experiments with groups of children by Lipitt and by Lipitt and Whiye, at the Iowa Child Welfare Research Station. The children were divided into homogenous groups based on socioeconomic characteristics, as well as according to the results of psycho-social tests. The aim was to create equivalent groups on such qualities as leadership and interpersonal relationships. The task of the groups was to make theatrical masks. The scientists kept the activities and instruments of the groups constant while they varied the atmosphere of the groups with the help of a leader assigned to each group. The leaders created a group with a *democratic* atmosphere, a group with an *autocratic* atmosphere and a third one with a *laissez-faire* atmosphere. For the democratic group many paths of actions and behaviours were open; for the autocratic only one, namely the path determined by the leader. In autocracy the leader determined not only the kind of activity but also who should work with whom (Lewin, 1948, p. 77). In the *laissez-faire* atmosphere the group was left to its own devices. The results obtained showed a striking difference in the performance and quality of the masks: the democratic groups developed a wider sense of cohesiveness and sense of belonging, what Lewin calls the 'we' feeling.

Overall, the three experimental conditions proved that authoritarian groups are more productive at the beginning but soon are affected by internal struggles and aggression among members. The scapegoat is a well-known phenomenon when one member is singled out and bullied by the others, and is an exemplification of group aggression in authoritarian group conditions. The *laissez-faire* atmosphere tended, instead, to create apathy.

This, and other studies, became important because they were considered to demonstrate that certain psycho-social needs, such as that of belonging and social acceptance, can be satisfied by groups that are managed in a democratic style. Groups can take some time to 'learn' democracy, as they need to learn how to take decisions out of the many alternatives, and how to accommodate differences. But, in the long run, the outcome of their work is higher both in qualitative and quantitative terms.

Teams for learning: Continuous improvement and innovation

The issue of learning and knowledge creation and diffusion has increased in importance in recent decades (see Chapter 6), with many asserting that knowledge is the source of competitive advantage. A flourishing literature has developed that analyzes, describes and often prescribes strategies, ideas and models for understanding, creating, facilitating and supporting organizations that learn to improve or innovate by creating, transferring and managing successfully new and existing knowledge (Drucker, 1993; Senge, 1990; Nonaka and Takeuchi, 1995; Davenport and Pusak, 1998). The level and quality of creativity and problem-solving required to innovate or improve on existing business solutions is very high. An individual working alone rarely produces the creative ideas or solutions required, for example, for complex or discontinuous innovation (Tushman and Nadler, 1998). If this seems blindingly obvious at an intuitive level, it should also be appreciated that theoretically the creation and transfer of knowledge – in the form of learning – has been increasingly recognized as a social phenomenon rather than an individual cognitive endeavour. This is why teams/groups, as a basic social unit, can be considered as media of knowledge creation and diffusion. Specifically, learning and knowledge creation occur:

- in the social context
- in interaction and participation in shared practices
- in processes of reflection and feedback
- in freedom to explore and implement new and daring concepts.

For all these reasons, many studies are concentrating on team learning and how this can be favoured and nurtured in organizations (Argote *et al.,* 2000, 2001; Wood and Bandura, 1989; Gibson and Vermeuler, 2003; Edmonson, 2002; Bogenrieder and Nooteboom, 2004). As Peter Senge (1990, p. 236) puts it, 'there has never been a greater need for mastering team learning in organization than there is today'. According to Senge, areas and issues that should be considered for facilitating team learning are:

- *Discussion and dialogue.* These are two different modes of communication, both important. Discussion enables members to dissect a topic or a problem from various points of view. Dialogue is a 'free flow of meaning' through which people can observe their own thinking, understand how it developed and enable it to cohere in a collective meaning.
- *Dealing with conflict and defensive routines.* Defensive routines are entrenched in often unacknowledged habits that we use to defend ourselves from the embarrassment and threat that comes with exposing our thinking. Reflection and mutual inquiry are skills employed for dealing with conflictual situations and defensive routines.
- *Practise team learning.* Create space and time (with specific sessions or learning laboratories) to practise discussion and dialogue and to develop skills for dealing with defensiveness.

You might have already recognized the possibility that if a team can be a medium of knowledge creation, learning as a social phenomenon does not occur exclusively within the restricted, officially prescribed formal boundaries of

Dr Peter M. Senge is the founding chairperson of the Society for Organizational Learning (SOL) and a senior lecturer at the Massachusetts Institute of Technology. Dr Senge is the author of *The Fifth Discipline: The Art and Practice of the Learning Organization.* He has lectured extensively throughout the world, translating the abstract ideas of systems theory into tools for better understanding of economic and organizational change. He has worked with leaders in business, education, health care and government. The *Journal of Business Strategy* (September/October 1999) named Dr Senge as one of the 24 people who had had the greatest influence on business strategy over the last 100 years.

Source: www.solonline.org/aboutsol/who/Senge/

Box 4.2
Peter Senge

Exercise 4.1

You can engage with your seminar group in a 'learning laboratory' to improve your skills at dialogue and negotiation. Centre your discussion on the question: 'How do we deal with conflicts?' The ground rules that everyone has to respect are:

- *Suspension of assumptions*. Do not hold on to your position at any cost but try to understand your own and all the others' views.
- *Act as equals*. There might be differences between you – some people have better marks than others, or are considered more knowledgeable. Suspend these differences for the time you are in this 'learning laboratory'.
- *Spirit of enquiry*. Try to understand what are the deep assumptions beyond the positions you and others hold. Probe by asking what is the evidence or reason that justifies the positions people hold? Ask the question: How have we come to accept these views?

specific, formal or functional team membership. Some authors (Lave and Wenger, 1991; Brown and Duguid, 1991) have suggested we should also concentrate on what they call 'communities of practice' (COPs), which are made up of people clustering around a specific practice (such as the design of digital solutions as in the case of AML) they are involved in, and for which they share a keen interest.

By participating in these communities, people develop new ways of doing or improving on existing practice, and the activities comprising the practice itself. In this process of participation they develop a certain identity (in the case of AML as web designers, for example), and become active and recognized members of that wider community. Learning occurs in the participation in the practice, as members engage and develop a specific language, share stories that help make sense of the practice and produce artefacts that are meaningful for all the members. We can be members of many COPs. In some we might be at the periphery, whereas in others we might be at the centre, recognized as competent members, even experts of that practice.

Thinkpoint 4.3

To which COPs do you belong? Can you identify the key aspects, such as specific language, stories and artefacts, of each of the COPs you belong to?

If learning occurs at various levels and dimensions and it is not restricted to specific business units like formal teams, then we need to consider the implications for organizations. One of these implications is that multi-membership (see Figure 4.3) should be noted and managed (Wenger, 1998; Wenger and Snyder, 2000; Wenger *et al.*, 2002), for example, by identifying the existing COPs, and by fostering and nurturing COPs and the members' freedom and ability to tap into the different levels and dimensions of learning and innovation.

Exercise 4.2

Deploy the model of multi-membership and the concept of COPs to analyze the AML case study.

Key problems and open questions

Much of the mainstream literature on teams at work has been dedicated to understanding how they behave and how they can be made more effective with a view to enhancing various aspects of organizational performance. In particular, team effectiveness has been studied in terms of productivity and members' attitudes and behaviours (Kirkman, 2000). Some research strengthens the claims that teams increase productivity (Cohen and Ledford, 1994; Trist *et al.*, 1977; Wellins *et al.,* 1991). Other research has been less positive as experiments have not demonstrated a correlation between teamworking and higher productivity (Wall *et al.*, 1986; Cordery *et al.*, 1991). This has resulted in a general ambiguity about teams at work. What makes them perform at their full potential is still an open question, but there are some areas that have consistently being addressed as significant. Team effectiveness is linked to elements such as team development, design, leadership and resistance. We shall look at each of these in turn.

Figure 4.3 The multi-membership learning circle
Reprinted by permission of Harvard Business School Press. *Cultivating Communities of Practice*, Wegner, Dermott and Snyder, Boston, MA, 2002, p. 19. © 2002 Etienne Wegner, Richard R. McDermott and William Snyder. All rights reserved.

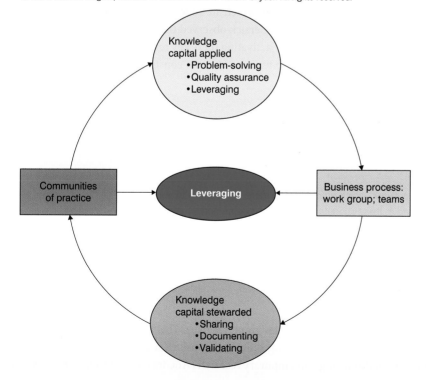

HOW DO TEAMS DEVELOP?

One of the oldest and better known models of how teams evolve and develop over time was proposed by Tuckman (1965) and slightly modified in Tuckman and Jenson (1977). These later stages are indicated in *italics*.

- *Forming*. This is the stage when people start to know each other and start understanding their activity and the task to be accomplished. A general consensus starts emerging, which is identified as the *conforming stage*.
- *Storming*. Conflicts among people emerge due to frustration or difficulties with the task and different personalities, styles of working and ideas.
- *Norming*. Norms and patterns of acceptable and recognized behaviour of conduct, work objectives and style emerge. A *reforming stage* sets in when people assess their behaviour according to the new standards established in the norming stage.
- *Performing*. This is the stage when team members as a team concretely engage with the task and the activities required for its accomplishment. Two final stages – *adjourning* and *mourning* – have also been added. The first is the moment of concluding the task with the accomplishment of the team objectives. The second signals a certain reluctance to 'let go' of the team and engage actively with new activities and new tasks in new teams.

As Poole (1983) put it, 'for 40 years researchers on group development have been conducting the same study with minor alterations' (cited in Gersick, 1988, p. 11). This model is very popular, particularly in management training and development. However, are we sure that all teams all the time move in such a linear, hierarchical progression? Do we know anything about the timescale and factors involved in the progression? Nothing certain. Even Tuckman was critical of applying his model to all groups (Reynolds, 1994). It was Gersick's (1988) research that finally challenged the idea that team development is only conceivable as a set of necessary stages the team must go through.

Gersick's (1988) qualitative study, which was part of wider research into team effectiveness, suggested that teams do not follow specific and necessary stages. Rather, they proceed in the accomplishment of their task by what she calls 'punctuated equilibrium'. This expression comes from biology and it is based on the observation of fossils, which indicate that, in nature, change (evolution) does not occur in long continuous processes of development. Rather, it is characterized by periods of relative stability (*equilibrium)* which are suddenly interrupted and disrupted (*punctuated)* by a revolutionary period where new forms emerge. Gersick observed the same type of development with her team experiments. Aspects she found to be important for activating these key revolutionary moments were (i) the continuous relations with the external environment of the team and (ii) the constant awareness of time and deadlines.

Thinkpoint 4.4

Reflecting on your experiences of teamwork, which model seems more appropriate to you? Why? What issues are not considered in these models that you have come across in your experiences of teamwork?

HOW SHOULD TEAMS BE DESIGNED?

Many authors point out how difficult, and delicate, the task of designing teams is. This also includes the problem of allocating and matching proper technical and problem-solving skills to the task (Katzenbach and Smith, 1993; Hackman, 1987; Hackman and Morris, 1975). Promising contemporary research (Ancora and Caldwell, 1992, 2000;

Carroll *et al.*, 2006; Stewart, 2006; Oh *et al.*, 2004; Reagans *et al.*, 2004) is exploring two key aspects for designing effective teams: **team human capital** and **team
social capital**.

However, it is Meredith Belbin's model of team design (see Belbin, 1993, 2004)
that is widely employed in training and development. Belbin's model for team
management concentrates on the importance of designing teams that are balanced
in terms of personal characteristics and abilities of members. In a nine-year
research project, Belbin and his research group identified nine 'roles' that are seen
to be crucial for team effectiveness (see Table 4.1). A 'role' is defined as a tendency
to behave, contribute and interrelate with others in a particular way. Each of these
roles is considered significant for team effectiveness because it helps to provide a
good balance for achieving the task.

Team human capital The
resources (knowledge, time,
know-how, attitude, etc.)
individual members make
available to the team.

Team social capital The
quality and quantity of social
relations inside the team but
also between the team and
the broader organizational and
social field.

The success of this model could be explained by the fact that Belbin's model claims predictive capacity. This
means that by applying the instruments provided to test and score people, it is possible to design the best team
(in the given circumstances) to perform a specific task. Such a promise is very appealing and might explain the
interest in Belbin's model shown by managers and students. However, the validity of Belbin's model and his team-
role self-perception inventory has been questioned and retested, with mixed results. For example, Furnham *et al.*,
(1993, p. 254) found that there is little psychometric support for the structure of Belbin inventories. Yet, as a
learning tool in training and development this still has its uses as it facilitates discussions and reflections on the
'team human capital'.

In 2012, Google embarked on Project Aristotle, an initiative that studied hundreds of Google's teams to understand how to design the 'perfect team'. Dubey, a leader of the project, summarizes: 'We looked at 180 teams from
all over the company, we had lots of data, but there was nothing showing that a mix of specific personality types or
skills or backgrounds made any difference. The "who" part of the equation didn't seem to matter' (Duhigg, 2016).
As in Furnham *et al.*,'s study (1993), Google findings seem to suggest that a team's success is not much related
to members' roles, hierarchical structure, and composition, but rather, to how team members treat each other.
Specifically, they found two main components for a 'good team': a) an equality in distribution of conversational
turn-taking; and b) an average social sensitivity. What emerged in this study is that it does not matter whether leadership shifted in each assignment, as long as at the end of the day people speak roughly the same amount of time.
Also what emerged as important was to be able to understand how members of the team feel – whether they are
upset or feel left out – based on their tone of voice and non-verbal cues. This ability seems also to be fundamental
for successful teamworking.

These two elements can be summarized as 'team psychological safety' (Edmondson, 1999). The term refers to
'a shared belief that the team is safe for interpersonal risk taking [...] a sense of confidence that the team will not
embarrass, reject, or punish someone for speaking up. This confidence stems from mutual respect and trust among
team members' (*ibid*, p. 354). For Project Aristotle's researchers, psychological safety, more than other elements such
as clear goals, culture of dependability, seems to be key to teamworking.

HOW DO YOU MAKE TEAMS WORK?
Addressing resistance

Students and advocates of teams at work report that creating 'real teams' is difficult because there is often resistance to
their implementation. Bernstein (1992, p. 359), for example, reports that in the experiments at Volvo discussed earlier, 'to
everyone's surprise some workers resisted changes because they preferred the traditional approach of doing a single task
all day'. Weisbord (1992), in recounting his attempt to implement participative work design and teams in his company,
points out that some ex-supervisors, as well as some workers, could not adapt to the self-managing teams: 'Sidney, our
best shipper, a world class miracle of efficient distribution had about as much interest in participation as a gourmet chef
would have in McDonald's. "I don't want more responsibility. Why can't I just pack orders?"' (Weisbord, 1992, p. 98).

Do the quotes reported above signal a resistance to teamwork? This is anecdotal evidence, you might think, and you would be right. Mainstream researchers have rarely undertaken in-depth explorations of employees' experiences of teamwork. Some studies have attempted to identify the factors that intervene in producing resistance to working in teams. Kanter (1983), for example, considers that teams are not immune from organizational politics as people pursue personal agendas, internal competition, etc., resulting in a disruption of team cohesiveness and effective task accomplishment

Some of the factors intervening in generating resistance that have been studied are: perceptions of fairness and trust; attitude towards change; and cultural values.

Table 4.1 Belbin's model for team management

Rules and descriptions – team role contributions	Allowable weaknesses
Plant	
Creative, unorthodox, imaginative; solves difficult problems	Ignores details; too preoccupied to communicate effectively
Resource investigator	
Extrovert, enthusiastic, communicative; explores opportunities; develops contacts	Over-optimistic; loses interest once initial enthusiasm has passed
Co-ordinator	
Mature, confident, a good chairperson; clarifies goals, promotes decision-making; delegates well	Can be seen as manipulative; delegates personal work
Shaper	
Challenging, dynamic, thrives on pressure; has the drive and courage to overcome obstacles	Can provoke others; hurts people's feelings
Monitor evaluator	
Sober, strategic and discerning; seeks all opinions; judges accurately	Lacks drive and ability to inspire others; overly critical
Teamworker	
Co-operative, mild, perceptive and diplomatic; listens, builds, averts friction, calms the nerves	Indecisive in crunch situations; can be easily influenced
Implementer	
Disciplined, reliable, conservative and efficient; turns ideas into practical actions	Somewhat inflexible; slow to respond to new possibilities
Completer	
Painstaking, conscientious, anxious; searches out errors and omissions; delivers on time	Inclined to worry unduly; reluctant to delegate; can be a nitpicker
Specialist	
Single-minded, self-starting, dedicated; provides knowledge and skills in rare supply	Contributes on only a narrow front; dwells on technicalities; overlooks the big picture

Note: Strengths of contributors in any one of the roles is commonly associated with particular weaknesses. These are called allowable weaknesses. Executives are seldom strong in all nine team roles.

Source: Reprinted from *Team roles at work*, Belbin (ed.), 1993, p. 23 with permission from Elsevier. Reproduced by kind permission of Belbin Associates – www.belbin.com

Perception of fairness and trust

If one perceives teamwork as fair then people tend to show less resistance. Researchers, in fact, have concluded that trust and fairness of treatment in the perception of employees is an important element in avoiding or engendering resistance to teamwork. More specifically, according to Kirkman (2000), the aspects of work that are significant for employees' perception of fairness (Kirkman *et al.*, 1996; Jones and Lindley, 1998) are:

- pay
- distribution of workload
- criteria for decisions
- interpersonal treatment.

However, Kirkman (2000, p. 7) argues that one should not believe that fair management will *necessarily* reduce resistance. In the first place, there should be a desire of the worker to be self-managing or 'self-leading', as Manz (1992, p. 486) also stresses. There must be, these authors maintain, a certain personal philosophy, a belief that teamwork is important, for the employees to be willing and productive members of a team. It is a certain view and meaning of their work that makes working in teams personally meaningful and appealing for them. These non-fairness issues are related to **dispositional factors**, such as stable attitudes towards change and cultural values. These dispositional factors are clarified below.

> **Dispositional factors** Internal personality aspects, traits and beliefs that are specific to each individual and may be seen to motivate a person to behave in a certain way. They are opposed to situational factors where the behaviour is due to factors or circumstances external to the individual.

Tolerance for change

As Kirkman (2000) suggests, low tolerance towards change is negatively associated with the introduction of self-managing teams. In other words, if you do not like change then you are more likely to resist working in teams. People may well understand intellectually that change is required but they can have negative emotional responses that can be unconscious or conscious, such as a fear of not being able to develop the skills and behaviours required, or of not understanding the task. They can find it extremely difficult to cope with the novelty and ambiguity that, for example, working in self-managing teams might mean for them intellectually, physically and emotionally.

Gender diversity

As Dwyer *et al.*, (2003) suggest, gender diversity in teams has the potential to bring novel insights, perspectives, creativity, and experiences that foster and support a firm's expansion.

Yet, there is no consensus on whether gender diversity enhances teams' effectiveness. Some research suggests that mixed groups do not necessarily perform as well as single-gendered groups (Maznevski,1994). Other works found that teams with more women than men outperform groups with other gender compositions, and specifically all-male groups (Fenwick and Neal, 2001).

Dwyer *et al.*'s (2003) research outlines that the organizational culture has an impact on the benefits of gender diversity in teams. For example, when the organizational culture emphasizes informal organizational processes, such as flexibility and spontaneity, and focuses inward on the firm and employees, placing high value on integration and teamwork, a diverse gender group is likely to enhance firm's performance.

Women are found to be more co-operative than men, encouraging participation, and leading through inclusion, thus avoiding competition; men, conversely, are driven by competitive individualism (Eagly *et al.*, 1992; Grant, 1998). These contrasting styles affect firms' performance differently according to the organizational culture in place. For example, different styles can hinder performance within an organizational culture, which places focus on competition and interaction with the external environment.

Cultural values (See Chapter 10)

Cultural diversity in teams is on the increase, and there are contradictory findings on how this impedes or facilitates team effectiveness (Hambrick *et al.*, 1998; Swann *et al.*, 2004; van Knippernberg, De Dreu and Homan, 2004; Harrison and Humphrey, 2010). Hofstede (1980, 1983) indicated that cultural values are based on durable, desirable conduct deemed proper to certain societies (Kirkman and Shapiro, 1997, p. 11). Some cultural values may facilitate self-managing teams while others may induce resistance.

- *Collectivism–Individualism.* This is evident in the attitude towards teamwork as a process that requires interdependency. It regards how much a person finds it desirable to share, collaborate and depend on others for results, thereby valuing the benefit of the group (collectivism) over self-interest (individualism). Individuals embedded in a collectivist culture are understood to be less likely to resist teamwork than those steeped in an individualist culture.

The following considerations also have a bearing upon the attitude towards self-management:

- *Power distance.* This is the level (high or low) of acceptance of an unequal distribution of power. Individuals with high power distance expect their managers to lead them and respect those who do. Those with low power distance are more comfortable with a high degree of autonomy and responsibility and are more inclined to bypass bosses, status and formality in order to get the job done. High power distance is expected to create resistance to self-management.
- *Orientation.* Doing versus being. This is the orientation towards work and non-work activities. Being-oriented people have a tendency to emphasize non-work activities, while doing-oriented people emphasize the accomplishment of goals at work. The being-oriented people are expected to have a higher resistance to self-managed teamwork because this may require a continuous process of goal-setting, higher commitment and effort at work.
- *Determinism versus free will.* This concerns the belief of whom or what controls one's life. Determinists believe that outcomes and life's difficulties are controlled by forces outside oneself (God, fate, management, etc.). They are thought more likely to resist self-management.

Limiting and containing resistance, for example by selecting the individuals with the 'right' dispositions, is therefore advisable, if not easily done. Another of the main aspects related to team effectiveness is leadership. We discuss next how this relates to teams at work.

ADDRESSING LEADERSHIP

(See Chapter 8) Should teams, and especially the so-called self-managing teams, have a leader? What type of leadership should be utilized in organizations based on teamwork? It is true that self-managing and self-leading teams would not require, in principle, a leader or supervisor because this role is internal to the empowered team? Research

Cartoon 4.1
'Helen, you're the Team Leader, why don't you jump first?'

'Helen, you're the Team Leader, why don't you jump first?'

(Wall *et al.*, 1992) has shown that self-managing teams reduce cost by removing traditional supervisory hierarchical levels. Employees are empowered to be autonomous and responsible in how they organize, co-ordinate and improve their work. This creates strong demands upon managers who are under pressure to maintain systems of direction and control. As Manz (1992) argues, following a study by Mulder (1971), employees lack the managerial knowledge and education, and thus lack the 'expert power' attributed to managers. Therefore many management writers point at the fundamental role of leaders in companies where work is organized into teams. Hackman (1992; 2002) has argued that team leaders should focus on critical aspects of the team's performance: clear direction, enabling structure, supportive organizational context, available coaching and adequate material resources that the leaders must constantly monitor and take action as required. Manz and Sims (1987) delineate what is the actual role and specific behaviour in order for such leaders to be effective and useful to the team. They suggest that the 'external leader' is one who is able to make the team lead itself. They call this 'SuperLeadership' (Manz and Sims, 1993; Manz, 1992). They consider it ineffective, and even dangerous, for the performance of the self-managing team to have traditional leadership (e.g., a foreman) using a top-down approach. In Table 4.2 you can see the set of behaviours associated with traditional leadership and you can compare it with that of the 'SuperLeader' (Manz and Sims, 1993, p. 209).

Table 4.2 Traditional versus 'SuperLeadership'

Traditional leadership	SuperLeadership
• Direction	• Encourage self-goal-setting
• Instruction	• Encourage self-evaluation
• Command	• Encourage high self-expectancy
• Assigned jobs/tasks	• Facilitate self-problem-solving
• Assigned goals	• Develop self-initiative and responsibility
• Hierarchical conflict resolution	• Encourage within-group conflict resolution
	• Provide training
• Reprimand	• Encourage opportunity thinking

Exercise 4.3

Using Table 4.2, analyze and discuss leadership in the case of AML. Who is leading the team? What type of leadership can you identify? Illustrate your arguments with examples from the vignette.

In SuperLeadership, external managers and superiors are supposed to facilitate the team to lead itself. But how does a team specifically develop leadership? Glaser (1992) suggests that self-leadership is obtained through a process of progressive empowerment of the team – a shift of power and authority from the supervisors to the team itself. Self-leadership is the last stage of a four-stage process:

- *Stage 1.* The team is unempowered. Glaser calls this an underdeveloped group. The groups follows the direction of the facilitator, who deploys a top-down leadership style very similar to the traditional one of planning, directing and controlling.
- *Stage 2.* The team starts questioning aspects of its work through dialogue and requests feedback. The role of the leader starts being more that of a coach, offering counsel and advice in a continuous, open communication with the team.

- *Stage 3*. The team is, as Glaser defines it, 'somewhat empowered'. This is a team able to contribute with possible strategies and to engage in some critical thinking regarding the planning, controlling and directing of its work.
- *Stage 4*. An effective, self-managing team is established. It is 'fully empowered' as the team itself takes responsibility for planning, direction and control. The team leader has the role of a SuperLeader, facilitating the members of the team to lead themselves, while control of the teamwork is, for the most part, in the hands of the team.

WORKING ACROSS DIFFERENT KNOWLEDGE DOMAINS

Cross-functional or multidisciplinary teams comprise members from different knowledge domains who work together to accomplish a joint task (Kotlarsky *et al.*, 2015). As Contu (2014) highlights, differences of skills, ideas and ways of seeing a task/problem, and status in cross-functional teams can generate significant creative abrasions within a team. Cross-functional teams face challenges in balancing and integrating different knowledge domains to achieve a joint outcome (Majchrzak *et al.*, 2012; Oborn and Dawson, 2010). Whereas specialization (differentiated knowledge) is essential for carrying on a complex task, some degree of common knowledge (of who does what) is needed to co-ordinate the different knowledge domains (Lewis and Herndon, 2011; Ren and Argote, 2011).

As Carlile (2004) suggests, when integrating knowledge from different domains, members of cross-functional teams face issues of communication created by knowledge boundaries. These knowledge boundaries refer to (1) syntactic boundaries (differences in vocabulary and lexicon); (2) semantic boundaries (differences in interpretations across different practices; and (3) pragmatic boundaries (differences in interests). Cross-functional teams bring together different knowledge domains; their members might have different professional backgrounds. For example, in AML, John is a computer scientist, whereas Laura is a designer. Differences in specialized knowledge enable a team to have a wide range of potential knowledge at their disposal. However, this might also bring negative consequences. Diversity of expertise may impede knowledge sharing across team members (Mitchell *et al.*, 2011). Additionally, members might resist forms of accountability for the entirety of the project, beyond the responsibility for the implementation of their own technical expertise (Contu, 2014). Political infighting, factionalism, a silo mentality, and egos of members who are suddenly thrown together to complete a task, might impede the achievement of the team's objectives (Legare, 2001).

Different knowledge domains within a team might encounter some external opposition as well. In the case of AML, Amber's intervention (Case Study 4.1) in the crafting of the document for S4, is an example of how a team's cross-functional capabilities are disciplined by the managers in the attempt to conform the product to the company's expectations.

TEAMWORKING IN THE GLOBAL ERA

Virtual organizations and teams are increasingly becoming part of the contemporary business landscape. Time, space, cultural and organizational boundaries are crossed by team members thanks to electronic communication systems that enable co-operation and co-ordination among diverse geographical positions.

What are virtual teams? Townsend *et al.*, (1998, p.18) propose this definition:

'Virtual teams are groups of geographically and/or organizationally dispersed co-workers that are assembled using a combination of telecommunications and information technologies to accomplish an organizational task.'

According to Townsend *et al.*, (1998) and Powell *et al.*, (2004), virtual teams:

- Rarely meet in face-to-face settings
- Preponderantly – and at times exclusively – rely on IT to communicate with each other
- Can be set up as temporary structures, to accomplish a specific task, or be more permanent, such as when addressing ongoing issues (e.g., strategic planning)
- Have fluid memberships, often evolving according to changing task requirements.

Organizations tend to adopt virtual teams for the many benefits of virtual collaboration, such as the reduction of time and travel expenses, access to a wide range of expertise, possibility to engage in multiple, geographically-dispersed teams (Cascio, 1998), and to address the increasing globalization of trade and corporate activity (Townsend *et al.*, 1998). Research (e.g., Jarvenpaa and Leidner, 1999; Kayworth and Leidner, 2000; Maznevski and Chudoba, 2001) has been interested in a specific type of virtual teamworking: the 'global virtual team'. In this type of virtual team, members work and live in different countries, and are culturally diverse. Case Study 4.4 represents an example of such a global virtual team.

Case study 4.4
Virtual teamworking in HP

Between the early and mid-1990s, Hewlett-Packard's Medical Products Group used cross-functional virtual teams to deliver health care industry solutions (Legare, 2001). An example of such implementation was the MPG'S Patient Monitoring Division within HP, which developed and rolled out the Viridia Patient Care System. The system comprised medical equipment products (e.g., diagnostic workstations, remote computer and communications links, and health care telemetry system) designed for caregivers in order to help them manage and monitor their patients. The system was developed by 200 MPG employees from six different virtual cross-functional project teams.

From the beginning of the project, HP engaged in initiatives that would facilitate the development of a relation among the geographically dislocated members. An off-site planning meeting for all 200 team members at a resort in New Hampshire was designed as a kick-off event. Thereafter, the virtual team members co-ordinated and reviewed their progress through weekly video conference calls, which started with a small talk about families and hobbies. The Viridia program manager would also travel monthly from Massachusetts to Germany in order to spend time with other project team members. This virtual and cross-functional teamworking was highly successful: the product research and development cycle at HP shrank by 50 per cent (from 5 years to 2.5 years); the system was launched into the marketplace in 1997, with no delays; MPG revenues increased by 10 per cent, and MPG customer satisfaction levels by 25 per cent.

Source: Adapted from Legare (2001)

Whereas these are some of the advantages for an organization to implement virtual teamworking, there is a darker side of this picture. Shared understanding (a communality in beliefs, expectations, processes, tasks, and members' knowledge), integration (ways differentiated systems and structures can work together for creating value), and mutual trust (of others in the team) are the key conditions for virtual team effectiveness (Gibson and Cohen, 2003). For example, synchronization of information systems is fundamental for virtual team effectiveness: if organizational units across different locations have different IT infrastructures, connectivity might be affected (e.g., a team member might be unable to send an email to another business unit's member located in another country). Powell *et al.*, (2004) identify four potentially problematic areas for virtual teamworking: inputs (design, culture, technical, and training), socio-emotional processes (relationship building, cohesion, and trust), task processes (communication, co-ordination, and task-technology-structure fit), and outputs (performance and satisfaction). How can team members, who have never met in person, succeed in developing trust amongst themselves? Early face-to-face meetings, such as the one developed by the MPG division in HP, can be designed to facilitate trust and cohesion building among members.

Thinkpoint 4.5

Can you use any of Powell *et al.* (2004)'s or Cohen and Gibson (2003)'s elements to analyze and reflect on the potential issues faced by MPG team members in HP? How do they relate to both the virtual and the cross-functional nature of the Viridia project team?

SUMMARY OF KEY MAINSTREAM CONTRIBUTIONS AND EMPIRICAL STUDIES

In the first part of this chapter we have provided some definitions and discussed the distinction between *team* and *group work* as they are defined in management theory. We have also considered some of the insights developed in psychology and psychoanalysis for understanding the experience of being in a group. We have seen that there are many group phenomena and that some of these are not necessarily positive for performance, such as the free-riding tendency and the groupthink.

In mainstream management theory teams are considered fundamental for today's organizations. It has been suggested that teams are important because they activate/enhance three organizational dimensions that are considered central for healthy and wealthy work organization: flexibility, motivation and learning. We have analyzed and discussed many different empirical studies that are important for studying teams at work in the mainstream management literature. These included traditional industries such as the automobile industry. With the case of NUMMI we illustrated teams working in regimes of 'lean production', 'learning bureaucracy' and 'continuous improvement'; with Volvo, we discussed participative work design and self-managing teams. We also presented a case of a knowledge-intensive SME, AML, which develops, designs and builds 'perfect digital solutions'. This helped us in illustrating what are often referred to as post-bureaucratic organizational forms, with only two organizational hierarchical layers, and where interdependent members working in self-managing teams are fundamental for getting the job done.

The notions that sustain the positive view of teams at work for increasing morale, flexibility and ultimately productivity, we have argued, are not entirely a new phenomenon but belong to a long tradition of studies that gave origin to the 'human relations school' (Mayo, 1933, 1945), the socio-technical tradition of work design (Trist and Bamforth, 1951) and studies in social psychology devoted to understanding and facilitating social change and democratization through groups (Lewin, 1948). The empirical studies we have referred to are summarized in Table 4.3, where it is indicated how each of these has contributed to the debate on teams at work. Then we looked at aspects and issues that management theorists consider important for enhancing and perfecting team effectiveness and efficiency. Group development, roles design, resistance and leadership, it is suggested, are some of the areas that need to be attentively managed in order to obtain high-performing and successful teams.

Contribution and limitation of mainstream

CONCEPTUAL AND METHODOLOGICAL CONTRIBUTIONS AND LIMITATIONS

One of the main contributions of the mainstream literature is that it appears to offer a solution for everything: it explains how teams work, why they work and how you can make them work more effectively, and even how you can yourself become a successful team member. This can be useful in so far as it helps to reduce the anxiety of what to do when faced with a teamwork situation. Yet, if you have experienced it, team life is rarely as rosy as the mainstream literature seems to imply, and the prescriptions do not necessarily help in improving the situation. It is not always, or not 'just', a matter of 'wrong implementation' of teams at work. Too often, mainstream knowledge creates an overenthusiastic and simplistic view of organizational life that pictures team-work as a **panacea** (Jenkins, 1996; Dunphy and Bryant, 1996; Sinclair, 1992; Yevu and Reedy, 2012). The categories and the prescriptions offered in the mainstream are often detached from the complexities and messiness of organizing people and resources. A list of bullet points that is mechanically applied without regard to the particularities of the situation can create more problems than it solves.

Panacea A remedy that cures all complaints. Teamwork, for example, might be commended as a technology of work organization that solves all production problems from control, to productivity, to retention and commitment.

Table 4.3 Summary of empirical studies (1)

Authors	Key concepts	Key contributions
Mayo (1933, 1945)	• Social needs • Group norms and rules	• Informal groups have an impact on motivation and conduct in organizations. They need to be managed.
Lewin (1948)	• Group cohesion: we-ness • Group dynamics • Group atmosphere	• A democratic participative atmosphere increases quality and quantity of output. • Social relations can be changed and improved by intervening with/in group dynamics.
Trist and Bamforth (1951)	• Autonomous responsibility • Socio-technical system	• Social systems can produce groups that show high levels of responsibility even when they have high autonomy. • When introducing organizational change we need to intervene, not only on the technical, but also on the social system.
Adler (1993) Adler and Borys (1996) Womack, Jones and Roos (1990)	• Lean production • Just In Time (JIT) • Learning bureaucracy	• Teams' responsibility for a practice increases flexibility, motivation and learning. • Standardization, formalization and continuous improvement can also be obtained with team-based production.
Berggren (1992) Bernstein (1992)	• Self-managing teams • Participative design and organization	• Democratic, participative design is feasible. • Social and political factors intervene in favouring the success or failure of a new design.

Much of the mainstream literature centres on the classification of what teams are and how it is possible to improve team effectiveness. The aim is to establish – by limited, often anecdotal and methodologically dubious studies – the basis for models that can establish conceptual differences (such as the distinction between 'real teams' and 'group-work') and predict behaviours and results (for example, by limiting the number of individuals with cultural values that are not conducive to self-managing teams; or recruiting people to fill required roles). However, the possibility of finding comprehensive and universally predictive models is, as Berders and van Hootegem (2000, p. 7) put it, a 'mission impossible'. Many have pointed out that when we leave the field of prescriptions (i.e., the magic bullet points) it is very difficult to make comparisons between different plants and experiences (Mueller, 1994; Berders and van Hootegem, 1999, 2000; van Amelsvoort and Benders, 1996; Buchanan, 2000). In the concrete experiences of work, the variances we can find are enormous and the issues at work numerous and awkward.

Thinkpoint 4.6

Can you employ any of the concepts of the mainstream to analyze and compare teams at work in NUMMI, VOLVO and AML? What limitations do you find?

In the case of AML, many elements that are suggested in the mainstream, such as assessing employees for relevant roles and identifying resistances, and matching people to obtain role balance, are impossible given the resources available. Including the elements suggested in the literature in the recruitment and selection process could be a sensible thing to do, but it would be very costly – an aspect little considered in the mainstream literature where there is a silence on costs issues as well as the broader feasibility of introducing the prescriptions for 'proper' teamwork (Dunphy and Bryant, 1996; Sinclair, 1992). Their universal, one-size-fits-all prescriptions do not take into consideration the specificity of the industry and the realities of a small enterprise. In order to understand teams at work, we need to include a much wider set of issues based on a 'detailed examination of historical, technological and socio-political internal and external conditions of teamworking practice' (Knights and McCabe, 2000). Teamwork, in other words, should not be considered as a well-defined, fixed package but, rather, it is dependent upon, and influenced by, a set of dynamic circumstances: 'issues of the extent and nature of delegated power, or whether socialization of teams' members plays an important role, are contingent on a variety of national, corporate and local factors' (Thompson and Wallace, 1996, p. 105).

EMPOWERMENT, CONTROL AND POWER RELATIONS

Many authors, as we have seen, enthusiastically assure us that control is 'pushed down' to the workers; that with empowerment there is a power transaction from the management to the workers by means of letting the workers participate and make decisions regarding the planning, co-ordination and method of their work (Glaser, 1992; Manz and Sims, 1987). Yet some authors in the mainstream literature seem to be worried by this aspect of teams at work, signalling that, perhaps, this devolution would not be entirely desirable; at least if it happened to the extent that is often rather loosely advocated. The anxiety is due to the possibility that 'pushing down' responsibility and autonomy at work might be 'too literal' and, to a certain extent, 'too real'. For authors in the mainstream there is a danger of this happening as it could have undesirable consequences. Power devolution might result in loss of control, or in over-confidence and, in turn, misjudgements on the part of subordinates (Conger and Kanungo, 1988, p. 480). Others point to how empowerment can become an 'agency problem', which refers to the problem of reconciling loss of top-down control with the organizational requirement for goal congruence (Mills and Ungson, 2003). More simply, this means that there is a danger that empowered employees follow different goals and ends from those that are called 'organizational' ones. Then the question becomes, you might think, what are the organizational goals or ends? Also, who is to decide what they are and how to pursue them? If you are asking these questions you are entering the terrain of values, and who decides what the dominant values are to be and why. You are asking ethical and political questions.

Mainstream thinking refers to organizations (and teamwork) as neutral and apolitical entities with specific 'needs', just as if they were organisms. The term 'organizational need' is widely invoked as a shorthand for the aims of owners (shareholders) and managers of an organized system of production. This system is not only (re)producing wealth, but it is also (re)producing (unequal) social relations. Some people, the workers, are subordinated to others – that is, to managers (and owners) who, it is suggested, are the ones who are 'supposed to know', as they have acquired a monopoly of expert knowledge. Manz, we have seen earlier, calls this 'expert power', which is what helps in guaranteeing the dominant position of management in the system itself. But, as we have seen, this is exactly what is potentially subverted if teams at work (with their autonomy, empowerment and learning) are taken too literally.

For the mainstream, this would be evidence of irrationality, or, at least, a lack of managerial knowledge and know-how. But this is a naive interpretation. The creative director intervenes in the practice in very effective ways to facilitate the team in achieving its task, when she sees fit or when she can. She is neither irrational nor lacking in managerial knowledge. The mainstream, in other words, does not offer us ways for studying such paradoxes and ambiguities. It is these points of paradox and ambiguity that critical perspectives can help us to understand. These are studied and elaborated as the means and effects of relations of power that shape and reproduce both the identities of those involved and the field of work, including what is possible to do and also not to do.

To summarize, mainstream knowledge is mainly an instrumental knowledge devoted to prescribing how to make teams more efficient and effective in search of higher productivity. This approach takes for granted that this end

Case study 4.5
AML (2)

AML work organization seems to be centred around a team that participates in a community of practice designing 'perfect new media solutions'. This practice shapes their identity as new media designers. The directors, such as Amber, are some of the experts of this practice. AML, with its mixed-team organization, seems to favour organizational learning. But this explanation does not seem to tell us much of the situation, as Laura – a novice to the company and to the practice – found herself at the 'centre' of AML's practice of design, with much responsibility and unclear and ambiguous autonomy. You would have thought that, being a novice, she would be participating only at the periphery of the practice. In fact, Laura lacked the identity of a competent member, her colleagues did not recognize her as such. Yet the team *had* to work in this paradoxical situation: with spurious leadership, lack of guidelines or templates and with a key figure in the practice being a novice.

is right and universal. This knowledge has various consequences. First, it legitimizes shareholders' and managers' positions of authority, in particular of a masculine kind (see Metcalfe and Linstead, 2003), and second, supports and reinstates the social and material resources that these managers (particularly senior managers) enjoy in contemporary capitalist societies. Perhaps, it is in order to gain access to these positions and resources that you are now studying management at university.

Expert knowledge also helps in reducing the anxieties of managers (and management academics) in the face of the uncertain, open nature of everyday life. As the anxiety of losing control demonstrates, managerial identity and the knowledge and practices that support it, are not established once and for all. Managers depend on others, the subordinates, to accept and reproduce their position of subordination. Hence, there is a continuous search for new ideas and new prescriptions that help this reproduction. But, at the same time, this relation is also constantly under threat. New practice, new relations and knowledge – such as team 'empowerment' – which are intended to improve and maintain the status quo can, if taken too literally, threaten the status quo itself (see Case Study 4.6), as Conger and Kanungo (1988), Mills and Ungson (2003) and Manz and Sims (1991) have all, with a degree of uneasiness, noted.

CRITICAL PERSPECTIVES ON TEAMS AT WORK

Introduction to critical approaches to teams at work

Critical perspectives approach (and conceptualize) teams at work not as a neutral technology of work design, but as a practice that intervenes in creating, maintaining and reproducing unequal social relations. To signal this shift, we can now use the term 'teamworking' rather than 'teams at work', to emphasize that we are no longer talking about a neutral tool in pursuit of unproblematic and universal organizational goals. A critical view implies that the meaning, value and existence of these social relations (work relations), the practice that sustains them (like teamworking) and the identities (such as 'team members', 'SuperLeader', etc.) they sustain (and by which they are sustained), are not 'naturally given'. They are not given by some external authority (God, the market, the state) or internal entity (human nature). Rather, they can be thought of as the result of **sedimented power relations** (Laclau, 1990).

Sedimented power relations Sedimented power relations are decisions taken (and routinely reproduced) which establish what something is (and what it is not). The result is a state of things, a situation so normal, so constant, that we take it to be natural – so much so that it becomes difficult to look at it as anything but entirely normal and 'given', e.g., having food every day to eat or having to find employment once university is finished.

Idealized picture Description of a situation in a way that portrays only positive elements and is cleansed of any negative aspects.

Critical writers therefore contest the **idealized picture** of teamwork painted in the mainstream literature. This idealization can be seen in the somewhat benign nature of teamwork as creating a win–win work situation (Ezzamel and Willmott, 1998): employees are more satisfied and their work is 'smarter' because they have been treated like adult human beings with respect and they are given responsibility and autonomy. This makes it possible for the 'organization' to be more flexible, innovative and capable of sustaining and building its future.

The idealized, rosy picture is obtained by dismissing behaviours, ideas and issues that do not fit the creed sustained in the mainstream – what Sinclair (1992) calls the 'team ideology'. The mainstream promises a better organizational reality for managers and for workers alike. But, as we have seen, things often 'do not fit'. There are 'leftovers' – that is, elements that disrupt the nice, clear picture of teams at work.

Thinkpoint 4.7

How is the idealized picture sustained and maintained? Behaviours that 'do not fit' are quickly dismissed, if even noticed, in different ways in the mainstream. For example:

- As *irrational aberrations,* as in the case presented earlier of the Volvo operator who actually stated he preferred to be told what to do. The suggestion is that it is irrational to prefer the inhumane and alienating repetition of Taylorist organization to the empowering and democratic self-managing teams. What do you think?
- As *personal shortcomings or idiosyncrasies,* as in the example of the order filler who was fantastic at his job but just could not understand how good and amazing the whole new system based on teamwork was.
- As *unfortunate individual/cultural predispositions,* as in the case of the Kirkman model (page 133) whereby if you are individualist and being-oriented and high in power disposition you are hopeless because the likelihood that you are going to be a bad team player is high.
- As *perceptions* of fairness, trust and justice, which makes these issues a subjective matter to be addressed and seemingly resolved by means of ethical codes of conduct and regulations.

Critical perspectives on teamworking question what, in the mainstream literature, are taken-for-granted 'truths' of teams at work, pointing out the contradictions of such teamwork theory and practice. First, we delve into contributions that aim to show another, arguably darker, side to teamwork. This section is entitled 'The other side of the coin', which specifically highlights issues of inequality and autonomy/freedom. Concepts and ideas will be illustrated by reference to the NUMMI case study presented earlier. As a significant part of the critical debate centres on the concept of control, a second section is dedicated to understanding teamworking by considering how issues of identity are of relevance for its critical analysis. Other empirical studies, including AML, will be used to illustrate these ideas.

The other side of the coin

WORKING SMARTER *AND* HARDER

One of the key considerations pointed out by critical writers is that teamworking is generally a top-down, management-driven process. Many classical studies of teams at work, particularly those of the socio-technical tradition, are examples of employees' self-organization (see also Ezzamel *et al.*, 2001), while mostly today teamwork is introduced by management as part of a managerial strategy (Procter and Mueller, 2000, p. 8). This strategy has specific stated aims, one of the most important being to increase the efficiency of the workforce – as the slogan goes, 'by working smarter not harder'. Yet, many contend that often teamwork means working smarter *and* harder (Adler, 1993; Parker and Slaughter, 1988b; Berggren, 1992; Garrahan and Stewart, 1992; McCabe and Black, 1996). In other words, teamworking can produce (and it often does) work intensification. Voices from the union movement have been extremely critical of practical applications of teamwork, specifically in regimes of 'lean production', so much so that it has been recast as **mean production** (Parker and Slaughter, 1988b; Parker and Slaughter, 1994; Kamata 1983; Grenier, 1989).

> **Mean production** Describes how critical theorists interpret lean production. They see it as having subtle controls and forms of surveillance over workers that result in work intensification.

Production is 'mean' because of the negative effect upon the employees of minimizing stockpiles of parts and other forms of duplication in production. These are considered as waste in the lean, JIT design. Yet they function as 'buffers', which, Parker and Slaughter argue, make the system more bearable for the workers as they give them a breathing space lacking in the highly regimented lean design. Buffers also give managers a certain leeway, enabling them to keep things going, covering for problems or emergencies if they arise. CYA ('cover your ass'), by building in some elements of slack and redundancy, has often been considered a prudent operating procedure, as Parker and Slaughter (1988b, p. 16) observe. Lean production has also been defined as a 'very sophisticated prison' (James and Jones, 2014, p. 2176), to emphasize the dehumanizing effects of the system and the sacrificing of human safety and dignity for productivity purposes.

By aiming to eliminate waste of all kinds, lean production pressurizes all the 'components' of the system continuously, reducing a steady and tolerable pace. The pace of production is relentless and stressed to higher and higher degrees, in many different ways, for example, by speeding up the line. Parker and Slaughter call this management-by-stress (MBS) as, when following the principles of *kaizen,* new standards are created that assign additional activities to the workers of a team that must also keep up with a faster assembly line. But higher stress is also felt every time there is an absentee from the team, or a new, novice worker is assigned to the team. Given that workers in the NUMMI teams are interchangeable, and a team is completely responsible for a certain area of work, then it is the team that is responsible for covering for slow workers, novices or absentees. Each worker has to continue with their normal tasks and all the team members are called on to do a bit of the work of the novice or the absentee. In other words, the cost is on the team and the team leader and, as Parker and Slaughter (1988b, p. 21) put it, 'no department's budget is hurt by absenteeism'.

Thinkpoint 4.8

What problems do you see with this system? Do you think this system ensures equality in the distribution of effort/cost? Do you think this system of work respects human dignity? What is human dignity for you?

Parker and Slaughter (1988b) contend that this intensification of work is less humane than traditional forms of work organization. In the name of empowerment, this system cuts the possibility of breathing space and personal autonomy that 'buffers' of different kinds made possible. Teamworking in these conditions then induces unprecedented levels of responsibility, since the main objective of the system is to develop higher and higher degrees of efficiency (and productivity). It, therefore, requires strict adherence to its own rigid methods and procedures (Klein, 1989, pp. 60–61) limiting the possibility of genuine autonomy and freedom.

Box 4.3
'Human dignity' and inequality

Human dignity might appear an uncontested concept, but the example of what is understood by 'human dignity' in the context of the advocates of teams in lean production is enlightening. Human dignity is central for the 'empowered' workforce yet, as Parker and Slaughter (1988) point out, the whole teamwork rhetoric employs a peculiar notion of humanity. They give the example of the answer given by Monden (1983), an advocate and popularizer of the practices of Toyota, to those who criticize the lack of buffers and slack. Monden suggests that allowing for slack 'does not give the opportunity for the worker to realize his [*sic*] worth. On the contrary, that end can be better served by providing the worker with a sense that his work is worthwhile and allowing him to work with his superior and his comrades to solve problems they encounter.' This example, apart from showing the gendered organization of work, also succinctly points out how human dignity and human fulfilment is defined within a mainstream perspective, namely, to exercise one's abilities to solve problems with others. This view is *defined by management,* and somewhat 'given', ready-made, to the workers who simply have to accept and actualize 'this dignity' in the terms and in practices that are established by management. A narrow view of human dignity established by a particular section of the population, namely management, is taken to stand for a universal and necessary view of human dignity. This instrumental view of human dignity at once poses a particular view as universal and also reproduces and legitimizes the structured system of inequalities in wealth and status that are normal features of capitalist societies.

Source: www.solonline.org/aboutBol/who/senge/

These considerations are important and represent a departure from the mainstream for two reasons. They point to the other, ugly face of teamworking as an intensifying and stressful practice of work, which does not really square with mainstream images of teams as a more playful and fulfilling co-operation in achieving harmonized organizational ends. More fundamentally, it questions who is benefiting from the working smarter and harder logic. For Parker and Slaughter, the workers are not necessarily benefiting from this process of intensification of their labour, which instead serves the ends of 'those' exploiting the workers' capacity for labour, as they get more labour for less money and less managerial overheads, in a regime in which 'participation' is mostly on management's terms (Chapter 7).

TEAMWORKING AS CONTROL AND CONSENT OVER LABOUR EFFORT AND COST

With the shift to a critical view of teamworking, we pay attention to its role in the perpetuation of a particular socio-economic order – that of liberal capitalist societies. In liberal capitalism, the owners of the business organization (the 'shareholders') and its controllers and enactors (management) are, broadly speaking, concerned to maximize profit at the minimum cost. This is obtained by dividing and co-ordinating a set of productive activities where the surplus (income minus expenditures) generated in these activities (which, as we have seen earlier, are made natural and normal by the use of comparatively impersonal organizational ends) is privately appropriated (by the owners themselves).

Karl Marx, a political thinker, developed the understanding that, in capitalism, the planning, division and co-ordination of work are intended to ensure control of the workers in a process that is alienating and exploitative (Chapter 7). While wages are paid for the workers' *capacity* to engage in purposeful activities, the transformation that adds value to a given process of work happens only in the moment of its actual application. *Without control, this application is at the discretion of the workers,* and that is why management is employed to control workers in order to get the maximum application at a minimum cost. Control is needed to make sure that workers submit to the logic of capital accumulation, so as to eliminate what are considered 'unproductive' time and practices – what we called 'waste' in JIT. This understanding of work organization – which highlights the role of management (and management-driven systems) in controlling workers in order to produce a surplus that can be distributed to shareholders – questions something that for us all is entirely normal. It is so normal, in fact, that we take it for granted as our existence is routinely seen within the co-ordinates that this system produces and maintains. We expect and also wish to enter wage relations with an employer, with the inequalities and the subordination to, or over, others that this relation implies. We generally regard this as an unexceptional, even natural progression in life, signalling independence and the entrance into adulthood.

Thinkpoint 4.9

Do you think there are alternatives to this organization and division of labour and resources? How could those alternatives be realized? What problems do you foresee?

In other words, critical perspectives suggest that, even if teamworking moves away from the fragmenting, individualizing logic of Taylorism, it maintains the same fundamental logic of workers' exploitation. But this is accomplished in a different way as the workers are given the means to influence, within narrow limits controlled by management, part of how the application of their labour should be accomplished. The logic (and the power relations that are sustained by it) is much the same, as the co-ordinates are that of maximum application of labour at minimum cost. This, in the case of NUMMI, was accomplished by work intensification so as to achieve maximum input per unit of work. But it can be accomplished in different ways. In AML, we saw how workers 'feel responsible' for finishing the detailed content design of the email system address book. They stay at work late to get the job done. This means that they continue to work beyond 'normal working hours' – a concept that has become almost obsolete in many (e.g., knowledge-intensive) firms – and far beyond the working hours for which they are paid. This effort, then, is literally (money) and figuratively (time that could be spent doing other things in their life) at the workers' expense.

This example of AML illustrates what Friedman (1977) calls control by 'responsible autonomy' (Chapter 11), in which workers are encouraged and rewarded by management to exercise their discretion in ways that are responsible for attaining management's goals (e.g., greater productivity). Friedman suggests that, not only managers exercise control face-to-face, but also by manipulating workers' engagement and self-motivation (Price, 2015).

Teamworking facilitates this feeling of involvement, and a sense of ownership of their practice that increases the responsibility they have for their work. Through teamworking, they actively **consent** to furthering their own exploitation and subordination. It is in this sense that teamworking is considered a subtle form of control, not least because it is clothed in the rhetoric of participation and employee involvement. It is intended to enhance work effort, thereby increasing productivity but saving on labour costs (see Poliert, 1996; McCabe and Black, 1996; Buchanan, 2000).

Consent Widescale agreement relating to authorities and their decisions. For example, where production workers assent to, and approve of, managerial strategies and mechanisms of work organization.

Thinkpoint 4.10

Why do people consent to this form of control? How is it that teamworking facilitates this consent?

Some writers, such as Parker and Slaughter (1988), have argued that the utilization of the team concept – what, as we have seen, Sinclair calls 'team ideology' – is a manipulation that 'cons' workers because they believe that the managerial strategies for intensification and consent are good, desirable and serve their interests both as workers and as individual human beings. In other words, teamworking is regarded as a managerial strategy that realigns (most of the time successfully) 'individual motivation' with 'organizational need' (see Mueller, 1994); it reduces conflict and resistance at work; and it marginalizes or neutralizes the need for, and the role of, unions, as the employees' material and psychological needs are met through their (managed) identification within their team.

But does this not imply that the workers are a bit stupid because they cannot see their 'real' interest while others such as, let us say union leaders, or indeed a cunning management can, and therefore use this knowledge to exploit workers? Also, do workers really have a 'real' interest only? Something that never changes in all time and places that can be easily masked by practices such as teamworking?

A murkier picture of teamwork

Many critical writers suggest the picture is much murkier than the one where teamworking is simply fooling workers into believing that teamworking is good for them. Teamworking is more of a contested and complex practice rather than a whole-encompassing official ideology that is readily and effectively applied by a cunning management applied to a naive workforce.

Garrahan and Stewart (1992), for example, contend that at Nissan workers willingly consent to their own subordination and further exploitation and they are not fooled by the rhetoric of teams at work. And yet they mostly submit to it in practice. There is something in the practice itself that facilitates consent. Yet this is not the case all the time and in all places.

Poliert (1996) and McCabe and Black (1996) suggest that teamworking can create a set of ambiguities for the workers, which does not necessarily lead to consent (see Ezzamel et al., 2001). But also managers themselves experience conflicting demands that make the contradictions of teamworking more evident and often give reason 'for the union to retain a foothold' (Poliert cited in McCabe and Black, 1996, p. 114). Most times teamworking is messy; it does not correspond to the rosy picture detailed in the mainstream literature and reflects local dynamics where its principles are partially implemented, imperfectly adopted and inconsistently applied.

However, we should avoid slipping into a form of 'contingency analysis' where a detailing of the context forgoes theoretical reflection altogether' (Knights and McCabe, 2000, p. 6).

We need additional theoretical resources to question teamworking and understand why it is that people may not buy the managerial rhetoric of teamwork and yet embrace teamworking in practice. Many authors (see, for example, Ezzamel and Willmott, 1998; Ezzamel et al., 2001; Knights and McCabe, 2003; Knights and McCabe, 2000; McKinlay and Taylor, 1996; Sewell and Wilkinson, 1992; Sewell, 1998) have attempted to address these issues, in particular by considering how workers' *subjectivity,* i.e., their sense of self, is central to resistance and consent. These views draw upon theoretical sources that we explore and illustrate next.

SELF-DISCIPLINE AND SURVEILLANCE

Detailed studies of actual people at work, the words they say, the gestures they make, the artefacts they use, which are called ethnographies, may enable us to make sense of how it is that workers' sense of identity comes to be shaped in a conduct that secures willing consent and compliance to working smarter *and* harder.

The main point conveyed by these studies is that teamworking itself is a social practice through which workers discipline themselves, and each other, by continuous surveillance and by creating, as well as enforcing on themselves and on others, the identity of 'team mate' (see Barker, 1993, 1999; Sewell and Wilkinson, 1992; Sewell, 1998).

By working together in a team, people develop knowledge of themselves as team members and therefore they start to see and understand themselves as such. This knowledge exerts power (see power/knowledge Chapter 6) because it is also self-knowledge, i.e., a way by which workers talk about themselves and rationalize their conduct, i.e., considering what it means to be a good team player and what it takes to be one. As a conduct emerges as the 'right one' a worker who has identified with the team, i.e., has developed a team identity, would find it very difficult to disobey.

Barker's study of ISE (see Case study 4.6), a US electronic company, is exemplary of the specificities of this power/knowledge mechanism developed when self-managing teams are introduced. In this case we can see how self-discipline and surveillance facilitate the emergence of compliant team identities. Barker called this 'concertive control' (see also Tompkins and Cheney, 1985), because workers act in concert to develop the means of their own control (Barker, 1993, p. 4).

Case study 4.6
Teamwork and concerted control: self-discipline and surveillance

Barker's ethnography of an electronic board assembly factory, ISE, started at the beginning of the 1990s and lasted two years. ISE's CEO had read the popular management writers (such as Drucker), praising the importance of teamwork and the recognition of employees' participation. He was fascinated and persuaded by this knowledge. He studied the system based on self-managing teams, and then implemented a new organizational design.

First he conducted a 'pilot', and then the whole production activity was organized into self-managing teams. Each individual was assigned to a team that became responsible for the manufacture or configuration of two or three electronic boards. The teams had to decide how to share the work, how to assign responsibilities, the ground rules of their work, etc. The company offered training in teambuilding and interpersonal skills and provided supporting advice. They were never told what to do but were guided, notably by the mission statement that was prepared for them by the ISE president. This expressed the values that the company expected from the team, and from each individual as a self-manager: personal initiative, responsibility in doing the work, commitment to the team, quality of individual and team contributions. Barker describes how team members at first experienced confusion and uncertainties because they did not know what to do. Yet, they soon realized it was 'really' up to them to decide how to do the work!

In an impressive number of meetings, teams started discussing closely what their work meant for them, what good quality was, what they expected from each other and so on. Barker notes how the team members started to talk about a sense of ownership and extreme commitment to the work they were doing, feeling that delivering the product on time was their responsibility. For example, there was an incident where some material arrived late, which then required the team to stay late if they were to get the order out to the customer as scheduled. Lea Ann, one of the team members, called the team and put it to everyone that it would take two hours' overtime to accomplish the task. Some people had various commitments, but they discussed the issue and eventually all agreed to stay. One of them, they agreed, could leave at the normal time because she wanted to attend her children's play at school, but she promised that she would work late the next time it was required.

This is a compelling example of how a team translated into practice the values indicated by the company. The team acquired a set of values that became translated, particularly when new employees joined, into more and more visible signs of commitment. The teams created a series of mechanisms that facilitated and disciplined workers into forms of conduct that reproduced and reinforced their identity as proper, valuable and respected members of an effective and efficient team. Mutual surveillance was part of the conduct of team members. The rules of the team became progressively clearer and more explicit and were enforced in many different ways. For example, some teams had time set aside in their meetings to confront members whose behaviour did not conform to the team rules.

But there were also more subtle means of mutual surveillance – for example, in relation to lateness. Before teamworking, the supervisors might have turned a blind eye to lateness. But teams developed a zero tolerance for tardiness so that everyone's arrival was ranked every day with a colour-coded card system. If a worker collected too many red dots, a sanction would be given. As one of the employees put it, 'Now the whole team around me is observing what I am doing'. The constant surveillance promoted self-discipline and compliance as it implied that to be a team member one has to follow the conduct expected, the standards of which are agreed and monitored by the team itself.

What is fascinating about Barker's study of ISE is that the final result of the team activity has a strong resemblance to the traditional bureaucratic form of control – i.e., the card checking and ranking of performance. Nonetheless, the source of authority and the enforcement of this control is not the abstract impersonal rule of bureaucratic order but a diffuse set of mechanisms devised by the teams themselves and sustained by the team power/knowledge. Teamwork power/knowledge is also composed of the rules identified and recognized by team members as establishing and summarizing the proper conduct of a rightful teamwork ethic.

Self-discipline and surveillance of the concertive control produced an even tighter 'iron cage' as it's being used metaphorically/figuratively. than the traditional bureaucracy. Some have called this type of control 'chimerical control' exactly because it is not traditional top-down but is diffused and has hybrid and monstrous characteristics (Sewell, 1998, p. 12). The team members daily construct, reproduce and maintain a power/knowledge of what they are, and what their work is, that makes them their own masters and their own slaves: 'ISE teamworkers are both under the eye of the norm and in the eye of the norm, but from where they are, in the eye, all seems natural and as it should be' (Barker, 1993, p. 435).

According to this view, teamworking is a social practice that institutes, maintains and creates certain power relations by means, as Knights and McCabe (2000) put it, of constituting particular kinds of subjectivities – in short, transforming individuals into teamworking subjects who assume a self-identity as team mates or face problems or expulsion. For example, Barker points out that 'uncommitted workers' – that is uncommitted according to the team power/knowledge – do not last in the concertive system: 'If they wanted to resist their team control, they must be willing to risk their human dignity, being made to feel unworthy as "team-mates"' (Barker, 1993, p. 436).

RESISTANCE IS FUTILE (?)

We seem to have painted a rather bleak picture of teamworking. We have suggested that considering teamworking as mere managerial rhetoric that fools workers in to believing that teamwork is good for them is problematic. Power/knowledge, concertive control, surveillance and self-discipline were proposed to unpick the issue of consent and resistance, but we have still reached what appear to be similar conclusions, i.e., total consent to teamworking. The bars of the 'iron cage' are even stronger than in traditional forms of work as people are entrenched in what makes them what they are: their own self-identity as team members. Teamworking power/knowledge seems comparable to the technology of the Borg in *Star Trek,* the famous sci-fi series. The Borg pursues the quest for knowledge and for perfection by assimilating in the collective mind all the alien cultures encountered, so all the differences are maintained in a perfect whole. The collective changes all the time, but it always stays the same imperturbably, just like capitalism, which has to change in order to avoid collapse. 'Resistance is futile!' states the Borg in front of the terrorized subject, to whom perfection and knowledge is given when the assimilation is completed. Are the Borg right – resistance is futile?

Critical writers suggest that resistance is not futile. But, again, it is not a matter of finding or even proposing a single solution or recipe. One might start with acknowledging the studies where forms of resistance are visible. Garrahan and Stewart (1992) studied Nissan's work practices and culture. They show us that not all employees totally identify with the 'team-mates' ethos and identity. There is resistance to practices that were intended to strengthen the Nissan culture and its values, such as the sponsoring of sports events, family events and holidays for employees' children. Many employees would not, or could not, identify with such values, and many were cynical towards teamworking (see also Ezzamel *et al.*, 2001; Knights and McCabe, 2000, 2003). Some of the workers (but arguably also some of the managers) would consider themselves to have no alternative other than to 'shut up and put up' because resistance may lead to losing employment – not a real option for these workers and managers. In such cases it is their sense of identity as providers for their own family or homeowners or consumers that made it impossible for them to consider risking losing their jobs. But how can such differences in the meaning and consequences of teamworking be understood so that we avoid the 'it depends on the context' type of argument?

Critical authors suggest that social practices (such as teamworking) never totalize nor exhaust the field of what is possible. In other words, it is impossible to ever determine the meaning, the results and the possibilities offered by a particular practice, including that of teamwork. Teamworking then operates neither once and for all according to the aims of the managers nor the workers, but it establishes what the identities of both might be. Fundamentally, here we must challenge the binary logic (the either/or), that is at the basis of such a discussion – teamwork *either* produces consent *or* produces resistance; *either* it is a managerial tool for exploitation *or* it is an empowering tool that enhances equality and well-being. Given that, as a social practice, teamworking is never determined once and for all, then it is open to contestation and its closure is constantly under threat and open to rearticulations – new ways, new meanings are possible.

The aim of critical studies in such a view becomes that of making explicit the ambivalence and ambiguity of teamworking, and in making explicit the antagonism in the social relations reproduced by and in teamworking. As we said earlier what we take for granted is the result of sedimented power relations and the results of the many acts we reproduce every day. Teamworking is the same, it requires a constant set of acts that need to be reproduced in a certain order by a lot of people at once to become what it is; in it there is nothing naturally given.

We can illustrate this openness and ambiguity of teamworking with reference to McKinlay and Taylor's (1996) study of Pyramid (see Case Study 4.7).

In summary:

- As a social practice, teamworking is 'owned' neither by the managers nor by the workers. What is a 'manager' and what is a 'worker' is realized and reproduced in the teamworking practice, as well as by other practices, which create and maintain the meaning of self and the meaning of work in our lives.
- Teamworking as a social practice is not a monolith established once and for all at the service of management, but is constantly open to rearticulations that can disrupt and subvert the status quo.

Case study 4.7
Resistance and teamworking

In Pyramid, a technological company, teamwork power/knowledge came to play a role that compromised the expected aims for which empowered teams were introduced. A clue to the role of teamworking in dislocating managerial expectations and design can be seen in the adoption of the system of peer reviews for the teams. This was introduced by the management as a way of obtaining knowledge about the shop floor, as well as a forum for the teams to reflect on themselves and their team-building processes. It was, in other words, a disciplinary mechanism.

This practice of peer review proved largely unpopular at first, and it was resisted by many employees, who, for example, started to use retaliatory scoring to get at each other. Eventually, however, the equalizing of scores became widespread, which, of course, made this technology useless. Interestingly, the equalizing was made possible by the mobilization of the team ethos itself. It was argued that if the team is reaching the target, why should different people be scored more highly than others if the overall result was good? This makes explicit how teamworking is open to constant rearticulation, which also establishes the interests it is serving. Rather than creating consent it created a sense of resistance to the scoring system and the differences this was designed to establish among workers. In other words, it shows us how the system of inequalities, on which capitalist work relations are based, are actually subverted by taking teamworking 'too seriously' as the workers did in this case by over-identifying with the team ethos.

As a disciplinary mechanism, the peer review was supposed to classify, divide and rank the workers so that bonuses could be allocated to 'deserving' workers. The fact that this was done by the workers themselves should have tied them to their own self-evaluation. This also would have provided the effect of a 'consensual' basis for bonus payments. But the workers disrupted these intended truth effects of the self-assessment exercise. They subverted the idea of consensual ranking and classification, as well as that of equitable 'bonuses'. Managers faced with the impossibility of equality – because if bonuses were paid equally the profitability of the operation would be hurt – assigned the bonuses randomly. This response became a nodal point for the constitution of a clear antagonistic move, with teams going on a silent strike – what the employees called three weeks of 'go slow' – and a devastatingly high number of complaints filed against the managerial decision. This occurrence made evident the inequalities built into the system and shows us the contradictory and ambiguous features of teamworking. In this articulation teamworking worked against the desired managerial outcomes.

Summary of key contributions, empirical studies and limitations in the critical approach

In the second part of this chapter we have analyzed critically the concept and practice of teamwork. We referred to a number of empirical studies that have approached teamwork from a critical perspective. These studies are summarized in Table 4.4 and their main contribution to the debate in questioning teamwork is highlighted.

We have suggested that teamwork is often considered an ideology that, under the seductive slogan of 'working smarter not harder', in reality forces workers to work both smarter *and* harder. In other words, there is another, darker side to the rosy picture we have seen presented in the mainstream literature. By revisiting the NUMMI case and the AML case we have discussed how teamwork is a process that increases work intensification and furthers workers' exploitation, participating in eroding workers' rights and conditions. We have considered how one of the limitations of this view is that it assumes that workers are 'conned' by management into believing that teamwork is good for them. This view implies that workers are determined in their conduct and their beliefs by the managerial strategies and the manipulations they are able to engender, while both managers and critical social theorists are able to see what the workers' real interests are, or should be. However, some critical writers suggest that this privileged insight cannot be justified because, empirically, we observe that production, including teamworking, is very contested and not a monolithic terrain totalized by a whole encompassing official ideology that fools workers.

Workers and managers are ambiguous in their understanding of teamwork and the way they participate in these practices. It is suggested that we can understand and address better the complexities and ambiguities of the experiences and realities of teamworking if we move away from essential notions of identity. One's sense of self is not determined solely by managers' official strategies but is produced, maintained and elaborated in the many practices, diffused mechanisms and technologies in which we participate, and in which we are constituted as subjects, such as in the case of teamworking, where workers develop a knowledge about themselves and their conduct as team members.

One of the limitations of this approach is that it appears to create a bleak picture of working practices because disciplinary mechanisms seem to produce entirely consenting subjects, excluding any sense of resistance. However, we have suggested that these mechanisms of power, of which teamworking is an example, cannot be considered to be owned by anyone in particular (for example, managers) and cannot ever be defined in their meaning and consequences once and for all. In other words, even if teamworking can be intentionally introduced in order to intensify workers' output this does not mean that it will produce what top managers wish for. The practice of teamworking can actually be disruptive for both managers and workers. This indicates that discipline and surveillance of teamworking can also be a subverting force. Pyramid workers over-identified with the teamworking ethos of equality and this brought to bear some of the inequalities on which the capitalist system of production is based. This sparked resistance and open antagonism towards management rather than facilitating the creation of an obedient and consenting workforce.

Table 4.4 Summary of empirical studies (2)

Authors	Key concepts	Key contributions
Parker and Slaughter (1988)	• Mean production • Management by stress	• Teamwork is a managerial strategy of work intensification
Barker (1993, 1999) See also Sewell (1998) Ezzamel and Willmott (1998) Sewell and Wilkinson (1992)	• Concertive control • Self-discipline • Surveillance • Consent	• Teamwork is itself a social practice that produces and maintains a self-identity • This enhances control and consent
McKinlay and Taylor (1996) See also Knights and McCabe (2000, 2003) Ezzamel and Willmott (1998) Ezzamel et al. (2001)	• Openness of social practices • Resistance	• Teamwork as a social practice and its subject cannot be determined once and for all • Teamworking can also provoke resistance and antagonistic behaviour

Conclusion

Teams and good performance are inseparable; you cannot have one without the other. But people use the word 'team' so loosely that it gets in the way of learning and applying the discipline that leads to good performance. For managers to make better decisions about whether, when or how to encourage and use teams, it is important to be more precise about what a team is and what it isn't (Katzenbach and Smith, 1993, p. 163).

Some of my students and I love this quote because it condenses the taken-for-granted truth about teams and teamwork in mainstream management studies. But there is another truth that oozes from this quote on which I want to concentrate.

Some of my students find the quote appealing because they want to become managers. Arguably, they believe that if someone tells them precisely how they are supposed to manage properly, they will get it right and will be successful managers. This belief is directly attended by Katzenbach and Smith (1993), who propose to 'repair' the shortcomings of woolly thinking and bring in the due precision that will lead to good performance.

Who would not like that? If there were clear, sure recipes telling us what to do and how; if there was something of an indubitable descriptive precision; if there was a natural Truth, we would all know what to do at all times. How great that would be! No more uncertainties and doubts, nor that stomach-churning anxiety we occasionally or often feel but rarely mention. A template would describe and dictate our behaviour, working life and even family life and leisure. It would all be perfectly determined and we would be living in a world of ... automatons. Yes, with a template for everything, everything would already be decided so we would be like sophisticated robots. We would not decide anything as the decision would be dictated by principles – of teamwork or total quality management, etc. Actually we would not even think of such a thing/concept as a decision. A decision requires an utter not-knowing. A real decision is a crazy step because it is something we take out of undecidability. It is after we have taken it that we find reasonable motives for taking 'this' decision rather than 'that' one. In other words, always it is the present that gives us a sense of the past and the future and not vice versa.

The whole point of much of what we call 'knowledge' is about telling us what to do, when and how. Much of management and organization theory is about explaining how things are organized in systems and how these systems help us to predict and control what we do. In organizations there are job descriptions, financial charts, business plans, procedures and contracts. All these indicate, and even prescribe, the role and behaviour of managers, workers, customers, clients and suppliers, and what these 'stakeholders' are supposed to do. You are reading this book because, most likely, you are a student in a university and your professor said you should read it, and because you are a conscientious student or because your family expects you to do your best at university, and perhaps, because you want to get a good mark and get a top, highly paid job.

So much is directed, ruled, regulated, decided. Yet there are things (ideas, behaviours, elements) that do not fit. As we have seen earlier, if employees really followed completely their job description or the implications of things such as teamworking, probably their units would arrive at a standstill. And, yes, your family may want you to be a conscientious student; but they also want you to be a rounded person, and have friends and keep fit and eat well and be a good citizen. So they probably would not want you to be over-conscientious! But when is the line reached? So many things are often contradictory and, anyway, you do not only do what your family wishes!

It is because things never fit perfectly, because there are some remains of what we are supposed to be and do, that there are so many different views on life and interpretations and theories and cultures. Procedures, templates, desires, etc. can never tell us 'the truth' of what we are and what the world is about. We are not automatons. This is the sense of freedom that is at once appealing, seductive, chastening and terrifying. There are alternatives to the way things are; they are not naturally given; they are not written in stone. They are 'sedimented' constructions, so much so that too often we forget that they are constituted. They are sedimented power relations, and power is not 'natural' – power is 'social'. That, in a nutshell, is the fundamental assumption upon which the critical knowledge discussed here is constructed.

Alternatives are possible. Suspecting and undermining those who claim to have the truth, those who do not even consider that 'truth' is problematic, and showing and proposing alternatives that mobilize the values of equality and freedom, is part of what a radical and democratic project is about. And this is what this chapter, in showing mainstream and critical views, has tried to do in relation to the meaning and valence of teamwork. This is a way of making sense of the politics of one arena of management knowledge, and, as such, this knowledge itself, and your reading of it, is a political act.

Discussion questions

1 What are the main differences between mainstream and critical views of teams at work?

2 Why are teams deemed fundamental in contemporary organizations?

3 What are the key factors one must consider to manage teams successfully?

4 Why is identity important in establishing the success of teamworking?

5 In what sense is teamworking a form of control? Why?

6 In what ways is it possible to talk about resistance to teamworking?

Further reading

Barker, J. R. (1999) *The Discipline of Teamwork: Participation and Concertive Control,* London: Sage.

Forsyth, D. R. (2010) *Group Dynamics,* fifth edn, Wadsworth: Cengage Learning.

Foulkes, S. H. and Anthony, E. J. (1957) *Group Psychotherapy: The Psychoanalytic Approach,* London: Penguin Books.

Hackman, J. R. (ed.) (1990) *Groups That Work (and Those That Don't): Creating Conditions for Effective Teamwork,* San Francisco, CA: Jossey Bass Business and Management Series.

Procter, S. and Mueller, F. (eds) (2000) *Teamworking,* Basingstoke: Macmillan Business.

Wetherell, M. (ed.) (1996) *Identities, Groups and Social Issues,* London: Sage.

Useful websites

Social psychology, group and cultural studies sources:

www.socialpsychology.Org/social.htm#group

www.sgr.sagepub.com/

Radical and critical sources:

www.marxists.org/index.htm

www.workersworld.net/

www.forumsocialmundial.org.br/

Examples of teams and COPs consultants' sites:

Belbin: www.belbin.com/

Katzenbach: www.katzenbach.com/

COPs: www.solonline.org/

www.ewenger.com/

Portals and sites with resources, games and exercises on teambuilding and development:

www.grouprelations.com/

www.wilderdom.com/games/lnitiativeGames.html

reviewing.co.uk/toolkit/teams-and-teamwork.htm

References

Adler, P. (1993) 'Time and motion regained', *Harvard Business Review,* 71(1): 97–108.

Adler, P. S. and Borys, B. (1996) 'Two types of bureaucracy: Enabling and coercive', *Administrative Science Quarterly,* 41(1): 61–89.

Albanese, R. and van Fleet, D. D. (1985) 'Rational behaviour in groups: The free-riding tendency', *Academy of Management Review,* 10(2): 244–55.

Alvesson, M. (1993) 'Organizations as rhetoric: Knowledge-intensive firms and the struggle with ambiguity', *Journal of Management Studies,* 30(6): 997–1015.

Ancora, D. and Caldwell, D. (2000) 'Compose teams to assure successful boundary activity', *Blackwell Handbook of Principles of Organizational Behavior*, pp. 199–210.

Ancora, D. G. and Caldwell, D. F. (1992) 'Bridging the boundary: External activity and performance in organizational teams', *Administrative Science Quarterly*, 37(4): 634–655.

Argote, L., Gruenfeld, D. and Naquin, C. *et al.* (2001) 'Group learning in organizations', in M. E. Gurner (ed.) *Groups at Work: Advances in Theory and Research*, New York: Erlbham.

Argote, L., Ingram, P., Levine, J. M. and Moreland, R. L. (2000) 'Knowledge transfer in organizations: learning from the experience of others', *Organizational Behavior and Human Decision Processes*, 82(1): 1–8.

Barker, J. R. (1999) The discipline of teamwork: Participation and concertive control. Sage Publications.

Barker, J. (1993) 'Tightening the iron cage: Concertive control in self managing teams', *Administrative Science Quarterly*, 38(3): 408–437.

Belbin, M. (1993) *Team Roles at Work*, Oxford: Butterworth-Heinemann.

Belbin, M. (2004) *Management Teams: Why They Succeed or Fail?*, second edn, Oxford: Butterworth-Heinemann.

Berders, J. and van Hootegem, G. (1999) 'Teams and their context: Moving the team discussion beyond existing dichotomies', *Journal of Management Studies*, 36(5): 609.

Berders, J. and van Hootegem, G. (2000) 'How the Japanese got teams', in S. Procter and F. Mueller (eds) *Teamworking*, Basingstoke: Macmillan Business.

Berggren, C. (1992) *The Volvo Experience: Alternatives to Lean Production in the Swedish Auto Industry*, Basingstoke: Macmillan Press.

Bernstein, P. (1992) 'The learning curve at Volvo', in R. Glaser (ed.) *Classic Readings in Self-Managing Teamwork*, Pennsylvania: Organization Design and Development, Inc.

Bion, W. R. (1961) *Experiences in Groups and Other Papers*, London: Tavistock Publications.

Bogenrieder, I. and Nooteboom, B. (2004) 'Learning Groups: what types are there? A theoretical analysis and an empirical study in a consultancy firm', *Organization Studies*, 25: 287–313.

Brown, J. S. and Duguid, P. (1991) 'Organizational learning and communities-of-practice: Toward a unified view of working, learning and innovation', *Organization Science*, 2(1): 40–57.

Buchanan, D. (2000) 'An eager and enduring embrace: The ongoing rediscovery of teamworking as a management idea', in S. Procter and F. Mueller (eds) *Teamworking*, London: Macmillan Business.

Campion, M. A., Medsker, G. J. and Higgs, A. C. *et al.* (1993) 'Relations between work group characteristics and effectiveness: Implications for designing effective workgroups', *Personnel Psychology*, 46: 823–850.

Carlile, P.R., (2004), 'Transferring, Translating, and Transforming: An Integrative Framework for Managing Knowledge across Boundaries', *Organization Science*, 15(5), pp. 555–568.

Carroll, J., Hatakenaka, S. and Rudolph, J. (2006) 'Naturalistic decision making and organizational learning in a nuclear power plant: Negotiating meaning between managers and problem investigation teams', *Organization Studies*, 27: 1037–57.

Cascio, W. F. (1998) 'On managing a virtual workplace', *Occupational Psychologist*, August, 5–11.

Cohen and Gibson (2003) *Virtual Teams That Work: Creating Conditions for Virtual Team Effectiveness*, San Francisco: John Wiley and Sons, Inc.

Cohen, S. G. and Ledford, G. E. (1994) 'The effectiveness of self-managing teams: A quasi experiment', *Human Relations*, 47(1): 13–43.

Cohen, S. G., Ledford, G. E. Jr. and Spreitzer, G. M. (1996) 'A predictive model of self managing work team effectiveness', *Human Relations*, 49(5): 643–675.

Conger, J. and Kanungo, R. (1988) 'The empowerment process: Integrating theory and practice', *Academy of Management Review*, 13: 471–482.

Contu, A. (2014) 'On boundaries and difference: Communities of practice and power relations in creative work', *Management Learning*, 45(3): 289–316.

Cordery, J. L., Mueller, W. S. and Smith, L. M. (1991) 'Attitudinal and behavioural effects of an autonomous working group: A longitudinal field of study', *Academy of Management Journal*, 34: 464–476.

Davenport, T. H. and Pusak, L. (1998) *Working Knowledge: How Organizations Manage What They Know*, Cambridge, MA: Harvard Business School Press.

Drucker, P. F. (1993) 'Knowledge-worker productivity: The biggest challenge', *California Management Review*, 41(2): 812–856.

Drucker, P. F. (1992) 'The new society of organisations', *Harvard Business Review*, Sept–Oct: 95–104.

Duhigg, C. (2016) 'What Google Learned From Its Quest to Build the Perfect Team', available at: www.nytimes.com/2016/02/28/magazine/what-google-learned-from-its-quest-to-build-the-perfect-team.html?_r=1. Accessed on 29/02/2016.

Dunphy, D. and Bryant, B. (1996) 'Teams: Panaceas or prescriptions for improving performance?', *Human Relations*, 49(5): 677–99.

Dwyer, S., Richard, O. C. and Chadwick, K. (2003) 'Gender diversity in management and firm performance: the influence of growth orientation and organizational culture', *Journal of Business Research*, 56(12), 1009–1019.

Eagly, A. H., Makhijani, M. G. and Klonsky. B. G. (1992) 'Gender and the evaluation of leaders: a meta-analysis', *Psychological Bulletin*, 111(1): 3–22.

Edmondson, A. C. (1999) 'Psychological safety and learning behavior in work teams', *Administrative Science Quarterly*, 44(2): 350–383.

Edmonson, A. C. (2002) 'The local and variegated nature of learning in organisations: A group-level perspective', *Organization Science*, 13(2): 128–146.

Ezzamel, M. and Willmott, H. (1998) 'Accounting for team work: A critical study of group based system of organizational control', *Administrative Science Quarterly*, 43(2): 358–397.

Ezzamel, M., Willmott, H. and Worthington, F. (2001) 'Power, control and resistance in "the factory that time forgot"', *Journal of Management Studies*, 38(8): 1953–1981.

Fenwick, G. D. and Neal, D. J. (2001) 'Effect of gender composition on group performance', *Gender, Work & Organization*, 8(2): 205–225.

Flores, F. and Gray, J. (2000) *Entrepreneurship and the Wired Life: Work in the Wake of Careers*, London: Demos.

Friedman, A. (1977) *Industry and Labour: Class Struggle at Work and Monopoly Capitalism*, London: Macmillan.

Furnham, A., Steele, H. and Pendleton, D. (1993) 'A psychometric assessment of the Belbin Team-Role Self Perception Inventory', *Journal of Occupational and Organizational Psychology*, 66: 245–257.

Garrahan, P. and Stewart, P. (1992) *The Nissan Enigma: Flexibility at Work in a Local Economy*, London: Mansell.

Gersick, C. (1988) 'Time and transition in work teams: Toward a new model of group development', *Academy of Management Journal*, 31(1): 9–41.

Gibson, C. and Vermeuler, F. (2003) 'A healthy divide: Subgroups as a stimulus for team learning behavior', *Administrative Science Quarterly*, 48(2): 202–239.

Gibson, C. and Cohen, S. G. (eds) (2003) *Virtual teams that work: Creating conditions for virtual team effectiveness*, San Francisco, CA: John Wiley & Sons.

Glaser, R. (1992) *Moving Your Team Towards Self Management*, King of Prussia, PA: Organization Design and Development Inc.

Grant, J. (1998) 'Women as managers: what they can offer to organizations', *Organizational Dynamics*, 27(3): 56–63.

Grenier, G. (1989) *Inhuman Relations: Quality Circles and Anti-Unionism in American Industry*, Philadelphia: Temple University Press.

Hackman, J. R. (1987) 'The design of work teams', in J. Lorsch (ed.) *Handbook of Organizational Behavior*, Englewood Cliffs, NJ: Prentice Hall, pp. 315–342.

Hackman, J. R. (1992) 'The psychology of self managing in organizations', in R. Glaser (ed.) *Classic Readings in Self-Managing Teamwork*, Pennsylvania: Organization Design and Development, Inc.

Hackman, J. R. (2002) *Leading Teams: Setting the Stage for Great Performances*, Massachusetts, MA: Harvard Business School Press.

Hackman, J. R. and Morris, C. G. (1975) 'Group tasks, group interaction process and group performance effectiveness: A review and proposed integration', in L. L. Berkowitz (ed.) *Advances in Experimental Social Psychology*, 8: 47–100, New York: Academic.

Hambrick, D. C., Davison, S. C., Snell, S. A. and Snow, C. C. (1998) 'When groups consist of multiple nationalities: Towards a new understanding of the implications', *Organization Studies*, 19: 181–205.

Harrison, D. and Humphrey, S. E. (2010) 'Designing for diversity or diversity for design? Tasks, interdependence and within-unit differences at work', *Journal of Organizational Behaviour*, 31(2–3): 328–337.

Heller, F., Pusic, E., Strauss, G., Wilpert, B. *et al.* (1998) *Organizational Participation Myth and Reality*, Oxford: Oxford University Press.

Hofstede, G. (1980) *Culture's Consequences: International Differences in Work-related Values*, Beverly Hills, CA: Sage.

Hofstede, G. (1983) 'National culture in four dimensions: A research-based theory of cultural differences among nations', *International Studies of Management and Organization*, 13: 46–74.

Huczynski, A. A. (1996) *Management Gurus*, London: Thomson Business Press.

James, R. and Jones, R. (2014) 'Transferring the Toyota lean cultural paradigm into India: implications for human resource management', *The International Journal of Human Resource Management*, 25(15): 2174–2191.

Janis, I. L. (1972) *Victims of Groupthink*, Boston, MA: Houghton Mifflin.

Janis, I. L. (1982) *Groupthink: Psychological Studies of Policy Decisions and Fiascos*, Boston, MA: Houghton Mifflin.

Jarvenpaa, S. and Leidner, D. (1999) 'Communication and Trust in Global Virtual Teams', *Organization Science*, 10(6): 791–815.

Jenkins (1996) *Social Identity*, London: Routledge.

Jenkins, A. (1994) 'Teams: From ideology to analysis', *Organization Studies*, 15(6): 849–860.

Jones, R. G. and Lindley, W. D. (1998) 'Issues in the transition to teams', *Journal of Business and Psychology*, 13(1): 31–40.

Jonsson, D., Medbo, L. and Engstrom, T. (2004) 'Some considerations relating to the reintroduction of assembly lines in the Swedish automotive industry', *International Journal of Operations and Production Management*, 24(8): 754–762.

Kamata, S. (1983) '*Japan in the Passing Lane: An Insider's Account of Life in a Japanese Auto Factory*', London: Allen & Unwin.

Kanter, R. M. (1983) *The Change Masters: Innovations for Productivity in the American Corporation*, New York: Simon and Schuster.

Katzenbach, J. R. and Smith, D. K. (1993) *The Wisdom of Teams*, Boston, MA: Harvard Business School Press.

Kayworth, T. and Leidner, D. (2000) 'The Global Virtual Manager: A Prescription for Success', *European Management Journal*, 18(2), 183–194.

Kell, J., Lorenzetti, L., Kowitt , B. and Fry, E. (2015) 'You want collaboration? We'll show you collaboration', *Fortune* Magazine. Available at: www.fortune.com/2015/06/05/teams-of-the-fortune-500/. Accessed on 15/02/2016.

Kirkman, B. L. (2000) 'Why do employees resist teams? Examining the "resistance barrier" to work team effectiveness', *International Journal of Conflict Management,* 11(1): 74–93.

Kirkman, B. L. and Shapiro, D. L. (1997) 'The impact of cultural values on employees' resistance to teams: Towards a model of globalized self managing work team effectiveness', *Academy of Management Review,* 22(3): 730–757.

Kirkman, B. L., Shapiro, D. L., Novelli, L. Jr. and Brett, J. M. (1996) 'Employee concerns regarding self managing work teams: A multidimensional justice perspective', *Social Justice Research,* 9(1): 47–67.

Klein, J. A. (1989) 'The human costs of manufacturing reform', *Harvard Business Review,* March–April: 60–66.

Knights, D. and McCabe, D. (2000) 'Bewitched, bothered and bewildered: The meaning and experience of teamworking for employees in an automobile company', *Human Relations,* 53(11): 1481–1517.

Knights, D. and McCabe, D. (2003) 'Governing through teamwork: Re-constituting subjectivity in a call-center', *Journal of Management Studies,* 40(7): 587–619.

Kotlarsky, J., van den Hooff, B. and Houtman, L. (2015) 'Are we on the same page? Knowledge boundaries and transactive memory system development in cross-functional teams', *Communication Research*, 42(3): 319–344.

Kramer, R. M. (1998). 'Revisiting the Bay of Pigs and Vietnam decisions 25 years later: How well has the groupthink hypothesis stood the test of time?', *Organizational Behavior and Human Decision Processes,* 73(2): 236–271.

Laclau, E. (1990) *New Reflections on the Revolution of Our Time,* London: Verso.

Lammers, C. J. and Szell, B. (1989) *International Handbook of Organizational Participation, Vol. 1 Organizational Democracy: Taking Stock,* Oxford: Oxford University Press.

Lave, J. and Wenger, E. (1991) *Situated Learning: Legitimate Peripheral Participation,* New York: Cambridge University Press.

Legare, T. L. (2001) 'How Hewlett-Packard Used Virtual Cross-Functional Teams to Deliver Healthcare Industry Solutions', *Journal of Organizational Excellence*, 20(4): 29–38.

Levine, D. I. (2004) 'The wheels of Washington: Groupthink and Iraq', *San Francisco Chronicle,* 5 February, A23 [sfgate.com/article.cgi?file=/chronicle/archive/2004/02/05/EDGV34OCEPl.DTL].

Lewin, K. (1948) *Resolving Social Conflicts: Selected Papers on Group Dynamics,* London: Harper & Row.

Lewis, K. and Herndon, B. (2011) 'Transactive memory systems: Current issues and future research directions', *Organization Science*, 22: 1254–1265.

Majchrzak, A., More, P. H. B. and Faraj, S. (2012) 'Transcending knowledge differences in cross-functional teams', *Organization Science*, 23: 951–970.

Manz, C. C. (1992) 'Beyond self managing work teams: Towards self-leading teams in the workplace', in R. Glaser (ed.) *Classic Readings in Self-Managing Teamwork,* Pennsylvania: Organization Design and Development, Inc.

Manz, C. C. and Sims, H. P. (1987) 'Leading workers to lead themselves: The external leadership of self-managing work teams', *Administrative Science Quarterly,* 32(1): 106–128.

Manz, C. C. and Sims, H. P. (1991) 'Superleadership beyond the myth of heroic leadership', *Organizational Dynamics,* 19(4): 18–35.

Manz, C. C. and Sims, H. P. (1993) *Business Without Bosses: How Self-Managing Teams are Building High-Performance Companies,* New York: John Wiley & Sons Inc.

Mayo, E. (1933) *The Human Problems of an Industrial Civilization,* New York: Macmillan.

Mayo, E. (1945) *The Social Problems of an Industrial Civilization,* New York: Macmillan.

Maznevski, M. L. and Chudoba, K. (2001) 'Bridging Space Over Time: Global Virtual Team Dynamics and Effectiveness', *Organization Science,* 11(5): 473–492.

Maznevski, M. L. (1994) 'Understanding our differences: Performance in decision-making groups with diverse members', *Human Relations,* 47(5): 531–552.

McCabe, D. and Black, J. (1996) '"Something's gotta give": Trade unions and the road to teamworking', *Employer Relations,* 1992: 110–127.

McKinlay, A. and Taylor, P. (1996) 'Power, surveillance and resistance: Inside the "Factory of the Future"', in P. Ackers, C. Smith and P. Smith (eds) *The New Workplace and Trade Unionism,* London: Routledge, pp. 279–300.

Metcalfe, B. and Linstead, A. (2003) 'Gendering teamwork: Re-writing the Feminine', *Gender, Work and Organization,* 10(1): 95–119.

Mills, P. K. and Ungson, G. (2003) 'Reassessing the limit of structural empowerment: Organizational constitutions trusts controls', *Academy of Management Review,* 28(1): 143–151.

Mitchell, R. J., Parker, V. and Giles, M. (2011) 'When do interprofessional teams succeed? Investigating the moderating roles of team and professional identity in interprofessional effectiveness', *Human Relations,* 64: 1321–1343.

Monden, Y. (1983) *Toyota Production System,* Norcross: IIE Press.

Mueller, F. (1994) 'Teams between hierarchy and commitment: Changes strategies and the "internal environment"', *Journal of Management Studies,* 31(3): 383–403.

Mulder, M. (1971) 'Power equalization through participation', *Administrative Science Quarterly,* 16(1): 31–40.

Nonaka, I. and Takeuchi, H. (1995) *The Knowledge Creating Company,* Oxford: Oxford University Press.

Oakland, J. C. (1996) *Total Quality Management: A Practical Approach,* University of Bradford Management Centre: European Centre for Total Quality Management.

Oborn, E. and Dawson, S. (2010) 'Knowledge and practice in multidisciplinary teams: Struggle, accommodation and privilege', *Human Relations,* 63: 1835–1857.

Oh, H. S., Chung, M. and Labianca, G. (2004) 'Group social capital and group effectiveness: The role of informal socializing ties', *Academy of Management Journal,* 47(6): 860–75.

Parker, M. and Slaughter, J. (1988a) 'Management by Stress', *Technology Review,* 91(7): 36–44.

Parker, M. and Slaughter, J. (1988b) *Choosing Sides: Unions and the Team Concept,* Boston, MA: South End Press.

Parker, M. and Slaughter, J. (1994) 'Lean Production Is Mean Production', *Canadian Dimension,* 28(1): 21–22.

Peters, T. (1988) *Thriving on Chaos: Handbook for a Management Revolution,* London: Pan Books.

Peters, T. and Waterman, R. H. (1982) *In Search of Excellence,* London: Harper and Row.

Pfeffer, J. (1998) *The Human Equation: Building Profits by Putting People First,* Boston, MA: Harvard Business School Press.

Plunkett, L. C. and Fournier, R. O. (1991) *Participative Management,* New York: Wiley.

Poliert, A. (1996) '"Team work" on the assembly line: Contradictions and the dynamic of union resilience', in P. Ackers, C. Smith and P. Smith (eds) *The New Workplace and Trade Unionism,* London: Routledge, pp. 178–209.

Poole, M. S. (1983) 'Decision development in small groups III: a multiple sequence model group decision development', *Communications Monographs,* 50: 206–232.

Powell, A., Piccoli, G. and Ives, B. (2004) 'Virtual teams: a review of current literature and directions for future research', *ACM Sigmis Database,* 35(1): 6–36.

Price, R. (2015) 'Controlling routine front line service workers: an Australian retail supermarket case', *Work, Employment & Society,* 15: DOI: 0950017015601778.

Procter, S. and Mueller, F. (2000) *Teamworking,* London: Macmillan Business.

Reagans, R., Zuckerman, E. and McEvily, B. (2004) 'How to make a team: Social network vs demography as criteria for designing effective teams', *Administrative Science Quarterly,* 49: 101–33.

Ren, Y. and Argote, L. (2011) 'Transactive memory systems 1985–2010: An integrative framework of key dimensions, antecedents, and consequences', *Academy of Management Annals,* 5: 189–229.

Reynolds, R. (1994) *Groupwork in Education and Training: Ideas in Practice,* The Educational and Training Technology Series, London: Kogan Page Limited.

Senge, P. (1990) *The Fifth Discipline: The Art and Practice of the Learning Organization,* New York: Doubleday/ Currency.

Sewell, G. (1998) 'The discipline of team: The control of team-based industrial work through electronic and peer surveillance', *Administrative Science Quarterly,* 43(2): 397–429.

Sewell, G. and Wilkinson, B. (1992) '"Someone to watch over me": Surveillance, discipline and the just-in-time labour process', *Sociology,* 26(2): 271–298.

Sinclair, A. (1992) 'The tyranny of team ideology', *Organization Studies,* 13(4): 611–626.

Stewart, G. (2006) 'A meta-analytic review of relationship between team design features and team performance', *Journal of Management,* 32(1): 29–54.

Swann, W. B. Jr, Polzer, J. T., Seyle, C. D. and Ko, S. J. (2004) 'Finding value in diversity: Verification of personal and social self views in diverse groups', *Academy of Management Review,* 29(1): 9–27.

Tannenbaum, S. I., Beard, R. L. and Salas, E. (1992) 'Team building and its influence on team effectiveness: An examination of conceptual and empirical developments', in K. Kelley (ed.) *Issues, Theory, and Research in Industrial/Organizational Psychology* (Vol. 82), Amsterdam: Elsevier Science, pp. 117–153.

Thompson, P. and Wallace, T. (1996) 'Redesigning production through teamworking: Case studies from the Volvo Truck Corporation', *International Journal of Operations and Production Management,* 16(2): 103–118.

Thrift, N. (2001) '"It's the romance, not the finance, that makes the business worth pursuing": Disclosing a new market culture', *Economy & Society,* 30(4): 412–432.

Tompkins, P. K. and Cheney, G. (1985) 'Communications and unobtrusive control in contemporary organisations', in R. D. McPhee and P. K. Thompkins (eds) *Organizational Communication: Traditional Themes and New Directions,* Newbury Park, CA: Sage, pp. 179–210.

Townsend, A. M., DeMarie, S.M. and Hendrickson, A. R. (1998) 'Virtual Teams: Technology and the Workplace of the Future', *The Academy of Management Executive,* 12(3): 17–29.

Trist, E. L. and Bamforth, K. (1951) 'Some social and psychological consequences of the Longwall method of coal-getting', *Human Relations,* 4(1): 3–38.

Trist, E. L., Susman, G. I. and Brown, G. R (1977) 'An experiment in autonomous working in an American underground coal mine', *Human Relations,* 30: 201–236.

Tuckman, B. W. (1965) 'Developmental sequences in small groups', *Psychological Bulletin,* 63(6): 384–399.

Tuckman, B. W. and Jenson, M. A. (1977) 'Stages of small group development revisited', *Group and Organization Studies,* 2: 419–427.

Tushman, M. and Nadler, D. (1998) 'Organizing for innovation', in K. Starkey (ed.) *How Organizations Learn,* London: Thomson Business Press.

van Amelsvoort, P. and Benders, J. (1996) 'Team time: a model for developing self-directed teams', *International Journal of Operation and Production Management,* 16(2): 159–170.

van Knippenberg. D, De Dreu, Carsten K. W., Homan, A. C. (2004) 'Work group diversity and group performance: An integrative model and research agenda', *Journal of Applied Psychology,* 89(6): 1008–1022.

Wall, T. D., Kemp, N. J., Jackson, P. and Clegg, C. (1992) 'Outcomes of autonomous workgroups: A long-term field experiment', in R. Glaser (ed.) *Classic Readings in Self-Managing Teamwork,* Pennsylvania: Organization Design and Development, Inc.

Wall, T. D., Kemp, N. J., Jackson, P. R. and Clegg, C. W. (1986) 'Outcomes of autonomous workgroups: A long term field experiment', *Academy of Management Journal,* 29: 280–304.

Wallace, T. (2004) 'The end of good work? Work organisation or lean production in Volvo organisation', *International Journal of Operations and Production Management,* 24(8): 750–753.

Waterson, P. E., Clegg, C. W., Bolden, R., Pepper, K. *et al.* (1999) 'The use and effectiveness of modern manufacturing practices: A survey of UK industry', *International Journal of Production Research,* 37: 2271–2292.

Weisbord, M. R. (1992) 'Participative work design: A personal odyssey', in R. Glaser (ed.) *Classic Readings in Self-Managing Teamwork,* Pennsylvania: Organization Design and Development, Inc.

Wellins, R. S., Byham, W. C. and Wilson, J. (1991) *Empowered Teams,* San Francisco: Jossey-Bass.

Wenger, E. (1998) *Communities of Practice: Learning, Meaning and Identity,* Cambridge: Cambridge University Press.

Wenger, E. and Snyder, W. (2000) 'Communities of practice: The organizational frontier', *Harvard Business Review,* Jan–Feb: 139–145.

Wenger, E., McDermott, R. and Snyder, W. M. (2002) *Cultivating Communities of Practices,* Boston, MA: Harvard Business School Press.

West, A. (2004) *Effective Teamwork: Practical Lessons from Organizational Research,* Oxford: Blackwell.

Womack, J. P., Jones, D. T. and Roos, D. (1990) *The Machine that Changed the World,* New York: Rawson Associates.

Wood, R. and Bandura, A. (1989) 'Social cognitive theory of organizational management', *Academy of Management Review,* 14: 361–384.

Yevu, S. M. and Reedy, P. (2012) 'A Critical Evaluation of Teamworking Literature: A Critique from a Poststructural-Social Constructionist Healthcare Perspective', *International Journal of Multidisciplinary Thoughts,* 2(1): 217–228.

5 Managing people: Contexts of HRM, diversity and social inequality

DEBORAH KERFOOT AND DAVID KNIGHTS

Aims of the chapter

This chapter will:

- Present a selection of mainstream ideas about the management of people in contexts of diversity and inequality.

- Explore the problems of these ideas as well as expose some of their underpinning assumptions.

- Discuss critical approaches to the management of people and problems of diversity.

- Develop case study material in order to illustrate debates on the management of people and issues of diversity in organizations.

Key concepts and learning objectives

By the end of this chapter you should be able to:

- Describe some of the main approaches to managing people and diversity at work.

- Understand the evolution and development of HRM and diversity management.

- Critically evaluate the contribution of selective HRM and diversity management mainstream literatures.

- Explore key themes in critical approaches to managing people and diversity at work.

- Assess the value of critical approaches in the management of people and diversity.

Overview and key points

This chapter is concerned with the management of people at work. Two perspectives are taken that offer quite different understandings of how people are being managed in the context of contemporary organizations. One approach that

Managerialism or managerialist Term applied by critical academics to describe the type of social science output that serves the objectives of managers, as these critics see them, rather than offering an independent or alternative perspective. Managerialism usually entails the idea that effective management is the solution to an array of socio-economic problems.

we can generally define as mainstream is concerned with developing research which directly contributes to managerial goals and objectives. A second, critical perspective describes the first approach as **managerialist** for taking the side of power rather than endeavouring to be detached or independent of sectional interests. The first part of the chapter focuses on the mainstream way of understanding and exploring managing people and how they behave in organizations. Later we focus on the critical perspective.

Any attempt to understand human behaviour must recognize the part that diversity and inequality play. In particular, we are concerned with how diversity and inequality relate to issues of identity, insecurity and power. The chapter suggests that how people behave is a consequence of the tensions and conflicts that pervade many work situations. At the same time, people's behaviour in organizations contributes to those tensions and conflicts. So we explore how human behaviours, both those of managers as well as employees 'lower down' the hierarchy, are interlinked with their surroundings. In this respect, behaviour in organizations is not simply a product of individual or group interests in ways that much managerialist literature suggests. Indeed, our contention is that behaviour in organizations is inescapably a *social* phenomenon and, therefore, that human behaviour is conditioned and changes according to the socio-political and economic circumstances or contexts in which it occurs. Consequently, how people behave in organizations is, in part at least *an outcome of the way that they are managed*.

As we have shown in previous chapters, the overriding concern of the managerialist perspective, at least within the private sector, is to improve performance, productivity and profitability. The widespread adoption of this perspective in the public sector is a comparatively recent development. In the UK, for example, its increase has increased rapidly since the late 1970s. In the public sector (often referred to as the state sector or as state employment), managerialism has been adopted largely to achieve similar aims to those in the private sector – that is, by emulating private sector methods but replacing concerns with profitability and financial returns to shareholders with those of cost efficiency and value for money. The concern of a managerialist perspective is to know about people - how and why they act the way that they do – in order to increase profitability or drive down costs with as little resistance as possible. In the public and private sectors alike, managerialism is applied to gain more effective control of employees and/or to develop productive forms of collective and individual self-discipline.

The task of controlling and/or directing the efforts of employees has historically shifted from groups of workers and/or gang bosses to become the responsibility of professional managers (see Chapter 7). The managerial agents of private capital expanded as companies grew in size and scope beyond the confines of owner control. Thus, the body of people whose work we now refer to as 'management', emerged. While legally obliged to increase value for the owners (shareholders), managers enjoy hierarchical authority, relative material security (e.g., high income and other financial benefits) and significant symbolic privileges (e.g., superior status). Most students of business and management, for example, prefer to see themselves as managers of people rather than being subjected to management by others. Student's perceptions of managerial work and of life as a manager are often shaped by the expectation of ultimately sharing the material and symbolic privileges enjoyed by senior managers. Contemporary media representations of business management activities and the lifestyles of notable business figures often reinforce this seductive ideal. Indeed, popular television and other media portraits of business as conveyed in, for example, television's 'The Apprentice', create an image of managerial work that is far removed from the realities of everyday activities of the majority of managers. That managerial careers appear so seductive to students of business and management indicates how pervasive is the idea of managerial work as privileged, and therefore desirable as a career choice for students, despite the realities of daily work in most management jobs where managers find themselves as pressured by 'the system' as those whom they manage. In large part this is because controlling people's behaviour is far more complex and difficult than the managerialist perspective might suggest. From a managerialist perspective, the relationship to knowledge is underpinned by a single question: one centred on knowing or finding out how best to manage people in order to achieve organizationally defined goals. This question, often asked by many managers or would-be managers at all levels is: 'what works?' In other words, how can knowledge about people and their diversity be identified, and then applied, in the achievement of the assumed shared goals of the enterprise? (See Chapters 7 and 8).

From this perspective, the 'successful' manager is the one who can most closely control his or her subordinates and direct their effort in the desired way in order to achieve organizational goals. Obviously, the term 'successful' here is not neutral in that it refers to success as defined by managers rather than those subordinates who carry out managerial instructions. Even within the managerialist perspective, there is no universal agreement about *how to* manage people, despite the strength of the desire to find this elixir. What exists is a range of ideas that offer many different definitions, models and theories as to the best way it could be done (see Chapter 7). Despite the fact that none of these ideas has been proven to be 'the best method', some are clearly more popular amongst managers – something that is confirmed by our own experiences of being managed in organizations. Yet ideas about the best way to manage people shifts in time and place and according to fashion in management thinking. Consequently, what appears to be the truth about managing people at one time may not appear so compelling or appear to offer such potency a few years thereafter. However, whilst there are multiple ideas within the mainstream, what is shared among these different approaches is a commitment to prevailing managerial aims, norms and values. This chapter explores a selection of these ideas.

By contrast, a critical perspective is not directly or principally concerned with improving organizational efficiency, the achievement of performance targets or profitability. Critical perspectives enable us to analyze what goes on in the name of managing people and diversity by way of producing knowledge about some of the implicit, unintended or wider social effects of management action or inaction. What this means is that critical perspectives can enable us to 'see' beyond the immediate considerations that most managers have in seeking success for their organizations. Critical perspectives provide a different way of understanding how we are managed in organizations than presuming a simple consensus. Contributions to a critical perspective can provide us with an understanding of what managers do in the name of managing, both their intended *and unintended* consequences. They are uniquely useful in that they enable us to make visible the often unrecognized and uncontrolled effects of management policy and practice. Critical approaches therefore bring to the surface issues of management and aspects of organizational life that might otherwise go unacknowledged or be denied.

Critical approaches produce knowledge about the management of people and their diversity that is markedly different from the mainstream. Broadly, the underlying relationship of critical perspectives to knowledge centres on concerns that extend beyond the instrumental pursuit of performance, productivity and profit. Insights are sought about the background to and the effects of managers' preoccupation with the instrumental pursuits of profit or efficiency. So, for example, one of the conditions for minimizing costs in many Western organizations has been the employment of migrant labour, who have often, and for a variety of reasons, accepted work on wages lower than those expected within the indigenous or home labour force. Organizations then can become a 'melting pot' of mixed ethnicities, races, religions and cultural diversities and this often generates additional managerial problems. Diversity management has evolved to 'deal' with these problems. However, critical approaches do not unquestioningly regard this as necessarily beneficial to the different groups of workers at whom diversity management is targeted. As with the mainstream, a critical approach is not one single unified theory or a coherent body of thought. Rather, critical approaches represent different ways of 'seeing', and understanding, the management of people and their diversity in ways that are not limited by concerns about the 'what works?' question of many practitioners. Here, the concern is not with the output or efficiency considerations that govern managers for much of their time. Critical approaches address the questions: *'what are the foundations of knowledge?'* about managing people and diversity and *'what are the consequences?'* of the application of this knowledge in organizations.

MAINSTREAM APPROACHES TO HRM AND DIVERSITY

Because human resource management (HRM) is often examined in mainstream texts separately from diversity, we treat them individually in the first part of this chapter. We then proceed to provide a mainstream analysis of how they can be seen as integrated. In the mainstream literature HRM has always been understood as a broader field of theory and practice than diversity. HRM is concerned with every aspect of employment – recruitment, selection and induction; training and development; job evaluation and appraisal; performance and pay; employee relations and collective negotiations; and equal opportunity. From a mainstream perspective, diversity is much more narrowly concerned with equal opportunity and with limiting the potential disruptions or conflicts that may arise because of ethnic, religious, sexual or other divisions within the workforce. In the second part of the chapter, we focus on more critical approaches to HRM and diversity and here we find that there is a tendency to reverse the priorities of the mainstream. Diversity and the inequalities associated with it are treated as the central focus. HRM is then expected to radicalize itself to remedy the disadvantages and discriminations that are the result of these inequalities.

While the practices of HRM and diversity are straightforwardly focused on the above, theory in the mainstream is varied (see Figure 5.1). Broadly, there are **unitarist** accounts that perceive there to be a consensus that reflects management goals versus **pluralist** accounts that see differences and conflicts of interest between

Unitary Form of management in which the views of top management are assumed to be shared by everyone. Conflict is treated as pathological rather than a reflection of different interpretations and interests.

Pluralist A recognition of diverse legitimate viewpoints, interests or approaches. A pluralist vision of organizational politics emphasizes the free interplay of interest groups as operating to check and balance the potentially authoritarian tendencies of governing bodies.

diverse groups of stakeholders. By stakeholders we might include, for example, shareholders, employees, suppliers, environmentalists, government, etc. Another division is between 'hard' and 'soft' views of HRM. Hard HRM is focused on treating the human resource as an asset to be exploited. Soft HRM seeks to harness the creative and productive capacities of labour by treating employees more empathetically or humanely. Soft HRM and its associated techniques purport to be a more effective way of securing better performance and so indirectly benefits the goals of management for profitability and/or efficiency. The concern to manage organizational culture and 'involve' employees by gaining their commitment to work is closely related to soft HRM. Probably the most common approach is to understand HRM and the management of diversity as integrating with the corporate, business or organizational strategy. Traditionally, diversity issues were largely driven by legal requirements to at least provide the appearance of complying with laws against discrimination. Diversity was, and to some extent continues to be, seen by managers as a problem to be managed. Alongside this pragmatic concern, however, is the increasingly widespread belief that diversity provides an opportunity to integrate more closely the management of employees with the attainment of organizational goals. Diversity is, in this way, gradually becoming more closely linked with strategic issues and long term planning in the organization rather than merely a response to legislative requirements on equal opportunities.

HRM

HRM emerged as a practice and academic sub-discipline long before it was named in this way, for the term only began to be used in the mid-1980s (Storey, 1995). Up until this time, the task of managing people was the prerogative of personnel departments and its study was called personnel administration or personnel management (PM). In that form, the function was largely responsible for organizing activities relating to employees in a uniform, equitable and standardized manner. Its main tasks were personnel record maintenance, recruitment personnel specifications, job descriptions, induction, training, employee benefits, equal opportunity, health and safety, appraisal, job evaluation, promotion, welfare facilities, and ultimately displacements either in the form of retirement, redundancy or dismissal. In many companies the personnel manager also had responsibility for industrial relations (IR) issues and would be the chief negotiator for the employer in collective bargaining with local employee representatives or the trade union at a regional or national level. Figure 5.1 sets out some of the key differences between PM and HRM. However, in Western economies at the height of union power in the 1960s and 1970s, industrial relations were seen as too important for the personnel manager and appropriated by a specialist IR function, usually with board of director status. This was an indication of the relatively low esteem in which the PM function was held and may partly account for the emergence of HRM as a function that sought to be a part of the strategy as well as the operations of the business.

In her classic study of HRM, Karen Legge (2005) raises the question as to what HRM is and how it differs from personnel management (PM). She suggests that in normative terms (or what is prescribed as opposed to what actually happens) HRM differs from PM in that the former is expected to integrate the management of people with the strategy of the organization as defined by senior management. We refer to this from a different perspective later in the chapter (see p. 184) where the transition from PM to HRM is seen to reflect a much wider and more universal cultural transformation of human life (Costea, 2010). Legge (2005) finds how the expectation that HRM integrates people management with strategy is rarely realized in practice and she therefore concludes that essentially HRM is little more than a rhetorical device for elevating the status of the activities formerly performed by personnel managers. This is not surprising because it is common knowledge, not least amongst managers themselves, that PM has traditionally been the 'poor relation', having something like a Cinderella status (Huczynski and Buchanan, 2001, p. 667), with respect to other management functions like accounting and finance, marketing or information systems. Its association with managing people, rather than being directly related to the bottom line of business, contributed to PM's lowly image amongst managers and amongst a wider public, who have grown accustomed to denigrating activities associated with personnel administration as mere 'pen pushing'. In response to this, there have been attempts to elevate PM by creating HRM centres that develop a central strategic approach to the management of people and treat employees as potentially driving forward, rather than merely supporting, organizational outcomes.

Thinkpoint 5.1

Why do you think that HRM has a comparatively lower status than other management functions? Is this lower status justified? What does this tell us about the priorities of managers in organizations?

While there is controversy over the differences between HRM and PM, there is also no single unitary model of how HRM itself is practised or defined in the literature (see Figure 5.1 below).

In the mainstream, however, an approach widely deployed in the USA is dominant. This links closely with the view that HRM must be directly aligned with corporate and business strategy. Despite the lack of a coherent or universal set of management practices associated with HRM (Keenoy, 1990; Legge, 1989), it is distinct in seeking, although not necessarily achieving, an alignment with the strategic operations of the corporation or the organization (Guest, 1990, pp. 378–9). There are, however, different ways to view the human resource. It may, for example, be seen as an asset whose variable cost of production needs to be constrained, or it may be viewed more as a creative and innovative asset to be nurtured and developed in order to advance the productive power of the organization.

Thinkpoint 5.2

Which of these two views about human resources do you think the most appropriate? Why?

Exercise 5.1

Divide into two groups. Group 1 should choose a large commercial retailing organization and Group 2 a public sector service organization. Discuss the appropriateness for your chosen organization of each of the following two views of the human resource:

- Employees are a cost to be controlled in our organization.
- Employees are a creative asset to our organization.

Hendry and Pettigrew (1990) raised the issue of what is to be emphasized in HRM – the human or the resource element (p. 21). If the human element is stressed, we are closer to the PM or 'soft' version of HRM (Storey, 1989, p. 10) which gives greater emphasis to the care of employees and engaging them in the development of the organization through engendering their commitment, flexibility and prioritizing of quality (Collings and Wood, 2009). By contrast, what is termed a 'hard' version of HRM (Storey, 1989) focuses on employees as an 'asset' that can be exploited instrumentally to secure productivity and profit. At its extreme, the resource approach prescribes keeping employee rights, job security and wages as low as the labour market will allow (Collings and Wood, 2009, p. 2) thus facilitating competitive success in the product and capital markets. This enables companies to achieve comparatively high profit margins, high share prices and to fend off potential aggressive predators that might seek to initiate takeover bids. However, critics argue that it leads to high staff turnover, low morale and poor performance thereby undermining long-term competitive survival (ibid.).

In addition to, but overlapping with the distinction between 'soft' and 'hard' versions, there are four models of HRM that are widely engaged in the literature. All of them regard HRM as linked to strategy but each has a different emphasis. Two of them definitely subscribe to a 'hard' definition of HRM. The first, established by

Thinkpoint 5.3

Thinking about your own work experience, what might be some of the consequences of managers viewing you as a cost to be controlled?

Fombrun *et al.* (1984), considers business strategy to be the determinant of how the resource represented by human beings is deployed in a flexible and cost-effective manner. The second 'hard' approach, developed by Schuier and Jackson (1987), focuses more on the operational and competitive strategy and is concerned with two aspects of the human resource – its capacity to cut costs and its power to innovate. Following a contingency approach in which it is argued that the content of a HRM strategy is conditioned by the particular context of operations in any given organization (see Chapter 7), the authors link the two central aspects of HRM competitive strategy to specific human resource behaviours demanded of employees (p. 209). Not unexpectedly, innovation involves the following and can be seen to align with McGregor's (1969) Theory Y (see Box 5.1 and Chapter 2).

1 A high degree of creative behaviour
2 A longer-term focus
3 A relatively high level of co-operative, interdependent behaviour
4 A moderate degree of concern for quality
5 A moderate concern for quantity
6 An equal degree of concern for process and results
7 A greater degree of risk taking, and
8 A high tolerance of ambiguity and unpredictability.

Box 5.1
McGregor's Theory Y

The authors stress how corporations seeking to secure competitive advantage through a cost cutting strategy must reduce their staff and wage levels partly by outsourcing to low cost labour markets often overseas, and through automation, work simplification and measurement procedures. Appropriate employee role behaviour is summarized as follows. Here again there is a similarity to McGregor's Theory X (See Box 5.2 and Chapter 2).

The other two HRM models are closer to the 'soft' version but do not depart from all aspects of a 'hard' approach. Beer *et al.* (1984; 1985) were the first academics to introduce HRM into their teaching programmes at Harvard. While seeking to link HRM with strategy, they subscribed to a humanistic philosophy that drew on organizational psychology and the human relations perspective (see Chapters 2, 7 and 8) concerning the development of employees as people, and their full involvement in the 'progress' of the organization (Kerfoot and Knights, 1992, p. 654). They take a stakeholder approach whereby in addition to shareholders (ordinarily pre-eminent in 'hard' versions of HRM),

1 Relatively repetitive and predictable behaviours
2 A rather short-term focus
3 Primarily autonomous or individual activity
4 Modest concern for quality
5 High concern for quantity of output (goods or services)
6 Primary concern for results
7 Low risk-taking activity, and
8 A relatively high degree of comfort with stability (McGregor, 1969, p. 211).

Box 5.2
McGregor's Theory X

Exercise 5.2

How are you expected to behave in university? Working in small groups, draw up a table from Box 5.1 and Box 5.2 that you think reflects the behavioural requirements for a typical student in university.

If you think there are behavioural requirements not included in the two lists, add these but distinguish them by using italics.

other interests such as employees and their trade unions, managers and their associations, government and the community are expected to be taken into account. While not ignoring 'bottom-line' concerns with cost and organizational effectiveness, these authors are attentive to the quality of working life and social well-being.

All three of the above models are from the USA. Another prescriptive model (see Hendry and Pettigrew, 1990) that has achieved recognition, this time developed in the UK, seeks to combine the best aspects of the **strategic contingency** and the human development approaches. In their model, Hendry and Pettigrew sought to avoid *a priori* prescription by refusing to define HRM in advance of conducting case study research of the 'range of things' that affect 'the employment and contribution of people, against the criteria of coherence and appropriateness' (Hendry and Pettigrew, 1990, p. 24). Their resulting model (see Figure 5.1) revolves around linking the content of both strategy and HRM to a range of internal and external contexts.

Strategic contingency
Theory suggesting that uncertainty for an organization stems from its systems of operation, which include technology and work operations from its environment.

Exercise 5.3

When reading different texts or articles on HRM, see if you can place them somewhere in this 2 × 2 dimensional table. Remember some may overlap more than one box, as do Hendry and Pettigrew. Some may not fit at all and so you could elaborate the table to include them.

Figure 5.1 HR and HRM: The differences
Source: Storey, J. (1992) 'HRM in Action: The Truth Is Out at Last', *Personnel Management*, April: 28–31.

HR and HRM: The differences		
Dimension	Personnel and IR	HRM
Beliefs and assumptions		
Contact	Careful delineation of written contracts	Aim to go 'beyond contract'
Rules	Importance of devising clear rules/mutuality	'Can do' outlook impatience with 'rule'
Guide to management action	Procedures/consistency control	'Business need'/flexibility/commitment
Behaviour referent	Norms/custom and practice	Values/mission
Managerial task vis-a-vis labour	Monitoring	Nurturing
Nature of relations	Pluralist	Unitarist
Conflict	Institutionalized	De-emphasized
Standardization	High (e.g., 'parity' an issue)	Low (e.g., 'parity' not seen as relevant)
Strategic aspects		
Key relations	Labour-management	Business-customer
Initiatives	Piecemeal	Integrated
Corporate plan	Marginal to	Central to
Speed of decision	Slow	Fast
Line management		
Management role	Transactional	Transformational leadership
Key managers	Personnel/IR specialists	General/business/line managers
Prized management skills	Negotiation	Facilitation
Key levers		
Foci of attention for interventions	Personnel procedures	Wide-ranging cultural, structural and personnel strategies
Selection pay	Separate, marginal task job evaluation: multiple fixed grades	Integrated, key task performance-related: few if any grades
Conditions	Separately negotiated	Harmonization
Labour-management	Collective bargaining contracts	Towards individual contracts
Thrust of relations with stewards	Regularized through facilities and training	Marginalized (with exception of some bargaining for change models)
Communication	Restricted flow/indirect	Increased flow/direct
Job design	Division of labour	Teamwork
Conflict handling	Reach temporary truces	Manage climate and culture
Training and development	Controlled access to courses	Learning companies

MANAGING DIVERSITY

Diversity is simply the recognition that there are numerous differences between people in terms of their social characteristics (e.g., gender, race, age), their backgrounds (e.g., education and skills) and their values (e.g., cultural, moral and political beliefs). These differences often intersect such that a person may, for example, experience advantages or disadvantages in multiple ways. In a famous early study of culture and social class, it was suggested that 'working-class kids get working-class jobs' (Willis, 1977). Willis's study has been drawn on subsequently to explore how, for example, many black working-class kids get different jobs – in terms of status, pay and conditions – than many white working-class kids. Willis draws on in-depth ethnographic research of people that is directly concerned to understand cultural and class differences and how they are generated and reproduced. Other studies demonstrate how low-skill manual workers are heavily over-represented amongst the long-term unemployed and economically inactive men in Britain, while men with high-level skills and educational qualifications continue to have far better employment prospects (Alcock *et al.,* 2003; Nixon, 2006). Similarly, the experience of working in, say, a large organization like the police force may well be different for a white person than for a black person and also for a black woman than a black man, or for a young black Muslim man and a young black Muslim woman and so on. These differences alert us to the disadvantages that can occur *between* specific social groups alongside those that can happen *within* such groups. Similarly, Adib and Guerrier's (2003) research on women in hotel work explores the effects of nationality, race, ethnicity and class in shaping women's experiences of work and calls attention to differences amongst women rather than viewing women as if they were one homogenous group of people.

On the surface, one of the most 'obvious' distinctions in our society is that between men and women, but an effect of the introduction of a concept of diversity is to increase awareness of how there are probably just as many differences amongst women and amongst men as there are between women and men as a whole. Indeed, much of the academic and policy study of the experiences at work of gay men and women, and on lesbian, gay, bisexual and transgendered persons (LGBT) has underscored this point. This highlights the distinctions between how gay men and gay women are employed in organizations compared to their 'straight' colleagues. In a study of a group of gay men in the NHS for example, Rumens and Kerfoot, (2009) conclude that, even within so-called 'gay friendly' organizational settings, creating and maintaining a professional identity, and displaying 'competence' – often defined in terms of rationality and objectivity – can entail continuous negotiation and struggle on the part of gay men.

Managing diversity is about respecting the differences of people in work organizations and adapting policies and practices so as to accommodate them and to enable diverse employees to participate fully in workplace activities. The basic concept of the management of diversity:

> accepts that the workforce consists of a diverse population of people. The diversity consists of visible and non-visible differences, which will include sex, age, background, race, disability, personality and workstyle. It is founded on the premise that harnessing these differences will create a productive environment in which everybody feels valued, where their talents are being fully utilized, and in which organizational goals are being met (Kandola and Fullerton, 1994, p. 19).

Exercise 5.4

List as many pieces of anti-discriminatory legislation as you can.
In each case, think about who this legislation was designed to protect.

Earlier discussion of equal opportunity, and especially equal opportunity legislation, found its origins in the requirement not to behave towards or treat anyone in an obviously discriminatory manner:

> Equal opportunities is about treating everybody fairly and equally regardless of lifestyle. (Collins, 1992, p. 3)

Within the managerial and organizational vocabulary, diversity became established around the end of the 1990s however, with renewed impetus following the emergence of the Equality Act 2010. Prior to this, 'managing diversity' was partly a response to the assessment of some academics and progressive practitioners that the legalistic and negative tone of earlier equal opportunity and anti-discrimination literature had, in some respects, become counter-productive. The anti-discrimination focus tended to concentrate exclusively on areas for which there was legislation and, in particular, gender and race. However, legislation was widening to include other aspects of discrimination such as age, culture, disability, religion and sexual preference. Many studies concentrated on one or other of these modes of discrimination rather than packaging them together. More problematically, studies of equal opportunity and anti-discrimination often failed to identify the interrelationships between different aspects of disadvantage and discrimination. A black woman confronted by sexism, for example, is highly likely to be doubly disadvantaged as she is almost bound to suffer some racial discrimination as well (Bagilhole, 2009). It is not just that one source of discrimination is added to another but that each affects the other. The outcome is disadvantage that is greater than the sum of the parts seen separately. This has become known as the problem of intersectionality (Crenshaw, 1991, 2015). The term originally sought to illustrate the inadequacy of legal frameworks in dealing with inequality and discrimination that resulted from the ways that race and gender had intersected to constrain the employment experiences of Black women. As the work by Rodrigues et al (2016) point out, intersectionality aims to capture the social, economic, employment and other disadvantages that multiply in complex and often unpredictable ways. This will be discussed in more detail in Section 2, 'Critical approaches to HRM and diversity', of this chapter.

As a counterbalance for a long history of discrimination (Ashkanasy *et al.*, 2002), the USA included in its legislation what is called affirmative action or preferential treatment. Through affirmative action, quotas were given to employers to ensure that disadvantaged gender and ethnic groups were employed in proportion to their representation in the population at large. Consequently, disadvantaged groups had to be given priority in situations of equal qualification for a job, for example. By contrast, preferential treatment follows the same goal but by privileging the disadvantaged regardless of qualifications (Blommaert and Verschueren, 1998). This has not happened in Europe despite institutionalized racism and sexism, although the legislation has been modified in an effort to eliminate this form of discrimination, at least in the public sector. Institutionalized racism and sexism is a situation where discrimination is embedded in the culture and structure of organizations. Insofar as it is reflected and reproduced in everyday organizational practices, norms and routines, it renders equal opportunity legislation largely ineffective (Collinson *et al.*, 1990; Green, 2000; Bagilhole, 2009). Legislation can support quotas for employers either as voluntary codes or backed by statutory force. Other non-legislative interventions take the form of assimilation and attempts to integrate diverse cultures into the dominant national one; cultural pluralism where tolerance of difference is promoted; or multiculturalism in which cultural difference are celebrated (Blommaert and Verschueren, 1998).

As a feature of organizational theory and practice, an interest in diversity first emerged in the USA in the 1980s (e.g., Nkomo and Cox, 1996; Pringle and Scowcroft, 1996; Lynch, 1997; Prasad and Mills, 1997; Kelly and Dobbin, 1998; Ivancevich and Gilbert, 2000; Lorbiecki and Jack, 2000; Lorbiecki, 2001; Ashkanasy *et al.*, 2002; Janssens and Zanoni, 2005; Jack and Lorbiecki, 2007). Ever since the Civil Rights Act (1964) in the USA, and the anti-discrimination legislation in Europe that followed shortly afterwards, corporations have been legally constrained to demonstrate that they have procedures in place to enable equal opportunity. In the USA, this extends to having internal legal codes inscribed in their human resources manuals (Dobb, 2009, p. 2). However, in the 1990s in the USA, employers and certain federal states began to challenge affirmative action programmes. More generally, it was claimed that the impact of the 1960s equal opportunity legislation worldwide had been extremely limited (Collinson *et al.,* 1990; Kelly and Dobbin, 1998).[1]

Exercise 5.5

Working in small groups, decide whether you think affirmative action and/or preferential treatment should be introduced:

- in the country where you are studying
- in other parts of the world.

Give your reasons why, or why not.
If you wish to follow up this discussion, you could consult Parekh (1992).

Equal opportunity and anti-discrimination legislation was seen as bureaucratic and negative in imposing external constraints on what managers could do. Perhaps largely as a consequence, legislation met with minimal compliance. The solution of the diversity management thinkers and specialists, particularly in the context of the USA has been to transform equal opportunity and affirmative action programmes into a practice that would contribute significantly to the production of profits, efficiency, effectiveness and other organizational benefits. In other words, it has been trans-lated from a moral question of equity to an instrumental issue of efficacy. In this sense, advocates of diversity drew inadvertently on what Foucault (1982) has described as the positive and productive aspects of power, rather than just its negative and constraining features. Compliance with the law was redefined as providing an additional and partly unintended benefit to corporations rather than the driver of change that would drive out discrimination. We will return to the contribution that Foucault's work makes to the study of diversity later in the chapter when we discuss disability.

One of the principal arguments for the shift towards diversity and away from equal opportunities was that corporations themselves often had a very diverse base of customers. To reflect and address this diversity in the organization was thought to secure some competitive advantage for the companies that moved in its direction, over those companies that did not (see for instance, Cox, 1994; and Robinson and Dechant, 1997). The development of diversity was welcomed by many advocates of equal opportunity as it meant that the promotion of equal opportu-nity could get 'off the back foot' in the sense of falling back on legislation for legitimacy. It was also of tremendous assistance to management consultants specializing in this field as they could now sell the productive and competi-tive advantages of greater employee diversity.

As a practice, diversity management soon began to displace more radical demands for eradicating discrimina-tion and of stimulating organizational change in pursuit of gender, race, sexual and other equalities. Diversity appealed to the instrumental interests of managers to secure efficiencies and/or profits. As Omanovic (2011) has pointed out, a majority of mainstream studies are concerned to link diversity to the performance of individuals, groups or the organization as a whole (see Watson *et al.*, 1993; Robinson and Dechant, 1997; Hambrick *et al.*, 1998; Harrison *et al.*, 1998). Methodologically, they advance a position in which relations of diversity are reduced to quantitatively measured variables – such as race, gender, age, sexual orientation – that can be linked with perfor-mance. In contrast to critical perspectives on diversity (see Section 2, 'Critical approaches to HRM and diversity'), these variables are treated as if they are 'independent of managers' and researchers' own interests in managing or promoting diversity as an object to be managed' (Knights and Omanovic, 2010, p. 10).

Exercise 5.6

Think about the distinctions between equal opportunity and diversity. The following example serves as a useful discussion topic:

Ahmed worked for the same company in Yorkshire for 20 years, and had expe-rienced racial remarks and jokes from time to time. He let these comments ride over him until his colleagues began to abuse him on a regular basis. He ignored them for around six weeks and then made a complaint to his manager. Eventually Ahmed left work in a traumatized state. He has not returned to work and the company never disputed the fact that he was not fit to do so. The CRE assisted Ahmed in taking his case to an employment tribunal who unanimously agreed that he had suffered discrimination on the grounds of his race, which is Pakistani. (Commission for Racial Equality, March 2006)

To what extent could equal opportunity and diversity each be seen as having a moral underpinning?

To what extent are both equal opportunity and diversity instrumental with respect to employees?

Managing people and diversity: Integrating HRM and diversity

Thinkpoint 5.4

Why do you think there are more women than men in HRM?

For a number of reasons, the HRM function in business has been dominated by women. This is in spite of the fact that Business Studies as a subject is studied by more men than women. The phenomenon of women's numerical dominance in HRM is illustrative of what is called the feminization of an occupation whereby, for example, in the so-called 'caring' professions (e.g., human resources or personnel management, nursing, teaching, welfare) attract a disproportionate number of women recruits. Usually these occupations are of a comparatively lower status and pay which deters many men from considering this kind of work. Earlier in this chapter, we discussed the way that personnel management had become associated with the administrative aspects of organization and management, away from central or 'bottom-line' business functions in an organization, and it was this that led to many mangers referring to personnel as the Cinderella of managerial functions, indicating what was held to be its peripheral status. Further, because of sex discrimination, the preponderance of women in feminized occupations serves to reinforce their low status. With respect to the history of personnel management in the UK, the downgrading and devaluation of the sex-typed 'female' role of caring within personnel work (Legge, 1989) stems in part from its early association with the 'women welfare workers' of factory production in the late nineteenth and early twentieth centuries. In the history of factory work, such women were usually 'respectable' middle class 'ladies' whose presence patrolling the factory floor was thought to deter the lewd or inappropriate behaviour of the working classes, brought together en masse for the first time in large scale factory systems. Not only might such conduct distract from production and offensive to paternal employers, but also governmental bodies felt it their wider social obligation to restrain the perceived lack of moral character among lower class male employees. The presence of these 'lady social workers' was reinforced during world war one, when large numbers of women workers replaced men in factory work, especially in munitions and related production. As men were drafted to war service, maintaining the health and well-being of the nation's women became a concern for welfare workers, who directed their attention to maintaining the health and moral compass of legions of 'factory girls'.

So, the history of personnel management is gendered. This history has left a legacy that relegates the HRM function to what is often little more than a sidelined or peripheral position with minimal authority. This, coupled with what is often regarded still as a lack of 'bottom line' financial considerations in HRM, identifies personnel management and HRM as predominantly 'women's work'. Studies of the career profiles of personnel specialists, including their education and training, career progression, reasons for working in personnel, and the differences in male and female careers, continue to show that career progress in the field is more rapid amongst men, especially those with higher level qualifications: such careers often divide between those whose daily work is dealing with industrial relations disputes and those who deal with administrative support systems, with little movement between the two career paths (Monks, 1993; Gatrell and Swan, 2008).

Given the feminization of HRM, its integration with diversity ought to be just a matter of course. However this is not the case and although many organizations have diversity or equal opportunity programmes, women and minority groups invariably suffer lower pay and prospects than their white male counterparts. UK research, for example, found that the average female earns 18% less than her male equivalent (Guardian, 2016) whilst for graduates and women with A-levels, there has been little improvement in the ten years to 2013 (ONS, 2013). For mid-level and higher educated women, the gender pay gap is broadly the same as it was 20 years ago. For more than a decade after a child is born, women earn a third less pay per hour than men pointing to a continued penalty for women in having children

(Joseph Rowntree Foundation, 2015). It has been argued that HRM has a different impact depending on whether you are a man or a woman because the model is itself gendered. 'The implementation of apparently gender-neutral – but in reality gendered – HR concepts and policies perpetuate rather than challenge gender inequality' (Dickens, 2006, p. 23). Moreover, with limited exceptions, research reinforces this practice because 'women are invisible and men are not identified as men' (ibid.) but simply seen as the generic model for all workers, regardless of gender and, it might be added, other identities deriving from age, disability, ethnicity, race or sexuality – all of which are discriminated against.

Exercise 5.7

There is plenty of data on the Internet about gender and other inequalities. Divide up into three teams. Two teams should compile a report on the current state of equality between the sexes. Each can then present their report to the third group who will judge the quality of each team's report.

The growth in part-time, contract or temporary service work, coupled with a decline in so-called 'traditional' patterns of male employment in full-time uninterrupted careers, forces us to reconsider embedded stereotypes of the gendered division of labour and the sex composition of the workforce.

In the past, working-class men tended to enjoy full-time, permanent employment and a status as family 'breadwinners', whereas nowadays they are as likely to be in part-time, temporary work or be unemployed as are women. This is because of the decline in manufacturing and the growth of service industries, which have tended to favour women employees.

The extent to which this has led to a reconfiguration of managerial work by gender – colloquially referred to as a 'shattering of the glass ceiling' for women in management – is debatable, despite the existence of a few prominent exceptions. In addition, we are left to speculate on the consequences for male workers, not least in terms of the traditional archetype of the male breadwinner in all areas of work. For example, the unemployed low-skill men in Nixon's (2009) study rejected low-skill customer-oriented interactive service jobs because this work required of them skills and behaviours that they saw as oppositional to (that is, disconfirming) their male working-class social and cultural status. It is reported that unemployed low-skill men rejected female-dominated service occupations that required a customer focus because they struggled to associate themselves with what they saw as feminized work. The men in Nixon's research were called upon to manage their emotions and be passive and deferential as part of the service encounter and because such work denied them the opportunity to relieve their stress in their usual ways – through 'shouting', 'swearing', 'taking the piss' and 'having a laugh' (2009, p. 314), they refused or resisted the work. Despite declining levels of work in low-skill manual occupations, the men remained attached to this form of work and the masculine identities that it sustained (see Collinson, 1992).

Declining populations as a consequence of lower birth rates, the effects of migration, and a demographic shift toward an ageing population through increased life expectancy, all have implications for policymakers in arenas such as pensions planning and health and welfare provision, but also for the composition of the workforce. Some service and retail companies in particular have expanded the pools from which labour is recruited by including so-called 'third-age' workers. In the case of the US owned-ASDA supermarket chain, the skills and abilities of workers that have been secured as a result of such life experience are directly capitalized upon. The following example from some of their recruitment literature demonstrates implicitly what ASDA expects of its workforce:

... most days we hear a story about a colleague who has behaved exceptionally well in a challenging situation, or excelled against some demanding targets. Let's take a quick look at some recent hero stories from across the country. There was the lady from Horwich who whipped out her needle and thread to mend some George underwear for a disabled boy – and did it free of charge. A colleague from Kilmarnock who bought jump leads with his own money to help a customer jump start their car in the ASDA car park or the Stafford store which received a special award for its commitment to providing excellent customer service to deaf and blind customers. Everywhere you look at ASDA you'll see evidence of our exceptionally positive way of working with each other – whether it's the ASDA chant during huddles at the beginning of the shift or the ABCD badges. But don't just take our word for it – we have consistently ranked in the top 10 of the *Sunday Times* '100 Best Companies To Work For' for the past three years, being cited for our 'ground-breaking maternity, paternity and adoption packages'. *(ASDA website, accessed 10th March, 2008)*

Exercise 5.8

Discuss the following question:
  Should organizations expect workers to bring their all-round life skills to work? What might be the consequences for management when they do?

In respect of age and demographics, the concept of managing diversity finds immediate resonance with those who would seek to find ready solutions to the problems both of filling available vacancies, and finding staff that can meet the skill needs of contemporary organizations. This is where managing human resources and diversity come together in particular solutions of which the mainstream literature approves.

We now turn to a case study, located in a company given the pseudonym 'FinanceCo'. The study presents a selection of research material drawn from several larger projects designed to investigate management and employment practice in the UK financial services sector over a period of years. Here, we look at the operation of a specific employment policy for older women workers in the context of a medium-sized life and pensions company. Just by way of methodological background to this case study, the authors and their colleagues spent several years with this company and the chief executive gave us pretty well an 'open book' to research any part of the organization including sitting in on, and recording the discussions in, board meetings. Numerous articles were published, a small selection of which are listed in the references to this chapter.

The case is useful as it enables us to explore the ways in which several factors in relation to HRM and the management of diversity cross-cut. With reference to our case illustration, these factors in the management of diversity are:

- age
- sex
- gender identity
- social class.

USING THE CASE STUDY

As you read the case study, think about how the new employment practices discussed in the text expand to other areas of working life, and consider their effects on managers and staff in organizations. As has been said in the introduction, we all have experience of organizations, whether in the form of paid work or in our relationship to organizations (for example, as students in education). You are also asked to reflect on your own experiences of being managed in organizations in the light of the topics raised, and in relation to the larger questions surrounding HRM and diversity.

OVERVIEW – ABOUT FINANCECO

This section draws on research conducted in the UK financial services sector to explore the topic of managing people. The research consisted of group and individual interviews. Research access was also given to some management meetings and all company training exercises. The main focus of attention was on the head office administration division where large numbers of clerical staff were employed: at the time of the research, 620 individuals worked in the division, predominantly in clerical posts. In addition, a small number of staff was interviewed informally outside working hours and away from the company. A total of 135 FinanceCo managers and staff took part in the research; 24 of the staff were older females, and 16 of the overall total were employed on management grades up to the level of Assistant General Manager (AGM).

Our concern is not specifically with the operation of financial services or financial markets: rather the purpose is to explore aspects of the way in which people are managed in this area of employment in the service sector. Moreover, as the service sector has grown to become the largest employer in Britain, it is therefore doubly relevant that we consider the management of people in this area of the economy. The financial services sector is, therefore, used in the chapter as a site for empirical research on management and employment practices specifically in relation to the concepts of HRM and diversity.

MANAGING PEOPLE: A CASE FROM THE FINANCIAL SERVICES INDUSTRY

Simultaneous to the growth and expansion of financial services as an employer, the language and ideas of HRM emerged. Companies sought to harness what was felt to be the creative and productive potential offered by the labour resource and find new means of managing often depleted and demoralized workforces. The spread of the idea of HRM as a solution to the problems in the sector serves in part as the background for events in the case study organization. As often large scale redundancies began in the financial services sector, the trend towards downsizing in some areas gave way to expansion and an increase in recruitment of key staffs. The recruitment of one group of these key staffs is explored in detail through the empirical material featured here.

The case study highlights the way that the company developed a policy to expand the recruitment of certain workers who were thought to be able to meet a shortage of key skills in sales and marketing. This concerns the employment of older women recruited partly in response to the tight labour market brought about by an increase in the demand for clerical workers in an expanding service sector. Moreover, their demand was sustained also by the decline in the numbers of school leavers seeking employment as a result of specific demographic factors. For many managers, the process of (often sustained) contraction and expansion is one of the most uncertain aspects of daily life in their own work, not least in terms of their own job prospects and the knowledge base drawn on to sustain managerial functions. The precariousness of being a manager signalled here alerts us to the uncertainly and insecurity of managerial work at all but the highest levels. We return to this point in the discussion in Section 2, 'Critical approaches to HRM and diversity'.

Case study 5.1
HRM and diversity in a UK financial services company

FinanceCo is an insurance company in the UK. Local school leavers have usually satisfied much of the company's need for 60 to 70 young people each year as new recruits to the existing clerical workforce of 'about three-quarters' of the whole company labour force numbering over 6500 people. A number of factors coincided to disrupt what had for the personnel officer, been a relatively straightforward task of finding an appropriate number of 'bodies' at each intake. These factors included: accelerating competition for product markets, and a demand for labour from other finance companies in the region, following government deregulation and expansion of the industry; a concern for labour productivity and efficiency in the company, linked to accelerating salary costs and high staff turnover; recent reorganization and restructuring of the company and a concern at the top of the new management structure that the company should be managed more 'professionally'. Moreover, expansion of the clerical function within FinanceCo itself, higher salaries in competitor companies in a nearby city, and demographic changes in the region, as elsewhere, had combined to produce a situation whereby the company could not fill a substantial proportion of available vacancies from its usual school leaver sources.

'THEY'RE WHAT WE CALL "BUCKET JOBS"' – THE MATURE ENTRANT SCHEME AT FINANCECO

Men and women of all ages worked in FinanceCo and in the administration division, yet women were primarily concentrated in the clerical grades with around two-thirds of all women employed in some form of clerical capacity. Low graded posts were occupied almost entirely by women with a decreasing number of females towards the top of the grading hierarchy. A few women were employed in junior supervisory positions and a smaller number still were employed on the mid-supervisory grades. In the administration division there were no female managers whilst the very few who existed throughout the company as a whole were found in personnel-related work or in the personnel division. The administration division was staffed by a mix of broadly three categories of employee: school leavers in their first job, young people in their late teens or early twenties, and a significant minority of older women, most of whom had been married for several years and had returned to work after a period of childrearing. The ages of the latter group of women returners varied from the late twenties to mid-fifties, although the average age of most was approximately 35 to 45. Length of service ranged from school leavers who had less than one year with the company to older women whose work with FinanceCo began many years previously, was interrupted for childcare and then resumed for anything between 1 to 15 or 20 years.

'Mature ladies' then, were nothing new in the administration division or in FinanceCo: what was new was the scale of their recruitment on the mature entrant scheme. The scheme appeared under that name around the time that senior managers in the company decided to address the organization's problems, and when recruitment difficulties arose.

No exact figures were available anywhere in the company as to the number of mature entrants. Throughout the period of research under discussion, HR managers could not produce or estimate a close figure, but a minimum of over 70 people had been recruited on to the scheme and supplied to the administration division alone. There was no detailed job description or job specification for those on the scheme: job content was largely at the discretion of immediate line management with a minimal degree of intervention by the HR division. Some of the women worked part-time, either permanently or during school term time only, but most mature entrants worked full-time and were permanent staff, although a handful of full-timers worked term time only. No two staff could be found who were paid at exactly the same point on the same scale: often scales overlapped and annual individual merit payments calculated on a percentage basis and added to basic pay created extra difficulties in determining who earned what. Throughout the duration of the research, no clerical worker was found who could estimate the earnings of fellow employees or give an exact figure for their own salary.

Most managers and staff promoted the image of FinanceCo as being a progressive, forward-looking employer because of its recruitment of older women, and the mature entrant scheme was often cited as indicative of the liberal pioneering anti-discriminatory practices that the company was said to adopt. Yet mature entrant labour was useful for the company in a number of ways: it cost less to hire, directly and indirectly reduced turnover, alleviated problems of tight labour supply, increased productivity, possessed tacit skills that reduced the training load, was self-disciplinary and performed a disciplinary function over the remainder of the clerical workforce.

QUESTIONS

1 Can we understand inequality at work independently of the study of gender?
2 To what extent does gender identity undermine or reflect wider social and economic inequality?
3 To what extent is the concept of intersectionality helpful in understanding the management of contemporary organizations?

Key problems

It is important that when we discuss the management of people, we consider a variety of wider, contextual factors. In this respect, we can explore two significant trends:

● the changing nature of the workplace, and
● shifting composition of the workforce.

Each of these trends is the subject of considerable debate. It depends which writer you read as to the significance attached to specific factors. Some writers suggest very little has changed over history in what remains a capitalist economic marketplace for labour, and where management always has the 'upper hand'. From this perspective, the management of people has shifted only insofar as the names of the techniques used to manage people have changed: the underlying purpose of controlling labour and exploiting it for profit is the same. We will return to this argument in more detail later.

HOW DO WE STUDY THE MANAGEMENT OF PEOPLE?

What is undisputed is that the composition of the workforce is shifting. The direction that this takes in the UK is broadly in line with other countries in Western Europe and the USA. The demographic shift of the population in the West has resulted in an increasing potential number of older workers. For many companies and organizations, this means that a non-traditional source of labour is created. Organizations now look beyond what are often 'traditional' sources of recruitment, frequently school or college leavers, and extend the scope of their recruitment to encompass mature workers.

Age

Certain high-profile cases like the UK do-it-yourself chain B&Q, and the American organization Walmart, have achieved notoriety by targeting post-retirement workers. As mentioned above, in Britain the Walmart-owned supermarket chain ASDA has sustained a deliberate practice of targeting groups of potential employees who are in the age range 40-plus to the mid-60s for their customer service posts of checkout operator and 'greeter'.

The ageing population similarly impacts elsewhere in service organizations, for example, in financial services and other retail outlets. For a variety of reasons, including improved health care and nutrition, which in turn brings about increased life expectancy, there are more 'older' workers in the marketplace for jobs. Together with the much-publicized underfunding of several pension schemes in the private and public sectors, and the collapse of some company pension schemes entirely, employees are forced to remain in work longer. They must keep working in order to maintain a level of income that will sustain them. As retirement pensions fall with declining annuity rates (the percentage pension income that can be had from the 'pot' of accumulated savings) employees are required to work further into later life.

Whereas age is one factor in the shifting composition of the workforce, a second is women's relationship to paid work. The age for marriage for women in the West has increased from an average of early to late 20s, far later than in previous generations. As many as 40 per cent of twenty-first century teenage women are predicted never to marry if present trends continue. A large proportion of births are outside marriage and an increasing number of women are likely to remain childless. It is suggested that, in combination, women's greater average life expectancy, late marriage and birth of children, or childlessness, shapes women's relationship to the workplace. Whilst it is undisputed that women form a significant part of the workforce, some of the effects of this in the contemporary context are that a proportion of, usually middle-class, women on average have higher disposable income and are in work for longer. Women's participation in the workforce can be interpreted in different ways. Given that almost half of marriages end in divorce, women's foothold in the workplace arguably enables them to retain a degree of security and financial independence.

Women workers

Women at work are, however, concentrated in segregated or separate areas of employment. One of the purposes of the case study was to explore in detail an example of an employment strategy pursued by an organization. In the case study company, women workers were confined to low pay jobs in work that was considered by the company to be an expression of the women's femininity rather than their skill as workers.

Thinkpoint 5.5

Consider jobs like nursing and secretarial work. To what degree are these jobs usually associated with women? Why do you think this is so?

Whatever weight we want to put on different factors, when we discuss the management of people it remains important to recognize the emergence of certain employment practices in relation to changes in the wider workplace. The service sector of the economy provides a useful illustration.

In Australia, Britain, Europe and the USA, the growth of that part of the economy devoted to services has been the subject of great interest and much speculation by many commentators. Glenn Morgan in Chapter 13 touches on the debate in relation to his discussion of globalization. In order to illustrate the point in this chapter on people management, we can take banks as an example of service corporations. Our relationship with the economy revolves around money (our pay, spending, credit, savings, etc.) and banks have been in the public eye following the global financial crisis of 2008, and subsequent discussion of bankers pay and rewards, particularly (high) bonuses, in a period of contrast with so-called austerity budgets in the public sector. So the illustration is also useful in that it enables us to make links across the chapter with a sphere of life that most, if not all of us at points in our lives, will have a sustained connection.

Illustration

Most of us have a bank account at some point and are at least reasonably familiar with financial services as consumers. In common with many other organizations, service corporations are increasingly concerned to control capital costs (land, buildings and equipment) and operating costs (staff) in order to maximize profit for their shareholders. Often this is in the face of what is regarded as a more competitive marketplace for their products in the wider economy. Most notably in Britain, Australia, the US and other countries in Western Europe, the deregulation or loosening of controls that restrict how we all handle our money and who can manage it for us, has meant more organizations wanting to become involved, and gaining a profit for so doing. We can now get a bank account just as easily from the supermarket at the same time as we buy groceries whether online or in person.

In pursuit of the greater efficiencies thought to improve value to shareholders and sustain or increase market share, many high street banks have adopted practices which aim to 'downsize' or 'delayer' the corporation. In practice, this has meant the redeployment or, most often, redundancies for large numbers of staff and many lower hierarchy managers. When you contact your bank by phone, you frequently find yourself connected to a call centre often outsourced to an operator in one of the developing countries and most often India. A major reason for this development is that labour in developing countries can be as little as 10 per cent of the cost in the West. The turn towards 'flat' structures (fewer layers of command) described here, is thought in many managerial and practitioner literatures to give rise to greater possibilities for adaptability and speed of response in the face of changing markets as well as to reduce costs. For some companies, this has been interpreted as needing to sell off or close down areas of their business to focus on the delivery of a narrower range of service products, or to increase flexibility and response times in servicing customers. You can look in many national newspapers and find these trends reported in connection with banking on a regular basis.

Thinkpoint 5.6

Think of the way your banking is conducted. To what extent does it illustrate the characteristics described above?

Perhaps the most significant effect of the process of change for our purposes has been the reduction in the size of the workforce in many companies. In our illustration of banking, what this means is that there are fewer jobs in banking and in the financial services sector generally than has been the case in recent history. Of course, having fewer staff impacts on the banks' customers, who have given a mixed response to the use of call centre staff. The reduction in staff also affects those who seek employment with the banks too. As an entry point for graduates, students can often find that companies are now far less willing to employ them. Financial services companies no longer offer guaranteed employment: work that could be termed 'a job for life' with the security that it brings in the form of regular income and a long-term career with prospects of promotion and a pension on retirement.

Companies trying to create flexibility in their workforce have moved towards creating pools of workers from alternative sources: casual or short-term labour drawn from, for example, students on holiday jobs, older workers, or parents of young children. Contract and part-time labour has flourished, at the same time as companies have reduced the number – and thus the cost – of full-time, permanent staff. Case Study 5.1 looks in detail at one of these strategies by an employing organization.

Exercise 5.9

How can your experience of work, in any field, be interpreted in the light of the changes described here? Discuss what similarities exist in the accounts of work experiences amongst your fellow students.

A further point concerns the jobs that remain within banking and other financial services. At one and the same time as staff numbers have been declining, there has been a marked shift towards greater responsibility and accountability for people in the posts that remain. Financial services employees have become heavily relied upon not just to operate the clerical 'paperwork' but to achieve performance targets set by their employer. Targets can include the sale of a set number of other services the organization offers, such as car or travel insurance. Further, redundancies and restructurings facilitated by waves of offshoring, online technology and smartphone banking, have been accompanied by streamlined management functions so that the number of managers deemed necessary to control the enterprise is also reduced. The reduction in what are often middle and junior managers has meant that employees are themselves required to take responsibility for achieving the targets given to them. These trends have been further intensified by the global financial crisis of 2008 for in the boom years of excessive lending and risk taking, staff numbers increased exponentially only to lead to large-scale redundancies as banks came close to collapse.

Summary – what does it all mean?

We have developed an illustration from the financial services sector to show the changing nature and shifting composition of the workforce. However, it is important to remember that what is happening in the banking and financial services sector firms is useful in illuminating wider trends. What is happening in this sector of the economy is not something peculiar to services or to finance, but is indicative of a wider shift in both the public and private sectors. We go on to discuss this point further in Section 2, 'Critical approaches to HRM and diversity'.

CRITICAL APPROACHES TO HRM AND DIVERSITY

For many people who study management and organization as university or college students, the trend towards downsizing and restructuring has become doubly problematic. Some of you may have witnessed these trends within your own university or college as a consequence of cuts in funding, in response to pressures to reduce the public deficit following the global financial crisis. At one level, your everyday experience of life in a university will be immediately affected, not just by tuition fees and the prospect of interest-bearing student loan repayments, but by the delivery of the education infrastructure system within which learning takes place. Many of the central services to students in a great many UK universities across the sector for example, are now being delivered, either in whole or part, through online technologies and with reduced face-to-face staff-student contact. In the case of library resources, the flexibility offered by online access to a full range of library and learning materials, books, journals and reports etc., is often headlined by universities seeking to attract students in what is by now a heavily competitive marketplace for student numbers. Whilst this feature may of course be welcomed by students with respect to enabling wider access to available library resources, there may be less student satisfaction as a result of reductions to (or reconfigurations of) central student services budgets and fewer face-to-face learning experiences. The increasingly dominant avatar-led guidance tutorials, or web-based features may never fully compensate for 'live' student services and learning experiences with staff on campus.

With respect to life beyond university, as well as stimulating academic interest in describing and developing ideas surrounding the causes of workplace change, this change has reduced the number of openings for graduate entry on in-house management training programmes. What this means in practical terms is that there are fewer job opportunities for graduates. So, do all graduates with the same qualification have an equally good chance of securing available jobs?

Organizations in both the public and private sectors have become increasingly selective in their choice of entrants to management or, in some instances, have completely closed off some of their entry points for new management trainees. The changing nature of the workplace directly affects students of management insofar as career and promotion opportunities for would-be managers are reduced in number. Furthermore, if we scan media advertisements for employment in managerial work, we find that the skill requirements of many organizations for managers encompass more abstract or broad-ranging talents of 'creativity' and 'vision' in addition to, and sometimes over and above, conventional technical skills of management as, for example, knowledge of accounting, finance or systems.

Thinkpoint 5.7

When you read a newspaper recruitment section, look at managerial jobs in a range of organizations. What skills are being asked of managers?

What are the implications of these changes for issues of diversity in employment? When labour markets become tight in this way, there is a strong possibility that those who are positioned outside the so-called mainstream of employment – including minorities from diverse ethnic, religious or sexual groups – will be further marginalized. There may not be open discrimination but employers can hide behind notions of merit to employ those who are similar to themselves; that is, on the whole, white, middle-class men (Collinson *et al.*, 1990). The term 'homosociality' was used by Kanter as early as 1977, before consideration of diversity had achieved prominence. In using homosociality to characterize organizations and their managements, Kanter refers to managers appointing people who appear to be 'in their own image' in other words, that recruiters are likely to favour those prospective recruits who share, for instance, their background, education and social class, as well as being the same sex. In many companies and organizations, this is referred to as 'fit' with the organization or discussed in colloquial terms as an aspect of the organization culture and what is conceptualized by managers as enabling the new recruit to succeed within it. In some industries and sectors, it has been argued that the place of 'fit' in recruitment decisions is so dominant as to have become an oblique screening process that works wholly counter to diversity initiatives. Following our earlier example of banking and financial services (and prophetically perhaps, more than a decade before the financial crisis of 2008) the work of academic geographer Linda McDowell produced a study of gender in the city and the financial services industry in London (1997). She explored the role of gender in constructing imagery of how men in banking and investment conducted themselves with respect to gendered and sexualized narratives that explicitly acted to exclude women and 'the feminine' whilst at the same time elevating or privileging men. Subsequent work (McDowell, 2010) followed the financial crash to re-examine the role of gender in risk-taking.

Elsewhere, the Financial Times (1st September, 2016) reports on a recent academic study demonstrating that appearance and presentation of oneself at interview were construed as evidence of social class acceptability and as a series of subtle and convoluted markers of 'polish' on the part of the prospective recruit. The signals that were derived from dress – interpreting a candidate's appearance as an expression of social background – were often enough to shape, if not determine, recruitment decisions. For example, the wearing of brown shoes or 'the wrong tie' was reported to be sufficient to exclude a candidate from employment when recruiting to certain areas of banking and financial services:

'An interviewee was advised after an interview that he had performed well but was not the right fit for that particular bank. He looked at me and said: 'see that tie you're wearing? It's too loud. Like, you can't wear that tie with that suit.''

Thinkpoint 5.8

S tudent recruitment: High Flyers 'Graduate Market in 2016'

'The six universities currently targeted by the largest number of leading graduate employers are Manchester, Nottingham, Warwick, Bristol, Cambridge and Oxford (see Table 5.8). These institutions have attracted the largest number of top graduate recruiters for campus fairs, recruitment presentations or other local university promotions during 2015-2016.' http://www.highfliers.co.uk/download/2016/graduate_market/GMReport16.pdf

Discussion point: How far do you think can we see homosociality operating in graduate recruitment? How far do you think discriminatory management and organizational practices continue in graduate recruitment, despite attempts at diversity initiatives?

Exercise 5.10

S o how does this relate to students? Aside from those who seek banking and finance as a career of course, many graduates look for their first substantive post within a competitive graduate labour market via the university they attended. Campus fairs, recruitment presentations or other regional university promotions can be important since they attract graduate recruiters for whom the 'fit' of a potential recruit may be a consideration. In contrast to dress code as a proxy for social class acceptability, or perhaps along with it, how does a student's choice of university affect their recruitment prospects? In the competitive marketplace for students and for courses, how might your selection of the university where you are obtaining your degree affect your chances of employment from a 'top' graduate recruiter?

Whilst there have clearly been changes in employment and the nature of the workforce, the shift in Western economies toward service industries has been of some benefit to women and older workers by virtue of what is seen as their greater adaptability and flexibility – for example, their need to work part-time around other responsibilities and their greater preparedness to fill temporary jobs as a consequence. It remains to be seen whether, in the present period of economic downturn and its outcrop of redundancies, downsizing and delayering, women workers will continue to bear the brunt of some of these changes in, for example, the public sector where they have been hitherto been comparatively numerous. Recent research (Conley and Page, 2016) has documented the effects of the 2010 UK coalition government's attachment to austerity budgets and a cuts agenda which has led to a significant reduction in the numbers of staff in public sector employment, disproportionately affecting women workers.

The changing nature of business

The broad sweep of writing on organizations of the last 20 or 30 years has documented, and debated, diverse changes in the political context of Western democracies towards a neo-liberal economic and political faith in 'free' markets. Although these exploded in the wake of the global financial crisis of 2008, faith in free markets has far from been abandoned. The period around the 1980s and 1990s marked something of a watershed. Organizations began to be regarded as increasingly uncompetitive in relation to a growing, and more globalized, marketplace for goods and services. Partly in response to the perceived inadequacies of production, governments sought to deregulate labour markets.

Critical HRM

Critics of HRM have suggested that it amounts to little more than empty rhetoric or is simply a reflection of broader neo-liberal movements in Western economies towards free market and managerialist solutions to human resource problems. Legge is so sceptical of HRM as to suggest that it could be described as 'macho-management dressed up as benevolent paternalism' (Legge, 1995, p. 48 quoted in Keenoy, 1997, p. 826) Keenoy's (1997) extended review of Storey's edited book *HRM: A Critical Text,* provides interesting material for challenging Storey's claim to offer 'by far the most authoritative source available' with regard to critical HRM (Storey, 1995, p. xi). Keenoy acknowledges that some chapters make a solid contribution to a critical view of HRM but contends that, overall, the text is neither critical nor free of managerial prescriptions and the occasional unreflective hyperbole. We agree that there is a paucity of analytical critique and drive from the editorial position, resulting in the absence of a central critical argument or theme running through the book.

Another reflection of this comparatively conservative ethos is an edited book on HRM (Collings and Wood, 2009) in which, despite claiming to be offering a critical approach, its critical agenda rarely extends beyond a support for stakeholder theory as it is argued that management should take a range of conflicting interests – employees, suppliers, customers, environmental groups, government as well as shareholders – into account when making decisions. This conforms to what has been seen as a pluralist rather than a unitary approach where the former has been exposed as only slightly different from the latter in that it serves to legitimize the unequal relationship between labour and capital (Fox, 1973).

One of the problems of a pluralist perspective is that it presumes management can act as an independent referee arbitrating between the diverse and conflicting interests (Knights, 2008, p. 541). This overlooks how management's priorities tend to be aligned fairly closely to shareholders' concern with increasing profits, or at least with the pursuit of profitable growth. The critical credentials of Collings and Wood (2009) would seem limited to a concern for HRM to adopt a more pluralist view and to accommodate industrial relations issues in ways that were being criticized as highly conservative 40 years ago. Their focus primarily on classification and typologies and the absence of any discussion of diversity and gender (women are mentioned only occasionally) hardly supports their claim to offer a critical approach.

That said, it is almost contradictory to link HRM with critical approaches. Critical studies are likely to approach HR only indirectly as a focus of critical studies tends to be upon gender or feminist analysis, diversity more generally or organization theory. HRM in theory and in practice tends to take for granted the idea that managing people is principally about securing more effort and productivity so as to increase the efficiency or profitability of the organization. Although they do not necessarily discount the importance of efficiency in public organizations and profitability in private organizations, critical perspectives challenge their relentless single-minded pursuit of these aims, and suggest that issues of inequality, discrimination, power and privilege need to be given equal attention in relation to people at work.

Thinkpoint 5.9

Some have attributed the 2008 global financial crisis to this preoccupation with profit regardless of benefits to society. Do you think a broader view of the organization in society may have prevented the collapse of major financial institutions?

As Marx (1887/1976) made clear, the contract of labour is comparatively vague. All that it specifies is the potential to make labour available between certain hours of work, not the actual productive effort. The labour contract sets out what *should* happen by way of employees' effort but it cannot determine what actually happens – that is, whether employees actually work in the way that managers want them to, or to what extent labour works with the same productive goals that managers intend (see also Chapter 7). In this respect, managers are always at the mercy of their own lack of knowledge as to the 'perfect' solution to the conundrum of how to control employees. Indeed, it has been argued that managers can never develop knowledge of a genuinely predictive nature (McIntyre, 1984/2003) and are therefore always facing situations of uncertainty beyond their control. So, do managers really know what they are doing after all? Do the media images of managerial work portrayed in popular culture really match the reality of being a manager? When speaking to managers, they will often declare that it is not the technical aspects of their jobs but the human dimension that is so taxing. To transform labour power into outputs – to get people to do what you want them to do, that is – requires various managerial techniques, and of course, managers to apply them. Although this is the task of line management, HRM is involved in organizing work in such a way as to narrow the gap between managers and workers, or rather, the gap between the potential and the actual performance of employees. In other words, HRM offers the potential to make management more effective in rendering employees controllable.

Case study 5.2
Managing the shop floor

We turn now to an ethnographic study of a workplace culture where gender is at work. In *Managing the Shopfloor*, Collinson (1992) develops an illuminating analysis of power and identity through his study of workplace culture in a motor manufacturing corporation. This study departs radically from the mainstream's concern with performance and profit. Nonetheless, while focusing primarily on cultural issues of masculine identity, power and inequality, it has relevance for the performative aspects of organization. At the time of the research, the organization had just been taken over by a US international corporation and the new management had become persuaded of the importance of a humanized management style and structure, as advocated by the human relations school of organization (see Chapter 11), as a means of raising productivity.

Open and friendly management was the new style, so that managers could be spoken to on first name terms regardless of hierarchical position. 'Call me Barney' and 'my door is always open' was the mantra of the new managing director from the USA. But this did not go down well with the manual workers who quickly caricatured the message as 'bullshit from Barney'. The 'softer' HRM approach was not something they respected because they were not steeped in a (middle class) culture of assumed consensus and superficial humanism, and therefore preferred the straightforward and 'down to earth' policies of a 'harder', 'no nonsense' management system. That 'harder' approach chimed with their masculine self-images (i.e., identities) and associated view of their work as 'tough', physical, material and predictable.

The more 'open', 'softer' and symbolic aspects of the new managerial culture were regarded as effeminate. Such 'niceties' belonged in office culture where predominantly 'pen pushing' women went around in circles, as the men saw it, not contributing anything to the actual production of physical output. The shop floor men were more respectful of the 'hard' figure work performed by accountants, even when their accounts were the basis for a redundancy programme. The shop floor seemed to identify with figures in a manner that was similar to their identification with physical and material reality; numbers were perhaps more 'real' because of their association with mathematics and the natural sciences. Masculine identity could be reinforced by the certainty of physical and mathematical reality but its reproduction depended on its ability to undermine that which it is not – effeminate symbolic reality.

The irony, of course, is that, in accepting the accounting numbers, these workers participated in their own labour demise (i.e., redundancy), thus removing one of the principal sources of masculine identity – physical work and 'breadwinner' wages. We cannot ascertain the extent to which these shop floor workers saw redundancy pay and escape from work as adequate compensation for the loss of employment. There is little doubt that their experience of inequality and insecurity makes such payouts seem large *but,* when spread over the period that they and their dependents might suffer unemployment, they are pitifully small.

A classical approach to management style might, perhaps, have been the most effective for this factory where, on the shop floor at least, there was little appetite for a more 'flexible', 'humanized' or 'soft' HRM approach. This was not due to some universal sense of a 'one best way' (Taylor, 1911) or because it necessarily correlated with effective performance for a mass assembly line production system (Woodward, 1958). Rather, its appropriateness is in relation to its fit with the shop floor culture where workers appeared to be preoccupied with sustaining or embellishing their masculine identities. What remains in doubt, of course, is whether this classical approach would have been compatible with the ideology of the company or indeed with the demands of a changing product market in which flexibility of response through close co-operation, relying upon 'soft' skills, between managers and workers was becoming of increasing importance. There is also the issue of whether 'indulging' the macho culture of the shop floor was sustainable in terms of employment law and what is acceptable to customs and shareholders.

What Collinson's study shows is not dissimilar to Paul Willis's (1977) research on working-class kids who were found to distance themselves from education because it failed to support their masculine identities. Ending up with no qualifications and few aspirations, these kids were found to reproduce the conditions of their own deprivation as unskilled workers. Partly because it helped reinforce their masculine identities, Collinson's shop floor workers accepted the 'hard' figures of the accountants as if they could not be challenged. In doing so, they participated in their own eventual redundancy, which is not to say that challenging the figures would have resulted in them keeping their jobs. However, if the men had questioned the figures, the union would not have been placed in such a weak position to fight the redundancy. In short, it can be argued that the masculine identities of these shop floor workers contributed significantly to the legitimacy of power-knowledge relations (accounting and management) that reproduced the conditions of their own inequality and loss of economic freedom that, ironically, then undermined the sense of security that they sought to defend.

Exercise 5.11

The UK labour market is among the most segregated in Europe: Scott (1994) found that 66 per cent of men worked exclusively or mainly with other men, and 54 per cent of women worked exclusively or mainly with women. Half of women in employment are in just three occupational groups: clerical and secretarial, personal and protective services, and sales, as compared to about one-fifth of men. On the other hand, women are very under-represented in areas such as engineering and the sciences (Knights and Richards, 2003).

Provide a brief explanation of this segregation from your own point of view. Compare your account with those of other students carrying out the same exercise. Are there any patterns in the explanations, particularly in relation to the gender of the student providing the explanation?

Thinkpoint 5.10

C an you think of anything in your experience that reflects the view of masculinity expressed in this brief case study?

Masculine discourses are extremely dominant in a majority of organizations and while humorous (see Cartoon 5.1 below), the cartoon captures the way in which men often behave and think such that discrimination is difficult to eradicate.

In a way that parallels the observations in the case study, critics of 'human relations' have argued that its emphasis on co-operation is overly optimistic. The idea of co-operation glosses over deep-seated differences of power and inequality, and that improving labour prospects and influence rests 'not on spontaneous co-operation but upon the legitimization of industrial conflict through collective bargaining and strikes' (Perrow, 1972, p. 72).

Townley (1993; 1994) has developed the insights about power and knowledge of Michel Foucault to provide a radical interpretation of HRM. She argues that the discipline of HRM is largely informed by functionalism or systems theory (see Chapter 7). By this she means that the primary concern is to identify and give 'scientific' credibility and legitimacy to those features of an organization or society that may be seen to facilitate its smooth functioning and orderly stability. As we have argued, the languages and practices of HRM are preoccupied with HRM as a tool of managerial efficiency and effectiveness. In short, mainstream HRM discourse aims to help managers reproduce or transform the social arrangements already in place within the organization of labour. Its intent is to contribute significantly and more effectively to the organization's goals, as defined by managers, rather than lower hierarchy employees. It is important to note here that these goals are not confined to the private sector in the form of, for example, profit. HRM can be seen as equally appealing to managers in the public services where considerations of efficiency are expressed in forms other than profit, such as cost-effectiveness or value for money. Two significant questions underpin Townley's analysis in *Reframing HRM*. First, what gives the group of practices commonly known as HRM their coherence? Second, how can the critical academic study of HRM help people at work and not just the managers? In this regard, Townley is unusual amongst writers in that her analysis is explicitly aimed at providing a politics of change at the level of the workplace.

Townley's use of Foucault centres on how his analysis of the operation of localized mechanisms and practices of power can reveal aspects of the management of the workplace under HRM that would otherwise remain hidden. Following this line of argument, *Reframing HRM* starts with the task of first revealing, and then developing, a critical analysis of the means by which the body of techniques, procedures and knowledges commonly known under the umbrella term HRM constitutes a nexus of disciplinary practices. In other words, HRM operates as a point of connection for a number of disciplinary practices that ensure control over the workforce by 'transforming individuals into subjects that secure the sense they have of themselves, their identity and meaning through engaging in the practices' that the power of HRM invokes (Knights, 2006, p. 732). We should therefore be mindful of the effects of HRM, as well as being sceptical of its intentions. For Townley, HRM represents a number of mechanisms (such as job analysis, performance appraisal, etc.) that have the effect of disciplining employees. HRM is to be understood as much more than a package of 'neutral' techniques for improving the management of people and organization. Instead, HRM is understood as an exercise of power over those who are subjected to it.

The emphasis is on how HRM techniques – job appraisal and evaluation, recruitment, promotion, teamworking – 'fix' individual employees in time and space, thus transforming them into manageable objects of the power-knowledge that constitutes HRM as a practice. HRM discourse provides a rational means of classifying, grading, measuring, ordering and regulating the population of employees so that they are within the systematic disciplinary and controlling gaze of HRM (Townley, 1993).

Exercise 5.12

List the ways in which you are classified, graded, measured, ordered and regulated in education. Does this list surprise you?

It is not so surprising that HRM can be seductive to managers. Its appeal, in part at least, lies in the possibility of making managers' own knowledge more secure. HRM consists of a series of practices that promise to transform organizations and their members into objects of calculable knowledge. It is this process that renders employees more amenable to being managed. As Townley (1993, p. 223) puts it, HRM helps to organize 'labour into a productive force'.

At one and the same time, the techniques of HRM classify and order labour. Moreover, by classifying and ordering labour, the techniques also individualize employees so that they are less likely to collaborate collectively against managerial control and the ways that they are governed. What is meant here is that employees become far less likely to imagine themselves as part of a collective ('the workforce') as a base for the organization of labour in various forms, such as unions. It is by individualizing employees that the practices of HRM make more likely employees' internalization of managerially defined goals than the goals of any potential collective resistance or opposition. For managers this proposition is highly attractive as it offers the potential to displace more or less explicit forms of non-co-operation and resistance – strikes and other forms of collective action – that repeatedly have proved to be problematic for the day-to-day activity of managing. This analysis of the power-effects of HRM also provides the basis for reorienting contemporary, historical and comparative analyses of HRM.

Processes of individualization have had the effect of transforming workers into subjects whose behaviour can be analyzed, documented and recorded and thereby readily controlled by management. Because employees are aware that the processes and practices of their labour are under the direct surveillance of management, they become self-disciplined thus facilitating an 'economy of power' where management need only exercise power on rare occasions. As an approach, this allows HRM to be understood as a system of knowledge and a mode of power that not only provides details at the localized level in the day-to-day management of employees but also connects these to a larger framework *of power relations* within the organization and the wider society.

Historically, HRM has gone through a number of changes the first of which was its evolution out of personnel management, as discussed earlier. In the 1980s along with general trends in business and organization, the HRM function was distributed down the line so that department or divisional managers were more directly responsible for recruitment, promotion, training and career development (Cornelius, 2001). HR would then just provide an advisory role and training for line managers especially on legally sensitive issues related, for example, to equal opportunity, human rights or grievance procedures. It may seem that this development rendered HR more critical of line management but it was much more a matter of protecting members of the organization from acting illegally – for example, by producing documentation and following procedures that could provide the basis of a defence if an organizational action led to a prosecution. It was not necessarily about ensuring that the company complied with the law so much as generating procedural evidence that ticked the appropriate boxes and so provided the appearance of doing so. It is often the case that corporations with well-publicized and sophisticated equal opportunity policies and procedures, are in practice inferior as equal opportunity employers to companies that lack this formal compliance, but are substantively in closer touch with the concerns of women or minorities (Hoque and Noon, 1999).

HRM varies across national and cultural boundaries. Managing the human resource in the USA is seen predominantly as a matter of motivating the individual, whereas in Europe there is a greater history of collective management through trade union negotiations (Guest, 1990). This reflects a significant divergence of respective 'business systems' between the USA where capital is predominant and contracts of employment are more readily terminated, than in

Europe where there is more protection by legislation (Leidner, 2002). There have also been criticisms of the view that there is some kind of homogeneity within national cultures (Jack and Lorbiecki, 2007, p. S82). Indeed, diversity itself places in question the assumption of homogeneity of national cultures, the argument being that there are numerous 'intranational workplace "differences" with respect to gender, race, ethnicity, age, values, experiences and social class' (ibid.).

The way that we are managed is clearly not 'naturally' occurring, although we may have grown to think of it as in some way inevitable. Management practices involve socially embedded *constructions* (e.g., about the nature and value of 'human resources') that develop over time. Such constructions are dependent upon prevailing ideas about people, human nature and the ways that knowledge about people can be used to manage them. This understanding invites us to consider the management of people as grounded not in a supposedly objective 'science' but in an ever-shifting range of different cultural and political ideas and opinions from various groups. Both historically and in the context of contemporary organizations, these groups have included for example, academics, practitioner managers, so-called 'guru' writers and management consultants. What is questionable, however, is the diversity of their membership, which has tended to be male, white and highly educated, and 'middle class'.

It has been argued that HRM reflects a cultural change in thinking about managing people. It extends back to human relation theorists (see Chapters 2 and 8) and then expanded dramatically in response to cultural, economic and political crises in the 1970s and 1980s (Costea, 2010). In very broad outline, it was the energy crisis of the 1970s that precipitated an extended period of 'stagflation' – a stagnant economy with 'soaring prices, high unemployment and low economic growth' (The Energy Crisis, 1973–2000) – in many advanced economies. In some of these economies, there was increased industrial conflict, which eventually produced a shift from Keynsianism towards a stronger reliance upon neo-liberal 'free markets' and economic deregulation as a means of reducing deficits and stimulating growth. Trades unions were weakened by successive waves of legislation and by mounting unemployment arising from policies of de-industrialization. This process involved the withdrawal of state subsidies to manufacturing that was suffering competition from low wage developing economies but the result was the displacement of manufacturing by services. Of crucial importance, accompanying these shifts in political and economic ideology, was a transformation of ideas about work and employment. It was felt that traditional approaches, which relied heavily on bureaucratic labour contracts, close supervision and/or collective negotiations with employees, were responsible for competitive failure and that an alternative – more market-based and flexible – approach was necessary to beat stagflation.

It was not only the economy that was a target of deregulation but also the subject or employee. Their labour power could no longer be taken for granted as a simple exchange of effort for reward or productive output for income. New ways of motivating workers were required. Ways had to be found for subjectively engaging the worker – reinvented as the employee – *in the activity of work*. And this was to be accomplished through programmes of personal development, employee participation, quality, teamworking and self-management. A new emphasis on commitment at work, as a kind of group or individual subjective self-discipline, was commended as greater emphasis was placed on the 'attributes of human subjectivity' (Costea, 2010, p. 6). This meant developing the potential of the individual employee, securing their subjective identification and engagement with the organization (their commitment), and generating the conditions of self-affirmation where their sense of personal well-being is secured. The value of this approach was justified by reference to the Japanese 'miracle' where, at least in the primary sector, employees were seen to be strongly committed to quality and continuous improvement but also saw their organization as central to their sense of self (Vogel, 1979).[2] What tended to be conveniently overlooked was the distinctive Japanese tradition, exemplified in guaranteed lifetime employment (for those in the primary economy) that had few parallels in Western workplaces. Unabashed, advocates of HRM believed that cultures could be designed that would emulate Japanese practice (a movement that was called **Japanization**) and thereby secure an equivalent level of employee commitment.

Japanization Process of adopting practices associated with Japan. In particular, it refers to the adoption in the West of certain production practices such as team meetings based on quality improvements.

Thinkpoint 5.11

Market-based approaches to HRM rely on the price mechanism (wages) in relation to supply and demand of labour, whereas Japanization was about how employees might more closely identify with their organization and then be more productive. In what ways are these two approaches compatible or incompatible with one another?

Critical diversity perspectives

It is perhaps surprising to find that much of the diversity literature is as conservative and managerialist as HRM. It is generally concerned with diversity as a problem to be managed, and thereby reduce if not eliminate the risk of disharmony and instability at work. The appeal of diversity for managers, then, lies in substantial part in its promise to provide a means of more readily managing, reducing the tensions that arise in the workplace, and achieving organizational goals. Diversity is also attractive as a way of alleviating some of the insecurities of managers who are unsure of how to manage staff. Arising out of a reaction against reverse discrimination and statutory quotas, diversity management presents a more positive approach, which HR managers can 'sell' more readily to their sceptical managerial colleagues.

Promoting equal opportunity and diversity at work can be seen to contribute to organizational goals and performance because employees from a multiplicity of diverse backgrounds, cultures and range of life experiences can often better understand the diverse customer base in the marketplace. As we noted earlier, this advantage provided an even stronger 'business case' for promoting equal opportunity and diversity than the negative ones of legal compliance and avoiding disharmony and disruption. Consider the following examples drawn from mainstream managerial practice in large commercial organizations where organizational goals and performance clearly dominate:

Example 1: Ernst & Young

Diversity and inclusiveness is key to the culture of Ernst & Young. It enables our people, our clients and our wider communities to achieve their potential and make a difference, wherever they come from and whatever their characteristics. A sustainable, inclusive culture helps enable us to deliver a high quality service to our clients, create competitive advantage and drive market leadership. [...] We believe that it is the responsibility of all employers to recognize that the traditional models of work have changed. In order to recruit and retain the best people, working practices need to be adapted according to the needs of a twenty-first century workforce. (www.ey.com)

Example 2: American Express

Creating an environment that enables American Express to be inclusive, both internally and externally is a business imperative. To get there, we champion our diverse talent efforts and support the business lines to understand and engage the broadest base of current and potential employees and customers worldwide. (*Kerrie Peraino, Chief Diversity Officer.* www.AmericanExpress.com)

Example 3: Deutsche Bank– 'our commitment to diversity'

We believe that diverse teams are smart teams; that success comes from many perspectives and that diversity is vital to delivering innovative solutions for our clients. Diversity matters to us because our employees perform at their best when they are in an inspiring and inclusive environment and this enables us to provide outstanding solutions for our clients. By recognizing and respecting individuality we create a diverse and inclusive work environment that allows us to:

1 Recruit and retain the best talent from a variety of backgrounds and perspectives which reflect the growing diversity of the places where we do business and the clients that we serve.

2 Deliver innovative and creative solutions to our clients. A diverse workforce stimulates innovation by promoting creative thinking, inspiring new ideas from different perspectives and motivating employees to perform to the best of their ability.

3 Succeed in a globally integrated and competitive market. Our refined cultural understanding allows us to reach a wider spectrum of clients and diverse segments of the market which is essential to realize our vision and provide strong value to our shareholders. (www.db.com)

From a more critical perspective, however, the very perception of 'diversity as a problem' is itself problematic. Indeed, it has been suggested that 'the fact of the debate may be more of a problem than diversity itself. In other words, a major part of the problem consists precisely in viewing diversity as a problem' ... and this is ... 'what the "tolerant majority" tends to share with the extreme right' (Blommaert and Verschueren, 1998, p. 3). This leads us to ask whether many efforts to 'manage diversity' are more about sustaining divisions than limiting their damaging consequences. If this question is answered in the affirmative, it suggests that *managers themselves reproduce and sustain relations of power and inequality.* By this we mean that managers are active in (re)producing the conditions within which, despite ostensibly having a commitment to diversity at work, inequality continues to be maintained. Managers are thus part of the problem of (a lack of) diversity in the workplace. There are parallels here between our discussion of the problems with the 'turn to diversity' and the continued maintenance and production of what Acker refers to as inequality regimes. As she puts it:

All organizations have inequality regimes, defined as loosely interrelated practices, processes, actions and meanings that result in and maintain class, gender and racial inequalities within particular organizations. (Acker, 2006, p. 443)

Understood in this light, diversity management is an outcome of an attachment by managers to ideas and ideals of the diverse workforce for its commercial value – for example, for its capacity to mirror or target a particular customer base. In this process, inequalities within organizations are effectively maintained as diversity is celebrated. From this critical perspective, we are able to see managers not as neutral arbiters or brokers who mediate between the demands of complex organizations in which they are employed, the markets in which they operate and the available labour supply or between different stakeholders. Rather, a critical perspective regards managers as active agents in the process of sustaining social divisions in the name of equality of opportunity. This is to problematize the role of managers in the management of diversity and implicate them, as well as their managerial discourses and practices, in sustaining the very divisions they purport to manage or reconcile.

The case of disability at work

In 2009, the Guardian newspaper reported the case of a West London woman student who had been working part-time in a branch of the clothing retailer Abercrombie & Fitch. The student had been born without a left forearm and had worn a prosthetic arm since infancy. Her wearing of a cardigan to cover the connection between her upper arm and the prosthetic device was deemed by her manager to be in contravention of the firms' 'look policy', that is, not consistent with the all-American natural/outdoor style that the company aims to portray. Her appearance was considered to be so at odds with the brand image of the organization that the student was asked to work away from customer-facing responsibilities on the shopfloor and was allegedly sent on duties in the stockroom instead.

Our concern in relating this vignette lies less in deciding whether the employer was guilty of discrimination, but with the image of the ideal worker that the case illuminates and the relationships of power with respect to disability, in which the student was embedded. The effect of disability on workplace outcomes differs between groups, such as by gender and race (Danieli and Wheeler, 2006) and it is, important to note the discussion of intersectionality elsewhere in this chapter, and how experiences of disability in relation to other aspects of identity affect the experience of work and employment.

Since the Equality Act 2010 brought together existing pieces of legislation into a more coherent whole, disability has occupied the attention of managers to a greater extent than other forms of 'difference'. For the purposes of legislation, broadly, someone may have a disability if he or she has 'a physical or mental impairment and the impairment has a substantial and long-term adverse effect on his or her ability to carry out normal day-to-day activities'. This means that the person must have an impairment that is either physical or mental, the impairment must have adverse effects, which are substantial, the substantial adverse effects must be long-term; and the long-term substantial adverse effects must be effects on normal day-to-day activities. As such, disability is a 'protected characteristic' under the Act (2010, Code of Practice). Organizations are required to make 'reasonable adjustments' so that all their members can fully participate. The need to make reasonable adjustments as defined by the Equality Act means that it is unlawful to discriminate against disabled people by failing to make these adjustments. In the case of universities as organizations, if disabled students face barriers to using university services because of their disability, the university may be guilty of discrimination by failing to provide reasonable adjustments, as determined by an assessment of the student's needs within the university. Further, students should not face 'unreasonable difficulty' in using services, in terms not just of physical barriers but also the time, inconvenience, effort, discomfort, anxiety and loss of dignity entailed in accessing services. The duty of making reasonable adjustments exists for a range of conditions such as physical and mobility difficulties, hearing and visual impairment, learning difficulties, as well as medical conditions and mental health problems. Whilst what constitutes reasonable is not fully defined, any adjustment can only be determined to be reasonable (or not) in relation to specific circumstances so there appears to be something of a grey area in defining exactly what might be reasonable, although several principles shape the definition of whether an adjustment is reasonable, based on effectiveness, how practical or costly the adjustment might be and whether there is assistance available, for example.

The study of disability, its experiences and effects on life chances and employment prospects has not just occupied legislators of course. Policy makers, practitioners, academics and theorists, as well as business and industry, have all occupied different positions with respect to disability. Whatever the range of contributions to the debate, Williams and Mavin (2012) suggest that "disability remains inadequately theorized as a constructed difference" (p. 159). By this the authors refer to the socially constituted understandings and expression of how difference is produced and maintained in our society: in short, how difference comes to be seen as such. How is it that we draw attention to certain features of being human, over and above others? How do we reproduce the idea of disability as disabling to the life chances and work experience of those employees categorized as disabled? A useful contribution and interrogation of disability can be developed from the work of Foucault. We drew on Foucault in the discussion of Townley's work on HRM but his theory has perhaps more immediate application and explanatory potential with respect to disability and the body. For Foucault's contribution lies in enabling us to examine the ways in which the body, and its categorization as 'disabled', is implicated in the relations of power that maintain difference. Managers, and the technologies that they employ in the name of managing, are key actors in the construction of difference. From this perspective, managers are active in the production of a division between the able-bodied and the disabled worker. The store manager who allegedly discriminated against a student with a prosthetic forearm by asking her to work 'behind the scenes' in service work, both mobilized and sustained a concept of disability as otherness that had the effect of reproducing the students' disability. It was the manager's action that led to the student being treated differently and being seen as different. The manager also drew upon an explicitly western, Euro/American understanding of corporeal 'appeal' developed from the company's desire to project a particular brand identity. In so doing, the company sought to project brand image through the corporeality of its employees – *at the level of the body* as a site of power. In this respect, the body is implicated in relations of power and does not exist prior to those relationships within which it is constituted. The organization sought to make real its brand image, *through the body of the worker*.

Different groups have sought to explore disability, and in so doing, have mobilized different concepts of power and politics. The disabled persons 'movement' over the last few decades from the 1970s onwards has sought to politicize disability and its definitions as part of a larger project of action for change and resistance. Drawing on a critical discussion of a *social model* of disability, writers examined the ways in which disabled people became disabled not by their impairment but by the social oppression they experience as a result of it. From this perspective, those who are physically or mentally impaired are categorized as disabled through their participation in, or exclusion from, society and this label affects all their relations with others. As Oliver (1996) expresses it:

> Disability is something imposed on top of our impairments by the way we are unnecessarily isolated and excluded from full participation in society. Disabled people are therefore an oppressed group in society. To understand this it is necessary to grasp the distinction between the physical impairment and the social situation, called 'disability', of people with such impairment." (Oliver, 1996, 22).

The social model of disability sits in contrast to the *medical model* of disability that had come to dominate much thinking and practice. The medical model of disability conceives of the disabled person as 'lacking' and in need of cure or 'treatment' and so it is perhaps not surprising that the social model of disability found favour amongst those who had hitherto found themselves being defined as, and by, disability. That the social model offered a possibility for social change that the medical model did not – identifying and thence dismantling the barriers to people with impairments – created the conditions under which disability could be tackled and barriers removed. The perceived potency and immediate political appeal of this model led to pressure to remove barriers so as to create a 'level playing field', not least through legislation and policy change. Yet writers such as Shakespeare and Watson (2002), whilst acknowledging their own active support for an 'identity politics' offered by the social model, are critical of the separation between the medical and social models. They contend that the social model side-stepped the physical and material consequence of impairment and was thus counterproductive since it left behind the real lived experience of the impaired body. Whilst recognizing the historical conditions under which the social model achieved such prominence, gave voice to disabled people, and facilitated a political movement – it also recognized the limitations of displacing medical accounts of impairment with wholly social interpretations of processes of exclusion, discrimination and their development.

Their contribution lies perhaps in calling our attention to the 'messy reality' of bodies and the way that bodies have been, and continue to be represented, in all forms of debate, even when such debate aims to support people with disabilities. As an example of the importance of this injunction, the question as to how (disabled) bodies are included and represented, and with what consequences, has recently found further problematic expression. The 2016 Paralympic games in Brazil drew world attention to the often extraordinary capabilities of sports people. What also drew attention, although of a far less supportive persuasion, was a series of media images used by Brazilian Vogue for their Paralympic publicity campaign (BBC, 26th August, 2016) depicting not Paralympic athletes but 'attractive' models posing as Olympic athletes and whose physical disability, amputation or prosthetic was the result of computer Photoshopping. The ideal in contemporary culture of the elite sportsperson sits at odds with the reality of the bodies of disabled athletes but perhaps, more importantly, of the majority of those suffering from some kind of impairment.

Even though Foucault does not explicitly theorize disability as such, his deployment of the concept of 'biopower' (1982) is useful in advancing the study of diversity as it relates to disability. A strength of Foucault's work lies in his conceptualization of power. It is important to note that Foucault's understanding is that power is positive - for it creates possibilities - not that power is repressive. Dominant in much disability studies debates discussed above, a *juridical* concept of power imagines that the individual possesses power, that power is a commodity, as it were. It is this idea of juridical power that underpins the idea of barrier removal through policy change and in legislation to reduce or dismantle the obstacles to equality that disability creates. By removing barriers, so the argument goes, we can 'give power' to disabled people. By contrast, Foucault's idea is not in seeking to define power – for him, this would be the wrong question – but in seeing how power is exercised and by what means. Here, power is seen not as the exclusive prerogative of a minority and something that is done *to* the majority but as more broadly distributed and *enabling* people more generally to act as they would wish. The conception of disability as a 'handicap' can be seen to be underpinned by the medicalized model, that can be traced to earlier periods in history where knowledge about bodies, demographics, fertility rates, births and deaths began to be used as means and measures of governing populations through what is called bipower (Foucault, 2008). At one and the same time, power and knowledge was used as a basis for 'educating' the public and medicalizing the population in ways that would lead to its own self-management and self-surveillance. In this regard you may want to consider how social media has resulted in an extension of this self-surveillance beyond the sphere of merely government intervention. This categorizing, classifying and sorting process that Foucault identifies enables us to see how the very construct we call 'disability' came about: Foucault identifies the emergence of 'the problem' of bodies and how 'the body' came to be regarded as an object to be managed and controlled.

Viewed this way, the management of diversity in organizations with respect to disability can be seen as less to do with social justice and inclusion than with regulating the body as an object to be managed and controlled. Clearly, whilst central governments in developed economies drive forward austerity budgets, reconfigure services and reduce or remove some of the welfare benefits supporting people with disabilities amongst others, there remains an immediate imperative for a greater degree of financial self-sufficiency on the part of disabled people who may hitherto in many cases, have been economically far less active. The 'business case' for diversity can thus be seen as a response by management to the emergence of this new and growing section of the labour force. The business case is at the same time, an expression of the (managerial) idea that people are economic units of production, that organizations are best managed and their goals more readily achieved by the use of methods that will harness, under the guise of 'inclusion', the productive advantage that can be had by employing a hitherto largely untapped group of workers. Organizations respond to the legal requirement to create, through for example mechanisms such as reasonable adjustments, the conditions under which the disabled employee can more fully participate in work: the disabled worker is included, but not under conditions of her or his own choosing. Indeed, there are studies in Sweden that identify previously marginalized groups of mentally or physically impaired people as particularly well suited to certain forms of highly routinized work and who actually perform more effectively than the non-impaired (Maravelias, 2016). In this way their productive contribution well exceeds their welfare cost.

Practitioner studies of diversity management are geared towards enhancing the effectiveness of managerial practice, as defined by managers. At the heart of a critical approach to analyzing management and organization, by contrast, is a focus on themes of power, control and inequality. Exploring 'diversity' provides a way of illuminating and problematizing the social relations through which processes of management are accomplished. Critical perspectives examine exercises of power that underpin these processes. In sum, instead of expanding the toolkit of managers or would-be managers, critical approaches to diversity look at 'what gets done in the name of managing' and seek to transform the processes that further disadvantage those already disadvantaged.

Intersectionality

Since the 1990s theories and methodologies of intersectionality have developed within feminism and have increasingly gained support among students of diversity (Acker, 2006). Although heavily critical of more mainstream perspectives, intersectional approaches are not just of theoretical interest. They also have policy implications and have had an impact on the equal opportunity and diversity programmes of European Union (EU) legislators (Bagilhole, 2009). As indicated in Section 1, 'Mainstream approaches to HRM and diversity', intersectionality is concerned with the multiplicity of identities that are held simultaneously and how group-based disadvantages are not merely additive but also constitutive of one another. That is to say, the nature of disadvantage is qualitatively different as a result of the interaction of its varied elements (e.g., age, class, ethnicity, gender, physical or mental impairment, or religion). So, for example, a gay Muslim woman experiences disadvantage in a way that is greater than the sum of the parts of this disadvantage.

Although the stereotyping of groups that are disadvantaged sees only homogeneity, there are numerous differences that merit closer attention in diversity research. Bagilhole (2009) uses intersectionality as a theme for exploring equal opportunities and diversity in chapters on statistical evidence of disadvantage, on theories that help to elucidate the adoption of equal opportunity and diversity, particularly by the EU, as a policymaking tool and methodology for generating social justice. It is clear that through notions of intersectionality, diversity has become more sophisticated theoretically as well as having certain practical and policy implications. It readily builds on concepts of identity, which although of tremendous importance to us all (Knights and Willmott, 1999; Collinson, 2003) have been seldom analyzed by means of intersectionality. We now return to our own case study, introduced in Section 1 above since this allows us to develop a critical approach to diversity in relation to a specific illustration from business and industry.

Case study 5.3
Analyzing the themes

We can now revisit some of the ideas connected to diversity and its management described in Case Study 5.1. In doing so, we consider whether Acker's concept of inequality regimes is perhaps a better descriptor of practice in the company. We focus on a practice, known as the mature entrant scheme, which began as an expedient, or firefighting, response by two comparatively junior HR managers who were wrestling with recruitment difficulties in the clerical processing sections of the company.

In the management practice under examination here, several themes are noteworthy, including gender and age. Throughout FinanceCo, the issue of age was prominent. The mature entrant scheme as an HR policy for women returners was deployed to alleviate recruitment problems that had resulted initially from a shortage of supply of school-leavers. When the established labour supply of 16-year-olds had all but 'dried up', two of the company's HR managers sought to find new labour markets of supply to satisfy the demand for clerical labour required in the company's administrative processing sections. Women returning to work from a period of absence, usually for reasons of childcare and raising a family, were considered to be useful 'pairs of hands'. They were also seen by the managers as particularly cheap to employ. As a new, unconventional source of workers, FinanceCo had instigated a revision to its payment structure to accommodate these new workers. This change took account of mature entrants who worked full time (term time only); part time, permanent (school hours); or part time, permanent (school hours, term time only). One manager explained the complicated pay structure in simple language:

> They get paid less than they otherwise would, less than the normal for a clerical assistant, which is what you'd expect. Their rates are less. (Rick: Department Manager)

Furthermore, the job options of older women were circumscribed by the scheme on which they were employed as their pay bands fell outside the mainstream clerical grades and career structure. In order to enter a higher grade they had first to be transferred or promoted onto the core pay bands leading to the position. So, anyone employed on the mature entrant scheme was effectively immobile. Directly and indirectly, this restriction helped to reduce the longstanding problem of high staff turnover. During the period of research, turnover levels in the administration division averaged around 50 per cent and were concentrated mainly at the lower clerical end. Another manager summarized the company's position on how mature entrants helped to alleviate the turnover problem by being another source of clerical 'fodder' in the tight labour market facing the company:

> It's a panic measure to resolve the demand for people we can't get ... What else can one do? Personnel found themselves in a hopeless situation. (Julian: Department Manager)

Mature entrant labour was regarded as reducing staff turnover in several ways. Older women with families were seen as less ambitious, less likely to leave or to want to progress within the company, and their job tenure was better than school leavers. The ideal clerical employee was seen as:

The mature entrant who's got no real ambitions, who just wants to come here for a job. They'll do the same work year in and year out. They won't want to move on and they will stay. (Julian: Department Manager)

Mature entrants were seen to reduce turnover directly by staying put, remaining in post either through personal choice or through difficulties in overcoming barriers to grade progression (see above). Furthermore, older women were considered to be more willing to adapt to the specific demands of the repetitive monotony of work in the administration division. They were thought to have a higher boredom threshold for inputting information into computer terminals, for example. School leavers, in contrast, were viewed as having short attention spans, in contrast to older women who were 'so grateful to be given a job' and could be 'just put at a desk and given a lot of menial work to do and told to get on with it' (Cindy: HR manager). This was reflected in and replicated by the team-organized structure of clerical production in FinanceCo. Small groups of staff were hierarchically ordered in task-related groupings. In the family-like structure of work groups or 'teams', there were one or two older women, and these 'mature entrants' were seen to have a positive influence upon the school leavers in their team:

They come in and say 'My God, you've got it cushy' to all these kids who are whingeing ... and they start to realize that they're doing quite well.... (Cindy: HR Manager)

Older women were described as affecting productivity in two ways. First, they worked efficiently since they were felt to be 'more accurate, more conscientious' and were seen to motivate others to do likewise. Second, most mature entrants had some form of previous clerical or office work history enabling them to bring a range of skills to the workplace. At recruitment, candidates who had worked for FinanceCo in the past, or those with previous insurance or office experience in other organizations, were considered to be especially suitable for recruitment by the scheme. Partially as a result of their prior working lives, mature entrants were recognized as reaching peak efficiency faster and so reduced the training load within departments, thereby freeing the individuals who would normally have to supervise them. This lowered staffing and unit costs and released much needed training resources.

Mature entrants were seen as self-disciplined as a consequence of being mature and experienced workers and also by virtue of other 'innate' personal characteristics linked to their biological definition as women, including their identity and responsibilities as wives, carers, helpmeets and mothers. It was expected that, by their nature, the mature entrants would perform a maternally disciplinary role in relation to younger elements of the clerical workforce. Managers described the most efficient workgroup as composed of both sexes and a range of ages, but always with one or two older women present, depending on the size of the team. Given the implicit conditions of their employment and the explicit conditions of their work situation, the women themselves frequently reproduced the expected, maternal behaviour by 'mothering' the younger members of their work group. In the eyes of management, this confirmed the success of the family-team strategy and the wider efficacy of the scheme, as demonstrated by falling turnover levels and increased productivity. At the time of the research, a human resource manager with ultimate responsibility for all clerical appointments was engaged in constructing and reorganizing teams in accordance with the family model. To do this, she exercised her discretion when recruiting and deploying staff appointed under the mature entrant scheme.

Case study 5.4
Discussion of analytical frameworks

The hiring of older women as clerical workers at FinanceCo takes on a gendered character as what are in effect 'new jobs' are defined for the women concerned. We need to remember that these jobs were designed implicitly with the category of 'older' worker in mind. This points to the construction and constitution of age as a significant aspect of analysis of diversity, and highlights how gender and age cross-cut and overlap in the diversity mix. The intersectionalities of age and gender emerge as key themes that are relevant in alerting the reader to age (as well as gender and other elements of diversity) as an issue that is overlaid with social meaning. The contemporary concern with age and an ageing population in advanced economies is not just a preoccupation with the increasing number of people who are over 60 or 65 years of age and the economic impact that their demands in prospective old age represent, such as care, financial, medical and other needs. It is also an outcome of reconsidering and revisiting age as a social construction whereby particular meanings associated with age are, as it were, 'mapped' onto bodies.

In this respect, age is a double-edged sword. On the one hand, an ageing population makes demands on organizations and public services (for welfare needs and the like). On the other hand, there is a business imperative to recognize both the spending power of affluent sections amongst older people and an interest in the contribution that age and experience can make in the running and management of organizations. So whilst age is 'a problem' for employers and policymakers alike, it is also an asset, when maturity and familiarity with a range of life experiences is assessed as a source of potential competitive advantage. Workers can, in the service of the organization, use an extensive range of previous employment and life experiences that are available without the employer having to provide costly training resources. The mature worker may be denigrated and dismissed as 'out of touch' with the demands of the 'modern' workplace with respect to, for example, the use of technology. But he or she mobilizes social and interactive service skills that have a capacity to facilitate increased profitability and production. The point here is that management and its practices sustain diversity as the production of difference.

Within our case study organization, we are not suggesting that mature entrant work is new work in the sense of generating more jobs, better jobs or increased numbers. Rather, old jobs are defined and redefined in new ways contingent upon a fluid, amorphous and dynamic concept of what clerical work is, and who does it. What shapes the design and content of the jobs under examination is not a pre-existing or emerging requirement for a specific technical function or component of clerical operations. Instead, the shaping of jobs is conditioned by a stereotypical and common sense notion of who 'is good at' different types of work, and why. Our case study here has illustrated the process by which the content of a job comes to define the type of person doing it and, simultaneously, how the type of person doing the job begins to confirm the nature and content of that job, the post itself, and the rationale for discriminating in favour of recruiting mature women. By this we mean that managers do not just manage difference, they produce and reproduce difference in their practices.

Disembodied Analysis that relies purely on the cognitive aspects of human conduct, completely ignoring how bodily and emotional life is central to human existence.

In our case study, the women were drawn into certain clerical posts not as a consequence of their possession of a gender-neutral **disembodied** service capacity, the ability to process paperwork or a skill in maintaining mathematical accuracy, for example. What made them employable was their identity as women at a particular life cycle stage related to age. In other words, the mature entrant scheme is articulated through and within a highly gendered and ageist framework, which acts to reinforce and reproduce gender difference in the workplace and to sustain clerical work in the company as 'women's work'. Drawing on a stereotypical image of mothering, the mature entrant scheme created an informal matriarchal leadership and supervision role formally unacknowledged and unrewarded in the pay structure. Originally a response to the declining local labour supply, the recruitment of older women became a deliberate hiring policy within the company; one which drew on an image of matriarchal leadership, 'mothering' and nurturing which was thought to echo domestic life but was assessed to be relevant and useful for improving a variety of performance indicators (e.g., turnover, productivity) in the organization. For the older women, this capacity translated into a disparate collection of low status, low grade tasks known colloquially in the company as 'bucket jobs'. These jobs were drawn together under informal job titles such as 'correspondence clerk' and encompassed a range of 'duties' that effectively serviced the day-to-day running of 'her group'. In the organization hierarchy, the mature entrant woman in FinanceCo was, in effect, the female equivalent of an odd-job man, but at the same time through her definition as an older woman, provided a key, formally valued but materially and symbolically unrewarded, function by smoothing and facilitating clerical production.

Conclusion – managing people

Managing people through what is called HRM has been and continues to be dominated by a mainstream approach both in the academic literature and in everyday practice. It has, however, transformed itself from a focus largely on the details of employment procedures, personnel records, employee rights and welfare when it was seen as personnel management. Under the auspices of HRM, managing people is generally more strategic in terms of ensuring that the appropriate staffing and employee development is secured in relation to present and future corporate plans. However, whether it is personnel management or HRM, whether unitarist in seeing only consensus or pluralist in acknowledging conflicting interests that have to be reconciled, or whether attached to 'soft' HRM in being focused on people as a creative human asset or on 'hard' HRM where they are seen as a cost to constrain, the mainstream supports managerialist objectives of efficiency, productivity, performance and/or profit. Hard HRM does this by, for example, restraining employee rights, job security and wages. Softer approaches seek to develop the creative and innovative capacities of people by investing in quality programmes, teamworking and customer service training, for example. In the chapter we discussed four different models of HRM, two of which adopted a hard approach in focusing on strategic and cost cutting issues and the other two a soft approach, where either a pluralist view of seeing a diversity of stakeholders that HRM is expected to manage, or seeing HRM as both strategic and having a concern to develop the creative skills of employees, but recognizing how the internal and external context in which HR operates affects priorities. Within the mainstream, there may be some focus on equal opportunities insofar as it is necessary for corporations at least to be seen as not violating the law and this may carry more weight where organizations have adopted policies of diversity management. However, diversity management has been more concerned with exploiting diversity to facilitate strategic goals within the corporation rather than for purposes of radically eradicating discrimination. Both HRM and diversity management provide opportunities to integrate more closely the management of a diversity of employees with the attainment of organizational goals.

The principal contribution of critical approaches to HRM and diversity is to stimulate reflection upon some of the rarely explored conditions and consequences of managing people at work. Consequences such as power asymmetries and most notably, social and economic inequalities have been highlighted. Critical perspectives are less concerned with the prescriptive or normative question of *how to* manage. Instead, they provide us with a commentary on actions, policies and beliefs that can provide greater insight into the management of people. Echoing Townley's theoretical discussion of HRM, the contemporary concern with diversity and people management is not straightforward *as it turns on moral as well as social issues*. For example, how far is it acceptable to incorporate older workers into the workplace? On what, and in whose, terms is that incorporation conducted? How should we view the turn to diversity with respect to people with disabilities? How is it possible to reconcile competing views of people as economic units of production at one and the same time as regarding them as human beings? How should we view the turn to diversity?

Whilst recognizing that diversity offers the possibility of examining the unequal treatment of both individuals and groups, an emphasis on intersectionality suggests one means by which we can offer insights into the ways in which social relations interact and combine. We can see that, for example, there are as many differences amongst women and men as there are between women and men. The women in our case study had particular work experience on the basis of both their sex *and* their age. Recognizing and understanding intersectionality has the potential to move analyses of managing people away from essentialist, biologically-grounded notions of difference that informed earlier equality debates. As Kirton and Greene (2000) suggest:

> The shift away from conceptualizing social groups as homogenous hermetically sealed groups, leads towards a perspective which views social groups as heterogeneous, overlapping and non-fixed. From this perspective, a diversity paradigm has the important ability to highlight infra-group as well as inter-group difference, enabling issues of social identity to be drawn out which have been neglected in equality debates. (Kirton and Greene, 2000, p. 4)

It has long been recognized that the management of people is problematic. Employees resist designs to control them. Partly as a consequence of continued employee resistance and the elusiveness of a 'golden ticket' or 'silver bullet' that might finally resolve management's problem of predicting and controlling human behaviour, management knowledge remains largely uncertain. The management of diversity is perhaps symptomatic of a larger struggle to achieve management control in the face of contemporary changes in organizations and their markets; the ways people work, and the methods by which people are managed. We should also remind ourselves of Bagilhole's (1997) contention that certain members of organizations – (some) men for example – continue to benefit from the maintenance of inequality. As a consequence, they are hostile to measures, including the encroachment of equal opportunities and diversity initiatives that are perceived, rightly or wrongly, to threaten their position of privilege.

As we argued earlier, what the mainstream fails to recognize is how HRM and diversity management subscribe to a model that often reproduces rather than challenges inequalities (Dickens, 2006), partly because of the unconscious tendency of practitioners and academics in the field, to see work from the standpoint of white men (the universal worker). Yet there is an even more insidious way in which HRM and diversity management reproduce inequalities; that is through legitimating them in the name of neo-liberal, meritocratic equal opportunity. In other words, we simply transfer the inequalities surrounding different diversities to impenetrable inequalities of so-called merit – a normative consensus organized around educational qualifications, competitive performance and middle-class social skills.

Our focus has been to examine HRM and diversity and to explore the ways in which diversity – difference – is produced and reproduced in workplaces rather than just treating managers as functionaries performing their roles as if they were neutral arbiters of complex relations and events. While in mainstream diversity and HRM, managers are seen as merely providing solutions to organizational problems. In a more critical approach they are seen not just as part of the solution but also as part of the problem.

Discussion questions

1   Can managers manage diversity?

2   Do you think that the management of people can ever be successful? What might this look like?

Further reading

Acker, J. (2006) 'Inequality regimes: Gender, class, and race in organizations', *Gender & Society,* 20(4): 441–464.

This is a journal article that most students will be able to access online or in hard copy. A surprisingly readable article that summarizes key ideas and themes with respect to intersectionality and shows how barriers to workplace equality can be identified. The author also looks at why attempts to redress inequality in workplace organizations so often fail.

Dow, B. J. and Wood, J. T. (2006) *The Sage Handbook of Gender and Communication,* London: Sage.

The rationale for this handbook is that communication lies at the centre of social life and that gender relations are shaped by the processes of identity formation within the social structure. It focuses on gender and communication through five sections: interpersonal; organizational; rhetoric; media; and intercultural/global.

Ely, R. J., Foldy, E. G. and Scully M. A. (eds) (2003) *Reader in Gender, Work and Organization,* Oxford: Blackwell.

This reader provides students with an alternative conceptual approach to gender in the workplace and in doing so provokes us into thinking differently about conventional management topics, such as leadership and negotiation.

Gatrell, C. and Swan, E. (2008) *Gender and Diversity in Management: A Concise Introduction,* London: Sage.

A short and accessible book, deliberately aimed at those with no prior knowledge of the field. Although the specific focus is on gender and diversity in management, other intersections such as race and sexuality are discussed. www.bookshop.blackwell. co.uk/jsp/id/ Reader_in_Gender_Work_and_ Organization/9781405102568.

Konrad, A. L, Prasad, P. and Pringle, J. (eds) (2005) *Handbook of Workplace Diversity,* London: Sage.

Jeanes, E., Knights, D. and Yancey Martin, P. (eds) (2011) *Handbook of Gender, Work and Organization,* London: Wiley Blackwell.

These handbooks include commissioned articles by international authors reporting on the theoretical and empirical developments in the field of diversity and gender respectively. While gender is a focus in both handbooks, Jeanes *et al.* seek to link gender with organization and work as is the case in this chapter.

Powell, G. N. (Ed.) (1999) *Handbook of Gender and Work,* London: Sage.

This handbook draws on 24 separate contributions that together demonstrate how the workplace is skewed in favour of men. While gender is the principal focus of the book, explanations of inequalities extend also to issues of race and ethnicity, as well as other aspects of work such as group, interpersonal and organizational processes. It contains a good bibliography.

Townley, B. (1994) *Refraining HRM: Power, Ethics and the Subject at Work,* London: Tavistock.

A thought-provoking text which sets out a critical perspective on HRM and opens some useful discussion on the ethics of HRM and management in its final chapter. The main contribution of this book lies in its ability to communicate aspects of Foucault's theory very clearly and in a manner that forces us to rethink how people are managed in workplace organizations.

Advanced further reading

Alcock, P., Beatty, C., Fothergill, S., Macmillan, R. and Yeandle, S. (2003) *Work to Welfare: How Men Become Detached from the Labour Market,* Cambridge: Cambridge University Press.

Bacchi, C. (1990) *Same Difference,* London: Allen & Unwin.

Blakemore, K. and Drake, R. (1996) *Understanding Equal Opportunity Policies,* London: Prentice Hall.

Chemers, M., Oskamp, S. and Costanzo, M. A. (eds) (1995) *Diversity in Organizations: New Perspectives for a Changing Workplace,* London: Sage.

Cockburn, C. (1991) *In the Way of Women,* London: Macmillan.

Connerley, M. L. and Pedersen, P. B. (2005) *Leadership in a Diverse and Multicultural Environment,* London: Sage.

Cornelius, N. (2002) *Building Workplace Equality: Ethics, Diversity and Inclusion,* London: Thompson.

Dingle, A. (2003) *Managing Diversity in the Workplace: An Introduction for Voluntary and Community Organizations,* London: NCVO.

Ely, R. J., Foldy, E. G. and Scully, M. A. (eds) (2003) *Reader in Gender, Work and Organization,* Oxford: Blackwell.

Harvey, C. and Allard, M. (1995) *Understanding Diversity,* London: HarperCollins.

Itzin, C. and Newman, J. (eds) (1995) *Gender, Culture and Organizational Change: Putting Theory into Practice,* London: Routledge.

Kirton, G. and Greene, A. (2005) *The Dynamics of Managing Diversity: A Critical Approach,* Oxford and Burlington: Butterworth Heinemann.

Knights, D. and Willmott, H. (eds) (2011) *Organizational Analysis: Essential Readings,* London: Cengage Learning.

Konrad, A. L. (2006) *Cases in Gender and Diversity in Organizations,* London: Sage.

Kossek, E. (1996) *Managing Diversity: Human Resource Strategies for Transforming the Workplace,* Oxford: Blackwell.

McGregor, D. (1969) *The Human Side of Enterprise,* New York: McGraw-Hill.

Marshall, J. (1995) *Women Managers Moving On: Exploring Career and Life Choices,* London: Routledge.

Monks, K. (1993) 'Careers in personnel management', *Personnel Review,* 22(1): 55–66.

Nixon, D. (2009) '"I can't put a smiley face on": Working-class masculinity, emotional labour and service work in the "new economy"', *Gender, Work & Organization,* 16(3): 300–322.

Prasad, P., Mills, A. J., Elmes, M. and Prasad, A. (eds) (1997) *Managing the Organizational Melting Pot Dilemmas of Workplace Diversity,* London: Sage.

Wrench, J. (2005) 'Diversity management can be bad for you', *Race & Class,* 46(3): 73–84.

Young, I. (1990) *Justice and the Politics of Difference,* Princeton: Princeton University Press.

References

Acker, J. (2006) 'Inequality regimes: Gender, class, and race in organizations', *Gender & Society,* 20(4): 441.

Alcock, A. *et al.* (2003) *The Union: The Past, Present and Future,* Colourpoint Books.

Allen, Katie (2016) 'Gender pay gap: women earn £300 000 less than men over working life', available at www.theguardian.com/money/2016/mar/07/gender-pay-gap-uk-women-earn-300000-less-men-lifetime [Accessed on 3rd November 2016]

Ashkanasy, N., Härtel, C. and Daus, C. (2002) 'Diversity and emotion: The new frontiers in organizational behaviour research', *Journal of Management,* 28(3): 307–338.

Bagilhole, B. (1997) *Equal Opportunities and Social Policy,* London: Longman Press.

Bagilhole, B. (2009) *Understanding Equal Opportunities and Diversity,* Bristol: The Policy Press.

Beer, M., Spector, B., Lawrence, P., Quinn Mills, D. and Walton, R. (1984) *Managing Human Assets,* New York: Free Press.

Beer, M., Spector, B., Lawrence, P., Quinn Mills, D. and Walton, R. (1985) *Human Resource Management: A General Manager's Perspective,* Glencoe, IL: Free Press.

Blommaert, J. and Verschueren, J. (1998) *Debating Diversity,* London and New York: Routledge.

Collings, D. G. and Wood, G. (2009) *Human Resource Management: A Critical Approach,* London: Routledge.

Collins, H. (1992) *The Equal Opportunities Handbook,* London: Blackwell.

Collinson, D. (1992) *Managing the Shopfloor: Subjectivity, Masculinity, and Workplace Culture,* Berlin and New York: de Gruyter.

Collinson, D. (2003) 'Identities and insecurities: Selves at work', *Organization,* 10(3): 527–47.

Collinson, D., Knights, D. and Collinson, M. (1990) *Managing to Discriminate,* London: Routledge.

Commission for Racial Equality (March 2006).

Cornelius, N. (2001) *Human Resource Management: A Managerial Perspective,* London: Thomson Learning.

Costea, B. (2010) *The Vitality of HRM: Comments on its Cultural History,* Unpublished paper, University of Lancaster.

Cox, T. (1994) *Cultural Diversity in Organizations: Theory, Research and Practice,* San Francisco, CA: Berret-Koehler.

Crenshaw, K. (1991) 'Mapping the margins, intersectionality, identity, and violence against women of color', *Stanford Law Review,* 43(6): 1241–1299.

Dickens, L. (2006) 'What HRM means for gender equality', *Human Resource Management Journal,* 8(1): 23–40.

Dobb. (2009) 'An Essay on Economic Growth and Planning', New York: Monthly Review Press

Fombrum, C. J., Tichy, N. M. and Devanna, M. A. (eds) (1984) *Strategic Human Resource Management,* New York: John Wiley.

Foucault, M. (1982) 'The subject and power', in H. L. Dreyfus and P. Rabinow (eds) *Beyond Structuralism and Hermeneutics,* Brighton: Harvester Press, pp. 208–226.

Foucault, M (2008) *The Birth of Biopolitics,* trans by G. Burchell, London: Palgrave Macmillan.

Fox, A. (1973) 'Industrial relations: A social critique of pluralist ideology, in J. Child (ed.) *Man and Organization: The Search for Explanation and Social Relevance,* London: Allen and Unwin, London.

Gatrell, C. and Swan, E. (2008) *Gender and Diversity in Management: A Concise Introduction,* London: Sage.

Green, D. G. (ed.) (2000) *Institutional Racism and the Police: Fact or Fiction,* London: The Institute for the Study of Civil Society.

Guest, D. E. (1990) 'Human resource management and the American dream', *Journal of Management Studies,* 27(4): 378–379.

Hambrick, D. C., Davison, S. C., Snell, S. A. and Snow, C. C. (1998) 'When groups consist of multiple nationalities: Towards a new understanding of the implications', *Organization Studies,* 19(2): 181–205.

Harrison, D. A., Price, K. H. and Bell, M. P. (1998) 'Beyond relational demography: Time and the effects of surface- and deep-level diversity on work group cohesion', *Academy of Management Journal,* 41(1): 96–107.

Hendry, C. and Pettigrew, A. (1990) 'Human resource management: An agenda for the 1990s', *International Journal of Human Resource Management,* 1(1): 17–43.

Hoque, K. and Noon, M. (1999) 'Racial discrimination in speculative application: New optimism six years on?', *Human Resource Management Journal,* 9(3): 71–82.

Huczynski, A. and Buchanan, D. (2001) *Organizational Behaviour: An Introductory Text,* fourth edn, London: Financial Times/Prentice Hall.

Ivancevich, J. M. and Gilbert, J. A. (2000) 'Diversity management time for a new approach', *Public Personnel Management,* 29(1): 75–92.

Jack, G. and Lorbiecki, A. (2007) 'National identity, globalization and the discursive construction of organizational identity', *British Journal of Management,* 8: S79–S94.

Janssens, M. and Zanoni, P. (2005) 'Many diversities for many services: Theorizing diversity (management) in service companies', *Human Relations,* 58(3): 311–334.

Kandola, R. and Fullerton, J. (1994) *Managing the Mosaic: Diversity in Action.* London: CIPD Publishing.

Keenoy, T. (1990) 'HRM: Rhetoric, reality and contradiction', *International Journal of Human Resource Management,* 1(1): 363–384.

Keenoy, T. (1997) Review article: 'HRMism and the languages of re-presentation', *Journal of Management Studies,* 34(5): 825–841.

Kelly, E. and Dobbin, F. (1998) 'How affirmative action became diversity management', *American Behavioral Scientist,* 41(7): 960–984.

Kerfoot, D. and Knights, D. (1992) 'Planning for personnel? HRM reconsidered', *Journal of Management Studies,* 29(5): 651–668.

Kirton, G. and Greene, A. M. (2000) *The Dynamics of Managing Diversity,* London: Heinemann.

Knights, D. (2006) 'Authority at work: Reflections and recollections', *Organization Studies,* 27(5): 723–744.

Knights, D. (2008) 'Myopic rhetorics: Reflecting epistemologically and ethically on the demand for relevance in organizational and management research', *Academy of Management Learning and Education,* 7(4): 537–552.

Knights, D. and Omanovic, V. (2010) 'Diversity at Work: A Reassessment', Unpublished paper presented at the 7th International Critical Management Studies Conference, Naples, July 11–13.

Knights, D. and Richards, W. (2003) 'Sex discrimination in UK academia', *Gender, Work and Organization,* Special Issue on Gender and Academic Employment edited by L. Krefting and W. Richards, 10(2): 213–238.

Knights, D. and Willmott, H. (1999) *Management Lives, Power and Identity in Work Organizations,* London: Sage.

Legge, K. (1989) 'Human resource management: A critical analysis', in J. Storey (ed.) *New Perspectives on Human Resource Management,* London: Routledge.

Legge, K. (1995) *Human Resource Management: Rhetorics and Realities,* London: Macmillan.

Legge, K. (2005) *Human Resource Management – Rhetorics and Realities,* Anniversary Edition, Basingstoke: Macmillan Press.

Leidner, R. (2002) 'Fast-food work in the United States', in T. Royle and B. Towers (eds) *Labour Relations in the Global Fast Food Industry,* New York: Routledge.

Lorbiecki, A. (2001) 'Changing views on diversity management. The rise of the learning perspective and the need to recognize social and political contradictions', *Management Learning,* 32(3): 345–361.

Lorbiecki, A. and Jack, G. (2000) 'Critical turns in the evolution of diversity management', *British Journal of Management,* (Special Issue), 11(3): 17–31.

Lynch, F. R. (1997) *The Diversity Machine. The Drive to Change the 'White Male Workplace',* New York: The Free Press.

Maravelias, C (2016) Immaterial labour and biomedical regulation of functionally impaired jobseekers' presented at the 2nd Stockholm-Lancaster Symposium, Lancaster Management School, 22nd Sept.

Marx, K. (1887/1976) *Capital,* Volume 1. Harmondsworth: Penguin.

McGregor, D. (1969) *The Human Side of Enterprise,* New York: McGraw-Hill.

McIntyre, A. (1984/2003) *After Virtue,* London: Duckworth.

Monks, K. (1993) 'Models of personnel management: A means of understanding the diversity of personnel practices?', *Human Resource Management Journal,* 3(2): 29–41.

Nixon, D. (2006) 'I just like working with my hands: Employment aspirations and the meaning of work for low-skilled unemployed men in Britain's service economy', *Journal of Education and Work,* 19(2): 201–217.

Nixon, D. (2009) '"I can't put a smiley face on": Working-class masculinity, emotional labour and service work in the "new economy"', *Gender, Work & Organization,* 16(3): 300–322.

Nkomo, S. M. and Cox, T., Jr. (1996) 'Diverse identities in organizations', in S. Clegg and C. Hardy (eds) *The Handbook of Organization Studies,* Thousand Oaks, CA: Sage, pp. 338–356.

Omanovic, V. (2011) 'What is diversity in organizations? Critically examining the assumptions in the literature on diversity in organizations', in E. Jeanes, D. Knights and P. Yancey Martin (eds) *Handbook of Gender, Work and Organization,* London: Wiley Blackwell.

Parekh, B. (1992) 'A case for positive discrimination', in B. Hepple and E. M. Szyszak (eds) *Discrimination and the Limits of Law,* London: Mansell Publishing.

Perrow C. (1972) *Complex Organizations: A Critical Essay,* New York: McGraw Hill.

Prasad, P. and Mills, A. J. (1997) 'From showcase to shadow – Understanding the dilemmas of managing workplace diversity', in P. Prasad, A. Mills, M. Elmes and A. Prasad (eds) *Managing the Organizational Melting Pot – Dilemmas of Workplace Diversity,* Thousand Oaks, CA: Sage, pp. 3–30.

Pringle, J. and Scowcroft, J. (1996) 'Managing diversity: Meaning and practice in New Zealand organizations', *Asia Pacific Journal of Human Resources,* 34(2): 28–43.

Robinson, G. and Dechant, K. (1997) 'Building the business case', *Academy of Management Executive,* 11(3): 21–31.

Schuier, R. S. and Jackson, S. E. (1987) 'Linking competitive strategies with human resource management practices', *The Academy of Management EXECUTIVE,* 1(3): 207–219.

Scott, A. M. (ed.) (1994) *Gender Segregation and Social Change,* Oxford: Oxford University Press.

Storey, J. (1995) 'Human Resource Management: still marching on or marching out?', in J. Storey (ed.) *Human Resource Management: A Critical Text,* London: Routledge.

Storey, J. (ed.) (1989) 'Introduction: From personnel management to human resource management', in J. Storey (ed.) *New Perspectives on Human Resource Management,* London: Routledge.

Taylor, F. W. (1911) *The Principles of Scientific Management,* New York: Harper.

The Energy Crisis, Deindustrialization, and the Service Economy (1973–2000) wwwtheomahaproject.org/module_display.php?mod_id=85&review=yes. Accessed 19 March 2011.

Townley, B. (1993) 'Foucault, power/knowledge, and its relevance for human resource management', *Academy of Management Review,* 18(3): 518–545.

Townley, B. (1994) *Reframing HRM,* London: Tavistock.

Vogel, E. F. (1979) *Japan As Number One: Lessons for America,* London: Harvard University Press.

Watson, W. E., Kumar, K. and Michaelsen, L. K. (1993) 'Cultural diversity's impact on interaction process and performance: Comparing homogeneous and diverse task groups', *Academy of Management Journal,* 36(3): 590–602.

Willis, P. (1977) *Learning to Labor: How Working Class Kids Get Working Class Jobs,* Gower Press.

Woodward, J. (1958) *Management and Technology,* London: HMSO.

Notes

1 Clearly the quota system in the USA was more effective since it could be more readily legally enforced. Dobb (2009), however, argues that it was the personnel managers rather than the Act per se that ensured anti-discriminatory organizational change.

2 Employment in the secondary sector was always more precarious and less privileged to the point at which some authors described conditions as not dissimilar from late nineteenth century sweatshops in London and New York where employers exploited the vulnerability of their often immigrant labour.

6 Knowledge and learning: Consuming management?

ANDREW STURDY

Aims of the chapter

This chapter will:

- Introduce the different perspectives and debates surrounding knowledge and learning.

- Enable readers to reflect on their own learning, including through reading textbooks such as this one.

- Show how some common sense views of knowledge as an object or commodity are challenged by both mainstream and critical perspectives.

- Argue that it is only through an understanding of the critical perspectives that a broader view can be developed – that knowledge and its use are essentially political.

Key concepts and learning objectives

By the end of this chapter you should be able to:

- Critically assess the relevance and value of learning objectives in textbooks.

- Illustrate different views of knowledge, connect them with theoretical perspectives on learning and apply them to practical approaches that may facilitate learning in organizations.

- Understand why management knowledge, in the form of 'new' management ideas, is adopted in organizations.

- Apply the idea that the relationship between power and knowledge is not simply associated with the view that those with knowledge have power.

Overview and key points

Until fairly recently, knowledge would not have featured as a core management textbook topic. Of course, learning might be covered in relation to organizational behaviour (OB), in terms of human development, or the acquisition of skills through training, for example. Equally, and as in this book, it might be discussed as part of an introductory chapter – how do we learn and what is the best way to use this text as a 'learning resource'? However, today knowledge has become fashionable, making it sometimes seem more like an object or commodity to be consumed, like a car or a new pair of trainers. Indeed, even though it has always been present and important, knowledge and its management are now seen as key to the competitiveness of organizations and even nations, and a whole 'knowledge industry' and set of associated concepts has emerged.

Management knowledge
Often associated with apparently discrete management ideas such as human resource management, but more generally linked to different types of knowledge used or claimed by management.

In this chapter we shall explore some of these concepts, but focus on the key concerns with knowledge in organizations, especially **management knowledge** – what it is and how and why it is acquired and, in particular, transferred from person to person and place to place. In one sense, we can address these questions quite easily – knowledge can be seen as one major source of a person's capability. It includes certain theoretical and/or practical skills, and is acquired and transferred through a process of education, learning, training and application. However, and as we shall see, it is not quite so simple, not least because, as with all phenomena, there are different ways of looking at knowledge and different aspects to it. Also, knowledge is not something peculiar to organizations, nor is it simply created and acquired to serve organizational ends. In the second half of the chapter, we shall explore some of these important, but neglected critical features of knowledge and learning.

Thinkpoint 6.1

Stop and think why you are reading this chapter. What do you hope to gain from doing so ... a good assignment mark ... a better understanding ... avoiding the embarrassment of being seen as uninformed/unprepared or ...? Note down your first few thoughts and return to them when you have finished reading.

Chapter structure

In the first part of the chapter, the mainstream approaches to knowledge and learning are explored in terms of the key perspectives and issues. In particular, we examine the different types of knowledge and the different theories of learning. We then focus on management knowledge and management ideas in particular, how they are promoted, selected, adapted and evaluated – how and why they are 'consumed'.

In the second half of the chapter, critical perspectives are introduced and explored. Here, alternative accounts of the nature of management knowledge and the reasons why management ideas are adopted are set out, suggesting that the popularity of specific management ideas – such as those discussed in textbooks like this one – is no guide to their organizational effectiveness when put into practice.

Finally, the importance of acknowledging that knowledge is adapted according to context and political dynamics is highlighted. This suggests that knowledge and learning need to be understood in terms of the core concepts of the book, especially those of power, insecurity and inequality. In short, management knowledge can be seen to be used and abused, sometimes at the same time.

MAINSTREAM APPROACHES TO KNOWLEDGE AND LEARNING
Introduction

The most successful companies and the most successful countries will be those that manage *human capital* in the most effective and efficient fashion – investing in their workers, encouraging workers to invest in themselves, provide a good learning environment, and yes, include *social capital* as well as skills and training. (Becker, 2001, p. 1)

Why has knowledge begun to be seen as a new and important focus for organizations? Surely, knowledge has always been important in terms of producing goods and services, innovating and keeping up with the competition? It has. But even if we temper some of the hype or **rhetoric**, which is typical of those

Rhetoric Art of persuasion and may encompass a range of techniques aimed at changing views or behaviour. It is also sometimes seen as meaning false or exaggerated, and is contrasted with reality or truth – 'that's just rhetoric' or someone trying to convince you of their beliefs. Others see no distinction.

wanting to promote ideas, there have been some changes, in many Western contexts at least, which warrant a change in focus:

- There has been a shift away from manufacturing industries in terms of the numbers employed. Here, manual skills were deemed of central importance but have been either automated or exported (Sennett, 2000). While, as we shall see, manual skills can be viewed as a form of knowledge, it is argued that the growth of service employment and 'knowledge-based sectors' (e.g., professional services, software and bioscience) are a source of greater **competitive advantage** (Hislop, 2013). They have been comparatively more profitable, partly because the knowledge they depend upon cannot easily be emulated and therefore new organizations find it difficult to enter the market in which they operate. This can provide partially monopolistic conditions and this usually means higher profits.

- It is often claimed that the global economy has become more competitive, connected and dynamic. Therefore, knowledge becomes more available and plentiful, but its advantages are short-lived. At the same time, pressures to innovate – to create and apply new knowledge – are more intense. Knowledge needs to be continually updated therefore.

- The boundaries perceived between organizations are becoming more fluid, giving rise to an opening up of sources of knowledge (from suppliers, customers, alliance partners and new or geographically distributed employees, for example) and therefore also the danger of losing knowledge, or **leakage** (Monteiro *et al.*, 2015).

- While technology in the past was designed to mimic (control, cheapen and/or replace) the knowledge of many manual and office workers, it is now also being developed with the hope of capturing the expertise of professional and managerial individuals and groups and disseminating it selectively throughout the organization as quickly as possible. This is what is seen as **knowledge management**. For example, in management consultancy, what has been learned from a client or project is often input into an IT database so that others in the consulting firm can draw on this information when working with the same or similar clients in future (Boussebaa *et al.*, 2014). But, as we shall see shortly, knowledge is not exactly the same as information.

Competitive advantage What is deemed to make an organization or nation more competitive or economically successful than another, such as access to important resources.

Leakage The unintended loss or flow of knowledge such as commercially sensitive material.

Knowledge management Process of capturing and codifying knowledge for management (e.g., profitable) purposes. It is often linked with information systems that store 'knowledge' in databases, but has become associated with the broader activity where management seek to appropriate the tacit as well as the explicit knowledge of their employees (see also **tacit skills**) (Hislop, 2013).

Knowledge-economy Not based upon producing physical things, but on using knowledge to deliver services. Consultancies like Universal, advertising agencies, software development houses, even universities, are all examples of organizations that make up the knowledge-economy – knowledge-intensive firms, knowledge-sectors and knowledge-workers.

This view of the emergence of **knowledge-economies**, knowledge-workers, knowledge-sectors, knowledge-management and knowledge-intensive firms presents a potentially exciting (or frightening) scenario. Traditional practices of learning a trade or profession with great emphasis on early intensive and formal learning – a degree in business administration for example – followed by gradual personal development, sometimes through formal training, may now seem anachronistic or at least insufficient. Indeed, we are increasingly called upon to engage in regular and lifelong learning. Furthermore, traditional classroom-based instruction – first started because of a shortage of books! – is not only seen as having limited effectiveness (see Freire, 1972 for example), but inappropriate, given emerging, busy lifestyles and the declining 'shelf-life' of knowledge. Moreover, and as we shall see, it is not just the profile of knowledge that has changed, but also our views of it and how to develop it. For example, in a short space of time, it was hoped that the limitations of the classroom would be addressed by the rise of self-directed, Internet-based e-learning which was seen as being cheaper. However, its limitations soon gave rise to the importance of participating in informal networks or **communities of practice (COPs)**. Now, perhaps unsurprisingly, attention is focused on a mix of approaches or 'blended learning' (Porter and Graham, 2015).

While knowledge is now seen as key for the success of businesses and orga-nizations, it is obviously not a new phenomenon. For example, it is inherent in activities such as innovation; organizational change; applying different manage-ment ideas or practices; crossing organizational and national cultures; learning new skills as well as other everyday organizational activities. Indeed, it can be argued that knowledge and learning are core human processes – 'all individu-als and all organizations ... are knowledgeable' (Blackler, 1995, pp. 1022, 1026). It should certainly not, therefore, be seen solely as a topical area of study. For example, an understanding of knowledge in organizations and how it moves and develops in general is helpful in making sense of future developments, which we do not yet know about, such as new management ideas. Indeed, helping to develop this type of understanding is one aim of this chapter. Before exploring knowledge and learning in more detail, however, the beginning of a short case is presented (see Case Study 6.1), which should shed light on the issues raised in the rest of the chapter.

Communities of practice (COPs) Refers to groups of people who interact (through meeting personally or electronically) and in so doing share knowledge and learn from each other through the interaction. Precise definitions vary, but emphasis is typically placed on the informality of such groups and interactions (Handley *et al.*, 2006).

Thinkpoint 6.2

If knowledge is changing so fast what are the implications of studying for a degree over three or four years or using textbooks, most of which change very little in terms of content? (When next in the library, pick a topic and compare it in two editions of the same textbook.) What type of knowledge is likely to have long-term relevance to the understanding and practices of organizations?

Case study 6.1
Learning to love the customer: customer relationship management

Rohan Pryce is studying management at the 'college of knowledge', or so it is jokingly known to the students there. His first piece of assessed work is an essay on learning.

His cousin Cathy has a new job in the local call centre of a car insurance company, DK-Line, as a 'learning manager'. Rohan is curious about what this job means and thinks that, with a title like that, she should be able to help him produce an original and inter-esting essay.

It turns out that she is helping to set up an approach to service based on a school of thought in marketing – **customer relationship management (CRM)**. Cathy explains that the reason for this initiative is that the firm is losing their existing custom-ers to cheaper competitors and so they want to develop good long-term relationships with their customers in order to retain their business. Her role is to ensure that staff have the appropriate skills and knowledge to do this and then evaluate whether the CRM initiative was effective. Apart from trying to ensure that staff are motivated, the first part of this role involves staff recruitment, training and development.

Although most new recruits knew nothing about technical, insurance issues, this was quite easy to teach, not least because most of them were quite literate and numerate and also had their own cars and so knew something about insurance already. Also, the more they knew, the higher (pay) grade they achieved. But even if staff often forgot things that were not used frequently when dealing with customers, the IT system had lots of information available at the press of a few buttons.

Customer relationship management (CRM) A broad management approach that emphasizes the financial value of developing long-term relationships with, and detailed knowledge of, customers. For example, through the use of information systems' databases, it is assumed that customers can be 'captured' so that customized goods and services may be targeted appropriately to them.

It was more difficult to train other things like how to deal with people, to be generally sociable, and, with angry customers, remain calm and yet efficient. Indeed, Cathy knew from her own experience and from things said by a group of managers she occasionally met up with at conferences, that some things were best learned from experience and through one's colleagues. Also, people should be given space to develop their own solutions. She had put these ideas into practice by introducing frequent team meetings for problem solving, assigning experienced mentors to new recruits and 'empowering' staff to create their own call scripts and coping mechanisms. The problem was trying to ensure that within the team meetings staff stuck to the agenda and produced solutions acceptable to their manager.

Rohan was beginning to see how he could use this account or 'case study' in his essay. He tried to bring the conversation to an end – the essay was due in the next day – but Cathy was so clearly 'into' her job and CRM, it was difficult to cut it short. He hadn't seen her like this before. She also seemed to get annoyed when Rohan said that it all seemed to fit with his lectures and books. She said that it was 'not that simple you know!' Rohan began to feel uncomfortable and made a sharp exit home to write his essay.

Key problems

Now that knowledge is seen to be so important to organizations, the difficulties in understanding what it means and how it can be captured and used are increasingly recognized. Indeed, paradoxically and as with so many phenomena, the more attention it receives, the less clear it becomes. There is nothing new in identifying types of knowledge, but

Classify Places ideas, phenomena, practices or events into categories that are then named. Most sciences begin by classifying the types of objects they study (e.g., types of plants in botany).

Innovation The process of imagining something new in a given context (e.g., invention), combined with developing that idea into an applied form.

Non-rigorous Usually a pejorative term meaning the absence of in-depth analysis or systematic research procedures.

distinctions have been quite basic and fail to recognize that knowledge is multiple and diverse. Therefore, there have been numerous attempts to **classify** knowledge and the relationships between different types. However, this runs alongside a more pressing and practical concern of how knowledge can be created, acquired and transferred to others.

Again, there is a long tradition in other fields such as education, **innovation** and training, and these have been drawn on in the field of management But traditional approaches have been seen as lacking the necessary sophistication or the appropriate contexts for the kind of speed and flexibility seen as necessary in competitive and changing markets. Also, and as we shall see, there are different views on how people learn – which are the best methods and what are their practical implications? In addition, it is increasingly recognized that sources of knowledge are as likely to be outside the organization as inside and, either way, extracting and retaining knowledge is difficult to achieve. It is hoped by some that new communication technologies will be able to help in this regard as a repository, fast transmitter and editor or translator of information.

Finally, a more specific concern within the study of knowledge and learning is that of how management knowledge is promoted, adopted and evaluated. Here, there is some recognition that managers seem to be adopting the latest ideas in a **non-rigorous** way – as fashion victims – regardless of whether the ideas have been proven to be useful for the organization. Also, the transfer of ideas across cultures is seen to pose problems. How can **cultural barriers** to universally relevant management ideas be overcome, or is knowledge and learning more bound to – embedded in – particular contexts? Overall then, mainstream thinkers in management are seeking to help, know, capture and transfer management knowledge to achieve organizational goals. We shall now explore some of these issues in more detail.

> **Cultural barriers** Are seen to prevent the transfer of ideas and practices because of differences in what is viewed as acceptable in different cultural contexts (e.g., teamworking in individualistic cultures).

Key ideas and contributions

WHAT IS KNOWLEDGE?

In everyday talk, knowledge is often seen and treated as being like an object or **commodity**, something of value, which can be transferred from one place to another. For example, knowledge of different theories of learning might be gained from this text and applied in an assignment or in a seminar discussion. This view is also common in organizations, especially in knowledge management, where it is believed that experts' 'knowledge' of, say, a particular client or market, can be written onto an IT system (i.e., **codified** and captured), such as the customer database at DK-Line in the case study. However, and as we shall see, this view is problematic and can be misguided. For example, this book does not contain knowledge, but something more like codified information. Furthermore, reading it does not necessarily result in learning or an increase in knowledge. Learning may occur, depending on how you think about what you read, connecting it with things that you already know (not least your knowledge of the English language) and whether you try applying the ideas, even if only in your mind. Before going further into the nature of these processes, it is worth unpacking views of different types of knowledge, but note that this can reinforce the view of knowledge as being like an object.

> **Commodity** Something that can be exchanged for a price. While normally seen in terms of physical goods or services, the term is sometimes extended to human beings where they are treated in a dehumanized manner purely in terms of their economic value (price) as labour.

> **Codified knowledge** Knowledge in the form of information that has been deliberately and explicitly written down in a book or stored on a computer, for example.

Knowledge, information and data

Knowledge is often, especially in IT circles, distinguished from data (discrete facts) and information (categorized, summarized, contextualized data, used in decision-making for example) in that it reflects a higher level of abstraction and ability. Data, and even information without knowledge, is meaningless. Think of the three different colours in a traffic light or those colours in the context of a crossroad. Without the knowledge of how they are there to direct the traffic so as to avoid accidents, the data and the information are meaningless. When information is infused with analysis, insights from experience, judgement, values and associated capabilities or skills, it may become knowledge (see Malone, 2003).

For example, imagine demand for textbooks on OB in the UK is 30 000 copies (*data*). This is presented to a new marketing manager as 35 per cent of the total market of students studying OB (*information*). The manager uses this to bid for a higher budget next year in order to grow sales. But this request is rejected by her boss who *knows* from experience and a recent conversation with the production team that not only does the 35 per cent market share figure typically remain unchanged (most students do not buy the recommended text), but the production department is at full capacity. The point is that the decision to reject the increase in budget is based on a more developed and nuanced understanding or construction of the data and information. It is not necessarily the correct decision – production might be outsourced and more students could be persuaded to buy the book.

Knowledge to knowing

A more common way of classifying knowledge is to distinguish between 'knowledge that' (or 'about') and 'knowledge how' (Ryle, 1949; see also Polyani, 1966). The typical example given is that of driving a car: *knowing that* you have to depress the clutch before changing gear does not mean that you *know how* to do it in practice. But it can be applied to all types of activity – knowing and applying types of knowledge for a start! This distinction is close to another, which distinguishes between knowledge that can be made *explicit* (e.g., described, written down) such as that suggested in textbooks, and that which can be so only partially, which is implicit, elusive or tacit (see Lam, 2000; Chia, 2003). In the case study, for example, Cathy realized how some things could be taught quite easily, but others, such as social skills were more tacit.

These distinctions are very useful, but do not reveal some of the different characteristics of knowledge or the 'grey' areas between types. For example, some knowledge is clearly linked to individuals while other knowledge is also held in groups or networks of people and their activities – i.e., collective knowledge. Also, as knowledge has assumed greater importance in business, people have tried to capture it even more precisely (i.e., make knowledge of knowledge explicit). Blackler (1995) for example, identified five overlapping types of knowledge and Lam (2000) developed this schema in terms of whether they were primarily tacit or explicit and individual or collective:

- *embrained* (e.g., expertise in accounting principles): cognitive, individual and explicit
- *embodied* (e.g., craft skills): practical, individual and tacit
- *embedded* (e.g., who does what in a system of routines – beyond individual skills): collective, tacit and relational
- *encultured* (e.g., group norms): collective and tacit or explicit
- *encoded* (e.g., information in expert systems software): explicit and collective.

Thinkpoint 6.3

Take the knowledge involved in an occupation, job or activity (e.g., sport or playing a musical instrument) you are familiar with, and try and identify examples of Blackler's five knowledge types. How difficult is it to distinguish them?

The above classification of knowledge types is now commonly used in the literature and even some workplaces. Like categories generally, they help us feel as if we know something about the subject – knowledge itself in this instance – and we may feel reassured by this. They also help us have conversations about the topic and learn more (e.g., the difficulty in distinguishing them).

Paradoxically, after setting them out, Blackler himself shows them to be rather static and, ultimately, flawed. He opts for a focus on 'knowing as a process', something we (all) *do*, rather than knowledge as something we have (see Chapter 10 for the source of this distinction in organizational culture analysis). This is quite a complex and unconventional, but important, view of knowledge. It undermines or, at least, challenges the knowing-doing (knowledge that/how) distinction mentioned above, and highlights the fluid, communal and emergent or contested nature of knowledge. In other words, knowledge is far from being tangible and fixed, but emerges in real time through social interaction, and this makes it subject to challenge and disagreement.

There are then two broad perspectives on knowledge. The **processual** view of Blackler and others can be contrasted with a more **objective, cognitive** (mental) and **static 'structural'** perspective, where knowledge types can be classified (see Newell *et al.*, 2002, p. 8). These views are evident in the different ways of understanding learning to which we now turn.

WHAT IS LEARNING?

People learn in a combination of different ways – from novelty, experience/doing and social interaction, for example. This may depend on the situation, including what they are learning (a foreign language, a poem, etc.). For example, learning to ride a bike or drive a car cannot be achieved through books or manuals alone. We acquire the skill largely through doing it, but we also rely on other knowledge, such as knowing that it will be possible, that the ground is solid (hopefully!) and that pushing the pedals makes the wheels go round. Also, and more generally, we may have personal/cultural inclinations or 'preferences' for particular types of learning, borne out of individual experiences – **learning styles**. This variation partly explains the range of different theories of learning, although perspectives also differ in their assumptions about people's behaviour in general and these rise and fall in popularity. We now examine groups of theoretical approaches to learning (see also CIPD, 2002).

Learning as behaviour

This approach is associated with 'behaviourism', but is not restricted to this rather specific perspective in that the focus is on *learning by doing*. Behaviourism is a theory that explains human behaviour in terms of its pleasurable or painful consequences (Skinner, 1953, 1971). In responding to some stimulus in the environment, we learn which kinds of response have a pleasant effect and thereby seek to repeat such behaviour. Where a response has brought about pain, we seek to avoid it. Over time, 'appropriate' behaviour becomes automatic to us or habitual – it is then said to be **internalized** within us so that it is done without necessarily thinking about it.

The desired behaviour (desired by parents, teachers, friends, managers, etc.) is positively reinforced by receiving valued rewards, such as praise, promotion, a good test score, feeling satisfied or having something disliked withdrawn. This process is clearly evident in a number of situations, especially as we learn basic things as a child, but also in the development of skills through formal training or instruction from experts. In the case study, learning was encouraged by the prospect of the reward of promotion through the grading system.

Processual Theoretical approach that focuses more attention on the political, but also cultural and strategic processes within organizations, than their content or structure.

Objective Free from bias, prejudice, judgement and emotion.

Cognitive Associated with thinking or mental processes such as perception; or traditional views of understanding such as those that are gained by reading or classroom learning.

Static structural A way of understanding that does not allow for processes of change over time and which presumes that the phenomenon can be divided into layers or structures. For example, knowledge can be classified as different types that do not change over time.

Learning styles Variations in approaches to learning attributed to individual, cultural or other background differences, and subject to change.

Internalized When an idea, norm or value is completely embedded in individual consciousness such that there is often no awareness of its existence and influence on behaviour.

Thinkpoint 6.4

Behaviourism is illustrated well in the training of pet dogs, teaching them to behave in an acceptable manner or to do tricks by providing rewards. In what ways does this apply to how we learn to behave, as children and subsequently, and how, if at all, do we differ?

Another behavioural view of learning, closely linked to behaviourism, places emphasis on learning by doing, tacitly, through repeating or practising behaviours until they become perfected. Here, there is less emphasis on rewards. Both views remain influential and continue to be applied in organizations (e.g., reward systems for desired behaviour). However, partly because of its association with rewards and power, the behaviourist view of learning is much maligned by many academics. It is not fashionable. But also, it does not come near to telling the whole story –

Action Behaviour that is socially meaningful or purposeful; it is influenced or interpreted by oneself or others. Thus, moving one's leg might be seen as behaviour (unless agreed as a pre-arranged signal), whereas kicking a ball in a football match might be seen as action (unless as a deflection).

perceptions, feelings and motivations, for example, are not considered. Indeed, reinforcement may just prompt other learning processes, such as reflection on the task in hand when practising, or be facilitated by discussions with others. As we shall see, these additional activities may also make it more likely that reinforced skills can be applied in different situations or adapted and thereby help to become more creative. In short, behaviourism and the behavioural view more generally, are associated with a view of people as (trainable) automatons – rewards as well as unthinking repetition of acts are seen as the basis of learning. It has little to do with what we might see as an explicit or meaningful understanding, which has a much wider applicability since this is typically associated with creative thinking and **action**.

Learning as understanding

This is another dominant perspective on learning and it is associated with cognitive views and more closely with knowledge in the sense of a commodity to be internalized, like the contents of a textbook or insights of a

Double-loop learning (DLL) Involves highly reflective and creative actions that, through continuous feedback processes of self-learning, testing and exploration, facilitate organizational change. DLL is contrasted with single-loop learning (SLL), which is more incremental and mechanical and often likened to the role of a thermostat that regulates a domestic heating system in accordance with external temperatures.

case study – 'knowing that'. At its crudest or most 'rational', this view is associated with passively acquiring and correcting explicit knowledge, rather like a traditional view of school learning and revising for exams. However, rather than simply responding to stimuli or digesting established facts, cognitive learning can refer to more active, complex, adaptive and creative processes – it is more thoughtful or cognitive (Piaget, 1950). Based on our perceptions, we create mental models to make sense of the world and learn by using and adapting these in and to novel situations (e.g.,'double-loop learning' (DLL)). Indeed, novelty is a key area of learning – if something is not novel, then it is already known. However, sometimes the novelty is too extreme to adapt to – there are no obvious connections with existing knowledge or behaviour – and so new information, such as the latest management idea, is either ignored or denied (Sturdy *et al.*, 2009).

Translated Changed from one form to another. This might be in the sense of a complete transformation, as an idea is adapted to a particular context, or a more modest change such as a (good) linguistic translation. (See also knowledge diffusion and cultural barriers.)

Cognitivism Psychological perspective on human behaviour that emphasizes the mental processes of thinking and perception rather than other influences, such as the subconscious or social factors.

Learning as knowledge construction

This view presents people as even more active and creative in their learning than the previous perspective allows – constructing meaning from interaction with the environment and peers, for example. Also, and importantly, from this perspective there is no knowledge that is independent of the knower – it is all tacit. Explicit knowledge only becomes useful when it is **translated** so that it has meaning for people – i.e., relates to their experiences. In practical terms, this means that instruction (behaviourism) or help from others with learning techniques, materials or frameworks (**cognitivism**) are not especially helpful. Rather, learning occurs best in stimulating contexts such as new work projects, through discussion, **brainstorming** and self-directed activities (e.g., 'learning logs'), which use and transform explicit knowledge. In Case Study 6.1, Cathy implicitly sought to use this perspective in empowering the staff to develop their own scripts, for example.

Learning as social practice/interaction

As with most topics, actual research studies and the theoretical perspectives used in them are not usually pure types that can be easily fitted into boxes or classifications such as 'behaviour', 'understanding' or 'knowledge construction'. Social learning theories often draw on aspects of behavioural, cognitive and/or constructivist views, or recognize their relevance, but place particular emphasis on the importance of a social (interactive) setting for effective learning and application. Learning is seen either as a result, or **integral** feature, of interaction (Brown and Du Guid, 2001). This is clear from the importance of learning through observing others (especially friends, family, peers and people we respect or admire) and modelling or adapting ourselves (and identities) accordingly. Sometimes this occurs directly, but we may also do this through imagining what significant others would do or think in a particular situation (**anticipatory socialization**). We are especially conscious of this when we enter new social situations or groups such as a new work or seminar group – we tend to think 'what is the appropriate way to act in this context?'

Brainstorming Involves people in a group exercising their creative skills to generate new ideas or innovations. The key aspect of it is that, in the early stages, all ideas put forward are considered valid and no criticism or selection is allowed until later on when ideas are evaluated.

Integral A necessary or inherent part of something.

Anticipatory socialization A process of learning to behave in ways appropriate to particular future roles, relationships or occupations. An example would be anticipating what is the expected behaviour of a student prior to starting university.

Thinkpoint 6.5

If research and ideas are not readily classifiable into boxes, tables, diagrams or bullet points, why are such devices so common in textbooks and why are they less so in other academic texts? What theory of learning does their use imply and why?

Learning through interaction can also be an especially effective form of learning. For example, it has been observed how children (and others) can perform above their individual learning potential through direct contact with more 'knowledgeable' others such as older children or adults (Vygotsky, 1962). Similarly, in work situations, the practice of 'brainstorming', where groups 'free think' about addressing a particular problem, may result in far more creative and numerous solutions than if the same people had worked on the problem individually (synergy). Again, this view is evident in Cathy's practise in the case study with the use of mentoring and team problem solving. Interaction in different activities with other people and things, such as IT systems or objects (e.g., a new product or a diagram), can also help iron out inconsistencies or smooth out processes that might not happen if people were left to themselves to learn (Engestrom and Middleton, 1996; Wilson *et al.*, 2008). For example, this is where (when it works) the seminar can be far more effective than sitting in a lecture.

Social learning theories have become fashionable in management, academic and, perhaps to a lesser extent, practitioner circles as the difficulty of codifying organizational knowledge is increasingly recognized. For example, the notion of 'situated learning' (Lave and Wenger, 1991) places emphasis on the fact that social practices *naturally* lead to learning, but they do so incidentally as much as through formally structuring learning groups (Handley *et al.*, 2007). In this way, knowledge becomes a collective phenomenon, shared or embedded (see Blackler's knowledge types above) among participants – it is 'co-produced'. Here, we can talk about 'organizational learning'. However, relationships may vary in their learning potential. For example, relatively close or familiar relationships with fellow employees, might be most effective for learning *complex* knowledge. By contrast, *new* knowledge is more likely to arise from other, more distant relationships. Granovetter (1973) referred to this latter phenomenon as 'the strength of weak ties', such that sometimes (e.g., searching for knowledge for a change in career), you learn more from people you know less well.

In an organizational context, new knowledge is associated with innovation and change and it is for this reason that the idea of communities of practice (COP) has come to prominence (e.g., Lave and Wenger, 1991). These are

Project teams Groups of people working together on a particular task with a discrete objective and time frame. Often such groups include different specialists, perhaps drawn from different departments, for the purpose of achieving the project task.

largely informal and open-ended groups (i.e., not assigned **project teams**) through which we learn, create and share tacit knowledge or 'know-how' especially. They are based on common practice, rather than necessarily, say, shared geographical location, employer or friendship. We are all members of COPs and may be seen as expert in some and a novice in others. For example, in an office context people who are called out to repair photocopiers formally work largely on their own, but may meet colleagues over coffee and lunch and learn far more in these conversations or 'war stories' than in a training session of the same duration (Orr, 1996; cf.

Contu and Willmott, 2003). Equally, email and other Internet-based communication has facilitated the more or less informal interaction of more dispersed groups (Newell *et al.*, 2002). In Case Study 6.1, Cathy learned about effective training from her conversations with peers she met at a conference.

But COPs are not a new phenomenon as such (we all learn through informal groups); only a newly recognized potential source of innovation and change for managers. The key dilemma here, however, as it has been in tapping the productive potential of informal work groups more generally, is that their strength lies in their informal and relatively voluntary or spontaneous nature. Imagine being told that you should now see the people who you hang out with on a management course as a COP and that you should learn something from it or, even report back on what you learned while you were at lunch! Also, and with social learning more generally, while most would concede the learning potential of COPs, there are other pressures or constraints: work tasks need to be completed and, in particular, not everyone wants to share their knowledge or be in communities.

Thinkpoint 6.6

Think of how COPs relate to your learning about management and OB. Why might people be reluctant or unable to share their knowledge or see their informal groups as something to extract knowledge from? What other obstacles might there be? How might you go about addressing the obstacles in order to cultivate your COP?

More generally, the view of knowledge as embedded and as inherently social makes practical suggestions on how to facilitate learning in general very difficult. Added to this is the range of possible factors which influence learning, sometimes in opposite directions. Let us take the example of working in project teams (see also Chapter 4), something often seen as particularly good for learning (Tempest and Starkey, 2004). Indeed, a sub-field of study has emerged called project-based learning (see Box 6.1 and Sturdy *et al.*, 2009).

WHAT IS MANAGEMENT KNOWLEDGE?

The above discussion of knowledge and learning has been rather general. We now look at *management* knowledge specifically, and the different ways of classifying it, before exploring some of the processes associated with new management ideas. First, of course, we need to be clear about the nature of management. This is being explored elsewhere in this book (see Chapter 8) and is, surprisingly perhaps, no easy task. If we focus on management as an activity, rather than as an occupation or hierarchical level for example (Hales, 1993), we can see that conventional views distinguish between the formal or 'espoused' views, and what actually happens in practice – knowledge *in use*

Box 6.1
Project teams and other practical suggestions to facilitate learning

The advantages claimed for projects:

- By bringing together people with different experience, projects are seen to draw on the 'strength of weak ties' and support tacit learning.
- By focusing on an explicit goal, project members can learn in a way which is more difficult to achieve in functionally structured arrangements – through *learning-by-absorption* and *learning-by-reflection* (Scarbrough et al., 2004).
- The relatively transient nature of projects can mean that the knowledge they produce poses a lesser threat to vested organizational interests than that arising from individual departments (Sydow et al., 2004).

However, counter arguments can be put forward:

- A neutral status of the project team in the organization (not associated with a department of power base) can diminish the legitimacy and credibility of knowledge it produces.
- A new boundary can develop around the team and other parts of the organization – the project boundary becomes a barrier.
- The demands of the immediate task – of doing – may take priority over or inhibit reflection and deeper understanding (Sydow et al., 2004).
- The one-off or non-recurring nature of project activities provide limited scope for drawing out any generalized insights.
- Knowledge bases among members can be too diverse for learning to occur – people and ideas are too different (Bogenrieder and Nooteboom, 2004).

These polar arguments suggest that project teams are by no means a panacea for encouraging knowledge flow or generation among members. This also applies to other prescriptions for learning such as: joint working; networking; the use of intermediaries and boundary objects; facilitating communities of practice; the development of trust and shared values, and interpersonal styles. As Orlikowski (2002) points out, prescriptions are typically double-edged and can have unintended 'negative' consequences:

> … *sharing identity becomes organizational groupthink, interacting face-to-face leads to burnout, aligning effort discourages improvisation, learning by doing is lost through (staff) turnover, and supporting participation is immobilizing because of conflicts and time delays* (2002, p. 257).

In effect, context is all important and universal, 'checklist' solutions to the problems of learning in organizations are not tenable. This is not to say that prescriptive accounts have no value, for many tend to be based on similar broad (e.g., Western, 'knowledge-intensive') contexts. However, it does place the situated view of knowledge at the boundary of critical and mainstream perspectives and so we shall return to it in the second half of the chapter.

Exercise 6.1

As you did with the different types of knowledge earlier, reflect on how you learned how to do a particular job or activity (e.g., sport, playing a musical instrument, speaking a language) and connect this with the different approaches and perspectives on learning: as behaviour (practice and rewards), understanding (thinking, frameworks), knowledge construction and social practice/interaction. Can you make connections with all the approaches? Which seem most relevant? Are there any overlaps? What do your reflections imply for theories of learning and their changing popularity? Are we in the best position to assess how we learned something? What would be the best way to find out how people learn?

(see Argyris and Schon, 1974; also Tengblad, 2012). Together, this gives rise to three dimensions of management activity (see also Watson, 1986):

- The 'art' of meeting organizational objectives through others.
- Systematic or rational planning and control.
- A messy, sometimes reactive, political, emotional and frenetic mix of activities.

We shall return to these later when considering the adoption of management ideas, but, for now, they suggest that the knowledge (and skills) involved in management is multifaceted. Alvarez (1998), for example, set out a number of forms of management knowledge, which can be seen to roughly correspond to Blackler's classification discussed earlier:

- Technical *or* instrumental knowledge such as specific marketing techniques (embrained and encoded).
- Habits and a sense of intuition, such as that which might be involved in routine decision-making (embodied).
- An understanding of what is acceptable, both formally ('professional' behaviour) and informally (e.g., who is in and out of favour). Indeed, all types of knowledge are embedded in local, e.g., national, settings (encultured).

This classification is also useful in that it combines both explicit and tacit forms of management knowledge. By definition, the latter is more difficult to unpack and transfer, as we have seen. For this reason perhaps, attention is typically focused on explicit management knowledge or what might be described as 'management ideas'. These will now form the focus of our discussion, but it will become clear how this does not exclude more tacit and informal aspects of management activity.

Explicit knowledge: management ideas

Studying management (and most other topics) we are faced with a mass of ideas, concepts, theories and prescriptions. Following the cognitive view of learning and the explicit view of knowledge, these are presented in lectures and textbooks in the form of lists, diagrams and written accounts. This is often experienced as overwhelming, not least because people are always updating, adapting and creating new ideas (Rigby and Bilodeau, 2015). In the same cognitive tradition then, it should be useful to construct classifications – 'mental pigeon holes' – of the ideas themselves. This should be helpful, not only as a way of organizing existing ideas, but making sense of (i.e., classifying, framing, comparing, understanding) seemingly new ideas as they come along after a formal period of study. The alternatives are: to continue studying with further courses or reading; assume that nothing changes; or ignore new ideas and continue to draw on and adapt those that we learned in the past.

There are various ways to organize management ideas. These are informed by, and tell us something about, management (see Huczynski, 2006). First, management ideas are typically known in terms of the role they perform (e.g., change management, leadership) and therefore can often be grouped in terms of management functions (e.g., marketing, strategy, human resource management (HRM), finance, etc.). Sometimes similar ideas are combined or coalesce into a 'school of thought' or movement (e.g., CRM, HRM, entrepreneurship).

Thinkpoint 6.7

Many management ideas are represented as a three-letter acronym (TLA) (Grint, 1997). How many can you think of? Look for TLAs in the index of a management textbook. Why do you think they are so popular?

These might be presented historically. For example, in OB, we might learn that bureaucracy (see Chapter 14) and scientific management (see Chapters 8 and 9) were followed by human relations, the more psychological (see Chapters 2 and 3) 'neo-human relations' and culture management, and entrepreneurialism. Typically, each approach would be seen as incorporating, and/or an improvement on, the previous one (cf. Guillen, 1994). For example, in Case Study 6.1, CRM is seen to be a development of customer service ideas more generally in that it focuses on developing long-term relationships.

An earlier and now less common form of classification in OB is one where the prescribed action is focused – organization, group, individual, customer. (Can you connect these with the above list of dominant OB schools of thought?) How else might management ideas and practices be classified? (Huczynski, 2006)

HOW IS MANAGEMENT KNOWLEDGE ADOPTED AND EVALUATED?

While being aware of the different types of knowledge and how theories and approaches to learning can help in identifying and acquiring new knowledge, it does not help in assessing the value of that knowledge, nor does it reveal how management ideas are disseminated and adopted by managers. This is a huge topic, linked to studies of innovation and organizational change for example (see Rogers, 1983/1995; Mol and Birkinshaw, 2014), but we introduce some key themes here. In particular, we focus on the channels of knowledge transfer, the reasons for adoption and methods of evaluation.

Diffusion channels

New ideas and, usually, their associated practices are introduced to individuals and organizations in many different ways:

- teaching/training/conference presentations
- alliances/joint ventures/relations with suppliers/mergers
- Internet, books, magazines, videos, training packages and other media
- new staff (e.g., chief executive officer (CEO) brings in new practice)
- management consultancy
- innovation/adapting existing practices
- compliance to professional/state requirements
- social networks (e.g., COPs)/word of mouth.

The ideas are then often implemented or applied – although typically only partially and with some difficulty – and eventually may become normal practice, taken for granted or 'institutionalized'. Then, of course, they may become inappropriate in new circumstances, or new, improved, ideas come along and the cycle starts again (cf. Strang *et al.,* 2014).

Selection and adoption: The rational approach

But why are new ideas of interest to organizations and their managers? If we take the first of the three themes of management activity outlined above – addressing organizational objectives – then the answer lies in issues such as solving organizational problems or improving organizational efficiency, effectiveness or competitiveness. For example, a company may be experiencing falling profits, be losing customers or suffering a costly level of staff turnover. In response, it will seek out solutions. This may involve thinking of different ways to adapt existing procedures, devising new approaches or seeking out solutions from a range of external sources or channels (as above). This was clearly the situation in Case Study 6.1, where CRM was seen by Cathy as a way to solve the problem of losing customers.

If we take the second theme of management activity – systematic planning and control – then approaches and ideas such as CRM in the case study are selected and evaluated against these aims in a rational way. For example, evidence of its effectiveness will be sought and a quantitative cost-benefit analysis may be carried out to assess whether or not the returns are worth the investment compared to other possible solutions. Alternatively, if the solution is not known, management consultants may be asked to tender (compete) for a project and a choice is made on the basis of an 'objective' assessment of their bids and references. Such procedures are sometimes required by regulations, in the public sector for example. More generally, it has been argued that with increased competitive pressures and the potentially high costs of failure, organizations are becoming more 'objective' in their assessment of new ideas (Beer and Nohria, 2000; O'Mahoney *et al.*, 2013).

Selection and adoption: satisficing

Such techniques and prescriptions fit with the view of management as seeking 'objective' solutions to specific organizational problems in a rational manner (i.e., by systematic measurement). In practice, and in keeping with more general critiques of managerial rationality (e.g., see Simon, 1960), the best that might be expected given limited time and/or available information, is **satisficing** – making an acceptable, but not necessarily ideal decision/assessment. For example, in undertaking an assessment on the likely return on investment (ROI) in a new practice, it is often difficult to quantify some outcomes (**intangibles**) such as employee innovativeness, and to isolate or control the impact of the new idea from other influences on performance, including the experience of being measured itself (see Chapter 9 on decision-making in this volume). In the case study for instance, customer retention might have increased after the impact of CRM, but this might have been due to the failures of a competitor and/or the fact that employees improved their performance while it was being measured.

Satisficing A situation where a satisfactory resolution to a problem is adopted, rather than an optimum one.

Intangibles Difficult or impossible to measure accurately yet remain important. For example, a new procedure or system might be seen to increase productivity or employee satisfaction, but the benefit is difficult to isolate and measure.

However, it is not simply the fact that making objective assessments is technically difficult or imperfect. If we take the third dimension of management activity as being messy, sometimes reactive, political, emotional and frenetic, it becomes clear that in practice, selecting and evaluating ideas is not a completely rational process. We shall explore this later in the chapter, but it is generally recognized that managers adopt ideas for a range of informal reasons, which can be classified as psychological (e.g., stress leads to adopting ideas impulsively), political (a new idea serves career or departmental interests) and cultural (ideas are adopted because they fit one's values). For example, in the case study, it appeared that Cathy was feeling under pressure and that this might influence her decision-making and view of the success of CRM. What this means is that, not only may potentially effective ideas be rejected, but also flawed ideas may be adopted. This is clearly a real threat to the role and expertise of management. Indeed, this is not just true of management. There is a long history of inventions that were rejected despite technical and other advantages (e.g., see Rogers, 1983/1995). What, then, can be done?

There is considerable attention being given to helping ensure that management can identify, adopt and implement the most effective ideas. One view is to improve the sophistication and implementation of objective assessment techniques. Another is to recognize such rational procedures as being flawed, but also as not only better than doing nothing, but serving an important function, providing some 'immunity' from pressures to adopt ideas in a non-rational way (e.g., Abrahamson, 1991). We shall return to this theme later in the chapter.

Thinkpoint 6.8

Compare the process of adopting new management ideas to that of buying a new car or bike. You might be having problems with performance or a better model becomes available. To what extent do you adopt a rational and systematic approach to this activity? For example, do you choose on the basis of technical evaluations on consumer websites or on recommendations from friends, or what is considered fashionable?

Continuing debates

The above discussion set out why knowledge and learning have come to be seen as so important in organizations, and then explored some of the main perspectives. The particular case of management knowledge and explicit management ideas was then looked at, particularly in relation to how they are adopted and evaluated. These issues remain a feature of debates among and between academics and practitioners (Volberda *et al.*, 2013). Sometimes, however, the terms change. So, for example, the **transferability of knowledge** might now be seen in terms of its **stickiness** and the 'absorptive capacity' of the receiving organization or person, rather than a question of tacitness and motivation or cognitive ability (Szulanski, 2003). Also, while the above account is (hopefully) presented in quite a balanced way, there is sometimes fierce debate between people adopting different perspectives on knowledge and learning. At the same time, some perspectives are more pervasive and dominant in practice, even if the newer approaches receive more attention in articles and academic courses. Overall, behavioural and cognitive perspectives of learning continue to dominate, as does the view of knowledge as object-like and capable of transfer from one place to another.

Transferability of knowledge The capacity to move knowledge from one context or form to another. This may vary according to the people involved. For example, it might be easier to help another engineer learn a new theory of mechanics than it would be to teach an engineering novice (see also **knowledge diffusion** and **cultural barriers**).

Stickiness Sometimes used to denote how difficult it can be to transfer knowledge from one context to another – e.g., the tacit skill of a craft worker developed over years of practice (Szulanski, 2003).

Thinkpoint 6.9

Management ideas, theories and practices are like items in the daily news. Those that receive media coverage or academic attention do so because they are seen as relatively new or unusual. Hence, in the same way that it is easy to get the wrong impression about the likelihood of being murdered in your bed or the street, one can assume management innovations to be more common than they really are. For example, a large-scale survey reported that only around 20 per cent of UK firms had engaged in organizational and management innovation in recent times (Battisti and Stoneman, 2010). This suggests that the adoption of new management ideas and practices is very much a minority activity in organizations, in the UK at least – not the impression one gets when listening to consultants or management academics.

While some debates continue, new ones also emerge or come to the fore. In particular, it is increasingly recognized that knowledge is not easy to classify, capture, control and transfer, especially through information systems. Here, the social and constructivist theories have gained ground, but uncertainty remains as to how, and the extent to which, they can be applied or managed. For example, if *knowing* (i.e., a process) is preferred to knowledge, how can one assess learning outcomes? A related issue for management is that of aligning what individuals learn with the needs or demands of organizations. For example, Cathy (in Case Study 6.1) had this problem when she empowered her staff to develop their own solutions, but they did not always stick to the agenda. Is this a potential source of innovation or misbehaviour?

Within the realm of explicit management ideas, similar issues remain unresolved. For example, if the adoption of ideas by managers is not always wholly rational (in the sense of objective assessment against organizational objectives), how can this be achieved or improved in practice? Can managers become less prone to psychological and political influences? Similarly, with the continuation of globalization, a long-standing debate about the local specificity or embeddedness of knowledge continues to trouble and divide people. At one time, and for many, even currently, management knowledge was seen as of universal relevance, applicable everywhere (e.g., assembly line technology, CRM, knowledge management (KM)) (Hislop, 2013). The adaptations that people made as ideas travelled to different sectors or countries were seen to distort or corrupt the idea and its associated practices. Now, such modifications might be seen, not as distortions so much as inevitable constructions of knowledge in action – as innovation (Ansari *et al.*, 2010). Here, knowledge is not simply *in* context but *made by* the context, so cannot be transferred or moved (Orlikowski, 2002). This might seem reasonable enough, but it raises a number of issues when it comes, not only to ownership of knowledge or **intellectual property rights (IPR)**, but also to the teaching and learning of management.

Intellectual property rights (IPR) A legal term referring to ownership of knowledge or ideas. For example, the copyright assigned to authors, editors or publishers means that others have to ask permission and, often, pay to reproduce material. Likewise, inventions might be patented.

Selected studies

The references used above point to some of the key names associated with different views of knowledge and learning for example. Here we highlight three particular studies that are commonly referred to.

KOLB'S EXPERIENTIAL LEARNING CYCLE

Most of us would agree that we learn a lot through experience, but not all experience leads to learning. It depends on how we think about the experience. Kolb's (1984) model presents learning as an active (cognitive and experiential) process of perception and mental processing. Faced with direct (e.g., sensory) experience, we reflect on it and generate mental or visual concepts and conclusions, which we then test out in practice for feedback and, as we continually repeat this cycle, we develop our understanding. Think of an example of this process in the context of (a) travelling on a new foreign transport system, and (b) learning to play a new computer game.

NONAKA AND TAKEUCHI: LEARNING AS KNOWLEDGE TRANSFORMATION

This integrative approach to learning emphasizes facilitating processes. Using the tacit-explicit knowledge distinction, Nonaka and Takeuchi (1995) describe complex, independent, simultaneous or sequential processes through which knowledge is changed (see Figure 6.1).

First, tacit-tacit knowledge transfer ('socialization') refers to the traditional 'master-apprentice' relationship where skills are learned through observation, imitation and practice. Second, tacit-to-explicit transfer ('externalization') – the aim of much KM refers to attempts to unlock or capture knowledge through words, pictures or metaphors/analogies, for example. It is, by definition, often impossible and always partial (e.g., writing golf coaching books). Third, the opposite transfer of explicit to tacit knowledge ('internalization') relates to the application of representations of knowledge (e.g., manuals, diagrams and models) to develop abilities and understanding through practice and reflection. Finally, 'combination' is the use of existing explicit knowledge to create a 'bigger picture', such as is the case in formal learning situations like writing an essay and combining models.

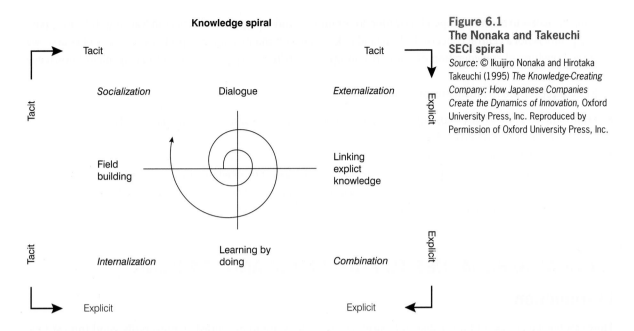

Knowledge spiral

Figure 6.1
The Nonaka and Takeuchi
SECI spiral
Source: © Ikuijiro Nonaka and Hirotaka Takeuchi (1995) *The Knowledge-Creating Company: How Japanese Companies Create the Dynamics of Innovation*, Oxford University Press, Inc. Reproduced by Permission of Oxford University Press, Inc.

ABRAHAMSON'S 'FADS AND FASHIONS'

Abrahamson (1991) is interested in helping managers make more rational decisions when adopting new management ideas. He recognizes that assumptions of rational management – free choice and clear organizational goals and criteria for assessing efficiency – are rarely appropriate or evident, especially in conditions of high uncertainty (cf. Simon, 1960). Rather, he shows how adoption of ideas can be 'forced' (e.g., government bodies requiring use of safety or quality protocols) or subject to the influence of 'fashion' (e.g., from consultants/gurus, media and business schools). Also, this can lead to copying others such as 'in-group' or peer companies. He calls this the 'fad' perspective, although most writers do not distinguish between fads and fashions. See Abrahamson and Michigan (forthcoming) for a more recent take on this topic.

Core concepts and the mainstream

Aside from the obvious case of knowledge, there has been little mention of our core concepts in the discussion so far. This does not mean that they are wholly absent in mainstream approaches. Indeed, if we had been able to go into more detail, some would have featured quite prominently. Identity, for example, is very important to social theories of learning in the sense of learning through others with whom you identify, and of knowledge and interests being associated with what it is to be a consultant, plumber, etc. Similarly, freedom is evident in the notion of self-directed learning and empowering staff to develop their own knowledge, perspectives and approaches, either individually or through communities of practice.

More generally, some learning theories are founded on a humanistic view, whereby we develop and become 'free' and creative thinkers through lifelong learning and self-improvement. On the other hand, according to such a view, a lack of **self-esteem** or confidence might hinder learning potential and this is quite close to the notion of insecurity. This is most evident in relation to the non-rational adoption of management ideas – grabbing at the latest technique for 'psychological' reasons. Similarly, power is evident in relation to the influence of rewards and of experts over others and in terms of a recognition that some may be reluctant to share their knowledge with others in the organization as a result. This clearly sets up the possibility of an inequality in terms of expertise and access to knowledge. While some mainstream thinkers are concerned with

Self-esteem A psychological term referring to how one thinks or feels about oneself in an evaluative (i.e., positive or negative) way.

opening up access to learning – open innovation for example – and recognize differences in learning styles or capacity, inequality is not a central concern. Indeed, and in keeping with mainstream perspectives generally of course, we shall see how limited consideration of our core concepts results in a very partial view of management knowledge and learning.

Key concepts from the mainstream include:

- From skills to knowledge (-economies; -sectors; -intensive firms; -workers; and -management).
- Data, information and knowledge.
- From knowledge types to knowing as a process.
- Learning as behaviour, understanding, knowledge construction and social practice/interaction.
- Adoption of management ideas and practices – a question of rational decision-making or satisficing?
- Knowledge as manageable and movable and/or as local and adaptable?

CRITICAL APPROACHES TO KNOWLEDGE AND LEARNING

Introduction

How can one be critical of knowledge and learning? Surely they are to be valued as universally good things? One might debate the direction in which they are channelled – what knowledge is to be learned and how – but they are unavoidable social processes or outcomes. Even if this is the case, there are important questions of:

- how knowledge and learning are conceived, prescribed and practised
- in whose name and interests
- with what consequences, and
- who and what are silenced or marginalized through them?

These help not only in terms of our understanding of the subject and its **contestability**, but also as regards the way in which our lives are shaped and can be altered (Contu *et al.,* 2003); how knowledge and learning can be used for particular ends that are seen as desirable or can be abused in the pursuit of undesirable or harmful ends. In this way, a critical view of learning can be seen as one that not only critiques learning theories and practices, but directs learning towards particular **emancipatory** processes and goals (Freire, 1972). This is especially clear in the particular case of management knowledge, our focus here, and is evident even from a cursory look at the particular way in which our core concepts – power, identity, freedom, inequality and insecurity – are *absent* from much of the mainstream debate.

Contestability Extent to which something can be disputed and debated.

Emancipatory Political term associated with emancipation or freedom from control. An example is freedom from slavery, but freedom remains an important issue in other contexts, even where control may be less visible.

Truth A common-sense term relating to that which is accepted as factual or verified beyond doubt, but also a philosophical issue, or claim, of some complexity. A core theme here would be the contrasting views on whether there can only be one truth or many truths.

We have now seen how knowledge has become a key focus in mainstream studies of management and organizations. However, it is generally a particular view of knowledge that is used, one that is largely cognitive and suggests its transferability and market or commodity value, for example. Implicit in the mainstream account has been the fact that knowledge and learning have been directed at improving organizational performance. What of other forms of knowledge, such as that of the 'whistle-blower' who reveals unethical or illegal practices or knowledge that would be generally useful, but is withheld to protect the organization's interests – i.e., an abuse of knowledge by silencing it? And what of 'knowledge for its own sake' rather than that which is developed for particular instrumental motives?

Even in more sophisticated (e.g., processual) accounts, knowledge is largely divorced from a broader politics of **truth** or how reality is made (and silenced) by knowledge. For example, in relation to learning, the prevailing truth is that

COPs are effective, but this may close off other approaches (Handley *et al.*, 2006). Similarly with identity, where broader issues of power are neglected, the self is seen as an individual possession rather than a partially shared story or narrative. And freedom also remains limited, as if achieved largely through self-knowledge and reflection or personal development. It is as if we can all become who we want to be without constraint or consequences for others. Inequality is not an issue either, except insofar as management's primacy is taken for granted – the right to select people and set the parameters of, and access to, knowledge and methods of learning. Insecurity too tends to be seen outside of a political context, either as a universal trait or one induced by work pressures and 'curable' through training or insistence on rational procedures for the adoption of new management ideas. Indeed, emotion more generally has been marginalized or commodified in mainstream approaches (Vince and Gabriel, 2011). For example, it has been translated into something else, like motivation, or a measure such as 'emotional intelligence' (basically, social skills) rather than recognized as central to all processes, including the most 'rational' – scientists can be seen as having, or even needing, a *'passion'* for objectivity for example (Sturdy, 2004).

Overall then, the key point is that mainstream approaches tend to celebrate the rational and objective and under-play the political. Where the political is considered, it is only in terms of minor differences in individual or small group interests, say between different departments or teams, rather than in a more critical or fundamental sense. Sometimes, these themes are combined in the sense of legitimate power, such as in the view that the most powerful or influential ideas (or people) are so because they provide the most effective or rational solutions to organizational problems. We shall see how this view seriously distorts the practice of management. First however, we continue with our case study and present an alternative view of management learning with a focus beyond, but including, immediate cognitive and social interaction processes (see Case Study 6.2).

Case study 6.2 Learning to love the customer: an alternative view of CRM

After hurriedly leaving Cathy's office, Rohan bumped into an old friend, John Melia. It turns out that John has been working at the DK-Line call centre for a year or so. John knew all about customer relationship management (CRM) of course, but he had a different story to tell. His version, from the 'front-line' as it were, was that the company wasn't especially interested in developing relationships with customers so much as selling other products such as car breakdown and loans because these were more profitable. Also, they had only adopted this approach when it was realized that all their competitors were doing it. Most of these firms had used a firm of CRM consultants and they had come in to DK-Line after its CEO had seen a presentation of theirs promising all kinds of savings, especially staff costs. But there was no way that this could be checked now as they didn't know what the output figures were before CRM was introduced at DK-Line.

As to the skills needed and the support given for this, John's view was that the mentors were effectively supervisors, checking up on mistakes and standards, and although staff had some leeway in the way they spoke to customers, this was quite restricted. For example, even if it was clear that customers didn't want any other service, staff still had to offer the full range of additional products in every call. He agreed that much could be learned from colleagues, especially about how to deal with angry customers. The training on 'handling irates', as it was known, was useless, as it gave standard approaches that customers saw through and it used examples from what John called the 'have a nice day' approach. Also, being able to relate to customers was taken for granted in the firm. It was only technical insurance skills that helped get you promoted, and most didn't have the necessary time to study for the exams, especially those with family responsibilities. Finally, with the new IT system, although it was easier having information available, you no longer needed to use your judgement. It was all set up for you in the 'frequently asked questions' page. They didn't need technically experienced recruits anymore ... Rohan sat down at his computer to start his essay. It was going to be a long night!

Key problems

BEYOND LEARNING THEORIES?

In the first half of the chapter, we saw how mainstream approaches have become critical of traditional views of knowledge as an object. A range of perspectives were drawn upon, including learning as behaviour and as understanding, and learning as the interactive construction of knowledge. While this shift is evident in many written accounts, it was also noted how this is not always reflected in organizational and management practice. Indeed, this observation can be made more generally about management ideas and practices – espoused theories and theories in use (see above). Rather, knowledge continues to be seen as an object or possession, which can be categorized into types, managed and acquired through the appropriate reward system and forms of instruction. However, there are more critical views of even the more **progressive** (and espoused) theories of knowledge and learning.

Progressive Favouring and believing in progress or moving forward by improving on the past.

These critical views can be divided into two types (for a detailed outline of the literature see Grey and Antonacopoulou, 2004; Easterby-Smith and Lyles, 2011). First, there have been some sustained assaults on the detailed contents of mainstream learning theory. Thus, and in a similar tradition to more longstanding critiques of learning (e.g., Freire, 1972), Vince and Martin (1993) explore the way that conventional approaches neglect considerations of power, emotion and gender (see also *Management Learning,* 1997; 2009). By presenting or configuring individuals (us) as 'learners', the details of how such an identity is constructed and enacted are simply ignored. This is problematic because the 'learner' is a deeply individualized notion that consequently marginalizes or silences the sociological and structural ways which – in other contexts – are widely recognized as configuring individuality. For example, individual assessment or appraisal encourages people to look upon themselves as separate from others and even in competition with them. It also encourages them to see their strengths and weaknesses and even their character or identity as wholly of their own doing and making. It helps in a broader process, through, which we deny or play down our interdependence with others for who we are and what we do. It 'individualizes'.

This one-sidedness is most evident in the widespread use of the notion of 'learning style' (Honey and Mumford, 1986). Learning style is an unusual concept in that it simultaneously individualizes and classifies. The learner is indeed an individual with his or her own particular relationship with what is learnt: yet the learning style approach always parcels that individual into some kind of predetermined category – as a 'theorist' or 'pragmatist' for example – usually captured by a traditional two-by-two matrix. Such 'models' can be seen as abuse, not only of the processes involved in learning, which are typically multidimensional, but of the individual learner as an object. Yet they are the staple of just about every management development course run in organizations or by consultants, as well as of academic learning models upon which they typically build. These make up evermore complex ways of linking learning to assorted 'variables' (e.g., work environment and personality), but this complexity can blind us to the underlying assumptions entailed by the paradox of the learner as individual and the learner as 'type' (see Reynolds, 1997, for a rare and systematic critique of learning styles within its own terms).

The second kind of critical view is less concerned with this or that detail of mainstream learning theory, but instead focuses on the general 'hoopla' or hype that infests writing on learning in organizations. One of the earliest and most incisive of these critiques was provided by Coopey (1995), where learning organizations are considered in terms of the way that they individualize and discipline their members. For example, by transforming *organizational* responsibilities for training into *individual* needs and responsibilities for (lifelong) 'learning', employees are pressured to develop in such a way that any failures in development or even advancement are deemed to be solely of their own making. This is an important critique, not just for what it says about '**learning organizations**' or 'societies', but because it links the fashion for learning with the rise of new organizational forms (see Chapters 4, 10 and 14 in this volume). In other words, preoccupations with learning cannot be separated from a much wider swathe of claims about organizations. More generally, it is simply invalid to separate calls for

Learning organization A term to describe organizations that value collective and not just individual learning. May be reflected in more participative structures and a managerial emphasis on continuous learning (i.e., organizational improvement).

learning from their wider social and organizational context (see Contu *et al.,* 2003 in the 'Important studies' section below).

Thus, mainstream learning theories have begun to be critiqued, especially in terms of how their neglect of context results in a 'naturalizing' of particular approaches to organizing and being (i.e., making them seem inevitable). The individual becomes a 'learner' with a particular style and a personal responsibility for learning and the organization becomes an entity focused on the acquisition of knowledge for the benefit of owners and others. Here, we can now see how learning is not unequivocally or unquestionably good as suggested by mainstream approaches. For does it not make a difference what is learnt? In this sense, any evaluation we make of learning cannot be separated from knowledge and/nor its consequences, and it is to this theme that we now turn.

FOUR ALTERNATIVE VIEWS OF MANAGEMENT KNOWLEDGE

We have seen how, in the conventional view, management can be looked at as an activity that is directed towards the rational achievement of organizational objectives, even if minor political, cultural or psychological factors may sometimes interfere with these processes. This gives rise to a particular view of management knowledge as that which achieves those rational ends. The means and ends are not questioned, but seen as neutral or legitimate.

Critical perspectives on management knowledge differ from this view. Needless to say, they do not appear in management guru presentations or most textbooks. (Why is this?) And even when they do appear in textbooks, they are often marginalized, labelled as being 'critical' and even separated off into a specific section in each chapter (as in this book.). In addition, while critical writers do not always promote their ideas as clearly as they might, the fact that these ideas are less familiar means that they resonate less with our existing (learned) ways of seeing the world. This may make them seem less persuasive – they are 'too new' or 'too different' or 'too abstract', regardless of their validity or clarity!

The ideology of a privileged male elite

All of us carry out activities that might be associated with 'management' (e.g., running a household; planning tasks; organizing an event), but we are not all called 'managers'. While the activities of organizing are long-standing, management as an elite group is a comparatively recent phenomenon, derived largely from appropriating ('buying' or 'stealing') and monopolizing knowledge of how to do tasks from craft labour (Braverman, 1974; see also scientific management in Chapters 7, 11 and 14).

What is the basis of managers' claimed 'right' to manage? Aside from formally acting on behalf of the legal owners of organizations (i.e., property rights gave rights of control), the authority and growth of management was founded on a claim to expertise, much like that of the professions such as lawyers and accountants, although without their formal associations and regulation. In this way then, management knowledge can be seen not only as associated with various activities, but as constructing and serving the interests of an elite, as *ideological* (Hales, 1993). Management qualifications are a good illustration – they help justify or legitimize expertise, higher salaries and positions in the hierarchy, while the majority are excluded (Willis, 1977). Would people study management in such large numbers if they were simply seeking a better understanding of business and organizations? What management ideas do you know that challenge the relatively privileged position of managers?

The notion of ideology is not solely a point about hierarchy, however, but about who occupies management positions. For example, the traditional emphasis in management on rationality, planning, measurement, competition and logical thinking can be seen as favouring attributes nurtured in the upbringing and education of males (see Chapter 5 on Diversity and HRM) – management as masculine (see Morgan, 1988; Collinson and Hearn, 1996; Wilson, 1996). Women can, of course, and do emulate these masculine forms of behaviour, but usually this involves a break with how they have been brought up and silences how broad-ranging sexual identities reinforce less instrumental relationships. More generally as well, knowledge is valued differently according to whether it is associated with dominant groups. If not, it may be taken for granted, as natural and not warranting special reward. This has long been the case where jobs become gendered – seen as the domain of one particular sex. In the case study above for example, John mentions how social skills are not recognized as highly as technical ability and that some groups are effectively denied access to the latter.

Neo-imperialism and/or religious conversion

Similarly, there is a cultural bias to management (and rationality more generally), founded, for the most part, on the economic dominance of the West. Here, the spread of North American management ideas and practices can be seen as **neo-imperialism**. Indeed, Western consultants, managers and lecturers working in South East Asia (*New Oxford Dictionary for Writers and Editors*, p361) and Eastern Europe have been likened to missionaries, involved in a process of conversion to the *true* way of managing/organizing (e.g., 'free' market capitalism) (Kostera, 1995). This view draws attention, not only to issues of power in terms of control over resources, but also claims to truth and whose knowledge is given voice and who are silenced or marginalized (O'Mahoney and Sturdy, 2015).

> **Neo-imperialism** Colonization other than by military force, typically associated with the spread of a particular dominant set of ideas such as religious beliefs or consumerism.

For example, it has been argued that a preoccupation with *explicit* management knowledge is a peculiarly Western notion and silences the wisdom and contribution of Eastern business practices (see Chia, 2003).

A discourse of our time

The same issues are evident in the concept of management as a dominant discourse more generally. Here, in contrast to the above view that management knowledge is restricted to an elite few, recent critiques of hierarchy from within management and calls for de-layering and (limited) 'empowerment' suggest that 'we are all managers now' or should be (see Burrell, 1996; Chapter 14 on post-bureaucracy). Indeed, the legitimacy and relevance of management knowledge has spread way beyond business organizations into government and even how we personally 'manage' our health and personal relationships (Grey, 1999; Hancock and Tyler, 2009). In this way, management is political, not so much simply by association with having power and privilege, but by shaping the way we all think about, talk about and do things and silence other (e.g., more radical or traditional) ways of organizing (Parker, 2003).

We have seen how this is the case in relation to learning itself – we might see ourselves as having a particular learning style. But how management knowledge comes to shape how we think and feel, our identity, is evident more generally. For example, Rose (1989) shows how the organizational behaviour concepts of attitudes and personality were developed in the Second World War in public and private sector programmes to 'govern' citizens and employees. Now, we take for granted that we have a personality and attitudes and may see ourselves in this way. This highlights how what might seem to be a shared view is itself the product of power. For example, the idea of a sense of time discipline – a concern with punctuality or not wasting time – and that of the consumer emerged and developed, partly to ensure greater work effort from employees (Thompson, 1967).

A market commodity

The combination of its importance, claimed universal relevance and its own focus on markets as key arbiters of value, makes management probably one of the most commoditized forms of knowledge. It is converted into an object-like form for transmission at a price in different markets – like 'milk into dairy products' (Huczynski, 2006). Although, as we know, explicit or codified knowledge may be merely the 'tip of the iceberg' when it comes to management, this view corresponds to many of the processes of managing knowledge (O'Mahoney *et al.*, 2013).

The 'products' are all very familiar from the management guru talk, text, training programme, DVD and vodcast; through various graphical representations such as the classic two-by-two matrix used by consultants and management lecturers; to the management degree and, of course, textbook (see also Sturdy and Gabriel, 2000). In the latter case, it is important to note that they are seen by many publishers and authors as first and foremost a product in a market, just like any other (see Box 6.2).

Box 6.2
OB textbooks and the cost of packaged knowledge – Where does your money go?

The current market price for an introductory OB book such as this one in the UK is now around £50.00. From the first print run, say 5000, the income of £250 000 will be distributed approximately as follows:

Bookshop (c.35 per cent discount for university stores)	£87 500	(£17.50 per copy)
Author(s) (commission at c.10 per cent receipts of £130 000)	£16 250	(£3.25 per copy)
Marketing and sales reps (c.5 per cent of receipts)	£ 8 125	
Distribution and warehousing (c.5 per cent of receipts)	£ 8 125	
Publisher overheads (e.g., staff) (c.30 per cent of receipts)	£48 750	
Publisher (retained surplus)	£81 250	(£16.25 per copy)

Clearly, for the publisher, there is some risk that the book will not sell well and the above costs partly reflect an unknown investment. But costs will decline in subsequent years and print runs. For subsequent 'new' editions such as this one, profits will be greater still, not least because the price is likely to be higher and relative costs lower, especially as only minor changes to content are usually made.

How else might publishing textbooks be organized and rewarded? How can the value and ownership of knowledge be decided upon? Google 'open access publishing'.

FOUR ALTERNATIVE VIEWS OF THE ADOPTION OF MANAGEMENT IDEAS

Cartoon 6.1
'He's a great manager because he has extra dimensions.'

'He's a great manager because he has extra dimensions.'

'Management ideas do not work!' If this is the case, you may wish to stop reading at this point, and even stop studying management, certainly critically. You might also wonder about all the ideas in this and other texts. What is the point?! Alternatively, you might be intrigued about why some ideas become and remain popular and important and what some of their consequences are.

Of course, management ideas, when applied or even talked about, have numerous and often highly significant effects (Walker *et al.*, 2015), but they can never work *exactly as intended,* and certainly do not often meet the expectations and promises associated with them (see Kotter, 1995). They are, then, necessarily imperfect. This is one reason why there seems to be a constant stream of seemingly new management ideas or fashions. This transience of management ideas is typically explained by changes in the business environment – new ideas are needed for new times – or the need to keep ahead of rival companies. Alternatively, there are core dilemmas, in structuring organizations for example, which can never be resolved fully. For example, too much centralization of decision-making can stifle creativity and too little can lead to a lack of focus (see Child, 1981). As a consequence, Mintzberg (1979) for example, compared the changing preferences for (de)centralized organizations to changes in fashion for clothes (also Abrahamson, 1991). While there is some merit in these accounts, they cannot fully explain the apparent rate of change of management ideas.

A more radical view is that the demand for new ideas is almost constant because of the persistence of a forlorn hope that problems can be solved, a hope which is enhanced by economic pressures on managers to achieve results. This hope might be seen as reflecting a naive (unitary) view of everyone in organizations sharing the same interests, whereas management ideas are often resisted by those who are subjected to them (Edwards, 1979). Conflict is inherent in organizations, not least because of the degrees of inequality. Here, unless the underlying causes of conflict are addressed, new ideas will never work and only treat the symptoms. Alternatively, the hope could be seen as a **modernist** faith (in the power of rationality and scientific knowledge to control the world), which is especially problematic in relation to managing people's behaviour, values and emotions (e.g., their motivation) – the unmanageable organization (Gabriel, 1995). (Why might employees be ultimately unmanageable?)

Modernist Label attached to a range of phenomena, including art and architecture. Here, it is a set of beliefs associated with the historical period of modernity. These beliefs value progress and include a faith in the rationality of science to discover truth and control nature. Things like ambiguity, chance, play, fun, unmanageability and multiple truths or rationalities (e.g., based on custom, religion, lifestyle) are denied or subjected to scientific scrutiny in modernism. For example, under modernist thinking, emotion might be seen as a quantitative measure of emotional intelligence. By contrast, such things are not denied, but celebrated or brought to the foreground in what has come to be known as postmodernist views.

Mentors Those assigned the task of supporting others by providing advice and assistance to help in their personal and career development.

Power

In the first half of the chapter we saw how the process of adopting new explicit forms of management knowledge matched two of the claimed dimensions of management activity – meeting organizational objectives and rational planning (e.g., evaluation) – although in practice an approximation or 'satisficing' might often occur. A more critical view would place greater emphasis on the third dimension of management, especially in terms of its emotional and political nature. We now take each of these in turn and then develop a more social approach to management knowledge in general.

While it is comforting to think that managers adopt ideas and use knowledge for the good of their organization (indeed, they are unlikely to admit otherwise), championing the latest idea in marketing, human resources (HR), finance or whatever, is likely to be helpful in getting noticed by superiors and helping advance one's career. Who gets promoted these days for saying that 'Things are fine as they are. We don't need new ideas.'? Given the difficulty in assessing the true impact of implemented ideas, this means that the emergence of ideas can be seen in terms of competition between different managers. Indeed, this can be seen at a broader level in terms of competition between management functions (e.g., accountants, consultants, marketers, etc.) both within individual organizations and generally (Armstrong, 1986 and Chapter 9 on decision-making in this volume). Apart from pursuing personal or functional advancement, ideas can be adopted and ab/used to legitimize or mask other, often sensitive, motives such as reducing headcounts or increasing control over employees (Braverman, 1974). For example, in our case study, CRM was adopted to increase cross-selling rather than improve relationships, and **mentors** were introduced, more to check up on than develop staff.

It is also important to consider those whose knowledge is not valued, whose voice is not heard and who are effectively denied access to valued (and valuable) ideas and practices. This raises the whole issue of how some knowledge is valued highly and the criteria against which knowledge is valued in society. For example, we have seen how management knowledge can be seen as a form of ideology that silences other (e.g., Eastern, feminine, **labourist**) views. As noted earlier, this can be regarded as neo-imperialism in that, unlike imperialism based on the use of military force, colonization is achieved through ideas and market power.

Labourist That which is seen to reflect, represent or celebrate the views of manual labour especially, but the working classes more generally.

Thinkpoint 6.10

Who decides which skills and forms of knowledge are valued most highly in an organization or society? Is this reflected in salaries and should it be? What other criteria might be used in assessing rewards?

Exercise 6.2

Rank the following skills in terms of their value (1 is highest, 8 is lowest):

- keyboard skills
- prioritizing activities
- driving a car
- social skills
- manual dexterity
- memory
- team leading
- foreign language fluency

Now reflect on what criteria you used to value them. Using these criteria, compare two different jobs that you are familiar with. How do your evaluations compare the relative status and income of these jobs?

Psychodynamics

Managers turn to management ideas in the same way that the Ancient Greeks turned to myth-makers and legends – to help them create a sense of order in the face of the potential chaos of human existence. (Watson, 1994, p. 10)

Psychodynamics refers to the 'anxieties, fears and yearnings' and corresponding psychological 'need' for a reassuring sense of order, *identity* and control, which underpins much behaviour. We have already referred to this in the sense of how managers act 'emotionally' and 'impulsively' in adopting or copying ideas in an effort to achieve psychological security, and that this may blind them to the organizational effectiveness of those ideas. The mainstream approach sees such 'non-rational' behaviour as pathological or something to be eradicated. Alternatively, it can be treated or 'immunized' against, by following systematic evaluation procedures (Abrahamson, 1991). However, more critical perspectives regard these issues as inescapable or, at least, as exacerbated by certain **individualizing** contexts,

Individualizing The process through which people come to see themselves as separate from others and personally responsible for their actions and life chances rather than interdependent.

whether in terms of the organization (e.g., career hierarchies) or beyond (e.g., capitalism or consumerism). These conditions create underlying and sometimes overt pressures and anxieties, such as a fear of failure and a sense of isolation (see Jackall, 1988; Gill and Whittle, 1993). However, such dynamics do not only account for how managers might be seen as gullible victims of the latest fad, desperate to avoid being left out of the 'gang'. They also provide an important basis for energy and action – imagine an organization where there were no pressures or uncertainties about the future or our identity. Insecurity then, is a condition and consequence of management. But it is also reflected in managers wanting to be seen as innovators and leaders and as the creators of ideas (Huczynski, 2006; Jackson, 1996).

Explaining the adoption of management ideas and knowledge in terms of political and psychological motives and the inevitability of these dynamics, provides an important counter to the mainstream rational view, but all three tend to generalize the processes. Why, for example, do some forms of management knowledge appear to spread (e.g., to different companies, sectors, countries) while others do not, or do so at a different time and in a different sequence?

Institutions and networks

There has always been **knowledge diffusion** across groups and societies (e.g., neighbouring interactions, exploration, colonization, trade, media) (see Rogers, 1983/1995), often, but not always, from the most to the less powerful or 'effective'. The crucifix and Coke bottle are said to be the two most recognized objects in the world. This has been facilitated (and fuelled) by technologies (e.g., print, telegraph, telephone, TV, computer, mobile technology). However, working or travelling in different parts of the world clearly shows how business, organizations and management are both similar (e.g., bureaucracies; assembly lines) and different (see Chapter 13).

Institutional theory broadly seeks to demonstrate and explain the variety of societal influences on organizational/management structures and practices – their institutional 'embeddedness'. It is concerned with variations *between* contexts – why one management practice is adopted in organizations in one sector, country or region and not another. These are explained in relation to a number of social institutions or categories of established patterns of behaviour – economic (company), political (parliament), kinship (family), occupational (professional and industry associations), educational (school, university), etc. What this means in practice is that, although the demand for new management knowledge and ideas might be based on economic reasons (e.g., falling profits) for particular ideas to be adopted, objective technical superiority is less important than institutional conditions (Guillen, 1994). These have to be conducive to idea adoption, which means, for example, that the business elites of opinion makers and relevant government and professional bodies have to be supportive and that their ideas are taken up by educational and training institutions. Indeed, sometimes new ideas (e.g., quality management) are imposed by **standard-setting bodies** such as the European Union.

In other words, ideas and practices (e.g., HRM, outsourcing, etc.) are adopted for largely symbolic reasons, as managers seek support and legitimation from different *institutional* sources or belief systems. The result is that organizations in the same context become more and more alike – **isomorphic** – such as in the case study of DK-Line call centre and its adoption of CRM on the basis of copying competitors (see Kostova and Roth, 2002; Strang, 2010). For this to occur, social networks of different actors are important in promoting and adapting ideas (see Robertson *et al.*, 1996; Alvarez, 1996; Tregaskis *et al.*, 2010). This parallels the mainstream literature on communities of practice, although, as already noted, differential access to those networks and communities is rarely highlighted (Handley *et al.*, 2006).

Knowledge diffusion The spread of knowledge across contexts such as between organizational or national boundaries, as if knowledge acts like a gas. Recent challenges have been made to this traditional view, such that knowledge does not exist independently, but is produced and adapted or translated in context. See contextual embeddedness on page 31.

Standard-setting bodies Regulatory organizations that set and monitor standards of practice for organizations, such as those in health and safety or accounting.

Isomorphic A term associated with the institutional approach that means 'takes the same or a parallel form'. In particular, it refers to the ways in which organizations adopt the same practices as their peers in a given social context, because they are required to do so by standard-setting bodies, see it as 'best practice' or are uncertain of what to do and so copy others.

Cultures

The institutional approach incorporates aspects of culture (see Chapter 10) in terms of knowledge which resonates with the prevailing values of business elites and managers (e.g., 'being progressive'). The cultural perspective is more focused and we have already referred to it in relation to mainstream approaches. For example, management practices such as individual and team-based payment systems are likely to fare differently in predominantly individualistic, compared with collectivistic, contexts, at whatever cultural level (e.g., regional, national, occupational, organization, functional department). In Case Study 6.2, we saw how John was critical of the new 'have a nice day' approach to service – it did not resonate with his sense of identity, culturally. In this sense then, cultures and associated social identities can act as barriers or bridges in the adoption of ideas (Cagliano *et al.*, 2011).

The cultural perspective is critical in the sense that it challenges the rational view that knowledge is adopted on the basis of its objective usefulness for the organization. However, it is incorporated into mainstream approaches in that cultural sensitivity training is recommended for employees or consultants to help them smooth the transition of ideas into new contexts. A more critical view would be to adapt the idea to fit the culture better, not least because most management ideas arise from relatively few (masculine, middle-class, Western) cultures (see p. 217). A related issue is that the importance of cultural resonance is exaggerated and power relations downplayed. For example, some knowledge is welcomed precisely because it is alien, if its source is associated with success (e.g., Japanization in the West in the 1980s). Similarly, many management practices are imposed without conforming to *all* prevailing norms and values (Wilkinson, 1996). Thus, the assembly line was widely diffused, but did not conform to the culture and institutions of skilled craft workers whose jobs it often threatened. At the same time, new ideas may be resisted, not simply because they are new or clash culturally – the 'have a nice day' approach at DK-Line – but because they are being used as a technique of control (Sturdy, 2001).

INTEGRATING PERSPECTIVES AND THE ART OF PERSUASION

We have seen how there are a range of different approaches to explaining the adoption of management ideas – power, psychodynamics, institutions and cultures (see also Chapter 2 on motivation and Table 6.1). They share the view that the mainstream or rational view is necessarily problematic, but what makes them critical is the extent to which power is important. However, while we might wish to attach reasons to the actions of managers, other critical views point to the dangers of such certainty, arguing that ambiguity is widespread. Sometimes, they even celebrate this lack of clarity or reason.

Table 6.1 Perspectives on the adoption of management ideas

Reason	Perspective
Organization effectiveness	Rational
Help career, function and/or control	Political
Relieve anxiety/fear	Psychodynamic
Provides legitimacy/imposed	Institutional
Fit values	Cultural
Well promoted	Rhetorical
Not sure there was one!	'Muddling through'

Note: See also Sturdy, 2004.

In practice, studies tend to adopt multiple or combined perspectives, perhaps because there are often multiple reasons for adoption. For example, an idea may be beneficial for the organization as well as for the manager who champions it, both psychologically and in terms of his/her career.

A recognition of the multiplicity of reasons for adoption is evident in studies of those who promote and sell new management ideas, such as management consultants, gurus, professors and textbook writers. In fact, this might be seen as another reason or perspective on why ideas are adopted – because they are presented in ways that appeal to people.

We might call this the rhetorical perspective. The basic tenet of this approach is that management knowledge is ambiguous – its value is impossible to prove absolutely or objectively. Therefore, its adoption crucially relies on how it is constructed, packaged and presented, not its objective merit (Grint, 1997). This is not simply a cynical view because even a good idea, like a good product, needs to be communicated or promoted well, but it does mean that the popularity of a management idea is no indication of its value.

Thinkpoint 6.11

A common way in which new management ideas and practices are promoted is to point out how they are used by very successful organizations (see Strang, 2010). The assumption we are being asked to make is that they are successful because of their adoption of the idea. A question rarely asked is 'might they have been more successful still if they had not adopted the new innovation?' If it is difficult to prove the effectiveness of management ideas, on what basis can they be judged?

There is not the space here to explore all the different ways in which ideas are promoted (see Cleverley, 1971; Kieser, 1997; Grint and Case, 1998; Jackson, 2001; Fincham, 2002). However, a useful starting point is to see how the perspectives discussed so far can be applied rhetorically. Imagine you were the management consultant in Case Study 6.2 wanting to convince DK-Line management (the client) to adopt CRM. How would you have done this?

- Taking the rational view, you might have explained the logic of CRM – keeping customers is cheaper than getting new ones – and offer statistics of the results achieved by others who use CRM. Here, citing 'independent' academic research would be helpful, using lots of references, for example. Of course, in a culture where science and rationality is valued, this would also provide a sense of reassurance, order and control (psychodynamic view) as well as a legitimate basis for furthering the career of the client and the profile of his/ her particular management function or department (political view).

- Drawing more explicitly on the other perspectives, you might have tried to scare ('unfreeze' – see Chapter 11 on change) the audience by stories of how, if they did not adopt CRM, they would go out of business and that all the 'best', 'leading' companies are already using CRM, especially the main competitor of DK-Line (psychodynamic and institutional views). You might have also pointed out to the manager concerned that, at the same time as helping the business with customer retention, CRM would be especially useful in influencing the CEO or in improving control of staff in terms of service quality, for example (political view).

- In countering some of the reluctance about the US origin of CRM, you might have pointed out that, although it is a different approach to current practice, it is merely what you normally do in everyday life – keeping in touch with valued friends for example (cultural view). Also, appealing to the client's identity as a marketing manager, for example, you might have pointed out that CRM is now a core element in the latest marketing qualification or course at a leading business school. Finally, you might have considered the visual way in which the idea is presented (rhetorical view) – a two-by-two matrix would be a good start, if a little clichéd – as 'the content (e.g., packaging) is itself part of the performance' (Grint, 1997, p. 733).

Exercise 6.3

What rhetorical techniques are used in textbooks to persuade the readers of the validity or value of their content (see also Fineman and Gabriel, 1994; Hackley, 2003)? How might promotion techniques be adapted to different learning theories?

Of course, much of this promotional packaging work may have already been done for you as management ideas are constructed and adapted at different stages (by consultants and academics for example) with their subsequent adoption by other managers in mind (see Huczynski, 2006; O'Mahoney *et al.*, 2013). Indeed, it is important to highlight that management ideas are not simply invented by others (e.g., academics, consultants, gurus), but typically derived from the practice of managers and other employees (see Abrahamson and Fairchild, 1999). This is a key criticism of the rhetorical approach as an approach to the development of ideas. It presents managers as gullible victims of the clever tricks of management consultants and gurus – organizational 'witch doctors' (Micklewait and Wooldridge, 1996) – rather than as co-producers in a more (inter)active process involving both insiders (managers, staff) and outsiders (e.g., consultants, academics) developing and applying ideas, techniques and practices (Groß *et al.*, 2015).

Exercise 6.4

Promoting/selling a 'new' management idea Your task is to plan how to promote or market a new idea in a country (or sector) that you are familiar with using one or more of the frameworks and ideas discussed here, and others you can think of.

Thinkpoint 6.12

Do the perspectives/reasons in Table 6.1 apply to your own interest in, or attraction to, particular management ideas? How would you rank them in importance? Why the differences?

IDEAS, TRANSLATION AND PRACTICE

Outlining critical views of management knowledge and of the adoption of ideas by managers, highlights how management is not a neutral, technical and objective process, but embedded in power relations, whether these are seen in psychological, institutional, cultural or rhetorical terms. However, the focus has been on management ideas more than management in practice. While there is a close connection between the two (see Sturdy and Fleming, 2003), not least in the promotion and adoption of practices, there is a danger of neglecting the application of ideas. For example, while ideas might be recognized by managers as being of value, this does not mean that others will be persuaded, or that the ideas will be applied in practice. In one respect we are considering the difference between cognitive/affective and behavioural learning or between espoused theories and theories in use – what people think and say and what people do.

We have noted how management practices (e.g., the assembly line) can sometimes be imposed on employees regardless of whether or not they 'buy into' them and the ideas that support them (Guillen, 1994). More generally, within all the management disciplines, there is a concern to identify whether or not the latest idea has been applied, regardless of how popular it seems (see also Kostova and Roth, 2002; Groß et al., 2015). Such an approach is useful, not least because it gets behind a media focus on the latest ideas to what is actually practised in organizations (Benders and van Veen, 2001), but it does suggest that ideas do have *pure* ideational and practical forms. (Are the practices at DK-Line 'really' CRM?) This neglects the active and inevitable way in which both ideas and practices are amended in use – *translated*. Even relatively 'dogmatic' knowledge such as religion is adapted to local contexts and hybrid forms emerge (Lillrank, 1995). In other words what, say, Business Process Re-engineering (BPR) means, differs from one person/organization/context/OB essay to the next (Ansari et al., 2010). More generally, and in keeping with social views of learning and processual views of knowledge mentioned earlier, it can be argued that knowledge is never fixed, but always and necessarily interpreted so that it has meaning in a particular context (Latour, 1987; Orlikowski, 2002). However, meanings are not simply free-floating and random, but channelled through power relations. This channelling is especially clear in relation to management knowledge as we shall see in the following section.

TRANSLATING THE CRITICAL TO THE MANAGERIAL

If a manager is persuaded of the utility of an explicit management idea, it is simply one point in a continual process of adaptation. Clearly, if the idea is to develop into an established practice in the organization, other managers and employees will need to be convinced, persuaded and taught. In doing so, the idea and its associated practices will change, as we have seen. We have also seen how ideas are moulded and packaged prior to being presented to managers in written or verbal presentations. For example, think of the process of producing this text. Who decided the structure? How was it written and edited, by whom and with what thoughts or motives in mind?

A key difference with this text, compared to most others, is not that it breaks any convention in relation to the process whereby books are written, edited, marketed or produced. Its difference is largely based on the choice to include critical perspectives on management and organizations. As intimated when management was discussed as an **ideology**, management ideas will not explicitly challenge management interests. For example, imagine trying to make a management idea popular, however valid it was, which gave no role or status to managers. Indeed, this is a key challenge for this textbook, and critical ideas more generally – how can those interested in management (or being managers) be persuaded of ideas that challenge management and its privileges (see also Chapter 5 and Chapter 9)? Now, some cite empowerment as a popular idea, which appears to undermine management's role by ceding power to subordinates. However, it does not significantly challenge hierarchy and certainly not ownership patterns in industry, only the middle layers in an organization (Burrell, 1996; Sturdy et al., 2015). Moreover, there is good reason to do this for cost-cutting purposes because middle management has proliferated over recent years.

Ideology A set of ideas and beliefs sometimes used to justify particular political or sectional interests. A patriarchal ideology, for example, justifies male domination. However definitions differ in the extent to which ideology is seen as reflecting or distorting the truth.

The difficulty of promoting critical or challenging ideas does not mean that they never emerge of course, for there are still other, albeit relatively marginalized, social contexts (e.g., universities and, in particular, political domains) or conditions that make them possible (see Parker, 2003). Indeed, numerous groups develop ideas that pose at least some challenge to management. Many of these are not heard (i.e., not published or read), but others are adapted in a way that silences or neuters that challenge, however slight. Indeed, Jacques (1996) shows how, when something genuinely novel and radical emerges, it tends to be adapted – or cut to size as in the Greek myth of **Procrustes** – to better fit current (modernist) arrangements and interests. For example, **post-modern** ideas might be more appropriate to present times. However, where they have been promoted, it is in a diluted, conservative form (e.g., Peters, 1992) and barely applied in practice. Hence, any potential challenge disappears in this translation or abuse of ideas (Willmott, 1992).

The **neutering** of ideas may be quite explicit. For example, when you read case studies or research that names the organization(s) in question, you are unlikely to see much criticism of the organization or its management unless they have left or heroically solved the problem at hand (compare this with O'Mahoney and Sturdy, 2015 where they study the consulting firm, McKinsey and Co.). This is partly an outcome of explicit censorship – who would allow such potentially bad publicity after all? But more often, it is self-censorship and author/publisher fear of litigation. But being critical is not pointing out that a particular individual or organization is managed badly; it is not so much personal, but potentially far more unsettling than that.

As the existence of this text suggests, critical ideas, if not practices, have some visibility. However, in textbooks for example, authors are constrained to present them in a largely commodified form (see Box 6.1 above) and alongside 'mainstream' approaches in order to reach large audiences. Equally, those with a commercial (e.g., consultancy) and, increasingly, academic interest tend to dilute or omit anything that is really critical. They may not even see it. This is evident generally, but also in the particular case of learning theory. For example, Contu and Willmott (2003) show how the situated learning theory associated with Lave and Wenger (1991) actually has important critical dimensions, which are lost in subsequent accounts of it by others and in its application. Power relations are central in their notion of 'legitimate peripheral participation' in terms of access of particular social groups to COPs and how seemingly consensual relations are produced **hegemonically** rather than naturally. These critical dimensions of Lave and Wenger's ideas are lost in others' adaptations and broader debate, such that situated learning comes to be known as a mainstream approach (see also Handley *et al.*, 2007). Thus, the Procrustean process continues in translating the critical into the managerial. When this occurs even in the realm of management ideas and writing, the possibility of developing critical *practice* becomes an even greater challenge.

Procrustes An ancient Greek mythological character who either stretched his guests to fit the bed or chopped off their legs if they were too tall. Eventually, the same fate befell Procrustes himself!

Post-modern Has two broad meanings – a historical era following modernity and a philosophical/theoretical perspective. Both are seen to celebrate what modernism devalues and/or represses – surface appearances, emotion, play, chance and indeterminacy in life – the value of different rationalities (e.g., based on experience) rather than a single authoritative science or **truth**. See also **modernist**.

Neutering Rendering impotent or ineffective.

Hegemonic Form of control that includes, if not focuses on, the control of people's ideas and values, their 'hearts and minds'. An example would be the instilling of a sense of respect for authority or for property rights or a commitment to the organization. All these may help ensure that we do what we are supposed to do and want what we are supposed to want by those in authority, such as employers and governments. This renders control through more overt reward or punishment (e.g., job loss) less necessary.

Important studies

BRAVERMAN AND DE-SKILLING

Much of the above text has applied to managers' adoption and use of management ideas and the privileged status of management. Relatively little attention has been given to how management first came to acquire and apply this knowledge, and with what consequences for other employees. Braverman's (1974) classic study shows how both shop floor and office work in the twentieth century was subjected to a rigorous process of de-skilling through the application of scientific management. This is quite a well-documented process whereby skills were effectively appropriated by management (and supporting academics) with the consequence that work tended to become more intensive, poorly paid and alienating, if also often more productive. For example, in Case Study 6.1, much of the judgement required on the job had been incorporated into the IT system. However, Braverman's key contribution was to place this in the context, not of improved efficiency, but the ideological nature of management. What was claimed as neutral, objective science was more about securing management control over labour and cheapening the costs of production, as a necessary condition for capitalism and continued growth in profitability – what many might see as an abuse of knowledge. This critique of capitalism has been itself criticized for focusing only on de-skilling, failing to recognize any re-skilling (e.g., use of computing) and ignoring gender divisions and the subjective

Scientism A view where ideas and techniques that comply with scientific protocols are believed to be objective and politically neutral and widely applicable.

experience of de-skilling. However, it remains important as a challenge to the **scientism** of management where its ideas and techniques are presented as objective and politically neutral. For example, and as already intimated, it could be argued that knowledge management is a contemporary approach to de-skilling, but further up the hierarchy. Now, it is professionals and managers whose knowledge is targeted for capture and abuse.

GUILLEN'S MODELS OF MANAGEMENT

Guillen's (1994) work explores key streams of management thought (scientific management, human relations, systems theory, etc.) in different countries (e.g., the USA, UK, Spain and Germany) and demonstrates a recognition of the range of factors involved in the adoption of ideas. It is an important counter to the rational-economic

Institutional approach A perspective that highlights the social shaping of activities at a broad level whereby institutions such as the state, education, professions and the church are seen to condition how things are done in a similar way within these contexts. Emphasis is placed on the importance of practices (such as managing employees) being seen as socially legitimate rather than necessarily technically efficient. When such practices and their legitimacy become taken for granted and established, they are said to be institutionalized. It is less useful in explaining variations within contexts or human agency.

Politics of truth The process of giving voice to ideas that compete over what is taken to be accepted knowledge or ideology.

Utilitarian Useful, especially in a practical way, but also refers to utilitarianism, which is a doctrine that judges actions on their outcomes in terms of overall increases in 'good' or happiness, for example.

approach in that he showed how new knowledges and practices are not adopted universally, to the same extent, nor, necessarily, in the same sequence or for the same reasons across nations or sectors (see also Djelic, 1998). In Spain, for example, management elites and practitioners adopted the human relations ideas or ideology. However, only managers in large organizations (electronics and petrochemicals) implemented the actual practices because smaller companies did not have the necessary resources (e.g., training departments) and were less in need of more effective supervision and control. This **institutional approach** also places emphasis on the role of employee resistance to control in shaping how particular practices emerge.

CONTU ET AL. (2003): AGAINST LEARNING

This is one of the few systematic attempts to critique learning, or, more accurately, the contemporary discourse of organizational learning. It uses the notion of a **politics of truth** in challenging hidden and explicit claims of this discourse, not least that learning is necessarily a good thing for all and is open to all. For example, contemporary learning discourse assumes that the content will not challenge managerial control and yet claims empowerment and post-bureaucratic structuring. Likewise, it shapes governmental agendas and broader politics in a manner that is difficult to contest as other voices are silenced. In short, learning organizations and societies enable one to learn only that which is good for them (rather than their members) and do not so much create knowledge as access it and seek to control it for **utilitarian** purposes (see also Fenwick, 2000).

Contribution to thinking about the field

This section of the chapter began by posing the question – how can one be critical of something as valuable as knowledge and learning? Hopefully, this has now been answered, at least in part. Critical perspectives overall place knowledge and power close together, but not simply in terms of knowledge as a commodity that brings power in the sense of influence over others. In the particular case of management knowledge, we have seen how a critical view challenges the idea of management as an objective, technical activity solely directed towards achieving organizational goals. At the same time, insofar as it does address and construct organizational aims, it is problematic in that these are also not **value-free**, nor without consequences in terms of inequality of resources and status, for example. Equally, regardless of issues of occupational privilege and management control over labour, management knowledge, like other forms, helps shape what we think and feel. In this sense, then, the issue, from a pluralistic or democratic point of view, is a concern over the increasing dominance of management as a **discourse** and the commodified or market form it takes (Chia, 2003). Such concerns are reinforced in the light of the association of management knowledge with other (e.g., Western, masculine, middle-class) discourses of privilege.

Attention has been focused on management knowledge rather than learning as traditionally defined, but similar criticisms can be made of the particular form of knowledge surrounding management learning. For example, we have seen how approaches to learning that focus on relations of power are few and far between and continually censored, either by default or design. They tend to ignore the context in which learning, shapes and individualizes identities, in terms of learning styles for example (cf. Contu *et al.*, 2003; Contu and Willmott, 2003). Overall, the principal contribution of critical approaches to management learning to date is in drawing attention to how management knowledge is engaged with or produced and with what consequences. Here, we have seen a number of approaches that point to fundamental limitations of the mainstream, rational view of management knowledge as a universal and explicit tool that can be used and assessed for the control of organizations. For example, the continual emergence of waves of ideas are better seen as a reflection of their inherent limitations than environmental change, not least because there is little variation in the (modernist) nature of management ideas. Moreover, their limitations are extended by intended and unintended political outcomes such as resistance from those who are subjected to their application.

We have seen that mainstream approaches sometimes recognize that organizational life is not simple or 'rational' and that anxieties, identities, politics and culture are important. However, we have also seen that consideration of such issues tends to be couched in a unitary or consensus view, or it fails to recognize power relations beyond local interpersonal or departmental conflicts. Moreover, even where such broader issues are recognized, we have seen how, over time, they may be edited out. Indeed, this abuse is almost a necessary condition for ideas to be disseminated beyond the confines of academic articles or 'critical' sections in textbooks. Nevertheless, we have also seen how culture, institutions and 'insecurity-identity' are not only important, but channelled within, and productive of, power relations. In particular, what is taken as normal and natural – the relative value of management knowledge for example – is, on the contrary, historically and socially produced. It is therefore contestable and changeable. Likewise, what might be seen as abnormal, managerial anxiety or stress for example, certainly should not be regarded as individualized or **pathologized**. In short then, a key element of the critical (and sociological) view of the world is scepticism or questioning things that are taken for granted, especially those beliefs that support inequitable relations of power (see Chapter 5). However, it should also be self-critical and, here, we can point to areas where critical approaches such as those outlined above are developing or may do so in future.

Value free That which is seen to be **objective** – i.e., detached from particular personal values. Critical theory questions its existence.

Discourse Often taken to mean the same as language or the spoken word and written text, but may also refer to a broad category of talk or text such as *managerial* discourse. Some approaches extend the meaning of the term to what is possible in a given context or era and to meaningful behaviour as well (discursive practices). Here, the term can be summarized as what can be said (and done).

Pathological Derives from psychology or psychiatry to refer to mentally disturbed individuals. Emile Durkheim used the term 'social pathology' to describe a situation where individuals failed to see society as an objective reality. Managers tend to regard workers as pathological ('awkward', 'bloody-minded', 'uncooperative', etc.) when they fail to comply with the logic and reason of management.

Experiential Pertaining to direct experience rather than thought or imagination.

Much of the discussion of management knowledge centres on explicit ideas. There is a danger here that cognitive and commodified views of knowledge are privileged and reinforced at the expense of **experiential** and processual views. Moreover, there is a division between those who are interested in knowledge and its emergence and those who are concerned with practices and their consequences. For example, one might be concerned with the tension inherent in CRM, which was evident in the case study (establishing relationships versus extracting more sales) and not the consequences for employees in coping with this. This issue is a problem not just in terms of focus, but analytically. Here, mainstream theories might even be useful in drawing out how social practice and knowledge are intimately connected. This is also hinted at with a focus on how ideas are necessarily translated or 'in motion' and by a growing attention to knowledge as produced through action and social activity, including talk (Chia, 2003; Sturdy and Fleming, 2003).

Finally and relatedly, conceptual divisions may distort what is experienced. Recent critical approaches have sought to challenge some of these separations. For example, the above account of perspectives on the adoption of management ideas presents critical views in direct opposition to rational accounts. This clearly draws out some important limitations of the mainstream view, but perhaps goes too far conceptually. Thus, being rational is seen as *not* being anxious or emotional, or political or cultural, for example. While this may conform to a common and classic distinction between emotion and rationality, heart and mind, informal and formal organization, in practice rationality is sustained (as well as threatened) by feelings, values and power (Sturdy, 2004). The crucial issue then is how these are channelled in particular directions and with what consequences. This returns us to some more basic questions that might act as a starting point for those wishing to pursue a critical view of knowledge and theories of knowledge: who makes claim to them; who is silenced or excluded; who assesses their value; what are their conditions and consequences, and how are these distributed or dispersed? In other words, what are the uses and abuses of management knowledge? Where such questions are directed at mainstream ideas and practices, they may go some way in reversing the typical translation process by converting the managerial *to the* critical.

Conclusion

Our core concepts – *identity, power, freedom, insecurity, inequality and knowledge* – have been evident to varying degrees throughout the chapter. Clearly, knowledge has been of central concern, but we have seen how this can be viewed in various ways. Similarly, power is recognized in some mainstream views, but in a very limited fashion, whereas a broader conception of power is what distinguishes critical perspectives. For example, insecurity and social identity are both important to some mainstream views of learning, but they are divorced from the power relations, which constrain and enable them.

Freedom and inequality have been largely implicit in the discussion, except insofar as access to valued knowledge is concerned, and the ways in which critical approaches draw attention to those who are privileged and silenced. Nevertheless, both concepts are central to the subject of learning and knowledge. Indeed, both mainstream and critical approaches often present the pursuit and acquisition of knowledge as a route to freedom. However, they would differ in the view of knowledge and the ways in which it is valued and distributed in societies.

These are important distinctions, but those with opposing views often neglect what they may hold in common. Indeed, the structuring of the chapters in this textbook into mainstream and critical views serves to strengthen this limitation. For example, in the same way that mainstream views ignore or, at best, edit out critical knowledge, critical writers may readily dismiss the empirical findings of mainstream research on the basis of their flawed or conservative theoretical assumptions. For example, the assumptions and claims associated with behaviourism and cognitivism are highly problematic, but do have some validity and resonance with learning in practice. This is not necessarily to argue for some kind of middle ground or compromise, but more for the translation of mainstream into critical ideas and practices.

In this chapter, I have sought to present selectively both mainstream and critical approaches to knowledge and learning in the particular context of management. In the first part of the chapter, emphasis was placed on learning in general, while in the second part the focus was on learning in the sense of the adoption of management ideas and practices. In both cases, different perspectives were presented within what have been organized as mainstream and critical approaches. Whatever position(s) adopted, this is one of the most important issues – the plurality of available perspectives. This is important because it shows how an understanding of a topic is limited if it is restricted to a single approach. Indeed, in practice most researchers adopt a number of approaches or combine them. However, this does not mean that one gets closer to the truth the more perspectives one adopts. First, perspectives are sometimes quite incompatible and, second, there is no one truth. Indeed, an important lesson drawn from recent critical approaches, but with a long tradition, is that one should be sceptical of all claims to truth, even critical ones – the 'point is not that everything is bad, but that everything is dangerous' (Foucault, 1984, p. 343).

Discussion questions

1   Return to the notes you made at the start of the chapter about why you were reading it. Now that you have reached the end, have those aims been addressed? How would you now amend the learning objectives?

2   In a small group, agree and then list what you consider to be the main themes of the chapter. Then, take each one in turn and discuss what you understand them to mean, by thinking of examples. Note down any differences in views. Finally, discuss the implications of different understandings for the study of management.

3   Management ideas do not work as intended. Discuss/consider the implications of this for (a) the practice of management, and (b) studying management.

4   In what ways can one be critical of learning and knowledge? What practical implications does this have for organizations and for the design of courses and the presentation of ideas and theories?

Further reading

Easterby-Smith, M. and Lyles, M. A. (eds) (2011) *The Handbook of Organizational Learning and Knowledge Management,* New York: Wiley.

Dierkes, M., Antal, A. B., Child, J. and Nonaka, I. (eds) (2001) *Handbook of Organizational Learning and Knowledge,* Oxford: Oxford University Press.

Both these are large and comprehensive volumes with high quality chapters from well informed contributors – not all chapters will be relevant, but both should be consulted as further reading when it comes to assignments, and as useful sources of other references as well, although obviously not the most recent ones.

Hislop, D. (2013) *Knowledge Management in Organizations – A Critical Introduction,* third edn, Oxford: Oxford University Press.

The book's title pretty much says it all except that it covers knowledge processes more generally rather than being restricted to the active management of knowledge. Interestingly, it addresses the topic of unlearning in some detail.

Huczynski, A. A. (2006) *Management Gurus,* second edn, London: Routledge.

Despite its title, this book focuses on explicit management knowledge or ideas and is an excellent and uniquely accessible account of the popularity of management ideas. It covers a range of perspectives to show how ideas become and are made popular.

Malone, S. A. (2003) *Learning About Learning,* London: Chartered Institute of Personnel and Development.

This is described as an 'A–Z of training and development tools and techniques' and provides readable and concise accounts of key terms and concepts in mainstream learning practice. It is also very useful for numerous website references on individual learning topics, but does not really engage with critical perspectives.

Newell, S., Robertson, M., Scarbrough, H. and Swan, J. (2009) *Managing Knowledge Work and Innovation,* second edn. Houndmills: Palgrave.

This is a popular, useful and more advanced text with a focus on knowledge and its management more than learning theories. It also covers some critical perspectives, especially in terms of the critique of knowledge manageability.

Advanced further reading

The following are mostly academic journal articles and therefore not especially accessible, but they are particularly insightful and therefore worth exploring, even if only in terms of identifying their central points and arguments. As we have seen, more critical perspectives are not typically presented to mass markets. Hence the value of this textbook. In addition, you should take a look at the journal, *Management Learning,* as well as more general management journals which publish critical work such as *Organization, Gender, Work and Organization, Organization Studies* and *Human Relations.*

Abrahamson, E. and Michigan, R. (nd) 'The Interrelation between Supply and Demand in the Market for Business Fashions', Columbia University, Department of Management, Graduate School of Business, Working Paper.

Blackler, F. (1995) 'Knowledge, knowledge work and organisations: An overview and interpretation', *Organisation Studies,* 16(6): 1021–1046.

Birkinshaw, J., Hamel, G. and Mol, M.J. (2008) 'Management innovation', *Academy of Management Review,* 33(4): 825–846.

Brown, J. S. and Du Guid, P. (2001) 'Knowledge and organization: A social-practice perspective', *Organisation Science,* 12(2): 198–213.

Chia, R. (2003) 'From knowledge creation to the perfecting of action: Tao, Basho and pure experience as the ultimate ground of knowing', *Human Relations,* 56(8): 953–981.

Contu, A. and Willmott, H. (2003) 'Re-embedding situatedness: The importance of power relations in learning theory', *Organisation Science,* 14(3): 283–296.

Contu, A., Grey, C. and Ortenblad, A. (2003) 'Against learning', *Human Relations,* 56(8): 931–952.

Easterby-Smith, M. (1997) 'Disciplines of organizational learning: Contributions and critiques', *Human Relations,* 50(9): 1084–1113.

Easterby-Smith, M., Lyles, M. A. and Tsang, E. W. K. (2008) 'Inter-organizational knowledge transfer: Current themes and future prospects', *Journal of Management Studies,* 45(4): 677–690.

Fineman, S. and Gabriel, Y. (1994) 'Paradigms of organizations: An exploration in textbook rhetorics', *Organisation,* 1(2): 375–399.

Fox, S. (1994a) 'Debating management learning I', *Management Learning,* 25(1): 83–93.

Fox, S. (1994b) 'Debating management learning II', *Management Learning,* 25(4): 579–597.

Freire, P. (1972) *Pedagogy of the Oppressed,* Harmondsworth: Penguin.

Furusten, S. (1999) *Popular Management Books: How They Are Made and What They Mean for Organisations,* London: Routledge.

Grey, C. and Antonacopoulou, E. (eds) (2004) *Essential Readings in Management Learning,* London: Sage.

Grint, K. (1997) 'TQM, BPR, JIT, BSCs and TLAs: Managerial waves or drownings', *Management Decision,* 35(10): 731–738.

Jacques, R. (1996) *Manufacturing the Employee: Management Knowledge from the 19th to 21st Centuries,* London: Sage.

Levitt, B. and March, J. G. (1988) 'Organisational learning', *Annual Review of Sociology,* 14: 319–340.

Perkmann, M. and Spicer, A. (2008) 'How are management fashions institutionalized? The role of institutional work', *Human Relations,* 61(6): 811–844.

O'Mahoney, J. and Sturdy, A. J. (2015) 'Power and the Diffusion of Management Ideas: The Case of McKinsey & Co.' *Management Learning.* (Online first –DOI: 10.1177/1350507615591756).

Prichard, C, Hull, R., Chumer, M. and Willmott, H. (2000) *Managing Knowledge: Critical Investigations of Work and Learning,* Basingstoke: Macmillan.

Scarbrough, H. (ed.) (2008) *The Evolution of Business Knowledge,* Oxford: Oxford University Press.

Starkey, K. (1996) *How Organisations Learn,* London: Thomson.

Sturdy, A. J. (2004) 'The adoption of management ideas and practices: Theoretical perspectives and possibilities', *Management Learning,* 35(2): 155–179.

Sturdy, A. J. and Gabriel, Y. (2000) 'Missionaries, mercenaries or car salesmen? MBA teaching in Malaysia', *Journal of Management Studies,* 37(7): 979–1002.

Sturdy, A J., Handley, K., Clark, T. and Fincham, R. (2009) *Management Consultancy, Boundaries and Knowledge in Action,* Oxford: Oxford University Press.

Willis, P. (1977) *Learning to Labor: How Working Class Kids Get Working Class Jobs,* New York: Columbia University Press.

Useful websites

www.learning-theories.com/

www.cipd.co.uk/hr-topics/learning-development.aspx

www.wenger-trayner.com/introduction-to-communities-of-practice/

www.mlq.sagepub.com/

See if you can find useful links of your own for topics such as communities of practice and organizational learning.

References

Abrahamson, E. (1991) 'Managerial fads and fashions: The diffusion and rejection of innovations', *Academy of Management Review,* 16(3): 586–612.

Abrahamson, E. and Fairchild, G. (1999) 'Management fashion: Lifecycles, triggers and collective learning processes', *Administrative Science Quarterly,* 44(4): 708–720.

Abrahamson, E. and Michigan, R. (forthcoming) 'The interrelation between supply and demand in the market for management fashions', *Academy of Management Review.*

Alvarez, J-L. (1996) 'The international popularization of entrepreneurial ideas', in S. R. Clegg and G. Palmer (eds.) *The Politics of Management Knowledge,* London: Sage.

Alvarez, J-L. (1998) 'The sociological tradition and the spread and institutionalisation of knowledge for action', in J-L. Alvarez (ed.) *The Diffusion and Consumption of Business Knowledge,* London: Macmillan.

Ansari, S., Fiss, P. and Zajac, E. (2010) 'Made to fit: How practices vary as they diffuse', *Academy of Management Review,* 35(1): 67–92.

Argyris, C. and Schon, D. A. (1974) *Theory in Practice,* San Francisco: Jossey-Bass.

Armstrong, P. (1986) 'Management control strategies and inter-professional competition', in D. Knights and H. Willmott (eds.) *Managing the Labour Process,* Aldershot: Gower.

Battisti, G. and Stoneman, P. (2010) 'How innovative are UK firms?', *British Journal of Management,* 21: 187–206.

Becker, G. S. (2001) 'Talking human capital with Gary S. Becker', *Learning in the New Economy,* Spring (at www.linezine.com), cited in CIPD, 2002.

Beer, M. and Nohria, N. (2000) *Breaking the Code of Change,* Boston: HBS Press.

Benders, J. and van Veen, K. (2001) 'What's in a fashion? Interpretative viability and management fashions', *Organisation,* 8(1): 33–53.

Blackler, F. (1995) 'Knowledge, knowledge work and organisations: An overview and interpretation', *Organisation Studies,* 16(6): 1021–1046.

Bogenrieder, I. and Nooteboom, B. (2004) 'Learning groups: What types are there? A theoretical analysis and an empirical study in a consultancy firm', *Organization Studies,* 25(2): 287–313.

Boussebaa, M., Sturdy A. J. and Morgan G. (2014) 'Learning from the world? Horizontal knowledge flows and geopolitics in international consulting firms', *International Journal of Human Resource Management,* 25(9): 1227–1242.

Braverman, H. (1974) *Labor and Monopoly Capital,* New York: Monthly Review Press.

Brown, J. S. and Du Guid, P. (2001) 'Knowledge and organisation: A social-practice perspective', *Organisation Science,* 12(2): 198–213.

Burrell, G. (1996) 'Hard times for the salariat?', in H. Scarborough (ed.) *The Management of Expertise,* Basingstoke: Macmillan.

Cagliano, R., Caniato, F., Golini, R., Longoni, A. and Micelotta, E. (2011) 'The impact of country culture on the adoption of new forms of work organization', *International Journal of Operations & Production Management,* 31(3): 297–323.

Chia, R. (2003) 'From knowledge creation to the perfecting of action: Tao, Basho and pure experience as the ultimate ground of knowing', *Human Relations,* 56(8): 953–981.

Child, J. (1981) *The Challenge of Management Control,* London: Kogan Page.

CIPD (2002) *How Do People Learn? Research Report,* London: Chartered Institute of Personnel and Development.

Cleverley, G. (1971) *Managers and Magic,* London: Longman.

Collinson, D. and Hearn, J. (eds) (1996) *Managers as Men,* London: Sage.

Contu, A. and Willmott, H. (2003) 'Re-embedding situatedness: The importance of power relations in learning theory', *Organisation Science,* 14(3): 283–296.

Contu, A., Grey, C. and Ortenblad, A. (2003) 'Against learning', *Human Relations,* 56(8): 931–952.

Coopey, J. (1995) 'The learning organization: Power, politics and ideology', *Management Learning,* 26: 193–213.

Djelic, M-L. (1998) *Exporting the American Model: The Post-war Transformation of European Business,* Oxford: OUP.

Easterby-Smith, M. and Lyles, M. A. (eds) (2011) *The Handbook of Organizational Learning and Knowledge Management,* New York: Wiley.

Edwards, R. (1979) *Contested Terrain,* New York: Basic Books.

Engestrom, Y. and Middleton, D. (eds) (1996) *Cognition and Communication at Work,* Cambridge: CUP.

Fenwick, T. (2000) 'Questioning the concept of the learning organisation', in C. Paechter, M. Preedy, D. Scott and J. Soler (eds) *Knowledge, Power and Learning,* London: Paul Chapman.

Fincham, R. (2002) 'Charisma v technique: Differentiating the expertise of management gurus and management consultants', in T. Clark and R. Fincham (eds) *Critical Consulting,* Oxford: Blackwell.

Fineman, S. and Gabriel, Y. (1994) 'Paradigms of organizations: An exploration in textbook rhetorics', *Organisation,* 1(2): 375–399.

Foucault, M. (1984) *The Foucault Reader,* Harmondsworth: Penguin.

Freire, P. (1972) *Pedagogy of the Oppressed,* Harmondsworth: Penguin.

Gabriel, Y (1995) 'The unmanaged organization: Stories, fantasies and subjectivity', *Organization Studies* 16(3): 477–501.

Gill, J. and Whittle, S. (1993) 'Management by panacea: Accounting for transience', *Journal of Management Studies,* 30(2): 281–296.

Granovetter, M. (1973) 'The strength of weak ties', *American Journal of Sociology,* 78(May): 1360–1380.

Grey, C. (1999) 'We are all managers now?', *Journal of Management Studies,* 36(5): 561–586.

Grey, C. and Antonacopoulou, E. (eds) (2004) *Essential Readings in Management Learning,* London: Sage.

Grint, K. (1997) 'TQM, BPR, JIT, BSCs and TLAs: Managerial waves or drownings', *Management Decision,* 35(10): 731–738.

Grint, K. and Case, P. (1998) 'The violent rhetoric of re-engineering: Management consultancy on the offensive', *Journal of Management Studies,* 35(5): 557–577.

Groß, C., Heusinkveld, S. and Clark, T. (2015) 'The active audience? Gurus, management ideas and consumer variability', *British Journal of Management,* 26: 273–291.

Guillen, M. F. (1994) *Models of Management: Work, Authority and Organisation in a Comparative Perspective,* Chicago: University of Chicago Press.

Hackley, C. (2003) '"We are all customers now …": Rhetorical strategy and ideological control in marketing management texts', *Journal of Management Studies,* 40(5): 1325–1352.

Hales, C. (1993) *Management Through Organisation,* London: Routledge.

Hancock, P. and Tyler, M. (eds) (2009) *The Management of Everyday Life,* Basingstoke: Palgrave-Macmillan.

Handley, K., Clark, T., Fincham, R. and Sturdy, A. J. (2007) 'Researching situated learning: Participation, identity and practices in client-management consultant relationships', *Management Learning,* 38(2): 173–191.

Handley, K., Sturdy A., Clark, T. and Fincham R. (2006) 'Within and beyond communities of practice: Making sense of learning through participation, identity and practice', *Journal of Management Studies,* 43(3): 641–655.

Honey, P. and Mumford, A. (1986) *Using Your Learning Styles,* Berkshire: Peter Honey.

Huczynski, A. A. (2006) *Management Gurus: What They Are and How To Become One,* London: Routledge.

Jackall, R. (1988) *Moral Mazes: The World of Corporate Managers,* Oxford: OUP.

Jackson, B. (1996) 'Re-engineering the self: The manager and the management guru', *Journal of Management Studies,* 33: 571–590.

Jackson, B. (2001) *Management Gurus and Management Fashions,* London: Routledge.

Jacques, R. (1996) *Manufacturing the Employee,* London: Sage.

Kieser, A. (1997) 'Rhetoric and myth in management fashion', *Organisation,* 4(1): 49–74.

Kolb, D. A. (1984) *Experiential Learning,* Englewood Cliffs, NJ: Prentice Hall.

Kostera, M. (1995) 'The modern crusade: The missionaries of management come to Eastern Europe', *Management Learning*, 26(3): 331–352.

Kostova, T. and Roth, K. (2002) 'Adoption of an organisational practice by subsidiaries of MNCs: Institutional and relational effects', *Academy of Management Journal*, 45(1): 215–233.

Kotter, J. P. (1995) 'Leading change: Why transformation efforts fail', *Harvard Business Review*, 73(2): 59–67.

Lam, A. (2000) 'Tacit knowledge, organisation studies and societal institutions: An integrated framework', *Organisation Studies*, 21(3): 487–513.

Latour, B. (1987) *Science in Action*, Cambridge, MA: Harvard University Press.

Lave, J. and Wenger, E. (1991) *Situated Learning: Legitimate Peripheral Participation*, New York: Cambridge University Press.

Lillrank, P. (1995) 'The transfer of management innovations from Japan', *Organisation Studies*, 16(6): 971–989.

Malone, S. A. (2003) *Learning About Learning*, London: Chartered Institute of Personnel and Development.

Management Learning (1997) 'Special issue: Emotion and learning in organisations', 28(1).

Management Learning (2009) Special issue: Teaching from critical perspectives', 40(1).

Micklewait, J. and Wooldridge, A. (1996) *The Witch Doctors: What the Management Gurus Are Saying, Why It Matters and How to Make Sense of It*, London: Heinemann.

Mintzberg, H. (1979) *The Structuring of Organisations*, New York: Prentice Hall.

Mol, M. J. and Birkinshaw, J. (2014) 'The role of external involvement in the creation of management innovations'. *Organization Studies*, 35: 1287–1312.

Monteiro, L. F., Mol, M. J. and Birkinshaw, J. (2015) 'Ready to be open? Explaining the firm-level barriers to benefitting from openness to external knowledge'. INSEAD working paper (forthcoming in *Long Range Planning*).

Morgan, G. (1988) *Images of Organisation*, London: Sage.

Newell, S., Robertson, M., Scarbrough, H. and Swan, J. (2002) *Managing Knowledge Work*, Houndmills: Palgrave.

Nonaka, I. and Takeuchi, H. (1995) *The Knowledge Creating Company*, Oxford: Oxford University Press.

O'Mahoney, J. and Sturdy, A. J. (2015) 'Power and the diffusion of management ideas: The case of McKinsey & Co.', *Management Learning*. (Online first – DOI: 10.1177/1350507615591756).

O'Mahoney, J., Heusinkveld, S. and Wright, C. (2013) 'Commodifying the commodifiers: The impact of procurement on management knowledge', *Journal of Management Studies*, 50(2): 204–235.

Orlikowski, W. (2002) 'Knowing in practice: Enacting a collective capability in distributed organizing', *Organization Science*, 13(3): 249–273.

Orr, J. (1996) *Talking About Machines: An Ethnography of a Modern Fob*, Ithaca, NY: IRL Press.

Parker, M. (2003) *Against Management*, Cambridge: Polity.

Peters, T. (1992) *Liberation Management: Necessary Disorganisation for the Nanosecond Nineties*, New York: Knopf.

Piaget, J. (1950) *The Psychology of Intelligence*, London: Routledge.

Polyani, M. (1966) *The Tacit Dimension*, London: Routledge.

Porter, W. W. and Graham, C. R. (2015) 'Institutional drivers and barriers to faculty adoption of blended learning in higher education', *British Journal of Educational Technology*. doi: 10.1111/bjet.12269.

Reynolds, M. (1997) 'Learning styles: A critique', *Management Learning*, 28: 115–133.

Rigby, D. and Bilodeau, B. (2015) *Management tools and trends 2015*, New York: Bain & Co.

Robertson, M., Swan, J. and Newell, S. (1996) 'The role of networks in the diffusion of technological innovation', *Journal of Management Studies*, 33(3): 333–359.

Rogers, E. M. (1983/1995) *Diffusion of Innovations* (third/fourth edns), New York: Free Press.

Rose, N. (1989) *Governing the Soul: The Shaping of the Private Self*, London: Routledge.

Ryle, G. (1949) *The Concept of Mind*, Harmondsworth: Penguin Books.

Scarbrough, H., Bresnen, M., Edelman, L., Laurent, S., Newell S. L. and Swan, J. (2004) 'The processes of project-based learning: An exploratory study', *Management Learning*, 35(4): 491–506.

Sennett, R. (2000) *The Corrosion of Character*, New York: W. W. Norton and Co.

Simon, H. (1960) *The New Science of Management Decisions*, New York: Harper and Row.

Skinner, B. F. (1953) *Science and Human Behaviour*, New York: Macmillan.

Skinner, B. F. (1971) *Beyond Freedom and Dignity*, Harmondsworth: Penguin.

Strang, D. (2010) *Learning by Example*. Princeton: PUP.

Strang, D., David, R. J. and Akhlaghpour, S. (2014) 'Coevolution in management fashion: An agent-based model of consultant-driven innovation', *American Journal of Sociology*, 120(1): 226–264.

Sturdy, A. J., Handley, K., Clark, T. and Fincham, R. (2009) *Management Consultancy, Boundaries and Knowledge in Action*, Oxford: Oxford University Press.

Sturdy, A. J. (2001) 'The global diffusion of customer service: A critique of cultural and institutional perspectives', *Asia Pacific Business Review*, 7(3): 73–87.

Sturdy, A. J. (2004) 'The adoption of management ideas and practices: Theoretical perspectives and possibilities', *Management Learning*, 35(2): 155–179.

Sturdy, A. J. and Fleming, P. (2003) 'Talk as technique: A critique of the words and deeds distinction in the diffusion of customer service cultures', *Journal of Management Studies*, 40(5): 753–773.

Sturdy, A. J. and Gabriel, Y. (2000) 'Missionaries, mercenaries or car salesmen? MBA teaching in Malaysia', *Journal of Management Studies,* 37(7): 979–1002.

Sturdy, A. J., Wylie, N. and Wright, C. (2015) *Management as Consultancy: Neo-bureaucracy and the Consultant Manager,* Cambridge: Cambridge University Press.

Sydow, J., Lindkvist, L. and DeFillippi, R. (2004) 'Project-based organizations, embeddedness and repositories of knowledge: Editorial', *Organization Studies,* 25(9): 1475–1490.

Szulanski, G. (2003) *Sticky Knowledge – Barriers to Knowing in the Firm.* London: Sage.

Tempest, S. and Starkey, K. (2004) 'The effects of liminality on individual and organizational learning', *Organization Studies,* 25(4): 507–527.

Tengblad, S. (2012) *The Work of Managers: Towards a Practice Theory of Management,* Oxford: Oxford University Press

Thompson, E. P. (1967) 'Time, work discipline and industrial capitalism', *Past and Present,* 38: 56–97.

Tregaskis, O., Edwards, T., Edwards, P., Ferner, A. and Marginson, P. (2010) 'Transnational learning structures in multinational firms: Organizational context and national embeddedness', *Human Relations,* 63(4): 471–499.

Vince, R. and Gabriel, Y. (2011) 'Organizations, learning and emotion', in: M. Easterby-Smith and M. A. Lyles (eds) *Handbook of Organizational Learning and Knowledge Management* (2nd edn), Chichester, UK: Wiley, pp. 331–348.

Vince, R. and Martin, L. (1993) 'Inside action learning: The psychology and the politics of the action learning model', *Management Education and Development,* 24(3): 205–16.

Volberda, H. W., van den Bosch, F. and Heij, C. V. (2013) 'Management innovation', *European Management Review,* 10: 1–15.

Vygotsky, L. S. (1962) *Thought and Language,* Cambridge, MA: MIT Press.

Walker, R., Chen, J. and Aravind, D. (2015) 'Management innovation and firm performance', *European Management Journal* 33: 407–422.

Watson, T. (1986) *Management, Organisations and Employment Strategy,* London: Routledge.

Watson, T. J. (1994) *In Search of Management: Culture Chaos and Control in Managerial Work,* London: Routledge.

Wilkinson, B. (1996) 'Culture, institutions and business in E. Asia', *Organisation Studies,* 17(3): 421–447.

Willis, P. (1977) *Learning to Labor: How Working Class Kids Get Working Class Jobs,* New York: Columbia University Press.

Willmott, H. (1992) 'Post-modernism and excellence: The de-differentiation of economy and culture', *Journal of Organisational Change Management,* 5(1): 58–68.

Wilson, F. (1996) 'Organisation theory: Blind and deaf to gender', *Organisation Studies,* 17(5): 825–842.

Wilson, J. M., O'Leary, M. B., Metiu, A. and Jett, Q. R. (2008) 'Perceived proximity in virtual work: Explaining the paradox of far-but-close', *Organization Studies,* 29(7): 979–1002.

The organizational dimension

7 Organization, structure and design

8 Management and leadership

9 Politics and decision-making in organizations

10 Culture

11 Change and innovation: New organizational forms

12 Technology

PART II

Part II covers a wide, though far from exhaustive, range of topics. Each chapter shows how they are examined in mainstream analysis, but also challenges the conventional assumption that organizations function as coherent and self-reproducing systems. In the mainstream, the consideration of politics, conflict or cultural diversity is fleeting and/or is seen as a disruptive element that needs to be cauterized or contained. More critical approaches explore the recurrence and proliferation of such disruptions and the integral nature of their relationship to organizational and technological life, as well as their significance for continual processes of change as well as resistance to it.

7 Organization, structure and design

DAVID KNIGHTS AND HUGH WILLMOTT

Aims of the chapter

This chapter will:

- Introduce key mainstream and critical contributions to the study of the structure and design of organizations.

- Explore the difference between classical and modern thinking about organization, highlighting the importance of open systems theory to contemporary organizational design.

- Clarify the nature of, and relationship between, 'formal' and 'informal' features of organizing.

- Explain and illustrate the basis of criticisms of mainstream thinking about organizational structure and design.

- Show how concepts of inequality, knowledge, power, freedom, identity, inequality and insecurity can provide a different way of considering issues of organizational structure and design.

- Review diverse contributions to the critical analysis of organization structure.

Key concepts and learning objectives

By the end of this chapter you should be able to:

- Develop an understanding of the assumptions and theories underpinning mainstream thinking.

- Show how ideas about the structure and design of organization are developed and applied in practice, with particular reference to a case study.

- Explore some alternative approaches and tensions associated with the design and control of organizations.

- Understand a number of key concepts that are relevant to mainstream and critical analysis, such as effectiveness and efficiency, and performance and control.

Overview and key points

> The concept of organization structure is at the heart of organizational studies, historically and contemporaneously ... understanding organizational structure is central and the thrust of the discipline of organization theory is to understand effective and efficient organizing, through structural design. (Hinings, 2003, p. 275)

Suppose that you want to set up an organization. You might ask yourself: What exactly is it for? What difference do I want it to make? How do I go about it?

Very likely, you would base your organization on a familiar model. A dominant, common sense way of designing an organization involves drawing a chart comprising a set of linked boxes, with the boxes indicating the positions or roles played and the lines identifying the main relationships – lines of authority and communication. As a first stab at a design, you might draw such a chart. When deciding on the number and type of boxes and the nature of the links between them, the chances are that you would more or less copy a model that you already know, such as a company you have worked for or your university, and then make a few modifications.

Whatever method you use, the outcome will be an organizational design with a distinctive structure that you believe will serve the purpose and strategy you ascribe to the organization. But what exactly does 'structure' mean? It is widely used to describe the *form* of an organization. For example, if in an organization of 100 members, 99 report individually to one boss, then that would be called an extremely simple and autocratic structure; but it is also one that is likely to overwhelm the boss because nothing is **delegated**. The boss probably wants to retain complete control by ensuring that he or she takes every decision, perhaps because he or she does not have the confidence or trust in anyone else taking them. A possible outcome is that he or she is worked into the ground and/or there are long delays while everyone waits for decisions to be made. In which case, he or she may decide to design and introduce an alternative structure with a longer and perhaps more bureaucratic chain of command.

> **Delegated** The process of passing the responsibility to make management decisions down the hierarchy to those in less senior positions.

Thinkpoint 7.1

Have you ever experienced an autocratic organization, as a member or as a customer? What was it like? Why was it like that?

In an alternative structure, the other 99 people will be *grouped* in some way (e.g., by specialist activity, such as production or sales) and will report to a manager to whom the owner-cum-boss has delegated some authority/responsibility for overseeing that task. Here, then, we are moving towards a more elaborate, or less simple, structure. There is a horizontal division of labour into different specialist tasks (e.g., sales) and a vertical division that comprises three, rather than two, levels of a hierarchy – the big boss, some managers and the workers. The managers to whom authority for their specialist areas of responsibility has been delegated now make many decisions. But the selection of the managers continues to be made by the boss who is accountable only to him or herself. The boss may continue to control things in the organization (e.g., by making the hiring, firing and allocation decisions and restricting the autonomy of employees) in ways that are inefficient or ineffective, as well as morally questionable, at least from the perspective of the workers and/or the managers.

Mainstream thinking can be divided into 'classical' and 'modern' variants. Advocates of the *classical* approach believe in the possibility of identifying *principles* of organization that have *universal* applicability. By applying these principles, this approach seeks to replace what it regards as non-rational, ill-disciplined, wasteful muddle – what is sometimes described as **custom and practice** – with a more efficient and effective way of mobilizing productive effort. So, for example, in an organization with 100 members, classical thinking would say that the span of control – roughly speaking, the number of people who report to a single boss – should be limited and would therefore suggest introducing several layers or tiers of management within a hierarchy. To repeat, the assumption of classical theory is that the

> **Custom and practice** Workplace behaviour that has been repeated over a lengthy period and is therefore routinely taken for granted.

same, avowedly rational, efficient principles of organization can be successfully applied regardless of the cultural context or operating environment. It does not contemplate the possibility that in some circumstances (e.g., where the other 99 workers believe fervently in the superhuman powers of the big boss and/or refuse to take orders from anyone else) the creation of a tier of managers might be counterproductive. It could be counterproductive, for example, if the managers are likely to be ignored or bypassed by workers, or where the specialist managers lack a broader overview of the implications of their decision-making for other parts of the organization. Yet even autocratic football managers, such as Jose Mourinho and Sir Alex Ferguson, have always employed deputies and training staff.

Advocates of the **modern** approach share the concern to make organizations more efficient and effective. But, crucially, it stresses the importance of adapting the design of organizations to the particular, *contingent* demands and opportunities of the context, or wider system, in which organizations are embedded. Additionally, it incorporates the understanding that some employees respond positively to particular arrangements or styles of management (e.g., material incentives, the authority of 'experts') while others do not, and that these responses may themselves be reversed with changes of circumstance. Such considerations, modern thinking contends, should be built into the design of organizations so as to ensure their most effective operation.

It is a mistake to believe that classical (or modern) thinking is uniform. Some classical thinkers believe that a top-down approach to design will be effective as long as it includes a more economically rational approach to the remuneration of effort. This belief assumes that people come to work primarily if not exclusively to earn a wage, and an improvement in wages would be made possible by the productivity gains achieved by imposing a more rational design of work organization. Other classical thinkers assume that material compensation alone will be insufficient to secure productive co-operation, and therefore stress the importance of creating an **esprit de corps** among employees. An equivalent emphasis may be given to managing the psychological 'engagement' of employ-

Esprit de corps Positive morale – strong sense of belonging and purpose shared by a work group or organization.

ees as to 'controlling' them (e.g. through incentives, such as payment-by-results). Management is then charged with developing a design of organization – by establishing a corporate culture, for example – that will encourage employees to identify with the workplace in a way that goes beyond a purely material, instrumental dependence upon it.

Exercise 7.1

Diversity and responsiveness From your own experience, identify some examples where particular arrangements or incentives have elicited a positive reaction (in terms of motivation and activity) from some people but a more negative one from others. You might, for example, think of the reactions of different students to contrasting styles of instruction and learning; or the reactions of different employees to particular management styles. (See also Chapter 3.)

Modern mainstream thinking is distinguished by its concern to take account of complexities in the organization–environment relationship that are ignored or inadequately appreciated by classical thinkers' approach to the

One best way Refers to anything that is regarded as the one solution for all organizational ills.

design of organization structures. The classical idea that there is a single, universal **one best way** is replaced by a view that the effectiveness of an organization's structure depends upon adapting it to deal with the demands and opportunities of the situation.

When considering mainstream approaches, we have identified a basic difference between classical and modern variants. But it is perhaps more important to recognize similarities, especially as we are concerned ultimately to compare and contrast them to critical analyses of organization structure and design (see Table 7.1). Classical and modern mainstream thinking share (i) a rejection of traditional or haphazard ways of structuring economic organization that have no virtue other than familiarity, typified by the view that 'this is the way we have always done things around here'; (ii) a top-down approach in which it is assumed that those at the top of the hierarchy need only order things to be done and their expectations will be fulfilled; and (iii) a restricted way of appreciating the significance of the environment as an objective reality, to which the organization can readily adapt as long as the appropriate structure is in place.

Table 7.1 Comparison of mainstream and critical knowledge

Mainstream approach (classical and modern)	Critical approach
Conceives of structure and design as an impartial, rational process	Conceives of structure and design as a cultural and political process
Minimal attention to issues of power, inequality, etc.	Attentive to issues of power, inequality, etc.
Assumes consensus underpins organizations	Assumes conflicts are endemic to organizations
Preoccupied with improving control through better design	Concerned to illuminate and question control

Whether in its classical or modern form, mainstream thinking is indifferent to how the structure of organizations reflects and often reproduces the distribution of power and the wider social inequalities in society. Little or no consideration is given to how history, culture, politics or economics are involved in conditioning an organization's design and development. In our example of the organization with 100 members, attention would be focused upon the horizontal and vertical divisions of labour (or the lack of them), and not upon the cultural values or political struggles that have shaped its formation or guide its reform.

Critical analysis, in contrast, understands the theory and practice of organization to be deeply embedded in particular politico-economic social systems. From this perspective, mainstream thinking does not approximate objectivity or neutrality. Rather, it is infused by dominant values and priorities. Yet it is largely blind to their influence, and is incapable of acknowledging or examining their effects. Our very knowledge of organizations – including how concepts such as 'structure' are used to convey their reality in particular, limited ways – is considered , from a critical perspective, to be conditioned by particular, mainstream and critical, perspectives.

MAINSTREAM APPROACH TO STRUCTURE AND DESIGN
Introducing structure and design

Cartoon 7.1   'What we've done is make it dramatically easier to navigate the corporate hierarchy.'

**'What we've done is make it dramatically easier
to navigate the corporate hierarchy.'**

Mainstream thinking about organizations has been preoccupied with the design of their structure as a means of facilitating the efficient achievement of the goals ascribed to organizations, such as generating profits or providing public services. The idea of structure conveys cohesiveness and regularity:

> ... a focal interest of organization theory must inevitably be the understanding of how to organize people and resources in order to collectively accomplish desired ends ... Design drives the way strategies are formulated and determines whether and how they can be implemented ... only appropriate organizational designs can configure resources to achieve the desired end. An organization's structure comprises a set of hierarchical and/or horizontal positions and relationships. (Greenwood and Miller, 2010: pp. 78–9)

Activities in contemporary work organizations are generally divided and co-ordinated by more formal mechanisms, such as legal contracts of employment, written job descriptions and so on. For example, when it is announced that an organization is to 'restructure', there is an intention to reconfigure the vertical and/or horizontal divisions – perhaps by **de-layering** or by removing or **rationalizing** one or more areas of activity.

De-layering Reducing the number of levels in the hierarchy so as to have fewer managers.

Rationalizing Measures intended to increase the efficiency and/or improve the effectiveness of work practices. See **rationality** in Glossary.

Components of the structure of organizations have been identified to include:

- The way people are grouped into teams or departments.
- Strategies and tactics involved in allocating activities and responsibilities.
- Forms of accountability such as the line(s) of reporting from subordinate to superordinate (boss), and the number of subordinates that report to any one boss.
- The lines of communication between employees and the means of integrating different activities.
- Monitoring of performance and the design of reward systems.

There are differences of emphasis within mainstream thinking with regard to the importance of these elements. Some analysts concentrate primarily upon the design and allocation of tasks. Others take a broader view of the means of their integration, which may include, for example, reference to some basic values that maintain motivation. What they frequently share is a disembodied and de-personalized understanding of structure and design. Consider the following definition of organization structure:

> The structure of an organization can be defined simply as the sum total of the ways in which it divides its labour into distinct tasks and then achieves co-ordination between them. (Mintzberg, 1979, p. 2)

In this definition of organization structure, it is *as if* organizations determine their own structure: we are told that '*it* divides its labour into distinct tasks' (our emphasis). This definition of structure also assumes the division and co-ordination of labour to be an established fact, rather than as something that is introduced and continuously maintained or modified through a process of conflict and struggle in which managers as well as employees selectively accommodate or resist different pressures and forms of control. The absence of this broader appreciation of politics in the formation, reproduction and representation of 'structure' is why we identify such thinking as 'non-critical' or mainstream.

The emphasis in mainstream thinking is upon tasks. As our list of components of structure suggests, however, its meaning can be extended to include such things as performance monitoring and systems of reward where there is likely to be more or less visible tensions and stress. Even where such considerations are incorporated, however, mainstream thinking about organization, structure and design takes established structures of organization and power as given and necessary. It produces knowledge that operates to conserve and refine, rather than question, prevailing organizational structures and designs. A critical perspective, which departs from the managerialist mainstream of organizational analysis is developed in the second half of the chapter. For the moment, we further explore mainstream thinking on organization structure and design by illustrating its relevance through a case study.

Case study 7.1
Bar Mar

In this and the following chapter, we draw on a case study of Bar Mar (a pseudonym). Bar Mar was established 20 years ago and has expanded to become an international chain of multi-award-winning bar-bistros. This case is intended to help illustrate ideas and concepts as well as to demonstrate the relevance of ideas presented in this and the following chapters.

Figure 7.1 shows the vertical and horizontal division of labour in the very first Bar Mar. Three staff are employed, each of whom has primary responsibility for a defined area of activity. The chart shows that selection and deployment of staff is determined and supervised by the owner-manager, Margaret.

To establish the first Bar Mar, Margaret took the risk of sinking her personal savings, together with a substantial windfall arising from the death of a relative, to set up and run a small bar – a dream she had nurtured for a few years. As the owner-manager, Margaret controlled key decisions, such as the nature and pricing of drinks and food, opening hours, working hours, furnishings and so on. One thing that had appealed to her about running a bar was the opportunity to create a total experience for her customers – a key part of which is their interaction with Bar Mar staff, herself included.

She liked the idea of working with a small number of staff – co-workers and friends, as she thought of them – with whom she could provide and develop a distinctive atmosphere and a range of drinks, snacks and light meals.

Figure 7.1 Organization chart for an owner-managed bar

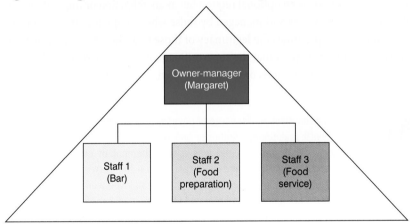

Exercise 7.2

Linking theory and practice Thinking over the ideas that have been presented in this chapter so far, identify those that have relevance for analyzing the initial organizational structure of Bar Mar.

Margaret based Bar Mar on a familiar structure of organization – a hierarchical design with herself at the apex. She decided how activities were to be allocated to her employees. Staff would report to her and she would ensure that their work was adequately co-ordinated. She would monitor and evaluate their conduct, and she decided how they were to be motivated and rewarded. At the same time, Margaret did not want to 'boss' her staff. Instead, she wanted them to learn how to take responsibility for delivering an exceptional standard of customer service. The last thing she wanted was to follow the example of McDonald's, where a highly detailed set of rules and procedures dictates how each activity is to be undertaken. What she had in mind was recruiting a type of employee who would connect with and embrace her vision for Bar Mar, and so 'automatically' work the way that she wanted, with the minimum of training, surveillance and intervention on her part. She wanted to hire staff who required very little supervision and were concerned to make Bar Mar a success, even though this benefited Margaret more than them.

An employee who does *only* what the rules permit – who 'works to rule' – is likely to be viewed as rather inflexible, and so insufficiently 'co-operative'. Much modern management theory is about developing styles of leadership among managers, as well as forms of commitment among employees, that *incorporate* productive elements of the 'personal' and 'informal' *within* a formal, impersonal contract of employment (see Chapter 8). There have been repeated efforts to find ways of softening a rigid, 'command-and-control' approach that ultimately demands compliance with instructions or established rules (see Chapter 10) – for example, by shifting to a 'coach-and-empower' philosophy, and by favouring flatter, less rigid and regimented forms of structure in which employees are more engaged, more adaptable and so 'add more value'. In this respect, Margaret's thinking reflects the ideas of Mary Parker Follett (see Box 7.1), one of the classical writers on management. She believed that management must be 'civilized' in order to minimize frictions and, more specifically, to avoid problems of personal identity, such as the loss of dignity or status ordinarily associated with being 'bossed around' (see Chapter 8).

Follett advocates 'depersonalization' which does *not* mean *im*personalization, where the relationship loses all personal qualities. Instead, depersonalization involves relating to other staff as occupants of legitimate roles, but not as personal friends or enemies (see Chapter 1). Depersonalization occurs when employees respond to an instruction or request issued by a manager not as a casual favour or as an optional request but as an obligation or imperative – an obligation which arises from the roles played by managers and managed by those who occupy functionally necessary positions, or offices. To put this another way, it presumes the legitimacy of those in authority as functional for the organization, rather than oppressive or exploitative, such that the superordinate (e.g., Margaret) is understood by the subordinate to have a legitimate right to have instructions or requests fulfilled.

Management is a responsible discharge of necessary functions, not the privilege of elites, [Follett] maintained. Authority and responsibility derive from function, not privilege ... What was required was a reinstatement of civility, society, and fellowship in and through work and its organization if the corrosive effects of competitive individualism on the moral character of the employee were to be halted. People needed to think not just of themselves and the individual benefit to be gained through competition at work but how they fitted into an overall pattern of functions, responsibilities and authoritative entitlements to command and to obey (Clegg *et al.*, 2005, p. 31).

Box 7.1
Mary Parker Follett
on authority and
civility

In practice, 'depersonalization' may be difficult to establish and sustain, perhaps because managers are 'unprofessional' (for example, Margaret might ask a member of staff to do something, like clean her car, which lies outside contractual duties), or because their subordinates are 'bolshy' (for example, one of Margaret's staff ignores her requests or does not do anything unless told very specifically what is required). Establishing and maintaining 'depersonalized' relationships requires a measure of willingness and co-operation that cannot be taken for granted. Often, it requires some inducement, which may take a symbolic (e.g., change of job title) as well as a material form. If

Thinkpoint 7.2

Why is it that we are (often) willing to comply with, or obey, 'authorities'? When are we not so willing to comply?

Margaret did not pay her staff, it is unlikely that they would continue to work at Bar Mar. But even if Margaret paid them very well but treated them badly in other ways (e.g., harassing or bullying them) it is probable that they would look for work elsewhere. It is precisely the symbolic dimension of the employment relationship (e.g., making her staff feel valued and part of a team with a special *esprit de corps)* that Margaret sought to foster. At its core, the willing co-operation of employees depends upon them interpreting hierarchies and their associated rules and social divisions as functionally necessary, rather than as a means of establishing and maintaining forms of power and privilege.

The first Bar Mar comprised a simple, hierarchical structure with a short span of control. Margaret has only three staff reporting to her, and she manages by relying upon her ability to recruit and train staff who identify with her vision. This simple structure can be contrasted with the structure of a much larger, multinational organization in which the differentiation is not only between factories (or business units comprising a cluster of operations), but also by product divisions and geographical area. The company is organized into several divisions, each of which is divided into sites or units within which a range of functions (e.g., production, accounting) and tasks (e.g., assembly, costing) are undertaken (see Figure 7.2).

At first glance, the organization chart of the multinational organization looks quite different to Bar Mar, but the basic structure remains – a hierarchy with a division of labour. In fact, as Bar Mar expanded and diversified into an international chain, it came to resemble the structure of the multinational automotive company, with its separate but related areas of activity, each of which has become a division within the Bar Mar Group (see Figure 7.3; see also Chapter 13). The most significant difference between the first Bar Mar and the current Bar Mar structure is that there is now no direct reporting relationship between the chief executive officer (CEO) (e.g., Margaret) and the 'front-line' staff. Instead, there is an extended set of reporting relationships, or **chain of command**, in which areas of responsibility are delegated, and then delegated again, through a series of layers of management.

Chain of command Links within a hierarchy between the most senior and least senior of managers or supervisors.

Figure 7.2 Structure of a multinational automotive company

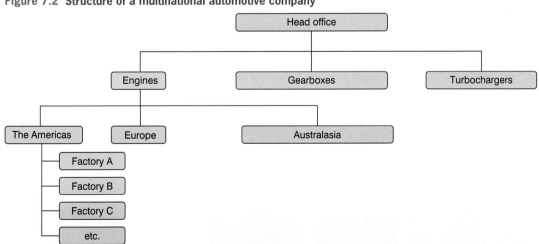

Figure 7.3 Bar Mar as one division within the Mar Group

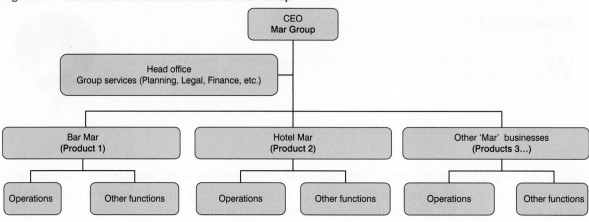

In a hierarchy with numerous levels, it becomes impossible for the CEO to keep a direct eye on all the staff. Margaret can no longer see what they are doing, or even know them personally or be responsible for their recruitment and training. Even if CCTV cameras were installed in each Bar Mar (assuming this was compatible with the company ethos and acceptable to its staff), it would be impossible for Margaret to keep track of all of the branches all of the time. As a consequence, each manager in the hierarchy, from the CEO down, is obliged to rely upon more indirect forms of monitoring and control that increasingly are provided by information and communication technologies (ICTs) which, for example, track the revenues generated by each bar, or even by each member of the serving staff. Unless the manager can depend upon those further down in the hierarchy to act as clones, doing precisely what he or she would do in the circumstances, he or she must depend upon other means of controlling their behaviour. That is where the introduction of (bureaucratic) rules, procedures and performance measures (see Chapter 14) as well as training programmes and forms of 'hoopla' (e.g., uniforms, catchphrases or party tricks) that encourage staff identification with Bar Mar, provide substitutes for more direct forms of monitoring and control (see Chapter 10).

Even where a CEO succeeds in establishing a 'strong' culture – where employees are hired and trained who embrace a distinctive corporate vision – it is impossible to rely upon face-to-face ways of monitoring employee behaviour (see Figure 7.4). That does not necessarily mean that there will be very detailed control of employee behaviour (e.g., 'McDonaldization') by using standardized procedures, including the scripting of interactions with customers, to produce standardized outputs so that everything is, in principle, predictable. Instead, employees may be evaluated primarily by outcomes (e.g., production targets; service quality levels). They may also be allowed, and

Figure 7.4 Four forms of control

Direct control of behaviour	Control through rules/ procedures	Control through culture	Control through performance
(Supervision of operations)	(Manuals of procedures)	(Shaping of attitudes and values)	(Measurement of outcomes)
e.g. 'management by walking about'	e.g. scripting of operatives in call centres	e.g. selection based upon social attributes	e.g. monitoring of customer satisfaction

indeed encouraged, to exercise initiative and discretion in ways that are consistent with some overarching values. What is controlled is not task behaviour but the outcome of that behaviour. Satisfactory performance is rewarded through retention; unsatisfactory performance is punished through dismissal.

When Margaret set up the business, her preference was for something 'unique' and 'relaxed'. She wanted to create an organization in which 'the situation', rather than a rule book, would determine how, for example, staff would interact with customers. She would create 'the situation', and expected her staff to follow her example. Instead of giving detailed instructions about how each activity (bar, food preparation, food service) should be performed, Margaret preferred to pick the staff that she believed would do the right thing (in her eyes).

Margaret wanted a flexible, adaptable set of staff guided by a shared commitment to her vision of Bar Mar. She sought to inspire her staff with this vision so that they would exercise discretion in ways that were consistent with her dream – in terms of maintaining a distinctive atmosphere, helping each other out and so on. And, broadly speaking, Margaret succeeded.

Exercise 7.3

Comparing organization structures Compare and contrast the Bar Mar structure with other organization charts (this may involve a little research but the Web may provide most of the answers) with which you are familiar (perhaps café or bar chains that you visit). Why do you think there are diverse organization structures, such as franchises? What are the advantages and disadvantages of simple, in contrast to more complex, designs of organization structure, and vice versa? Discuss and debate your views with student colleagues.

We have seen how it is possible to map out the vertical and horizontal division of labour with the use of an organization chart. But such diagrams, and their associated conception of structure, cannot do justice to how, in practice, activities in organizations are co-ordinated and shared, let alone illuminate how staff do their work. To understand the everyday structuring of activity at Bar Mar, it is necessary to take account of how 'structure' functions in practice, how communication is organized, how information is shared, and how the exercise of discretion is circumscribed and monitored. But even this is still limited, as we shall show in the second part of this chapter.

Key contributions of mainstream thinking

In this section we look at the thinking that laid the foundations of contemporary organization design. Known as a 'classical' approach, it seeks to establish universal principles through which organizations are designed and tasks undertaken. Two of the most pre-eminent of classical theorists were the Frenchman, Henri Fayol and the American, Frederick Taylor both of whom believed, in their own way, in methods of organizing that could be identified as having very extensive applicability, summed up in the phrase 'one best way'.

CLASSICAL THINKING ABOUT ORGANIZATIONAL DESIGN

Classical theorists of management developed a model of organizations as well-oiled machines. They sought to replace ways of organizing dominated by tradition and rules of thumb with what they considered to be a much more systematic and rational approach to organizational design and operation. To this end, universal principles were identified that, it was anticipated, would provide a comprehensive guide to management practice.

Fayol's principles of administration

Henri Fayol (1841–1925) had a direct and intimate knowledge of many aspects of work organization as a consequence of working his way up through the company in which he became the managing director. His focus was upon administrative work, in contrast to Frederick Taylor who, as we shall see, directed his attention to the shop floor. Fayol became famous for turning around what had been a near-bankrupt company, and then for publishing a book that recorded his experience and drew key lessons from it. In *General and Industrial Management* (1949, first published in 1916), Fayol distilled 14 key principles of organizational structure and design. These include, for example, the idea of a unified command structure in which each employee reports to one superordinate, and where attention is given to *esprit de corps* so as to ensure good morale and motivation. Huczynski and Buchanan (2001, p. 502) boil down Fayol's lengthy list of principles to five basic imperatives. We summarize these in Table 7.2, together with some reflections on their application in Bar Mar.

The classical interest in establishing principles of organization design and representing these in organizational charts is today undiminished but there has also been a concern amongst advocates of classical thinking to overcome

Matrix A form of organization where there are parallel lines of authority criss-crossing one another so that staff are accountable simultaneously to managers in a hierarchy and other specialists horizontally.

perceived shortcomings ('dysfunctions'), such as those associated with the limited attention given by Fayol to the *integration* of activities. It has been suggested, for example, that there are circumstances in which employees should report to more than one boss so as to ensure that adequate attention is given to competing considerations (e.g., reporting to a product or service manager as well as to the head of the function that provides support to that activity). We examine such a design when we consider **matrix** organization.

Table 7.2 Fayol's key principles and their application at Bar Mar

Fayol's basic principles of administration	Bar Mar
• Functional division of work	Division into specialist activities. In the first Bar Mar, Margaret distinguished bar staff, food preparation and service
• Hierarchical relationships	Chain of command. Each of the staff at the first Bar Mar reported to Margaret
• Bureaucratic forms of control	Kept to minimum but increased as scale of operations made direct control an impossibility
• Narrow supervisory span	Initially limited to three staff. Later extended to more staff but deliberately kept narrow in order to facilitate direct forms of control
• Closely prescribed roles	Loosely prescribed roles not favoured when it leads to confusion and hampers accountability

Thinkpoint 7.3

The effectiveness of many of Fayol's principles has been questioned in recent years when the emphasis has been upon flexibility and agility. What do you consider to be the advantages and disadvantages or risks of *not* applying Fayol's ideas? Do you detect areas in which his principles are weak or could usefully be extended? Discuss with other students your distinctive lists and defend your choice.

Taylor's scientific management

By contrast, Frederick Taylor (1856–1915), the founder of 'scientific management', sought to demonstrate experimentally how a series of principles (see Table 7.3) could be applied to deliver increased productivity. He drew upon experience as an engineer, manager and consultant to devise what he commended as a more rational system of organizing production. He was convinced that management had failed to gain adequate control of the division of labour and especially the detailed design and planning of work. Taylor's focus was primarily on the design of jobs rather than the grander concern with organizational structure. He had observed how labourers had been allowed a great deal of autonomy in the workplace, which meant that they did not always perform their tasks in the most efficient manner. Consequently, he ascribed to management responsibility for designing work tasks (although he based this on careful observation of a model worker who had high rates of productivity) and introduced a piecework system of paying the labourer directly for the amount of output achieved.

Table 7.3 Taylor's principles and their application at Bar Mar

Taylor's scientific principles of organization	Bar Mar
• Separation of design and planning of work from actually doing it	In the first Bar Mar, Margaret determined the structure, and planned activities
• Detailed division of labour	After the expansion into an international chain, there was a division into specialist areas of activity such as operations, marketing, etc.
• Based on observation of working practices	Identification of 'best practices' and training of staff to adopt them

From unified chain of command to a matrix structure

One obvious limitation of classical thinking is its emphasis upon vertical, top-down reporting can pose problems for horizontal communication. In principle, a single chain of command means that there is no reporting relationship across organizations. Indeed, it is to minimize conflicts and confusion arising from such 'horizontal' relationships that the unified chain of command is prescribed. But such clarity can have its shortcomings. For example, a university business school consists of academic subject areas (e.g., accounting and finance, organizational behaviour, information systems, marketing and strategy) usually headed by a professor (equivalent in industry to specialist functions). There are also educational programmes headed by someone equivalent to a course or programme director (the industrial equivalent being a manager responsible for a product line). Lecturers within subject areas provide services (e.g., lecture courses) to programmes but also report to their 'line manager' – the professor who heads the subject area. So, what does the programme manager do if he or she is concerned about the contents of a lecture course being delivered by a member of staff? Recall that the lecturer does not report to the programme director but to the subject area head. The lecturer may, indeed, refuse to be 'bossed around' by the programme director, arguing that the programme director lacks the formal authority to determine course content. In principle, then, where there is a single, unified chain of command, the programme director must speak to the head of the subject area who then raises the issue with the lecturer concerned so that the communication is indirect and this can result in distortions due to different interpretations of the message.

This is an example of how a unity of command comprising a single, vertical chain encounters limitations with respect to *horizontal* forms of communication. It is this limitation that has been addressed by a matrix structure of organization where there are two reporting lines – one to the manager of the specialist function (e.g., the subject area head) and the other to the user of this function (e.g., the programme director). This is illustrated in Figure 7.5 with the example of a series of projects (equivalent to teaching programmes) to which different specialisms (equivalent to subject groups) contribute. The basic difference is that an employee (e.g., a lecturer) occupying a position at the intersection of the vertical and horizontal lines is required to report to both the functional (e.g., subject area) and project (e.g., programme director) heads. The intention is that the delivery of products/services/projects receives as much attention as the development of functional expertise (and vice versa), thereby securing greater integration. The matrix design runs counter to Fayol's principle of a unity of command. Similarly, trends towards 'flatter' organizations (at least in principle and as presented in organization charts), where hierarchical layers are removed, require an extension of a span of control beyond the optimal number recommended by Fayol (see below).

Parallel problems have been identified with the relevance of the standardization generated by Taylor's Scientific Management. When it has not been shunned on moral or religious grounds for its tendency to treat employees like imbeciles, robots or machines, it has been criticized for undermining morale, and hence productivity, through de-skilling work and/or failing to fully harness the unique capacity of workers to be creatively involved in improving the production process. In short, advocates of *modern* thinking have questioned the capacity of their *classical* predecessors adequately to appreciate and address the complexity and diversity of issues confronted by the designers and adapters of organizational structures.

Figure 7.5 Matrix arrangement within a functional organization structure

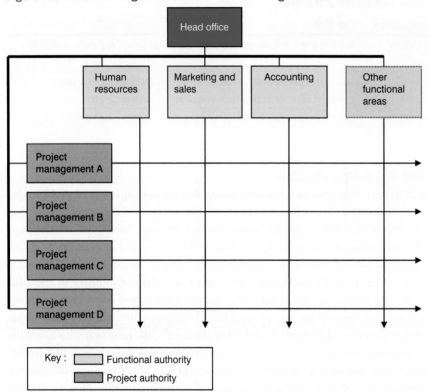

Modern thinking

While classical thinking conceives of organizations as closed systems in which the environment is harnessed and conquered by following singular, standardized principles, a modern approach to organization design and structure abandons the idea of finding the ideal, universal, one best design. The consistent application of universal principles is replaced by a concern to adapt the design of the organization to the contingencies of the context, such as the stability or volatility of the market for its goods or services. Organizational designs and structures are then expected to ensure a good 'fit' with the demands or constraints of the **environment**.

Environment What exists external to the organization, such as available technologies, markets and government.

SYSTEMS THINKING

Many modern theories of organization rely, more or less implicitly, upon systems thinking where organizational activities are analyzed in terms of inputs, conversion processes and outputs. At Bar Mar inputs include labour and raw materials (foodstuffs); conversion processes involve cooking and serving, etc.; and the outputs include prepared

Thinkpoint 7.4

What ideas and arguments would you use to justify abandoning Fayol and Taylor's classical principles? Once you have identified these ideas and arguments, try to distinguish the values that render these ideas coherent and the arguments credible.

meals and potentially satisfied customers. We have noted earlier how classical thinking assumes a closed *system* in which no attention is given to any factors – such as changing lifestyles or customer tastes. Classical thinking commends the continuous perfection of what is assumed to be a universally effective formula of organizational design and operation. This is rather like a car producer developing a single model that is intended to be suitable for any customer, terrain or climate.

Open systems thinking analyses activities in terms of inputs, processes and outputs and takes account of how each system is interdependent with others in the wider system. Organizations are seen as similar to organic bodies where all the parts (e.g., brain, heart and lungs) are functionally integrated to secure stability or equilibrium in relation to external conditions. Consequently there is sensitivity to how changes external to one system impact upon, and so affect, its operation and effectiveness. Returning to the car producer analogy, a variety of models, including **hybrids**, would be developed to take account of diversity and change in relation to customer taste, running costs, climates and regulations. Open systems thinking favours greater experimentation and innovation as a way of adapting to changing circumstances.

Hybrid Combination of two or more elements or characteristics that are normally separate.

Exercise 7.4

Comparing closed and open systems thinking Can you draw up a list of points that support a modern, open systems view of organization in contrast to a more closed, classical approach?

Modern open systems thinkers adapt the design of organizations to the contingencies of the situation (see Box 7.2). Partly, variation is generated 'internally' with the increasing size of the modern corporation that arises from mergers and acquisitions as well as growth. The *simple* hierarchical structure favoured by the classical theorists makes little allowance for such contingencies. Conglomerates (combinations of different kinds of businesses) and multinationals have tended to allow their constituent companies and divisions a greater level of independence than allowed, for example, by classical thinking. Adherence to classical principles is selective as contingencies are encountered and accommodated.

Different product or regional divisions may exercise discretion as to which markets they enter and the products they develop but they are also accountable to the centre for results that flow from their decisions (see Chapter 13). In the multi-divisional form, each national, regional or divisional operation may become a 'business unit' with its own cost and profit centre. Each operation is required to make profit from its operations as if it were an independent company. It is 'however' accountable to the head office for its performance and, of course, dependent on it for future investment unless allowed to retain some of its profits for that purpose. In short, there are recurrent attempts to manage complexity in ways that harness the benefits of *diversity* (of product or location) and *integration* (e.g., centralized setting and monitoring of performance targets). The chart (Figure 7.3) that sets out Bar Mar's product divisions illustrates this approach. Other criteria used for structuring larger organizations, whether of a regional, national or international form, include those based on product differences, process or function, project, or some hybrid variation, such as a matrix design where there are two or more lines of authority rather than one.

Another way in which a correction to the disadvantages of classical organization design may be attempted is by reducing the number of levels in the hierarchy through creating what is called 'flatter' organization. Not only are there fewer middle managers to whom employees are accountable, but some measure of responsibility and power is seen to be delegated to operational functions in what has been called a process of

Empowerment The distribution of power to people lower down the hierarchy so that they can feel a degree of autonomy and sense of personal identification in the decisions they make.

empowerment (see Chapters 2, 3, 4 and 11). This process of empowerment means that lower hierarchy staff are able to take some initiative and make some decisions without seeking permission from more senior staff. They are also responsible for the decisions made, and are therefore expected to engage in a greater degree of *self*-management. Often the organizational structure is 'softened', not merely by flattening the hierarchy and empowering the workforce but also by mediating the flows of management control through the introduction of teams of workers who have a

degree of autonomy for particular tasks or specialisms in the production process (see Chapters 2 and 4). Teams provide for a more intimate set of work relations and sources of identification with the team and its leader (see Chapter 8), thus enabling, in principle, members to feel a sense of identity with their tasks that is more difficult to foster in relation to the more remote organization as a whole. Structuring an organization around teams can facilitate internal co-operation within the team and may induce competitive rivalry between teams that can have positive productive organizational outcomes in terms of meeting performance targets. Just as with the league tables in sport, striving to be higher up the league or avoid relegation to a lower league may stimulate extra effort and dedication.

Box 7.2
Applying systems thinking

In a sports team, such as in netball, a closed system view assumes the possibility of selecting and training players according to one method of organization that can beat all challengers. It assumes the possibility of identifying the perfect approach for outwitting the opposition, irrespective of their strategy and tactics. An open system approach, in contrast, considers the specific qualities of the competition, and then decides upon the choice of team members and relevant formations. In principle, open systems thinking can enable a team of players with a limited stock of individual talent to outsmart teams that possess more talent on paper, yet struggle to respond to the challenges presented by resourceful opponents.

In the world of football or English soccer as it is termed in the USA, an example of this open approach was occasioned by the European Cup Final of 2005: Liverpool's capacity to adapt against a better AC Milan team that at half time was winning by three goals. By changing their formation, Liverpool clawed back all three goals to force a penalty shootout in extra time, and they went on to win. As an organization, this flexibility of structure allowed for a change of strategy. Open systems theory helps to explain why AC Milan's formula or system succeeded brilliantly in the first half but was less effective in the second once Liverpool had changed their game plan. A system does not necessarily produce the same level of performance when applied in a different place and/ or time. Although eventually knocked out, a more recent example of this flexibility was offered by Arsenal in the 2010/11 Champions League who in the first leg managed to beat a much better Barcelona by putting all their players behind the ball and hitting them on the break. In the second leg, this strategy did not succeed but might have done had one of their players not been red-carded when they were winning on the away goal rule.

Open systems thinkers perceive organizations to be like organic bodies, which are expected to maintain themselves in 'good health' by being adaptive to changes. The assumption is that they tend towards equilibrium, each part works co-operatively to maintain the whole, with each member or department sharing similar values and objectives. In this sense, modern (open) systems thinking is not very different from classical (closed) systems thinking in presuming a prevailing consensus in organizations. It differs, however, in giving much more attention to the organization–environment interface, arguing that organizations are not closed to the world, they cannot be fully protected or isolated from its influences, and so their design must be adapted to secure a productive exchange with the wider world. This is the basic proposition of open systems thinking, and it presents a direct challenge to classical theory, which assumes that universal principles should be applied irrespective of the circumstances.

Box 7.3
Open and closed systems – spans of control and organization methods

Classical theorists sought to identify the optimal span of control – that is, the number of people reporting to a given manager. The contemporary view is that there is no universally applicable optimal number. What is optimal will depend upon so many factors, including the environmental demands, the nature of the activity and the skills of the manager. Where behaviour is already well disciplined and/or where there is much regularity and predictability, extended spans of control may work well and be cheaper in terms of managerial overheads. Conversely, in more volatile and uncertain conditions, control is more problematical and a wide span may become unmanageable. Alternatively, other arrangements may be favoured, such as a matrix structure (see Figure 7.5) where integration is pursued through more than one reporting line.

Thinkpoint 7.5

Consider an experience of your own as a participant in, or supporter of, a group activity, such as sports, music or drama.

- Can you identify elements of 'closed' and 'open' systems thinking in how the activity was organized and performed?
- What benefits and what costs were associated with each type of thinking?
- In what circumstances might 'closed system' thinking be effective, and 'open system' thinking be counterproductive, in terms of formulating aims and achieving objectives?

Contingency theory

Open systems thinking underpins various forms of contingency theory. This thinking conceives of organizations as engaged in processes of continuous and somewhat experimental adjustment (e.g., through successive restructurings) to changing circumstances or contingencies. Organizations are seen as adaptive systems where changes in the 'environment' are accommodated to ensure their effective functioning. Each organization is regarded as a

Figure 7.6 Organizations as complex open systems
© Adapted from model ascribed to Leavitt, Huczynski and Buchanan, 2001, p. 450.

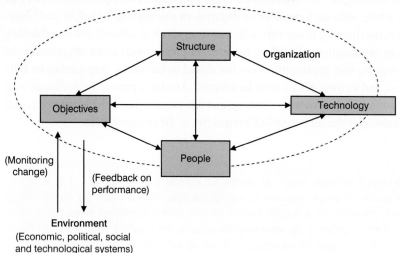

Subsystem One part (e.g., the heart) of numerous interdependent elements that comprise the wider system (e.g. the body).

subsystem of a wider system that comprises all the systems that make up its environment (see Figure 7.6). As indicated by the dotted line between the organization and its environment, the boundary is regarded as permeable and shifting. Superior performance is attributed to the goodness of 'fit' between the elements of subsystems (e.g., people, technology, etc.) and the environment in which they are located. Contingency theory seeks to take account of changing environmental demands and opportunities – such as legislative requirements (e.g., employment regulations), availability and costs of people and natural resources (e.g., energy), developments in technologies, etc. – when acquiring and matching all the parts of the system (e.g., technology, people, objectives) and designing the structure to ensure their effective interdependence. Note how people and technologies span the organization and its environment.

Attention is paid by contingency theory to the interdependence of system components. For example, the identification of appropriate or realistic 'objectives' is conceived to depend upon the capability of people, technology and the effective means of their combination. In turn, the attainment of these objectives is considered to be conditional, or contingent, upon (strategically) combining people, technology and structure in ways that effectively match and address the opportunities and demands – economic, political, social and technological – presented by the environment. This is indicated by the arrow that points to the organizational monitoring of change in the environment and the arrow that shows the feedback on performance provided by the organization (e.g., through annual reports).

Exercise 7.5

Draw a diagram that presents a view of a university lecture as a system.

- How do its components interact?
- What are its input–output interfaces?

Compare and contrast this with a similar diagram of a seminar or tutorial. Which is closer to a closed system and which to an open system?

From structure to process: Informal understandings and practices

Classical and modern thinking tends to be preoccupied with establishing formal order and advocating the substitution of rational planning for custom and practice. Structure, as we have noted, is conceived predominantly in terms of the specification of positions and reporting relationships that have official or administrative legitimacy (e.g., they are in job specifications), rather than with all manner of practices and processes that, in comparison, are 'informal' and which may be tolerated or even encouraged but lack *official* recognition and sanction. What is largely excluded from such thinking is recognition of informality in organizations.

The very term 'informality' is potentially confusing, however, as there is often a mixed view of its value. In principle, when following classical and modern theory, any productive 'informal' practice should be incorporated and institutionalized into officially agreed, formal arrangements and procedures. Consequently, any remaining forms of 'informality' are, at best, of dubious legitimacy. In practice, however, elements of informality – such as a preference for casual forms of communication and the presence of networks and ad hoc groups – may be tolerated and perhaps actively encouraged by some designers of organizational structures without seeking their incorporation within the formal structure. Indeed, even in a rigid bureaucracy, there will be a degree of dependence upon informal understandings and practices in order to 'get the job done'. Invariably, organizations depend upon some 'informal' understandings and practices that exist alongside officially sanctioned rules and procedures, even where strenuous efforts are made to eliminate them.

Classical and modern designers of organizations have sought to replace fuzzy, 'informal' arrangements with clear reporting lines and detailed job descriptions. They seek to remove ambiguity and replace loosely negotiated agreements with clearly demarcated boundaries and precise rules and procedures. Such **formalization**, however, is often accompanied by rigidity as action becomes dependent upon a rule or procedure that permits it. As a consequence of this rigidity, employees may become demoralized or demotivated as they experience themselves as a part of the (bureaucratic) machinery over which they can exert little or no control (see Chapter 14). Alternatively, greater informality – often described as 'flexibility' or a 'can do' attitude – may be valued as a key resource for securing the effective functioning of organizations (see Chapter 14) by minimizing unproductive effort and waste. (See Table 7.4.)

> **Formalization** The process of codifying what was previously tacit or informal. Typically, it refers to the introduction of formal rules and procedures in place of custom and practice.

Table 7.4 Formal and informal aspects of organization

Formal	Informal
Planned, procedural	Emergent, pragmatic
Officially sanctioned	Officially illegitimate but may be unofficially tolerated or encouraged
Comparatively fixed and rigid	Comparatively dynamic and flexible
Based on authority	Based on trust or reciprocity
On the record	Off the record
Reliant upon position	Reliant upon personal affinity or political allegiance

Working to rule

When union members engage in industrial action by **working to rule**, the shortcomings of formally endorsed methods of working rapidly becomes apparent. Reliance upon various **tacit skills** and informal understandings is then shown to be extensive and indispensible. Some deviation from the letter of formal rules is routine because, when employees comply strictly with the rules, productive activity is impeded rather than enabled.

> **Working to rule** The way employees, when in dispute with employers, may revert to formally prescribed ways of working that disrupt efficiency and effectiveness by replacing informal practices with rigid and often time-consuming procedural requirements.

Tacit skill A form of knowledge that cannot be made fully explicit, such as in a training manual or through verbal instruction. Examples include riding a bike or changing gear in a manual car.

You might expect that formal rules would be changed to reflect actual practice. But this would require a further elaboration of the rules that, in all likelihood, would reduce flexibility and responsiveness to changing conditions and thereby hamper productivity. Here we encounter a contradiction of formalization. Greater formality is introduced to eliminate the uncertainties and inefficiencies of custom and practice. But, in the process, unintendedly it creates some of the problems that it is designed to overcome and is thus detrimental to productive performance.

A recognition of informality points to the limitations of a predominantly formal approach to design. For one thing, officially sanctioned methods are rarely sufficiently comprehensive to cover every possible eventuality. In practice, employees may ignore them, overlook them, short-circuit them, or even find better – more acceptable and/or efficient or effective – alternatives to them. Such workarounds do not reflect well upon those who designed, or who seek to enforce, formalization measures.

Take the submission of student coursework. A formal procedure or channel of communication may require you, as a student, to submit an assignment by a certain date. Informally, however, you have discovered 'through the grapevine' that it is possible to 'negotiate' some extra time with certain lecturers. Such informal arrangements may facilitate or impede effectiveness in organizations. It may, for example, enable you to write a better essay as you have more time to prepare it and/or feel less stressed. But it may also make it more likely that a lecturer's time is taken up negotiating extensions with students who, in any event, will often leave writing their essays until the last minute and, as a consequence of being granted an extension, do not acquire the discipline to meet deadlines. On the other hand, students may regard a lecturer who is inflexible with respect to deadlines as overbearing and unreasonable, especially when the hand-in date seems to be, and often is, quite arbitrary. But the exceptions to the rule associated with such practices will tend to increase the workload of administrators charged with the task of recording the submission of essays. The practice of allowing extensions may also create conflicts with other academic staff who come under pressure to be 'accommodating', or risk a slump in their teaching ratings with potentially damaging consequences for their career progress.

Exercise 7.6

Supposing that you were a lecturer (or any other person in authority, such as a police officer who is expected to enforce rules), how would you ensure that students comply with formal rules in relation to, for example, attendance at classes, coursework submission dates, chatting in lectures, participating in seminars, etc.?

In considering this question, think about the *practicalities* and possible unforeseen consequences of different courses of action.

In defence of formality, it is also relevant to note how the substitution of informality for formality runs the risk of allowing those who occupy a superordinate position in the hierarchy to abuse their position by stepping outside what is officially allowed (see Chapter 14). Without formal rules and procedures, subordinates may also be in a weaker position to take issue with the inappropriate exercise of authority – for example, in the form of bullying and harassment.

SUMMARY

Our consideration of mainstream thinking has concentrated, first, upon the 'closed system' approach favoured by classical thinkers and, second, upon the more open, contingency approach developed by modern thinkers. Closed system thinking seeks to identify and promote universal principles of organizational design that are effective independently of their context. By contrast, open systems theory is attentive to the interface between organizations and their environments (including other organizations). One kind of dependence is upon people who bring aspects of the environment with them to work, in the form of their values, expectations and so on. Imposing formalization, in the guise of rules and procedures, in order to eliminate culturally specific, 'informal' understandings and practices can arouse hostility and so become counterproductive. It may, for example, estrange and demotivate employees, and it may create rigidities that impede, rather than facilitate, effectiveness.

Classical organization thinking suggests that organizations can be improved by adopting universally rational, formalized ways of dividing labour and ensuring its integration. Modern mainstream organization theory continues to be preoccupied with performance but suggests that an over-reliance upon universal principles of design can be self-defeating. From this perspective, performance improvement is seen to depend upon a careful assessment of the environment and then a development of the organization to match its opportunities and constraints. Sometimes, a blind eye may be turned to informal practices, or an effort may be made to incorporate and channel them. But such practices inherently present a challenge to formal authority, including its sense of order and predictability.

Other perspectives: Organizations as complex institutions

We now briefly review a number of other important, but rather less dominant and pervasive contributions to mainstream theory. In different ways, these contributions further develop or illuminate a number of the ideas found in classical and modern theory. While in some ways stretching the mainstream, they mainly endorse rather than challenge its presuppositions and priorities. These contributions are:

- institutional economics
- institutional theory
- resource dependency theory
- population ecology theory
- network theory
- virtual organization

INSTITUTIONAL ECONOMICS: MARKETS AND HIERARCHIES

Institutional economists, such as Williamson (1975), who draw upon the earlier work of Coase (1937) in economics and Chandler (1962) from business history, believe that the key to understanding the formation and adaptation of organizations resides in their capacity to operate more cost-effectively than market-based forms of economic activity. According to institutional economists, organizations come into existence when the cost of business transactions, conducted through buying and selling in markets, becomes greater than can be achieved through the alternative structure of an organizational hierarchy. This preference for 'hierarchy' rather than 'markets' results from price volatility, problems of reliability and quality, and the opportunism of those constrained only by the market. Hierarchies of control in organizations emerge and survive by competing successfully against markets in providing economic returns that are greater than the costs of managing, producing, controlling and distributing their outputs. Implicitly, this echoes the view of classical theorists who assume that the formalization of economic relationships within hierarchies can provide the most competitive, cost-effective way of organizing economic activity. Conversely, the demise of organizations is understood to occur when the costs of internal hierarchical transactions exceed those of market exchanges, and it is seen as better or cheaper to 'buy' from the market rather than 'produce' in-house.

Returning to our case study of Bar Mar, Margaret could have hired staff on a casual, market basis – for example, on an hourly or daily rate, employing the very cheapest available. Such a market-based approach would have been highly risky. Some days many people might arrive seeking work; other days there might be no one. And even if there had been a reliable supply of casual labour, Margaret might not be able to select anyone who she believed would

Outsourcing Business practice involving greater levels of intermediation. Producers of goods and services establish contracts with other companies or specialists (e.g., payroll, web management, call centres or distribution) to supply essential parts of their business. It has a long tradition stretching back to the early nineteenth century when producers bought their labour from contractors, but became less common in the twentieth century as companies directly employed their labour forces.

share her vision for Bar Mar. She might have hired the kind of employees that she wanted but it would have been a matter of chance. In short, the transaction costs would have been prohibitively high and, in the extreme case, she might have all the costs of the business to bear but no staff to generate revenues. So, an alternative economic institution, in the form of a minimal hierarchy, offers a way of address-ing the issue (of labour supply) (see Figure 7.1). In fact, the very normality of a simple hierarchical design probably meant that Margaret did not even consider a market alternative.

An increasingly popular example of shifting away from retaining activities in-house is **outsourcing**, involving the transfer of some activities to an external supplier, prompted by the calculation that this offers a more cost-effective, market-based way of securing particular goods or services. In recent times, many corporations have chosen to buy-in services from overseas (e.g., India, China) where labour can be as low as 10 per cent of the costs in the domestic Western economy.

Exercise 7.7

Think of some product or service examples where an organization has turned to the market to buy services from the cheapest supplier rather than provide them in-house. Discuss these with members of your fellow students.

Economic self-interest is assumed to be the basis of transactions in institutional economics. It is taken for granted that unless these transactions are managed or constrained by structures, individuals will be opportunistic, devious and manipulative. In pursuing their interests, they will create risks and costs. Organizational structures are intended to control or channel their members' individual economic self-interests towards the goals of the organization. What institutional economics tends to ignore – an oversight seized upon by critical thinkers – is that organizations can be established or developed to control markets (at least in the short to medium term and possibly in the longer term too) by creating various barriers (such as heavy advertising) to market entry, and so impede competition (see Resource Dependency, p. 258). Once in a dominant position, organizations may extend their domination by, for example, discounting goods in order to further undercut and destroy weaker competitors, and thereby secure their own growth. This logic is reflected in the widespread existence of **oligopolistic** markets in which a few large firms are dominant, and where smaller firms struggle to survive, let alone grow.

Oligopolistic Market where a small number of very large suppliers of a product or service have removed the competition and are thereby able to dominate the consumer since there are few alternative sources of supply.

INSTITUTIONAL THEORY

Institutional theory offers an alternative to an economics-led approach focused on minimizing transaction costs (DiMaggio and Powell, 1991; Rowlinson, 1997, Chapter 4). Institutional theory conceives of organizations as embedded in, and emergent out of, broader historical and cultural relations. People, including the founders and managers of organizations, are seen to do things primarily on the basis of established practice, tradition, habit and familiarity, and not simply in accordance with economic calculation. From an institutional theory perspective, orga-nization structure is not a product of purely rational design in any consistent or impartial sense, even though it may, nonetheless, be represented and legitimized in terms of rationality.

Thinkpoint 7.6

Think of something that you buy (e.g., trainers, jeans) and examine the various alternative products that would fulfil the same use. Why did you buy the ones you did? Discuss your explanations with other students.

To return to the example of Bar Mar, Margaret took it for granted that she would employ staff on a permanent contract, with one month's notice on either side. Had she attended business school, she might have thought of using a recruitment agency to find her staff. This never crossed Margaret's mind, but nonetheless she would have defended her decision as 'rational' despite this behaviour being conditioned primarily by established norms of employing staff on a non-casual basis. Her approach to staffing was reinforced by a (largely implicit) 'business model' that relied heavily upon her direct involvement in the identification of suitable staff. In other words, her values and common sense beliefs, rather than economic calculations concerning a series of options, guided the establishment of Bar Mar and the manner of its everyday operation.

Transactions and even calculations need to be seen, then, as conditions and consequences of numerous relations – cultural, economic, social, political, etc. Institutional theory extends back to the work of Philip Selznick (1949, 1957) who was concerned to demonstrate how organizations are embedded in their local communities, connected through a whole range of personal and inter-organizational relations, through which negotiations occur often with a view to co-opting support and avoiding conflicts.

This focus upon negotiation and accommodation between groups with divergent objectives shifted as 'new' institutional theory, developed during the 1970s, placed greater emphasis upon how organizations must comply with established expectations if they are to have credibility and legitimacy. More recently, 'neo-institutional theory' has sought to reintroduce the earlier focus upon conflicting expectations but in a way that is also routinely, rather than calculatingly, attentive to the issue of ensuring consistency between organizational design and established institutional practices. Regardless of its particular strands, however, the recurrent theme of institutional theory is its departure from thinking that is founded upon 'rational choice' (See Box 7.4), as narrowly defined by neoclassical economists.

Box 7.4
The assumptions of rational choice

- Individuals exist as discrete entities.
- Act rationally with respect to a range of freely available choices.
- Choices are made in order to fulfil conscious intentions.
- The aggregate effect of individual rational choices ensures the efficiency of competitive organizations.

A critical perspective on rational choice theory, shared to a degree by institutional theory, suggests that it is particularly appealing to elites. Why? First, this is because rational choice theory regards high levels of social inequality (e.g., the heavily skewed distribution of material goods and status symbols) as no more than outcomes of the choices or preferences of individuals. Second, it justifies the market as the main stimulus for corporate efficiency, conceived as a set of rational choices. Third, rational choice theory ignores or denies the role of corporations and other institutions (e.g., government, the media, education) in shaping the preferences of consumers through, for example, advertising, fashion and indeed promoting the ideology of individual rational choice. Overlooked, too, is the way that established inequalities and forms of privilege are preserved in this process.

Rational choice thinking effectively denies or ignores how institutions, cultures and society pre-exist individuals. Institutions do not simply place constraints upon individual choices. For they also generate the conditions that make possible the identification and fulfilment of these choices. This idea can be difficult to understand precisely because rational choice theory is so dominant in contemporary society. It floods our common sense thinking and it forms the actual or *post hoc* basis of so much corporate and government action. In order to seem legitimate such action has to be seen to accord with rational choice theory. In this sense, an institutional theory perspective allows us to appreciate how the idea of rational choice is now so widely accepted as to have become a dominant norm that regulates behaviour.

RESOURCE DEPENDENCY

In common with contingency theory, resource dependency theorists (e.g., Pfeffer and Salancik, 1978) owe a debt to systems theory but abandon its assumptions of equilibrium and consensus. Instead of the interdependency drawn from organic analogies, the emphasis is upon the organization's dependency upon, and hence vulnerability to, unpredictable supplies of resources (e.g., labour, capital, raw materials, customers, distribution outlets, etc.) in an often hostile environment. From a resource dependency perspective, the basic challenge for organizations, and the key to understanding their structural design, is uncertainty. Organizational structures are seen to emerge in an effort to reduce and/or manage uncertainties associated with their dependence upon diverse resources.

A common way of reducing dependency on the environment is to control suppliers through vertical integration along the **supply chain**. An alternative strategy is to acquire or merge with competitors so as to limit the ability of customers to switch suppliers. In such cases, the incentive is not so much to reduce transaction costs, as institutional economists maintain, but to gain control over sources of uncertainty. **Barriers to entry** may arise as a consequence of growth, for example; or they may be deliberately created through other means, such as branding, in order to deflect potential competition. These barriers cannot therefore be seen as the outcome of the operation of impersonal market forces. From a more critical standpoint, resource dependency theory signals how relations of power and dependence are relevant for understanding the formation and elaboration of organization structures. Structures that endure are those that enable organizations – or, better, those who derive the greatest material and symbolic benefit from organizations – to enhance and preserve their power and autonomy relative to other organizations and actors. Resource dependency theory points to, but does not actually develop, the idea that organizations are not merely or even generally the outcome of rational calculations

Supply chain Stages through which materials and other resources are passed in the process of their being combined, assembled and delivered to their ultimate customer.

Barriers to entry Corporate practices that develop or are deployed to deny or deter potential competitors entering the market.

Thinkpoint 7.7

Think of the various goods that you buy:

- How many of them can you say are products or services of companies that control resources in the ways described above?
- Are there other ways than mergers and acquisitions to control resources?

whose purpose is to make them more efficient and effective. Instead, they are an outcome of (political) struggles to reduce uncertainty and dependency especially for those who have the most to lose from such divergence. Included in such struggles are the contests with employees (labour) over issues of pay, representation (union recognition) and control over key decisions (e.g., investment, outsourcing, etc.).

POPULATION ECOLOGY THEORY

Population ecology theory is concerned with the birth and death of populations of organizations, and contends that their structures largely reflect what is supportable within (changing) environments (Hannan and Freeman, 1989). At the risk of oversimplifying, the nature and fate of organization structures is seen to depend primarily upon the environment as it is understood to have the decisive influence. A negligible role is ascribed to managers' powers of interpretation and adaptation. Instead, it is the ecology of the environment that promotes the development or the demise, and so seals the fortune, of organizations.

From this perspective, only structures that are found to be supportable by the (changing) environment survive. Unless the structure of an organization matches environmental requirements, it will disappear much like a species (e.g., the dinosaur) that has been rendered non-viable through evolutionary processes of natural selection (e.g., inability to adapt sufficiently quickly to a changed environment). As environments alter, the attributes favoured also change, resulting in the demise of some organizations and the flourishing of those with more congruent features. As the environment changes in a way that selects and supports a new form of structure, such as the Internet for delivering a product (e.g. Amazon), the new business model flourishes and the established, but increasingly outmoded, one declines.

Population ecology points to the difficulty for organizations in adapting to new circumstances – for example, the challenge faced by bookstores that attempt to copy and compete with the likes of Amazon, or airlines struggling to compete with the 'no frills' operations of budget providers – as they suffer from the legacy of structures (e.g., limited electronic infrastructure, inflexible bureaucratic rules, generous pay and conditions packages) that lack congruency with the new environment (notably, the Internet) and the ability to respond to it

From a critical standpoint, population ecology is one-sided in that it simply ignores or bypasses key questions concerning how organizations might not just respond to, but also be active in, the creation and interpretation of environments. In population ecology theory, environments appear to exist and change independently of the organizations that constitute them. Population ecology focuses upon outcomes – births and deaths – without consideration of the processes that select or reject certain structures. What, from a critical perspective, are viewed as politically charged processes of organizational reproduction and transformation are represented by population ecology as largely inevitable outcomes of the impersonal forces of environmental selection.

NETWORK THEORY

Powell (1990) describes network theory as follows:

> In network modes of resource allocation, transactions occur neither through discrete exchanges nor by administrative fiat, but through networks of individuals [or organizations] engaged in reciprocal, preferential, mutually supportive actions ... the basic assumption of network relationships is that one party is dependent upon resources controlled by another, and that there are gains to be had by the pooling of resources.

Network theory introduces a form of economic organization that departs from the classic, hierarchical, vertically integrated model, and also reduces the uncertainty and potential anarchy of exclusively market transactions (Castells, 1996). The network notion emphasizes the importance and potential of interdependencies within and between organizations. It takes a more modular view, with organizations forming more or less temporary alliances or partnerships to develop or produce services and products in ways that are, for example, more cost-effective than undertaking the equivalent activities in-house. Structures are understood to permit and support arrangements that are more or less transitory.

Networking is therefore something of a hybrid between the flexibility of 'markets' where, in principle, an alternative supplier can be found, and the reliability of 'hierarchies' where dependence on suppliers is replaced by direct, internal controls. Like market relations, alliances and partnerships can be replaced if they prove unsatisfactory; but like hierarchical relations, they offer greater certainty than purely market relations. Increasingly, larger companies (e.g., vehicle assemblers, hypermarkets) are creating networks of preferred suppliers with whom they 'co-operate' to supply at the price and to the specification that they demand. In return, the supplier receives some 'assistance' to ensure that deliveries to the required specification arrive just-in-time; and these suppliers have a guaranteed trade rather than relying on the precariousness of sales in the marketplace (see Table 7.5).

From a critical perspective, network theory neglects to examine the political and career processes that lie behind the development and maintenance of alliances, and how the power and dominance of an alliance might result in inefficiencies for the economy as a whole. An example is the big supermarket or hypermarket retailers who control their suppliers by making 'alliances' with them; and because of their dominant (oligopolistic) position, they chase out other sources of supply, at the same time as squeezing the margins of the suppliers that are increasingly dependent on them. Because they occupy a dominant position in a network, such organizations are able to avoid passing on the lower prices to consumers except through single-item loss leaders that are promoted to attract customers whom they know will buy non-discounted items as well.

Table 7.5 Comparing markets, hierarchies and networks

Key features	Markets	Hierarchies	Networks
Tone or climate	Precision and/or suspicion	Formal, bureaucratic	Open-ended, mutual benefits
Methods of conflict resolution	Haggling – resort to courts for enforcement	Administrative fiat — supervision	Norm of reciprocity – reputational concerns
Degree of flexibility	High	Low	Medium

Source: Adapted from Powell (1990)

VIRTUAL ORGANIZATION

Electronic technologies are commonly viewed as enabling (and even requiring) innovation and experimentation with new forms of organization, as we indicated when referring to Amazon and budget airlines. The role that technologies of 'virtual distribution' may play in facilitating new practices of organizing and management is frequently apprehended in the literature through the loosely defined concept of the virtual organization (Handy, 1996; Mowshowitz, 2002) that can be summarized as follows:

- Co-ordination across time and space through continuous electronic connectedness between suppliers, employees and consumers.

Disintermediation
Abandonment of intermediaries (e.g., wholesalers, retailers) that facilitate the distribution of goods and services so that producers trade directly with consumers. Mail order and Internet trading represent common examples of disintermediation.

- Ability to 'switch' between resources via vertical **disintermediation** and outsourcing of facilities, and fluid participation of personnel.
- Freedom from constraints imposed by time and distance – 'time–space compression' – making possible
- an ethos of flexibility and adaptability through permanent innovation, that is further enabled by
- 'flattened hierarchies', employee empowerment and fostering an organizational culture of trust and responsibility.

In this literature, organizations are identified as close to the 'virtual' ideal as a consequence of their possession of some or all of the above characteristics. There is little question that the Internet and information and communication technologies have broken down the time–space distances between people in the electronic age, but the new channels do not necessarily or significantly undermine 'traditional' channels. Internet banking, in particular, is supplementary and often stimulates dependence on, and increases business through, other

**Box 7.5
Virtual
organizations**

If one ignores the technology, there is nothing new, conceptually, in the idea of an activity without a building as its home. Where information is the raw material of work, it has never been necessary to have all the people in the same place at the same time. A network of salespeople is the most common example – an ordinary and everyday example that we would not think of giving it such a grandiose title as a virtual organization. Yet salespeople operate on their own, out of no common place – out of sight but not, one hopes, out of touch or, for that matter, out of line.

Journalism provides other examples. I myself fill an occasional slot on the BBC morning radio programme *Today*. For many years, I did not meet my director, nor have I ever met any members of the production team. I communicate by telephone from wherever I happen to be, and my contributions are often broadcast from remote, unmanned studios. It is not in any way unusual.

Source: C. Handy, Trust and the Virtual Organization (2000).

channels, especially the telephone. Rather than a movement towards the virtual organization, we encounter a multiplication of hybrid forms.

Morally charged notions such as flexibility, adaptability, etc., certainly figure prominently in the promotional discourses of technology companies, consultants and other purveyors of 'virtuality'. Despite this encouragement, examples such as the (short-lived) purely Internet-based Security First Network Bank (SFNB), which had no branch network for its customers, are infrequent. Instead, many established institutions have created independent, stand-alone 'virtual' operations and others have sought add-ons at minimal cost. Here there is often little, if any, integration between remote distribution and traditional 'bricks and mortar' operations. The establishment of stand-alone organizations for new channels gives more freedom to experiment with developing the special skills and competencies required without the encumbrance of **legacy systems** and traditional culture. It also means that the established brand can be protected from such experimentation if the new channel fails or has teething troubles. Another important reason is that the new operation can provide discounted (and usually unprofitable) rates in order to attract a particular segment of the market without having to make the same offer to existing customers:

> **Legacy systems** Old technology practices that have been superseded but still have to be serviced or managed since the cost and effort involved in merging all of the data files and procedures to the new system is greater than the benefits of just allowing it to be 'run down' until extinct.

> The last thing we want is someone coming in to a branch to tell us 'I saw this Internet rate advertised on TV. I have been with this bank for 20 years. Give it to me or I walk.' (Interview with technology manager in a major bank.)

Those adding on a new channel have largely been operating defensively against the erosion of quality business by new entrants. Internet operations like phone banks, for example, have lower costs and a more progressive image so that the traditional banks see no alternative but to emulate them. However, this increases their cost structure in the medium term as they still have a costly branch network. Consequently, they have sought to avoid excessive costs, and this precludes either the strategy of setting up a greenfield site or fully integrating the operations within the business. Technological integration has typically proven to be both difficult and expensive. Each new operation, merger and acquisition potentially contributes not to the seamless and frictionless electronic traffic prophesied in the virtual organization literature but to a multiplicity of complex systems.

Many of the criticisms levelled against the other forms of analysis presented in this section are also applicable to virtual organization. In addition, virtual organization can be criticized for exaggerating the difference between established and virtual forms of organizing. So, for example, telephone communications and even memos that are commonplace in established organizations could be characterized as 'virtual' in the sense of having no face-to-face encounter. It is probably best to conceive of 'virtuality' as a way of signalling the presence and impact of ICTs in organizations and their use to communicate between organizations, rather than to think of particular, novel organizations as 'virtual' (Woolgar, 2002). The failure to recognize this led to the dot.com bubble burst in the 1990s just in the same way as the undue faith in algorithmic-based new financial instruments contributed to bringing down the major banks in 2007/08.

Thinkpoint 7.8

R eviewing criticisms that have been made of the five kinds of organization theory sketched in this section, consider how they apply to network theory and virtual organizations.

Reinvention of 'one best way': Business process re-engineering and total quality management

Business process re-engineering (BPR) and total quality management (TQM) are two examples of techniques that have been developed to bring improvements to established, hierarchical forms of organizational design. In each case, the commended techniques of organizational improvement are considered to have a universal application. In this respect, they are appropriately regarded as 'neoclassical'.

BPR and TQM illustrate ways in which mainstream thinking has been preoccupied with the question of how the benefits of a more rational, or rationalized, approach to the design of work and organization can be engineered without provoking individual and collective forms of resistance to their respective demands. This quest has proceeded along two intersecting paths. First, there have been recurrent efforts to refine 'hard' methods of measurement and control, in the form of performance indicators, benchmarking, scorecards and so on. Such methods pay minimal attention to questions of how they are likely to be received and interpreted by employees.

A second path implicitly challenges the assumption that the application of 'hard' methods will mechanically improve performance by inducing more productive behaviour. Instead of striving to design a technically perfect system into which people are expected to fit, the second path pays greater attention to existing arrangements and expectations and considers how, by going 'with the grain', these can be adapted and managed to improve performance and, in this respect, some concession is made to the modernist mantra of contingency.

Business process re-engineering (BPR) An approach to organizational redesign that proposes information technology should be the catalyst for revolutionary organizational change, leading to improved measures of performance in terms of costs, speed, quality and service.

Silos Discrete functions, departments or divisions within an organization that through the routines of repetition have become ossified and self-absorbed.

BUSINESS PROCESS RE-ENGINEERING

Business process re-engineering (BPR) has followed the first path, promising to transform the internal structures of businesses using information and communication technologies to convert sequential into parallel processing of tasks (see Box 7.6).

Central to BPR is the intended destruction of the **silos** that result from the organization of work around specialist departments. Silos are seen to organize employees' activities to expand and preserve their specialisms rather than to develop processes necessary to produce competitive products and services. ICTs are identified as providing the means of ensuring horizontal co-ordination and

- *From function to process.* BPR aspires to produce radical, quantum-leap change by reorienting businesses around key processes. It demands the complete replacement of bureaucratic and functional silos by units organized around delivering customer requirements.
- *Entrepreneurialism.* The aim is to transform organizations so that all staff are driven by a competitive desire to provide the 'best' and most profitable customer service.
- *Information technology.* Advocates the widespread use of information and communication technologies to enable the shift from function to process, combined with some, apparently universally applicable, human resource management (HRM) techniques that are intended to empower employees and facilitate teamworking.

**Box 7.6
What is business process re-engineering?**

vertical control (through remote monitoring of activity). Notably, ICTs are expected to facilitate a process of self-managing in which unproductive, non-value-adding activities are stripped out, with attendant gains in profitability and associated loss of jobs.

In the majority of cases, BPR has failed to fulfill its promise principally because insufficient attention is given to the human dimension of bringing about radical, step change (although it may also be doubted whether simply giving this greater attention would have made the bitter pill of lay-offs any more acceptable). Management has often lacked the capability and authority, and sometimes also the inclination, to impose BPR upon employees who regard it as disruptive of their established routines and positions, and threatening insofar as it openly advertises its capacity to cut costs by 'downsizing'. This is managerial code for axing jobs, including the jobs of many managers who, in principle, also face redundancy as a consequence of the promotion of empowered, *self-managing* teams (see Chapter 4). For its advocates, failures of BPR to deliver on its promises are attributed to its partial or bungled application, rather than to its limited or negative and mechanistic understanding of the complexities of organizations as institutions.

The second path takes fuller account of the *social* dimensions of organizations as systems. No matter how well an organization is designed or structured, it is only people, not organizations, who 'behave' – that is, engage in activities that may be more or less 'productive'. As discussed in Chapter 2, 'human relations' has been an influential variant of this thinking. It appeals to the common sense view that all human beings have concerns for social recognition and identity and value a sense of belonging to a wider group, even though such group membership can constrain an individual's freedom and potentially be oppressive.

TOTAL QUALITY MANAGEMENT

A version of this thinking is present, in a more focused and self-managing form, in the quality management movement, which became full-blown in the development of **total quality management (TQM)**, where individuals or teams of employees co-operate to identify areas for improving their practice.

Early quality management programmes revolved around 'quality circles' (Hill, 1991) where teams of employees meet regularly to discuss work and production problems and suggest practical ways of improving the quality of processes and outputs. In contrast to BPR, which advocates a more radical transformation of established practice, quality management, including TQM, favours a process of incremental change. While insisting that there is always room for improvement, TQM assumes that the basic design of work and organization is sound. It does not seek to substitute

Total quality management (TQM) A system of quality control that is designed to build in quality at every stage of production to minimize waste and defective parts that would otherwise be detected at the end of the production process.

its own 'one best way' of reforming existing practice but, rather, aspires to work with the grain of the particularities of such practice with the aim of removing unnecessary impediments to the quality as well as the quantity of productive activity. Instead of a 'one best way' approach, TQM is based upon a set of broad points of reference (see Box 7.7).

Box 7.7
What is total quality management?

- *Continuous improvement.* TQM is concerned with improving internal processes through, for example, quality circles, where groups of employees are brought together to discuss how working practices can be improved. Various technical means have also been devised to achieve the improvements, including **statistical process control** and 'zero defects', which involve the quantification and monitoring of quality outputs that aims to remove all obstacles to perfection.

Statistical process control
A statistical technique used by quality managers to ensure that product quality standards are maintained.

- *Customer orientation.* The aim of TQM is to transform the culture of an organization such that products or services will be characterized by their 'fitness for use' and thus 'meet the expectations of the customers'.
- *Teamworking.* Combined with a notion of employee empowerment and participation, which involves assigning greater discretion to team members, teamworking has become a central means of securing quality objectives.

A broad based quality approach has enjoyed a long period of widespread managerial support and continues to attract management practitioners. This may well be because it is an amalgamation of a number of moderate and incremental innovations – culture change, empowerment, quality circles and teamworking – and it is permissive in the sense that it does not dictate to managers that all its elements must be simultaneously and fully adopted. It also gives encouragement to managers to involve employees in its implementation, in contrast to BPR where there is a suspicion of employee involvement and an insistence upon its top-down application, with the anticipation that employees will be released from their confinement within silos and become empowered as a result. With TQM, it is more likely (but by no means inevitable – see Chapter 11), that employees will interpret aspects of the (incremental) changes as bringing some benefits to them, and for this reason there is rarely strong or sustained resistance, whether in the form of covert withdrawal of co-operation or open hostility, to its introduction.

Case study 7.2
Structure and technology

A study conducted in the late 1950s, when research into industrial organization began to flourish, continues to have relevance for illustrating a number of the ideas presented in this chapter. Led by Joan Woodward (1958, 1965), the study broke new ground by providing a research-based analysis of organization design and structure and was important in demonstrating the value of systems theory and supporting a contingency approach to organization design.

Prior to the 1950s, ideas about structure and design principles had been based mainly on the personal experience of classical writers (e.g., of Taylor and Fayol). Max Weber's writings on the legal formalism and rationality of bureaucracy (see Chapter 14) provided a more theoretical explanation of the appeal of such principles, but it was in the post-war period that social scientists began to test out and evaluate the rationality and efficiency of particular organizational designs. Statistical analyses of the relationship of structure and performance were pursued by developing measures of levels in the hierarchy, spans of control, proportions of indirect labour, etc. Woodward was primarily interested in the question of whether the type of technology used in industrial organizations has an effect upon the design of organizations, as this would lend empirical support to those who doubted the applicability of principles that advocated 'one best way' irrespective of the technology involved.

Woodward's work was theoretically informed by the growing interest in the power of technology to determine structure and behaviour. To apply and test her thinking, she grouped technologies into three types:

- Unit and batch production technologies, which created single or small quantities of product (e.g., custom-built machines for manufacturers).
- Mass or assembly line production (e.g., cars).
- Process production (e.g., chemicals).

One finding was that process technology firms had longer hierarchical chains, with a correspondingly large number of managers and support staff. It was also discovered that the span of control of CEOs was greater with process production but that proportionately smaller spans of control for first-line supervisors occurred in process as well as batch production, with much larger spans occurring in mass production. An important conclusion of Woodward's research was that firms that most closely matched the norm for the type of production were more successful in terms of their profitable performance.

Two implications of Woodward's research are that, first, universally applicable or 'one best way' solutions take inadequate account of the variability of technologies; and, second, firms not taking account of this variability (e.g., by deviating from the industry norm) were least likely to be successful.

Woodward's work can be seen to challenge, but also to reproduce in a more nuanced form, the classical faith in a 'one best way' of organizational design. There was no universal single design appropriate for industry as a whole, but there was one best way within firms using particular types of technology. Woodward's research also stimulated an academic industry of quantitative research on organizational design, structure and behaviour, which set out to identify the configurations that produced the best performance.

For example, studies sought to specify and measure the elements of organization structure in respect of degrees of 'formalization', 'standardization', 'specialization', etc. This research examined how such aspects of organization structure interrelate, as a system, to the context, to interaction patterns within organizations and to performance – with the prospect that desired outcomes might be predicted and controlled by establishing forms of structure and behaviour best fitted to the context.

Although much of this research proved inconsistent and inconclusive, it has been sufficiently persuasive to contribute to a growing disillusionment with simple, universally applicable models of the relationship between technology, structure and performance (see Chapter 12 for a more detailed analysis of organization and technology and critique of technological determinism).

Organizations and technologies

Organizations are readily regarded as combinations of technical and social systems. In Woodward's (1958) research on industrial organization (see Case Study 7.2), technology is seen as key in determining the design and development of an organization (see Chapter 12). Yet, the technology is treated like a 'black box' whose content is never interrogated to reveal how it is necessarily interpreted and given meaning and significance only through the activities and interactions of those working in, and others trading with, the organization. Whatever the relationship between technology and structure, or between structure and behaviour, it is mediated by the sense-making activities of members of the organization.

Consider Woodward's finding that the most successful firms, grouped by type of technology, tended to share a similar structure (see Case Study 7.2 above). This finding does not demonstrate the determining nature of technology. Rather, it suggests that many managers have made parallel interpretations in relation to the significance of the technology and the effectiveness of different organizational arrangements – perhaps by learning from, or copying the more successful companies – when working on the design of their structures (see Chapter 12). It is not just the design of *organizations* that is social, and therefore to be understood as the outcome of human action, but *technology* as well. When we concentrate upon technology as a determinant of change or organizational (re)design, we may neglect how the development of technology as well as its effects on society are themselves conditioned by various human, cultural and organizational influences. And, of course, the same can be said of the treatment of organization as (if it were) a technology – that is, as a technical artefact or instrument that can be designed or reformed in much the same way as a machine (see Chapter 1).

Thinkpoint 7.9

The technology needed for an electrically propelled motor car has been available for much longer than that for mobile phones. Think of the reasons why the latter has been a mass consumption product whereas the former has so far been restricted to a few environmentally friendly trendsetters.

The understanding that the influence of technology upon performance (for example) is mediated by social considerations is a focus of 'socio-technical systems' thinking within mainstream analysis. The basic idea is that disregarding the established social order (e.g., a tightly knit work group) in an organization can have detrimental effects when a new technology, or technical system (e.g., appraisal), is introduced that is poorly aligned to that order. It may disturb the social balance and risk resistance, demotivation and labour turnover.

A socio-technical systems framework would suggest that the architects and implementers of BPR (see above) are often insufficiently attentive or sensitive to the social dimensions of organizational life. That is to say, they treat organizations as if they are purely technical systems, without adequate regard for the norms and sensibilities of employees and their managers. The cautious and conservative quality of socio-technical systems thinking is derived from the human relations philosophy (see Chapter 2) that is its guiding light. Here the maintenance of balance is given priority over more radical kinds of proposals favoured by root-and-branch reformers. The radical reformers have little hesitation in 'throwing out the baby with the bath water', particularly with respect to displacing the tacit skills and knowledge on which organizations so depend.

THE IMPORTANCE OF 'TACIT KNOWLEDGE' AND 'USER INVOLVEMENT'

'Tacit knowledge', although having no formal standing or recognition, is the lifeblood of an organization. Tacit knowledge consists of the numerous routine, sometimes idiosyncratic, and often subconscious ways through which we carry out work tasks, and that we have acquired through long periods of familiarity with those tasks. These ways may not comply with any rational model of how things should be done, and indeed it is this 'idiosyncrasy' that the advocates of BPR and similar programmes seek to eliminate. The problem, however, is that the eradication of certain routines can be highly disruptive because the designers of (re-engineered) systems rarely appreciate how what they are replacing addressed various crucial contingencies and eventualities. It is the vital importance of implicit understandings, often ignored by engineers or those seeking to re-engineer, that results in the mantra of 'user-involvement' and 'user-friendliness' being increasingly rehearsed. But even if this mantra is heeded and followed, it is often extremely difficult for the users themselves to articulate their tacit knowledge or to communicate willingly and effectively with consultants and (re)designers whose temporary and transient status is not conducive to generating the kind of trust that would be necessary to support such communication. Users may be reluctant to share this information if they fear that it will enable others to redesign their jobs, and so risk their work becoming more demanding, less interesting or even surplus to requirements.

If, following a redesign, the tasks and/or personnel executing them change dramatically, the informal culture and tacit skill erodes, with attendant difficulties for addressing unforeseen problems. In such circumstances, and in the absence of control over the process of change, employees may become fearful and insecure. At best, they may become resigned and disaffected about their jobs and the material and symbolic security that employment ordinarily provides. In short, their work identities are more vulnerable than before, often leading to highly defensive behaviour in response to management power. They are much less likely to trust managers and in this sense a greater polarization between them may result in which power and inequality, rather than productive collaboration, frames the relationship.

The kinds of criticisms levelled against the study of technology in organizations can be generalized to many mainstream studies which attempt to isolate and measure variables, including structure. These studies disregard how the very identification and specification of the variables, quite apart from the (determining) effects attributed to them, are the constructions of, and are mediated by, organizational members and/or social scientists. 'Technology', for example, cannot be known except by identifying it in particular, interpretation-dependent ways. Its effect upon other 'variables', such as structure or performance, depends not upon the technology in itself but upon the specific, favoured meaning, or interpretation, of technology. This meaning is mediated by organizational members as well as by researchers. Unfortunately, much mainstream thinking excludes consideration of this interpretive process. As a consequence, statistical correlations are frequently spurious in the sense that they claim outcomes that are a consequence of something (e.g., cultural, social, political or economic relations) that is outside of, or very poorly registered by, the 'variables' that are their focus. It is partly for this reason, but also to avoid restricting analysis to linear causal factors, that the very term 'variable' is avoided in critical studies. For such mainstream thinking operates routinely to deflect attention from a host of important human and relational issues that are the focus of critical organization studies.

Contributions and limitations of the mainstream

CONTRIBUTIONS

We can summarize the contribution of the mainstream as follows:

- The structure of organizations is seen largely to determine behaviour so that it is vital to ensure that it is designed, redesigned or re-engineered to be more consistent with its intended purpose (e.g. improved performance in terms of efficiency and/or effectiveness) or more compatible with the particular contingencies of its environment.
- The analytical framework most commonly drawn upon is some variant of systems theory (closed or open) where inputs (labour, resources, policies) are processed to produce the required outputs (e.g. profitable or cost-effective products and services).
- Generally, a consensus is presumed to exist within organizations and management whereupon 'good' design is understood to be a matter of creating and sustaining a rationally defensible ordering of hierarchical work relationships.

Mainstream thinking about management and organization is firmly wedded to the view that knowledge that has any relevance and value is properly and exclusively concerned with *enhancing performance within the ideological and political parameters of the status quo*. Performance is therefore closely coupled to profitability and growth, rather than to any wider measures of human advancement or sustainability. Knowledge that challenges the status quo, or is not perceived to be relevant for its functional reform, as framed by senior managers, is identified as irrelevant if not outright dangerous.

LIMITATIONS

Despite, or perhaps because of, its rather narrow focus, the mainstream agenda enjoys widespread credibility and legitimacy. It seems so eminently sensible and acceptable to seek out those organizational structures that are assessed to be the most efficient and productive for maintaining and renewing the status quo – and thereby preserve established hierarchies of power and inequality. Yet, questions of whether the pursuit of a mainstream agenda is necessarily beneficial or sustainable (e.g., **work–life balance**; Third World labour that lacks basic legal protections in terms

Work–life balance General term to refer to how far work dominates people's lives over and above any other considerations.

of working conditions, age restrictions, hours worked, etc.), non-human life (e.g., factory farming) or the future of the planet (e.g., global warming) tends to be marginalized or dismissed as 'moral' or 'ethical' matters beyond the core domain of management. At best, these questions are couched and re-described in business-friendly terms as 'corporate social responsibility' (CSR) or they are placed in the sphere of government. In this scenario, the 'efficient' organization is obliged to find ways of accommodating restrictions upon its operations. As we have seen in recent corporate scandals, it is often more a matter of being seen to conform to the letter of the law, or just calculating the business risk of deliberately evading regulations, than of actively welcoming reforms that place quality of life before profitable production. Even after the global financial crisis of 2008, only lip service was paid to ethics as opposed to constraining the excesses of capitalism through increased government regulation such as enforcing higher capital reserves and lower asset/lending ratios on financial institutions (Knights and McCabe, 2015).

In *The Organization of Business*, Stephen Ackroyd (2002) concludes that the orthodox approach to organizational structure should be discarded because it is incapable of understanding contemporary patterns of organizational change. The argument that designs or structures are simply functional for organizations to survive – by facilitating their adaptation to the environment – is, he contends, a one-sided and highly partial view. It deflects attention from the power relations that underlie such structures and precludes any understanding of how organizations constitute and enact their environments rather than simply respond to them. To this we would add that organizations are historically and culturally embedded so that their design and operation articulate the values and priorities of their particular contexts.

We may recall that an important element of mainstream thinking, in the form of institutional theory, also rejects the systems or contingency approach. Institutional theory invites us to appreciate how non-rational considerations colour the design of organizational structures in ways that may enhance their effectiveness as well as their legitimacy. This points to some permeability of boundaries between 'mainstream' and 'critical' approaches. Indeed, as in all spheres, history has no respect for the status quo. What is groundbreaking today becomes mainstream tomorrow so that elements of a critical approach are now gradually becoming accepted as part of the mainstream. For example, a mainstream scholarly institution – the American Academy of Management – has incorporated a substantial Critical Management Studies Division. Its significance for the central theme of this chapter is that this division has been required to fit within and be compliant with the (mainstream) form and protocols of the organizational structure of the Academy. From a mainstream standpoint, this accommodation would be viewed as functionally necessary (the Academy acquires a new set of members and demonstrates its capacity to adapt to new developments/innovations in the field). From a more critical standpoint, in contrast, the accommodation could be regarded as indicative of a hegemonic imposition that is intended to incorporate and domesticate critical voices. In practice, such developments (e.g., mergers and acquisitions) can have unintended consequences – for example, as the ostensibly incorporated party begins to exert pressures upon its 'host' in ways that may or may not be intended as, but can be, disruptive.

Thinkpoint 7.10

C an you think of an example drawn from your own experience where one group has sought to enrol the members of other groups that were apparently antagonistic, at least in some respects, to its values and priorities? How was this process managed, and what was the outcome?

Although mainstream approaches make passing reference to some of our key concepts (e.g., power and identity), their meaning and relevance is defined in ways that do not challenge the status quo and its structures of organization. Social inequalities – of income, status, gender, ethnicity, etc. – are largely unacknowledged and unquestioned. It is assumed that equilibrium and consensus are core features of the prevailing system and, conversely, that deviation from this continuity and stability is detrimental rather than productive of innovation and needed change.

Taking the example of power, the mainstream tends to view power as the property of persons, groups or institutions. Power is regarded as something to ensure decision-making is routine, and unbroken by disruptions. Or power is viewed negatively as a factor that constrains or limits operations. An understanding of power is considered relevant only for purposes of enhancing managerial control. Accordingly, its meaning is framed and circumscribed by the significance it has for preserving the status quo and parrying challenges to it. In other words, mainstream thinking defines the nature and operation of power in a way that maintains its boundaries. Likewise, it provides a limited domain of knowledge that is attentive to diverse issues of identity, inequality or freedom only insofar as they are assessed to be instrumentally useful for enhancing performance. Here performance is itself equated primarily with profitability and growth, and where other considerations, such as customer satisfaction or employee motivation or ecological sustainability, are conceived and justified only, or primarily, as means to this end.

CRITICAL APPROACH TO STRUCTURE AND DESIGN

INTRODUCTION

Throughout this chapter as in others, a critical approach has been repeatedly referred to when pointing to various limitations in mainstream thinking. In broad terms, a major limitation of mainstream approaches is their failure to appreciate the importance of inequality and power in the formation and maintenance of organizations. They also have a weak and narrowly instrumental grasp of the significance of identity, freedom and insecurity in the reproduction of features of organizational life, characterized as 'structure' in mainstream analysis. These limitations are connected to a particular conception of knowledge that attempts to map the sense of reality conveyed by common sense without reflecting upon how the realities of organizing and managing are formed historically. Nor, relatedly, is there much reflection upon how common sense thinking has been forged, or organized, in power-invested ways, within relations of domination in which social technologies of oppression are represented as benign mechanisms of functional necessity. Our common sense understandings of organizations and management have been shaped and disseminated predominantly by the people who occupy positions of relative material and symbolic advantage – the owners and managers of organizations and, increasingly, management consultants (see Chapter 9). Unsurprisingly, they have developed or supported bland, ostensibly apolitical ideas about organization, including its structure. The blandness and seeming impartiality of these ideas are important insofar as it allows them to be routinely invoked and enacted without provoking a backlash or any kind of challenge.

We will focus upon two key strands of critical thinking that, by deviating from the mainstream, necessarily appear partial and challenging. *First*, there is analysis that is critical of the mainstream for its failure to incorporate an appreciation of power and inequality in the understanding of how organizations are structured. The basic concern is that the hierarchical design of organizations reflects and reinforces an unequal distribution of material and symbolic goods. Far from promoting greater freedom, most work organizations are seen to place a brake upon opportunities for self-development and self-management, increasingly by seeming to promote it – for example, by encouraging employees to 'just be themselves' (Fleming and Sturdy, 2011), an injunction that, if taken seriously, would result in behaviour unacceptable to managers (e.g. texting friends).

Pressures and incentives at work encourage people to absorb and reproduce dominant values and established priorities, and not to reflect critically upon them as to do so threatens to open up other directions and institutions for productive activity. From this standpoint, the concern to introduce or develop structures that are more efficient and/or effective is seen to be driven by a desire to preserve the status quo, or a fear of the consequences of its loss (e.g., for security and identity). Their design is seen to mask more fundamental preoccupations with the operation and exercise of power and the retention of its associated privileges.

Second, and relatedly, critical analysis seeks to expose how employees' sense of identity and their insecurities are exploited to establish and tighten control in organizations in ways that curtail employee freedom while claiming to extend it. Control is accomplished through the managed acquisition of self-knowledge (e.g., the production of desirable identities through lifestyle marketing) to which the individual's sense of meaning and security becomes tied.

What these strands of critical analysis share is an antagonism towards how 'organizational structures' become frozen as reified entities in mainstream analysis. 'Structures' are represented as if they have a life of their own, and capacity to act independently of the people that participate in the activities and relationships to which the term 'structure' is attributed. Critical analysis challenges the common sense knowledge that enables 'structures' to be so widely defined and examined in this way. It invites students of organization to undertake a radical rethink of the basis and credibility of forms of knowledge and common sense thinking that are (mis)construed as self-evident.

A critical approach to organization and structure

We have drawn attention to the centrality in mainstream thinking of:

1 Closed and open systems thinking.
2 The distinction between formal and informal elements.

Critical approaches begin by inverting these ideas, arguing that within mainstream thinking:

3 Systems thinking produces an abstracted set of concepts about organization that marginalize the human, political and process dimensions of organization and management.
4 Even when some idea of the human, political and process dimensions (e.g., through the distinction between formal and informal elements) is introduced, this is narrowly channelled and dimmed by a belief that they must be eradicated or contained to prevent them disrupting the formal system and management's goals.

What fundamentally distinguishes these contrasting approaches is a different perception and orientation towards consensus and conflict in organizations and society.

The diverse elements of mainstream thinking tend to share an assumption of consensus and social balance as the norm in organizations. Conflict is therefore regarded as an aberration that managers or leaders must either remove or somehow divert and direct into productive channels. There is widespread adherence to closed or open systems theory in which organizations are represented as interdependent elements that seemingly develop and operate independently of the processes through which organizational members (re)produce organizational realities. From a critical perspective, systems theory is seen to 'neglect the ways in which [organizational members'] purposes and perspectives intervene in the interpretation and contesting of goal-related prescriptions for action' (Elger, 1975, p. 94). In other words, whatever (functional) purpose is attributed to the elements comprising the closed/open system of organization(s), its significance is invariably interpreted from within the particular frames of reference of different groups of organizational members.

Mainstream neglect of how organizational realities are an ongoing outcome of processes of interpretation and negotiation is reflected in the assumption that 'an over-arching consensus informs all organizational processes' (ibid). Critics are sceptical about such claims, arguing that consensus is often *forced*, rather than determined through informed debate under conditions of an equality of participation; and that the absence of tension and conflict is more credibly interpreted as a product of effective control rather than a sign of underlying harmony.

Thinkpoint 7.11

Consider an occasion where, beneath the surface, there were major conflicts brewing but there was very little visible evidence of these. How would you account for their invisibility? Were there any tell-tale signs of the conflicts? If your example was drawn from outside the sphere of organizations, can you think of some examples within them, again drawing upon your experience?

Once the presumption of consensus is challenged, the notion that organizations have a single, shared goal is also placed under critical scrutiny. It is understood that different groups and individuals have *diverse* agendas and 'goals', and that these cannot sensibly be equated with a *single* organizational goal. Accordingly, the notion that organizations, rather than their members, have goals is no longer conceived as a self-evident fact but, instead, is viewed as a misleading fantasy, or cynical claim, of a dominant group that has acquired widespread, commonsensical plausibility.

That it is possible for a particular view to become deeply ingrained in common sense thinking is explained, from a critical perspective, by the differentials of power between dominant and subordinate individuals and groups. For some groups – those who have access to channels of communication within organizations or the media more generally – exert greater influence upon the formation of what becomes received wisdom or common sense, and/or ensure that dissenting voices are suppressed or marginalized by more or less covert threats to withdraw resources from them. In this way, a questionable claim – such as the idea that organizations have goals, or that roles within organizations are determined by functional imperatives 'untouched by personal concerns or collective interests' – becomes, in the absence of critical reflection and/or countervailing discourses, taken-for-granted as a 'common **normative** standard' (Elger, 1975, p. 94).

One way in which the presumption of consensus can be sustained with minimal challenge is through the design and structure of an organization. This is so especially where the structure is represented and accepted as the most rational, cost-effective and even 'one best way' of organizing. Only at times of crisis or when there are major disruptions – due perhaps to a takeover, a change of government or regulatory reform – is it likely that the structure of an organization becomes a focus for critical re-examination or radical redesign. From a critical perspective, mainstream approaches do not provide impartial or neutral knowledge, but instead reflect senior management's interest in control by assuming the legitimacy and functionality of the structure of inequality. Mainstream approaches lend credibility to knowledge that supports the status quo by presuming, rather than interrogating, organizational consensus. Through the engagement of critical approaches, we can identify how organizational structure is a condition of, but also has consequences for, the reproduction of power and inequality.

Normative What is commonly accepted as normal and/or appropriate to an organization. Critical political analysis draws attention to the evaluation of behaviour using normative criteria, often the criteria favoured by supporters of the status quo (e.g. managers), as an exercise in classification and control. See **normative control**.

A fundamental aspect of economic organizations is that a majority are privately owned and thereby designed principally to make profit for their owners. In speaking about the structure and design of organizations, mainstream texts rarely mention that our economy is capitalist, let alone discuss the implications of it being so. Even when considering the public sector, there is a concentration upon the efficiency of the means of attaining current objectives rather than any questioning of them. Mainstream texts take for granted that profit and/or efficiency are the sole and necessary drivers of organizations and assume a managerialist focus where the major purpose of studying organizations is to discover ways of facilitating the achievement of efficiency and/or the attainment of profits. How far they are ever successful in doing this is debatable; but critical researchers challenge the legitimacy of managerialism and the knowledge that sustains it. For example, the balance between prevention and treatment of illness in the health sector might be questioned; and a parallel in schools and universities might be between education and training, with the former being viewed as a basis for self-training – for example, in the form of **transferable skills**.

In the following analysis, it is understood that the capitalist market economy is the context in which organizations operate. Penetrated and guided by neo-liberal thinking, governments increasingly identify competition as the driver of efficiency, with correspondingly less concern for public accountability. Over recent years, much of what was in the public sector, such as energy, transport and telecommunications, has been targeted for **privatization** (see Chapter 1). In local authorities, hospitals and educational institutions, many governments have sought to introduce competition, and thereby drive down unit-costs, by applying key performance measures (KPIs), conducting audits and/or publishing league tables.

Transferable skills Employee skills or knowledge that can be readily applied to a wide range of tasks.

Privatization Selling off public corporations, in part or in full, to individuals or corporations that anticipate increasing their wealth or value from this acquisition. See **New Right**.

Exercise 7.8

Reflect upon the use of grades in education, such as the grading of performance (e.g., qualifications to enter university or assessment of assignments), to consider the consequences of their use, both intended and unintended, and positive as well as negative.

1 List the consequences in terms of what you consider to be their importance.
2 Compare and contrast your list with those of other students.
3 Identify points or areas of agreement and disagreement.
4 Analyze the basis of any disagreements.

The model for an increasing number of organizations – public, private and not-for-profit – is increasingly the private corporation in a competitive market. External competition for resources between organizations – for example, between hospitals, schools or universities – is undertaken using common measures to assess their performance and justified level of reward. Internal to these organizations, individuals are encouraged to treat their performance like a commodity that can be used to compete for scarce resources and positions. In other words, the provision of public goods begins to resemble the world of sport where, for example, teams (e.g., soccer, netball, baseball) or individuals (e.g., tennis, golf) compete for top positions in their respective league tables or official rankings.

The challenge to a mainstream stance on knowledge production runs, for example, something like this:

THE PRODUCTION OF KNOWLEDGE

1 Universities are charged with the task of developing and disseminating research-based knowledge. Often they are also fully or partially funded by the State. In which case, knowledge produced in universities should not be predisposed to the business of making money but, rather, should be geared to challenging, and advancing upon, received wisdom. To the extent that the work of university staff contribute directly to the profitability of private organizations, there is effectively a redistribution of funds from the taxpayer to the private investor.

2 Against the above argument, it could be said that when organizations operate more efficiently and profitably, they contribute to the success of the economy as a whole and everyone, including publicly funded researchers, benefits.

3 Critics of (2) contend that it is impossible to evaluate the effectiveness of prescriptions because they cannot be separated from the power relations through which they are developed and implemented.

4 It is therefore better for university staff to generate ideas, understandings and insights about organizations that practitioners would not ordinarily produce; and this should include critical as well as more conventional views. Practitioners can then decide which are of value and applicable to them.

5 Even (4) would encounter censure from other critics who would say that the population of 'practitioners' is often narrowly restricted to senior managers, or even managers, and excludes a majority of people – citizens, taxpayers – who are directly or indirectly affected by prescriptions about the design and structure of organization.

6 Finally, some critics would argue that there should be no direct relationship between the content of public goods (e.g., education, health) and the funding of them. This is on the grounds that it creates an inappropriate dependence that may compromise the quality and dissemination of the output.

Major issues and controversies

Critical approaches challenge the idea that consensus is the prevailing norm within organizations and focus more attention on domination and exploitation, if not overt conflict. Domination occurs when employees are required to comply with directions that are not democratically established or maintained. Where there is an absence of conflict, or 'consensus' apparently prevails, critical studies are inclined to suspect or question whether it is imposed or forced on employees by coercive means, rather than freely and openly accepted. From this critical standpoint, lack of overt conflict or dissatisfaction does not necessarily imply active agreement or fulfilment, as it may be the product of institutionalized domination that has come to be seen as entirely normal. The term 'structure' may then more appropriately be seen as a medium and outcome of diverse modes of domination, such as the exploitative subordination of labour to capital, of women to men, and/or of one ethnic group to another.

To understand why, in the context of work organizations, critical analysis focuses upon domination and exploitation, it is necessary to consider how it accounts for the historical formation of economic organization. In other words, it is relevant to ask: if the quest for greater efficiency is rejected as the explanation of modern economic organization, what is the alternative explanation? The answer is the development of new forms of *control* and *institutionalized domination* – not as ends in themselves but as a means of private wealth accumulation that is based upon the *exploitation of labour*. Its point of departure is that modern economic organization is based primarily upon specifically capitalistic principles and associated notions of rationality that have fostered its development. Capitalist principles include the pursuit of profit and the freedom of people to exchange their labour as a commodity in return for a market-determined wage. In this context, what is rational is what is deemed to facilitate the pursuit of profit for private wealth accumulation and the removal of restrictions upon the equilibrium achieved by the (seemingly impartial) operation of markets, including the free exchange of labour. In this way, labour can be systematically exploited as the wealth generated by its creative power is appropriated by capital, thereby increasing and institutionalizing social inequality.

Thinkpoint 7.12

In your experience, when has control been exercised (e.g., by a supervisor at work or a teacher at school) to maintain the status quo (e.g., the status hierarchy) rather than for any 'good' or defensible business or educational purpose? What were the consequences?

In mainstream analysis, the presence and virtue of capitalist principles of economic organization and a market-centred, calculative notion of rationality are taken as given and justified in terms of materialism – economic growth and wealth – that, it is claimed, is universally valued and so is legitimate. In critical analysis, close attention is given to this context as the impartiality or even efficiency of capitalism is challenged. The operation of markets, for example, is seen to be most beneficial to those who have the 'market power' – in the form of material resources and know-how – to play markets (e.g. for labour) to their own advantage.

Conversely, those with least market power are found to struggle to participate in markets and, at the extreme, are simply unable to secure a minimal level of subsistence from their operation. Indeed, markets simply fail to cater for such people. When people lack the resources – 'purchasing power' – to participate as consumers, for example, they become dependent upon direct or indirect forms of charity. It is difficult to see how capitalist principles are 'rational' from the point of view of people (e.g., women, ethnic and religious minorities, and other socially excluded or deprived groups in the rich world and the mass of people living in poverty elsewhere) who are *systematically* disadvantaged by their application.

From a critical standpoint, capitalist economies systematically disadvantage a *majority* of people – consumers as well as employees, or what recently has been described as the 99 per cent. How can that be, since over recent decades a majority of the population, in many developed economies at least, have normally experienced a progressively improving material standard of living? Excluding pensioners and members of the so-called 'underclass', spending power has increased or at least been maintained. In most cases, people consider themselves to be paid appropriately for the work that they do, and do not regard themselves as badly treated by their employers. And yet, at the same time, many feel little enthusiasm for, or have a sense of control over, the work they do or their long-term future. There is a feeling of being a cog in a machine whose work is continuously measured and evaluated, and where the primary meaning of work is to become a bigger, better paid cog – just as Taylor advocated (see above and Chapter 14). In effect, exploitation and domination have become institutionalized.

As Max Weber, quoted in Mayer (1956, pp. 126–127) put it:

> The performance of each individual worker is mathematically measured, each man becomes a little cog in the machine and aware of this, his one preoccupation is whether he can become a bigger cog ... as it were to become men who need 'order' and nothing but order, who become nervous and cowardly if for one moment this order wavers, and helpless if they are torn away from their total incorporation in it.

The structure of work organization

How, then, is sense to be made of this? The form of critical analysis that responds to this challenge draws originally from Marx's ideas and, more specifically, from his analysis of the organization of labour processes in the distinctive context of capitalist economic organization.

In examining how work is organized in capitalist enterprises, Marx shifts analysis away from the idea that every commodity, including labour, secures its fair price in the market where demand and supply find their equilibrium. That assumption underpins so much of mainstream thinking, particularly analysis that takes its lead

Neoclassical economics A form of economics that emphasizes free markets and non-intervention by the state. It contrasts with the post-war consensus around Keynes's ideas of state intervention and public spending to maintain economic growth.

from **neoclassical economics**. In its place, Marx seeks to understand the status of labour in capitalist economies and, in particular, how it is organized within workplaces to ensure that an adequate surplus, or profit, can be extracted and privately appropriated from the productive efforts of labour.

Marx illustrates the capitalist–worker relationship by giving it a personal dramatization, imagining how a shift occurs when we leave the 'sphere of circulation' where commodities, including labour, are exchanged fairly and impersonally in market transactions, and enter the 'sphere of production' where there is a more overt relationship of domination and exploitation:

> When we leave the simple sphere of circulation or the exchange of commodities ... a certain change takes place ... He [sic] who was previously the money-owner now strides out in front as a capitalist; the possessor of labour power follows as his worker. The one smirks self-importantly and is intent on business: the other is timid and holds back, like someone who has brought his own hide to market and now has nothing else to expect but a tanning. (Marx, 1973, p. 280)

Marx's key point is that when each party is involved in agreeing a payment for the worker's productive capability (i.e., 'labour power'), the contract is 'freely' entered into. Crucially, Marx acknowledges how it is based upon agreement, rather than feudal obligation, slavery or some other form of overt coercion. As a market transaction, the worker is at liberty to terminate the contract, just as 'he' freely accepts it. Or so it seems, at least, from what Marx identifies as a *particular*, 'bourgeois', mainstream perspective where the freedoms associated with market relations are abstracted from a wider structure of (capitalist) social relations in which markets are promoted and supported as their key and dominant institution. So, why, as the workplace is approached, does the possessor of labour power become timid and 'hold back'? Marx's answer is that when exchanging the power of labour for an agreed wage, the worker effectively *surrenders control* – that is, he or she becomes enslaved and subordinated to the employer – for the duration of employment. The worker enters a situation where, in principle, he or she is obliged to work in whatever ways will secure an adequate level of profit for the employer.

Such subordination, Marx contends, is integral to the structure of capitalist economic organization. It may be more or less relaxed or tightened – some employees receive training or education sufficient to become (internally) self-disciplined and therefore require less direct supervision, whereas others will apply themselves only if they are coerced or closely monitored. Others may successfully resist efforts to control them; and yet others may be too important to the employer – because their labour is so scarce and/or because the added value that they create is so great – to risk losing them by imposing counterproductive controls. So, in some cases, the subordination may be mainly what Marx calls 'formal': a relationship of exploitation exists but it is something of a formality. The employer does not directly exercise control over the employees' labour process. The planning and organization of work on a day-to-day basis remains the responsibility of the employee. With the development of scientific manage-ment, however, the subordination changes from being 'formal' to becoming increasingly 'real' as the employer intervenes to organize and control the detail of how employees work, such that they are required to execute tasks designed and strictly monitored by management. A similar process occurs when professionals – such as lawyers or accountants – are required to complete time sheets, which account for their contribution to the profitability of service firms.

SUBORDINATION – FORMAL AND REAL

In many situations, there is a difference between what is 'formally' required (e.g., the requirement to attend the workplace between certain hours) and what degree of control over labour is 'really' secured.

- *Formal subordination of labour,* where in order to increase productivity (and profitability) the working day is lengthened, or cheap labour (e.g., children, women, immigrants, students) is hired.
- *Real subordination of labour,* where there is an intensification of production (e.g., capital investment, new tech-nology, strict job specifications, productivity schemes, targets, bonus systems, etc.).

This difference is illustrated by the quip-cum-slogan: 'We are employed here 9–5, you surely don't expect us to work as well!' What this signals is how formal subordination, in terms of the obligation to be at the workplace, is bad enough without adding insult to injury by forcing employees to work hard (e.g., on the assembly line) while there.

As subordination becomes progressively 'real', the employee is told what to do, how to do it and when to do it. There may then be some relaxation of control as the employer becomes more trusting of 'loyal' employees and/or calculates that the production process is adequately profitable only if employees are allowed to exercise greater discretion within boundaries that continue to be set and policed by employers. But this more flexible situation is understood to remain one of 'real' subordination of labour, rather than to be a return to a 'formal' position, as the employee is now seen to internalize the control logic of the employer (see Chapter 10).

EXPLOITATION AT BAR MAR?

What might an analysis of Bar Mar (the case study presented earlier in this chapter) which focuses upon exploita-tion look like? Suppose that Margaret's staff were working overtime but not being paid the extra hours worked. In common sense terms, that would be viewed as 'exploitative'. Why? Because it breaks the formal or informal contract that Margaret has with her employees. She agreed to pay them so much per hour and she is now expecting them to work additional hours for nothing.

From a more critical standpoint, it would be argued that Margaret's staff are exploited *every hour that they work*, and not just when they put in overtime without extra pay. That is because the very structure of their relationship is seen to be exploitative, regardless of how well staff are treated and how promptly they are paid. Margaret extracts money (a 'surplus') from the labour of her staff by paying them less than the revenues minus costs that she derives from their work. The differ-ence between the revenues and the costs of her business are not distributed among those whose labour has produced this surplus. Instead, the surplus is appropriated and accumulated by Margaret as her (personal) capital.

Margaret treats her staff well. She pays them more than the market rate. She does her very best to accommodate their family responsibilities. She has always paid them a handsome Christmas bonus. So, how can she possibly be

Normalize A term to describe how discourses and practices are defined or perceived as proper and normal such that they become unquestioned; it serves to control or discipline individuals by transforming them into subjects that obey certain cultural or political norms or rules.

exploiting them? They are content; they would not dream of working for anyone else. But, that, arguably, is because they have come to **normalize** and accept the capitalist basis of contemporary economic organization. They take it for granted, and do not mind, that Margaret hires them and tells them how they should behave, not the other way around. Should *they* become unhappy with the way Margaret is running the business, they have no basis for sacking *her*. They are in no position to do so. It is difficult for them even to approach her to object to her attitude, tactics or strategy. At base, it is suggested, the relationship is one of domination and exploitation, founded upon Margaret's ownership of Bar Mar and the dependence of staff upon her for their employment. It is this basic arrangement, above all, that is understood to condition how they relate to each other.

In the absence of counter logics, such as the welfare or well-being of the community, capitalist economies endorse 'free' markets where everything is viewed as a commodity – art, education; even religion, air or water – that

Bourgeois Critics of capitalism use this term to denote the privileged complacency of the relatively affluent middle classes.

has its price and/or becomes a business. Such thinking, characterized by Marx as **bourgeois**, is so widespread and institutionalized, as a common sense truth, that it is widely embraced by the sellers of labour (i.e., employees) as well as by its buyers (i.e., employers). Jobs become valued primarily on the basis of the economic wage, not whether they are meaningful or rewarding either for the worker or for the wider community. It is the credibility and authority of this thinking that Marx challenges as he invites us to turn our attention from the marketplace to the workplace. In doing so, he seeks to show why the institution of the market and its associated ideology of freedom, to which many workers commonsensically subscribe, is so important for the development and maintenance of capitalist economies but also for restructuring or repressing welfare or any democratic control.

What, then, does Marx have to say about how labour processes are designed and organized within capitalist workplaces? The analysis hinges upon the understanding that the accumulation of wealth is fundamentally dependent upon the application of workers' productive capability, or labour power. In the context of capitalist workplaces, employees are seen to be denied control of the application of this labour because, above all, the capitalist must ensure that an acceptable level of profit is generated by the activities that create products or deliver services.

THE FACTORY SYSTEM

The growth and development of capitalist work organization(s) in the nineteenth century depended on the success of the factory system as a structure for harnessing labour and this was attributed to its greater efficiencies – workers could be trained and supervised more effectively and could also be combined with the most productive technologies. For its architects and investors, the appeal of the structure of the factory system resided in its promise, and its subsequent demonstration, that it could be a reliable and sustainable means of *controlling* labour so that greater and more dependable profits could be extracted from its productive activity.

Often, draconian measures and penalties were introduced to force and contain workers within the factory system. Abject poverty drove many reluctant workers into the factories where they would find themselves corralled like cattle. But with the rise of trade unions and an associated labour movement, workers mobilized some resistance, or at least a voice of opposition, to the worst exploitative excesses of their employers. As Hobsbawn (1975, p. 214) observes, collective action through the union was, for many, more than a 'tool of struggle: it was a way of life'. For it enabled workers to construct an alternative identity to that of the disposable commodity that was treated by most employers in a manner directly comparable to other, inert factors of production, such as cotton or machinery.

Agency The sense of acting from an individual's own volition.

This 'way of life' was 'collective, communal, combative', where a sense of **agency** was recovered and asserted, giving workers' lives a renewed 'coherence and purpose' (ibid.). Today, this struggle continues as employees working in diverse organizations endeavour to resist efforts to cheapen or de-skill their labour or to intensify their work – for example, by outsourcing public services to the private sector that hires cheaper labour and provides inferior terms and conditions (e.g. pension entitlements).

For employers, ensuring the attendance of workers in workplaces was, and remains, only part of the challenge. The larger part is to *convert the potential* of labour to be productive into products and services that can be sold for a profit. For it is one thing to buy the labour, it is quite another to organize it in ways that renders its production adequately profitable. It is this challenge that continues to face the designers and managers of organization who are employed to ensure that labour is marshalled and controlled in ways that secure sufficient surplus.

It is here that we return to the earlier examination of classical thinking about organization and, more specifically, to Taylor's ideas about scientific management. It should be acknowledged that few factories or offices have adopted Taylor's ideas in their entirety. As we noted earlier in this chapter, 'pure' Taylorism encounters the virtually insuperable obstacle of established social practices and traditions. While it aspires to sweep these aside, it necessarily relies upon people – notably managers – who are themselves steeped in these traditions. More obviously, its demands for change encounter resistance from workers who fear that more efficient production methods will bring redundancies and/or are not convinced that compliance with design requirements imposed by management will be adequately compensated by higher wages. So arguably, the importance of Taylorism lies less in its direct application than in its distillation and articulation of a (technocratic) way of thinking that has shaped the development of industrial capitalism. More specifically, Taylorism has served to justify the exclusion of workers from participation in key design decisions that affect their working lives.

Braverman's Labor and Monopoly Capital

The major contribution to a critical analysis of work organization has been Harry Braverman's *Labor and Monopoly Capital* (1974). Just as Taylor's thinking had the greatest influence upon the design of work in the twentieth century, Braverman's critique of Taylorism has inspired and provoked critical analyses of its effects. Braverman identifies Taylor's writings on scientific management as the key to understanding the transformation of work during the past two centuries and, more specifically, within industrialized economies. What Braverman singles out, and finds to be the pivotal feature of Taylorism, is the progressive separation of 'thought and action, conception and execution, mind and hand' (Braverman, 1974, p. 171).

Table 7.6 Key ideas in Braverman's (1974) *Labor and Monopoly Capital*

Braverman contends that applying Taylor's principles of scientific management demanded:

1. A separation of conception (i.e., design, planning, organization of work) from its execution (i.e., carrying out the work tasks). Braverman describes this as de-skilling.

2. A detailed division of labour, which Braverman describes as job fragmentation and simple 'monotonous', repetitive work tasks. Braverman labels this the 'degradation' of work.

3. Payment-by-results, often, though not necessarily, taking the form of piecework rates of pay based on time and motion studies.

Source: Powell, W.W. (1990) *Research in Organizational Behaviour*, 12: 295–336 London, Elsevier. © Elsevier 1990.

Following the broad contours of Marx's analysis sketched earlier, Braverman's view is that the determination of the structure and design of work has been transferred to managers and 'experts'. In the name of 'scientific management', these experts have monopolized control of labour processes. Work has been widely de-skilled and degraded as workers are left with the execution of highly specialized, repetitive tasks designed by those senior in the hierarchy. Managers have become 'the sole subjective element', in the sense that they alone are active in making the decisions about organizational structure and the design of jobs. Workers are expected to be compliant and passive. Routinely, corporations place profit and/or managerial self-interest above employee priorities or community welfare. It is workers' sense of oppression and unfairness that can ignite individual and collective forms of resistance and ultimately generate labour movements, general strikes and revolutionary change. Employees are often smoulderingly resentful in having to execute what managers and other self-styled experts have planned.

Exercise 7.9

Think of an occasion when, in no uncertain terms, you were told what to do. Reflect on what that felt like, and how you responded or might have responded if you had not been concerned about the consequences of contradicting the command. Discuss your own experiences of this with those of other students to see whether there are any common features.

Of course, the exact opposite can also occur. Where employees have been used to undertaking routinized tasks designed by others, and are then asked to engage their mind in some redesign of work, they may refuse to assume greater responsibilities, especially when they can expect to receive no equivalent payment despite the increased stress or work intensification that the redesign creates. They may resent the imposition of such demands, arguing that they are not paid to think and/or to do management's job for them. Management innovations such as teamworking, quality initiatives or re-engineering that have been introduced into a previously Taylorized work regime have come unstuck because of such attitudes.

It is not difficult to find examples of repetitive, closely supervised, assembly line work or the scripting and electronic surveillance of some contemporary call centres that lend relevance and credibility to Braverman's analysis. More generally, it is possible to see how all kinds of supervisory, managerial and professional work is subjected to disciplines of the kind commended by Taylor – specialization of tasks, work measurement, payment by results, etc. Take, for example, the labour process of leading accountancy and law firms. There is a specialist division of labour including a 'managing partner', there are time sheets for charging customers with targets for billable hours, and there are bonuses for meeting and exceeding targets. So, even the most prestigious and ostensibly unindustrialized work exhibits key features of Taylorism. On the other hand, many who are broadly sympathetic to Braverman's analysis have identified a number of limitations:

1 *The subjectivity of labour.* By suggesting that management has become 'the sole subjective element', Braverman minimizes the extent to which managers have had to address the **subjectivity** of labour. Historically, managers

Subjectivity The sense of being-in-the-world that includes but is not reducible to the sense of identity and meaning that is associated with it.

have had to anticipate, and to a degree accommodate, the values and priorities of labour in order to transform the potential of labour power into productive activity. As Burawoy (1985, p. 48) notes, 'the advance of mechanization must be seen as a response not just to increasing costs of labour but also to labour's increasing power' as machines offered a means of employing less skilled workers, of which there was a greater supply, and also the use of machines to pace their work.

Workers' values have included social divisions of gender, ethnicity, age, etc., and employers have sought to exploit these differences. But Braverman has rather little to say about the presence and influence of these divisions. Precisely because managers depend in numerous ways upon the subjectivity of labour, they are obliged to attend to this dependence – for example, by acting to preserve ethnic and gender inequalities even when they personally disagree with them – if conflicts are to be minimized and co-operation is not to be withdrawn by significant (e.g., white/male) sections of the workforce. Management never has been all-powerful, nor can managers expect to become so, as they are constrained by values and priorities that extend into the wider society. For this reason, forms of capitalist work organization exhibit considerable variation across sectors and economies around the world.

2 *The limits of specialization.* A highly specialized, fragmented division of labour is not necessarily the most effective, nor even the most controlled, way of organizing work. Allowing employees to exercise a degree of discretion, rather than subjecting them to close, direct control, can bring benefits of commitment and motivation as well as flexibility, thereby limiting the requirement for, and cost of, managerial oversight. Management innovations (e.g., teamworking) have been promoted as ways to facilitate a *reintegration* of conception (i.e., organizing production) and execution (i.e., completing well-defined tasks) rather than its further separation.

3 *Dependence upon labour.* In order to ensure the optimum quality of the product or a more effective method of production (or service delivery), it may become necessary to re-involve employees (e.g., through quality circles) in decision-making about the structure and design of their work. Workers and 'users' at the 'coal face', or 'sharp end', of the business are increasingly seen as sources of tacit knowledge about the complex practicalities of work that are alien and/or inaccessible to managers remote from day-to-day practices.

4 *Profitability overrides control.* The structure of work organization in capitalist economies is not designed to maximize control per se, but rather to ensure an acceptable level of profitability in the face of numerous issues, including the co-operation and productivity of labour, that can derail it. An important element of this co-operation is the legitimation of capitalism through its regulation and redistribution of wealth by the state, in the form of public services (e.g., education) that are provided through the taxation of economic activity. Legitimation is by no means automatic as there are frequently tensions between what people want (e.g. employment, housing, health care) and what employers and politicians are willing and/or able to deliver.

5 *A romantic view of craft.* Braverman has a rather romantic view of the skills of the craft worker that skates over the operation of guilds as monopolies and their creation of an aristocracy of labour that has often been hostile to the aspirations of, and dismissive of, the importance of non-artisan skills. He pays only passing attention to how the level and value of a skill is socially defined through a series of historical and cultural evaluations and legitimations, rather than simply given by its exercise. He does not, for example, appreciate how, historically, the association of skill with masculinity has tended to raise its value; and how work predominantly carried out by women (e.g., nursing, secretarial, teaching) tends to be less valued at least in terms of economic reward if not also status. Braverman also overlooks how 'unskilled' and 'semi-skilled' work generally involves the application of considerable tacit knowledge and unacknowledged skill.

6 *Managerial divisions* Braverman implies that managers are unified in their intent to de-skill and degrade labour. But managers too are divided by their own specialisms as well as through hierarchical differences. While Braverman recognizes that middle management are increasingly subjected to Tayloristic forms of accountability and control (e.g., management by objectives, payment by results), he does not consider how divisions within management are reflected in differential degrees of enthusiasm for varying aspects of Taylor's thinking.

Braverman's analysis focuses upon Taylor's classical ideas rather than modern, open systems thinking that allows for variation in the approach to job and organizational design according to the contingencies of the situation. Does that mean that Braverman's insights and criticisms have little relevance for interrogating contemporary forms of theory and practice? Let's first acknowledge that the limitations of Braverman's analysis (as listed above) have equal, if not even greater, applicability to much modern organization theory. That said, his analysis does not adequately appreciate how managers are pragmatic rather than doctrinaire in adapting scientific management principles as they wrestle with the political realities of powerful suppliers and fickle customers as well as mobile or recalcitrant employees. Defenders of Braverman's basic thesis would point to the extent to which, in the very process of addressing these conflicting pressures, managers continue to favour procedures and mechanisms of control that have strong affinities with Taylorism. When designing and operating organizational structures that are intended to address the contingencies of the environment, managers are generally loath to take the risk of trusting employees to work without monitoring their activity or incentivizing them. And, whenever there is an opportunity to 'rationalize' work – for example, by removing the cost and unpredictability of (skilled) labour – managers are under pressure to seize it by, for example, cutting **headcount**, outsourcing to lower-cost suppliers or moving production to locations where labour is cheaper and regulation is weaker.

Headcount Staff or employee numbers in an organization.

Thinkpoint 7.13

What is the appeal of outsourcing? Does it have any benefits for employees?

Braverman died shortly after *Labor and Monopoly Capital* was published, so he did not have the opportunity to respond to his critics in any detail. Had he done so, he might have conceded in a number of areas – notably, his audacious claim that management has become the sole subjective element or agent in the development of contemporary organization structures. But it is unlikely that he would have abandoned his central thesis. That is, an insistence in the historical trend of capital to degrade the 'subjectivity' of labour as management assumes power to determine the design of work and its organization by appropriating (Taylorist de-skilling) dissolving (self-discipline), or removing employee control over work. If, however, attention is turned to the dependence of capital upon labour, it is questionable whether a linear process of degradation is necessarily viable or productive in terms of maintaining the structure of inequality that routinely privileges capital over labour. What would appear to be an arrangement (e.g., legal contract of employment) introduced by 'the powerful' to work exclusively to their advantage can be turned into a resource by 'the powerless' to improve their conditions. In other words, as long as capital needs to mobilize labour to ensure its reproduction, in principle workers are able to expose and even challenge their dependence, regardless of the various instruments of management control designed to weaken or prevent this.

Critical thinkers who broadly share Braverman's concerns about the unnecessarily divisive and destructive features of capitalist economic organization have sought to redress his disregard of the subjectivity of labour by exploring its significance within the development of organization structures in the context of capitalist economic organization. *From a critical standpoint, organization structure arises out of a dialectic of control involving an interdependence between actors – individuals and groups – with differential access to resources.* This process is strongly conditioned by structures of inequality that it reproduces. Workplace co-operation cannot be taken for granted as it is a product of interdependent yet unequal relations. The 'free' labour contract introduced with the advent of capitalism, as Marx showed in his critique of classical political economy, served to consolidate the power of employers over workers, but the workers succeeded in turning the labour contract into a resource of their own through the collective withdrawal of labour (Giddens, 1979, pp. 149–150).

From a critical standpoint, any sense of order or permanence is attributed predominantly to the dominance of 'the powerful' and the compliance of 'the powerless', rather than to an underlying consensus. An example is to be found in the organizational structure of teaching in higher education. A lecture involves interdependence between student and teacher. It might appear that the lecturer has a monopoly of control as he or she decides the content, and also the fate of the student, in terms of assessment. But the lecturer depends on the student attending and co-operating with the process of delivery and assessment resulting in the students' class of degree. This becomes obvious when even a small number of students disrupt a class by refusing to co-operate by, for example, making a noise or in other ways violating the conventions of the lecture theatre. So the existence and reproduction of the organizational structure – in this case, the relationship between lecturer and student – is as much dependent on the behaviour of students, who may appear 'powerless', as it is upon lecturers who seem 'powerful'.

Exercise 7.10

Consider the lectures that you attend. If a lecture is boring or non-engaging, it is likely that the noise levels rise. But it is also unusual for the level of noise to become so loud as to terminate the lecture.

- How would you account for how the lecture format survives even in conditions when many students in the class, and perhaps the lecturer also, find no point in being there?
- Should such a failure of communication be attributed solely to the lecturer?
- If so, give your reasons. If you disagree, explain why.

In order to illustrate the complexities of the **dialectic of control** through which organizational structures are reproduced, it is helpful to appreciate the relevance of identity and insecurity with regard to collaboration and co-operation in workplace relations. Collaboration can be motivated by a concern to sustain conditions that make us feel more secure because they are orderly and familiar. In this way, feelings of anxiety that may be aroused by actions that disrupt convention and routine (e.g., the established lecture format) are minimized. To elaborate upon the significance of identity and insecurity for understanding the dialectic of control, we turn to Michael Burawoy's (1979) *Manufacturing Consent.*

Dialectic of control Contested process whereby work and other activities are socially accomplished. Every activity is seen to involve an interdependence between diverse individuals and groups, such as managers and workers. While exercising differential power associated with their access to scarce and valued resources such as income, status and qualifications, none of these bestow a monopoly of control. This is because each individual or group has a degree of dependence on the other.

MANUFACTURING CONSENT: OBSCURING EXPLOITATION

Distancing himself from the analysis provided by Braverman, and drawing upon his experience as a machine operator working in a multinational corporation, Michael Burawoy (1979) argues that the key to understanding the development and reproduction of capitalism is not the separation of conception (organizing work) from execution (work practices) upon which Braverman places much emphasis. Rather, it is workers' involvement in the practices (e.g., **piecework** machining of diesel engines), through which organizational structures are reproduced, that obscures the extraction of surpluses (i.e., profit) from employees. Burawoy's analysis stands as a corrective to Braverman's deliberate exclusion of the role of

Piecework Payment on the basis of what is produced rather than the time taken to produce it.

workers' consciousness in reproducing as well as resisting forms of organizational structure and control. Whereas Braverman concentrates on evidence of what he regards as an inevitable trajectory of de-skilling and degradation, Burawoy examines how shop floor activity simultaneously articulates an imperfect form of management control and a compromised expression of workers' resistance (see Chapter 2).

At the centre of Burawoy's analysis is the notion that shop floor resistance to management control rarely turns into revolt because the exploitation of employees' labour is obscured by their absorption in everyday work realities – for example, the activities and 'games' that make working life more meaningful and less oppressive – that they construct in the process of participating in their own subordination. To explain the importance of such games and rituals, Burawoy contrasts the situation of the employee with that of the serf. For serfs, the extraction of a surplus from their labour – that maintains the materially and symbolically privileged lifestyle of the feudal lord – is comparatively transparent. Feudal **relations of production**

Relations of production The basic set of social relations that allow production to take place. Typically they are the relations between those who own property and their agents (managers), and those who are dependent on them for a way, or means, of subsistence.

openly require a proportion of what the serf produces (e.g., food) to be handed over to the lord. What justifies this *social* arrangement and holds it in place is the ideology that presents it as a system of domination and exploitation as a *natural* order in which the lord has a natural obligation to ensure a minimum level of well-being for the serfs in return for their service and loyalty.

In capitalist societies, in contrast, comparatively underprivileged groups have, through processes of struggle, established democratically elected governments which fund basic public services and welfare provisions with taxation revenues. For most people, the gravest impacts of inequality are averted, and this is facilitated by the free exchange of labour for a wage. Unlike the serf, the worker is in principle free to sell his/her labour to whichever buyer (i.e., employer) he or she chooses.

According to Burawoy, however, it is at the very point of production or service delivery – where people are engaged in productive labour – that the (exploitative) extraction of surplus value from the labour of working people is *obscured*. He notes how forms of 'making out' at work, including participation in competitive, productivity games among workers:

> [h]ad the effect of generating consent and of obscuring the conditions that framed them ... as we slaved away on our machines trying to make our **quotas** we manufactured not only parts of diesel engines, not only relations of co-operation and domination, but also consent to those activities and relations. (Burawoy, 1985, p. 11)

Quotas Limits placed on something; in trade, quotas usually refers to limits placed on the number of goods, for example cars, which can be exported from one country to another. In the workplace, quotas refer to the amount of units (or services) produced/provided in a given time period (e.g. a shift).

In such ways, the exploitative nature of capitalist relations *of* production is masked by employees' lived experience of relations *in* production. Much industrial work is physically demanding (e.g., tiring) and/or mentally draining (e.g., monotonous). But, even in the most physically and emotionally demanding conditions, employees are creative and skilful in developing diverse coping and compensating mechanisms that render such work minimally bearable and provide relative satisfactions in the sense that they offer a degree of 'temporary relief from the discomfort of certain work realities' (Baldamus, 1961, p. 53, cited in Burawoy, 1985, p. 37). Burawoy follows Marx and Braverman in conceiving of the design and structure of capitalist work organizations as inherently oppressive and exploitative, but emphasizes that it is necessary to appreciate what happens in the mundane, lived processes of production in order to arrive at an adequate understanding of how this structure of work organization operates and is maintained.

Thinkpoint 7.14

Think of a time when immersion in some aspect of an activity diverted or distracted your attention from appreciating the bigger picture and the place of such activity within it. To what extent did others encourage your involvement in this activity? And what were the consequences?

In mainstream analysis, shop floor and office games are associated with obstructive restrictions of output as workers, rather than managers, actively police each other's productivity; or such games are understood to counter demoralization and disaffection, and thereby limit psychological withdrawal, unproductive time and labour turnover. For Burawoy, however, such games and other practices are central for understanding the manufacture of consent that supports the smooth reproduction of capitalism. Participation in them, he argues, 'generates the legitimacy of the conditions that define [the] rules and objectives' (Burawoy, 1985, p. 38) of capitalist economic organization. In other words, they are fundamental to the process of reproducing organizational structure. They are not deliberately 'designed in' to this structure but, nonetheless, they are critical for its operation and preservation. By valuing and pursuing such games and practices, employees routinely and unintentionally take as given, and so reproduce, the wider set of production relations in which capital systematically extracts surplus from their labour.

COMMENT

Burawoy's analysis is valuable in drawing attention to how employees' participation in games reproduces the organizational structures without any necessary intention to do so. His assumption is that employees' consent is simply an unintended consequence of their concerns to transform the grinding routines of shop floor work into something more pleasurable and minimally bearable. Here we can see some similarities with Collinson's (1992) study of shop floor workers who participated in a subculture that had the effect of enhancing their masculinity, but Burawoy sees no gender element in the preoccupation of his workers with competition, even though this is a feature of so many aspects of contemporary capitalist economic organization. Nonetheless, Burawoy does point to, although he does not elaborate upon, the extent to which employees '*develop a stake* in those rules and objectives' (ibid., p. 38) that form part-and-parcel of game playing and related informal practices, 'as can be seen when management intervenes to change them or somehow infringes them' (ibid., p. 38). In other words, it is not simply the existence of the games but employees' *identification* with their rules that ensures their contribution to the maintenance of organizational structures, which dominate them, and, if the thinking of Marx or Braverman is accepted, exploits them.

It may be argued that a limitation of Burawoy's analysis arises from his core assumption of extraction of surplus being *obscured* as well as secured through relations in production. Equally possible, and arguably more likely, is the view that (1) the issue of exploitation *per se* is not a live one for most employees, and so does not require concealment; and (2) that, in many cases, employees are not unaware of how investors and managers systematically organize productive activity to ensure that an adequate profit is appropriated. Despite this knowledge of their own exploitation and the unnecessary degradation of their work, employees may calculate that their own earnings power, and the material standard of living that accompanies this, is likely to be greater within a capitalist economic system than in any system that replaces it. It may be that they are systematically exploited but that does not mean that they believe, or anticipate, that they would be better off in any way under some other system. Indeed, as Burawoy (1985) himself acknowledges, there is no *imperative* that workers will even come to regard themselves as economically exploited (rather than, say, psychologically dissatisfied). That is because their understanding of themselves and their situation is mediated and organized through 'political and ideological processes' (ibid, p. 35). As a consequence of these processes, in which employees are active participants, they *may* come to regard the structures of capitalist economic organization, including competition, as normal and broadly beneficial, rather than as unacceptably exploitative and/ or oppressive. Put at its basest, an identification with the anticipated benefits of increased consumption may override the costs of demeaning production.

Controversies and debates

SELF-DISCIPLINE AND THE PANOPTICON

It is relevant to appreciate how efforts to address feelings of insecurity and the associated desire to maintain or reinforce an established sense of identity serve to reproduce the status quo. Any identity is precarious and vulnerable to challenge, a precariousness that produces insecurity. From this perspective, it is not simply game playing, or other broad political and ideological processes, that serve to explain how organizational structures are reproduced. In addition, and perhaps more fundamentally, it is the process of stimulating and then addressing feelings of insecurity that holds the key to maintaining the status quo. Identification with the disciplines of organization, to which Michel Foucault's analyses have made a lasting contribution, is compelling insofar as it provides the practical means of holding insecurity in check. Most relevant and accessible are Foucault's ideas about discipline and his discussion of the panopticon as a dramatic way of conveying how control operates in modern organizations.

The panopticon (all-seeing apparatus) was a design for a prison developed in the nineteenth century by Jeremy Bentham in which guards occupied a central tower so that they were able to see into the prisoners' cells without themselves being seen. In this way, prisoners had to assume that they were continuously under surveillance, rather than watched over only when a guard checked their door. The broader significance of this arrangement is that it encourages individual prisoners to engage in a process of continuous self-surveillance and related self-discipline as they anticipate that they may be being watched. A contemporary equivalent is the use of CCTV cameras, which have proved effective in deterring crime within their sphere of operation, just as open plan offices deter certain forms of unproductive activity.

The panopticon example has direct parallels for work organizations where there is a replacement of the direct control by gang bosses or supervisors with other, less personal and immediate forms of surveillance and discipline that operate at a distance. So, for example, even when behaviour cannot be directly observed, the use of performance measures and targets enables managers to make outcomes visible and, of course, to compare performance levels. Crucially, the significance of such measures does not reside in their existence per se but rather it depends upon the amenability of employees to internalizing their direction.

DESIGNING TODAY'S PRISONS – LOS ANGELES TWIN TOWERS JAIL

While direct supervision was the hot new trend 15 years ago, today, high-tech circular designs dominate the punitive cutting edge. Chief Barry King, who runs Twin Towers, is convinced that the round design of the jail, coupled with its reliance on technology, is the only thing that makes the 4000-bed, maximum security jail affordable to operate. 'In an old jail, everything was designed in blocks – you needed more people to walk the rows of cells. Over here, you can have one guard watch the whole area,' he says, gesturing at the stylish new jail that rises outside his window.

To develop efficient plans for people like King, designers have looked all the way back to Jeremy Bentham, the eighteenth-century British utilitarian philosopher and grandfather of the hottest trend in prison design today. Bentham, a social reformer, drew up plans for his ideal prison, the panopticon – a circular cell-house with a central guard station where a few officers could watch over hundreds of inmates stacked many stories high. Prison administrators following Bentham believed that the spectre of constant surveillance would make prisoners more apt to follow rules and help them integrate into society when they were released. Bentham's plan also required fewer guards – a fact that has not been lost on today's prison designers. (Rendon, 1999)

The panopticon is an example of what Foucault (1977) terms 'hierarchical observation', whereby a privileged group (e.g., jailors, managers) exercises power through its surveillance of a subordinate group. 'Hierarchical observation' is accompanied by 'normalizing judgement' involving the punishment of those who stray from the norm and the rewarding of those who respect it. Finally the 'examination' combines 'hierarchical observation' (the difference between the examiner and the examined) and 'normalizing judgement' that is exercised by the examiner who assesses and classifies the examinees in a series of reports. Its intent is to produce particular, *self-disciplining* individuals whose very perceptions of reality are governed by such discipline. Discipline, however, is not conceived as inherently negative or repressive, or as something that individuals would necessarily avoid or resist. Instead, discipline is recognized to be enabling as well as constraining, as something that may be as much welcomed as resisted. Prisoners might regard panoptical control as less intrusive than the closer and less predictable form of attention provided by a guard's tour of the cells. Nonetheless, to the extent that discipline is internalized, it is far-reaching in its effects as it 'resides in every perception, every judgement, every act. In its positive sense it enables and makes possible; and negatively it excludes and marginalizes' (Deetz, 2004, p. 29). So, for example, it enables prisoners to escape the *personal* attentions of their guards by making surveillance a more distanced, impersonal process. But it also reduces, if not excludes, the possibility of influencing how they are treated.

One thing that such discipline tends to 'exclude and marginalize' is forms of knowledge that encourage critical reflection upon the presence and pervasiveness of disciplinary power. Foucault (1980) describes this as 'subjugated knowledge' – it occupies the margins of visibility in a society and only surfaces once it has already begun to be taken account of by the established powers. Examples of such knowledge, which have assumed a marginal status, include knowledge of the ecological damage perpetrated by industry, feminist resistance to the gendered aspects of management and organization and claims for equality on the part of ethnic minorities, age cohorts and sexual preference. Consideration of the operation of discipline offers a possible way of understanding how capitalist relations of production and, more specifically, the design of capitalist work organization through which surplus is routinely extracted from labour. But this knowledge has become widely normalized and taken for granted. It requires a critical reactivation if it is to challenge or subvert the operation of 'hierarchical observation', 'normalized judgement' and forms of 'examination'.

Conclusion

Contributions

The critical approach challenges the mainstream view that knowledge of structure and design is relevant and valuable only when it contributes to the productivity, performance and/or profitability of organizations. The critical approach:

- Demonstrates how power and knowledge as well as concepts of inequality, insecurity, identity and freedom can help us to understand the way that organizations are designed and structured.
- Appreciates how organizations are embedded in societies.
- Resists legitimizing the status quo.
- Develops an awareness of how ideas about organization and management help to constitute the world that analysts of organization aspire to know and control.

Organizations are more complex and contested than, in its search for 'quick fixes' or simple causal patterns, mainstream analysis presumes. So for example, understanding the part that identity plays in employees' lives, or how some level of insecurity can be productive, yet incapacitating if excessive, is probably of more value than fantastical beliefs about the perfect organizational design.

The design and structure of an organization is not independent of wider economic, social and political relations. Mergers and acquisitions affect organizations not just when they occur but, in a capitalist society, by their very possibility, presenting a continual threat to the continued existence of those organizations. Going international or global (see Chapter 13) can be a strategy that challenges some features of established organizational designs and structures. Since organizations are so dynamic it makes sense to challenge much conventional thinking about them. We should also be aware that while the direct relationship between theory and practice, or ideas and their adoption, is not always obvious, academic research and writing indirectly, and perhaps quite slowly but deeply, enters the consciousness of those who are studied. It is in this sense that knowledge of management and organization comes to construct the world that it may merely claim to describe (Latour, 2005).

Moreover, when considering the wider (e.g., global) context of economic and political relations it is possible that organizations – principally in the form of industrial and commercial corporations – have become more powerful in their effects upon societies than the other way around (Ackroyd, 2002). Two explanations are offered for this: first, organizations are in the direct control of wealthy elites; and, second, those who do not have access to, or are excluded from powerful work organizations, become, in effect, second-class citizens. These developments are linked to broad-ranging changes in the socioeconomic structure of society in which there is an 'increase in the importance of the economic, as opposed to the political or civil, institutions in shaping the life-chances of people' (ibid., p. 250). In this context, it is those who, collectively, occupy the top positions in the largest corporations who are seen to shape our destiny by, for example, deploying their resources to fund political parties and/or lobbying governments so that policies broadly supportive of corporations are pursued. The complex, often unaccountable European Union (EU) decision-making procedures and the lack of a truly European public debate are obstacles to democracy, but provide fertile ground for corporate lobbyists, says the Corporate Europe Observatory (CEO), an Amsterdam-based campaign group that monitors the political influence of business.

'Lobby groups succeed all too frequently in postponing, weakening or blocking sorely needed progress in EU social, environmental and consumer protections,' Olivier Hoedeman, research co-ordinator at the Corporate Europe Observatory told IPS. 'We believe such groups are leading the EU to becoming self-centred in international negotiations, including the EU's negotiating strategies within the World Trade Organization (WTO) trade talks.'

The European Parliament website lists 5039 accredited lobbyists working for a range of familiar names such as McDonald's and Visa. The Corporate Europe Observatory puts the total number of lobbyists at somewhere between 15 000 and 20 000, and says two-thirds of these represent big business (Bianchi, 2004).

In a mainstream approach to the study of organizations, little attention is given to the wider politico-economic context, such as the lobbying of governments, that conditions the formation and reproduction of organization structure, or to the significance of the micro-politics of 'game playing' in the workplace that serves to reproduce employees' participation in the maintenance of established structures. The critical approach is concerned to take analysis beyond the mainstream boundaries as it examines the design and structuring of organizations as a historical and political process. This process is understood to involve struggles between groups pursuing differing priorities, and accruing benefits and penalties – consequences that are themselves widely promoted and delivered through the medium of organizations. The critical approach is concerned with scrutinizing what mainstream thinking takes for granted or excludes from its field of vision. It favours an interrogation of what we commonsensically know and value about organizations, with the possibility that their design and priorities might be radically changed to ensure greater equality and human well-being.

Limitations

As supporters of critical approaches, our inclination is to defend rather than to attack them. But if we are to be consistently critical, then we must also be self-critical. Here then are some of the limitations of critical approaches:

- Can be too human-centred.
- May neglect the global nature of capitalism.
- May neglect the domination of financial power.
- Can be theoretical and idealistic rather than practical and applied/pragmatic.

Because critics are seeking to challenge the domination of concerns with productivity, performance and profitability found in the mainstream, they may tend to focus too heavily on human-centred and environmental issues. The focus of this chapter on the structure of organizations leads to a critique that emphasizes how formal structures depend upon human beings for their design, development and implementation. It follows from this that neglect of the human dimension is self-defeating. Much mainstream thinking has gradually incorporated some appreciation of this insight – from human relations to more contemporary attention to forms of 'empowerment'. But it does so by modelling human nature in a way that is malleable to 'enlightened' forms of management control. It is assumed that there is an essential underlying consensus within organizations, and that applying progressive techniques will be positively received and ensure employee commitment. Critical approaches have regarded such techniques as manipulative. But this assessment has itself often been based upon an inadequately examined humanistic philosophy. That is to say, much critical analysis has taken insufficient account of how humanism, and especially its preoccupation with the autonomy of the individual, can be oppressive, or what Foucault (1984) termed the 'greatest confinement'. Humanism, its critics argue, forces individuals back on themselves, makes them reliant on their own devices for a sense of self, and it is this that fuels the insecurity we all tend to have about our identity that then renders us vulnerable to authorities (e.g., managers) who offer ways of mitigating it – notably, by investing ourselves in practices that reproduce prevailing hierarchies, power and inequalities. This has given way increasingly to what is seen as a post-humanist approach that challenges the power of management in organizations through engaging with it rather than seeking to displace it (see Chapter 8).

Focusing on the human dimension may also lead us to neglect broader structures of power such as global capitalism, international regulation and finance capital. Recent protests about global capitalism have proliferated. International economic and political events have been skilfully targeted and lampooned, thereby generating massive media coverage and considerable public sympathy. Effective use of global communication has been made through the Internet, which has, to date, probably served the cause of anti-globalization protesters and sympathizers better than it has the corporations and international institutions that they seek to criticize for their exploitation of developing countries, labour and the environment. Global corporations and the finance capital that sustains them have been depicted as exploitative of the comparatively weak, and as dominators of other organizations, especially suppliers and distributors. Inasmuch as governments have often sided with the largest corporations and financiers, established party politics has become discredited, and activists who pursue single-issue politics have become increasingly linked together by a common antagonism towards the divisive and damaging policies of global capitalism and its corporations. Critical approaches have yet fully to rise to the challenge of developing analyses that resonate with, and provide academically credible studies of, these contemporary issues and movements.

Despite what has been claimed above regarding the indirect and often unintended benefits of critical analyses to practitioners, another problem is that there is a tendency to be abstract, idealistic and over-theoretical. This is partly because the immediate audience for critical research is more likely to be other academics rather than practitioners or even students. Obviously, this text is intended to challenge and redress this situation by counter-posing critical to mainstream perspectives in a way that reaches out to an audience of students as aspiring practitioners.

To conclude, the design and structure of organizations is discussed in mainstream texts predominantly through the lens of a systems model where the parts of an organization are seen as similar to the parts of a body or a machine. Like a car, the organization is seen to work most efficiently when designed properly. Hence, even when it is recognized that designs and structures are contingent on the context in which they are to be applied, theorists find it difficult not to search for the holy grail of a technique, or set of techniques, that will remedy organizational problems as they assume that nothing more fundamental requires attention.

Notably, mainstream literature gives scant attention to how power is relational. Senior managers are seen to possess power, much like someone owns a house. When others are seen to exercise power, such as subordinates or unions, this is not a trigger for appreciating its relational quality but, rather, a stimulus for seeing how it can be either suppressed (scientific management) or harnessed (human relations) to managerial ends according to the circumstances (contingency theory). There is an associated tendency to believe that decisions at the top will, and should, be automatically executed lower down the hierarchy, much like we expect the car to move once it is started, a gear is engaged and the accelerator is pressed.

To avoid such simplistic thinking, it is necessary to conceptualize power as a relationship, and thereby to see it as only fully effective when its exercise transforms people (e.g., managers and subordinates) into subjects that secure a sense of their own purpose, meaning, identity and reality through behaving in accordance with its demands. This, of course, is not to accept this self-disciplining process uncritically since it dominates subjects more deeply than the visible controls of traditional authority. A critical approach does not take power for granted and will always seek to understand how organizations are more than the sum of their structural parts and therefore have to be interrogated rather than accepted as given and incapable of being transformed.

Since almost all organizations in contemporary society are designed or structured around a hierarchy, there is no escape from exercises of power. But it has been argued throughout this chapter that the structure of an organization can never guarantee to deliver what it is designed to do. This is because power is a relationship and depends on those subjected to it consenting or complying with its demands. Often the structure of an organization will be sufficient to secure consent or compliance insofar as it embodies authority and legitimacy, or simply because there seems to be no realistic alternative. Subordinates, as well as superordinates, also desire benefit from their membership of an organization. Mostly this takes the form of some economic benefit (e.g. a wage) or salaries but work is far more than a mere economic activity – it is also social. As members of organizations, we derive some degree of meaning and purpose from our work, and this enables us to fashion a sense of identity and security. While our knowledge is of value to an organization and it enables us to gain employment, we also learn a great deal from work; and this practical knowledge enhances our sense of freedom or self-determination, for example, to advance in the hierarchy or to move elsewhere.

Although there is much inequality in organizations and this is reflected in their hierarchical design and structure, it is constrained by the necessity to secure the consent, co-operation, creativity and collaboration of those engaged in production. This is made easier by the institutionalized pressure of values – such as respect for authority and property, the law, the legitimacy of management, and the belief that inequality is a function of just rewards for ability and effort, etc. Mainstream organization theory trades on these values but rarely addresses their impact and significance. A critical approach raises them as important issues to understand, challenge and debate – with the prospect of contributing to a process of more informed and democratic change.

Discussion questions

1 How does the design and structure of an organization affect people?

2 What do classical and modern forms of mainstream thinking share? What makes them different? Construct a brief list to identify their common concerns and the differences between them.

3 Are the main assumptions underlying a systems approach valid?

4 What are some of the contingencies that need to be considered in relation to an appropriate organization structure?

5 What are the main differences between a classical and an open systems approach to organizational design and structure?

6 What does a critical view of organizational design and structure add to our understanding of organizations?

Further reading

Important empirical studies

Barker, J. R. (1999) *The Discipline of Teamwork,* London: Sage.

Barnard, C. (1938) *The Functions of the Executive,* Cambridge, MA: Harvard University Press.

Beynon, H. (1973) *Working for Ford,* Harmondsworth: Penguin.

Burawoy, M. (1979) *Manufacturing Consent,* Chicago: Chicago University Press.

Frankel, S., Korczynski, M., Shire, K. and Tam, M. (1999) *On the Front Line: Organization of Work in the Information Economy,* New York: Cornell University Press.

Kondo, D. (1990) *Crafting Selves: Power, Gender and Discourses of Identity in a Japanese Workplace,* Chicago, IL: University of Chicago Press.

Kunda, G. (1996) *Engineering Culture,* Philadelphia: Temple University Press.

Nichols, N. and Beynon, H. (1977) *Living with Capitalism,* London: Routledge.

Annotated texts

Daft, R. L. (various editions) *Organization Theory and Design,* New York: West Publishing Company.

A mainstream textbook that has gone through several editions, this book provides a useful summary of the different theoretical frameworks and models in relation to empirical findings and cases about changes in the design and structure of actual organizations. As well as using a diverse range of pedagogical (teaching) techniques, the book also seeks to provide an integration of different perspectives rather than treating them discretely. The most recent edition of this book (Daft, Murphy and Willmott, 2017) incorporates elements of critical thinking.

Ackroyd, S. (2002) *The Organization of Business: Applying Organizational Theory to Contemporary Change,* Oxford: Oxford University Press.

This book summarizes the mainstream approaches to the diverse ways in which British organizations are designed and structured. Identifying these approaches as informed primarily by contingency theory, where there is an absence of any focus on the human dimension, the author offers an alternative view of organizations as designed and structured through processes of negotiation.

Kanter, R. M. (1993) *Men and Women of the Corporation,* New York: Basic Books.

Based on concrete observations of organizations in action, this book examines the structure of US corporate organizations as a reflection of white male dominated power relations. In this sense, it is an empirical example of how the design and structure of an organization are an outcome of negotiations and career struggles largely between men, but it also pays attention to the increasing demands of the global economy.

Du Gay, P. (2001) *In Praise of Bureaucracy,* London: Sage.

Most modern texts have been critical of bureaucratic organizational structures on the basis that they are too inflexible and rule-bound to respond adequately and speedily to the dramatic levels of change in contemporary society. This book bucks the trend, defending bureaucratic forms of organization design and structure as necessary to good government in democratic societies. Following Weber, the author contends that the bureaucratic ethos encompassing impersonal and detached, rule-based decision-making can be defended as the most ethically and technically appropriate mechanism for managing socially responsible organizations.

More general reading

Ackers, P. and Wilkinson, A. (eds) (2003) *Understanding Work and Employment: Industrial Relations in Transition,* Oxford: Oxford University Press.

Barley, S. and Kunda, G. (1992) 'Design and devotion: Surges of rational and normative ideologies of control in managerial discourse', *Administrative Science Quarterly,* 37: 363–399.

Burrell, G. and Morgan, G. (1970) *Sociological Paradigms and Organisational Analysis,* London: Heinemann.

Dawson, P. (2003) *Understanding Organizational Change,* London: Sage.

Hancock, P. and Tylker, M. (2001) *Work, Postmodernism and Organization,* London: Sage.

Jacques, R. (1996) *Manufacturing the Employee: Management Knowledge from the 19th to the 21st Centuries,* London: Sage.

Kanigel, R. (1997) *One Best Way: Frederick Winslow Taylor and the Enigma of Efficiency,* New York: Viking.

Knights, D. and Willmott, H. C. (eds) (2000) *The Re-engineering Revolution? Critical Studies in Corporate Change,* London: Macmillan.

Lennie, I. (1999) *Beyond Management,* London: Sage

Littler, C. (1982) *The Development of the Labour Process in Capitalist Societies: A Comparative Study of the Transformation of Work Organization in Britain, Japan, and the USA,* London: Heinemann.

Marchington, M., Grimshaw, D., Rubery, J. and Willmott, H. C. (2005) *Fragmenting Work: Blurring Organizational Boundaries and Disordering Hierarchies,* Oxford: Oxford University Press.

McDowell, L. (1997) *Capital Culture,* Oxford: Blackwell.

Roberts, J. (2004) *The Modern Firm: Organization Design for Performance and Growth,* Oxford: Oxford University Press.

Rowlinson, M. (1997) *Organizations and Institutions,* London: Macmillan.

Salaman, G. (1979) *Work Organizations: Resistance and Control,* London: Longman.

Thompson, P. (1983) *The Nature of Work,* London: Macmillan.

Willmott, H. C. and Wilkinson, A. (eds) (1995) *Making Quality Critical,* London: Routledge.

References

Ackroyd, S. (2002) *The Organization of Business: Applying Organizational Theory to Contemporary Change,* Oxford: Oxford University Press.

Bianchi, S. (2004) 'EU: Corporate lobbying grows', *Inter Press Service,* 22 December.

Braverman, H. (1974) *Labor and Monopoly Capital,* New York: Monthly Review Press.

Burawoy, M. (1979) *Manufacturing Consent,* London: Routledge.

Burawoy, M. (1985) *The Politics of Production,* London: Verso.

Castells, M. (1996) *The Rise of the Network Society,* Oxford: Blackwell.

Chandler, A. D. Jr. (1962) *Strategy and Structure: Chapters in the History of Industrial Enterprise,* Cambridge, MA: MIT Press.

Clegg, S., Kornberger, M. and Pitsis, T. (2005) *Managing and Organizations: An Introduction to Theory and Practice,* London: Sage.

Coase, R. (1937) 'The nature of the firm', *Economica,* 4: 386–405.

Collinson, D. (1992) *Managing the Shopfloor: Subjectivity, Masculinity and Workplace Culture,* Berlin: de Gruyter.

Deetz, S. (2004) 'Disciplinary power, conflict suppression and human resource management', in M. Alvesson and H. Willmott (eds) *Studying Management Critically,* London: Sage.

DiMaggio, P. and Powell, W. (1991) *The New Institutionalism in Organizational Analysis,* Chicago, IL: University of Chicago Press.

Elger, A. (1975) 'Industrial organizations: A processual perspective', in J. B. McKinlay (ed.) *Processing People: Cases in Organizational Behaviour,* New York: Holt, Rinehart and Winston.

Fayol, H. (1916/1949) *General and Industrial Management,* London: Pitman.

Fleming, P. and Sturdy, A. (2011) '"Being yourself" in the electronic sweatshop: New forms of normative control', *Human Relations,* 64(2): 177–200.

Foucault, M. (1977) *Discipline and Punish: The Birth of the Prison,* Harmondsworth: Penguin.

Foucault, M. (1980) 'Power/knowledge: Selective interviews and other writings 1972–1977', (ed. C. Gordon, trans. C. Gordon *et al.*), Brighton: Harvester Press.

Foucault, M. (1984) 'What is enlightenment?', in P. Rabinow (ed.) *The Foucault Reader,* Harmondsworth: Penguin.

Giddens, A. (1979) *Central Problems in Social Theory,* London: Macmillan.

Greenwood, R. and Miller, D. (2010) 'Tackling design anew: Getting back to the heart of organization theory', *Academy of Management Perspectives,* November, 78–88.

Handy, C. (1996) *Beyond Certainty: The Changing Worlds of Organizations,* Boston, MA: Harvard University Press.

Handy, C. (2000) *Understanding Organizations,* Oxford: Oxford University Press.

Hannan, M. T. and Freeman, J. (1989) *Organizational Ecology,* Cambridge, MA: Harvard University Press.

Hill, S. (1991) 'Why quality circles failed but total quality management might succeed', *British Journal of Industrial Relations,* 29(1): 541–568.

Hinings, B. (2003) 'Organizations and their structures', in R. Westwood and S. Clegg (eds) *Debating Organization: Point-Counterpoint in Organization Studies,* Oxford: Blackwell.

Hobsbawn, E. (1975) *The Age of Capital 1848–1875,* London: Weidenfeld and Nicholson.

Huczynski, A. and Buchanan, D. (2001) *Organizational Behaviour: An Introductory Text,* London: Prentice Hall/FT.

Knights, D. and McCabe, D. (2015) '"Masters of the Universe": Demystifying leadership in the context of the 2008 Financial Crisis', *British Journal of Management,* 26: 197–210.

Latour, B. (2005) *Reassembling the Social*, Oxford: Oxford University Press.

Marx (1887/1973) *Capital: A Critique of Political Economy.* Volume I, Trans. Samuel Moore and Edward Aveling, edited by Frederick Engels, London: Lawrence & Wishart.

Mayer, J. P. (1956) *Max Weber and Germany Politics*, London: Faber and Faber.

Mintzberg (1979) *The Structuring of Organizations*, Englewood-Cliffs, NJ: Prentice Hall.

Mowshowitz, A. (2002) *Virtual Organization: Toward a Theory of Societal Transformation Stimulated by Information Technology*, New York: Quorum Books.

Pfeffer, J. and Salancik, G. R. (1978) *The External Control of Organizations: A Resource Dependency Perspective*, New York: Harper and Row.

Powell, W. W. (1990) 'Neither market nor hierarchy: Network forms of organization', *Research in Organizational Behaviour*, 12: 295–336.

Rendon, J. (1999) *Inside the New High-Tech Lock-Downs* www.archive.salon.com/21st/feature/1998/09/cov_08feature.html.

Rowlinson, M. (1997) *Organizations and Institutions*, London: Macmillan.

Selznick, P. (1949) *TVA and the Grass Roots*, Berkeley, CA: University of California Press.

Selznick, P. (1957) *Leadership in Administration*, New York: Harper & Row.

Taylor, F. W. (1911) *The Principles of Scientific Management*, New York: Harper.

Williamson, O. E. (1975) *Markets and Hierarchies: Analysis and Anti-Trust Implications – A Study in the Economics of Internal Organization*, London: Macmillan.

Woodward, J. (1958) *Management and Technology*, London: HMSO.

Woodward, J. (1965) *Industrial Organization: Theory and Practice*, Oxford: Oxford University Press.

Woolgar, S. (2002) *Virtual Society? Technology, Hyperbole, Reality*, Oxford: Oxford University Press.

8 Management and leadership

DAVID KNIGHTS AND HUGH WILLMOTT

Aims of the chapter

This chapter will:

- Introduce the nature and significance of management and leadership and explore the linkages between them.

- Identify the assumptions and values underpinning and framing mainstream thinking about management and leadership.

- Consider personal and impersonal modes of control, and the use of forms of 'mutual adjustment' within both.

- Provide an overview of the diversity of mainstream thinking about management and leadership.

- Describe and illustrate some basic criticisms of mainstream thinking about management and leadership.

- Show how ideas about inequality, knowledge, power, freedom, identity, inequality and insecurity can provide a different way of considering issues of management and leadership.

- Examine different aspects of a critical approach for analyzing organization management and leadership.

Key concepts and learning objectives

By the end of this chapter you should be able to:

- Show how ideas about organization, management and leadership are developed and applied in practice, with particular reference to a case study.

- Explore some of the tensions associated with managing and leading staff.

- Present and define a number of key concepts that are relevant to mainstream and critical analysis, such as type of leadership and styles of management.

- Develop an understanding of the assumptions and theories underpinning mainstream thinking on management and leadership.

- Understand some important concepts relevant to mainstream and critical analysis, such as effectiveness and efficiency, and performance and control.

Overview and key points

This chapter is concerned with an appreciation of the overlaps, interconnections as well as the differences between management and leadership in both a conceptual or theoretical, and a practical or empirical, sense. In everyday conversation, in the media, in workplaces and even among academics, the terms are often used interchangeably. This is acknowledged but the chapter also points to their difference and distinctiveness. In developing this knowledge, we trace the development of thinking about management from closed to open system theory, and from the control of factors of production to the shaping of culture and values. By contrast, when thinking about leadership, the emphasis is upon directing others through inspiration and drive, rather than through hierarchical control. Mainstream theories and practices of leadership draw on an understanding of a range of personal(ity) qualities or traits, from authoritarian or transactional to democratic and transformational styles and by taking into account various situations, contexts and contingencies. In the second part of the chapter these mainstream views of management and leadership are examined critically to expose the assumptions that, while they are routinely taken for granted, can be questioned.

MAINSTREAM APPROACHES TO MANAGEMENT AND LEADERSHIP

Management and leadership are central to studying behaviour in workplaces. Both concepts have been adopted and elaborated to make sense of, and also to control, what goes on in organizations. As a concept, the term 'management' identifies responsibility for maintaining the division and co-ordination of tasks, often through the development of a hierarchy to regulate the allocation and flow of work. 'Leadership' is concerned less with allocating work tasks than with energizing employees/staff with a sense of direction and commitment. For example, acts of leadership are expected to foster a collective/communal sense of purpose to which members of the organization are encouraged to commit their 'hearts and minds'. The role of management in organizing and controlling the labour of others is said to account for 'the proportion of output that cannot be explained by the growth of input' (Chandler, 1977, p. 490). 'Management' supplements and may even replace 'leadership' to the extent that hierarchical arrangements, whether formal or informal, become pre-eminent. To illustrate this understanding; as a business expands, responsibility often passes from the founder-as-leader to a group of 'professional' managers who sustain the continuing division and co-ordination of productive effort.

As a modern technology of organization, management has been celebrated as something of importance and impact is equivalent to the most influential of world-changing innovations:

> What were the most important innovations of the past century? [Make your own list – antibiotics, contraceptives, computers, mobile phones, etc.] All of these innovations transformed our lives, yet none of them could have taken hold so rapidly or spread so widely without another. That innovation is the discipline of management, the accumulating body of thought and practice that makes organizations work. When we take stock of the productivity gains that drive our prosperity, technology gets all of the credit. In fact, management is doing a lot of the heavy lifting. (Magretta, 2002, p. 1)

Of course, there are many contextual factors besides technology, not least of which is the health or otherwise of the general economy, so that even incompetent managers can be successful in thriving economies,

Distinctions have their limits. However, at what point does black become white? In the case of management and leadership, it might be argued that the 'leader' who founds an organization probably exercises some 'management' skills, such as the ability to plan and co-ordinate. Equally, management involves some of the skills associated with 'leadership', such as the capacity to inspire respect. It would be a mistake to think of 'leadership' as *simply* coming before 'management' or for it *merely* to supplement management. Following the development of more management activities and the formalization of procedures, the initial sense of direction and inspiration may diminish – something that makes the call for 'leadership' a recurrent concern (see Box 8.1).

It has become fashionable recently to elevate leadership over management. An interest in, and preference for, 'leadership' often indicates a desire to move away from 'bureaucratic', command-and-control approaches associated with 'management' *(see Chapter 14)*. Leadership is linked with processes of organizing in which (in principle) greater emphasis is placed on inspiring, listening, facilitating and involving people, rather than instructing them to act. Leadership is linked to communication and innovation. Grint (2005) associates management with the solving of 'tame' or routine problems, whereas leadership is required for more difficult, 'wicked' problems that defy any clear-cut solution. An example of a comparatively tame problem, which can also be complex, is teaching a young adult to pass the driving test. Being a good or 'successful' parent of this young adult is, in contrast, an ill-defined and

'... the world's most admired manager, GE's legendary leader Jack Welch... consciously rejected the word *manager*. It carried too much bad baggage. It smacked of control and bureaucracy. Welch was on a crusade. His call for *leaders* struck a responsive chord' (Magretta, 2002, p. 5). What might Welch do with managers who were unresponsive to this call? What does that tell us about the standing of most managers in such organizations? For those of you who may be interested in reading more about Welch and GE, see N. M. Tichey and S. Sherman (1993), *Control Your Destiny or Someone Else Will*, New York: Doubleday.

Box 8.1
Management is 'out', leadership is 'in'

recurrently tricky endeavour. 'Management might be focused on solving complex but essentially tame problems in a unilinear fashion: applying what worked last time. But leadership,' Grint suggests, 'is essentially about facing wicked problems that are literally "unmanageable"' (Grint, 2005, p. 9).

There is, of course, a difference between preaching an approach to leadership and practising it. As we shall suggest, when considering more critical studies of management, what accounts for this difference is the politics of organizing (see Chapter 9) where issues of identity, inequality, power and insecurity are entangled in the advocacy of leadership (and management) as well as resistance to its realization. A self-aware, facilitative approach to leadership may sound like a good idea, only to be rejected by managers who have invested their careers, and their very selves, in a 'bossier', more overtly hierarchical kind of relationship with their 'subordinates'. Or managers may be deeply sceptical about the value of a participative style in highly demanding and contradictory contexts where it is difficult to maintain a consistent approach, and where greater involvement from subordinates seems to risk loss of control. They may believe that effective leadership demands a more 'hard-headed', aggressive and coercive approach – one that has been emphasized in a number of recent business-related TV shows, such as *The Apprentice* (www.bbc. co.uk/apprentice/). In the USA, where the show originated, it was Donald Trump who took on the role of the business 'master' (see www.nbc.com/nbc/The_Apprentice/) whereas in the UK, it was Alan Sugar. Like other reality TV shows, the principle that operates to hook the audience to watch the show to the end of the series is that one person is eliminated or 'fired' each week until only one person remains to secure the prize of employment with the managerial/leadership hero. Both Trump and Sugar professed great success in business, but in the show they adopt a highly aggressive and coercive stance as if the only effective strategy of leadership is autocratic, and the 'stick' is preferred to the 'carrot'. However, the context is clearly one of a big carrot or incentive in the possibility of working for the organization that these leaders head up, not to mention securing fame and opportunities through media exposure that more than compensates for the humiliation of being continually demeaned by Trump or Sugar. We have seen how this kind of aggressive and even offensive behaviour has gained Donald Trump political popularity as the USA has responded defensively, as elsewhere in the West, to pressures of economic migration in the twenty-first century.

Those wedded to an autocratic style are likely to experience great difficulty in shifting from a 'hire and fire' mentality to one in which 'coaching' and engaging staff is seen as more appropriate. At best, the security provided by a veneer of charisma and charm may make bullying tolerable. In the effort to 'change their spots', autocratic managers may lose their capacity to lead those who are admirers, or at least willing consumers of 'strong (wo)men'. That is because their ability to provide a degree of certainty and security in confusing and contested situations is what, despite their bullying tendencies, can make them seductive, if not necessarily attractive, figures of authority.

Fuzzy boundaries: Management and leadership

We have noted how definitions of, and boundaries between, management and leadership can be useful but also somewhat loose, arbitrary and potentially misleading (see Box 8.2). Each tends to be defined in relation to the other, and a notion of 'good management' may well incorporate leadership skills. There are further complications. 'Management' is a term used to describe a comparatively privileged (in terms of pay and status) occupational group or elite, as well as an organizational function or role. This adds a layer of complexity in terms of developing an analysis; it also creates difficulties in practice, as the issue of privilege can undermine the 'legitimacy' of management decisions. The meanings attributed to management and leadership are fluid, and vary with the contexts in which they are used and, indeed, the terms may be used almost inter-changeably, as in the exhortation: 'There is a need for better management/ leadership around here'.

A recurrent complaint of senior executives is the lack of 'leadership' in middle and supervisory levels of management. Because they are judged ultimately on the basis of their subordinates' performance, executives generally want to see more productivity, effectiveness and innovation within 'their' organizations; and they often regard 'better leadership' from their subordinates, including middle managers, as the key to such change (see Chapter 11). This desire is understandable but it fails to appreciate how identification with, and commitment to, the organization often declines as you pass lower down the hierarchy in a way that renders redundant demands for 'better leadership' (see Chapter 7).

At DipPep (a pseudonym), the meanings of 'manager' and 'leader' were virtually interchangeable. Leadership was regarded as an integral and essential element of management (even if, in practice, the motivation and scope for 'leading' was restricted by the manager's position in the hierarchy). At CaseCo (a pseudonym), in contrast, the chief executive officer (CEO) repeatedly emphasized the difference between management and leadership in order to highlight what he perceived to be missing (i.e., 'leadership') from his management team.

Box 8.2
Manager or leader?

Securing commitment is by no means straightforward. Lower levels of staff are generally much less well paid and provided for; they also lack any direct accountability to the owners or senior executives. Whether the organization performs exceptionally may be of limited consequence to them, in terms of their sense of self-esteem, career prospects or returns on stock options. Employees may therefore be unresponsive to calls to exercise greater leadership (for example, in teams, see Chapter 4), or to commit themselves beyond the call of duty (i.e., to do more than is formally written into their job description). Where employees are fearful of losing their jobs, they may comply superficially with new expectations without being committed to them. In conditions where staff lack a strong identification with the organization for which they work, qualities characterized as 'leadership' are less likely to emerge among them. Managers may also find it more difficult to be effective leaders. In other words, we are pointing to how issues of power, inequality, identity and insecurity (i) shape how we organize, (ii) stimulate calls for, and (iii) prompt different responses to, demands for more or better 'management' and 'leadership'.

To summarize:

- Conventionally 'management' is seen to be primarily concerned with the maintenance of existing organizational arrangements, whereas 'leadership' is associated with their development, revitalization or transformation.
- The meaning of the terms 'management' and 'leadership' is often fluid – for example, the latter may be incorporated into the former.

- Issues of limited commitment to the organization can frustrate as well as stimulate efforts to improve management and/or leadership both among managers and staff.
- Power, identity, inequality and insecurity are intimately related to leadership (and management), as also is resistance to what it seeks to achieve.

Thinkpoint 8.1

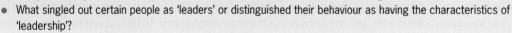

Management and leadership: Your experience Think of an example of leadership drawn from your own experience – perhaps a job you have worked in, participating in a collective activity, playing a sport, or simply going out with mates.

- Can you identify elements of this experience that comprise some part of 'management'?
- What singled out certain people as 'leaders' or distinguished their behaviour as having the characteristics of 'leadership'?

Reflecting upon your experiences of leadership (see Thinkpoint 8.1) has probably shown you how ideas about leadership, and what we think of as management (and organization), overlap. A person identified as a leader, or as exhibiting leadership behaviour, may also be regarded as a good organizer or manager – someone who is able to 'pull together' or 'harness' the diverse skills of a group. Without this leader, the group may become 'disorganized', perhaps resulting in the quest for a replacement leader. Or the failure of a particular leader may demand a different way of organizing that reduces the risk of dependency upon a single leader. One way to limit this risk is for rules and routines of organization to emerge, and for a managerial hierarchy to be created, whereupon conformity to the bureaucracy substitutes for leadership (see Chapter 14). Behaviour is then organized without a heavy reliance upon leadership that recurrently provides inspiration and direction, but with possible adverse consequences for harnessing the energies of those involved.

Exercise 8.1

Identify some of the different ways in which management and leadership overlap, interconnect, or are substitutes for each other.

Needless to say, activities identified as management and leadership extend well beyond the world of work. In other spheres – at home or in leisure pursuits – we often find ourselves being 'managed' by, or we end up 'managing', others – such as our partners, close relatives, friends and acquaintances. We also identify, and perhaps more readily admire, 'leadership qualities' in others and occasionally have these qualities attributed to our own actions. On reflection, we recognize that 'management' and 'leadership' connote prized qualities in modern organizations and societies, often because they are associated with competent individual or organizational performance, or they are attributed to different ways of organizing our activities. Not surprisingly, then, management and leadership are found to connect to each other, with management often signifying more structured, impersonal aspects of organization and leadership pointing to the importance of nurturing interpersonal relations as well as a shared sense of purpose.

Case study 8.1
Bar Mar

In the previous chapter, we introduced the case study of Bar Mar. It will be recalled that Margaret was the owner-manager of the first Bar Mar who, before the venture expanded to become an international chain of multi-award winning bar-bistros, controlled key decisions, such as the nature and pricing of drinks and food, opening hours, working hours, furnishings and so on. One of the things that had appealed to Margaret about setting up Bar Mar was the opportunity to create a total experience for her customers, a key part of which involved the interaction with Bar Mar staff, herself included. She liked the idea of working with a small number of staff – co-workers and friends, as she thought of them – with whom she could provide and develop a distinctive atmosphere.

Margaret hand-picked her initial trio of staff by 'poaching' them from other local bars in which she drank and ate regularly. She successfully tempted them away by enthusing them with her concept for a new kind of bar, and also by offering them better pay. Working closely with them, Margaret found that she was able to run Bar Mar highly successfully with the very minimum of formal instructions or communications. Whatever issues came up were quickly resolved through a process of discussion or 'mutual adjustment' (Mintzberg, 1979, p. 3), albeit one in which it was understood and accepted that Margaret would always have the final word.

Margaret had the final word as a consequence of her legal position as the owner of Bar Mar, a position that also underpinned her authority on the premises, and not as a result of her considerable charisma, or her reputation as a minor pillar of the local community. It is this relationship of control to other members of her staff that lends plausibility to the pyramid shape of the organization chart (Figure 8.1). Margaret's position as owner-manager also allowed her to determine how and when her own labour was flexibly deployed – in the bar or in the kitchen, depending upon the demand for drinks or food. And if she felt like taking a break to do some shopping, or to see what was happening in other bars in her neighbourhood, she just informed her staff that she was going out for an hour or two.

The situation has now changed substantially. Today, Margaret is CEO of what has become an international chain of bar-bistros but she owns only 10 per cent of the shares in the business of which she was once sole owner. Funding for the ambitious expansion of the business came primarily from venture capitalists who, in return for their investment, secured a 51 per cent stake in the company, thereby giving them ultimate control. They were attracted to Bar Mar's proven business model. Its uninterrupted growth had demonstrated a capacity to manage relationships with all the key stakeholders – suppliers and employees as well as customers. The highly successful operation of Bar Mar in a competitive marketplace had demonstrated the robustness of its distinctive formula, or strategy, for delivering greater (perceived) value to its customers than its direct competitors.

A substantial string attached to the venture capital funding, however, was the imperative to strengthen Margaret's management team by recruiting a group of senior managers with expertise in key functional areas (e.g., operations, finance, human resource management (HRM), etc.), and a proven track record in taking businesses through a period of rapid growth. Management expertise was the area where the venture capitalists identified the greatest challenge and risk. The creation of an experienced senior management team was identified as the way to manage the risks associated with sustaining Bar Mar's strategy, and associated position of competitive advantage, during a potentially turbulent and disruptive process of expansion. In common with her fellow directors. Margaret's authority as CEO is now effectively delegated to her by Bar Mar shareholders, who, legally, are in a position to replace her and any other members of the board of directors if they fail to manage this risk. However, Margaret has become so identified with the Bar Mar brand, and is so respected in financial circles for her flair for anticipating trends and ceaselessly innovating, that her immediate future looks pretty secure. Privately, however, Margaret considers that her position as CEO is vulnerable. This is not least because any faltering of the company's peerless performance may be attributed to the lack of a 'professional' manager at the helm of the company. Not infrequently, she has felt out of her depth, and only her disarming willingness to admit her ignorance, her humour, and ability to learn quickly from others has saved her from more critical and potentially damning scrutiny; and one or two of her senior executive team have made no secret of wanting her job.

Figure 8.1 Organization chart for an owner-managed bar

```
              Owner-manager
               (Margaret)

    Staff 1        Staff 2        Staff 3
     (Bar)         (Food          (Food
                 preparation)    service)
```

Thinkpoint 8.2

Is Margaret a leader? What attributes of Margaret prompt you to think of her in this way? Do you think she would be identified as a leader in many different situations?

Reflecting upon her 20 years at the top of Bar Mar, Margaret takes satisfaction from how her methods of managing the company have adapted to its growth. When she was owner-manager of the first Bar Mar, she relied upon a personal relationship with her three staff. There was little need for formal rules and procedures as she could easily guide and coach them by word of mouth. Frequently, she was working alongside them and could readily see how they were performing and offer encouragement and 'advice' about how to do things better. As these staff told her, they tended to regard her more as a colleague than a boss, and were particularly impressed by her willingness to listen to their suggestions, as well as to their occasional grievances. What they perhaps did not realize, and this is something that Margaret did not share with them, is the extent to which they taught her about how to manage successfully as she carefully observed and reviewed their responses to her interventions and prompts as the owner-manager.

As Bar Mar expanded and additional bars were added to the chain, Margaret reluctantly discovered that she had to rely increasingly upon more impersonal methods. She could no longer keep a direct eye on Bar Mar staff, yet she was determined to ensure that all Bar Mar employees maintained and continuously improved the standards that she had set in the first Bar Mar. She feared that introducing rules and procedures – for preparing food and interacting with customers, for example – would undermine the spirit of continuous improvement and friendly, upbeat ambience that she wanted to nurture in the bars. This ambience, above everything else, is what she wanted to preserve and enhance. This is what she wanted to create when opening her first Bar Mar, and she believed passionately that it would differentiate Bar Mar from its competitors. The special ambience of Bar Mar, she anticipated, would also enable her to pay better staff wages and provide excellent conditions of work, as customers would willingly pay a slight premium for the special experience and treatment they received.

Ideally, Margaret wanted to recruit a set of 'carbon copies' of herself as managers of each newly opened Bar Mar, who would then lead and inspire by example as she had always done. She wanted Bar Mar staff, and especially the managers, to be as enthusiastic about, and committed to, the Bar Mar concept as she was herself. She expected Bar Mar managers at all levels of the organization to provide a broad sense of direction for their subordinates. Staff would then know what was required in every area of activity without having to be given a very detailed set of instructions, comply with a series of procedures or even achieve a set of financial targets. Margaret believed that commercial success would inevitably follow from upholding and refining the basic Bar Mar concept and ambience, eventually condensed in two, low-key and somewhat upmarket slogans: 'Meet, Absorb and Recharge' and 'Lively Ambience, Exciting Food, Affordable Prices'. Instead of hiring managers to act as trainers who would drill their staff to obey the commands set out in the corporate rule book, Margaret wanted managers to recruit and train staff who would enthusiastically embrace and live out the basic, guiding values of Bar Mar. She wanted and expected all Bar Mar staff to use their initiative and exercise discretion to ensure that these values were communicated and fulfilled in every aspect of its operations. Margaret discovered, however, that it is not easy to find or retain staff showing the degree of dedication and commitment that she required. It seemed to Margaret that Bar Mar staff – managers at different levels as well as their staff – were often going through the motions of embracing Bar Mar values without fully grasping, or indeed caring, how to put them into practice. When asked about the company's values, they said 'all the right things' but they did not necessarily or faithfully act them out when serving drinks or interacting with customers. Instead of showing that they could not be more concerned for the customers, they unintentionally communicated an attitude of not caring less.

Thinkpoint 8.3

What dilemmas is Margaret facing? As Margaret expands the Bar Mar chain, she encounters a number of unforeseen difficulties of organization, management and leadership. How would you describe and diagnose these problems? What remedies would you consider in similar circumstances?

Margaret believed that more careful selection and training of staff could solve the problem. The human resources (HR) budget in these areas was substantially increased. This had mixed but generally disappointing results, however. According to reports from 'mystery shoppers' who regularly visited each Bar Mar, little difference could be detected between the experience of visiting bars where staff had been given additional training compared to staff in bars who had yet to receive it.

Thinkpoint 8.4

The limits of training Margaret believed that training would solve what she identified as a key problem for the reputation and future of the Bar Mar chain. What might have led her to place her faith in this remedy? What might explain its limited success? What solutions would you suggest?

Margaret was reluctant to abandon her faith in the Bar Mar concept. She believed that there must be some way of managing the staff that would enable them to 'do things right'. She continued to give much thought to this issue but, at the same time, she conceded that an alternative approach was required if the standards she had set for the company were to be realized and, ideally, surpassed. Against all her instincts, Margaret accepted that exemplary leadership was insufficient, and that it would have to be supplemented and perhaps partially displaced, by a closer specification of requirements, more effective forms of surveillance and ultimately by disciplinary procedures for staff found breaching company rules. She comforted herself with the thought that this was simply a 'stopgap' measure that could be dropped, or at least trimmed back, once the HR specialists identified a more effective way of training staff to embrace Bar Mar's defining values. But, half-consciously, she had her doubts about whether a 'magic bullet' would ever be found.

The mainstream agenda

The mainstream agenda is preoccupied with how to manage and lead in order to maximize performance; and it tends to assume an underlying consensus of values and objectives between members of society and organizations (see Chapter 7). Where there are some difficulties of alignment, it is assumed that a technical remedy, such as improved staff selection or training, will resolve the problem. Organization, management and leadership are conceived as three interrelated elements of a system that is routinely and legitimately treated as an object of manipulation and control. The mainstream particularly in textbooks is 'managerial' in the sense that it *assumes* the legitimacy of management; and it is focused on how to help managers meet their existing goals rather than enabling them to reflect critically upon how these goals are identified and pursued (see for example, Mullins, 2002, p. 4).

MANAGEMENT: DISCIPLINE, FUNCTION, SOCIAL GROUP

As a discipline, the term 'management' is used to indicate a measure of responsibility, deliberate planning and control. This discipline was developed in work organizations – church, army, factory, etc. – but has increasingly become an integral part of modern everyday life. For example, the idea of self-management suggests the acquisition of a discipline that enables the individual to direct their own life (e.g., career choices and development), which they plan, review and control. Margaret's decision to establish the first Bar Mar, and her continuing efforts to retain her vision during its expansion into an international chain, requires considerable skills of self-management, such as allocating her time and focusing her effort. This effort to manage activities and processes occurs, to some degree, at all levels within organizations. The shop floor worker or the clerical assistant may have minimal formal authority and exercise little discretion, but they have some involvement in managing themselves and others to perform tasks that have been identified, but not exhaustively specified, by superiors within the hierarchy. Today, management as a discipline has been disseminated into almost every institution (e.g., charitable foundations, voluntary groups, personal health, etc.) in contemporary societies. As an ostensibly rational discipline and way of thinking, management is advocated to deal effectively with all kinds of personal and social problems, including the control of scientific work.

> Keith Waldron of the Institute of Food Research suggests a more balanced approach to managing research establishments could be developed through a closer relationship with business schools ... Dr Waldron writes that the expertise to tackle the problem [of performance] could be found in business management schools. 'Perhaps now is the time to exploit these with a view to clarifying the roles and responsibilities of scientists in relation to organizational management and strategic intent.' (Farrar, 2004)

As a function, management is conceived in relation to an understanding of how collective forms of activity are organized (see Chapter 7). 'Management' is thought of as an essential and necessary component of such activity. Without this function, there is the threat of chaos or, at least, a suboptimal use of resources involving unnecessary wastage of human and/or material resources. The function of management is understood to ensure effective forms of division and integration of tasks among elements – people and technologies – that comprise organization. It may be identified as a function for which there is collective responsibility (e.g., through mutual adjustment or a democratic election of managers) but it is more often conceived as an area of specialist expertise to be undertaken by those with relevant qualifications who are appointed by an elite. In the Bar Mar example, the management function was assessed to be weak by the venture capitalists who made their investment conditional upon the recruitment of senior executives who would introduce management discipline as well as their specialist knowledge of key areas.

Finally, management is conceived of as a social group that acquires and applies specialist expertise, and to which differential power and privileges are often attributed. The term 'management' is used to identify a stratum of people who occupy positions of comparative seniority and advantage within work organizations. Initially, Margaret was the sole member of this group, though she was reluctant to identify herself as hierarchically distanced from 'her' staff. Later, as the chain expanded, more managers were appointed (by Margaret) and eventually an elite group of executives joined the business as a condition of obtaining the financing for further expansion (see Table 8.1).

Exercise 8.2

Work in a small group to construct a table in which you list and illustrate some key elements of management as a discipline, as a function and as a social group.

Table 8.1 Summary: Three common meanings of management

Management as discipline	Practices directed to increasing output for a given input. Employed by many people but institutionalized in work organizations
Management as function	Conceived as an essential and universal component of organized activity
Management as a social group or elite	A social and organizational stratum that is positioned between a small number of owners of property and land and a mass of comparatively unqualified and unskilled employees

Central to the mainstream view on management is an assumption that, as a function, as a discipline and as a social group, management plays an essential, impartial and legitimate role in improving human welfare. Those who are most closely identified with 'management' are understood to apply their specialist expertise in an impartial manner for the common good. Disciplined expertise is a hallmark of their functional contribution that is manifest in the strategies, structures and systems devised by them to transform raw materials and human labour into needed outputs (see Chapter 7); and it is the scarcity of this expertise that accounts for their formation as an elite social group. A rather different view of management is explored in the second half of this chapter, where we suggest that their expertise is shaped and applied in specific ways that are valuable for maintaining capitalist enterprise and/or the comparatively privileged place of managers within it.

MANAGEMENT AS EVER-PRESENT?

The capacity to 'manage' – to plan, review and control – *may* be seen as a universal human capability that has been applied, more or less systematically and widely, in all societies. In pre-modern societies, however, other influences, notably the weight of tradition or the dominance of myth, were more powerful in directing and legitimizing human behaviour. An acceleration of the discipline of management, involving the spread of calculating, secular, this-worldly reasoning, occurred during the nineteenth and twentieth centuries when it was harnessed to the development of capitalist organizations:

> Like generals of old [managers in eighteenth-century Britain] had to control numerous men, but without powers of compulsion ... Again, unlike the builders of the pyramids, they had not only to show absolute results in terms of certain products of their efforts, but to relate them to costs, and sell them competitively. While they used capital like the merchants, they had to combine it with labour, and transform it first, not merely into saleable commodities, but also into instruments of production embodying the latest achievements of a changing technology. And above it all there lay the heavy hand of a hostile State and an unsympathetic legal system, which they had to transform, as they had to transform so much of the rest of their environment, in the process of creating their industrial capitalism. (Pollard, 1965, pp. 6–7).

Prior to the emergence and consolidation of capitalist economic organizations, management as a discipline had been developed, in comparatively embryonic form, in religious, military and governmental forms. It was then augmented, further rationalized and embroidered in the process of developing and governing commercial as well as public sector organizations so that, today, it is a pervasive discipline that extends well beyond work organizations and into everyday life.

Box 8.3
The development of management in capitalist economies – a two-stage process

Historically, owners of capital – in the form of buildings, tools and machinery – emerged as a distinctive group who used skilled labour that previously worked in guilds and owned their own means of (craft) production but did not employ it directly. These owners developed and applied some basic management disciplines as they decided which tools and raw materials to purchase, what outputs would be required and where these would be sold. But these owners did not hire labour directly or take responsibility for how it was organized. Instead, they paid 'gang masters' who gathered together groups of workers. The gang masters were paid by the owners for whatever output they produced that met the agreed standard. In effect, during this first stage, owners 'outsourced' responsibility for work organization to the gang bosses. There was minimal direct intervention by owners in the organization of production, largely because this was contracted out to an external supplier of labour.

During the second stage, owners took a closer, substantive interest in how production was organized (see Chapter 7). The owners employed their own staff – managers – to undertake the task of deciding when, where and how labour was to be deployed, in an effort to improve its reliability and productivity. Employees were hired directly by managers who decided how their effort was to be deployed and rewarded. Today, this second stage has become so institutionalized as to be largely taken for granted. Increasingly, this system of 'managerial capitalism' (Chandler, 1977) renders the owners almost invisible, in part because ownership has been extended through wider participation in savings and pension schemes. Despite their withdrawal from day-to-day management, the interests of owners has rarely suffered partly due to managers' legal obligations to shareholders but also because profit in the private sector is the clearest measure of managerial competence.

CLASSICAL THINKING ABOUT MANAGEMENT

We have noted how, in mainstream considerations of management, there is an assumption that the objectives or 'goals' of organizations are readily identified, understood and shared; and that the responsibility of management is to establish a framework of policy and practice that ensures their effective realization. Mainstream knowledge of management also assumes the value and legitimate place of management as a social elite.

A distinguishing feature of 'classical thinking' in management is its belief in the possibility of specifying a single way of organizing, managerial style or mode of leadership that would have universal efficacy (see Chapter 7). Conceived as a system of expertise that is technically adept, politically neutral and morally benign, classical thinking about management assumes the existence of a set of principles whose application will ensure the smooth operation of any collective endeavour. The possibility that management could be, like anything else, a manifestation of its time and place – a product of struggles between those who believe in, and value, its claims and those who are neither convinced nor seduced – is unacknowledged or brushed aside. Instead, it is assumed that more management – as discipline and/or function – inevitably produces a better world. With extraordinary self-confidence, its advocates have urged its adoption in every sphere of human activity.

One of the most celebrated efforts to catalogue the constituent parts of management was produced by Henri Fayol (see Table 8.2). Versions of this list have reappeared in numerous guises (e.g., Barnard, 1936; Drucker, 1974; Koontz *et al.,* 1984) since its publication in *General and Industrial Administration* (1916/1949). Classical management theory presupposes that any institution can benefit from attaining its objectives by identifying and enhancing its methods in five respects – planning, organizing, co-ordinating, commanding and controlling. The discipline of management subjects the five components to systematic analysis in order to pinpoint deficiencies and devise a remedy. Fayol and other 'classical' theorists believed that the application of universal principles of management would serve to transform work organization based upon custom, prejudice and favouritism into rational, balanced, well-integrated entities from which unproductive frictions, misunderstandings and conflicts are progressively eliminated (see also Chapter 7).

Table 8.2 Fayol's principles of management

1	Division of work	Reduces the span of attention or effort for any one person or group. Develops practice and familiarity
2	Authority	The right to give orders. Should not be considered without reference to responsibility
3	Discipline	Outward marks of respect in accordance with formal or informal agreements between firm and its employees
4	Unity of command	One man, one superior
5	Unity of direction	One head and one plan for a group of activities with the same objective
6	Subordination of individual interests to the general interest	The interest of one individual or one group should not prevail over the general good. This is a difficult area of management
7	Remuneration	Pay should be fair to both the employee and the firm
8	Centralization	Is always present to a greater or lesser extent, depending on the size of company and quality of its managers
9	Scalar chain	The line of authority from top to bottom of the organization
10	Order	A place for everything and everything in its place; the right person in the right place
11	Equity	A combination of kindliness and justice towards employees
12	Stability of tenure of personnel	Employees need to be given time to settle into their jobs, even though this may be a lengthy period in the case of managers
13	Initiative	Within the limits of authority and discipline, all levels of staff should be encouraged to show initiative
14	*Esprit de corps*	Harmony is a great strength to an organization; teamwork should be encouraged

One absentee from Fayol's catalogue of components of management is any direct reference to motivation and to related, human aspects of work organization. Motivation is something that more recent management writers have repeatedly considered (see Chapter 2), and which is central to the study of leadership where the focus shifts from functions to relationships. In Fayol's thinking, motivation is apparently assured by the smooth operation of the five components (planning, organizing, co-ordinating, commanding and controlling). In addition, he commends forms of 'good practice' that may be associated with the positive motivation of staff, such as equality of treatment and developing an *'esprit de corps'* (communal solidarity) so that strife and division is minimized. Other related elements marginalized by Fayol, though emphasized by later, 'modern' thinkers, include the development of staff, the importance of communicating with them and, finally, the wider social responsibilities of management (see Chapters 11 and 15).

Of the classical theorists, Mary Parker Follett was more conscious of the human dimension of management and how, at least within her own US culture, subordinates dislike being 'bossed about'. She proposed that management and leadership should be depersonalized so that authority is related to its context, and compliance is contingent upon what she represents as *the demands of the situation,* not the instruction of a manager or the inspiration of a leader (see also Chapter 7). Modern management and leadership has sometimes achieved this state of affairs – for example, by securing consent to some activity or set of symbols, such as achieving a bonus, identifying with the culture or the corporate brand, thus obscuring the management control that lies behind this achievement.

Modern thinking about management

More recent thinking emphasizes the particular circumstances or context (of culture, technology, history, etc.) in which management disciplines and functions are applied. Notably, open systems thinking (see Chapter 7) indicates how, for example, a style of leadership that 'fits' and performs well with one particular combination of people and technologies will not necessarily succeed when applied in a different context or to other groups. There is greater attentiveness to how cultural differences and established ways of doing things – comprising practices of organizing, managing and leading considered 'normal' and 'acceptable' within particular environments – exert an influence upon people as they work. Employees are recognized to bring diverse elements of their 'environments', such as their habits, prejudices and expectations, to work; and open systems thinking suggests that such elements have to be managed in ways that are sensitive to, and appropriate for, the particular organization. In this way, open systems thinking can, in principle, incorporate some awareness of the 'importation' and impact of norms and values within organizations – ways of thinking and acting that can enable, but also may constrain, efforts to impose universal, formal rules and procedures.

Thinkpoint 8.5

Think of an occasion in which a person in authority (e.g., a teacher or manager) was insensitive to the particular circumstances of their actions. How was their behaviour received? What difference might appropriate preparation or skills 'training' have made?

In lay terminology, open systems thinking prompts consideration of a wide range of factors that interact to affect the situation and, therefore, the rational choice of 'strategies', 'structures' and 'processes' for its managing. Open systems thinking may extend to include 'flexibility' in which certain teams or players are managed and led, depending upon variations in the way in which they respond to different approaches. Simultaneously, open systems thinking may attend to the negative effects upon morale if such flexibility is interpreted as favouritism or inconsistency rather than an effective means of improving performance. Such thinking commends the scanning of environments to select a philosophy and design that matches what the environment has to offer (e.g., technologies, levels of skill) with what is demanded by it (e.g., speedy responses, reliability). So, even when a generic formula or prescription is embraced – such as 'strong corporate culture' (Chapter 10) or 'lean production' (Chapter 11) – open systems thinking stresses how the particularities of the context should be taken into account and the formula thereby adjusted or modified to fit with the specific conditions in which it is being applied. But, at the same time, such 'modern' thinking continues to hanker after guidelines that are conceived to have widespread efficacy, sometimes described as 'best practices'.

Modern management guidelines include:

- Being attentive to customers and anticipating, or even initiating, shifts in demand (e.g., through branding and associated customer loyalty schemes).
- Paying attention to current and potential competitors so as to establish a distinctive market position where improved profits can be made.
- Attending to costs through careful monitoring and control (e.g., by harnessing the power of information and communication technologies).
- Contracting out activities that can be done more cheaply elsewhere.
- Establishing closer relationships with suppliers.

Such thinking commends attending to processes as much as outputs so as to achieve continuous improvements in quality and productivity; and paying attention to staff (e.g., by fostering greater openness and trust) especially in knowledge-intensive industries where their knowledge and skills are critical to performance.

These guidelines do not necessarily depart markedly from classical principles. But they suggest a more holistic approach that is simultaneously mindful of the immediate (business) and wider contexts of its operations. Such 'modern' thinking has been applied in the private sector and is increasingly being introduced into public sector organizations.. 'Business disciplines' are introduced in both sectors in an effort to 'modernize' and 'streamline' what are viewed as inefficient, excessively labour-intensive, customer-unfriendly and/or inflexible practices (see Box 8.3).

Major issues/controversies in this field: Mainstream debates

THE HUMAN DIMENSION OF WORK

Classical thinkers paid minimal attention to complex issues of motivation. They focused primarily upon structures and systems (see Chapter 7) without much consideration of how employees would respond to such (impersonal) methods and measures. It was believed that a positive – co-operative, productive – response would follow naturally from the application of classical principles of 'good management'. In Frederick Taylor's (2011) *Principles of Scientific Management,* for example, it was assumed that better pay would compensate for the imposition of narrowly drawn and repetitive tasks. For Taylor firmly believed that economic reward is the primary, if not the sole, purpose of going to work. From this assumption it followed that any change in working practices would be accepted as long as earnings increased as a result. It is questionable, however, whether Taylor's assumption about work and industrial workers' purely economic interest in wages is universally correct or is a 'self-fulfilling' prophecy in the sense that money is likely to become the major concern if workers lack, or are denied, any alternative set of meanings at work.

The notion of a self-fulfilling prophecy applies to many features of human behaviour where those exercising power constitute how others make sense of, and act in, the world. When managers believe that workers are only motivated by money, they organize the workplace in such a way as to marginalize any other possible meaning or interests (e.g., planning the work, innovating methods, social recognition, camaraderie between workers) such that only the size of the wage can matter. Lo and behold, the assumption about economic interests is confirmed. It is a self-fulfilling prophecy because managers' application of the principles of scientific management has generated the conditions through which it would become true. Of course, an understanding that the prophecy is self-fulfilling does not make the basic belief incorrect. Rather, it suggests that its effectiveness depends upon the creation of conditions that act either to confirm or to deny its claims.

That said, Taylor, in common with Fayol and others (e.g., Urwick), also believed that employees should be treated 'decently' by training them to acquire those work methods that were 'scientifically proven'. What classical thinkers shared was an adamant opposition to reliance upon some arbitrary (e.g., personal threat) basis for giving instructions. This, of course, placed a significant burden of responsibility upon managers who had previously relied upon their power to hire and fire employees in order to make them work harder. Not surprisingly, there was considerable resistance from managers to Taylor's principles as applying the principles placed new demands upon them. Managers had not previously been burdened by the responsibility of introducing new methods but, instead, habitually relied upon personal (e.g., favouritism) and despotic (e.g., punishment-based) ways of securing employee productivity.

Largely absent from both despotic and classical approaches to management was any careful or close consideration of employee psychology. When Taylor challenged custom and practice, he did so by assuming a direct relationship between productivity and reward, in the form of payment by results. It did not occur to him that employees might place a greater value upon other concerns, such as solidarity with their fellow employees, their dignity or the comforts of habitual ways of working. Resistance to classical methods of organization, and especially to the demands (and privations) of classical, closed systems thinking, resulted in this assumption being questioned.

Thinkpoint 8.6

If Taylor were considering the work of students, how might he seek to apply his principles? To what extent do you think that academic credentials (i.e., degree results) have a tendency to perform the same function in university as money in scientific management? Can you identify areas of higher education that have been 'Taylorized'? (Some commentators have described contemporary universities as McUniversities.) Why might Taylor's ideas have limited application in this context?

Resistance to the application of the principles of scientific management was both individual and collective. As individuals, many workers disliked and resented the redesign of their jobs, which eroded any scope for imagination or personal identification with the task. Workers often experienced the uniformity of the new methods as alien and degrading as their effect was to remove individuality and minimize the scope for exercising discretion or creativity. Employees may have strongly disliked the 'irrationality' of 'unscientific', tyrannical bosses who managed according to personal whims and arbitrary prejudices, rather than by the seemingly impartial logic of 'scientific' principles. However, managers' disinclination to manage consistently and closely creates spaces and provides scope in which employees can more readily develop and control meanings about their work (that is 'subcultures') that are not reducible to a calculation about output and wages (see Chapter 7).

Collectively, workers subjected to classical principles of management became homogenized and fragmented as their jobs were mechanized and de-skilled through a process of specialization in which each task tends to become narrower and more repetitive. A sense of control over the nature and pace of work is lost when 'scientific' experts apply the new disciplines of management. By design, its 'scientific' principles exclude workers from involvement in the development and application of this instrument of management control. Workers are entirely its targets or objects, not its architects or subjects. Not surprisingly, then, for many workers, the classical principles of management were not experienced as a neutral and progressive technology but as a political and socially divisive weapon that posed a threat to their sense of identity, solidarity and interests. To the extent that forms of scientific management encounter organized resistance, they provoke opposition to the aim of rationalizing the workplace rather than operate to expose and remove irrational deviations from it.

Theories 'X', 'Y' and 'Z'

Throughout the history of management thinking and practice, there have been recurrent efforts to understand and manage the 'softer', more complex aspects of organizational behaviour. The emphasis is upon getting employee motivation right. The underlying assumption is that properly motivated staff, from the bottom to the top of an organization, will develop appropriate and effective ways of organizing, including the use of 'harder', more rational and quantitative methods of assessing and rewarding staff. It is believed that the complexity of human motivation can, if managed effectively, enable organizations to be more productive as well as less heartless. This distinction between 'soft' and 'hard', parallels that later articulated by HRM (see Chapter 5).

The introduction of more 'enlightened' or 'humanistic' management is understood to require a deep appreciation of individual and especially group psychology. It necessitates, for example, an understanding of how the norms of work groups can exert a stronger influence upon worker identity and behaviour than the rules and incentives imposed by managers. This is the central message of Human Relations thinking popularized by Elton Mayo, a Harvard academic. Mayo studied the influence of social factors, such as recognition of contribution and the operation of group norms (e.g., the socially acceptable level of effort and co-operation) upon the productivity of factory workers. According to him, 'Human collaboration in work ... has always depended for its perpetuation upon the evolution of a non-logical social code that regulates the relations between persons and their attitudes to one another.' (Mayo, 1933, p. 120)

Even when there is a strong material incentive to be more productive (e.g., payment by results), Mayo observed that the effectiveness of such inducements may be dampened by the strength of a group norm about what is an acceptable level of output. In such circumstances, the material incentive does not elicit a high level of productivity where there is a strong desire to avoid being excluded or stigmatized by fellow workers as a consequence of exceeding an established workgroup output norm. Instead of operating against the grain of such norms and values – a stratagem that is seen to risk a loss of morale and/or increased opposition to management – the 'humanizing' approach pays close attention to employees' 'non-logical' or 'irrational' psychological 'needs'. They are termed 'non-logical' or 'irrational' because, in purely economic terms, they are seen to obstruct the individual's maximization of earnings. Instead of ignoring or dismissing such 'needs', managers are encouraged to acknowledge, address and, indeed, 'exploit' the 'need to belong' – for example, by making the organization, and not the work group, the primary source of satisfaction of workers' 'irrational' needs – by developing schemes and styles of management that demonstrate how the corporation is taking care of their psychological as well as their material welfare. Human relations thinking suggests that while economic incentives cannot be ignored, employees also seek to have their sense of identity developed and confirmed at work. For the advocates of human relations thinking, worker resistance to management control is surmountable by training managers in interpersonal, leadership skills. To put this another way, employees are no longer to be treated as mere 'hands' but are complex elements within an 'open system' – elements that import values into the organization that managers ignore at their peril but, with the benefit of social science, may harness to their advantage.

Building upon the insights of human relations ideas, 'modern' thinking shifts from a model of the worker as an appendage to the machine – writ large in Fordism (see Chapter 4) where the pacing of the assembly line was deployed to dictate the speed of each worker's task (see Chapter 13) – to an idea of the worker as a more complex creature who is malleable. However, human relations thinking falls short of recognizing how workers can come to resemble how they are treated; in short, to behave in the way expected of them thus providing evidence that the theory is correct while this may not be the case. This is because, as noted above, assumptions about workers that inform management strategies can affect the very behaviour they seek to control in self-fulfilling ways. Of course, the workers are diverse but, if treated like machines, will tend to feel frustrated and resentful, and therefore become the mulish, inflexible individual who is motivated to work harder only by the incentive of more pay because that is the only value on offer. Conversely, if the complex and diverse character of workers' interests, values or orientations is recognized and met, the worker feels appreciated, grows in confidence and self-esteem, becomes more co-operative and therefore more productive.

McGregor (1960) summarized this difference of philosophy by coining the terms 'Theory X' and 'Theory Y' (see Table 8.3). Common to variants of Theory Y is the understanding, or assumption, that the need to belong enables the integration of individual and organizational goals; and that organizations can be managed in ways that motivate individuals by providing opportunities to fulfil their other needs, such as self-esteem and self-actualization (see Box 8.4). Only then, advocates of Theory Y contend, is it possible to design the content of jobs and the activities of work groups, as well as relevant systems of reward, that harness human potential to the realization of organizational goals. In effect, a psychological remedy is advocated which, it is claimed, can reconcile the 'needs' of the individual worker with the 'needs' of the organization. We have placed these terms in inverted commas because it is far from clear that needs can be so readily identified or taken for granted – an issue to which we will return in the second part of this chapter.

Table 8.3 Comparison of Theory X and Theory Y

Understanding of	Theory X classical	Theory Y modern
Human nature	Lazy. Must be induced or coerced into productive activity	Potentially self-motivating. Will respond positively to opportunities to take responsibility and exercise discretion
Employee's attitude towards work	Negative. Extrinsic rewards (money) compensates for effort expended	Positive. Intrinsic rewards (enjoyment, fulfilment), such as the opportunity to learn and develop, are important
Role of management	Supervise and direct to ensure that work is done	Support to enable learning and development

Management by objectives (MBO) is a widely used technique in which common goals and targets are mutually agreed between superior and subordinate, and then subsequently reviewed to assess performance and identify changes necessary to make further improvements. This is consistent with Theory Y as subordinates are not given detailed instructions for performing their tasks but, rather, are permitted to use initiative and discretion to achieve the agreed goals.

Box 8.4
Theory Y
in practice:
'Management by
objectives'

Exercise 8.3

Complete the following table by listing some of the key differences between 'X' and 'Y' theories of management.

Table 8.4 Differences between X and Y theories

	Theory X	**Theory Y**
Challenges the idea that		
Focuses upon		
Assumes that		

Theories X and Y have their parallels in management styles. A 'managerial grid' (see Figure 8.2) constructed by Blake and Mouton (1964; see also Blake and McCanse, 1991), which takes as one of its axes the results-orientation, is largely indifferent to human psychology and is therefore a variant of Theory X, but combines it with a people-centredness approach that is very reminiscent of Theory Y. This grid produces five distinctive styles and, of course, numerous less extreme mixes of them:

- low X, low Y = impoverished management
- high X, high Y = team management
- low X, high Y = country club management
- high X, low Y = authority-compliance management
- medium X, medium Y = middle-of-the-road management.

Management is described as 'impoverished' where there is a lack of attention both to people and production; in effect, where management is 'hands off'. Often in such circumstances, both managers and workers exert the minimum of effort to sustain the organization. In contrast, 'team management' combines maximum concern with employees and production by aspiring to ensure that individual 'needs' and organizational goals are fully integrated. Here there is an emphasis upon building trust and mutual respect. In 'Country club management', there is much attention to employee needs, but limited attention to production. The atmosphere is relaxed, and maintaining harmonious relationships is more important than raising output. Finally, high concern for production combined with minimal concern for people is described as an 'authority-compliance' approach. It is a form of management associated with arranging work in ways that are designed to minimize human intervention.

Not surprisingly, the 'team management' combination of concern for people with a concern for production is viewed as the most desirable. Blake and Mouton's 'team management' is similar to Likert's 'System 4' (see Table 8.5), where management develops and welds the contributions of individuals into an effective, mutually supportive and productive (synergistic) group.

For champions of Theory Y, the primary task and responsibility of managers is to enable and educate employees into seeing how the desire to satisfy their own 'needs' can be aligned with the attainment of organizational goals. Managers might be invited, for example, to locate their 'style' on the axes of the 'managerial grid', and then to reflect upon how they can develop themselves to move in the direction of the optimal 'team management' approach. Blake and Mouton developed their grid in the early 1960s but it took another 20 years before the value of 'teamworking' became widely applauded and applied in forms of leadership (see below), total quality management (TQM), business process re-engineering (BPR) and culture management (see also Chapters 2, 4 and 7).

Figure 8.2 A management grid
Source: Adapted from Huczynski, A. and Buchanan, D. (2001)

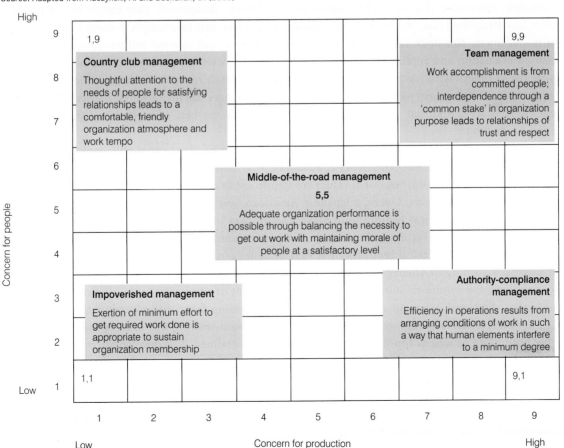

Table 8.5 Likert's 'System 4' approach to management: Key features

Management characteristic	Management behaviour
Share knowledge and insights	Be attentive and approachable
Acknowledge and reward success	Provide guidance and coaching
Recognize and address personal issues	Support career advancement

Source: Adapted from *New Patterns of Management* by Rensis Likert, 1961. © The McGraw Hill Companies, Inc.

Thinkpoint 8.7

● How would you describe Margaret's changing approach to management, using the categories developed by Likert?
● What limitations do you detect in the Theory Y prescriptions for improved employee motivation and productivity?

One limitation of a focus upon the 'needs' of individuals as the key to motivation is the scant attention paid to the wider context of managing people in organizations. It does not consider, for example, how national or regional culture or dominant organizational values may condition not only the response of employees to different styles of management but also the very construction or development of those styles in the first place. So, for example, employees who are used to 'authority-compliance management' may simply be less productive and/or less disciplined (i.e., 'slacken off', 'take advantage') in response to attempts to move in the direction of team management. Nor does Theory Y take account of external and internal influences upon managers' appreciation, evaluation and application of different approaches. After all, managerial and non-managerial employees always inherit what has gone before – they do not completely reconstruct the positions they occupy in an organization. Yet the theory assumes that the individual manager has the power and discretion to select the most effective style, and that 'team management' is obviously the best as it combines attentiveness to people and production.

Concerned to demonstrate that Theories X and Y are not exhaustive of potential philosophies of management, an alternative approach, labelled Theory Z, advanced by William Ouchi (1981), is somewhat responsive to the observation that wider organizational values are significant in constraining and enabling the styles and decisions of individual managers. Ouchi, a Japanese American, was researching at a time when, in the late 1970s, 'the Japanese miracle' was beginning to make a significant impact upon global US competitiveness. He invited his readers to reflect upon the success of Japanese companies in penetrating Western markets with goods (e.g., cars and electrical products) that were of better quality, more reliable and cheaper. The key to such success, according to Theory Z, resides in the distinctive culture of large Japanese corporations. In such corporations, the culture encouraged the active involvement of employees in developing forms of lean production and shortened design-to-manufacture times by providing them with a combination of job security (e.g., lifetime contracts of employment) and a mode of decision-making that is more inclusive by being somewhat bottom-up as well as top-down. The Japanese, it was claimed, had developed corporate cultures that provided economic security and a real sense of belonging. This had enabled them to maximize the involvement and contribution of workers not just through their hard work but, crucially, by incorporating their ideas, knowledge and skill into the process of innovation and manufacturing development. This has also been described as a form of 'distributed leadership' where shop floor workers play their full part in 'leading' the development of corporations (see Box 8.5).

Box 8.5
Distributed leadership for the networked economy

The organizational theory that will successfully dominate the world of networking has less to do with management and more to do with leadership – not leadership in the charismatic sense that comes from the top, but leadership that exists and operates all throughout the organization. Such leadership is frequently not 'scientific', nor the result of a formal planning process, but more results from a 'hands-on' relationship with particular work processes – what Shoshana Zuboff has called informating the workplace.

'The information age demands, and will enforce, a transition to empowered employees throughout the organization. The organization will be successful to the extent that employees are free and have the capacity, to exercise leadership. The organizations faced with the most difficult transition to the information age are likely to be those that never really bought into the industrial age management paradigm – the public sector, with higher education and health care being the two most obvious examples ... they tend to be far more inertia-bound than their aggressive private sector cousins, particularly than the high-tech industries that currently drive the economies of developed countries.'

Source: Heterick, (1996).

Theory Z suggests the importance of the context of management. The limited duration of the Japanese success story and its subsequent 'unravelling' also confirms the view that any 'best way' is limited by time as well as place. 'Fordism', founded primarily upon Theory X with a gloss of paternalism, is another example. Fordist manufacture, which was adopted by all the mass automobile manufacturers, combined Taylor's philosophy of job specialization and simplification with an automated line that effectively paced the work (see Chapter 12). This proved to be a highly successful approach until the system developed by Toyota, which unified elements of Theory Z with a greater responsiveness to consumers' developing interest in greater customization and better quality, demonstrated that Fordism was not, or was no longer, the 'one best way'.

Thinkpoint 8.8

Consider a situation in which you have been strongly motivated to perform a task or achieve a goal. How might Theories X, Y and Z be applied to account for the strength of your motivation?

It was not just Theory Z but a whole range of management thinking – including innovations such as culture management, teamworking, the learning organization, TQM, BPR and knowledge management (KM) – which embraced and promoted the view that employees responsible for daily production have numerous skills and largely underutilized but invaluable tacit knowledge (Knights and McCabe, 2003). Discounted by Theory X, mass assembly automation could, in principle, be transformed into a resource for improving productivity and achieving greater profitability. In a market for mass-produced goods that is reaching saturation point, it is also becoming increasingly important to develop ways of differentiating products in terms other than mere functionality. It is recognized that cars and other consumer goods can be a status symbol – an expression of one's place in the social order (see Exercise 8.4) or a statement of a particular lifestyle; and it also has become clearer that product competition is less likely to be successful if customer service fails to be of a high standard.

Exercise 8.4

Take a car manufacturer like Mercedes or some other of your choice and note one of its models that appeals to you, and how it differentiates itself from the equivalent models of other manufacturers. In the case of Mercedes, explore how surveys of reliability and customer satisfaction compare with the image projected by the manufacturer and reflect upon how any discrepancies are managed.

In *The Art of Japanese Management,* Pascale and Athos (1982) present a '7-S' framework, devised by the consultants McKinsey, that combines elements of Theories X, Y and Z. The '7-S' framework retains a classical emphasis upon structure, systems, skill and strategy but incorporates, and makes central, an attentiveness to staff, style and, most importantly, shared values. As with Theory Z, the focus in the '7-S' framework, which is also central to Peters and Waterman's (1982) highly influential *In Search of Excellence* (see Box 8.6), is upon developing a strong organizational culture. As we have seen, Theory Y anticipates that individual and organizational needs will be reconciled if individuals are given the opportunity to fulfil their multiple needs. Theory Z, and especially *In Search of Excellence,* makes no such assumption. Instead, management is urged to 'create a broad, uplifting, shared culture' (Peters and Waterman, 1982, p. 51) where 'the real role of the chief executive is to manage the values of the organization' (ibid., p. 26), and where employees 'either buy in to their norms or get out' (ibid., p. 77). While some might want to describe the ideal Theory Z worker (see Box 8.6) as displaying obsessive behaviour that requires psychiatric attention, advocates of strong cultures seek to make all workers as devotional and obsessive about their companies as cult members are about their values.

One of our favourite stories is about a Honda worker who, on his way home each evening, straightens up windshield wiper blades on all the Hondas he passes. He just can't stand to see a flaw in a Honda! Now, why is all of this important? Because so much excellence in performance has to do with people being motivated by compelling, simple – even beautiful – values.

Source: Peters and Waterman (1982), p. 27.

Box 8.6
The ideal theory
Z worker

In a chapter entitled 'Man Waiting for Motivation', Peters and Waterman (1982) contend that the key to delivering 'better relative performance, a higher level of contribution from the "average" is to establish a "strong culture" reinforced by "transforming leadership"'. It is this combination of culture and leadership that, according to Peters and Waterman, differentiates the 'best-run companies' from the 'also-rans'. Their claim is that a strong culture provides the final solution to the long-lamented problem of motivating employees as it demonstrates that what (classically trained) managers 'have been dismissing for so long as the intractable, irrational, intuitive, informal organization *can* be managed' (ibid, p. 11). Contemporary thinking about management provides a linkage to identify and connect the basic sequence of managerial work where, in the case of Theory Z, objectives and policy are gathered around a few core values.

A normative orientation

Common to the variants of classical and contemporary thinking is a *normative* orientation. That is to say, there is an enthusiasm or impatience to prescribe – to say what *ought* to be done – in advance of any sustained effort to detect or diagnose what *is* being done.

Associated with this drive to prescribe is a tendency to identify simplistic, universal remedies – such as 'one best way' solutions or 'best practice' guidelines. These may be attractive to practising managers, and, indeed, to students, because they may seem to provide an authoritative, reassuring answer to the bewildering, 'wicked' difficulties of managing unpredictable and awkward 'human resources' in dynamic and uncertain conditions. Such solutions appeal to a so-called 'need' for security that has been a recurrent theme of management thought. However, the relevance and adequacy of any prescription is dependent upon the quality of the diagnosis. Instead of concentrating upon solutions that can be sold to 'needy' managers, some researchers have emphasized the importance of first investigating and seeking to understand what managers do.

WHAT DO MANAGERS DO? BEHAVIOURAL APPROACH

To move beyond approaches that prescribe methods and styles of management, some researchers have undertaken observational studies of managers that investigate what they do. On the basis of such a study of senior managers, Mintzberg (1973) concluded that their work could be described in terms of the performance of three major, overlapping roles that comprise diverse forms of activity. The three roles are 'interpersonal', which includes liaison and figurehead activities in addition to general leadership; 'informational', which embraces the tasks of disseminating information, monitoring activity and acting as a spokesperson; and, finally, 'decisional' roles, which include those of negotiating, dealing with conflicts, allocating resources and taking entrepreneurial initiatives. In short, Mintzberg's study shows managers to be undertaking a number of roles that frequently overlap in the manner of a Venn diagram (see Figure 8.3). So, for example, activities as a figurehead may involve the dissemination of information about how resources are to be allocated; or processes of negotiation may involve liaison and the monitoring of others' performance and/or stance.

Figure 8.3 The roles and activities comprising managerial work
Source: Mintzberg, H., *The Nature of Managerial Work* © 1980, p. 59, Fig. 8. Adapted by permission of Pearson Education, Inc.

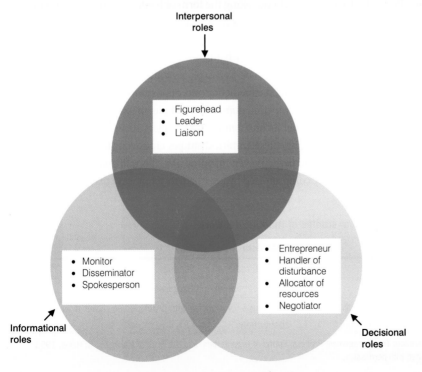

In addition to identifying the breadth of activity undertaken by managers and its conceptualization as the performance of three major roles, Mintzberg's analysis paints a picture of managers rapidly shifting between activities, operating as 'disturbance handler' one moment, then acting as a 'spokesperson' or playing the role of 'ceremonial figurehead' the next. In the process, they are seen to manage boundaries within organizations and with their environments. The proportion of time spent playing the different roles is said to depend largely upon the position occupied by a manager: he or she may be required to play one or two of the roles more frequently than some of the others. Some managers are centrally involved in monitoring, disseminating and prioritizing information, while others are primarily engaged in the entrepreneurial activity of initiating change and developing innovative solutions to problems. The key point to be appreciated is that the practicalities of managerial work are more *complex, contingent and dynamic* than is implied by both classical and modern prescriptions for management. Managerial work, according to Mintzberg, is often fragmented, with much time being devoted to immediate concerns and problems, and rather little time being devoted to broader strategic issues. That said, it is also important to recognize that it was not the intention of classical writers, like Fayol, to describe how *individual* managers fulfil their responsibilities but, rather, to specify what components comprise the *collective* function of management.

Common to Fayol and Mintzberg's analyses, nonetheless, is a formulation of managerial work that associates it only with functions and roles that are seen as independent of the demands upon their time and attention – for example, from subordinates and superordinates, suppliers and customers. Their focus is upon the components of management as a function or upon the activities of individual managers. Neither considers managerial work as a medium and outcome of wider institutional and politico-economic forces.

Other observational studies of managerial work suggest that interactions with other people are not only often brief but also charged with many multiple, cross-cutting issues and agendas (Kotter, 1982) that are rich in both local knowledge and political 'baggage'. Managers are seen to be involved in a process of continuously making sense of what is going on, and divining its implications. They are also seen to be engaged in deliberately shaping the sense-making of their staff, but not necessarily in ways that are consistent from one day to the next, or that suggest a conscious and/or sustained attempt to 'manage culture'. Instead, managers are shown to be continuous 'scanners' of their work context, seeking out information that is valued for providing a *richer*, real-time picture of the threats as well as opportunities that are posed for their tasks and career prospects. Much managerial work is also shown to be about 'influencing' others in ways that are expedient and pragmatic. In this process, activities uncharted by Fayol or Mintzberg, taking the form of bantering, swearing and joking, form part-and-parcel of the process of forming and maintaining alliances as well as attaining some degree of personal popularity (Collinson, 1988; see also Chapters 9 and 11).

Such contemporary understandings of management are equivalent to what is now seen as 'soap opera' or the 'kitchen sink' drama that cuts through images of how managerial work 'ought to be' as it explores some of its practical complexities, contrariness and even absurdities (see Table 8.6). Politically charged expediency and opportunism are seen to be central to managing in practice, as managers wrestle with numerous competing demands, multiple uncertainties, and endeavour to communicate, network and motivate simultaneously but often inconsistently (see Chapters 10 and 11). While Theories 'X', 'Y' and 'Z' each seek to identify a 'one best way' of managing, these empirical studies endeavour to provide a window upon management practice, serving to show how difficult, and perhaps even inappropriate, it is to manage using any single formula as, in practice, any consistent approach is routinely compromised by pressures to act in ways that contradict it.

Table 8.6 Key findings of contemporary empirical studies of managerial work

Character	Behaviour
Frenetic, fragmented and disjointed	Reactive rather than initiating
Preoccupied with ad hoc, immediate matters	Much negotiating and bargaining
Decisions and plans emergent in process of dealing with immediate matters	Preference for working with practicalities rather than abstractions

Source: Adapted from *Managing through Organization: The Management Process, Forms of Organization, and the Work of Managers*, C. Hales, 1993 p. 14, © Cengage Learning EMEA Ltd, reproduced with permission.

Recent empirical studies show how established – classical and modern – theories of management tend to promote an idealized conception of, and set of prescriptions for, management. That is to say, they abstract 'management' – as a set of principles, functions or roles – from the specific context in which it is practised. Even when the context is not entirely ignored, the importance of social institutions in shaping the development of management is under-estimated. These institutions are also downplayed in studies that directly address the question of 'what managers do' where there is little consideration of the wider context – politico-economic as well as cultural – in which, and through which, managerial work is undertaken. Such studies do not, for example, consider how the very meaning of 'management' and aspirations of 'managers' have emerged through struggles to establish their credibility and exert influence in the teeth of opposition – for example, from owners who have been reluctant to trust them; from employees who have not been guaranteed to obey them; from politicians who think they fail to deliver on expectations for the economy; from regulators who seek to constrain them; from consumers who might feel marginalized by being ignored except at the point of sale; and from a wide range of commentators, such as journalists, academics and various special interest groups, who alternatively idolize or lampoon them.

Thinkpoint 8.9

Consider the work of a CEO like Margaret at Bar Mar. In what ways would you expect her activities to illustrate the findings of studies undertaken by Mintzberg and Kotter?

Key ideas and contributions on leadership

We noted earlier how the idea of 'leadership' is distinguished from 'management' by a greater emphasis upon directing others through inspiration and motivation, rather than command-and-control reliance upon hierarchical position. Leadership also tends to be associated with personal qualities, such as charisma, drive, determination, focus, dedication, etc.; but it has also been associated with ruthlessness, obstinacy, autocracy and obsessiveness. In any event, ascribing the virtues of leadership to an individual suggests that their power or capacity to 'get things done' does not depend purely, or even primarily, upon the occupancy of (managerial) position but, rather, upon qualities summed up as 'leadership' that may take a variety of forms and 'styles'.

Thinkpoint 8.10

Identify a person whom you have known and you regard as a leader. Attempt to create a list of characteristics that distinguish this person from other people. Would *anyone* exhibiting these characteristics be viewed as a leader? Can you think of situations in which such characteristics would be viewed negatively rather than positively?

Classical thinking about leadership

LEADERSHIP AS A PERSONALITY TRAIT

The traits approach to leadership concentrates upon identifying the qualities attributed to individuals who are widely viewed as leaders. Traits of leadership have included such qualities as initiative, intelligence and self-assurance. The difficulty is that few leaders have been found to share many of these traits and/or non-leaders are also deemed to possess them in equal measure. Such traits do not appear to discriminate sufficiently between leaders and non-leaders to be of analytical use. Nonetheless, a variant of the traits approach has resurfaced in the form of 'transformational' leadership (Burns, 1978; Bass, 1985) – a kind of leadership capable of meeting the challenge of re-energizing or reinventing organizations during periods of turbulence and uncertainty. 'Transformational leaders' are conceived to possess the qualities, or traits, needed to inspire and redirect staff to solve problems and attain ambitious objectives – objectives that are rarely achieved by relying upon a 'transactional' approach where co-operation relies upon narrow calculations of self-interest ('if you do/don't do this, you will/won't get this', as exemplified by bonus schemes, pay and promotion systems, etc.). In contrast to mere managers who lack transformational traits and, as a consequence, fall back upon more mundane, transactional techniques to secure compliance, transformational leaders are seen to exhibit behaviours that energize and enthuse others. As a consequence, it is claimed that their followers come to care as much or more about realizing the visions or mission of the leader as they do about any personal gain that may result. Key features attributed to transformational leaders are set out in Table 8.7.

In common with trait theories of leadership, the idea of transformational leadership assumes that exhibiting its key features delivers the intended results irrespective of the circumstances, such as the nature and scale of the task at hand, the established systems and culture of the organization, or the readiness of followers to respond to the calls of a leader who aspires to be transformational.

We can conclude that classical approaches perceive leadership broadly to be an attribute of the individual – an individualized and therefore bastardized version of the ancient Greek image of leadership as honourable and heroic, so well represented by Odysseus in Homer's narratives. By contrast, modern approaches begin to see leadership more in relational terms and in the context of followers or with respect to the contingencies that are the medium and outcome of its impact.

Recent leadership as practice approaches are more concerned to locate leadership in the collective organizational practices that are a condition and consequence of any individual action (Raelin, 2016).

Table 8.7 Transformational leaders

• Clear and compelling sense of vision	• Admiration and/or respect from followers	• Ability to communicate and persuade
• Capacity to provide and stimulate		• Engendering of confidence and optimism
• Creativity and innovation	• Clear linking of strategies to vision	

MODERN THINKING ABOUT LEADERSHIP

In modern contingency thinking, leadership is seen as a product of an interaction between a number of variables that form a collective activity comprising diverse elements shared by, or passed among, various people at different times. This is in contrast to understanding leaders as individuals who possess the appropriate traits or display the relevant behaviours. When leadership is conceived of as a (distributed) function that occurs within any group engaged in a task, it is no longer seen as the preserve of a single individual but, rather, may be spread across a number of group members or simply executed as part of a group process. Numerous components of leadership as a function have been suggested (see Table 8.8), many of which bear a marked resemblance to the set of roles ascribed by Mintzberg to managers (see Figure 8.3), except that they are conceived as a property of a group and may therefore be undertaken by one or more individuals at different points in time.

Table 8.8 Elements of the leadership function

• Father-figure	• Opinion shaper	• Planner
• Role model	• Policymaker and implementer	• Anxiety absorber
• Expert	• Arbitrator and mediator	• Figurehead
• Purveyor of rewards and punishments	• Distributor of tasks and responsibilities	• Scapegoat for failure

Source: Adapted by the uuthor from Krech, Crutchfield and Ballachey, 1962.

Situational theories conceive of different elements or aspects of leadership – such as the provision of expertise or the implementation of policy – shifting between individuals over time. Considered in this way, a person who emerges as a leader, and may be identified by the group as their leader, is the one who is perceived by others to perform the most significant of these elements or to be the best exponent of key leadership tasks, the importance of which may itself shift with changing circumstances. In short, leadership needs to reflect the situation in which it finds itself.

According to Adair (1979), the function of leadership, whether undertaken individually or collectively, involves not only the achievement of tasks but also the maintenance of group processes (e.g., building morale, maintaining focus) and addressing the particular 'needs' of group members (e.g., self-esteem). Individuals are understood to exhibit leadership characteristics whenever they take opportunities to practise the skills associated with delivering the elements of the leadership function. This understanding challenges the view that leadership is a manifestation of personality traits possessed by individuals. Instead, it is seen to be an outcome of opportunities, willingness and capacity to master its constituent elements. In this sense, there are no born leaders but more, like Doc in Case Study 8.2, they are considered to develop through an unfolding process of 'mastery'.

Case study 8.2
Cornerville street-corner society

Participant observation Method of research originating in social anthropology where the researcher engages with the subjects of their study by attempting to live like them for some time.

In his classic **participant observation** study of street-corner gangs in Cornerville (a pseudonym – an American slum), Whyte (1943/1993) demonstrated the centrality of leadership and organization regardless of whether the activity has a purpose in relation to work or the formal economy. The study concentrated on one of the gangs and discovered that unemployment, poverty and marginality were no obstacles to a highly organized life based on hanging around with the gang. These gangs were formed on the street where they can be found almost every night of the week. Membership continued well beyond teenage life into adulthood, even after marriage. Doc, the leader of the gang with whom Whyte spent most of his time, was either more proficient in all the activities (e.g., alley bowling, fighting, gambling, womanizing) or at least made to appear so. He would promote those activities where he excelled and discourage those in which he was less skilled. Whyte (ibid., p. 23) found a 'very close correspondence between social position in the gang and bowling performance': bowling had become the main activity of the gang and, more importantly, the vehicle for maintaining, gaining or losing prestige. Several other social psychological regularities or norms were discovered relating to group behaviour. Among these were: the leader spends more money on his followers than they on him; the gang has little collective coherence in the absence of the leader; the leader is more decisive and his decisions are more satisfactory to the group and therefore usually considered 'right'; and he is better known and more respected outside his group than any of his followers, and is expected to represent the interests of the group externally whether in conflict, competition or co-operation (ibid., p. 260). Whyte concludes that a major benefit of his study is to help inform social workers about leadership. Rather than relying on the so-called leading figures in the community – those middle class 'respectable business and professional men' – Whyte recommends that social workers mobilize the informal leaders in street-corner gangs that Cornerville people recognize. Potentially, these leaders could be harnessed to forms of community development – an orientation that has its parallels in the appropriation of informal shop floor behaviour for managerial purposes.

Leadership *style* characterizes differences in how elements of leadership are undertaken. One possibility is for all members of a group to refuse to take responsibility for the leadership function such that no single leader arises – in effect, the style of 'abdication'. Another possibility is for the group or a leader to decide that each member will assume responsibility for all elements of the leadership function. Rather confusingly, this has been described as *laissez-faire,* which implies that each individual is left to 'do their own thing', whereas it is clear that very considerable responsibilities are imposed upon each individual by a leader or actively embraced by all members of a group.

Leaving aside the rather rare and exceptional options of abdication and *laissez-faire,* a basic division in styles of leadership is generally between those that are consultative or participative (widely described as 'democratic'), and others that are imposing and dictatorial (widely called 'authoritarian'). A dictatorial style generally relies exclusively upon personal conviction, the force of personality and the power to favour, or to dispense with, followers. This may be accompanied by giving trusted lieutenants considerable discretion to act in ways that realize the broad direction and goals set by the leader as well as unqualified confidence in the ability of the mass of followers to excel in their work. Churchill, and more especially Hitler, provide examples of what House (1971) terms a 'path-goal theory' of leadership in which the central function of leadership involves identifying a route to the achievement of desired goals but largely omits any detailed specification of how the goals are to be realized. While authoritarian leaders may not always be 'control freaks', they often get by with a minimal degree of co-operation from followers. Unconditional commitment may be the desired outcome but lip service rather than active consent or devotion to the leader may be sufficient to sustain their leadership. An authoritarian style is, however, more vulnerable to disenchantment and rebellion if the leader's grip on power is seen to slip – ironically in Churchill's case by his strategic role in winning the war and in Hitler's case by losing it (see Box 8.7).

Box 8.7
Hitler and churchill: born leaders?

The association of inspiration and direction with leadership explains why Hitler and Churchill are widely identified as leaders. Were Churchill and Hitler born leaders, or did they learn to master key elements of the leadership function? Would they have emerged as leaders at any time or place, or did circumstances 'conspire', as it were, to identify them as popular, and seemingly 'natural', leaders? Especially through their speeches, each articulated a set of beliefs and policies that served to remove doubts and establish resolve in the masses who became their followers. Churchill and Hitler depended upon the co-operation of others – not only for the organization and management of the political and military apparatus they commanded, but also for a continuing belief in their leadership capabilities – something that was greatly tested when war propaganda was unable to conceal defeats and setbacks. In Churchill's case, qualities of leadership that were an inspiration to most of the population during a period of national crisis (i.e., the Second World War) were shown to lack popular appeal and relevant direction during the subsequent period of reconstruction, as evidenced by the rejection of his party at the general election of 1945. Hitler was seen as a charismatic leader but chose to consolidate his power through totalitarian methods intended to scare any doubters into submission. Yet had he not entered political life at a time of economic crisis due to hyperinflation in Germany, his message would probably have secured support only from a fringe of ultra-nationalists and racists. Followers can readily destroy as well as make leaders, since each process is dependent upon the situation or circumstances that render ideas (e.g., fascism) credible or at least supportable, and thereby confer leadership upon their most articulate and persuasive champions.

Thinkpoint 8.11

How would you characterize Margaret's style of leadership at Bar Mar?

A consultative style or mode of leadership necessitates a process of discussion in which followers participate in shaping opinions, making policies and making decisions about the distribution of tasks and responsibilities. In principle, the consultative style harnesses the collective wisdom of the group, rather than assuming that an individual leader possesses a monopoly of truth and good judgement. The consultative style risks paralysis induced by endless discussions resulting in costly delays, procrastination and compromises. Discussion may ensure a degree of harmony, but at the expense of dealing effectively with issues faced by the group. Styles of leadership can be related and contrasted by considering the extent to which group members take responsibility for the leadership function and the extent to which they rely upon a leader to perform this function.

Exercise 8.5

Above we have discussed the various approaches to leadership. Respectively, leadership is seen as consisting of:

- personality traits
- transformational capacities
- functions and styles.

In a seminar or tutorial group divide into three groups, each of which is required to support and defend the merits of one of the three approaches. Each group should elect a spokesperson at the beginning of a discussion in which you seek to develop arguments to defend the approach designated to you. This is a role-play exercise so you do not necessarily have to be actually committed to the approach you are supporting, except for the purpose of this exercise. It will help to support your arguments with examples of leaders from the case studies of Bar Mar and Cornerville, the world of politics, sport, the media, soaps, history or whatever else may help to render your case more convincing. When you return to the whole seminar group, the spokesperson should present the defence after which there will be space for questions and comments from the group as a whole.

LEADERSHIP AND CONTINGENCY

Contingency theories relate the effectiveness of leadership behaviours to the demands and possibilities presented by a specific situation or context. The success of a leader or leadership style is understood to be contingent upon the circumstances that support its effectiveness. Hickson *et al.* (1971) found that the power of a leader increases in direct proportion to their indispensability (difficult to replace) and their ability to manage uncertainty *(see also Chapter 9)*. Other aspects of the situation that are regarded by Fiedler (1967) as influential include the nature of the task, the make-up of the followers including their assessment of the leader, the culture of the group and the formal position occupied by the leader. Fiedler's contingency model of leadership suggests that the effectiveness of a leader depends upon the adoption of a style that is appropriate to (i) the status of the task – is it structured or unstructured?; (ii) leader–member relations – is the leader trusted and respected? and (iii) position power – does the leader occupy a formal position of authority? (See Table 8.9.)

Table 8.9 Fiedler's contingency model of leadership

Style of leadership	Leader–group relations	Task	Position
Authoritarian	Good	Structured	Strong
Authoritarian	Bad	Unstructured	Weak
Participative	Mixed: Not consistently or unambiguously positive or negative		

Source: Fiedler, F. E. (1967) *A Theory of Leadership Effectiveness.* New York: McGraw Hill. Reproduced with permission from F. E. Fiedler.

Fiedler distinguishes between styles of leadership that are more or less participative. A directive style, he contends, is more effective when there is little inconsistency and ambiguity about these three contingencies: they are either highly positive or completely negative. A directive, authoritarian style is said to deliver results in situations where the task is either highly structured or completely unstructured; where the leader is highly respected or totally disparaged; and where there is very strong or very weak position power. Conversely, where there is greater ambiguity or inconsistency in the contingencies – for example, where position power is high and the task is structured but trust in leader–group relations has not been fully established – then a more participative style is conceived to have a better chance of success. In turn, this suggests that for maximum effectiveness, the selection of a leader by an organization or a work group should be made on the basis of the contingencies of the situation. For example, only where there is ambiguity and inconsistency with respect to the three contingencies is it recommended that a person with a participative style be selected.

Thinkpoint 8.12

On what basis is Fiedler's assessment and recommendation of the appropriateness of different leadership styles being made?

A recurrent theme of contingency theories of leadership is the relationship between the leader and the group, and students of follower behaviour take up this aspect. They focus upon the readiness of followers to be led – are they willing, able and/or confident in their leader? Hersey and Blanchard (1993) suggest that the effectiveness of a leadership style depends critically upon its compatibility with followers' preparedness to accept and respond to it.

When followers are unable, unwilling or insecure about the task, then 'telling' by giving strong guidance on tasks is commended as the most effective style. This coincides with the view, sketched earlier, of a leader being more powerful when he or she demonstrates an ability to manage uncertainty (see Chapter 9). At the other end of the continuum of 'follower readiness', 'delegating' is most likely to succeed when followers are able, committed and confident. In between, there are followers who have the ability to follow (e.g., to perform a task) but are unwilling or insufficiently confident to have the task delegated to them, and who therefore require support through 'participating' but need little guidance on the task. Another group in the middle are those with low to moderate readiness who lack the ability to perform a task independently of the leader. Nevertheless, they are willing and (over)confident so that 'selling', in the form of guidance on the task, justifying the instruction and providing support for its accomplishment, is advised (see Exercise 8.6).

Major issues/controversies in this field: Mainstream debates

Contingency theories of leadership, including Fiedler's, are based upon matching a style of leadership to the demands attributed to the current situation – in respect of the task, the relations with the group, the environment and so on. Vroom and Yetton (1973) and Vroom and Jago (1988) develop the contingency model to incorporate a consideration of the future consequences of adopting a particular style – an approach that extends beyond an assessment of its probable effectiveness in achieving a current goal. The choice of leadership style, this theory suggests, should take account of its longer-term effects upon the motivation and commitment of individual employees and/or group members (see Chapter 2), such as the development of competencies and capacities to undertake future tasks. Balanced against this, the theory includes consideration of the time available to address a problem, which may, for example, make a more consultative approach untenable. Different types of problems are conceived to be best addressed with different leadership styles – autocratic, consultative or 'group', the latter being descriptive of a style where the leader acts as a chairperson or facilitator of a group discussion in which the objective is to achieve consensus among its members (see Chapter 4).

Exercise 8.6

What are the key similarities and differences between Fiedler's and Hersey and Blanchard's ideas about leadership?

Table 8.10 Vroom and Jago's (1988) contingency model of leadership style

Type of problem	Leadership style
Principally affecting a single individual: tough time constraints	Autocratic Leader makes decision for subordinate or obtains information from subordinates and provides a solution
Principally affecting a single individual: manager wishes to develop employee	Consultative Problem explored with individual subordinates: decision taken by leader which may reflect influence of subordinates
Principally a group-level problem: tough time constraints	Autocratic Leader makes decision for subordinate or obtains information from subordinates and provides own solution *or* Consultative Problem explored with subordinates as a group, then takes decision
Principally a group-level problem: manager wishes to develop employees' capabilities	Group Problem explored with subordinates, with leader facilitating this exploration to achieve consensus

Source: Reproduced with permission of Victor H. Vroom.

Vroom and Jago's (1988) contingency approach seeks to link particular styles of leadership (revolving around the autocratic–democratic polarity) to different contexts (see Table 8.10). Three kinds of context have been discussed:

1 Where democratic/participatory styles of leadership are presumed appropriate, there is generally uncertainty and ambiguity regarding relations with the led, the task structure and/or the power of the leader. An autocratic style is suited to all other situations, where the dimensions are clear-cut either in a positive or negative direction.
2 Followership studies concentrate more on the relations with the led, simply providing more detail as to the capability, willingness and confidence of followers to carry out tasks independently of the leader. These should inform the selection of the style of leadership.

3 Attention to personal and organizational development extends consideration of the context beyond the present to anticipate the consequences of a style of leadership for the future motivation, commitment, capability and competence of followers.

Contribution and limitations of the mainstream approaches

The mainstream approaches to management and leadership are extremely varied and provide numerous insights. We can summarize our review as follows:

- 'Management' and 'leadership' are often used interchangeably and their meaning changes in accordance with circumstances and fashion. Currently, leadership is enjoying a new lease of life among both practitioners and theorists, which we will examine in the second part of this chapter.
- Management is generally associated with maintaining existing organizational arrangements whereas 'leadership' is more linked to change, innovation and transformation.
- Management can be seen as a discipline of modern society, an organizational function and a privileged social group, whereas leadership is associated with an individual attribute, or a style appropriate to particular contingencies or contexts, that may be extended to characterize a collective function.
- While management is associated with planning, administrative co-ordination and control, leadership is linked with inspiring and motivating people, whether by autocratic or democratic means, to develop and realize their individual and collective capabilities.
- Most modern approaches to management and leadership have drawn on some variant of open systems or contingency theory.

The limitations of the mainstream approaches to management and leadership stem from taking for granted the prevailing form, structure and knowledge of organizations. The sense that mainstream thinking makes of management and leadership tends to assume and reinforce ways of organizing that have developed within this structure, even when they aspire to challenge them.

For example, more participative styles of management and leadership may be prescribed but basic inequalities of earnings are maintained or increased. Hierarchies are preserved even if they are de-layered. Leadership is associated with preserving, or bringing reform to, established forms and structures not with their transformation in any radical sense. Managers are largely unaccountable to their subordinates even if subordinates are 'empowered'. The very term 'transformational' when applied to leadership (or management) is an oxymoron as its intent is to renew or streamline established practices, not to transform them. While democracy in society is trumpeted as a defining feature of modern, civilized societies, democracy in organizations is usually absent from the agenda. Forms of participation and involvement that operate within the framework of prevailing hierarchies, with management at the helm, effectively displace their substantive realization. In short, mainstream thinking implicitly adopts, endorses and legitimizes the values of the status quo and the distribution of material and symbolic (e.g., status) goods that flow from it. It plays upon, rather than addresses the roots of, the insecurities that are engendered by patterns of domination – with regard to gender and ethnicity as well as wealth.

We have noted how modern thinking about management and leadership is inclined to favour an open systems or contingency approach. By conceiving of organization, management and leadership in such terms, the existence and necessity of the 'system' and its subsystems is taken for granted. The challenge is to control or manipulate its elements in ways that achieve existing objectives and priorities even more effectively. Disregarding the presence of inequalities and power in the formation of practice and theory, consensus is assumed, and attention is concentrated on adapting the organization to its environment. The problems with it are numerous. It assumes, for example, that:

- Managers or leaders are rational actors effectively applying their knowledge of the organization and its environment in pursuit of a consensual set of goals, yet knowledge is not only imperfect but often unavailable; behaviour is diverse and unpredictable; and goals are variable and often conflicting between different members of an organization.

- Managers or leaders possess the power to implement their decisions and have them executed by lower hierarchy staff without leakage or even disruption, yet these staff frequently have a very low regard for the competence and integrity of their seniors and often vice versa.
- Managers or leaders are assumed to focus exclusively upon the goals of the organization and not upon their own personal interests in power and identity, or a concern with freedom and/or security that might conflict with such goals.
- Managers or leaders tend to adopt a linear causal understanding wherein one or a small number of determinants of desired behaviour can be discovered. This relies upon sharp boundary distinctions between so-called independent variables (e.g., managers or leaders) and dependent variables (e.g., the managed or led); that is, a natural scientific model is deployed that is of dubious relevance and merit since, unlike material objects, humans live through meaning and interpretation and their behaviour is not the product of 'variables' to which causal power is attributed. Moreover, this presumed knowledge of causal chains ignores any understanding of them as constructions that, in self-fulfilling ways, reflect and reinforce the power, interests, knowledge and identity of those that construct them.
- Managers or leaders need not concern themselves with a whole range of 'environmental', social and other interests and pressures that might conflict with the straightforward preoccupation with the economic goals of performance, productivity and profit.

Critical approach to management and leadership

INTRODUCTION: OVERVIEW OF A CRITICAL APPROACH TO MANAGEMENT AND LEADERSHIP

Critical analysts are sceptical about the assumptions upon which mainstream accounts of management and leadership are based. Major parts of the critical analysis of management have already been covered, so here we will concentrate primarily upon the area of leadership. In any event, as we noted, in doing so, it is relevant to recall the considerable overlap between 'managing' and 'leading', with the term leadership being used to identify the more dynamic and innovative features of management.

The assumptions made in mainstream leadership and management literatures are generally taken-for-granted, and so are not made explicit. Take, for example, the assumption of consensus. Few, if any, mainstream thinkers directly acknowledge that they assume consensus in organizations. They simply proceed as if this is the case. How do we know that? We deduce it from the fact that little attention is given to conflicts; and when conflict is addressed it is analyzed as something pathological or attributed to factors such as 'resistance to change'. The possibility that there might be underlying, endemic conflicts, associated with inequalities of wealth, status or power, is simply not contemplated.

The assessment of critical analysts, in contrast, is that organizations may *appear* to be consensual but this is because managers occupy positions in the hierarchy that enable them to suppress conflict and/or because subordinates have a 'realistic' understanding that compliance or consent is in their own 'best' interests. In other words, the absence of *overt* conflict is often a consequence of relations of *dependence*. Subordinates are usually dependent on managers for a variety of workplace terms and conditions – for example, retaining their jobs, the allocation of tasks and responsibilities, increments in pay, overtime, promotion, future employment references, etc. Given this relative dependence, it is perhaps surprising that there is ever any conflict, especially of the kind that directly challenges management/leadership.

Thinkpoint 8.13

Think of an occasion – at home or university – where conflict has been suppressed; that is where a potential antagonism has not surfaced or been expressed. Does that mean that it does not 'come out' in other ways? Think of examples of how 'buried' conflicts are articulated, more or less consciously, in a covert or subtle manner.

Figure 8.4 'Bullshit Bingo'

Do you keep falling asleep in meetings and seminars? What about those long and boring
conference calls? Here is a way to change all of that!

How to play: Check off each block when you hear these words during a meeting, seminar, or
phone call. When you get five blocks horizontally, vertically, or diagonally, stand up and shout
BULLSHIT!!

Synergy	Strategic fit	Gap analysis	Best practice	Bottom line
Revisit	Bandwidth	Hardball	Out of the loop	Benchmark
Value-added	Proactive	Win-win	Think outside the box	Fast track
Result-driven	Empower [or] Empowerment	Knowledge base	Total quality [or] Quality driven	Touch base
Mindset	Client focus[ed]	Ball park	Game plan	Leverage

The suppression of something does not mean that it is eradicated. Instead, it is driven 'underground' and manifests itself in acts of more or less subtle forms of subversion. Often dissent and opposition are expressed in the form of humour directed at management practices. In 'Bullshit Bingo' (see Figure 8.4), it is the very basis of managerial expertise that is challenged. Management's self-importance – manifest in the obsession with holding meetings that often make little contribution to productive activity – is lampooned by redefining the content of its communications as 'bullshit'. Managers are seen to be slaves to, and mindlessly dependent upon, demonstrating their credentials as managers by puffing themselves up with self-serving platitudes and vacuous catchphrases.

At the very least, 'Bullshit Bingo' offers a form of tension release from the boredom and hypocrisy of routine managerial work where managers themselves often fear to say what they think, deliberately mislead subordinates or are highly selective in what they communicate in order to gain some kind of tactical, competitive advantage. Problems of management are frequently described and diagnosed in terms of 'poor communication'. Yet communication is often poor because 'power games' are being played (i.e., monopolizing information; keeping others in the dark because they 'don't matter'), and other priorities are being pursued.

Critical analysis assumes that conflicts of priority and 'interest' are endemic and deeply engrained, not sporadic or superficial. Forms of humour and gossip frequently are understood to expose the underside of organizational life by articulating feelings of grievance or absurdity. Humour – notably, irony and satire – offers a comparatively subtle and ambiguous way of signalling issues and grievances that are otherwise difficult or dangerous to expose or express. There are difficulties and dangers precisely because relations of dependence make the anticipated sanction or punishment following an overt challenge (in terms of employment prospects or reputation) too great. In effect, there is a climate of fear, often masquerading as one of openness (e.g., the 'open door' policy that no one dare take up) which operates to suppress dissent, and thereby produces the impression that no significant conflict exists (see Chapter 5, Case Study 5.2).

A critical analysis of management and leadership also assumes that manifestations of conflict cannot be adequately explained away in terms of awkward, militant or pathological 'personalities'. Individual differences (see Chapter 3) are not denied, but their 'positive' (e.g., 'Sam(antha) is a brilliant, charismatic leader/manager') or 'negative' (e.g., 'Sam(antha) is an incompetent, indecisive manager/leader') evaluation is related to the particular social situations in which such differences are shaped (socialization) and assessed (organizational setting). From a critical analytical standpoint, Sam(antha) is not essentially 'charismatic' or 'indecisive' but is understood to have developed ways of interacting with other people (i.e., he/she has been socialized) that are characterized in such terms by admirers or detractors. Mainstream thinking often equates such ways of interacting with personality differences. Such thinking is itself a potent way of glossing over social differences and conflicts by attributing them to *essential* personality traits or differences. In doing so, it takes for granted and acts to solidify and sanctify the *particular* circumstances that, in principle, could be changed.

Despite the best efforts of managers to suppress tensions, remove 'troublemakers' and placate dissenters, collective industrial action occasionally erupts as employees withdraw their labour or refuse normal co-operation in attempts to have grievances settled. Or, more frequently, individuals simply offer minimal compliance rather than real consent or, if the option is available, seek employment elsewhere. For employees, the existence of a trade union can provide a degree of legitimacy and some protection against managerial victimization.

One task for the critical researcher is to expose the extent to which an apparent consensus conceals or diverts attention from seething discontent, dissent and disarray that bubbles beneath the surface of organizational serenity. This is to express the point rather colourfully. Yet most of us would recognize that organizations harbour forms of antagonism, resentment and fear that are either unknown to, or are ignored or exploited by, management. Mainstream analysis is, of course, not unaware of imperfections of morale and motivation in the informal system of organizations. Efforts to build 'strong cultures' (see Chapter 10) or 'cohesive teams' (see Chapter 4) are responses to this. But the response is limited to developing 'better' styles of 'professional' management (as designers of effective cultures and teams) that, in principle, remove the sources of disaffection (e.g., by eliminating favouritism, bullying, sexism, racism, etc.). The critic, in contrast, is more likely to interpret conflict as an indication of employees' capacity to challenge, or at least subvert, the imposition of self-serving management control, including its seemingly benign forms (e.g. programmes of 'empowerment') rather than seek instantly to repair or eliminate it.

Thinkpoint 8.14

Think of your experience of working in an organization or simply being a student. How often have you been (or have you noticed others being) polite and co-operative to your (their) 'boss' or your teacher, and thought secretly – what a 'bastard'? Reflect on what made you or others have thoughts that were inconsistent with your (their) actual behaviour. What was their source – were they related to problems concerning managers as people, inadequate leadership, inequality at work, the nature of authority or something else?

Case study 8.3
Strife at the dog and duck

Conflict that is evident in organizations is often a reflection of the inequalities of income, status, hierarchical position and gender, ethnic or other diversities (see Chapters 2 and 7), but this is not always obvious. To illustrate this, we will return to our introductory chapter and the case of Jackie and Christine falling out behind the bar at the Dog and Duck pub. Jackie, a student, is asked by the landlord to act as manager for an evening. This upsets Christine because she has worked at the pub for much longer and regards Jackie as an upstart. In everyday language, Christine feels snubbed. Feelings of injustice and resentment boil over into overt conflict between them.

Someone coming into the pub for the first time that evening who witnessed the dispute between Jackie and Christine may have reasonably concluded that this was a conflict between staff of similar status. Yet, as we know, Christine was angry with Jackie for having been given a temporary management position. Christine felt that her experience and career ambitions in bar work qualified her better for the role. The situation was clearly explosive, just waiting for an 'accident to happen', and the ensuing row could have been anticipated, assuming knowledge of the background. Without this knowledge, it would be easy to describe this, and many other disputes, as just personality conflicts or poor communications (in this case between the landlord and Christine), and therefore relatively trivial. Such descriptions are often favoured in mainstream thinking because they do not represent a threat to the often taken-for-granted presumption of an underlying consensus within organizations. Conflict is represented simply as a clash between individuals that is seemingly unrelated to differences of values, priorities, politics and so on.

Thinkpoint 8.15

Do you think it would have made any difference if Jackie had been Jack or Christine had been Christopher? What if Jackie and Christine had been from very different ethnic backgrounds? Would such differences have been irrelevant, or would they have made the conflict less or more likely, or take a rather different form? Of course, we cannot know. But such questions can encourage us to reflect upon how everyday working relationships are conditioned by wider social contexts, expectations, 'prejudices' and power relations.

What do you think a mainstream management view would be of this conflict, and of the landlord's decision to ask Jackie to manage the pub? Is it possible to act objectively or impartially in such situations?

Case study 8.4
CaseCo and leadership

Here we return to CaseCo (pseudonym) presented briefly earlier in this chapter. At CaseCo, the CEO emphasized the difference between management and leadership in order to highlight what he perceived to be missing (i.e., 'leadership') from his management team. He subscribed to a view of leadership that he had learned on a management course in which leadership was understood to be synonymous with personality traits or qualities, which though possible to improve, are broadly inherited characteristics. Consequently, most attention had to be focused on recruiting 'good' leaders – that is, people who were assessed to have natural talent as leaders.

Some more junior managers whose management training was more recent were highly sceptical of this approach to leadership. They recognized that the trait approach produces an almost endless list of leadership characteristics (e.g., extroversion, vision, initiative), which have little correlation with one another or with 'successful' practice. The trait approach attributes essences to individuals, thus ignoring the social context and the importance of followers in any leadership practice. Being convinced of the correctness of his views, the CEO as the leader of CaseCo was in a position to ignore the views of his subordinates. Fear of contradicting their 'leader' led the junior managers to comply with his views, thereby confirming the CEO's false belief that consensus prevailed. The cartoon here illustrates both the normality and absurdity of claims that difference of pay and status are largely irrelevant because each person has an equally important role to play in ensuring the success of the organization.

Cartoon 8.1   'I didn't mean to jest about your dictatorial leadership style.'

'I didn't mean to jest about your dictatorial leadership style.'

Box 8.8
Blurring any
distinction
between self and
organization

'... more leaders are attempting to bind employees to the corporate ideal, while curtailing forums of debate. They project an image of charismatic leadership, stress a compelling vision, depict their companies as surrogate family and attempt to blur any perceived difference between the interests of managers and non-managers... Such approaches seek to re-engineer the most intimate beliefs of employees, so that they are aligned with whatever the leader deems is helpful to the corporate enterprise. It makes it even less likely that employees will ask awkward questions of their leaders, and so be capable of correcting their inevitable misjudgements. These may constitute fertile conditions for the emergence of other Enrons in the future.' (Tourish and Vatcha, 2005, p. 476).

A critical perspective on leadership

Before he became an academic, Keith Grint (2000) was a senior representative of a trade union. In that capacity, he had been management/leadership practitioner for at least 10 years before he began studying it. After some 14 years of study and having written many books and research articles on leadership, Keith concluded that his understanding had 'decreased in direct proportion to his knowledge' (ibid., p. 1). The more he read, the less he felt he understood. Instead of enriching or extending his insights, the literature was dulling and diffusing them. In this assessment, Grint echoes sentiments that had been expressed almost half a century earlier by Warren Bennis (1959), one of the top researchers in leadership studies. He suggested that 'probably more has been written and less is known about leadership than any other topic in the behavioural sciences' (ibid., p. 259). Having become critical of the mainstream approaches, Grint offers an alternative, constitutive approach. This approach contrasts with the three mainstream approaches – trait, contingent and situational – each of which is understood to have a distinctive identity in relation to whether leadership was *essentially* an individual matter or one that was *essentially* determined by the context (see Figure 8.5).

Figure 8.5 Essentialist and non-essentialist leadership
Source: The Arts of Leadership, K. Grint (2000). © Reproduced by permission of Oxford University Press, Inc.

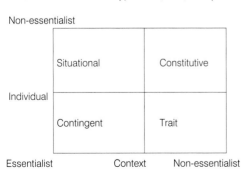

Before discussing these approaches from a critical perspective, the term 'essential' is in need of clarification. In essentialist thinking, it is assumed that the world comprises a series of 'essences', and that the purpose of reflection is to discover the fundamental or universal aspects of whatever is being examined. So, for example, it would seek to identify what is *essential to human nature* as the basis of all human and social life. Take the phrase, or claim, 'it's just human nature'. It is frequently invoked as an explanation of a person's behaviour when nothing more specific comes to mind. It may, for example, be used to excuse a person or an action of which you disapprove, often because they behave in a way that is irresponsible or is seen to exhibit extreme self-interest. The excuse is built into a notion that it is natural, and therefore perfectly normal if not necessarily commendable, to look after yourself first. It is clearly a universal explanation. But it is developed within a particular context. In other words, its plausibility as a universal explanation is context-dependent. It is precisely this dependence that is unacknowledged by such explanations. That is why 'it's just human nature' can appear to be a self-evident truth when, arguably, it is a *claim* that acquires the status of truth only because it resonates with context-specific, deeply ingrained, individualistic and Judaeo-Christian attitudes. Such attitudes are tied up with notions of original sin and Darwinian ideas about the survival of the fittest. They take no account of either the awesome 'openness' of human existence (as the New Testament puts it: the birds have their nests but the son of Man has no place to rest his head); and, relatedly, they disregard the deeply social quality of human development.

Exercise 8.7

The following questions could provide a focus for discussion in a small student group:

- If self-interested behaviour is 'human nature', does it mean that someone who sacrifices their own interests to the interests of others is not human?
- Would it ever be possible to disprove an explanation of behaviour that resorts to the notion of human nature?

Hint: There is always a danger of replacing one essentialism (human nature is 'X') with another essentialism (human nature is 'Y'). Think for example of McGregor's distinction between Theory X and Theory Y conceptions of management. Is there a way of avoiding such essentialist thinking?

Comparing Approaches to Leadership

When we revisit the trait approach in the light of our reflections upon essentialism, we can better see how the context is ignored in favour of a more universal individual 'essence' – a personality or character that is seen to be the foundation of their leadership and/or transformational powers. The trait approach emphasizes selection as most crucial since if you get it wrong at that stage then there is no escape short of dismissing the leader. By contrast, the situational approach perceives the context as essential. It assumes that there are no universal modes or styles of leadership but only ones appropriate to different contexts or situations. The situational approach commends the training and development of leaders by developing and applying the appropriate skills for the specific context in which they lead. It assumes that the characteristics of the context can be pinned or boiled down into their essential features. Managers or leaders 'grow' into the job when they make a competent analysis that discloses the essence of the situation and act accordingly. Wherever an essence is sought – whether it be in the person or in the context – a deterministic stance is implicitly taken. That is, some essential factor – the personality (trait approach) or the environment (situational approach) – is seen to cause or determine leadership.

The contingency approach seeks to combine both the trait and the situational approaches: it considers individual characteristics and the context to be equally important elements of an adequate explanation, and associated technology, of good leadership. Certain types of leaders are appropriate to certain contexts and it is just a matter of matching the two. A major limitation of such mainstream thinking is its reliance on open systems or contingency theory where a number of assumptions go unchallenged. For example, as we noted earlier, a linear conception of causation is favoured where one, or at least a small number, of prime determinants of the object of study can be established. In order to deliver on this model of causation, hard-and-fast distinctions – between say the behaviour of leaders and the led and between the organization and its environment – are sustained so that clear-cut causal relationships can be made between them. So, in contingency approaches, the environment is depicted as the source of uncertainties, the reduction of which determines the effectiveness of leadership. Yet the environment, let alone the uncertainties that it is seen to create, is not a self-evident, transparent or readily accessible entity. Rather, its existence is defined, described or constructed by members of organizations and therefore the uncertainties are not independent of the interests, identities and politics of those that mobilize them as resources in their organizational pursuits. The same point is illustrated in the 'Small Cog' cartoon where the subordinate is encouraged or instructed to think of himself in a distinctive way – not as someone who occupies a small but key part in the bigger machine but, instead, as someone who costs the organization and therefore is a key, 'important' target of cost reduction. Here it is the worker rather than the environment that is being assigned an identity. In this case, the message is intended to concentrate the minds of employees to demonstrate how their production of benefits, or value, is at least equivalent to the costs, or drain, they impose on the organization.

This takes us to a more recent 'constitutive' approach (Putnam et al., 2016)[1] to leadership (see also Knights and Willmott, 1992; Knights and Morgan, 1992), which not only questions the idea of essential leadership qualities or traits but also the idea that the context or environment is a self-evident, readily accessible truth or 'objective' reality. It is important to appreciate how both leadership and the environment are constituted socially through particular definitions of the situation that have more credence when supported by exercises of power. What is seen as a 'good leader', or a description of the context or environment, is conceived to be unavoidably open to interpretation, and any shared view, or 'consensus' about this is not independent of the exercise of power. Crucially, those who fill leadership positions or functions are expected to provide definitions of the context – indeed that is one of the common sense tests of a 'real' leader – and therefore have a greater effect upon others, including others' propensity to accept, in public at least, that their leaders are suited to lead. From this standpoint, 'leadership' is less a matter of matching a style with a context than about 'the management of meaning' (Pfeffer, 1981; Smircich and Morgan, 1982) – of educating potential followers about (the 'real' or 'objective' naming of) the context so that they accept this definition of the situation and therefore, come to identify its author as their leader. The constitutive approach suggests that the very acquisition of positions of leadership involves managing others' definitions of reality, particularly those of potential and existing followers. Gaining the support of followers is often about power and identity even though it is presented in the language of leadership.

If a manager mobilizes resources (e.g., finance, material artefacts or other organizations) and enrols people (e.g., politicians, celebrities or the public), whether unintentionally or purposefully, he or she is likely to assume a leadership position but is also better placed to sustain this position once it is attained (the actor-network perspective discussed in Chapter 12 shares this view). Interpretations of reality tend to be more appealing and convincing when they facilitate people in maintaining their identities or making them feel free, less insecure and more respected (less unequal).

Exercise 8.8

Identify examples of leaders that you know, and examine them in terms of the four approaches discussed above.

What is distinctively critical about the constitutive approach?

So far we have sought to elaborate the distinction between a critical and a mainstream approach. In the process, we confess to having committed one of the sins that critics often direct towards the mainstream. For we have tended to treat complex, diverse and multiple forms of knowledge (of leadership, for example) in a universal fashion as if all studies converged upon the four, readily identifiable conceptions of leadership – trait, situational, contingency and constitutive.

It would be more consistent with our critical thinking to conceive of the division of research on leadership into four types of approach as *itself* constitutive. Like any other schema, it is inviting you to adopt its definition of the situation. It is asking you to make sense of the world in a particular, power-invested, way. Implicitly, it is encouraging you not only to think about leadership in a particular way, but also inviting you to engage in the practices associated with leadership in a different way as a consequence of being subjected to this knowledge. This process of constructing meaning for others, forms part of what Gramsci (1891–1937) called 'organic' intellectual leadership, which is where thinkers do not simply describe social life in accordance with scientific rules, but rather 'express', through the language of culture, the experiences and feelings that others (who do not have the education, time or inclination) are unable to articulate for themselves. Few descriptions are entirely innocent of human intention but the difference between mainstream and critical scholarship is an acknowledgement of the politics of knowledge. Critical scholarship openly offers an alternative to the content and form of intellectual leadership supplied and supported by those who are wedded to the values of the status quo, yet pretend merely to be reporting the 'truth' or doing science independently of ethical/moral and political values.

LEADERSHIP AND ETHICS

Various corporate scandals and disquiet about the trustworthiness and propriety of top corporate leaders, culminating in the global financial crisis of 2008 that disrupted the economies of Western societies for several years, combined with media attention through films such as the *Margin Call* (2012), *The Wolf of Wall Street* (2013) and *The Big Short* (2015) has stimulated interest in the relationship between ethics and leadership. The mainstream response to financial scandals and crises was one of attempting to link conventional studies of leadership with those on business ethics even though the latter is invariably perceived as a competitive, brand-image management tool (see Chapter 15).

A basic assumption of the mainstream is that 'poor leaders' are a primary cause of current scandals and crises and therefore that better leadership will restore confidence. The problem underlying this response is that the continued faith in heroic leaders, whose perceived immense capabilities will enable them to adopt ethical standards to render the corporation socially responsible, is at best, naïve and at worst, a licence to legitimize their traditional practices of outwitting or outmanoeuvering the regulators. However, during the global financial crisis, no one was prosecuted since although everyone in society was convinced of irresponsibility, moral misdemeanours, an overwhelming hubris and a lack of concern for the well-being of society, no laws/rules were actually breached. Consequently it is not clear that social responsibility or complying with the rules can offer any protection against those who pursue economic self-interests independently of any ethical concerns. Some feminists have sought to encourage more embodied engagements with organizational activity as an alternative ethic to either rule compliance or CSR (Pullen and Rhodes, 2014) and as a way of challenging macho masculine modes of leadership (Knights, 2015).

Drawing on the case of the Salomon Brothers (see Box 8.9 below), Sims and Brinkmann (2002) blame the leader John Gutfreund for moulding an organizational culture that resulted in unethical and illegal behaviour by its members. The focus of their research is on the character of Gutfreund, his absolute attention to a short-term business focus, his alleged willingness to cover-up illegal behaviour and the ease with which he allegedly betrayed his mentor in his rise to power.

Treviño *et al.* (2003) are also concerned at the absence of empirical studies of ethical leadership and are critical in the sense that they wish to understand how ethical leadership is 'perceived and attributed to executives' (ibid., p. 7). But their concerns are voiced from within a taken-for-granted, common sense notion of

Salomon Bros had been a highly respected Wall Street investment bank for a century until in the 1990s it was found guilty of rigging the vast US Treasury security market in its favour. Treasury rules forbid any of the primary dealers who buy and resell the bonds and notes issued by the Treasury to take more than 35 per cent of a single issue. The assumption is that if any dealer owns more than that amount, it would be in a position to manipulate prices. By placing bids in other people's names, Salomon, on several occasions throughout the first half of the year, controlled much larger shares of the market – once as much as 57 per cent. The traders responsible for the false bids have been fired and John H. Gutfreund, Salomon's blunt, aggressive chairman, was forced to resign along with a number of other top executives.

Box 8.9
Banking fraud

leadership. They favour an attribution theory approach that seeks to show how the qualities of ethical leadership are defined and attributed to managers by other members of the organization. This may *reveal* the dependence of such attributions on common sense reasoning but it fails to problematize this dependence, as would a critical perspective. A main problem is that it tends to attribute leadership to managers of organizations that are deemed to be conventionally successful, and a lack of leadership to organizations that fail in some way. In other words, if an organization is deemed to be successful in common sense terms, there is a tendency to see it as being 'well led'. You may see parallels here with the mainstream systems approach discussed earlier in the chapter, where parts of an organization were explained in terms of their consequences for, or function in, maintaining its stability. It fails to focus on how the very topic of leadership and methods of researching it are socially constituted or constructed.

FEMINIST SCHOLARSHIP AND LEADERSHIP

Feminist scholars who see organizations as deeply gendered have explored what is meant by the topic of, and research on, leadership as being 'socially constituted' . Sinclair (2005, p. 1), for example, contends that there is a 'close connection between constructs of leadership, traditional assumptions of masculinity and a particular expression of male heterosexual identity' (see also Knights and Tullberg, 2012). The basic idea here is that what we understand as 'leadership' is deeply conditioned by its development over the past several hundred years in societies where men have dominated senior positions of leadership. Indeed, the very identification of only some positions (those generally occupied by males, such as President and CEO) as exhibiting qualities of 'leadership', downplays the possibility of women being leaders in other spheres. This effect is illustrative of how leadership has been socially constituted.

For Sinclair, an alternative way of 'doing leadership' involves an avoidance or renunciation of a 'macho' view of leadership, where the leader feels compelled to be 'hard' and 'controlling' so that respect is based upon fear and blind loyalty rather than a sense of mutual valuation and trust. This 'macho' approach, Sinclair suggests, is often counterproductive in terms of winning the trust and full co-operation of subordinates. It is also damaging, emotionally and spiritually, as well as to the body. The leader is obliged to repress or hide those impulses and aspects of social and bodily identity that are incompatible with being, or at least giving the appearance of being, 'macho'. And, of course, this applies as much, if not more, to women who feel pressured by the dominant expectations of leaders to be tough, combative in their relationships with subordinates. Interestingly, leaders may often be gentle, subtle and even seductive; but it has been suggested that such features are rarely visible in the literature on leadership (Calas and Smirich, 1991). Acknowledging the presence of seduction, for example, can facilitate the development of innovation in leadership theory – something that is evident in Sinclair's theory of leadership and sexuality (2005, Chapter 9) where she explores the varied ways in which sexual identities are brought to leadership.

DOING LEADERSHIP DIFFERENTLY

For men and women in organizations, being different as leaders sometimes means asking what is the purpose of their leadership work. It involves taking a stand for work that is valuable and important, and insisting on doing it in a reflective and compassionate way, not simply capitulating to the imperatives generated by an overpowering boss, truculent client or invented sense of urgency. Leadership of this kind risks the individual being used as a scapegoat, being singled out as an 'odd-ball', 'not a team player', or not 'on board' with the interests of the organization. Yet, in a wider sense, taking such a position is exactly what leadership is often about (Sinclair, 2005, p. x).

Sinclair cautions about the managerial appropriation of elements or trappings of this alternative conception of leadership to 'strengthen the status quo'. She foresees the way in which people, especially men, who are captivated by the idea of '*life as a contest*', may mouth 'the language of care and consultation' in order to sound fashionable and/or advance their careers. This is a manipulative use of the alternative conception of leadership as a weapon for managing a favourable impression so as to secure the status quo and/or pursue self-interest under the guise of transcending it.

More generally, as individuals, managers (men or women) may privately harbour doubts about the moral value and integrity of their actions. But, in order to hold down their jobs and/or meet their family responsibilities, they tell themselves and others, with greater or lesser conviction, that it is necessary to dilute or suspend personal values or their embodied existence as fully human. They are encouraged in this by the tendency of corporate managers to punish those who take issue with their corporate practices, such as 'whistle-blowers' who are regarded as 'disloyal' and risk instant removal.

Exercise 8.9

Can you think of people or occasions that illustrate an alternative form of leadership? Were there 'risks' and how were these dealt with?

LEADERSHIP AND MANAGEMENT DEVELOPMENT

One area in which management and leadership come together is in the sphere of management development where good management is conceived to rely upon the honing of interlinked mindsets. Gosling and Mintzberg (2003, p. 2) suggest a framework of management development that comprises five interventions that are necessary for improving the leadership of managers and the managing of leadership:

- Managing self: the reflective mindset.
- Managing organizations: the analytic mindset.
- Managing context: the worldly mindset.
- Managing relationships: the collaborative mindset.
- Managing change: the action mindset.

The identification of five mindsets emerged mainly through the authors' own practice in developing and delivering management programmes, and it is not intended to be exhaustive. The emphasis upon managing rather than leading is precisely because 'nobody aspires to be a good manager anymore, everybody wants to be a good leader' (ibid., p. 1). Echoing our earlier discussion of how the meanings of management and leadership are differentiated, Gosling and Mintzberg argue that management without leadership is uninspiring and that leadership without management produces a disconnected style. This view of leadership nonetheless is somewhat unconventional as, in their own words, they believe that 'leaders don't *do* most of the things that their organizations get done, they do not even make them get done. Rather they help to establish the structures, conditions, and attitudes through which things get done' (ibid., p. 7, original emphasis). In other words, Gosling and Minzberg are suggesting that leadership comprises those elements of management which are concerned with establishing and enabling ways to get things done – with respect to creating 'structures', nurturing conditions and shaping attitudes. This requires the interlocking of the various mindsets. The action mindset is alert to, and facilitative of, change. In order to develop an effective patterning or structure of activities or to manage change, contexts and relationships are examined analytically. Finally, Gosling and Mintzberg's framework recalls that every intervention by the manager/leader is contingent upon the managing of self, which involves a reflexive mindset capable of reviewing, challenging and developing the other mindsets.

This is a potentially useful way of framing key aspects of activities identified as managing and leading. It locates these activities in a wider context that is attended to by the worldly mindset. It also appreciates that leading and managing in the context of organizations involves collaboration that necessitates the managing of relationships. But perhaps the key question concerns the boundaries of the knowledge that inform this process. Does the 'analytic mindset', for example, encompass the kinds of critical ideas about leadership and management that have been discussed in this and other chapters? To return to Amanda Sinclair's assessment of the boundaries of mainstream thinking about leadership, does the Gosling and Mintzberg framework itself exemplify a rather masculinist, if not macho, approach? We think it does insofar as it is very performative in terms of achieving end results that are often seen as logocentric and linear outputs that can be causally linked to their rational inputs. How far does their reflective mindset stretch – just as far as is thought functional for getting the job done? Or does it allow for the possibility, even if it does not commend it, of reflection resulting in the rejection of mainstream thinking and methods of leading and managing? The framework is an example of how critical thinking can be selectively appropriated to advance more sophisticated mainstream accounts of leadership/management.

To take up the focus of the reflective mindset, it is relevant to acknowledge how many managers are aware or reflective about the pressures and contradictions of their work (Watson, 1994; Clarke et al., 2009). Notably, they detect the tensions between the official, formally stated objectives and policies of their employing organization and the demands and evaluations of them from those immediately above them in the hierarchy. Needless to say, the obvious way to survive and succeed is to pay closest attention to the immediate priorities, expectations and criteria of evaluation applied by superiors (see Jackall, 1988; Dalton, 1959), and to minimize the risk of incurring the emotional and financial penalties of being scapegoated or ostracized for 'rocking the boat' and failing to be a 'team player'. Here is another instance of how conflict is suppressed through self-censorship occasioned by reflection upon the likely consequences of being genuinely open and communicative. Given these dynamics, it is unsurprising that managers frequently feel frustrated and abused by the systems that they supposedly control, and bemoan the difficulties encountered in gaining unequivocal co-operation and commitment from their staff.

Managers routinely experience these contradictions and problems, but mainstream knowledge provides them with very limited resources for making sense of their situation (Alvesson and Willmott, 2011, especially Chapter 8). Management education and development tends to substitute prescription for diagnosis. That is to say, it rushes to provide a bullet point plan of action without first examining in depth the nature of the problem for which the plan is presented as a solution. Such lists may supply managers with some reassuring prescriptions as well as a comforting sense of their own importance. Managers may even believe that, on the basis of this knowledge, they can develop or enhance a mindset for (strategically) analyzing contexts or (operationally) managing change. Insofar as mainstream thinking marginalizes or trivializes discussion of the complex politics of managerial and leadership work, however, the consumers of mainstream knowledge are denied access to critical thinking that, arguably, would enable them to make more incisive sense of their predicament. In particular, it would challenge the tendency to diagnose difficulties in terms of personal failings (for which attendance at management development seminars is often the recommended solution), and place in doubt any inclination to address these difficulties by redoubling their efforts (e.g., by becoming even more calculating or macho). In general, management development courses that are intended to improve managerial or leadership skills shy away from diagnosing and addressing the conditions that impede their development and application. Their contents may be plausible enough in principle, but within a couple of weeks of taking the course, the pressures of work frustrate or overwhelm any good intentions to put them into practice.

Managers find themselves juggling competing demands for resources (e.g., jobs) and recognition – demands that come as much from other managers as from their subordinates. In mainstream thinking, this is interpreted as inter-group politics as if such conflicts are unrelated to deeper social divisions, which include those of gender and ethnicity as well as those between employers and employees and managers and workers. It makes *ideological* sense to exclude from critical scrutiny the mainstream view that managerial authority is firmly founded upon objective expertise; and to ignore how this expertise is compromised by a concern to maintain the status quo and to preserve the distribution of privileges associated with it, including the lack of accountability of the managers to the managed. In this way, management is sanitized as it is distanced from the political conditions of its own formation and development (see Chapter 7).

Case study 8.5
In search of critical reflection

Tony Watson (1994) studied a group of senior managers. Following interviews with their new Managing Director, Paul Syston, these managers suspected that Syston had been hired as a hatchet man and feared for their jobs. In principle, such unsettling situations can stimulate a process of reflection on the conditions that make such episodes and responses possible. The managers might have reflected upon the rationality of an economic system that results in its participants, even its more privileged members, feeling deeply mistrustful and threatened. However, for this process of reflection to develop, there must at the very least be access to a (critical) theory that provides an interpretation of such episodes which goes beyond the personalities involved and the probable consequences for the individuals concerned, significant as they may be (see Willmott, 1997). Given their lack of access to such knowledge, it is understandable that the managers concerned were exclusively preoccupied with discussing Syston's motives, his personal style and inclinations, and were uninterested in analyzing the conditions that make it possible for a boss to treat subordinates in a distant, intimidating manner. Had they avoided personalizing the problem – by overcoming their preoccupation with Syston's distant personal style or his appearance as 'a bit of a miserable sod' (Watson, 1994, p. 103) – they might have reflected on how the hierarchical relationship between managing directors and senior managers as well as between managers and their subordinates tends to produce such disorientating and demoralizing encounters.

Syston's coolness might be read as the nervousness or defensiveness of an outsider who is brought in by his own superiors, perhaps against his own preferences. In this light, Syston's distant, non-communicative style can be interpreted as symptomatic of how the wider system of employment relationships is organized. By declining to enter into any kind of personal relationship with his senior managers, Syston minimized his moral relationship to them. It was probably this impersonal distance, above all else, that made the senior managers anxious as they experienced Syston as a cold fish and a closed book; and they anticipated that they would encounter great difficulty in exerting any personal influence over such a 'miserable sod'. The outcome of this anxiety was inaction, rationalized by the comforting idea that perhaps Syston would be willing to listen to them and therefore that they would 'wait and see' rather than, say, resolve collectively to defend and develop more open and democratic processes of corporate governance where, in principle, those occupying positions of authority, such as Syston, would be under much greater pressure from below to communicate the plans of the company, including any possible job losses.

THE PREROGATIVE AND POLITICS OF MANAGEMENT

These observations call into question the legitimacy of managerial prerogative – that is, the right of management alone to manage, to make the key decisions so that all other stakeholders, including employees, have no voice in decision-making processes. In the mainstream literature, Child (1984, pp. 15–16) offers the following assessment when commenting upon the issue of managerial prerogative. Problems arise, he suggests, when the way that the organization is structured 'becomes a victim of politics [because] it does not reflect political forces within the organization'. The implication is that politics are seen to be present *only* when the established political forces are disrupted – for example, when managerial prerogative is challenged or undermined.

An unfortunate consequence of this narrow sense of politics – where it is conceived as pathological with regard to the status quo – is that any structural design, however oppressive or coercive, is understood to be legitimate as long as it does not exhibit (or successfully suppresses) 'politics'. Such accounts of management soft-peddle on any sustained critical scrutiny of the conditions and consequences of management theory and practice. An image of the manager as a dispassionate technocrat is preserved. There is a failure to register how managerial work is politically charged on a continuous basis because, in capitalist work organizations at least, managers are *socially* distanced from, and are largely unaccountable to, those whom they manage, even when they succeed in deploying their charm and skills of communication to encourage a strong identification of employees with what are conceived as the shared goals of the corporation.

Acting as dispassionate technocrats does not, however, protect managers from the vulnerabilities of their position. The logic of neutrality 'demands' that managerial work be subjected to the same rationalizing processes that it has visited upon less powerful groups. Notably, employee involvement and corporate culture programmes promote the internalization of supervisory responsibilities among multi-skilled, self-disciplined operatives, and thus 'flatten' the organization by reducing the number of levels and ranks among supervisory staff and middle management (see Chapters 11 and 14). Middle and junior management are increasingly the targets of de-layering in 'lean', 're-engineered' organizations (Willmott, 2012). When they endorse technocratic ideology, they are not well prepared to make sense of, let alone resist, the contradictory operation of dominant 'logics' that pose a threat to their very existence. As employees, managers too are expendable. Managers, as Anthony (1977, p. 310) has observed, are likely to find themselves being treated as 'the unwitting victims of reorganization' as they are transferred, trained or dismissed at the behest of more senior managers who frequently employ consultants (arch-technocrats) to guide and/or justify their decisions. Like other employees, they find themselves subjected to the indignities of being 'regarded as human resources, shuffled and distributed by specialists in management development and planning' (ibid). Increasingly, managers are the victims and not just the perpetrators of a rationality that inhibits reflection upon, and transformation of, a design and structure of organization that impedes efforts to develop more ethically defensible and morally sound forms of management theory and practice.

We now turn to a small selection of empirical case studies that reflect a critical approach to understanding management and leadership.

Selection of important studies within the critical approach

DOING MANAGERIAL WORK

In the following extract from Theo Nichols and Huw Beynon's (1977) study of an ICI plant, Colin Brown, a comparatively young and inexperienced manager describes how he uses a case of poor timekeeping to manage his relationship with a shop steward:

> Every man is born to do something and my function in life is to manage. I think this is a problem that most managers have failed to get to grips with. Now take an example. As far as I can see, any man who takes on the job of shop steward wants his ego boosting. But you've got to boost his ego in the proper manner. Now, if I get a bit of trouble – now take an example, perhaps of a serious case of a man who has been perpetually late. Now, I'm the manager, and it's my function to manage. It's my function to discipline this particular man. But I have to deal with the steward. So, what do I do? I take the shop steward aside and tell him that in half an hour's time this man Smith is going to walk into this room. That I'm going to stamp and bang the table and tell him that I'm going to put him out on the road with a caution. Then I'll say to the shop steward, 'And what you can do will be to intervene at this time. Make a case for the man. And we'll agree to let the man off.' Now the man comes in and I bang the table and the steward says 'Come on, Mr Brown. Couldn't you give him one more chance?' I relent. The shop steward gets out of the meeting and says to him 'I've got you off this bloody time but don't expect me to do it again.' You see the shop steward gets his ego boosted. He gets what he wants and I get what I want. That's what good management is about. (ibid, p. 122)

Colin Brown begins by employing the notion that everyone is born to do something, and that his predetermined mission, for which he is naturally fitted, is to manage. This (essentialist) view includes the understanding that in any organization there will be a separation between managers (who are born to manage or trained to be managers) and those who are managed. It is this inevitable fact, Brown suggests, that most managers have 'failed to get to grips with'. Brown's belief in the division between managers and managed within the natural order of things is also reflected in his view that shop stewards aspire to quasi-managerial positions because they have a need to get their egos boosted. This, Brown observes, presents the manager with a challenge: to boost the steward's ego in a way that is 'proper' for the effective execution of the management function. The notion of 'proper' reflects Brown's view that good management is about the calculated contribution and negotiation of situations in ways that produce the maximum benefit for the minimum cost.

It is views like this that enable Brown to make sense of, and to organize, his work. They underpin and are supported by his skilful management of the interaction with the steward and Smith, the poor timekeeper. He takes the steward aside in order to rehearse his performance and generally stage-manages the disciplinary scene. Brown makes the most of his apparent capacity to put Smith 'out on the road': he identifies a low-cost opportunity to reinforce the relationship of domination over the steward. Brown stage-manages the situation so that, in the process of getting his ego boosted, the steward becomes both incorporated into the management process and indebted to Brown for enabling him to play out his (managerially defined) role as shop steward. And at the same time, Brown enjoys the game that demonstrates to himself as well as to others how he can move these pieces around the board.

On this occasion, the steward seemingly accepts the right of the manager to discipline Smith, and Brown 'recognizes', and indeed exploits, the right of the steward to make out a case for his union member. The positive sanction of the ego boost is used by Brown to ensure that the steward follows his script to the letter, and with gratitude. As long as it works – and this depends appreciably upon the interpretation(s) that the steward invokes to make sense of the situation – the asymmetrical relationship of power between the manager and the steward is hegemonically maintained and concealed in the very process of its reproduction.

Thinkpoint 8.16

What gives Colin Brown the right to discipline Smith? Why might managers find it useful to deal with a unionized workforce?

LEADERSHIP PROCESSES IN A FINANCIAL SERVICES COMPANY

This study (Knights and Willmott, 1992) took place in the early 1990s when the UK financial services industry was experiencing a revolution in its markets due to major regulatory changes. This resulted in the CEO at Pensco (pseudonym) seeking to change the leadership style of his senior management team. In writing up this study, we were concerned to step outside of the orthodox paradigm, where the objective was to identify effective leadership in terms of specific traits, styles or contextual factors. Instead we observed senior executives in board meetings seeking to construct their own reality but often having their reality constructed for them by the CEO. We drew on different analytical frameworks to examine leadership practice as a lived-experience but one that is embedded in the CEO's construction of reality. To sustain this reality the CEO stigmatized any signs of divergence as evidence of individual incompetence, if not disloyalty. The CEO made effective use of his structural position at the apex of the hierarchy to assert his definition of the situation and to undermine the identity of anyone who sought to challenge it. Take the following extract from a board meeting where the Assistant General Manager of Customer Services (CS) challenges the CEO:

> CS: 'I think the point that I would like to make is that I think that one needs to distinguish between direction, which is clearly your prerogative and the more detailed decision-making, and I've felt that there's been a tendency to move down to a more detailed decision-making ...'
>
> CEO: 'Oh, certainly, I think the idea of being in the City office and taking everything that is going just isn't on. Not with me and my temperament. I intend to be right there and I will stay there as long as I find, taking New Business as an example, that there have been "hot line" cases for two and half weeks and they still haven't left the office. That sort of thing will just drive me mad. And if anybody wants to get rid of me on jobs like that, there's a simple answer: don't let me see ...'

In this transcript, the CS finds himself reprimanded for his rather mild attempt to persuade the CEO to focus less on the detail and more on the bigger picture of overall 'direction'. In response, the CEO picks on precisely a weakness in the area that the CS is responsible for – processing New Business so that clients have their policies speedily. He argues afterwards that while he is prepared to listen to those who think he is interfering too much (yet clearly he was not prepared to listen to the CS), 'My interests are quite calculated. They're not random.' But there is a broader context to the CEO's interventions, which is his concern to ensure decision-making is more sensitive and responsive to its strategic significance for the company's competitive position. That is why he is unwilling to tolerate New Business taking more than two and a half weeks to process a policy.

Mainstream analyses of traits, styles or the characteristics of followers have proven less than informative since they fail to capture the lived experience and the politico-economic and cultural contexts of 'management' and 'leadership' as a practical accomplishment. A more critical approach is less concerned with providing technical prescriptions than highlighting some of the hidden processes to show how leadership is accomplished in daily encounters such as the brief excerpt illustrated above.

'MAKING OUT'

We examined in Chapter 7 the ways in which productivity targets and bonus schemes were transformed by shop floor engineering workers into a competitive game whereby their function as a form of management control was obscured (Burawoy, 1979). Management designed the bonus scheme with its targets and rewards for achieving them and did not anticipate how it could provide a framework for a game called 'making out':

> 'Making out' can be seen 'as comprising a sequence of stages – of encounters between machine operators and the social or nonsocial objects that regulate the conditions of work. The rules of making out are experienced as a set of externally imposed relationships. The art of making out is to manipulate those relationships with the purpose of advancing as quickly as possible from one stage to the next' ... 'The games workers play are ... played within limits defined by minimum wages and acceptable profit margins. Management, at least at the lower levels, actively participates not only in the organization of the game but in the enforcement of its rules' (Burawoy, 1985, p. 80). Much of the stimulus to engage in such games 'derives from the inexorable coercion of coming to work, and subordination to the dictates of the labour process once there' (ibid, p. 81). In short, turning work into a game relieves workers of the numbing routine and the indignity of subordination; it almost becomes fun. It is also what best accounts for the huge amount of humour and practical joking that occur in factories. (Collinson, 1992)

Such game-playing displaces the need for managers as leaders because the workforce led itself – there is a kind of collective self-discipline that removes any necessity for management or leaders to intervene. According to Burawoy, the significance of creating a game out of the labour process extends well beyond the particularities of 'making out': 'The very activity of playing a game generates consent with respect to its rules' (Burawoy, 1979, p. 80). Management no longer needs to be visible as leaders, or as the embodied manifestation of control and direction for the workforce. Involvement in the competitive game of achieving targets and bonuses means that workers manage themselves, thus removing what the classical writer Mary Parker Follett (see page 305) saw as the greatest vulnerability of managers – having to tell employees what to do. The case study demonstrates how the 'trick' of management or leadership is to dissolve into the background as those whom it seeks to manage are enabled to become self-managing in ways that more adequately realize management's priorities.

Gideon Kunda's (1991) study of 'Engineering Culture' shows how highly educated employees can become self-disciplining. There was a comprehensive system of 'normative control' wherein employees were symbolically entrapped within the reality defined by management in terms of the corporate interests (ibid., pp. 219–20). Management recognized the importance of identity for employees; they sought to make the organization more of a community, allowing individual concerns to be addressed. Management and leadership were focused on managing identity through sustaining a strong organizational culture (see Chapter 10). However, Kunda finds that employees remain fairly ambivalent and relate to corporate efforts to involve an internalization of company values with some irony and symbolic distance. But, of course, such 'distancing' can be a safety valve or a means of boosting the egos of staff who consider themselves smart enough to see through, and poke fun at, the corporate culture. The generation of a corporate culture that seeks to secure the commitment and loyalty of employees through appropriating their identities can, argues Kunda (ibid., p. 222), also create the very conditions of its own dilution. That is to say, by providing the conditions through which employees generate a sense of community, such solidarity can in principle be turned against the corporation and management interests just as easily as in support of them.

Contributions and limitations to thinking about the field

CONTRIBUTIONS

Critical thinking is concerned to link larger social and political issues with the theory and practice of managing, leading and organizing. It also focuses more directly on human, political and process dimensions of management and leadership. To the extent that the mainstream recognizes these aspects of life in organizations, the human, political and process dimensions of organizations are domesticated by treating them as an informal system to be manipulated to secure more effective management control. Or, if this proves too difficult or costly, these dimensions are viewed as an aberration to be eradicated. By contrast, critical studies regard human and political processes as integral to the 'lived reality' of organizations and view attempts to eradicate them as self-defeating.

Critical analysis of management and leadership may also provide practitioners with insights into how management and leadership are possible since it is only through their acceptance as legitimate activities by the managed and the led that they can be in the least bit effective. In particular it:

- Gives close consideration to the political and processual character of (practices that are identified as) 'management' and 'leadership'.
- Applies a number of key concepts, including identity, inequality, insecurity and freedom to explore management and leadership as problematical *social* phenomena rather than taking them as self-evident objects of examination and improvement.
- Gives attention to the historical formation of management and the way leadership involves the management of meaning, including the meaning of management.
- Moves away from knowledge of management as assuming the adequacy of common sense thinking and the legitimacy of the status quo.
- Invites a more sceptical assessment of the claims made in the name of management and leadership and thereby opens up a space for different notions of what they could mean.

In mainstream thinking, 'management' and 'leadership' tend to be widely viewed as unquestionably valuable and therefore desirable. Leadership, in particular, has a very seductive appeal. Each is assumed to be something that is obviously 'needed' and, in principle, easily identified and improved. Books and courses on leadership instantly attract attention and gain a large audience. Critical analysis contributes to stripping away the gloss and hype.

In this chapter we have concentrated on issues less connected with productivity, performance or profitability than is usual in the mainstream. Critical approaches, we believe, can provide managers and leaders with knowledge and insights that are excluded or diluted in mainstream thinking. This is particularly relevant when there is a proliferation of stakeholders making demands on organizations. Organizations exist within society and increasingly managers find themselves harried by predatory competitors, let down by unreliable suppliers, rebuffed by discriminating customers and deserted by footloose staff, not to mention pressured by fund managers who demand the impossible of 'above average' financial performance from all companies. A parallel picture applies to public and not-for-profit sector managers who are under relentless pressure to introduce changes that promise to produce more for less. Today, managers probably have less discretion to pursue a narrow range of interests, especially as the media will expose any management that is discovered or deemed to behave dangerously or without due care and attention. Many organizations are caught up in increasingly global relations (see Chapter 13) where an apparently insignificant local action can have massive worldwide repercussions, much like a whisper turning ultimately into a hurricane (e.g., the Global Financial Crisis, 2008[2]; the News International hacking scandal of 2012[3] or the manipulation of Libor foreign exchange rates 2009–2015[4]). This goes for academic analyses every bit as much as the interventions of practitioners, since actions and words are always affecting the actions of others and this can multiply into global proportions.

While we cannot ultimately control for the unintended consequences of our actions, we can endeavour to think ethically and to be as responsible as possible for what we say and do. It is clear from critical research that organizations are much more complex than the mainstream literature, in its search for 'quick fixes' or simple causal patterns, presumes. Understanding, for example, what part identity plays in managers' and employees' lives, or how some level of insecurity can be productive but becomes incapacitating if excessive, is of greater value than fantasies about perfect leadership or profound management. While the direct relationship between theory and practice or ideas and their adoption is not always obvious, academic research and writing, indirectly and perhaps quite slowly, filters into the consciousness of those we study. At the time of writing, there has been a fashion for leadership, and this is why we have sought to question and counter any tendency for management to become neglected. A critical approach tends to foster scepticism about panaceas or fashions, which is no less relevant to the fashionable advocacy of 'leadership' than it is to the longer established preferences for 'one best way' approaches to management, such as Theories X, Y and Z (see Chapter 7).

LIMITATIONS

One of the strengths of a critical approach is that it is both self-reflexive and reflexive about broader relations both internal and external to organizations. It follows that it is self-critical about critical approaches as well as the mainstream, both in terms of the value of our theory and its implications for practice. We identify the following limitations of critical approaches, which are often excessively centred on managing people and may, as a consequence:

- Neglect the global nature of capitalism.
- Neglect the domination of financial power.
- Act in a theoretical and idealistic rather than practical and applied/pragmatic manner.

Insofar as it compensates for the domination of concerns with productivity, performance and profitability in the mainstream, one version of the critical approach is its rather exclusive concern with issues of managing people or, to be more accurate, managing relations between people. More caution must be taken in assuming that relations can be managed or controlled since that is rarely the case. Managing or leading is about facilitating the conditions that enable people to manage their own relations in ways that benefit one another and ultimately the productive power of an organization, but in ways that are responsible and ethical for others (e.g., customers, the public, environmentalists, the developing world, minorities or government) who are not direct stakeholders.

Of course, the focus of this chapter on management and leadership necessarily means that we cannot avoid a strong focus on the human dimension as it is impossible to manage and lead without inspiring, engaging or driving human beings to pursue their tasks creatively, collaboratively and competitively. That said, the human dimension outside of organizations might lead us to focus on the broader structures of power such as global capitalism, international regulation and finance capital, especially given the success of recent protests about global capitalism and demands for global justice that have captured media attention. It is interesting to note how radical movements have made as much use of global telecommunications as have the corporations and the international institutions that they seek to criticize for their exploitation of developing countries, labour and the environment. Not only are the global corporations and the finance capital that sustains them exploitative of the comparatively weak, but also they tend to dominate other organizations, especially suppliers and distributors. Typical examples have been the way that supermarket chains in Western economies have forced prices down for suppliers and not always passed these on to their retail customers.

Finally, despite what has been claimed above regarding the indirect, and often unintended, benefits of critical analyses to practitioners, much of it remains abstract, idealistic, and over-theoretical. For example, many critical theorists are prone to draw on esoteric theories drawn from philosophy, partly perhaps to display their intellectual credentials and scholarly credibility. Whereas the mainstream justifies itself on claims to advancing a science of behaviour or make appeals to pragmatism and expediency, the critics seek a philosophical self-justification that aspires to disrupt and radically change the status quo rather than to protest and sustain it.

Conclusion

Theories of 'leadership', it is believed, enable us to identify 'leaders' and perhaps train them and others to become better leaders. For many practitioners and for mainstream theorists of leadership, this way of understanding leadership makes good sense. The challenge is to develop or identify a way of conceptualizing and studying leadership (or management) that detects its existence and, if possible, enhances it. This process of detection and prescription necessitates developing a view, concept, or *theory*, of leadership (or management) that accurately reflects the realities of leadership 'out there'.

Can 'leadership' be understood in another way? Attempting to do so is not easy as it necessitates some bracketing or suspension of belief in common sense ways, or habits, of thinking. How else might 'leadership' be understood, if not as an effort to capture and upgrade the realities that it aspires to reflect? To develop a different understanding requires the questioning and abandoning of the assumption of a neat *separation* between, on the one side, thought (or theory) and, on the other side, the reality (or practices) that concepts of organization, etc. are assumed to reflect, more or less adequately. Challenging this assumption is necessary because it underpins established thinking, and knowledge about organization, management and leadership.

Rarely do we find organizations, other than families and friendship groups, not organized through a division of labour in which managers and leaders are in the senior hierarchical ranks enjoying the power to allocate scarce rewards and resources (e.g., wages, bonuses, promotions, status, etc.). In addition, these managers and leaders enjoy several of their own material (economic) and symbolic (status) privileges associated with their position. We live in a hierarchical and competitive society that is grounded in an ethic of success and achievement. In Chapter 5 the ideology of equal opportunity was critically challenged as providing legitimacy to existing inequalities. In this chapter, we have focused more on the difficulties that managers and leaders have in securing the consent or compliance of employees that are partly a result of major inequalities. While the mainstream takes this consent and compliance as unproblematic, the critical literature has sought to demonstrate how consent may be secured by management appearing *not* to manage and lead. The extent to which employees are routinely coerced and controlled is then obscured. Sometimes this occurs accidentally as when employees become preoccupied with achieving their bonuses as a competitive game; at other times, managers foster and facilitate forms of employee collective and individual self-discipline as the most effective managerial and leadership strategy. Conditions are created in which subordinates find their work sufficiently meaningful for the sense they have of themselves (i.e., their identity and associated aspirations and responsibilities). In effect, the institutionalization of such meaning engenders a self-disciplined commitment to fulfilling their tasks in ways that displace feelings of subjugation and grievances associated with exploitation.

Management and leadership are discussed in mainstream texts predominantly through the lens of a systems model where the parts of an organization are seen as similar to the parts of a body or a machine and/or through individualistic conceptions of the leader who is heroic, possesses appropriate personality traits, is constrained by the situation, or adapts to contingent factors. The organic or mechanical analogy largely remains unquestioned in the mainstream despite it being known how organizations are populated by human beings who think for themselves, interpret their experiences and may challenge or contest, just as well as collaborate and comply with, the demands that leaders make of them. Similarly, the way in which the contexts and attributions of leadership are constituted through relations of power and knowledge is not considered by the mainstream. Of course, critical ways of understanding management and leadership completely undermine any possibility of a 'one best way' of 'managing' or 'leading'. Management and leadership are terms used to frame untidy and unpredictable activities within uncertain and continually changing circumstances. By focusing on power, knowledge, identity, insecurity, freedom and inequality, we are continually confronted by their precarious and unpredictable contexts.

The critical approach does not follow the mainstream in legitimizing the status quo or providing managers with ready-made solutions that are intended to make organizations more efficient or profitable. This is what throughout this book we have called a narrow managerialism in the approach to the study and practice of organizing production. Rather, the critical analyst incorporates into the study of organization, management and leadership consideration of much broader issues in society such as equality, justice and freedom. This extends to an examination of the extent to which managers, leaders and their work organizations contribute to, or constrain and deflect attention from, such ideals. It also has to be said that even though it is not their direct intention, critical studies of organization can be beneficial to management in providing alternative insights and visions that would be unlikely to arise from the mainstream. Indeed, an unintended consequence of critical work may be that it helps managers pursue their performance and/or profit objectives more effectively than the mainstream, if only because the examination of issues – from work processes to their corporate governance – provides managers with a broader and fresher perspective. In turn, this perspective may enable them to develop innovative approaches and/or avoid self-defeating methods of management control. Our hope, of course, is that it may enable managers to think beyond current conventional wisdoms in ways that directly address and help to overcome needless sufferings associated with the social divisiveness and ecological destruction that is perpetrated and legitimized by mainstream managerial work.

Discussion questions

1 How do managers and leaders make a difference to organizations?

2 Are the main assumptions underlying a mainstream approach to management and leadership valid?

3 Is management likely to be effective in the absence of leadership, and vice versa?

4 What are some of the contingencies that managers and leaders have to consider in carrying out their work?

5 What are the main differences between a classical and an open systems approach to organizational design and structure?

6 What does a critical view of management and leadership add to our understanding of organizations?

Further reading

Empirical studies

Burawoy, M. (1979) *The Manufacture of Consent,* Chicago, IL: Chicago University Press.

Burns, T. and Stalker, G. (1961) *The Management of Innovation,* Oxford: Oxford University Press.

Collinson, D. (1992) *Managing the Shopfloor,* Berlin: de Gruyter.

Kanter, R. M. (1977/1993) *Men and Women of the Corporation,* New York: Basic Books.

Kidder, T. (1981) *The Soul of the New Machine,* Harmondsworth: Penguin.

Knights, D. and McCabe, D. (2003) *Organization and Innovation: Gurus Schemes and American Dreams,* Milton Keynes: Open University Press/McGraw Hill.

Kondo, D. (1990) *Crafting Selves: Power, Gender and Discourses of Identity in a Japanese Workplace,* Chicago, IL: University of Chicago Press.

Kunda, G. (1991) *Engineering Culture,* Philadelphia, PA: Temple University Press.

Annotated readings

Yukl, G. (2002) *Leadership in Organizations,* Upper Saddle River, NJ: Prentice Hall.

Presents a comprehensive review of mainstream approaches to leadership in organizations. Also includes a chapter on the nature of managerial work and a final chapter that overviews a number of 'biases' and 'controversies' in the field. For students who want to gain a close understanding of what 'mainstream analysis' looks like, this is to be strongly recommended.

Grint, K. (2005) *Leadership: Limits and Possibilities,* London: Palgrave.

A text that takes a more critical approach to the claims made by theories of leadership.

Sinclair, A. (2005) *Doing Leadership Differently,* Melbourne: Melbourne University Press.

Takes an explicitly feminist line on leadership. Connects with mainstream preoccupations but addresses them in a more critical way. Provides something of a bridge between mainstream and critical approaches. Written in a personal and engaging manner.

Alvesson, M. and Willmott, H. C. (1996) *Making Sense of Management,* London: Sage.

Reviews critical contributions to the study of management including its specialist areas of activity such as marketing and accounting. Illustrates how critical analysis can be applied to develop an alternative way of making sense of the development of management.

Anthony, P. (1986) *The Foundations of Management,* London: Tavistock.

An accessible and thoughtful reflection upon the basis of management's claim or prerogative to manage. Pays close attention to the morality of management.

Parker, M. (2002) *Against Management,* Oxford: Polity Press.

An entertaining polemic that draws together the numerous strands of criticism that can be levelled against management. Includes a critique of 'critical management'.

More general reading

Academy of Management Executive (2003) 'Retrospective: The practice of management', 7(3): 7–23.

Ackroyd, S. and Thompson, P. (1999) *Organizational Misbehaviour,* London: Sage.

Bryman, A. (1999) 'Leadership in organizations', in S. R. Clegg, C. Hardy and W. R. Nord (eds) *Managing Organizations,* London: Sage.

Burnham, J. (1941) *The Managerial Revolution,* Harmondsworth: Penguin.

Casey, C. (1995) *Work, Self and Society: After Industrialism,* London and New York: Routledge.

Fulop, L. and Stephen Linstead, S. (eds) (1999) *Management: A Critical Text,* London: Macmillan Business.

Hales, C. (1993) *Managing Through Organization,* Routledge: London.

Harding, N. (2003) *The Social Construction of Management: Texts and Identities,* London: Routledge.

Heterick, R. C. (1996) *Getting Organized,* Sequence: 31(2) net.educause.edu/apps/er/review/reviewArticles/31260. html Consulted 6.8.11.

Jackson, N. and Carter, P. (2000) *Rethinking Organizational Behaviour,* London: Financial Times/Prentice Hall.

Knights, D. and Morgan, G. (1992) 'Leadership and corporate strategy: Toward a critical analysis', *Leadership Quarterly,* 3(3): 171–190.

Pollard, S. (1965) *The Genesis of Modern Management,* London: Edward Arnold.

Rhodes, C. (2002) 'Coffee and the business of pleasure: The case of Harbucks v. Mr Tweek', *Culture and Organization,* 8(4): 293–306.

Shorter, J. (1992) 'The manager as a practical author: Conversations for action', in J. Shotter (ed.) *Conversational Realities: Constructing Life Through Language,* London: Sage.

Willmott, H. C. (1984) 'Images and ideals of managerial work', *Journal of Management Studies,* 21(3): 349–368.

References

Adair, J. (1979) *Action-Centred Leadership,* Aldershot: Gower.

Alvesson, M. and Willmott, H. C. (2011) *Making Sense of Management,* London: Sage.

Anthony, P. (1977) *The Ideology of Work,* London: Tavistock.

Barnard, C. (1936) *The Functions of the Executive,* Cambridge, MA: Harvard University Press.

Bass, B. (1985) *Leadership and Performance: Beyond Expectations,* New York: Free Press.

Bennis, W. G. (1959) 'Leadership theory and administrative behaviour: The problem of authority', *Administrative Science Quarterly,* 2: 42–48.

Blake, R. R. and McCanse, A. A. (1991) *Leadership Dilemmas: Grid Solutions,* Houston, TX: Gulf Publishing.

Blake, R. R. and Mouton, J. S. (1964) *The Managerial Grid,* Houston, TX: Gulf Publishing.

Burawoy, M. (1979) *The Manufacture of Consent,* Chicago, IL: Chicago University Press.

Burawoy, M. (1985) *The Politics of Production,* London: Verso.

Burns, J. M. (1978) *Leadership,* New York: Harper & Row.

Calas, M. and Smircich, L. (1991) 'Voicing seduction to silence leadership', *Organization Studies,* 12(4): 567–602.

Chandler, A. D., Jr. (1977) *The Visible Hand: The Managerial Revolution in American Business,* Cambridge, MA: The Belknapp Press of Harvard University.

Child, J. (1984) *Organization,* second edn, London: Harper and Row.

Clarke, C. A., Brown, A. D. and Hope-Hailey, V. (2009) 'Working identities: Agonistic discourse resources and managerial identity', *Human Relations,* 62(3): 323–352.

Collinson, D. (1988) '"Engineering humour": Masculinity, joking and conflict in shop floor relations', *Organization Studies,* 9(2): 181–199.

Collinson, D. (1992) *Managing the Shopfloor,* Berlin: de Gruyter.

Dalton, M. (1959) *Men Who Manage,* New York: Wiley.

Drucker, P. (1974) *Management: Tasks, Responsibilities, Practices,* London: Heinemann.

Farrar, S. (2004) 'Research policy put on back burner', *Times Higher Education,* 14 January, available at

www.timeshighereducation.co.uk/story.asp?story
Code=186345&sectioncode=26.

Fayol, H. (1916/1949) *General and Industrial Management,*
London: Pitman.

Fiedler, F. E. (1967) *A Theory of Leadership Effectiveness,*
New York: McGraw-Hill.

Gosling, J. and Mintzberg, H. (2003) 'The five minds of a
manager', *Harvard Business Review,* November, 1–9.

Grint, K. (2000) *The Arts of Leadership,* Oxford: Oxford
University Press.

Grint, K. (2005) *Leadership: Limits and Possibilities,* London:
Palgrave.

Hales, C. (1993) *Managing through Organization: The
Management Process, Forms of Organization, and the
Work of Managers,* p. 14, London: Cengage Learning
EMEA Ltd.

Hersey, P. and Blanchard, K. H. (1993) *Management of
Organizational Behaviour: Utilising Human Resources,*
sixth edn, Englewood Cliffs, NJ: Prentice Hall.

Heterick, R. C. (1996) Getting Organized, *Sequence,* 31(2),
www.educause.edu/pub/er/review/reviewArticles/31260.
html).

Hickson, D., Pugh, D. and Pheysey, D. (1971) 'Operations
technology and organisation structure: An empirical
appraisal', *Administrative Science Quarterly,* 14: 378–398.

House, R. J. (1971) 'A path–goal theory of leadership
effectiveness', *Administrative Science Quarterly,* 16:
321–338.

Huczynski, A. and Buchanan, D. (2001) *Organizational
Behaviour: An Introductory Text,* London: Financial
Times/Prentice Hall.

Jackall, R. (1988) *Moral Mazes: The World of Corporate
Managers,* New York: Oxford University Press.

Knights, D. (2015) 'Binaries need to shatter for bodies
to matter: Do disembodied masculinities undermine
organizational ethics?', *Organization,* 22(2): 200–216.

Knights, D. and Tullberg, M. (2012) 'Managing masculinity
/mismanaging the corporation', *Organization,* 19(4):
385–404.

Knights, D. and McCabe, D. (2003) *Organization and
Innovation: Guru Schemes and American Dreams,* Milton
Keynes: Open University Press/McGraw Hill.

Knights, D. and Morgan, G. (1992) 'Leadership as corporate
strategy: Towards a critical analysis', *Leadership
Quarterly,* 3(3): 171–190.

Knights, D. and O'Leary, M. (2006) 'The possibility of
ethical leadership', *Journal of Business Ethics,* 67(2):
125–137.

Knights, D. and Willmott, H. (1992) 'Conceptualising
leadership processes: A study of senior managers in
a financial services company', *Journal of Management
Studies,* 29(6): 761–782.

Koontz, H., O'Donnell, C. and Weihrich, H. (1984)
Management, eight edn, Tokyo: McGraw-Hill.

Kotter, J. (1982) *The General Managers,* New York:
Free Press.

Krech, D., Crutchfield, R. S. and Ballachey, E. L. (1962)
Individual in Society, New York: McGraw-Hill.

Kunda, G. (1991) *Engineering Culture,* Philadelphia, PA:
Temple University Press.

Likert, R. (1961) *New Patterns of Management,* New York:
McGraw Hill.

Magretta, J. (with N. Stone) (2002) *What Management Is,*
London: Profile.

Mayo, E. (1933) *The Human Problems of an Industrial
Civilisation,* New York: Macmillan.

McGregor, D. (1960) *The Human Side of Enterprise,* New
York: McGraw Hill.

Mintzberg, H. (1973) *The Nature of Managerial Work,* New
York: Harper and Row.

Mintzberg, H. (1979) *The Structuring of Organizations,*
Englewood Cliffs, NJ: Prentice Hall.

Mullins, L. J. (2002) *Management and Organizational
Behaviour,* sixth edn, London: Financial Times/Prentice
Hall.

Nichols, T. and Beynon, H. (1977) *Living with Capitalism,*
London: Heinemann.

Ouchi, W. (1981) *Theory Z,* Reading, MA: Addison-Wesley.

Pascale, R. T. and Athos, A. G. (1982) *The Art of Japanese
Management,* Harmondsworth: Penguin.

Peters, T. and Waterman, R. H. (1982) *In Search of
Excellence,* London: Harper and Row.

Pfeffer, G. (1981) 'Management as symbolic action: The
creation and maintenance of organizational paradigms',
in L. L. Cummings and B. M. Staw (eds) *Research in
Organizational Behaviour,* Vol. 3, Greenwich, CT:
JAI Press.

Pollard, S. (1965) *The Genesis of Modern Management,*
London: Edward Arnold.

Pullen, A. and Rhodes, C. (2014) 'Corporeal Ethics and the
Politics of Resistance in Organizations', *Organization,*
21(6): 782–796.

Putnam, L., Fairhurst, G. T. and Banghart, S. (2016)
'Contradictions, dialectics, and paradoxes in
organizations: A constitutive approach', *The Academy
of Management Annals,* 10(1): 65–171, DOI:
10.1080/19416520.2016.1162421.

Raelin, J. A. (ed.) (2016) *Leadership-as-Practice: Theory and
Application,* London: Routledge.

Sims, R. and Brinkmann, J. (2002) 'Leaders as role models:
The case of John Gutfreund at Salomon Brothers',
Journal of Business Ethics, 35: 327–339, cited in Knights
and O'Leary (2006, op. cit.).

Sinclair, A. (2005) *Doing Leadership Differently,* second edn,
Melbourne: Melbourne University Press.

Smircich, L. and Morgan, G. (1982) 'Leadership: The
management of meaning', *Journal of Applied Behavioral
Science,* 18: 257–273.

Taylor, F. W. (2011) *Principles of Scientific Management,*
New York: Harper.

Tourish, D. and Vatcha, N. (2005) 'Charismatic leadership
and corporate cultism at Enron: The elimination of

dissent, the promotion of conformity and organizational collapse', *Leadership,* 1(4): 455–480.

Treviño, L. K, Brown, M. and Pincus, L. (2003) 'A qualitative investigation of perceived executive ethical leadership: Perceptions from inside and outside the executive suite', *Human Relations,* 56(1): 5–36.

Vroom, V. H. and Jago, A. G. (1988) *The New Leadership: Managing Participation in Organizations,* Englewood Cliffs, NJ: Prentice Hall.

Vroom, V. H. and Yetton, P. W. (1973) *Leadership and Decision-Making,* Pittsburgh: University of Pittsburgh Press.

Watson, T. (1994) *In Search of Management,* London: Routledge.

Whyte, W. F. (1943/1993) *Street Corner Society: The Social Structure of an Italian Slum,* fourth edn, Chicago, IL: University of Chicago Press.

Willmott, H. C. (1997) 'Critical management learning', in J. Burgoyne and M. Reynolds (eds) *Management Learning,* London: Sage, pp. 161–176.

Willmott, H. C. (2012) '"Spirited away – all mouth and no trousers"; Reflections on Boltanki and Chiapello's "New spirits of capitalism"', in P. du Gay and G. Morgan (eds) *New Spirits of Capitalism?: Crises, Justifications, and Dynamics,* Oxford: Oxford University Press.

Notes

1   While Putnam *et al.* (2016) describe their constitutive approach as encompassing four types of metatheory relating to organization studies in general – process-based systems, structuration, critical, postmodern, and relational dialectics, we follow a narrower view of it as relating to the types of approaches to leadership (see text on page 331).

2   www.britannica.com/topic/Financial-Crisis-of-2008-The-1484264

3   www.ft.com/indepth/leveson-phone-hacking

4   www.nytimes.com/interactive/2015/04/23/business/dealbook/db-libor-timeline.html?_r=0#/#time370_10900

9 Politics and decision-making in organizations

DAVID KNIGHTS AND PAMELA ODIH

Aims of the chapter

This chapter will:

- Give an account of pluralist models of political organizations and decision-making as part of the mainstream perspective.

- Examine several significant mainstream studies.

- Discuss a selection of major critical studies.

- Explore the strengths and weaknesses of critical approaches.

Key concepts and learning objectives

By the end of this chapter you should understand:

- The key conceptual and theoretical ideas that form the pluralist model of organizational decision-making.

- The disputes about their value with regards to effectively explaining the power dynamics of decision-making, conflict resolution and goal achievement.

- The ideological issues that inform mainstream perspectives.

- The contribution of a critical perspective in outlining the importance of treating power and its operation in decision-making as problematic, and not as given or taken for granted.

Overview and key points

This chapter examines a familiar concept – politics. A political analysis highlights organizations as systems of governance, inclined either towards authoritarian (totalitarian) or liberal (democratic) forms of rule. Of course, as with nation states, there are hybrid forms that are mixtures of these two polar extremes – neither wholly authoritarian nor fully liberal. Indeed, most organizations adopt some in-between form of governance. It is through governance that organizations become orderly or not, and how diverse individuals and groups are directed to follow common organizational pursuits. However, formal governance cannot preclude members of organizations from challenging, competing and conflicting, as well as co-operating with one another, as they seek to advance – collectively as well as individually – their own careers, competitive advantage and claims to power, wealth and status. Indeed, it is these internal and not formally acknowledged practices that we call organizational politics.

To the extent that mainstream writers have acknowledged, let alone researched, organizational politics (e.g., Pettigrew, 1973), they tend to comprehend it pejoratively as something negative that needs to be eradicated (Knights and Murray, 1994). Both organizational practitioners and theorists go about their activities as if organizational politics do not exist, or as if it is found only on the margins or in the **interstices** of organizations. Arguably, however, politics is at the very core of how organizations 'tick'. Politics is the way of 'sorting out' problems, generating new ideas and innovations, and promoting as well as sometimes undermining the organization. Writers and researchers have struggled to come to terms with the idea that organizational life is as much about differences as similarities, conflict as collaboration, and competition as co-operation. This is why classical theorists frequently made reference to **authority** and **power** in organizations without recognizing them to be political issues, which establish specific forms of superior–subordinate relations.

MAINSTREAM APPROACH TO POLITICS AND DECISION-MAKING

Introduction to the mainstream approach

People are recruited into work as individuals, but they bring with them a collection of social experiences, beliefs and values that help define their informal relations with other organizational members (see Chapter 5). Although individuals might not formally be aware of their links to groups within organizations, they will inevitably share a degree of commonality with certain colleagues. Imagine that you have been recruited, on a temporary basis, by a local council office. Due to the huge public deficit following the global financial crisis (see Chapter 8), the council is suffering reduced funding from central government as part of the politics of austerity. Given the complexity of local council resourcing, the initiative is likely to generate disagreements. Discussions during lunchtime and around the water cooler are rife with speculation and counter speculation of cuts in services and inevitable redundancies. You might wish to remain blissfully oblivious to the wider processes of recruitment. But your appointment has already aligned you with the interests of those that recruited you even if their rationale for recruiting you is likely to be superseded by the demand for savings.

Your appointment is likely to have been an outcome of competition between groups for limited organizational resources, power and influence. In a climate of austerity and retraction, those who recruited you may find it difficult to claim that the service you provide, or your performance, is sufficient to retain your employment. On the basis of a well-established industrial relations norm of 'last in first out', your position is highly vulnerable. All is not lost, however. As a new recruit fresh out of college, you are likely to be significantly less expensive than more established workers. If your contribution is held to be as good or better than other staff, whose longevity in the job may have eroded their enthusiasm, commitment and productivity, you may be retained. It might also be argued that your temporary status acts as an incentive to be 'on your toes' and perform better as a result. The more established staff will, of course, make counterclaims of experience and competence to protect their jobs. Prior to the cutbacks, you could have felt a sense of camaraderie and co-operation with your colleagues. But now you are all in competition with one another for a share of significantly reduced resources. Even in 'normal times' there is competition for comparatively scarce resources but the new circumstances result in politics becoming more manifest or explicit. An alternative to individual competition over reduced resources is a political strategy of collective resistance on the part of those threatened by the cuts, which involves collaborating to prevent management delivering their demands for austerity and potential redundancies. At the time of writing this revised text (May, 2016), France was experiencing widespread national industrial disruption as the government's austerity plans involved reforming the labour laws. Workers 'blockaded power plants, petrol stations, and oil refineries' (see www.bbc.co.uk/news/world-europe-36387492, consulted 3.6.16).

Interstices That which exists in-between two 'objects'.

Authority Legitimate *right* to control, prohibit and judge the actions of others. It is when someone has the right to exercise power over you (e.g., tell you what to do). It is often distinguished from power, where there can be physical coercion or force, for that is based on 'might' not 'right'. Authority establishes rights recognized by subordinates as well as exercised by superiors.

Power Often conceived as ability of A to influence B to do something that B would not ordinarily have done without A's influence. The attribution of power to individuals or groups as their 'possession' has been challenged by a view of power that is 'relational' – such as the disciplines and ideologies that operate to constrain as well as enable those to whom power is attributed by the 'possessive' view.

Here the collective power of the trade union is called upon to threaten industrial action as a way of preventing the rationalization enforced by central government. Politics enters a new phase of extending beyond the local organization as it represents a challenge to the government itself. The diversity of views and their implications concerning an individual appointment illustrate how decisions in organizations are always steeped in politics – that is, differences about their consequences in terms of security, rewards, status and prospects for individuals and groups. Indeed, the concept of organizational politics stems from the view that conflicts and power occupy centre stage in the ebb and flow of organizational decision-making (Knights and Murray, 1994).

Thinkpoint 9.1

I n 2011 the Manchester United footballer, Ryan Giggs, brought out a super injunction in order to prevent media publicity about a recent extra-marital affair with an ex-contestant in a TV reality programme, *Big Brother*. He did not expect this to result in a UK constitutional crisis that put him clearly in the political limelight in the UK, if not worldwide. Can you think of any other examples where private matters are so quickly and dramatically transformed into political events?

A definition of political behaviour in Box 9.1 is intended to draw your attention to key conceptual ideas. First, that political behaviour extends far beyond the formal authority of one's specified job requirement. Second, that political behaviour involves cultivating influential allies, controlling the flow of information and influencing decisions through the informal use of one's power basis (Robbins, 1998). And finally, that political behaviour is directly linked to organizational decision-making, which is inescapably intertwined with the political strategies of bargaining, compromising and trading support for information and other scarce resources.

P olitical behaviour is defined as those private activities, which may not be consistent with the interests of the organization, but that influence, or attempt to influence, the distribution of advantages and disadvantages within the organization. (Robbins, 1998, p. 410)

Box 9.1
'Political behaviour' – a mainstream definition

Mainstream account of political activity in organizations

Cartoon 9.1
'We're not hibernating this year.
Too much cultural change to keep
up with.'

'We're not hibernating this year.
Too much cultural change to keep up with.'

To illustrate the mainstream approach, this section provides an adapted case study of Burns and Stalker's ([1961] 1968) account of politics and organization within the Scottish electronics industry during the 1950s. Entitled *The Management of Innovation,* Burns and Stalker's classic study is a highly insightful example of mainstream political analysis. The research was originally motivated by a desire to study an industrial company as a 'community of people at work' (ibid., p. 1). The proposed aim was to research into organizational conduct and relationships using the same terms of reference as would be applied to urban neighbourhoods and small communities. Despite changes to this original remit a committed interest in 'the adaptation of relationships between individuals' continued to guide the focus of their research. Consequently, Burns and Stalker (ibid.) set about studying the organizational relations, which in the mid-1950s defined firms involved in the Scottish Council's innovative 'Electronics Scheme'.

The Scottish Council was, at that time, a voluntary body financially sustained by industrial firms, the local government and trade unions. The Electronics Scheme was a joint venture involving the Scottish Council, the Scottish Home Department and the Board of Trade. It operated as an incentive scheme, to actively encourage the growth, in Scotland, of industries willing to adopt new technologies. The declared agenda of the scheme was to provide firms with assistance necessary to build up technological expertise so as to attract suitable contracts from the defence ministries. Companies that entered the scheme would be assisted in setting up a laboratory team dedicated to advancing the company's technological expertise. To this end the scheme was intent on instigating a rapid change in the rate of electronic development in the Scottish electronics market. It was this condition of rapid change and development that attracted Burns and Stalker's (ibid.) research interest. For their part, they hoped to observe 'how management systems changed in accordance with changes in the technical and commercial tasks of the firm' (ibid., p. 4).

Burns and Stalker's (ibid.) initial findings produced curious anomalies. They analyzed the major incentives that encouraged firms to enter the scheme. Most firms entering the scheme were prompted by a fear of market competition. Only a few firms were prompted by a desire to expand their technological know-how and enter into new markets. The reticence of firms to embrace an 'expansionist urge' was reflected in the role and status firms ascribed to the laboratory teams, which they were required to form as part of their entry into the Scottish Council's scheme. Firms generally appeared less inclined to exploit the team as a technical resource, often sidelining their efforts or confining them to specific activities. Burns and Stalker (ibid., p. 4) describe how 'in half the cases, laboratory groups were disbanded or disrupted by the resignation of their leaders'. In other instances laboratory groups were 'converted into test departments, "trouble-shooting" teams or production departments' (ibid). Three features were common to all these predicaments. First, the dire fate of the laboratory group was often sealed from the outset. Established organizational members were, in many cases, determined to exclude the laboratory group from decision-making in the rest of the organization. Burns and Stalker (ibid., p. 139) provide verbatim evidence of this intention to exclude the laboratory group:

> These 'cultural' differences were openly accepted by the senior managers with whom we were first in touch. "Physicists", we were seriously told by one managing director, 'are very difficult people to work with.' But the same differences showed up in remarks to the effect that a good production engineer was a person who would tackle any problem given to him and solve it unaided, while a good design engineer in a laboratory was a person who could say 'I don't know'; again they appeared in references to 'long-haired types' and to 'the production clots'.

Burns and Stalker's observation here illustrates the conflicts of power that constituted, for them, a second noticeable response by existing organizational members to the introduction of the laboratory group. A third noticeable response was evident in the tendency for senior managers to convert what were clearly management problems into difficulties defined as caused by the 'ignorance and obstructiveness' of opposing interests. Burns and Stalker (ibid., p. 140) defined this latter course of action as, 'The price of adapting the working organization – and refusals to pay it'. They had observed that for some managers adapting to the rate of commercial and technical change carried with it too many demands on their existing relationships and 'heavier mental [cognitive] and emotional commitments' (ibid., p. 7). For these managers a method of coping was either to control their personal situation or claim exemption from a problem so as to protect the special conditions attached to their status. But such manoeuvres were problematic as they compounded the company's 'inability to adapt the management system to the form appropriate to conditions of more rapid technical and commercial change' (ibid., p. 5).

Political structure Balance of competing pressures from interest groups seeking to realize, or gain recognition of, their own particular concerns.

The difficulties encountered by these firms in adjusting to rapidly changing technology and commercial situations led the researchers to identify the **political structure** of a company as a vital determinant of effective organizational management. They defined the concept of political structure as follows: 'The political structure of a [company] is the balance of competing pressures from each group recognizing a common interest for a larger share of all or some benefits or resources than they have now or think they may have in the future.' (ibid., p. 145)

What Burns and Stalker (1968) sought to establish was, first, that political systems and status systems exist within firms, and, second, that they do not exist as isolated entities: 'political and status considerations constantly influence the working organization, and influence it so as to reduce its effectiveness' (ibid., p. 146). It needs to be recognized that Burns and Stalker's (ibid.) position here is firmly committed to a mainstream account of politics and organizations. Notably, they fall well short of claiming the existence of endemic irreconcilable power struggles within organizations – in contrast with, for example, a critical perspective of political analysis. Instead they suggest that the political structure of specific types of organization has detrimental consequences in the sense that these may be dysfunctional for the realization of organizational goals. At no point do they argue, as critical theorists are inclined to do, that the goals themselves are the outcome of political struggles.

Burns and Stalker (1968) set about elucidating two divergent forms of organizational structure operating within the sample of Scottish firms studied. The first of the two ideal types is the **mechanistic organization**. In an early example of contingency thinking (see Chapter 7), they describe this system as appearing 'appropriate to an enterprise operating under relatively stable conditions' (ibid, p. 5). This mechanistic form of organization is very similar to Weber's model of rational-legal bureaucracy (see Chapter 14). It includes a specialized **division of labour** within which each individual carries out an assigned and precisely defined task. This takes place within a clear hierarchy of control where senior persons take responsibility for major decisions, the direction of operations and the co-ordination of specialized tasks. Communication is mainly vertical (i.e., between superiors and subordinates): instructions are directed downward through the chain of command. Information flows upwards and is processed at specialist levels before reaching the top. As they describe it:

> This command hierarchy is maintained by the implicit assumption that all knowledge about the situation of the firm and its tasks is, or should be, available only to the head of the firm. Management, often visualized as the complex hierarchy familiar in organization charts, operates a simple control system, with information flowing through a succession of filters and decisions and instructions flowing downwards through a succession of amplifiers. (Burns and Stalker, 1968, p. 5)

Burns and Stalker (ibid.) contrast this bureaucratic structure with the **organic organization**. They describe how this system 'appeared to be required for conditions of change' (ibid, p. 5). A rigid hierarchical structure was far less evident in the organic organization and the authors claim that this makes it better able to respond quickly to changing and unpredictable conditions. For this reason, organic organizations 'are adapted to unstable conditions, when problems and requirements for action arise which cannot be broken down and distributed among specialist roles' (ibid, pp. 5–6). In rapidly changing, unstable conditions it is difficult to operate mechanistically and break down new emerging difficulties into precisely allocated tasks. When a problem arises within an organic organization all those who have relevant knowledge and expertise contribute to its resolution. An emphasis is placed on knowledge as a contributive resource rather than restricted to a specific job specification. Consequently there exists a continuous adjustment of tasks as they are shaped by the nature of the problem. Although a hierarchy exists, interaction and communication may occur at whatever level is (functionally) required by the process and conditions at hand. Organizational charts detailing the requirements of specific jobs are therefore less prevalent or relevant in the organic organization. For such formal organizational charts hamper the flexibility necessary for an efficient flow of communication and co-operative participation.

Mechanistic organization Similar to Weber's model of rational-legal bureaucracy. Includes a specialized division of labour within which each individual carries out an assigned and precisely defined task comparable to the discrete parts that comprise a machine. It is the opposite of **organic organization**.

Division of labour The way that people divide up different tasks or jobs between one another to achieve greater levels of efficiency and productive output. Emile Durkheim (1947) argued that the division of labour was not only economically efficient but also socially effective in that it made clear how we are all dependent upon one another and this knowledge would help to generate social solidarity – a necessary condition of social survival.

Organic organization An emphasis is placed on knowledge as a contributing resource rather than restricted to a specific job specification. There exists a continual adjustment to tasks as they become shaped by the nature of the problem rather than predefined. Opposite of **mechanistic organization**.

Thinkpoint 9.2

Going back to our example of the footballer, Ryan Giggs, whose private extra-marital affair was quickly transformed into a major political event as a result of Twitter and hence thousands of people breaching a judicial order not to reveal his name, it could be argued that this was because the law and especially human rights legislation is mechanistic rather than organic and therefore cannot adapt to a rapidly changing situation such as social network innovations on the Internet. Can you think of any other examples where mechanistic organizational arrangements are inappropriate?

Ideal-type An ideal-type is the purest, most fully developed version of a particular thing (usually a concept). It does not mean that the thing itself is ideal. The ideal-type of a sadistic serial killer would be someone with all the characteristics of the cruellest mass murderer imaginable – but that does not mean that there is anything desirable about serial killers! It does not mean that the 'ideal' is good or bad. Instead it simply refers to an abstract, exaggerated image or a benchmark by which actual behaviour (e.g., the acts of an actual serial killer) can be assessed.

The significance of Burns and Stalker's (1968) identification of two **ideal-types** of organization for the present chapter is its relevance for understanding the politics of conflict within organizations. They were particularly interested in the question of why some of the Scottish firms did not change their system from 'mechanistic' to 'organic', even though this would have been more consistent with the increasingly unstable conditions that these firms faced. Only some of the firms in their study even attempted to adopt an organic system. Why?

The answer which suggested itself was that every single person in a firm not only is (a) a member of a working organization, but also (b) a member of a group with sectional interests in conflict with those of other groups, and (c) one individual among many to whom the rank they occupy and the prestige attaching to them are matters of deep concern (Burns and Stalker, 1968, p. 6).

Burns and Stalker highlight how political systems and status structures coexist with the more formal structures of the working organization. The authors describe how the political and status structure of the organizations studied was directly threatened by the introduction of the new laboratory group. Organizational members were particularly wary of the technical information available to the newcomers as this was perceived as a source of 'political control' (ibid., p. 6).

Consequently the 'laboratory engineers claimed or were regarded as claiming élite status within the organization' (ibid.). Individuals within mechanistic organizations were observed to be committed to the organization as a whole but also political players with affiliations to their departments, stable career structures and sectional interests. As Burns and Stalker (1968, p. 6) describe it:

> Neither political nor status preoccupations operated overtly, or even consciously; they gave rise to intricate manoeuvres and counter-moves, all of them expressed through decisions, or discussions about decisions, concerning the internal structure and the policies of the firm. Since political and status conflicts only came into the open in terms of the working organization, that organization became adjusted to serving the ends of the political and status system of the [company] rather than its own.

Such practices are political in reflecting and reproducing career and sectional interests to the detriment and/or displacement of what might be characterized as the overarching organizational goals. Burns and Stalker (ibid.) show how the realization of those goals is impeded as established interest groups are preoccupied with retaining status and power, thus preventing the required transformation of the mechanistic systems into an organic form.

Three of the 'pathological' systems, which developed as part of the determination of established groups to sustain their status position and power, are autocracy; elites in the mechanistic jungle; and committee systems.

- *Autocracy.* This refers to the development of an 'autocratic system' constituted by the official hierarchy and non-official pairings between chief executives and senior managers. As the mechanistic organization tenaciously tries to cope with rapidly changing conditions, an accumulation of information flowing upwards (i.e., as subordinates encounter new conditions) begins to consume the activities of executive management. Burns and Stalker (1968, p. 6) describe how 'the individual manager became absorbed in conflicts over power and status because they presented him with interests and problems more immediately important to him and more easily comprehended than those raised by the new organizational milieu and its unlimited liabilities'. Many of the managers found it difficult to maintain control of the stream of new information pouring into their occupational lives. Autocratic rule provided a means of managing the information overload and seemingly preserving the status attached to their managerial role. But these practices persistently involved manoeuvres that mitigated against the development of an organic system in response to the changing external environment.

- *Elites in the mechanistic jungle.* A second pathological system generated by the mechanistic organization's attempts to operate in unstable conditions is the emergence of an **elite**. Many of the electronic firms in Burns and Stalker's (ibid.) study had employed technologically adept scientists and technicians to respond to the new information required by the market. These newly recruited employees were sometimes seen as a threat to the established order of rank, power and privilege. Existing personnel feared seeming inept as the currency of knowledge within the organization shifted away from their traditional areas of expertise. Concerns were raised about a loss of status and power in decision-making. In an attempt to hold on to power some managers tried to distance the new department operationally and administratively from the rest of the organization. Elsewhere, whole new departments were created to respond to the changing conditions. But this also proved conflictual as these departments clearly depended for their existence on the perpetuation of the existing difficult conditions. For these departments, success in resolving the conflicts would be like turkeys voting for Christmas.

> **Elite** Selected group of presumably gifted or otherwise distinguished individuals.

- *Committee systems.* A third pathological response, as discussed by Burns and Stalker, is the proliferation of **committee systems**. The establishment of committees is the traditional method for dealing with new conditions while not upsetting the balance of power of existing structures. But the formation of committees is only effective as a temporary measure. When used as a permanent device the committee begins to compete with the loyalty demanded, and career structure offered, by the established departmental structure.

> **Committee system** Where decisions are taken by committees rather than individuals – a situation that can lead to a proliferation of committees dominating the decision-making process of an organization.

In terms of a political analysis, several other important issues arise from Burns and Stalker's study. First and foremost their research draws attention to the form and function of the organization as subject to the internal politics of the organization. The failure of the Scottish companies to adapt to an organic system was seen as the consequence of the strength of political status structures. Burns and Stalker's study also emphasizes the importance of conceiving organizations as operating at three levels or social systems. The first refers to the formal authority structure, which is defined by the organization's goals, technology and **organizational chart**. This is a clear systematic representation of the organization and a clear basis for the analysis of decision-making processes. Political analysis also reveals organizations to be constituted by covert 'co-operative systems' based on negotiation and bargaining. The tendency for organizations to be simultaneously systems of co-operation and competition means that decisions taken in the formal structure inevitably have differential effects on members' interests. As sites of both conflict and co-operation, a third level or system of organizational relationships is its **political system**.

> **Organizational chart** Stylized but clear representation of the organization that may provide a basis for the analysis of decision-making processes.

> **Political system** Boundaries, goals, values, administrative mechanisms and hierarchy of power, which constitute a particular organization.

Exercise 9.1

KEY ISSUES RAISED BY THE BURNS AND STALKER CASE STUDY

1 Discuss how Burns and Stalker's ([1961] 1968) case study draws our attention to the form and function of the organization as largely defined by internal politics.
2 Discuss how Burns and Stalker's ([1961] 1968) case study draws our attention to the many interactions that take place between different parts of an organization.

Political analysis reveals all organizations to be at one and the same time formal structures and political systems. Decisions in the formal structure impact on co-operative relations and set the scene for political activity. But it would be naive to assume only a downward flow of forces that instigate political activity from the most senior ranks.

Politics occur at all levels of the organization and 'the politics of organizational decision-making often involves preventing crucial decisions from being made, as well as fostering those that one actually desires' (Morgan, 1986, p. 166). It is also the case that effective politics depends on the consent or at least compliance of those over whom power is exercised (Burawoy, 1979).

Thinkpoint 9.3

Can you think of examples where particular political decisions have been undermined by the absence of consent on the part of those who are expected to translate policies into practice? Would various forms of discrimination or environmental detriment continue to exist if there was a real consensus in organizations and society regarding equal opportunity and environmental sustainability?

Typologies Form of classification that involves grouping together entities or subjects with like themes and ensuring that these groups are mutually inclusive and mutually exclusive from all other groups. For example, cars and aeroplanes might be different groups of entities within a typology of transportation.

Legitimacy Condition in which decisions or practices are widely acceptable to those whom they affect because there is a broad level of consensus about the form or process of their adoption.

Rule system System of governance based on rules.

Action-based A concept used to describe the dynamics of organization. It assumes that political rule is dependent on the practices of organizational members and limited by the norms, values and foresight of informed actors.

Purposeful actors Belief that individuals retain rational control (e.g., in their pursuit of self-interest and sectional loyalties) throughout the processes of organizational decision-making.

Central problems in the mainstream agenda

The analysis of organization as a process of government provides unique opportunities to understand the day-to-day political dynamics of organizations. Mainstream political analysis focuses on explaining:

- **typologies** of political rule
- how *rules* are maintained
- how *conflict* is contained, and
- how **legitimacy** is sustained.

CONSTRUCTING TYPOLOGIES

Implicit parallels between the nature of organizations and political systems have enabled writers to construct useful political rule typologies and the processes through which rules are maintained. Organizations, like governments, trade upon **rule systems** as a means of sustaining order among members. Political rule involves goals, interpersonal influence, skills and tactics of negotiation. In other words, it is **action-based**, dependent on the practices of organizational members and limited by the norms, values and foresight of informed actors (Kakabadse *et al.*, 1988). Organizational members are **purposeful** in their actions (Fincham and Rhodes, 1996/1999), retaining their pursuit of self-interests and sectional loyalties throughout the processes of organizational decision-making.

HOW RULES ARE MAINTAINED

Political analysis reveals organizations as constituted by a plethora of interests, each with the potential for conflict, agitation and manipulation. Interest groups have the capacity to exploit the legitimate authority bestowed on them by virtue of their formal position and the power drawn from controlling resources, forming alliances and managing boundaries. This mainstream image of politics and organization relates directly to what is generally recognized as the 'pluralist' frame of reference. The pluralist vision of organizational politics emphasizes the free

Exercise 9.2

IDENTIFYING RULE SYSTEMS IN EVERYDAY SITUATIONS

Organizations, like governments, operate according to 'rule systems' as a means of sustaining order among members. These rule systems relate to the existence of formal and informal procedures/structures for managing decision-making. The following are organizational events that you might be familiar with. Discuss each event and identify the formal rules that generally characterize these decision-making instances. In each case, try to identify some of these rules and the norms and values they reflect and reproduce.

1 *Student union elections.* The election of a student representative depends on the adherence by delegates and voters to predefined norms, values and rules. Try to identify some of these rules and the norms and values they reflect and reproduce.
2 *Implementation of work assignment deadlines and penalties for non-compliance in your courses.*

interplay of interest groups, as operating to check and balance the potentially authoritarian tendencies of governing bodies. This approach is evident in the following quotation drawn from Bacharach and Lawler's (1980) account of decision-making as a 'politically negotiated order'. In adopting this view they describe how:

> We can observe organizational actors in their daily transactions, perpetually bargaining, repeatedly forming and reforming coalitions, and constantly availing themselves of influence and tactics ... politics in organizations involve the tactical use of power to retain or obtain control of real or symbolic resources. In describing the processes of organizations as political acts, we are not making a moral judgement: we are simply making an observation about a process. (Bacharach and Lawler, 1980, pp. 1–2)

Exercise 9.3

Conflict management Recollect a time when you or someone you know has been involved in some conflict with mates or in a more formal situation and think how events unfolded.

1 Did the conflict end in outright aggression?
2 If so, how did it end? Did someone seek to arbitrate? Alternatively, did it end through a stand-off in which the parties refused to acknowledge each other?
3 If not, were there some compromises made through negotiation?
4 Can you think of other ways in which the conflict might have evolved?
5 How do these processes compare with politics as you know it?

Discuss and analyze your various answers with other students in your group.

HOW CONFLICT IS CONTAINED

Pluralist perspectives perceive organizational relations as defined by bargaining, competition and the use of politics to achieve a 'negotiated order that creates unity out of diversity' (Morgan, 1986, p. 185). The strength of this perspective is that it places emphasis on diversity, conflict and power. Indeed, it regards power as a crucial medium through which conflicts and divergent interests are managed and resolved. The pluralist model differs considerably from a unitary, classical perspective, which assumes a consensus of values, priorities, interests, etc. In a classical perspective, expressions of conflict are viewed as an aberration, a source of trouble, a dangerous but temporary deflection from the quest to sustain synergy between the interests of individuals and the goals of the organization. Here conflicts are brushed under the carpet rather than acknowledged and managed.

Thinkpoint 9.4

Think of a time when you have fallen out with a friend or friends. Did you resolve the conflict by talking about it or did you pretend it didn't exist? What were the consequences? Are these two alternatives equivalent to the pluralist and the classical models described above and if not how do they differ?

HOW LEGITIMACY IS SUSTAINED

The classical approach to organizational analysis trades upon a notion of willing compliance between organizational members. When translated into management practice, the notions of 'unity' and 'working together' provide elements of a powerful discourse through which to adapt organizational relations to meet management goals. In effect, the concept of a 'team', whether as an entire organization or as a work group, conspires to eliminate any acknowledgement of difference. Instead, individuals subordinate themselves to the service of the team. Table 9.1 provides a brief summary of the features of unitarism and pluralism.

Rational process Process that incorporates goals and a mechanism calculated to achieve agreed aims largely irrespective of its consequences for other dimensions of social existence (e.g., community well-being).

Decision-making is perceived in unitarist theory as a **rational process** in which managers act jointly and consensually to resolve problems. Senior management in the formal hierarchy of the organization is attributed the responsibility of producing consensus and preserving unity (see also Chapters 7 and 14). This approach has little basis for addressing chaotic political systems operating in many directions. Conversely, pluralist approaches recognize that management is about balancing and co-ordinating difference. Rather than disrupting organizational goals, conflict and its political resolution can function as both a positive and negative force. The pluralist manager is positioned as the arbiter of conflict management and is assigned the duty of facilitating positive conflict. He or she is involved in managing conflict through reconciling the diverse interests between, for example, employees, shareholders, the state, suppliers, consumers and other interest groups such as environmentalists. The political arena is a context in which positive conflict is to be facilitated and negative conflict is managed.

Table 9.1 Comparison of political analysis in classical and pluralist traditions

Classical tradition	Pluralist tradition
Emphasis on formal structure	Emphasis on informal structure
Achievement of common interests	Organization as loose coalition of diverse interests
Principles of decision-making	Decision as outcomes of political bargaining
Eradication of conflict	Conflict as inherent and ineradicable
Power as formal authority	Power drawn from myriad of sources and groups
Hierarchical structure as disciplinary	Free interplay of interests as a check to power
Rationality in decision-making	Rationality through communicative discussion
Unity through adherence to rules	Politically negotiated unity

Mainstream concepts

Decision-making is a political process in which power is exercised and a range of tactics deployed by people or groups seeking to gain particular advantage. Political analysis highlights eight key concepts with (in brackets) their connection to the theoretical concepts that frame this book. These are relevant to the study of interpersonal relations in organizational analysis, and are examined in the following subsections.

1. MICRO-POLITICS (FREEDOM)

Pluralist perspectives highlight the relevance of micro-politics to organizational relations. The concept of micro-politics refers to those strategies and activities that groups (and individuals) within an organizational context are free to seek in order to secure their preferred outcomes in a situation in which there exists dissent.

2. DECISION PROCESS (KNOWLEDGE)

Pluralist perspectives situate knowledge as a valuable resource in decision-making. Knowledge limitation and restriction provide for crucial conditions for the manipulation of power in organizations. Pluralist discourse attempts to demonstrate the relevance of knowledge in its account of the decision process. It distinguishes three interrelated elements that have relevance as a point of entry for micro-politics and control. The first element is the **decision premises**. Morgan (1986, p. 166) observes how 'one of the most effective ways of getting a decision is to allow it to be made by default'. He describes how, as a consequence, much of the activity in organizations involves controlling the structures and processes within which decisions take place. These are defined as the decision premises. An example of a decision premise is the agenda for business meetings. Control of the agenda enables manipulation of how a decision is approached.

The second element concerns **decision processes**. This refers to the formal systems through which a decision travels and the authorized controls on its passage. For example, the decision within an academic institution to elect a new student representative to sit on a number of departmental committees has to progress through a formal system dictated by rules of procedure, such as nominations and elections. The final of the three elements of decision-making is 'decision issues' and **objectives**. These features refer to the process of focusing and defining the outcomes of a decision. All three elements provide avenues for what has been termed the **mobilization of bias** where desired outcomes are made more probable by shaping agendas, designing procedures and conditioning outcomes.

Decision premises
Structures and processes that constitute the apparatus of decision-making. An example of a decision premise is the agenda for meetings. Control of this agenda can enable one to manipulate how a decision is approached.

Decision process Sequential processes and structures involved in the deliberation of a decision.

Decision objectives Aim/goal of a decision and the criteria through which outcomes can be evaluated.

Mobilization of bias Manipulation of decision-making premises, processes and objectives so as to ensure that a specific point of view or intention is supported.

Thinkpoint 9.5

C an you think of occasions when instead of demanding what you want from others (parents, siblings, friends or mere acquaintances) you have defined the circumstances in such a way as to make your preference probable if not inevitable? Is this similar to the mobilization of bias described above and if not how is it different?

3. NEGOTIATED ORDER (IDENTITY)

Pluralist perspectives describe organizations as arenas of political struggle. Formal structures remain of significance, but are of marginal consideration when compared to the significance ascribed to informal relations. Taking the example above, long before the formal procedure of elections, students will probably have encouraged or provided support informally for someone to be a student representative. The person who is particularly keen to become a student rep will also usually canvass informal support from other students before standing in an election.

4. PLURALITY OF POWER

Pluralists perceive organizational relations to be defined by bargaining, competition and the exercise of power to resolve conflicts and represent conflicts of interest. Power is pluralistically dispersed throughout the organization and operates to prevent any one group or individual monopolizing influence. But the problem with mainstream concepts of power is that they are based on the ideas of power as possessed by individuals rather than a more precarious outcome of social relations that are continually subject to negotiation and change.

5. CONTINGENCY

Pluralist accounts of organizational processes are predicated on a belief that **uncertainty**, for an organization, stems from external conditions or events such as technological developments, market competition or government legislation. Reducing uncertainty is a vital precondition of effective management and those groups deemed capable of controlling uncertainly gain power and status. The concept of contingency appears in the Burns and Stalker

Uncertainty Branch of political analysis which argues that leadership and influence within organizations tends to be enjoyed by those perceived as dealing with the sources of greatest ambiguity.

(1968) case study as it is the dynamic market that is seen to be the determinant of whether an organization should become more organic in its operations. To be fair, the authors do see career conflicts and competition generating uncertainty and preventing organizational change consistent with a changing market environment. However, insecurity is an unacknowledged resource in this mainstream form of analysis; it is not examined as a driving force that rivals the market in generating change.

6. MOBILIZATION OF BIAS (KNOWLEDGE)

This refers to the process whereby groups (and individuals) manipulate core beliefs in such a way as to prevent potentially threatening ideas and alternative positions being presented. In the USA and Europe, for example, critical challenges to the Iraq war were marginalized by an ideology about weapons of mass destruction, that eventually were proven to be entirely fictitious.

7. CONFLICT (INEQUALITY)

Classical perspectives in decision-making are predicated on the existence of harmony of interests. This is reproduced in classical decision-making models that emphasize rationality and unity as achieved through the adherence, by employees, to formal rules. The existence of conflict is either neglected in classical theory or marginalized by treating consensus as if it were natural, like the very air we breathe. This is a process that is termed reification where the status quo is seen as natural or inevitable and not subject to change. Pluralist perspectives challenge the tendency of classical theory to reify organizational relations into a model of harmonic co-ordination and shared goals. Instead, pluralists emphasize the significance of implicit and explicit conflict, which arises as a consequence of technical specialization and divisions of labour within organizations. Members are enticed into co-operative relations to maximize their abilities to mobilize interests in their favour. It follows from this that organizations are political coalitions, in the sense that allegiances are formed to enhance the bargaining power and influence of individual members.

8. POLITICAL RULE SYSTEMS (POWER AND INEQUALITY)

Pluralist analysis depicts organizations as constituted by definable modes of power mobilized into a rule system. Examples of political rule systems include the following:

- **Autocracy** is a term used to describe a political regime or person that rules by coercion rather than consent, as is expected in democratic regimes (discussed later). The Murdoch media empire has always been seen to operate in a fairly autocratic fashion such that anyone disagreeing with the boss rarely survives or succeeds in the organization. Coercion is possible largely because the regime or person is able to punish deviants or withdraw rewards from those who fail to comply with its rule. It signifies absolute modes of governing where power operates dictatorially through the intentions of an individual or small group.

- **Bureaucratic** power equates with rational-legal authority. It refers to the legitimate use of authority based on an acceptance of hierarchy and rules that are believed to result in rationally organized or efficient activities and thereby a willingness of people to consent to them or at least be compliant with them (see Chapter 14).

- **Technocratic** rule is exercised through expertise, technical aptitude, knowledge and experience. Power and accountability are directly linked to the perceived relevance and marketability of an individual's technical knowledge and expertise. French and Raven (1959) describe this form of influence as 'expert power' that is highly specific and limited to the particular area in which the individual has expert knowledge (see Chapter 12).

- **Co-determination** refers to a form of influence predicated on the co-operation of parties with possibly opposing or competing interests in the pursuit of a mutual or common outcome. Clear parallels exist here between the coalitions that define the world of politics, and the politicking that may be an essential aspect of achieving a collective organizational goal.

- **Representative democracy** also draws closely upon political reality to describe a form of democratic influence predicated on legitimate forms of electoral selection, accountability and representation.

- **Direct democracy** refers to a system of collective decision-making in which everyone participates and has equal rights in influence. Morgan (1986) describes how 'self-organization' and 'active citizenship' are key modes of organizing direct democracy.

Differences between these forms of political rule relate mostly to the different principles of legitimacy that they draw upon and which transforms their rule into authority rather than crude power. It is this authority that the mainstream takes for granted, refusing to contemplate power and politics as anything other than disruptive and thus to be eradicated.

Autocracy A political regime or person that rules by tradition or coercion rather than consent, as might be expected in a democratic regime.

Bureaucracy Describes a form of business administration based on formal rational rules and procedures designed to govern work practices and organization activities through a hierarchical system of authority. Bureaucratic organization is often thought to be rigid, inflexible and overburdened by hierarchical rules sometimes pejoratively referred to as 'red tape'.

Technocratic Form of governance, which is exercised through the technical knowledge of experts.

Co-determination Form of influence predicated on the co-operation of parties with possibly opposing or competing interests in the pursuit of a mutual or common outcome.

Representative democracy A form of political reality in which democratic influence is predicated on legitimate forms of electoral selection, accountability and representation.

Direct democracy System of collective decision-making in which there is an opportunity for everyone to participate and influence how 'things' get done or are organized.

Exercise 9.4

Role playing political rule systems Refer to the Burns and Stalker ([1961] 1968) case study discussed earlier. The authors identify several 'pathological systems' that developed as part of the established group's determination to sustain status position and power. Drawing upon the key concepts in the mainstream approach (outlined here) match a mode of political rule system to each of Burns and Stalker's 'pathological systems'.

Major controversies

FLEXIBILITY AS AN EFFECTIVE POLITICAL RESPONSE TO EMERGENT SECTORS?

Contemporary applications of Burns and Stalker's (1968) typology converge around management analyses of the particular organizational structures emerging within the information communication technology sector. In revisiting this classic study, Sine *et al.* (2006) provide indication of its continuing relevance yet challenge Burns and Stalker's proposition that in dynamic volatile economic sectors, organizations with 'organic' systems of management are more likely to flourish than firms with rigid 'mechanistic' operational structures. Their empirical evidence of venture capitalist organizations performing in the emergent Internet sector found that these opportunistic enterprises operating in fluctuating commercial conditions suffer from an excess of flexibility, change and a structural 'liability of newness' (Sine *et al.*, 2006: p. 129). They therefore counter Burns and Stalker's hypothesis with the supposition: 'That new ventures with greater founding team formalization, functional specialization, and administrative intensity would outperform those firms that had less of these attributes' or exhibiting a more organic structural formation (ibid.). Empirical data to support the hypothesis was sourced from a sample of Internet-based service ventures established in 1996 and operating in the USA during the survey period of 1996–2001.

This clearly has implications for Burns and Stalker's contribution to the politics of organizations and thus requires brief elaboration. First and foremost, the concept of 'Role Formalization in Founding Teams', was hypothesized in contradiction to Burns and Stalker's supposition that formalization undermined the rapid decision-making needed to respond quickly to a changing environment. For, Sine *et al.* (2006, p. 123) the converse is true, whereby in the absence of a delineation of role specialism and role formalization, organizational members flounder as they scrabble together improvised individual responses to situations that require coherent group initiatives. While improvising gives way to some degree of collaboration, this according to Sine *et al.* (ibid.) remains an impoverished response to the challenging 'environmental changes' manifest in dynamic sectors; for in the absence of 'clear boundaries of responsibility' the political machinations of organizational members 'will be forced to rely upon decision-making by consensus, thereby decreasing the speed and increasing the cost of any particular decision'. Conversely, in turbulent conditions of dynamic change, knowledge of organizational member formal roles, provides a coherent delineation of tasks; and when embedded into the organizational structure of the foundational team: 'These boundaries empower particular individuals to make decisions on behalf of their organization and result in both decreased co-ordination costs and increased decision-making speed' (ibid.). This and similar narratives affirming structure over intuitive flexibility, informed the processes of operationalization and coding of Sine *et al.*'s (2006) empirical data. Indeed, their statistical analysis focused on ascertaining whether the designated indicators of 'role formalization', 'functional specialization' and 'administrative intensity' (i.e., indicators of formality in organizational structure) are advantageous for new ventures operating in highly volatile economic sectors. Their results confirmed the initial hypothesis concerning the beneficial outcome in performance, for new venture enterprises that adopt formal operational structures as a response to the challenges presented by a dynamic and volatile Internet sector. Additional findings identified: 'that the impacts of formalization, specialization, and administrative intensity were greater for larger new ventures' (ibid., p. 129). This study provides further evidence to support recent challenges to the discrediting of bureaucracy (du Gay, 2000; see also Chapter 14).

Sine *et al.* (2006) proffer their results as directly contradicting Burns and Stalker (1961); for the latter supposed that mechanistically formal organizational structures are to the detriment of organizations operating in dynamic volatile industries. Sine *et al.* (2006, p. 129) nevertheless, are reluctant to undermine the continued relevance of Burns and Stalker's supposition, but rather they emphasize the need for readers to situate the effect of political structure and flexibility within the context of the industry's stage of development. As Sine *et al.* (2006, p. 129) express it: 'Our results suggest a new scope condition for Burns and Stalker's structural theory – namely, that the effects of structure are contingent on an organization's and industry's stages of development'. When considering the implications of Sine *et al.*'s (2006) findings our attention is directed towards enterprising political decision-making within new ventures and the stabilizing of this dynamic force through the existence of foundational teams with formal role structures. Of significance is the guidance that establishing a new venture, in a volatile emergent sector, is often a busy and haphazard period of time, in which issues of organizational structure are detrimentally sidelined. While Burns and Stalker's advocacy for organically structured flexible organizational arrangements are befitting of established new ventures, fledgling ventures, in emergent sectors, require immediate attention to the development of formal organizational structures. As Sine *et al.* (2006, pp. 130–131) describe their results: 'Demonstrate that new ventures that have greater role formalization and specialization in founding teams, as well as administrative intensity, also show better future performance'. While it is necessary to impose critical judgement on absolute assertions pertaining to the best form of organizational management, we concur with Sine *et al.* (ibid., p. 131) in their pronouncement that their study 'is only a first step in exploring how the relationship between particular types of formal structure and organizational performance is contingent on both environmental and organizational factors'. Additional pathways made evident by their research include: 'examining the relationship between structural attributes … life cycle stages, transitions between life cycle stages, and environmental stability' (ibid.). Comprehending these associations will be particularly relevant to analyses of politics and decision-making within the rapid start-up times, and intensely concentrated life cycles of dot.com Internet companies operating in the dynamically turbulent emergent sector of information communication technology.

POLITICAL ACTIVITY AS A RATIONAL PROCESS?

Although rational procedure is emphasized in mainstream theory, the actuality of decision-making in everyday circumstances involves significant elements of irrationality. Table 9.2 contains a list of conditions that contribute to irrational decisions.

Managerial decisions are never totally rational; they are better characterized by what March and Simon (1958) termed **bounded rationality**. Limitations in the human capacity to process information are defined as restricting individuals *to simplified models that extract the essential features from problems* without capturing all their complexity as is evident in the retail case study (see Exercise 9.5).

Bounded rationality
Stipulates the existence of limitations in the human capacity to process information without resort to some arbitrary or non-rational selection. It suggests that these limitations restrict individuals to constructing simplified models that extract only the basic elements of a problem and thereby neglect its complexity.

Table 9.2 **Potential contributors to irrational decisions**

Ideal rational decision-making model	Potential contributors to irrationality
Problems identification	Conflicting goals
Problem definition	Changing goals
Data collection	Limited information
Seeking alternatives	Misinformation
Analysis	Errors in logic
Authorization	Personal ambition
Deliberation	Jealousies
Compromising	Personality domination
Evaluation	Power struggles
Sub-decision	Rationalization
Decision/action	Time pressure

Source: From Willam, Bubrin and Sisk, *Management & Organization*, 5E, © 1985 South Western, as part of Cengage Learning, Inc. Reproduced by permission www.cengage.com/permissions.

Exercise 9.5

Bounded rationality Think back to when you were considering which university to attend. Recall the wealth of choices available to you. The concept of 'bounded rationality' recognizes that with so many options available an individual might not consider every viable alternative. Rather, when faced with a complex problem – such as selecting a university – most people reduce the problem to a level at which it can be easily comprehended and managed. These constraints on rational decision-making are effectively summarized in Table 9.2. In small groups, identify the potential contributions to irrational decision-making that influenced your choice of university.

Key mainstream studies

Groups – particularly specialist groups – coalitions, networks and sponsors all provide a source of power from which to control the process of decision-making. One common power strategy, based on group formation, is the

Sponsor–protégé relationship Informal relationships between senior and junior personnel, often motivated by mutual advantage.

Cliques Small exclusive group of friends and associates who constitute part of the **informal** structure of an organization.

Coalitions Informal liaison between two or more interest groups intent on increasing their joint power and control with respect to another group or groups.

sponsor-protégé relationship. These are informal relationships between senior and junior personnel and motivated by mutual advantage. The junior organizational member might provide the senior with direct access to sensitive information or alert him/her to relevant events. In return the senior will guide the career development of the protégé. Burns (1963) provides some indication of this phenomenon in his account of organizations as interlocking **cliques** and **coalitions**. The skilled organizational politician actively cultivates informal allegiances with powerful interest groups operating in his/her field. A 'coalition' refers to a special type of power resource.

DIFFERENTIATING CLIQUES AND COALITIONS

To recap, a clique or coalition is 'an informal relation between two or more interest groups for the purpose of increasing their joint power in relation to some other group or groups' (Fincham and Rhodes, 1996, p. 445). This definition takes for granted coalitions as premised on an alliance between employees with shared interests. But coalitions and other forms of alliance are not necessarily based on shared identities. That is to say, members of a coalition may not identify with each other except for the opportunistic activity that has brought them together. Rather, their recruitment may be motivated by disparate aims and objectives, tenuously converged around a similar interest. Organizations reflect this definition of coalition when they comprise formal and informal groupings united by an interest or stake but whose ultimate intentions and preferences might differ (Morgan, 1986, p. 154). Political analysis often makes contrasts between cliques 'that become aware of common goals' and coalitions who 'unite to pursue a joint interest, often working against a rival network' (ibid). Given the potential power of coalitions to advance specific interests and pursue particular objectives, it is important to reflect upon their formation (see also Chapters 7, 8 and 11).

FACTORS MOTIVATING GROUP FORMATION

Relative power Assumption that power exists in relation to the will and objectives of both superordinates and subordinates.

Fincham and Rhodes (1996) identify three distinct factors relevant to the formation of coalitions. The first condition, which might encourage a coalition group forming, is the **relative power** of the interest groups. If a single interest group is deemed sufficiently powerful to gain advantage in the decision-making process, they might well decide that a coalition is not worth forming. A second feature, which plays a part in coalition formation, is managerial differentiation. If interests within the organization are extremely diverse, any coalition will be unstable and subject to factious tensions. In these circumstances, the interdependent co-operation required for the successful operation of the coalition will be so difficult that the very existence of the coalition will be jeopardized. A third feature relevant to the formation of a coalition is the issue itself. If an objective is suitably realizable through the one-time pooling together of interests, this might tempt unlikely groups into a temporary coalition. In summary, conditions relevant to coalition formation are as follows:

1 Coalition attracted by relative power of the respective interest groups.
2 Limited amounts of managerial differentiation.
3 Likelihood of coalition formation as issue-based.

Contributions and limitations of mainstream approaches

Political analysis clearly encourages us to recognize that organizational decisions are often made by coalitions of individuals and groups. Organizations are constituted by a diversity of individual and group interests, each with the potential of influencing decision-making. Limited organizational resources precipitate ceaseless competition between individuals and groups. Although many mainstream thinkers prescribe strategies for preventing such competition bursting into uncontrollable conflict, sometimes it heralds the conflict as stimulating innovative change. The intended imagery is one of vibrant political behaviour and ongoing processes of change and development.

Decision-making in the pluralist model is conceptualized as operating through the continual resolution of conflict. Political analysis often converges towards a model of decision-making predicated on negotiation and bargaining between divergent interests. Conflict takes centre stage in this bargaining model, because it is conflicting interests that motivate actors to draw upon tactics and skills in advancing their position (Fincham and Rhodes, 1996). Figure 9.1 provides a diagram that simplifies the conditions in which conflict tends to arise. The diagram is particularly pertinent as it highlights the possibilities as opposed to **dysfunctions** of conflict.

> **Dysfunctions** Action, procedures and processes that impede or disrupt the ability of an entity to achieve its aims.

In summary, the pluralist approach offers:

- A primary focus on examining the micro-politics of everyday organizational life to reveal the plurality of political processes through which decision-making is performed. In contrast to the classical theorists' image of stable formal structures, pluralist analyses depict organizations as 'organized anarchies'. Coherence and order in organizational life emerges out of the accommodations, compromises and negotiations that reflect and reproduce political activity.

- An understanding of organizations as **negotiated orders**. Order and stability within an organization is the negotiated outcome of relations between the interest groups and coalitions, which contain and manage overt conflicts.

- The adoption of a contingency approach, which rests on the view that an organization is constituted by informal subsystems and boundaries, which delineate it from its wider environment. The contingency approach seeks to identify the subsystems that define the organization and the conditions that foreground their interrelationships.

> **Negotiated order** The idea that social reality is open to a degree of interpretation and mutual adjustment between actors (e.g., between members of a team or between a boss and a subordinate). This element of negotiability makes possible a process of manoeuvring to influence other actors.

- A rejection of a universal and unitary model of organizations. Rather, the form an organization adopts is framed by how it copes with specific contingency factors, group dynamics and political negotiations.

- A concept of power that acknowledges how diverse interests, competition and conflict characterize decision-making in organizations.

Figure 9.1 The conflict process in mainstream pluralist theory
Source: Adapted from Robbins, S. and Judge, T. A., *Organizational Behaviour*, 14th edn, p. 457, © 2011. Adapted by permission of Pearson Education, Inc. Upper Saddle River, NJ.

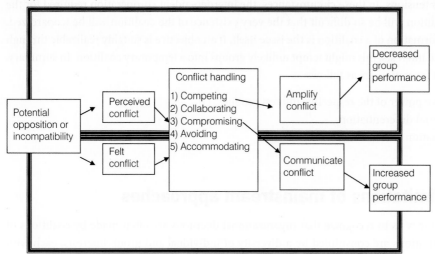

Limitations of the pluralist approach include:

- Politics and negotiations are restricted to minor issues and conflicts within accepted or agreed rules of the game, so that the prevailing structure of power, inequality, freedom and identity cannot be challenged.
- Managers are presumed not to have their own interests above and beyond a concern to reconcile diverse and conflicting interests.
- Power is still seen to be located in persons or groups rather than in the relations between them.
- While rationality is seen as bounded or limited, it is not itself recognized as political such that power defines what can be accepted as rational.
- When satisfactory rather than optimal outcomes are seen as the new form of rationality, big issues of conflict, say over world poverty, the environment, the faith in 'free' markets, consumerism, etc., are marginalized.

The pluralist framework fails to take account of how prevailing structures of inequality are a limitation on any shared decision-making. Different interest groups may influence decisions but only so far as this does not challenge the structure of power and inequality. Although recognizing how organizations are adaptive, even structural theorists are extremely reticent about the potential for group activities to dramatically change enduring procedures and normative values. The enduring nature of organization structure means 'only a few elements of the system are adaptive at any one time; the remainder are, at least in the short run, "givens"' (March and Simon, 1981, p. 148).

Mainstream accounts of politics and organization focus on explaining: (1) typologies of political rule; (2) how rules are maintained; (3) how conflict is contained; and (4) how legitimacy is sustained. A perspectival link to each of these concerns is the acceptance that co-ordination and co-operation between members constitutes a vital condition for organizational survival. No one would deny that co-operation is a legitimate topic of organizational analysis. But mainstream analysis focuses predominantly on the dynamics and strategies that sustain the political status quo or organizational stability. Consequently, although conflict is examined it is as a temporary aberration that can readily be reconciled to secure organizational stability and management control. Moreover, the rules and regulations that sustain existing political relations are seen as politically and morally neutral devices. An image is developed of a complex network of political actors jostling for power and, somehow, largely unaffected by the deep-rooted structural features of class, gender, sexuality and race (Jeanes *et al.*, 2011). A degree of myopia is clearly evident here, in that a concentration at the micro-level of interaction underestimates the extent to which the practices of dominant power groupings may have the effect of reproducing wider inequalities of power, status and wealth (see Chapter 5).

CRITICAL APPROACH TO POLITICS AND DECISION-MAKING
Broad overview of the critical approach

Critical perspectives have been keen to locate decision-making within the political and economic context in which organizations operate. Critical theorists refuse to focus only on the micro-relations internal to organizations, but also demand to reflect on broader configurations of power and inequality in society, which simultaneously constrain and enable the political activities of organizational members. A clear example of this perspective is embodied in Marxist political analysis (see also Chapter 7).

Marxist political analysis emphasizes the necessity to be historical and contextual when studying organizational relations. Work organizations are uniquely linked to the capitalist productive economy and thus require an analysis that appreciates the dynamics of capitalist accumulation and the labour process (Thompson and McHugh, 1991, p. 40). In this sense the structures and everyday processes of organization can only be comprehended in terms of control initiated by class-based interests (Reed, 1992, p. 95). Organizations are social arenas in which wider social and political inequalities of power are played out. While groups display differences of interests and thereby behave in distinctive ways, these differences present limited challenges to the enduring structures of capitalist production. Organization relations, structures and processes do indeed have political significance. But political analysis, according to the Marxist perspective, needs to extend beyond the confines of the physical organization and embrace the wider 'political economy' (Thompson and McHugh, 1991). Organizations are perceived as mechanisms through which dominant groups secure conditions necessary for the reproduction of their economic, political and cultural advantage. It could be argued that the structure and design of organizations are designed and structured in such a way as to reflect and reinforce the interests of owners or those senior in the hierarchy (see Chapter 7).

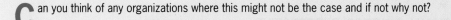

Thinkpoint 9.6

Can you think of any organizations where this might not be the case and if not why not?

RETHINKING THE PLURALIST ACCOUNT OF DECISION-MAKING DYNAMICS

Critiques of the pluralist tradition in political analysis draw attention to a shortfall in the theoretical analysis of deep-rooted social cleavages. This radical view, influenced by Marxist theory, introduces a political focus on the social and cultural reproduction of endemic inequalities. Pluralist accounts of political activity regard conflict as an inherent characteristic of organizational life. Conflict stems from a multiplicity of sources drawing upon an innumerable plurality of power resources. The negotiations, coalitions and alliances, which characterize the organization as a political system, are with difficulty contained by reference to a single focal point of power. Critiques of the pluralist tradition emphasize the inherent oppositional and irreconcilable conflicts that define the nature of power in capitalist society. Conflict theory identifies how incompatible class-based interest mediates organizational politics.

While the mainstream has made often-exaggerated claims about the partici- | **Critical structuralist** Critical
pation and involvement of lower hierarchy staff in decision-making, **critical** | theory that identifies
structuralist approaches see employee participation schemes as primarily means | the political activity of
of manipulating the consent of staff. Important decisions still remain with senior | organizations to be directly
management, leaving only minor operational decisions as the prerogative of | linked to the capitalist
| productive economy.

Structuralist approach
Concentrates on the complexity of the design or structure of an organization independently from the human dimension. It tends to see organizational structures as determined by external conditions characterized as the environment.

Capital In Marxist critical theory, capital is defined as assets (e.g., property, machines, money) used to finance the production of commodities for the private gain of the capitalist classes. Capitalists invest their capital in the production of commodities and accumulate profits by selling goods at a value exceeding the costs of their production.

Labour People or class of people involved in productive work who can be distinguished from those who manage the processes of productive work.

employees. **Structuralist approaches** define unresolved conflict as a conspicuous feature of organizational decision-making. Organizations are constituted here as arenas of power struggle between diverse ranges of incompatible interests. The pluralist model of loosely aligned, shifting coalitions is assumed to deny the existence of incompatibilities between the interests of **capital** and those of **labour**, between men and women or different ethnic groups. These endemic differences of interest translate into deep-seated oppositions between the interests of management and workers.

Following the analyses of Marx and Weber, structuralist approaches argue that decision-making practices and outcomes are, at least partly, controlled by factors external to the organizations themselves. According to Marxist analysis, economic conflict between management and labour demonstrates how decision-making processes are 'instruments of capital' (Braverman, 1974; Clegg and Dunkerley, 1980). Decision-making is defined in these Marxist terms as enabling the owners of the means of production to further exploit workers through paying them much less than the value of their labour (see Chapter 7). In contrast to this Marxian analysis, Weberian approaches (see Chapter 14) identify how organizational roles might conflict with systems of authority, formal and informal operating procedures, and patterns of expertise (Fligstein, 1992; Perrow, 1973; March and Simon, 1958). Weberian approaches shift the structuralist emphasis from the experience of being oppressed by broader economic factors to a focus on oppression in terms of a worker's internalized obligation to comply with company directives. Decision-making is thus defined in Weberian structuralist theory as compelling workers to submit to authority through rules and regulations that have secured some legitimacy. This legitimacy, however, has been achieved largely through the ability of those exercising power to define the situation for others.

A CRITICAL 'ORGANIZATIONAL POLITICS' PERSPECTIVE

This perspective does not presume order and consensus, and insofar as there are claims within organizations about adapting to their environments, it identifies these very claims as inherently political. The environment is merely a linguistic description whose content has to be articulated and perhaps mobilized as a way of enrolling others to a particular definition of reality for the purposes of pursuing specific political objectives. This political activity concerns individuals or groups securing power to advance not just their material interests in terms of career, income and security but also their symbolic interests in relation to identity, social recognition and status. From this perspective, management and leadership are seen to be inescapably political, as may be seen in Case Study 9.1 (Knights and Murray, 1994) of a medium-sized UK mutual life insurance company, where organizational politics is seen to have determined the direction followed by the company.

By contrast to processual theorists, this research identified organizational politics not as 'aberration or pathological condition' but 'as the motor of organizational life' (ibid, p. 245). Clearly, the participants are struggling not merely to have their ideas or knowledge accepted by significant others in the organization, although that does enhance the sense of their own identity, but they are also competing for career progress (power, wealth, freedom and status) and seeking to achieve greater levels of security. While not entirely obvious from this brief synopsis of the research, it also challenges the over-rational view of organizational processes that is common both among theorists of organizational behaviour and practitioners themselves. It is this belief in rationality that precludes an admission that organizational outcomes are often the relative arbitrary result of political processes of competing career and identity-securing strategies that are anything but rational. From this perspective, management activity is a political process constructing a reality that denies its own political character – to paraphrase Oscar Wilde, 'a politics that dare not speak its name'. Were it to be recognized, let alone admitted publicly, that management is arbitrary and accidental rather than rational and planned, this would be to threaten the very basis of its power and privilege. If organizational outcomes cannot be perceived as a result of managerial competence, then why are managers rewarded so much more than their staff? By avoiding blowing the cover, as it were, the mainstream contributes to reproducing the myth of management rationality and the maintenance of existing power relations. In this sense, it reflects and reinforces the identity of managers as indispensable to organizations and thereby helps to sustain their security.

Case study 9.1
Pensco

At the time of the research in the mid-1990s, a fundamental political struggle was occurring between managers in marketing and those in other divisions but, in particular, Information Systems (IS). Ostensibly it was over how the environment was to be understood, but the effect of having one definition of the environment accepted as opposed to another had major political consequences. The IT division interpreted the environment as one in which competition had made the provision of good customer service vital and this was dependent on adequate administrative procedures, which in turn required a complete overhaul of IT systems. The marketing division, however, interpreted the environment somewhat differently. In response to a new government initiative to persuade consumers to contract out of the state earnings related pension scheme (SERPS) and make private arrangements, the marketing division was convinced that competition would be focused more on providing the most attractive products – one being a group pension product. While there were many complex shifts of position of the various parties that would take up too much space to record here, the outcome was that marketing was more forceful regarding its position because of resilient arguments but due to enrolling the chief executive officer (CEO) on their side. In order to deliver a new suite of pensions products, IS was forced to 'botch up' a number of systems rather than completely overhaul them, which was its preference. Customer service was sidelined in this struggle and just had to hope that the administration of policies would not be too severely affected by the deflection of IS resources away from routine administrative tasks towards a concentration on new products.

Thinkpoint 9.7

Modern organizations have been described as cultivating forms of political rivalry between human interest groups. This assumption is based on the premise that modern organizations are designed as systems of simultaneous competition and collaboration (Kakabadse, 1983). In the above case study, marketing was effective in defining the situation in accordance with its interests. Can you think of reasons why this may have been the case?

CONSIDERING LIMITATIONS OF THE CRITICAL ALTERNATIVE

Having set an agenda for the study of structure and institutional conflict within organizations, we do not want to fall into the theoretical trap of dismissing all that went before. Indeed the critical structuralist approach has significant limitations – namely its neglect of the individual. In pluralist political analysis, conflicts result from a plurality of divergent interests among individuals as well as groups. This micro-politics of organizational decision-making provides at least some opportunity to focus on the individual or group interest. Conversely, structuralist analysis describes how conflict in organizations rests on ideological foundations and fundamental questions of structural relations and power. Both positions insufficiently acknowledge how organizational members are engaged in the pursuit of their own personal interests and their own commitments related to beliefs and values. Purely structural forms of analysis tend to obviate the experiences, views and interpretations of the individual actors that make up any organization (Ball, 1987).

**Box 9.2
Key issues and processes in the control of information flows within organizations**

1 *Formal and informal communication networks.* Information is a scarce and valued resource within organizations. Access to information can increase the power and influence of group members. Consequently, hierarchies often emerge according to who has access to important sources of information.
2 *Gatekeepers.* Informational flow is invariably controlled through restrictions on access and interpretation.
3 *Partiality.* Information held and transmitted by people is often partial and reflects their interests and resources.
4 *Suppression.* Some information may be consciously or subconsciously excluded from consideration if it questions or counters the dominant view.

Source: Adapted from Dawson, S. (1986) Analysing Organisations, London: Macmillan.

Thinkpoint 9.8

Think of the number of situations in your own life that have been defined for you by others – parents, teachers, police, the government, peers, etc. Often, especially when you completely agree with what is defined, it may seem like it is your own definition of the situation so you may have to think deeply to trace the source. Compare this list with another list where you have most definitely defined a situation for yourself. How do the two sets of situations differ in terms of your commitment and feelings about them?

Masculine discourses
Communication consciously or unconsciously reflects and reproduces a sense of being analytical and technical, and masterly and in control, generated largely but not exclusively by men.

Rationality in our society is a highly valued concept. It is at the heart of science, administration and business and it is reinforced in all three by dominant **masculine discourses** (Collinson and Hearn, 1996) that privilege 'cold', 'hard' and calculating rationalities against 'warm', 'soft' and intuitive emotional relations. Consequently, there is a conspiracy of silence regarding the existence of bodies and emotions, in addition to cognition and calculation, in management and leadership. Theory and practice present management in a 'disembodied' fashion. In *Beyond Management,* Ian Lennie (1999) carried out his research while acting as a full-time manager in public welfare. He was aware that management was a messy, fully embodied process; and yet all the literature seemed strangely disembodied, speaking only cognitively and at a distance from the everyday experience of managing. He writes of this as the difference between management and managing, and admitted that managers seeking a professional status and through their training were increasingly made to feel that management was technical, abstract and completely separate from what it means to be bodily as well as mentally involved in work on an everyday basis. He is convinced that a disembodied manager cannot manage well since managing is largely about social relations and we only know whether we have managed well through the quality of those relations: 'The results of managing well are not control and accumulation, but civilization.' (Lennie, 1999, p. 141)

Exercise 9.6

1   Critically review the classical model of decision-making.
2   Provide fictional examples of the pluralist model of organizational decision-making.
3   Provide fictional examples that illustrate the limitations of the pluralist model.
4   Discuss the limitations of the mainstream structuralist model of decision-making.
5   Discuss the limitations of the critical structuralist approach to organizational politics.

Conclusion

Classical models of decision-making place less emphasis on individual action, focusing instead on the operation of collective norms, values and social structures. They describe decision-making as a response to organizational structures rather than directed by political activities and interest groups. Many writers within this tradition base their theories of decision-making on the premise that members of organizations share common interests. Successful decision-making is defined by its ability to achieve organizational goals, so that all its members can be more highly rewarded.

Conversely, pluralist approaches recognize political behaviour as a crucial feature of decision-making. Political behaviour involves cultivating influential allies, controlling the flow of information and influencing decisions through the informal use of one's power base. The imagery invoked in pluralist analysis is that of loosely connected coalitions vying for limited resources in an organizational context, characterized by contested cultures and shifting alliances. The pluralist model is indeed a vibrant, optimistic account of power and its distribution throughout the organization.

However, structuralist analyses raise considerable doubts about the pluralist conception of power. There are assumed to exist significant limits on the degree to which incompatible interests can be articulated and reconciled within decision-making processes. Questions are raised concerning the extent to which informal groups cut across formal divisions (Etzioni, 1964; Dubin, 1954). Questions are also raised concerning the scope of informal groups (Etzioni, 1964). Whether mainstream or critical, structuralists have a propensity to neglect individual behaviour, thus transforming the complexities of interpersonal influence into nothing more than the outcome of structural processes.

Possibilities, however, exist in the synthesis of structuralist and pluralist approaches within those critical perspectives that emphasize individual identity and insecurity as the medium and outcome of the exercise of power conditioned by structures of inequality generated by global and national capitalist, gender and race relations.

Discussion questions

1 How are we to understand organizational politics in contemporary organizations?

2 What are the similarities and differences between a classical, pluralist and a mainstream structuralist view?

3 How does organizational politics affect people?

4 Which in your view of the various perspectives studied in this chapter provides the best account of conflict and politics in organizations?

5 What does a critical view of organizational politics add to our understanding of organizations?

Further reading

Clegg, Stewart (1989) *Frameworks of Power*, London: Sage.

This book provides an overview of power in organizations drawing on Weber who focuses largely on authority or legitimate power that contingency and resource dependency theory also subscribe to, and Marx whose focus is on class conflict and the exploitation of labour. Clegg's favoured approac h, however, is to focus on actions and decisions that are a function of the struggles between different agents with competing objectives and calculations.

Edwards, Richard (1979) *Contested Terrain: The Transformation of the Workplace in the 20th Century*, New York: Basic Books.

Edwards' major contribution is to make a distinction between three types of management power or control. Simple control involves a personal and informal exercise of power typical of paternalistic management in owner-managed organizations. Technical control is where the machine, as in mass production, controls the flow and pace of work. Finally, complex or bureaucratic control enforces detailed rules and regulations allowing managers to exercise power at a distance rather than through close supervision.

Jackall, Robert (1988) *Moral Mazes: The World of Corporate Managers,* New York: Oxford University Press.

This empirical study focuses on two conflicting management techniques of exercising power – centralization and decentralization – because with bureaucracy they allow power to be exercised economically. Through allowing negotiations about output and profit targets and then imposing a rigorous reporting system, subordinates disciplined themselves.

Jermier, John M., Knights, David and Nord, Walter R. (eds) (1994) *Resistance and Power in Organization,* London: Routledge.

This edited book contains several chapters which draw on the work of Michel Foucault to describe situations

similar to that in Jackall's study where self-discipline facilitates an 'economy of power'. These chapters also show that resistance is never far away when power is being exercised in organizations.

Lukes, Steven (1975) *Power: A Radical Approach,* London: Macmillan.

Steven Lukes developed an analysis of three different conceptions of power that many organizational theorists have adopted. First, a one-dimensional view perceives power to exist when individuals or groups can assert their will in situations of conflict. A two-dimensional perspective keeps potential conflicts off the agenda so that power is exercised prior to decisions being made. Finally, a third dimension is one where the situation is defined for others so that they internalize the norms and comply even when it is against their interests to do so.

Key sources for this chapter

Crazier, M. (1964) *The Bureaucratic Phenomenon,* Chicago, IL: University of Chicago Press.

Fincham, R. and Rhodes, P. S. (1996/1999) *Principles of Organizational Behaviour,* Oxford: Oxford University Press.

Handy, C. (1976) *Understanding Organisations,* Harmondsworth: Penguin.

Kakabadse, A., Judlow, R. and Vinnicombe, S. (1988) *Working in Organisations,* Harmondsworth: Penguin.

Knights, D. and Murray, F. (1994) *Managers Divided: Organisational Politics and Information Technology Management,* London: Wiley.

March, J. and Simon, H. (1958) *Organization,* New York: John Wiley and Sons.

Morgan, G. (1986) *Images of Organization,* London: Sage.

Pettigrew, M. (1973) *The Politics of Organisational Decision-Making,* London: Tavistock.

Reed, M. (1992) *The Sociology of Organizations: Themes, Perspectives and Prospects,* London: Harvester Wheatsheaf.

Sine, W., Mitsuhashi, H. and Kirsch, D. (2006) 'Revisiting Burns and Stalker: Formal Structure and New Venture Performance in Emerging Economic Sectors', *The Academy of Management Journal,* 49(1): 121–132.

Thompson, P. and McHugh, D. (2002) *Work Organisations,* third edn, Basingstoke: Palgrave.

More general reading

Ball, S. (1987) *The Micro-Politics of the School,* London: Routledge.

Burns, T. (1961) 'Micropolitics: Mechanisms of institutional change', *Administrative Science Quarterly,* 6(3): 257–281.

Castles, F. G., Murray, D. J. and Potter, D. C. (1971) *Decisions, Organizations and Society,* Harmondsworth: Penguin Books.

Hall, R. (1999) *Organizations: Structures, Processes and Outcome,* Englewood Cliffs, NJ: Prentice Hall.

Handy, C. (1976) *Understanding Organisations,* Harmondsworth: Penguin.

Hassard, J. and Pym, D. (1990) *The Theory and Philosophy of Organisation: Critical Issues and New Perspectives,* London: Routledge.

Lawrence, P. R. and Lorsch, J. W. (1967) *Organisation and Environment,* Harvard: Graduate School of Business Administration.

Mangham, I. (1979) *The Politics of Organisational Change,* London: Associated Business Press.

Pettigrew, A. (1975) 'Towards a political theory of organisational intervention', *Human Relations,* 28(3): 191–209.

Pugh, D. and Hickson, D. (1996) *Writers on Organisations,* fifth edn, Harmondsworth: Penguin.

Reed, M. (1992) *The Sociology of Organizations: Themes, Perspectives and Prospects,* London: Harvester Wheatsheaf.

Sofer, C. (1972) *Organisation in Theory and Practice,* London: Heinemann Educational Books.

Thompson, P. and McHugh, D. (1991) *Work Organisations,* Basingstoke: Palgrave.

Sine, Wesley D., Mitsuhashi, H. and Kirsch, David A. (2006) *Burns And Stalker: Formal Structure and New Venture Performance in Emerging Economic Sectors,* Academy of Management Journal 49, 1: 121–132

Zald, M. (1970) *Power in Organisation,* Nashville, TN: Vanderbilt University Press.

References

Bacharach, S. and Lawler, E. (1980) *Power and Politics in Organizations,* London: Jossey-Bass.

Ball, S. (1987) *The Micro-Politics of the School,* London: Routledge.

Braverman, H. (1974) *Labour and Monopoly Capitalism,* New York: Monthly Review Press.

Burawoy, M. (1979) *Manufacturing Consent: Changes in the Labor Process Under Monopoly Capitalism,* Chicago, IL: University of Chicago Press.

Burns, T. (1963) 'Industry in the new age', *New Society,* 31 January, 17–20.

Burns, T. and Stalker, G. ([1961] 1968); *The Management of Innovation,* London: Tavistock Publications.

Clegg, S. and Dunkerley, D. (1980) *Organization, Class and Control,* London: Routledge and Kegan Paul.

Collinson, D. and Hearn, J. (1996) *Men as Managers, Managers as Men: Critical Perspectives on Men, Masculinities and Management,* London: Sage Publications.

Dawson, S. (1986) *Analysing Organisations,* Basingstoke: Macmillan.

du Gay, P. (2000) *In Praise of Bureaucracy: Weber, Organization, Ethics,* London: Sage.

Dubin, R. (1954) *Human Relations in Administration: The Sociology of Organization, With Readings and Cases,* New York: Prentice Hall.

Durkheim, E. (1947) *The Division of Labour in Society,* New York: Free Press.

Etzioni, A. (1964) *Modern Organisations,* Englewood Cliffs, NJ: Prentice Hall.

Fincham, R. and Rhodes, P. S. (1996/1999) *Principles of Organizational Behaviour,* Oxford: Oxford University Press.

Fligstein, N. (1992) 'The social construction of efficiency', in M. Zey (ed.) *Decision Making: Alternatives to Rational Choice Models,* Newbury Park, CA: Sage, pp. 351–376.

French, J. and Raven, B. (1959) 'The bases of social power', in D. Cartwright (ed.) *Studies in Social Power,* Ann Arbor, MI: Institute for Social Research.

Jeanes, E., Knights, D. and Yancey Martin P. (eds) (2011) *A Handbook on Gender, Work and Organization,* London and New York: Wiley.

Kakabadse, A. (1983) *The Politics of Management,* Aldershot: Gower.

Kakabadse, A., Judlow, R. and Vinnicombe, S. (1988) *Working in Organisations,* Harmondsworth: Penguin.

Knights, D. and Murray, F. (1994) *Managers Divided: Organisational Politics and Information Technology Management,* London: Wiley.

Lennie, I. (1999) *Beyond Management,* London: Sage.

March, J. and Simon, H. (1958) *Organization,* New York: John Wiley and Son.

March, J. and Simon, H. (1981) 'Decision-making theory', in O. Grusky and G. Miller (eds) *The Sociology of Organisations,* London: Macmillan.

Morgan, G. (1986) *Images of Organization,* London: Sage.

Perrow, C. (1973) 'The neo-Weberian model: Decision making, conflict, and technology', in S. Graeme and K. Thompson (eds) *People and Organisations,* London: Open University.

Pettigrew, A. M. (1973) *The Politics of Organisational Decision-Making,* London: Tavistock.

Reed, M. (1992) *The Sociology of Organizations: Themes, Perspectives and Prospects,* London: Harvester Wheatsheaf.

Robbins, S. (1998) *Organizational Behaviour,* eighth edn, Englewood Cliffs, NJ: Prentice Hall.

Robbins, S. and Judge, T. A. (2011) *Organizational Behaviour,* 14th edn, p. 457. Upper Saddle River, NJ: Pearson Education, inc.

Sisk, H. L., Willams, J. C. and Dubrin, A. J. (1985) *Management & Organization,* Cincinnati : SouthWestern Pub Co.

Thompson, P. and McHugh, D. (1991) *Work Organisations,* Basingstoke: Macmillan.

10 Culture

JOANNA BREWIS WITH HUGH WILLMOTT

Aims of the chapter

This chapter will:

- Identify the origins of the interest in culture in the field of organizational behaviour.

- Outline the mainstream perspective on culture.

- Identify the extent to which the key claim of this perspective stands up to empirical and conceptual scrutiny.

- Outline the critical perspective on culture, and the ways in which it departs from its mainstream counterpart.

Key concepts and learning objectives

By the end of this chapter you should be able to:

- Outline the origins of the interest in organizational culture.

- Understand the 'culture is something that an organization has' perspective.

- Critique the central link made in mainstream perspective between the 'right' culture and high levels of organizational performance.

- Understand how the 'culture is something that an organization is' perspective challenges the orthodoxy.

Overview and key points

Organizational behaviour (OB) as a discipline seeks to understand why people behave as they do in organizations. The literature on **culture** is no exception. Borrowing from anthropological studies of societal cultures, students of organizational culture focus on the values, beliefs and norms about what is important and how things should be done in particular organizational settings. 'Organizational culture' is seen to represent some kind of shared commitment to particular ways of relating to the organization, to superiors, to colleagues and to the role.

For example, you are likely to share a certain kind of organizational culture with fellow students. You might share, to some degree, a belief that higher education is important, that your university will deliver a relevant education for the future you have planned, that your tutors are qualified to deliver such education, that your task is to participate in lectures and seminars, study independently outside of these sessions, abide by coursework deadlines and so on. And you will undoubtedly be expected to comply with such beliefs even if you are not committed to them. The key argument here is that values like these influence behaviour in organizations, and so are worthy of study in their own right.

Culture An anthropological term that refers to the shared values, beliefs and norms about key priorities and ways of undertaking particular tasks, or relating to colleagues among members of a particular organization.

This interest in organizational culture emerged in the late 1970s as a result of a series of challenges facing Western management practitioners and theorists at the time. These have been said to include the following:

- *A general decline in religious belief.* This can be linked to the long-standing claim that modern society is disenchanting if not alienating – as discussed in a number of the preceding chapters. Westerners, it seems, began to look to work as a source of 'identity'. 'Organizational culture' offers a way to find answers to questions like 'Who am I?', as well as 'What is my job for?', 'What is my organization for?' and so on (see also Chapter 2).

New Right Political development or strategy popular in the final quarter of the twentieth century where the 'free market' is advocated and state intervention stigmatized. New Right policies favour the neo-liberal privatization of public sector corporations such as gas, electricity, the railways, etc.

- *The expansion of highly technical work and the growth of service industries.* These developments have meant that workers require more skills and expertise (and therefore cannot be managed by using a traditional authoritarian approach); they are required to behave in 'customer-pleasing' ways. **New Right** politics has emphasized individualism (e.g., Thatcherism in the UK and Reaganomics in the USA). Workers have become more educated and expect more autonomy, partly as a result. 'Culture' here can be understood as a way to give employees more day-to-day discretion or freedom – the idea being that there is no need for strict rules and/or management surveillance if workers have acquired the 'correct' (e.g., customer-facing) values, such as 'the customer is always right'.

- *Limitations of a mechanical, 'Theory X' approach to managing people.* The 'management science' approach, which dominated theory and practice during the 1960s and 1970s, had become discredited because employees could not in fact be managed purely through 'objective' and mathematical analysis of organizational operations (see Chapter 6). This led to a renewed focus on the 'soft', 'human' elements of organizations. The culture literature represents part of this backlash in its emphasis on managing what Peters and Waterman (1982, p. 11), as we shall see later, call 'the intractable, irrational, intuitive, informal organization'.

- *Innovative production methods.* Techniques like 'just-in-time' were making organizational operations more efficient (see Chapters 4 and 11). But this required increased flexibility and therefore greater commitment from workers. Given that culture supposedly provides a reservoir of meaning for the individual worker and also enhances a sense of collectivity among workers, a strong set of shared cultural values should – it was argued – enhance their commitment.

Globalization Notion that countries are becoming economically, politically, technologically and culturally closer to each other. Examples of this process include the European Union, the Internet and the worldwide popularity of branded products including Coca-Cola, Nike shoes and Mercedes cars.

- *The Japanese 'miracle'.* The emergence of Japan following the Second World War as a world economic power was seen to have something to do with the cultural values informing Japanese management techniques. **Globalization** – the breaking down of economic, political, cultural and technological barriers between countries (see Chapter 13) – meant that the West was paying more attention to other countries. And if Japan could create such dramatic success through underpinning its economic activities with a strong value system, why couldn't this also work elsewhere?

In this chapter we will discuss both mainstream and critical approaches to organizational culture. First we review the mainstream perspective, which sees culture as something that an organization *has,* as something that managers can shape and modify. This 'has' perspective, urges managers to make every effort to ensure that employees have the 'right' values, beliefs and norms. Creating culture 'at the top' in this way is said to engender harmony and stability in the organization, as well as ensuring that employees behave in the 'appropriate' ways, as defined by senior management. The 'has' perspective on culture draws a strong link between the management of culture and organizational success, but there is controversy as to whether there is 'one best culture' that fosters excellence, or whether the development of an effective culture is a matter of contingency (see Chapter 7). In this part of the chapter we also review some of the (many) mechanisms that the mainstream approach suggests can be used to manage culture. It ends with a more critical look at the empirical and conceptual support for its key claim – for instance, whether a strong culture always leads to excellent organizational results.

In the second part of this chapter we discuss the critical alternative. This approach argues that culture is something that an organization *is:* in other words, everything in the organization, from the market segment it targets to the number of people it employs, speaks in some way of underlying values, beliefs and norms in that environment. From this perspective, culture is seen to emerge organically as workers learn together to cope with what their jobs require of them. Because workers differ both in terms of what they face within the organization and their experiences outside work, the 'is' perspective argues that any one workplace is likely to house a number of potentially antagonistic *subcultures.* For these reasons, this perspective is much more sceptical about the management of culture, and it anticipates that such initiatives will be resisted, more or less overtly, by employees; or that they involve an unethical use of management power that comes close to attempted brainwashing.

Introduction

Anyone who has spent time with any variety of organizations, or worked in more than two or three, will have been struck by the differing atmospheres, the differing ways of doing things, the differing levels of energy, of individual freedom, of kinds of personality. For organizations are as different and varied as the nations and societies of the world. They have differing cultures – sets of values and norms and beliefs – reflected in different structures and systems. (Handy, 1993, p. 180)

Despite OB's relatively recent interest in culture, it has nonetheless become a major focus of attention in the area. We already know broadly speaking what culture is – shared organizational values, beliefs and norms – but it is worth breaking the concept down a little before we embark on the chapter proper. Aspects of organizational culture might include some or all of the following:

- Mission and goals: what is the organization aiming towards? – e.g., to be the market leader in a particular product, or to expand into markets in other parts of the world.
- The **psychological contract**: what employees can expect of the organization beyond the formal employment contract (e.g., job security, exciting work) and what the organization can expect in return (e.g., long hours, customer responsiveness).

  > **Psychological contract** The invisible or implicit set of expectations that employees have of their organizations (e.g., challenging, stimulating work that allows for career progression) and that their organizations have of them (e.g., loyalty and flexibility), but are not laid down in the formal contract of employment.

- Authority and power relations: these are not the same thing. Someone can have formal authority but no real power to influence what others do, and vice versa (see Chapter 9). This is nicely illustrated in Ackroyd and Crowdy's (1990) study of abattoir workers, where the authors suggest that teams in this environment were *formally* led by chargehands, but in reality the chargehands were often fairly low down (and so comparatively powerless) in the *informal* hierarchy that had developed.
- The qualities or characteristics that members should have (or not have): some organizations, for example, stress innovation, initiative and risk-taking; others emphasize caution, conservatism and attention to detail. The latter qualities might be more actively sought by a firm of undertakers, for example.
- Communication and interaction patterns: do staff address managers by their first names? Do they see colleagues as competitors or collaborators? Do they see co-workers in the evenings or at weekends?
- Rewards and punishments: how is 'good' behaviour rewarded – praise or something more tangible like a bonus or a promotion? What kind of sanctions are available for 'bad' behaviour? Is it OK to be late three days in a row? How far does an employee have to go to get the sack?
- Ways of dealing with the outside world: how committed is the organization to protecting environmental resources? Are recycling schemes, electricity saving policies or car sharing arrangements in place, and how seriously are they taken? Moreover, is information shared with competitors or are all organizational processes shrouded in a veil of secrecy?

Organized activity demands that people work together in co-ordinated ways, whether they are in a university, a shop, a factory, a call-centre, a publishing house or wherever. So it would be impossible if the individuals concerned did not agree, at least to some extent, on issues like those identified above. Culture is a source of organizational 'common sense' (see Chapter 1) upon which members draw when deciding where, when and how to act. And if organizational structures, strategies, regulations and policies frame the possibilities for behaviour formally and explicitly, culture could be argued to bring the organization to life. Much of what is presented in bullet points above is codified in written documents like strategic plans, job descriptions and disciplinary procedures. But if cultural values, beliefs and norms in any way contradict these documents, then members will probably subvert or ignore the formal rules in their real-life workplace activities – as we have already seen in the abattoir example (see bullet point above).

Thinkpoint 10.1

How do some of the questions in the bullet points above relate to your university? For example, what do lecturers guarantee to students – prompt feedback on assessed work, perhaps, or maybe they have an open door policy so you can see them whenever you want to? What do they expect in return – essays always being handed in on time or thorough preparation for seminars maybe? Do you ever socialize with your lecturers? To what extent are you encouraged to work with other students on assessed essays or presentations? How would your department deal with plagiarism? And what might the answers to these questions say about the values, beliefs and norms that exist at this institution?

Thinkpoint 10.2

Can you think of instances in your university where what happens in practice goes against institutional rules? For example, perhaps assignment extensions are sometimes granted over the phone when the rules state that forms must be filled out in order for students to make such a request, or attendance registers are not always kept for seminars.

Cultural artefacts
Phenomena accessible to the senses, including architecture, myths, rituals, logos, type of personnel employed and so on, which signify the values in an organization's culture.

Since organizational culture consists of values, beliefs and norms that exist in people's heads, we can only actually identify it at what Schein (1992) refers to as **cultural artefacts**. These are tangible phenomena that embody organizational culture, such as types of people employed (personalities, levels of education, etc.), traditions and rituals, technology, architecture, logos, heroes, stories, myths and so on. Schein argues that there are three levels of culture, and that artefacts represent the tip of an iceberg in the sense that the other two levels (explained below) are hidden from view.

Values incorporate answers to questions like 'What are we doing this for?' and 'Why are we doing it?' So an organization's values might include a commitment to equality of opportunity, to solving human problems through the application of technology or to profit maximization for shareholders – but these can be brought to light only through careful and directed questioning.

Basic assumptions on the other hand are almost impossible to surface. These are unconscious and taken for granted ways of seeing the world and are *the source of values and artefacts*. They concern questions about:

- Our relationship to our environment (should we seek to master nature or to live in harmony with it?) and to each other (should our prime orientation be to ourselves as individuals, or is it more important to be a member of, and offer loyalty to, a group?).
- Reality and truth (is there such a thing as a universal, timeless human truth or reality, or do we live in dynamic worlds that are largely of our own making?).
- Human nature (are we essentially good, bad or a mixture? Is it appropriate to place our trust in others or do we need to take steps to avoid being exploited by them?).
- Human activity (should we focus on measurable achievement and see our activities as a means to an end, or is it more appropriate to live for the moment and enjoy the actual process of our activities?).

With the context for the chapter now established, we turn to the mainstream perspective.

MAINSTREAM PERSPECTIVE ON ORGANIZATIONAL CULTURE

Introduction to the mainstream perspective, aka culture is something that an organization 'has'

Most literature portrays organizational culture as, in Smircich's (1983) words, something that an organization *has*. From this perspective, culture is understood to be:

- *A variable.* Like capital or other assets such as information technology, culture – how employees think and feel – is something that can be delineated and manipulated by managers.
- *Integrating and stabilizing.* Because culture is shared between organizational members, it is seen to provide a '"natural" force for social integration' (Meek, 1988, p. 455). Culture brings people together: it ensures that they all think, feel and act in relatively similar ways, that they all develop similar workplace identities. Thus it creates consistency and reduces conflict. The 'has' theorists suggest that culture simplifies choices about how things work, what is important and how to behave in organizations.
- *Created at the top.* Culture is set by senior management and disseminated downwards throughout the organization. This can be referred to as **cultural engineering** (Jackson and Carter, 2000, pp. 27–28) – creating the 'right' kind of organizational culture such that management-imposed values rule out discrepant courses of action and/or narrow the range of options for a decision.

Taking this mainstream approach, culture is understood as a management 'lever' for improving control and/or performance – a means of enabling employees to direct their efforts towards organizational goals. Such 'performance' may extend to any form or aspect of organizational activity, such as the 'greening' of organizations where it has been argued that ecological sustainability is 'dependent upon the

Values Has a variety of meanings in organization studies, but in the specific sense intended by Schein it encompasses his 'middle level' of organizational culture, located between basic assumptions and cultural artefacts. Values derive from basic assumptions and inform cultural artefacts. They involve shared organizational responses to questions such as 'What are we doing?' and 'Why are we doing it?', and might include a commitment to profit maximization or a focus on equal opportunities.

Basic assumptions A term used by Schein to refer to the origins of values and cultural artefacts in organizations. Basic assumptions are shared and deeply embedded presuppositions about issues such as whether human beings do or should live for the moment (immediate gratification) or see their activities as a means to a future end or goal (deferred gratification).

Cultural engineering Attempt to change an organization's culture to accord with the interests or values of managers. It depends on a view that a culture is something that an organization 'has' rather than 'is'. If organizational relations are defined by culture, it is more difficult to impose a unified set of values, beliefs and norms that are designed to provide the basis for all organizational actions and decisions.

institutionalization of environmental beliefs ... into the very fabric of modern organizations' (Purser, 1994; Harris and Crane, 2002: p. 220). Peters and Waterman (1982, p. 11) sum up what is being characterized here as the 'has' perspective in their suggestion to managers that:

> All that stuff you have been dismissing for so long as the intractable, irrational, intuitive, informal organization *can* be managed. Clearly, it has as much or more to do with the way things work (or don't) around your companies as the formal structures and strategies do ... you [are] foolish to ignore it.

So what might such cultural engineering look like in practice? Case Study 10.1 describes a classic case of an apparently successful cultural change, which took place at British Airways. We ask you to read this before continuing.

Key issues and controversies

In the BA case, we see fairly striking evidence of how the 'has' theory account of organizational culture is plausible in terms of the link it forges between the management of culture and organizational effectiveness. Indeed, this claim – that 'a culture has a positive impact on an organization when it points behaviour in the right direction ... [al]ternatively, a culture has [a] negative impact when it points behaviour in the wrong direction' (Kilmann *et al.*, cited in Alvesson, 2002, p. 43) – is probably the most important one that it makes. This 'has' theory sees the 'appropriate' culture as leading to organizational effectiveness in two ways. First, it provides meaning for employees so that their work makes more coherent and appealing sense to them, which can be seen as motivating. Second, it establishes particular ways to think, feel and act, which are linked to the achievement of organizational goals. The 'has' theorists believe that the strength of an organization's culture – the extent to which employees buy into management-directed values, beliefs and norms – has a direct impact on performance.

Case study 10.1
Cultural engineering at British Airways, 1982–1996

British Airways was the result of a merger in 1974 between British Overseas Airways Corporation (BOAC) who offered long-haul flights, and British European Airways (BEA) specializing in flights to continental Europe. In its early years, BA was very bureaucratic and rules-oriented (see Chapter 14). At that time, BA was reported to have had an introspective, inflexible culture where over-staffing was routine, hierarchy was all-important and little attention was paid to customer service, employee opinion or profitability.

Substantial cultural differences continued post-merger. BOAC staff tended to look down on their BEA counterparts, believing they provided flights for 'tradesmen' whereas their own services were for 'gentlemen'. BEA employees on the other hand regarded the BOAC staff as snobs who had no real sense of the cut-throat world of commercial competition. The result was disastrous in terms of performance. In 1980, BA was voted the airline to avoid at all costs; and, at the time, it was also the most unpunctual European carrier flying out of the UK.

When John King was appointed by Prime Minister Margaret Thatcher as BA Chairman in 1981, he saw a need for drastic action, not least because the company was suffering huge financial losses. His 'survival plan' resulted in nearly 20 000 staff redundancies, closed routes and disposure of BA's cargo-only service. When Colin Marshall took over as CEO in 1982, an operating surplus had been created for the first time since the merger. Marshall's objective was to build on this by encouraging all BA staff to take responsibility for customer satisfaction, and also to develop a more holistic outlook on the company, bridging functional and cultural divides. An extended training initiative was developed. Marshall was quoted at the time as talking about 'designing' BA staff to deliver good service, just as BA already designed the seats on its planes, its inflight entertainment and its airport lounges to do the same.

The first of these training events was launched in 1983. Two days long, it was called 'Putting People First', and was eventually attended by 40 000 staff. The course focused on encouraging effective personal relationships, the idea being that if staff felt good about themselves they would also feel good about interacting with customers. A senior director was present for question and answer sessions at these events and Marshall himself frequently attended. Other programmes followed, including 'Managing People First' for BA's 1400 managerial and supervisory staff, launched in 1985. Its objectives were to foster a more caring and trusting relationship between managers and their teams, and to improve communication and staff motivation. Another – 'Day in the Life' – was introduced in the same year to improve co-operation and break down barriers between BA's various functions.

Other more tangible changes were also afoot, including privatization in 1987 and a takeover of British Caledonian Airways in 1988. Both marked the progress BA had made towards becoming a market-oriented, customer-facing organization. The organization's structure changed as Marshall revamped BA into 11 profit centres. This streamlined its bureaucracy and allowing for greater cross-functional communication and cohesion. Executives who he felt weren't up to the changes were removed. Performance-related pay, linked to the new BA values, was introduced.

But the developments didn't end there: in 1987, 'Awards for Excellence' were brought in to recognize high levels of performance among staff, and the suggestion scheme 'Brainwaves' was introduced. In 1988 BA began to offer an in-house MBA in conjunction with Lancaster University; and the initiative 'Winning for Customers', consisting of a training event to signal that every staff member makes a difference to the customer experience, and an associated course for supervisory and managerial staff, was launched in 1992.

All in all, this lengthy and expensive programme seems to have transformed a loss-making public organization colloquially known as 'Bloody Awful' into a profitable private company, which won the *Business Traveller* 'World's Best Airline' award for seven years up to and including 1995. Indeed, former CEO Bob Ayling (who took over from Colin Marshall in 1996, when Marshall became Chairman) suggested in a BA magazine that the organization 'has been one of the great turnaround stories of the late twentieth century. The image this airline has built for itself in the past 14 years has stood it in great stead' *(Business Life,* 1997, p. 45). The BA example therefore suggests that culture can indeed be engineered, and that a substantial hike in performance can be achieved by managers embarking on this kind of initiative.

The socialization of new staff into a particular company's culture, suggests that this amounts to asking them to swear an oath of allegiance to hard work, turning up on time and putting in extra hours as and when required. The 'has' literature takes these possibilities very seriously. It believes that taking on board the 'right' values will guide employee behaviour without the need for costly and demotivating direct supervision. Indeed Deal and Kennedy (1988, p. 15) go as far as to claim that it is possible to increase every worker's productivity by one or two hours a day if culture is managed effectively.

Reflecting on 'has' thinking, we can say that it is functionalist and technical in outlook. Its **functionalism** can be seen in the claim that culture performs a function in establishing and/or strengthening organizational equilibrium and consensus. The 'has' perspective is also **technical** as it seeks to develop knowledge about organizations which enables managers to manipulate specific variables (workers' values, beliefs and norms) in order to achieve a specified outcome (organizational effectiveness). Of course, the suggestion that culture might be the solution to an age-old problem of getting people to work hard by encouraging them to identify with it, has a populist appeal. Perhaps that is why there are so many subscribers to the 'has' camp. As we shall see in the second half of this chapter, however, there are reasons to be sceptical and directly critical of the sort of conformist world that champions of 'culture', as something that an organization has or could aquire, are inclined to promote.

Functionalism Theoretical model or framework that presumes organizational consensus and posits that activities continue to exist only because they perform the indispensable function of maintaining a coherent integration of the organization. Consensus is presumed to be the natural state of affairs.

Technical In an organization studies context, this term refers to theories or ideas intended for application by managers so that they can improve the organizational 'bottom line'.

Exercise 10.1

Investigate the culture of Southwest Airlines and compare and contrast this airline with the development of British Airways. In addition to much Internet information on the airline, the following sources are directly relevant:

> The Southwest Airlines Way: Using the Power of Relationships to Achieve High Performance', Available at www.digitalcommons.ilr.cornell.edu/cgi/viewcontent. cgi?article=1089&context=ilrreview&sei-redir=1#searclWsouthwest+airlines
>
> Milliman, J., Ferguson, J., Trickett, D. and Condemi, B. (1999) 'Spirit and community at Southwest Airlines: An investigation of a spiritual values – based model', *Journal of Organizational Change Management*, 12(3): 221–233.
>
> Quick, J. C. (1992) 'Crafting an organizational culture: Herb's hand at Southwest Airlines', *Organizational Dynamics*, 21(2): 45–56.
>
> Taylor, F. (2008) 'How Southwest's Culture Drives Cost Leadership', www.southwest .com/swamedia/speeches/fred_taylor_speech.pdf

Leaving to one side the suggestion that getting the culture 'right' results in high levels of performance, there are two areas on which there are disagreements in the 'has' literature. The first concerns the question of whether there is one kind of culture, which, if implemented in any organization, will result in high performance (the 'one best culture'/'one size fits all' argument) or whether the right kind of culture is a question of the variables affecting the organization (the contingencies/'horses for courses' argument). So that you can get to grips with this debate, this section begins by reviewing each side of the debate, identifying the best known contributions and suggesting which one is probably more plausible.

Before exploring these 'sides', it is relevant to consider a controversy within the 'has' perspective. This surrounds the mechanisms that should be used by managers to change, consolidate or establish organizational culture. We explore the central points of this discussion in order to draw attention to the many cultural tactics that managers may have at their disposal, and to focus on some of the key decisions that the 'has' literature suggests managers need to make in this regard. We end the section by acknowledging that, although those in the 'has' camp are not universally optimistic about the end result of cultural management strategies, this doubt has had little discernable impact on wider public demand for its prescriptions and advice – perhaps because of the aforementioned attractiveness of the primary link that it makes between culture and organizational performance.

ONE BEST CULTURE VS HORSES FOR COURSES

In terms of the *'one best culture'* argument, Peters and Waterman (1982) – whose work is discussed in more detail in the 'Important empirical studies' section later in this chapter – and Ouchi (1981) are probably the most notable proponents. Their position suggests a kind of magic formula for organizational success. Peters and Waterman identify eight cultural values that they say exist in America's best performing companies, and which should be introduced into all organizations to ensure 'excellence'. Indeed, the subtitle of their best-selling text *In Search of Excellence* is *Lessons from America's Best-Run Companies*.

Ouchi analyzes what he sees to be a distinctive form of culture in Japanese organizations. Ouchi calls this approach Theory Z, after Maslow's claim that type Z is the highest form of self-actualization (see Chapter 2). It is based on the assumption that, instead of the competitive ethos of the 'market' organization or the rules-driven bureaucracy, workers in a Theory Z organization behave in appropriate ways because they share a commitment to the same value system. This also helps them to counter the apparently alienating characteristics of the modern world – something we have already touched upon. Ouchi recommends that US managers should try to socialize their employees into just such a culture. The subtitle of his book, *How American Business Can Meet the Japanese Challenge,* – a 'challenge' that 40 years ago was perceived as a major threat to Western economies and the USA especially (before the Japanese economy overheated and then stagnated) – again makes his message very clear.

More common in 'has' thinking, however, is the contingencies/'horses for courses' argument. These theorists pick and mix a range of different internal and external variables to which, they argue, managers should attend when deciding what kind of culture best fits their particular organization. The best known of these writers are Deal and Kennedy (1988) and Handy (1993), who borrows extensively from earlier work by Harrison (1972). Deal and Kennedy, whose ideas are also developed in the 'Important empirical studies' section, identify a four-fold 'typology' of organizational culture. The suitability of each cultural type is seen to depend on the level of risk involved in an organization's activities and how quickly it receives feedback on those activities. Handy, similarly, identifies four key forms of culture to fit a range of organizational situations, as follows:

1 *The power culture (represented by a web)*
   - Depends on a central power source, usually the founder or owner.
   - Trust between centre and 'outlying' staff is key to effectiveness, as is personal interaction.
   - The central figure needs to select staff who have similar ways of thinking so they can be left to get on with their work: thus members have a lot of freedom.
   - Few rules and routines; decisions depend on balance of power rather than procedure.
   - A strong, cohesive and flexible culture where politically minded risk-takers thrive.
   - Centre's influence declines as organization grows bigger (and the web weaker), which may prompt break-up into smaller divisions or a shift towards role culture (see below).
   - Tough and competitive, possibly causing low morale and high labour turnover.
   - Replacement of the centre at the end of their career is a key challenge because 'a web without a spider has no strength' (Handy, 1993, p. 184).
   - Likely to be found in small entrepreneurial organizations such as trading, finance or property companies, new businesses and/or family firms.

2 *The role culture (represented by a Greek temple)*
   - Reason and logic are key values here.
   - A bureaucratic and highly structured organization; temple's pillars are specialist departments like marketing or production, and roof is senior management team.
   - Organizational operations controlled by job descriptions, reporting procedures, communications policies, etc.
   - Staff are selected on basis of capability/expertise and are not required to do anything more than their roles require.
   - Power comes from hierarchical position, not personal charisma.
   - Works well where the market is predictable or a **monopoly/oligopoly** exists. Provides security and predictability for workers, who are able to climb the 'career ladder'.
   - 'But Greek temples are insecure when the ground shakes' (Handy, 1993, p. 186 – emphasis added): they do not respond quickly to changing circumstances, and can be frustrating for those who seek freedom.
   - The civil service, car manufacturers, oil companies, life insurance companies and high street banks are all likely to be role cultures.

Monopoly A market where only one supplier of a product or service exists. There is no competition and thus no other sources of the commodity, so the supplier is able to completely dominate the consumer. See also oligopolistic and oligopoly.

Oligopoly The noun that describes the type of market discussed above.

3 *The task culture (represented by a net or a matrix)*
   - Centres on getting the job done, bringing the right people and resources together at the right time to work on a project; staff may be simultaneously involved in several different projects.
   - Key values are expertise and teamwork.

- Overall control maintained by central allocation of resources and people to projects.
- Suited to competitive and volatile markets with short product cycles, where responsiveness, co-operation and creativity are vital.
- Project teams can be formed and abandoned rapidly and decision-making is often faster, being devolved to team level.
- But no real attention to economies of scale and staff may have little opportunity to develop expertise when working across a range of projects (can also generate confusion and insecurity).
- May be found in venture capital firms, management consultancies and advertising agencies.

4 *The person/cluster culture (represented by a galaxy of stars)*
- Key value here is individuality or freedom.
- Organization exists only for its members' benefit; it comes into existence when people find that sharing office space, desks, an IT network, etc. helps them, but there are no collective goals as such.
- Overall control is only possible by mutual consent, and power is shared.
- Tends not to last: 'Too soon the organization achieves its own *identity* and begins to impose on its individuals. It becomes, at best, a task culture, but often a power or role culture' (Handy, 1993, p. 191 – emphasis added).
- Unusual but may be found in 'start ups', including social media businesses as well as barristers' chambers or architects' partnerships, or in small organizational enclaves like consultants in a NHS hospital.

Handy identifies size, market and individual worker preference as the key variables in identifying the best culture for a particular organization. Other contingencies that render a particular type of culture more or less effective include:

- National culture – see, for example, Hofstede's (2001) discussion of differences between IBM subsidiaries in various parts of the world.
- Political environment – such as Tayeb's (1988) comparison of industrial relations legislation and government attitudes to market regulation in the UK and India.
- Founder/leader – like Henry Ford, whose approach to management is discussed by Corbett (1994, pp. 123–132), and Konosuke Matsushita of the Matsushita Corporation, analyzed by Pascale and Athos (1981).
- Technology – Anthony's (1994) discussion of production processes in coal mining, for instance.

The contingency stance might well seem to be more credible when organizations vary so widely in terms of size, sector, ownership, location, staff and so on. As Handy (1993, p. 183) points out: 'It must be emphasized that [any culture] can be a good and effective culture; but people are often culturally blinkered, thinking that ways that worked well in one place are bound to be successful everywhere. This is not the case.'

Subculture A set of values, beliefs and norms that is specific to one group in the organization, and may be at odds with the 'official' culture as promoted by senior management. See also cultural differentiation and multiculturalism.

Cultural differentiation Refers to differing sets of values, beliefs and norms which co-exist in one organization. Also see multiculturalism and subculture.

More sophisticated variants of the contingency literature also acknowledge that organizations may house **subcultures** because of the particular circumstances facing different departments or functions (see Chapter 7). Such **cultural differentiation** may prompt managers to work to integrate these various groups of employees, to encourage them to understand each other despite their differing values, beliefs and norms. Typologies – such as the four cultures identified by Handy – might indeed be best understood as 'ideal-types' for benchmarking or analyzing aspects of actual organizations. In other words, the four cultures could be taken up to analyze and manipulate dimensions that are important in understanding why particular values exist and whether these values come together to 'form a coherent [organizational] ... whole' (Brown, 1998, p. 72).

Exercise 10.2

If you are a student who is studying abroad, think about how educational practices in universities at home differ from those in the country where you are doing your degree (you might have to email a friend at home for information). If you are a 'home' student, ask a friend who comes from elsewhere. Some examples might be:

- How essays are marked (some higher educational cultures typically award much higher marks in general than others).
- How degrees are graded (some use grade point averages, others prefer 'bands' like the British class first upper second/lower second/third system).
- How students treat academic staff and vice versa.
- The extent to which you are expected to write in your own words or submit course work as part of your assessment and so on.

When exploring differences, consider if there is 'One Best' culture of higher education. What are the arguments for and against?

Thinkpoint 10.3

Think about the different departments or functions in a 'typical' manufacturing organization – marketing, R&D, production, finance, human resources and so on. Using Handy's typology, identify the kind of culture you would expect each department to have and suggest why this might be.

The second controversy in the 'has' literature centres on the most appropriate ways to manage organizational culture. These discussions generally focus on changing an existing culture – as in the BA case study. But it is worth remembering that cultural initiatives may also involve managers trying to preserve the status quo, which can be particularly challenging in the face of large numbers of staff leaving or joining the organization. Alternatively, they could be trying to build a specific type of culture in a new organization. Daymon (2000), for example, discusses efforts to encourage commercial values around high profit and low costs as opposed to 'traditional' broadcasting values of creativity, artistic merit and production excellence among incoming staff at Countrywide Television.

The **cultural transmission mechanisms (CTMs)**[1] that are used tend to be the

Cultural transmission mechanism (CTM)
Techniques used by managers to build, maintain or change a particular organizational culture, to encourage employees to adopt specific values, beliefs and norms. Examples include management by example (MBE) and deliberately recruiting new staff who embody the desired culture.

same whether managers are trying to change, maintain or build a culture. Since change, as in the BA example, is probably more difficult than the other types of cultural engineering, '[b]ecause it entails introducing something new and substantially different from what prevails in existing cultures' (Trice and Beyer, 1993, p. 393), we concentrate on cultural change.

Exercise 10.3

E valuate the BA case study in terms of what it suggests about how many people and how much of their behaviour needed to change in this organization; how different the new culture was from the old; and whether there were any external or internal role models for the new ideas and behaviours. How might it have felt to be an employee experiencing this series of interventions?

There are many empirical examples of the CTMs that managers have deployed to change (or maintain or build) a culture. These have been claimed to fall into two main categories:

* Devices that are the responsibility of the human resources department and focus on employee resourcing (getting the 'right' people into the organization and ensuring that they perform in a particular way once there, as well as 'disposing' of the 'wrong' people), employee development (training staff in 'appropriate' ways) and employee relations (encouraging 'suitable' forms of communication between management and staff).
* 'Symbolic leadership' devices – the ways in which senior members of the organization go about managing the rank-and-file employees and how these tactics embody various values, beliefs and norms to those employees.

These measures are said to be more effective when used in a kind of package because they are unlikely to have much impact when used on their own. A 'consistent cues' approach is said to be necessary such that 'all aspects of every ... programme must unequivocally promote the desired state culture' (Brown, 1998, p. 166). An example of the use of *human resource devices* to change a culture is the British Airways case study where employee resourcing, employee relations and employee development tactics were all used to shift the prevailing values towards an emphasis on customer service and internal staff co-operation.

Thinkpoint 10.4

C an you classify the various CTMs used at BA into the categories of resourcing, relations and development? Some may fall into more than one.

Management by example (MBE) A symbolic leadership device, or cultural transmission mechanism, which involves managers embodying the values, beliefs and norms they wish employees to adopt in everything they say and do.

In terms of *symbolic leadership devices,* **management by example (MBE)** is probably the epitome of such techniques. It involves, quite literally, 'walking the talk', acting out the organization's cultural vision because, in the old adage, actions speak louder than words. Indeed, according to the 'has' theorists, managers should 'be seen as spending a lot of time on matters visibly related to the values they preach' (Deal and Kennedy, 1988, p. 169). A potent example of such 'embodiment leadership' in cultural change projects is chief executive officer (CEO) Lee Iacocca's refusal to draw more than US$1 a year salary until he got General Motors on its feet. Another is BA's Colin Marshall's acting as check-in staff on the first day of the company's Super Shuttle service when the airline found itself overrun with customers.

Box 10.1
Management by example

❝ If he saw that the service counter was buried knee deep in customers, Larry would jump in and help out. Afterwards he would help us realize that it wasn't about us ... it was about the customer and their perceived wait time. In the best of ways a little situation like this was used to teach me to be proactive and keep the customer front and centre. Larry made sure we all saw the people in our store as "our customers" and their shopping experience was paramount. He taught us the importance of good customer service. After all, happy customers come back. Through teaching and managing by example, Larry taught us all that the relationship between our co-workers and our customers was imperative to our success. Larry managed by example. His employees would follow him anywhere because of his demonstrated work ethic and respect for the people who worked for him.❜

Source: Extract from G. Petz, 'Management by Example' accessible at http://ezinearticles.com/7lvlanagement-by-Example&id=1359445.

Thinkpoint 10.5

Which values do you think 'Larry' (see Box 10.1) is exemplifying? Why might such behaviour not impress or influence everyone?

In sum, then, advocates of 'has' thinking disagree on (a) whether one culture fits all organizations, and (b) how managers ought to go about changing, maintaining or constructing cultures. In other words, no consistent message emerges here about the appropriate combination of cultural transmission mechanisms.

We should also note the cautionary tales that appear periodically in the 'has' literature with regard to the realities of managers embarking on a cultural intervention. Many initiatives of this kind are seen to fail when any initial enthusiasm on the part of staff fades and training is not used to support the changes. It has also been suggested that change initiatives fail when insufficient time and space is given to employees to voice their resentment about the changes and 'grieve' for what has been lost. Managers contemplating changes of this kind are also counselled to attend to organizational **multiculturalism** (see Chapter 5). They are encouraged not to assume that the organization has one culture through and through.

Multiculturalism In the organization studies context, another term for cultural differentiation or the existence of subcultures in an organization.

Overall, then, it would be unfair to say that the 'has' literature necessarily regards cultural change as a 'quick fix' or a panacea for all managerial problems. As Deal and Kennedy (1988, p. 163) have it, 'let us summarize the dismal economics of effecting real and lasting cultural change: it costs a fortune and takes forever'. They suggest that achieving even half the change in values, beliefs and norms that management propose in any one initiative necessitates spending between 5–10 per cent of the salaries of the staff being targeted. They strongly recommend that managers ask themselves whether embarking on cultural change is either necessary or worth it.

Such warnings emphasize the possibility of cultural change but also alert managers to the potential pitfalls along the way. Yet, seemingly, they do little to sap the enthusiasm of the corporate market for 'how to' texts and programmes for organizational culture. It is to two such texts – the key empirical contributions to the 'has' literature – that we now turn.

Important empirical studies

In this section we briefly review two of the central empirical texts in the 'culture is something that an organization has' school: Peters and Waterman's (1982) *In Search of Excellence: Lessons from America's Best-Run Companies* and Deal and Kennedy's (1988) *Corporate Cultures: The Rites and Rituals of Corporate Life*.

Peters and Waterman gathered their data by interviewing managers in 43 top performing US companies, all Fortune 500 listed. They began with a list of 62 of McKinsey's[2] 'star' clients and subtracted 19 – including General Electric – on the basis of specific performance measures. The organizations left included Hewlett Packard, McDonald's, Procter & Gamble, and Disney. From this they derived a list of tenets characteristic of the strong culture that, according to Peters and Waterman, distinguished these 'best-run' companies:

- *A bias for action.* Instead of discussing and planning everything in minute and pernickety detail, go out and make things happen – use the trial and error approach.
- *Close to the customer.* Listen to what the customer wants and tailor business activities accordingly.
- *Autonomy and entrepreneurship.* Empower employees and encourage innovation, creativity and risk-taking.
- *Productivity through people.* Regard employees as the organization's most important resource and the source of quality goods and services.
- *Hands-on, value-driven.* Managers must get involved in the work that their staff do as well as demonstrate their own commitment to the central corporate values (referred to above as management by example).
- *Stick to the knitting.* Stick to producing whatever it is that the organization is good at; don't be distracted by diversification.
- *Simple form, lean staff.* The organization's structure should be as flat and flexible as possible; top-heavy bureaucracies are inimical to excellence.
- *Simultaneous loose-tight properties.* Employees should have a great deal of discretion all the way down to the shop floor (loose properties), as management exercises control through a strong set of centralized values (tight properties).

Of course this list sounds almost commonplace now. But *In Search of Excellence* is probably the most influential management book of recent times, having sold millions of copies worldwide and been translated into many different languages. It would be surprising, then, if it had not had some effect on managerial thinking. And in the early 1980s it was certainly heady stuff, given the aforementioned backdrop of management-by-numbers (Parker, 2000, pp. 10, 12 and 16). In sum, Peters and Waterman's key message is 'My way or the highway' – i.e., there is 'one best way' to business excellence via cultural management.

Deal and Kennedy stress that 'people make business work' (1988, p. 5). Their research encompassed 80 US companies, 18 of which had strong cultural values and were all high performers. The latter group included DuPont, the chemical, energy and materials giant, and vehicle component manufacturer, Dana Corporation. But unlike Peters and Waterman, Deal and Kennedy argue that the type of culture that is most likely to breed business success depends on particular features of that business's environment – specifically the level of risk that the business faces and the speed of feedback it receives. On this basis, they develop a four-part typology:

1 *Tough-guy culture*
- Key values are speed (making decisions quickly) and emotional resilience (living with the consequences).
- A high-pressure, individualistic, all-or-nothing culture, nicely illustrated by 'rogue trader' Nick Leeson's claim that he needed 'balls of steel' to survive the Baring's Bank trading floor; it respects risk-takers and mavericks.
- Suits organizations, particularly new ones, where operations are risky (e.g., millions of dollars invested in a film) and feedback rapid (e.g., when using dynamite to explode the last stretch of a tunnel under construction).
- But has a short-termist outlook, plus there is little co-operation between members and no real incentive to learn from mistakes.

- Constant pressure also makes employee burnout likely.
- Those who thrive are tough and competitive, want to do well on their own merits and prefer to work alone.
- The police force, construction companies, management consultancies, advertising agencies, television, film and publishing companies, and sports teams might all be tough-guy cultures.

2 *Work hard/play hard culture*
- Values customers, trying to meet their needs and solve their problems.
- Also emphasizes action, or what Deal and Kennedy (1988, p. 114) call the 'try it; fix it; do it' ideology, and teamwork.
- Performance measured by results, such as sales generated.
- As its name suggests, a friendly culture where having fun (e.g., staff parties) is as important as hard graft.
- Suited to organizations where the risks are small (e.g., no one sale makes or breaks a retail organization like Tesco, Marks and Spencer or Next, a car salesroom or an estate agency) but feedback is quick (e.g., you either close the sale or you don't).
- Manufacturing companies may also fall into this cultural category: workers here know when mistakes are made but checks along the production line mean no single error is a disaster.
- Good for extroverts.
- But emphasis on volume can override attention to quality, not always adaptive to change and has a tendency to prefer quick fix solutions.

3 *Bet-your-company culture*
- Attention to detail and precision are key values here. Has a long-term orientation and believes in giving a good idea the chance to work.
- A relentless 'drip drip' pressure culture where technical expertise is emphasized because errors are costly.
- Knowledge is shared and staff interdependence seen as important.
- Suitable for high-risk, slow-feedback environments where running a business 'means investing millions – sometimes billions – in a project that takes years to develop, refine, and test, before you find out whether it will go or not' (Deal and Kennedy, 1988, p. 116), and a quick fix ideology could be disastrous.
- Produces high-quality inventions and breakthroughs.
- But vulnerable to short-term fluctuations: always waiting for the 'pay-off'.
- Survivors have character, confidence and the stamina to 'wait it out'.
- Oil companies, the nuclear arms industry, mining corporations, investment banks and the forces (who spend considerable time and money preparing for wars they may never have to fight) could all exhibit this culture.

4 *Process culture*
- Very bureaucratic; the emphasis is on caution and getting processes right.
- Status-oriented and formal; hierarchy is visible in artefacts like size of desks, office space, etc.
- Suited to low-risk, slow-feedback environments: 'This lack of feedback forces employees to focus on *how* they do something, not what they do' (Deal and Kennedy, 1988, p. 119).
- Organizes and routinizes work when required, and may allow other sorts of organizations to survive.
- Survivors are orderly, attend to detail and work by the book.
- But an inflexible and potentially stifling culture.
- May be found in insurance companies, government departments, public utilities and highly regulated industries like pharmaceuticals.

Deal and Kennedy's key message is 'It depends' – i.e., there are several different routes to excellent performance via cultural management, according to the circumstances that organizations face. The challenge is to match the culture to the circumstances.

Exercise 10.4

Compare Deal and Kennedy's cultural types to Handy's. Where are the similarities and the differences?

Despite their differences, contributions to the 'has' perspective make fairly unequivocal and empirically grounded claims about the connection between culture and organizational performance. Rather than just accepting these claims, however, we should subject them to scrutiny. Before we do so, we will briefly revisit the British Airways case, because developments following Colin Marshall's apparently successful re-engineering of culture in this organization foreshadow both this and later critical discussion of the 'has' perspective.

Case study 10.2
Cultural engineering at British Airways: what happened next?

British Airways had apparently been 'turned around' in the 1980s and early 1990s. Yet, there were signs that all was not entirely well. In 1993, for example, Richard Branson of Virgin Atlantic won a libel case against John King and Colin Marshall. This arose from Marshall's claim that Branson had lied in alleging that BA was engaging in 'dirty tricks' (i.e., forms of unfair/illegal competitive activity). Branson's accusations included the suggestion that after Virgin's relocation from Heathrow to Gatwick in July 1991 where it began to compete directly with BA, BA sought to steal Virgin customers by encouraging their staff to pose as Virgin employees. Branson also said that BA had gained access to confidential Virgin files, and that the BA public relations guru Brian Basham had been deliberately spreading detrimental stories about him and Virgin in the City and in the media. Branson was eventually awarded £500 000 in damages. Virgin won £110 000 and BA were also held liable for some £3 million in legal costs as well as being forced to make a humiliating and commercially damaging public apology.

In addition, there was conflicting evidence regarding just how far the customer service ethos had been taken on board. Heather Höpfl tells an anecdote about a BA flight attendant who offered passengers six leftover cartons of milk after a flight. This gesture could be seen to suggest that this employee was going out of her way to 'delight' customers, even though her actions were in fact against company rules. On the other hand, Bob Ayling claimed in the aforementioned *Business Life* (1997, p. 47) interview that:

I believe we already have a caring team working for us ... who make every effort to make our passengers feel as comfortable and at at home as possible. But somehow we haven't been able to communicate that properly and I don't know why ... Perhaps because, up to now, we've concentrated on projecting the more macho side of the company, how strong we are, how powerful and business-like.

These are fascinating claims from the Chief Executive of a company that had spent the previous 15 years or so (and enormous sums of money) trying to promote customer care in all aspects of its operations! But, then again, perhaps Ayling's comments can be read as reflecting back on the dirty tricks episode?

Ayling himself was to create his own controversies during a stormy four years at the BA helm. After a very healthy first 18 months, the announcement in June 1977 of a new corporate identity caused a not-so-positive stir. The changes included a brand new livery for BA, dubbed World Images, which appeared on plane tailfins, cabin crew scarves, business cards and ticket jackets. World Images featured 50 new designs commissioned from artists all over the world to replace the traditional red and blue BA logo. The key intention was to revamp BA (yet again) into something more cosmopolitan, diverse and friendly, to reflect its growing numbers of both overseas staff and customers and play down the potentially offputting associations of the organization's introverted 'Britishness'. But shareholders were appalled, calling the rebranding unpatriotic and extravagant. In a public drubbing of the livery, Margaret Thatcher demonstrated her own feelings when she draped a hanky over a model BA plane tailfin featuring a World Images design at a Tory party conference.

The announcement of this initiative coincided with two ballots on strike action by BA staff. One, concerning the sale of the inflight catering division, was resolved without industrial action being taken. The other related to an aspect of Ayling's cost-cutting Business Efficiency Programme (BEP) which meant that cabin crew stood to lose out financially. This ballot – for a 72-hour strike – was successful by a majority of 3 to 1. In the event, and arguably due to what was widely regarded at the time as intimidation by BA management,[3] only 300 staff went on strike but a further 1500 called in sick. The action ended up costing the airline £125 million. In the aftermath of the strike, Ayling did begin to put restorative measures in place, such as an internal task force focusing on staff motivation and patching up relations with customers.

1998 also proved to be somewhat of a curate's egg for Ayling and BA. It featured, among other things, the decline of the 'Asian Tiger' economies, rising levels of customer dissatisfaction and more legal action by Branson, this time alleging that BA's recent performance and 'dirty tricks' meant that it had no business using their 'World's Favourite Airline' slogan. Of course, this was all good, free publicity for Branson's Virgin and the Advertising Standards Authority found in BA's favour in the end. Nonetheless, it did more damage to BA, and a Consumers' Association survey published at the same time suggested that the airline had lost considerable ground in terms of being a carrier that people recommended to each other. By late 1998 Ayling had had to declare BA's first ever third-quarter loss.

In 1999 an internal opinion survey entitled 'It's Your Shout!' proved rather damning – staff apparently did not believe BA directors could cut costs and still maintain quality, were cynical about their commitment to honest and straightforward communication with employees and also did not believe that the board cared about them. 'Putting People First' was therefore rejuvenated as 'Putting People First Again', involving all 64 000 staff. BA's financial performance began to improve after the announcement of a six-year low in annual profits in May, but was not helped by the decision in June 1999 to cease using the World Images designs on its planes.

In August 1999, Ayling was forced to announce 1000 job losses. However, things started to look up again later in the year as new service innovations (such as flat beds in business class) and an e-commerce initiative to increase online sales were publicized. Customer satisfaction measures began to improve and BA's low-cost airline Go was also doing well – somewhat ironically when its parent company was moving strategically away from the economy end of the market and focusing its attentions on 'front cabin' passengers.

Nonetheless, a further 6000 job losses were made public in February 2000 and the BA share price then nosedived as part of wider market trends. By March, Ayling had been forced to resign. The CEO had apparently failed to persuade BA customers or staff of the viability of his vision.

Exercise 10.5

Focusing upon developments that are directly relevant to BA culture change, examine the following sources to deepen, extend and update the BA story.

Höpfl, H. J. (1993) 'British carriers', in D. Gowler, K. Legge and C. Clegg (eds) *Cases in Organizational Behaviour*, London: Paul Chapman, pp. 117–125.

Colling, T. (1995) 'Experiencing turbulence: competition, strategic choice and the management of human resources in British Airways', *Human Resource Management Journal*, 5: 18–32.

Mills, A. J. (1995) 'Man/aging subjectivity, silencing diversity: Organizational imagery in the airline industry. The case of British Airways', *Organization*, 2(2): 243–269.

Mills, A. J. (1998), 'Cockpits, hangars, boys and galleys: Corporate masculinities and the development of British Airways', *Gender, Work & Organization*, 5(3): 172–188.

Grugulis, I. and Wilkinson, A. (2002) 'Managing culture at British Airways: Hype, hope and reality', *Long Range Planning*, 35(2): 179–194.

Before moving on to examine some of the limitations of the 'has' perspective on organizational culture, it is relevant to recall that contributors to this body of thought broadly agree that culture:

- Is an organizational variable that managers can manipulate.
- Integrates and stabilizes organizations because it ensures that everyone thinks, feels and acts in the same way.
- Is created at the top and disseminated down through the organization.
- If properly managed, generates excellent organizational performance.

They disagree, however, on:

- Whether there is 'one best culture' for all organizations.
- The best way to change, maintain or build a culture.

Limitations and contributions

Groupthink Term used by Janis to refer to situations in which groups make problematic decisions because individuals over-conform to the group ethos and fail to express personal doubts. There is comfort in groupthink in that the group as a whole feels protected given that the decision is collective, but silence is presumed to imply consent whereas it may signify a fear of resistance.

One area of contention over whether the claims made by the 'has' perspective stand up to scrutiny is the issue of whether *strong* cultures are always *good* cultures. Here we could note, for example, the argument that while strong cultures enable stability, co-ordination and rapid decision-making, they may also encourage complacency, lack of creativity, inflexibility and **groupthink** (see Chapter 4). So a strong culture might actually harm performance when it inhibits fresh thinking or is inflexible. Indeed, work by Kotter and Heskett (1992) suggests organizations with strong cultures are no more likely to perform well than organizations whose value systems are relatively weak. 'Strong culture' organizations which performed poorly during the US economic boom years of 1977–1988 include Sears, General Motors and Goodyear, whereas some of their 'weak culture' counterparts – such as GlaxoSmithKline and McGraw-Hill – did well. Likewise, Miller (cited in Trice and Beyer, 1993, p. 380) suggests that overly strong cultures create 'paths of deadly momentum ... [so] productive attention to detail ... turns into an obsession with minutia; rewarding innovation turns into gratuitous invention; and measured growth becomes unbridled expansion'.

Thinkpoint 10.6

Thinking back to Bob Ayling's comments about BA showing a rather 'macho' face to its public, and the 'dirty tricks' campaign waged by BA against Virgin, how might these episodes suggest that BA's new culture had by the early 1990s begun to demonstrate some of the problems relating to strong cultures discussed above?

There is the related question of whether cultural change programmes produce *long-term* organizational success. Some commentators suggest that all we have available are 'brief, anecdotal stories of the dramatic impact of founders, leaders, heroes, in establishing or rescuing their enterprises' (Anthony, 1994, p. 15) – and we could also reflect on 'what happened next' at BA in the light of this argument.

More generally, the validity and reliability of the texts establishing the culture–excellence link have been heavily criticized. Peters and Waterman, for example, have been accused of carrying out most of their interviews with senior managers who would be expected to sing the praises of their organizations. The companies they researched were also all high growth and employed large numbers of professional staff. Both conditions could be argued to make management-by-values more feasible, at least in terms of the required investment of resources and the likely reaction of the workforce.

Perhaps most damningly, by 1985 nearly a quarter of the firms surveyed by Peters and Waterman were in economic difficulties or decline – a point which is taken up by Chapman (2003) in the wryly titled *In Search of Stupidity*. The platform for Chapman's discussion is that it was the high-tech firms in particular in the Peters and Waterman sample that subsequently began to struggle. Chapman claims that these firms (perhaps *because* of their cultures – bearing in mind the argument above about strong cultures and complacency) often fail to learn from past mistakes and therefore continue to repeat avoidable errors. One example is Lotus' misguided 18-month long project to enable Lotus 123 to run on 640kb computers, by the end of which such machines were virtually obsolete.

Not surprisingly, it has been suggested that the 'has' theorists over-privilege culture as *the* factor that leads to business success. Consider this claim, taken from a biography of IBM founder, Tom Watson. Here a former colleague responds cynically to Watson's proposition that IBM's success was founded on its distinctive corporate philosophy, and not its capital investments, its R&D and so on:

> Well, what the hell could he say? He couldn't very well [say] that IBM had the money, recruited the scientists or was ready to spend half a billion dollars ... to take over the computer market by making everything in it, including IBM's own machines, obsolete. He couldn't very well say that it didn't make any difference what the company, or the employees, believed if they got 80 per cent of the market. (Cited in Parker, 2000, p. 25)

It is possible to level several empirical and conceptual critiques at the 'has' camp claims about the connection between culture and business excellence. Nonetheless, as Parker (2000, pp. 12, 20 – emphasis added) suggests, 'these gurus *were* attempting an interesting reformulation of organizations and organizing' in their reinterpretation of the manager as committed champion of the organizational cause, not boring, numbers-obsessed cipher (see Chapter 7). It is also worth remembering with regard to the BA case study. The cultural change effected by Colin Marshall did to some extent transform a moribund organization with a very formal and 'people-unfriendly' style of management into an outfit where staff apparently felt more valued, and this translated into an improved service to customers, albeit from a pitifully low base.

The emphasis on how organizational life can be constructed and reconstructed reminds us that it is *people* who make organizational processes happen or fail, not machines or money or information technology. It is only through human creativity, vision, efforts and interactions that goods are produced, services delivered, profits made, government targets met, budgets adhered to, shareholders satisfied and so on. That said, there are other issues we need to consider when analysing the contribution of the organizational culture orthodoxy. These relate specifically to what we might call its **ontology** – the assumptions about workplace reality on which its key assertions are based, and the various anthropological, sociological, political and ethical implications of those assertions. It is to these issues that we now turn in considering an alternative reading of organizational culture. Instead of simply suggesting that 'has' theory exaggerates the claims that it makes – as we have in this subsection – this perspective takes critical issue with *the ideas that lie behind* these claims.

Ontology Theories of reality; claims about the nature and contents of the natural and social worlds. It includes a concern with the nature of human existence or what it is to be human, so it is about our relationship to the world as a whole person, not just in terms of some aspect such as personality, motivation or attitudes.

THE CRITICAL PERSPECTIVE ON ORGANIZATIONAL CULTURE

Introduction to the critical perspective, aka culture is something that an organization 'is'

The broad alternative to understanding culture as something that an organization 'has' is the claim that culture is something that an organization 'is'. This perspective is closer to the original anthropological conceptualization of culture than its mainstream counterpart. Indeed some 'is' theorists argue that 'has' theories have gone too far in their analysis of culture, claiming that 'Most anthropologists would find the idea that leaders create culture preposterous: leaders [according to anthropology] do not create culture, it emerges from the collective social interaction of groups and communities,' (Meek, 1988, p. 459).

On a related point, and emphasizing how 'is' thinking shies away from the functionalist, technical, managerialism of 'has' theory, Alvesson (2002, p. 25) suggests that 'Advocates of the ["is"] ... view of culture are inclined to play down the pragmatic results that can help management increase effectiveness in favour of more general understanding and reflection as the major emphasis of cultural studies.' That is to say, 'is' thinkers are interested in interpreting organizations rather than generating a series of management prescriptions regarding improvement of the bottom line, as favoured by 'has' theorists. The focus of the 'is' perspective, then, is primarily a **practical hermeneutic** one. In particular, it directs our attention to how co-ordinated action (without which, as we saw in the introduction to the chapter, organizations would not exist) becomes possible among disparate aggregates of individuals with varying aspirations, views, experiences and so on.

Practical hermeneutic Describes theories that seek to understand and reflect on organizations as opposed to reporting them or issuing prescriptions as to how to manage them more effectively. Can be contrasted to managerialist theories and in some instances also to emancipatory theories.

'Is' theorists begin from the claim that culture is *not* a variable – i.e., it is not just one organizational element. Instead they see it as a metaphor of, and for, organization(s). If culture is something that an organization is, then everything in the organization is in some way cultural, evoking prevailing values, beliefs and norms:

> Seemingly 'objective' things, such as numbers of employees, turnover, physical products, customers, etc. become of interest (almost) only in terms of their cultural meanings. The size of a company may be seen as 'small is beautiful' ... [or l]imited size may ... signal exclusiveness and elitism. (Alvesson, 2002, p. 25)

Alvesson here clarifies how numbers of employees, for example, may be interpreted by 'is' theorists as signifying particular values. In the same way, the significance of turnover figures, product range, target market segment(s) and so on is seen to reflect something about the organization's culture. 'Is' theorists, then, focus on the symbolic nature and significance of even the most mundane organizational phenomena as a way of understanding them.

The 'is' perspective conceives of organizational culture as a *jointly but not equally produced* system of **intersubjectivity**. It examines how shared assumptions emerge and are passed on in day-to-day organizational activity. Culture is seen to be an ongoing product of 'learning the truce' (Mills and Murgatroyd, 1991, p. 62).

The principal values in any one workplace come about as the result of a collective accommodation between organizational requirements and individual members' aspirations. Here we see a particular understanding of freedom and identity: the common sense of culture allows workers to come to terms with what is asked of them at work, to arrive at a compromise between their own personal desires and the demands of their employment.

Intersubjectivity The existence of consensually shared ideas, values, beliefs and norms. Organizational cultures are a form of intersubjectivity.

Dirty job A job that carries with it some form of social stigma and so may require its incumbents to reconcile this with their sense of themselves as 'decent' human beings. Examples include jobs that deal with literal dirt (e.g., refuse collection, lavatory cleaning) or involve what is regarded as morally problematic behaviour (e.g., prostitution, crime).

Ashforth and Kreiner (1999), for example, discuss what are usually referred to in the OB literature as **dirty jobs** in an attempt to understand the occupational cultures that grow up around this type of employment. They categorize such jobs as 'physically' dirty – where individuals deal with literal dirt, do dangerous tasks or work in areas that bring them into contact with death (e.g., refuse collectors, deep sea divers or mortuary attendants); 'socially' dirty – necessitating association with stigmatized groups or having to be servile in the job itself (e.g., prison warders and personal maids); and 'morally' dirty – the job is regarded as morally problematic or requires some form of 'cheating' (e.g., prostitution or professional gambling). Those involved in occupations like these, argue Ashforth and Kreiner, work to reconcile their sense of themselves as upright and functional human beings with what they do for a living.

Thinkpoint 10.7

Think of examples where you have engaged in the process of reconciliation – maybe during your studies at university – or have observed others striving to do the same.

One example of this process of reconciliation, referred to earlier, is Ackroyd and Crowdy's (1990) study of abattoir workers (see Box 10.2). Their work is both physically and morally dirty – it involves contact with blood, organs and excreta and centres on killing 'innocent animals' (p. 4). In the face of these exigencies, abattoir workers celebrate their toughness and resilience – stressing, for example, that 'Only one in a thousand has the stomach for this job' (p. 8) – and attributing the highest status to those who actually kill the animals. Their pride in what they do is also visible in the fact that they bring their sons to the plant for visits. Moreover, the men (and it is only men at the abattoir studied by Ackroyd and Crowdy) rarely shower before leaving work – indeed some deliberately splash themselves with blood before departing – and only change their overalls and hats when they are absolutely filthy. This culture therefore turns external social values upside down and prizes exactly what it is about the work that others view as negative. As Ackroyd and Crowdy (1990, p. 5) put it, 'the occupational culture of the slaughtermen grows out of the barrel of polluted products they are seen to handle' – it therefore insulates those who participate in this culture from wider society's moral condemnation and disgust.

For 'is' theorists, then, *everyone* participates – although, as we shall see, not necessarily as equals – in the ongoing construction of an organization's culture. It is not a matter of values being transmitted by managers and passively accepted by the lower ranks. The 'is' understanding of culture is more organic and 'socially emergent': organizational culture is a product of the ways in which groups of people come to accept the limitations on their freedom or the challenges to their identity that working for a living entails. In short, culture here is understood to be a mechanism for negotiating one's way in the world, including coping with forms of adversity, rather than a handy management tool. It involves the collective (re)production of a particular form of organizational reality, which allows workers to accommodate what they do for a living, however demanding or restrictive it might be.

Box 10.2
Abattoir work

If the meat you buy is sliced and ready-portioned; wrapped in clean, sterile, plastic; bears no obvious resemblance to the animal it came from, then, like most of us, there's probably not much chance that you think about the important transition from live animal to dead meat. Why would you?

When you buy your meat from the butcher, you see more realistic signs that your Sunday joint was once a grazing creature. We don't have to think about it too much though: because someone else does it all for us ...

Like the certification of an x-rated film, employees should be at least 18 years of age and abattoir operatives must also be licensed by the Meat Hygiene Service. This is not a job for the squeamish ...

Employment opportunities

There was a time when most areas had one or two small abattoirs, most of these have since closed and been replaced by larger businesses.

No academic qualifications are needed but some experience of handling animals/ butchery, or food safety procedures, is helpful. English and Maths at GCSE level are useful if would-be-employees wish to train further in this sector. Training is provided on the job, as is the necessary protective clothing ... Further training and experience may lead to the position of supervisor, manager, trainer, product development and work related to food marketing. Salary increases apply to these positions.

Work involved

An abattoir operative's first contact with the animals scheduled for slaughter is made when the livestock is unloaded from the trailer, or lorry, they've been transported on. This crucial stage should be handled with calm sensitivity and the animals kept under control. A Government approved veterinarian is on site to ensure that the animals don't suffer and that the meat is suitable for human consumption. Animals are humanely slaughtered once they are unconscious. A captive bolt stunner (stun gun) or electrical equipment is used efficiently and painlessly to 'knock out' the animal.

Further stages include:

- Eviscerating (removing internal organs)
- Skinning
- Boning
- Cutting.

High standards of cleanliness are essential throughout and between each stage of processing. The importance of food hygiene is paramount at all times, as is safety with knives, handling, carrying and the lifting of carcasses. Operatives need to be physically fit and are expected to work quickly and efficiently. Some areas of an abattoir are cold to work in because of the need to keep the meat refrigerated. Strong chemicals may be used during the cleaning processes of equipment.

The average working day starts at 6am and lasts for 8–9 hours. There are occasions when longer working days will be required. Managers oversee their staff and each stage of work in the abattoir. They strongly encourage greater efficiency: to improve yield and reduce waste during meat processing.

This may be a career entered into by personal circumstances, rather than choice; but all the time consumers demand meat products there will be employment opportunities for those that can do it!'

Source: Extract from *Careers with Animals – Working in an Abbatoir.* Available at www.careerwithanimals. co.uk/working-abattoir.html

Exercise 10.6

Another example of 'learning the truce' can be seen in the 'dirty job' of prostitution. For example, sex workers rarely allow their punters to kiss them, and will almost always insist on the use of condoms at work when they may not bother in their personal relationships. How might selling sex for a living threaten a woman's identity, and how might these coping mechanisms allow her to deal with this threat? Compare this with how working in an abbatoir might enhance a man's identity.

'Is' theory therefore focuses on:

Explor[ing] the phenomenon of organization as subjective experience and ... investigat[ing] the patterns that make organized action possible ... When culture is [seen as] a root metaphor, attention shifts from concerns about what do organizations accomplish and how may they accomplish it more efficiently, to how organization is accomplished and what does it mean to be organized? (Smircich, 1983, pp. 348, 353)

As already stated, at least a measure of cultural agreement, even if it is manipulated, is necessary in order for organizations not simply to descend into anarchy. The example of abattoir work (Box 10.2) illustrates how this is sought by requiring employees to handle animals with 'calm sensitivity' and comply with high standards of cleanliness throughout the process. From a 'has' perspective, such values are impressed upon staff by managers who establish or maintain culture in order to enhance competitive advantage, improve quality, increase productivity and so on. The 'is' camp, in contrast, understands the values and norms of organizational culture as the ongoing outcome of process of negotiation which develops jointly and gradually. Culture comprises much more than the prescriptions and urgings presented in Box 10.2, as Ackroyd and Crowdy's study graphically demonstrates. In practice, and from an 'is' perspective, culture is understood to turn on the daily accomplishment of an organizational reality within which members can feel psychologically 'safe' – where their identities are protected and they have come to terms with restrictions on their freedom. Perhaps, then, we should use different terms when referring to 'has' and 'is' readings of culture; 'corporate culture', or the corporatization of culture, when we are discussing interpretations based on the possibility of management-led cultural engineering initiatives, and 'organizational culture', or cultures of organizing, for the 'is' claim that culture develops more organically (Linstead and Grafton-Small, 1992).

We now discuss the implications of 'is' theory's claims in more detail, as well as exploring a key debate around power and inequality within this area of the cultural literature.

Key issues and controversies

As it sees culture as a day-on-day social product, enacted by all the members of the organization, the 'is' concept of 'culture-from-everywhere' emphasizes both the fragility of organizational life and its dynamics. 'Is' theorists attend closely to the ways in which *rank-and-file* members of organizations produce and reproduce systems of values, beliefs and norms – and therefore also amend and adapt them.

In addition, 'is' analysts emphasize 'cultural traffic' – the ways in which cultures shift 'with the flow of meanings and values in and around organizations'. For example, as new recruits join a firm, they may bring different ways of seeing with them, especially given the increased probability in our globalized world that these newcomers originate in another country. So culture here is understood as fluctuating in accordance with changing organizational circumstances (Alvesson, 2002, pp. 191–192).

Exercise 10.7

British Airways apparently attempted to accommodate 'cultural traffic' – its growing numbers of non-British staff and customers – through its World Images rebranding exercise. But the initiative lasted only two years. Bearing in mind 'is' theory's suggestion that culture is an organic, collective product, can you suggest why it was so short-lived?

Cartoon 10.1   'A good team leader inspires intense loyalty.'

'A good team leader
inspires intense loyalty.'

'Is' theory is also much more attentive than 'has' theory to the diverse, multicultural nature of organizations (see Chapter 5). It suggests that:

> ideas within a social group are not homogenous but plural and often contested ... An organization's culture could thus be viewed as a struggle for *hegemony* with competing factors attempting to define the primary purpose of the organization in a way that meets their perceived definitions. (Parker, 2000, p. 75 – emphasis added)

'Has' theory does, as we have seen, accept that different cultures may exist in different organizational departments or functions as a consequence of the different technical challenges that they face. But it then tends to confine its analysis to the question of how managers can devise ways of overcoming the resultant differentiation. For 'is' theory, this approach does not go far enough. For 'is' commentators, the organization represents a site in which there is an ongoing *contest* between various groups to make their voices heard, to control or have power over the overall direction that is taken, to shape activities in ways that meet their particular desires and aspirations. We now expand upon this way of thinking.

First, and reflecting its understanding that culture comes from 'everywhere' in an organization, 'is' theory contends that different sets of values, beliefs and norms (i.e., subcultures) *inevitably* develop at different loci within the organization, and for reasons that are not reducible to the different technical or functional challenges that they face. It may be, for example, that members of a particular ethnic minority or gender or age group are recruited into certain sections of the organization because their lack of qualifications means that they provide the most plentiful supply of cheap and reliable labour. Cultural heterogeneity is 'situation normal' – especially given power structures within organizations and the fact that ordinary employees' experience of work may therefore be rather different from that of managers. This heterogeneity and the consequent 'struggle for hegemony' often become very visible when workers feel their interests are being ignored or marginalized by management. The two episodes of industrial action at BA in 1997 and 2003 are examples. 'Has' theory only rather grudgingly accepts that such heterogeneity *may* exist *despite* managers' best efforts. As Willmott (1993, p. 525) argues, 'has' theory is 'responsive to the presence of value conflicts within modern (capitalist) organizations' but sees them 'as a sign of cultural weakness that can be corrected'. 'Is' theory, by way of contrast, suggests that organizations are *always* highly internally differentiated in terms of values – that they are almost mosaic-like in this respect.

Second, 'is' theory asserts that cultural differences are not just a product of varying experiences *inside* the organization. It adds to these considerations the issue of 'extra-organizational' identity. In other words, for 'is' theory, subcultures do not just spring up among those who participate in specific activities within the organization, but also among those who share things 'outside the factory gates'. In addition to more obvious considerations such as ethnic identity, gender or age (see Chapter 5), these might include membership of an occupation (e.g, accountancy), socio-economic or educational similarities and so on. Such affiliations will further cut across, dilute or undermine any connection employees have with the values, beliefs and norms that management attempts hegemonically to impose.

Thinkpoint 10.8

Think about the students in your year at university. To what extent would you say that they tend to 'split off' into subcultural cliques based on gender, racial, ethnic, religious, class or educational differences? If such 'divisions' are noticeable, how do they manifest themselves? How are they different in terms of values?

Shared 'external' experiences may well be *reinforced* by internal organizational processes, perhaps creating subcultures that span organizational boundaries. An example is the professional women's networks that bring together women from various organizations to discuss and advise each other on the challenges they face within traditionally masculine workplace hierarchies.[4] This broader and deeper consideration of culture suggests further complications in that one person may simultaneously be a member of several organizational subcultures, the values, beliefs and norms of which potentially contradict each other. For example, at the time of writing, the lead author of this chapter is a UMIST graduate, a Professor in Management, a lecturer in OB and research methodology, someone who researches the intersections between the body, identity and processes of organizing, a course leader for a Master's degree and Caucasian as well as Geordie[5] – all at the same time. Such complexity means that individual employees may 'switch' between or emphasize specific cultural allegiances at different times in their working lives – for instance, when they receive a promotion or decide to blow the whistle (see Chapter 15 on the latter issue). Awareness of this complexity makes the lines of 'Them' and 'Us' much more difficult to draw. In this understanding of organizational multiculturalism, then, 'Individuals are nodes on the [workplace] web, temporarily connected by shared concerns to some but not all the surrounding nodes' (Meyerson and Martin, 1994, p. 124).

So the 'is' version of multiculturalism means that organizational values, beliefs and norms are just as much the source of organizational *dis*agreement as they are of harmony and consensus. As Figure 10.1 indicates, for instance, some groups may buy into the culture that management wishes to impose, fervently and without reservation ('enhancing' subcultures that bolster the management message), others ('orthogonal' subcultures) accept the basic corporate culture but have an independent set of values of their own and still others ('counter' cultures) may be resistant to what management is attempting to instil.

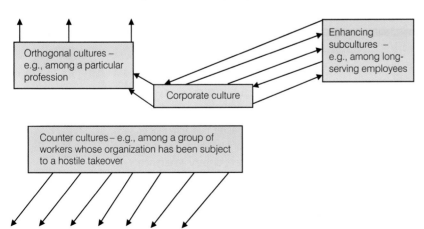

Figure 10.1
Different subcultures and their relationship to corporate culture
Source: Based on *Organizational Dynamics*, Vol. 12 (1983) J. Martin and C. Siehl (1983) Copyright Elsevier; *Journal of Management Studies*, D. Meyerson and J. Martin. Copyright Blackwell Publishing (1994). Reproduced with permission of Blackwell Publishing.

Thinkpoint 10.9

Thinking back to the early days of the BA cultural change initiative, how would you classify the former BOAC employees and the former BEA employees using the above framework (Figure 10.1) – are these groups enhancing, orthogonal or counter cultures? Or are the lines not that easy to draw?

The argument here is that, instead of being passive recipients of management hegemony, employees will 'accept, deny, react, reshape, rethink, acquiesce, rebel, conform, and define and refine the[se] demands and their responses' (Kunda, 1992, p. 21) in various ways. This point is evident in the contrast that can be drawn between the representation of abattoir work in Box 10.2 and the graphic account of the culture of abattoir workers provided by Ackroyd and Crowdy (see above). This then raises the question of the extent to which it is actually possible for managers to change, maintain or build organizational culture – a capacity, which, as we know, is a central tenet of 'has' theory. 'Is' theory is sceptical. Golden (cited in Brown 1998, p. 93) argues, for example, that there are at least four possible reactions to corporate culture as 'sold' by senior management:

- *Unequivocal adherence.* Unquestioning acceptance of management values, which is likely, as Brown asserts, 'to be the exception rather than the rule'. *Strained adherence.* Employees have concerns about the ethics or effectiveness of these values, but for the most part 'buy in'.
- *Secret non-adherence.* Wor*kers outwardly comply* with management values, usually because management have more power than they do and thus they fear for their jobs. But underneath this workplace 'act' they do not accept these values and will demonstrate this non-acceptance when it is safe to do so. Höpfl's (1993) BA research, for example, highlighted the potential flipside of the friendly greeting we receive when we board an aeroplane. One flight attendant told her that, while the staff are verbally wishing us 'Good morning', in their heads they are saying 'fuck you'. The 'fuck you' preserves some measure of personal identity and individual freedom in the face of corporate demands.
- *Open non-adherence.* Out-and-out resistance to management values, such as the profound resentment displayed by certain brewery workers in Aktouf's (1996) research. Their dislike of colleagues who conformed to the corporate culture was manifest in insults including 'traitor', 'brownnose', etc. These epithets seem to demonstrate that these workers felt so strongly about their individuality, identity and freedom that they were not prepared to put on a workplace front even for the sake of a quiet life. Here Parker's struggle for hegemony (see above) again becomes very visible, as it did in the various forms of industrial action discussed above.

Thinkpoint 10.10

Drawing on your experience of situations (at university or elsewhere) in which you were expected to behave according to particular values – e.g., respect for your seniors or neatness and tidiness – can you think of times when you have demonstrated secret non-adherence? An instance might be to have private, derogatory nicknames for disliked tutors to whom you show deference in public. You could also reflect on the following question: if workers display adherence to corporate values in public, does it matter whether they have actually taken them on board as part of their 'identities' or not?

In short, 'has' theory is seen by 'is' theory to take a rather naive view of the extent to which culture can be managed. 'Is' theory regards meanings as contested within organizational settings. It emphasizes the multicultural character of organizations and suggests that different groups within a workplace constantly work to make their voices heard, to persuade others of the legitimacy of their interpretations of the organization. Here culture is the ongoing, dynamic product of contests of power that revolve around efforts to establish and contest favoured meanings, in which the advantage routinely rests with managers because their control over symbolic (e.g., status) as well as material (e.g., promotion) resources is institutionalized with the organizational structure. Except in highly unusual situations of 'unequivocal adherence', managers' hegemonic attempts to persuade workers to take particular values on board are likely to encounter more or less overt and organized forms of resistance.

For example, Kunda's (1992) fascinating study of High Technologies Corporation (Tech) suggests that management in this organization remorselessly reinforce their corporate message (see also Chapter 6). Tech employees were encouraged to invest in the company in terms of time, effort and identity, indeed to cease to think of themselves and their employer as separate entities. These forms of cultural control seemed to be successful: most Tech workers put in long hours and enjoyed what they did for a living. But many of them also distanced themselves from the organizational ideology, describing it as 'the bullshit that comes from above', for instance (p. 158). At best, their 'adherence' was 'strained'.

Nonetheless, while their distancing may seem to undermine the Tech ethos, it actually served as a safely valve through which employees could express their frustration with management attempts at manipulation, thereby forestalling more damaging forms of dissent (such as industrial action). Workers at Tech also knew that in order to *really* get on in the company they had to 'buy in' – morose behavioural compliance was not enough. Senior Tech managers required Tech employees to give their hearts and souls, not just their time. Staff dealt with this tension by managing a convincing impression of commitment whilst maintaining a distance, and by making ironic comments to one another. So, there was a measure of resistance to management 'bullshit' but this was routinely tempered by the influence that managers, as controllers of valued resources, could exert to shape and control their staff's working lives. Managers were prepared to accommodate this limited measure of 'token' resistance as it was seen not only to provide a safety valve for venting frustrations but also because it reinforced an image of Tech as a liberal, caring workplace where employees were allowed to express themselves by poking some fun at its culture (as long as this nurtured their commitment rather than undermined it!).

In relating culture to power and inequality, some 'is' theorists begin to pose some further questions. In doing so, they go beyond critiquing 'has' theory for its naiveté in ignoring or downplaying organizational multiculturalism, contested meanings and worker dissent to focus on what they regard as its problematic aspirations. Willmott (1993), for example, claims that cultural management is similar in its objectives, though not necessarily in its consequences, to the activities of the totalitarian.[6] Oceania government in George Orwell's famous novel *1984*. Notably, they are both seen to operate on the basis of what Orwell calls 'doublethink'. Cultural management initiatives, Willmott suggests, effectively promise greater autonomy for the individual employee by subscribing to the company ideology. For example, *In Search of Excellence,* Peters and Waterman (1982, p. 322) contend that the discipline provided by 'strong culture' provides 'the framework in which practical autonomy can take place routinely'. Such arguments can be heard to celebrate an idea (autonomy) while simultaneously rejecting it (through requiring submission). In other words, says Willmott, the 'has' gurus are recommending doublethink as a management tool, advocating that managers create a situation in which employees *believe* that they determine their corporate existence yet have no real freedom to make choices for themselves because such choices are restricted to what is dictated by the framework. So the basic 'has' theory message to managers is reinterpreted by this strand of 'is' thinking as follows:

> A stupid despot may constrain his slaves with iron chains; but a true politician [/manager] binds them even more strongly by the chain of their own ideas; it is at the stable point of reason that he secures the end of the chain; this link is all the stronger in that we do not know of what it is made and we believe it to be our own work. (Servan, cited in Foucault, 1977, p. 35)

What this quote means is that overt forms of management control or open displays of management power – use of rules, reward and punishment, direct supervision and so on – are much more obtrusive and likely to be resisted than the subtle manipulation of employee values, especially where workers really do buy into what is being 'sold' to them. Authors like Willmott see this as the central tenet of 'has' theory. In this hard-edged version of 'is' thinking, then, the emphasis is less on organizations as pluralist arenas in which a cacophony of different cultural voices can be heard, and more on the ways in which managers attempt to exercise their superior power to silence these voices, and impose their own hegemony. Our attention is thus drawn to the ways in which management values – such as the idea that 'the customer is always right' – might conceivably assume an organizational normality that is difficult to question. Instead, they may simply become what the organization and its members 'are all about'; just 'the culture'. 'Is' theory here becomes more explicitly political, more 'emancipatory', more to do with identifying the organizational forces that 'prevent [workers] from acting in accordance with their free choices' (Alvesson, 2002, p. 8).

Exercise 10.8

A bad manager says
  'I'm sorry. You'll have to work all the hours that God sends.'
A good manager says
  'I'm proud. This is a 24/7 organization.' (Beaton, 2001, p. 17)

Why might this extract from Beaton (2001) be considered an 'emancipatory' 'is' theory joke about organizational culture?

We can reconsider the apparent 'success' stories told by 'has' theory in this light – like the one about the Honda worker who adjusts all the windscreen wipers on the Hondas he passes on his way home because he wants them to look perfect, or the Procter & Gamble employee who bought an entire range of P&G products in his local supermarket because the labels were wrongly positioned.[7] Colin Marshall's comments about the need to 'design' BA staff so that they give good customer service just as the organization designs seats, lounges and in-flight entertainment are also relevant here. Perhaps these examples now begin to seem just a little sinister, a touch more like organizational cloning. Perhaps Honda, P&G and BA are examples of what Coser (1974) calls the **greedy institution**, demanding unswerving loyalty and enormous amounts of employee effort, such that its members have little time or energy for anything outside work, given the strength of the bond with their employer. Perhaps strong cultures such as these are apt to produce Whyte's (1957) **organization man** (/woman); employees who put what the corporation demands before their own needs, maybe without realizing that this is what they are doing. And then there is Kanter's (1983, p. 203) claim that strong corporate cultures offer workers 'a high' akin to that derived from alcohol or drugs – perhaps they are just as addictive as these substances, with equally problematic results? Here in fact the management of culture begins to look very much like a perpetuation of organizational inequalities and an abuse of management power.

Greedy institution Coser's term for organizations that require unstinting effort and immense dedication from their employees.

Organization man The term used to refer to a worker who is so committed to the organization that he or she automatically and perhaps even unconsciously prioritizes their job demands above what they themselves require or want.

Relatedly, we can consider what 'is' theory tends to identify as a gulf between the values senior management claim to promote in their public relations literature, annual reports, recruitment brochures and so on, and what it is actually like to work in that organization – what kind of values really shape organizational behaviour. A real-life example is the fact that most large organizations – and many smaller ones – now claim to be equal opportunities employers. They say they recruit, reward and promote all employees on the basis of merit and not ascribed characteristics like gender or race. But there are still marked inequalities between, for example, men and women in terms of their organizational experiences. According to the Equal Opportunities Commission (2003, p. 11), full-time women workers in Britain were paid only 81 per cent of what their male counterparts earn. Findings of this kind are only really explicable if we accept that sexism is still at large in many workplaces, not least because it is more profitable to operate in this way (see also Chapter 5).

Exercise 10.9

Following the launch of BA's 'Putting People First Again' initiative in 1999, one commentator wrote: 'Admirable though this may be, it does rather beg the question of where BA has been putting people recently' (*The Times*, 1999, p. 23). We know that the impetus behind this training intervention and its 1980s predecessor was to make staff feel good about themselves so they would also feel good about their dealings with customers. But then there are the various cost-cutting and redundancy exercises that have been characteristic of BA management practice since 1981. What might all of this suggest about BA management's claim regarding the organization's culture, versus what it is actually like to work there?

In sum, the 'is' perspective is not functionalist or technical. Rather, it considers organizational culture as a negotiated order of meaning and this understanding is extended to a refusal to accept things at their face value, and to appreciate the role of power and inequality in establishing organizational cultures. Advocates of an 'is' understanding of culture are more inclined to emphasize how organizational values, beliefs and norms are both multiple and contested, and that workplaces are environments where there is an ongoing struggle over meanings as well as material resources. An equally strong motif within the 'is' camp is how the management of culture generally involves a problematic attempt by the senior members of the organization to clamp down on this multiplicity, to impose ways of thinking and feeling – in effect, to 'brainwash' employees sufficiently so that they accept the official organizational 'line' as an exclusive cognitive framework. 'Is' analysts adopt a practical hermeneutic stance on organizational culture as their interest is to appreciate how working lives are rendered meaningful though active participation in culture(s), as contrasted with the treatment of culture as a variable that may be engineered to enhance the corporate bottom line. Amongst these 'is' analysts, some have moved to critique the purpose and effects of culture – strengthening programmes in ways that are avowedly emancipatory. This later emphasis is even more at odds with 'has' theory as it views management activities as potentially oppressive. In order to illustrate some of the issues discussed above in more depth, we now consider two key empirical studies within 'is' theory: Collinson's (1988) 'Engineering humour' and Ackroyd and Crowdy's (1990) 'Can culture be managed?'

Collinson's factory workers

Collinson's study was set in the components division of a lorry-making factory in north-west England, where 250 men were employed. It examined humour in this context, and suggests that the various ways in which the men joked with each other 'reflected and reinforced the central values and practices of these male manual workers and contained elements of resistance and control, creativity and destructiveness' (p. 184). Examples included:

- Nicknames like 'Electric Lips', who couldn't keep a secret.
- Initiation rites – e.g., being sent to another colleague for 'a long stand'. The initiate would then be asked, after standing waiting for some time, 'Is that long enough?' (p. 189).
- Jokes at each other's or the management's expense, such as one colleague sending a rate-fixer (who set the payment rates for the men's work) to examine another rate-fixer's job, the implication being that he was not working hard enough.

The men's humour was generally unforgiving, macho, highly sexual and peppered with curses. Collinson suggests that it was a product of what we referred to earlier as 'learning the truce'. These men did repetitive, mundane work and also worked the longest hours in the company, in insecure jobs with very poor terms and conditions. This employment situation sent a clear message that they were both disposable and of little value. In the face of this challenge, not least to their masculine pride, the men established a culture that preserved their identities. Their humour emphasized that, while they could laugh at themselves, they were also different from the managers and the white-collar workers, the 'twats and nancy boys' who didn't have the freedom to joke around (p. 186).

'Having a laugh' helped the men to get through dull working days. Humour was also a means of achieving group acceptance. Being able to withstand humiliation by one's colleagues as well as meting it out (i.e., by being a 'real man') was, in effect, a passport to becoming 'one of the gang'. But jokes were also directed at those who were seen as skiving (e.g., the rate-fixer gag in bullet point 3 above), because an element of the men's wages was calculated using a collective bonus system. As Collinson points out, these men worked in a creative culture of resistant shop floor humour that was an edgy, competitive experience but permitted no real basis for a sense of belonging in the form of collective action. This was illustrated when, following the announcement of the closure of the components plant, these workers voted to accept a lump-sum redundancy payout without resistance. Collinson's key argument is that culture in this environment had evolved to allow the male shop floor employees to deal with the demands of their working lives. Yet, humour did not produce a cohesive or supportive community of co-workers or any basis for collective resistance to an oppressive regime in which these workers effectively colluded. It enabled them to nurture and confirm a macho sense of identity and offered an outlet for some creativity, in the form of improvised joking, but, like the employees at Tech studied by Kunda who distanced themselves from the corporate culture through the use of irony, it contributed little to a sense of solidarity necessary to mount an effective, organized challenge to the threat to their jobs.

Ackroyd and Crowdy's slaughtermen

Ackroyd and Crowdy (1990) note how the work of slaughtermen, like that in Collinson's lorry-making factory, is monotonous and partly remunerated using team-based bonuses. The men emphasized hard and fast work, often not taking scheduled breaks, and taking pride in completing tasks in the shortest time possible. Anyone reading the description of abattoir work provided by careerwithanimals.com (see Box 10.2, Abattoir Work) would probably not envisage a macho and aggressive culture in which every man had to measure up in terms of output as well as being able to withstand and/or participate in certain production line rituals. These included:

- 'Harassments' and 'degradations', where the men might speed up their own efforts such that work piled up at the stations of slower colleagues, or throw entrails at 'inadequate' workers.
- 'Demonstrations', where individual workers expressed boredom in acts such as spraying excreta from an animal's intestine and yelling 'It's raining' – identified here as a manifestation of that worker's individual toughness (p. 7).
- 'Set pieces', which were 'targeted', but 'also statements of [personal] effectiveness' (p. 7). These necessitated groups of workers co-operating to, for example, fill the boots of another with blood, having judged its temperature so that the unfortunate victim would not notice until it was too late.

Ackroyd and Crowdy note how much merriment hinged around a (bullying) desire to show others up – a more sinister motivation that lurks beneath what, superficially, may be passed off as jolly workplace japes. They also note that there was little resistance from the lower status workers (usually the targets) to such 'japes'. Their central point, however, is to question 'the extent to which a culture is something a management can create or control' (p. 4). At the same time, and echoing Kunda's observations of Tech, they argue that some distancing or deviation from corporate rules and values – in the abattoir case, slaughtermen's contravention of health and safety regulations and formal abattoir hierarchies – actually suits management very well because the work gets done, workers feel that they have some measure of independence or freedom from the employer and their dedication to work as a means of (macho) identity confirmation means that there is less need for direct supervision. Ackroyd and Crowdy's key argument is that the organizational culture of the abattoir developed organically in a way that has enabled the workers to accommodate the exigencies of their employment, and that this accommodation is managerially tolerated, if not explicitly valued, as it is highly competitive. Management had little need to intervene because the prevailing values among the men guaranteed that they worked extremely hard. What such findings imply, of course, is that attempts by management to impose or strengthen a homogeneous organizational culture may act to demoralize rather than motivate employees when it is experienced as damaging or destroying their (subcultural or occupational) values. In turn, this suggests that efforts by management to establish a totalizing culture are unlikely to succeed, short of replacing the workforce, in situations where alternative values are well entrenched.

In summary, contributors to the 'is' perspective are in broad agreement that culture:

- Is a metaphor for the organization – every organizational phenomenon says something about the prevailing values, beliefs and norms in that workplace.
- Is jointly produced by everyone in the organization, representing a means of coping with the demands of members' working lives.
- Is multiple and fragmented in complex and conflicting ways – different subcultures inevitably emerge in different organizational loci because of varying external and internal influences.
- Can therefore be very difficult to manage.

They disagree, however, on the extent to which managers are able to impose a culture on their employees. Some emphasize the similarities between cultural management and brainwashing, whereas others suggest that groups of employees will detect and find ways of resisting management attempts to manipulate them even if the methods of resistance ultimately contribute to their impotence in the face of managerial power.

Conclusion

In drawing the chapter to a close, it is plausible to conclude that some organizational values will be shaped by management, and taken on board in different ways by different member subgroups, and others will be a product of collective or subcultural accommodation to the slings and arrows of organizational life. Although managers tend to act as what Hines (1988, p. 255) calls 'Official Communicators of [Cultural] Reality' ('has' theory), this does not mean that other groups within the organization do not try to influence the ways in which the organization operates ('is' theory).

We should pay attention to what 'has' theory says as it offers an explanation of organizational success and failure: we can add 'culture' to more obvious factors such as technological innovation, high-quality products and market dominance. 'Is' theory, in contrast, asks us to acknowledge that workers are not simply embedded in a culture where they passively accept what management feeds them. Even senior managers do not have this much power, and those further down the organization have even less in terms of their overall visibility, control over resources, numbers of people they interact with and so on – however much it may appeal to their vanity to believe the contrary.

Indeed, the more reflective analysis offered by the 'is' perspective – which seeks to understand how, in practice, people in organizations come together to work in more or less co-ordinated ways – is probably a precondition of any effective cultural initiative by management, as would be recommended by 'has' theorists. That said, a difficulty for many managers is that 'is' views are more complex, less accessible and do not take for granted the legitimacy of managerial values. As a consequence, 'is' thinking is more likely to threaten managerial identity, or appear irrelevant to it, than to enhance and inflate it.

Finally, it is worth pondering Smircich's (1983, p. 355) claim that thinking about organizational culture may encourage us 'not to celebrate organization as a value, but to question the ends it serves'. She reminds us that organizations and management as we know them today are in themselves cultural (and relatively recent) phenomena. They are not natural, historical human activities. With this in mind, we can also think about the outcomes of modern organization and the disciplines of management – which include space travel, university education (hurrah!) and the cure for smallpox, but also nuclear arms, developing world sweatshops and environmental destruction – and consider possible alternatives.

Discussion questions

1 What does it mean to say that culture brings an organization 'to life'?

2 Can you identify key differences between the 'has' perspective and the 'is' perspective on organizational culture?

3 What are some of the contingencies that might help managers to identify the 'right' culture for their organization?

4 Is a strong organizational culture always a good thing in terms of achieving business excellence? What problems might such a culture create?

5 To what extent do you think it is possible to manage organizational culture?

Further reading

Important empirical studies

Ackroyd, S. and Crowdy, P. (1990) 'Can culture be managed? Working with raw material: The case of the English slaughtermen', *Personnel Review,* 19(5): 3–13.

Collinson, D. L. (1988) '"Engineering humour": Masculinity, joking and conflict in shopfloor relations', *Organization Studies,* 9(2): 181–191.

Deal, T. E. and Kennedy, A. A. (1988) *Corporate Cultures: The Rites and Rituals of Corporate Life,* Harmondsworth: Penguin.

Fleming, P. (2009) *Authenticity and the Cultural Politics of Work,* Oxford University Press.

Peters, T. J. and Waterman, R. H., Jr. (1982) *In Search of Excellence: Lessons From America's Best-Run Companies,* New York: Harper and Row.

Reading highlights

All the texts below represent good overviews of the organizational culture literature. You may find some more challenging than others.

Alvesson, M. (2002) *Understanding Organizational Culture,* London: Sage.

Anthony, P. D. (1994) *Managing Culture,* Milton Keynes: Open University Press.

Brown, A. D. (1998) *Organizational Culture,* second edn, London: Financial Times Pitman Publishing.

Linstead, S. (2004) 'Managing culture', in S. Linstead, L. Fulop and S. Lilley (eds) *Management and Organization: A Critical Text,* Basingstoke and New York: Macmillan, pp. 93–122.

Parker, M. (2000) *Organizational Culture and Identity: Unity and Division at Work,* London: Sage.

Smircich, L. (1983) 'Concepts of culture and organizational analysis', *Administrative Science Quarterly,* 28(3): 339–358.

References

Ackroyd, S. and Crowdy, P. (1990) 'Can culture be managed? Working with raw material: The case of the English slaughtermen', *Personnel Review,* 19(5): 3–13.

Aktouf, O. (1996) 'Competence, symbolic activity and promotability', in S. Linstead, R. Grafton-Small and P. Jeffcutt (eds) *Understanding Management,* London: Sage.

Alvesson, M. (2002) *Understanding Organizational Culture,* London: Sage.

Anthony, P. D. (1994) *Managing Culture,* Milton Keynes: Open University Press.

Ashforth, B. E. and Kreiner, G. E. (1999) '"How can you do it?": Dirty work and the challenge of constructing a positive identity', *Academy of Management Review,* 24(3): 413–434.

Beaton, A. (2001) *The Little Book of Management Bollocks,* London: Pocket Books/Simon and Schuster.

Brown, A. D. (1998) *Organizational Culture,* second edn, London: Financial Times Pitman Publishing.

Business Life (1997) 'The way ahead', July/August, pp. 44–47.

Chapman, M. R. (2003) *In Search of Stupidity: Over 20 Years of High-Tech Marketing Disasters,* Berkeley, CA: Apress.

Collinson, D. L. (1988) '"Engineering humour": Masculinity, joking and conflict in shopfloor relations', *Organization Studies,* 9(2): 181–1910.

Corbett, J. M. (1994) *Critical Cases in Organizational Behaviour,* London: Macmillan.

Coser, L. A. (1974) *Greedy Institutions: Patterns of Undivided Commitment,* New York: Free Press.

Daymon, C. (2000) 'Leadership and emerging cultural patterns in a new television station', *Studies in Cultures, Organizations and Societies,* 6(2): 169–195.

Deal, T. E. and Kennedy, A. A. (1988) *Corporate Cultures: The Rites and Rituals of Corporate Life,* Harmondsworth: Penguin.

Equal Opportunities Commission (2003) *Facts about Women and Men in Great Britain 2003,* January. Online. Available at: www.eoc.org.uk/cseng/research/factsgreatbritain2003.pdf (accessed 18 December 2003).

Foucault, M. (1977) *Discipline and Punish: The Birth of the Prison,* A. Sheridan (trans.), London: Allen Lane.

Handy, C. (1993) *Understanding Organizations: Managing Differentiation and Integration,* New York: Oxford University Press.

Harris, L. C. and Crane, A. (2002) 'The greening of organizational culture: Management views on the depth, degree and diffusion of change', *Journal of Organizational Change Management,* 15(3): 214–234.

Harrison, R. (1972) 'Understanding your organization's character', *Harvard Business Review,* 50 (May–June): 119–128.

Hines, R. (1988) 'Financial accounting: In communicating reality, we construct reality', *Accounting, Organizations and Society,* 13(3): 251–261.

Hofstede, G. (2001) *Culture's Consequences: Comparing Values, Behaviors, Institutions, and Organizations Across Nations,* Thousand Oaks, CA: Sage.

Höpfl, H. J. (1993) 'British carriers', in D. Gowler, K. Legge and C. Clegg (eds) *Cases in Organizational Behaviour,* London: Paul Chapman, pp. 117–125.

Jackson, N. and Carter, P. (2000) *Rethinking Organisational Behaviour,* Harlow, Essex: Financial Times Prentice Hall.

Kanter, R. M. (1983) *The Change Masters,* New York: Simon and Schuster.

Kotter, J. P. and Heskett, J. L. (1992) *Corporate Culture and Performance,* New York: Free Press.

Kunda, G. (1992) *Engineering Culture: Control and Commitment in a High-Tech Corporation,* Philadelphia: Temple University Press.

Linstead, S. A. and Grafton-Small, R. (1992) 'On reading organizational culture', *Organization Studies,* 13(3): 331–355.

Martin, J. and Siehl, C. (1983) 'Organizational culture and counterculture: An uneasy symbiosis', *Organizational Dynamics,* Autumn: 52–63.

Meek, V. L. (1988) 'Organizational culture: Origins and weaknesses', *Organization Studies,* 9(4): 453–473.

Meyerson, D. and Martin, J. (1994) 'Cultural change: An integration of three different views', in H. Tsoukas (ed.) *New Thinking in Organizational Behaviour: From Social Engineering to Reflective Action,* Oxford: Butterworth-Heinemann, pp. 108–132.

Mills, A. and Murgatroyd, S. (1991) *Organizational Rules: A Framework for Understanding Organizational Interaction,* Milton Keynes: Open University Press.

Ouchi, W. G. (1981) *Theory Z: How American Business Can Meet the Japanese Challenge,* Reading, MA: Addison Wesley.

Parker, M. (2000) *Organizational Culture and Identity: Unity and Division at Work,* London: Sage.

Pascale, R. T. and Athos, A. G. (1981) *The Art of Japanese Management: Applications for American Executives,* New York: Warner Books.

Peters, T. J. and Waterman, R. H., Jr (1982) *In Search of Excellence: Lessons From America's Best-Run Companies,* New York: Harper and Row.

Purser, D.M. (1994) Guest editorial: '"Shallow" versus "deep" organizational development and environmental sustainability', *Journal of Organizational Change Management,* 7: 4–14.

Schein, E. (1992) *Organizational Culture and Leadership,* second edn, San Francisco, CA: Jossey Bass.

Smircich, L. (1983) 'Concepts of culture and organizational analysis', *Administrative Science Quarterly,* 28(3): 339–358.

Tayeb, M. H. (1988) *Organizations and National Culture: A Comparative Analysis,* London: Sage.

The Times (1999) 'Not such a bad air day for Ayling', 10 February, p. 23.

Trice, H. M. and Beyer, J. M. (1993) *The Cultures of Work Organizations,* Upper Saddle River, NJ: Prentice Hall.

Whyte, W. H. (1957) *The Organization Man,* London: Jonathan Cape.

Willmott, H. (1993) 'Strength is ignorance, slavery is freedom: Managing culture in modern organizations', *Journal of Management Studies,* 30(2): 515–552.

Notes

1 Exercise 10.1, when you identified ways in which the staff at your university attempt to convey their 'philosophy', teach newcomers the 'rules of the game' and so on, would have identified some of the CTMs in use in this organization.

2 The management consultancy that Peters and Waterman – and indeed Deal and Kennedy – worked for at one time.

3 Management apparently threatened anyone planning to strike with removal of their staff perks, a block on promotion, dismissal or even being sued for damages.

4 See for example the Business and Professional Woman UK website at www.bpwuk.org.uk/.

5 In other words I hail from the north-east of England.

6 Controlling all aspects of its citizens' lives and quickly and mercilessly suppressing any resistance.

7 He was, the story runs, reimbursed at a later date.

11 Change and innovation: New organizational forms

FRANK WORTHINGTON

Aims of the chapter

This chapter will:

- Examine the nature of organization innovation and change.

- Explain how mainstream thinking accounts for the rise and development of new organizational forms.

- Analyze how and why new forms of production and organization have come to replace previous forms.

- Demonstrate how new forms of production are designed to release the productive potential of employees in organizations in novel ways.

- Explain how new organizational forms are viewed from a critical perspective.

Key concepts and learning objectives

By the end of this chapter you should understand:

- The terms 'Fordism' and 'post-Fordism' as key concepts for describing the rise and development of contemporary forms of production and work organization.

- How and why post-Fordist forms of production and organization have supplemented or replaced conventional Fordist forms.

- How new, post-Fordist organizational forms are conceived to release the creative and competitive potential of employees in organization.

- How new organizational forms are seen by critical organization and management theorists as subtle forms of power, control and surveillance.

Overview and key points

During the last quarter of the twentieth century the nature and organization of work in advanced industrial society is said to have undergone a radical transformation, resulting from the emergence of forms of organizational innovation that are both quantitatively and qualitatively different to those that existed at the beginning of the century (Delbridge, 1998). These innovations are seen to have brought about major changes, not only in the way in which goods and services are produced, but also in business practices, management control methods and management–labour relations.

Bureaucracy Describes a form of business administration based on formal rational rules and procedures designed to govern work practices and organization activities through a hierarchical system of authority. Bureaucratic organization is often thought to be rigid, inflexible and overburdened by hierarchical rules sometimes pejoratively referred to as 'red tape'.

Mass production The large-batch/mass assembly line/conveyor belt systems of production, often referred to as Fordism because of its association with Henry Ford's production line.

Direct management control Describes conditions where workers have little or no scope to decide how work is organized and conducted.

Work intensification Working conditions in which workers are subject to constant pressures to increase output and productivity levels.

Over the past two decades or so, this change has been widely celebrated in mainstream management literature. Business organizations and their employees are said to have benefited considerably from these changes. The changes are said to provide businesses with the means to operate more flexibly to improve productivity, product quality and reliability, and therefore customer satisfaction, and the ability to respond more rapidly to shifting economic and market conditions (Child, 2005). Employees also are understood to benefit because these changes have given rise to new working practices that provide opportunities which allow them to be much more centrally involved in the day-to-day planning and organization of production in ways that make their work more interesting.

According to the leading advocates of these new organizational forms, employees in organizations today no longer face a life at work governed by regimented working practices, simplified and repetitive work tasks, narrowly defined roles and responsibilities, and 'low-trust' management control methods associated with **bureaucracy** and **mass production** (see Chapters 7 and 14). Instead, it is claimed, in both the public and private sector, employees at all levels can now enjoy a very different and much improved lived-experience of work that is based on 'high-trust', 'employee involvement' practices rather than **direct management control**.

Critical organization and management theorists, on the other hand, have a rather different view of these developments. They acknowledge that the contemporary workplace has changed considerably in recent decades in terms of job design, the nature and organization of production, business practices and the management and control of employees. But, from their perspective, fundamentals have not changed. Today's ostensibly progressive 'high-trust' flexible organizational forms are no less exploitative, or necessarily less alienating and degrading, than those that existed before the advent of this apparent 'brave new' world of work (Sewell, 1998). As many commentators, especially labour process and critical theorists, have shown, the view among mainstream management theorists that contemporary innovative forms of organization, production methodologies and working practices release employees from direct control, is largely based on a somewhat 'selective perception' of these arrangements (Alvesson and Thompson, 2005; Thompson and Smith, 2010). This view fails to acknowledge the subtle forms of managerial power and control through surveillance (Sewell and Wilkinson, 1992), which far from releasing employees from direct control, have in reality intensified control in ways that have a tendency to lead to **work intensification** (Graham, 2005).

In this chapter you will become familiar with these two perspectives as we examine how mainstream and critical organizational and management theorists reach these very different assessments of the transformational changes that are said to have taken place. Specifically, we will examine the mainstream account of the reasons for the rise and global expansion of contemporary flexible systems of production and work organization, the competitive advantages they afford manufacturing and business organization, the improvements in the lived-experience of work that is said to have accompanied these changes, and how and why critical organization and management theorists contest these claims. Before we consider these two perspectives, let us first take a brief look at a case study as a way of gaining an insight into management efforts to operationalize the new forms of production. In particular, we will examine how these new forms are actually received by employees and some of the difficulties managers can face in attempting to translate theory into practice (see Case Study 11.1).

Case study 11.1
Northern plant: 'the factory that time forgot'

*C*oming here has been an absolute nightmare and a career disaster. Everyone talks about Northern Plant as being militant. But militancy is normally associated with formal trade union activity. Well it doesn't mean that here. This is one of the most militant shops I've ever seen but none of it is union led.

This statement was made by Mike, a senior manager from Northern Plant's North American Corporate Headquarters, who had been drafted in as a member of a human resource management (HRM) 'change' team charged with facilitating the full introduction of an innovative approach to work production, called 'lean production' (see Box 11.1), at Northern Plant. Lean production was viewed by Northern Plant's parent company as the most competitive form of manufacturing within the high-tech sector of the automotive industry in which the company operated. Prior to Mike's arrival, Northern Plant had experimented for over a decade with a number of 'new wave' flexible manufacturing and production methodologies, including just-in-time (JIT), teamworking and total quality control, but with little success. Workers at the plant resisted lean production because in their view it was designed not simply to improve productivity but to enable their managers to gain greater control over working practices, which they believed would lead to work intensification. The ways in which they resisted new working practices, however, was not something that managers at the plant found easy to understand or to explain. As a long-standing senior human resource specialist, who had joined the plant some years earlier, explained to members of Mike's change team: 'When you join this plant you quickly come to realize that it's not managed properly, that there are no basic rules and professional human resource standards in place that managers should be working to, which has resulted in workers becoming ill disciplined.'

Senior managers at the plant attributed this problem of ill-disciplined workers to the poor man-management skills of first-line managers, which, over time, had accustomed them to 'getting away with "murder"' in terms of their approach to their work and their attitude to authority. What frustrated managers at Northern Plant most, however, was that workers never actually *openly* challenged their authority. As long as managers left them to their own devices, the workers at Northern Plant were in fact highly co-operative. It was only when managers interfered in the 'informal' organization of production and working practices (see Chapter 7) that they became uncooperative.

What these managers didn't fully explain to Mike's change team was that prior to the plant's interest in lean production, workers had been given considerable autonomy from management control, and had in effect been encouraged to 'manage' themselves. This situation had come about because of the extremely strong market demand for the company's products. In 1980, Northern Plant's parent company was the major competitor in a rapidly expanding world market, which by the early 1990s had almost trebled in size. Meeting customer demand became a Herculean task. Even with 24-hour production in operation, shipments of products to customers were seldom dispatched on time. As one senior manager put it, although Northern Plant was 'never touched by recession, it was a very difficult period. We were of course facing "problems" most other companies would have been *delighted* to have, but we simply couldn't make the parts fast enough, and our customers were constantly complaining about late deliveries.'

This situation gave rise to an informally negotiated arrangement between first-line-managers and shop floor workers whereby, in exchange for management 'turning a blind eye' to how they organized themselves and how they chose to spend their time once output targets had been met, the workers would meet production quotas in the fastest way possible. Moreover, they would guarantee the 'quality' of all parts, components and finished products in accordance with the needs and requirements of what the 'Total Quality Control' movement in manufacturing would later refer to as 'right-first-time' production. Workers valued this arrangement because it gave them a considerable measure of autonomy from direct management control. In more colloquial terms it got management off their backs. As long as their output was of a sufficient quantity and quality, and that each day's production of finished products was 'right first time' and dispatched to customers on time, workers were allowed to take as many unofficial rest times as they liked during the working day itself, and also to build up considerable 'free time' at the end of each working shift, time which they were allowed to spend in various leisure activities. These activities included reading books or newspapers, chatting to friends, playing table tennis, cards, darts or chess, studying the day's race card and placing bets with the plant's bookie, sleeping during the night shift, taking leisurely strolls around the plant or the surrounding area, and even making the occasional visit to a local pub during working hours.

Although many of them pretended that they did not know what was going on behind the scenes, and obviously could not afford to openly condone what was going on, the first-line managers went along with this arrangement in response to the constant high market demand for the plant's products and the tight delivery schedules they were required to meet, and some first-line managers even participated in many of the workers' leisure activities. Without giving workers 'responsible autonomy' from direct management control in this way, and without encouraging them to complete production quotas in the fastest time possible, and rewarding their efforts with 'time off for good behaviour' during working hours, targets would not have been achieved as readily. This kind of give-and-take arrangement between managers and workers is not so unusual. Indeed, the organization studies literature provides lots of similar examples. But at Northern Plant the negotiated control arrangements and informal output and productivity agreements went far beyond what most managers in manufacturing would normally be willing to accommodate, or likely to condone. Indeed, it is worth considering for a moment the unanticipated outcomes of these arrangements, as they help explain why these workers would later resist the introduction of new working practices under lean production, which strangely were not in fact so dissimilar to the kinds of practices that were already in place – and which they themselves had helped initiate, or at least had tacitly supported!

As well as enabling the plant to meet deadlines, the relaxed shop floor control arrangements and informal productivity 'deal' between first-line managers and workers had, unbeknown to them at the time, cultivated the kind of 'high-trust' flexible teamworking practice and level of worker responsibility for 'total quality control', normally associated with lean production, that managers at Northern Plant were now keen to introduce. In other words, these kinds of practices were operational in Northern Plant, albeit on an informally negotiated basis, long before they were championed within the industry. Managers saw Northern Plant as ideally suited to lean production, and, not surprisingly, confident in the belief that they had in fact *already* evidently established their own peculiar version of it. They automatically assumed they would have little if any difficulty formally introducing the principles of lean production in real terms. How wrong could they be?

Box 11.1
Lean production

The term 'lean manufacturing' describes a system of production, first used in Japan in the 1950s, that is designed to maintain the smooth flow of operations by using minimum resources. This saves costs by reducing work-in-progress, waste, factory and warehouse space, labour, money and other overheads. The ultimate goal of lean manufacturing is to 'do more with less': use less time to produce and assemble parts and final products with less inventory, which is normally delivered 'JIT' by suppliers, and dispatched to points in the production process precisely at the time required. Its success relies upon firms re-engineering their manufacturing arrangements into small loosely-coupled 'product-focused' production areas, often referred to as 'cells', and reorganizing their personnel into small, integrated, flexible teams of workers who, ideally, operate high-tech multipurpose machines and automated assembly lines that require less physical effort, less manufacturing and factory space, less machine hours, fewer tools and less inventory.

There can be very few, if any, managers with experience of managing people in work organizations who would not expect to encounter at least *some* resistance to change. Workers' resistance to lean production faced by managers at Northern Plant, however, came not only as a surprise to them, it left them totally at a loss in terms of how to deal with it, and how to overcome it. Even after the company announced its plans to invest in lean production, workers were *still* prepared to work 'flexibly' to 'make the number' in the fastest time possible and were *still* meticulously attentive to product quality requirements, and *still* willing to produce more than the official daily output quotas, to meet customer delivery requirements on time, as they had done previously. That is: they acted as model lean production workers as long as the existing unofficial arrangements for 'time off for good behaviour' *in work* remained untouched! Because of the high market demand for their product, the situation left managers between a rock and hard place: between corporate demands to capitalize on the principles of lean production to increase the plant's productivity and performance, and workers' refusal to allow them to abandon more or less *the same* kinds of practices that, ironically, were already unofficially in place, and had been for years.

In an attempt to satisfy corporate expectations, policy statements were drawn up espousing the plant's investment in lean production, 'total quality management' (TQM), and the philosophy of 'continuous improvement' in product quality and reliability, to achieve 'total' customer satisfaction. The shop floor was divided up into 'customer-focused' business units, comprising a series of 'product-focused cells'. Workers were organized into teams attached to dedicated customer production lines. Training seminars, 'quality circles' and team briefings were introduced to *educate* them about the aims of the principles of lean production. Achievements in these areas were communicated to corporate headquarters, suppliers and customers alike, and to the shop floor through a company magazine, office and shop floor wall-displays, notice boards, 'visual' productivity and performance charts displayed in each product-focused cell, and through information bulletins during team meetings. On the rare occasions when corporate managers and customers visited the plant, what they saw would have appeared to them as a fully-functioning lean production system, operated by a flexible, co-operative and committed workforce led by a competent management team.

Behind the scenes, however, little had changed. Management had hoped that the training seminars, quality circle meetings and team briefings would harness workers' commitments to lean production. Workers on the other hand saw these simply as 'time out' from their established flexible work routine. They were perceived as a welcome respite from the monotony of shop floor work and, as we will see below, as an opportunity to entertain themselves by 'goading' management about the inability to manage the shop floor, to show, in no uncertain terms, who was really in charge! Although Northern Plant's manufacturing resources had been reconfigured into lean production arrangements, and workers had accepted training, and were willing to attend 'quality circles' and cell team briefings, any serious attempt to operationalize lean production in real terms outside of these meetings was vigorously resisted. Any first-line management interference in how the 'numbers were made', and how workers spent their *hard earned* 'free' time after targets had been reached, was automatically met with threats of retaliation that would be used to expose management's introduction of a lean production system for what it was: an elaborate 'charade' designed purely for corporate management's consumption that bore absolutely no resemblance at all to what really went on. Both managers and workers were, indeed, acutely aware of the latter's 'situational power' (Ackroyd and Thompson. 1999) by reverting to 'normal' working arrangements and producing only the official hourly output quotas *by* the hour, and *on* the hour over an eight-hour shift, as opposed to producing eight hours work in less than six hours,[1] declining invitations to work overtime,[2] and by abdicating their responsibility for in-process quality assurance, leaving this to the plant's quality-patrol inspectors.[3] Workers could at a stroke effectively slash daily productivity by up to 25 per cent.

The situation in which first-line managers at Northern Plant found themselves illustrates how those who we assume hold power in organization, by virtue of the authority role they perform, can in certain circumstances quite easily find their power and authority neutralized by those normally considered less powerful.

Thinkpoint 11.1

From what you have read so far about Northern Plant, how would you account for managers' failure to understand the differences between what workers at Northern Plant had been used to, and what 'lean production' required and involved?

We have seen how, when attempts were made to introduce new working practices associated with lean production, workers at Northern Plant refused to co-operate with managers, by distancing themselves from any involvement in its planning and organization (see Collinson, 1992, 1994). The workers did this by claiming that, although not objecting to its introduction, as far as they were concerned it stood to reason that *responsibility* for its success ultimately lay with management, not themselves. We will explore the reasons why workers employed this particular form of resistance when we revisit this case study later in the chapter.

For now, to give you an indication of what it is like to face this kind of resistance, imagine for a moment you are a member of Mike's human resource 'change team'. Like Mike, you arrive at Northern Plant to help re-engineer the plant into a lean production facility. You are informed how management at the plant has been attempting to fully introduce lean production for some years, but without much success. You have been briefed about the workers' ill-discipline. You see the problem as a challenge, as a difficult barrier to change that obviously needs to be overcome, but this does not faze you. From your experience as a 'change agent' elsewhere, you already have a good idea what the likely problem is: *a lack of leadership and poor communication.* You know this from studying for your 2.1 BA Human Resource Management Degree at a reputable university. As your favourite 'change management' lecturer pointed out to you and your classmates many times, 'scratch below the surface of any "change management" problems in organizations and what you will undoubtedly find in almost every case is lack of leadership and poor communication'. You will also recall how it was explained to you that you may of course come across the odd militant worker, or a few 'bad apples', who seem to have a chip on their shoulder, and because of this tend to go out of their way to resist management's prerogative to manage, and how resistance is almost always due to a 'fear of change' to which everyone is susceptible when facing the unknown.

You make these points at Mike's first team meeting. You are consequently perceived by your colleagues to have a clear understanding of the problem and how to solve it, and you are given the task of tackling these problems. Pleased with having been given this responsibility, you arrange a series of small group meetings with the plant's workforce. In these meetings you give an excellent presentation, drawing upon your lecture notes on the topics of lean production and change management, about the aims and objectives and benefits of lean production, both in terms of its competitive advantage for the company and also, in particular, in terms of the benefits for workers themselves.

You feel confident from these presentations that workers at the plant will at least appreciate that lean production is essentially about working *smarter* not *harder*, and how they will be empowered to make decisions and have the opportunity to take greater responsibility for the planning and organization of production, 'quality control' and customer satisfaction. You feel quite confident that this will put their 'fear of change' to rest.

The response of your audience to your account of the benefits of lean production is, however, not quite what you expect. Not only are the workers apparently unconvinced that lean production will give them a greater say in decision-making, they totally refuse to accept that it will make their work more interesting. In any case, they say, they are quite happy with the way things are at present and don't particularly want to work differently. You try to convince them that their views are misguided, by recounting how lean production offers them job enrichment and skill enhancement. This doesn't seem to get you very far. They just become more hostile, not only to your ideas but also to you personally. They even claim that your attempt to convince them to accept new working practices is motivated purely by your own personal ambitions. As they put it, getting them to 'buy into' lean production will probably get you a 'bonus' of some sort, and help you to move up the corporate ladder as a reward for your efforts, while they will be left to work much harder than they did before within a system of production that does not offer them the same rewards and opportunities. They also claim that you know very well that the proposed changes are designed not to empower them but to subjugate them to greater management control, for no other reason than to increase productivity.

You refute these claims emphatically. You admit that yes, as a management graduate, you certainly do want one day to progress to the top of your profession – who wouldn't? You also concede that ultimately lean production is obviously designed first and foremost to increase productivity. But you also insist that it does not achieve this by 'sweating labour'. A chorus of laughter erupts from around the training room. As the laughter dies down you're told to 'come clean', to be honest with workers and with yourself. You are told that if you want to be taken seriously as a manager you need to stop insulting their intelligence by treating them 'as if they were born only yesterday'.

You begin to realize that you are being drawn into a situation in which these workers are claiming that your own selfish, personal, professional goals and interests are the *real* motives behind your attempts to induce them to accept new working practices. Your attempts to counter these accusations serve only to produce further gales of laughter that imply that you are simply digging a deeper hole for yourself. They then finish their attack on you by claiming that everyone – including yourself – knows that first and foremost management's job is to 'screw' workers as much as they can to get as much productivity out of them as possible! At this point you lose your composure, you blush and become lost for words, not quite sure what's going on, but you have a sinking feeling that you're getting nowhere and that you have 'the challenge of your life' in front of you.

Summary of the issues raised by this case study so far

This is just a brief insight into a number of subversive forms of misbehaviour (see Ackroyd and Thompson, 1999) that workers at Northern Plant employed to resist lean production. Having read Box 11.1, you will appreciate how workers did not openly challenge management's right to re-engineer the plant's manufacturing arrangement. Instead, they questioned managers' integrity as a way of 'spoiling' their professional and personal identity to undermine the legitimacy of their power and authority. Conventional organizational behaviour and management textbooks rarely acknowledge this kind of misbehaviour, and when they do they seldom examine it in any real critical detail. And yet, as Ackroyd and Thompson (1999) and Collinson (1992, 1994) show, misbehaviour of this kind, which is commonplace in many organizations, is generally ignored or downplayed in most case studies that fill the textbooks used on so many management courses.

Exercise 11.1

- Make a list of the challenges that you think Mike's change team faced at the lean production briefing meetings described in the case study.
- Make a separate list of what you think are the likely reasons for worker resistance to lean production at Northern Plant.
- Sketch out a strategy that Mike's change team might adopt to counter worker resistance at the plant.
- Assess the workers' strategy of resistance that involves questioning managers' integrity and 'spoiling their identity'.

We will return to these issues when we revisit the case study later in the chapter. What we need to do first is to look in more detail at how 'new organizational forms' have come to replace conventional ways of producing goods and services in advanced industrial society during the late twentieth century.

MAINSTREAM APPROACH TO CHANGE AND INNOVATION

Introduction to the mainstream approach

The new organizational forms that emerged during the latter part of the twentieth century have acquired a wide variety of labels. The following are widely used:

- 'just-in-time' (JIT) (Schonberger, 1986)
- 'lean production' (Womack *et al.*, 1990)
- 'innovation-mediated production' (Kenney and Florida, 1993)
- 'cellular manufacturing' (Alford, 1994)
- 'product-focused manufacturing' (Alford, 1994)
- 'the integrated factory' (Bonazzi, 1994).

Along with these various terms and concepts, new theories have also been developed that are used to describe their nature and characteristics. The most common include:

- 'flexible specialization' (Piore and Sabel, 1984)
- 'post-Fordism' (McKinlay and Starkey, 1992; Wood, 1989)
- 'Toyotaism' (Imai, 1989)
- 'Japanization' (Bratton, 1992; Oliver and Wilkinson, 1992)
- 'neo-Fordism' (Agglietta, 1979).

What all of these terms and concepts have in common is the notion that in advanced industrial societies in recent decades a radical change has been occurring (or must occur if 'the West' is to remain competitive) in the way that work is organized and experienced.

Fordism System of mass production based on hierarchical management control pioneered by Henry Ford during the early twentieth century, adopted throughout most Western economies up until its decline in advanced capitalist economies in the 1970s when product differentiation and changing markets demanded more flexibility.

Post-Fordism Describes flexible systems of production that are designed to produce differentiated goods and services for niche markets.

Lean production/ manufacturing System of production, first used in Japan, to maintain the smooth flow of production by using minimum resources to reduce cost, work-in-progress and other overheads. It is associated with JIT services and stock inventories where companies do not retain excess labour or stocks of goods but use information technology to ensure recruitment or reordering of stocks when actually needed.

Here we will concentrate primarily upon 'lean production', an innovation that is intended to revolutionize the organization and productivity of shop floor work. As Womack *et al.* (1990), leading champions of lean production, explain, in contrast to traditional **Fordist** mass production arrangements, **post-Fordist** organizational forms, such as **lean production**, comprise small dedicated multi-skilled and multi-functional teams of workers who operate high-tech, multi-purpose machines and automated assembly operations that require less physical effort, less manufacturing and factory space, less machine hours, fewer tools and less inventory. Within this new, high-tech manufacturing environment workers are *empowered* to take greater responsibility for decision-making, problem solving, product quality control and production maintenance. According to Womack *et al.* (*ibid.*), directly involving workers in the day-to-day running of production and the planning and organizing of work, not only makes work more interesting for workers, it also makes organization more competitive.

One of the most popular forms of flexibility found in many organizations today is JIT. This technique forms an integral part of most lean production systems. JIT is essentially a system of production that is designed to improve productivity and competitiveness by reducing waste. According to JIT enthusiasts, forms of waste include idle machine time, waiting time, lost production due to machine breakdowns, defective parts, poor-quality finished products, high levels of inventory and work-in-progress, late deliveries, the need for overtime to meet output quotas not achieved within normal working hours and so on. JIT is designed to eliminate these various forms of waste by controlling stock levels and the level and flow of work-in-progress through each of the various stages of production. The key aims of JIT are to:

- Reduce stock and work-in-progress to the minimum possible level.
- Prevent large quantities of work-in-progress from building up within the production system.
- Reduce the level of finished goods held by the organization, by dispatching them to the consumer as soon as they are produced.

All of this rests on the capacity of organizations to buy in small batches of materials from suppliers, delivering them to the point of production *just in time* for when they are needed, and to arrange for finished goods to be dispatched to, or collected by, customers immediately they reach the end of the production process. This requires close buyer-supplier co-operation, simple workflows, fast machine set-up and changeover times, rigorous in-process quality control methods designed to guarantee that things are made 'right first time', and, most importantly, a workforce that is both aware of, and committed to, the principles of JIT (see Schonberger, 1986). Workers are the most important resource in this system because JIT ultimately relies on them to keep the flow of production going by addressing problems quickly, as and when they occur, in order to minimize stoppage time and avoid faults or breakdowns within the system. The underlying rationale behind this is to 'build in' quality at each stage of production rather than 'inspect out' defective or substandard parts or products at the end of the production process.

There are various accounts of the origins of JIT. One of the most popular states that it was first introduced at Toyota in the 1950s after one of the firm's senior executives visited an American supermarket where he observed workers restocking shelves immediately after customers had purchased goods rather than when shelves became empty. According to Schonberger (1986), it was following its introduction at Toyota that JIT became widely adopted in other post-war Japanese manufacturing industries, especially shipbuilding, car plants, and later, in other high-tech industries. Its introduction and subsequent widespread popularity in North American and Western European industries, as you will see below, came about as a result of spiralling production costs triggered by economic crises in the 1970s, which left Western industries unable to compete with their Japanese counterparts.

Many industrial sociologists, especially those working within the labour process tradition for example, contest the claim that new organizational forms, such as those promoted by JIT and lean production, make work more interesting and rewarding. Oliver and Wilkinson (1992) demonstrate how under lean manufacturing arrangements workers are often simply required to do several boring and monotonous jobs instead of just one. Diane Sharpe (1998), who worked for a full year on the shop floor in a Japanese manufacturing company in the UK, shows how 'so-called' **multiskilling** rarely involves little more than **multitasking**. She also notes how, more often than not, workers merely acquire *company-specific* skills as opposed to genuine *transferable skills* that are applicable to other organizational settings.

Multiskilling Working arrangements in which workers acquire the full range of necessary skills required to perform a number of jobs, tasks and duties efficiently under minimum supervision.

Multitasking Working arrangements where it is claimed that workers acquire the various skills needed to perform a number of jobs, tasks and duties.

Thinkpoint 11.2

On what basis would you assess the claims made by the advocates of lean production, bearing in mind the case study of Northern Plant? How would you defend this basis?

Researchers working within the labour process tradition have shown how so-called multiskilling, along with teamworking and total quality control methods, not only fail to live up to their promise to make work more interesting and rewarding but lead to work intensification. Delbridge and Turnbull (1992), Delbridge *et al.* (1998), Garrahan and Stewart (1992) and Sewell and Wilkinson (1992) show how under lean production, which they refer to as 'mean' production, workers are subject to new subtle forms of managerial surveillance that extend rather than reduce management control. As they show from their research, **flexibility**, **teamworking** and TQM operate to eliminate what has given workers some respite from the boredom and monotony and fatigue of the production line. These new forms of work organization, they observe, are not more empowering in any meaningful sense. They are instead designed first and foremost to increase output and reduce costs. Needless to say, advocates of lean production reject these criticisms as entirely unjustified.

Flexibility Systems of production and working arrangements that allow material and human resources to be utilized speedily to meet the fickle and fluctuating demands of the market and customer taste.

Teamworking Working arrangements in which workers themselves are given responsibility for the planning and coordination of some aspects of their work and the roles and tasks they are required to perform.

In this opening section, we have looked at how new organizational forms are viewed from two perspectives. On the one hand, mainstream theorists have celebrated the advent of post-Fordism as a radical departure from the past, from traditional Fordist organizational structures based upon rigid hierarchical and bureaucratic management command and control regimes. They also celebrate it as the beginning of the end of the problem of workplace alienation and degradation. On the other hand, critical commentators challenge this rosy view by arguing that post-Fordist production methods and working practices do not deliver what they promise.

Key controversies surrounding the mainstream approach

So far, we have talked mainly about the advent of new forms of organization in manufacturing. However, it is not only manufacturing industries that have been subject to change in recent decades. Similar major changes in organization structures, working practices, job design and management control methods have taken place in other private and public sector organizations. As in manufacturing, changes have been driven, or at least justified, in light of the emergence of highly complex and competitive economic and market conditions, which some would say have been brought about by the forces of globalization (see Chapter 13). To cope with these conditions, managers across diverse sectors and across the world have all turned to 'new wave' management ideas and novel organizational forms.

In the name of competitiveness and commercial success – which could equally be interpreted in terms of a response to a crisis in profitability, or a determination to reassert control over value-producing activities – managers have sought to re-engineer their business processes and human resource practices. In many cases, this involves the formation of alliances and complex inter-organizational relationships as firms co-operate with one another to minimize their individual limitations and vulnerabilities or to capitalize upon synergies. As Child (2005) has pointed out, many firms no longer compete solely on a national basis. They operate globally, distributing products and providing services across national and cultural boundaries. For example, firms that previously operated independently of each other now operate in 'clusters' within retail or technology parks (Wilson, 2004), or within Japanese style spatially concentrated, preferred buyer–supplier production sites (Oliver and Wilkinson, 1992).

Box 11.2
The benefits of lean production

Job enrichment Work arrangements that are designed to expand the number of tasks and roles workers perform to provide opportunities for them to gain greater satisfaction, reward, recognition and achievement.

Womack *et al.* (1990) argue that first and foremost lean production is simply a system that combines the advantages of mass production with the benefits of craft production, and claim that whether this actually leads to genuine skill enhancement is not important. In their view, the more important issue, which they claim their critics fail to appreciate, is that lean production is undoubtedly a far 'better way of making things', which organizations have no choice but to adopt given today's highly competitive global markets (ibid., p. 225). Even if this reading of the nature of JIT and lean production is accepted, we can see from the 'mean' production perspective that we should be very careful about automatically viewing new post-Fordist organizational forms as a radical departure from the demands placed upon workers and the levels of control under Fordism. As Womack *et al.*'s response to their critics indicates, even leading advocates of such new organizational forms are willing to concede that flexible production arrangements and working practices do not necessarily lead to skill enhancement and **job enrichment**. It is difficult to resist the conclusion that their advocacy of lean production is based upon its cost-effectiveness and ultimately upon its inevitability in the face of global competition, and not on its enrichment of the experience of work, even when it does fortuitously bring such benefits.

Note how at the same time, new information and communication technology has played a part in forging new forms of organization and business relationships. Zuboff (1988), for example, shows how advances in information and communication technologies and knowledge transfer capabilities have enabled, if not compelled, business organizations in general to transform the way they operate, in terms of their business and customer relationships and their use of material and human resources.

RE-ENGINEERING IN THE PUBLIC SECTOR

Public sector and voluntary service organizations have similarly sought ways to achieve ambitious improvements in performance (McNulty and Ferlie, 2005) by re-engineering their organizational structure and human resource functions and capabilities (Legge, 2005). Attempts include the introduction of leaner, flatter, flexible organization practices (Beattie and McDougall, 1998), business process re-engineering (BPR) (Hammer and Champy, 1993), quality audit systems (Morley, 2003), 'new public management' (Corby and White, 1999) and cultural change initiatives (Hope-Hailey, 1998) (see also Chapter 6). In the UK, as in other advanced industrial societies, these investments are designed to erode the rigidities and inefficiencies associated with traditional post-war welfare state hierarchical and bureaucratic organizational structures, which are seen as having made public sector services 'wasteful and bloated' (Ferlie *et al.*, 1996), and to provide taxpayers with more value-for-money public services that better serve consumer needs and expectations (Howkins and Thornton, 2002).

Here again, critical management and labour process theorists draw out important differences between the rhetoric and reality of the outcomes of new organizational forms in the public sector (e.g., Dent, 1998; Ferlie *et al.*, 1996; McNulty and Ferlie, 2005; Wilson, 2004; Worthington, 2004). These studies show how, BPR and TQM (see Chapter 7), for example, have resulted in widespread dissatisfaction, discontent and alienation. To take the example of health care, it has been found that clinicians, nurses, medics, auxiliary and catering and cleaning staff alike have tended to experience the new working practices resulting from these investments as '*dis*-empowering' rather than 'empowering', and relying on work-intensification rather than work enrichment (Wilson, 2004).

In further and higher education a similar picture emerges. The application of quality methodologies to job role analysis, output requirements and performance targets, teaching and learning methods, student support and methods of assessment has also resulted in widespread employee discontent, stress and alienation. So much so that university vice-chancellors, teachers' trade unions and academics have all expressed concerns about the purpose of quality assessment in higher education, both in terms of its financial cost and also its drain on time and resources (see Howie, 2002; Harley, 2001; Morley, 2003; Strathern, 2000). But what most concerns them is how the notion of quality in higher education has led to the marketization of education (Willmott, 1996), and with this the subordination of academic work to managerial priorities resulting in work intensification.

Benefits of new organizational forms

It should be apparent from what we have covered thus far that lean production and flexible working practices are attractive to organizations because they promise to improve productivity. But do these organizational forms benefit workers? As we have noted, lean production enables organizations to use their manufacturing, financial and human resources in more cost-efficient ways. John Atkinson's (1984) flexible firm model (sometimes referred to as 'flexible specialization') is widely used to illustrate the benefits of flexibility not only to firms but also to their employees.

THE FLEXIBLE FIRM

Atkinson's flexible firm model has three distinct but interrelated characteristics: (i) *functional* flexibility; (ii) *numerical* flexibility; and (iii) *financial* flexibility.

- Functional flexibility refers to how firms assign (multiskilled) employees to different roles, activities and work tasks to meet changes in market demand and customer requirements.
- Numerical flexibility refers to how firms adjust the size of their workforce in relation to fluctuations in output requirements and market demand by using employment agencies, such as Manpower, or 'non-standard' employment practices such as part-time, short-term and fixed-term employment contracts.
- Financial flexibility refers to how firms adjust their wage costs to make savings by moving away from uniform and standardized pay structures, or by introducing performance-related pay in keeping with the objectives of functional and numerical flexibility.

Box 11.3
Supply chains and the clustering of firms

Spatially concentrated business clusters, as they are referred to, comprise small- to medium-sized firms located in close proximity to each other, or to larger (often) multinational manufacturing and business organizations for whom they are contracted to supply outsourced small sub-assembly and sub-component parts and accessories delivered on a JIT basis to the buyer organization. The underpinning rationale of preferred buyer–supplier relations is to allow (large and small) firms to collaborate to 'continuously improve on cost savings by reducing transport and distribution costs, smoothing the flow of production, reducing lead times, eliminating waste, sharing the costs of investment in new technology, research and development and maintaining quality control' (see Oliver and Wilkinson, 1992).

Within this flexible firm model, workers fall into one of two distinct groups: *core* or *peripheral* employees. Core employees normally perform what Atkinson refers to as 'functionally flexible' roles. Workers who fall into this category are usually highly skilled (e.g., craft workers, and research and design engineers), experts in a particular field (e.g., computer technicians and technical sales staff), or essential to the firm's core operations. Given their importance to the firm, this group normally enjoys relatively secure terms and conditions of employment, higher salaries than other workers, good company benefits such as bonus payments, generous holiday pay, sick pay and company pension rights. Peripheral employees (e.g., part-time, contract and agency workers, and public subsidy trainees), on the other hand, perform what Atkinson calls 'numerically flexible' roles. Workers who fall within this category are easily replaceable, tend to have rather less secure employment conditions and more often than not receive less pay and less access to the company benefits enjoyed by functionally flexible workers.

For many mainstream theorists the 'flexible firm' model captures some of the key benefits of new forms of organization. However, they tend only to flag up how 'flexibility' reduces costs and improves organizational performance. They rarely look beyond these priorities at the potential implications of the flexible firm for core and peripheral employees, in terms of job security, skill development and career opportunities. One way of exploring this issue is to imagine for a moment what it might be like to be a core or peripheral employee. Smith and Poliert, who critique Atkinson's flexible firm model from a labour process perspective, provide a good starting point (see Box 11.4).

Box 11.4
A critique of the 'flexible firm'

According to Poliert (1988) and Smith (1991), it stands to reason that flexible firms will try hard to attract, and keep, their *core* workers by offering them good terms and conditions of employment: good pay, attractive company benefits, and opportunities for education and training, etc. *Peripheral* workers, however, as Poliert and Smith note, normally perform mainly routine tasks that require only generic skills. This makes them easily replaceable, and therefore less important to the firm. Not only does this disadvantage them in the workplace itself – in terms of the limited opportunities for genuine skill development, training and education and career development – but their contracted conditions of employment have a detrimental effect on their economic, social and personal well-being.

When it comes to taking out a mortgage or a loan, for example, which many of us (until recently) were able to take for granted, we need to demonstrate our creditworthiness by being in regular (relatively) secure employment. Peripheral workers do often work for one firm for long periods of time, but this does not mean they are in secure employment. On the contrary, the nature of the roles they perform and their position within the firm, especially when they are recruited through employment agencies, means that they can easily find themselves out of work at very short notice. Another issue that is also ignored in mainstream literature is that women and ethnic minorities are over-represented in many peripheral employment groups (see Warhurst *et al.*, 2004).

The important point to draw from this is that the mainstream literature gives an impression that training, education and skill enhancement are a priority in all organizations, irrespective of the employees' position and role within the firm. The reality of employment conditions in the flexible firm, however, shows clearly that this is not the case. Only *certain* workers, those who are valuable or cannot be easily replaced or disposed of, are likely to receive good pay and conditions, and have access to training and education. Others, who are not as valuable to the firm, for the reasons outlined above, are generally denied these opportunities. Changes in the technical and social organization of production, and the flexible utilization of labour, in other words, do potentially create opportunities for multiskilling and job enrichment, but not for all employees. By focusing mainly on the technical superiority and competitive advantages of new organizational forms over older forms of production, mainstream theorists fail to recognize how the trend towards flexibility in organizations has different outcomes for different employee groups, and how this can just as easily lead to 'skill-polarization' as 'skill expansion' (Warhurst *et al.*, 2004). The problem is that investments in new flexible organizational and working practices that provide firms with genuine opportunities for skill expansion are driven first and foremost by managerial priorities concerned with cost reduction, profit maximization and market share.

Exercise 11.2

- Make a list of the advantages of *functional, numerical* and *financial* flexibility for organizations. Make a list of the advantages and disadvantages of being a *core* worker.
- Make a list of the advantages and disadvantages of being a *peripheral* worker.
- Are firms likely to be concerned about skill polarization, and to what extent are they likely to seek ways to address this 'problem'? Is it a problem for employers?
- Make a list of how the 'problem' of skill polarization would be addressed from: (i) a management perspective; and (ii) an employee perspective.

The skill polarization versus skill expansion issue discussed in this section, along with the issues you may have considered in carrying out Exercise 11.2, may well have raised some doubts about the claim that new flexible post-Fordist organizational forms represent a radical break from the past, and the related claim that they (can) significantly improve the lived-experience of work. As we have seen, flexibility brings some benefits for 'core' elements of the workforce, but such improvements are largely a coincidental outcome of the drive to gain competitive advantage. So how different are Fordist and post-Fordist working practices? The following section deals with this question by assessing the reasons for, and outcomes of, the apparent shift from Fordist to post-Fordist work regimes.

The shift from Fordism to post-Fordism in context

The term 'Fordism' refers to a form of manufacture and work organization that was developed at the beginning of the twentieth century by Henry Ford at the Ford Motor Company in the USA. Fordism can be loosely defined as a system of mass production for mass consumption. Its principal feature is a moving production line, along which a highly detailed division of labour is governed by rigid hierarchical command and control structures, comprising 'low-trust' inflexible management control methods based upon the principles of 'scientific management' (see Chapters 2 and 7). An underlying premise of this system is the view that workers 'should be paid to work not to think', and that it should be management alone that determines how work is organized and how jobs and work tasks are performed.

THE POLITICS OF SCIENTIFIC MANAGEMENT

According to the mainstream literature, 'scientific management' came into being as a result of the rapid expansion of mass markets in North America at the turn of the twentieth century (Burnes, 2002; Huczynski and Buchanan, 2003; Mullins, 2001; Watson, 2002). Scientific management provided a practical solution to two basic problems. Many workers employed in large-scale manufacturing organizations at that time were from agricultural regions in the USA, or were immigrant workers who had little knowledge of the English language, few job skills and little or no experience of factory work. By simplifying manufacturing processes, scientific management overcame these problems by making it easier for managers to train workers to perform simplified repetitive jobs and monitor their performance. This implies that Ford and Taylor were only concerned with discovering better ways to increase productivity and efficiency. Finding new ways to raise productivity through more efficient use of resources was certainly important to them, but it was not their only priority. In their view, the key to raising productivity and efficiency lay not only in management being able to exercise a greater level of control over the production process, work design and the flow of materials to work stations, but also the extent to which managers could directly control workers and the tasks they were required to perform. Both Ford and Taylor saw direct control methods not only as a means for achieving productivity and efficiency gains, but also as a method that would enable management to instil in workers a more ordered and disciplined attitude to work (Anthony, 1977). Their methods for achieving this consisted of four basic principles:

1 Replacing traditional rule-of-thumb work methods with more systematic methods based on a scientific study of the work tasks.
2 Scientifically selecting, organizing, training and developing each individual employee separately rather than allow them to organize and train themselves.
3 Providing detailed instruction and exercising close constant supervision over each worker to ensure they perform a set number of discrete tasks in accordance with management's instructions.
4 Divide the work of managers from that of workers, so that managers can apply scientific management principles to the planning and organization of work to ensure that each individual worker actually performs the tasks in the required fashion.

Labour discipline was a particular concern for Ford and Taylor. Having passed up the opportunity to go to Harvard in order to work on the shop floor, Taylor had been appalled by what he saw as the lack of management knowledge and control of working practices, and, moreover, what he referred to as 'soldiering'. This term describes what Taylor saw as the natural tendency among workers in organizations to use any opportunity available to 'take it easy' by working no harder than was absolutely necessary. What most concerned Taylor, however, was what he referred to as '*systematic* soldiering'; the tendency of both individuals and work groups to find ways to exercise informal means of controlling the pace and duration of work in order to reduce the effort needed to perform tasks, so as to make the working day as comfortable as possible. What alarmed Taylor was management's apparent inability to address this problem.

In Taylor's view, soldiering would be overcome by directly employing workers instead of relying upon subcontracting to 'gangs', organized by 'gang masters', by bringing order and discipline to the shop floor, and by preventing workers, especially craft workers, from keeping their knowledge to themselves. What Taylor failed to appreciate is that restrictive practices, such as soldiering, and other forms of misbehaviour and resistance to management control, are not simply due to laziness. As Littler (1982) explains, systematic 'soldiering' was, at the time, a by-product of nineteenth-century craft production arrangements, which Taylor, whose middle-class background impeded any knowledge of such traditions, attributed to laziness.

Before the 1880s, factory, mill and mine owners employed workers indirectly through subcontractors who took responsibility for the selection, recruitment, training and disciplining of workers. In this period it was 'master craftsmen' and 'gang masters', rather than management, who determined how work was to be organized, and the speed at which tasks were to be completed (Littler, 1982). Under this system there was no real incentive for workers or their 'gang masters' to seek to improve productivity for its own sake. Higher levels of output, they believed, would reduce the market demand for their labour, and thus lead to periodic bouts of unemployment. They also held many other very different views about work, and shared very different economic values than those held by Ford and Taylor. As Anthony (1977) points out, workers in this period, unlike today, saw work as essentially a means to an end, not an end in itself: a way of sustaining personal economic well-being, rather than maximizing earnings or acquiring personal wealth. Maintaining control of their labour and regulating output and productivity, to avoid over-production, and the risk of lay-offs, was to them common sense.

From Ford and Taylor's perspective these practices were unnecessary and unacceptable constraints of productivity and efficiency, and barrier to economic growth. Taylor saw these attitudes as a result of non-incentive wage systems that effectively encouraged low productivity. If workers received the same pay, irrespective of what they produced, and believed that *doing more* would lead to management *expecting more* from them without receiving sufficient reward for their efforts, it becomes perfectly understandable why workers would erect and defend 'restrictive practices'. However, we know from early factory studies conducted during Ford and Taylor's time (see Schwartzman, 1993), and many other studies conducted throughout the twentieth century (e.g.: Burawoy, 1979; Eldridge, 1971; Lupton, 1963; Roy, 1952; Turner, 1971) and right up to the present day (see Smith, 2010), that 'restrictive practices' are about more than basic pay and other financial incentives (Thompson, 1989).

Understanding resistance

'Restrictive practices' as well as many other acts of misbehaviour are common in organizations, and take many forms. Management control, management–labour relationships, working practices, formal rules and regulation and instructions governing how workers are required to perform tasks, job performance measures and appraisal criteria, time-and-attendance requirements, and everyday social norms and behavioural expectations at work are all susceptible to resistance. Middle and senior managers and other occupational and professional groups also resist change. In the mainstream literature, resistance is often simply attributed to employee 'fear of change'. This may be true to some extent. But even so, surely there is more than just one single factor that accounts for resistance to change? If 'fear of change' is *the* single causal factor that accounts for why it is often resisted, how do we account for other wider acts of resistance to management's basic prerogative to manage *per se,* in periods of relative stability, that have nothing much to do with change? The simple answer is that resistance is not merely a defensive, psychological or emotional response to 'fear of the unknown'. It is a political act used to defend perceived interests: employment rights, such as pay and conditions, and pay bargaining agreements and procedures, holiday, sickness, maternity, redundancy and pension entitlements, promotion criteria, the erosion of formally agreed and informally established working practices and demarcation lines and so on. As we have seen at Northern Plant, it is also motivated by a defence of occupational and professional values, as well as gender, age, race and social class discrimination, and not least of all exploitation and work intensification.

Exercise 11.3

- Consider some of the everyday acts of resistance or misbehaviour you may have witnessed or been involved in from time to time, such as the ritual teasing, chiding 'wind-ups' and other joking behaviour enacted among classmates at school, peer groups and friendship networks. For example, did you or any of your classmates at school occasionally playfully or wilfully misbehave to disrupt lessons to challenge or undermine teachers' authority; or secretly send and receive 'under the desk' derisory text messages about lesson content, learning and teaching aims and goals, teachers' and other pupils' clothes and appearance, views, attitudes, character or general demeanour? Were there occasions when you or one of your classmates sabotaged a lesson, a science experiment; or set off the school's fire alarm for a laugh, or to annoy certain teachers and other school authority figures? Recall the celebration and 'hero status' afforded to the perpetrators of such misbehaviour by other pupils as the classes were paraded out to the fire assembly points in the school yard, to enjoy a welcome break from a particularly boring lesson, especially on a sunny day – or the sheer frustration you and your teachers felt and the anger you may have expressed towards them when this occurred in poor weather. Also recall how overly conscientious, diligent, studious or conformist classmates or 'teachers' pets' may have been treated. And also consider why you or your classmates more often than not made a hasty 'bee line' to secure a place on the back seats of the bus on school visits to the theatre, museums, local or national historic sites of interest, or whatever. Was it not to escape the teachers' authority by distancing yourself from the normal reach and scope of their 'disciplinary gaze'?

- These and other forms of 'counter-cultural' school deviance and misbehaviour have traditionally been particularly prevalent in schools located in working class areas (see Willis, 1977; 2000). They are practices that Northern Plant's shop floor workforce would likely recognize. They are forms of (mis)behaviour that, as you and they will know from experience, normally tend to be summarily dismissed as acts of an immature, childish, juvenile, deviant minority lacking personal self-respect, as well as a basic respect for authority. What Willis's analysis of 'oppositional culture' practices at school, which sits firmly, and self-consciously, in a critical sociological tradition informed by a close Marxist reading of how working class males (in particular) view the nature and condition of work in a capitalist society, is how classroom deviance at school is a sort of 'training ground'. To use Willis's original term, it prepares 'working class kids' for 'working class jobs' and what they will actually encounter once they enter the workplace. That is, it is what Henry Thoreau (a nineteenth-century American poet, abolitionist and tax-evader!), referred to as a 'life of quiet desperation', a sentiment echoed on Pink Floyd's 'Dark Side of the Moon', and what another sociologist from Willis's era calls the 'not enough world of work' (Gouldner, 1971), characterized by long hours in often noisy, dirty and essentially boring and monotonous work environments. Such environments offer very little in terms of individual self-determination, reward, job satisfaction, gratification, or personal dignity (Hodson, 2001). As Thoreau put it:

  '(In modern society) the mass of men [and women] lead lives of quiet desperation. By a seeming fate, commonly called necessity, they are employed, as it says in an old book, laying up treasures, which moths and rust will corrupt, and thieves break through and steal. It is a fool's life, as they will find when they get to the end of it, if not before.' Henry Thoreau (1817–1862).

Exercise 11.4

- How does Ford and Taylor's explanation of the causes of 'restrictive work practices' and recalcitrant behaviour towards management in organizations differ from those of Willis and Gouldner?
- How does Willis's account of 'oppositional school culture' help us understand why workers at Northern Plant resisted new working practices under lean production?
- How much does Gouldner's term, the '*not enough world of work*', and Thoreau's somewhat morbid characterization of work as a '*life of quiet desperation*' apply to other work outside of manufacturing: i.e., leisure, retail, entertainment, tourism, transport, film and music industries, fast food outlets, newspaper, advertising and publishing companies, financial services, accounting firms, law firms, teaching, nursing, social care and other professions, libraries, museums, charity shops and other voluntary sector organizations?

Changes associated with progress and the transition to new flexible organizational forms that have emerged in many different contexts in recent decades impact on the position and the interests of employees at all levels. Child (2005) notes how senior managers see downsizing as reducing their 'positional power', influence and status (Thompson and McHugh, 1998) in terms of their control over employees, budgets and other resources as well as opportunities for promotion. The power and status of middle and first-line managers are similarly affected by the introduction of flatter organizational structures, self-managing teamworking arrangements and the concept of empowerment, which they automatically see as a threat to their role and job security (see Oliver and Wilkinson, 1992). Trade unions resist change for the same reason. For them, however, change represents a serious threat to traditional management–trade union relations, pay and conditions, bargaining rights, job security, and consequently their ability to represent worker interests (see Poliert, 1996). Workers also seek to resist change, as our case study shows, when its potential impact on established structural arrangements, production methods and working practices is seen to result in downsizing and/or work intensification.

Many mainstream theorists, Child (2005) included, tend to interpret and dismiss these responses as irrational manifestations of the general 'fear' of the unknown, which is felt by employees at all levels, whenever significant and sometimes even simple changes to established organizational structures and traditional ways of doing things occur. Negative employee reaction to change is also often caused by misconceptions of the aims, goals and purpose of change. As Child and others argue, without full and effective communication it is understandable why employees will fail to recognize, acknowledge and accept the need for change, and of the benefits of new organizational arrangements and working practices. Lack of proper communication is also seen to account for how and why employees often fail to appreciate the effects of wider external competitive market pressure facing organizations, brought about by 'naturally' occurring changes in the economy, or the build up of competitive pressures in the business environment, which demand responses that ultimately compel an organization to change. At the same time, Child claims that managers can overcome 'fear' of the unknown and any resistance this may cause. As most mainstream theorists argue, although some resistance to organizational change is more or less inevitable, as long as management recognize this inevitability they will always be in a strong position to deal with it. It is worth pausing for a moment to note how the terms '*change*' and '*resistance to change*' are being used in this context.

For mainstream theorists, organizational change is a naturally occurring phenomenon, a condition and consequence of persistently occurring changes in the economic, business environment and product market conditions in which an organization operates. And resistance is a reaction to the necessary organizational responses to, and outcomes of, what businesses need to accomplish in order to survive. This reified view of the change-resistance dynamic, leaves out important factors that shape employee understanding, and subsequent reactions to the potential detrimental, personal and professional implications and outcomes of 'organizational survival' strategies. This reified managerial perspective, which fails to acknowledge how change impacts on workers' real or perceived interests and how new organizational arrangements effect job security, for example, rests on, and reinforces, the somewhat naive mainstream assumption that what is good for the organization is good for the employee. In other words, that the employers and their employees have shared priorities and interests which coincide with the needs of the (reified) firm, and the pursuit of the business and management strategy and associated operations arrangements it may need to implement to ensure its survival. From this perspective, it stands to reason that, when faced with resistance, managers need only to fully explain to workers the underlying reasons and rationale for change, and how by doing this, and by involving them as much as they can in the change process, 'disturbances' caused by employees' natural 'fear' of the unknown, can be minimized and eventually overcome. In other words, by following this simple formula, managers can turn 'resistance into commitment to the change so people contribute their knowledge and experience to working out its details and ensuring its successful implementation' (Child, 2005, p. 299).

Thinkpoint 11.3

What does Child's recommended formula for dealing with resistance ignore? Is adequate attention given to how the outcome and potential consequences of change can result in individuals experiencing intense feelings of powerlessness, angst and insecurity?

How are we to make sense of this resistance from employees? Is it because they do not understand the goals and underlying rationale for change? Or is it because of the sudden realization that 'downsizing' may reduce their job security, status and power and position within an organization, and with reduced job security and opportunities for career advancement that may even lead to their unemployment? It is worth pondering that:

- Both 'victims' *and* 'survivors' of downsizing often feel betrayed by organization.
- Both are also prone to feelings of angst and guilt.
- For victims, this is because they can find themselves unable to account for, or come to terms with, why they and not others were made redundant.
- For survivors, this is because they feel guilty about the fact that others have lost their jobs when they themselves have kept theirs.

Critical management and labour process theorists view the mainstream lines of reasoning behind the assumption that fear of change is irrational, and that all that managers need to do to get employees 'on board'. As Ackroyd and Thompson (1999) show, workers often resist both change and management's right to manage as a way of 'getting back' at management – either as compensation for the psychological and emotional depravation of boring and monotonous work, or for 'fun' that provides a respite from the 'dull compulsion' of monotonous shop floor work in manufacturing.

NON-FORDIST ORGANIZATIONAL FORMS

Not all organizations and management practices in the twentieth century were Fordist, nor did all Fordist-type organizations fully embrace scientific management. Systems and contingency theorists show how certain business environments limit the scope and reach of *direct* management control methods (see Chapter 7).

Box 11.5
Direct control versus responsible autonomy

The term 'responsible autonomy' (RA) is used to differentiate organic forms of organization from mechanistic forms that rely upon 'direct control' (DC). These two terms, coined by Andrew Friedman (1977, 1990), a labour process theorist, are used to show how all management control strategies tend to fall somewhere along a 'continuum' between DC and RA. Freidman has been criticized for overly simplifying management strategy. Nevertheless, the DC/RA typology is useful for understanding the contingent nature of management control in organization.

These two 'ideal types' of control, Friedman argues, are determined by the level of skill needed to perform tasks in any given industry or work setting. DC, which he associates with 'low-trust' Taylorist management thinking, is found normally in low-skilled work, whereas RA is normally found in work with more high-skilled content. In short, whereas DC, as the term indicates, is used to exercise close detailed control over the production process and working practices, RA is used to give workers leeway and encourage them to be proactive in decision-making and problem solving to help assist managers to achieve organizational goals. In essence, the aim of RA in releasing workers from DC is to harness their creative powers and adaptability to achieve organizational goals.

What is particularly noteworthy about this typology, as Friedman points out, is that management can find it extremely difficult to shift from RA to DC, and vice versa, once either practice has become embedded in organization over time. Both DC and RA, in other words, create their own habits and rules and related inflexibilities. As Friedman shows, employees subject to RA are usually reluctant to automatically surrender the relative freedom and self-determination they enjoy under this system of control. By the same token, those subject to DC are often disinclined to embrace a shift to RA, and are often suspicious about management's motivation for introducing it, believing that management would support or initiate (ostensibly) autonomous work practices if they did not ultimately serve the firm's interests, and erode workers' interests.

Strengths and limitations of the mainstream approach

Mainstream literature sees organizational transformation as a smooth process from one organizational form to another, and assumes that all that is required to achieve this change is good management communication and leadership. It also assumes that change is always a positive thing for both organizations and employees, and that resistance occurs only when the rationale for change is not explained. However, a shift from one organizational form to another is fraught with contradictions and challenges that are often beyond management's control and understanding. Mainstream thinking can provide managers with a degree of guidance and comfort in undertaking their work as work designers and employee motivators, but their capacity to address fundamental problems is limited both by their dependence upon mainstream knowledge as well as upon the social distance (of inequality and power) between themselves and their subordinates.

Managers cannot always anticipate problems. Good communications cannot always alleviate employees' concerns about the outcome of new organizational arrangements. In part, this is because mainstream accounts of the unitization of new forms of organization take inadequate account of the implications of change for employees – of how leaner organizational structures and downsizing, for example, reduce job and career opportunities and in many cases lead to redundancy. Mainstream thinking assumes the legitimacy of established institutions, however it fails to contemplate how the organization limits and impedes the 'good communication' that it assumes can be instilled.

Mainstream thinking also fails to recognize and explain why change is resented and resisted. Teamworking and notions of empowerment may well lead to work enrichment in some cases, but in others may amount to little more than job enlargement. Mainstream thinking does not take into account how employees, including managers themselves, become attached to established working arrangements and valued work routines, from which they gain a sense of purpose and self-identity, and that irrespective of the rationale for change, they are unlikely to want to forfeit.

Having said this, it is worth noting how the challenges facing organization brought about by globalization, the emergence of new organizational forms, ideas about cultural management and employee involvement, etc. have unsettled many traditional ideas about how best to manage organizations. The rhetoric surrounding these new ideas about improving the quality of the lived-experience of work, and its talk about treating people more as 'human beings' rather than simply 'human resources', though seldom practised in most cases, has had the unintended consequence of opening up a space in management education for more critical thinking about the nature of work (as we know it).

Critical thinkers are concerned with seeking ways of making work more meaningful and rewarding. However, what they detect in many, if not most, change management programmes is the exercise of subtle forms of management power and surveillance that produces new kinds of subjugation rather than the promised benefits of empowerment. It is healthy to question the claims of the 'new wave' management literature. Otherwise, it is impossible either to improve upon them or to rethink their application. But it is also important to acknowledge that 'new wave' criticisms of established management theory and practice usefully draw attention to, as well as promote, the contingent nature of traditional management control methods. The literature on new organization forms assumes that it *is* possible to organize differently. It invites us to think about how to avoid, and possibly (one day) eliminate conditions of exploitation, alienation and excessive work degradation. But instead of developing ways of enabling such reflection, it displaces and impedes it by declining to consider whether the elimination of these conditions is possible without a radical transformation of economic activity.

Much of the 'new wave' literature incorporates, or resonates with, other 'progressive' thinking that attributes importance to business ethics, greater corporate responsibility and a need to ensure employee social and economic welfare. How much guru management ideas can, or are really intended to, challenge conventional management theory and practice in any *meaningfully radical* sense is open to interpretation. Critical commentators are sceptical, arguing that such ideas are more influential in comforting practitioners and placating opponents of big business and globalization than in disrupting the managerial status quo in organizations. Seemingly enlightened consultants and executives are heard to call for the re-engineering of organizational management practices, but do *not* really promote a radical rethink about the fundamental causes of alienation and work degradation, nor do they address head on, the wider socioeconomic, ecological and environmental problems associated with global industrialization. Nor, finally, do they address the challenges and dilemmas facing workers and managers in organizations, the need to earn a living and sustain a sense of purpose and dignity in work conditions where managers and employees alike are treated as a resource to be bought or disposed of as and when required. Very little consideration in all of this, in other words, is given to the underlying logic and rationality of contemporary management thinking.

CRITICAL APPROACH TO CHANGE AND INNOVATION
Introduction to the critical approach

In this section we will look at the claims about new forms of organization made by mainstream management theorists in more critical detail. Following, among others, Thompson and Warhurst (1998), the section shows how many of their claims are based on rather weak evidence. Before doing this, we will look in a little more detail at where the claims originate in terms of the management thinking and ideas that lie behind them. We will then move on from the example of innovation in manufacturing to change in the provision of public services and, more specifically, the delivery of health care. For change and innovation are by no means confined to the private sector or the shop floor. We will consider the case of 'professional workers', such as doctors, and the processes of change and resistance associated with efforts to subject their activities to 'external', managerial performance criteria.

Searching for excellence in the new workplace

Many of the ideas about the utilization of new organizational forms and management practices that we have examined in the first section of this chapter on the 'Mainstream approach', relate to a particular brand of management thinking that emerged during the 1980s, generally referred to as the 'excellence movement' (e.g., Deming, 1982; Imai, 1986; Ouchi, 1982; Pascale and Athos, 1982; Peters and Waterman, 1982). The excellence movement has been most influential in promoting calls for organizational culture change as a prerequisite for successful work and organizational transformation (see Chapter 10). Its emphasis on the importance of culture change as a way of improving employee performance, productivity and competitive advantage in organizations was precipitated by a series of distinct but related social, political and economic events that took place during the last quarter of the twentieth century:

- The flagging performance of North American and Western European industries in the wake of global economic crises triggered by the 1973 and 1979 OPEC 'oil shocks'.
- The rise of new, strong Southeast Asian economies, mainly the Japanese economy, that in the 1970s and 1980s were suddenly outperforming Western organizations in world markets.
- The rise of highly competitive global capitalist market conditions, and increasingly diverse socio-cultural and consumer trends, within and between newly emerging supranational political-economic trading blocs.
- The emergence of new organizational forms, comprising novel complex 'customer/consumer-driven' flexible production regimes and business practices, pioneered by Japanese organizations, designed to meet these challenges (Oliver and Wilkinson, 1992; Storey, 1994).

Turning Japanese

For many theorists it is the Japanese economy and Japanese management and business practices that, directly or indirectly, have had the most influence on the emergence of new organizational forms, especially in manufacturing. During the 1970s Japan's phenomenal post-war economic growth was considered an 'economic miracle' (Whitehill, 1990). Its continued growth and competitiveness in the wake of a severe global economic downturn in the 1970s earned it unprecedented Western management attention (McKinlay and Starkey, 1992). One need only consult any current textbook on organizational behaviour (e.g., Huczynski and Buchanan, 2003; Mullins, 2001), human resource management (HRM) (e.g., Legge, 1995; Redman and Wilkinson, 2002; Storey, 1994), change management (Burnes, 2002) and employee relations (Hollinshead et al., 2002) to appreciate the extent to which Japanese management and organizational practices were seen in the 1970s and early 1980s as a new way of improving productivity and competitiveness. As the 'excellence theorists' claim, Japanese managers were doing something 'right' – that is, effective and successful – in the face of these severe economic conditions that Western organizations had failed to recognize and incorporate. Japan's dominance within the emerging global economy was attributed to a number of factors that were identified as peculiar to the Japanese post-war economy (Whitehill, 1990):

- Closely integrated and highly efficient family-owned and controlled co-operative business cartels.
- Japanese state supported capital investment in key strategic domestic and export industries.
- Novel manufacturing and market-responsive production regimes and a customer-driven business strategy.
- Japanese organizational culture and flexible teamworking practices and total quality control methods.

For the excellence theorists, the most important of these factors is Japanese organizational culture (Morgan, 1986; Ouchi, 1982; Whitehill, 1990). In the early 1980s, belief in the link between Japanese organizational culture and Japanese economic competitiveness gained widespread Western attention (McKinlay and Starkey, 1992). Japanese organizations were said to comprise highly motivated and committed employees who shared a common sense of purpose, encouraged by clearly articulated corporate values and organizational goals. In contrast, Western organizations were seen as overly bureaucratic, rule bound and governed by low-trust, inflexible, top-down, typically Fordist command-and-control management styles (McKinlay and Starkey, 1992) that tended to create conflict rather than co-operation between management and workers. It is worth noting that different theorists use the term culture in organization and management studies differently. As Smircich (1993, p. 339) points out, the term has been applied in a variety of ways, and there is no generally agreed view of what cultural analyses of organizations means. Even in social anthropology, from where this term originates, there is no real consensus on its meaning. As Clifford Geertz (1973, p. 3) observed, every so often 'certain ideas burst upon the intellectual landscape with a tremendous force. They resolve so many fundamental problems at once that they seem also to promise that they will resolve all fundamental problems.' This is certainly the case in Western organizations and management studies in the wake of the so-called 'Japanese economic miracle'. The 'culture concept' was snapped up with great enthusiasm by the 'excellence theorists' as the '*open sesame*' answer to all of the competitive economic problems and management challenges facing Western businesses in the 1980s. Definitions of the term culture in social anthropology include:

> '(i) the total way of life of people, (ii) the social legacy an individual acquires from his group, (iii) way of thinking, feeling and believing, (iv) a theory about how a group of people behave, (v) a storehouse of pooled learning, (vi) a set of standardized orientations to recurrent problems, (vii) learned behaviour, and (viii) a mechanism for the normative regulation of behaviour' (*Geertz, 1973, p. 5*).

We can see how anthropological descriptions of the meaning of culture map on to the notions of corporate culture. How they have been borrowed by organizations as ways to influence employees' thinking, feelings and beliefs; ways of shaping their behaviour; ways of tapping into the storehouse of pooled learning among employees; ways of releasing them from management control; ways of engaging them in solving recurrent operational and organizational human and material resourcing and quality control problems; and how they have sought to use these practices as normative regulations for governing employee behaviour, beliefs and values. In Japanese organizations teamworking is considered key to achieving these goals. It is *the* crucial feature of normative corporate cultural control (Kamata, 1979). As a number of observers have pointed out, Japanese-style management control systems also rely on several other important related features that are linked to the team concept. These include:

> '(i) suggestion programmes used for continuous improvement; (ii) highly standardized and recorded work processes with each workstation electronically connected to a mainframe computer for purposes of surveillance; (iii) just-in-time production that eliminates buffers of inventory stock; (iv) a corporate culture of "co-operation" intent on mobilizing workers to identity their interests with company goals rather than identifying with their co-workers; and finally (v) a rigorous system of pre-employment screening with ongoing training in quality control and work standardization' (*Graham, 2006, p. 342*).

Differential terms and conditions of employment are also crucial for ensuring and maintaining employee engagement in, and commitment to, these practices. Japanese corporations, as well as many Western companies who have adopted the Japanese 'model', tend to employ non-standard 'peripheral' personnel, often on temporary and fixed-term contracts, who are excluded from the normal employment benefits and entitlements enjoyed by 'core' workers (Atkinson, 1984). This enables companies to perfectly match their human resourcing needs to the market demand for their products, and to assess the 'suitability' of non-standard personnel – those who show commitment, demonstrate they are 'good team-players', embrace corporate cultural rhetoric, and extol the virtues and values of the 'TQM' philosophy – for standard employment. As Barker (1993) Delbridge (1998) and Gottfried (2000) have shown, corporate cultural discourse is widely used to instil in workers the sense that they are in a permanent 'competitive battle' for market share, and that by committing themselves to 'winning' this battle they will not only increase company profits, and therefore their own job security, but also reduce the likelihood of facilities possibly being transferred to more 'competitive' lower-wage economies (Graham, 2005). As Willmott (1993, p. 516) explains, corporate culture is effectively a form of 'social engineering' at work that is designed to win the hearts and minds of employees', generate loyalty and commitment to the organization, to shared values about what the organization is, and what it stands for, and to encourage employees to *internalize* these values as their *own* values; but its ultimate aim is to improve productivity and performance.

Thinkpoint 11.4

I f Japanese organizational culture is strongly rooted in Japanese national culture, distinctly differ-
ent social values from those of Western cultures, what implications does this have for learning from Japan? As Dore (1976), Morgan (1986) and Whitehill (1990) show, Western cultures hold dear the belief that self-worth and social recognition is gained essentially by *individual* enterprise and personal achievement. Japanese culture, on the other hand, rests on a belief that self-respect and social recognition at work and in society at large are achieved through collective and co-operative involvement with others, personal sacrifice, and a strong sense of commitment to the system as a whole, however much particular aspects of the system can be highly oppressive (see Kamata, 1979; Kondo, 1990). Indeed, echoing questions raised by Thoreau about the nature of work in modern society, Kamata invites us to look closely at the reality of the nature of work in post-war Japanese automotive manufacturing industries: at 'not only its inhumanity but also the unquestioning adherence to such a system'; and to ask ourselves if indeed 'the prosperity of modern, industrial society is worth such a cost, such a cruel compulsion of robot-like work'. He also invites us to consider if 'the production of cars – mere machines – necessitates such a sacrifice of human freedom, just what does this say about the paradox of modern civilization' (1982, p. viii).

Japanese organizational and management practices and values are in many ways anathema to the ideology of individualism that pervades traditional Western societal and organizational cultural beliefs and values (Morgan, 1986). That said, following an extended period of economic stagnation and scandals, there is less confidence in Japan about the long-term effectiveness of their form of economic organization. Reforms have been slowly and unevenly introduced. At the same time, there is a break with tradition by new generations of urban Japanese who have not acquired the commitments (e.g., work ethic) and collective orientations that were so taken for granted by their parents. In the West, techniques that were once applauded simply because they were applied in Japan are now assessed on the basis of notions of 'best practice' – notions that are no longer equated with what goes on in Japanese companies.

BUT WHY LET THE FACTS GET IN THE WAY OF A GOOD STORY?

The discovery of the apparent 'secret' of Japan's success led to calls for, and efforts by consultants and managers to engineer, a wholesale shift in (Western) management thinking during the 1980s. This cultural turn, as it has been referred to, coincided with a significant loss of faith in traditional Western modes of production and management (Burnes, 2002). Japanese-style organizational forms and organizational cultural practices, it seemed, suddenly held the key both to greater organizational effectiveness and human resource efficiency.

Critical management theorists challenge this. They show how cultural management is much more problematic than the picture 'excellence theorists' present (see Chapter 10), how it downplays the complexities of organizational culture and ignores, in particular, the politics of organizational culture change. As Edwards (1979) argues, management–employee relations is a 'contested terrain'. Conflict over culture change and work transformation arises not simply because of employees' fear of change, ignorance, weak management, inadequate leadership or poor (visionary) management communication, etc., as mainstream management theorists and practitioners argue. Conflict occurs, as noted already, because employees anticipate that it will be detrimental for them. It is a manifestation of more deep-seated tensions – what some would call contradictions – that are built in to capitalist work organizations. Conflict occurs also because of its real or perceived threat to the norms, values and identity concerns of the various professional and occupational groups within organizations upon whom managers rely in order to secure productive work and output. Moreover, these norms, values and identity concerns are developed within an institutional context (see Chapter 1). As they are endemic to this context, it is necessary to transform the entire context – including the established relations of inequality and power – in order to bring about a deep and sustained change in the 'culture'.

Occupational identity

Resistance to change in organizations occurs, in its various forms, for a whole host of reasons. As noted earlier, these include the real or perceived threat of unemployment, disempowerment, de-skilling, work intensification, loss of autonomy, and the erosion of traditional professional boundaries and demarcation lines that so often accompany organizational restructuring (see Scarborough and Burrell, 1996). Change, however, is also resisted in order to defend the symbolic realms of the organization, and to maintain prized working practices and occupational values (Ezzamel *et al.*, Willmott and Worthington, 2001). This is because work in modern society is not just a means of producing goods and providing services. It is also an important site of social identity.

Deal and Kennedy (1982), along with most 'excellence theorists', contend that a strong organizational culture can provide employees with a valued sense of purpose and self-identity. This claim completely overlooks the presence and potency of other occupational and organizational *sub*cultures in shaping employees' priorities and identity concerns. Occupational as opposed to organizational culture, in other words, is more often than not the bedrock shaping identity (Trice, 1993). As Trice illustrates, occupational cultures mediate how members of an organization relate to each other, and also to how they make sense of their role and status in relation to others, especially to 'outsiders'.

Becoming a member of an occupation or profession involves not only acquiring formal training and education and entry qualifications through examination, professional licensing and accreditation or other formal 'rites of passage'. New entrants are also taught to act in ways deemed appropriate to a profession, to recognize and internalize its values, by observing its rituals, ceremonies and codes of practice and to protect the profession from interlopers. New entrants to a profession not only learn professional knowledge, skills and expertise from established members; at the same time, they learn how to conduct themselves towards client groups and others within organizations (including management and other non-management employees) who are not of their group or profession. As Trice (1993) points out, new entrants to a profession are only required to learn that which gives them entry to their chosen career; they are also taught to observe and to internalize the new values and ideology and to defend the occupational ethos, from being undermined, transgressed or eroded by 'rogue' in-group members or 'outsiders'. It is all 'part of the package' of becoming a competent, credible member within a particular institutional context.

Change and conflict at work in the UK National Health Service (NHS)

Government and NHS managers are clearly aware that re-engineering the NHS has had a considerable negative effect upon motivation and morale within the medical profession (Department of Health, 2003). What doctors themselves object to is the way change has led to demands for them to adopt a managerial attitude to health care, to take on new roles and responsibilities and to meet government performance targets when, as they see it, they are already overworked and underpaid. However, by far their overriding concern behind the strength of their stance against organizational re-engineering is the question of their professional autonomy.

As a way of overcoming this problem, the NHS has sought to harness what they refer to as the 'creative tension' that they believe exists between doctors and managers in innovative ways. That is, rather than seek to erode tension they have sought to exploit it to release 'its creative potential', which they see as a means of reaching a genuine consensus for change, one in which both doctors and managers openly acknowledge and respect professional values and priorities. This is contingent upon creating a climate of 'responsible autonomy', whereby doctors maintain prime responsibility for clinical decision-making, unhindered by management control, in exchange for acting *responsibly* towards the roles and responsibilities of management (Dent, 1998). What is remarkable here is the level of faith the NHS has in the ideology and principles of HRM. It is remarkable because this is also the actual *source* of doctors' distrust of the NHS modernization agenda.

The problem for doctors is that the call to enhance performance through 'more staff working differently' (Department of Health, 2003) to achieve higher standards of health care that privilege the sovereignty of individual consumer/customer expectations bears little resemblance to their lived-experience of change. As this Department of Health report shows, doctors perceive change in the NHS to have led only to increasing stress and feelings of alienation and degradation due to a loss of social recognition, compounded by ever-increasing workloads, and constant pressure to meet government performance targets. Thus, far from winning doctors' 'hearts and minds' for change (Thompson and Warhurst, 1998), cultural management in the NHS has led to widespread disaffection. From the point of view of doctors, cultural management has severely ruptured the psychological contract between doctors and society, for example, by distorting traditional clinical priorities and by disregarding the sense of responsibility that clinicians have to the needs of individual patients, rather than financial budgets.

FROM PROFESSIONAL TO RESPONSIBLE AUTONOMY?

The NHS uses the term 'responsible autonomy' to capture the kind of working practices they are trying to instil in doctors and other health care workers. We have discussed this concept earlier (see Box 11.4). In this context, however, the NHS is not attempting to create a shift from direct control to responsible autonomy – rather it is attempting to create a shift from *professional autonomy* to *responsible autonomy*. Friedman's concept of responsible autonomy does not include consideration of 'professional autonomy' (PA), although there are certain parallels between the two, the main difference being the degree of top-down managerial control present in RA compared to PA.

Both forms of autonomy give certain groups in an organization special status that differentiate them from others, and also certain 'situational power' in relation to management. Friedman's notion of RA originates from his analysis of private sector problems of labour control in relation to the competitive pressures of capitalist political-economic market conditions and the possibility of worker resistance. PA, in contrast, is the outcome of competition and conflict between professional and managerial groups and, in the public sector, their relationship to the state, rather than in relation to a struggle between 'capital' and 'labour', as in Friedman's original analysis (Dent, 1995).

Of relevance in this context, nonetheless, is Friedman's point that management find it extremely difficult to shift from RA to DC, and vice versa, once either strategy is embedded in organizational practices. Friedman shows how employees subject to RA are usually reluctant to surrender the relative freedom and self-determination they enjoy under this system of control. By the same token, those subject to DC rarely take at face value the introduction of autonomous work practices, designed (ostensibly) to harness their commitment to the pursuit of new organizational norms, goals and values. Both systems of control, in other words, create their own *cultural* inflexibilities. That being the case, it follows that professional groups, in this case the medical profession, as Friedman's typology indicates, are reluctant to surrender their PA to closer managerial scrutiny and state control.

Dent argues that RA is not a new concept within manager–doctor relations in the NHS. In his view RA has 'long been the preferred control strategy of the British State towards the medical profession' (Dent, 1995, p. 87), but one which it has been unable to establish because of persistent countermeasures by the medical profession to prevent themselves from 'being incorporated into the state apparatus of health care' (ibid., p. 88). As he points out, contemporary attempts to renegotiate the medical profession's relationship to the state is just the latest in a long line of similar attempts stretching back as far as the advent of the UK post-war welfare state. What has prevented the state from realizing this goal has been the medical profession's determination to maintain the privileged status of their professional right to 'clinical autonomy' as *the* principal mechanism for governing the 'frontier of control' (Friedman, 1977) between doctors and the state, doctors and managers and other occupational and professional groups supplementary to medicine within health care.

New organizational forms

Critical organization and management theorists acknowledge that employees in many organizations today do work in ways that differ significantly from traditional Fordist work practices. However, they also point out that hierarchy, rigid bureaucracy, command-and-control management practices, low-skilled detailed divisions of labour, strict demarcation and unequal rewards, recognition and remuneration determined by class, gender, race and social inequalities have far from disappeared in the new workplace (Thompson and Warhurst, 1998). There is a wealth of empirical evidence suggesting that there is a considerable difference between the espoused values of post-Fordist organizations and the extent to which its values and beliefs are actually embraced, let alone internalized, by their members (Casey, 1996; Kunda, 1990). Many commentators also question the claim that cultural management alone can raise employee performance and productivity, change values and reshape beliefs and attitudes.

As Burnes (2002) points out, there is an assumption in culture change literature that 'attitude change' leads to voluntary 'behavioural change', and that individuals will willingly (want to) put aside their concerns for the greater good of their organization. The mainstream literature assumes that good management communication and effective leadership will always overcome internal conflict and struggles between individuals or occupational or professional groups over the outcomes of change. Hope-Hailey (1998) shows how such assumptions ignore the influence of hierarchy, specialist organizational, departmental and occupational boundaries, etc., on organizational culture change. These writers also show how new organizational forms are heavily reliant on new forms of accountability and surveillance techniques that are concerned with more than simply attempting to win employees' hearts and minds (see Thompson and Warhurst, 1998).

The assumption that culture change leads to behaviour change ignores the spatial and temporal domains of organizations and cultures. There is evidence that improvements in productivity and employee performance through cultural management programmes, in so-called 'excellence' organizations, have rarely been sustained over time (Burnes, 2002). Power, politics and conflict are widely ignored or trivialized. This is because a fundamental assumption in 'excellence' cultural management theory is that organizational cultures are essentially unitary and apolitical (Anthony, 1995; Hatch, 2002; Martin, 2000; Thompson and Warhurst, 1998; Willmott, 1993). As labour process theorists in particular demonstrate, workplace cultures comprise a complex web of competing occupational and organizational cultural and subcultural work groups, whose norms, values, beliefs and behaviour patterns are conditioned by particular occupational and professional values and interests rather than those of the organizations that employ them (Knights and Willmott, 1990; Thompson and McHugh, 1998; Thompson and Warhurst, 1998). In this context, the idea that organizations are open to change through top-down strategic human resource intervention is highly questionable.

Here we return to 'lean' production and to the argument made by Delbridge (1995, p. 803), for example, that it is a subtle system of managerial power, control, surveillance and accountability that could hardly be more distant from its humanistic image of empowering employees (Delbridge and Turnbull, 1992). Empowerment within and between teams in the new workplace takes place only in accordance with narrowly defined boundaries that closely monitor and control, rather than expand the scope for workers to exercise discretion (Delbridge, 1995; Delbridge and Turnbull, 1992; Sewell, 1998; Sewell and Wilkinson, 1992). Even where scope for increased levels of worker involvement and decision-making does exist, ideas put forward that go beyond those that offer up productivity gains or cut costs are largely ignored or marginalized (see Buchanan and Preston, 1992; Kamata, 1979). In short, their conclusion is that 'total quality control', 'teamworking' and 'flexible' working practices do not really empower workers to play a more active and autonomous role in production. And, for this reason, it should come as no surprise to us when workers fail to respond positively to efforts to introduce it.

Resistance in the new workplace

Cartoon 11.1   'And that is what happens when we resist change.'

'And that is what happens when we
resist change.'

There are many studies within the literature that have examined how and to what extent new forms of work organization, whether on the factory floor, in the office or in the public sector domain of health care, can be resisted. In opposition to the view that resistance is minimal or even impossible because the power of management, supported by the state's employment laws, is ultimately overwhelming, it is shown how resistance of one form or another is always possible. McKinlay and Taylor's (1998) research in the UK microelectronics industry shows that, even under conditions that could hardly be more favourable for close management control methods to flourish uncontested, resistance still occurred. A considerable number of critical case studies support McKinlay and Taylor's findings (e.g., Graham, 1994; Poliert, 1996; Rinehart *et al.*, 1996; Stephenson, 1996). Even those studies that proclaim the 'end of worker resistance' (e.g., Zuboff, 1988) argue that, through the use of information technology, the contemporary workplace is now a site of consolidated managerial disciplinary power, control and surveillance by management supported by information and communication technologies; however, there is evidence of worker resistance. Sakolsky (1992) notes how the workers studied by Zuboff were able to avoid the disciplinary 'power effect' of computer surveillance by cheating on certain working practices and operational procedures, and how even managers manipulated output and productivity records in a way that could not be detected. Sewell and Wilkinson (1992, p. 293) talk about the inescapability of 'panoptic' power, control and surveillance under lean production, but at the same time also note evidence of workers falsifying output and productivity figures. It is also worth noting that resistance is often not so much an attempt to *escape from work* as an attempt to *escape into work* (Sturdy, 1997). This term, escape into work, refers to how workers deal with boring and monotonous work by establishing routines and rituals that enable them to 'turn off' and perform tasks without actively thinking about the work being performed and what is taking place around them.

Case study 11.2
Resistance at
Northern Plant

At the beginning of this chapter it was shown how workers at Northern Plant refused to accept management's claim that lean production would provide more interesting and satisfying work, and how they resisted new working practices through misbehaviour rather than through industrial action.

When Northern Plant first invested in lean production in the early 1980s, it comprised five main manufacturing sections. Over the ten years prior to Mike's (the new HR manager) arrival these sections were re-engineered a number of times, and given different labels each time: lean manufacturing cells, product-focused cells, customer-focused cells, autonomous business units, strategic business units and then finally profit centres. Workers themselves were also organized into teams: manufacturing teams to begin with, then autonomous production teams, self-managing teams, and finally 'high-commitment teams'. Yet, from their point of view, the work they performed remained what it had always been, a dull and tedious process of operating drilling, boring, grinding, turning, de-burring and spot-welding machines that turned out various parts and sub-components which were assembled into finished products along traditional Fordist assembly lines.

When lean production was introduced managers were at a loss to understand why workers resisted it and saw it as work intensification. What these managers failed to appreciate was that it was not simply the opportunity to work independently of direct management control that motivated workers to work 'smarter', and, indeed, *harder* to 'make the numbers'. What they valued most was the opportunity to earn 'free time' during working hours. They resisted lean production, therefore, not just because it was perceived as work intensification, in the normal sense of the term, but because they saw it as an attack on the 'free time' and leisure activities they had become accustomed to, which they believed they earned and were rightfully entitled to in exchange for their efforts to meet production targets.

Thinkpoint 11.5

Earlier in this chapter (p. 411), you were asked to imagine that you were a member of Mike's change team who had been given responsibility for calming workers' fears and concerns about lean production. What should Mike do to address the problems you faced?

As you think about this question you might like to reflect on the situation facing Mike's change team. Imagine now that you are a first-line manager who had worked at the plant prior to Mike's arrival, and who had subscribed to the informal system of production described earlier.

For years, you had condoned the unspoken agreement that once output quotas had been reached shop floor workers could spend their time as they saw fit. From time to time you and some of your first-line management colleagues had taken part in various leisure activities, including sleeping on nightshift and occasionally spending time in the local pub during working hours. Then, overnight, following the launch of lean production at the plant, you find yourself charged with the responsibility for introducing the new teamworking practices and quality control methods.

No longer can you continue to accommodate previous informal agreements whereby you trade time for output and then turn a blind eye to how workers spend their time once they have reached the agreed output quotas. At team briefings you explain the need for change, the need for workers to accept new working practices and the benefits these can offer them in terms of skill enhancement. You are required to 'sell' these new ideas to workers, and convince them that the 'old way of doing things' can no longer continue. In response, both the shop stewards and workers remind you that any proposed changes in working practices are ultimately subject to trade union agreement, which can only be reached through formal negotiations with senior management, and, therefore, although they are willing to listen to what you have to say, you should not assume that this means that they are willing to accept new ways of working. At the end of your briefing the shop stewards and shop floor workers claim that you have done a very poor job in selling lean production to them. This is because, they say, you have made it more than apparent that it will undoubtedly lead to work intensification and possibly redundancies.

Fearful of what senior managers will make of these claims, which, of course, you do not accept, you respond by trying again to explain that 'working smarter rather than harder' and 'doing more with less' does not mean doing more with fewer shop floor personnel. You remind them again that the old ways of doing things cannot continue, and that whether they like it or not, corporate management is determined to introduce new systems and work practices.

Then, out of the blue, you find yourself being denounced as a hypocrite. Along with the other first-line managers, you are reminded of your own 'misbehaviour' under the old system: your poor timekeeping and attendance, the extended lunch breaks and rest allowances you were happy to take, and how, like workers themselves, you also enjoyed participating in card schools, sleeping during nightshifts and how you (with other first-line managers) occasionally accompanied workers to the pub during working hours. In the light of this, you are asked how you have the nerve to now condemn these activities, and how you are going to explain to Mike's change team why you have completely lost your credibility as a manager.

You witness other similar instances of workers using tactics designed to discredit first-line managers. What you find particularly frustrating and humiliating is the enjoyment workers get from ridiculing and threatening you and your colleagues, by reminding you of how you previously failed to manage workers properly and allowed them to 'skive off' so much during working hours, and how you yourselves also regularly 'skived off'.

You then hear a cell manager, who, when he was a shop floor worker, had regularly slept in a comfortable cardboard construction made while working the nightshift, being told during a briefing session, that 'people who live in cardboard houses shouldn't throw stones'! Similarly, a first-line manager who had acquired the nickname 'Disco Dave', as a consequence of making regular visits to a local nightclub during his nightshift, is told by workers that they do appreciate that things may well need to change, but that there is still no need to make a 'song and dance' about it!

Above and beyond this kind of barbed banter, workers presented 'reasonable' arguments against the proposed new working practices, which they know you, as a first-line manager, cannot accept. Certain workers, for example, who claimed that they recognize the benefits of teamworking, argue that, in practice, teamwork would be unworkable due to the age of certain workers and also because of personality differences. To support this claim they point out that, as they see it, under lean production the stamina of younger workers would put undue stress upon older workers. Others argue that workers who are fundamentally 'lazy' would end up being 'carried' by other team members. Carrying lazy workers, they explain, would not only impede team performance but also possibly lead to 'hard-working' team members also being perceived as 'lazy'. Others claim they are 'loners', who are unsuited to teamwork, who would therefore rather work on their own and have their *own* individual output targets. Some simply question the need for change, and argue that if it is true that lean production empowers them to have a 'say in things', they would prefer things to stay as they are! Others exercise their 'say in things', by identifying fellow workers who they could perhaps work with within a team, those who they believe they would find it difficult to work with, and those who they are not prepared to work with at all. Some others announce that they intend to refuse to work in teams with certain workers because they simply don't like each other. To further ridicule the situation, others openly announce in each other's presence that they 'do in fact like each other', but that they had better not be allowed to work together because their shared interests would distract them from 'getting on with the job'.

All these comments and arguments are used to point out to you that it stands to reason that if management were to put certain workers together in teams this would undoubtedly undermine discipline and impede performance, and therefore it was only right that responsibility for any subsequent poor performance should ultimately lie with those – that is, you – who have decided to put them together.

When you attempt to counter these arguments you are told that although you obviously have considerable management experience, you still don't really understand the shop floor. For you clearly lack a grasp of the problems teamworking can cause. In the end, like Mike's change team, you are challenged to come clean and admit that all you (as a member of management) *really* want is to regain control of the shop floor – something that has been lost over the years because of your inadequate 'people management' skills and of course your own 'shenanigans'. In the process you are also asked how you are going to explain to senior and corporate managers why flexibility, teamworking and total quality control methodologies had *seemingly* been introduced but are not really in place because you have merely gone through the motions of introducing them ('the charade') whereas, in practice, you have allowed things to continue as before.

Exercise 11.5

- How would you counter the claim that you are a hypocrite?
- How would you explain to Mike why you subscribed to, and why you sometimes took part in, the plant's leisure activities?
- Do you think the way you ran the shop floor and managed production before Mike's arrival makes you a 'bad' manager?

Summary of the issues raised in this case study

These episodes of resistance at Northern Plant show how workers in organization use humour and misbehaviour to expose what they see as the inconsistencies and contradictions in the effort to engineer change, such as the change to lean production, including 'teamworking' and 'continuous improvement'.

It might be argued that this account of resistance at Northern Plant shows how discrediting teamworking and new organizational practices and working arrangements in this way, and with them the credibility and authority of those presenting them, is simply a tactic used by workers to entertain themselves and to inflate their own sense of self-importance. But we should be aware that such misbehaviour is also a 'consciousness-raising' exercise. That is to say it is an engaging device used by shop stewards and 'politically astute' workers to alert others to what is at stake in 'change management' programmes. By using humour, it is possible to demonstrate, in an accessible and enjoyable way, how these programmes are ostensibly human-centred, yet on closer examination are perhaps more to do with management's concern to gain control of production and working practices. Greater control is needed in order to improve productivity, rather than to empower workers to have a greater say in the organization and management of production. The promise of empowerment is, at best, a means to the end of productivity because, in a leaner, more flexible manufacturing system, it is necessary to obtain the ('responsible') involvement and co-operation of workers in order to make the system function effectively.

It is worth mentioning that this is not a fictitious account of resistance through misbehaviour. Northern Plant does, or rather *did* exist. The plant was closed down by MotorCo, its multinational parent company, in 2007 and relocated to an Eastern European country where labour costs are much lower than in the UK (see Chapter 13). Plans to shift production to this new location were drawn up by corporate management even as they were vehemently claiming that the introduction of lean production, which would improve the plant's productivity and competitiveness, would serve to guarantee the plant's future within the industry and, with this, security of employment for its workforce.

We can draw several conclusions from this, including the capacity of managers who seek the respect and trust of employees to engage in forms of deception and disingenuousness that subvert this quest. But what is perhaps most noteworthy is that profit maximization above all else ultimately governs (corporate) management thinking and decision-making even if this is tempered by career ambitions, insecurities, and the unintended consequences of pursuing apparently profitable strategies. For all the talk about employee-centric work organizations, empowerment, enlightened management thinking and the rhetoric of workers being stakeholders in the organizations they work for, labour nevertheless is regarded primarily as a resource to be exploited and then disposed of when more promising opportunities to reduce costs and/or to increase returns on investments for shareholders are calculated to exist elsewhere. Likewise, in the case of the NHS, doctors have suddenly found themselves being treated more like workers (or wage labourers) who are required to record their achievement of targets, set by politicians and managers. They, too, are the recipients of lectures from management designed to entice them to reorganize the need to 'modernize' their working practices, but which paid little or no regard to their workers' well-being or the logic of their organization of work. Instead, their way of working tends to be viewed by (mainstream) management as, at best, irrational and, at worst, entirely self-serving.

Strengths and limitations of the critical approach

The critical view of the shift from 'low-trust' Fordist organizational forms and work practices, to flexible 'high-trust' employee conditions questions the mainstream claim that under these conditions managers genuinely utilize not only the physical but also the subjective and intellectual capacities of the human subject. The critical approach, then, is to challenge the credibility of mainstream thinking and expose its limitations. It also anticipates the possibility of organizing work differently but without providing any prescriptive blueprint for such change. Indeed, to do so would be rather contradictory as it would assume or promote the existence of an intellectual elite, equivalent to a managerial elite, that would tell everyone else what to do. Not only would this simply reinvent the division between managers and workers, it would also likely produce the same kinds of difficulties, tensions and frustrations that currently exist.

The critical approach raises questions about the contradictions and oppressive outcomes of new organizational forms, but it does not show how they may be overcome. In other words, it does not demonstrate how more democratic and emancipatory conditions of employment could be realized so as to replace dominant market-driven management priorities and the overriding importance given to growth and corporate profit. This is not to say that understanding organizations in a critical context is a fruitless exercise. It leaves open important questions about how organization might (one day) shift to more genuine human-centred organizational conditions and practices. As our case study shows, people in organization are capable of 'messing with power' to protect valued working practices. Such behaviour and practices, however, are not to be conflated with real challenges to managerial power and control (Alvesson and Willmott, 1996) that have a radical intention behind them. As we can see, worker resistance at Northern Plant, which is the case in most organizations, had no clear or explicit political or emancipatory aim or purpose. It was, above all, a 'game' that enabled workers to retain a degree of self-respect at management's expense. The game was played out in a context of resignation to the overwhelming capacity of big business to move its manufacturing capability elsewhere. Critical analysis can, in principle, challenge and counter such resignation and defeatism by suggesting how, for example, struggles in different workplaces and across different domains of society (e.g., gender relations, environmentalist movements) can be linked together through an appreciation of their relatedness as aspects of subordination within a wider totality of modern capitalist economies.

By way of drawing this chapter to a close, it is worth giving some thought to how, during the past three decades, many organizations, many commentators, gurus and mainstream academics have created the impression that the contemporary world of work in advanced industrial society is moving towards more creative and competitive human-centred organizational forms. In contrast, what concerns the critics of new 'leaner' organizational forms and work practices is how paid employment for the vast majority of people at the point of production is an essentially monotonous and unrewarding existence; a 'not enough world of work' as Gouldner (1971) so eloquently puts it. Critical management theorists call for managers to recognize this, to think about how labour is organized, used and abused in organization, as a way to help them to critically reflect on the contradictions of the system and ideology it upholds, as a means of developing more credibly 'human-centred' organizations.

What might help make this possible? This is a challenging question. One way to think about it is to imagine Schonberger or Womack *et al.,* Peters and Waterman along with the corporate managers who read their books and put their ideas into practice, being employed to write and rewrite and read and reread respectively *just* one and *only* one chapter, section, paragraph, sentence from just *one* and *only* one of their books over and over again, hour by hour, minute by minute, without ever needing to make sense of the meaning of the words, and with no respite from this monotonous repetitive process other than one or two 10 or 15-minute coffee breaks and one 30-minute lunch break in an eight, ten or possibly 12-hour working day or night.

Faced with these conditions they would no doubt quickly come to recognize what Gouldner is alluding to. Imagine these guru's working under such conditions for their entire working lives, with no alternative employment choices except those that involve writing or reading, rewriting and rereading bits of other books in other similar 'book reading' facilities. Imagine if someone were to then come along after years of drudgery in a system of production governed by Taylorist and Fordist management control and surveillance methods, to introduce them to more efficient *lean ways of working* that promise to increase their productivity.

How might they react to being invited to subscribe to suggestion schemes, 'quality circles' and *Kaizen-type* initiatives and techniques to help them devise new 'creative capabilities' to turn the pages of the parts of the text assigned to them faster so as to reduce 'waste' and 'increase' throughput – so they could 'read more in less time'. Is it not highly likely that they would look differently at the outcomes of such ideas?

Conclusions

In this chapter we have considered the rise and development of various new organizational forms in both public and private sector organizations. In the 'Mainstream approach' section we considered how mainstream theorists assess them as a positive development that has created new opportunities and possibilities for both organizations and their employees. As the mainstream theorists see it, efficiency, competitiveness and profitability continue to be of key importance to organizations, but what has become more important is continuous innovation and adaptability to ever-changing global market conditions and business environments. This, managers increasingly believe, can only be achieved through people who are highly motivated and committed; and this 'enlightened' approach to work necessitates employees being allowed to exercise greater discretion so as to achieve organizational goals.

In the 'Critical approach' section, we explored a very different interpretation of change and innovation. Without denying that employees in many organizations today evidently work in ways that depart significantly from those of traditional modernist organizations, critical students of organization suggest that new organizational forms and work practices are not adequately represented in mainstream accounts. Hierarchy, rigid bureaucracy, command-and-control management practices, low-skilled detailed divisions of labour, strict demarcation and unequal rewards, recognition and remuneration are hardly swept away in contemporary organizations. At the very least, there is reason to believe that a considerable difference exists between the *espoused* 'excellent' (e.g., lean production) management ideas, values, beliefs and control methods in (so-called) post-modern organizations, and how these ideas and values are worked out in practice.

Mainstream theorists seem to think that employees are passive yet enthusiastic recipients of 'excellence' management jargon, and are likely to 'buy into' new working practices without looking critically at what empowerment and teamworking, for example, mean in practice in terms of workloads, career prospects and job security. But, equally, we should not assume that employees will always, automatically resist change. It suggests only that employees are unlikely to take what managers say at face value and that they may be somewhat reluctant to put aside individual personal advancement and individual self-interest for the greater good of their organization. As Flemming and Spicer (2003) show, employees in organizations who are mistrustful of management promises often adopt a cynical distance from the normative control and behavioural expectations of the rhetoric of empowerment, teamworking and notions of self-management. They may, for example, conform outwardly while doing the absolute minimum to implement or facilitate the desired change. Cynicism and other 'distancing' strategies of resistance (Collinson, 1994), do not prevent employees in organizations from performing their roles. On the contrary, a weakness of cynicism can allow workers (and managers in some cases) to deal with the contradictions and superficiality of 'new wave' management philosophies and values.

So where do we go from here? Change and innovation, in the form of lean manufacturing, 'new public management' and many other 'advances' in work organization have given rise to ostensibly new structures, networks, business and management practices and new ways of working. And people in organization have adapted to them – to the new roles, relationship and responsibilities they have brought with them. What mainstream theorists ignore, or prefer to downplay, is how the cultivation of new roles, responsibilities and relationships in organizations has been driven as much, if not more, by politico-economic pressures – notably, the pressure to maintain or increase a return to investors (**shareholder value**) in the face of intensifying national and international competition – rather than changes of values and ideas. Without a change in the structure of inequality and power that conditions the generation of ideas, it is likely that new forms of accountability, surveillance techniques and performance indicators will deviate little from traditional managerial means of securing productivity, profitability and control. Looking to create ways of 'winning employees' hearts and minds' may well be what managers today claim to be a more effective way of running an organization. But

Shareholder value Associated with the idea that the first responsibility of firms is to deliver value to shareholders. Therefore, the interests of employees, consumers and communities are secondary. Most associated with US and UK firms.

when we look more closely at some of these methods, we see a rather different and darker picture from the one portrayed by advocates of innovation in manufacturing, public service and elsewhere.

Further reading

Ackroyd, S. and Thompson, P. (1999) *Organizational Misbehaviour,* London: Sage.

This book offers a rich insight into various forms of misbehaviour in organization from an interdisciplinary perspective, drawing on industrial sociology, deviance studies and labour process theory. It illustrates in detail how and why misbehaviour is an inescapable problem for managers in organizations that is poorly recognized, ignored or downplayed in most mainstream management textbooks.

Child, J. (2005) *Organization,* Oxford: Blackwell.

This book offers a detailed insight into the kinds of changes taking place in organization examined in this chapter. The reasons for the rise of new organizational forms since the 1970s are considered in detail from a range of perspectives that address the challenges involved in introducing new organizational arrangements and working practices in the contemporary public and private sector workplace.

Jackson, N. and Carter, P. (2000) *Rethinking Organizational Behaviour,* London: Financial Times/Prentice Hall.

This book offers an alternative insight into the study of behaviour in organizations from a critical standpoint, to illustrate how mainstream textbooks fail to appreciate the complexities of organizations and society. It deals in detail with the kind of theoretical developments in the study of behaviour in organization that are addressed in this textbook in clear and accessible language.

Jermier, J., Knights, D. and Nord, W. (eds) (1994) *Resistance and Power in Organizations,* London and New York: Routledge.

This book provides detailed theoretical and case study accounts of conflict, struggle and resistance practices in organizations in diverse contexts, and how resistance is understood and theorized from Marxist, labour process and post-structuralist standpoints.

Strangleman, T. (2004) *Work Identity at the End of the Line,* Basingstoke: Palgrave/Macmillan.

This book provides a detailed case study account of the impact of change in the UK railway industry on employee subjectivity and identity from a labour process perspective.

Sturdy, A. and Grey, C. (2003) 'Special issue on organizational change management', *Organization,* 10(4).

This special edition on change in organizations brings together a collection of critical papers that examines the complexities of change management from a critical management standpoint.

Thompson, P. (1989) *The Nature of Work: An Introduction to Debates on the Labour Process,* second edn, Basingstoke: Macmillan Education Ltd.

This book offers a very comprehensive and accessible introduction to the study of work and organizations from a labour process perspective. Although many of the labour process issues and debates dealt with in this book have moved on since its publication, this is still an excellent text for students new to labour process studies.

References

Ackroyd, S. and Thompson, P. (1999) *Organizational Misbehaviour,* London: Sage.

Agglietta, M. (1979) *A Theory of Capitalist Regulation: The US Experience,* London: New Left Books.

Alford, H. (1994) 'Cellular manufacturing: The development of the idea and its application', *New Technology, Work and Employment,* 9(1): 42–57.

Alvesson, M. and Thompson, P. (2005) 'Post bureaucracy', in S. Ackroyd, P. Thompson and P. S. Tolbert (eds) *The Oxford Handbook of Work & Organization,* New York: Oxford University Press, pp. 485–608.

Alvesson, M. and Willmott, H. (1996) *Making Sense of Management: A Critical Introduction,* London: Sage Publications.

Anthony, P. (1977) *The Ideology of Work,* London: Tavistock.

Anthony, P. (1995) *Managing Culture,* London: Sage.

Atkinson, J. (1984) 'The changing corporations', in D. Clutterbuck (ed.) *New Patterns of Work,* Aldershot: Gower.

Barker, J. (1993) *The Discipline of Teamwork,* London: Sage.

Beattie, M. and McDougall, R. S. (1998) 'Inside or outside HRM? Lateral learning in two voluntary sector organizations', in C. Mabey, D. Skinner and T. Clark *Experiencing Human Resource Management,* London: Sage.

Bonazzi, G. (1994) 'A gentler way to total quality? The case of the "integrated factory" at Fiat Auto', in T. Elger and C. Smith (eds) *Global Japanization? The Transformation of the Labour Process,* London and New York: Routledge.

Bratton, J. (1992) *Japanization at Work: Managerial Studies for the 1990s,* London: Macmillan.

Buchanan, D. and Preston, D. (1992) 'Life in the cell: Supervision and teamwork in a "Manufacturing Systems Engineering" environment', *Human Resource Management Journal,* 2(4): 221–238.

Burawoy, M. (1979) *Manufacturing Consent. Changes in the Labor Process under Monopoly Capitalism.* Chicago, IL: The University of Chicago Press.

Burnes, B. (2002) *Managing Change: A Strategic Approach to Organizational Dynamics,* London: Pitman/Financial Times.

Casey, C. (1996) *Work, Self and Society,* New York: Routledge.

Child, J. (2005) *Organization: Contemporary Principles and Practices,* Oxford: Blackwell Publishing.

Collinson, D. (1992) *Managing the Shopfloor: Subjectivity, Masculinity and Workplace Culture,* Berlin: Walter de Gruyter.

Collinson, D. (1994) 'Strategies of resistance: Power, knowledge and subjectivity in the workplace', in J. Jermier, D. Knights and W. Nord (eds) *Resistance and Power in Organizations,* London and New York: Routledge, pp. 25–68.

Corby, S. and White, G. (1999) 'From the New Right to New Labour', in S. Corby and G. White (eds) *Employee Relations in the Public Services,* London and New York: Routledge.

Deal, T. and Kennedy, A. (1982) *Corporate Cultures: The Rites and Rituals of Corporate Life,* New York: Addison-Wesley.

Delbridge, R., Kenny, M. and Lowe, J. (1998) *Manufacturing in Transition,* Routledge: London and New York.

Delbridge, R. (1995) 'Surviving JIT: Control and resistance in a Japanese transplant', *Journal of Management Studies,* 32(6): 803–817.

Delbridge, R. (1998) *Life on the Line in Contemporary Manufacturing,* Oxford: Oxford University Press.

Delbridge, R. and Turnbull, P. (1992) 'Human resource maximization: The management of labour under a JIT system', in P. Blyton and P. Turnbull (eds) *Reassessing Human Resource Management,* London: Sage.

Deming, W. E. (1982) *Quality, Productivity and Competitive Position,* Cambridge, MA: MIT Press.

Dent, M. (1995) *Doctors Peer Review and Quality Assurance: Health Professionals and the State in Europe,* London: Routledge.

Dent, M. (1998) 'Hospitals and new ways of managing medical work in Europe: Standardization of medicine in the public sector and the future of medical autonomy', in P. Thompson and C. Warhurst (eds) *Workplaces of the Future,* Basingstoke: Macmillan Business Press.

Department of Health (2003) 'Why British Doctors Are So Unhappy?' The National Health Confederation.

Dore, R. (1976) *British Factory, Japanese Factory,* London: Allen and Unwin.

Edwards, R. G. (1979) *Contested Terrain: The Transformation of the Workplace in the Twentieth Century,* London: Heinemann.

Eldridge, J. (1971) *Sociology and Industrial Life,* London: Michael Joseph Ltd.

Ezzamel, M., Willmott, H. C. and Worthington, F. (2001) 'Power, control and resistance in "the factory that time forgot"', *Journal of Management Studies,* 38(8): 1053–1080.

Ferlie, E., Pettigrew, A., Ashburner, L. and Fitzgerald, L. (1996) *The New Public Management in Action,* Oxford: Oxford University Press.

Flemming, P. and Spicer, A. (2003) Working at a distance', *Organization,* 10(1): 157–179.

Friedman, A. (1977) *Industry and Labour,* London: Macmillan.

Friedman, A. (1990) 'Managerial strategies, activities, techniques and technology: Towards a complex theory of the labour process', in D. Knights and H. Willmott, (eds) *Labour Process Theory,* London: Macmillan, pp. 177–209.

Garrahan, P. and Stewart, P. (1992) *The Nissan Enigma: Flexibility at Work in a Local Economy,* London: Mansell Publishing Ltd.

Geertz, C. (1973) *The Interpretation of Cultures,* New York: Basic Books.

Gottfreid, H. (2000) 'Compromising positions: Emergent neo-Fordism and embedded gender contracts', *The British Journal of Sociology,* 52(2): 235–259.

Gouldner A. (1971) *The Coming Crisis of Western Sociology,* London: Heinemann Educational Books Ltd.

Graham, L. (1994) 'How does the Japanese model transfer to the United States? A view from the line', in T. Elger and C. Smith (eds) *Global Japanization: The International Transformation of the Labour Process,* London: Routledge.

Graham, L. (2005) 'Manual workers: Conflict and control', in S. Ackroyd, R. Batt, P. Thompson and P. Tolbert (eds) *The Oxford Handbook of Work & Organization,* Oxford University Press.

Graham, L. (2006) 'Workers: Conflict and control', in S. Ackroyd, P. Thompson and P. S. Tolbert (eds) *The Oxford Handbook of Work & Organization,* Oxford and New York: Oxford University Press, pp. 338–356.

Hammer, M. and Champy, J. (1993) *Reengineering the Corporation: A Manifesto for Business Revolution,* London: Nicholas Brealy.

Harley, S. (2001) 'Accountants divided: Research selectivity and academic accounting labour in the UK', Working Paper. De Montfort University Business School.

Hatch, M. J. (2002) *Organization Theory: Modern Symbolic and Postmodern Perspectives,* Oxford: Oxford Books.

Hodson, R. (2001) *Dignity at Work,* Cambridge: The Press Syndicate of the University of Cambridge.

Hollinshead, G., Nicholls, P. and Tailby, S. (2002) *Employee Relations,* London: Financial Times/Prentice Hall.

Hope-Hailey, V. (1998) 'Managing culture', in L. Gratton, V. Hope-Hailey, P. Styles and C. Truss (eds) *Strategic Human Resource Management*, Oxford: Oxford University Press.

Howie, G. (2002) 'A reflection of quality: Instrumental reason, quality audits and knowledge economy', *Critical Quarterly*, 44(4): 140–148.

Howkins, E. and Thornton, C. (2002) *Managing and Leading Innovations in Health Care*, Ballière Tindall: Royal College of Nursing.

Huczynski, A. and Buchanan, D. (2003) *Organization Behaviour: An Introductory Text*, London: Financial Times/Prentice Hall.

Imai, M. (1986) *Kaizen: The Key to Japan's Competitive Success*, New York: McGraw-Hill.

Imai, M. (1989) *Kaizen*, New York: Random House.

Kamata, S. (1979) *Japan in the Passing Lane*, London: Pantheon.

Kenney, M. and Florida, R. (1993) *Beyond Mass Production: The Japanese System and Its Transfer to the US*, New York and Oxford: Oxford University Press.

Knights, D. and Willmott, H. (1990) *Labour Process Theory*, Aldershot: Gower.

Kondo, D. (1990) *Crafting Selves: Power, Gender and Discourses of Identity of a Japanese Peripheral Worker*, Chicago, IL: Chicago University Press.

Kunda, G. (1990) *Manufacturing Culture*, Philadelphia, PA: Temple University Press.

Legge, K. (1995) *Human Resource Management: Rhetorics and Reality*, London: Macmillan Press Ltd.

Legge, K. (2005) *Human Resource Management*, London: Macmillan.

Littler, C. (1982) *The Development of the Labour Process in Capitalist Societies*, London: Heinemann.

Lupton, T. (1963) *On the Shopfloor*, Oxford: Pergamon Press.

Martin, J. (2000) *Organization Culture: Mapping the Terrain*, London and New York: Sage.

McKinlay, A. and Starkey, K. (1992) *Strategy and the Human Resource*, Oxford: Blackwell Business.

McKinlay, A. and Taylor, P. (1998) 'Through the looking glass: Foucault and the politics of production', in A. McKinlay and K. Starkey (eds) *Foucault, Management and Organization*, London: Sage.

McNulty, T. and Ferlie, E. (2005) *Reengineering the NHS: The Complexities of Organizational Transformation*, Oxford: Oxford University Press.

Morgan, G. (1986) *Images of Organizations*, London: Sage Publications.

Morley, L. (2003) *Quality and Power in Higher Education*, Milton Keynes: Open University Press.

Mullins, L. (2001) *Management and Organizational Behaviour*, London: Pitman/Financial Times.

Oliver, N. and Wilkinson, B. (1992) *The Japanization of British Industry*, Oxford: Blackwell.

Ouchi, W. (1982) *Theory Z*, Reading, MA: Addison-Wesley.

Pascale, R. T. and Athos, A. G. (1982) *The Art of Japanese Management*, Harmondsworth: Penguin.

Peters, T. and Waterman, R. (1982) *In Search of Excellence: Lessons from America's Best-Run Companies*, London: Harper & Row.

Piore, M. and Sabel, C. (1984) *The Second Industrial Divide*, New York: Basic Books.

Poliert, A. (1988) 'Dismantling flexibility', *Capital and Class*, 34: 445–567.

Poliert, A. (1996) 'Team work on the assembly line: Contradiction and the dynamics of union resilience', in P. Ackers, C. Smith and P. Smith (eds) *The New Workplace and Trade Unionism*, London: Routledge.

Redman, T. and Wilkinson, A. (2002) *Contemporary Human Resource Management*, London: Financial Times/Prentice Hall.

Rinehart, J., Robertson, D., Huxley, C. and Wareham, J. (1996) 'Reunifying conception and execution of work under Japanese production management? A Canadian case study', in P. Ackers, C. Smith and P. Smith (eds) *The New Workplace and Trade Unionism: Critical Perspectives on Work and Organization*, London: Routledge.

Roy, D. (1952) 'Quota restriction and goldbricking in a machine shop', *American Journal of Sociology*, 5(5): 427–442.

Sakolsky, R. (1992) 'Discipline, power and the labour process', in A. Sturdy, D. Knights and H. Willmott (eds) *Skill and Consent: Contemporary Studies in the Labour Process*, London: Routledge.

Scarborough, H. and Burrell, G. (1996) 'The axeman cometh: The changing role and knowledge of middle managers', in S. Clegg and G. Palmer (eds) *The Politics of Management Knowledge*, London: Sage Publications.

Schonberger, R. (1986) *World Class Manufacturing*, New York: The Free Press.

Schwartzman, H. B. (1993) *Ethnography in Organizations*, Newbury Park: Sage Publications.

Sewell, G. (1998) 'The discipline of teams: The control of team-based industrial work through electronic and peer surveillance', *Administrative Science Quarterly*, 43(2): 397–428.

Sewell, G. and Wilkinson, B. (1992) '"Someone to watch over me": Surveillance, discipline and the just-in-time process', *Sociology*, 26(2): 271–289.

Sharpe, D. (1998) 'Changing Managerial Control Strategies and Subcultural Processes: An Ethnographic Study of the Hano Assembly Line'. Paper Presented at the 14th Annual Labour Process Conference, Aston.

Smirchich, L. (1993) 'Concepts of culture in organizational analysis'. *Administrative Science Quarterly*, 28: 339–358.

Smith, C. (1991) 'Automation to flexible specialisation: A déja vu of technology panaceas', in A. Poliert (ed.) *Farewell to Flexibility*, Oxford: Blackwell.

Smith, V. (2010) 'Ethnographies of work and the work of ethnographers', in P. Atkinson, A. Coffey, S. Delmont, J. Loftland and L. Loftland (eds) *Handbook of Ethnography*,

London and Los Angeles, CA: Sage Publications Ltd, pp. 220–234.

Stephenson, C. (1996) 'The different experiences of trade unions in two Japanese plants', in P. Ackers, C. Smith and P. Smith (eds) *The New Workplace and Trade Unionism: Critical Perspectives on Work Organisation,* London: Routledge.

Storey, J. (ed.) (1994) *New Wave Manufacturing Strategies: Organizational and Human Resource Management Dimensions,* London: Paul Chapman Publishing.

Strathern, M. (2000) *Audit Cultures: Anthropological Studies in Accountability, Ethics and the Academy,* London: Routledge.

Sturdy, A. (1997) 'The consultancy process: An insecure business?', *Journal of Management Studies,* 34(3): 389–413.

Thompson, P. and Smith, P. (2010) *Working Lives: Renewing Labour Process Analysis,* London: Palgrave Macmillan.

Thompson, P. (1989) *The Nature of Work: An Introduction to Debates on the Labour Process,* 2nd edn, Hampshire: MacMillan Education Ltd.

Thompson, P. and McHugh, D. (1998) *Work Organization: A Critical Introduction,* London: Macmillan.

Thompson, P. and Warhurst, C. (1998) *Workplaces of the Future,* London: Macmillan Press.

Trice, A. (1993) *Occupational Culture,* Chicago, IL: Chicago University Press.

Turner, B. (1971) *Exploring the Industrial Subculture.* London: The Macmillan Press Ltd.

Warhurst, C., Grugulis, I. and Keep, P. (2004) *Skills That Matter,* Basingstoke: Macmillan Press

Watson, T. (2002) *Organising and Managing Work,* 2nd edn, Financial Times/Prentice Hall.

Whitehill, A. (1990) *Japanese Management: Tradition and Transition,* London: Routledge.

Willis, P. (1977) *Learning to Labour: How Working Class Kids Get Working Class Jobs,* Farnborough: Saxon House.

Willis, P. (2000) *The Ethnographic Imagination,* Oxford: Blackwell Publishers.

Willmott, H. (1993) 'Strength is ignorance, slavery is freedom: Managing culture in modern organizations', *Journal of Management Studies,* 30(4): 681–720.

Willmott, H. (1996) 'Managing the academics: Commodification and control in the development of university education in the UK', *Human Relations,* 4(9): 993–1027.

Wilson, F. (2004) *Organization at Work: A Critical Introduction,* Oxford: Oxford University Press.

Womack, J., Jones, D. and Roos, D. (1990) *The Machine That Changed the World: The Triumph of Lean Production,* New York: Rawson Macmillan.

Wood, S. (ed.) (1989) *The Transformation of Work,* London: Unwin Hyman.

Worthington, F. (2004) 'Management change and culture in the NHS: Rhetoric and reality', *Clinicians in Management,* 12(2): 55–68.

Zuboff, S. (1988) *The Age of the Smart Machine,* Oxford: Heinemann.

Notes

1 Under the informally agreed system, output that should officially take eight hours to produce was normally produced in less than six hours. The lead-time between components leaving the product-focused cell and reaching final assembly lines was two hours. Hence, working 'normally' trapped up to two hours production per day in the system.

2 Northern Plant shift system comprised five Monday to Friday, 8am–4.30pm, day shifts, and four Monday to Thursday, 11.15pm–8am, night shifts. The hours between shifts were normally filled by overtime and weekend work.

3 Responsibility for quality assurance in Western manu-facturing, prior to the advent of lean production, lay with specially-trained quality patrol inspectors. Their role involved periodically visiting workstations in the produc-tion line, to measure sub-assembly parts and component specification, and to check for faults. At Northern Plant workers themselves performed this role in collaboration with inspectors to reduce the possibility of faulty parts and components building up between patrols. This helped limit the possibility of the workers *and* the inspectors facing the unwelcome prospect of having to face rework-ing any faulty parts during their 'free time'.

12 Technology

THEODORE VURDUBAKIS

Aims of the chapter

This chapter will:

- Introduce the different strands in mainstream and critical thinking on the issue of the interrelationship between technology and organization.

- Present, explain and illustrate the key concepts that are relevant to mainstream and critical analysis, such as technological determinism and the social shaping of technology.

- Present a number of major studies that show mainstream and critical thinking on this topic 'in action'.

- Evaluate the assumptions and values underpinning mainstream and critical perspectives associated with technology, management and organizations.

Key concepts and learning objectives

By the end of this chapter you should understand:

- Why the role of technology in organizations has received so much attention.

- The main different approaches that have been used to analyze the complex interrelationship between technology and organizational behaviour.

- A number of major studies that illustrate the strengths and limitations of these approaches.

- The main disputes and debates about the value of the different approaches in explaining the patterns of potential relationships between human behaviour and technology.

- How the concepts of power, knowledge, freedom, identity, inequality and insecurity can be used in the analysis of these relationships.

Overview and key points

Technology plays a key role in the ways we organize ourselves and in the ways we work and live our lives. This chapter will review and evaluate the main approaches that can be used to understand the complex interrelationship between technology and organizational behaviour. **Technological determinism**, while somewhat out of favour in certain academic circles, is still prevalent in mainstream and in media accounts of technology and organization. At the core of technological determinist thinking is the assumption that the technical properties of particular technological devices are the cause of corresponding developments in organizations or even society. Therefore, a crucial question for much of the mainstream literature is how organizations can best adapt to the demands placed upon them by new technologies. More critical approaches, however, condemn this perspective as rather too simplistic and one-sided. To counter the dominance of technological determinism a number of alternative forms of explanation have been

Technological determinism
Determinism is the view that there is an inevitable direction in which events move. For technological determinists, the cause is technology. According to technological determinists, certain key technologies are the primary movers in developments in organization, the economy or even society itself.

Social shaping of technology
A sociological approach that rejects the technologically determinist view of technology as being distinct from the rest of society. It focuses on social and economic interests as key influences on the eventual shape of the technology. For those who follow this approach, technology is just one aspect of the way we live socially (and is not inherently different to organizations, art or politics).

Social construction of technology (SCOT) A more radical variant of the approach known as the social shaping of technology. According to constructivists, in order to understand technological developments we need to study the social interpretations that have produced the definitions of what problems can or should be solved by a given technology. These interpretations, SCOT argues, guide the choices made by the designers, manufacturers and users. Technical choices in other words are not merely the application of an abstract technologic but are also vehicles for the expression of perspectives and ideologies of those social groups (including designers, opinion formers, users, non-users, etc.) that have a stake in the development of a particular technology. Technologies are therefore the offspring of alternative constructions and compromise.

Actor-network theory or analysis (ANT or ANA)
A theory that does not restrict action to that performed by humans but also involves non-human action as performed by material artefacts such as cars, phones or social institutions insofar as they and humans affect one another. Every technological device is dependent on a heterogeneous network, which supports the specific ways in which this device has been designed and used.

proposed, among them the **social shaping of technology**, the **social construction of technology (SCOT)** and **actor-network theory**. What most of these approaches have in common, apart from their rejection of technological determinism, is the desire to redress the balance by bringing to the fore the role that organizational, social and cultural factors play in the making (and un-making) of technology 'itself'.

Introduction

It is a truth universally acknowledged that the use of technology in any contemporary organization has now become so prevalent that it makes little sense to discuss the one without reference to the other. At the same time, social scientists, including sociologists, psychologists, economists, historians, management theorists and organization analysts, have been arguing for decades over what is the most appropriate theoretical framework for integrating the organization's 'human' and 'technological' dimensions. Social scientific debates often appear far too esoteric and therefore of little interest to anyone who is not a fully paid-up member of the academy. Be that as it may, a look at today's papers will show that disputes over the role technology plays in the ways we choose to organize our lives are not confined to some ivory tower but are a prominent feature of public discourse. Disagreements over say technologically facilitated unemployment, nuclear power, surveillance and privacy, genetic engineering or robotic weaponry, echo across political, managerial, academic and public spheres. In the twenty-first century, increasing awareness of the many ways various technologies are shaping how we organize our activities and how we conduct our lives, has made the need to better understand what is going on around us all the more urgent. This chapter aims to provide you with some of the rudimentary theoretical tools necessary to develop such an understanding. But first, let's attempt to clarify what we actually mean when we speak of **technology**.

Definitions: Making sense of 'technology'

At the most basic level, 'technology' (derived from the Greek *techne* meaning art, craft or skill) may be said to refer to 'the entire set of devices, whether mechanical, chemical, or linguistic', which facilitate the adaptation of human collectivities to their environments: 'Ploughs, clubs, radios, airplanes, fertilizers, drugs, breakfast cereals, grammars and concepts are each implements and instances of technology, which influence and are influenced by one another' (Aaronson and Osmond, 1971, p. 3).

We might call this a 'hardware' focused definition of technology. At the same time, as MacKenzie and Wajcman (1999) point out, devices are useless if divorced from the set of human activities necessary to activate them. Technological change involves not only new gadgets but also new practices, new ways of doing things. 'Technology' therefore includes what people do as well as what they use. An airplane becomes but a lump of metal and fertilizer but a pile of dirt if we lack the required know-how to put them to use. Any meaningful definition of technology must therefore also include what people *know:* devices are meaningless without the necessary know-how to construct, operate or repair them. Such knowledge and skills typically have elements (e.g., tacit, visual, tactile, etc.) that are not easily captured in words but require hands-on engagement with the technology in question.

In sum, in order to have an adequate understanding of what a technology is or does we need to pay close attention to at least three different sets of issues:

- devices
- human activities
- knowledge and skills.

Put like that, the term 'technology' effectively embraces the whole of the human-built world (Williams, 2000). This approach may go somewhat against current organizational behaviour (OB) textbook convention, where analyses of the role of 'technology in organizations' tend to narrow down the focus of the discussion to the role that information technology plays in the workplace. It is easy to see why this is the case, as the importance of information and communication technologies (ICT) for contemporary organizations can hardly be exaggerated. Nevertheless, in what follows we will take a broader view of technology and try not to lose sight of the wide range of technologies that are employed in the organization of human activities. For some OB writers, such as Alan Fox, technologies worthy of attention in this respect include not only what he terms 'material technologies' but also 'social technologies'. Fox's 'social technologies' cover organizational arrangements such as corporate communications, reward and control systems, job specifications and 'all the many other rules and decision-making procedures which seek to govern what work is done, how it is done and the relationships that prevail between those doing it' (Fox, 1974, p. 1). In this chapter, for the sake of simplicity and in order to keep within manageable bounds, we will focus primarily on 'material technologies'.

> **Technology** At the most basic level the term 'technology' is used to refer to the 'entire set of devices' that facilitate the adaptation of human collectivities to their environments. A fuller definition of technology includes the human activities, knowledge and skills that are necessary in order to create, understand and operate such devices.

Thinkpoint 12.1

List the technological developments that you think will most affect your life in the near future. From your point of view, will these developments be positive or negative? What do you think is the driving force behind them? Who controls technological developments and their consequences? Does anybody? Are such developments inevitable and outside our control?

The 'just so story' in Box 12.1 narrates a typical encounter between new technology and organization. For as you know from personal experience a university lecture is a remarkable feat of organization. The one or two hours it takes to attend this particular lecture represent but the tip of a (bureaucratic) iceberg. Months ago, syllabuses and curricula were compiled, scrutinized and approved by the relevant academic decision-making bodies. University timetables were compiled, time-slots and rooms allocated, lecture notes were prepared and presentational aids assembled. Registration and option forms were filled in and submitted to specified deadlines. Even the room itself could be understood as but the material expression of a set of 'social technologies' in Fox's (1974) sense. A lecture room embodies a particular set of organizational relationships, for instance, between the lecturer and her audience or between those who have the right, and often the obligation, to be there and those who do not. (Remember how tough it was to gain admittance to university?) Many people have to carry out particular tasks in prescribed ways (including students and lecturers but also administrators, cleaners, security staff, etc.) in order for this particular lecture to take place. The mobile phone's merry ringtone could be a sign that this picture is about to be dramatically transformed. To paraphrase Philip Agre (2000) (from whose work this little vignette has been inspired), anyone in the world can now reach into the controlled space of the lecture theatre and via a technological device communicate

**Box 12.1
Mobile phone troubles (1) – an encounter between technology and organization**

Picture this. There is a lecture going on. The semi-darkness of the lecture theatre is relieved only by the glow of the lecturer's PowerPoint presentation. Other than the voice from the podium, there is no other noise save that of rustling paper and the pecking of keyboards. Suddenly, a mobile phone plays a jaunty tune, downloaded only the previous evening from the official Top 40 ringtone chart. The lecturer interrupts her elaboration of a particularly subtle theoretical point in mid-sentence. Jackie, the embarrassed owner of the phone, desperately rummages among her belongings to retrieve and silence the offending device. Meanwhile, the tune plays on. Some of the other students giggle. *Schadenfreude?* And what a naff ring tone! None is more amused than Jon who has spent the last few minutes texting his mates under the desk – one of whom (Raj) is himself attending a different lecture in the same building – on the subject of their forthcoming tour of the local watering holes. Raj, however, is not responding. 'Ten out of ten for dedication', Jon thinks.

Jon is wrong. For nearly an hour now, Raj has paid as little attention to what the lecturer has been droning on about as to Jon's insistent text messages. Far more important matters preoccupy him at the moment. Just as his lecture started, a picture had appeared on the Facebook page of his Significant Other who is currently on an exchange visit to Florida, USA. In the picture, two unknown (to him) guys at the beach are holding her aloft. The pose conveys an air of easy familiarity between the members of this group, which he finds rather unsettling. The picture is not very clear. He can't see their hands. Where are their hands?

The phone has been retrieved and switched off. 'One missed call'. The lecturer casts a censorious look. Perhaps she might remind the offender of the University policy – clearly stated in the Student Handbook (not to mention the laminated notice on the door of this very room) – that mobiles must be switched off during lectures. Jackie mumbles an apology. The lecturer resumes: 'As I was saying before we were interrupted ...'

with any of the attendees. Similarly, anyone in the lecture can 'reach out' to anyone outside. Suddenly the whole of the 'outside' world of activities and relationships can no longer be kept out of the lecture room. A sign of the times?

In the days before mobile communication every social activity and relationship had its place. You would interact with your friends at Bar Mar or down the pub, with your bank at your local branch and with your boss at work. You could conceivably run into someone from your bank in Bar Mar but you would not attempt to do your banking there. Your Significant Other could always ring you on the telephone, but telephones were located in specific places. Insofar as communication devices have now become truly mobile, the close correspondence between activities, relationships and places is starting to break down. Boundaries between inside and outside previously marked by the lecture theatre walls are now permeable. Boundaries between home and work, work time and leisure time, are also increasingly blurred. Indeed, recent surveys (e.g., Worrall *et al*, 2016) have claimed that managers' after-hours emails now effectively cancel out their annual leave allowance.

It is evident that the many relationships (family, partners, friends, work colleagues) that traditionally made up a person's life can no longer be kept as separate as they used to be. They now, so to speak, follow you around in a form of electronically mediated continual presence. Furthermore, more and more people conduct more and more of their friendships and other social relationships via what we have come to call 'social media'. Many see in such trends symptoms of the imminent **death of distance** (Cairncross, 1998). Arguably however, these changes are also transforming the *temporal* patterns which characterize our lives. Once upon a time, friends and acquaintances would, as it were, drift in and out of your life. As you moved on from school, to college, to university to work, to another city, you would in all likelihood lose touch with many

Death of distance View popularized by Cairncross (1998), that, for the purposes of organizing, the importance of physical location and geographical distance is no longer a constraint because of the developments in ICT.

of the people you knew, even some you may have been close to. Keeping in touch required effort. Now, in the age of social media, you do not have to lose touch unless you want to (and, perhaps, not even then). Through, say Facebook you can, in principle, maintain all these relationships, as you (and they) move on with your lives (Miller, 2011). We certainly appear to be witnessing 'a tremendous shift in human relationships: from episodic to always-on' (Agre, 2000, p. 10).

Thinkpoint 12.2

Let's note at this point that Jon or Raj's activities during the lecture may be hidden from the lecturer but are of course visible to the networks which 'know' where they are and what they are doing. Indeed our work (and out of work) activities and interactions are increasingly technologically mediated and generate as a matter of course a multitude of electronic traces – a version of the phenomenon Zuboff (1989) describes as the 'information panopticon' (see Chapter 7; Lyon, 1994). Some view these developments as opportunities for enhanced management control, better organization, more effective marketing and more transparent government (e.g., Garfinkel, 2001; Baker, 2008; Jarvis, 2011). For instance, Class120™ (see www.class120.com/) is a US commercial notification service which for $199 a year offers to track in real time the location of students via their smartphones. If a student is not 'within a geofence mapped around the classroom where they are supposed to be', then their parents (who presumably pay their tuition fees) are alerted (Belkin, 2015).

Many however, view the surveillance capabilities of electronic technologies as a major threat and raise the spectre of the imminent 'death of privacy' (*The Economist,* 1999; Froomkin, 2000; Albrecht and McIntyre, 2005; Keen, 2011). For a flavour of this debate currently in the media see Keen (2011), Johnson (2011) and Jarvis (2011). Can you identify the electronic traces you generated today? Facebook? Mobile phone? ATM? CCTV?

Go to **www.aclu.org/pizza/images/screen.swf** and watch the clip. Make sure you pay attention to the cursor movements. Is this the future? Are we witnessing as some suggest the 'death of privacy? Is that a bad thing? What, if anything, can be done and by whom?

For those of a techno-optimistic disposition these technological advances bring in their wake positive developments including individual empowerment and new freedoms of association. For others, they herald the erosion of leisure time, intensified surveillance and increasingly shallow social relationships. Organizations as we know them (universities, theatres, places of worship) tend to be dependent upon, and a reflection of, the (until now) episodic and place-specific character of social life. The way that the mobile phone disrupted the organization of the lecture could be seen as an example of that. Note also, however, that mobile communications also enable new practices of co-ordination – recall for instance Jon's organizing of his little excursion. Indeed, many media commentators have proclaimed the decisive role played by social media in the protest movements of the last decade including the so-called 'Facebook revolutions' which in 2011 rocked Tunisia, Egypt and various other countries in North Africa and the Middle East.

Students of social behaviour routinely note that the proliferation of social networking tools have dramatically diminished the (administrative) costs of group organization. However obscure an interest, however eccentric a pastime, however bizarre a predilection, such tools allow like-minded individuals to find one another and to create social groups and communities that share tips, provide mutual support and publicize their views to potential members. This is particularly evident in the case of groups whose views or practices – ranging from the promotion of anorexia among teenagers to racism and other forms of intolerance – are subject to social disapproval (Shirky, 2009). The controls which governments, media corporations and educational institutions formerly exercised over the collection, accumulation and circulation of information have been gradually loosened. Today, as the ever-expanding blogosphere and the immense popularity of services such as Facebook, Twitter, Instagram or YouTube testify, (nearly) everyone believes they deserve an audience. Press has increasingly become 'free' in the sense that the dramatically diminished costs of (online) broadcasting allow everybody (that is those with access to social media technologies) to publish their views bypassing the restrictions, as some would argue, and 'quality controls', as others would put it, of more traditional print and broadcast media. Some even claim that one of the most noticeable impacts of the Internet has been to render us more susceptible to misinformation, conspiracy theories, fake history and bogus science (Thompson, 2008) with highly detrimental effects upon contemporary culture and economy (Keen, 2008). Be that as it may, we appear to be in the midst 'of a remarkable increase in our ability to share, to co-operate with one another, and to take collective action, all outside the framework of traditional institutions and organizations' (Shirky, 2009, p. 21).

Some commentators claim that it is the very nature of our engagement with knowledge that is changing and not just its modes of circulation. For instance, in 'Is Google Making Us Stupid?' Nicholas Carr (2008) argues that the Internet is changing the way we read, remember and even think. According to Carr (2008; 2010), extensive Internet usage has inculcated new habits in users. Compared to the days when books and other print media were our main sources of information, current expectations of quick access have shrunk users' attention spans and left them unable to read texts 'in depth'. 'Surfers' as the word hints, shallow read, skimming and jumping through hyperlinks instead of immersing themselves in the text. If, as many scientists believe, our brains are relatively plastic and change depending on how we habitually use them, then new media like the World Wide Web are strengthening those parts that handle skimming, surveying and multitasking (the 'juggler brain') while allowing the parts that handle engagement, concentration and contemplation to atrophy (e.g., Greenfield, 2008).

Technology and organizational behaviour

As these few introductory remarks indicate, there is a pressing need to better understand the role that the various technologies play in the 'changing fabric' of contemporary organizations and of social life (Zammuto *et al.*, 2007; Orlikowski and Scott, 2008). And yet, as will become apparent, there is within management studies (and in the social sciences more broadly), considerable disagreement as to how this task might be best accomplished. As is often the case, lurking beneath social scientific disagreements over how best to make sense of the relationship between 'society' and 'technology', organizing's 'human' and 'technological' dimensions, is the venerable philosophical dispute between determinism and freedom.

Determinism presumes that one factor (e.g., technology) can be seen to cause a series of effects independently of context or human intervention. Critics of determinism argue that while such a view may be applicable in natural science where, for example, the force of gravity will always determine that an apple falls to the ground, in human life this is not so. Here, much depends on the meaning attributed to 'things' and the freedom of humans to alter their behaviour in accordance with their particular interpretations and interests. In the words of Langdon Winner (1977, p. 46):

> On the one hand, we encounter the idea that technological development goes forward virtually of its own inertia, resists any limitation and has the character of a self propelling, self sustaining ineluctable flow. On the other hand, there are arguments that human beings have full and conscious choice in the matter and that they are responsible for choices made at each step in the sequence of change.

It is not the objective of this chapter to provide the ultimate resolution of such disagreements, but rather to point out their *consequences* for our understanding of the organization–technology relationship. The most common alternative frameworks for understanding this relationship are technological determinism, the social shaping of technology, the social construction of technology, and actor-network theory. We shall examine each in turn.

MAINSTREAM PERSPECTIVES: TECHNOLOGICAL DETERMINISM

You will have read, or heard people express, views along the lines: 'Technological developments X and Y are all but inevitable. The best people can do is try to adapt to them'. Such views are typically espoused by both those who are exceptionally optimistic and those particularly pessimistic about current technological advances. It is the theoretical outlook of choice for both those who dream that technology will ultimately deliver a society of freedom and plenty *and* for those who fear that out-of-control nano-robots will someday munch the world into grey goo. For large sections of the mass media it is something of a commonplace that the *existence* of a technology will inevitably lead to its use, whether for good or ill. Technology, we are told, will transform our jobs, 'educate our children, revolution-ize our families, erode our privacy and modify our genes' (Winner, 1997, p. 1).

Such views are also quite common in the literature on management and organiza-tions and the theoretical perspective behind them is **technological determinism**. Determinism is the view that there is an inevitable direction in which events move determined by some cause. For **technological determinists**, that cause is technol-ogy. In other words, certain key technologies are the primary movers in developments in organizations, the economy or even society itself:

> **Technological determinism** The view that there is an inevitable direction in which events move determined by some cause.

> **Technological determinists** Those who adopt technological determinism.

> In technological determinism, research and development have been assumed as self-generating. The new technologies are invented as it were in an independent sphere, and then create new societ-ies or new human conditions. (Williams, 1979, p. 13)

It follows from the viewpoint of technological determinism that the key problem for OB is to understand a technology's – positive or negative (depending on one's point of view) – impact upon individuals and groups, orga-nizations and society. Countless studies have thus focused upon the impact of computers on employment patterns, the distribution of skills, spans of control, firm strategies, competitive advantage, managerial decision-making and worker alienation.

Figure 12.1 Technological determinism

Technology → Society

For technological determinism (TD) then, social and organizational changes are caused (or at least shaped) by technological developments. But what are the causes of these technological developments themselves? For TD, tech-nological developments are determined by technological superiority in a manner resembling a Darwinian 'survival of the fittest'. Sociologist William Ogburn (1950), for example, suggested that if collectively people select the same technology, it must be because it is that technology that best satisfies their needs. In the words of Ralph Waldo Emerson, the American writer, if you invent a better mousetrap, the whole world will beat a path to your door. How does the invention of a better mousetrap come about according to the proponents of TD? Ogburn and Thomas (1922) have claimed that since technologies follow an inherent internal logic of their own, once all the necessary elements are present, an invention will become inevitable: 'given the boat and the steam engine, is not the steamboat inevitable?' (quoted in MacKenzie and Wajcman, 1999, p. 9). The fact that the same invention may be made almost concurrently in geographically dispersed locations adds weight to this argument. In sum, new technologies emerge out of older technologies by means of (techno-scientific) 'breakthroughs' which *subsequently* have social and orga-nizational consequences – whether intended or unintended. For TD technology is the engine of organizational and social change. It is what takes us from the Stone Age, to the Bronze Age, to the Iron Age, to the Age of Steam, to the present Information Age and forever onwards. The transition from say the Bronze Age to the Iron Age came about because of the technological superiority of iron tools and weapons over bronze ones, and all other aspects of this changeover are consequences of this technological superiority rather than causes of the change in their own right. The key ideas in the deterministic outlook are summarized in Box 12.2.

Box 12.2 Key ideas in technological determinism (TD)

- Technology is seen as extraneous to the rest of society, an autonomous force that causes social and organizational changes.
- TD concentrates on the impacts of technology on human organization and action.
- Key mainstream problem: How can organizations best adapt to new technologies?

Key issues and controversies

In other chapters, various determinisms (biological, economic, etc.) come in for a fair amount of criticism. It should then be clear by now that determinism is on the whole considered an intellectual gaffe. Thus, in social scientific debates, 'technological determinism' is more often than not an accusation, employed to show that one's intellectual adversary has an irredeemably naive perspective on technological and organizational change. That is not to say that social scientists are unlikely to harbour deterministic views (quite the opposite), but rather that writers very rarely explicitly identify their own arguments with that school. Technological determinism is, so to speak, the theory that dare not speak its name.

Among the more explicitly determinist arguments we should include Joan Woodward's (1965) view, also discussed in Chapters 7 and 14, to the effect that organizational structures will reflect the type of technology being employed. As Woodward argued, 'there are prescribed and functional relationships between [organizational] structure and technical demands' (ibid., p. 51). There is, in other words, 'a particular form of organization [that is] most appropriate to each technical situation' (ibid., p. 72). Similar arguments were (and are) made concerning what we might call the more informal aspects of work organization. In their classic study, Walker and Guest argued in 1952 that the impact of technology upon assembly line work meant, among other things, that social interaction among workers decreased and that work groups were now difficult to form. Therefore, the social needs of employees were not met under the 'Fordist' (see Chapter 8) organization of work. In the same vein, Blauner (1964) claimed that the particular production technologies employed in car assembly and chemical processing resulted in alienated workforces. Blauner described this experience of alienation in terms of feelings of powerlessness, meaninglessness, isolation and self-estrangement. Nevertheless, Blauner believed that the gradual introduction of new, more advanced technologies would eventually rid the workplaces of the future from the malady of alienation. Jaques Ellul (1967, p. 138) on the other hand, did not share the (techo-)optimism of Blauner. For him 'there can be no human autonomy in the face of technical autonomy'. Technological autonomy, he claimed, means that the human individual is reduced to 'a slug inserted in a slot machine' (ibid., p. 135; cf. Kelly, 2010).

As described in Chapters 11 and 14, more recent TD inspired contributions to management literature and practice have argued that bureaucratic forms of organization reflect the technological imperatives of a previous (Industrial) Age and are therefore totally unsuited to the requirements of the present Information Age (e.g., Evans and Wurster, 2000; Kelly, 1999; 2010).[1] New computer technologies are indeed widely regarded as the impetus for fundamental changes in the scope and range of organizational activities. The call to urgently adapt our behaviours and associated forms of organizing and enterprise in line with the new technological imperatives has, for instance, been a common refrain in the literature and practice of business process re-engineering (BPR). As you will recall from Chapter 7, BPR proposes that information technology should be a catalyst for revolutionary organizational changes leading to 'dramatic improvements in critical contemporary measures of performance, such as cost, quality service and speed' (Hammer and Champy, 1993, p. 32; cf. Grint, 1994). Indeed, much theoretical and empirical work in a wide range of management disciplines has routinely claimed that contemporary societies are in the throes of a new and fundamentally different phase of development (Toffler, 1980; Kelly, 2010; Ford, 2015; 2016). The ongoing ICT revolution, many argue, signals a fundamental shift in the underlying dynamics of societal and organizational change, pushing inexorably in the direction of flatter more decentralized and dispersed forms of organizing (e.g., Negroponte, 1995; Peters, 1997; Kelly, 1999; Tapscott and Williams, 2010). 'Network' forms of organization are said to be in the process of replacing bureaucratic ones as the dominant structure in the Information Age (Davidow and Malone, 1992; van Aken *et al.*, 1997; Friedman, 2005; Kanter and Fine, 2010; Brynjolfsson and Saunders, 2013; Brynjolfsson and Mcafee, 2011; 2016; see also Chapters 6, 10 and 13). Tapscott (2008) argues along similar lines that the generational impact of ICT applications such as Google, FaceBook, Twitter and YouTube has created a 'net generation' of 'digital natives' or 'Screenagers', who are currently in the process of 'changing the world' and with whom contemporary businesses must engage (whether as employees or as consumers) in radically new ways.

Most of the works mentioned in this section are significantly more complex than the more 'straightforward TD' one finds in many media accounts of new technologies, while at the same time still in debt to particular deterministic assumptions.[2] TD themes typically permeate arguments concerning organizational change without being named as such. As an even cursory examination of the many works currently crowding bookshop shelves that claim to guide management through the actions necessary in order to ride the latest wave of technological change will show, technologically deterministic assumptions tend to underpin much of mainstream management thought and practice.

In many ways, technological determinism has achieved the status of a common sense perspective on matters technological. As Rosalind Williams (2000, p. 652) of the Massachusetts Institute of Technology (MIT) has put it:

> Most historians condemn technological determinism as a dangerous fallacy, but my MIT colleagues are convinced it is simply true ... Over and again people talk about the inevitability of change ... understood as a series of [technologically originated] shocks, an endless catch-up game.

Nevertheless, and as various chapters in this book have argued, when critically investigated, 'common sense' views often turn out to be neither common nor to make much sense. This turns out to also be the case with TD. At the same time, we must resist the temptation many textbooks succumb to of treating TD as nothing more than an intellectual error, thus leaving the causes of its popularity an incomprehensible mystery. Rather, in order to gain a clearer view of its strengths and limitations, we need a better understanding of how it 'works' as a mode of explanation. For this see Case Study 12.1.

The events discussed in Case Study 12.1 happened so long ago that the relevance of White's analysis to the world of modern technology and contemporary organizations may appear obscure. And yet, from a TD point of view, what matters is what we might call the *mechanics* of technological and social change. In modern management-speak, the introduction of a new technology, the stirrup, radically altered the cost/benefit equation of medieval armies by introducing remarkable efficiency gains (Darby, 2001). It was a cheap, easy to implement technology, which offered the irresistible competitive advantage of economy of effort, combined with increased productivity. The stirrup brought within the grasp of the average rider levels of control of his mount hitherto only achievable by the most talented and highly skilled riders. A process not dissimilar you might say to the way graphical user interfaces (GUI) brought computing power within reach of the least technically adept, thus launching the so-called PC revolution. Or the way in which search engines and the World Wide Web have made the resources of the Internet, until relatively recently accessible only by the highly computer literate, available to the many millions, thus initiating the so-called Internet revolution. In TD accounts then, the *dramatis personae* may change but the plot remains much the same.

Case study 12.1
The stirrup

By way of illustration of how technological deterministic explanations 'work' analyti-cally, we can point to Lynn White's (1962) influential analysis of the relationship between medieval technology and social change, a key case in the development of the TD perspective. Briefly, White claimed that the diffusion westwards of an Asian invention, the stirrup, brought about a new form of military and social organization in Western Europe: feudalism. Up until that time fighting on horseback had been severely constrained by the ever-present danger of falling off. The stirrup gave the medieval rider a far more secure grip on the horse, welding them together into a single fighting unit capable of an entirely new level of violence in combat.

White illustrates the argument about the social and organizational effects of this technological device by recounting the story of Charles Martel (c.689–741 AD). In the early eighth century, Charles Martel created a new type of cavalry force in order to repel Moorish incursions into France. A mounted warrior (knight) is depicted in the image accompanying this case study. Note the stirrup. Note also how the mounted warrior is holding his lance: the long lance is held under the arm in the 'couched position'. The medieval knight enjoys the benefit conferred by the stirrup, an advantage that ancient mounted warriors lacked. The former can strike home with the combined momentum of horse and rider, the latter with little more that the force of his arm. 'The new knightly tactic of charging with the lance couched – tucked firmly under the arm to unite the impact of man and horse – proved a battle-winner' (Holmes, 1988, p. 34).

Charles Martel's battlefield successes, marked, or so the TD argument runs, the emergence of the mounted knight as the specialized practitioner of a new kind of 'mounted shock combat' – made possible by the stirrup. A strike force of knights thus conferred a competitive advantage that no European ruler or potentate could do without. The armoured knight would therefore dominate European battlefields for centuries to come. At the same time the maintenance of such a force posed some acute economic problems: armour was expensive, horses were costly to acquire and main-tain, while the acquisition of horsemanship skills takes a long time. In order to ensure the ready availability of such a strike force in their domains, Western European rulers granted knights fiefs of land in return for military service. A new mounted warrior nobility was thus created, endowed with land, castles, retainers and all the other accoutrements we now associate with chivalry, and upon whom European monarchs grew increasingly dependent. According to TD then, a new form of military, social and economic organization comes about not because of the whims of kings and queens, nor

Figure 12.2
After the stirrup

out of the operation of 'social forces', but as the direct result of the introduction of 'a simple mechanical device' (Darby, 2001). As White put it:

Few inventions have been so simple as the stirrup, but few had so catalytic an influence in history. The requirements of the new mode of warfare which it made possible found expression in a new form of Western European Society, dominated by an aristocracy of warriors endowed with land so that they might fight in a new and highly specialized way.

The story of the knight ends the way it began, with yet another technological device – gunpowder – revolutionizing European warfare: increasingly accurate firearms were the knight's undoing. Firearms can penetrate armour at a distance, so the infantry gains the upper hand in the battlefield over the mounted warriors. As Cervantes' Don Quixote bitterly lamented, the gun was:

An invention which allows a base and cowardly hand to take the life of a brave knight.

A new technologically-induced transformation of both military organization and of society was afoot. Useless against cannon, the knightly castles dotting the European continent were either demolished or transformed into what we now call 'stately homes' devoid of any military function. The title 'knight' became an essentially honorific one. It no longer described a mounted warrior but a courtier. Feudalism was no more and the Early Modern Age was upon us (Cameron, 1999).

How much space do technological determinist accounts allow for human choice? White himself was careful to state that 'a new device merely opens a door, it does not compel one to enter' (1962, p. 28). The acceptance or rejection of a technological invention therefore appears to remain a matter for society to decide. Nevertheless, one could claim with some justification that what TD explanations give with the one hand, they take with the other. Since as you will recall, for technological determinists technological change has as its cause the technological superiority of one device or technique over another, individuals, organizations and societies that choose *not* to adopt a new and more effective technology will not survive long against competitors who *did* choose to adopt the technology in question. One example that can be used to illustrate this point concerns the knight's Japanese counterpart, the samurai warrior. Competition for power among the nobility in Japan had by the beginning of the sixteenth century erupted into all out civil war in which cannon and firearms often played a decisive role (Turnbull, 1996).[3] During the civil wars Japan built itself a substantial firearms industry to keep the combatants supplied. By the seventeenth century, however, the civil wars having been concluded, the seemingly inexorable spread of the gun was put into reverse. The population was disarmed and weapons collected to be melted down (it was said) for the construction of a giant statue of the Buddha. After the experience of the civil wars, guns came to be seen as a recipe for social disorder and forever tainted by their association with European Christianity. They were considered as incompatible with samurai martial virtues and with the culture of Japan. By the end of the seventeenth century the use of guns had effectively been eliminated in Japan (Perrin, 1979). From then on, the samurai warrior class would only carry swords (Turnbull; 1998). This then could be seen as an example of – in White's terms – a society's refusal to enter the door opened by the technological innovations of gunpowder and the gun. We could therefore say that the Japanese made the choice *not* to undergo the changes in military and social organization necessary for effective exploitation of the destructive power of guns. This choice, however, appears to have been open only for as long as Japan remained isolated from the Western world. In 1853, ships of the US navy entered Tokyo Bay and forced the Japanese government to open up trade with Western nations thus ending – at gunpoint – centuries of Japanese isolation. The door was, so to speak, reopened and entry forced at gunpoint. Western technologies, including firearms, were introduced as part and parcel of Japanese modernization. The modernization of Japan meant that the samurai were now essentially redundant and their social privileges withdrawn. This led to sporadic uprisings against the new order by some samurai who still persisted in fighting the old way (without firearms), only to be mown down by conscripted peasants armed with guns (Turnbull, 1996).[4]

Implications of technological determinism

If the assumption of a neutral, 'self-propelling, self-sustaining' technology, which is made in the advocacy of technological determinism is open to criticism, it also has its attractions, particularly for those who despair of making sense of the complexity and confusion of human affairs. Among other things, TD fits well with mechanistic views of organization and management (see Chapter 9; Morgan, 1986; Tsoukas, 1994). Furthermore, for those particularly enthusiastic about TD, most of the problems afflicting human existence – whether they be poverty, war, alienation or overpopulation – appear capable of being fixed or eradicated through the progress of science and technology. Countless are the examples of technologies that have at some point or another been proclaimed as the miracle cure for this or that social ill. The term 'technological fix' was coined by physicist Alvin Weinberg (1966), who claimed that rather than engage in ultimately futile efforts to solve our problems by attempting to change people's attitudes or behaviour, it makes far more sense to look for technological solutions to those same problems. New production technologies, he argued, would eliminate poverty in developed countries, free contraceptive devices would reduce overpopulation in developing ones, nuclear-powered desalination would reduce conflict over access to fresh water (thus bringing an end to the Arab–Israeli conflict), free air–conditioning would reduce riots in inner cities, cheap computers would compensate for the shortage of teachers in the classroom, while nuclear weapons would reduce the likelihood of war. The ideology of the 'technological fix' therefore represents an optimistic take on the relationship between technology and human choice.

Digital divide Disparity between those who have access to the new information and communication technologies and those who do not.

It is not all good news, however. Over the past few decades, policymakers have grown increasingly concerned about the emergence of a new form of inequality: the so-called **digital divide**. The 'digital divide' refers to the disparities between those who have access to the new ICTs and those who do not – and are therefore excluded from the brave new digital economy. Research and debate on the subject typically focus on whether the social impact of computers and the Internet reinforces or reduces existing social and economic inequalities (both within and between nations). Policy discussions thus typically focus on how social policy can be employed most effectively for the purpose of ameliorating any such technological imbalances. At the same time as the *Scientific American* points out:

> The big problem with the *digital divide* framing is that it tends to connote digital solutions, that is, computers and telecommunications, without a consideration of the context into which that hardware would be put. This line of reasoning led some to assume that the dearth of digital access of nations, communities and individuals could be easily tackled by an infusion of computers and Internet connections. (Warschauer, 2003, pp. 42–43)

Case study 12.2
OLPC

Perhaps the most high profile initiative in recent years is the One Laptop Per Child (OLPC) initiative (see www.laptop.org/en/). OLPC is a US-based non-profit organization that has as its objective the building of a low cost (ideally under US$100) laptop computer so that every child growing up in the less developed world can own one. OLPC aims:

> [t]o eliminate poverty and create world peace *by providing education to the poorest and most remote children on the planet by making them more active in their own learning, ..., connected to the Internet, with their own laptop, as a human right and cost free to them* (**/www.olpcnews.com/people/negroponte/ nicholas_negroponte_windows_xp.html**, *emphasis added*).

OLPC was launched in 2005 by Nicholas Negroponte, a former director of MIT's Media Lab, at the World Economic Forum in Davos, Switzerland. It was funded by a number of corporate sponsors including AMD, Brightstar, eBay, Google, News Corporation, Red Hat and until 2007, Intel), who each donated $2 million (Silva and Westrup, 2008). OLPC developed a highly innovative laptop computer, the XO series, which utilized a Free/Open Source operating system and used a novel graphic user interface (Sugar) that is not based on a 'desktop' metaphor, which the designers considered less relevant to children living in the developing world. Considerable technological innovation has also gone into the XOs' 'power supply, display, networking, keyboard, and touchpad' in order to create a durable laptop that is resistant to dirt and moisture and which could therefore operate in the most remote areas of the planet (Kraemer *et al.*, 2009, pp. 68–69).

Nevertheless, at the time of writing, success appears elusive with OLPC plagued by rising costs, budget cuts, ideological clashes, the loss of key staff and the defection of sponsors. For example, Intel left to develop its own more conventional (and more expensive) laptop, the Classmate, which it proceeded to market aggressively. Intel subsidies were thus 'instrumental' in persuading the Libyan government, which was planning to participate in the OLPC scheme by funding 1.2 million XO-1s, to choose the Classmate instead (Kraemer *et al.*, 2009, p. 69). Overall, we might say, the OLPC project has prompted something of a 'backlash' from the big players in the computer industry who are themselves increasingly targeting consumers at 'the bottom of the pyramid' (op. cit., p. 72).

The innovative nature of the XO was itself perceived to be a problem. For instance, 'the opportunity cost or the foregone investment in teachers, facilities, or other educational materials [was] cited by India's education ministry as its main reason for not joining OLPC' (op. cit., p. 73). In response to such concerns, Negroponte endorsed Microsoft's offer to put Windows XP onto the XOs at a reduced price ($3). At the same time, this endorsement immediately created dissent within OLPC. Its president, Will Bender has publicly rejected the move, while the UK Green party has accused OLPC of 'selling out' to Microsoft rather than sticking to the principled use of Free/Open Source Software (Silva and Westrup, 2008, p. 10).

It is perhaps ironic that 'technical fixes' rather than resolving social conflicts and problems – as Weinberg (1966) had envisaged – appear to become entangled in them.

Furthermore, there is a widespread view that technologies tend to advance at a much faster pace than organizations and society can adapt to them. Thus, today's social arrangements and organizational forms are bound to be destabilized in the wake of the introduction of ever-newer technologies (e.g., Toffler, 1971). Study after study have warned that new generations of cheap, efficient and increasingly smart robots are currently ushering in a society of increased inequality and mass unemployment, where even professional jobs are not ultimately immune to robot competition (Brynjolfsson and Mcafee, 2011; 2016; Brynjolfsson and Saunders, 2013; Susskind and Susskind, 2015; Ford, 2015). Such technological developments, warns celebrated physicist Stephen Hawking (CNN, 2015) are 'driving ever-increasing inequality'. 'Machines' argues Martin Ford (2016, p.11) are even:

> encroaching on the fundamental capability that sets us apart as a species: our ability to make complex decisions, to solve problems – and, most importantly, to learn … In the coming decades … widespread unemployment … has clear potential to tear society apart … in a world with far too few jobs, who will have the income and confidence to purchase the products and services produced by the economy?

In a widely cited report Frey and Osborne (2015) estimate that '47 per cent of the US workforce is at risk of automation as a result of these trends' (p. 58). Similar numbers have been suggested for the UK and for other developed economies arguing, for instance that '54 per cent of European Union jobs are at risk of automation' (ibid., p. 61). 'We are completely unprepared', argues Ford (2016, p. 11), 'for the robot revolution: If we fail [to] … develop workable ways in which to adapt our economies and societies, then … frightening volatility is sure to arrive before too long'.

Thinkpoint 12.3

The Henn-Na Hotel which opened in Nagasaki in July 2015 describes itself as the world's first robot hotel. The publicity for the hotel, which is located in a theme park, claims that it is (*almost*) entirely staffed by automata (Figure 12.2 is of one of the hotel's robot receptionists).

In your view, is this a sign of Ford's (2016) 'robot revolution'? An early example perhaps of the robot-run economy (the imminent arrival of which technological determinists have long prophesied) at work? Or something else?

If you do not happen to be in Nagasaki you can find more information at the hotel website: www.h-n-h.jp/en/. Also visitors to the hotel have posted a number of videos from their stay on YouTube which might give you an idea of the 'Henn-Na experience'. You can also check out guest reviews on TripAdvisor: www.tripadvisor.co.uk. For a traditional newspaper review see Rajesh (2015) online at: www.theguardian.com/travel/2015/aug/14/japan-henn-na-hotel-staffed-by-robots.

Figure 12.3
Welcome to the New Economy: Robot receptionist at Henn-Na

Contributions and limitations of technological determinist approaches

Technological deterministic accounts tell a simple and powerful story about the place of technology in human behaviour and organization. Technologies they claim, 'affect all patterns of social existence and technological change is the single most important source of change in society' (Winner, 1977, p. 76, Marx and Smith, 1994). In our technologically saturated age this appears to be a highly plausible explanation for many of the changes that engulf us (Knights *et al.*, 2002). It is not altogether surprising then, that TD is as common in the literature on management and organizations as it is in the media or advertising, and that a central preoccupation of this literature is with the power of key technologies to shape what happens in organizations. Optimists look forward to freedom from drudgery, worker empowerment, decentralization and self-actualization (technophilia). Pessimists fear de-skilling, unemployment, universal surveillance, work regimentation and intrusive management control (technophobia).

Technological determinists accept that technological changes often have uneven implications for different groups. For instance, a technology that enables the attainment of particular management goals – say increased efficiency, higher profitability or enhanced control – may have adverse consequences for the workforce. A technology that benefits a particular firm, industry or community may have devastating effects for other firms, industries or communities. At the same time, the notion of technology as an autonomous force that TD perspectives promote, assumes that the burden of adaptation to technological advance has to be borne by human communities and organizational stakeholders. It is they who will have to 'conform' one way or another to whatever new requirements technological progress might impose. Failure to accept this self-evident truth invites accusations of being a **Luddite**. 'Luddites'[5] is the name given to those British textile workers who in defence of their livelihoods set out to resist the mechanization of their trades. Between 1811 and 1816 in particular, the Luddites were blamed for outbreaks of machine breaking that were only brought to an end by executions and the deployment of large numbers of troops in the affected areas of the country. The term 'Luddite' has had a bad press ever since, being employed as convenient shorthand for all those misguided individuals who attempt to stand in the way of technological progress. While this picture of the Luddites reinforces the view of new technology as the proverbial offer you can't refuse, TD advocates argue that technologies are 'neutral' or 'apolitical' since it is technological superiority rather than socio or political considerations that dictates the fate of a given technology – though a technology may well be 'superior' because it is cheaper. Like a knife, technology is seen as something that can be used for good or ill.[6]

Luddites Name originally given to late eighteenth and early nineteenth century textile workers who, in defence of their livelihoods, set out to resist the mechanization of their trades. 'Luddite' is often employed as a term of abuse to describe those who attempt to stand in the way of 'progress'.

Technological determinist perspectives are sometimes subdivided into strong and weak variants. While the 'strong' or 'hard' version may portray a particular technology (say IT) as a kind of autonomous irresistible force, 'weak' or 'soft' variants of the same argument may portray it as one important influence among many. Clearly, weak TD can be seen as a significant improvement on the 'hard' variety, and people are therefore more likely to own up to it (Miles, 1989). In practice, however, the distinction between weak and strong is often lost as 'it is easy to slide from one to the other' in the course of an argument, 'without realizing quite where one is being led' (Finnegan, 1975, p. 105).

Let us note in passing that TD perspectives, whether 'strong' or 'weak', typically conceptualize technological innovation and the emergence of new technical devices in terms of a common scenario. Technological innovations are said to move through a succession of logically distinct stages, something along the lines shown in Figure 12.3.

Figure 12.4 The linear model of technological innovation

Scientific research → Application → Design and development → Production → Marketing → Diffusion → Use → Impact

Thinkpoint 12.4

Some years ago Paul Allen was granted a US patent for the 'Programmable Subcutaneous Visible Implant' (PSVI) a watch that was surgically implanted into the user's wrist. Its liquid crystal display, visible under the user's skin, displayed time and date. For all its obvious advantages over normal watches – for instance PSVI could neither be mislaid nor stolen – the gizmo was not a commercial success and its disappointed inventor went on to new things, co-founding Microsoft (van Duiken, 2004).

The story of PSVI as outlined here is the story of a failed technology. Consider the life cycle of PSVI in terms of the model presented in Figure 12.3. In your view, at which stage or stages did things go wrong for PSVI? (For instance, was it a problem of bad design, inadequate marketing or something else?)

Technological determinists, of all persuasions, readily agree that 'human factors' or 'people issues' are of central importance. At the same time, these tend to be conceptualized in a rather restricted manner, either in terms of how the functioning of a technology may be complicated by the unpredictable behaviour of its users, or else in terms of the impact of technology on organizations and society (Bloomfield and Vurdubakis, 1994). Critical approaches tend to condemn this narrow view for failing to account for the ways technology is *itself* shaped by the social world. We will have more to say on this topic since all of the alternative approaches to technology we will be considering in this chapter started life as critiques of technological determinism. For the time being, it will suffice to say that of the various criticisms typically levelled at TD, the following are among the most common:

- Technological devices cannot compel their adoption on unwilling organizations and societies. Rather, the characteristics of a particular society play a crucial role in determining which technologies it will adopt. (For example, the Amish, a fundamentalist Christian community in the USA, eschew modern farming methods and equipment but are nevertheless remarkably successful farmers (Selby, 2004); similarly, native American warriors often eschewed the use of the stirrup but were nevertheless remarkably successful mounted combatants.
- The idea that social and organizational impacts are ultimately the logical consequences of the characteristics of a given technology provides a very shaky theoretical foundation for unravelling the relationship between technology organizations and society. The impacts of the same technology can vary widely with the different social, economic or organizational specificities of different times and places. For example, the nomads of central Asia may have invented the stirrup but did not adopt the knights' heavy armour nor – needless to say – feudalism.[7]
- Technological determinism fails to pay due attention to the dynamic reciprocal relationships in which technical, economic, social, political, cultural and organizational phenomena are simultaneously causes and effects in the relationship between technological and organizational change (more on this later).

Let's briefly revisit this book's key concepts of knowledge, power, freedom, identity, inequality and insecurity (see the Appendix) as they appear through the lens of technological determinism. We have already referred, or alluded to, the key role that *scientific* (including engineering) knowledge plays in TD accounts. A typical TD view is that technology is applied science.[8] An inscription in the 1933 Chicago Century of Progress exposition summed up the credo of TD well: 'Science Finds, Industry Applies, Man [sic] Conforms' (Williams, 2000). Science is held to be concerned with the discovery of physical reality and thus be ultimately unaffected by society or culture. This view of scientific knowledge and the role it plays in shaping technology is not without some problems of its own. Suffice to say that there is by now a considerable body of scholarship showing that society and science are in practice so intimately interconnected that it makes no sense to consider the one as if it were 'external' to the other (e.g., Kuhn, 1970; Barnes, 1985; Barnes *et al.*, 1996; Woolgar, 1988). The rather narrow view of the role of knowledge is in many ways typical of TD's limited consideration of our core concepts, which can be said to result in a very partial view of technology and of the ways in which technological systems and devices participate in the organization of human activities.

As we have seen, technological determinists tend to talk about power, freedom, identity, inequality or insecurity mainly in terms of the intended or unintended *effects* of various technologies. You will probably recall the role the stirrup is said to have played in the creation of particular social relations and identities (knights, serfs) with their corresponding patterns of power and inequality in medieval Europe. You may also remember how these same patterns were undone – both in Europe and in Japan – by the introduction of even more effective technologies of warfare. Furthermore, as you are no doubt aware, hardly a day goes by without new claims being made concerning the critical role of various ICTs in bringing about greater worker empowerment (Peters, 1997), opportunities for forging new identities (online)[9] (Rheingold, 2000), or alternatively, as increasing job insecurity for both workers and managers (Rifkin and Heilbroner, 1996).

To counter the dominance of technological determinism, a number of alternative forms of explanation have been proposed, which we will consider in the next section.

CRITICAL PERSPECTIVES: TECHNOLOGICAL DETERMINISM

For those who remain unconvinced by technologically determinist accounts of the way the world works, TD's chief theoretical vice is the sin of reification, which, as you will recall from Chapter 6, describes the tendency to treat a human creation (say technology) as if it had an independent existence of its own rather than being the product of human thought and work. Critical approaches tend to regard talk of technology as an autonomous force in human affairs as suspect. Critics argue that TD theories amount to little more than highly convenient cover stories (Pippin, 1994). Indeed, as Daniel and Hogarth (1990) have shown, organizational changes resulting in job losses are less likely to be resisted by employees when they piggyback onto technological changes. As the eminent MIT computer scientist Joseph Weizenbaum (1984, p. 241) has put it: 'Today even the most highly placed managers represent themselves as innocent victims of a technology for which they accept no responsibility'. From a critical viewpoint then, TD is a political resource for justifying inequality and powerlessness in organizations and beyond. It allows, for instance, those who occupy positions of dominance in organizations and society to represent bad technological developments, as inherent in technological progress, rather than as social changes sponsored by, and of benefit to, themselves (Schaefer, 2003). Powerful organizational actors can thus denounce opponents of such technological projects and developments as enemies of progress ('Luddites') and therefore not worth listening to (e.g., Head, 2003).

By contrast, critical approaches tend to highlight the role of power relations and of inequality in their explanations of technological developments. They tend to reject the TD view that social science (including OB) should restrict itself to the identification and monitoring of the social and organizational adaptations necessary to smooth the path of technological advance. Instead, they argue, the social sciences should aim higher: they should investigate the reasons *why particular technologies take the form they do*.[10] It is not therefore accidental that, as we shall see below, attempts to develop a more critical perspective on matters technological have sought to expand social scientific investigations to domains commonly left to engineers and other technical experts.

The social shaping of technology

There is a Soviet-era Russian joke about the worker who would every day go past the factory gates pushing a wheelbarrow. The security guards would inspect the contents and finding it full of dirt would let him pass. The man, it turns out, was stealing wheelbarrows. Critics argue that like the factory guards of the tale, technological determinists focus on the wrong thing and thus miss what is really going on. By directing attention on technological 'impacts' – just one part of a far more complex whole – they fail to recognize the intricate ways in which social, organizational and cultural processes are shaping the technologies themselves.[11] The social shaping of technology (SST for short) perspective was therefore developed as a corrective to the prevailing notions of technological determinism. Roughly, SST researchers argue that the relationship between technology, organizations and society is not the unidirectional one portrayed in Figure 12.1, but rather the two-way process depicted in Figure 12.4. Thus, rather than impacting on organizations and society from the outside, technologies are themselves outcomes of the deep entanglement of technical, social and cultural processes.

What does it mean to say that 'technologies are socially shaped'? Let's consider a mundane example, buildings.[12] As Rapoport (1969) notes, the variety of building styles we can observe around us demonstrates that what and how we build cannot be explained solely in terms of technical factors such as extant technologies, available construction material, climate or the unchanging biological needs of humans.[13] While all these factors do limit our choices in important ways, for Rapoport the primary determinants of what and how we construct buildings are socio-cultural factors such as attitudes to the family, privacy, pollution and the social position of women. In northern Europe for instance, private houses tend to look out though windows and doors visible from the street,

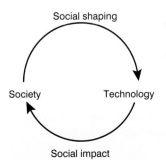

Figure 12.5
The social shaping of technology
Source: Reproduced by permission of SAGE publications, London, Los Angeles, New Delhi and Singapore, from Peter Dicken (2003), *Global Shift: Reshaping the Global Exonomic Map in 21st Century* fourth edn.

while in many other parts of the world we often encounter more 'inward' building styles where houses face towards an inner courtyard shielded from the street by a wall. Both building styles appear to have strong links with social attitudes, customs and religious beliefs concerning, for instance, the question of whether there is a need (or not) to protect the women of the household from the eyes of strangers. Our buildings are thus 'shaped' by our society and our culture (Dant, 1999).

Essentially, SST perspectives view technologies as the materialization of our social, economic and cultural arrangements. As such, technologies are not neutral but on the contrary mirror our society, reinforce and to some extent legitimize the dominant socioeconomic forms. As MacKenzie and Wajcman (1999, p. 5) put it: 'in adopting a technology we may be opting for far more – economically, politically, even culturally, as well as technically – than appears at first sight'.

Box 12.3
Key ideas in the social shaping of technology

- Technology is not separate from the rest of society; on the contrary, social, cultural and political issues are inherent in technology.
- Technology in other words, is just one aspect of the way we live socially (not unlike organizations, art or politics).
- Key question: how can we best identify the effects of social relations and institutions on particular technologies?

Case study 12.3
Numerically controlled machine tools

SST researchers seek to identify the ways in which relations of power and inequality can shape the direction and rate of innovation and the overall form of a technology. In his classic study on the development of automatically (numerically) controlled machine tools, David Noble (1999) has pointed out that the various impacts we commonly ascribe to this technology, such as increased industrial concentration (the high initial costs of automatic tools driving smaller metalworking firms out of business) and greater managerial control over the production process (numerical tools enabling management to bypass the machinist's skills altogether as the source of the production intelligence), are not the straightforward consequences of technological advance as the industrialists who promoted the technology in the name of 'progress' had claimed. Rather, he argues, the key question is why was this particular technological option chosen over other equally technically effective and economically viable alternatives? For instance, one alternative was record playback technology where the machine recorded and replicated the manual actions of a skilled machinist. Numerically controlled machines on the other hand control operations by means of elaborate mathematical programs. According to Noble, the reason automatically controlled tools were seen as preferable to record playback technology is that the latter entailed continued reliance upon the traditional machinist's knowledge and skills. In other words, Noble claims that automatically controlled tools were developed not primarily as a technology to improve metal cutting but as a management tool to decrease management dependence on the workforce. You may have noted the similarities here between Noble's view and Harry Braverman's (1974) thesis discussed earlier in this book. Two physicists promoting this technology in *Fortune* described the new tools' advantages in the following terms:

These devices are not subject to any human limitations. They do not mind working round the clock. They never feel hunger or fatigue. They are always satisfied with working conditions ... In short they cause much less trouble than humans doing comparable work (Cited in Noble, 1999, p. 118)

The technology was thus shaped by the preoccupation with promoting management control, a preoccupation that was if anything particularly prominent in the early post-war decades, further fuelled by fears that communist workers acting as Russian spies might steal sensitive blueprints.

Similarly, Cockburn's (1983) study of typesetting technology in Britain has described how in an effort to exclude female workers, men redesigned certain aspects of hand typesetting around the use of heavy mechanical equipment. This strategy rebounded however as male workers themselves were to find that this work was beyond their strength when they got older. The connection drawn by Noble, Cockburn and others between power and technology highlights how what might appear to be an inevitable product of technological progress – say automated machine tools – is itself a product and vehicle of very specific power relations.

For example, it may be in the interest of industrial capitalists to invent and introduce new generations of labour saving devices but not in the interest of workers. According to this view then, the reason 'technological progress' has not delivered the 15 hour working week predicted by Keynes (1930) but has instead institutionalized mass unemployment – whilst forcing those 'lucky' to (still) be in employment to work ever longer hours – has to do with the *particular* technological choices sponsored by powerful social actors.

For SST then, the key research question is precisely *how* and *why* particular technologies are adopted, refused or ignored in specific social and organizational contexts. As Ruth Schwartz-Cowan (1985) notes, many technically sound technologies have been abandoned for non-technical reasons, or rejected in favour of inferior ones: waterless toilets and central vacuum cleaners (self-cleaning rooms) being just a few examples of such technologies. She argues, for example, that the compression (electrical) fridge originally came to dominate the market at the expense of an alternative technology, the absorption (gas) refrigerator, not because it was technically superior (indeed, gas refrigerators were far less noisy, easier to maintain and had lower operating costs than their electric counterparts), nor even because consumers preferred one machine over the other, but because the production and marketing of electric fridges was backed by 'very large, very powerful, very aggressive and very resourceful companies', which the gas refrigerator companies were not. She draws attention to the fact that: 'the machine that was best from the point of view of the producer was not necessarily best from the point of view of the consumer' (ibid., p. 214).[14] The secret of the success of the electric fridge, in other words, was not that it was technically superior, but that it had powerful backers: the coalition of commercial interests backing it was stronger than the coalition of interests backing the gas refrigerator. Thus society ended up with a refrigerator that was more expensive to run and more prone to breakdowns.

It is clear from what has been said so far that SST constitutes an attack on the technological determinist view that technological developments are determined by technological superiority in a manner resembling a Darwinian 'survival of the fittest'. The notion that a given technology may triumph in the marketplace, not because it is technically better than its competitors but because it had the more powerful sponsors, should not come as a surprise to anyone who ever had to grapple with the MS-DOS operating system. MS-DOS which tyrannized generations of PC users, compared very unfavourably with other available operating systems (such as the one used in Apple computers). In fact, it has always been notorious for its user-unfriendliness. The general public, however, did not have much say in the matter since the vast majority of personal computers depended on MS-DOS. This dependence was the result of commercial agreements between powerful actors, such as IBM and a certain Bill Gates.

Thinkpoint 12.5

Environmentalists often blame the power of oil companies and other vested economic interests for society's failure to develop efficient non-fossil fuel energy technologies such as solar power. In your opinion, does SST provide support for this view? In what way might such 'vested interests' operate to prevent more environmentally friendly technological innovations?

Case study 12.4
Edison's invention

Increasingly, we encounter technological devices as parts of a whole system rather than as separate isolated objects. For example, for a washing machine to work, it must be successfully integrated into a functioning system of electricity supply, water supply and drainage (MacKenzie and Wajcman, 1999, p. 12). A washing machine taken away from this system has mainly curiosity value. A television that works perfectly well in the USA will probably be useless in Europe. The need for each device to integrate into the relevant system, then, imposes specific constraints upon design and use.

In fact, Thomas Hughes (1983) has argued that a successful invention is not simply the invention of a new device but rather of a new system. Thomas Edison, for example, did not conceptualize the (incandescent) light bulb as an isolated device but as part of a whole new system of electricity generation and distribution. It was the (commercial) requirements of that system that dictated the technical design of the light bulb. In fact, Edison publicly revealed his plans to bring electric lighting to New York homes more than a year before he had worked out the light bulb's technical design. Edison, in other words, first visualized the system of electricity generation and consumption as a whole, then sorted out the design of the light bulb that would best fit the requirements of that system. For instance, he recognized that in order to persuade the public to have electric rather than gas lighting in their homes, electricity needed to be at least as cheap as its main rival, gas. His key objective therefore was to minimize costs. Edison quickly realized that the high cost of copper conductors would significantly raise the price of electricity distribution. He thus set out to reduce copper usage by making the copper wires thinner and by seeking densely populated consumer areas, such as New York. However, the thinner the copper wires the higher the energy loss – a problem that he eventually overcame by increasing the resistance of the filament in the light bulb (Ohm's Law). Edison's commercial choices are thus embodied in the technical design of the light bulb we still use.

Ohm's Law describes the relationship between voltage and current in an ideal conductor and is given by $V = I \times R$ (where V is voltage, I is current and R is resistance).

According to Thomas Hughes, Edison's real invention (Case Study 12.4) was not the light bulb, as folklore would have it, but rather the electricity *system*. The phases in the history of this or any other socio-technical system he argues: 'are not simply sequential; they overlap and backtrack ... invention, development, innovation, transfer and growth, competition and consolidation, can and do occur throughout the history of a system *but not necessarily in that order*' (Hughes, 1987, pp. 56–7; emphasis added).

Of course, as Hughes notes, such systems hold together only so long as favourable conditions prevail. There is always the potential for a disastrous dissociation into their component parts. The stability of systems is frequently – as the travails of OLPC (relayed in Case Study 12.2) remind us – a rather precarious achievement. If the case made by Hughes, Schwartz-Cowan and other SST writers is accepted then we could argue that the traditional linear model, which, as we have seen in Figure 12.3, treats development–marketing–diffusion as separate stages in a one-way technologically determined process, is oversimplified and severely limited. In its place, SST research seems to suggest a spiralling socio-technical process, where crucial innovations take place not only at the design stage, but also in the implementation and use of technology, providing important feedback that helps shape future rounds of technological change (e.g., Hughes, 1987; Bijker, 1992).

Thinkpoint 12.6

Consider the automobile. What would you identify as the main components of the socio-technical system of the car?

If we shift our focus from the design of technological artefacts and technological systems to their use, we again find a more complex picture than the straightforward 'impacts' invoked by determinists.

> From the point of view of the users, technologies come with a set of properties crafted by designers and developers. ... However, *how* these properties will actually be used in any instance *is not inherent or predetermined*: rather it depends on what people do with them in particular instances. (Orlikowski, 2000; p. 409; emphasis added)

For instance, Japanese companies have been known to use machinery identical to their US competitors but to operate it 'in dramatically different ways' (Thomas, 1994, p. 233). Similarly, Robey and Sahay's (1996) study of geographic information systems has shown that organizations often use identical information systems in radically different ways (see also Barley, 1986). Orlikowski therefore asks us to focus on users' *practices* in order to better understand the ways in which particular technologies are '*enacted*' by their users in different organizational settings. 'We know that when people appropriate technologies into the workplaces, they end up using them in all sorts of ways that go way beyond what the designers ever anticipated' (Orlikowski, 1999).

SOCIAL SHAPING OF TECHNOLOGY: REVIEW AND IMPLICATIONS

It is clear from what has been said so far that SST constitutes an attack on all the central pillars of technological determinism. As we have seen, SST technology is *not* an autonomous causal force for change largely outside the realm of conscious organizational or social control (Thomas, 1994). SST proponents do not dispute that technologies play a significant role in social and organizational change. They argue however that social and organizational 'impacts' should not be understood as inevitable consequences of the technical characteristics of a given device. This is because technologies are not products of immaculate conceptions in research laboratories cut off from the social world, but are from their inception part of society. It is therefore not technological superiority pure and simple that makes a technology successful (UNPD, 2001). SST work shows that the life cycle of a technological device is as likely to be driven by an agenda of power and politics, which does not exclude the possibility that technologies may impact on society in unforeseeable ways. SST researchers do not deny that while technology may not be an external influence upon society, 'it is often *experienced* by people and organizations as an exogenous force' (Thomas, 1994, p. 8). For SST, however, the experience of technological determinism – that is the experience many people have of technology as something outside their control – is the experience of *powerlessness* over the nature and direction of technological change. Technology may indeed be 'socially shaped' but we must not forget that the opportunities to shape technology are not equally available to all.

It is easy to imagine what technological determinists might find wrong with SST. From the point of view of TD, social shaping research underplays the fact that technologies do exist 'out there' and do fundamentally constrain and transform the range of possible forms of organization in more or less predictable ways.

Beyond TD, however, the SST perspective has other critics who consider the following to be among its main weaknesses:

- That the SST approach's focus on social and economic interests as the key influences on the eventual shape of the technology leaves it ill-suited to explore the accidental, unintended and often contradictory nature of the social and institutional context within which technological and organizational changes take place.
- That, despite its good intentions, social shaping research has relatively little to say about the technical characteristics of the technologies it examines.

It might not come altogether as a surprise that, not unlike technological determinism, the social shaping of technology can also be said to be available in 'weak/soft' and 'strong/hard' variants. (Hard variants make stronger claims concerning the role of social factors in determining the technical content of a given technology.) So far we have mostly focused upon 'soft' SST. The next section discusses SST's 'strong(er)' variant, or to call it by its proper name, the social *construction* of technology.

Cartoon 12.1
Source: Copyright The Daily Telegraph.

The social construction of technology

We have seen in our discussion of SST that in any given situation there is often more than one way to design and construct a given technological device (e.g., a bridge, a refrigerator) or a technological process. The social construction of technology (SCOT) approach attempts to take this insight a step further, no longer speaking of the social *shaping* but of the social *construction* of technology. (You shape something that is already there but you construct something more or less from scratch.) This is clearly a much more radical claim than that of mainstream SST. The SCOT argument is that the technical characteristics of a given technology cannot be divorced from the interpretative frameworks that people use to make sense of what it is for or what a device can or cannot do.

SCOT in other words seeks to explain how and why specific technologies emerge and are adopted at particular times. It suggests that in order to understand what technologies an organization or society ends up with we need to study the meanings that the various technologies have for those social groups with a stake in their development, promotion and use. Advertisers of course never cease trying to persuade us that what we buy, whether clothes, mobile phones or magazines, expresses something important about our identity, our values and ourselves. It is a view deeply held among marketing professionals that we acquire particular products not just to use them but also in order to create meaning in our lives. Nevertheless, SCOT's central claim that the various socially constructed meanings of technological objects provide the key to understanding not only their uses but also their design and technical characteristics is for many rather hard to swallow. The role of meaning in SCOT therefore requires some elaboration. Our everyday understanding of 'meaning' is that it may be attached to technical devices but in no way affects their technical characteristics. Marketing practitioners may argue for instance that we associate sports cars with (male) sexual attractiveness. We can also readily accept that such interpretations may even influence design and use. For example, Peter Horbury, executive director of design at Ford, claims that a popular truck model originally failed to sell in China because the 'face of the vehicle had Western proportions. Raising the base of the windshield – which lessened the area occupied by its "eyes" – made an immediate difference [in sales]' *(Connect,* 2004, p. 1). Similarly, the spectacular marketing failure of the 1958 Ford Edsel has been attributed to the widespread perception among US (male) drivers that its grill 'looked like a vagina' (Wernwick, 1994). The Edsel was, in other words, a victim of male insecurities (see also Chapter 5).[15]

Figure 12.6
Like a Vagina?
Reproduced courtesy of edsel.Com

Clearly, we see technological devices not merely as functional objects but also as expressions of ourselves (e.g., Figure 12.5). Take a simple device, a chair. Chairs are clearly meaningful objects. They are also very visibly *shaped* by society in order to fulfil various functions and social roles. We have armchairs, dentist's chairs, rocking chairs and so on. A chair may be a mark of authority. Seating plans are often ways of acting out hierarchical relationships in organizations (Cranz, 1996). We normally have little trouble with the deciphering of the 'meaning' of a chair. A dentist's chair in the lounge would be as socially inappropriate (except as a joke) as a rocking chair at the dentist's. You immediately realize that armchairs in a seminar room are meant to put you at ease, while less supportive chairs mean you have to remain physically alert (Dant, 1999). But can we go further than that? Surely, one might object, all chairs share a basic 'technical design' reflecting straightforward physical requirements. Think about it. The way a chair is put together roughly reflects human anatomy (Scarry, 1985). Chair legs, for example, imitate your legs and are meant to bear your weight so your legs don't have to carry it. The back of the chair is meant to do the same for your back and so on. All perfectly straightforward?

Box 12.4
Key ideas in the social construction of technology

- Technology is but a set of solutions to the problems that a given society poses for itself.
- To understand technological developments, we need to study the social interpretations that have shaped the definitions of what problems can or should be solved by a given technology – and thus guided the choices made by the designers, manufacturers and users.
- Technical choices are not merely the application of an abstract techno-logic but are also vehicles for the expression of the world-views and ideologies of those social groups (including designers, opinion formers, users, non-users, etc.) that have a stake in the development of this particular technology.
- Technologies are therefore the offspring of conflict and compromise.
- Key question: how and why do technologies actually take the form they do? (In other words, how 'might [they] have been otherwise'?)

Thinkpoint 12.7

Afterthought 1

When asked to reflect on the career of the Programmable Subcutaneous Visible implant (PSVI, animated tattoo) a while ago, some of you may have concluded that the device was pointless, painful to install and why would anyone want it anyway. Let's not forget, however, that not too many years ago, the currently popular facial and body piercings and tattoos would have struck most observers as equally pointless and absurd (not to mention infection-prone). Nevertheless, their present popularity is good evidence that particular social groups now consider them meaningful expressions of their lifestyle and identity. Could this be where PSVI went wrong?

Afterthought 2

A similar, SCOT-influenced, answer one that emphasizes the *meaning* particular technologies hold for specific social groups, can be given to the questions asked in Thinkpoint 12.3 concerning the Henn-Na Robot Hotel. A constructivist analysis would place emphasis on the role of the hotel *as a theme park attraction*, not unlike Sleeping Beauty's Castle in Disneyland. They would thus seek to identify the human effort invested by the hotel's human staff (who have to check passports, do the cleaning, make the repairs, answer difficult questions and deal with awkward guests – e.g., see Rajesh, 2015). But also the self-service labours of hotel guests, which are equally necessary in order to realize the 'robot-hotel' experience for those who seek it, in order to live out, as it were, the technological fairy tale.

Figure 12.7 Meaningful devices: Manuela & Marcus forever

'Could it have been otherwise?' If one wanted to be awkward (or subscribed to SCOT) one could argue that historically speaking large sections of humanity – including Arabs, native Americans or the Japanese to mention but a few – did not use chairs nearly as much as we do. In these cultures the far more natural thing to do would have been to sit cross-legged on the ground on mats or cushions. In many ways this promotes a healthier body posture compared with the 'C' shape that most people almost automatically adopt when sitting on chairs. (Probably you too as you are reading these lines?) Furthermore, in many non-Western cultures squatting is regarded as a restful pose (Ingold, 1996). For most Westerners however, who have grown up in a world of chairs, this is a position they find painful to sustain over any length of time.

The question to ask then is why did those groups change their ways and embrace the chair (and sometimes a lifetime of back problems)? The answer probably lies in the cultural dominance of the West (Cranz, 1996). The sad truth was that if you wanted to be taken seriously by Westerners you had to sit like them, dress like them and behave like them, however inconvenient or nonsensical these habits might have been in the eyes of others. Thus the chair, SCOT writers would argue, is 'socially constructed'. Its commonsensical 'natural' status is an illusion (Bloomfield *et al.*, 2010, p. 421).

If this sort of argument is accepted, then it has implications for organized life that go far beyond the status of chairs. It implies for instance that an organization's technologies are more than merely functional devices but are also symbolic artefacts, which will incorporate, reflect and enforce particular assumptions and world-views. We have already had a hint of that for instance in the struggle (mentioned in Case Study 12.2) over whether OLPC's XO laptop computer should, or should not, incorporate Windows XP.

Case study 12.5
The bicycle

Consider the penny-farthing, a popular bicycle type of the Victorian era. To us the reasons for this popularity may be something of a mystery. In our eyes the high front wheeled penny-farthing may appear as a hilarious example of a design so bad that it is dysfunctional: difficult and dangerous to ride. What could these Victorians have been thinking off? A tempting answer would be to see the penny-farthing as an inept predecessor to the modern bicycle we all know and love. However, Pinch and Bijker (1984) in their influential account of the social construction of the bicycle, seek the answer in the study of the *relevant social groups* that were involved in 'negotiating' and 'stabilizing' the *meaning* of the bicycle. From the point of view of one such group – adventurous young men – the penny-farthing was essentially a sporting machine. The fact that it was difficult and hazardous to ride was for them part of its attraction:

Young and often upper-class men could display their athletic skills and daring by showing off in the London parks. To impress the rider's lady friends, the risky nature of the [penny-farthing] was essential. Thus the meaning attributed to the machine by ... [its] users made it the macho bicycle. (Bijker, 1995, p. 75)

In other words, we cannot understand the *technical* design of the penny-farthing unless we also understand its *cultural* connections with particular late-Victorian ideas about male (often upper-class) 'youth culture' and identity. It follows that for those social groups who did not share that culture or identity, the penny-farthing would have been a highly dysfunctional device. Its design functioned to exclude particular groups, including women (impossible to ride in a skirt) and the elderly. For Pinch and Bijker (1984) these people constitute another relevant social group – the 'non-users'. In the eyes of this group, the very same characteristics that made the penny-farthing attractive to the young 'macho' riders were reasons to avoid it. The machine 'was difficult to mount, risky to ride and not easy to dismount. It was in short the unsafe bicycle' (Bijker, 1995, p. 74). The 'macho bicycle' and the 'unsafe bicycle' are thus descriptions of the same machine. What were advantages from the viewpoint of one social group were disadvantages from that of the other:

The macho bicycle was ... radically different from the unsafe bicycle – it was designed to meet different criteria; it was sold, bought and used for different purposes; it was evaluated to different standards; it was considered a machine that worked whereas the unsafe bicycle was a non-working machine. (Bijker, 1995, p. 75)

**Figure 12.8
The Penny-Farthing – a difficult
design to understand**

The moral of the story then, is that the questions of whether a machine works or not or whether one technological device is superior to another are not straightforward technical matters as TD might lead us to expect, but are socially determined. Pinch and Bijker (1984) use the example of the penny-farthing to illustrate a key SCOT concept – that of the *'interpretative flexibility'* of technological devices. What it means in practice is that there tend to be as many different machines (macho bicycle, unsafe bicycle) as there are relevant social groups. That is why an engineering understanding can never be by itself sufficient, and what makes a social scientific investigation of how over time we might come to share a common interpretation of the artefact essential.

Here enters another set of key SCOT concepts: *closure* and *stabilization*. Bijker (1995, p. 270) describes them in terms of 'the process by which interpretative flexibility decreases, leaving the meaning attributed to the artefacts less and less ambiguous'. In the case of the penny-farthing (also known at the time as the 'ordinary bicycle'), social agreement (closure) was achieved and it was the non-working/'unsafe' and not the working/'macho' interpretation that stuck. As a result, the penny-farthing has now become a museum exhibit. The 'ordinary bicycle' is now considered to be extraordinary, a technological curiosity. 'Stabilization' is represented by another machine, called at that time the 'rear-driven safety bicycle'. This had not been conceived as a sports machine but as a means of transportation. It is now known simply as the bicycle.

Thinkpoint 12.8

Is the skateboard a kind of penny-farthing for the present age? Identify and make a list of the relevant social groups of the skateboard.

As Case Study 12.5 shows, the application of the SCOT analytical framework involves a number of key steps. The first involves the identification of the relevant social groups (RSGs) associated with, or which have had a stake in, the development and use of a given technology. SCOT argues that a new technology may mean different things to different social groups. More specifically, a device may be seen as a response to different problems, represent a variety of solutions and be associated with a range of social impacts. Hence we use the concept of 'interpretative flexibility'. This may be defined as the different meanings various relevant social groups give to a particular technology. For example, the views held by young clubbers on the properties of 'recreational' drugs may be very different from those held by parents, the medical profession or law enforcement authorities. When a technology is relatively new, there is a higher degree of flexibility in how people may think of it or interpret its artefacts and in how those artefacts are designed. It is not therefore surprising that if we go back far enough in the history of any technological process or device, we are likely to find interpretations of 'what this technology is for', and what it can and cannot do that may appear bizarre to us now.

For example, in his study of the history of radioactive waste,[16] Bruhèze (1992) describes how the Atomic Energy Commission's (ATC's) Division of Military Application considered radioactive waste, not as waste but rather as a useful by-product of the nuclear industry that could be used as raw material in weapons construction or in the irradiation of food. In the ATC's Division of Reactor Development, radioactive waste was perceived as an essentially economic problem (waste was expensive to store). The ATC's Division of Biology and Medicine saw it in terms of risks to human health while the ATC's headquarters considered radioactive waste to be a relatively normal problem, to be solved in due course through technological advances and therefore not requiring immediate attention. Even within the same organization then, different relevant social groups hold radically differing interpretations of the 'same' thing.

This interpretative flexibility associated with a technological innovation can be curtailed by various means, including force, agreement and compromise on a particular design, standard, or specification. 'Closure' may be reached in many different ways – including rhetorical closure where the relevant social groups perceive (or are persuaded) the problem as being solved; the obscuration of alternatives; the redefinition of the problem, and so on. Misa (1992, p. 109), for instance, defines 'closure' as 'the process by which facts or artefacts in a provisional state characterized by controversy are moulded into a stable state characterized by consensus (...) it is how artefacts gain their hardness and solidity'.

The decrease in interpretative flexibility typically leads to one variant of the technology becoming dominant (e.g., the 'rear-driven safety bicycle' becomes 'the bicycle'). The dominant artefact will then develop an increasing degree of stabilization within the various RSGs. Processes of closure are almost irreversible – but not quite. Clearly not all rival interpretations will necessarily vanish; instead we may see the development of distinct devices that meet different groups' needs. 'Closure' tends to be a two-sided process. It tends to involve the stabilization of both technological device *and* relevant social groups. As Bijker (1995, p. 273) argues, 'all stable [socio-technical] ensembles are bound as much by the technical as by the social'. Organizations and other social arrangements and institutions are stabilized by the technical means as much as they stabilize the technologies. 'The technical is socially constructed and the social is technically constructed (...) social classes, occupational groups, firms, profession, machines – all are held in place by intimate social and technical links' (ibid., p. 273).[17]

Exercise 12.1

Below you will find a brief description of a technology called AWOL™, which, its makers claim, can change the way alcohol is consumed. On the basis of this information, you are invited to consider whether you would recommend the installation of such a device in any of the following establishments:

- a 'hip' urban bar
- a traditional family pub or the Dog and Duck (discussed in Chapter 1)
- an 'ethnic' restaurant
- Bar Mar (discussed in Chapters 7 and 8).

AWOL™ (Alcohol With Out Liquid™) is a machine that mixes spirits with oxygen. A cloudy alcohol vapour is created that can be inhaled or snorted. As the makers of the device put it:

> Up the nose or breathe in the mouth, straight to the brain. Finally, a solution to the two greatest problems today's drinkers have: hangovers and calories. This is the dieter's dream, this is the Atkins diet alcohol and diabetes alcohol, low carbohydrates, low calorie and low sugar alcohol. The AWOL machine includes the hand held diffuser into which the booze of choice is poured; this, in turn, is connected to an oxygen generator the size of a school backpack. The drink is then snorted up the nose like a nasal decongestant or breathed through the mouth – instead of swallowed down the throat with a sweet mix like Cola or ginger ale.

Once inhaled, the alcoholic vapour enters the 'bloodstream to give an instant buzz'. Its promoters claim that the device offers among other things (source: **www.awolmachine.com**):

- A very mild way to enjoy the aromas and flavours of fruit-infused spirits.
- The Ultimate Facelift! Oxygen facials are the natural alternative to Botox and surgery, instantly reducing lines and wrinkles.
- The Ultimate Workout! Oxygen workouts will make your routine easier, improve your endurance, speed recovery and reduce post-workout stiffness.
- The Ultimate Urban Cure! Beat pollution and stress with extra oxygen. Nature's antidote for revitalizing, rejuvenating and re-energizing your mind and body.

On the other hand, a number of medical experts and alcohol concern groups have condemned AWOL™, fearing it is an unsafe machine that could lead to brain damage and have called for an investigation by the UK Trading Standards officers (e.g., *The Daily Telegraph,* 19 February 2004; BBC 2004b; *The New York Times* 2006; Glatter, 2013; Castillo, 2013). Indeed, AWOL has been banned in a number of US states: Arizona, California, Colorado, Connecticut, Florida, Idaho, Illinois, Indiana, Iowa, Kansas, Kentucky, Louisiana, Maine, Michigan, Minnesota, Nevada, New York, North Carolina, Ohio, Pennsylvania, South Carolina, Tennessee, Virginia and Wyoming.

Whether you remember the earlier discussion of SCOT or not, it is still likely that in attempting to answer the question you began by reflecting upon the *meaning* of this particular technology. Chances are that using the sparse cues provided in the above description, you set out to identify the relevant social groups – that are relevant to the various establishments – including publicans and different categories of drinkers and non-drinkers (e.g., students, families, diabetes sufferers, etc.) and the ways they may relate to the various 'technical' claims (and counter-claims) made about this machine. You may have considered how these groups of people do things and what the things they do mean to them. Are they potential as user or non-user groups? A family outing 'means' different things to the participants than a pub-crawl or a hen/stag party. You may have reflected for instance upon current drinking rituals and their place in what is understood as 'student behaviour' and (if you have read the rest of this book), upon how they ultimately figure in the construction of what we might call 'student identity'. Or more accurately the construction of a *particular* student identity – given that many students may not share it or wish to share it (more non-users?). However unsystematic, such musings are inescapably tied up to the interpretative flexibility that still characterizes this particular machine. We may speculate that were the machine to become successful, this interpretative flexibility would diminish. Perhaps one day it might appear as a self-evident piece of pub equipment as the beer pump looks now ('closure' and 'stabilization'). If it is unsuccessful, for instance through lack of interest or if 'closure' is achieved around the 'unsafe machine' interpretation instead, the machine may appear one day at least as bizarre in our eyes as the high-wheeled penny-farthing now does.

SOCIAL CONSTRUCTION OF TECHNOLOGY: REVIEW AND IMPLICATIONS

Social constructivists could be described as the 'radical wing' of SST (Pinch, 1998). SCOT is concerned to demonstrate how various social processes influence the technical characteristics of a technology. SCOT's key claim is that

Social constructivists or constructivists Those who adopt the constructivist approach.

the meanings of a technology, including the facts about how or whether it works, are socially produced. Hence, there is no such thing as a 'pure technology' developing under its own immanent logic independent of its creators' world-views, cultural assumptions, prejudices or biases. Rather, technological processes and devices are outcomes of social conflicts, negotiations and compromises. Clearly the meanings of a technology are not simply free-floating and random, but more often than not, are channeled through power relations. This channeling is especially evident in relation to organizations where there is contention as to which world-views or interpretive frameworks 'will be employed to guide the definition and choice of technologies' (Thomas, 1994, p. 212). SCOT thus provides a useful perspective on socio-technical change that allows us to highlight how culture, social arrangements and institutions – and the patterns of power, inequality and identity that comprise them – are important influences upon, or even constitutive of, technology. At the same time SCOT is subject to a number of different criticisms from both mainstream and critical perspectives:

- From a mainstream perspective, it is often argued that SCOT accounts over-stress social choice and human factors at the expense of technological ones. SCOT is thus accused of having *replaced technological with a social determinism.*
- For TD critics, SCOT is in fact pernicious, as it sets out to obscure the (to them) self-evident fact that the study of society may indeed be about differences in interests, values, world views and the like, but the study of technology is about indisputable facts and observable relationships (Thomas, 1994, p. 246). Furthermore, technologies are not infinitely plastic – technological design is constrained in fundamental ways by the physical, chemical, or in the case of software, logical properties of its material: 'We are not dealing with ectoplasm here nor the stuff that dreams are made of' (Miles, 1988, p. 1).
- From a critical viewpoint, SCOT is often seen as inattentive to the broader social context and the role of inequalities of power between social groups. For instance, how do particular groups become relevant? What of those social groups that do not have a voice?
- SCOT is also said to be inattentive to the social *consequences* of technological choices, including an apparent lack of concern for the ways in which we might judge whether particular technologies make the world better or worse.

From a number of critical points of view then, including that of many feminist, Marxist and post-colonial authors, SCOT appears politically disengaged, debilitating and insipid and of little use to those seeking to transform society and organizations. Some of these criticisms are more justified than others. The debate appears destined to run and run (for criticisms and responses see, for instance, Pinch, 1998; Grint and Woolgar, 1999). Over the last few decades, a number of researchers originally associated with SST/SCOT (such as Bruno Latour and John Law) have developed yet another theoretical alternative that is critical of both TD and SST/SCOT. This is commonly known as actor-network theory or actor-network analysis, and we will consider this next.

Actor-network theory

The third alternative to technological determinism is actor-network theory (ANT for short), from the viewpoint of which the arguments between TD, SST and SCOT over the role of technology in society and organizations are in essence chicken and egg debates: various perspectives propose different answers to the question of what comes first, the social chicken or the technological egg (Bromley, 1994). For ANT the solution is to stop viewing technology and society as two separate but related domains and see them instead as different *phases* in the same action. We cannot, ANT claims, draw hard and fast distinctions between what is social and what is technological in order to try and find out which one determines the other: the social and the technological already presuppose and contain one another. As MacKenzie and Wajcman (1999, p. 23) note, the various 'material resources – artefacts and technologies, such as walls, prisons, weapons, writing, agriculture – are part of what makes large scale society feasible. The technological, instead of being a sphere separate from society, is part of what makes society possible – in other words, it is constitutive of society'. We cannot, in other words, have a society without technology any more than we can have a technology without society.

Researchers, ANT insists, *should not* switch registers and use different types of explanation when they move from the analysis of the technical to that of the social aspects of the problem studied (Callon, 1986a, p. 200). They should in other words *resist* the temptation of providing (purely) social explanations (say in terms of social group interests, social values or cultural world-views) for social phenomena, while giving (purely) technical explanations (say in terms of physical or chemical) properties for technological ones. Instead, technological (and organizational) processes are both to be understood as processes of network building. Such networks are constructed through the enrolment of both human and non-human actors[18] by various means including negotiation and conscription. The idea of an actor-network then refers to the bringing together of various actors – whether human individuals, groups, technical standards, money or natural forces – whose *actions* are to be somehow aligned for a particular purpose. A car cannot function without roads, petrol stations, car mechanics, traffic codes or qualified drivers (recall Thinkpoint 12.6). Drivers need cars and cars require drivers. Petrol stations need roads and roads need petrol stations (Stalder, 2002). All these actors give one another specific identities and roles in the network. Each is influenced by, and in turn exerts influence upon, all other actors, playing an active part in the eventual outcome of every process of network building and maintenance. ANT is therefore the study of the creation, maintenance and demise of actor-networks. It makes the claim that the creation of both technology and organization (or for that matter society) involves the building of such heterogeneous networks (see Box 12.5).

Box 12.5
Key ideas in
actor-network theory

- The creation of both technology *and* organization involves the creation and maintenance of *heterogeneous* actor-networks involving both human and technological actors.
- 'Actors' therefore may be either persons or things. It should not matter to researchers whether the various actors assembled in a network (say cars, drivers, roads) should be classified as 'social' or 'technological'. What matters is such entities' ability to *act* on one another.
- Every technological device is dependent on a heterogeneous network that supports the specific ways in which this device is being used.
- The different elements in a technology's actor-network are held together by chains of 'translations'. Translations build actor-networks out of otherwise unrelated entities.
- Key question: how can we best explain the processes whereby such relatively stable networks of aligned actors are created, maintained and dissolved?

If what this 'actor-networking' entails is not altogether clear, then the example in Box 12.6 might help. Even in a relatively simple situation like the one described there, the *act* of 'switching off' the mobile phones of the audience is carried out (or resisted) by a number of different configurations of human and non-human actors (including lecturers, air-stewards, mobile users, texts, building materials, etc.). As we have seen, the various networks involve diverse acts of delegation between the human and non-human entities that comprise them. The delivery of an instruction for instance ('switch off your mobile'), can be delegated to a human actor, a written notice and so on. Similarly, the physical act of 'switching off' can be performed by a human actor or, alternatively, delegated to particular insulation materials. In fact, delegations to non-human actors are frequently initiated in order to overcome perceived deficiencies in human actors.

Box 12.6
Mobile phone troubles (2)

Suppose you were asked to devise a strategy for preventing the use of mobile phones in lectures. How would you proceed? Take a moment or two to devise your strategy.

Clearly there are many strategies you could adopt. Let's for the sake of simplicity discard from the outset those that are too unreasonable or intrusive to implement (such as employing staff – 'human actors' in ANTspeak – to search everyone at the door and confiscate their mobiles, a tactic used in prisons but which is clearly not suitable for deployment in the classroom or the theatre). Let us look instead at some of the strategies actually used in such situations. A notice on the door and/or in the student handbook to the effect that 'all mobile phones must be switched off' is by far the most typical of these. We will call this Strategy 1. It should be largely successful in 'enrolling' most mobile users. Everyone, that is, except the forgetful (such as Jackie in our Box 12.1 story), and those intent on contravening this regulation (such as Jon and Raj) who might put their phones on 'silent' and continue using them. Together, these two groups constitute what we might call 'anti-network 1' (see Figure 12.6).

Figure 12.9 Actor-networks and anti-networks

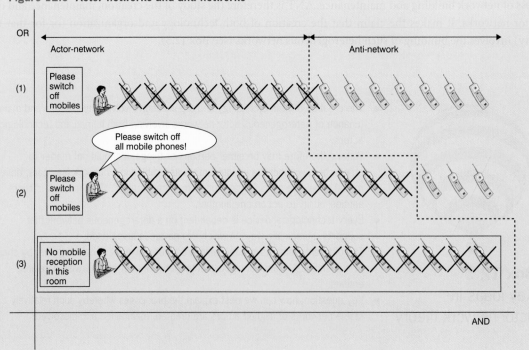

What can be done about them? The addition of a verbal reminder from the lecturer at the start of the session might take care of all but the most brazen and the extremely absent-minded (Strategy 2). This is the typical strategy used in, for instance, examinations in order to prevent cheating or disruption. This means that using your mobile is now not merely a distraction, likely to attract censorious looks, but an offence. The university disciplinary code can now be enrolled to discipline offenders. You will also find this strategy in use in air travel.

We have perhaps now reached the limit in terms of the number of mobile users we can enrol without employing more drastic measures and recruiting more powerful allies. Facing us is the real hard core of mobile users, perhaps including the type of person who will attempt to use a mobile during a flight. We could, of course, recruit further (non-human) allies to our cause. We could, for example, seek to insulate the room with material that would prevent the transmission of the signal – to cut off, so to speak, phone-from-phone network (Strategy 3). There is, for instance, special wallpaper containing a metallic mesh that will screen out mobile phone signals (e.g., Howell, 2004). When we employ this strategy, the task of 'switching off mobiles' is no longer performed by the users (the human actors) but is delegated instead to the insulating material (a non-human actor). This is a strategy that might prove useful in theatres, the opera or in other sites where it is considered worth making the investment in order to ensure that performers can perform their roles without distractions. (It is also a possibility in aircraft where, as we know, mobile usage might interfere with flight instruments.) There are reports, for instance, that a number of Chinese provinces have ordered the installation of 'mobile telephone blocking devices' around University entrance examination halls to prevent answers being sent in by text message (Spencer, 2006). Similarly, the French Ministry of Trade has authorized the installation of equipment in theatres and cinemas which is able to jam mobile phone calls in the premises while permitting emergency calls (Randall, 2004, p. 12). The three strategies described here and the actor-networks and anti-networks (enrolled versus resistant actors) are illustrated in Figure 12.6 (based on Akrich and Latour, 1992).

From an ANT perspective, a working technological device is dependent on the operations of the heterogeneous network that supports the ways in which that particular device functions (Callon, 1993). A working mobile phone, for example, presupposes functioning handsets, competent users, a telephone network plus a network of masts (in tall buildings or concealed behind billboards and petrol station signs) to supply coverage. It requires the signing of legal contracts and the establishment of business relationships between the user and the various organizations and institutions that provide coverage, sell upgrades, or are otherwise involved in the development, distribution and maintenance of the technology. Changes in actor-network are also changes in what a device does and how it is being used. The stabilization of a technological device is therefore at the same time as the stabilization of its actor-network. All this may sound rather esoteric but is well understood by those involved in the design, production or marketing of a device.

Consider the following example (quoted in Fox, 2003):

'Software which causes illegal copies of computer games to self-destruct has been unveiled. Just as the player gets hooked, fragments of a subversive code begin making it impossible to fire [weapons] or steer cars' (*Metro,* 9/10/03, p. 11). According to the developers, '[t]he beauty of this is that the degrading copy becomes a sales promotion tool. People go out and buy an original version.'

The software called Fade is therefore a new (non-human ally) in the struggle between two actor-networks. The legal network of game designers, manufacturers and retailers versus the 'piratical' one. The problem exercising the human members of the official actor-network is that of 'defection': games can be copied and used illegally. Copyright laws and law enforcement agencies have so far proved themselves weak allies in the prevention of such defections. The hope of the developers is therefore that Fade will prove a more effective ally in this struggle. Not only will the defection of the product be prevented but also illegal users, once suitably hooked, may themselves desert the piratical for the legitimate network. Is this then the ultimate 'technical fix' to the longstanding 'problem' of software piracy? A note of caution is in order. The 'pirates' are not themselves devoid of potential technological allies. Indeed, a quick Internet search will show a wide range of software products and fixes dedicated to the disablement of the anti-copying features of commercial software, including video games and DVDs. The tug-of-war goes on.

Thinkpoint 12.9

The following story was circulated by the Reuters news organization on 1 April 2001:

> Police in Amsterdam, the Netherlands, sick and tired of cell phone thefts, have launched a new weapon against the culprits. As soon as thefts are reported, stolen phones are sent a Short Message System text message every three minutes noting 'This device is pinched. Purchase or sale is an offence', and signing the note 'the police'. A police spokesman admitted 'the idea is to drive the thieves mad' and make the phones virtually unusable.

What would an actor-network account of this technology look like? Do you think or can you think of any strategies or devices that can prevent or impede the 'defection' of *your* mobile?

The 'social' and 'technological' elements of a technology's actor-network are tied together by processes of translations.[19] In translations one actor assigns another actor a new identity, a new role to play or new projects to carry out in order to reach its own goal, which however may change in the course of the translation process (Stalder, 2002). Translation can be analyzed by means of a number of interrelated concepts, which, for reasons of simplicity, are presented here as sequential 'moments' in a serial process[20] (Latour, 1987; Grint and Woolgar, 1999):

- *Problematization.* Where the 'problem' that a technological device is meant to address is re-defined in terms of the solution one wants to promote.
- *Interessment.* The drumming-up of interest as those who profess a particular solution seek to persuade others that the solution to their *own* problems lies with the enrollers. It aims towards the (gradual) dissolution of existing networks and their ultimate replacement by the new network.
- *Enrolment.* Represents the stage whereby various agencies and actors become tied in to the means of producing particular solutions and come to occupy specific roles in the emerging network. Whether through coercion, seduction or consent, the new network is starting to achieve a common identity.
- *Mobilization.* The mobilization of the enrolled members of the network towards the objectives, while sustaining commitment and making withdrawal difficult.

Some of this terminology may be rather unfamiliar but its meaning is straightforward enough. Take for example the case of AWOL™ discussed in the previous section. Recall what *problem* the machine is supposed to address: 'Finally, a solution to the two greatest problems today's drinkers have: hangovers and calories' (www.awolmachine.com). To the extent that the backers of AWOL™ are successful in arousing *interest* in their machine and in persuading others (e.g., drinkers, publicans, licensing authorities) that yes, this *is* the solution to their (perceived) problems, then *enrolments* will take place. Success in actor-networking rests on the ability to translate (reinterpret, represent or re-appropriate) others' interests to one's own: e.g., buying or using *my* machine means that for *you* the era of the head-splitting hangover and the beer-gut are at an end. This trick crucially relies on the enrollers' ability to prevent *different* definitions of the situation from effecting alternative translations of the machine in question (e.g., 'this could lead to brain damage'), thus preventing enrolment or causing defections from the emerging network. Finally, a successful *mobilization* would see the machines installed in the establishments run by those who are enrolled and customers using them such that profits could be generated: the reward due to successful translators-entrepreneurs. Alternatively, if the network fails to come together – say publicans are afraid of incurring moral disapproval or being sued and/or drinkers are indifferent – then the machine joins the Programmable Subcutaneous Visible Implant in the Hall of Fame of technological curiosities.

A central concern of ANT has been to stress the contingent nature of networks and network-building (Grint and Woolgar, 1999). Actor-networks can be fragile and the translations they effect precarious. How can networks gain stability and obduracy?

The ANT concept of 'irreversibility' attempts to describe how translations are made durable over time and able to resist assaults from alternative translations. For example, Bruno Latour (1988b, pp. 36–37) tells the tale of how, in early twentieth century Paris, the privatization of the metro system was successfully thwarted by the radical Paris government. The solution the Paris government came up with was to reconstruct the subway tunnels making them too small for the rail coaches of the commercial operators:

> They shifted their alliance from legal or contractual ones, to stones, earth and concrete. What was easily reversible in 1900 [i.e., contractual obligations and social commitments] became less and less reversible as the subway network grew. The engineers of the Railway Company now took these thousands of tunnels built by the Subway Company as destiny and as an irreversible technical constraint.

Thus the takeover was prevented and the actor-network gained a new obduracy with the Paris government's (contingent) political control being made permanent.

For ANT, power is exercised through the construction and maintenance of actor-networks (Law, 1986a, 1986b). Actors typically construct 'programmes of action' (Akrich and Latour, 1992) perhaps with the intention of maximizing the number of actors that behave in a prescribed way (Underwood, 1999). Some actors, however, may resist this by generating and following 'anti-programmes' (see Figure 12.6). It is clear that the success or failure of actor-networking projects crucially depends upon the ability of a technological device to cope with the variety of users and user environments. ANT thus pays particular attention to the ways technological devices are designed in order to elicit specific behaviour from their users. The concept employed by ANT to describe the behaviour expected from people by specific technical devices is that of the 'script': 'Like a film script technical objects define a framework of action together with the actors and the space in which they are supposed to act' (Akrich, 1992, p. 208).[21]

The 'scripts' of some devices may be fairly simple. For example, 'child resistant closures' (CRCs – i.e., the 'child-proof packaging used for medications and other hazardous substances), use scripts that adults can perform relatively easily but children cannot. For instance, young children are said to be unable to perform two different motions simultaneously such as pushing down and turning a bottle top. At the same time there is always the possibility of a bad fit between the script of a device and some groups of actors. To stick with the CRC example, there is evidence that the elderly and the infirm (heavy users of CRC packaged medications) often have difficulty in performing the actions or exerting the amount of force required by this 'script' (Winder et al., 2002). Such users may in turn refuse to follow the script and attempt to evade it by, for instance, transferring the contents into non-CRC containers – thus unwittingly making them accessible to children (BBC News, 2004a; Sheffield University Packaging Research Group, n.d).

Clearly, more complex technologies will require their users to perform much more elaborate scripts. Enterprise resource planning (ERP) systems for instance, are mostly off-the-shelf computer packages that currently comprise the IT infrastructure in many contemporary organizations – including most *Fortune* 500 companies (Kumar and van Hillegersberg, 2000; Knox et al., 2012). ERP systems aim to integrate all major business functions (including production, finance, sales, human resource management) across the organization. A single ERP system can (in theory) meet the information needs of an organization replacing a wide range of legacy systems. However, in order to be able to construct this kind of package it is necessary to define in advance and standardize (script) elaborate procedures to be followed in the performance and documentation of organizational tasks (Kallinikos, 2004). Deviation from the correct 'script' can easily disrupt the operation of the system (e.g., Knox et al., 2008). An organization therefore does not merely buy, but also buys into an ERP system. Although such 'scripting' is said to represent the industry best practice for each particular process designed into the system, it can also cause problems, particularly in areas of the world with business practices that are different to the USA and Europe where most systems originate. For example, in a study of ERP use in a Middle Eastern manufacturing company, El-Sayed and Westrup (2003) found that haggling over prices was commonplace and valued customers expected prices *not* to be fixed until after the receipt of goods. This was not a notion of business supported by the company's ERP system so staff only entered sales order data *after* payment was received so that they could then create an invoice that satisfied the ERP system. Company accountants had in other words found a way to evade the ERP script in order to preserve established practices.

Actor-network theory: Review and implications

Actor-network theory helps us understand the course of technological *and* organizational innovations (these are but different *phases* in the same action). Actor-network theory proposes that technologies and organizations are both enacted through networks of actors (where the actors can be both human and non-human). ANT allows us to investigate issues such as 'How did it come to turn out this way?' (through the changing alliances of [heterogeneous] actors), 'Who is influencing it?' (who has been doing what scripting?) or 'Why are some actors acting this way?' (what scripts are they enacting?). These are not questions with deterministic answers but allow a rich interpretation of the situation (Underwood, 1999). On the other hand, ANT has had its fair share of criticism, with the following being among the most common:

- ANT has been criticized for generating jargon-ridden accounts that describe but do not explain. ANT analysis is said to offer a 'homogenous model, where everything is part of everything else and mutual influence is effective everywhere at once, [which] may be less misleading, but at the cost of offering little guidance: how do you proceed and where do you look first?' (Bromley, 1994, p. 14).

- One symptom of ANT determination to make no analytical distinctions between human actions and the behaviour of objects is, as we have seen, the symmetrical treatment of human and non-human 'actors'. Critics find this intellectually and morally problematic, as reducing people to the status of objects (e.g., Collins and Yearley, 1992a, 1992b). While this flattening of human/non-human differences might make analytical sense it is not without political implications.

- ANT, critics have argued, seems to view and describe 'networks' from the standpoint of the manager, the innovator, the victor, the entrepreneur. From a critical viewpoint then, ANT has been criticized as 'apolitical' or even insensitive to those social structures and institutional sources of power and inequality and oppression – such as gender inequalities (see Chapter 5) – which severely limit the spectrum of social actors' choices and behaviours.

At the same time we need to acknowledge that ANT is not a stable body of knowledge that can be used in an unproblematic way, but still very much a work in progress, subject to regular revision (and even criticism) by its developers.[22] Unavoidably then, many of the above criticisms have different applicability for different ANT authors.

Exercise 12.2

Revisit the case of OLPC and of the XO laptop computer briefly described in Case Study 12.2. How would you describe the OLPC actor-network? What would an Actor-Network analysis highlight as key issues in the project's troubles?

(For additional information see Kraemer, K., Dedrick, J. and Sharma, P. (2009) 'One laptop per child: vision vs reality', *Communications of the ACM,* 52(6): 66–73 also available at **http://cacm.acm.org/magazines/2009/6/28497-one-laptop-per-child-vision-vs-reality/fulltext**. See also the project website at **http:// laptop.org/en/**).

Conclusion

The role technologies play in the ways we organize our affairs is a topic that can provoke heated discussions. The aim of this chapter has been to selectively present the main interpretative frameworks that provide the 'toolkit' for both mainstream and critical investigations of this topic. In the mainstream literature, the influence of technological determinism has long been dominant. As a result, much of what has been written about technology and organizational behaviour has often tended to focus on the power of technology to determine what happens in organizations and society. Social shaping, social constructivism and actor-network theory have also had their share of influence on critical approaches concerned with the ways technology can become a vehicle for relations of domination in the workplace and elsewhere.

It should by now be apparent that these 'toolkits' can be used to construct a variety of stories about technology. What stories we choose to tell about this topic *is* important because stories about technology are never just that. They are also stories about human behaviour and have implications for the ways we act in the world. What do these stories tell us? Do they tell us that technology determines the ways we organize and co-ordinate our activities or even the ways we live our lives? Or do they tell us that we have the freedom to do things differently, to do technology differently? To what extent and in what way does our identity, our vision of who 'we' are, influence what technologies we end up with? What do these different stories hide, obscure or leave unsaid?

Perhaps there are no single answers to such questions. All the frameworks reviewed in this chapter have their strengths and weaknesses and we have devoted some space to discussing those. It may well be that our understanding of the topic would be unduly limited if our knowledge was restricted by the viewpoint afforded by a single theory. Maybe we need to consider such issues from *multiple* perspectives. Perhaps again, this is a piece of advice that is easy to dispense but less easy to follow.

Discussion questions

1   Go back to the list you were asked to compile in the opening section of this chapter (p. 447) of those future technological developments that you thought will most affect your life. Review the answers you gave to the questions about who/what have control over or bear responsibility for those technologies. Did the reading of this chapter cause you to revise your answers and if so in what way?

2   What do you understand by the term 'technological determinism'? What are the main strengths and limitations of that approach to understanding the role technologies play in the ways we organize our activities?

3   What does it mean to say that a technology is 'socially shaped'? Illustrate your answer with examples.

4   What does it mean to say that a technology has been 'socially constructed'? In what way – if at all – does 'social construction' differ from 'social shaping'?

5   What do you understand by the term 'actor-network' and how can a 'theory' based on this concept help us better understand technology? Illustrate your answer with examples.

6   What, in your view, is the best theoretical approach to understanding the role that *management* plays in deciding what technologies we get and how they are implemented? Illustrate your answer with examples.

7   In your judgement, which of the theoretical approaches outlined in this chapter best helps us understand the role of technology in relations of power and inequality?

8   Take a technology with which you are familiar (say music downloading). Then pick *two* of the frameworks presented above and try to sketch out what an analysis of this technology conductive from these two different perspectives might look like. For instance, which aspects of this technology each approach focuses on.

Further reading

Mainstream approaches

Recent examples of work heavily influenced by TD include Ford (2015) *The Rise of the Robots – Technology and the Threat of a Jobless Future* (Basic Books); Brynjolfsson and Mcafee (2016) *The Second Machine Age* (W. W. Norton & Company); Brynjolfsson and Saunders (2013) *Wired for Innovation: How Information Technology Is Reshaping the Economy* (MIT Press) all very readable accounts of how technology is transforming work organization, the economy and society. Brynjolfsson and Mcafee (2011) *Race Against the Machine: How the Digital Revolution is Accelerating Innovation, Driving Productivity, and Irreversibly Transforming Employment and the Economy* (Digital Frontier Press) is a shorter version of the same argument. An earlier contribution from a TD perspective can be found in Evans and Wurster's (1997) article 'Strategy and the new economics of information', *Harvard Business Review*, September–October, 71–84. A decidedly more pessimistic take on the same developments can be found in Rifkin and Heilbroner (1996) *The End of Work: The Decline of the Global Labor Force and the Dawn of the Post-Market Era* (J. P. Tarcher). Among the most influential mainstream texts in recent times has been Hammer and Champy's (1993) *Re-engineering the Corporation: A Manifesto for a Business Revolution* (Nicholas Brealey). The gist of their argument can be found in Mike Hammer's (1990) 'Re-engineering work: Don't automate, obliterate', *Harvard Business Review*, July–August, 104–112.

Alternative approaches

An alternative perspective on these same developments can be found in Soshana Zuboff's (1989) *In the Age of the Smart Machine*. Zuboff's argument is closer to 'social shaping' approaches to the role of technology in that she puts emphasis on the role that managerial choices play in determining the role of technology in organizations. Among the classic studies of the shaping role of managerial choices and (through them power and inequality) in determining the characteristics of a technology is David Noble's classic, article 'Social choice in machine design: The case of automatically controlled machine tools' in D. MacKenzie and J. Wajcman (eds) (1999) *The Social Shaping of Technology* (Open University Press). Harry Collins' and Trevor Pinch's (1998) *The Golem at Large* (Cambridge: Cambridge University Press) contains a number of very readable empirical studies from a SCOT perspective. For those in search of a more demanding read, check out Wiebe Bijker's and John Law's (eds) (1992) *Shaping Technology/Building Society* (MIT Press), which contains a range of empirical explorations of SCOT and related matters.

For an introduction to the actor-network approach, see Bruno Latour (1988a) 'Mixing humans and non-humans together: The sociology of a door-closer', *Social Problems*, 35, pp. 298–310. For demonstrations of how ANT might be used in empirical work, see Barbara Czarniawska and Tor Hernes (eds) *Actor-Network Theory and Organizing* (Copenhagen Business School Press). For those in search of something shorter and less demanding, Felix Stalder's (2002) 'Failures and successes: Notes on the development of electronic cash', *The Information Society*, 18(3), pp. 209–219, is another good illustration of ANT-influenced empirical work.

For an overview of the different approaches to technology see the different contributions to William Dutton (ed.) (1996) *Information and Communication Technologies: Visions and Realities* (Oxford University Press). See also the introduction to Donald MacKenzie and Judy Wajcman (eds) (1999) *The Social Shaping of Technology* (various editions, Open University Press). Keith Grint and Steve Woolgar's (1999) *The Machine at Work* (Polity) is another interesting, albeit more demanding overview – this time with a constructivist flavour. For ANT, see Bruno Latour's (2005) *Reassembling the Social: An Introduction to Actor-Network-Theory* (Oxford: Oxford University Press).

For an overview of current thinking on, and debates about, technology see the January 2010 special issue of the *Cambridge Journal of Economics* Volume 34 Issue 1.

For an overview and discussion of the role of information technology in social life contemporary organizing see Jannis Kallinikos's (2007) *The Consequences of Information: Institutional Implications of Technological Change* (Edward Elgar).

Important empirical studies
Technological determinism

Woodward, J. (1980) *Industrial Organization: Theory and Practice,* Oxford: Oxford University Press.

Hammer, M. and Champy, J. (1993) *Reengineering the Corporation: A Manifesto for Business Revolution,* London: Nicholas Brealey.

Frey, C. B. and Osborne, M. (2015) *Technology at Work: The Future of Innovation and Employment*, Oxford Martin School & Citi Bank.

Social shaping of technology

MacKenzie, D. and Wajcman, J. (eds) (1999) *The Social Shaping of Technology,* second edn, Milton Keynes: Open University Press.

Zuboff, S. (1989) *In the Age of the Smart Machine: The Future of Work and Power,* New York: Basic Books.

Social construction of technology

Bijker, W. (1995) *Of Bicycles, Bakelites, and Bulbs: Towards a Theory of Sociotechnical Change,* Cambridge, MA: MIT Press.

Collins, H. and Pinch, T. (1998) *The Golem at Large,* Cambridge: Cambridge University Press.

Actor-network theory

Latour, B. (1996) *Aramis, or The Love of Technology,* Boston, MA: Harvard University Press.

Law, J. (1994) *Organizing Modernity,* Oxford: Blackwell.

Useful websites

http://www.wired.com/
Wired magazine is a good source of technologically deterministic reflections on 'cutting edge' technological developments.

http://www.lancs.ac.uk/fass/centres/css/ant/ant.htm
You can find additional information about SST, SCOT and ANT – including frequently asked questions and further readings at Centre of Science Studies (CSS) website.

http://www.bruno-latour.fr/
For more on actor-network theory and its recent evolution, Bruno Latour's website has a number of accessible articles and opinion pieces on the topic. See also John Law's webpage:

http://heterogeneities.net/

References

Aaronson, B. and Osmond, H. (eds) (1971) *Psychedelics: The Uses and Implications of Hallucinogenic Drugs,* Boston: Schenkman Publishing.

Agre, P. (2000) 'Welcome to the Always-On World', *IEEE Spectrum Online.* Online at: www.spectrum.ieee.org.

Akrich, M. (1992) 'The description of technical objects', in W. Bijker and J. Law (eds) *Shaping Technology/Building Society,* Cambridge, MA: MIT Press, pp. 205–222.

Akrich, M. and Latour, B. (1992) 'A summary of a convenient vocabulary for the semiotics of human and nonhuman assemblies', in W. Bijker and J. Law (eds) *Shaping Technology/Building Society,* Cambridge, MA: MIT Press.

Albrecht, K. and McIntyre, L. (2005) *Spychips: How Major Corporations and Government Plan to Track Your Every Move with RFID,* Nashville, TN: Nelson Current.

Baker, S. (2008) *The Numerati,* London: Jonathan Cape.

Barley, S. R. (1986) 'Technology as an occasion for structuring: Evidence from observations of CT scanners and the social order of radiology departments', *Administrative Science Quarterly,* 31: 78–108.

Barnes, B. (1985) *About Science,* London: Basil Blackwell.

Barnes, B., Bloor, D. and Henry, J. (1996) *Scientific Knowledge: A Sociological Analysis,* London: Athlone Press.

BBC News (2004a) 'Child-proof packs baffle adults', 25 April, available at http://news.bbc.co.Uk/l/hi/health/3652607.stm.

BBC News (2004b) 'Inhaling alcohol may "harm brain"', 16 February. Online at: http://news.bbc.co.uk/1/hi/england/bristol/3493487.stm.

Belkin, D. (2015) 'Cracking down on skipping class: high-tech trackers aim to boost attendance, as colleges seek higher graduation rates' *The Wall Street Journal,* 14 January. Online at: http://www.wsj.com/articles/cracking-down-on-skipping-class-1421196743.

Bennett, W. (2004) 'Expert who told Bond to hang up his "lady's gun"', *The Daily Telegraph,* 6 September, 6.

Bijker, W. (1992) 'The social construction of fluorescent lighting or how an artifact was invented in its diffusion stage', in W. Bijker and J. Law (eds) *Shaping Technology/Building Society,* Cambridge, MA: MIT Press.

Bijker, W. (1995) *Of Bicycles, Bakelites, and Bulbs: Towards a Theory of Sociotechnical Change,* Cambridge, MA: MIT Press.

Bijker, W. and Law, J. (1992) 'Postscript: Technology, stability and social theory', in W. Bijker and J. Law (eds) *Shaping Technology/Building Society,* Cambridge, MA: MIT Press.

Blauner, R. (1964) *Alienation and Freedom: The Factory Worker and His Industry,* Chicago, IL: Chicago University Press.

Bloomfield, B. P. and Vurdubakis, T. (1994) 'Boundary disputes: Negotiating the boundary between the social and the technical in IT systems development', *Information Technology and People,* 7(1): 9–25.

Bloomfield, B. P. and Vurdubakis, T. (2008) 'IBM's chess players: On artificial intelligence and its supplements', *The Information Society,* 24(2): 69–82.

Bloomfield, B. P., Latham, Y. and Vurdubakis, T. (2010) 'Bodies, technologies and action possibilities: When is an affordance?', *Sociology,* 44(3): 415–433.

Braverman (1974) *Labor and Monopoly Capital,* New York: Monthly Review Press.

Bromley, H. (1994) 'The Social Chicken and the Technological Egg', paper presented at the American Research Association Annual Meeting, April.

Bruhèze, A. de la (1992) 'Closing the ranks: Definition and stabilization of radioactive waste in the US Atomic Energy Commission, 1945–1960', in W. Bijker and J. Law (eds) *Shaping Technology/Building Society,* Cambridge, MA: MIT Press, pp. 140–174.

Brynjolfsson, E. and Mcafee, A. (2011) *Race Against the Machine: How the Digital Revolution is Accelerating Innovation, Driving Productivity, and Irreversibly Transforming Employment and the Economy*, Digital Frontier Press.

Brynjolfsson, E. and Mcafee, A. (2016) *The Second Machine Age,* second edn, New York: W. W. Norton & Company.

Brynjolfsson, E. and Saunders, A. (2013) *Wired for Innovation: How Information Technology Is Reshaping the Economy*, Cambridge, MA: MIT Press.

Cairncross, F. (1998) *The Death of Distance: How the Communications Revolution Will Change Our Lives,* London: Orion Business Books.

Callon, M. (1986a) 'Some elements of a sociology of translation: Domestication of the scallops and the fishermen of St Brieuc Bay', in J. Law (ed.) *Power, Action and Belief,* London: RKP.

Callon, M. (1986b) 'The sociology of an actor network', in M. Callon and J. Law (eds) *Mapping the Dynamics of Science and Technology,* London: Macmillan.

Callon, M. (1993) 'Variety and irreversibility in networks of technique conception and adoption', in D. Foray and C. Freemann (eds) *Technology and the Wealth of Nations,* London: Pinter.

Cameron, E. (ed.) (1999) *Early Modern Europe,* Oxford: Oxford University Press.

Carr, N. (2008) 'Is Google Making Us Stupid?', *The Atlantic* 301(6). Available at http://www.theatlantic.com/magazine/archive/2008/07/is-google-making-us-stupid/6868/.

Carr, N. (2010) *The Shallows: How the Internet is Changing the Way We Think, Read and Remember,* London: Atlantic Books.

Castillo, M. (2013) 'Inhaling alcohol vapor puts you at risk of overdose', CBS NEWS June 5. Online at: http://www.cbsnews.com/news/inhaling-alcohol-vapor-puts-you-at-risk-of-overdose/.

CNN Money (2015) 'Stephen Hawking: Technology is making inequality worse'. Online at: http://money.cnn.com/2015/10/12/news/economy/stephen-hawking-technology-inequality/index.html.

Cockburn, C. (1983) *Brothers: Male Dominance and Technological Change,* London: Pluto Press.

Collins, H. and Yearley, S. (1992a) 'Epistemological chicken', in A. Pickering (ed.) *Science as Practice and Culture,* Chicago, IL: Chicago University Press, pp. 301–326.

Collins, H. and Yearley, S. (1992b) 'Journey into space', in A. Pickering (ed.) *Science as Practice and Culture,* Chicago, IL: Chicago University Press, pp. 369–389.

Connect (2004) 'When cars become human', 65(5) January: 1–2.

Cranz, G. (1996) 'The Social Purpose of Chairs: Maintaining Hierarchy in Ancient Societies and Contemporary Institutions', paper presented at the AASA Conference, New York, August.

Daniel, W. W. and Hogarth, T. (1990) 'Worker support for technical change', *New Technology, Work and Employment,* 5: 85–93.

Dant, T. (1999) *Material Culture in the Social World,* Milton Keynes: Open University Press.

Darby, D. (2001) *How the Stirrup Changed Our World,* unpublished manuscript, Darby Consulting Group LLC.

Davidow, W. and Malone, M. (1992) *The Virtual Corporation,* New York: HarperCollins.

Dicken, P. (2003) *Global Shift: Reshaping the Global Exonomic Map in 21st Century,* fourth edn, London, Los Angeles, New Delhi and Singapore: SAGE Publications.

Ellul, J. (1967) *The Technological Society* (trans. John Wilkinson), New York: Vintage.

El-Sayed, H. and Westrup, C. (2003) 'Egypt and ICTs: How ICTs bring national initiatives, global actors, and local companies together', *Information Technology and People,* 16(1): 76–92.

Evans, P. and Wurster, T. (1997) 'Strategy and the new economics of information', *Harvard Business Review,* September–October: 71–84.

Evans, P. and Wurster, T. (2000) *Blown to Bits,* Boston, MA: Harvard Business School Press.

Finnegan, R. (1975) 'Communication and technology', in *Open University Course D101: Making Sense of Society* [Unit 8 of Block 3 Communication] Milton Keynes: Open University Press.

Ford, M. (2015) *The Rise of the Robots – Technology and the Threat of a Jobless Future,* New York: Basic Books.

Ford, M. (2016) 'We are completely unprepared for the robot revolution', *Financial Times,* 3 May: 11.

Fox, A. (1974) *Man Mismanagement,* London: Hutchinson.

Fox, B. (2003) '"Subversive" code could kill off software piracy', *New Scientist,* 10 October. Available at: http://www.newscientist.com/news/print.jsp?id=ns99994248.

Frey, C. B. and Osborne, M. (2015) *Technology at Work: The Future of Innovation and Employment,* Oxford Martin School & Citi Bank.

Friedman, T. (2005) *The World Is Flat: A Brief History of the Globalized World in the 21st Century,* Harmondsworth: Penguin.

Froomkin, M. (2000) 'The death of privacy?' *Stanford Law Review,* 52: 1461–1543.

Garfinkel, S. (2001) *Database Nation: The Death of Privacy in the 21st Century,* Sebastopol, CA: O'Reilly.

Glatter, R. (2013) 'The dangers of "smoking" alcohol', *Forbes,* June 21: Online at: http://www.forbes.com/sites/robertglatter/2013/06/21/the-dangers-of-smoking-alcohol/#58d81e447fd5.

Greenfield, S. (2008) *ID: The Quest for Identity,* London: Sceptre.

Grint, K. (1994) 'Reengineering history', *Organization,* 1(1): 179–202.

Grint, K. and Woolgar, S. (1997) *The Machine at Work,* Cambridge: Polity.

Hammer, M. and Champy, J. (1993) *Reengineering the Corporation: A Manifesto for Business Revolution,* London: Nicholas Brealey.

Head, S. (2003) *The New Ruthless Economy: Work and Power in the Digital Age,* Oxford: Oxford University Press.

Holmes, R. (1988) *The World Atlas of Warfare: Military Innovations That Changed the Course of History,* London: Viking.

Howell, J. (2004) 'Why wallpaper does a cracking good job', *The Sunday Telegraph (House and Home),* 8 August: 6.

Hughes, T. P. (1983) *Networks of Power: Electrification in Western Society, 1880–1930,* Baltimore, MD: Johns Hopkins University Press.

Hughes, T. P. (1987) 'Edison and electric light', in D. MacKenzie and J. Wajcman (eds) *The Social Shaping of Technology,* Milton Keynes: Open University Press.

Ingold, T. (1996) 'Situating action V: The history and evolution of bodily skills', *Ecological Psychology,* 8(2): 171–182.

Jarvis, J. (2011) 'Your life torn open, essay 3: Get over it', *Wired,* 3 February: 92–93. Also available at http://www.wired.co.uk/magazine/archive/2011/03/features/get-over-it?page=all.

Johnson, S. (2011) 'Your life torn open, essay 2: Zuckerberg's next move', *Wired,* 3 February: 89–91. Also available at: http://www.wired.co.uk/magazine/archive/2011/03/features/zuckerbergs-next-move?page=all.

Kallinikos, J. (2004) 'Deconstructing information packages: Organizational and behavioural implications of ERP systems', *Information Technology and People,* 17(1): 8–30.

Kanter, B. and Fine, A. (2010) *The Networked Nonprofit: Connecting with Social Media to Drive Change,* San Fransisco, CA: Jossey-Bass.

Keen, A. (2008) *The Cult of the Amateur: How blogs, MySpace, YouTube and the Rest of Today's User-generated Media are Killing our Culture and Economy,* London: Nicholas Brealey.

Keen, A. (2011) 'Your life torn open, essay 1: Sharing is a trap', *Wired,* 3 February: 86–89. Also available at http://www.wired.co.uk/magazine/archive/2011/03/features/sharing-is-a-trap?page=all.

Kelly, K. (1999) *New Rules for the New Economy,* Harmondsworth: Penguin.

Kelly, K. (2010) *What Technology Wants,* London: Viking Books.

Keynes, J. M. (2010 [1930]) 'Economic possibilities for our grandchildren', in L. Pecchi and G. Piga (eds) *Revisiting Keynes,* Cambridge, MA: MIT Press, pp. 17–26.

Knights, D., Vurdubakis, T. and Willmott, H. (2008) 'The night of the bug: Technology, risk and (dis)organization at the *fin de siecle', Management and Organizational History,* 3(3–4): 289–309.

Knights, D., Noble, F., Vurdubakis, T. and Willmott, H. (2002) 'Allegories of creative destruction: Technology and organization in narratives of the e-economy', in S. Woolgar (ed.) *Virtual Society? Technology, Cyberbole, Reality,* Oxford: Oxford University Press, pp. 99–114.

Knox, H., O'Doherty, D., Vurdubakis, T. and Westrup, C. (2008) 'Screenworlds: Information technology and the performance of business knowledge', in H. Scarbrough (ed.) *The Evolution of Business Knowledge,* Oxford: Oxford University Press, pp. 273–294.

Knox, H., O'Doherty, D., Vurdubakis, T. and Westrup, C. (2012) 'Enacting the global in the age of enterprise resource planning', *Anthropology in Action,* 19(1): 32–46.

Kraemer, K., Dedrick, J. and Sharma, P. (2009) 'One laptop per child: Vision vs reality', *Communications of the ACM,* 52(6): 66–73.

Kuhn, T. (1970) *The Structure of Scientific Revolutions,* Chicago, IL: University of Chicago Press.

Kumar, K. and van Hillegersberg, J. (2000) 'ERP experiences and revolution', *Communications of the ACM,* 43(4): 23–26.

Latour, B. (1987) *Science in Action,* Milton Keynes: Open University Press.

Latour, B. (1988a) 'Mixing humans and non-humans together: The sociology of a door-closer', *Social Problems,* 35: 298–310.

Latour, B. (1988b) 'The prince for machines as well as for machinations', in B. Elliott (ed.) *Technology and Social Process,* Edinburgh: Edinburgh University Press.

Latour, B. (1992) 'Where are the missing masses? A sociology of a few mundane artifacts', in W. E. Bijker and J. Law (eds) *Shaping Technology/Building Society,* Cambridge, MA: MIT Press.

Latour, B. (1993) *We Have Never Been Modern,* London: Harvester Wheatsheaf.

Latour, B. (2004) *A Prologue in Form of a Dialog Between a Student and His (Somewhat) Socratic Professor,* available at: http://www.ensmp.fr/~latour/articles/article/090.html.

Law, J. (ed.) (1986a) *Power, Action and Belief,* London: RKP.

Law, J. (1986b) 'On power and its tactics: A view from the sociology of science', *Sociological Review,* 34(1): 1–38.

Lyon, D. (1994) *The Electronic Eye: The Rise of Surveillance Society,* Minneapolis: University Of Minnesota Press.

MacKenzie, D. and Wajcman, J. (eds) (1999) *The Social Shaping of Technology,* second edn, Milton Keynes and Philadelphia, PA: Open University Press.

Marx, L. and Smith, M. R. (eds) (1994) *Does Technology Drive History? The Dilemma of Technological Determinism,* Cambridge, MA: MIT Press.

Metro (2003) 'This game will self destruct in ...' Thursday, 9 October: 12.

Miles, I. (1988) 'On Technology', paper presented at PICT Network Conference, Edinburgh, 19–21 September.

Miles, I. (1989) 'Review of S. Hill, the Tragedy of Technology', *Sociology,* 23(3): 489–490.

Miller, D. (2011) *Tales from Facebook,* Cambridge: Polity.

Misa, T. (1992) 'Controversy and closure in technological change: Constructing "steel"', in W. Bijker and J. Law (eds) *Shaping Technology/Building Society,* Cambridge, MA: MIT Press.

Morgan, G. (1986) *Images of Organization,* London: Sage.

Negroponte, N. (1995) *Being Digital,* London: Hodder and Stoughton.

Noble, D. (1999) 'Social choice in machine design: The case of automatically controlled machine tools', in D. MacKenzie and J. Wajcman (eds) *The Social Shaping of Technology,* Milton Keynes: Open University Press, pp. 161–176.

Ogburn, W. F. (1950) 'Social evolution reconsidered', in W. F. Ogburn (ed.) *Social Change,* New York: Viking, pp. 369–393.

Ogburn, W. F. and Thomas, D. S. (1922) 'Are inventions inevitable?', *Political Science Quarterly,* 37: 83–98.

Orlikowski, W. (1999) *Awareness is the First and Critical Thing: Conversation with Professor Wanda Orlikowski MIT Sloan School of Management.* Available at http://www.dialogonleadership.org/interviews/Orlikowski-1999.shtml.

Orlikowski, W. J. (2000) 'Using technology and constituting structures: A practice lens for studying technology in organizations', *Organization Science,* 11(4): 404–428.

Orlikowski, W. J. and Scott, S. V. (2008) 'The entanglement of technology and work in organizations', *Information Systems and Innovation Group, Department of Management,* LSE. Working Paper Series, No. 168.

OU (1996) *Information Technology and Society,* Block 1 of course text for THD204, Milton Keynes: Open University.

Perrin, N. (1979) *Giving Up the Gun: Japan's Reversion to the Sword 1543–1879,* New York: David Godine.

Peters, T. (1997) *The Circle of Innovation,* London: Hodder and Stoughton.

Pinch, T. (1998) 'The social construction of technology: A review', in R. Fox (ed.) *Technological Change,* Amsterdam: Hartwood.

Pinch, T. and Bijker, W. E. (1984) 'The social construction of facts and artefacts: Or how the sociology of science and the sociology of technology might benefit each other', *Social Studies of Science,* 14: 399–441.

Pippin, R. (1994) 'On the notion of technology as ideology', in Y. Ezrahi, E. Mendelsohn and H. Segal (eds) *Technology, Pessimism, and Postmodernism,* Boston, MA: University of Massachusetts Press.

Rajesh, M. (2015) 'Inside Japan's first robot-staffed hotel', *The Guardian,* August 14. Online at: http://www.theguardian.com/travel/2015/aug/14/japan-henn-na-hotel-staffed-by-robots.

Randall, C. (2004) 'France silences cinema mobiles', *The Daily Telegraph,* 12 October: 10.

Rapoport, A. (1969) *House, Home and Culture,* Englewood Cliffs, NJ: Prentice Hall.

Rheingold, H. (2000) *The Virtual Community: Homesteading on the Electronic Frontier,* Cambridge, MA: MIT Press.

Rifkin, J. and Heilbroner, R. L. (1996) *The End of Work: The Decline of the Global Labor Force and the Dawn of the Post-Market Era,* New York: J. P. Tarcher.

Robey, D. and Sahay, S. (1996) 'Transforming work through information technology: A comparative case study of geographic information systems in county government', *Information System Research,* 7(1): 93–110.

Scarry, E. (1985) *The Body in Pain: The Making and Unmaking of the World,* Oxford: Oxford University Press.

Schaefer, S. (2003) *Tech Bubble: Who Benefited? An Interview with Michael Hudson.* Available at: http://www.michael-hudson.com/interviews/030830_counterpunch.html.

Schwartz-Cowan, R. (1985) 'How the refrigerator got its hum', in D. MacKenzie and J. Wajcman (eds) *The Social Shaping of Technology,* 1st edn, Milton Keynes: Open University Press, pp. 202–218.

Selby, A. (2004) 'Against the grain: The Amish are old-fashioned farmers but their approach is remarkably successful', *Financial Times,* 22/23 May: W7.

Sheffield University Packaging Research Group (n.d.) *User Capabilities and Problems.* Available at: http://www.shef.ac.uk/packaging/paper3.htm.

Shirky, C. (2009) *Here Comes Everybody: The Power of Organizing Without Organizations,* London: Penguin.

Silva, L. and Westrup, C. (2008) '(Un) objectionable Development? The One Laptop Per Child Project', Manchester Business School, mimeo.

Spencer, R. (2006) 'Mobiles blocked in exam crackdown', *Daily Telegraph,* June 8: 18.

Stalder, F. (2002) Failures and successes: Notes on the development of electronic cash, *The Information Society,* 18(3): 209–219.

Susskind, R. and Susskind, D. (2015) *The Future of the Professions: How Technology Will Transform the Work of Human Experts,* Oxford: Oxford University Press.

Tapscott, D. (2008) *Grown Up Digital: How the Net Generation is Changing Your World,* New York: McGraw-Hill.

Tapscott, D. and Williams, A. (2010) *Macrowikinomics: Rebooting Business and the World,* New York: Atlantic Books.

The Economist (1999) 'The end of privacy: The surveillance society', May 1: 19–23.

The New York Times (2006) 'Citing Safety, States Ban Alcohol Inhalers', October 6. Online at: http://www.nytimes.com/2006/10/08/us/08whiskey.html?fta=y&_r=1&.

Thomas, R. (1994) *What Machines Can't Do,* Berkeley, CA: University of California Press.

Thompson, D. (2008) *Counterknowledge: How We Surrendered to Conspiracy Theories, Quack Medicine, Bogus Science and Fake History,* New York: Atlantic Books.

Toffler, A. (1971) *Future Shock,* London: Pan.

Toffler, A. (1980) *The Third Wave,* London: Collins.

Tsoukas, H. (1994) *New Thinking in Organizational Behaviour,* Oxford: Butterworth-Heinemann.

Turnbull, S. (1996) *Samurai Warfare,* London: Cassell & Co.

Turnbull, S. (1998) *The Samurai Sourcebook,* London: Cassell & Co.

Underwood, J. (1999) 'Not another methodology: What ANT tells us about systems development', in T. Wood-Harper, N. Jayaratna and J. Wood (eds) *Methodologies for Developing and Managing Emerging Technology Based Information Systems,* London: Springer.

UNPD (2001) *Making New Technologies Work for Human Development,* Oxford: Oxford University Press.

van Aken, J., Hop, L. and Post, G. (1997) 'The Virtual Company: A Special Mode of Strong Inter-company Co-operation', paper presented at the XVII Annual International Conference of the Strategic Management Society, Barcelona, 5 October: 8.

van Duiken, S. (2004) *Inventing the American Dream: A History of Curious, Extraordinary and Just Plain Useful Patents,* London: British Library.

Walker, C. R. and Guest, R. (1952) *The Man on the Assembly Line,* Cambridge, MA: Harvard University Press.

Warschauer, M. (2003) 'Demystifying the digital divide', *Scientific American,* August.

Weinberg, A. M. (1966) 'Can technology replace social engineering?', *University of Chicago Magazine,* 59 (October): 6–10.

Weizenbaum, J. (1984) *Computer Power and Human Reason,* Harmondsworth: Penguin.

Wernwick, A. (1994) 'Vehicles for myth: The shifting image of the modern car', in S. Maasik and J. Solomon (eds) *Signs of Life in the U.S.A.,* Boston, MA: Bedford Books, pp. 78–94.

White, L. T. (1962) *Medieval Technology and Social Change,* Oxford: Oxford University Press.

Williams, R. (1979) *Television: Technology and Cultural Form,* Glasgow: Fontana.

Williams, R. (2000) '"All that is solid melts into air": Historians of technology and the information revolution', *Technology and Culture,* 41 (October): 641–668.

Winder, B., Ridgway, K., Nelson, A. and Baldwin, J. (2002) 'Food and drink packaging: Who is complaining and who should be complaining?', *Applied Ergonomics,* 33(5): 433–438.

Winner, L. (1977) *Autonomous Technology,* Cambridge, MA: MIT Press.

Winner, L. (1997) *How Technomania is Overtaking the Millennium.* Available at: http://www.rpi.edu/~winner/How%20Technomania.html.

Woodward, J. (1965) *Industrial Organization: Theory and Practice,* Oxford: Oxford University Press.

Woolgar, S. (1988) *Science: The Very Idea,* London: Routledge.

Worrall, L., Cooper, C., Kerrin, M., La-Band, A., Rosselli, A. and Woodman, P. (2016) *The Quality of Working Life: Exploring Managers' Wellbeing, Motivation and Productivity,* London: CMI.

Zammuto, R, Griffith, T., Majchrzak, A., Dougherty, D. and Faraj, S. (2007) 'Information technology and the changing fabric of organization', *Organization Science,* 18(5): 749–762.

Zuboff, S. (1989) *In the Age of the Smart Machine: The Future of Work and Power,* New York: Basic Books.

Notes

1   As Thornton A. May ('Chief Psychographer' for the US consulting firm Toffler Associates Inc., puts it (2002, p. 64) 'basically we have *Star Wars* technology, factory-level deployment and sit-around-the-campfire [i.e., Neolithic] human behaviour'.

2   Even Karl Marx is sometimes described (e.g., Ellul, 1967) as a technological determinist because of his remark to the effect that the hand-mill gave us feudal society and the steam-mill bourgeois society.

3   In the battle of Nagashino (1575), for instance, warlord Oda Nobunaga used 1500 men armed with firearms to unceremoniously mow down the mounted samurai of his opponents (the Takeda clan). The Portuguese had introduced firearms to Japan in 1542.

4   This particular historical episode (the Shimpūren rebellion) has been dramatized in Yukio Mishima's novel *Runaway Horses.* It has also received the Hollywood treatment in *The Last Samurai* (Edward Zwick, 2003).

5   The Luddites are named after a certain Ned Ludd or Ludlam from Leicestershire, said to be the first to smash his machine in 1779.

6   While many concede that technologies may well be put to political uses, they often argue that it is the *purposes* to which a society puts its technologies that are political, not their technical content. Technology, the United Nations' Programme for Development (2001, p. 27) report argues, 'is not inherently good or bad – the outcome depends on how it is used'.

7   For illustrations of this point within Management and Organization Studies see Orlikowski (1999; 2000).

8   Indeed technological determinist perspectives are sometimes described as 'science push' theories.

9   As the old joke has it, 'on the Internet nobody knows you are a dog'.

10 From a TD perspective, the explanation of technology itself should be left to technical experts: For TD the technical 'content' is beyond social scientific understanding – what engineers call a 'black box' (MacKenzie and Wajcman, 1999).

11 For instance, it is customary to see the factory system as the product of a technological revolution. However, the first factories 'contained the same machinery as had been used previously in the cottage production system'. It was only *after* such factories were set up, 'that there existed the demand for new technologies' (OU, 1996, p. 62).

12 Yes, buildings – machines for living as Le Corbusier would have it – do qualify as technologies according to the definition provided earlier.

13 For instance, the choice between building an apartment block or a number of semi-detached houses for private accommodation has a lot to do with fashion (tower blocks were very popular in the UK in the 1960s), socioeconomic class (it was the poor that often ended up in the tower blocks) and our ideas about identity or the good life (say urban versus suburban living).

14 Are there any lessons here for OLPC (Case Study 12.2) and the success or otherwise of its XO laptop?

15 For similar reasons, British novelist Ian Fleming was told to change the weapon of his secret agent hero James Bond from a Beretta – considered a 'lady's gun' – to a (presumably more 'masculine') Walther PKK (Bennett, 2004, p. 6).

16 Although some might argue that radioactive waste is not a technology as such, the perception of nuclear waste clearly influenced the development of both nuclear and waste disposal technologies.

17 SCOT analysts often employ the concept of 'technological frames' (TF) to describe the diversity of interactions among social actors in RSGs. If existing interactions tend to move members of an emerging RSG in the same direction, a technological frame will build up. If not, there will be no shared technological frame, the RSG will fall apart and interaction will decline. A TF includes elements such as goals, technological and scientific theories, testing procedures and design methods and criteria, which members of RSGs use to make sense of a technology. A technological frame is therefore a social space, a kind of arena, within which the meaning attributed to an artefact by the members of the social group is negotiated. It is where the problems of the technology are identified, and solutions proposed using the problem-solving strategies characteristic of that frame (recall for instance the Atomic Energy Commission's various deliberations over the problem of radioactive waste mentioned above). In other words, describing the TF of a relevant social group helps one explain a particular course of events (Bijker, 1995, p. 124).

18 One casualty of ANT determination not to indulge in the separation of what are social (i.e., human) factors from what are technological/material (i.e., non-human) factors appears to be all taken for granted distinctions between 'human actors' (people) and 'non-human actors' (such as technological devices, institutions, forces of nature) (Callon; 1986b). To underline this point, ANT writers often prefer to speak of 'actants' rather than actors. To keep things simple, this neologism has been avoided here. However, ANT is not intended as an exercise in anthropomorphism. ('Anthropomorphism' is the attribution of human qualities to non-humans. This is not what is intended here.) Rather it is a recognition that the boundary between what people do and what machines etc. do, is in constant flux across the whole spectrum of human life (Latour, 1992; 1993; Bloomfield and Vurdubakis, 2008). Flying a plane, for instance, requires inputs from pilots and the onboard computers. As accident investigations have shown it is very difficult to separate their activities (e.g., Latour, 2004; Knights et al., 2008).

19 ANT's concept of 'translation' is a deliberate departure from the more common concept of interaction. As Stalder (2002) puts it, whereas interaction presupposes 'two (or more) stable entities that are linked together in a stimulus response relation … translation instead focuses on the mutual (inter)definition of actors as they become linked together'. ANT is often called the 'Sociology of Translation'.

20 In practice these 'steps' may occur in a different order.

21 One could say that you explored various such scripts when attempting to decide upon an appropriate environment and clientele for AWOL™.

22 The central concerns and conceptual tools of ANT have remained relatively unchanged, thus allowing us to present a rather simplified version here.

Emergent issues

13 **Globalization and organizations**
14 **Bureaucracy and post-bureaucracy**
15 **Ethics at work**

PART III

Part III provides a review of wider, emergent issues that are of contemporary significance. The global economy is examined within the context of the strategic plans of corporate managers who increasingly have to take some, if rather a limited, responsibility for the consequences of their activities for sustained ecological and environmental stability. The characteristics of new forms of organization, the nature of regulation and the relevance of ethics are examined from mainstream and critical perspectives.

13 Globalization and organizations

GLENN MORGAN

Aims of the chapter

This chapter will:

- Explain the meaning of the term 'globalization'.

- Examine how globalization impacts on organizational behaviour and management.

- Identify the factors that lead to the development of multinational firms, their strategy and structure.

- Analyze how multinational firms respond to national cultural differences.

- Demonstrate the contribution that a critical approach to globalization and multinationals can make.

Key concepts and learning objectives

By the end of this chapter you should understand:

- The concept of globalization.

- The mainstream models of the factors influencing the structure of multinationals and the limitations of these models.

- The importance of understanding multinationals as concentrations of economic and political power.

- The multinational as a transnational social space in which groups from different local contexts bargain and negotiate.

Overview and key points

The twenty-first century will be the century of globalization. Organizations increasingly plan their production, their innovation and their marketing on a scale that goes beyond the national. There are profound economic drivers for this process that come from accessing resources, skills, labour and technology in the most efficient way. That means crossing national borders in order to create economies of scale and scope that will enable goods and services to be produced as cheaply and flexibly as possible in order to respond to customer demands. It is globalization that has brought us cheaper commodities and that has increased the pace of innovation as firms compete to gain market share and establish new products and services. Globalization has opened up opportunities for travel, for learning from different contexts, for creating new hybrid forms of art, music and culture. But, at the same time, the world becomes more interconnected through these processes. Events in one part of the world rapidly impact on other areas. As Giddens (1999) and others have argued, globalization creates 'global problems of risk' that cannot be solved by any one country, e.g., climate change and its impact on the environment, global epidemics of disease, and events, such as the financial crisis which began in 2008 and primarily centred on the activities of banks and financial markets in the USA and the UK but soon impacted across the world. It also makes more visible the impact of these economic processes on particular localities and on particular social groups, drawing attention to issues of power and inequality in the global economy.

In terms of the actors which press the process of globalization forward, multinational firms are hugely significant in connecting different parts of the world together, through their role in trade, in the transfer of capital, in the organization of production and labour, in their influence on government policy towards investment, taxation, labour market rules and other regulatory frameworks. However, there are other actors in the global sphere. Clearly governments combine together in various ways, e.g., in bodies like the United Nations (UN), the European Union (EU), the G20 group etc., to set the framework for globalization. Alongside these exist global organizations set up by governments but provided with some discretion to enable professionals and experts to swap information and rules that enable international co-operation and trade, e.g., the World Trade Organization (WTO) or the Basle Committee, that oversee global banking stability. Finally, there are what we call 'global civil society' organizations, made up of citizens from many different countries who join together to push a particular agenda. This may involve radical social objectives such as the World Social Forum, which originally met in Brazil in 2001 to provide a framework for groups committed to increased democracy, participation and improved social conditions for the 'poor' of the Global South.

'Globalization' is a process in which all these different actors are engaged, intensifying and deepening connections around the world, creating more wealth and opportunities but also creating more risks, and reinforcing social divisions between the rich and the poor. In this respect, globalization is not an end stage, something that can ever be considered as complete or an end-state; it is rather a way of describing the social, economic and political terrain in which we live in the early twenty-first century. It has multiple aspects and logics; it does not proceed in a straight line or at an even pace. Arguably, globalization can also reverse; foreign direct investment (FDI) flows can decrease as they did after the Global Financial Crisis. Regions or countries may decide to cut themselves off from global trade. In this respect, it is important to see globalization as a contested concept and phenomenon, as an arena of discourse in which different actors try to pin a very particular meaning on to it and its implications (see Fiss and Hirsch, 2005, for an interesting analysis of the discourse of globalization and its structural underpinnings in the US context). The contestation over the concept of globalization has become more intense with the development of perspectives from the Global South, such as post-colonial theory and subaltern theory. These theories challenge the way in which globalization processes are predominantly seen and interpreted from the perspective of the developed economies in the northern hemisphere; they also emphasize how globalization deepens inequalities and shapes identities and subjectivities in ways that divide people by gender, ethnicity, race and class (see Chapter 5).

A key issue here is how globalization as a discourse becomes a frame for making processes of interdependence and homogenization deeper and inevitable, for undermining the basis of local identities and local resistance to these processes. In much mainstream managerialist and policy discussion, it is assumed that globalization is one process that has an overall positive outcome in terms of increased productivity and consumption, and that local resistances are futile and irrelevant over the longer term. This is usually wrapped up in neo-liberal market discourse where 'free' markets and, in particular, the deregulation of capital markets and labour markets is seen as a necessary and inevitable condition and consequence of the globalization process. However, it is still possible to think in terms of globalization without accepting neo-liberal ideas of free markets, without accepting the inevitability of the destruction of local identities, without accepting a deepening of global inequalities and conflicts. By viewing globalization as an uncertain and complex process of deepening interdependence between localities, the issue becomes how the global and the local interact. For this, we have to refocus back to social, economic and political relations in local and particular contexts and to understand the rootedness of social life in specific places. In these terms, the most important category of place in the modern world is that of the nation-state, what Weber defined as the entity which has the monopoly of the legitimate use of force within defined territorial boundaries. For much of the nineteenth and twentieth centuries, social life in the industrial societies of the West was constructed in a predominantly 'national' way. The nation-state established legal systems relating to property, corporations, labour, consumption, etc., as well as individual rights that were common within its boundaries. It constructed school and education systems that taught individuals the rudiments of disciplines, such as timekeeping and obeying authority, that were essential to running large collective efforts such as the civil service, factories, offices and armies. It created national identity that subsumed or transcended various forms of local and regional identities without necessarily destroying them altogether. Nevertheless, internal differences were reduced by standard educational systems, standard national legal systems and increasingly the creation of a national cultural identity. These processes were reinforced culturally and economically in the nineteenth century through competition between these states, particularly in terms of establishing overseas empires. From the sixteenth century onwards, but culminating in the scramble for Empire in the nineteenth century (when Africa was carved up between the European powers), all the major European powers, and the USA and Japan imposed themselves either through formal or informal imperial domination on parts of the world and on peoples lacking the capacity for industrialized warfare. This imperialist rivalry eventually spilled over into Europe itself causing the First and Second World Wars. As subaltern peoples struggled to release themselves from Empire in the post-1945 period, they too sought to create nations with specific national identities as part of their resistance to imperialism, even though, in many cases, the nations they were creating were the products of the land-grab of the colonial powers and thus tended not to reflect any specific social unity. The result was that many states, particularly in Africa, were composed of different social groups who rapidly started to compete with each other over 'ownership' of the state, leading to civil war and in some cases, the complete collapse of the state, e.g., in Somalia in the period from the late 1990s. Post-colonial theory emphasizes that just because formal decolonization has occurred this does not mean that the effects of colonization on the politics of these societies, on the identities of individuals and groups in these societies and in the colonial powers have fundamentally changed, since political, economic and cultural power still resides massively in the hands of the former imperial powers. The struggle against colonialism therefore has to continue in order to overcome both economic and cultural subordination.

The collapse of the final world Empire, that of the Soviet Union in the late 1980s, saw a surge in the number of 'new' nation-states, joining the world community, new in terms of their independence and autonomy but claiming ancient roots in culture, language and social ties. States have remained a key source of political authority, economic organization and social and cultural identity in the modern world, and inside their boundaries distinctive patterns of social relations have survived. Over the last two decades, building on previous comparative studies, such as Bendix (1956), what has been variously called 'the varieties of capitalism' approach (Hall and Soskice, 2001), the 'national business systems' approach (Whitley, 1999) etc. has sought to emphasize the continued existence of these differences and their implications for the organization and management of business even in the face of globalization pressures.

The tension between the forces of globalization and the forces of national identity and differentiation are nicely characterized in the US journalist Tom Friedman's distinction between 'The Lexus and the Olive Tree'. The Lexus represents modernity and globalization – a global car for the wealthy of all countries, originally built and designed in Japan but now spread across the world as a global brand; the olive tree on the other hand represents history, longevity and tradition, the embeddedness of social relations in specific places and the resistance to change. The modern world is characterized by the tension between these two sets of principles. On the one hand, there is an economic logic of globalization that ties societies together and creates interdependencies that make autonomous decision-making increasingly impossible; we all feel in our different ways the impact of the global financial crisis and no country, firm or individual can act alone to overcome these impacts. In a later book, entitled *The World is Flat* (2005), Friedman emphasizes that the barriers to this interdependence have been increasingly 'flattened' and that the impact of events in one part of the world rapidly transmit themselves elsewhere because of the erosion of barriers. In *The Lexus and the Olive Tree* (2000), however, Friedman emphasizes also that political power, cultural identity and much of the day-to-day process of economic organizing still occurs within the boundaries of the nation-state and this creates a mismatch between economic processes and political actions. When economic logics are globalizing but political action is predominantly national, how can multinational firms be held to account?

How has the study of organizational behaviour and management responded to the challenges of the emergence of globalization and the existence of this tension between 'the Lexus and the Olive Tree'? In this chapter, you will be introduced to these debates and arguments. First, we will look at what we mean by globalization and place this in a broad historical context. In the following section we will look at how mainstream theories of international business and international management have examined these issues. We will see that the predominant approach is to consider globalization in terms of the working out of a particular model of economic efficiency and managerialism (cf. Knights and Willmott, Chapter 7, Grey, Chapter 14 in this volume) represented by the actions of, in particular, multinational firms. Whilst this perspective can provide valuable insights into some areas of globalization, it lacks any perspective on globalization as a contested process in which social actors are competing over fundamental goals and objectives. For this reason it is necessary to develop a critical approach to globalization. In the second part of the chapter, therefore, we look at globalization in terms of how particular actors are participating in the process and with what effect. In particular, the chapter examines how power is exercised to further a particular view of the globalization process and how resistance to this view has developed and with what effects.

Introduction

Cartoon 13.1   'I love the expansion, but we will lack a branch in the Arctic.'

'I love the expansion, but we still lack a branch in the Arctic.'

The term 'globalization' is now commonly used and familiar to everybody and yet, even as recently as the early 1990s, 'globalization' was not included in the list of keywords in the social sciences compiled by the cultural theorist, Raymond Williams (1992). Globalization has, in effect, become one of the key ways in which we define our sense of ourselves in the current era. On a simple, everyday level it is easy to understand why. We only have to check the labels in our clothes to see that in some basic way our lives are connected to those of others across the world. The shirt I am wearing as I type this was made in China, the jeans in Mexico, the shoes in India. The food that I ate last night included vegetables brought from Kenya and Guatemala. The computer I am using was probably assembled in the Far East from parts made in China, Taiwan, Malaysia and the USA. The car I drive was made in Japan. The drinks in the average British pub come originally from all over the world; Carlsberg from Denmark, Heineken from the Netherlands, Fosters from Australia, Tequila from Mexico, Tiger Beer from India, vodka from Russia, Jack Daniels from the USA, wine from Australia, South Africa and Chile.

Globalization is not just a matter of trade and economic interdependence. It also relates to our whole way of life. Who or what do we think we are? What do we aspire to be? In sport, we see this very clearly. Although 'our teams' compete on the basis of their local and/or national affiliations (Manchester United, Chelsea, Arsenal; England, France, Germany, etc.) what draws the biggest crowds and the highest media interest are events like the Olympic Games or the World Cup. What makes us more aware of being 'One World' than watching great performances in events like these? Even so-called local or national teams are in reality often multinational and global. Take the example of football teams in the English Premier League. Over recent years, many of the major Premier League clubs have acquired overseas owners – from the USA (Manchester United, Liverpool), Russia (Chelsea), the Gulf States (Manchester City), etc. Their revenues come mainly from the sale of television rights, which means that league matches are available to be seen all over the world, and from the sale of merchandise across the world.

The growth of cheap air travel together with the growing popularity of 'gap years' for students between school and university, have both contributed to high levels of travel in, and experience of, different countries. The flow of overseas students into UK and US universities impacts not just those countries but also the countries from which they come as graduates and to where they return with new ideas and approaches. Styles of life cross national borders easily. Shopping malls in London, New York, Shanghai, Delhi and São Paulo share the same list of global retail brands. The influence of TV programmes and films, such as the *Sex in the City* franchise, is to construct mythical views of what life can be like, which in turn become aspirational targets for young people in many parts of the world.

Of course, we can raise questions about such a picture both at the descriptive and the evaluative level. At the descriptive level, the great age of mass migration was in the eighteenth and nineteenth centuries when European populations spread into the Americas, Australasia and parts of Africa and when many Africans were forced into slavery and transported to the Americas. More recently, the upheavals created by the Second World War led to massive shifts in populations across borders, both within Europe and elsewhere. Population shifts in the current period are growing as a result of political instability in the Middle East and Africa leading to migration into Europe supplementing the already important movements from poorer parts of the EU (in the East and the South) to more economically prosperous countries in the North and the West. However, they are not unusual in themselves but part of a longer term process during capitalism when shifts in economic and political power have encouraged large scale population movements. Similarly, looking back, it is also possible to see that this flow of styles of life and accompanying material goods has often occurred. The Brighton Pavilion, for example, was built in the late eighteenth century under the influence of architectural styles from India and interior decoration patterns from China.

Everyday staples of the British diet for centuries originated from trade with other countries – potatoes, coffee, tomatoes, chocolate from the Americas, tea from China, spices from the islands that eventually became Indonesia. We have to be careful, therefore, not to exaggerate the uniqueness of the current era.

Nevertheless, many authors argue that the current era is distinctive and therefore globalization is something new. In one of the most important and detailed analyses of globalization, Held and his colleagues state that, 'Globalization may be thought of initially as the widening, deepening and speeding up of worldwide interconnectedness in all aspects of contemporary life' (Held *et al.*, 1999, p. 2). This is a useful definition in that it allows us to see that globalization is a process. In this respect, we can identify different degrees of globalization across different spheres of social life. We can also identify different authors in terms of the degree to which they believe this process has proceeded. Held *et al.* (1999, Chapter 1), for example, differentiate three categories of interpretation:

- *Hyperglobalizers* who tend to emphasize the decline of the nation-state under the pressure of economic processes and the development of cross-border trade and multinationals.
- *Sceptics* who argue that the extent of these processes has been much exaggerated. Nation-states remain crucial actors and even multinationals are dependent on their home state in many ways. Firms are predominantly regional in their orientation, i.e., focus on one or, at most, two of the main regions in what is known as the global Triad – Europe, the Americas, and Asia. From this perspective interdependence is increasingly regional rather than global (e.g., Hirst *et al.*, 2009).
- *Transformationalists* who argue that there are profound changes occurring but the direction of these processes is uncertain, uneven and often contradictory. Held *et al.* place themselves in the transformationalist camp and it is from a similar position that the current author writes in this chapter and elsewhere (Morgan, 2001a, 2001b, 2009, 2010).

Thinkpoint 13.1

What is your experience of globalization? How would you characterize yourself in terms of Held *et al*'s three positions?

If we see globalization as a process, it is clear that one of its key drivers over the last two decades has been the expansion of production of many standard commodities (such as clothes, toys, electrical components, etc.) into areas like China, Vietnam and India, where the costs of production are much lower than in the developed Western economies. In developing countries, the existence of large numbers of rural and urban poor provides a ready pool of cheap labour to manufacturers. Similarly, these countries do not have the same standards of health and safety in their factories, the same level of taxes on companies to fund employment relief or health care, the same legislation restricting hours of work for children, etc. that exist in the developed societies. People can be put to work at much cheaper costs than in Western countries. The result has been a profound improvement in the standard of living of the Western countries with prices of standard manufactured goods (from televisions to computers and toys) continuously falling relative to wages over the last two decades because of the expansion of production in these low wage economies. In this respect, the standard of living in the Western economies has become dependent on the low wages paid to workers in other parts of the world. At the same time, massive numbers of people in countries like China have been rapidly brought out of abject rural poverty by the provision of jobs in manufacturing in the main urban areas.

It is important to note that many developing countries are seeking to use their new found wealth to move out of low value production. In India and China, for example, economic growth is being used to fund increased investment in schools, universities and scientific infrastructure. From a relatively low base, the scientific and technological capacities of such societies are rapidly increasing, in part due to the creation of a highly educated, middle class and, in part, due to the efforts of government to set up and encourage research facilities and joint-venture activities with foreign capital and foreign experts. With massive home markets, these countries have the possibility of learning from Western companies and themselves becoming major players in high-value international markets. For example, the Chinese IT firm, Lenovo, took over the PC element of IBM and has used this to improve its technology and its own brand awareness. One of the biggest producers of short-haul jets in the world is Embraer, a Brazilian-based company.

The biggest group of developing countries – the so-called BRICS group (Brazil, Russia, India and China with the more recent addition of South Africa) – are therefore becoming increasingly diverse economies, not solely dependent on cheap manufacturing production or the exploitation of natural resources. As they move up the value-chain, low value-added production is shifting to countries such as Laos, Cambodia, Ecuador and Peru which have more limited capacities for extending into other areas. The result is therefore both growing diversity within and between emergent economies, consequent on their broader position in the global economic system.

Thinkpoint 13.2

Look at the labels on your clothes and shoes. What proportion of them were made in the country where you are studying or from where you originate? Do you see a difference in origins between your more expensive clothes items and your cheaper ones? Why do you think this is? Should you care about where your clothes are made?

Similarly globalization pressures draw societies into the world economy in ways that both threaten traditional ways of life at the local level and more broadly the global ecology. The increasingly industrialized nature of large scale agricultural production drives local people off the land and often leaves them marginalized and demoralized in shanty towns or reservations that become human sinkholes. They therefore extend the pool of labour available to employers thus keeping a downward pressure on wages from oversupply. The same processes also rob the world of unknown resources that come from the high levels of biodiversity that characterize rainforest environments that are being cut down to provide land and space for more industrialized agriculture. Deforestation and other environmental changes seem also to have impacts on global weather systems that are hard to predict, while locally it makes areas more susceptible to flooding and other natural disasters (such as happened in Haiti in the floods that Tropical Storm Jeanne brought to the island in September 2004, in New Orleans in September 2005 with Hurricane Katrina, in floods in Pakistan and India in 2010). In the short run the benefits of deforestation flow to the global corporations that organize and manage the process, the local landowners who sell the rights to timber, and to the companies and consumers of the affluent societies who purchase the goods made out of these trees. In his analysis of globalization, Giddens (1999, Chapter 2) has associated this with the idea of risk. Events in one part of the world are interdependent with those in another part, and thus risks become magnified. Global warming does not respect national boundaries.

Organizations are central participants in this process. Multinationals in particular scour the globe looking for new opportunities – to find new markets, to find new resources, to find a cheaper labour force, to find new ideas. Their restless search takes them anywhere that money can be made, subject only to the constraints of geo-political dynamics and public opinion as the headlong rush of US companies into Iraq after President Bush declared 'Victory' illustrated. Authors such as Giddens (1999) emphasize the contribution made to this process by new information and communication technologies. It is now simple enough for European and North American managers to be in instantaneous contact with factories in China and Brazil, call centres in India and Scotland, suppliers in Taiwan and Mexico, distributors in Australia and South Africa. Systems of transportation and logistics mean that products and people can move around the world quickly, efficiently and (mostly) predictably in planes, trains, lorries and massive container ships. Giddens argues that our notions of time and space have been changed as a result of these develop-ments. He refers to this as time-space distanciation, by which he means the collapse of the constraints of time and place so that we expect instant communication with others – achieved thanks to mobile phones and email technol-ogy – and that geographical space and the demarcation of time is a limited barrier to this communication thanks again to technology.

Thinkpoint 13.3

When you are in another country, how do you communicate with friends and family? How do you think you would have communicated if you had been travelling abroad in the 1970s? Most young people now have mobile phones. Do you know anybody who has not?! Access to the Internet is increasing and services such as Skype, WhatsApp, Instagram, Facebook, etc. which allow rapid communication over the Internet have further increased the possibilities. What are the limits to Giddens' idea of this collapse of time-space constraints in your experience?

Managers need no longer worry about their actual physical distance from a factory in China because they can get close to it through monitoring various output and performance indicators. Nor need they worry about how long it might take to deliver goods from one side of the world to the other. This can be planned and speeded up by modern technology. Time and distance are being conquered in the interests of the (Western) consumer and the market system.

For those of us who study organizations, however, this story is too simple. Of course, organizations can do amazing things. By bringing individuals together and co-ordinating their actions with inputs of capital, technol-ogy and other resources, organizations have contributed to a vast expansion in our material well-being. But as you are well aware from the previous chapters in this book, this process is highly conflictual, generates and rein-forces inequalities of power, income and wealth, and has unanticipated effects on individuals, groups, localities and the planet more generally. In this chapter, therefore, we want to look at these two sides to globalization and organizations:

- On the one side, there is the mainstream approach in which the expansion of the global market contributes directly to this improvement in living standards as firms become more efficient. From this perspective, the considerable problems of organization that arise from internationalization can be solved if we apply sufficient rational decision-making to the issues faced, such as that of national differences. Inequalities are outcomes of market processes; interfering in market processes, in this view, brings negative effects. It is therefore better to let market forces work as these will gradually bring more people into work, providing them with a better standard of living than previously, even if it remains significantly below the standards of advanced Western economies.

- On the other side is the critical approach, which uncovers the costs of this process in terms of the concentration of economic and social power and the fact that it is in the hands of a few who are unaccountable to the populations affected by their actions. In this view, inequality is not a natural outcome of neutral market processes but an outcome engineered and maintained by the rich and powerful. Resistance to these outcomes emerges in various settings even though the rich and powerful try to keep it down through various forms of overt coercion and more hidden ideological manipulation. The critical approach also dissects the rational model of the multinational, revealing how groups are struggling inside the organization to make a difference to how they live and how their localities are affected by these processes of globalization.

Structure of the chapter

The rest of the chapter is structured in the following way. First, we introduce a short case study of Nike. This presents what may be termed the economic logic of Nike's internationalization. From this, we will consider why and how firms internationalize. The economic imperatives that we identify answer this question but do not consider how to organize international firms. This draws us on to a different literature that is more organizational in tone; you will recognize here assumptions about how organizations need to 'fit' their environment and the foundations of the contingency approach to organizations (see Knights and Willmott, Chapter 7, in this volume). Complementing this economic approach in mainstream discourse is an effort to deal with the 'olive tree' problem, i.e., the existence of different national traditions of management and organization. In textbooks and course syllabuses, this is often linked to the difference between the label International Business (referring to predominantly economic analyses of how and why firms internationalize) and the label International Management (how management adapts to cultural differences inside multinational firms). We then return to the Nike case and explore it from a more critical angle – particularly in terms of inequality and power. This then opens up the issue of developing a critical approach to the study of globalization where issues of power and conflict between different social groups become central.

**Case study 13.1
Nike: A mainstream view**

The Nike corporation and its products are well known throughout the world. It is a brand that from early on has been global in its reach. Originally producing sports shoes, it now manufactures a whole range of sports clothing, all of which is instantly recognizable by what Nike call their 'swoosh' logo. Nike's origins lie in the US West Coast town of Portland, Oregon, where a college athletics coach decided to go into the production and sale of sports shoes. Sports shoes were initially highly functional objects. There was little **product differentiation** (all sports shoes were white and with the same padded sole) meaning that production was standardized and prices low. There were a number of things that were changing in the 1960s and 1970s that would affect how people saw sport and the products associated with sport. Nike was both shaped by these changes and in turn was a major participant in these changes.

Product differentiation
Refers to one way in which firms can maintain their competitive advantage; they differentiate their product, in ways that appeal to the customer, from all others on the market.

Two aspects can be distinguished, both of which relate to globalization. The first change was that sport became big business. In one sport after another, from tennis to athletics to cricket and rugby, sports that had traditionally been amateur became professional. Both a cause and a consequence of this process was the role the media played in this. The large amounts of money necessary for sports to professionalize came predominantly from broadcasters' willingness to purchase viewing rights, which in turn was dependent on the great spectator interest in sport and the advertising revenues that could be generated from it. In turn, this related to selling rights to international events such as the Olympics and the World Cups (in soccer, cricket, rugby, etc.) to other countries. So sport increasingly became global with a global audience open to common advertising and imagery.

The second feature associated with this is the way in which it also reinforced a renewed sense of the importance of the body and bodily appearance. Increasingly the cult of exercise, reflected in the growth of private health clubs, public events such as the London Marathon and the general moral obligation to be 'fit and healthy' has become a dominant feature of life, particularly among the middle class of affluent Western societies.

Nike has been central in building these two aspects into a whole series of profitable opportunities. First of all, it saw that in such a climate, sport shoes could become not just a functional purchase but a lifestyle choice. This implied that the shoes needed to be associated with a set of key images that consumers found attractive. In their global advertising campaigns centred around the swoosh logo and 'Just Do It' catchphrase, they used celebrities of world sport as icons of a certain style of life that could be aspired to by men and women of different ages and of different backgrounds. Footballers such as England's Wayne Rooney, Portugal's Ronaldo, Spain's Fabregas, etc. are contracted to Nike and have their own Web pages within the Nike site to advertise the Nike boots which they use. Nike has reinforced this in the past by sponsoring teams such as the Brazil national football team and Manchester United FC. It has similar lists of star performers from basketball, track and field, American football and golf amongst other global sports. Second, this was to be associated with a shift away from the mass production of a single type of shoe towards more limited runs of distinctive styles. Third, the production of the shoes could be shifted out of the USA. Here Nike faced a classic choice; should they establish their own manufacturing subsidiaries in other parts of the world or should they use existing independent firms in those parts of the world? After some experiments, Nike moved towards a subcontracting system, reaching agreements with independent manufacturers to produce the shoes and other goods. This gave Nike a high level of flexibility, as they could decrease or increase overall production according to market demand without carrying unnecessary overhead costs. It also meant that they could set very tight conditions on the contracts, as there were so many manufacturers who wished to do business with them given that barriers to entry were relatively low – i.e., the capital investment required for producing Nike products was not high, nor was the level of skill needed by employees. In efficiency terms, therefore, the system of subcontracting that Nike devised was highly productive and profitable as it kept overall costs low and maximized the firm's flexibility.

Nike therefore is a good example of the dynamics of creating a multinational. Its internal structure separates off manufacturing from design and marketing. Manufacturing is carried out overseas by subcontractors and the main effort of Nike employees themselves is in managing the brand at a global level so that the shoes sell at a high price even though they are relatively cheap to produce. We will return to some of these issues in the discussions that follow.

Exercise 13.1

Who do you think are Nike's main competitors? Look around you at the clothes and trainers that you and your friends buy to find the answer – alternatively have a look in a specialist sports shop. What are the factors that differentiate these brands for you and your friends? Check out the websites of Nike competitors. How, if at all, are they different from Nike? Why do you think that Nike tends to be the company in this sector that is most talked about?

CENTRAL PROBLEMS IN THIS FIELD: THE MAINSTREAM AGENDA

As has been stated previously, products have flowed across national boundaries for many centuries. Often these flows were managed by intermediaries, people known as merchants, who bought goods in one setting and then arranged for them to be carried via sea or land to another country. This process was often highly precarious, as both land and sea were unsafe and uncertain means of transport due to the hazards both of nature and of human making (political uncertainties, piracy, etc.). For this reason, merchants also became involved in insurance and banking; insurance to insure against any losses on journeys (the origins of the Lloyd's insurance exchange in the City of London), and banking to lend each other money until goods from overseas turned up (the origins of what were known as 'merchant banks' in the City of London).

Only as international law developed and national boundaries became more secure (not least as a result of the establishment of European imperialism in the nineteenth century) did firms and individuals begin to invest directly overseas. Thus, this period saw the establishment of some of the main multinationals that still exist. Often these were concerned with the extraction of raw materials, such as oil (Shell, BP, Esso), sugar (Tate & Lyle) and minerals (Rio Tinto Zinc, Anglo-American Mining). Alongside this, three other trends emerged. First, there was increased export of capital from Europe; often this went into the development of infrastructure such as railways and later the supply of gas, electricity and water. Second, there was increased export of manufactured goods from Europe into other parts of the world, often in payment for the raw materials extracted from these countries. Third, there was the gradual establishment of overseas production facilities.

Approaches to internationalization

From an organizational point of view, the key issues are those of control, predictability and profitability. Investing overseas brought with it risks as well as opportunities. International business as an approach developed as a way to understand the economic forces which led firms to take risks and develop overseas. In this framework, four broad approaches to internationalization are identified moving from the least to the most risky – selling, licensing and franchising, subcontracting and, finally, setting up production outside the home base.

SELLING: EXPORT STRATEGY

The least risky strategy for a firm which wishes to benefit from overseas demand for its products is to simply export from the home base. This requires very little investment in other countries. Sales might be handled by an international office in the home country with independent agents operating as intermediaries overseas. Traditionally, most small and medium-sized enterprises tend to become 'international' by exporting their products. Even large companies have been reluctant to move beyond this. Until the late 1980s, for example, German manufacturing companies, including some of their large car companies, tended to become international through exports rather than any more direct involvement in overseas contexts. The main disadvantages of such a strategy are:

1 The firm incurs high transport costs in shipping products overseas.
2 The products are made additionally expensive because of customs duties levied on entry to the foreign market.
3 It tends to limit the market overseas. This is for two reasons:
   - The firm is unlikely to be able to adapt its product to the specific consumer needs of the overseas market (at least partly because, without actually being in the country, it finds it hard to know what those specific needs are).
   - Because it relies on agents, it does not have direct access to knowledge about the scale of the market or how to develop it further (at least partly because agents may find it in their interests to keep the company ignorant of these specific details).

LICENSING AND FRANCHISING

In this system, the agent (i.e., the licensee or franchisee) pays a fee to the company in order to use its system/design/invention in its own country. The fee can be negotiated in various ways but often is set so that there is an incentive to build the market because each new sale directly brings in a reward to the franchise holder. The company that has the idea or product does not have to risk its own capital and managerial time in setting up overseas in this system. Instead it relies on the local knowledge and the capital of local investors to bear most of the risk. There are many variations on this model. McDonald's, for example, has grown through a franchising system. It sells the rights to become a McDonald's to investors in different countries. Part of the franchise is the commitment of the owners to follow the McDonald's model in terms of décor, menu, methods of cooking and customer service. This process enables McDonald's to be present in all parts of the world without having to find the capital or managerial expertise itself to make this work in a diversity of cultural and social contexts.

Exercise 13.2

Find five other global franchises besides McDonald's. Choose one of them and find information on how its franchising system works and how truly international it is. As an initial starting point for your research, you can look at the website of the British Franchise Association (www.thebfa.org).

Franchising has a number of disadvantages:

1 Loss of control over the brand, raising the risk that it may be undermined by the poor performance of franchisees.
2 Loss of control over the knowledge and processes that are transferred overseas, enabling franchisees to transfer that knowledge to other operations that may eventually change the competitive environment for the renewal of licences – what is referred to as 'opportunism', i.e., that people will act in ways that benefit themselves to the detriment of others in a contract if they think they can get away with it.
3 Loss of knowledge about market changes in different contexts and how this might be relevant to either the adaptation of the original product or the development of new products.
4 Loss of direct control over the production process; the franchisor is thus unable to squeeze maximum revenue out of employees through increasing the level of effort demanded of the employees. These decisions are left to the local franchisee.

These disadvantages can of course all be overcome by increased monitoring of the licensee, but this then begins to undermine the economic logic of the bargain. Increased monitoring and surveillance of the franchisee costs the franchisor in terms of money and managerial time. Clearly there will inevitably be a point where the costs of monitoring exceeds the benefits of franchising and therefore the franchisor or licence holder may withdraw the franchise and move to set up his/her own subsidiary operations in the country.

SUBCONTRACTING

In this system, the firm recognizes that it would be cheaper and more efficient to produce overseas but is unwilling to take the risk of setting up and managing its own production in a different context. It therefore searches for other independent firms which would be able to produce the goods and services it requires according to the terms of a carefully specified contract. Again the firm reduces its risk as it does not have to commit its own capital or its own managerial time to direct control and co-ordination of the labour process. Subcontracting of this sort is also popular because it increases flexibility for the firm and reduces its costs. Researchers who have been particularly concerned with the construction of international, cross-border supply chains have labelled these relationships 'global commodity chains' (Gereffi, 1996, 2001; Bair, 2009) or 'global production networks' (Dicken, 2014: Coe and Yeung, 2015). Global commodity chains are common in the retail industry. Supermarkets such as Tesco and Sainsbury enter into contracts with farmers in many parts of the world to ensure year-round supply of products like strawberries, asparagus, apples, etc., which have short harvests in the UK itself. Clothes stores such as Gap, H&M and Topshop contract with independent firms in India, China, Malaysia, etc. to produce according to designs supplied by UK designers aiming to keep up or develop fashion trends for the various seasonal collections of clothes and accessories. Any manufactured product is likely to contain within it components from many different subcontractors, often in different countries and even continents.

Exercise 13.3

Check out the computer you normally use. It may be branded as Apple or Dell or HP, but where was it actually assembled and by whom? Foxconn (owned by the Taiwanese firm HonHai) assembles all of Apple's products mainly in a number of huge plants located in China. There is great controversy about the conditions of work in Foxconn plants given extra publicity by a series of suicides amongst Foxconn workers that occurred in 2012 (see Ngai and Chan, 2012 for a discussion of Foxconn). In this system, some companies such as HP effectively buy everything from their subcontractor (having designed the requirements); the manufacturer/assembler is known as an OEM (own equipment manufacturer) – i.e., it is an independent company producing under contract for a buyer such as HP, which will brand the end-product. When firms sell their own products, we call this the development of own-brand manufacturing (OBM) capability. Acer in Taiwan have both OEM and OBM capability – i.e., they produce for HP (which sells these products under the HP label) and under their own brand name (at a cheaper price).

   Look at commercial websites for the retail sale of computer components (e.g., Maplins) and you will see the range of producers who specialize in various parts that the OEM and OBM assembler puts together, such as memory chips, microprocessors, flash memory devices, logic chips and screens. Follow through to manufacturer websites (such as Intel, AMD, Motorola, Fujitsu) and look at where their production facilities are located and how they themselves are embedded in global commodity chains.

Where products are simple and designs can be standardized, it is relatively easy to establish contracting relationships as there will be high amounts of competition between contractors. However, as products become more complex and more knowledge has to be transferred to the contractor involving more specific investments in order to meet the contracting firms' requirements, so the relationship becomes difficult (Gereffi *et al.*, 2005). Both sides become open to potential opportunism (i.e., they may be tempted to cheat each other). Thus the main firm may respond to this problem in the same way as in the previous case – i.e., by cutting the contract and setting up its own subsidiary.

OVERSEAS PRODUCTION

Levels of what are known as FDI – i.e., directly investing in buying or establishing production facilities overseas – have grown massively in the last few decades (though with some retractions as a result of financial crises in 2001and 2008/09) after a slower and more steady period of growth in the period since the 1950s. These figures reflect two things. First, they reflect multinational companies investing in the building and creation of new manufacturing or office facilities overseas. Second, they reflect cross-border mergers and acquisitions. In the latter case, no new productive facilities have been added to those already existing. It is simply a case of ownership being transferred so that, for example, a firm based in the USA is now owned by a firm based in the UK. FDI inflow totals reached a peak in 2007 of $2100 billion, falling significantly in 2008 and 2009 as a result of the financial crisis (see the World Investment Report 2010 for details). The bulk of these inflows continued to come in the form of merger and acquisition activity rather than greenfield investments, though the financial crisis has restricted funding for mergers and acquisitions (M+A) and has increased the proportion of total FDI inflows going to fund greenfield investments.

The big multinationals

Multinational companies (MNCs) are key mechanisms in the flow of inward and outward FDI. They establish overseas production facilities through the transfer of capital (and also technology and people). One of the most important measures of multinationals is one developed by the United Nations Conference on Trade and Development. UNCTAD has produced what it terms a **transnationality** index for MNCs. This aims to show in very broad terms which are the most multinational firms in the world. The transnationality index measures MNCs by three criteria. These criteria are the ratio of home to foreign in the following categories – assets, sales and employment. So by each measure it is possible to measure the percentage of 'foreign' as opposed to home activity in each category – e.g., what percentage of total employment is outside the home country, etc.? Weighting each of these dimensions equally, it is then possible to construct a table of the most transnational firms in the world. Table 13.1 ranks the top 10 MNCs in foreign assets in 2006, and from the point of view of the overall transnationality index; Table 13.2 does the same thing for 2012.

Transnationality Indicates that some or many of the assets, sales and employees of a firm are based outside its home base.

Table 13.1 Top 10 non-financial MNCs by foreign assets, 2006

Ranking by:				
Foreign assets	TNI	Corporation	Home economy	Industry
1	75	General Electric	USA	Electrical and electronic equipment
2	32	Royal Dutch/Shell Group	UK	Petroleum expl./ref./distr.
3	6	Vodafone Group Plc	UK	Telecommunications
4	20	BP Plc	UK	Petroleum expl./ref./distr.
5	74	Toyota Motor Corporation	Japan	Motor vehicles
6	42	ExxonMobil Corporation	USA	Petroleum expl./ref./distr.
7	27	Total SA	France	Petroleum expl./ref./distr.
8	67	E.On	Germany	Utilities (Electricity, gas and water)
9	90	Electricite De France	France	Utilities (Electricity, gas and water)
10	10	ArcelorMittal	Luxembourg	Metal and metal products

Source: UNCTAD World Investment Report 2010.

Recently, a strong argument has been made that the internationalization of firms is not so much global but more regional. In his book *The End of Globalization*, Alan Rugman (2000) argues that firms' activities are closely concentrated in their particular part of the world triad – i.e., the world conceived of as being divided into three powerful trading blocs, the EU, NAFTA (the North American Free Trade Agreement covering the USA, Canada and Mexico, and increasingly incorporating in various ways most of Central and Latin America) and Asia Pacific.

Table 13.2 Top 10 MNCs by foreign assets, 2012

Foreign asset ranking	Transnationality index ranking	Name of company	Home economy	Industry
1	79	General Electric	USA	Electrical and electronic equipment
2	32	Royal Dutch Shell	UK	Petroleum
3	22	BP	UK	Petroleum
4	77	Toyota	Japan	Motor vehicles
5	28	Total	France	Petroleum
6	45	ExxonMobil	USA	Petroleum
7	8	Vodaphone	UK	Telecoms
8	62	GDF/Suez	France	Utilities
9	61	Chevron	USA	Petroleum
10	64	Volkswagen Group	Germany	Motor vehicles

Source: UNCTAD World Investment Report 2013.

Exercise 13.4

Go to the UNCTAD website and find the latest *World Investment Report*. Look for the data on the world's top 100 non-financial transnational companies and also the top 100 non-financial companies from developing economies; for the data on 2013 top non-financial MNCs see unctad.org/Sections/dite_dir/docs/WIR2013/WIR13_webtab28.xls.

1 Which companies are highest on the transnationality index and why?
2 Which industries are most highly represented on the transnationality index and why?
3 Which industries are most likely to be high on the ratio of foreign employees to home-based employees and why?
4 Why do small countries like Switzerland, the Netherlands and Sweden have companies that are so high on the transnationality index?
5 How significant is the growth of MNCs from the developing countries? Which countries and industry sectors are most often represented?

Rugman follows a rigid methodological approach which conceals some important issues, such as the degree of distribution across different countries within the same trading areas. His methods also cannot show the degree to which components are sourced from outside the home trading area, so it may be that a car assembled in North America is significantly composed of components made in China. Nevertheless, these arguments are suggestive about the need to think carefully on what is meant by the term 'multinational' (see also Hirst, *et al.*, 2009).

The economic logic for the multinational firm

Why do firms decide to establish overseas production and incur the economic risks associated with this instead of making do with exporting, licensing and subcontracting? There are three broad answers to this question: (a) extending the **product life cycle**; (b) internalization advantages; and (c) the eclectic theory.

Product life cycle Refers to how products move from being new to being mature to being obsolete. This impacts on the pricing and marketing of goods as well as the degree of competition.

EXTENDING THE PRODUCT LIFE CYCLE

An early analyst of multinationals, Vernon (1966) argued that the internationalization of production was a way of extending the life cycle of particular products. In this logic, firms in one country invest in producing a particular commodity which soon becomes outmoded. The investment is then effectively lost and written off. However, there may be other countries where the market is not so advanced that would be willing to buy the product. The company can therefore extend the life cycle of its products and investments by selling its older products to these overseas markets. Thus its home base is characterized by a continual process of product upgrading and innovation while its overseas markets receive 'last year's model'.

Vernon's ideas may seem a little dated now when globalization suggests the idea of simultaneous global launches of new products, yet it remains important. Take, for example, the Japanese car industry and its subsidiaries in the UK. The UK subsidiaries have been built to produce a small handful of standard designs that have been established in Japan for some years. More innovative cars, such as variants of four-wheel drives, electric cars, sports cars, etc. are designed, developed and manufactured in Japan for export to the UK. Innovations such as satellite navigation or the placing of TVs and videos in cars have been developed first in Japan, not in their UK subsidiaries. In general, most firms still seem to do their key development work in their home base and their overseas subsidiaries concentrate on standard products.

INTERNALIZATION ADVANTAGES

The argument (developed by authors such as Buckley and Casson, 1976, 1985) is that a firm invests at home in developing assets such as production systems, routines of co-ordination and control, methods of innovation and research and design, systems of management and management development. If the firm licenses its products to overseas manufacturers or sets up subcontracting relationships, it runs the risk that its agents will act opportunistically. In other words, agents will try to conceal the benefits that they receive from the licence or contract and maximize the costs that they incur. Similarly, agents need to be carefully monitored to ensure that they keep to the standards the licence demands of them in order to prevent damaging the broader reputation of the brand. Thus the threat of opportunism and cheating on the part of agents creates costs for the originating company. To avoid these costs, it can 'internalize' the transactions; in other words it can take tighter control of its contexts, e.g., by setting up subsidiaries or buying ownership of existing independent contractors. Internalization theory therefore provides an economic account of the conditions under which firms set up overseas production facilities; they will only do this if the advantages of doing so and ridding themselves of the problems of opportunism and monitoring outweigh the advantages of subcontracting and using intermediaries.

Exercise 13.5

Visit the websites of two well-known Japanese companies such as Sony and Toyota. Can you see any radically new products that they are developing? Are they developing them mainly in Japan or overseas? Are they launching them in Japan before they launch them elsewhere? Does the product life cycle argument still seem valid in these cases? Do you think this is just a peculiarity of the Japanese MNCs? Check out Sony's QRIO robot as a possible example.

THE ECLECTIC THEORY

One of the most well-known commentators on the dynamics of multinationals, John Dunning, put these arguments together with others to construct what he termed the 'eclectic' theory of multinationals. Dunning's theory is also referred to as the OLI theory of multinationals (for summaries see Dunning, 1998, 2001). 'O' stands for ownership advantages, 'L' for locational advantages and I for internalization advantages. In Dunning's view, firms decide whether to set up overseas by calculating whether the costs and uncertainties of such an endeavour are larger or smaller than the advantages that can be gained from these three sets of advantages. Ownership advantages refer to the advantages derived from the firm's build-up of its own assets, expertise and knowledge. Building on Vernon's argument, this relates to the ability of the firm to reuse the same assets in other contexts and thus to increase the productivity of those assets. Locational advantages refer to being near to various sorts of markets – e.g., to product markets, to markets for raw materials, to labour markets (with low wage employees) and to markets of expertise. Internalization advantages refer to the ability to avoid the opportunism of agents and maximize internal economies of scale and scope.

In summary, we can see that internationalizing is a complex task for firms, requiring from the mainstream perspective highly rationalistic decision-making processes in order both to identify measures of advantage and disadvantage and to reach a final decision about the economic viability of the process (see Table 13.3).

The last two decades have seen a simultaneous intensification of each of these processes creating stronger webs of interconnections across national and organizational boundaries. These theories have provided a formidable set of tools for analyzing the development of multinationals. What they have told us less about is the organizational and management implications of this. Clearly, the internationalization of an organization, whatever form it takes, adds new layers of complexity to issues of management. What can we learn from the mainstream about how this complexity is controlled and managed? For this we need to turn to another group of authors for whom issues of organization and management have been central in their analysis of multinationals.

Strategy and structure in multinationals

Once a firm has decided to pursue a particular type of internationalization strategy, how does it ensure that it controls and co-ordinates these activities effectively? This concerns the relationship between the headquarters of the company, the overseas subsidiary and the market context of the activity. Two counteracting factors are influential here. On the one hand, there is the impetus arising from the achievement of economies of scale. The more a firm

Table 13.3 Modes of international activities

Types of international expansion	Advantages	Disadvantages	Organizational implications
Export strategy	Low on co-ordination costs	Low on learning possibilities; high dependency on agents	Minimal: establishment of 'international' division
Franchise and licensing	Improves income stream and spreads costs further	Dependence on local franchise owners – potential loss of and control of brand which may impact negatively; danger of opportunism and poor management	Requirement for established procedures for offering franchises monitoring performance
Subcontracting	Improves flexibility of supply while keeping costs low	Problem of co-ordinating across different firms and managing problems of opportunism and poor performance	Central importance of supply chain management and logistics linked to improved methods of co-ordination
Overseas production (FDI)	Production closer to markets enables stronger learning; also economies of scale and scope can be maximized	Problems of integrating overseas plants into broader system; issues of standardization, benchmarking and restructuring	Increasingly complex management system associated with problems of integration, co-ordination and differentiation

can standardize its products and manufacture them in large plants with continuous working, the lower the price at which it will be able to sell, thus the higher its market share. This argues for a 'global' decision-making process whereby the firm decides the best location for its production, and exports from this base to all its main markets. On the other hand, national markets are often subject to different consumer tastes and different regulations, thus making global standardization difficult. Furthermore, states may set import taxes at levels that equalize the price of products from outside its boundaries and in this way support and sustain employment internally. These two tendencies were analyzed by Prahalad and Doz (1987) in terms of the dynamic between integration (the global imperative) and responsiveness (adaptation to local markets). A product like Coca-Cola is highly standardized and can be produced in bulk, while many other products are affected by national preferences – e.g., in terms of taste (the sphere of consumer preferences) or in terms of what is socially acceptable (the sphere of governmental regulation).

Thinkpoint 13.4

Global integration and local responsiveness: The case of McDonald's We may assume that McDonald's is highly globally integrated. Its core products are the burger bun. Its 'golden arches' are ubiquitous across the world. Its business model of fast, reliable food with limited but clean and hygienic eat-in facilities is reproduced in all its branches. But McDonald's has been trying to change in response to national differences. Some changes have gone from a local adaptation to a common product across the world, such as the introduction of salads. Other experiments in the same direction eventually failed to become global products – e.g., the McDonald's pizza. Still others remain just local adaptations, like the lamb burger in India and the teriyaki burger in Japan.

For more details on McDonald's and how it has adapted in East Asian countries like Hong Kong, China, Korea and Japan see the fascinating collection of papers in Watson (1997), *Golden Arches East*.

BARTLETT AND GHOSHAL'S MODEL

What are the implications of this for how the firm is organized? Bartlett and Ghoshal (1989) identified four models of organization: multinational; global; international; and transnational firms.

Multinational firms

In these firms the emphasis is on a strong local presence through being highly responsive to national differences. Each subsidiary is run relatively independently as the different national markets require different variations in the products. For example, until very recently there were strong differences between European countries in terms of how they did laundry. Bartlett and Ghoshal (1989, p. 20) state that:

> As late as 1980, washing machine penetration ranged from less than 30 per cent of households in the UK to over 85 per cent in Germany. In northern European countries 'boil washing' had long been standard, whereas hand-washing in cold water represented an important demand segment in Mediterranean countries. Differences in water hardness, perfume preferences, fabric mix and phosphate legislation made product differentiation from country to country a strategic necessity.

Global firms

This describes firms where efficiency of production, and economies of scale are high because products can be standardized across different countries. Consumer electronics tend to have these characteristics, particularly at the component level (e.g., semiconductor chips that are increasingly produced in massive highly efficient plants according to standardized designs) and also at the consumer product level (e.g., standardized designs for TVs, videos, DVD players, etc.). There are no strong market pressures towards national differentiation and, on the contrary, high pressures towards global standardization, economies of scale and strong price competition.

International firms

This category refers to the ability of firms to transfer knowledge and competencies across national boundaries. Thus subsidiaries are neither totally based on local capabilities nor totally driven by global economies of scale. Subsidiaries utilize the knowledge generated in the head office to create distinctive products in varied national markets where local knowledge is important.

Transnational firms

For Bartlett and Ghoshal, this was the most interesting category of firm and also represented the direction in which firms were heading. The transnational firm is characterized by a wide variety of different subsidiaries that perform their own specialized role in the organization as a whole but are also interdependent and interacting. This enables the firm to learn from different contexts and to spread this information around different subsidiaries. Thus, in theory, best practice can be identified in one setting and transferred to another. All subsidiaries can be subjected to a form of benchmarking – e.g., how many mistakes or rejects and how long to do a certain process. By benchmarking subsidiaries against each other, high performers and low performers can be identified and there can be transfers of learning, knowledge and people across the boundaries, which will enable the low performers to catch up. Early innovations can be communicated to other parts of the firm more widely and this can contribute to further improvement and development. Thus the transnational firm is locally responsive, globally efficient and internationally innovative.

The management and organization challenges arising in these different models are distinctive (see Table 13.4):

- In the global firm, production becomes concentrated in large integrated sites. Managers tend to be international, moving around the organization with an expertise in production technology. The central task is co-ordinating and controlling the supply chain in order to achieve company goals. Broadly, one might expect a Taylorist work system, highly controlled and monitored in order to achieve standardized outputs.
- Multinationals (in the Bartlett and Ghoshal terminology) are quasi-federations of firms with national identities. The head office will monitor performance primarily on a financial basis. There will be few transfers of managers or technologies or practices either across subsidiaries or to or between head office and subsidiaries. Work systems will differ depending on the history of the subsidiary and the normal pattern of control in its particular national context.
- The international firm will have intensive contacts with local subsidiaries but this is primarily in an advisory capacity and will be reflected in the transfer of technology. This will involve some international assignments for both managers and engineers but there will be relatively little lateral communication or movement between subsidiaries.
- The transnational firm involves dense communication and movement across subsidiaries and the head office. This will be reflected in frequent overseas assignments for managers and the use of international project teams to ensure the transfer of ideas and processes across the firm.

Table 13.4 Bartlett and Ghoshal's model adapted

	Low global integration	**High global integration**
Low local responsiveness	*International* Skills and knowledge in headquarters transferred to subsidiaries in local markets	*Global* Highly efficient: production organized on a global scale to maximize economies of scale in standardized products
High local responsiveness	*Multinational* Main focus on the national markets; little integration of production, management skills or knowledge across national contexts	*Transnational* Production planned to maximize economies of scale but local contexts remain central, so that products are adapted to local contexts and learning is transferred across subsidiaries

Exercise 13.6

Select a well-known firm and, using the information from its website, analyze where it fits in terms of Bartlett and Ghoshal's model. The key things to look out for are:

1 Is its strategy to produce for global markets, national markets or regional markets?
2 Where are (a) its major production sites and (b) its main research and development sites located and are they serving global, national or regional markets?

   Try, for example, brewing. How do firms like Carlsberg, Heineken and Fosters fit into this model?

Bartlett and Ghoshal's model has been highly influential. It moves from the broad question of why do firms internationalize as posed in Dunning, etc., to the question of how do they organize themselves when they internationalize, with the answer arising from the market contexts in which firms are located. It is based, however, on a highly rational view of how managers and firms behave, in which it is economic incentives that are the dominant influence, and more social and political considerations are ignored (see Chapters 2, 7 and 9).

HARZING'S CONTROL FOCUS

Harzing (2000) has elaborated on these processes by focusing particularly on the ways in which headquarters seek to maintain control over their subsidiaries.

Personal centralized control

In this mechanism of control, all key decisions are taken by the head office and are then monitored by frequent personal visits to the subsidiary. This has obvious disadvantages in that as the number of subsidiaries grows and the number of decisions that need to be taken increases, it becomes impossible to sustain personal control. Such a system is therefore only likely to occur when the degree of internationalization is low and the complexity of decision-making limited.

Bureaucratic formalized control

These controls are impersonal and consist of sets of rules and procedures that must be followed in subsidiaries. The problem with this system is that it tries to impose a single set of rules across diverse environments and can therefore run up against the problem of national differences. Also, bureaucratic systems more generally are inflexible and make it difficult for managers to respond to new contingencies (see Chapter 14). Given the diversity of contexts within multinationals, this can be highly problematic.

Output control

This refers to setting targets for the subsidiary management to achieve. Frequently these are financial targets but they may also relate to sales, productivity, market share, etc. Many multinationals use this as a primary means of control as it relieves the headquarters of detailed involvement in work processes (allowing local managers to respond flexibly to local conditions), and provides an easy way to compare performance across subsidiaries as well as in relation to the performance against targets set. The difficulties of such systems relate first to the diversity of output measures and the problem of choosing which is the most important one (though in US and UK multinationals financial targets are usually given top priority) and, second, to the problem of information asymmetry. Information asymmetry refers to individuals having different amounts of information about the same thing and the problems that can follow in terms of economic relations. Economists frequently cite the example of the buying and selling of used cars. Almost inevitably the seller has more information about the quality of the car than he/she is willing to provide to the buyer. In organizational terms, this leads to the possibility of key actors in the firm distorting the figures in order to serve their own interests.

Control by culture and networks

This technique of control is more complex and difficult to create (see Chapter 10). It relates to bonding different levels of management together and creating a strong shared culture among managers of subsidiaries and managers in headquarters. International management training programmes supported by an integrated international programme of management career development are ways in which such a shared culture can be established across managers from different national backgrounds. In these contexts, expatriate assignments and international project teams between different parts of the organization can be systematically constructed in order to both strengthen and develop formal and informal networks within the multinational. Thus, while subsidiaries necessarily remain geographically distinct, the managers within them have access to wider networks in order to monitor and control the tension between the local and the headquarters.

Harzing's model of control mechanisms does not map directly on to Bartlett and Ghoshal's model of different types of MNCs but it is highly suggestive:

- Global firms are likely to be characterized by 'bureaucratic formalized control' to ensure efficiency.
- Multinationals are likely to be held together by a strong personal centralized control as the constituent parts of the firm share little else in common.
- International firms are concerned to ensure that national subsidiaries improve their performance with the help of the head office, which will be reflected in strong output control.
- Transnational firms, with their dynamic internal processes and structures, are likely to require a strong, shared culture and the frequent use of networks to ensure that common goals, standards and processes are continually renegotiated in line with developments in individual subsidiaries.

These arguments are basically a variant of the contingency model of organizations. In other words, if we know the market that the firm is aiming at we are able to assess the balance between efficiency considerations (price, in particular: generally lower prices will come from larger and more concentrated sites of production where economies of scale and scope can be realized) and responsiveness considerations (adapting to local tastes and local regulations). From this we can decide the type of firm that we have and we can then deduce the implications for management and organization. A solution to our problem of organization structure and strategy follows quite naturally from this. Is life so simple?

National cultures and universalist solutions: The problems for MNCs

The most important challenge within the mainstream to this idea comes from the cultural differentiation thesis. In broad terms, this argument states that the values and beliefs that people hold about themselves, their society, their work and their position in the world, are deeply embedded in particular social contexts, the most significant of which in the modern world is defined by the nation state. Of course, it is relatively simple to reduce this to the level of stereotypes – the English 'stiff upper lip', the French *'joie de vivre'* and the German *'schadenfreude'* (enjoyment of others' misfortunes) are just a few examples. It is also very easy to exaggerate the degree to which this model has spread to other contexts – e.g., the states of Africa may seem similar on the surface but they are often creations of the period of European imperialism and have found it difficult to establish a single national identity over strong religious, ethnic and regional differences.

Nevertheless, if we accept that there is something in some contexts that constitutes a national culture, this is a considerable challenge to any universal theorizing about management and organizations. You cannot motivate a Japanese person the same way in which you would somebody from the USA. Japanese groups work differently.

Box 13.1
Motivation and the Japanese employee

It is not unusual for office workers in Japan to work until nearly 11.00 pm in the evening. However, their overtime is almost always unpaid. Moreover, unlike workaholics in the USA and the UK, they will not receive a personal individualized bonus. There is, in effect, no material incentive for them to work such long hours. We cannot understand this on the basis of a single universal explanation of how people are motivated at work. We must understand how different societies place different values on work, family, participation, control, etc. In Japan, the employment relationship in the large firm sector is profoundly different to that in the UK. It is long term; there are expectations of commitment on both sides; the fates of the firm and the individual are intertwined. Employees are expected to demonstrate a lifelong loyalty to the employer and to the people with whom they work. This loyalty overrides the individual's loyalty to the family and even to him/herself. Japanese employees take few holiday days, preferring instead to reserve them for moments of sickness or ill-health. Some Japanese firms have been so concerned about this that they present prizes to employees willing to take holidays. This sense of loyalty is not a 'natural' characteristic of Japanese people; rather it is drummed into them from a very early age by schools, families, the media, employers and the state that they must conform to authority. Even in the twenty-first century when Japanese young people love to display themselves in outrageous dress and show their openness to Western influence, this seems still a temporary rebellion before the onset of the pressures of work and conformity.

This reflects the way in which Japanese society industrialized, with strong links between the state and firms in order to maintain social stability by making employees highly dependent on the firm and limiting the role of independent trade unions. In Japan, there is a phrase which reflects this process: 'the nail which stands out is hammered down'. This reflects the broader problem for Japanese businesses and Japanese society that this sort of conformity leads to 'groupthink' – i.e., a collective inability to disagree or be innovative – which in turn has implications for businesses more generally. In the UK, on the other hand, employees expect to have to move from one company to another over the course of their working lives. They expect to be treated as individuals rather than as part of a collective. Work is only one part of their wider life. People do not expect the firm to look after them forever and are used to the prospect of having to move between firms, either because they are searching for better wages and conditions or the firm has made them redundant. Management in the UK, faces much bigger problems than Japanese management in terms of getting employees to do as they are told!

How is it possible to create coherence and stability when people in different subsidiaries see the world differently depending on their cultural backgrounds.

But can we prove national cultures exist? There are plenty of national stereotypes which have circulated for centuries (see Box 13.2) but is there anything that can satisfy a more 'scientific' approach? The predominant framework within the study of organizations that has been established to answer this question derives from the work of the Dutch researcher and management consultant, Geert Hofstede. Hofstede initially developed his ideas through accessing a large database of questionnaires about job satisfaction, which had been collected from among its employees by IBM in the late 1960s (Hofstede, 2001). Altogether Hofstede had around 116 000 questionnaires to deal with, collected from a variety of levels of employees within IBM's 46 national subsidiaries. IBM was a classic global company in Bartlett and Ghoshal's terms. It manufactured mainframe computers from a number of research and innovation intensive centres in the industrialized world. These products, subject to some local adaptation, were sold all over the world by IBM's salesforce which was renowned for its uniformity, not just in terms of the way in which mainframe computers were sold but also in terms of its style of dress (navy-blue suit and white shirt) and their general approach to business. IBM was seen as a company with a strong central culture, enforced by the presence of US expatriates in subsidiary offices and by common training systems.

Box 13.2
Some views on 'national character'

'The Englishman likes to imagine himself at sea, the German in a forest. It is impossible to express the difference of their national feeling more succinctly.' (E. Canetti: Crowds and Power)

'German managers visiting France are appalled at finding that their French colleagues will spend much of their time deciding where to eat lunch. The German does not speak the French language of time, which requires evoking the whole gustatory apparatus and setting the proper interpersonal relationship before business can be taken up. If the German insists on adhering to a rigid schedule, the French will label the visitor as uncouth, someone with little appreciation for life and no feeling for people.' (Adapted from Hickson and Pugh, Management Worldwide)

'Wittgenstein had to abandon his plan to produce a book of philosophy written entirely from jokes, realizing he had no sense of humour. German wit, famously, is no laughing matter.' (J. Paxman: The English)

'There are three things that concern the loyal servant. The Master's Will, his own vitality and the condition of his death.' (17th century Japanese Samurai manual, Hagakure)

'The Japanese are to the highest degree, both aggressive and unaggressive, both militaristic and aesthetic, both insolent and polite, rigid and adaptable, submissive and resentful of being pushed around, loyal and treacherous, brave and timid, conservative and hospitable to new ways.' (R. Benedict: The Chrysantheum and the Sword, 1946)

For an amusing view of what constitutes the 'real England', have a look at the novel *England, England* by Julian Barnes. The book is based on the idea of creating a theme park along the lines of Disneyland, which encompasses the 'essence of Englishness'. Before that, the intrepid entrepreneur has to decide what that essence is. On the basis of market research across the world, the following top ten emerge as 'quintessences of England':

1 The Royal Family.
2 Big Ben/Houses of Parliament.
3 Manchester United Football Club.
4 Class system.
5 Pubs.
6 A robin in the snow.
7 Robin Hood and his Merrie Men.
8 Cricket.
9 White Cliffs of Dover.
10 Imperialism.

However, Hofstede argued that the research showed that there were significant national differences in relation to key attitudes towards work and that, therefore, multinationals had to decide how to adapt to these differences. At first, Hofstede identified and labelled four key attitudinal complexes; he later added a fifth following further research, and this is included in the discussion that follows.

- *Power distance.* Hofstede identified that there were significant differences in terms of how national cultures viewed power. In some societies, those at the bottom of the organization felt very separate from those at the top, those in power (e.g., France). Surprisingly high power distance was often accepted by those at the bottom;

they thought that it was legitimate. Other countries rejected the idea that there should be a big distance between bosses and others and felt there should be more equality and less hierarchy (e.g., Sweden). In high power distance contexts, there tended to be more levels in the hierarchy; authority centralized at the top and low involvement of employees. In low power distance settings, managers and employees were expected to work more co-operatively together; there were fewer levels in the hierarchy and decision-making was more devolved.

- *Uncertainty avoidance.* The extent to which 'the members of a culture feel threatened by uncertain or unknown situations'. In societies characterized by high uncertainty avoidances there is a highly formalized conception of management. The power of superiors depends on the control of uncertainties and managers are more involved in details. Overall there is strong loyalty to the employer and long average duration of employment as a means of managing uncertainly (e.g., Greece, Japan). In low uncertainly avoidance contexts, there is tolerance for ambiguity in structures and procedures, the power of superiors depends on position and relationships (rather than the direct control that they exercise). Managers are more willing to take risks recognizing that the consequences may be uncertain. This reflects the fact that employees and managers do not expect firms to provide them with lifetime employment and are prepared to go into the labour market to improve themselves even though this brings uncertainty (USA and UK).

- *Individualism/collectivism.* Are the ties between individuals loose, with everyone expected to look after him or herself and his/her immediate family only (high individualism) (e.g., the USA)? Are people from birth onwards integrated into strong, cohesive in-groups, which throughout people's lifetime continue to protect them in exchange for unquestioning loyalty (high collectivism) (e.g., Pakistan)? In individualistic settings, the employer–employee relationship is a business deal in a 'labour market'. Employees perform best as individuals. Direct appraisal of performance improves productivity. Treating friends better than others is nepotism and unethical. In collectivist settings, the employer–employee relationship is basically moral, like a family link. Employees are seen to perform best in in-groups. Treating friends better than others is normal and ethical. Direct appraisal of individual performance is a threat to harmony and the employee has to be seen in a broader family and social context.

- *The masculinity/femininity dimension.* This describes attitudes to work centrality. The work ethos in masculine cultures tends towards 'live in order to work', whereas the work ethos in feminine cultures tends to 'work in order to live'. This reflects the degree to which gender roles are segregated or overlap: where men and women share childcare responsibilities, there has to be a work–life balance (e.g., Sweden, the Netherlands); where men work and women stay at home, men tend to become very work-centred (e.g., Japan). Thus societies where there are high levels of female participation in the labour force tend to be characterized by what Hofstede calls a 'feminine' culture – i.e., one where people are expected and encouraged to take time out from work to look after family and more generally to balance their work commitments against their home life. In masculine countries, managers hold ambitious career aspirations and are expected to be decisive, firm, assertive and competitive. In feminine countries, managers hold modest career aspirations and are expected to use intuition, deal with feelings and seek consensus.

- *Long-term orientation.* Hofstede developed this dimension later in his researches following more work on cultural values in Asian contexts. Long-term orientation was identified in terms of 'fostering of virtues oriented towards future rewards, in particular perseverance and thrift', while a short-term orientation reflected the need to preserve 'face' (i.e., the respect of others) and fulfil social obligations in the present. The long-term orientation is linked to what Hofstede terms 'Confucian dynamism'. Confucianism is a significant cultural influence in Asian contexts. It is associated with the wisdom of age and the importance of the long-term development and prosperity of the family. Hofstede identifies this with a willingness to work extremely hard in the present in order to build for the future (a future that may be conceived in terms of generations of the same family, not just a single individual or a single generation).

Hofstede argues that countries can be placed on each of these dimensions, and by understanding where a particular country lies in the rankings, we can better understand how to develop organizations in those countries.

Thus the Scandinavian countries tend to be low on power distance, low on uncertainty avoidance and predominantly feminine in their orientation to work. A US multinational setting up in a place like Sweden or Denmark would find that certain of its normal ways of doing things would be accepted and others would not. So the US firm could expect to find conflict if it pursued its normal strategy of expecting high commitment, long hours, and short holidays (its highly 'masculine' culture in Hofstede's words) in countries that held a very different view of the life–work balance. French managers with their expectations of high power distance would find that this would clash with Scandinavian expectations of low power distance, etc.

Table 13.5 Selected examples of Hofstede's rankings (out of 53 where 1 equals highest and 53 equals lowest on the dimension identified)

	Power distance	Uncertainty avoidance	Masculinity index	Individualism index
USA	38	43	15	1
UK	42/44	47/48	9/10	3
Japan	33	7	1	22/23
Germany	42/44	29	9/10	15
France	15/16	10/15	35/36	10/11
Top-ranked country	Malaysia	Greece	Japan	USA
Bottom-ranked country	Austria	Singapore	Sweden	Guatemala

Source: Geert Hofstede, *Culture's Consequences: Comparing Values, Behaviors, Institutions and Organizations Across Nations*, second edn, Thousand Oaks, CA: Sage Publications © 2001, ISBN 0-8039-7323-3.

Exercise 13.7

Figures 13.1 and 13.2 show Hofstede's profiles comparing Japan and the USA and a comparison of Singapore and the UK. What do you deduce from this data? There is a website where it is possible to access profiles of any particular country on the four (or occasionally five) dimensions and also to compare the profiles of two countries from his sample. If you have any foreign friends or family, find out what their country profile is at (www.geert-hofstede.com) and discuss with your friends whether this is accurate or not, stereotypical or fair in its portrayal.

Figure 13.1 Hofstede's 5D model – USA versus Japan (Hofstede, 2001)
Source: Geert Hofstede, *Culture's Consequences: Comparing Values, Behaviors, Institutions and Organizations Across Nations*, second edn, Thousand Oaks, CA: SAGE Publications © 2001, ISBN 0-8039-7323-3.

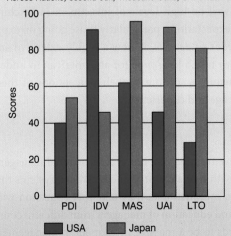

PDI Power distance index
IDV Individualism
MAS Masculinity
UAI Uncertainty avoidance index
LTO Long-term orientation

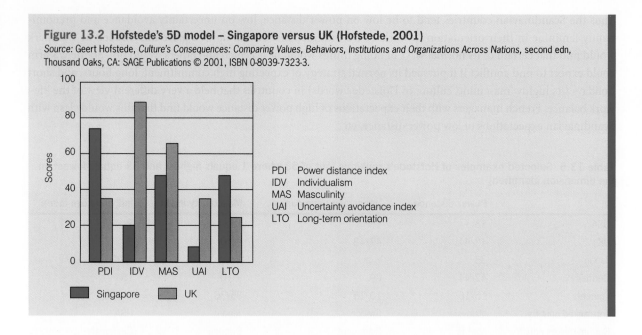

Figure 13.2 Hofstede's 5D model – Singapore versus UK (Hofstede, 2001)
Source: Geert Hofstede, *Culture's Consequences: Comparing Values, Behaviors, Institutions and Organizations Across Nations,* second edn, Thousand Oaks, CA: SAGE Publications © 2001, ISBN 0-8039-7323-3.

From this culturalist point of view, it is natural to expect conflict within multinationals as national cultural differences come into contact with each other. How local managers respond to output control mechanisms in Bartlett and Ghoshal's model of the international firm will vary depending on how they think of their status and position, what they consider their skills to be and how they relate to other parts of the organization. From this culturalist position, it is impossible to assume that all members of the firm will see these control mechanisms in the same way.

How does this culturalist approach supplement the more structural accounts of multinationals presented by authors like Bartlett and Ghoshal? Headquarters of multinationals may respond in a number of ways.

LEAVE ALONE

One way is to leave national subsidiaries as relatively independent entities and not seek to impose common practices and standards on to them. However, this is only feasible in what Bartlett and Ghoshal label as 'multinational firms' – i.e., where subsidiaries operate in highly distinctive markets and cannot make gains from a wider more global integration.

TRAIN MANAGERS IN CULTURAL AWARENESS

Where firms are global, international or transnational, there may well be high levels of investment in teaching managers from different contexts about different cultural values and expectations, particularly those going on expatriate management tasks. Cultural sensitivity training, using Hofstede's categories, is now a highly extensive and profitable business, but its problem is mainly its superficiality – it may take a long time for an American to understand why and how the Japanese rank people and alter their behaviour according to their perceptions of these rankings (which often derive from notions of age and the wisdom of age and experience).

CREATE AN INTERNATIONAL MANAGEMENT CADRE

This is where MNCs try to create a common culture through intensive training of a tier of international managers. This raises many questions and issues. Most managers are educated within one country in educational systems that reflect the history and inheritance of that country. When they join a multinational, they take that education with them and may find it difficult to understand the meaning of the skills and education of managers from different countries. In order to create a common culture within the firm, there needs to be a massive investment in management

Thinkpoint 13.5

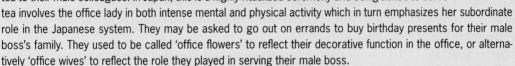

Women in Japanese workplaces and the impact of multinationals There are few women managers in Japanese organizations. Graduate women can aspire to the position of 'office lady' though they will be expected to leave when they have a child. As well as traditional office tasks such as typing, copying, filing, etc., office ladies are usually responsible for serving tea to their male colleagues. In Japan, this is a highly ritualized ceremony and being asked to serve tea involves the office lady in both intense mental and physical activity which in turn emphasizes her subordinate role in the Japanese system. They may be asked to go out on errands to buy birthday presents for their male boss's family. They used to be called 'office flowers' to reflect their decorative function in the office, or alternatively 'office wives' to reflect the role they played in serving their male boss.

These expectations have a long history in Japan and are part of the taken-for-granted reality of Japanese society even in an era when Japanese women are learning to rebel and reject these roles. However, senior Japanese managers are reluctant to deal with even foreign women as equals. How does this impact on Japanese firms when they set up offices in societies where the genders are more equal? How does it impact on US and UK multinationals when they set up offices in Japan? Women have come particularly to the fore in US multinationals in recent years. How therefore should US MNCs respond when deciding on expatriate assignments to Japan?

You can read more about the office lady in Japan in: Y. Ogasawara (1998) *Office Ladies and Salaried Men: Power, Gender and Work in Japanese Companies,* Berkeley: University of California Press.

training and development. Is this going to be worth it, especially given that there are high levels of mobility in many managerial tasks and any investment made can walk out of the door quite easily? Bartlett and Ghoshal (1989) try to anticipate these problems by their focus on diversity as a strength in the transnational firm so long as there can be communication across different people, different cultures and different units, but this simply assumes the problem away. Given the differences, how do we know that they can be productively, as opposed to destructively, harnessed?

Hofstede's results and his prescriptions have brought many plaudits, but equally many criticisms. Baskerville (2003, p. 1) summarizes her criticisms as follows:

(i) the assumption of equating nations with culture; (ii) the difficulties of, and limitations on, a quantification of culture represented by cultural dimensions and matrices; and (iii) the status of the observer outside the culture ...

A further problem is a general lack of confidence in the assumption of stability of cultural differences.

(See also McSweeney, 2002a and 2002b; and the replies by Hofstede to both authors, Hofstede, 2003a and 2003b; also Ailon, 2008, 2009.)

The idea that national cultural differences can help us understand the tensions within multinationals is therefore highly-contested; though, as we will see, the broader point that there are differences of perspective inside the MNC and this creates substantial problems for management can be developed much further and does not have to rely on an amorphous concept of national culture.

Contribution and limitations of the mainstream approach

These mainstream approaches have created a fertile field of study. Broadly speaking, we can summarize the research issues as follows:

- How and why do firms internationalize?
- How do firms organize the co-ordination between headquarters and subsidiaries?
- What impact do national cultural differences have on issues of managing multinationals?

In turn, we can make an initial identification of the weaknesses of these approaches. They are all basically variants of the contingency model of organizations, assuming that managers act rationally in the light of the information and knowledge that they have about how to ensure efficiency and market responsiveness. The contingency model relies on a number of presuppositions that are questionable and to which we will return:

- It assumes that it is possible to 'know' the market. However, as human beings our ability to process information is limited even when we supplement our decision-making with technology.
- It assumes that managers have the power to implement a particular model of organization. Yet it is clear from many of the chapters in this book that managers have limited knowledge and limited power.
- It assumes an economistic and rational view of internationalization with little concern for the unevenness of benefits presented in this process (inequality).
- There is little recognition of MNCs as constituted through social interactions of different groups and the power conflicts that arise (power). Little consideration is given either to other groups within the organization besides management or to how these might influence the process of internationalization and globalization. Nor are civil society groups outside the firm considered for their influence on globalization.
- The view of 'identity' and 'culture' that is used is highly static and over-deterministic. It lacks any reference to how subjectivities are constructed (see Roberts, Chapter 2, this volume).

In the following section, therefore, we present a critical alternative that builds on these themes.

THE CRITICAL APPROACH TO GLOBALIZATION AND ORGANIZATIONS
Introduction

How do we understand globalization and multinationals from a critical perspective? Broadly speaking, the following themes are crucial:

- Multinationals cannot be conceptualized separately from the impact they have on social relationships, political systems (at the national and the international level) and the global ecology.
- Multinationals cannot be conceived as single unitary rational actors. They are transnational social spaces in which ideas, people, knowledge, technologies, procedures, practices and capital flow across borders undermining simple unitary models of multinationals and national cultures.

Case study 13.2
Nike: A critical approach

From a critical perspective, Nike reveals the way in which multinational firms contribute to global inequality and how this relates to the emerging dominance of US style consumerism. It also reveals how both these processes promote resistance and conflict, as actors in different social settings seek to reassert control over their own lives in countering the forces of global capitalism.

As has already been described, Nike's strategy depends upon keeping the design, brand management and marketing in the USA and transferring manufacturing processes overseas. The rewards of this strategy are distributed highly unequally, with the bulk of them returning to US employees and US shareholders even though the actual material object is not produced in the USA. If Nike wanted to produce shoes in the USA, it would have to cut its profit margins substantially because US employees are (in world terms) paid quite high wages. They also have certain rights in terms of employment and union membership. The company would also be liable for contributions to pension schemes and health insurance. Producing the shoes in China or other countries in Southeast Asia reduces the costs significantly. Traditionally, regulations on hours of work, safety standards on machinery, and other aspects of labour discipline have been low. Nike's products are therefore manufactured overseas and well away from the high cost and high regulations of Western societies.

As described previously, this context enables Nike to squeeze its suppliers in terms of their costs. There are many potential suppliers to Nike in Asia, from India to China. Nike's representatives can bargain in this marketplace in order to get the lowest price possible for the manufacture of their shoes. In these circumstances, how do contractors keep their costs down and still make a profit? The answer is of course that they pay very low wages, make employees work long hours and keep other costs – e.g., health and safety, health care, sickness and pension rights – to a minimum. Exploring this further, who constitute the workforce of contractors for firms like Nike? The answer is that it is predominantly made up of young, single women. Carty states that in the early 1990s over 80 per cent of the women employed in factories in Southeast Asia making Nike products were under the age of 25. In the Indonesian factories, the average wage was US$2.20 per day (Carty, 1997, p. 193). It is easier for male supervisors to subject young women to mental and physical bullying than it is for them to do this to other men or older women. Carty reports frequent complaints about this in Nike-related factories. In these countries, demographic and land pressures often result in young women being forced to look for work in such factories where frequently they are housed in company barracks and subjected to further high levels of discipline.

As also discussed earlier, Nike moved from owning their factories towards subcontracting. At first sight this had another advantage (besides the economic one) for Nike. The actual conditions of work in its factories were set by contractors and not Nike itself. Thus, if Western observers saw child labour in Nike plants or watched young women working extremely long hours and suffering from poor working conditions and abusive employees, Nike itself could claim that it was not their fault. Such a defence was, of course, very superficial and over the last decade Nike has found itself having to defend its reputation more systematically. This is for the obvious reason that in its contracts with manufacturers it has the power to specify certain conditions in terms of labour, such as health and safety, wage levels, health and holiday entitlements, etc. The sorts of people that buy Nike products do not want to think that they are exploiting people in other parts of the world. Nike's website reveals their attempts to manage this part of their image and has much material relating to how they ensure employees in their contract manufacture work in acceptable conditions (www.nikebiz.com). However, this is an ongoing debate, and many commentators remain sceptical about the degree to which these goals are actually achieved and how systematically Nike inspects its contractors to ensure that they are put into place. Nike's argument is that it is bringing work and wages to people who would otherwise have a lot less. It is also encouraging the development of manufacturing facilities that can then be used to compete for other contracts and thus create a multiplier effect of gradually extending the range of employment opportunities in less-developed economies. Ideally this creates a virtuous circle of more FDI or contract work leading to a population with more wages to spend, thus encouraging further the development of the internal market of the country.

From a critical perspective, however, this argument can be countered with the view that whatever the limited local benefits (and these in turn can be contested), Nike reflects and reproduces inequalities within and across countries (see Box 13.1). Most obviously, there is the difference between the wages paid to the makers of its shoes and the salaries and other rewards received by its US management. For example, in 2010 Forbes Magazine reported that Nike's founder, chairman and chief executive Philip Knight, was the twenty-third richest person in the USA with a personal net worth of $11.1 billion. The shareholders of Nike are predominantly institutional investors, mostly controlled in the USA and the UK. These institutional investors control the pension funds and savings of millions of individuals in the USA, Europe and Japan, who in turn are beneficiaries of Nike's success. In 2003, return on equity in Nike was 18.9 per cent and in the period 2005–2010, it averaged 21.7 per cent. The price of Nike shares has moved up and down over the last 20 years and within the space of one year shifted from $132 in December 2015 to $53 in June 2016, reflecting the volatility of financial markets. The gains of Nike's success are nevertheless highly unevenly distributed, with the bulk of them flowing to their senior employees and shareholders in the USA and the advanced capitalist countries, and not to the people who actually make the shoes.

A further critical question pertains to the social constructions of identity that are central to the development of the Nike brand on a global scale. There are a number of aspects to such a discussion. One is to consider the messages that underlie the Nike adverts. The slogan 'Just Do It' relates to American traditions of individualism and individual ambition. Carty states that 'Nike clearly recognizes and plays upon American values which encourage and legitimate consumption, an ideology of personal hedonism whereby commodities display the symbols of individual achievement. Hedonism, authenticity, irreverence, narcissism and the pursuit of pleasure through hard work and performance are the backbone of Nike advertising' (Carty, 1997, p. 195; see also Goldman and Papson, 1998, for a more detailed analysis of Nike's adverts).

The power of Nike was also revealed in the US$200 million sponsorship deal which it set up with the Brazilian national football team in 1996. This required the Brazilian team not only to wear the swoosh logo and appear in Nike adverts (most famous of which was the football game conducted in Rio de Janeiro airport) but also for them to play five friendly matches a year featuring eight regular first team members. Following the defeat of Brazil by France in the World Cup final of 1998, it was rumoured that Nike had insisted that Brazil's star player Ronaldo play in the match in spite of the fact that he suffered a convulsive fit just before it was due to begin. Playing Ronaldo at less than his full fitness was seen by many commentators as a significant contributory factor to Brazil's defeat. A similarly huge deal worth over £300 million was to be made with Manchester United. The football team handed control of its global replica kit and merchandising business to Nike for the period 2002 to 2015. Manager Alex Ferguson was believed to have been offered an 'ambassadorial' role with the company when he retired. In 2016, Nike agreed to pay $100m per year for 10 years to be kit sponsor for Barcelona FC.

Thinkpoint 13.6

I n her best-selling book *No Logo*, Naomi Klein devotes a significant part of a chapter to an analysis of the resistance to Nike (Klein, 2000, Chapter 16). One of the most contentious areas has been in the relationship between Nike and the sportswear of famous US colleges and universities. College campaigns against firms accused of employing sweatshop labour have been recorded and stimulated by Klein's book. Would you be happy if your college had sponsorship from a company that employed sweatshop labour and how would you respond?

Exercise 13.8

W here does your student union or university buy its logo T-shirts, sweatshirts, caps and jackets from? Is it 'fair trade' or just the cheapest that it can find in the marketplace?

- David Boje's website at www.cbae.nmsu.edu/~dboje/nike/nikemain.html
- The adbusters website at www.adbusters.org/home/
- Behind the label website at www.labourbehindthelabel.org/

Box 13.3
Websites critiquing
Nike

The anger that many people feel about Nike reflects both the issue of sweatshop labour in its subcontractors and its role in shaping culture and claiming a right of ownership and control over popular institutions, particularly in the area of sports. Not surprisingly, therefore, Nike has been the object of attack in many ways. For example, there have been spoof adverts for Nike products appearing on the Internet reflecting what is called culture-jamming and ad-busting – 'the practice of parodying advertisements and hijacking billboards in order to drastically alter their messages' (Klein, 2000, p. 280).

Multinationals and power

In order to develop a critical approach, we proceed in two sections. First we consider the silences and absences in the mainstream approach. This relates primarily to a failure to reflect on the political, social and ecological significance of multinationals. Second, we consider the conceptual inadequacies of the mainstream model and present an alternative view of the multinational and global strategy.

Silences and absences in the mainstream approach

The mainstream approach generally limits its analysis within a framework of markets and the economic rationality of organizational forms. This ignores some key areas that have already been hinted at in the discussion of Nike. We can consider these under two main headings: economic power and political power. We then consider how resistance to this power is manifested.

THE ECONOMIC POWER OF THE MULTINATIONAL

A report in 2000 calculated that of the 100 largest economies in the world, 51 are corporations and only 49 are countries. Using a comparison of gross domestic product (for measuring country size) and annual sales (for measuring company size), General Motors (the largest company) is ranked at 23 above countries such as Denmark (24), Poland (29), Finland (34) and Singapore (54) (Anderson and Cavanaugh, 2000). In broad terms, the decisions made within these massive concentrations of economic power are reflected in patterns of FDI, labour adjustment and taxation payment, and in their global market management.

Patterns of foreign direct investment

FDI is crucial to all sorts of economic benefits, not just in terms of direct employment but also in terms of the indirect employment effects generated – e.g., in supplying firms with products and services, in the increased expenditure of the employees leading to increased consumption locally and knock-on effects on local business. States, regions and urban areas compete against each other to attract FDI, offering various deals on taxation and subsidies as well as on improving infrastructure. In this respect, multinationals' ability to shift investment around the globe places them in a very powerful position relative to most national governments. Governments become tied in to providing these benefits to MNCs in the hope that the investments will have spillover effects into the locality, by providing employment to local people and opportunities to local businesses. However, the evidence is mixed as to whether there are positive payoffs. Where MNCs simply locate assembly functions in a particular locality, they do not tend to put down deep roots and are easily able to shift their facilities if conditions change. Where, however, MNCs themselves make long-term commitments by placing expensive relatively immoveable assets in a location, and then over a period, there may be positive returns.

Patterns of labour adjustment

The ability of the multinational to move around also enables it to take advantage of different wage rates and employment conditions. This does not only work in terms of locating in cheap wage areas but also in terms of using such a threat to squeeze concessions out of unions and employees keen to keep jobs in their existing locations. This idea of the use of 'coercive comparisons' has become increasingly important in countries such as Germany where traditionally high levels of union organization and employee power have led to relatively high wages, short working hours and a welfare system that compensates employees at high rates for periods of unemployment or ill health. Trade unions, faced with the prospect of manufacturing moving out of Germany to eastern Europe or Asia have been willing to moderate wage demands and to co-operate with restructuring as a way of keeping employment in its traditional base. In the past decade German employers and managers have become increasingly demanding on their workforces. Now that it is relatively easy and safe to move production into eastern and central Europe, German employers are increasingly threatening to do this unless trade unions and employees agree to certain conditions. Both Siemens and VW, two of the largest and most important multinationals, have reached agreements with their employees to extend working hours from 35 to 39 per week with no additional money. The increasingly realistic threat that they will remove production from Germany has led the unions and employees to capitulate to these demands (Streeck, 2009).

Patterns of taxation payment

The multinational firm is highly complex in terms of its internal accounting system and the ways in which it calculates profitability and liability for tax. Such firms tend to have high levels of intra-firm trade; in intra-firm trade prices are set not by the market but by administrative decisions. Thus prices can be set so that profits appear higher in low-tax areas than in high-tax ones. Anderson and Cavanagh's (2000) report, for example, notes that of the 82 US corporations on the top 200 list, 44 did not pay the full standard 35 per cent federal corporate tax rate during the period 1996–98. Seven of the firms actually paid less than zero in federal income taxes in 1998 (because of rebates) including Texaco, Chevron, PepsiCo, Enron and General Motors. In recent years, the use of tax havens by MNCs has come under increased scrutiny (Palan and Murphy, 2009); tax havens allow firms and individuals to hide their earnings from the tax inspectors of their home countries. MNCs have also become notorious for their internal pricing systems which allow them to shift the point at which they declare profits to jurisdictions where tax rates are low. For example, Amazon's Luxembourg unit took £5.3bn sales from British Internet shoppers; this meant that its UK arm recorded profits of just £34.4m on which it paid £11.9m in taxes. The UK government lost out to what was essentially an accounting manoeuvre to reduce Amazon's tax bill. The use of tax havens and tax avoidance schemes by MNCs and wealthy individuals are under substantial scrutiny by the EU, the **OECD** and national tax authorities.

> **OECD** A forum in which the governments of 34 democracies with market economies work with each other, as well as with more than 70 non-member economies, to promote economic growth, prosperity, and sustainable development.

Managing global markets

Multinationals are able to use their power to manage global production networks in ways so that primary producers or subcontractors receive a very small part of the final retail price of whatever they produce.

Box 13.4
Commodity chain analysis: Primary products

Coffee

Coffee is a simple commodity crop, mainly grown in less-developed countries of Africa, Central and Latin America and Southeast Asia. It appears in the cafés, shops and restaurants of the developed world as the product of global multinationals. The four largest roasters of coffee are Kraft, Nestlé, Procter & Gamble and Sara Lee. Their brands include Maxwell House, Nescafé, Folgers and Douwe Egberts.

The chain of relationships whereby the coffee goes from being grown to being consumed has been analyzed in a recent report entitled *Mugged: Poverty in Your Coffee Cup*, published in 2004 and available on the Oxfam website. Taking the example of coffee grown in Uganda and sold in the year ended November 2002, the report shows the following stages and prices (in dollars):

- Stage 1: Farmer sells to middleman 1 kg of green coffee beans at a price of US$0.14.
- Stage 2: Middleman transports beans to local mill (US$0.05), bags and transports to capital city (US$0.02) and takes a margin of US$0.05, making the cost of 1 kg now US$0.26.

- Stage 3: Coffee is prepared for export and the exporter takes a margin (US$0.09); bagged and transported to port (US$0.10), giving a price of US$0.45 for the actual exported coffee.
- Stage 4: The price (which includes the cost of freight and insurance – US$0.07 – and the importers' cost and margin as well as delivery to the roaster – US$0.11) at which the importer sells the coffee to the roaster is US$1.64.
- Stage 5: The coffee is then roasted, prepared, packaged and delivered to the retailer who sells the coffee at US$26.40.

Apples

A report published by Oxfam and available on their website entitled *Trading Away Our Rights* looked at the export of apples from South Africa to the UK; of the price at which the apple was sold, the following shares were taken by the various elements in the chain:

- farm labour, 5 per cent
- farm income, 4 per cent
- farm inputs and packaging, 17 per cent
- shipping, 12 per cent
- UK handling, 7 per cent
- importer's commission and duty, 7 per cent
- supermarkets, 42 per cent.

THE POLITICAL POWER OF THE MULTINATIONAL

Concentrations of economic power on the scale that have just been described are inevitably political in their impact. We can distinguish here between (a) visible and invisible power in relation to political decisions; and (b) power exercised over national contexts and national governments versus power exercised over the development of international systems of economic regulation (see Table 13.6).

The use of visible power in national contexts

Multinationals have huge resources available for employing lobbyists who work on the doorsteps of governments and legislatures in order to protect the interests of their clients. The US political system is notorious for the extent to which 'special interest' groups lobby Congress to protect themselves. Lobbying in the US context means trying to persuade politicians to support the point of view of the interest group. This persuasion can stretch from providing figures and data that support the argument through to providing money to fund political campaigns. Other lobbying methods include buying advertising space, organizing demonstrations and supplying researchers and personnel to politicians. K Street in Washington, DC, an area a few blocks north of the White House, contains many of the firms employed by multinationals to act on their behalf. In 2016, $819 million was spent on lobbying in Washington, DC; the number of lobbyists which had peaked at 14 868 in 2007 was 9916 in 2016. The pharmaceutical industry was the highest spender on lobbying, determined to maintain its power and influence in the US health system; between 1998 and 2016, it had spent over $3.3 billion on lobbying (see www.opensecrets.org/index.php).

Table 13.6 Types of exercise of political power

	Visible	Invisible
National level	Governmental lobbying, e.g., in Washington DC	Covert involvement in political coups, e.g., in Chile 1973
International level	Lobbying at the EU or in the negotiations in the WTO	Formation of private interest agreement associations, e.g., international arbitration

A Centre for Public Integrity analysis of Senate lobbying disclosure forms shows that more than 1750 companies and organizations hired about 4525 lobbyists – eight for each member of Congress – to influence Obama's health reform bills in 2009. The number of lobbyists working Congress on health reform more than doubled throughout 2009 from more than 1400 in the first three months of the year to nearly 3700 in the final quarter (see www.publicintegrity.org/articles/entry/1953/). Alongside the issue of lobbying is the provision of financial support for political parties, particularly in the USA. The website **OpenSecrets.org** has drawn up a list of the corporate donors to US political parties. In 2015-16, AT&T, the telecoms company, donated over $2 million to Political Action Committees (PACs) in the USA with most of that going to the Republicans, with donations amounting to just over $45 million (55 per cent to the Republican party and 45 per cent to the Democrats). Not all systems are as open or visible about lobbying as that in the USA. Nevertheless, the important point is that such firms have many more resources to influence governments and legislatures than, for example, citizens' groups.

The use of visible power in international contexts

When it comes to international tiers of governance, the gap between democratic lobbying and paid lobbying by multinationals becomes even greater. In 2001, for example, the *Guardian* (3 September) reported that:

> Development campaigners have reacted with outrage to the news that American and European corporate lobby groups will outnumber organizations from Third World countries at the WTO's next summit at Qatar in November. Among the 200 accredited Western industry groups are a long list of US corporate lobbyists, including the Motion Picture Association, the American Sugar Alliance and the United Egg Producers Association. Twenty six of the groups are industry committees advising the US government on trade. Development campaigners, already furious that the WTO has told all observer groups to send a single representative, said corporate lobbyists outnumbered developing country groups by six to one.

Thinkpoint 13.7

The European Parliament has instituted a registration system for lobbyists. Under this system in 2016, 9215 organizations had the right to lobby in the parliament. 1076 were professional consultancies, law firms and self-employed consultants mainly lobbying on behalf of business. 4289 were in-house lobbyists for firms or business associations. 2365 were Non-governmental organization (NGOs) and the rest a mix of think tanks, religious communities and public authorities. As in the USA, the majority of lobbyists are directly serving the interests of business. Do you think that lobbying by corporate interests is 'good' for democracy?

The use of invisible power in a national context

US multinationals have frequently been accused of behind the scenes activities in order to elicit support from the US government and, in particular, the CIA to overthrow governments that have threatened their interests. In 1954, for example, the legally elected government of Guatemala was overthrown by an invasion force of mercenaries trained by the CIA. The President who was overthrown was Jacobo Arbenz, a left-of-centre socialist; four of the 56 seats in the Congress were held by communists. What was most unsettling to American business interests was that Arbenz had expropriated 234 000 acres of land owned by the US multinational United Fruit, offering compensation that United Fruit called 'unacceptable'. The new government gave the land back to United Fruit, abolished the tax on interest and dividends to foreign investors, eliminated the secret ballot and jailed thousands of political critics. A long list of other names could be added to this, of governments and leaders who were threatening the interests of US multinationals and therefore prompted intervention by the CIA to support anti-government forces. For example, in March 1964, Brazil's elected president, Joao Goulart, ordered the nationalization of all private oil refineries. By 1 April, a military junta brought down his government ushering in an era of an exceedingly brutal tyranny which introduced the use of death squads. The CIA was involved in a major way in bringing about the coup d'état in Brazil. Similar fates were met by Prime Minister Mossedeq of Iran (because he had nationalized the oil industry) and Salvador Allende of Chile (who also threatened nationalization of the property of US multinationals). Similarly, the US government, lobbied by US multinationals, has supported undemocratic regimes that have protected their property rights – e.g., right-wing death squad leaders in El Salvador, contras in Nicaragua, Suharto in Indonesia and apartheid in South Africa.

Exercise 13.9

The war in Iraq and its subsequent aftermath has led to a host of accusations that the US government was primarily interested in making sure that it had access to Iraqi oil. It was also accused of awarding contracts for the reconstruction of Iraq to certain favoured US multinationals, most particularly Haliburton, a company which used to be run by President Bush's vice-president, Dick Cheney.

Use the Internet to track down these allegations. Do you think there is any truth in them? Is this yet another example of US multinationals and the US government working hand-in-hand to create a government favourable to US interests rather than responsible to its own citizens?

The use of invisible power in an international context

In an era when international economic transactions increasingly cross borders, an important area of development that is almost totally invisible to public scrutiny concerns the establishment of private international law. In an interesting analysis of this phenomenon, Dezalay and Garth (1996) have revealed how companies that find themselves in dispute with each other are increasingly unwilling to reveal this in the public arena. As a result, a whole new area of law has begun to develop that is separate from normal, national jurisdictional contexts. A court has been set up by the International Chamber of Commerce (ICC) to deal with contract disputes between large companies or between countries and companies. In order to resolve these disputes by agreement, the parties are brought together in front of a neutral party to whom the facts of the case are presented. This neutral party then makes the decision in what is known as an 'arbitration'. This sounds like a normal legal procedure. The difference is that the parties to the contract decide which laws will apply and who will be the judge so they are not bound by the laws of the country in which the dispute takes place. With this flexibility, it is generally possible to structure a neutral procedure offering no undue advantage to any party. The website for the court states (amongst other things):[1]

- Judicial systems do not allow the parties to a dispute to choose their own judges. In contrast, arbitration offers the parties the unique opportunity to designate persons of their choice as arbitrators, provided they are independent. This enables the parties to have their disputes resolved by people who have specialized competence in the relevant field.
- Arbitration is faster and less expensive than litigation in the courts. Although a complex international dispute may sometimes take a great deal of time and money to resolve, even by arbitration, the limited scope for challenge against arbitral awards, as compared with court judgements, offers a clear advantage. Above all, it helps to ensure that the parties will not subsequently be entangled in a prolonged and costly series of appeals.
- Arbitration hearings are not public, and only the parties themselves receive copies of the awards.

Dezalay and Garth reveal how the arbitrators themselves are chosen from among establishment figures across a range of societies. These figures are generally highly-esteemed members of the legal elites sharing similar class backgrounds and connections. In these settings, multinational firms can ensure that their 'dirty linen' is not washed in public but kept discreetly behind closed doors. The rules that bind the sides in the arbitration can be chosen from many different jurisdictions; they do not have to reflect where the case is actually conducted or the national jurisdiction in which the case arose. Thus this sphere of international law emerges without any democratic accountability. In 2003, 580 requests for arbitration were filed with the ICC Court, concerning 1584 parties from 123 different countries and independent territories; the place of arbitration was located in 47 different countries throughout the world; arbitrators of 69 different nationalities were appointed or confirmed under the ICC rules.

Recent treaties negotiated by the USA – the TransPacific Partnership (TPP) with various Asian countries including Japan – and the Transatlantic Trade and Investment Partnership (negotiated with the EU but yet to be ratified) follow this model in that they allow national governments to be sued by foreign companies if they can be shown to have not allowed proper access to their markets, e.g., by constraining private participation in markets in health care or education. These rules are known as Investor-State Dispute Settlements (ISDS) mechanisms.

This has been just a small selection of the silences and absences of the mainstream. The key point is that this mainstream neglects issues of economic and political power. However, before we leave this topic it is necessary to reiterate that this power is continually opposed and contested. Any quick Internet search will reveal a massive list of websites devoted to anti-globalization.[2] It has been argued both by the opponents of globalization and its adherents that the communication possibilities among protestors have been improved by the Internet, enabling rapid and unexpected mobilization of protestors. Events such as the Occupy protests which began in 2011 have revealed both the strength of feeling and the role of the Internet in mobilizing such forces.

Moreover, there have been many efforts within existing international institutions to control multinationals. The International Labour Organization (ILO), which was originally founded under the Treaty of Versailles ending the First World War, and then became part of the UN, has been campaigning since 1919 for the promotion of fair labour standards across the world. The ILO has been active in developing conventions and regulations about the treatment of labour, many of which have been accepted by national governments, though much obviously remains to be done.

More recently, the UN itself set up a Global Compact bringing together multinationals, governments and labour organizations to discuss and agree forms of regulation and control.[3] The degree to which the Global Compact is effective in changing the behaviour of MNCs or merely a form of 'greenwashing' is hotly disputed (see Rasche and Kell, 2010). Resistance to globalization ranges from radical attempts to criticize and undermine the system (see e.g., Hardt and Negri, 2000) through to organizations that seek to reform multinationals and the process of globalization by creating public accountability systems (see Chapter 15).

Retheorizing the multinational

Many critical analyses of multinationals and their impact on globalization concentrate exclusively in issues of the concentration of power. However, another approach is to theorize in a different way the nature of multinationals. Here the emphasis is on attacking the vision of the multinational as an economically rational form, not just by emphasizing its political character but also by showing that the multinational in fact consists of multiple groups of actors involved in ongoing conflict and negotiation. One way to discuss this is in terms of the concepts of 'transnational social space' and 'transnational communities'. This terminology is initially drawn from the interface of ethnic studies, labour migration, economic globalization and cultural identities (see Morgan, 2001a, 2001b for a more extended discussion; also the contributions in Morgan, Whitley and Kristensen, 2001; Collinson and Morgan, 2009). Underlying it is the sense that forms of social action and identity are increasingly co-ordinated across national boundaries and it is therefore important to understand the modes of social organization, mobility and communication that enable these processes to hang together. This in turn is related to the idea of dialogues of communication that can emerge and be sustained across national boundaries, out of which new definitions of identity and interest can emerge. While these new definitions in themselves remain contested, they embody a dual movement. On the one hand, the importance of the local (in its cultural and social manifestations) is affirmed, but, on the other hand, the contrast between different 'locals' becomes the means whereby more general definitions of the collective become defined.

Such an approach turns the normal model of the MNC upside down as it means that the focus is on multiple local sites rather than a coherent hierarchical structure in which decisions are taken and implemented on the basis of an abstract, economically rational mode of acting. In this view, the multinational is not a 'thing' or an actor; rather it consists of multiple local sites that each have their own conditions of existence and their own type of embeddedness in local social relations, and that this produces a micro-political process in which different actors engage (see Becker-Ritterspach and Dörrenbächer, 2009; Blazejewski, 2006; Dörrenbächer and Geppert, 2006, 2009, 2011; Gammelgaard, 2009; Geppert *et al.*, 2003; Geppert and Matten, 2006; Geppert and Williams, 2006). By 'embeddedness' is meant work and authority relations reflecting the distinctive national and local history of the particular site (see the earlier discussion on 'varieties of capitalism'). From the point of view of senior managers and the capital markets, the multinational as an organization is a means of co-ordinating these local sites into a single legal and financial entity that can produce 'shareholder value'. The management headquarters of multinationals, within the constraints set for them by financial governance mechanisms operated through capital markets, develop specific sets of practices to bring order and co-ordination to these local sites. They seek to impose the terms of the debate in which 'general' and 'collective' interests are represented – e.g., profitability, shareholder value and efficiency. However, the degree to which these are imposed and accepted by local sites is clearly variable (see for instance the excellent studies by Belanger *et al.,* 1999 and Kristensen and Zeitlin, 2005 as well as the references above to micro-political studies). Also, the actors within the local sites may themselves seek to develop links across sites or with actors that are outside the multinational – e.g., the local state, local and international suppliers and customers, local, national and international social movements such as trade unions or other collective bodies. Other dialogues across national, organizational and institutional boundaries can potentially emerge in these contexts. These in turn may give rise to alternative definitions of the collective interest that may not be encapsulated in concepts of 'shareholder value' but may revolve around discourses of 'employee rights', **sustainable development**, 'respect for local communities', etc.

One aspect of such an institution is the European Works Council. Any company with subsidiaries in two or more members of the EU is supposed to establish a European Works Council (EWC). The EWC has the right to receive and be consulted about the company's strategy insofar as it affects employment and conditions of work. Employee representatives are nominated at national level and then meet in the EWC with other employees as well as managers. The EWC is a top-down institution emerging out of the EU rather than being the result of employees agitating for such a body. Nevertheless, it is one example of a formal institution that allows employees to make connections with each other and discuss common issues. It seems clear that when BMW management was discussing how to get rid of its loss-making Rover operation in the UK, employee representatives from both the UK and Germany strenuously opposed the closure of Rover in Birmingham.

Sustainable development
A term generally used to refer to a concern with balancing economic demands with a concern for future generations. For example, the use of timber is now controlled in many, but by no means all, parts of the world, so that for every tree cut down another is planted in its place.

Exercise 13.10
The growing significance of European Works Councils

In 2014, 980 MNCs were registered as having EWCs and 1061 were active. EWCs have been growing at a rate of 20–30 per year in recent years.

Using an Internet search engine, find two examples of EWCs based in MNCs from different countries in Europe. Can you find out what they have discussed? Do they have any power? What problems do you think emerge on the employee side co-ordinating their approach to these discussions?

In a critical approach to multinationals, local sites and subsidiaries can be seen as having their own social dynamics. They are not reducible to the outcome of the control measures undertaken by the headquarters. Two dimensions are relevant here. The first concerns the degree of autonomy and independence that the local site can exercise vis-à-vis headquarters control. The second concerns the nature of social relationships within the local subsidiary. With regard to the former, local sites will be more powerful if the following conditions apply:

- They have technical expertise that is unavailable elsewhere in the company and yet perceived as important.
- Their production system is perceived to be among the best in the company and therefore not easily replaceable.
- Their products and services are important for other sites and other products (i.e., rather than being only destined for local consumer markets).

This independence can be reinforced by conditions outside the firm itself. For example, where a local area constitutes what is called an 'industrial district' or an 'innovation cluster' in which there are multiple social relationships crossing firm boundaries and supported by local government, local training and innovation centres and local financial institutions, the subsidiary may be deeply embedded in these relationships (Solvell and Zander, 1998; Kristensen and Zeitlin, 2001). Moreover, the multinational may have set up or purchased the subsidiary precisely so that it can tap into these local resources. It cannot therefore act in a way that interferes with the operation of these local networks or it destroys what it set out to gain.

Exercise 13.11

Look in recent editions of the *Financial Times*. What examples can you find of multinationals doing the following?

- Closure of an existing subsidiary plant.
- Sale or divestment of a subsidiary plant. Acquisition of a subsidiary.
- New investment in an existing subsidiary plant.
- Setting up a new plant.

You will find it a lot easier to find examples of closures or the threat of closures. What reasons has the MNC given for its decisions? What have local political actors to say about these decisions? What impact will these have on the local community and/or the broader region/nation?

Whether and how a local site might exercise its power against the headquarters, however, depends on the nature of the social relationships within the local site. The most important issue in this context is the form of social cohesion in the local context. The literature on 'varieties of capitalism' has revealed that authority relationships within the firm can vary immensely depending on the nature of the national context. Simplifying this literature, one can distinguish on the one side local sites that are embedded in a social democratic or collectivist ethos of economic activity; on the other side are those systems based more on individual rights and responsibilities and/or in which collective organizations are weak.

In local sites within societies where social democratic movements have been strong and the outcomes of their activities have been put into the legal framework, a form of social cohesion exists that emphasizes the collective fate of the local economic activity and the rights of those concerned to be, at the least, consulted. Such systems would, for example, include Germany and the Scandinavian countries where trade unions and works councils have generally had access to high levels of information. These systems in turn are generally based upon a form of class compromise between labour and capital; in return for certain rights to consultation, stability of employment and high wages, workers accept managers' rights to continually upgrade technology and production processes. This class compromise

Box 13.5
The varieties of capitalism approach

In recent years there has been strong interest in how different forms of capitalism are structured. For example, in countries like Germany, Sweden and Japan, decisions about how firms should behave in relation to investments, how they treat employees and how they treat suppliers, tend to be decisions that are taken not just inside the firm but through co-ordinated action with others, such as their bankers, the state, their employees and their trade unions, and other employers in the same industry. Hall and Soskice (2001) refer to such systems as 'co-ordinated market economies'. Where these same decisions are taken primarily by the management of the firm on the basis of their perceptions of the market (for labour, for components, for capital, for products), this is referred to as 'liberal market economies' (the USA and the UK). These two models have profound implications for power and inequality as well as for how firms are managed and organized. Broadly speaking, co-ordinated market economies tend to be more consultative and participative both inside and outside the firm; they are often dominated by broadly social democratic politics. Liberal market economies tend to have firms that are led by managers who are keen to exercise power without restraint from other stakeholders. Liberal market economies are characterized by more flexible employment arrangements and higher disparities of reward than co-ordinated market economies. They tend to be dominated by more individualistic and market-dominated forms of politics.

The two systems tend to work better in different industry environments. Thus traditionally co-ordinated market economies have developed very strong capabilities in engineering, automotive and electronic products areas, while liberal market economies have tended to be more successful in rapidly evolving market areas where flexibility is important – e.g., software industries, professional services, entertainment and broadcasting.

In the 1980s, the co-ordinated market model was favoured by some commentators as it seemed to offer protection against the sort of 'deindustrialization' that the UK and the USA under Thatcher and Reagan suffered. In the 1990s as new industries sprang up in computing, Internet technology and biotechnology, the USA and UK seemed very much more successful than countries like Germany and Japan. However, in the early part of this decade, the dot-com crash and the subsequent fall of Enron, Arthur Andersen, WorldCom and a number of other companies seen as exemplars of the strength of US capitalism in the 1990s made people question US dominance.

As well as Hall and Soskice (2001) and Whitley (1999), see the collection of papers by Hancke (2009); also Morgan *et al.* (2010); Morgan and Whitley, 2012; Kristensen *et al.*, 2012.

is also reflected in wider social relations. In social democratic systems, welfare rights (e.g., unemployment benefit, sickness pay, pensions), tend to be the outcome of collective processes organized through the state or the trade unions.

Workers also accept the responsibility to learn and develop their own skills in the light of changing technological and competitive conditions (for the broader debate on skills and learning see Chapter 6). In its most worked out form, there exists a strong set of institutional links between the innovative capacity of local production sites, local government systems, forms of training inside and outside the firm and the legislative framework for labour and capital. These sites are locally embedded in a variety of ways, not least that employment in the locality is long term and has been built up on the basis of sustained collective investment in local training and research facilities. This is reinforced by strong links between local banks, local political institutions and the livelihoods of communities. It is also strengthened by the collective institutions at the national level in which the employee representatives of the local sites can access management information and form their own perspective on the 'collective good'.

In more individualist systems, on the other hand, collective institutions are weak and individuals have to develop their own responses to labour market conditions with little help from trade unions or the government. They are much more reliant on their own earning power to fund both gaps in employment or efforts at further training and their old age and retirement. Increasingly, the savings necessary for this tend to be invested in private sector investment management companies. All this reinforces the dependence of the individual and the family on movements in the stock market and reduces dependence on state provision of welfare. The power of capital in liberal market economies is relatively unconstrained by legal blocks or trade union power. Decisions about production and location are taken by managerial elites in response to 'market pressures'. Local objections to closures or rationalizations of production sites are treated as ill-informed and short-sighted about the conditions necessary for economic welfare. There are few strong institutional links between firms, local political institutions and the development of a social and training infrastructure for the workforce. The conditions for reproducing the locality as a community with a strong collective identity have been dismantled. The collective purpose is defined by unconstrained free markets, which will, in the end, supposedly, benefit all.

In collectivist systems, the local subsidiaries of multinationals are usually controlled at middle and lower management level (and sometimes higher) by managers who have long been associated with the local system. This is likely to lead to a stronger sense of solidarity and collectivism, binding managers and employees in a common 'community of fate', than where the managers have been put in by headquarters and see themselves as part of a global management cadre with their first loyalty to the company rather than the local site (Kristensen and Zeitlin, 2001). Therefore, local sites can exercise power and, within certain limited contexts, can create and sustain alternatives to the dominant managerial logic.

In any multinational, therefore, the degree to which the headquarters can enforce its power over the local sites will vary according to the degree to which a local site has some independence and also the degree to which there is a form of social solidarity/coherence among local managers and employees that enables that local power to be exercised (see e.g., the differences between sites in the study of a division of ABB by Belanger *et al.*, 1999; see also contributions in Morgan *et al.*, 2001; Geppert *et al.*, 2002).

Managing the multinational across national and institutional divides

Managers at various levels of firms (the divisional, the geographical business unit, the head office functions as well as those actually working within the local sites) attempt to bring order into the diversity of the localities. There are various ways in which control can be exercised. Among the most obvious are the quantitative controls that are placed on local sites. These may be financial measures, quality measures, productivity measures, manpower measures and other efficiency measures. Where such systems are in operation, the next tier of management is most concerned with the quantitative outcomes and less interested in how they are achieved.

This can have two obvious effects, though how this works out in practice will relate to issues of independence and solidarity as discussed in the previous section. The first effect is that the quantitative indicators themselves become sites of social construction and negotiation. What appear to be 'hard', quantitative indicators usually dissolve on further inspection into figures that have to be constructed and interpreted. What are taken as objective 'facts' are the outcome of processes in which actors negotiate over what is to count and what is to be 'discounted'. This is not to understate the importance of such quantitative targets and their use as a way both of co-ordinating across sites and providing the basis for management action. However, it is important to question within multinationals decisions, for example, about plant closures where the argument is made on the basis of so-called 'hard evidence' about lack of profitability, efficiency and so on.

This relates to the second effect of the use of quantitative indicators, which is the role of negotiation and meaning construction that occurs between local sites and various tiers of management at divisional and headquarters level. If multinationals hold to multiple quantitative targets, negotiation and power to define which are the most important measures becomes crucial. Senior management measures of productivity and efficiency may be challenged in themselves or even placed against other locally developed measures, such as 'serving the local community', 'innovating' and providing useful employment.

Control and co-ordination can also be exercised, as previously discussed, by positioning expatriate managers in the most important roles within subsidiaries. Expatriate managers can be expected to have been socialized within the headquarters and be strongly committed to achieving according to head office criteria. This will normally be their route to career advancement within the company. Even if their career expectations lie beyond the company, they will be more likely to rely on an assessment of their achievements by the head office for future advancement than by the local site. Expatriate managers act as 'the eyes and ears' of the head office. They exercise control and co-ordination by implementing practices defined by the head office as essential to its global functioning. However, there may be other sorts of managers who have developed their careers in the locality and are committed to this site. They are less likely to accept the logic espoused by the headquarters and can, in fact, be in a good position to debunk and challenge this approach on the basis of their knowledge of local conditions.

Instead of perceiving a multinational as a 'thing-like' object with goals that are determined by the necessities of market survival, the approach here has been to see the multinational firm as a transnational social space that binds together in various ways a variety of social contexts. The nature of these local sites, how they become bound together through processes of control and co-ordination, and how all of this fits into a broader process of capitalism becomes the focus of analysis. The approach is concerned with process, with 'becoming' rather than 'being'. From this point of view, the analysis of the multinational could be much more usefully concerned with analyzing these sites, in terms of how they relate to their local context, to other local sites, to social and political movements beyond their local boundaries and to the headquarters.

This has a crucial effect on issues of policy and strategy for those seeking to resist multinationals, because it emphasizes that local struggles can be successful. The multinational is not all powerful; it cannot simply close down a plant or reduce numbers employed. In order to do that, it has to be involved in some sort of negotiation and this negotiation is structured by the social relationships in the local site, the local community and the broader political context.

Box 13.6
The decline of Rover Cars in Birmingham, UK

When BMW saw that they would be continuing to lose money on Rover for some time, their senior management looked for ways to sever their ties. BMW saw that the simple closure of the site was not an option because the impact on the local area was too large in terms of jobs. Politicians, trade unionists and local community leaders would inevitably resist this. BMW therefore sought to pass on responsibility by selling Rover to a venture capitalist company, Alchemy partners. As it became known what Alchemy was planning, there was huge disquiet. Alchemy proposed to massively thin down production at Rover's main Longbridge plant. Trade union officials saw the implications and quickly moved to block this by threatening to take Alchemy and BMW to court for potential breaches of EU law in relation to the supply of information to employees, among other things. The coalition of local, national and international forces that had defeated BMW's initial moves to closure stayed together to defeat Alchemy. Instead, a new bid was put together by previous Rover managers under John Towers (who had left soon after BMW took over). They took over the Longbridge plant and other assets for a nominal sum and BMW made a less than graceful exit.

In April 2005 Rover Cars went into liquidation. The company had failed to generate sufficient revenue from its existing fleet of cars and needed substantial backing from another partner if it was to succeed. To that end, it had sought an alliance with a major Chinese car company, Shanghai Automotive Industry Corporation. These efforts were unsuccessful and Rover closed. There was a great deal of controversy because, while many thousands of employees in Rover and in the local area lost jobs, the owners of the company had managed to secure themselves large pensions that were not lost. For a comprehensive account of this see the report by the National Audit Office at www.nao.org.uk/pn/05–06/0506961.htm.

In comparison, other car plants have been effectively closed without this degree of opposition. Ford's earliest and biggest plant in the UK at Dagenham, Essex has been downgraded from assembly to engine work with a significant loss of jobs and very little resistance. In September 2004, Ford announced its intention to close one of its Jaguar plants in Coventry, and, in 2006, Peugeot decided to close its plant in Ryton, near Coventry.

Why are there such different reactions to factory closures? Is it simply a matter of scale or are some closures politicized in ways that others are not. Does it matter how strong a local community there is associated with the factory?

Conclusion

These arguments point to the role critical management theorists can play in developing alternative accounts of how multinationals work and showing how rationalist efficiency arguments are built on particular constructions and interpretations of social reality. These interpretations are not the only ones available and it is important to provide the possibility of alternatives by examining the different groups inside the multinational, with their different rationalities and logics of action. In fact, by virtue of its very structure, the multinational creates the space for new forms of dialogue across nations, across the developed and the less-developed regions of the world, and across different institutional contexts. Developing and using these spaces to create an emancipatory agenda is a fundamental challenge to critical theorists.

In conclusion, critical management studies can open up the sphere of international business and multinationals to much wider scrutiny than has previously been the case. It can shift the agenda away from technical and economistic analyses of these processes and link more closely with the critical social science literature that has emerged over the last few years in this area. It can do this best by building on its own strengths in terms of examining the conflicts and contradictions that emerge within multinationals as managers seek to control and co-ordinate different interests as well as different sites of production.

Discussion questions

1 Why do multinational firms exist?

2 How do the dynamics of different markets affect (a) how firms internationalize and (b) how international firms organize?

3 Should multinationals aim to create a single common culture among all their managers?

4 Do multinationals exert too much power? If so, who should control them and how?

5 Can and should local communities exercise influence over the decisions of multinationals to invest in or disinvest from an area?

6 Do you want to work in a multinational? If so, why, and how do you expect this would be different from working in a firm located in just one country?

Further reading

Collinson, S. and Morgan, G. (eds) (2009) *Images of Multinationals*, London: Wiley.

This edited collection provides a wide range of perspectives from both the mainstream and the critical alternative perspective on how multinationals are structured. It provides a series of useful contrasts that can be drawn on to make comparisons between different images of the multinational.

Dicken, P. (2014) *Global Shift*, seventh edn, London: Sage.

This is a vast source of information on how international production is organized within a variety of sectors. It provides detailed accounts both of the structure of multinationals and how global commodity chains are organized. As it is written by a geographer, it also contains some useful maps and illustrations of the dynamics of economic globalization and has been updated regularly since its first publication in 1986.

Hall, P. and Soskice, D. (eds) (2001) *Varieties of Capitalism*, Oxford: Oxford University Press.

Although many authors had already started to explore the idea of 'varieties of capitalism', this edited volume has become the essential reference point for subsequent debates. The Introduction sets out the basic model and further chapters explore how varieties of capitalism impact on firm strategies.

Held, D., McGrew, A., Goldblatt, D. and Perraton, J. (1998) *Global Transformations*, Oxford: Polity Press.

This book provides an overview of globalization in all its aspects, including economic production, regulation, labour migration and cultural issues, as well as considering the role of the state and other societal institutions. There are now a number of accompanying readers and collections that contain classic articles on these themes as well as a website www.polity.co.uk/global/default.asp.

Hirst, P., Thompson, G. and Bromley, S. (eds) (2009) *Globalization in Question*, third, Oxford: Polity Press.

This is the most comprehensive critical discussion of globalization from a sceptical perspective. It emphasizes the continued importance of states to the organization of the global economy as well as the role of the Triad regions in terms of the organization of firms and markets.

Locke, R.M. (2013) *The Promise and Limits of Private Power: Promoting Labor Standards in the Global Economy* Cambridge: Cambridge University Press

This book looks at how large MNCs in the West have been forced by consumer bodies and other NGOs to improve work conditions in their network of overseas sub-contractors. The author has conducted empirical research in a number of major countries such as Nike and their sub-contractors in Asia and Latin America. He shows the weakness of Codes of fair practice in labour standards due to problems of monitoring as well as the role that is played by the buyers in terms of their demands. He shows that it is only where there is strong engagement on the part of the buyer companies to upgrade the quality of work that serious improvement in labour standards begins to emerge.

References

Ailon, G. (2008) 'Mirror, mirror on the wall: *Culture's consequences* in a value test of its own design', *Academy of Management Review*, 33(4): 885–904.

Ailon, G. (2009) Mirror, mirror on the wall: *Culture's consequences* in a Value test of its own design', *Academy of Management Review*, 23(4): 885–904.

Anderson, S. and Cavanaugh, J. (2000) *The Top 200: The Rise of Global Corporate Power*, Washington, DC: Institute for Policy Studies.

Bair, J. (ed.) (2009) *Frontiers of Commodity Chain Research*, Stanford, CA: Stanford University Press.

Bartlett, C. A. and Ghoshal, S. (1989) *Managing Across Borders: The Transnational Solution*, London: Century Business.

Baskerville, R. F. (2003) 'Hofstede never studied culture', *Accounting, Organizations and Society*, 28(1): 1–14.

Becker-Ritterspach, F. and Dörrenbächer, C. (2009) 'Intra-firm competition in multinational corporations: Towards a political framework', *Competition and Change*, 13(3): 199–213.

Belanger, J., Berggren, C., Bjorkman, T. and Kohier, C. (1999) *Being Local and Worldwide: ABB and the Challenge of Global Management*, Ithaca, NY: Cornell University Press.

Bendix, R. (1956) *Work and Authority in Industry*, Berkeley, CA: University of California Press.

Blazejewski, S. (2006). "Transferring value-infused organisational practices in multi-national companies: A conflict perspective." In: Geppert, Mike & Mayer, Michael (eds.): *Global, national and local practices in multinational corporations* (pp. 63–104)

Buckley, P. and Casson, M. (1976) *The Future of the Multinational Enterprise*, London: Macmillan.

Buckley, P. and Casson, M. (1985) *The Economic Theory of the Multinational Enterprise*, London: Macmillan.

Carty, V. (1997) 'Ideologies and forms of domination in the organization of the global production and consumption of goods in the emerging postmodern era: A case study of Nike Corporation and the implications for gender', *Gender, Work and Organizations*, 4(4): 189–201.

Coe, N. and Yeung, H. W-C. (2015) *Global Production Networks: Theorizing Economic Development in an Interconnected World*, Oxford: Oxford University Press

Collinson, S. and Morgan, G. (2009) *Images of the Multinational Firm*, Chichester: Wiley.

Dezalay, Y. and Garth, B. (1996) *Dealing in Virtue*, Chicago, IL: University of Chicago Press.

Dicken, P. (2014) *Global Shift*, seventh edn, London: Sage.

Dörrenbächer and Geppert (2006) Micro-politics and conflicts in multinational corporations: Current debates, re-framing, and contributions of this Special Issue, *Journal of International Management*, 12(3): 251–265.

Dörrenbächer and Geppert (2009) A micro-political perspective on subsidiary initiative-taking: Evidence from German-owned subsidiaries in France. *European Management Journal*, 27: 100–112.

Dörrenbächer and Geppert (2011) Politics and power in the multinational corporation: an introduction, In: C. Dörrenbächer and M. Geppert (eds.): *Politics and power in the multinational corporation: The role of interests, identities, and institution* (pp. 3–38). Cambridge University Press: Cambridge.

Dunning, J. (1998) 'Reappraising the eclectic paradigm in an age of alliance capitalism', in M. Colombo (ed.) *The Changing Boundaries of the Firm*, London: Routledge, pp. 25–59.

Dunning, J. (2001) 'The key literature on IB activities: 1960–2000', in A. Rugman and T. Brewer (eds) *The Oxford Handbook of International Business*, Oxford: Oxford University Press, pp. 36–68.

Fiss, P. C. and Hirsch, P. M. (2005) 'The discourse of globalization: Framing and sensemaking of an emerging concept', *American Sociological Review*, 70(1): 29–52.

Friedman, T. (2000) *The Lexus and the Olive Tree*, London: Harper Collins.

Friedman, T. (2005) *The World is Flat: A Brief History of the Globalized World in the 21st Century*, London: Allen Lane.

Gammelgard, J. (2009) 'Issue selling and bargaining power in the intrafirm competition: The differentiating impact of the subsidiary management composition', *Competition and Change*, 13(3): 214–228.

Geppert, M. and Matten, D. (2006) 'Institutional influences on manufacturing organization in multinational corporations: The "Cherrypicking" approach', *Organization Studies,* 27(4): 491–516.

Geppert, M. and Williams, K. (2006) 'Global, national and local practices in multinational corporations', *International Journal of Human Resource Management,* 17(1): 49–69.

Geppert, M., Matten, D. and Williams, K. (eds) (2002) *Challenges for European Management in a Global Context,* London: Palgrave.

Geppert, M., Williams, K. and Matten, D. (2003) 'The social construction of contextual rationalities in MNCs: An Anglo-German comparison of subsidiary choice', *Journal of Management Studies,* 40(3): 617–41.

Gereffi, G. (1996) 'Global commodity chains: New forms of coordination and control among nations and firms in international industries', *Competition and Change,* 1(4): 427–439.

Gereffi, G. (2001) 'Shifting governance structures in global commodity chains: With special reference to the internet', *American Behavioural Scientist,* 44(10): 1616–1637.

Gereffi, G., Humphreys, J. and Sturgeon, T. (2005) 'The governance of global value chains', *Review of International Political Economy,* 12(1): 78–104.

Giddens, A. (1999) *Runaway World: How Globalization is Reshaping Our Lives,* London: Profile Books.

Goldman, R. and Papson, S. (1998) *Nike Culture,* London: Sage.

Hall, P. and Soskice, D. (eds) (2001) *Varieties of Capitalism,* Oxford: Oxford University Press.

Hancke, B. (ed.) (2009) *Debating Varieties of Capitalism,* Oxford: Oxford University Press.

Hardt, M. and Negri, A. (2000) *Empire,* Cambridge, MA: Harvard University Press.

Harzing, A.-W. (2000) 'An empirical test and extension of the Bartlett and Ghoshal typology of multinational companies', *Journal of International Business Studies,* 31(1): 101–120.

Held, D., McGrew, A., Goldblatt, D. and Perraton, J. (1999) *Global Transformations,* Oxford: Polity.

Hirst, P., Thompson, G. and Bromley, S. (2009) *Globalization in Question,* third edn, Oxford: Polity Press.

Hofstede, G. (2001) *Culture's Consequences,* second edn, Thousand Oaks, CA: Sage.

Hofstede, G. (2003a) 'What is culture? A reply to Baskerville', *Accounting, Organizations and Society,* 28(1): 811–813.

Hofstede, G. (2003b) 'Dimensions do not exist: A reply to Brendan McSweeney', *Human Relations,* 55(11): 1355–1361.

Klein, N. (2000) *No Logo,* London: Flamingo.

Kristensen, P. H. and Zeitlin, J. (2001) 'The making of a global firm', in G. Morgan, R. Whitley and P. H. Kristensen (eds) *The Multinational Firm:* *Organizing Across Institutional and National Divides,* Oxford: Oxford University Press, pp. 172–195.

Kristensen, P. H. and Zeitlin, J. (2005) *Local Pathways to a Global Firm,* Oxford: Oxford University Press.

Kristensen, P. H. Lilja, K. and Moen, E. (2012) *Nordic Capitalisms and Globalization,* Oxford: Oxford University Press.

McSweeney, B. (2002a) 'Hofstede's model of national cultural differences and their consequences: A triumph of faith, a failure of analysis', *Human Relations,* 55(1): 89–118.

McSweeney, B. (2002b) 'The essentials of scholarship: A reply to Geert Hofstede', *Human Relations,* 55(11): 1363–1372.

Morgan, G., Campbell, J., Crouch, C., Pedersen, O. K. and Whitley, R. (eds) (2010) *The Oxford Handbook of Comparative Institutional Analysis,* Oxford: Oxford University Press.

Morgan, G, Whitley, R. and Kristensen, P. H. (eds) (2001) *The Multinational Firm: Organizing Across Institutional and National Divides,* Oxford: Oxford University Press.

Morgan, G. (2001a) 'The multinational firm', in G. Morgan, P. H. Kristensen and R. Whitley (eds) *The Multinational Firm: Organizing Across Institutional and National Divides,* Oxford: Oxford University Press, pp. 1–24.

Morgan, G. (2001b) 'Transnational communities and business systems', *Global Networks,* 1(2): 113–130.

Morgan, G. (2009) 'Globalization', in P. Hancock and A. Spicer (eds) *Understanding Corporate Life,* London: Sage, pp. 96–113.

Morgan, G. and Whitley, R. (eds) (2012) *Capitalism and Capitalisms in the 21st Century,* Oxford: Oxford University Press.

Ngai, P. and Chan, J. (2012) 'Global capital, the state and Chinese workers: The Foxconn experience', *Modern China,* 38(4): 383–410.

Ogasawara, Y. (1998) *Office Ladies and Salaried Men: Power, Gender and Work in Japanese Companies,* Berkeley, CA: University of California Press.

Palan, R. and Murphy, R. (2009) *Tax Havens: How Globalization Really Works,* Ithaca, NY: Cornell University Press.

Prahalad, C. K. and Doz, Y. (1987) *The Multinational Mission: Balancing Local Demands and Global Vision,* New York: Free Press.

Rasche, A. and Kell, G. (eds) (2010) *The United Nations Global Compact: Achievements, Trends and Challenges,* Cambridge: Cambridge University Press.

Rugman, A. (2000) *The End of Globalization,* London: Random House.

Solvell, O. and Zander, I. (1998) 'International diffusion of knowledge: Isolating mechanisms and the role of the MNE', in A. D. Chandler, O. Solvell and P. Hagstrom (eds) *The Dynamic Firm: The Role of Technology, Strategy, Organization and Regions,* Oxford: Oxford University Press, pp. 402–417.

Streeck, W. (2009) *Re-Forming Capitalism,* Oxford: Oxford University Press.

United Nations Conference on Trade and Development (UNCTAD) (2010) *World Investment Report 2010: Investing in a low-carbon economy* Geneva: UNCTAD.

Vernon, R. (1966) 'International investment and international trade in the product cycle', *Quarterly Journal of Economics,* 80(2): 90–207.

Watson, J. L. (ed.) (1997) *Golden Arches East: McDonald's in Asia,* Stanford, CA: Stanford University Press.

Whitley, R. (1999) *Divergent Capitalisms,* Oxford: Oxford University Press.

Williams, R. (1992) *Keywords,* second edn, London: Fontana.

Notes

1 From www.iccwbo.org/court/english/arbitration/introduction.asp © The International Chamber of Commerce, reproduced with permission.

2 See e.g., www.anti-marketing.com/anti-globalization.html

3 See www.unglobalcompact.org/Portal/

14 Bureaucracy and post-bureaucracy

CHRISTOPHER GREY

Key concepts and learning objectives

By the end of this chapter you should understand:

- The two models of organizations – bureaucracy and post-bureaucracy – and what is claimed about the reasons for their existence and the benefits and limitations of each.

- The disputes about their value from the point of view of efficiency, but you should also understand that efficiency itself is a disputed concept.

- The different concepts of rationality in organizations and how these relate to the two models.

- The political and ethical issues that inform debates about the two models.

Key concepts and learning objectives

This chapter will:

- Explain bureaucracy and post-bureaucracy as models of organization.

- Explain the deficiencies of each model from mainstream perspectives.

- Examine some major mainstream studies.

- Identify critical approaches to each model.

- Examine some major critical studies.

- Explain the strengths and weaknesses of the critical approaches.

Overview and key points

Bureaucracy is a model of organization based upon rules, hierarchy, impersonality and a division of labour and has been the dominant form of organization for over a century. However, it suffers from problems such as poor employee motivation, producer-focus and inertia. In view of this, post-bureaucracy has been proposed as a new organizational model more suited to today's business environment. Post-bureaucracy is based on trust, empowerment, personal treatment and shared responsibility. But this brings its own problems in terms of loss of control, risk and unfairness.

These models and problems derive from mainstream thinking. Such thinking is concerned with narrow views of efficiency and is guided by a search for control and performance. Critical approaches provide a more radical analysis of bureaucracy and post-bureaucracy. From a critical perspective, bureaucracy is seen as dehumanizing and post-bureaucracy is interpreted as an extension of control. Moreover, both are criticized for seeking efficiency from the point of view of those with power, to the neglect of other people and of the ethical purposes and consequences of organization. However, among other limitations, critical approaches can be seen as Utopian.

Cartoon 14.1
'I'm in a paperwork mood, let 'er rip.'

'I'm in a paperwork mood, let 'er rip.'

MAINSTREAM APPROACHES TO BUREAUCRACY AND POST-BUREAUCRACY

INTRODUCTION

Imagine that you have been asked to manage student admissions to your course, and imagine that for some reason you have to do the job from scratch. What kinds of things would you do? The chances are you would set up some kind of system. As a minimum, you might set up a system that establishes a closing date for applications; which sends out a standard letter acknowledging receipt of applications; which sets a rule that once the closing date has passed you will accept the 100 best-qualified applicants; and which sends a standard letter of acceptance or rejection to each applicant, asking those you have accepted to confirm by a set date that they will take up your offer. You might well also employ other people to do some aspects of the job. For example, you might employ an administrative assistant to send out the letters, but make the decisions about the wording of the letters and about whom to accept yourself. And on what basis would you have the right to make those decisions? Obviously, the fact that you are the Admissions Manager.

Thinkpoint 14.1

What other kinds of procedures might you put in place?

No doubt there would be quite a lot of other aspects to the system you devised. What is sure is that you would devise a system, and that if you did not then you would be unlikely to do a very good job. Think for a minute about what would happen if you did not adopt a system similar to that just outlined. You might accept or reject applicants when later on you got better or worse qualified applicants; you would write a different letter each time you dealt with an application; you would accept applicants on the basis of something other than qualifications (at random? first come, first served? the sound of their name? where they were born?), and you would have no way of knowing who had accepted their places, because you had not asked them to confirm acceptance of your offer.

In order to perform this relatively straightforward task efficiently, you would have designed a system characterized by:

- rules (e.g., closing date)
- standardized procedures (e.g., letters)
- **rationality** (e.g., accepting applicants for a logical reason)
- division of labour (e.g., between you and your assistant)
- hierarchy (e.g., you are in charge of your assistant)
- authority (e.g., you have the right to make decisions).

Take any other task of any size and you will find that these kinds of systems will enable you to do the job better than any alternative. What does 'better' mean here? It means more efficiently (with less waste of time and resources) and more effectively (in terms of getting the result you require).

Rationality A commitment to reason, rather than faith, intuition or instinct. In the study of organizations, rationality is often claimed to consist of the adoption of optimally efficient means. However, critical approaches suggest that this is a one-sided view of rationality since it usually considers efficiency in terms of narrow goals such as profitability, without considering whether organizations are efficient for realizing the well-being of members of the organization, or for society more widely.

Exercise 14.1

Imagine another task you might be asked to organize. What system would you put in place and how does it illustrate the characteristics discussed? Can you design a system that would be effective that does not have these characteristics?

This example illustrates themes that have been at the heart of the theory and practice of organization for at least 100 years. One of the founding figures of organizational behaviour was Max Weber (1864–1920), a German social scientist who was interested in a wide range of social and political questions in his time. One of these was the question of what held societies together, and this, he thought, was to do with authority.

Authority comes in different forms in different societies at different times. It may be based on 'charisma' (the personal authority of particular individuals) or on 'tradition' (the established authority of institutions, such as the monarchy). But according to Weber, modern societies were increasingly based on rational-legal authority – that is, systems of rules (e.g., legal rules) devised for rational reasons. Hence the term rational-legal. People in society accepted that they had to follow the dictates of these systems. Hence they were a form of authority.

Rational-legal authority was the basis not just of the legal system, but the state, the civil service, industry and most other kinds of organization. We can see already how it relates to the example of setting up an admissions system, where terms such as 'rule', 'reason' and 'authority' appeared. Applied to organizations, rational-legal authority means bureaucracy. Nowadays we often use this word to imply something inefficient – **red tape** (and we will come back to that later). But in its pure form (which Weber called an 'ideal-type') it refers to a highly efficient form of organization. Indeed, this was the reason why, according to Weber, it was becoming more and more dominant from the late nineteenth century onwards. Bureaucracy, he said, was the most technically efficient and rational form of organization. It simply got the job done better than any other system, and this was why it was adopted.

Red tape A term of abuse applied to bureaucracies that enforce rules more elaborate and inflexible than is considered necessary.

Box 14.1
Characteristics of Bureaucracy

Let's take a closer look at what these bureaucracies consist of:

- *Functional specialization.* There is a formal division of labour so that some people are paid to do one kind of function as their official duty and they do not do anything other than their official duty. They are employed full-time within the context of a lifetime career structure and are appointed and promoted on the basis of qualifications and experience.
- *Hierarchy of authority.* There is a structure such that those holding a superior position have the authority, solely by virtue of holding that position, to give orders to those in subordinate positions. Subordinates, in turn, report upwards to their superiors.
- *System of rules.* Everything that goes on in the organization is based upon following a formal, written set of rules about procedures and practices that must be adhered to.
- *Impersonality.* Rules are followed and authority is held with regard for emotions, personality or personal preferences. Employees and customers are treated in accordance with these rules.

Some of these ingredients look pretty obvious to us. Does it really need to be said that people get paid in money? But Weber was trying to pin down all the features that separated bureaucracy from all other kinds of organization. Other features are familiar from the admissions system example – which isn't surprising because Weber's 'model' was based on his observation of what efficiently organized systems actually did. Some features look a little dated – full-time, permanent jobs for life, for example, are not necessarily a feature of modern bureaucracies. But overall, the reason why the list seems obvious is that Weber was right to think that these kinds of organizations were becoming dominant. Now, they seem so familiar that we hardly recognize them as anything other than 'the way things are'.

However, a bureaucratic way of organizing is one bound up with tasks of a particular kind. Specifically, it is effective in situations where very large numbers of identical, standard operations are needed – processing social security claims or mass producing cars, for example. It also suits situations where a rigid chain of command is favoured, where little training or initiative is required, since all that people need to do is to follow rules and orders.

Many commentators believe that these kinds of conditions no longer exist or, at any rate, are increasingly rare. Since at least the 1970s, but with a growing insistence, it has been claimed that such 'industrial' conditions are giving way to a 'post-industrial' era. This argument takes many forms, but in essence it says that the economy has moved from the mass production of standard products towards short product runs for niche markets. At the same time, it is suggested that people in organizations need – and perhaps want – to be more flexible and innovative, rather than simply following orders.

Thinkpoint 14.2

What do you regard as the benefits and costs of working in a bureaucracy from the point of view of the employee?

Against that background, there has arguably been the development of a range of new organizational forms. These are given many different names, but as an umbrella term we can call them 'post-bureaucracies'. Charles Heckscher (1994), one of the leading writers on post-bureaucracy, has devised a list of characteristics he calls the post-bureaucratic ideal-type, in contrast to Weber's ideal-type of bureaucracy.

- Rules are replaced with consensus and dialogue based upon personal influence rather than status. People are trusted to act on the basis of shared values rather than rules.
- Responsibilities are assigned on the basis of competence for tasks rather than hierarchy, and are treated as individuals rather than impersonally.
- The organization has an open boundary, so that rather than full-time, permanent employment, people come into and out of the organization in a flexible way, including part-time, temporary and consultancy arrangements. Work is no longer done in fixed hours or at a designated place.

Box 14.2
Characteristics of Post-Bureaucracy

Case study 14.1
Universal

Robertson and Swan (1998) explain the development since 1986 of a consultancy firm that specializes in advising high-tech companies and **start-ups** on innovation and the exploitation of intellectual property rights. The firm – which they call 'Universal' – is also involved in incubating (providing resource and assistance for new ventures) and taking equity shares in some client companies. The Universal case is an interesting one for illustrating aspects of the basic models of bureaucracy and post-bureaucracy and also some of the complexities of these models, which we will come to later in this chapter. Although over 20 years old, the dynamics of what happens in innovative firms that they grow is as relevant as ever.

Start-ups New small businesses that have just begun to trade.

To give a very brief summary, Universal grew from a charismatic founder and handful of consultants in 1986 until it employed around 120 consultants plus almost the same number again as associates in other countries. In the early years, Universal was explicitly egalitarian, non-hierarchical and non-bureaucratic. Many of the early members were recruited from more traditional consultancies and were attracted by the freer atmosphere. Project teams were self-organizing and trusted to do their work well and efficiently. Projects were initiated on the basis of their scientific value. People joined projects that interested them and rewards were fairly equally shared. Knowledge about projects was shared on a word of mouth basis. In short, bureaucracy was not much in evidence. From the early 1990s onwards, the combination of growth and also tougher market conditions led to the creation of divisions and divisional managers. Under a new performance management system, each division and each individual was given a revenue target, and this was linked to financial rewards. Projects were undertaken on the basis of their financial viability. Although there was still relatively little formal hierarchy, there was an informal pecking order among staff. There was an internal labour market for project staff, which used email systems to advertise opportunities.

Question
Imagine that you had joined Universal in 1986. How might you feel about the changes that happened afterwards?

Case commentary

This case is useful because it allows us to think about organizational changes over a long period of time. How we read it depends on where we look from. Entering Universal in 2016, we might see it as a good example of a post-bureaucratic organization. It is relatively flatly structured and project based, and it makes heavy use of 'virtual' organization. Looked at by someone who had worked at Universal since 1986 we might see it as a good example of an organization which has become more bureaucratically structured in order to compete in tougher market conditions by increasing efficiency. Although we will return to the case as we go through the chapter, the point to note for now is that bureaucracy and post-bureaucracy are to some extent relative terms. In other words, reality is usually less clear-cut than the models or 'ideal-types'. Robertson and Swan (1998, p. 561) make almost exactly this point when they show how cultural and systemic forms of control are interlinked at Universal.

Key problems

BUREAUCRACY

Although bureaucracy has been adopted in probably every large organization in every country in the world, organization theorists and analysts have always recognized that it poses problems. Some of these problems are to do with the social impact of bureaucracy, and these will be picked up in the 'Critical approach' section later in this chapter. But there are also problems from the more narrow perspective of organizational design and efficiency. Many of these are the kinds of problems that give rise to the everyday sense that bureaucracy equals 'red tape' – needless waste and pedantic obsession with rules. Later, we will cover some of the technical reasons for these problems, but for now we will just give a brief outline of them.

Bureaucracy can be thought of as a form of organization which is like a 'machine'. In principle, each part is perfectly designed to perform its task, and the whole thing operates 'like clockwork' in an entirely predictable, standard way. It is this that makes a bureaucracy efficient. But it also means that the people within the organization have to function as if they were mere 'cogs' within the machine. This leads to at least three key problems for bureaucracy.

One is the problem of motivation (see Chapter 2). Because people in bureaucracies have to follow rules, and have no choice or discretion about doing so, they may well have little personal commitment to the organization, and gain little interest or stimulation from their work. Theorists of motivation have long recognized that very often motivation is linked to factors such as job satisfaction and to a sense of achievement and responsibility at work. Bureaucracies rarely deliver this and *if* high motivation leads to better work performance then it follows that employees will perform suboptimally in bureaucracies. In this sense, they may not be as efficient as they seem at first sight.

Linked to this is the problem that bureaucracies, as rule-based systems, may not be very good at customer service. If the workforce are poorly motivated they are unlikely to care much about customer service but simply follow rules grudgingly or blindly. These rules are there for the good of the organization rather than customers, and will not be changed to suit the particular demands an individual customer may have. For this reason, bureaucracies are sometimes described as producer-focused. There is an expression – 'a jobsworth' – which describes the typical mindset of an employee of a bureaucracy. When asked by a customer to bend the rules in some particular case, such an employee replies 'that would be more than my job's worth'. They know that failing to follow rules will lead to their being punished, or even sacked. This can also lead to a situation where no decision is taken until it is passed up to the competent 'authority'. This 'buck-passing' leads to people 'hiding behind the rules' and is sometimes called 'bureaupathy'.

This kind of inflexibility is a microcosm of a third key problem for bureaucracy: it seems to be resistant to innovation and to change (see Chapter 11). Rules, once made, are enshrined for all time and will only change very slowly. This may not matter in contexts of, say, producing large quantities of standard products the specifications of which do not vary for long periods of time, perhaps several years. However, in more volatile and uncertain conditions, bureaucratic inertia will mean that these organizations fail to adapt and therefore will either disappear when faced with competition, or survive, only because of being protected by government from competition, to deliver goods and services in an inefficient way.

Thinkpoint 14.3

How does the system for student admissions, described at the beginning of this chapter, illustrate the problems of bureaucracy?

POST-BUREAUCRACY

Post-bureaucracy is very much a response to the kinds of problems believed to characterize bureaucracies and it proceeds, as we have seen, from the analysis that many or most sectors are in fact unstable and rapidly changing. This means that bureaucratic inertia will indeed be a problem. However, as an alternative model of organizations, post-bureaucracy generates its own set of problems, many of them, of course, being precisely those which bureaucracy seems to solve.

Case study 14.2
CompCo (Australia)'s Space 17 Project

CompCo (Australia) is a pseudonym for the Australian arm of one of the world's largest computer companies. It supplies hardware and support services for business and home computer users on a network or stand-alone basis, IT consultancy and also finance for its customers. It has been in business for many decades and is well-known for having a strong organizational culture, with shared values of technical excellence, customer focus and a sense of organizational 'belonging'. People talk about CompCo as being like a family. Over the years, it has acquired a large number of expensive offices in city centre locations throughout Australia. In order to make better use of these premises, CompCo (Australia) is launching the Space 17 project.

Traditionally, everyone employed in the firm has had a fixed desk space, either in an open-plan area or in a partitioned office housing one to four employees. All senior managers have had the use of their own office. At any one time 35 per cent of employees are away from their desk either at meetings on-site, or off-site, for example with consultancy clients or on sales trips in Australia or overseas, so that the offices are never full. Space 17 begins on 4 January, 2017. From that date, except for a few of the most senior managers, no one will have partitioned office space. The rest of the space will be open-plan (the necessary building work will be done during the Christmas and New Year holiday period, 2016). Within the open-plan area, staff who are always in the office will be allocated a fixed desk space. These staff account for 25 per cent of the workforce. The remainder of the staff will 'hot desk', that is, they pre-book a numbered desk and computer terminal (in whatever office is most convenient for that booking) via an online system and have use of it only for the booked period. Each terminal has identical software and gives access to the employee's network space. Those using hot desks will not be permitted to store possessions in the desk, instead they will have an allocated locker linked to their desk. They are not allowed to fix anything (papers, photos, etc.) to the hot desk area. Those with fixed desk space may store possessions in their desks and can pin papers and personal effects in the desk area. In addition to personal working space, all meeting rooms will be pre-booked in the same way.

By these means Space 17 expects to be able to reduce the total size of CompCo (Australia) premises and therefore to reduce rental and other costs by 35 per cent (compared with the previous year) by exactly matching space and employees.

Case commentary
The Space 17 project is an example of the kind of detailed ways in which an organization might put into practice the idea of post-bureaucracy. At its heart is a shift to flexibility in organizational arrangements, in this case by the literal shift from fixity to fluidity of workspace.

Thinkpoint 14.4

How does Space 17 relate to the characteristics of post-bureaucracy identified by Charles Heckscher?

If bureaucracy is like a machine, then post-bureaucracy is more like an organism – a living, growing, changing entity with a mind of its own. But this means that it is far less predictable than a machine, and prey to illnesses and malfunctions. Again, we can see at least three linked problems.

The first of them is that of control. Bureaucracies use detailed rules to control what goes on in organizations. Without such rules, how can control be exercised, especially in large organizations that may spread over many countries? In essence, post-bureaucracy proposes a different, normative, form of control based upon some version of culture management (see Chapter 10) and trust. But that is a rather fragile form of control, resting as it does on self-control rather than external monitoring. Trust may be difficult to sustain, especially over long distances and via the Internet where relationships are mediated 'virtually' rather than face-to-face, and trust, of course, may be betrayed. Since post-bureaucracies are also characterized by a 'porous' organizational boundary, this means that employees will be coming in and out of the organization on short-term and consulting contracts. These seem like particularly unpromising conditions to build shared values and trust. In short, there is a danger that post-bureaucracies will descend into anarchy.

Exercise 14.2

What impact might the Space 17 project at CompCo (Australia) have upon 'shared values'?

Related to this problem of control, there is the problem of risk. It is all very well to give people more freedom to innovate and to do away with rules, but what happens if this freedom leads to decisions that go wrong? The consequence will be failures of service delivery and lost money. Fixed rules may deter good ideas and improvements to products and services, but they also prevent bad ideas and damage. We can see that, in the case of Universal, these issues informed the development of more bureaucratic systems. Whereas, in the early days, projects were developed with little concern for their financial consequences, the later systems tried to ensure that these consequences were considered.

The third main problem is also linked to the issue of control. As well as the business risks of innovation there are also questions of fairness. Bureaucratic systems are impersonal; they do not discriminate between people except on the basis of experience and qualifications. Post-bureaucracy stresses individual treatment – again, a move away from rigid rules. But this opens up the possibility of all kinds of irrationalities and prejudices. For example, while you might want to be treated 'as an individual', would you want your promotion prospects to depend upon whim? Suppose a male project leader only chooses attractive young women to work on prestigious contracts. Wouldn't those of us who are not attractive young women (and, indeed, those who are) prefer to be chosen on the basis of a rational system? And the issues here are not only moral but also pragmatic, since businesses that allow discrimination may face legal penalties and also suffer suboptimal decisions about staffing. This also applies to the flexible treatment of customers. We might be delighted if an organization, say, rushed our order through and so responded flexibly to our needs. But what about the other customer whose order is therefore pushed down the queue? Would that customer be so pleased?

Thinkpoint 14.5

How does the development of Universal illustrate an attempt to deal with the problems of post-bureaucracy?

Key ideas and contributions

Because bureaucracy has had such a long history, there is a very wide range of studies that have tried to understand and refine it. Post-bureaucracy has a shorter history, but this has coincided with an upsurge in writing and thinking about organizations, so there is plenty of material to cover there as well. However, it would not be unfair to say that the earlier generation (say, 1945–1970) of organizational theorists, who were concerned with bureaucracy and its problems, contributed more to the key ideas in this area. This is partly because ideas about post-bureaucracy have actually been around for a long time (as we will see later) and so the earlier theorists had already developed several ideas about them. And it is partly because the later generation (say 1970 to the present) seem less to generate new ideas as to reformulate what has become something like an orthodoxy about the deficiencies of bureaucracy.

DOES SIZE MATTER?

In much of the earlier material, and explicitly in the case study of Universal, it has been implied that there is something significant in the impact of organizational size upon bureaucracy. And this is surely true. If we go back to the opening example of an admissions system for a university course, then it is fairly obvious that if, for the sake of argument, there were only three applications for the course, it would hardly be necessary to devise the systems described. There would be no need for standardization of letters, no need for a division of labour and no need for an authority structure. There might still need to be a rule on whom to accept (if, for example, there was only one place available) but this would hardly call for a bureaucratic system.

There can be no doubt that part of the reason Weber observed a growth in rational-legal, or bureaucratic, organization was because he also lived at a time that was witnessing a phenomenal growth in organizational size – whether that meant the army, the state or factories. Later studies confirmed this. Some of the classic work was done by Peter Blau (1955, 1970). In studies in the USA of over 50 government employment agencies involving over 1200 branches and 350 head offices, Blau found a consistent relationship between bureaucratization (which he measured in some technical ways that do not matter here) and organizational size, measured in numbers of employees. As employee numbers increased, so too did bureaucratization. An organization with, say, 10 000 employees was much more bureaucratized than one of ten, or even 100.

But, more than that, although bureaucratization increased with size, it did so at a declining rate. In other words, adding employee numbers to small organizations had a bigger impact on bureaucratization than adding the same numbers to large organizations. It is not difficult to see why. Imagine a firm employing ten people, which then expands to employ 510. That is likely to call for all kinds of new systems and rules. But imagine a firm of 20 000 people that expands to 20 500. That will have much less impact. So numbers of employees increase bureaucratization, but at a declining rate, and this observation gives rise to the 'Blau curve'.

Statistical probability
The chance of a given event happening across a population of events. For the probability to be robust, the population must be sufficiently large to be statistically significant.

That size was linked to bureaucracy was also supported by the Aston Studies, conducted at Aston University in the UK in the 1960s and 1970s (Pugh *et al.*, 1968; Pugh and Hickson, 1976). These studies asserted a causal relationship between size and bureaucratic structure. However, their explanation was different, and more complicated, to that of Blau. The Aston researchers proposed that in larger organizations there was a greater **statistical probability** of recurrent and repetitive events. This being so, such organizations were more likely to develop standardized rules since they were faced with standardized situations. And standardized rules are, of course, at the heart of bureaucracy. One way of understanding the developments at Universal consultancy is to see a growth in size as leading to the development of more standardized systems.

Although there is an obvious common-sense appeal in the idea that size is what drives bureaucracy, it is important to realize that the situation is less straightforward than common sense might suggest. First, there have been studies which argue that if there is a relationship between size and bureaucracy, then its causality may run against that proposed by the Aston Studies. In other words, it may be that sometimes size is a consequence, not a cause, of bureaucracy. Aldrich (1972) reanalyzed the Aston data and argued that this was so. Why? Imagine an organization setting up a new division (e.g., a personnel division or an overseas office). This is an increase in the division of labour, one of the measures of bureaucracy. This new division has to be staffed, so more people are employed. So an increase in bureaucratization has led to an increase in size, not vice versa.

Another classic study questions the size-bureaucracy link in a different way. Joan Woodward, who was not just one of the pioneers of organization studies but one of the few women among those pioneers, looked at the relationship between technology and bureaucracy. She studied around 100 manufacturing firms, of varying sizes, in the UK and argued that what affected the extent of their bureaucratization was not their size but the type of technology they employed (Woodward, 1965). Thus firms engaged in mass production of standard goods did indeed have bureaucratic structures, but those – even large firms – that were developing one-off products (e.g., hydroelectric turbines), or that had continuous high-tech production technologies (e.g., chemical refining), were far less bureaucratized.

Exercise 14.3

How might Woodward's analysis be updated to account for the changes at CompCo (Australia)?

How do these questions relate to post-bureaucracy? Is the implication that large organizations must be bureaucratic? This can be answered in two ways. First, the case for post-bureaucracy rests heavily on the proposition that new information and communication technologies have had a decisive impact upon ways of organizing. So the Woodward findings are relevant to this, because they suggest that there is not an iron law linking size and bureaucracy. Technology also comes in to the equation. Second, at least since Peters and Waterman's influential thinking on organizational culture, it has been claimed that organizations can 'be big' and 'act small' at the same time. They can use cultural norms, instead of bureaucratic rules, to combine personalized service and organizational control. Whether that is true remains, of course, an open question.

THE DYSFUNCTIONS OF BUREAUCRACY

Whatever it is that leads to bureaucracy, what are its effects? Classic studies here have focused on whether bureaucracy is really as rational as it appears. We have prefigured this question when, in discussing the problems of bureaucracies, we considered how efficient they were. A group of writers, sometimes called the 'bureaucratic dysfunctionalists', posed these issues with considerable sharpness, by probing some of the realities of bureaucratic life.

The American sociologist Robert Merton (1940) addressed a core theoretical and practical issue with his concept of **goal displacement**. He argued that, over time, people in bureaucracies came to see 'following the rule' as the goal or purpose, rather than the effect that the rule was supposed to produce. This is the theoretical way of talking about the 'jobsworth' mentality referred to earlier. What matters in goal displacement is, so to speak, 'doing the thing right' rather than 'doing the right thing'. A slavish adherence to the rules as an end in itself is central to the 'red tape' associated with bureaucratic life.

> **Goal displacement**
> Occurs when the pursuit of a secondary or marginal objective assumes greater importance than the primary objective and/or when the means (e.g., complying with a procedure) becomes more important than the ends (e.g., attaining the objective).

To see how it might work, let's return to the hypothetical admissions system discussed at the start of this chapter. Imagine that having set up the system described you receive an application from a student who has not filled in the application forms, but has provided evidence of already having achieved six 'A' grade A-levels at the age of 16. She also has an impressive record of non-academic achievement and a clutch of references attesting to her academic and personal qualities. But, for some plausible reason, she needs a decision on whether she will be accepted to the course before the closing date for applications has passed.

A reasonable response might be to offer her a place. You know that she fills the criteria and is almost certainly better qualified than any other applicant you will get. Yet the rules say that application forms must be completed and that no decisions will be made before the closing date. So, quite legitimately, you refuse to give a decision and she goes elsewhere. This is goal displacement. Goal displacement does not just mean that you have been inflexible. The point (or 'goal') of the rule is to ensure that the organization maximizes the quality of its student intake. Yet the effect of applying the rule has been to suboptimize the intake: the person who takes the place you might otherwise have offered the unorthodox applicant will not be as well qualified. You have acted as if the goal of the rule is to *follow* the rule.

Exercise 14.4

How would a post-bureaucratic organization deal with this applicant? What problems might this lead to?

A particular version of the goal-displacement thesis is found in the work of Philip Selznick (1949). His studies suggested that the divisionalized structures of a bureaucratic organization led inevitably to people identifying with the aims of their divisions, not the aims of the organization as a whole. Thus, they would pursue divisional interests at the expense of the organization. In this way, a bureaucracy not only could, but because of the divisionalization would, most likely deliver organizationally suboptimal outcomes. This line of thinking has opened up significant wider issues in organizational analysis, including the relationship between subcultures and organizational cultures (see Chapter 10) and the nature of organizational politics (see Chapter 9).

All this might seem to deal a fatal blow to the whole theory of bureaucracy. The key idea of this theory is that a system of rules enshrines the most efficient way of doing things. Yet goal displacement suggests that following the rules does not always lead to the best outcome. Someone might respond by offering this (sophisticated) defence of bureaucracy. The defence would be that bureaucracy offers not an optimum solution to each case it deals with but an optimum *average* solution. In other words, overall a bureaucratic system is more efficient even if, in particular cases, it is less than optimal.

Yet, against this, we would have to set the argument presented by Peter Blau. Apart from the Blau curve, this researcher also advanced a very elegant argument suggesting that bureaucracy *always* delivers suboptimal solutions to problems. Blau observed the trade union tactic called 'work to rule'. A work to rule falls short of a strike and consists of workers refusing to do anything other than follow the formal, established rules of their workplace. Anything that they do which is not in their contracts and not in the organizational rulebook, they refuse to do. If the rules say that they stop at 5.00pm, they stop at 5.00pm on the dot, for example. Similarly, if the rules fail to specify how a particular job should be done then they repeatedly ask for assistance or guidance before doing it. Blau explains that the reason why a union adopts 'work to rule' is in order to disrupt the organization (typically, in pursuit of a pay claim). Yet, if bureaucratic rules enshrine the most efficient way of organizing, then how could it be that following those rules to the letter made the organization less efficient? Blau's answer is that, in fact, following the rules exactly is *not* the most efficient way of organizing, just as goal displacement tells us that following the rules, rather than trying to meet the underlying purpose of those rules, is inefficient. But this means that bureaucracy is not the most efficient kind of organization. Therefore, the whole model of bureaucracy must be wrong.

These insights are very much in line with the case for post-bureaucratic organizations. This case invites us to 'tear up' the rulebook and allow individual discretion. Yet, although this is plausible in the light of Blau's analysis, it has its own problems. Workers may, in following the set rules, be less efficient than if they had used their own discretion. But it does not follow that, left to themselves, they would have adopted the most efficient way of working. They might have adopted an even less efficient approach than that enshrined in the rules. If so, a post-bureaucratic way of working would not only be less efficient during times of industrial action, it would be less efficient at all times!

Thinkpoint 14.6

Do you think that Universal is more or less efficient because it has adopted a more bureaucratic system? Do you think that the admissions system would be more or less efficient if it adopted a post-bureaucratic system?

The studies of Merton, Selznick and Blau show us that the close following of bureaucratic rules may not lead to efficiency. But there is also a second line of thought within the bureaucratic dysfunctionalist literature that advances a diametrically opposed set of problems. Here the issue is not one of an over-attachment to the rules but the observation that, very often, organizational rules are completely ignored. This was Crozier's (1964) finding – that employees in bureaucracies did, as a matter of fact, indulge all manner of prejudices whether or not the formal rules allowed it. These prejudices may be presumed to be sub-optimal from the point of view of organizational efficiency, but this is not necessarily so – as is the case of the Blau finding that ignoring organizational rules offers better outcomes than those delivered by the rules. But whether or not they are suboptimal, they certainly deal a blow to the idea that bureaucracies are impersonal.

The work of Alvin Gouldner elaborates Crozier's insights by introducing the concept of mock bureaucracy. Gouldner (1954) found cases of organizations that have elaborate rulebooks but, in practice, the rules are ignored. Examples include safety regulations. In many dangerous industries, from mining (discussed by Gouldner) to building sites, it is commonplace for the formal rules to exist but not to be followed – as the phrase has it, 'more honoured in the breach than the observance' – because people see them as inconvenient or getting in the way of the job. Other examples might include equal opportunities regulations or rules about cyber-security in organizations.

Thinkpoint 14.7

What kinds of 'mock bureaucracy' could you imagine developing at CompCo (Australia) once the Space 17 reforms are launched?

Mock bureaucracy and goal displacement are opposites – one is about following rules blindly, the other about ignoring rules – but both undermine the rational, machine-like picture of organizations found in the bureaucratic model. But their implications for post-bureaucracy are different. An over-attachment to rules vindicates the case for post-bureaucracy as a solution to this myopic inertia. But if bureaucracies ignore rules and find their own way of working then it might be argued that, in practice if not in theory, they end up being little different to organizations that dispense with rules, so why not stick with bureaucracy?

Key issues and controversies

Many key issues and controversies have already been indicated in the chapter, such as why do bureaucracies exist, whether they are efficient and what is the alternative? However, the major overriding controversy is whether bureaucracy is being, or should be, consigned to history to be supplanted by post-bureaucracy (see also Chapter 4).

The idea that bureaucracy is on the way out is one which has been touted for many decades – certainly since the mid-1960s when Warren Bennis (1966) proclaimed the imminent death of bureaucracy. His case for this was very similar to that heard today – namely that there was no longer the stable business environment within which bureaucracy made sense, and that more collaborative organizational relations rendered the rigid rules of bureaucracy obsolete. This analysis was disputed at the time, for example by Miewald (1970), and later by Perrow (1979), on the basis that bureaucracy, at least for large organizations, retained an efficiency advantage, and that the extent to which environmental turbulence had increased was exaggerated. More recently it has been suggested that bureaucratic ways of working persist in the public sector because of the advantages these bestow (Schofield, 2001), and that hybrids of bureaucracy and post-bureaucracy are the result (Josserand *et al.*, 2006).

Exercise 14.5

In what ways might the 'post-bureaucratic' change at CompCo (Australia) entail an extension of bureaucratic ways of organizing?

Despite this, there have been continual claims along the same lines as those of Bennis, although the vocabulary shifts over time. For example, Piore and Sabel (1984) advanced the idea that the world was moving from mass production and stable markets towards niche production in volatile markets. This in turn had the implication of a move from bureaucracy to '**flexible specialization**'. More recent outings of the argument have probably been more widely, or at any rate more vocally, made than ever before. In particular, management gurus such as Tom Peters and Charles Handy have been highly influential in proclaiming versions of the same basic claim. This analysis

Flexible specialization
Approach to production and the organization of work that emphasizes the need for adaptation rather than repetition. Companies following this strategy simply transform their production regularly as there is a demand for more distinctive, customized products and services. Flexibility can come in the form of producing non-standard products for niche markets; varying the number of employees according to fluctuations in demand; and/or requiring employees to undertake multiple tasks.

Network society A society composed of network organizations. More generally, a society in which there is a great deal of fluidity in social relations, multiple sources of information and multiple sources of authority, rather than fixed hierarchies and roles.

Network organization Organizations which are not structured hierarchically but which make lateral connections, and connections across functions. Usually associated with claims of increased flexibility and often claimed to be modelled on 'Toyotaism' rather than Fordism.

Contingency approach Way of analyzing organizations so that rather than there being a single way of doing things, there are different ways depending (or 'contingent') upon different situations. For example, technological determinists believe that organizations have to adopt different structures depending upon the technology that they use.

has also been popularized by more public policy-oriented writers such as Charles Leadbetter (1999) and in this way it has informed political debate in many countries, especially the UK and the USA. At the political level, the end of bureaucracy thesis links to attempts to reform public sector organizations and to devise education and training policies that are consistent with the emerging 'knowledge-economy' (see Chapters 6 and 13).

But it would be wrong to see all these arguments as deriving from the self-publicizing efforts of some influential popular writers. On the contrary, their claims are only accessible versions of some very sophisticated studies. For example, Manuel Castells has written several very detailed analyses (e.g., Castells, 1996) pointing to the rise of the **network society** and **network organizations**, which he links strongly to the information technology revolution of the last quarter of a century. More directly in the organization studies community, Heckscher and Donnellon (1994) have provided both a theoretical framework and several empirical illustrations of post-bureaucracy.

As with earlier predictions of the demise of bureaucracy, the more recent obituaries have also been met with a great deal of scepticism (see Chapter 4). Warhurst and Thompson (1998) have been particularly acute critics arguing that mass production and, for that matter, manufacturing are by no means in decline globally, and that new working practices based on trust and empowerment are more rhetorical than real. About the only attribute of the post-bureaucratic model that is unequivocally proven is an increase in the use of part-time and short-contract workers. But, even if increasing, this is not new, and it does not, of itself, demonstrate post-bureaucratization (see also Alvesson and Thompson, 2005). In a more recent thorough review of empirical studies of the subject, Johnson *et al.* (2009) suggest that there is some evidence that post-bureaucracy is more common than critics allow, but even so point out that its development is extremely uneven across sectors, regions and nations.

Later in this chapter we will return to some of these issues from a different perspective, but in terms of mainstream views, what is the answer to this controversy? In a sense, precisely because it is a controversy, there is no definite answer. It may be that it is just too early to tell. It may be that, as with Universal, there is no absolute answer because it depends on where, and when, you look at things. Thus it is possible to interpret Universal as being bureaucratic or as being post-bureaucratic. This perhaps reflects another important issue: both bureaucracy and post-bureaucracy as 'ideal-types' may not actually exist in practice. Instead, organizations may exhibit a range of characteristics, some of which are bureaucratic and others post-bureaucratic.

Finally, though, precisely because of the long history of this controversy, it is interesting to consider the now classic work of Burns and Stalker (1961). Their study suggested that organizations might be mechanical or organic (meaning roughly bureaucratic or post-bureaucratic) depending on 'contingencies' such as the nature of their business environment, the technologies they used and the skill levels of their workforces (a similar finding to the Woodward studies discussed earlier). This **contingency approach** might suggest to us that the idea that all organizations are, or will become, post-bureaucratic is simplistic. It is notable that most of the empirical examples given of such organizations are in high-tech business sectors, such as computing and biotechnology, which are yet to 'mature'. In the end, then, the mainstream answer to the current version of its main controversy may be a restatement of contingency theory.

Important studies

In the chapter so far, we have identified many of the main empirical studies in this area, all of which would repay closer attention. Because the theme of bureaucracy, in particular, has been present since the start of organization studies (indeed, in some ways, it is the bedrock of the subject), there are an almost literally endless number of studies we could examine. But the three discussed here are especially interesting.

The first study is Melville Dalton's (1959) classic *Men Who Manage*. This was in many ways a pathbreaking piece of research because it represents one of the first applications of **ethnographic** methods to the study of organizations. Although ethnography had been used from at least the 1920s to study social groups within Western societies, they had tended to focus on 'marginal' or relatively powerless groups, such as street gangs or prostitutes. Dalton's study was innovative because it was one of the first ethnographies of powerful elites.

> **Ethnography** A form of study where the researcher lives and works as a member of the group being studied. It aims to provide an 'insider' account but, because it is conducted by a researcher, it has a degree of 'outsider' detachment. Ethnography developed from the techniques used by anthropologists to study what were often seen as exotic cultures or societies outside their own.

Men Who Manage was a study of four bureaucratic organizations, code-named Milo, Fruhling, Attica and Rambeau, but the centrepiece of the book was the study of Milo, which was the most extensive of the four cases. Strictly speaking, we should in fact say that, as its title implies, this was a study of bureaucratic managers rather than of entire organizations. Apart from being methodologically innovative, this study was highly revealing about the realities of managerial work and did much to debunk the rational image of such work and, indeed, bureaucracy itself. Among other things, it illustrates some of the issues that Crozier discussed concerning how individual prejudices (e.g., about religious beliefs) were not left outside the office but played a central part in decision-making about, for example, who to employ and promote. The study also illustrates Selznick's point about how different divisions within bureaucracies pursue their own goals through political infighting, rather than there being a single, shared, organizational goal (see Chapter 9).

A second study in a recognizably similar tradition to Dalton's is Rosabeth Moss Kanter's (1993) book, *Men and Women of the Corporation*. The title itself seems to stand in some kind of relation to Dalton's work, published almost 20 years earlier. For not only had organizations become somewhat less male dominated in the intervening period but, more to the point, Kanter was one of the pioneers of applying feminist ideas to the study of organizations. Thus, while much of the detail of her study of the firm codenamed Indsco reveals some similar issues to that of Dalton, Kanter draws particular attention to how they relate to gender. For example, Kanter suggests that the relationship between (largely) male managers and (exclusively) female secretaries takes a form that is recognizably pre-bureaucratic and is quite resistant to the rational-legal ideal-type of bureaucracy. She suggests that the relationship is highly personalized and therefore unstandardized, and is in part bound up with displays of status on the part of both manager and secretary.

Good studies of this detailed type of post-bureaucracy are, as yet, more difficult to find. The 'afterword' to the second edition of Kanter's book is worth reading in this regard as it updates some of the Indsco story into the 1990s. A less academic study of post-bureaucracy is Ricardo Semler's (1993) account of his company Semco, a Brazilian engineering firm. Semler regards himself as a 'counsellor' rather than a chief executive, and this illustrates the idea that post-bureaucracy discounts hierarchy. Overall, Semco is characterized by an approach that rejects formal rules, employees set their own working hours and pay rates, and is relaxed about unionization and strike activity.

It is important to recognize that this study is the work of someone describing and justifying his own experience and activities: it does not purport to be detached or analytical, and it would be interesting to hear the voices of others within the firm to see how far they endorse Semler's account. Nevertheless, there is no doubt that Semco represents a departure from traditional bureaucratic models of organizing and, moreover, that it has been able to perform profitably and successfully and that it is no small high-tech start-up. From that point of view it offers a documented example of the existence and viability of something like the organizations that Heckscher and others argue are the future of work.

Limitations of the mainstream approach to bureaucracy and post-bureaucracy

Like most of the mainstream approach to organizations and management, a major limitation of its treatment of bureaucracy and post-bureaucracy is its one-sided and restricted focus on efficiency. Weber's ideal-type of bureaucracy has – wrongly, as we will see – been treated as if it were a design template for how organizations should be. In the process, this has elevated one particular kind of rationality – instrumental rationality – at the expense of others.

Why is this a limitation? There are two related reasons. One is that by its focus on *means,* instrumental rationality is only concerned with the 'how' of organizing and not with the 'why'. In the next section we will explore why this is such an important omission. Secondly, by seeing efficiency in terms of minimum inputs and maximum outputs, the mainstream only considers efficiency from the partial viewpoint of someone who has an interest in this kind of efficiency. Normally this means the powerful – the people who own and run businesses being the obvious example. As soon as we shift position, efficiency can look quite different.

Think of the now common way that all kinds of organizations use automated telephone systems. When we phone up, we are told to press different keys for different options and eventually, probably after waiting in a queue, we are connected to an actual person. This is efficient for the organization as it is a low-cost way of managing enquiries, partly because some of the work of transferring calls formerly done by a paid employee is now done, for nothing, by the caller. Sometimes, as with computer support lines, for example, the caller actually pays while they do this unpaid work for the organization. So from the caller's point of view it is not efficient because it involves a waste of time, sometimes a cost and, often, frustration. It also usually leads to a less personalized service (compare, for example, the traditional contact between a customer and a bank manager with that offered by national call centres).

Box 14.3
Whose Efficiency?

Thinkpoint 14.8

What other examples can you think of where things that are efficient for an organization are inefficient for you as a customer?

This one-sided view of rationality and efficiency can be seen to run through almost all of the debates about bureaucracy and post-bureaucracy discussed so far. For example, concerns about 'motivation' in bureaucracy are animated by the idea that demotivation will lead to employees working less hard – it is not concerned about happiness or well-being (see Chapter 2). Much of the bureaucratic dysfunctionalist literature is concerned with the alignment (or otherwise) between the formal rules of the bureaucracy and what actually happens. Something similar could be said of Dalton's preoccupation with politics 'getting in the way' of rationality.

As for post-bureaucracy, the whole basis of the shift towards these new organizational forms – if, indeed, the shift is occurring – is the fear that failure to do so will lead to declining competitiveness and shrinking profitability. The more trust-based ways of working, like traditional concerns with motivation, are animated by a belief that these will render employees more productive, which again reveals the underlying view of efficiency in the mainstream approach. It is surely no coincidence that moves away from bureaucracy are typically associated with harder work and more stress. So, again, we must ask the question: efficient for whom?

Exercise 14.6

Thinking of the admissions system, the changes at CompCo and the changes in the Universal case, for whom are they efficient and for whom are they inefficient?

In this sense, the limitations of the mainstream approach are, partly, to do with the partial picture it offers. But more fundamentally, it is to do with power. On the one hand, most mainstream approaches are concerned with deriving organizational methods – whether bureaucratic or post-bureaucratic – that best exert power and control over employees. On the other hand, by having this focus, mainstream approaches conform to and support the view that what 'matters' are the interests and perspectives of the privileged, the powerful and the elite.

CRITICAL APPROACHES TO BUREAUCRACY AND POST-BUREAUCRACY

INTRODUCTION

In many respects, the central dividing line between mainstream and critical approaches to bureaucracy and post-bureaucracy runs back to Max Weber. Perhaps we could even say that it runs 'through' him. For Weber on the one hand was persuaded that bureaucracy was becoming the dominant organizational form while, on the other hand, he bemoaned and even despaired of this fact. Weber did not use his term 'ideal-type' to mean that bureaucracy was a desirable ideal, or the ideal form of organization, but this is how mainstream approaches to organization studies have often interpreted it.

Weber's work (which was written in German) was for a long time not widely read in the USA, where the bulk of organization studies has been conducted. It became popular through the translation of eminent Harvard sociologist Talcott Parsons. Parsons' translation and interpretation of Weber put a 'spin' on it that emphasized bureaucracy as an 'ideal'. This had an impact on the development of the organization studies field in a general way, but more particularly on Merton, who was a student of Parsons. Merton in turn supervised Blau, Gouldner and Selznick. As we have seen, these authors provided the bedrock of the literature on bureaucracy.

Box 14.4
Spinning Weber

A different (and it is fair to say that most scholars would agree a more defensible) interpretation of Weber is to see his work as being concerned with two different kinds of rationality. One is the technical or instrumental rationality which, as we have seen, bureaucracy embodies. The second is value or **substantive rationality**.

Substantive rationality
Substantive rationality means whether the outcomes of an action are rational from the point of view of the actor, regardless of the efficiency of the action itself. Instrumental rationality is concerned with means. Substantive rationality is concerned with ends.

It is worth dwelling a little on the rather complicated issue of why substantive rationality is sometimes called value rationality. This is because deciding whether an outcome is rational involves a value judgement – is something good or not? Some people believe that this is not just a matter of opinion but can be decided on rational principles. Others would say that what is good or bad is a matter of what we generally agree is good or bad. So, for example, almost all people would accept that child pornography is bad (and those who think that these judgements have a rational basis might say that it is also irrational because it treats children as objects rather than people with rights). From this point of view, no matter how efficient an organization was in producing child pornography (that is, no matter how instrumentally rational it was), that organization would not have value or substantive rationality. If this seems complicated, there is an easier version of the definitions. We could say that instrumental rationality means 'doing the thing right' and substantive rationality means 'doing the right thing'. Of course, someone might object that instrumental rationality *does* embody a value – the value that efficiency is the sole criterion in deciding what to do. This is true, but it is present as a hidden value and one which, when made explicit, would then provoke debates about its ethical adequacy which are suppressed when it is simply assumed that instrumental rationality is 'a good thing'.

Actually, even when the theory seems obscure and abstract, in practice we are all familiar with the kinds of issues that are at stake. Is it right (or rational) for organizations to produce guns, cigarettes or instruments of torture? And outcomes of organizational actions are not just to do with their products but with their by-products. So, for example, is it right (or rational) for organizations to pollute the environment? This latter case is especially interesting because it does help to explain why there might be a link between what is right and what is rational. If it is the case that organizations need to live in a sustainable environment (e.g., because they need clean water to operate), then is it rational (let alone right) if they despoil that environment (e.g., by polluting water supplies)?

Exercise 14.7

What other examples of substantive irrationality can you think of?

A concern with substantive rationality is central to critical approaches to bureaucracy and post-bureaucracy, and later on we will return to it in several different ways. In one respect, it is another version of the question: efficient for whom? Is the efficient producer of landmines efficient for the Afghan child whose limbs are blown off? Is the efficient producer of cigarettes efficient for a Chinese peasant (who may never have heard about the risks) dying from lung cancer?

Thinkpoint 14.9

One of the big management problems facing the British National Health Service is 'bed blocking' – which normally happens when an elderly person is using a hospital bed because no suitable nursing home place is available. In 2004, Barbara Salisbury, a nurse, was convicted of attempting to murder such elderly patients. According to the prosecution, her motive was that she was trying to improve the efficiency of her ward. Was she a good bureaucratic manager?

Specific products aside, Weber's case for thinking that bureaucracy was substantively irrational was based upon his reading of the overall societal effects of its rise. These he described as creating an 'iron cage of rationality'. Here the idea is that, because bureaucracy is becoming dominant, more and more of people's lives are lived within the constraints of a rationalized (i.e., instrumentally rationalized) system. Living in a world in which every experience was organized, literally from the hospital in which we are born to the undertakers who take us to the grave, is there a sense in which bureaucracy undermines our very humanity? In particular, the experience of work within bureaucracies is, from a critical perspective, not just demotivating but actually dehumanizing. That is, by treating people as parts of a machine, bureaucracy denies everything that makes people human rather than inanimate objects – perhaps this was what made possible the hospital murders referred to in Thinkpoint 14.9? Again it can be said that this is both wrong and also irrational. Fundamentally, the functional reason for having organizations is to meet needs that no one could satisfy as an individual. But if the effect of organization (in its bureaucratic form) is to negate our human needs then there is a logical contradiction. Dehumanization, then, is not just wrong, it is irrational, and it is a profound negation of identity and freedom.

We will return to these issues shortly, but the final introductory point to the critical approach is to consider post-bureaucracy. In many respects it might be thought that, as an alternative to bureaucracy, this addresses some of the points made by the critics. Overtly, there is a stress on organizational values and a much less dehumanizing approach to work. However, as has been discussed in other chapters (e.g., Chapters 4 and 10), critical approaches are by no means reassured by such developments. At the heart of the problem is again the issue of power and control. Critical commentators believe that there is not an either/or opposition between the control of employees under top-down formal rule systems like bureaucracy and the freedom of employees under top-down value-based systems. Rather, both are seen as forms of control, the former operating at the level of behaviour and bodily actions; the latter at the level of belief and the mind. Indeed, many critical theorists regard the latter as the more insidious, because it seeks to exert control over the 'whole person'.

Thinkpoint 14.10

In a corner of the Dog and Duck, John and Richard are comparing their bosses. John is saying that his manager is inspirational: 'She just has a way of making you feel as if you want to do a really good job, for her and for the company.' Richard is impressed. 'Wow, you should have my boss – she's a real slave driver,' he complains.

Who do you think works the longer hours, John or Richard? Would you rather be coerced into doing something, knowing that it was coercion, or be manipulated into doing something, without knowing that you were being manipulated?

One way of thinking about these issues is in terms of employee skill levels. Bureaucratic organizations rely upon, and to some extent create, a situation where skill levels are low. They require that employees follow set rules and work in standardized ways. Skill is in many ways a form of power. If skill levels are low, then employees are easily replaceable and so reducing skill levels is an effective way of increasing organizational control. If the employees do not like the organization, well, there are plenty of people who can replace them. When skill levels are higher, then this gives more power to employees possessing these skills. In Joan Woodward's work, discussed earlier, it was assumed that the bureaucracy was linked contingently to the type of technology being employed. But perhaps a better way of rendering that link would be to say that technologies that required a skilled workforce gave more power to that workforce and, hence, they could not be managed bureaucratically.

By extension, post-bureaucratic organizations are obliged to create (or at least pay lip service to) employee responsibility because such organizations are predominantly in business sectors that need high levels of skill. These employees, who Reich (1993) calls 'symbolic analysts' and who have also been called (Kelley, 1990) 'gold-collar workers' (to distinguish them from blue-collar, or manual, workers and white-collar, or clerical, workers) have the power to command better treatment. Such employees are the consultants and professionals who possess a knowledge that resides in their heads. Craft workers had such knowledge, until it was broken down by Taylorism (see Chapter 7). And, wherever it can be achieved, symbolic analysts are similarly de-skilled, one example being attempts to replace accountants with IT-enabled audit factories. More generally, expert systems are used to replace professional employees. Even academics, traditionally a very difficult occupation to rationalize, are increasingly required to produce work in standard formats, such as this book, and perhaps eventually could be replaced with computer software.

Normative control Another term for the control of the 'hearts and minds' of employees. When a manager or professional 'chooses', apparently from free will, to work through the night to complete a task because of values of being responsible, then he or she is being controlled, by being self-controlled.

So, on this reading, post-bureaucracy reflects an accommodation with those occupations where skill level cannot be bureaucratized and it will only persist until such time as it can. In the meantime, post-bureaucracy uses the discipline of value-based or **normative control** to get the maximum amount of work out of its employees.

These kinds of ideas can sound, at first hearing, like pure nonsense. After all, control is about stopping people from doing what they want. So if people choose to do what they want to do then they are free, not controlled. But consider the haunting, and slightly scary, title of Nikolas Rose's (1999) influential book, *Governing the Soul*. Who we are, and what our choices signify, may not be as simple as we think. And, if recent work on consumer choice is right (Schwartz, 2004) having too much choice may also make us unhappy.

Thinkpoint 14.11

John has now left the Dog and Duck and is in the supermarket. There is an endless array of things to choose from. He buys some toothpaste because it gives him double reward points (he hasn't noticed that it is twice the price of the value brand). Then he considers whether to buy some traditional English sausages or the own-brand version – he chooses the traditional option because the packet is cardboard with a picture of a farmyard. The own brand are wrapped in cellophane. They are cheap and, frankly, look it (he doesn't know that both sausages are identical and come from the same factory) and, after all, he has been economical with his choice of toothpaste. He chooses some beer and, because everyone knows that German lager is passé, he gets a Hungarian brand (he doesn't remember that he saw an advert for it last night – it's just what he fancies). At the checkout there is a display of hand-cooked potato crisps with a Malaysian curry flavour and he puts one in the trolley – he wouldn't have thought of buying them if the supermarket hadn't helpfully put them there. Then he sees a sign that says he can have a second bag free, so he chooses to take two (he doesn't know it yet, but next time he goes to the supermarket he will seek out these crisps, even though they won't be on special offer).

John has made several choices. Is he free? Are you any different to John?

Key issues and controversies

One of the most remarkable books ever written about organizations is almost never mentioned, much less discussed, within mainstream literature on bureaucracy. The book in question is Zygmunt Bauman's *Modernity and the Holocaust* (1989). Bauman explores how the Nazi Holocaust, which murdered at least six million Jewish people as well as those from many other groups, was related to a highly-developed European civilization. He analyzes this in many ways, but in particular he explains how the genocide instigated by the Nazis represents the extreme application of a bureaucratic logic. What makes the Holocaust peculiarly horrifying is the way in which the mass extermination was conducted industrially – with a system of rules, impersonally applied, which made it as technically efficient as a genocide could be. The capacity to register and monitor populations so that Jews, communists, gypsies, homosexuals and the other categories to which the Nazis objected was itself a considerable administrative achievement. The shipping of these people to the camps was another, and their systematic extermination a third.

That bureaucratic practice, the impersonal, scientific, ethically-neutral pursuit of means made the Holocaust instrumentally rational while, clearly, not being substantively rational. This is perhaps the clearest illustration of how these two definitions of rationality differ. Bauman says that we should not, therefore, see the Holocaust as an aberration or anomaly when compared with mainstream Western culture: rather, it was a manifestation of the habitual ways of organizing within that culture.

The Holocaust example is very important, and not for emotive reasons. Almost everyone can agree that the extermination of a race of people is irrational on any meaning that might be given to that term. Yet the fact that (instrumentally) rational methods could be applied to it, as easily as to the production of toy cars or, for that matter, the distribution of food aid, serves to underscore the moral blindness of bureaucracy. It is not that bureaucratic techniques are necessarily 'immoral' but that they simply do not consider morality. So, if we want to live in a civilized society, we cannot simply be concerned with efficiency as envisaged by bureaucracy: we have to think about the purposes to which bureaucracy is put. Bureaucracy does not consider values: people do.

Thinkpoint 14.12

You are (probably) on a management course. Would you be willing to devise the most efficient way to exterminate people? If not, how is your course helping you to make moral judgements about how to use your skills?

Although the moral deficiencies of bureaucracy are a key issue within the critical approach, are they a key controversy? The British sociologist Paul du Gay (2000) has offered a sophisticated and important defence of bureaucracy although not, of course, one that would condone its genocidal use. It is worth pausing to reflect upon the context within which du Gay has made his arguments. It is a context in which the public sector within the UK (and elsewhere) has been accused of being far too bureaucratic, not in the sense of being amoral but in the traditional sense of being mired in 'red tape'. It stands accused of being characterized by goal displacement, producer focus and all the other mainstream complaints about bureaucracy. These complaints have their counterpart in other critical analyses which see bureaucracy as dehumanizing and morally blind (see also Chapter 15). Fighting on both flanks, du Gay argues, in the title of his book, *In Praise of Bureaucracy*.

Bureaucracy, du Gay explains, is actually imbued with morality, not because of Weber's concerns about substantive rationality but because of the demands of instrumental rationality for maximum efficiency. To satisfy these demands, du Gay argues, requires an ethic of impersonality and fairness so that employees and customers or clients are treated without prejudice. So, for example, bureaucracy does not care about an employee's gender or ethnic background – it only cares about qualifications since this is what will be most efficient. Clients, too, are treated the same, whoever they may be. Bureaucracy is a safeguard against discrimination. In this way it embodies, rather than ignores, a morality of fairness and due process. Post-bureaucracy or, as du Gay says, enterprise, has no such formal code.

Exercise 14.8

How does the admissions system example illustrate du Gay's point that bureaucracy is fair? In the last few years there have been many criticisms of the elitism of university admissions procedures, especially at Oxford and Cambridge. What would be better; a system based on A-level results, an interview system or, as some have suggested, a standardized aptitude test? In what ways might each approach relate to bureaucracy and post-bureaucracy? Would there be a conflict between efficiency and fairness in each of these approaches? Would it be greater in some than in others? Assuming you are at a university, do you feel that your application was dealt with efficiently or fairly or both?

In one way, there is no doubt that du Gay is correct. And his work has been important in answering the charge that bureaucracy is morally blind. Yet in another way it assumes far too much. It assumes that bureaucracies do, in fact, conform to Weber's ideal-type. Yet studies from the mainstream show how, in practice, bureaucracies allow all kinds of prejudice and discrimination – Crozier, Dalton and Kanter are all examples. Du Gay is right to say that the formal model of bureaucracy embodies an ethic. But it would be wrong to conclude that bureaucracy does invariably, in practice, exhibit this ethic.

Exercise 14.9

Jackie decides to rent a house with five other students. When they move in they draw up a rota to share the cooking, cleaning, shopping and so on. This is a (simple) kind of rule-based system with a division of labour. One of its features is that it divides the work up fairly. In your experience, is this likely to work in practice? What difference might it make if all Jackie's housemates are male?

du Gay's arguments are important because they question whether bureaucracy is discredited. Although he flies against mainstream thinking, he has a strong case. For all of the arguments against the death of bureaucracy advanced in the 1960s continue to hold true, and the basic advantages of bureaucracy, as illustrated by the admissions system example, are undeniable – both in terms of efficiency and those of fairness. But whether fairness is enough to offset the moral deficiencies of bureaucracy that Bauman illustrates is less clear – and remains a controversial issue.

Important studies

There are many ways in which bureaucracy and post-bureaucracy can be criticized. Studies have focused on the problems of the former, of the latter, or of the distinction between them. From the many possibilities, we have chosen some that represent a range of these positions and are the most articulate in advancing their analyses.

One of the more readable studies of bureaucracy is George Ritzer's widely praised book *The McDonaldization of Society* (2000). Ritzer's is in effect a reworking of Weber's concerns about the iron cage of rationality – the idea that there is no escape from the growing presence of bureaucracy. But Ritzer updates this analysis by focusing on McDonald's, the fast food chain, which he says is the template for contemporary forms of bureaucratization, with its standardized menus, architecture and even the words used by employees. At the heart of Ritzer's critique is the familiar complaint that bureaucracy dehumanizes both employees and customers. The impersonality that is central to the bureaucratic ethos may, as du Gay says, guarantee fairness, but it also means that the 'person' is irrelevant and subservient to the organizational machine. McDonaldization exemplifies the logic of standardization, which is what bureaucracy is all about, and Ritzer sees standardization as spreading into all kinds of areas of life: the national curriculum and modularization in education; package holidays and mass-build housing estates, for example.

Thinkpoint 14.13

When you eat at McDonald's, sit in a lecture theatre or go on a package holiday, do you feel dehumanized? And if you do not, does that mean that Ritzer is wrong or that you have become so tamed that you do not even notice the iron cage around you?

In a very different, but also highly readable, kind of study, the anthropologist and political activist David Graeber's *The Utopia of Rules* (2015) is also at pains to show how bureaucracy, in a variety of forms, remains supremely dominant. Indeed, at first sight paradoxically, he suggests that in the recent decades that have seen the supposed rise of a market logic over a bureaucratic logic, bureaucracy, especially corporate bureaucracy, has actually increased. Yet he offers an alternative in which bureaucracy is not simply discarded as 'bad' but works creatively with what he recognizes are the seductions of bureaucracy (for example the comfort and even liberation that can come from a system of rules).

Graeber and Ritzer, like Weber, are critical of the instrumental rationality of bureaucracy. Kathy Ferguson puts a particular spin on such a critique in elaborating *The Feminist Case Against Bureaucracy* (1984). Within the mainstream approaches we saw how Kanter's work indicated the male biases within bureaucratic organization, but Ferguson's arguments are much more radical. She sees the instrumental rationality of bureaucracy as being one that is in principle 'masculinist'. Whereas, for critics in the Weberian tradition, instrumentality is an expression of specifically modern and industrial ways of viewing the world and organizations, for Ferguson they embody something more – a masculine search for control and mastery. The structures of hierarchy are an expression of this both in the simple sense of being an example of such masculinism and, in a more complex way, by positioning employees and customers as passive and dependent in a way that Ferguson, borrowing the expression first coined by Simone de Beauvoir, sees as analogous to the traditional position of 'the second sex' or women.

In a wider ranging way, Ferguson sees the development of bureaucracy as being part and parcel of the way in which the modern world has been divided into a public and private sphere. The public sphere, where bureaucracy is located, is characterized by masculinity, competition, aggression and rationality, while the private sphere of families and households is characterized by femininity, co-operation, tolerance and emotionality. In this way, a range of archetypically feminine experiences and values are seen to have been excluded from the public sphere of bureaucracy and not just excluded but also disparaged and discounted.

Thinkpoint 14.14

Think about the ways you behave with your friends and family and compare them with how you behave at work or in classes. How are they different? Why? What would happen to you if you behaved in the same way in both settings?

The next study is one less concerned with theory and more focused on the lived-experience of, in particular, post-bureaucracy. Richard Sennett's *Work and the Corrosion of Character* (1998) looks at a series of lives affected by the changing nature of work. In many cases, Sennett returns to people and workplaces he had visited 25 years before as part of the research for an earlier book, giving a useful insight into these changes. For example, he revisits what was formerly a Greek bakery run along bureaucratic rules by a stable unionized workforce with intimate knowledge of baking techniques. It is now part of a huge multinational firm, and uses a shifting workforce of non-unionized migrant workers operating computer-controlled ovens. These latter allow production to shift flexibly from one type of bread to another, yet the operators know nothing at all of baking techniques: they simply click on icons on a computer screen.

This example is interesting because it shows how new post-bureaucratic working conditions of flexibility (in employment and production) do not imply an idyllic, empowered kind of organizational life. Rather, the new ways of working are as 'alienating' and dehumanizing as before, if not more so, because the bonds of community among the employees (and with customers) and the involvement of the workers with their work and product has been fractured. But it is also interesting because the loss of the traditional bureaucracy serves to point to the ways in which such organizations are not necessarily as dehumanizing as the work of someone like Ritzer claims, nor as devoid of emotionality as Ferguson's analysis might imply.

Something similar, albeit even more strongly expressed, can be found in Nancy Harding's book *On Being at Work* (2013). Here the author uses the life stories of people including Harding herself and her sister, Julie, a full-time carer for their father; Frank, a manager; Shakeel, a manual worker; Alex, an archaeologist; Kara and Saul, lecturers, to explore the nature of modern work. Organizations, she argues, typically (and perhaps increasingly) seek to render us less than human or even, to use one of her key expressions, 'zombie-machines'. This is so not simply in traditional dehumanizing bureaucracies but, even more, in post-bureaucracies that seek to enrol the 'whole self' into work so that there is no gap between work and pleasure or leisure.

Finally, a more conventional kind of empirical study, but one of the very best of its kind, is Rick Delbridge's *Life on the Line in Contemporary Manufacturing* (1998). Like Dalton's classic book on managers, this is an ethnography reporting on the author's time in two British factories. One is a Japanese-owned electronics plant (Nippon CTV), the other a European-owned producer of automotive components (ValleyCo). Although strictly speaking this is not a study of bureaucracy and post-bureaucracy, it does contrast the more traditional approach at ValleyCo with the 'Japanized' approach at Nippon CTV where there is a focus on lean production, just-in-time management, innovation, customer focus and human resource management. This is, at least, an adjacent theme to that of the present chapter.

While Delbridge found a number of contrasts between the plants, it is fair to say that his overall conclusion is that there is a considerable similarity between 'traditional' and 'new' forms of working in terms of things like hierarchy, participation or trust. His findings are very much in line with those in the various contributions to Thompson and Warhurst (1998) in relation to scepticism about post-bureaucracy: 'There is little to suggest that contemporary manufacturing is best characterized as "post-Fordist" and that the shop floor is a hotbed of worker autonomy and knowledge creation' (Delbridge, 1998, p. 192).

One feature of Sennett's, Delbridge's and Harding's studies which makes them 'critical' rather than mainstream is that they capture the experience and perspective of the front-line workers or just 'ordinary' people rather than being idealized and self-interested accounts written from a managerial perspective. In this regard they represent an antidote to some of the more hyperbolic claims made about the 'new economy' such as those found in the mainstream literature on post-bureaucracy.

Limitations of critical approaches

CONTRIBUTIONS

Perhaps the most important contribution of the critical approach is to move away from a narrow focus on efficiency and the techniques of bureaucracy and post-bureaucracy towards a recognition of the political and ethical values that come into play when organizations are designed (see also Chapter 15). The idea that managing and organizing are not 'neutral', technical issues is one that runs throughout critical approaches, as is clear from most other chapters in this book.

Post-bureaucracy, of course, is claimed by its advocates to be precisely an organizational form concerned with values. They argue that it liberates employees and consumers alike from the stifling 'red tape' and inflexibility of bureaucracy. Critical approaches are unpersuaded by such arguments. Crucially, as with culture management (see Chapter 10), the problem is that values are defined hierarchically and within an overall purpose of gaining control. Another way of saying this would be that post-bureaucracy, as much as bureaucracy, is defined by an instrumental – and, feminists would argue, masculinist – rationality. It may use a different set of techniques to get the job done, but it is still, essentially, an exercise of power, using people as instruments in pursuit of some other goal. The examples of Sennett's bakers or of customers' experience of automated phone systems both illustrate this, and Harding's notion of the 'zombie-machine' graphically captures it.

In any case, the other main contribution of critical approaches is to point out that the lived experience of post-bureaucracy is by no means the utopia that its advocates suggest. Bureaucracy dehumanized its employees, but at least offered the security of set routines. Post-bureaucracy marks an increase in insecurity and anxiety because it promotes job insecurity, an intensification of time pressures (the '24/7' society) and places the accent on the responsibility of individuals to manage their careers and lives without the collective protection that bureaucracies can offer. This, indeed, explains why post-bureaucratic reforms are often resisted, as in the case of the BBC (Harris and Wegg-Prosser, 2007).

Thinkpoint 14.15

Thinking about the people you know, particularly older people like your parents and their friends, do you think that they are anxious and insecure about work? Or do you think that people your age face more of a problem?

Thus critical approaches question a **binary** logic: either bureaucracy is 'right' or it is 'wrong'. A simple version of the mainstream-critical divide would be based on binary logic. Bureaucracy is good, post-bureaucracy is bad. Or post-bureaucracy is good, bureaucracy is bad. We have seen that many of the protagonists in the debate follow just this logic. Almost all of today's management gurus, and most policy-makers, say that bureaucracy is bad. Paul du Gay is one of the few examples of writers who say the opposite. However, in our discussions of the mainstream approach we found that evidence was split and we also found that the division between bureaucracy and post-bureaucracy was much less clear-cut. Critical approaches go further, though. It is not just a matter of trying to find evidence on one side of the argument or the other. Rather, it is to see that there are continuities, based on instrumental rationality, between both.

Binary Division into two and only two opposites as in body/mind, female/male, black/white, positive/negative, true/false or the code of 0 and 1 in computing. Criticisms of this way of thinking, sometimes described as dualistic, argue that there are other alternatives that lie in-between or beyond the two extremes.

Exercise 14.10

In what ways do the cases of both Universal and CompCo show that there is not a binary logic of bureaucracy and post-bureaucracy?

LIMITATIONS

Despite what was just said about a refusal of binary logic within critical approaches, it is also true that some individual studies within these approaches do have a tendency to oversimplify. Ritzer, in particular, seems to imply that because bureaucracy is 'bad' then anything that is not bureaucracy is 'good'. Thus some of the forms of resistance to McDonaldization that he proposes end up endorsing some of the niche marketing practices associated with post-bureaucracy. Defences of bureaucracy, too, can carry a danger of romanticizing such organizations as places of fairness and, even, communities. Studies like Delbridge's can be a useful antidote to this kind of danger.

A second difficulty with critical approaches, which seems to be present in Weber's discussion of the iron cage and again in Ritzer, is the problem of **determinism**. Many mainstream positions show this problem – for example,

Determinism View that there is an inevitable direction in which events move, as a result of some cause that is independent of the event. In organization studies and in everyday life, the idea that 'human nature' determines social arrangements is possibly the most common. See also **technological determinism**.

most cases for the rise of post-bureaucracy rest on the determinism of computer technologies – but so too do some critical approaches. The idea that bureaucratization is a 'juggernaut' that will inevitably sweep aside other forms of organization because of its technical efficiency is a common one in critical theory. The limitation of this view is that it pays no attention to the choices that people and societies make about how to organize themselves. In this respect determinism is a double problem. First, because it ignores choices, it is analytically problematic. Second, because it promotes the view that whatever choices are made they will have no effect, it encourages fatalism and quietism and is therefore a political problem as well.

Exercise 14.11

Politicians often use phrases like 'there is no alternative' or 'the fact of the matter is . . .'. Parents often respond to small children's favourite question ('why?') by saying 'that's just the way it is' or 'because I say so'. Many economists tell us that 'you can't buck the market' and some biologists say that 'it's all in the genes'. All these are, in different ways, deterministic arguments. How valid are they? Can you think of other examples?

Somewhat related to this is a third difficulty for critical approaches, especially the argument that post-bureaucracy is no more than the spread of even more intense forms of power and control. This then makes it very difficult to know what kinds of reform can be envisaged that would be acceptable to critics. If dehumanization and humanization at work are both versions of control, then what proposal for change does that leave? The answers typically seem highly Utopian, explicitly so in Graeber's work: for example, the suspension of masculinist and instrumental rationality. Given that this seems unlikely in the immediate future, does this mean that there is nothing to be done but bemoan the existing state of affairs until a complete social transformation has occurred?

Conclusion

In this chapter we have seen how a complex series of issues are involved in thinking about bureaucracy and post-bureaucracy. It is undoubtedly true that bureaucratic organizations have been one of the defining features of modern life. Weber was right to observe that they were becoming so in his time and right to predict that they would become more so in the future. Yet almost no one who has studied them seriously, whether from a mainstream or a critical perspective, has concluded that they are without problems. Mainstream and critical writers differ in the radicalism with which they explain these problems, however. As a broad generalization, mainstream approaches stress the ways in which reality diverges from the rationality of the bureaucratic model, while critics draw attention to the defects of the very rationality that underpins that model. Mainstream writers may be more likely to see possible reforms to bureaucracy but are perhaps over-optimistic about the likely efficacy of such prescriptions. Critics are likely to highlight the oppressive and dehumanizing consequences of bureaucracy and therefore will tend to want to reject it root and branch.

But of course things are never quite so simple. In recent years, there have been very pronounced rejections of the bureaucratic model from within mainstream thinking on organizations and, also, some defences of bureaucracy from critics. The mainstream proponents of post-bureaucracy, who repeat many earlier claims in their case, are in some senses 'critics' of bureaucracy, but not in the way normally implied by the term 'critical approaches'. This is because they make their case from within mainstream assumptions about efficiency and organizational purpose. They are saying, in effect, bureaucracy was fine for its time, but times have changed and now they favour post-bureaucracy. They do not question the underlying idea that organizations exist to deliver efficient outcomes for their owners, nor the need to maintain control. They just want to do it in a new way.

For that reason, critical approaches are critical of both bureaucracy and post-bureaucracy. They question the narrowness of the mainstream understanding of efficiency and the acceptability of pursuing control over others in pursuit of that efficiency. Although to polarize mainstream and critical approaches too much would be to fall into the trap of binary logic, there are some real and substantive differences between them. These differences reflect very serious and profound divergences of thinking, not just about organizations but about society as a whole. Critical approaches tend to be explicit that it is these political issues that are at stake, whereas mainstream approaches typically prefer to leave them implicit, and to treat organizational design as if it were simply a matter of developing and applying the most efficient technique. However, as we have seen, embedded within the very notion of efficiency there are some political assumptions, principally about the question of for whom organizations are efficient.

The mainstream approach is, in this regard at least, untenable, and its more reflective practitioners know it. Within the myriad of debates about bureaucracy and post-bureaucracy, what is ultimately at stake is how people choose to organize their collective activities and this goes to the heart of what we think those collective activities should be, and how we go about them. These are inescapably moral and political questions.

Discussion questions

1   Why did bureaucratic organizations come into existence?

2   Does the literature on 'bureaucratic dysfunctionalism' prove that bureaucracy is inefficient?

3   What kinds of contingencies could explain whether an organization will tend to be bureaucratic or post-bureaucratic?

4   Charles Heckscher says that the world is becoming more post-bureaucratic. George Ritzer says it is becoming more bureaucratic. Who is right? Could they both be right?

5   Is it substantively rational to make a profit? If so, then aren't private sector bureaucracies necessarily rational in all meanings of the word?

6   What kind of organizations would satisfy the critics of bureaucracy and post-bureaucracy? Do any exist?

Further reading

du Gay, P. (2000) *In Praise of Bureaucracy: Weber, Organization and Ethics,* London: Sage.

This is not an easy read, but it must stand as one of the most important books written in this area for many years. It offers what some might think is an audacious case for the virtues of bureaucracy, and challenges much conventional thinking in this regard. At its heart is a claim that bureaucracy embodies a specific ethic of impartiality that is of enduring value.

Ferguson, K. (1984) *The Feminist Case Against Bureaucracy,* Philadelphia, PA: Temple University Press.

Again not an easy book, but it should feature in any list of readings because it provides a fundamental challenge not just to bureaucracy but to the logic that informs many claims about post-bureaucracy. For Ferguson, bureaucracy exhibits a masculinist logic of control and this opens up the very fundamental terrain of the values underpinning any form of organization.

Graeber, D. (2015) *The Utopia of Rules. On Technology, Stupidity, and the Secret Joys of Bureaucracy.* New York: Melville House Books.

An unorthodox, lively book, really a collection of three essays, drawing examples not just from work but science fiction and wider culture. The first two essays depict a world dominated by bureaucracy and underpinned by violence. Then a redemptive possibility is offered in which bureaucracy does not disappear but is reimagined.

Ritzer, G. (2000) *The McDonaldization of Society: An Investigation Into the Changing Character of Contemporary Social Life,* second edn, Thousand Oaks, CA: Sage.

This is a provocative, well-written book that makes the case that modern society is becoming increasingly bureaucratized and standardized, with McDonald's as the defining example. It offers an interesting reworking of Weber's concerns about bureaucracy in a way that is much more accessible than the original writings.

Sennett, R. (1998) *Work and the Corrosion of Character: The Personal Consequences of Work in the New Capitalism,* London: WW Norton.

This book can be commended for its readability. It offers very personalized accounts of how shifts from traditional bureaucratic organizations to those of post-bureaucracy impact upon the lives of real people. Sceptics might say that Sennett offers us stories not analysis, but, carefully read, this book provides a convincing critique of contemporary organizational life.

Whyte, W. H. (1956) *The Organization Man,* New York: Simon & Schuster.

This classic work, which is available in many editions, was an early and perceptive critique of life in bureaucracy. Although over 50 years old, it still reads freshly, not least because many of the features described seem to apply to post-bureaucracy as well, which in itself should caution us against an overly polarized view of the two 'models'. Whyte's concern that individuals are subsumed within the organizational order has a disturbingly modern feel.

Alexander, J. K. (2008) *The Mantra of Efficiency. From Waterwheel to Social Control,* Baltimore, MD: Johns Hopkins University Press.

Much of the debate about bureaucracy, post-bureaucracy and rationality centres on the notion of 'efficiency' – but this itself is a complex and contested notion. Alexander's book traces its history with a particular emphasis on how this benign-sounding word is concerned with the pursuit of mastery through techniques of surveillance, discipline and control.

Clegg, S., Harris, M. and Hopfl, H. (eds) (2011) *Managing Modernity: Beyond Bureaucracy?* Oxford: Oxford University Press.

Useful websites

For the crucial segment of Weber's classic statement of bureaucracy see:
www.faculty.rsu.edu/felwell/TheoryWeb/readings/WeberBurform.html

For a brief overview of advantages and disadvantages of bureaucracy and alternative organizational forms:
www.uplink.com.au/lawlibrary/Documents/Docs/Doc11.html

For the political deployment of the post-bureaucratic idea, see this piece by David Cameron (the former British Prime Minister):
www.guardian.co.uk/commentisfree/2009/may/25/david-cameron-a-new-politics3

In a related vein, this group campaigns for post-bureaucracy as a democratic ideal:
www.pbage.org/

For a discussion of 'hot desking' (relevant to the CompCo case study), see:
www.bbc.co.uk/guides/zgjmtfr

References

Aldrich, H. (1972) 'Technology and organization structure: A re-examination of the findings of the Aston group', *Administrative Science Quarterly,* 17: 26–43.

Alvesson, M. and Thompson, P. (2005) 'Post-bureaucracy?', in S. Ackroyd, R. Batt, P. Thompson and P. Tolbert (eds) *The Oxford Handbook of Work and Organization,* Oxford: Oxford University Press, pp. 485–505.

Bauman, Z. (1989) *Modernity and the Holocaust,* Cambridge: Polity.

Bennis, W. (1966) 'The coming death of bureaucracy', *Think,* November: 30–35.

Blau, P. (1955) *The Dynamics of Bureaucracy,* Chicago, IL: Chicago University Press.

Blau, P. (1970) 'A formal theory of differentiation in organizations', *American Sociological Review,* 35(2): 210–218.

Burns, T. and Stalker, G. (1961) *The Management of Innovation,* Oxford: Oxford University Press.

Castells, M. (1996) *The Rise of the Network Society,* Oxford: Oxford University Press.

Crozier, M. (1964) *The Bureaucratic Phenomenon,* Chicago, IL: University of Chicago Press.

Dalton, M. (1959) *Men Who Manage,* New York: John Wiley & Sons.

Delbridge, R. (1998) *Life On the Line in Contemporary Manufacturing,* Oxford: Oxford University Press.

du Gay, P. (2000) *In Praise of Bureaucracy: Weber, Organization and Ethics,* London: Sage.

Ferguson, K. (1984) *The Feminist Case Against Bureaucracy,* Philadelphia, PA: Temple University Press.

Gouldner, A. (1954) *Patterns of Industrial Bureaucracy,* New York: Free Press.

Graeber, D. (2015) *The Utopia of Rules. On Technology, Stupidity, and the Secret Joys of Bureaucracy*, New York: Melville House Books.

Harding, N. (2013) *On Being at Work. The Social Construction of the Employee,* London: Routledge.

Harris, M. and Wegg-Prosser, V. (2007) 'Post bureaucracy and the politics of forgetting: The management of change at the BBC, 1991–2002', *Journal of Organizational Change Management,* 20(3): 290–303.

Heckscher, C. (1994) 'Defining the post-bureaucratic type', in C. Heckscher and A. Donnellon (eds) *The Post-bureaucratic Organization: New Perspectives on Organizational Change,* Thousand Oaks, CA: Sage, pp. 14–62.

Heckscher, C. and Donnellon, A. (eds) (1994) *The Post-bureaucratic Organization: New Perspectives on Organizational Change,* Thousand Oaks, CA: Sage.

Johnson, P., Wood, G., Brewster, C. and Brooks, M. (2009) 'The rise of post-bureaucracy. Theorists fancy or organizational praxis?', *International Sociology,* 24(1): 37–61.

Josserand, E., Teo, S. and Clegg, S. (2006) 'From bureaucratic to post-bureaucratic: The difficulties of transition', *Journal of Organizational Change Management,* 19(1): 54–64.

Kanter, R. M. (1993) *Men and Women of the Corporation,* second edn, New York: Basic Books.

Kelley, R. (1990) *The Gold-collar Worker: Harnessing the Brainpower of the New Work Force,* Reading, MA: Addison-Wesley.

Leadbetter, C. (1999) *Living On Thin Air: The New Economy,* London: Viking.

Merton, R. (1940) 'Bureaucratic structure and personality', *Social Forces,* May: 560–568.

Miewald, R. D. (1970) 'The greatly exaggerated death of bureaucracy', *California Management Review,* Winter: 65–69.

Perrow, C. (1979) *Complex Organizations,* Englewood Cliffs, NJ: Prentice Hall.

Piore, M. and Sabel, C. (1984) *The Second Industrial Divide,* New York: Basic Books.

Pugh, D. and Hickson, D. (1976) *Organisation Structure in its Context: The Aston Programme,* London: Saxon House.

Pugh, D., Hickson, D. and Hinings, C. R. (1968) 'Dimensions of organisation structure', *Administrative Science Quarterly,* 13(1): 65–103.

Reich, R. (1993) *The Work of Nations,* London: Simon & Schuster.

Ritzer, G. (2000) *The McDonaldization of Society: An Investigation Into the Changing Character of Contemporary Social Life,* second edn, Thousand Oaks, CA: Sage.

Robertson, M. and Swan, J. (1998) 'Modes of organizing in an expert consultancy: A case study of knowledge, power and egos', *Organization,* 5(4): 543–564.

Rose, N. (1999) *Governing the Soul,* London: Routledge.

Schofield, J. (2001) 'The old ways are the best? The durability and usefulness of bureaucracy in public sector management', *Organization,* 8(1): 77–96.

Schwartz, B. (2004) *The Paradox of Choice. Why More is Less,* New York: Harper Perennial.

Selznick, P. (1949) *TVA and the Grass Roots: A Study in the Sociology of Formal Organizations,* Berkeley, CA: University of California Press.

Semler, R. (1993) *Maverick,* London: Century.

Sennett, R. (1998) *Work and the Corrosion of Character. The Personal Consequences of Work in the New Capitalism,* London: WW Norton.

Thompson, P. and Warhurst, C. (eds) (1998) *Workplaces of the Future,* Basingstoke: Macmillan.

Warhurst, C. and Thompson, P. (1998) 'Hands, hearts and minds: Changing work and workers at the end of the century', in P. Thompson and C. Warhurst (eds) *Workplaces of the Future,* Basingstoke: Macmillan, pp. 1–24.

Woodward, J. (1965) *Industrial Organization: Theory and Practice,* Oxford: Oxford University Press.

15 Ethics at work

EDWARD WRAY-BLISS

Key concepts and learning objectives

By the end of this chapter you should understand:

- The core assumptions of mainstream writers on business ethics, and be aware of how these assumptions limit the ethical questions that mainstream writers have been able to ask of business.

- The connections between mainstream academic writing on business ethics and contemporary organization's socially responsible image.

- That there is a wealth of other, more critical approaches to ethics that enable us to question the appropriateness of this socially responsible image.

- How some of these critical approaches enable us to undertake a deeper examination of the values underpinning modern organizations.

Aims of the chapter

This chapter will:

- Examine the relationship between ethical values and organizational behaviour.

- Explore some of the key ideas and developments that have introduced ethics into the heart of the modern organization.

- Examine some key mainstream studies of business ethics.

- Explore some of the key ideas that mark the critical challenge to mainstream views of business ethics.

- Examine some key critical studies of ethics in organizations.

- Explore the linkages between ethics and the core concept of freedom, in order to better understand the issue of ethical values at work.

Overview and key points

Behaviour perpetrated within and on behalf of organizations affects all of us, every day. Thankfully, much of the time we experience positive effects. So for instance, we buy products made within organizations. We drink water and eat food processed by organizations. We are educated and employed in organizations. However, organizational behaviour is not always so benign. We are also ripped off by organizations. Our environment is polluted by organizations. Many people are exploited or abused, harmed or even killed as a result of organizational behaviour – indeed, as the *International Labour Organization*'s Director General reported in 2014, work kills more people than war each year. Much of the 'bad' organizational behaviour is regulated by the law. However, the law is often a very blunt tool. It can be limited in its reach. It is not always effectively enforced. It may be circumvented by the unscrupulous and the clever. It can even be blind to some seriously damaging events. Indeed, we have only to consider the global financial crisis of the last few years to see how legal, but irresponsible, practices by large financial institutions can prove so damaging to millions. There is, in short, potentially a large gap between how we may want organizations to behave and how the law ensures that they behave. As a result of this, society is increasingly asking management to make sure that their organizations not only refrain from breaking the law but also, and this is potentially much more radical and far-reaching though also less clearly defined, to ensure that organizations and their members behave *ethically*.

This chapter will examine this important way of thinking about organizational behaviour. In the first section we explore the work of theorists in the academic field of business ethics. We examine how such writers have attempted to integrate the apparently quite different arenas of 'ethics' and 'business'. We also explore how the managers of business organizations have come to appreciate how important it is for their organization to now be seen to behave ethically, or, in the new ethical language of business, to demonstrate corporate social responsibility.

In the second section we take a more critical look at these recent developments in both the study and practice of ethics in business. We re-examine the core assumptions of business ethics/corporate social responsibility and highlight how these are themselves ethically questionable. As part of this, we scrutinize the mainstream assumptions that organizations are or can be responsible; the desirability of employees' subordination to managerial control; and the reduction of ethics to the pursuit of profits. By exploring the theories of critical writers, and a number of compelling critical case studies, we see how such critical approaches to the subject can help to reclaim ethics as a concept that enables us to examine the values underpinning contemporary organizational behaviour.

Mainstream approaches to ethics at work

Introduction

The modern engagement with 'ethics at work' is conventionally described as having started in the UK and the USA in the 1980s. The 1980s were shaped by neo-conservative governments that pushed an aggressively pro-business, 'free market' agenda. The agenda centred upon **deregulation of markets**, reducing the legal restraints placed upon business, and an ideology of self-interest for both individuals and corporations. Crucially, for our account of the emergence of the modern engagement with ethics at work, this decade strongly promoted the idea and practice that business leaders should voluntarily *self-regulate*. The idea was that business leaders should be left alone to control their businesses rather than be more tightly regulated by the state or federal/national government. This was an ideology that the business community warmly welcomed then, and still jealously guards today.

Deregulation of markets
Process whereby greater competition is encouraged between commercial organizations through reducing regulations that previously restricted their behaviour or entry into certain markets.

Public faith in the effectiveness of business self-regulation was shaken, however, by a series of very public business scandals, disasters and frauds – much like our current era. People began to question the negative effects of business practice. Some even began to question the effectiveness of business self-regulation more generally. Of course, such scandals had occurred in the past, but in the 1980s more people (as a result of such things as the growth in small-scale share ownership) were directly affected by them, and social movements critical of business were better supported and had gained a greater visibility.

To regain public trust and ward off calls for more state regulation of business, the business community attempted to reassure the public and policymakers that it was capable of taking responsibility for the potentially negative effects of its practices. This reassurance took the form of ethics. The business community began to publicly present itself as concerned with the ethics of its actions and its effects upon the wider society. By drawing upon a discourse of ethics, business leaders could seek to reassure that they would take responsibility for their own actions. Business would be its own conscience if you like, and did not therefore need further governmental regulation. This modern concern by business leaders with issues of 'ethics' is generally given the shorthand title **Corporate social responsibility**.

Corporate social responsibility (CSR)
The practices and policies undertaken by organizations to promote the idea that they have concerns that extend beyond efficiency, performance, productivity and profit to embrace the public, customers, the environment and other stakeholders.

CSR is the term that has come to stand for the practices and policies undertaken by the business community to promote the idea that they are concerned with more than just profit and self-interest. CSR practices can include:

- Appointing managers or directors with responsibility for CSR.
- Developing and publicizing ethical statements, policies or codes of practice.
- Joining environmental or other public groups or forums.
- Publicizing a track record of good corporate governance.
- Making well-publicized donations of money, time or resources to charities and other good causes.
- Linking the business brand, through sponsorship, marketing, etc., with 'good' images such as ending child poverty, protecting the environment or inner city regeneration.

So widespread has the CSR movement now become that it is rare to find a large company these days that does not promote itself as socially responsible (see Table 15.1).

Business ethics The academic study and promotion of ethical practice in business.

However, just because business leaders now promote their organizations as 'socially responsible' does not mean that such claims are legitimate. One way the corporate world finds legitimacy for its claim to be socially responsible is through an association with the academic field of study called **business ethics**.

Business ethics may be understood as the academic study and promotion of corporate social responsibility. Business ethics explores the ethical legitimations for, and effects of, a wide range of business practices. These academic arguments are then widely disseminated to students and managers through, for example, business ethics modules on MBA and other university management courses, through the large market for business ethics textbooks, and through a sizeable and constantly growing volume of academic journals, conferences and symposia on business ethics and CSR.

The field of business ethics is, as a result, broad and diverse and can therefore seem difficult to get an overall sense of. Despite this variety and volume, however, it is possible to discern a common approach in most mainstream business ethics work, consisting of:

- *A pro-business agenda.* Business ethics critiques particular business practices, but does not question the ethics of business more generally.
- *A free market agenda.* Business ethics endorses voluntary self-regulation of businesses rather than, for instance, control from outside (e.g., state regulation) as the way to ensure ethical practices.
- *A belief in the compatibility of profits and ethics.* Business ethics sees good ethics as synonymous with good business.

Table 15.1 Examples of corporate social responsibility claims

Company	Practices
Shell	• Shell sustainable development 'At every stage of our operations we seek to reduce our impact on the environment and listen to the communities with which we work. This helps us to understand the indirect effects of our operations, both positive and negative, and to contribute where possible to the communities' needs.' (Shell Sustainability Report, 2014)
Ford Motor Company	• Ford of Britain Charitable Trust • Environmental policies 'As the number of motor vehicles around the world increases, so do environmental concerns. However, we have always aimed to be a model for the industry in this area. So we're working to reduce the environmental impact of our products, while providing the utility, performance and affordability customers demand. We want it to be easy for people to say, "I'm an environmentalist and a car enthusiast."' (www.ford.co.uk courtesy of Ford Motor Company)

Table 15.1 **Examples of corporate social responsibility claims (*continued*)**

Company	Practices
Nike	• Charitable donations • Code of conduct for subcontracted labour 'Nike's Corporate Responsibility mission is to be an innovative and inspirational corporate citizen in a world where our company participates. We seek to protect and enhance the Nike brand through responsible business practices that contribute to profitable and sustainable growth.' (www.nike.com)

Case study 15.1
The Cooperative Bank: A famous ethical organization

At the time of revising this chapter for the third edition of the textbook in 2016, the world is still reeling from the aftershocks of the global financial crisis of 2007/08, a crisis brought about by the irresponsible commercial practices of banks and other financial institutions in the USA and elsewhere. It may therefore seem surprising, at these times, that the celebrated 'ethical' company in the following case study is, in fact, a bank. The Cooperative Bank is a successful, medium-sized, UK financial institution that was publicly heralded throughout the 1990s as perhaps the best UK example of a successful ethical business: a business that seemed to demonstrate that good ethics was good business. This case study charts The Cooperative Bank's rise to this moral and economic high ground.

To start with some context, in the UK prior to the 1980s financial service organizations were prevented from engaging in cross-sector competition. The market for financial service products that the big banks (Barclays, Lloyds, National Westminster and Midland), along with smaller banks like The Cooperative Bank, were involved in was protected by law, and other financial service providers were prevented from supplying the banks' core products. Enjoying the benefits of a stable, protected and growing market, the big banks had entered into an unofficial agreement not to undercut each other's products and services, thereby keeping their profits inflated. As a result, relatively small institutions like The Cooperative Bank could carve out a profitable niche by offering service innovations that the big banks were reluctant to follow and other financial service institutions were legally prevented from providing.

In the 1980s, however, the UK conservative government radically changed the financial services market. The government embarked upon a programme of deregulating markets and freeing-up business from historical constraints. As part of this programme restrictions on banks and other financial service providers were lifted (e.g., The Building Societies Act 1986). The big banks now faced stiffer competition as other financial institutions could enter into their markets and undercut their products. They responded by providing new products and services, thereby competing more keenly against each other and against smaller companies like The Cooperative Bank whose profitable innovative product niche was suddenly under threat. Indeed, by 1990 The Cooperative Bank was making a loss of around £15 million. The bank had to do something, and fast. Its strategy was twofold. First, like many of the other banks, it cut costs. It rapidly shed over 1000 employees, closed branches, dramatically cut staff numbers in its branches (typically from 40 to eight), and rerouted most of its contact with customers from over-the-counter and face-to-face to telephone banking via remote **call centres**.

Second, the management of the bank decided to reposition it as an ethical bank – one that gave its customers the choice to invest their money ethically. The bank's management researched customers' opinions on ethical matters, and then formulated and widely publicized a 12-point ethical policy, detailing whom the bank would and would not do business with. The policy prohibited the bank from investing its customers' money in, or indeed having business customers who were involved in, for example, the tobacco trade, the testing of cosmetics on animals or operating in countries with oppressive regimes. As The Cooperative Bank ethical policy booklet expressed it: 'Do you know, do you approve of how your money is being used when you are not using it? Do you think you have a right to know at least in principle? ... Can you put up the Second World War defence – I didn't know?'

Call centres Offices where staff are employed principally to process telephone calls with customers. Such centres involve heavily routinized and disciplined work processes where staff often work at very high levels of intensity and under conditions of technological surveillance and close monitoring.

By so positioning itself as an ethical bank, The Cooperative Bank explicitly distanced itself from the big banks and the bad press that these banks had experienced through such practices as their involvement in providing finance to the racist apartheid government in South Africa and aggressive selling practices in the UK. For some business commentators and media analysts The Cooperative Bank's reinvention as an 'ethical' company was contentious. The *Financial Times* newspaper remarked at the time that: 'Sceptics have been quick to suggest that The Cooperative Bank is cashing in on ethics. A number also indignantly suggest that banks have no rights to preach to their customers or discriminate against potential recipients of loans.'

However, from this early scepticism, most detractors in the business world came to be converted to the good business sense of The Cooperative Bank's ethical policy. They came to understand it as an example of clever market positioning with little risk, that served to attract the custom of more affluent middle-class customers whose social conscience was matched with a solid bank balance. As the managing director of the bank expressed it: 'There's no denying this is a marketing initiative ... why else do it? But we are not part of the long-haired sandal brigade, we are socially concerned bankers.' Indeed the bank's own economic turnaround speaks for itself. The Cooperative Bank increased its market share year-on-year after this ethical turn. Deposits rose approximately 10 per cent in 1993, 16 per cent in 1994 and 20 per cent in 1995, with 44 per cent of new account openings being attributed to its ethical positioning. By 1996 the bank made a profit of almost £37 million, compared to its £15 million loss in 1990. Today, the bank still successfully positions itself as the ethical bank.

Questions

The case of The Cooperative Bank illustrates several elements that were also common to the emergence of CSR and business ethics more generally.

1 How does the case demonstrate connections between the free market economic context of the time and the emergence of the bank's ethical stance?
2 How does the case illustrate the self-regulatory/voluntary nature of the bank's ethics?
3 What relationship does the case suggest between the issues of ethics and profitability?

Key problems

Case Study 15.1 presented an example of one company's contribution to the problem of integrating ethics and business. In the next section some important academic contributions to business ethics are discussed, but first we look at some of the key problems facing the field. A field that focuses upon practical business issues as diverse as A(lcohol policies at work) to Z(imbabwe business bribery), and utilizes the framework of something as long-debated as ethical philosophy to do so, will clearly generate a number of debates. To illustrate the complexities of ethical issues in organization, Box 15.1 raises just some of the questions that we might need to consider when thinking about the ethics of one organizational issue that affects everyone of us: pollution (see also Chapter 12).

From just this one issue, it should start to become clear that any attempt to consider the ethics of almost any organizational practice is problematic. So business ethics is full of 'problems' – but perhaps it should be. Business ethics is after all concerned with questions of ethics – with what is right and what is wrong, with how to live a 'good' life and not just a 'comfortable' or 'profitable' life – and these are far from easy issues.

Underpinning all the problems associated with specific organizational practices and issues (like pollution, for instance), however, are a number of more general problems that the field of business ethics needed to find a way to resolve if it was to justify its existence to sceptical managers of business organizations. We focus upon three such problems here: relevance; conscience; and translation.

THE PROBLEM OF RELEVANCE

As an academic who works within the broad field of business ethics, the response that I invariably get when I tell people about my work is a look of bemusement followed shortly by the quip 'that's an easy job then ... there aren't any'.

The field of business ethics as a whole faces this same problem, that of connecting ethics with business in a context where many people see them as separate. Beaton's (2001) tongue-in-cheek advice to managers relies upon this commonly perceived disconnection between ethics and business for its humour: 'You cannot gain professional respect if your personal integrity is damaged. Prevent damage to your personal integrity by leaving it at home in the mornings.'

It is not just comics like Beaton, however, that reproduce such ideas. The US free market economist, Milton Friedman (1970), argued that *the only* social responsibility of business is to increase its profits. Friedman argued that the corporate executive or manager may *personally* feel responsibilities to particular charities, or good causes, but should only act on these responsibilities in the private sphere when at home or in the community. If, as an employee, he or she practises these or other expressions of social responsibility in the corporation's time or with the corporation's money, then far from being ethical he or she is being dangerously subversive, misspending the shareholders' money, and failing to act as he or she has been contracted to. For Friedman therefore:

> there is one and only one social responsibility of business – to use its resources and engage in activities designed to increase its profits ... so long as it engages in open and free competition without deception or fraud (quoted in White, 2000, p. 238)

Apart from pursuing profit as if it were itself a moral crusade, ethics has little or no place in the business world for Friedman. Instead ethics is seen as private and personal and should stay that way, and should stay out of business. It clouds and compromises the open, and *good,* pursuit of money-making.

How should we understand the question of pollution by business? As immoral or as inevitable? Should it be stopped or only limited? Who has rights in this case: the business, the community, the natural environment, the shareholders, or the workers whose jobs may rely on the company producing, and thereby polluting? Do these rights conflict or coincide? How do we decide between them? Is pollution an evil that we must accept for the greater good? Or does the community's right to clean air and good health outweigh all other moral appeals? And what health has a community without employment? Is it ethical to shift pollution-generating activities to other, poorer countries? Is it right to limit the goods that consumers can buy so that pollution is minimized? Who is to decide on each of these questions? On what ethical basis will such decisions be made?

Box 15.1
The complexities of ethics: The example of pollution

THE PROBLEM OF CONSCIENCE

Assuming that business ethicists somehow solve the above problem of making ethics seem relevant for business, who is to decide what ethics are relevant and how to enforce them? To encourage us to behave ethically, individuals have concepts such as conscience, or fear of God or gods; we have ideas such as damnation, karma, rebirth, salvation or enlightenment; we have the desire to please, or the desire to live according to our principles or precepts, and more, that encourage us to abide by what we understand to be ethical and good. But a business organization would seem to have none of these. Where is its god? Who is its conscience? Where is its desire to be principled? Who is to be its ethical authority, its guru, its lord, its cleric, its rabbi, its enlightened being? And, even supposing that such a figure or figures can be found, how are they to enforce the ethical conscience of the organization? And should this enforcement override other people's values in the organization and the values of those with whom the organization interacts?

Thinkpoint 15.1

- Who do you think should be the conscience of an organization, and why?
- Reflecting further upon your answer, what assumptions have you made regarding:
  (i) who you think has knowledge about ethical issues in organizations?
  (ii) and how this relates to the power you think these people should have to define an organization's ethics?

THE PROBLEM OF TRANSLATION

The third underlying problem facing business ethics is one of translation. Even if some body or bodies are identified as the conscience of the organization, are the languages of ethics and business commensurable? Ethics can seem to be all philosophical and abstract, concerned with goodness and virtue and justice, whereas business is practical and rational, concerned with efficiency, outputs, products, and costs. Business relies upon measurement and calculability – everything must have a cost, a value, a purpose. Business has profit and loss accounts, stock control systems, payroll systems, delivery schedules, contracts, human resource planning and a wealth of other management systems to plan and measure each tangible aspect of organizational behaviour. Surely a business cannot hope to plan or measure something as intangible, or even spiritual, as ethics. And anyway, isn't ethics essentially individualistic, a matter of conscience, one's personal relationship with the divine (however this is understood)? Whereas organization is, by definition, concerned with collective purpose and collective effort. How can business ethicists possibly hope to translate ethics into something intelligible to, and manageable for, business?

Taken together, these three problems of relevance, conscience and translation present a significant challenge for business ethics. In the next section we explore some of the key ideas and contributions in the field that have sought to address these issues.

Key ideas and contributions

OVERCOMING THE PROBLEM OF RELEVANCE

Business ethics academics have formulated both social and economic arguments to address the widely held belief that business and ethics are, and possibly should be, disconnected realms.

The social argument attests that business, its employees and management should be understood as part of the social world, rather than abstracted from it. They should be subject to similar expectations of ethical conduct that we would expect from other members of our communities. **Stakeholder theory** has been used to argue that shareholders are only one of the many groups of people whom business interacts with, and is therefore responsible for.

Stakeholder theory
The idea that business owes responsibility to more groups than merely its shareholders. Stakeholders may include customers, the environment, suppliers, the local community, future generations, etc.

While shareholders principally demand profit, stakeholder theory argues that other stakeholders have equally valid demands that it would be unethical for the business to breach. For example, employees have the right to demand payment for their work and a safe and suitable working environment; suppliers payment for their goods or services; the local community employment and a non-toxic environment; the nation state taxes; and consumers safe, trustworthy and reasonably priced goods. Such expectations can be seen to form an implied *ethical contract* between business and the community, such that it is only by abiding by this contract that society effectively gives business the right to consume resources and be rewarded with profit. Even in the early 1980s this hidden, ethical dimension of legal contracts was being emphasized in response to the spate of corporate scandals:

What is shocking about some of the current corporate scandals – bribery, falsification of records, theft, and corporate espionage – is that these acts violate the conditions for making contracts and market exchanges, conditions which are at the very heart of the free enterprise system. Such violations cannot be excused by saying that they do not appear on the contract. Such excuses are almost as absurd as someone defending the murder of a creditor by saying: I only promised to pay him back; I didn't promise not to murder him. Hence we can conclude that a company has moral obligations in the contract it makes with society and it has obligations to those moral rules which make contracts possible. (Bowie, 1983 in White, 2000, p. 245)

Business leaders must therefore ensure that their business is seen to be ethical, lest too many breaches lead us to start to question the usefulness of organizing our society according to the private profit-making, free market, business model. We can see here the beginnings of a self-interested argument for the business community to be ethical. This self-interested reason for being ethical is even more clearly seen in the second type of argument for connecting ethics and business, the economic argument.

The economic argument presents ethics, in one way or another, as a business opportunity waiting to be exploited. Thus the company that is seen to be ethical can attract more loyal staff and customers, can benefit from good public relations, can use their ethics as a unique selling point, can use ethics to develop a strong brand and can even charge a premium for its products because of its ethical image. To further impress upon business, and students of business, the link between ethics and the bottom line business ethics, textbooks are frequently peppered with stories of highly-profitable companies that have successfully traded upon a strong ethical image (such as The Cooperative Bank, Case Study 15.1, above). Overall, the message of many business ethics texts is that good ethics 'translates into increased profits' (Axline, 1990, p. 87).

Box 15.2
Being seen to be ethical versus being ethical

In 2004, Joel Bakan, Professor of Law at the University of British Columbia, published what became a bestselling book (and DVD) that critically examined corporations. This book says some interesting things about the moves by many companies towards ethics and corporate social responsibility. Bakan argued that such moves are not new. He shows how they surfaced on several other occasions throughout the twentieth century whenever corporations seemed to be losing the public's trust. He argues that, on each occasion, such attempts have represented corporation's desire to be *seen* to be good, rather than to actually *be* good. These moves represented the manipulation of the *appearance* of social responsibility that only masked, rather than changed, a naked self-interest in profits. Bakan asks then, what sort of personality treats ethics in this way, as something to manipulate so as to promote one's own selfish-interests? Drawing upon FBI psychological profiling, material on the legal constitution of corporations, and examples of corporate practices old and new, he argues that corporation's focus on being seen to be ethical so as to increase profits means that corporations have an amoral, *psychopathic*, personality type.

Thinkpoint 15.2

- What commercial organizations can you think of that have linked an ethical or socially responsible image with a profitable business?
- Can you think of organizations that have suffered or struggled because of an *unethical* public image?
- Your answers to these questions might illustrate further the ways that power, knowledge and ethics are related. By constructing in the public consciousness an image (knowledge) of being ethical, certain corporations have managed to become more economically powerful.

OVERCOMING THE PROBLEM OF CONSCIENCE

From the discussion above, we can see that business ethics makes a confident appeal to the business community's own commercial self-interest to justify the contemporary focus upon ethics. But who is to control the organization's new-found ethics? Who is to be, in effect, the conscience of the organization? Once we reflect upon the way that much of the field has now effectively rendered ethics a business resource, something from which profit and good public relations can be gained, then the answer that the business ethics field has come to might be fairly obvious: management.

Thinkpoint 15.3

- Can you think of any others, inside or outside the organization, who might question management's right to control what is defined as a matter of ethics? (We will pick up this point later in the chapter.)
- Your answer might illustrate the ways that the right to define the knowledge of what is ethical/ unethical in organizations is itself contested. This is because there are power effects that can arise as a consequence of such definitions. For instance, if working long hours is constructed as a marker of an employee fulfilling their ethical commitments to give their energy to their employing organization, then it will likely continue. However, if long working hours are constructed as an unethical infringement by employers on employees' right for leisure and family time, then there is likely to be a challenge to these expectations.

In choosing management as the ethical conscience of the organization, business ethicists are reproducing the dominant *managerialist* thinking of mainstream Western business thought. Since at least the time of F. W. Taylor's *Scientific Management*, we are used to understanding management to naturally bear the responsibility for all higher reasoning, all strategy and all important thinking in the organization (see Chapters 2 and 8; see also Parker, 2002). Business ethics reproduces this managerialism by assuming that management should necessarily have the right to define the organization's ethics and ensure other organizational members' compliance to these.

OVERCOMING THE PROBLEM OF TRANSLATION

If managers are to be the ethical agents or conscience of organizations, this still leaves the question of how the language and concerns of ethics can be translated into the rational or bureaucratic task of organizing.

Business ethics has managed this through simplifying ethics down to a process whereby management formulate and disseminate organization-wide ethical codes or policies. Through this mechanism the issue of ethics is reduced to a single, organizational-wide, series of rules. Ethics can now, in principle, be quite easily managed, with the manager merely having to decide whether the employee has broken the ethical rule or not.

Thinkpoint 15.4

- What ethical rules does your university or college have? (Does it have rules on cheating in exams, plagiarism, sexual harassment, bullying, discrimination?)
- What mechanisms are in place to enforce these rules, who enforces them and how effective do you think these are in regulating your behaviour?
- Some US universities, in response to worries about the safety of students, have started to introduce rules regulating students' sexual relationships. As part of this, some universities have started requiring students to obtain written consent from a prospective sexual partner before they have sex. If your university or college introduced this policy, would you consider this an unjustified exercise of power – interference into your private sexual relationships – or a responsible policy to ensure your freedom from possible sexual violence or accusations of such?
- Though not focused on sex, issues of ethics, managerial control and freedom of expression are explored well in Barry's (2007) article in *Business Ethics Quarterly*.

Key issues and controversies

So far, we have seen several problems with the attempt to integrate ethics and business and we have introduced the broad solutions to these problems presented by the business ethics field. These broad solutions are relatively uncontroversial within the field. There are gentle disagreements in this field, however, and often these centre around the question of which philosophical ethical framework should be applied to evaluate and make sense of behaviour in organizations. The main frameworks that business ethics texts draw upon are utilitarianism, stakeholder theory, deontology, justice and virtue (see Beauchamp and Bowie, 2012, for a useful summary, and Rorty, 2006, for a different perspective on the usefulness of philosophical ethics for business ethics).

> Originating in the work of philosophers David Hume (1711–1776), Jeremy Bentham (1748–1832) and John Stuart Mill (1806–1873), utilitarianism understands the ethical value of an act to be based on its *consequences*. Simply put, acts that lead to the greatest good for the greatest number of people are moral. This apparently straightforward proposition, however, hides much complexity. What exactly constitutes a good outcome, for instance, is very debatable. Is the good the same as happiness, or wealth, or personal growth, or alleviation of suffering? How are we to measure the sum total amount of good that each of a range of potential acts that we may undertake might lead to? How can a manager know, with any real certainly, the full consequences of his/her actions for others in a complex business situation?

One popular variation of utilitarian ethical approaches to business ethics is that of stakeholder theory. Stakeholder theory, as we have seen, argues that the management of an organization has responsibilities not just to consider the happiness or demands of shareholders, but to recognize that organizational behaviour affects a range of other stakeholders both inside and outside the corporation. Stakeholder theory can be understood to modify utilitarianism, reminding us that when we are considering the ethical consequences of particular organizational actions, we must consider the potentially quite different interests of different constituencies. These can include employees, shareholders, the environment, the local community, even an unborn generation that may be harmed by a company's products or the pollution it generates.

Clearly, trying to take into account all the possible consequences for all stakeholders of every organizational act could lead to a paralysis of indecision. Utilitarian thinking, including stakeholder variants, in the contemporary business world has recognized this and tends to focus upon the development of ethical rules to guide behaviour. Rules such as 'do not break contracts' and 'do not falsely advertise products' are argued to be those that business should always observe because the *consequences* of not doing so would be a loss of faith in business in general. However, even this rule-based utilitarianism, popular in business ethics, is not without its problems. For any rule formulated for organizational members to follow, we can always ask such questions as: Who decided on the rule? How can we be sure that this rule doesn't just reflect *their* self-interest? Why should we be certain that following this rule would indeed lead to the greatest sum of ethical outcomes?

Deontology, like rule-based utilitarianism above, is also based upon rules or laws. However, unlike utilitarianism, deontological ethics does not build its rules on the basis of anticipated consequences of actions. For deontology this would diminish ethics, reducing it to a means-ends calculation. To judge the ethics of an action on the basis of its contribution to, say, 'happiness' would be to elevate happiness *over* ethics – to, in effect, see ethics as a subset of happiness. According to deontology, ethics does not serve any such other ends, it is an end *in itself*. To act ethically an individual should not be attempting to second-guess the consequences of their actions, but rather should reason what *ethical duty* applies, and they should follow this without hesitation or regard to personal friendships, personal risks or any other contextual features. For deontology, these duties are worked out through reason on the basis of what German philosopher Immanuel Kant (1724–1804) argued was a 'categorical imperative' of 'universalizability'. Kant's categorical imperative can be understood as 'only act in ways that could in principle be made a general law for all human behaviour'. On the basis of this universalizable imperative, ethical duties can be worked out through a process of reason. Thus, for instance, murder cannot be moral because if murder was universalized as a moral duty, logically, not everyone could follow it (you can't follow a 'duty' to murder someone if you've been murdered yourself!). Therefore, refraining from murder is a logically universalizable moral duty.

This universalizable imperative translates into far more subtle moral duties as well. Perhaps most difficult to resolve in the context of today's organizations is the universal duty on all of us to respect the dignity and autonomy of others – a precondition if each person is to have the freedom to reason what their ethical duty is and to act accordingly. This universal duty is often translated as the duty not to treat other people as only a *means* (i.e., as a resource to achieve what you want), but always to treat people as an *end* in and of themselves. Some business ethics writers (e.g., Arnold and Bowie, 2003) have suggested that this last duty presents a difficult challenge for contemporary business organizations which use people instrumentally as disposable 'human resources'.

Another approach to ethics used in many business ethics articles is that of justice. Justice-based approaches to ethics, formulated by among others philosopher John Locke (1632–1704), focus upon rights and fairness (Snell, 2009). The *Universal Declaration of Human Rights 1948,* passed by the General Assembly of the United Nations, is perhaps the most famous attempt to formalize such a justice-based ethics and Amnesty International one of the best known examples of an organization attempting to turn these espoused rights into a reality (see www.amnesty.org/en/what-we-do/corporate-accountability/). Justice-based approaches to ethics have some similarities with deontology (for instance, the attempt to formulate universal rights, above); however, they can also be seen to depart in a crucial way. Whereas deontology focuses exclusively upon the observance of rational ethical duties, ethics of justice also focus upon the more emotional, and often emotive, issue of *fairness*. Thus, under an ethics of justice, punishment of infringements and compensation for victims, for instance, might be justified if members of an organization have acted in ways that deny others' rights.

If the talk of ethical consequences, ethical duties and ethical justice so far seems a little impersonal, the next ethical theory widely used in business ethics texts turns our attention right back to the individual. Virtue-based approaches to ethics are often traced back – in Western thought at least – to the work of Aristotle (384–322 BC). These approaches focus upon the *character* of the person who acts. After all, we could have all the information about the likely ethical consequences of our actions (as per utilitarianism) and we could know there to be clear ethical duties that we should not breach (as per deontology), but if we have failings in our character (if we lack 'virtue') we could still simply not choose to behave ethically. Within the business ethics field, this virtue-based approach to ethics can be seen in a range of material that focuses upon the moral education or character of individual managers (e.g., Hemingway and MacLagan, 2004). Occasionally, when being least critical, virtue approaches slip into a trap of individualism, where ethics seems to depend upon heroic individuals possessing the special qualities required to resist temptations or engage in selfless good deeds. This sometimes finds expression in business ethics texts celebrating charismatic senior managers as paragons of unimpeachable virtue, spreading purity throughout their organizations and it has resurfaced too in the Leadership Studies field in the concept of authentic leadership (see Caza and Jackson, 2011 and Ford and Harding, 2011 for reviews and critiques of authentic leadership).

Thinkpoint 15.5

- Think about some instance in your university, college, working life or earlier school life, where you believe that you acted ethically.
- Which of the approaches to ethics outlined above seems to best explain the reason why you acted this way? For instance was it because you thought about the consequences of your actions (utilitarianism); because you were obeying an ethical rule that you would never consider breaching (deontology); because somebody was owed something that you gave back (justice); because you are simply an ethical person (virtue); etc.?
- Could your evaluation of your behaviour as ethical be different if you applied one of the other understandings of ethics?
- The issue of ethics is central to our identity. We tend to justify our behaviour and selves using ethical arguments: 'I did what I thought was right in the circumstances'; 'I followed the rules'; 'I followed my conscience'; 'I am a good person'; etc. However, as the preceding section shows, there are different forms of knowledge about ethics. Not all of these would agree on what is the ethical course of action for any one situation. Given these disagreements, we might well begin to wonder just how secure any of our cherished ethical self-identities are?

Important studies

Two studies are reviewed here – Denis Arnold and Norman Bowie's (2003) 'Sweatshops and Respect for Persons', and Bill Richardson and Peter Curwen's (1995) 'Do Free Market Governments Create Crisis-Ridden Societies?' – that, in their different ways, both reproduce several familiar aspects of the mainstream business ethics discourse and also push the thinking of the field forward.

Arnold and Bowie's (2003) article, published in *Business Ethics Quarterly,* uses a Kantian (deontological) ethical theory of respect for persons to critique the ethics of exploitative 'sweatshop' employment practices of **multinational corporations** (MNCs). For Arnold and Bowie (2003, p. 222): 'Persons ought to be respected because persons have dignity. For Kant, an object that has dignity is beyond price. Employees have a dignity that machines and capital do not. They have dignity because they are capable of moral activity.' The authors draw upon evidence from trade unionists, labour activists and non-governmental organizations to argue that **subcontractors** working for MNCs routinely breach such respect for persons in the conditions of labour that they impose upon their employees.

Multinational corporations Very large corporations that have operations crossing multiple nations. Such corporations have been the focus of sustained criticism for the enormous economic and political power they wield.

Subcontractors Those working to provide goods or services for one company but who are employed by another company. See also **outsourcing**.

Such conditions include widespread and well-documented breaches of labour law relating to wages and benefits, forced overtime, health and safety violations, sexual harassment, discrimination and environmental protection. Psychological and physical coercion of workers also abounds. Such coercion can take the form of forced overtime through threat of job loss, and compulsion to work through verbal and physical assault. Working conditions are frequently appalling and include locking workers into overcrowded and unventilated factories to prevent them leaving, resulting in fatalities when fires break out.

For instance, the 10 000-person Tae Kwang Vina factory in Vietnam, producing Nike products, exposed employees to toxic chemicals at amounts up to 177 times those allowed under Vietnamese law in 1993. In another all-too-common example, a fire killed 200 employees and injured 469 in the Kader Industrial Toy Company in Thailand because the workers were locked into an unsafe environment from which they couldn't escape. The Kader Company produced toys for US MNCs such as Hasbro, Toys 'R' Us, J. C. Penney and Fisher Price (Arnold and Bowie, 2003, p. 231). Twenty years on, little seemed to have changed as over 1100 low-paid fashion factory workers were killed in the collapse of Rana Plaza in Bangledesh in 2013 after they were slapped and forced to return to work in the unsafe building or lose their jobs. Before they were killed, these factory workers made clothes for Benetton, Mango and Primark amongst other leading brands (www.theguardian.com/world/2015/dec/21/rana-plaza-24-suspects-abscond-before-trial).

In addition to unsafe, abusive and frequently illegal practices, these subcontractors, producing goods for some of the world's largest MNCs, fail to provide workers with wages high enough even to meet basic needs for food, clothing and shelter, and this despite the fact that a living wage may only be as much as US$30.00 per week in these regions (see also Klein, 2001).

Drawing upon such evidence in conjunction with Kantian ethical philosophy and a variant of stakeholder theory, Arnold and Bowie (2003, p. 239) argue that MNCs are failing to meet their ethical responsibilities to these employees: 'We have argued that **Multinational Enterprise (MNE)** managers who encourage or tolerate violations of the rule of law; use coercion; allow unsafe working conditions; and provide below subsistence wages, disavow their own dignity and that of their workers.'

Multinational Enterprise (MNE) A business that operates in more than one country.

Having criticized MNC treatment of their employees, the authors (ibid., p. 239) highlight MNCs as in a prime position to improve their ethics, thus reproducing the managerial focus of the mainstream business ethics field: 'MNE managers who recognize a duty to respect their employees, and those of their subcontractors, are well positioned to play a constructive role in ensuring that the dignity of humanity is respected.'

Thinkpoint 15.6

- Critics of MNCs' use of sweatshop labour argue that these companies are unethical in exploit-ing poverty and the stark inequalities in employment costs and conditions in developing countries compared to those in the West. Further, critics argue that MNCs are so large and powerful that they could, if they so wished, change these employment conditions and pay a sustainable wage.
- Imagine you are employed by one of the above companies and are given responsibility for improving your subcontractor's employment practices. What procedures would you recommend that the company undertakes?
- You may find it interesting to compare now what a company such as Nike says about its own international labour practices (www.nikebiz.com) with what critics, such as the anti-poverty charity Oxfam (www.oxfam.org.au/what-we-do/ethical-trading-and-business/workers-rights-2/nike/), say about the company.

Overall, Arnold and Bowie's argument is a powerful and important one. It blends traditional features of mainstream business ethics discourse with a powerful critique of the widespread exploitative practices from which the world's largest MNCs profit. It does, however, stop short of questioning the free market economic system that encourages business to put profit before such ethical considerations in the first place. In the paper reviewed next we see a rare example of an article published in the business ethics mainstream that does begin to question the prevailing free market economics.

Richardson and Curwen's (1995) article published in the *Journal of Business Ethics* is concerned with examining the causes of two fatal disasters, the *Herald of Free Enterprise* ferry disaster, and the King's Cross underground fire, both of which occurred in the late 1980s. The 1987 *Herald of Free Enterprise* roll-on/roll-off passenger and freight ferry disaster occurred in good weather when the ferry capsized at sea after she sailed with both her inner and outer bow (loading) doors open. As a result, 150 passengers and 38 members of the crew lost their lives and many others were injured. The King's Cross underground (below-ground passenger train) fire occurred in 1987, when grease and rubbish caught fire beneath the treads of the passenger escalators at the underground station level. The fire rapidly spread up the escalators and erupted into the ticket hall causing horrendous injuries and 31 deaths.

Analyzing the causes of these disasters, Richardson and Curwen criticize management's inappropriate beliefs as contributing to, if not causing, the disasters by creating inappropriate organizational cultures, structures, systems and behaviour. They give an example (ibid., p. 556) of such inappropriate beliefs:

> Despite the existence of theoretical and real world warnings about the dangers inherent in organizations, a domi-nant premise of the free-market philosophy is one of organizations as economic (and only indirectly as social) wealth creators/bestowers. A society which concentrates excessively on the assumption that organizations are only – or even predominantly – beneficial wealth-creators, tends to be disaster prone.

The authors suggest that these fatal disasters are not one-off examples of bad practice in an otherwise well-managed and safe economy. Rather, they highlight the free market economic system itself as strongly contributing to such inappropriate management beliefs: 'Free-market principles help sustain inappropriate beliefs about the nature of organizations and the kinds of cultures and systems which contribute to disasters' (ibid., p. 552).

So, we have in Richardson and Curwen what, for a mainstream business ethics article, is an unusually explicit criticism of top management's influence upon the organization *and* of the free market philosophy that has so increased top manager's control. Though unusual in voicing these criticisms, however, the article also falls back into reproducing the managerialism and voluntarism of the business ethics field. Though critical of management for contributing to these fatalities, the authors see the solution merely as *management voluntarily changing the way they manage.* Managers, the authors conclude, must learn to 'think-upside-down' and develop a 'wider belief base for the creation of contexts by management strategies' (ibid., p. 558).

Ultimately, then, we have in Richardson and Curwen (1995) a compelling and persuasive critique of organizational fatality. And while the authors reproduce the key assumptions of the business ethics field, they also extend beyond much of the field's thinking by examining more seriously the risks with management control and the free market economic system.

Although these studies are examples of some of the good work in the mainstream field of business ethics, critical approaches might suggest that they continue to display serious limitations. We begin exploring this next by focusing upon the contribution and limitations of mainstream writing on business ethics in relation to the core concept of 'freedom'.

Limitations of mainstream approaches to ethics at work

Ethics is intimately connected to the idea of freedom. Ethics is concerned with choosing between different paths. At its simplest, ethics is choosing right over wrong, good over bad. To choose, one must have the freedom to take different courses of actions, to make different choices. This core concept of freedom is illuminated in several different ways in the story of business ethics. First of all, the context of free market economics from which business ethics was born gave business more freedom from governmental control. Business self-regulation was to take the place of state regulation. With this freedom from state control came public examples of businesses abusing this freedom – leading to crises, frauds, abuses, and disasters (much like those discussed above by Arnold and Bowie, 2003, and Richardson and Curwen, 1995).

Business ethics then emerged as a response to the abuses of this freedom, a response that promised to encourage business managers to think about the effects and ethics of their actions. Importantly, business ethics does not seek to limit the freedom that managers have under the free market/self-regulating economic system, it does not tend to seek more state control, or stronger pressure groups, or more effective labour unions, for example. Rather, business ethics endorses and reinforces the freedom of management to self-regulate, to be free from outside control, and to use this freedom to voluntarily behave more ethically.

The links between business ethics and freedom do not end here, however. This is just the starting point of a whole series of questions regarding the nature of the freedom that business ethics promotes. For instance, has the rise of business ethics and corporate social responsibility actually made the world freer from business exploitation, industrial accidents, environmental destruction, etc.? Compelling evidence upon which to answer 'yes' to this question is in short supply. It does not take much effort to find example after example of disastrous business behaviour in the national and international media – despite most of these companies having glossy ethical policies and codes. Enron, the most infamously fraudulent US corporation of the last decade, for example, had a *64 page* Corporate Code of Ethics – which didn't seem to have any positive effect on curbing their fraudulent behaviour. Indeed, if the industrial crises, abuses and disasters of the 1980s arose, as the business ethics field states, from a context of management having new-found freedom to self-regulate, then why would it make sense to think that giving top managers even *more freedom,* freedom to define and police organizational ethics, was a plausible solution to these problems?

Finally, under the managerial focus of business ethics it is managers (and academics) only who have the freedom to define ethics – other employees and stakeholders seem to be cast in the subordinate position of merely submitting to these rules. Is their *unfreedom* the price that must be paid for more ethical organizations? Just how ethical is it for a small minority (in this case senior management) to impose their views and values upon the majority?

Such questions and issues are among those that critical approaches to the question of ethics at work address, and we turn to next.

Case study 15.2
A divine right to manage?

In previous centuries, the right to formulate and enforce codes of ethics was monopolized by Gods and their representatives on earth – be they priests, popes, bishops, rabbis, ayatollahs or various manifestations of royalty. Thus for instance, in the Christian tradition, God passed down his ethical commandments to Moses, the Son of God later passed his teachings down to his disciples, and the Church (one of the first large-scale hierarchical organization) enforced these upon the wider Christian and (through conquest, conversion and crusade) non-Christian populations. For centuries those who had control over formulating and enforcing ethics in the monotheistic, Abrahamic, societies of the West and the Middle East understood themselves to have a direct line to God. Returning to the present day: we now have a situation where distant and unreachable, quasi-mythical, heads of very large, hierarchical organizations formulate ethical codes, and their representatives on earth (directors and managers) enforce these on the mass populations of global corporations. Can we see parallels between past centuries and present times here? Well, in Wray-Bliss (2012) I suggested the answer here may be a worrying yes. Roberts (2001) too has argued that CEOs are at risk of starting to think and behave as if they were 'omniscient' and 'omnipotent', and Gabriel (1997) has suggested that CEOs may be coming to believe the messianic fantasies they, and those around them, project about them, and Kets de Vries has long argued that a form of destructive narcissism is a very real risk for those in the top jobs (e.g., Kets de Vries and Balazs 2011). Perhaps indeed those at the very top of global business organizations are starting to think that they have some sort of God-given, *divine right to manage?* Let's pause here to consider some of the language used by top executives at just one company, Enron, before its spectacularly-fraudulent collapse:

> 'If you walk around the halls here, people have a mission. The mission is we're on the side of angels ... We're bringing the benefits of choice and free markets to the world.' (Jeffrey Skilling, then CEO of Enron, *Business Week Online Extra*, 2001)

> 'There was one meeting in particular that everyone at Enron remembers as marking the moment Kinder became the boss. In Enron mythology, it came to be known as the Come to Jesus meeting.' (McLean and Elkind, 2003, p. 25)

> '"We saw things no one else could see," Amanda Martin, another former executive, added, "In the beginning, it was brilliant, we were riding a train, we were proselytizing. We were the apostles. We were right."' (ibid., p. 38)

> 'Skilling loved to say that in trying to create a new kind of energy company, Enron was doing "the Lord's work." Mark struck a similar tone in talking about her business. "We are brought together with a certain amount of missionary zeal," she told Harvard for a case study. "We are bringing the market mentality and spreading the privatization gospel in countries that desperately need this kind of thinking."' (ibid: 71, quoting Enron CEO Jeff and CEO of Enron International, Rebecca Mark)

> 'Skilling's handful of direct reports, noted Alkhayat, the Chief Operating Officer (COO) Egyptian-born aide, operated with his "blessed hand"; it was as if they'd been anointed by the leader as infallible and holy' (ibid: 124).

Questions

1 Could this use of explicitly religious, messianic language by executives in a company that so spectacularly and arrogantly disregarded laws to govern corporations, be a glimpse into the wider mindset of corporate managerial elites?
2 By giving these elites the right to define and enforce ethics, might we, as a society, inadvertently be elevating these business men and women to some sort of divine, quasi-celestial status?
3 Are we ready for (can we even imagine) the possible future repercussions of this?

Critical approaches to ethics at work

INTRODUCTION

One place to start an introduction to critical approaches to ethics at work would be to highlight the narrow range of ethical frameworks (utilitarian, deontological, justice and virtue) that mainstream business ethicists tend to draw upon. Business ethics tends to exclude or marginalize a wealth of contemporary, and more critical, ethical systems

Cartoon 15.1   'We have an agreement in principle. The question is, do we all have the same principles?'

'We have an agreement in principle.
The question is, do we all have the same principles?'

including those of **feminism** (Brewis, 1998; Derry, 2002), **Marxism** (Corlett, 1998; Wray-Bliss and Parker, 1998) and **post-modernism** (Phillips, 1991; Parker, 1998; Willmott, 1998).

Drawing upon such alternative ethical systems can provide us with fascinating and compelling different readings of ethics at work, readings that can make us radically question whether behaviour in today's organizations is indeed ethical. We start this section by questioning the ethics of organization; questioning the ethics of obedience; and questioning the corporate takeover of ethics.

QUESTIONING THE ETHICS OF ORGANIZATION

As we have seen, business ethics seeks to make organizations socially responsible by giving managers more power to define and control other organizational members' ethics. On the surface this seems like an effective way to bring ethics into the organization. However, by drawing upon the work of post-modern sociologist, Zygmunt Bauman (1989, 1993), this can be seen as potentially disastrous for ethics at work. It may provide the conditions to actually *increase* unethical organizational practices.

Organizations, like crowds, comprise a mass of people. Organizations differ from crowds, however, in that the behaviour of people in organizations is regulated and controlled so that it meets the collective purpose of the organization. By and large, employees do what they are expected to do and this harnessing of their collective effort is what makes organizations so powerful (Knights and Roberts, 1982). To achieve this, organizations must eradicate unpredictable behaviour. Thus we have rules, procedures, uniforms, targets, quotas and all manner of other bureaucratic and cultural mechanisms to control employee behaviour in organizations (see Chapters 10 and 14). Bauman argues that one effect of these organizational pressures towards conformity and uniformity is that individual ethical responsibility is squeezed out of the organization. Ethics for Bauman means doing what one feels to be right, not what may be profitable, what everyone else is doing, or what your boss or shareholders may want you to do. Organization and its leaders thus work, consciously or otherwise, to stop organizational members from feeling and acting upon their own individual moral impulse.

An example of such eradication of individual moral responsibility at work could be seen in the fact that we tend to apply different ethical standards to behaviour at work versus behaviour outside of work. For instance, while none of us would (I hope!) consider taking from a stranger on the street their wages, their car and their job, we might well,

Feminism The theory and politics associated with critiques of society that make gender and the oppression of women their central focus.

Marxism Theory and politics associated with the writings of Karl Marx. The principal focus is a critique of the oppressive effects of social class and structural inequality in a capitalist economy.

Post-modernism The theory and politics principally associated with contemporary French thinkers. Post-modernism may be understood as a critique of the faith that society and intellectuals have tended to have in notions such as truth, science, individual freedom and progress.

as managers, follow an instruction to make some employees redundant resulting in much the same effects for these people. While taking these things from a stranger would be outlawed as immoral and criminal, taking them from an employee, as happens in an organizational context and in an organized way, is typically not viewed in the same way. So we see here precisely what Bauman is alluding to, the same act is removed from ethical accountability because it happens to take place in an organization. For Bauman, the ultimate message to be drawn from examples like this is 'that the organization as a whole is an instrument to obliterate responsibility' (Bauman, 1989, p. 163).

The implications of this argument for how we should understand business ethics are profound. By promoting the idea that management should take responsibility for deciding and enforcing ethics, business ethics can be argued to be further *removing* ethical responsibility and freedom of conscience from individual organizational members (see also articles by Maclagan, 2007, and Schwartz, 2000, on this point). This explanation of Bauman's might help explain how modern organizations, populated with thoughtful and educated people who behave perfectly morally outside of work, can continue to reproduce unethical, fraudulent, and damaging outcomes in their work roles.

From the above, rather than promoting the idea of obedient organizational members following rules laid down by management, as mainstream business ethics does, perhaps we need to question such obedience and search for ethics instead in acts of *disobedience* and *dissent*. We turn to critical contributions on this issue next.

Thinkpoint 15.7

- Explain Bauman's argument that making more rules for organizational members to follow can encourage *less* personally responsible behaviour.
- What then might be the relationship between power, freedom and ethics suggested in Bauman's writing?

QUESTIONING THE ETHICS OF OBEDIENCE

A variety of ethical frameworks can be used to argue that requiring one person (e.g., an employee) to be subordinated to another (e.g., a manager) is unethical. For instance, it could be argued that employees' subordination is a breach of Kant's categorical imperative that states that a person cannot be used merely as a means by any other person. Alternatively, MacIntyre (1981) has argued that management can never be considered ethically virtuous because the concept and practice of management is inherently manipulative. Management is about manipulating employees to do what they otherwise may not want to do (see Chapters 2 and 8; also Roberts, 1984). However, perhaps the most powerful critiques of employees' subordination can be seen in Marxist writings on capitalist work relations.

Capitalist society
The dominant economic system around the world today. An economic system that concentrates the majority of wealth in private hands (capitalists) and requires the majority of people to sell their labour to secure a wage from this group.

Dehumanized A process by which human beings are treated like objects or things and thus their humanity is denied.

For Karl Marx what makes human beings unique is our potentiality and creativity. Through our collective creative effort (our *labour*) we transform ourselves, each other and the world around us. While the rest of life on earth operates predominantly through a limited range of instinctual patterns, we human beings fashion the world around us according to our own designs and conscious intentions. However, under conditions of work in **capitalist societies**, many of us do not experience our lives like this – despite the fact that our societies may well pride themselves on the freedom and opportunities they provide. Our labour – our creativity and energy – is bought by owners of corporations to service their self-interested search for profit. People are **dehumanized**, reduced to the status of things (e.g., 'human resources'), merely another factor of production to be used and exploited. Because of historical inequalities carried through the generations most people have to sell their labour for wages. Employees' creative energies – their labour – then comes to seem like an alien thing to them ('work'), something to avoid if possible. Work becomes resented – it turns into 'alienated labour' (Marx, 1844).

As the group with a vested interest in ending their own alienation and **exploitation**, Marx identified employees as those most likely to act to change these dehumanizing workplaces. However, this group is routinely excluded from the decision-making processes in organizations – despite being in the majority – with such processes reserved for management. Therefore, Marxist scholars of work and organization focus upon employee resistance to management control as an ethical and desirable act. Employee resistance is seen as employees' reactions against their alienation and exploitation. This understanding of employee resistance as ethical is in direct contrast to most of the mainstream business ethics field, which promotes increased managerial control as the only route to ethical renewal in organizations.

> **Exploitation** A process where people are used merely to further someone else's goals. In an economic context, 'exploitation' refers to using others for the purpose of creating a surplus that enables the exploiter to live without working or to supplement their income in this way.

To illustrate the usefulness of this understanding of the ethical nature of workplace resistance, let's return to Richardson and Curwen's (1995) article, 'Do Free Market Governments Create Crisis-Ridden Societies?', presented earlier in this chapter. You may remember that this article was concerned with exploring the reasons behind two UK fatal disasters, the King's Cross underground fire and the *Herald of Free Enterprise* ferry disaster. Throughout their paper the authors criticized top management as centrally contributing to both disasters. Despite this, the authors only identified management within the organization as providing any solution to such problems.

Drawing upon a critical understanding of the ethics of employee resistance, we can arrive at a less illogical solution. Taking the ferry disaster as an example, the investigation into this disaster discovered that it was caused as a result of the practice of ferries leaving port with bow doors open to save time on ferry turnaround and thereby maximize revenue. In this disaster 38 crew members lost their lives, and many more were injured. All of these employees on board the ferry clearly had an acute vested interest in the safety and security of the ship their lives depended upon. An obvious conclusion to be drawn from these facts would seem to be that to improve workplace conditions and health and safety, we should be promoting employee resistance to unethical and unsafe managerial demands. For example, by encouraging strong unions capable of voicing employee concerns, protecting them from victimization and generally exposing practices that put profit before people. This would seem to make more sense than, as the authors do, merely asking distant senior managers, who are under profound pressure to raise profits and reduce costs, to develop a 'wider belief base' or, indeed, to write a new ethical policy.

Thinkpoint 15.8

- What is alienation and why might employee resistance be seen as an ethical response to this?
- Your answer might illustrate the way that power even in a Marxist analysis does not just operate in one direction – i.e., *from* the powerful, *on* the powerless. Employee resistance demonstrates that employers are reliant upon employees behaving in productive ways. Once employees start resisting and not behaving in these expected ways, the workplace can be quickly transformed into a very difficult place to manage.

QUESTIONING THE CORPORATE TAKEOVER OF ETHICS

From the above, we are starting to have an image of ethics as something that could and should be radical. We have an ethics that can be drawn upon to fundamentally question, for instance, the ethics of the managerial monopolization of decision-making and authority and the capitalist economic system's exploitation of the majority of the population for the economic self-interest of a minority. Understanding ethics as informing such wide-ranging critiques, how would critical approaches read the emergence of mainstream business ethics and corporate social responsibility? Perhaps the description that would fit best would be the 'corporate takeover of ethics'. Business ethics could be regarded as ethics made safe for business, where ethics is reduced to a corporate image exercise in support of the business drive for profits (see e.g., Parker, 2002).

Case study 15.3
On the origins and ethics of management

What is a manager? What social function does he/she perform? For the mainstream business ethics field, management, as we have seen, is thought to be an ethically legitimate and essential role: one that can be entrusted with furthering the goodness and social responsibility of business. A Marxist reading of business organization clearly sees management quite differently – as part of an unjust social structure that seeks to ensure the continual exploitation of employees so as to generate profits for business owners. These views are quite divergent! Can we perhaps learn something further about management from considering its historical origins?

In most management textbooks and academic histories, the birth of modern management is presented as occurring on the US railroads from the 1860s onwards. This connects management with what seems to be a heroic, frontier-expanding time in American history. By association, management would seem to have cultural and social legitimacy right from its very birth – being associated with progress, technology and societal development, for example. In his 2003 article in *The Journal of Management Studies,* Professor Bill Cooke provides a very different account of modern management's birth. Cooke argues that the forgotten, or possibly deliberately denied, actual birth of modern management was not the US railways, but was the management of slaves on US plantations. He shows that 38 000 managers were managing 4 million slaves in the US by the 1860s. The people managing these slaves were *called* managers; they *understood* themselves to be managers; they had produced a body of techniques, technology and texts concerned with how to manage slaves; and they displayed *most of the classical management principles* that formed the basis of what we regard as modern management's conceptual beginnings. Cooke draws a number of powerful and persuasive conclusions from his historical research. Perhaps one of the most powerful is his argument that the history of slavery and white supremacist racism still overshadows a core aspect of contemporary management identity. Those managing the slaves on the plantations assumed, because of their racist ideology, that they had a 'natural' position of superiority over those slaves that they managed. For Cooke this 'imprint of slavery' can still be seen in contemporary management 'in the ongoing dominance from that time of the very idea of the manager with a right to manage' (Cooke, 2003, p. 1913).

By engaging in a few high-profile, charity causes, producing some glossy ethical statements, or marketing themselves alongside images of smiling children, happy communities or green fields of grass gently swaying in the breeze, business can apparently become wholesome and safe. For instance, according to their critics (e.g., Ritzer, 2010; Spurlock 2005; www.mcspotlight.org) giant fast-food organizations are complicit in reproducing health damaging obesity, environmental destruction, animal cruelty and the rise in poorly paid, temporary 'Mcjobs'. However these organizations publicly project a very different image – linking themselves with children's charities, sports events and images of happy communities and families. In short, ethics is reduced to another resource that business can exploit to attract the consumer and ward off criticism. This last point is illustrated well with an example from one of the world's largest defence (arms and weapons) contractors, Boeing (see Case Study 15.4).

In the Boeing case study we might have expected a business that is one of the world's leading sellers of weapons of warfare – the efficient and technologically advanced means to kill other human beings – to perhaps have some qualms about talking so boldly of high ethical standards. Clearly this is not so. (You can read Boeing's extensive statements on their ethics at www.boeing.com/principles/.) For critics of business ethics one possible reason why chief executive, Mr Condit, and Boeing itself, finds the language of ethics so safe to use would be because ethics has been bleached of much of its critical potential. Instead of questioning business in a serious way, business ethics has shied away from an analysis of the big picture, in favour of a blanket acceptance of capitalist society and the single-minded search for profit. Business ethics does not seem to require Boeing to question the deadly business it is profiting from. Instead, ethics has been reduced to the much safer and much narrower question of whether its self-defined ethical codes on recruitment have been followed. Instead of a serious ethical critique of the nature of business in general, business ethics instead too often focuses upon local, specific and comparatively minor issues. This means, as Parker (2002, p. 98) argues, that: '... business ethics is rarely utopian, or even moderately ambitious in its aims' and 'if so little is expected, then perhaps little is likely to be achieved.'

Case study 15.4 'Boeing sacks finance chief in ethics row'

Boeing, America's second largest defence contractor, yesterday dismissed Mike Sears, its chief financial officer, for unethical conduct in the hiring of a senior Pentagon official to run a $20 billion (£11.8 billion) refuelling contract for the US air force.'

The aerospace group admitted that Mr Sears had violated company policy by communicating with Darleen Druyun about her future employment when she was still acting in her official government capacity on matters involving Boeing.

Ms Druyun – in effect head of air force procurement before joining Boeing as deputy head of its missile defence division – and Mr Sears covered this up, an internal investigation found. Ms Druyun was also dismissed ...

Mr Sears, who joined McDonnel Douglas in 1969, becoming head of its aerospace business in advance of Boeing's takeover in 1997, was widely tipped to succeed Phil Condit as chief executive when he steps down in 2006 ...

Mr Condit said 'compelling evidence' of misconduct by Mr Sears and Ms Druyun had come to light 'over the last two weeks', leading the board to order their dismissal.

In July Boeing called in a former senator, Warren Rudman, from a prominent law firm to review its ethics programme and set up an office of internal governance. His work has now been extended to cover the hiring of government employees.

'Boeing must and will live by the highest standards of ethical conduct in every aspect of our business,' Mr Condit said. 'When we determine there have been violations of our standards we will act swiftly to address them.'

Question

1 Can you see anything slightly odd, or even disturbing, about the way the concept of ethics is being used in this case?

Source: David Gow, The Guardian, 25 November 2003, p. 17. © Guardian Newspaper Limited 1992.

This last point of Parker's is illustrated well by revisiting Arnold and Bowie's (2003) critique of the ethics of MNCs' use of **sweatshop labour**. This article, if you remember, made a powerful case against the dangerous and exploitative conditions under which employees who are subcontracting for MNCs work. A radical critique of the ethics of such practices would likely lead one to question more generally the ethics underpinning capitalism that have promoted such disregard for the value of human life in the search for profits. However, Arnold and Bowie's paper, limited by its uncritical acceptance of the profit motive, does not argue for the above. Instead they merely ask that: 'MNEs and their contractors adhere to *local* labour laws, refrain from coercion, meet *minimum* safely standards, and provide a living wage for employees' (Arnold and Bowie, 2003, p. 222, emphasis added).

Sweatshop labour
This term generally describes any form of labour in factories or smaller workshops that is done in conditions where labour is very poorly treated, lacks adequate rights, health and safely conditions are poor and wages low.

Critics of business ethics might suggest that we could be justified in feeling more than a little disappointed that an ethical critique of such exploitative business practices ends by asking for so very little. This last point is picked up in the following section, where we revisit the case study of the The Cooperative Bank, showing what, for those critical of business ethics, would be the shallowness of the bank's ethical claims.

Key issues and controversies

QUESTIONING THE COOPERATIVE BANK AS AN ETHICAL ORGANIZATION

The first of the critical approaches introduced above drew upon the post-modern ethics of Zygmunt Bauman. Bauman, if you remember, argued that organization exists by eradicating unproductive and unpredictable behaviour by its members, and especially behaviour arising from employees' ethical sentiments. But how can we reconcile this argument with an organization such as The Cooperative Bank, which is celebrated for having explicit ethical commitments?

A critical reading of The Cooperative Bank might highlight how the bank's ethical policy functions as a controlling device. By taking the monopoly right to construct the bank's ethical policy, The Cooperative Bank management can be understood to be taking this right *from* other organizational members. If others' concerns do not figure in what the bank's management has already defined as the ethical policy they are implicitly not a matter of ethics. The implications of these points can be seen in the history of the bank's successful reinvention in the 1990s. The bank is known now for only *one* of its strategies from the 1990s: the publication of its ethical policy. However, if we return to Case Study 15.1 we can see that its other major strategy at the time was a dramatic cost-cutting exercise:

First, like many of the other banks, it cut costs. It rapidly shed over 1000 employees, closed branches, dramatically cut staff numbers in its branches (typically from 40 to eight), and rerouted most of its contact with customers from over-the-counter and face-to-face to telephone banking via remote call centres.

By taking control of what constitutes ethics, The Cooperative Bank management effectively cast these redundancies as *not* an ethical issue. These redundancies, with their potentially devastating personal and social implications, are represented simply as a *financial* business decision. Returning to Bauman's arguments, we can see how this 'ethical organization' has effectively rendered redundancy outside of ethical discourse. As we will see below, this process of eradicating or removing issues from the status of ethics has occurred not only with the issue of redundancy at The Cooperative Bank. Other issues relating to conditions of employment are similarly absent from the organization's ethical policy.

Thinkpoint 15.9

- Do you think that redundancy should be regarded as an ethical, rather than a merely financial or legal issue? Why/Why not?
- Try to vividly imagine yourself in each of the following situations, and think whether your answer to the above question might have changed as a result:
  (a) Imagine that your parent, carer or family's main income earner was being made redundant.
  (b) Imagine that your job is merely to convey the financial figures to the board of directors explaining the need for redundancies.
- Reflecting upon your answers to (a) and (b) above, can you see how our *closeness* to the effects of an action can change how we think about and experience it ethically. It is very likely, for instance, that those who are made redundant and will experience the inequality of not having a job, immediately and personally will understand redundancy as an acutely (un)ethical issue and not merely a financial decision. Whereas it is likely that those who get no closer to redundancy than providing some figures on corporate profitability may not experience the subsequent redundancies of people they may never meet as an ethical issue at all.

QUESTIONING THE ETHICS OF OBEDIENCE

The second of the critical approaches to ethics and organization (introduced above) drew upon the writings of Marx. We saw how Marx's writings could be used to argue that one person's subordination to, and exploitation by, another is itself an ethical problem – it dehumanizes and alienates. Applying this critical ethical approach to The Cooperative Bank case provides an unsettling and important reinterpretation.

We know from the case study that, in addition to the widespread redundancies, many of the remaining employees were relocated in the bank's remote telephone banking call centres. These types of organization have been criticized as oppressive places to work.

Call centres are typically organized as large open-plan offices, where employees are permanently linked into a telephone and computer system that automatically distributes customers' calls to waiting staff. Staff have performance targets based upon number of calls answered per shift but little control over the automatic computerized allocation of their work. The work is high pressured and highly paced but routine, boring and repetitive. There is little chance for conversations and interaction among staff, so the social relationships that historically have been so important to the quality of working life are damaged. There is little chance to interact with customers. The nature of the targets, the impersonal telephone service and the lack of face-to-face interactions means that 'conversations' with individual customers typically last no more than a minute.

The chances for career progression are very limited, and salaries are not high. Timing on all of an employee's work (the number of calls they take, length of calls, actions between calls, time on breaks, time in the toilet, etc.) is recorded in the minutest detail by a central computer. Management can, at any time, examine each employee's statistics and make judgements about their performance, judgements that are linked to pay and/or discipline. So notorious has the quality of working life at call centres become that they have been described by some journalists and academics as the modern day equivalent of 'dark satanic mills' (Wylie, 1997).

For employees to experience their work so negatively, as so alien to their desires, and as so deadening of their potential, raises many ethical concerns about the nature of the work in The Cooperative Bank's call centres. For management, however, the working conditions were seen to be cost-effective – and matters of ethics just did not seem to figure. In fact, not one of the bank's celebrated 12 ethical commitments related to the conditions their staff were required to work under. This indication of where management's priorities lie also lends weight to the suggestion of the critical writers that it is to employee resistance, rather than management largesse, that we should look if we wish to see such ethically questionable employment practices challenged.

QUESTIONING THE CORPORATE TAKEOVER OF ETHICS

In Case Study 15.1 I showed how The Cooperative Bank was rebranded as an ethical business. Through developing and publicizing a 12-point ethical policy and combining this with a profitable business, The Cooperative Bank became one of the hottest ethical business brands. The above critiques demonstrate how a business can gain such a brand status despite serious questions that could be asked about shortcomings in its 'ethical' business practice. In particular, it has been argued here that it is often in the area of employment conditions that the contemporary business ethics discourse is most short-sighted. That so many redundancies and poor working conditions apparently do not affect a corporation's ability to brand itself as ethical, indicates just how successfully business has taken over the issue of ethics at work. What must be remembered from The Cooperative Bank case, and from similar celebrated ethical organizations, is that such organizations have not only deflected widespread public critical ethical scrutiny of such employment practices. More than this, they have been so successful in controlling what gets seen as an ethical issue at work that they actually profit from the image of having the highest ethical standards. For some critics, not only has business ethics removed its radical teeth, it is in danger of turning ethics into a tame lapdog of business (Banerjee 2007; Neimark, 1995; Parker, 2002).

Important studies

In contrast to the often toothless nature of mainstream business ethics texts, the selection of articles in this section illustrate and emphasize the power and significance of critical approaches to ethics at work.

In her (1995) article 'The Selling of Ethics: The Ethics of Business Meets the Business of Ethics', Professor Marilyn Neimark critiques mainstream business ethics. Neimark draws upon the example of the multinational shoe-ware manufacturer 'Stride Rite' that sells its products under the registered trademark brands of Keds, Grasshoppers and

Tommy Hilfiger Footwear. Like The Cooperative Bank, Stride Rite was celebrated for its ethical and socially responsible business practices, winning 14 social responsibility awards in the early 1990s – and presents to the public a socially responsible image up to the present day.

However, also like The Cooperative Bank, Neimark argues that behind the public eye Stride Rite engages in practices that have a far less convincing ethical justification. Alongside its ethical sentiments and numerous awards, Stride Rite has closed down production plants in deprived areas in the USA and shifted production to low-wage overseas plants, mostly in Asia. In addition to the financial exploitation of impoverished Asian employees, we already know from studies, such as Arnold and Bowie (2003) and Klein (2001), how appalling the conditions of work in low-cost overseas production facilities can be. The result of this cost-cutting is that Stride Rite has made very healthy profits indeed. As a result, Neimark argues, it can easily afford to channel a small percentage of this profit into high-profile socially responsible deeds, thereby creating a lucrative ethical brand image.

The conclusion that Neimark draws from such examples is interesting. She does not just argue that companies like Stride Rite are cynically manipulating an otherwise good business ethics discourse. Rather, she concludes that Stride Rite's behaviour is *acceptable* within the business ethics discourse because business ethics at its core endorses the profit maximizing, pro-business, free market agenda:

> Within that discourse there are no penalties for corporations like Stride Rite which, on the one hand, benefit from the positive public relations associated with doing good deeds and, on the other hand, act in ways that contribute to the increasing degradation and deformation of life in the USA and the exploitation of workers abroad.

For Neimark, business ethics does not represent the emergence of new ethical organizations or increased ethical scrutiny of business. Rather, as examples such as Stride Rite demonstrate, business ethics actually *deflects* such ethical scrutiny. Ultimately, business ethics risks turning ethics into just another resource to be cynically exploited in the construction of the corporate brand.

Neimark's article can be summarized as highlighting the danger of uncritically accepting corporations' claims to be ethical and thereby failing to question their less well publicized profit-seeking behaviour. The next study highlights the dangers with business ethics' promotion of obedience to managerial authority (see Box 15.3).

The (in)famous psychological experiments conducted by Stanley Milgram in the 1970s illustrate the importance of questioning authority (Milgram, 1974). Milgram and his colleagues explored the ethical limits of obedience to authority in the following way. They put up posters in a university asking for volunteers to take part in a study of memory and learning, for which the volunteers would receive a small payment for their time. People that responded to the advert were each given a time to turn up at a laboratory in the university. Here they were met by a scientist and another volunteer. The scientist gave both volunteers their payment, and then proceeded to give them a brief background to the study, explaining that it was concerned with the effects of punishment upon learning. Both volunteers then drew lots, to see who would be the teacher and who the learner. The learner is then taken into another room, strapped into a chair, and electrodes places on both wrists. The teacher sees all this, before being taken to a separate room, from which he or she can hear but not see the learner. He or she is seated in front of an electric shock generating machine with switches ranging from 15 volts to 450 volts in 15-volt increments.

The teacher is told to read a list of word pairs into a microphone to the learner. Having read through the list once, the teacher then starts with the first word of a pair and reads four possible second-word pairs. If the learner chooses the correct second word the teacher moves on to the next pair. If the learner gets it wrong they receive a shock and are told the correct answer. With every wrong answer the shock level increases. The scientist remains in the room with the teacher throughout the experiment and encourages them to continue where necessary.

There is, however, a catch. The teacher is a genuine volunteer. However, the learner is not actually a volunteer, but a trained actor. They are not being shocked. The volunteer teacher does not know this, however, and hears an escalating series of protests from the learner as the shock level rises. These protests range from a

Thinkpoint 15.10

- Imagine yourself in the position of being the 'teacher' and that experiment was being conducted at your university or college. At what level do you think that you would have stopped giving what you believed to be electric shocks to the learner'?
- Would you have stopped at the first exclamation of pain? Or the first demand from the learner to stop? Perhaps the first agonized scream would have been enough for you? Or do you think that you would have continued past the point that you thought the learner was seriously hurt?
- Remember your answer, and you can compare it to the results of the experiment, next.

grunt of pain at a fairly low shock level, through to a demand to be released, an agonized scream, complaints of heart problems, through to absolute silence (presumed death). The point of the experiment is not actually to test memory and learning at all, but rather to see how far ordinary people will proceed to administer pain to a protesting victim when told to.

The result of these experiments was extremely disturbing. For far from disobeying the command at a very early stage, as *all* psychiatrists Milgram surveyed prior to the experiment predicted (and you probably indicated as your likely behaviour), the majority of people continued administering shocks to the victim right to the end of the scale. As Milgram recorded:

> Many subjects will obey the experimenter no matter how vehement the pleading of the person being shocked, no matter how painful the shocks seem to be and no matter how much the victim pleads to be let out. This was seen time and again in our studies and has been observed in several universities where the experiment was repeated. (Milgram, 1974, p. 5)

In short, the subjects of this experiment continued to 'shock' the victim, even though they thought they were seriously hurting, even killing, another person who was pleading to be released. Why might this have been the case? A possible explanation might be that perhaps the subjects were, for some reason, unaware or uncaring of the suffering and harm that the other person was apparently feeling. The extract in Box 15.3 from the transcript of just one of these experiments (picked up at the 315-volt stage) shows this not to be the case.

As we can tell from the extract, Fred was neither unaware nor uncaring about the pain he believed he was inflicting. He clearly wanted to stop the experiment, indeed on numerous occasions he said that he would not continue the experiment any further. And yet he did continue right to the end of the scale. He continued even to the point that he thought he had killed the man next door, as did many others. Why? For Milgram, the explanation lies in Fred's and the other subjects' acceptance *of the decisions of those in authority*:

> 'it is the extreme willingness of adults to go to almost any lengths on the command of authority that constitutes the chief finding of the study and the fact most urgently demanding explanation'. (ibid., 1974, p. 5)

The Milgram experiments are a dramatic experimental illustration of the consequences of giving up control to a perceived legitimate authority. In the experiments the authority was a scientist, but it might have so easily been a manager demanding unethical behaviour from a subordinate. From these experiments, Milgram draws a very powerful conclusion. He argues that far from endorsing obedience to authority as an unquestionable good (as the *managerialist* assumptions of mainstream organizational behaviour and business ethics texts leads them to do) we should question any organizational members' subordination to another's authority. In such obedience there is always the potential for a loss or abdication of ethical responsibility, and ultimately, the possibility for inhumanity.

Thinkpoint 15.11

- To reflect further on the implications of the Milgram experiments, imagine that you are employed in a job that you really like and have worked hard to get. Now imagine that your manager insists that you carry out a task you believe to be morally wrong, and won't listen to your protestations that you don't want to do it. Imagine that your family, your house mortgage payments, your children, perhaps your health premiums, not to mention your relationship with your boss, all rely upon you following this direct order.
- Just how bad would the task have to be before you disobeyed and risked everything? Would you really throw your job away over the first, small immoral act? Or would you wait until the act you were told to do was very wrong? Just when would you draw the line?
- Thinking about these questions we can perhaps begin to see how, when illegal and immoral acts are perpetrated in organizational contexts, the perpetrators so often proclaim that 'I am not responsible, I was just following orders'. In such protestations, individuals are separating off their sense of self, their ethical identity, from their actions. They put responsibility for their actions on to those in positions of power. This is a dangerous process. Zygmunt Bauman (1989) pursues these points in Chapter 6 of *Modernity and The Holocaust* when he uses the results of the Milgram experiments to chilling effect, to explore the organizational dynamics behind the very worst example of organized immorality ever perpetrated.

Box 15.3
Fred Prozi, unemployed (transcript excerpt from Experiment 5) – from Milgram (1974, pp. 73–76)

The subject is about 50 years old, dressed in a jacket but no tie; he has a good natured, if slightly dissolute appearance. He employs working-class grammar and strikes one as a rather ordinary fellow. He begins the experiment calmly but becomes increasingly tense as the experiment proceeds...

SUBJECT: I think something's happened to that fellow in there. I don't get no answer. He was hollering at less voltage. Can't you check in and see if he's alright, please?

EXPERIMENTER *(with same detached calm)*: Not once we've started. Please continue, Teacher.

SUBJECT *(sits down, sighs deeply)*: 'Cool – day, shade, water, paint' Answer, please. Are you alright in there? Are you alright?

EXPERIMENTER: Please continue, Teacher. Continue please. (*Subject pushes lever*)

SUBJECT: *(swivelling around in his chair)*: Something's happened to that man in there. (*Swivelling back*) Next one. 'Low – dollar, necklace, moon, paint.' *(Turning around again)* Something's happened to that man in there. You better check in on him, sir. He won't answer or nothing.

EXPERIMENTER: Continue. Go on, please.

SUBJECT: You accept all responsibility?

EXPERIMENTER: The responsibility is mine. Correct. Please go on. (*Subject returns to list, starts running through words as rapidly as he can read them, works through to 450 volts*)

SUBJECT: That's that.

EXPERIMENTER: Continue using the 450 volt switch for each wrong answer. Continue please.

SUBJECT: But I don't get no anything!

EXPERIMENTER: Please continue. The next word is 'white'.

SUBJECT: Don't you think you should look in on him, please?

EXPERIMENTER: Not once we've started the experiment.

SUBJECT: But what if something has happened to the man?

EXPERIMENTER: The experiment requires that you continue. Go on, please.

SUBJECT: Don't the man's health mean anything?

EXPERIMENTER: Whether the learner likes it or not . . .

SUBJECT: What if he's dead in there? *(Gestures towards the room with the electric chair)* I mean, he told me he can't stand the shock, sir. I don't mean to be rude, but I think you should look in on him. All you have to do is look in on him. All you have to do is look in the door. I don't get no answer, no noise. Something might have happened to the gentleman in there, sir.

EXPERIMENTER: We must continue, go on please.

SUBJECT: You mean keep giving him what? 450 volts, what he's got now?

EXPERIMENTER: That's correct. Continue. The next word is 'white'.

SUBJECT *(now at a furious pace)*: 'White – cloud, horse, rock, house'. Answer please. The answer is 'horse'. 450 volts *(Administers shock)* Next word, 'Bag – paint, music, clown, girl'. The answer is 'paint'. 450 volts *(Administers shock)* Next word is 'Short – sentence, movie ...'

EXPERIMENTER: Excuse me, Teacher. We'll have to discontinue the experiment.

....

Contrary, therefore, to the business ethics field's practice of giving management sole moral authority to define ethical policies to which other organizational members should obey, we might look towards organizational members' *disobedience* as an ethical imperative. If only Fred Prozi, and all those others in the experiment like him, had simply *refused* to shock the protesting victim we could be far more confident that unethical acts are not being perpetrated as a result of organizational hierarchy and authority. The final critical article introduced here draws these points out strongly.

In their (1994) article, 'Whistle-blowing as Resistance in Modern Work Organizations', Joyce Rothschild and Terance Miethe demonstrate the importance of employee **whistle-blowing** in challenging unethical organizational practices. They define whistle-blowing as an organizational member's 'disclosure of illegal, unethical or harmful practices in the workplace to parties who might take action' (ibid., p. 254).

> **Whistle-blowing** When an organizational member tells the organizational hierarchy, and subsequently the wider world, of unethical or illegal practices being conducted inside their organization.

Whistle-blowers tend to be well-respected and conscientious employees. They tend to believe that once they have informed the appropriate managerial authority of these illegal or unethical acts the organization will take the appropriate measures to change its behaviour. In reality, what whistle-blowers often experience is that the organization's management do not see whistle-blowing as an act of good organizational citizenship. Instead, management tend to see the whistle-blower as a troublemaker, as a potentially dangerous and unpredictable organizational maverick, or just plain crazy. The result too often is that rather than investigating the unethical practices brought to their attention, management investigates the whistle-blowing employee. The whistle-blower is disciplined, victimized or even dismissed. The experience of being victimized reinforces a belief that their management has been morally corrupt. Undoubtedly, some who experience this unexpected victimization may be bullied or frightened into silence. However, some of these individuals go on to pursue the issue they raised with a stronger sense of moral purpose.

Rothschild and Miethe (1994) illustrate their study of whistle-blowers with empirical examples, such as that of 'Anne'. Anne, 37 years old, was grateful to be hired in the late 1990s as a casting operator for a company making rubber belts. Within just a few days of starting the job, Anne began to experience some strange physical reactions. However, she continued to work hard and got a special commendation from her supervisor as well as an expansion of her role to include training other employees. Only a few weeks later, however, Anne was experiencing worse physical symptoms, including burning in the nose and mouth, headaches and bone pain. She told her boss and said that she planned to send for the papers that by law should be displayed on the chemical drums they were using, which would give details of the nature of the chemicals in the drums. Her supervisor told her this was a good idea, but the next day she was dismissed. Anne refused to accept this treatment. She contacted other employees of the organization and found out they too had suffered similar health problems. She then contacted a local university. With their help Anne discovered that the company was exposing its workers, with no protective equipment or warning, to over 100 times the legal exposure to certain toxic chemicals, and further that it was dumping toxic waste illegally. As a result of her own short exposure, Anne now had tumours growing in her mouth, liver damage, her skull began to soften and she had irreversible lung damage. Despite these serious health effects, she continued to campaign to end the organization's unethical and illegal practices. She prepared a civil lawsuit against the company, provided witness testimony at a national level, and was interviewed by the national hard-hitting TV journalism programme *60 minutes*. Rothschild and Miethe quote Anne:

> I felt so completely victimized by the company. I had been such a trusting person. When they hired me, I thought they had picked me because they could see that I was an intelligent and responsible person. Now I know that when they picked me they were picking out a person to murder. (ibid., p. 263)

Rothschild and Miethe (1994) argue that for whistle-blowers such as Anne, a clear sense of ethics emerges that is in stark contrast to that of the managers of the organization. To quote the authors:

> To a person (whistle-blowers) come to see themselves as strong and moral. They have developed an understanding of how greed and self-aggrandizement can result in deceptive practices, harmful products and fraudulent services being built into the fabric of many organizations. They feel free of the abuse and above it. (ibid., p. 268)

Whistle-blowers' 'disobedient' ethics does not always mean that they are successful in changing organizational practices. Often the power and resources of the organization are just too vast for an individual, no matter how committed, to change. The conclusion that Rothschild and Miethe arrive at reflects this, and they call for more widespread and collective organizational resistance to unethical organizational practices. Rothschild and Miethe's work is thus in stark contrast to the endorsement of stronger managerial authority in mainstream business ethics texts. Rothschild and Miethe's research argues that, if we wish to have organizations that perpetrate less illegal and more ethical practices, we must look to and support those who *challenge* and *resist* managerial authority.

Thinkpoint 15.12

- Have you or someone close to you ever refused to do something you were instructed to do because you thought it was morally wrong?
- How difficult was it to refuse, and how did the person who told you to do it react to your refusal?
- What can your experience tell you about the relationship between ethics and power?

Rothschild and Miethe's research, alongside that of Milgram's experiments and Neimark's case study, demonstrate the significance of critical approaches to ethics and organizations. Such studies show that, despite many mainstream business ethicists' attempts to make ethics palatable and profitable for business, ethics can still be drawn upon to call organizations to account for their exploitative, dangerous or oppressive practices. Critically informed studies of organizational behaviour present an important challenge to unethical organizational practices.

Box 15.4
UK whistle-blowing legislation – The Public Interest Disclosure Act (PIDA) 1998

Following a number of high-profile organizational disasters, including instances of the abuse of vulnerable people in some care homes and children's homes, the collapse of the Bank of Credit and Commerce International and the Clapham rail disaster, legislation was introduced in the UK to protect whistle-blowers from being victimized by their organization in the kind of ways described by Rothschild and Miethe (1994).

The legislation (PIDA, 1998) makes it illegal to victimize or dismiss whistle-blowers where they raise genuine concerns about misconduct and malpractice, as long as certain conditions and procedures are followed. If a whistle-blower is victimized or dismissed as a result of his/her whistle-blowing they can take their case to an employment tribunal to seek compensation.

While clearly welcome, the actual usefulness and extent of this legislative protection must still be looked at critically. For instance, Dr David Kelly, the weapons expert and senior government adviser who whistle-blew on his concerns about the UK government's misrepresentation of evidence for engaging in the 2003 war in Iraq, seemed to be very poorly protected by this legislation. Dr Kelly's name was given to journalists by government representatives and a number of attempts were made by ministers to discredit him in the public perception by presenting him as paranoid and a fantasist. Dr Kelly committed suicide after these events, forcing a governmental inquiry. In addition to Dr Kelly's tragic case there have also been a number of other high-profile cases in the UK in recent years, where senior professionals have blown the whistle on practices ranging from child abuse within children's care homes, to medical malpractice (including the retention of the organs of dead children by a hospital without the parents' permission). Several of these whistle-blowers have also been victimized and dismissed by their employing organizations despite the 'protection' of this legislation.

Such cases perhaps serve to illustrate again the argument that formal ethical 'rules' (including laws and company policies on whistle-blowing) do not take away the need for our continual ethical scrutiny of organizational behaviour. To see current examples of whistle-blowing, both in corporate and government sectors, go to www.wikileaks.org.

Contribution and limitations of the critical approach to thinking about the field

Critical approaches to business ethics enable us to look again, and more deeply, at the ethics of business. Unlike mainstream business ethics, critical approaches are not tied to justifying their critiques in terms of what is profitable, comfortable or even necessarily sympathetic to business interests and managerial authority. Critical approaches enable us to understand that the consequences and conditions of work are far from wholly positive or benign. They remind us that exploitation, oppression, abuse and rampant inequality abound in the contemporary business world. Critical approaches help us realize that management and other organizational participants can often have different, even contradictory, agendas and interests. They remind us that management practices are not necessarily those that lead to the most ethical outcome.

Critical approaches help us to reclaim ethics as a language that can legitimize organizational members' right to radically question organizational behaviour. Overall, critical approaches help us to realize that ethical issues at work are far deeper, and more immediately pressing, than those contained within an organization's mission statement or 'code of ethics'. Importantly, critical approaches can also help us reflect more deeply upon our *own* behaviour within, and assumptions about, organizations.

A limitation of some critical approaches is that, perhaps because they do not merely reproduce more widely accepted mainstream knowledge about organizations, they can sometimes seem abstract and distant from the lived-experience of working in organizations. Indeed, critical writers do not always help themselves in this regard, with academic critics of organization sometimes seeming to prefer the company of dusty old books and long-dead philosophers than the problems facing working people in today's organizations. As a result, you might find that some critical writing on organization needs to be persevered with – it may take some time to understand the densely-packed arguments and concepts used. Persevere though, and your thinking about ethics and organization may be deepened, and changed, forever.

Thinkpoint 15.13

- Why would critical writers see management control as ethically problematic?
- Why might corporate social responsibility be viewed suspiciously from a critical perspective?

Conclusion

In this chapter we have explored the topic of ethics at work in a number of ways. In the first part of the chapter we examined the rise of business ethics as an academic subject area alongside the modern corporation's claim to be socially responsible. We have unpicked these concepts and highlighted key assumptions upon which they have been built. These included assumptions that business and organization are generally ethical; that managerial authority is good; and that ethics and profits are compatible rather than contradictory.

In the second part of the chapter we saw how critical approaches to ethics at work enable us to re-examine each of these assumptions. Through this critical lens we saw how, because it promotes and relies upon conformity, organization is dangerous for ethics; how employee resistance can reintroduce alternative ethical values into organization; and how critical approaches are trying to stop ethics from being just another part of the corporate brand.

So this is what the chapter has done, but why do I think it has been important to do this? As an introductory chapter to ethics at work, indeed as an introductory book on organizational behaviour, this text is unusual in dedicating much of its space to critical approaches. These critical approaches have been introduced not just to give you more 'theories' to think about and learn (even though we have done so!). Nor are they included simply because academics love to argue with each other (although we do!). Nor even are they included principally because critical writers think that mainstream authors have been guilty of presenting a very selective picture of organizations (although this could certainly be argued!).

Rather, as I understand it, critical approaches exist and have been presented to you principally because they signify an *ethical questioning* of, and unease with, the values and effects of organization. As I said at the start of this chapter, organizational behaviour affects all of us, every day. Organizations are powerful, and this power can be good and it can be terrible – indeed it may be both of these things *at the same time*. For critical writers especially, organization must accordingly always be judged on ethical and not just on financial criteria such as profitability or share dividends. Critical approaches attend to the ethics of organizational behaviour, and do so whether the specific topic is motivation, bureaucracy, corporate culture, technology or any of the other chapters in this book. Critical approaches are always underpinned by ethical questions. Questions such as:

- Whether, and how, organizations contribute to happiness or suffering?
- How should we judge this?
- Who is harmed and who is helped by organizational behaviour?
- Whose lives and values have we neglected in the way we both study and run our organizations?

Finally, and most importantly, such ethical questions and doubts should never be regarded as once-and-for-all resolved. Organizations do not stop being powerful and the ethical questions about work and organization do not therefore come to an end either.

Discussion questions

1 Outline how mainstream business ethics overcomes the three problems of 'relevance', 'conscience' and 'translation' when trying to argue for a greater role for ethics in business.

2 Does the rise of interest in business ethics and corporate social responsibility mean that business is becoming more ethical? Answer this question first from a mainstream and then from a critical perspective.

3 From a mainstream perspective, can ethics be managed? And if so, how?

4 From a critical perspective, what is dangerous with the idea of trying to manage ethics?

Further reading

Bakan, J. (2004) *The Corporation,* London, Constable.

A very readable critique of corporations and their claims of social responsibility.

Banerjee, S. B. (2007) *Corporate Social Responsibility: The Good, the Bad and the Ugly,* Cheltenham, UK and Northhampton, MA: Edwin Elgar Publishing.

A thought-provoking, critical examination of corporate social responsibility.

Beauchamp, T. and Bowie, N. (eds) (2012) *Ethical Theory and Business,* ninth edn, London: Prentice Hall.

Includes a wealth of classic and contemporary writings on most mainstream aspects of business ethics.

Crane, A. and Matten, D. (2016) *Business Ethics,* fourth edn, Oxford: Oxford University Press.

A good, broadly sympathetic review of current thinking in business ethics.

Frederick, R. (ed.) (2002) *A Companion to Business Ethics,* Oxford: Blackwell.

Edited book of original articles. Mainly dealing with mainstream approaches, but with some more critical work.

Jackall, R. (2009) *Moral Mazes: The World of Corporate Managers,* updated edn, New York: Oxford University Press.

The most extensive empirical research conducted to date critically examining the ethics of corporate managers.

Jones, C., Parker, M. and Ten Bos, R. (2005) *For Business Ethics,* Oxford: Routledge.

A thought-provoking critical discussion of business ethics.

McLean, B. and Elkind, P. (2003) *The Smartest Guys in the Room,* New York: Penguin.

A very well researched, and accessibly written, examination of the personalities, practices and policies behind that most famously fraudulent corporation: Enron.

Parker, M. (ed.) (1998) *Ethics and Organizations,* London: Sage.

Edited collection of critical writings on ethics and organizations. The first half reviews the main critical theoretical approaches to ethics, while the second half explores a number of organizational practices.

Solomon, R. and Martin, C. (2003) *Above the Bottom Line,* third edn, London: Wadsworth Publishing.

Thoughtful textbook introduction to mainstream business ethics.

Useful websites

www.corpwatch.org
An excellent website that pulls together critiques of contemporary business practices.
www.oxfam.org.au/what-we-do/ethical-trading-and-business/
Information from the respected independent anti-poverty charity and pressure group about sweatshop and other

exploitative employment practices of large multinational corporations.
www.wikileaks.org
A website that publishes whistle-blowing stories and leaks about governmental, business and other organizational illegal or unethical practices.

References

Arnold, D. and Bowie, N. (2003) 'Sweatshops and respect for persons', *Business Ethics Quarterly,* 13(2): 221–242.

Axline, L. (1990) 'The bottom line on ethics', *Journal of Accounting,* 170(6): 87–91.

Bakan, J. (2004) *The Corporation,* London, Constable.

Banerjee, S. B. (2007) *Corporate Social Responsibility: The Good, the Bad and the Ugly,* Cheltenham, UK and Northhampton, MA: Edwin Elgar Publishing.

Barry, B. (2007) 'The cringing and the craven: Freedom of expression in, around, and beyond the workplace', *Business Ethics Quarterly,* 17(2): 263–296.

Bauman, Z. (1989) *Modernity and the Holocaust,* Oxford: Polity Press.

Bauman, Z. (1993) *Post-modern Ethics,* Oxford: Blackwell.

Beaton, A. (2001) *The Little Book of Management Bollocks,* London: Pocket Books.

Beauchamp, T. and Bowie, N. (2012) *Ethical Theory and Business,* London: Pearson.

Bowie, N. (1983) 'Changing the rules', in J. White (ed.) *Contemporary Moral Problems,* London: Wadsworth, pp. 243–246.

Brewis, J. (1998) 'Who do you think you are? Feminism, work, ethics and Foucault', in M. Parker (ed.) *Ethics and Organizations,* London: Sage, pp. 53–75.

Business Week (2001) 'Online Extra: Q&A with Enron's Skilling', February 12th.

Caza, A. and Jackson, B. (2011) 'Authentic leadership', in A. Bryman *et al. The Sage Handbook of Leadership*, London: Sage, pp. 352–364.

Cooke, B. (2003) 'The denial of slavery in management studies', *Journal of Management Studies*, 40(8): 1895–1918.

Corlett, A. (1998) 'A Marxist approach to business ethics', *Journal of Business Ethics*, 17: 99–103.

Derry, R. (2002) 'Feminist theory and business ethics', in R. Frederick (ed.) *A Companion to Business Ethics*, Oxford: Blackwell.

Ford, J. and Harding, N. (2011) 'The impossibility of the "true self" of authentic leadership', *Leadership*, 7(4): 463–479.

Friedman, M. (1970) 'The social responsibility of business is to increase its profits', in J. White (ed.) (2000) *Contemporary Moral Problems*, London: Wadsworth, pp. 233–238.

Gabriel, Y. (1997) 'Meeting God: When organizational members come face to face with the supreme leader', *Human Relations*, 50(4): 315–342.

Gow, D. (2003) 'Boeing sacks finance chief in ethics row', *Guardian*, 25 November: 17.

Hemingway, C. and Maclagan, P. (2004) 'Managers' personal values as drivers of corporate social responsibility', *Journal of Business Ethics*, 50: 33–44.

Ket Vries, M.F.R. and Balazs, K. (2011) 'The shadow side of leadership', in Bryman, A., Collinson, D.L., Grint, K., Jackson, B. and Uhl-Bien, M. (eds), *The Sage handbook of leadership*, CA, Thousand Oaks, Sage

Klein, N. (2001) *No Logo*, London: Flamingo.

Knights, D. and Roberts, J. (1982) 'The power of organization or the organization of power?', *Organization Studies*, 3(1): 47–64.

Maclagan, P. (2007) 'Hierarchical control or individuals' moral autonomy? Addressing a fundamental tension in the management of business ethics', *Business Ethics: A European Review*, 16(1): 48–61.

MacIntyre, A. (1981) *After Virtue*, London: Duckworth.

Marx, K. (1844) 'Alienated labour', in L. Simon (ed.) (1994) *Karl Marx's Selected Writings*, Indianapolis, IN: Hackett Publishing.

McLean, B. and Elkind, P. (2003) *The Smartest Guys in the Room*, New York: Penguin.

Milgram, S. (1974) *Obedience to Authority: An Experimental View*, London: Tavistock.

Neimark, M. (1995) 'The selling of ethics: The ethics of business meets the business of ethics', *Accounting, Auditing and Accountability*, 8(3): 81–97.

Parker, M. (1998) 'Business ethics and social theory: Postmodernizing the ethical', *British Journal of Management*, 9(Special issue): S27–S36.

Parker, M. (2002) *Against Management*, Cambridge: Polity.

Phillips, N. (1991) 'The sociology of knowledge: Towards an existential view of business ethics', *Journal of Business Ethics*, 10: 787–795.

Richardson, B. and Curwen, P. (1995) 'Do free-market governments create crisis-ridden societies?', *Journal of Business Ethics*, 14: 551–560.

Ritzer, G. (2010) *The McDonaldisation of Society 6*, Thousand Oaks, CA: Pine Forge.

Roberts, J. (1984) 'The moral character of management practice', *Journal of Management Studies*, 21(3): 287–302.

Roberts, J. (2001) 'Corporate governance and the ethics of narcissus', *Business Ethics Quarterly*, 11(1): 109–127.

Rorty, R. (2006) 'Is philosophy relevant to applied ethics?', *Business Ethics Quarterly*, 16(3): 369–380.

Rothschild, J. and Miethe, T. (1994) 'Whistle-blowing as resistance in modern work organizations', in M. Jermier, D. Knights and W. Nord (eds) *Resistance and Power in Organizations*, London: Routledge, pp. 252–273.

Schwartz, M. (2000) 'Why ethical codes constitute an unconscionable regression', *Journal of Business Ethics*, 23: 173–184.

Skilling, J. (2001) 'Online Extra' in Business Week (12th Feb 2001 Issue) York PA: Bloomberg L.P.

Snell, R. (2009) 'Managing ethically', in S. Linstead, L. Fulop and S. Lilley (eds) *Management and Organisation: A Critical Text*, second edn, Basingstoke: Palgrave, pp. 357–407.

Spurlock, M. (Dir.) (2005) *Supersize Me: A Film by Morgan Spurlock*, Tartan Films.

White, J. (ed.) (2000) *Contemporary Moral Problems*, sixth edn, London: Wadsworth.

Willmott, H. (1998) 'Towards a new ethics? The contributions of poststructuralism and posthumanism', in M. Parker (ed.) *Ethics and Organizations*, London: Sage, pp. 76–121.

Wray-Bliss, E. (2012) 'Leadership and the deified/demonic: A cultural examination of CEO sanctification', *Business Ethics: A European Review*, 21(4): 434–449.

Wray-Bliss, E. and Parker, M. (1998) 'Marxism, capitalism, and ethics', in M. Parker (ed.) *Ethics and Organizations*, London: Sage, pp. 30–52.

Wylie, I. (1997) 'The human answering machine', *Guardian*, 26 July: 2–3.

Appendix
The conceptual framework

DAVID KNIGHTS AND HUGH WILLMOTT

The theoretical framework for analyzing management and organization in this book comprises six interconnected concepts: identity, knowledge, freedom, insecurity, power and inequality. In combination, these concepts offer a means of making sense of the complexity of social relations without involving excessive simplification, on the one hand, or student confusion and disorientation as a consequence of using obscure ideas or difficult esoteric language, on the other.

As a concept, *identity* draws attention to the importance of who we are – a preoccupation that we believe is unique to the human species. Of course, we can never be entirely sure whether other animals (e.g., dolphins) share *our freedom* to attribute an identity to others and ourselves. However, we are the ones that put dolphins into (aquatic) circus roles rather than the other way round. So it seems that we exercise *power* over them rather than the reverse, although it can be argued that the way in which they capture our attention, and thereby receive some privileges relative to other, 'lesser' animals, means that they do have some hold over us and, in this sense, exercise power over us. It only goes to show that power is a two-way relationship, but it is *we* who attribute 'captivating' qualities to dolphins and we train them to repeat these capabilities on our command, rather than the dolphins developing a sales pitch in which they make us an offer we can't refuse. In the social world, power is largely about securing the consent or compliance of another person, group or even a collection of people, such as an organization or institution, to behave in a given way. Power is exercised only because those over whom it is exercised are free. That may sound paradoxical. But if we could simply determine others to behave as we wish, there would not be a relationship of power but simply one of absolute and unending tyranny. The freedom that is a necessary condition of power relations, and which accounts for why everybody (even the lowest of subordinates) exercises some power, stems from our ability to reflect not only on what is outside of, but also on, ourselves – in short, our identities.

It is through our self-consciousness that we identify ourselves and are identified by others. Our actions are mediated by this *knowledge* of ourselves. Such knowledge can be highly complex; but it is grounded in the self-consciousness that makes us both free and concerned about our identities or about how other people see us. The concern with how other people see us, however, is symptomatic of *insecurity,* as human beings can rarely, if ever, exercise sufficient power to make others see and relate to us exactly how we would wish. Identity is always precarious. Think of some people who are generally considered or 'known' to be powerful – the President of the USA, for example. President Bush was repeatedly ridiculed for being a bit dumb; Clinton ended his presidency in disgrace for his sexual antics, and President Reagan was viewed as a 'B' movie actor who had lost his marbles. We can never control how people see or 'know' us, although we may turn such images to our own advantage as, arguably, each of these presidents was smart enough to do. As long as we are self-conscious and free, we will always suffer some insecurity about our identity. It can be argued that we often seek knowledge in order to address this insecurity. Not surprisingly, then, knowledge is widely considered to be of great value, but is perhaps most highly valued when it is perceived to have 'practical use' – which is generally understood to be useful for realizing our ambitions or allaying our fears.

Yet another source of our insecurity stems from forms of inequality between people. In addition to knowledge, material and symbolic wealth are highly valued. In pre-modern societies inequality is often more a function of birth as there is limited social mobility, whereas in modern societies it is more, but by no means entirely, a function of achievement (e.g., education or talent). That is because money can buy social advantages in terms of housing and health as well as education; and, conversely, poverty tends to be self-reproducing. Moreover, those who have wealth can more easily make more wealth than those who lack access to financial and other resources. In the absence of government intervention to redistribute wealth and establish genuine equality of opportunity, there is a polarization of access to material and symbolic (e.g., status) goods: a small number of people are extremely rich, and a larger number, but still a minority, are very poor. The vast majority end up somewhere in the middle, and this is one reason why there is not greater pressure to reduce inequality. Those not actually at the bottom of the hierarchy of wealth can in general feel a little less insecure, and even many who are at the bottom may aspire to be a little higher in the social hierarchy, where they anticipate occupying a more prestigious or dignified identity, rather than tearing it down.

Glossary

Action Behaviour that is socially meaningful or purposeful; it is influenced or interpreted by oneself or others. Thus, moving one's leg might be seen as behaviour (unless agreed as a prearranged signal), whereas kicking a ball in a football match might be seen as action (unless as a deflection).

Action-based A concept used to describe the dynamics of organization. It assumes that political rule is dependent on the practices of organizational members and limited by the norms, values and foresight of informed actors.

Actor-network theory or analysis (ANT or ANA) A theory that does not restrict action to that performed by humans but also involves non-human action as performed by material artefacts such as cars, phones or social institutions insofar as they and humans affect one another. Every technological device is dependent on a heterogeneous network, which supports the specific ways in which this device has been designed and used.

Agency The sense of acting from an individual's own volition.

Alienation Marx famously employed this concept to describe the experience of **labour** under capitalism; a condition in which individuals feel separated or estranged from some part of their existence (e.g., the product or process of their labour) because they are subjected to external controls.

Anticipatory socialization A process of learning to behave in ways appropriate to particular future roles, relationships or occupations. An example would be anticipating what is the expected behaviour of a student prior to starting university.

Anxiety Unlike fear, which has an identifiable source, anxiety has no specific object to which it responds. It is a *general* feeling of malaise or disease for no particular reason, and indeed cannot be understood. In extreme form, it may be associated with neurosis or psychosis

Ascribed Behaviour that is imposed upon people by virtue of their position or role. In earlier societies roles were often ascribed at birth rather than achieved through demonstrating competence.

Authority Legitimate *right* to control, prohibit and judge the actions of others. It is when someone has the right to exercise power over you (e.g., tell you what to do). It is often distinguished from power, where there can be physical coercion or force, for that is based on 'might' not 'right'. Authority establishes rights recognized by subordinates as well as exercised by superiors.

Autocracy A political regime or person that rules by tradition or coercion rather than consent, as might be expected in a democratic regime.

Barriers to entry Corporate practices that develop or are deployed to deny or deter potential competitors entering the market.

Basic assumptions A term used by Schein to refer to the origins of values and cultural artefacts in organizations. Basic assumptions are shared and deeply embedded presuppositions about issues such as whether human beings do or should live for the moment (immediate gratification) or see their activities as a means to a future end or goal (deferred gratification).

Binary Division into two and only two opposites as in body/mind, female/male, black/white, positive/negative, true/false or the code of 0 and 1 in computing. Criticisms of this way of thinking, sometimes described as dualistic, argue that there are other alternatives that lie in-between or beyond the two extremes.

Black box Metaphorical term for describing something that need not be or never is investigated. It is as if to uncover what is inside the black box would destroy its benefits, much like discovering the sleight of hand of magicians undermines their mystique.

Bounded rationality Stipulates the existence of limitations in the human capacity to process information without resort to some arbitrary or non-rational selection. It suggests that these limitations restrict individuals to constructing simplified models that extract only the basic elements of a problem and thereby neglect its complexity.

Bourgeois Critics of capitalism use this term to denote the privileged complacency of the relatively affluent middle classes.

Brainstorming Involves people in a group exercising their creative skills to generate new ideas or innovations. The key aspect of it is that, in the early stages, all ideas put forward are considered valid and no criticism or selection is allowed until later on when ideas are evaluated.

Bureaucracy Describes a form of business administration based on formal rational rules and procedures designed to govern work practices and organization activities through a hierarchical system of authority. Bureaucratic organization is often thought to be rigid, inflexible and overburdened by hierarchical rules sometimes pejoratively referred to as 'red tape'.

Business ethics The academic study and promotion of ethical practice in business.

Business process re-engineering (BPR) An approach to organizational redesign that proposes information technology should be the catalyst for revolutionary organizational change, leading to improved measures of performance in terms of costs, speed, quality and service.

Call centres Offices where staff are employed principally to process telephone calls with customers. Such centres involve heavily routinized and disciplined work processes where staff often work at very high levels of intensity and under conditions of technological surveillance and close monitoring.

Capital In Marxist critical theory, capital is defined as assets (e.g., property, machines, money) used to finance the production of commodities for the private gain of the capitalist classes. Capitalists invest their capital in the production of commodities and accumulate profits by selling goods at a value exceeding the costs of their production.

Capitalist society The dominant economic system around the world today. An economic system that concentrates the majority of wealth in private hands (capitalists) and requires the majority of people to sell their labour to secure a wage from this group.

Chain of command Links within a hierarchy between the most senior and least senior of managers or supervisors.

Classify Places ideas, phenomena, practices or events into categories that are then named. Most sciences begin by classifying the types of objects they study (e.g., types of plants in botany).

Cliques Small exclusive group of friends and associates who constitute part of the informal structure of an organization.

Coalitions Informal liaison between two or more interest groups intent on increasing their joint power and control with respect to another group or groups.

Co-determination Form of influence predicated on the co-operation of parties with possibly opposing or competing interests in the pursuit of a mutual or common outcome.

Codified knowledge Knowledge in the form of information that has been deliberately and explicitly written down in a book or stored on a computer, for example.

Cognitive Associated with thinking or mental processes such as perception; or traditional views of understanding such as those that are gained by reading or classroom learning.

Cognitivism Psychological perspective on human behaviour that emphasizes the mental processes of thinking and perception rather than other influences such as the subconscious or social factors.

Colonized Process where usually a larger, richer or more powerful unit (organization, country) takes control of a weaker one – as when, for example, in the eighteenth and nineteenth centuries, European states appropriated the wealth and labour of Africa, Far East Asia, the Indian subcontinent, Latin America and the New World.

Committee system Where decisions are taken by committees rather than individuals – a situation that can lead to a proliferation of committees dominating the decision-making process of an organization.

Commodity Something that can be exchanged for a price. While normally seen in terms of physical goods or services, the term is sometimes extended to human beings where they are treated in a dehumanized manner purely in terms of their economic value (price) as labour.

Common sense What is assumed to be self-evident, obvious and fundamentally correct. It is often used to silence all alternative understandings on the basis that common sense is clearly and universally authoritative and dependable.

Communities of practice (COPs) Refers to groups of people who interact (through meeting personally or electronically) and in so doing share knowledge and learn from each other through the interaction. Precise definitions vary, but emphasis is typically placed on the informality of such groups and interactions (Handley *et al.*, 2006).

Competitive advantage What is deemed to make an organization or nation more competitive or economically successful than another, such as access to important resources.

Conception What characterizes human creativity is that it begins with a mental process of imagination or conception.

Consent Widescale agreement relating to authorities and their decisions. For example, where production workers assent to, and approve of, managerial strategies and mechanisms of work organization.

Content theories of motivation These theories tried to identify the specific factors – individual needs, task factors, management styles – that shape individual motivation.

Contestability Extent to which something can be disputed and debated.

Contextual embeddedness Way in which any action on the part of, for example, managers or employees, is ascribed different meaning and significance depending on the context in which it occurs. Highlights the historical and cultural conditioning (and relativity) of what may appear to be normal and natural.

Contingency approach Way of analyzing organizations so that rather than there being a single way of doing things, there are different ways depending (or 'contingent') upon different situations. For example, technological determinists believe that organizations have to adopt different structures depending upon the technology that they use.

Corporate social responsibility (CSR) The practices and policies undertaken by organizations to promote the idea that they have concerns that extend beyond efficiency, performance, productivity and profit to embrace the public, customers, the environment and other stakeholders.

Critical structuralist Critical theory that identifies the political activity of organizations to be directly linked to the capitalist productive economy.

Cultural artefacts Phenomena accessible to the senses, including architecture, myths, rituals, logos, type of personnel employed and so on, which signify the values in an organization's culture.

Cultural barriers Are seen to prevent the transfer of ideas and practices because of differences in what is viewed as acceptable in different cultural contexts (e.g. teamworking in individualistic cultures).

Cultural differentiation Refers to differing sets of values, beliefs and norms which co-exist in one organization. Also see multiculturalism and subculture.

Cultural engineering Attempt to change an organization's culture to accord with the interests or values of managers. It depends on a view that a culture is something that an organization 'has' rather than 'is'. If organizational relations are defined by culture, it is more difficult to impose a unified set of values, beliefs and norms that are designed to provide the basis for all organizational actions and decisions.

Cultural transmission mechanism (CTM) Techniques used by managers to build, maintain or change a particular organizational culture, to encourage employees to adopt specific values, beliefs and norms. Examples include management by example (MBE) and deliberately recruiting new staff who embody the desired culture.

Culture An anthropological term that refers to the shared values, beliefs and norms about key priorities and ways of undertaking particular tasks, or relating to colleagues among members of a particular organization.

Custom and practice Workplace behaviour that has been repeated over a lengthy period and is therefore routinely taken for granted.

Customer relationship management (CRM) A broad management approach that emphasizes the financial value of developing long-term relationships with, and detailed knowledge of, customers. For example, through the use of information systems databases, it is assumed that customers can be 'captured' so that customized goods and services may be targeted appropriately to them.

Death of distance View popularized by Cairncross (1998), that, for the purposes of organizing, the importance of physical location and geographical distance is no longer a constraint because of the developments in information and communication technologies.

Decision objectives Aim/goal of a decision and the criteria through which outcomes can be evaluated.

Decision premises Structures and processes that constitute the apparatus of decision-making. An example of a decision premise is the agenda for meetings. Control of this agenda can enable one to manipulate how a decision is approached.

Decision process Sequential processes and structures involved in the deliberation of a decision.

Dehumanized A process by which human beings are treated like objects or things and thus their humanity is denied.

De-layering Reducing the number of levels in the hierarchy so as to have fewer managers.

Delegated The process of passing the responsibility to make management decisions down the hierarchy to those in less senior positions.

Deregulation of markets Process whereby greater competition is encouraged between commercial organizations through reducing regulations that previously restricted their behaviour or entry into certain markets.

Determinism View that there is an inevitable direction in which events move, as a result of some cause that is independent of the event. In organization studies and in everyday life, the idea that 'human nature' determines

social arrangements is possibly the most common. See also technological determinism.

Dialectic of control Contested process whereby work and other activities are socially accomplished. Every activity is seen to involve an interdependence between diverse individuals and groups, such as managers and workers. While exercising differential power associated with their access to scarce and valued resources such as income, status and qualifications, none of these bestow a monopoly of control. This is because each individual or group has a degree of dependence on the other.

Digital divide Disparity between those who have access to the new information and communication technologies and those who do not.

Direct democracy System of collective decision-making in which there is an opportunity for everyone to participate and influence how 'things' get done or are organized.

Direct management control Describes conditions where workers have little or no scope to decide how work is organized and conducted.

Dirty job A job that carries with it some form of social stigma and so may require its incumbents to reconcile this with their sense of themselves as 'decent' human beings. Examples include jobs that deal with literal dirt (e.g., refuse collection, lavatory cleaning) or involve what is regarded as morally problematic behaviour (e.g. prostitution, crime).

Discourse Often taken to mean the same as language or the spoken word and written text, but may also refer to a broad category of talk or text such as *managerial* discourse. Some approaches extend the meaning of the term to what is possible in a given context or era and to meaningful behaviour as well (discursive practices). Here, the term can be summarized as what can be said (and done).

Disembodied Analysis that relies purely on the cognitive aspects of human conduct, completely ignoring how bodily and emotional life is central to human existence.

Disintermediation Abandonment of intermediaries (e.g., wholesalers, retailers) that facilitate the distribution of goods and services so that producers trade directly with consumers. Mail order and Internet trading represent common examples of disintermediation.

Dispositional factors Internal personality aspects, traits and beliefs that are specific to each individual and may be seen to motivate a person to behave in a certain way. They are opposed to situational factors where the behaviour is due to factors or circumstances external to the individual.

Division of labour The way that people divide up different tasks or jobs between one another to achieve greater levels of efficiency and productive output. Emile Durkheim (1947) argued that the division of labour was not only economically efficient but also socially effective in that it made clear how we are all dependent upon one another and this knowledge would help to generate social solidarity – a necessary condition of social survival.

Double-loop learning (DLL) Involves highly reflective and creative actions that, through continuous feedback processes of self-learning, testing and exploration, facilitate organizational change. DLL is contrasted with single-loop learning (SLL), which is more incremental and mechanical and often likened to the role of a thermostat that regulates a domestic heating system in accordance with external temperatures.

Dysfunctions Action, procedures and processes that impede or disrupt the ability of an entity to achieve its aims.

Elite Selected group of presumably gifted or otherwise distinguished individuals.

Emancipatory Political term associated with emancipation or freedom from control. An example is freedom from slavery, but freedom remains an important issue in other contexts, even where control may be less visible.

Empowerment The distribution of power to people lower down the hierarchy so that they can feel a degree of autonomy and sense of personal identification in the decisions they make.

Entity Something that exists as a solid or concrete thing. May refer to human institutions, such as organizations, as well as to objects.

Environment What exists external to the organization, such as available technologies, markets and government.

Equity theory These ideas focus on the importance people attach to perceptions of fairness in how managers deal with them relative to others.

Esprit de corps Positive morale – strong sense of belonging and purpose shared by a work group or organization.

Essence That which is fundamental and unchanging in an 'object', situation or person and most commonly recognized in the phrase 'human nature' (see determinism). There is an assumption of some deep, inner essence that can be discovered and which defines the individual. Once an essence is attributed to an object, no further examination is seemingly required. That is why a phrase such as human nature or common sense gives the impression of providing the final and ultimate explanation of anything.

Ethnography A form of study where the researcher lives and works as a member of the group being studied. It aims to provide an 'insider' account but, because it is conducted by a researcher, it has a degree of 'outsider' detachment. Ethnography developed from the techniques used by anthropologists to study what were often seen as exotic cultures or societies outside their own.

Experiential Pertaining to direct experience rather than thought or imagination.

Exploitation A process where people are used merely to further someone else's goals. In an economic context, 'exploitation' refers to using others for the purpose of creating a surplus that enables the exploiter to live without working or to supplement their income in this way.

Externalization The process of creation through which what has been conceived in the mind comes to be embodied through work in an object.

Feminism The theory and politics associated with critiques of society that make gender and the oppression of women their central focus,

Flexibility Systems of production and working arrangements that allow material and human resources to be utilized speedily to meet the fickle and fluctuating demands of the market and customer taste.

Flexible specialization Approach to production and the organization of work that emphasizes the need for adaptation rather than repetition. Companies following this strategy simply transform their production regularly as there is a demand for more distinctive, customized products and services. Flexibility can come in the form of producing non-standard products for niche markets; varying the number of employees according to fluctuations in demand; and/or requiring employees to undertake multiple tasks.

Fordism System of mass production based on hierarchical management control pioneered by Henry Ford during the early twentieth century, adopted throughout most Western economies up until its decline in advanced capitalist economies in the 1970s when product differentiation and changing markets demanded more flexibility.

Formalization The process of codifying what was previously tacit or informal. Typically, it refers to the introduction of formal rules and procedures in place of custom and practice.

Functionalism Theoretical model or framework that presumes organizational consensus and posits that activities continue to exist only because they perform the indispensable function of maintaining a coherent integration of the organization. Consensus is presumed to be the natural state of affairs.

Globalization Notion that countries are becoming economically, politically, technologically and culturally closer to each other. Examples of this process include the European Union, the Internet and the worldwide popularity of branded products including Coca-Cola, Nike shoes and Mercedes cars.

Goal displacement Occurs when the pursuit of a secondary or marginal objective assumes greater importance than the primary objective and/or when the means (e.g., complying with a procedure) becomes more important than the ends (e.g., attaining the objective).

Greedy institution Coser's term for organizations that require unstinting effort and immense dedication from their employees.

Groupthink Term used by Janis to refer to situations in which groups make problematic decisions because individuals over-conform to the group ethos and fail to express personal doubts. There is comfort in groupthink in that the group as a whole feels protected given that the decision is collective, but silence is presumed to imply consent whereas it may signify a fear of resistance.

Headcount Staff or employee numbers in an organization.

Hegemonic Form of control that includes, if not focuses on, the control of people's ideas and values, their 'hearts and minds'. An example would be the instilling of a sense of respect for authority or for property rights or a commitment to the organization. All these may help ensure that we do what we are supposed to do and want what we are supposed to want by those in authority, such as employers and governments. This renders control through more overt reward or punishment (e.g., job loss) less necessary.

Hierarchy of needs Maslow suggested that individual needs were organized in a hierarchy from physiological needs, to safety needs, to needs for love, affection and belonging, to esteem needs and finally at the top of the hierarchy the need for self-actualization.

Hierarchy/Hierarchical levels Positions in an organization associated with different levels of status, power and economic reward.

Hybrid Combination of two or more elements or characteristics that are normally separate.

Idealized picture Description of a situation in a way that portrays only positive elements and is cleansed of any negative aspects.

Ideal-type An ideal-type is the purest, most fully developed version of a particular thing (usually a concept). It does not mean that the thing itself is ideal. The ideal-type of a sadistic serial killer would be someone with all the characteristics of the cruellest mass murderer imaginable – but that does not mean that there is anything desirable about serial killers! It does not mean that the 'ideal' is good or bad. Instead it simply refers to an abstract, exaggerated image or a benchmark by which actual behaviour (e.g., the acts of an actual serial killer) can be assessed.

Ideology A set of ideas and beliefs sometimes used to justify particular political or sectional interests. A patriarchal ideology, for example, justifies male domination. However definitions differ in the extent to which ideology is seen as reflecting or distorting the truth.

Idiographic approach to personality An approach that is suspicious of the value of generalized 'scientific' categories of classification and thereby understands personality in the terms used by individuals to describe themselves. It perceives individuals in terms of personal experience; their personality is learned through social and cultural interaction as opposed to biological or genetic determination.

Impersonal and disembodied Relates to the way that our relations with one another can lack any sense of personal intimacy and be so instrumental and calculative or cerebral and cognitive (i.e., linked to powers of the intellect and logic) as to deny any bodily and emotional content.

Individualizing The process through which people come to see themselves as separate from others and personally responsible for their actions and life chances rather than interdependent.

Informal or Informality Behaviour that is not officially recognized or approved.

Inhibition Inability to do or say something that one desires to say or do. There are numerous sources of inhibition from the fear of embarrassment of being wrong to the consequences of speaking your mind when in a position of subordination.

Innovation The process of imagining something new in a given context (e.g., invention) combined with developing that idea into an applied form.

Institutional approach A perspective that highlights the social shaping of activities at a broad level whereby institutions such as the state, education, professions and the church are seen to condition how things are done in a similar way within these contexts. Emphasis is placed on the importance of practices (such as managing employees) being seen as socially legitimate rather than necessarily technically efficient. When such practices and their legitimacy become taken for granted and established, they are said to be institutionalized. It is less useful in explaining variations within contexts or human agency.

Institutionalization Process whereby people are fully integrated into an institution (repeated and routine practices) so as to rarely think to challenge them.

Instrumental rationality Behaviour that is exclusively concerned with a self-interested end result such that the end always justifies the means. It seeks the most efficient (i.e., high output/effort ratio) means to achieve a given end. The two terms often (but need not) go together to emphasize how the behaviour is single-minded in its 'technical' and non-emotional pursuit of specific goals.

Intangibles Difficult or impossible to measure accurately yet remain important. For example, a new procedure or system might be seen to increase productivity or employee satisfaction, but the benefit is difficult to isolate and measure.

Integral A necessary or inherent part of something.

Intellectual property rights (IPR) A legal term referring to ownership of knowledge or ideas. For example, the copyright assigned to authors, editors or publishers means that others have to ask permission and, often, pay to reproduce material. Likewise, inventions might be patented.

Internalized When an idea, norm or value is completely embedded in individual consciousness such that there is often no awareness of its existence and influence on behaviour.

Interstices That which exists in-between two 'objects'.

Intersubjectivity The existence of consensually shared ideas, values, beliefs and norms. Organizational cultures are a form of intersubjectivity.

Invoked The drawing out, or encouraging, of some idea or action.

Isomorphic A term associated with the institutional approach that means 'takes the same or a parallel form'. In particular, it refers to the ways in which organizations adopt the same practices as their peers in a given social context, because they are required to do so by standard-setting bodies, see it as 'best practice' or are uncertain of what to do and so copy others.

Japanization Process of adopting practices associated with Japan. In particular, it refers to the adoption in the West of certain production practices such as team meetings based on quality improvements.

Job enrichment Work arrangements that are designed to expand the number of tasks and roles workers perform to provide opportunities for them to gain greater satisfaction, reward, recognition and achievement.

Just In Time An inventory strategy companies employ to increase efficiency and decrease waste by receiving goods only as they are needed in the production process, thereby reducing inventory costs.

Kaizen This is the process of continuous improvement developed in the Japanese organization of work and then introduced as an important element in Western organizational designs, such as total quality management.

Knowledge diffusion The spread of knowledge across contexts such as between organizational or national boundaries, as if knowledge acts like a gas. Recent challenges have been made to this traditional view such that knowledge does not exist independently, but is produced and adapted or translated in context. See contextual embeddedness.

Knowledge economy Not based upon producing physical things, but on using knowledge to deliver services. Consultancies like *Universal*, advertising agencies, software development houses, even universities, are all examples of organizations that make up the knowledge economy – knowledge intensive firms, knowledge sectors and knowledge workers.

Knowledge management Process of capturing and codifying knowledge for management (e.g., profitable) purposes. It is often linked with information systems that store 'knowledge' in databases, but has become associated with the broader activity where management seek to appropriate the tacit as well as the explicit knowledge of their employees (see also tacit skills) (Hislop, 2013).

Labour People or class of people involved in productive work who can be distinguished from those who manage the processes of productive work.

Labourist That which is seen to reflect, represent or celebrate the views of manual labour especially, but the working classes more generally.

Leakage The unintended loss or flow of knowledge such as commercially sensitive material.

Lean production/manufacturing System of production, first used in Japan, to maintain the smooth flow of production by using minimum resources to reduce cost, work in progress and other overheads. It is associated with just-in-time services and stock inventories where companies do not retain excess labour or stocks of goods but use information technology to ensure recruitment or reordering of stocks when actually needed.

Learning organization A term to describe organizations that value collective and not just individual learning. May be reflected in more participative structures and a managerial emphasis on continuous learning (i.e., organizational improvement).

Learning styles Variations in approaches to learning attributed to individual, cultural or other background differences, and subject to change.

Legacy systems Old technology practices that have been superseded but still have to be serviced or managed since the cost and effort involved in merging all of the data files and procedures to the new system is greater than the benefits of just allowing it to be 'run down' until extinct.

Legitimacy Condition in which decisions or practices are widely acceptable to those whom they affect because there is broad level of consensus about the form or process of their adoption.

Luddites Name originally given to late eighteenth and early nineteenth century textile workers who, in defence of their livelihoods, set out to resist the mechanization of their trades. 'Luddite' is often employed as a term of abuse to describe those who attempt to stand in the way of 'progress'.

Management by example (MBE) A symbolic leadership device, or cultural transmission mechanism, which involves managers embodying the values, beliefs and norms they wish employees to adopt in everything they say and do.

Management knowledge Often associated with apparently discrete management ideas such as human resource management, but more generally linked to different types of knowledge used or claimed by management.

Managerialism or managerialist Terms applied by critical academics to describe a type of thinking and kinds of social science output that serve the objectives of managers, as these critics see them, rather than offering an independent or alternative perspective, Managerialism usually entails the idea that effective management is the solution to an array of socioeconomic problems.

Marxism Theory and politics associated with the writings of Karl Marx. The principal focus is a critique of the oppressive effects of social class and structural inequality in a capitalist economy.

Masculine discourses Communication consciously or unconsciously reflects and reproduces a sense of being analytical and technical, and masterly and in control, generated largely but not exclusively by men.

Mass production The large-batch/mass assembly line/conveyor belt systems of production, often referred to as Fordism because of its association with Henry Ford's production line.

Matrix A form of organization where there are parallel lines of authority criss-crossing one another so that staff are accountable simultaneously to managers in a hierarchy and other specialists horizontally

Mean production Describes how critical theorists interpret lean production. They see it as having subtle controls and forms of surveillance over workers that result in work intensification.

Mechanistic organization Similar to Weber's model of rational-legal bureaucracy. Includes a specialized division of labour within which each individual carries out an assigned and precisely defined task comparable to the discrete parts that comprise a machine. It is the opposite of organic organization.

Mentors Those assigned the task of supporting others by providing advice and assistance to help in their personal and career development.

Mobilization of bias Manipulation of decision-making premises, processes and objectives so as to ensure that a specific point of view or intention is supported.

Modernist Label attached to a range of phenomena, including art and architecture. Here, it is a set of beliefs associated with the historical period of modernity. These beliefs value progress and include a faith in the rationality of science to discover truth and control nature. Things like ambiguity, chance, play, fun, unmanageability and multiple truths or rationalities (e.g., based on custom, religion, lifestyle) are denied or subjected to scientific scrutiny in modernism. For example, under modernist thinking, emotion might be seen as a quantitative measure of emotional intelligence. By contrast, such things are not denied, but celebrated or brought to the foreground in what has come to be known as postmodernist views.

Monopoly A market where only one supplier of a product or service exists. There is no competition and thus no other sources of the commodity, so the supplier is able to completely dominate the consumer. See also oligopolistic and oligopoly.

Multiculturalism In the organization studies context, another term for cultural differentiation or the existence of subcultures in an organization.

Multinational corporations Very large corporations that have operations crossing multiple nations. Such corporations have been the focus of sustained criticism for the enormous economic and political power they wield.

Multinational Enterprise (MNE) A business that operates in more than one country.

Multiskilling Working arrangements in which workers acquire the full range of necessary skills required to perform a number of jobs, tasks and duties efficiently under minimum supervision.

Multitasking Working arrangements where it is claimed that workers acquire the various skills needed to perform a number of jobs, tasks and duties.

Narcissism Preoccupation with self-image, and with making the world enhance this image. In the ancient Greek myth, Narcissus became fixated with his mirror image as he saw it reflected in a pool of water.

Negotiated order The idea that social reality is open to a degree of interpretation and mutual adjustment between actors (e.g., between members of a team or between a boss and a subordinate). This element of negotiability make possible a process of manoeuvring to influence other actors.

Neoclassical economics A form of economics that emphasizes free markets and non-intervention by the state. It contrasts with the post-war consensus around Keynes's ideas of state intervention and public spending to maintain economic growth.

Neo-imperialism Colonization other than by military force, typically associated with the spread of a particular dominant set of ideas such as religious beliefs or consumerism.

Network organization Organizations which are not structured hierarchically but which make lateral connections, and connections across functions. Usually associated with claims of increased flexibility and often claimed to be modelled on 'Toyotaism' rather than Fordism.

Network society A society composed of network organizations. More generally, a society in which there is a great deal of fluidity in social relations, multiple sources of information and multiple sources of authority, rather than fixed hierarchies and roles.

Neurosis Unhealthy compulsion and attachment to routines or behaviour patterns that if taken away stimulate feelings of nervousness and anxiety.

Neutering Rendering impotent or ineffective.

New Right Political development or strategy popular in the final quarter of the twentieth century where the 'free market' is advocated and state intervention stigmatized. New Right policies favour the neo-liberal privatization of public sector corporations such as gas, electricity, the railways, etc.

Nomothetic approach (to personality) Distinguished by the beliefs that there are underlying universals (e.g., of personality) against which everything and everyone can be measured and classified. Personality, for example, tends to be understood as an inherited phenomenon and one that is the product of biology, genetics and heredity. The nomothetic approach is based on large-scale quantitative and scientific study with the aim of discovering the mechanisms and 'laws' that explain human behaviour.

Non-rigorous Usually a pejorative term meaning the absence of in-depth analysis or systematic research procedures.

Normalize A term to describe how discourses and practices are defined or perceived as proper and normal such that they become unquestioned; it serves to control or discipline individuals by transforming them into subjects that obey certain cultural or political norms or rules.

Normative control Another term for the control of the 'hearts and minds' of employees. When a manager or professional 'chooses', apparently from free will, to work through the night to complete a task because of values of being responsible, then he or she is being controlled, by being self-controlled.

Normative What is commonly accepted as normal and/or appropriate to an organization. Critical political analysis draws attention to the evaluation of behaviour using normative criteria, often the criteria favoured by supporters of the status quo (e.g. managers), as an exercise in classification and control. See normative control.

Objectification The end point of the creative process at which point what has been produced comes to have an independent existence in the world.

Objective Free from bias, prejudice, judgement and emotion.

OECD A forum in which the governments of 34 democracies with market economies work with each other, as well as with more than 70 non-member economies, to promote economic growth, prosperity, and sustainable development.

Oligopolistic Market where a small number of very large suppliers of a product or service have removed the competition and are thereby able to dominate the consumer since there are few alternative sources of supply.

Oligopoly The noun that describes the type of market discussed above.

One best way Refers to anything that is regarded as the one solution for all organizational ills.

Ontology Theories of reality; claims about the nature and contents of the natural and social worlds. It includes a concern with the nature of human existence or what it is to be human, so it is about our relationship to the world as a whole person, not just in terms of some aspect such as personality, motivation or attitudes.

Organic organization An emphasis is placed on knowledge as a contributing resource rather than restricted to a specific job specification. There exists a continual adjustment to tasks as they become shaped by the nature of the problem rather than predefined. Opposite of mechanistic organization.

Organization man The term used to refer to a worker who is so committed to the organization that he or she automatically and perhaps even unconsciously prioritizes their job demands above what they themselves require or want.

Organizational chart Stylized but clear representation of the organization that may provide a basis for the analysis of decision-making processes.

Outsourcing Business practice involving greater levels of intermediation. Producers of goods and services establish contracts with other companies or specialists (e.g., payroll, web management, call centres or even distribution) to supply essential parts of their business. It has a long tradition stretching back to the early nineteenth century when producers bought their labour from contractors, but became less common in the twentieth century, as companies directly employed their labour forces.

Panacea A remedy that cures all complaints. Teamwork, for example, might be commended as a technology of work organization that solves all production problems from control, to productivity, to retention and commitment.

Participant observation Method of research originating in social anthropology where the researcher engages with the subjects of their study by attempting to live like them for some time.

Pathological Derives from psychology or psychiatry to refer to mentally disturbed individuals. Emile Durkheim used the term 'social pathology' to describe a situation where individuals failed to see society as an objective reality. Managers tend to regard workers as pathological ('awkward', 'bloody-minded', 'uncooperative', etc.) when they fail to comply with the logic and reason of management.

Piecework Payment on the basis of what is produced rather than the time taken to produce it.

Pluralist A recognition of diverse legitimate viewpoints, interests or approaches. A pluralist vision of organizational politics emphasizes the free interplay of interest groups as operating to check and balance the potentially authoritarian tendencies of governing bodies.

Political structure Balance of competing pressures from interest groups seeking to realize, or gain recognition of, their own particular concerns.

Political system Boundaries, goals, values, administrative mechanisms and hierarchy of power, which constitute a particular organization.

Politics of truth The process of giving voice to ideas that compete over what is taken to be accepted knowledge or ideology.

Positivism Term used especially by critical analysts to identify a method of social science research in which the differences between the 'natural' phenomena of the physical sciences and human phenomena are downplayed. Positivists are those who presume, and/or seek to emulate, the causal methods of the natural sciences. In doing so, they neglect the problems of meaning and interpretation, or how researchers are active agents (not merely passive recorders) in constructing the events and behaviour they may claim merely to report.

Post-Fordism Describes flexible systems of production that are designed to produce differentiated goods and services for niche markets.

Post-modern Has two broad meanings – an historical era following modernity and a philosophical/theoretical perspective. Both are seen to celebrate what modernism devalues and/or represses – surface appearances, emotion, play, chance and indeterminacy in life – the value of different rationalities (e.g., based on experience) rather than a single authoritative science or truth. See also modernist.

Post-modernism The theory and politics principally associated with contemporary French thinkers. Postmodernism may be understood as a critique of the faith that society and intellectuals have tended to have in notions such as truth, science, individual freedom and progress.

Power Often conceived as ability of A to influence B to do something that B would not ordinarily have done without A's influence. The attribution of power to individuals or groups as their 'possession' has been challenged by a view of power that is 'relational' – such as the disciplines and ideologies that operate to constrain as well as enable those to whom power is attributed by the 'possessive' view.

Practical hermeneutic Describes theories that seek to understand and reflect on organizations as opposed to reporting them or issuing prescriptions as to how to manage them more effectively. Can be contrasted to managerialist theories and in some instances also to emancipatory theories.

Privatization Selling off public corporations, in part or in full, to individuals or corporations that anticipate increasing their wealth or value from this acquisition. See New Right.

Procedural justice Like equity theory, procedural justice is interested in the effects, either positive or negative, that arise from how fairly and transparently managers implement decisions affecting their staff.

Process theories of motivation These theories look at motivation as the outcome of a dynamic interaction between the person and their experiences of an organization and its management. Such processes depend critically on the sense individuals make of their experiences at work.

Processual Theoretical approach that focuses more attention on the political, but also cultural and strategic processes within organizations, than their content or structure.

Procrustes An ancient Greek mythological character who either stretched his guests to fit the bed or chopped off their legs if they were too tall. Eventually, the same fate befell Procrustes himself!

Product differentiation Refers to one way in which firms can maintain their competitive advantage; they differentiate their product, in ways that appeal to the customer, from all others on the market.

Product life cycle Refers to how products move from being new to being mature to being obsolete. This impacts on the pricing and marketing of goods as well as the degree of competition.

Progressive Favouring and believing in progress or moving forward by improving on the past.

Project teams Groups of people working together on a particular task with a discrete objective and time frame. Often such groups include different specialists, perhaps drawn from different departments, for the purpose of achieving the project task.

Psychodynamic approaches Defined by a concern with internal processes and forces within the psyche that clash and conflict with varying degrees of intensity in each individual and in ways that take time to resolve. In this approach, individual behavioural routines, oddities or little peculiarities and idiosyncrasies are seen as surface acts of behaviour that are really 'symptoms' of more underlying, deep-seated and unconscious forces and desires. In the Freudian approach to analysis, psychodynamic forces are understood to reach eventual compromise or 'settlement' through the negotiation of a series of relatively well-defined stages – the anal, the oral and the oedipal, for example – the resolution of which help stabilize personality.

Psychological contract The invisible or implicit set of expectations that employees have of their organizations (e.g., challenging, stimulating work that allows for career progression) and that their organizations have of them (e.g. loyalty and flexibility), but are not laid down in the formal contract of employment.

Psychosis Breakdown of our normal ways of thinking and perceiving in which objects in the world lose definition and precision, merging and collapsing into one another in a surreal and agitated, highly charged riot of images. Objects in the world and even the sound of words can come to take on a seemingly malevolent force. In Freudian terms, psychosis is associated with the collapse of the distinction between the conscious and the unconscious so that our waking world takes on dream-like qualities.

Purposeful actors Belief that individuals retain rational control (e.g., in their pursuit of self-interest and sectional loyalties) throughout the processes of organizational decision-making.

Quality circles Meetings of group of workers committed to continuous improvement in the quality and productivity of a given line of production.

Quality of working life movements Denotes programmes of organizational design and development dedicated to improving productivity and workers' retention and commitment by bettering the relationship between employers and employees and the work environment.

Quotas Limits placed on something; in trade, quotas usually refers to limits placed on the number of goods, for example cars, which can be exported from one country to another. In the workplace, quotas refer to the amount of units (or services) produced/provided in a given time period (e.g. a shift).

Rational process Process that incorporates goals and a mechanism calculated to achieve agreed aims largely irrespective of its consequences for other dimensions of social existence (e.g., community well-being).

Rationality A commitment to reason, rather than faith, intuition or instinct. In the study of organizations, rationality is often claimed to consist of the adoption of optimally efficient means. However, critical approaches suggest that this is a one-sided view of rationality since it usually considers efficiency in terms of narrow goals such as profitability, without considering whether organizations are efficient for realizing the well-being of members of the organization, or for society more widely.

Rationalizing Measures intended to increase the efficiency and/or improve the effectiveness of work practices. See rationality.

Red tape A term of abuse applied to bureaucracies that enforce rules more elaborate and inflexible than is considered necessary.

Regression Compulsion to repeat or return to earlier patterns of behaviour and interaction as a way of avoiding the challenges associated with more adult or demanding situations and relations, such as returning to childish behaviour in adulthood.

Reification Describes the tendency to treat a human creation (say organization or technology) as if it had an independent existence of its own rather than being the product of human thought and work.

Relations of production The basic set of social relations that allow production to take place. Typically they are the relations between those who own property and their agents (managers), and those who are dependent on them for a way or other means of subsistence.

Relative power Assumption that power exists in relation to the will and objectives of both superordinates and subordinates.

Representative democracy A form of political reality in which democratic influence is predicated on legitimate forms of electoral selection, accountability and representation.

Rhetoric Art of persuasion and may encompass a range of techniques aimed at changing views or behaviour. It is also sometimes seen as meaning false or exaggerated, and is contrasted with reality or truth – 'that's just rhetoric' or someone trying to convince you of their beliefs. Others see no distinction.

Rule system System of governance based on rules.

Sabotage Conscious intention to disrupt 'normal service' or production. It is often considered a deviant activity.

Satisficing A situation where a satisfactory resolution to a problem is adopted, rather than an optimum one.

Scientism A view where ideas and techniques that comply with scientific protocols are believed to be objective and politically neutral and widely applicable.

Sedimented power relations Sedimented power relations are decisions taken (and routinely reproduced) which establish what something is (and what it is not). The result is a state of things, a situation so normal, so constant, that we take it to be natural – so much so that it becomes difficult to look at it as anything but entirely normal and 'given', e.g. having food everyday to eat or having to find employment once university is finished.

Self-esteem A psychological term referring to how one thinks or feels about oneself in an evaluative (i.e., positive or negative) way.

Shareholder value Associated with the idea that the first responsibility of firms is to deliver value to shareholders. Therefore, the interests of employees, consumers and communities are secondary. Most associated with US and UK firms.

Shop floor Location in factories where industrial or manufacturing workers are employed.

Silos Discrete functions, departments or divisions within an organization that through the routines of repetition have become ossified and self-absorbed.

Social construction – social constructionists (Similar to the definition of social construction of technology or SCOT) focus on social interpretations that produce and define given situations. Social constructs are seen as the result of human choices rather than being essentialist (i.e. having an underlying essence) or preordained. Social constructionism stresses the importance of perspective and ideologies of individuals and social groups that affect our understanding of situations and are socially shaped. The purpose of social constructionism is to understand how social phenomena are created and reproduced as part of the ongoing accomplishment of reality.

Social construction of technology (SCOT) A more radical variant of the approach known as the social shaping of technology. According to constructivists, in order to understand technological developments we need to study the social interpretations that have produced the definitions of what problems can or should be solved by a given technology. These interpretations, SCOT argues, guide the choices made by the designers, manufacturers and users. Technical choices in other words are not merely the application of an abstract technologic but are also vehicles for the expression of perspectives and ideologies of those social groups (including designers, opinion formers, users, non-users, etc.) that have a stake in the development of a particular technology. Technologies are therefore the offspring of alternative constructions and compromise.

Social constructivists or constructivists Those who adopt the constructivist approach.

Social shaping of technology A sociological approach that rejects the technologically determinist view of technology as being distinct from the rest of society. It focuses on social and economic interests as key influences on the eventual shape of the technology. For those who follow this approach, technology is just one aspect of the way we live socially (and is not inherently different to organizations, art or politics).

Social system Refers to a specific pattern of relationship, maintained by a certain flow of interactions and a common goal.

Span of control The number of people for whom a manager has responsibility.

Sponsor–protégé relationship Informal relationships between senior and junior personnel, often motivated by mutual advantage.

Stakeholder theory The idea that business owes responsibility to more groups than merely its shareholders. Stakeholders may include customers, the environment, suppliers, the local community, future generations, etc.

Standard-setting bodies Regulatory organizations that set and monitor standards of practice for organizations, such as those in health and safety or accounting.

Start-ups New small businesses that have just begun to trade.

Static *structural* A way of understanding that does not allow for processes of change over time and which presumes that the phenomenon can be divided into layers or structures. For example, knowledge can be classified as different types that do not change over time.

Statistical probability The chance of a given event happening across a population of events. For the probability to be robust, the population must be sufficiently large to be statistically significant.

Statistical process control A statistical technique used by quality managers to ensure that product quality standards are maintained.

Stickiness Sometimes used to denote how difficult it can be to transfer knowledge from one context to another – e.g., the tacit skill of a craft worker developed over years of practice (Szulanski, 2003).

Strategic contingency Theory suggesting that uncertainty for an organization stems from its systems of operation, which include technology and work operations from its environment.

Structuralist approach Concentrates on the complexity of the design or structure of an organization independently from the human dimension. It tends to see organizational structures as determined by external conditions characterized as the environment.

Subcontractors Those working to provide goods or services for one company but who are employed by another company. See also outsourcing.

Subculture A set of values, beliefs and norms that is specific to one group in the organization, and may be at odds with the 'official' culture as promoted by senior management. See also cultural differentiation and multiculturalism.

Subjectivity The sense of being-in-the-world that includes but is not reducible to the sense of identity and meaning that is associated with it.

Substantive rationality Substantive rationality means whether the outcomes of an action are rational from the point of view of the actor, regardless of the efficiency of the action itself. Instrumental rationality is concerned with means. Substantive rationality is concerned with ends.

Subsystem One part (e.g., the heart) of numerous interdependent elements that comprise the wider system (e.g. the body).

Supply chain Stages through which materials and other resources are passed in the process of their being combined, assembled and delivered to their ultimate customer

Sustainable development A term generally used to refer to a concern with balancing economic demands with a concern for future generations. For example, the use of timber is now controlled in many, but by no means all, parts of world, so that for every tree cut down another is planted in its place.

Sweatshop labour This term generally describes any form of labour in factories or smaller workshops that is done in conditions where labour is very poorly treated, lacks adequate rights, health and safety conditions are poor and wages low.

Tacit skill A form of knowledge that cannot be made fully explicit, such as in a training manual or through verbal instruction. Examples include riding a bike or changing gear in a manual car.

Team A small number of people with complementary skills who are committed to a common purpose, performance goals and approach for which they hold themselves mutually accountable. The team has a joint, specific 'collective work-products' such as experiments, reports, products, etc. An example can be a team report and presentation often part of the coursework in many university modules.

Team human capital The resources (knowledge, time, know-how, attitude, etc.) individual members make available to the team.

Team social capital The quality and quantity of social relations inside the team but also between the team and the broader organizational and social field.

Teamworking Working arrangements in which workers themselves are given responsibility for the planning and co-ordination of some aspects of their work and the roles and tasks they are required to perform.

Technical In an organization studies context, this term refers to theories or ideas intended for application by managers so that they can improve the organizational 'bottom line'.

Technocratic Form of governance, which is exercised through the technical knowledge of experts.

Technological determinism Determinism is the view that there is an inevitable direction in which events move. For technological determinists, the cause is technology. According to technological determinists, certain key technologies are the primary movers in developments in organization, the economy or even society itself.

Technological determinism The view that there is an inevitable direction in which events move determined by some cause.

Technological determinists Those who adopt technological determinism.

Technology At the most basic level the term 'technology' is used to refer to the 'entire set of devices' that facilitate the adaptation of human collectivities to their environments. A fuller definition of technology includes the human activities, knowledge and skills that are necessary in order to create, understand and operate such devices.

Theory X McGregor used this term to characterize a set of negative assumptions by managers about the attitudes and capabilities of employees; people are passive and need to be persuaded, rewarded, punished and controlled if they are to align their efforts with the needs of the organization.

Theory Y McGregor used this term to characterize a set of positive assumptions by managers about employees; that people are co-operative, able to take responsibility and set their own goals if managers provide the conditions under which they can do this.

Total quality management (TQM) A system of quality control that is designed to build in quality at every stage of production to minimize waste and defective parts that would otherwise be detected at the end of the production process.

Transferability of knowledge The capacity to move knowledge from one context or form to another. This may vary according to the people involved. For example, it might be easier to help another engineer learn a new theory of mechanics than it would be to teach an engineering novice (see also knowledge diffusion and cultural barriers).

Transferable skills Employee skills or knowledge that can be readily applied to a wide range of tasks.

Translated Changed from one form to another. This might be in the sense of a complete transformation, as an idea is adapted to a particular context, or a more modest change such as a (good) linguistic translation. (See also knowledge diffusion and cultural barriers.)

Transnationality Indicates that some or many of the assets, sales and employees of a firm are based outside its home base.

Truth A common sense term relating to that which is accepted as factual or verified beyond doubt, but also a philosophical issue, or claim, of some complexity. A core theme here would be the contrasting views on whether there can only be one truth or many truths.

Typologies Form of classification that involves grouping together entities or subjects with like themes and ensuring that these groups are mutually inclusive and mutually exclusive from all other groups. For example, cars and aeroplanes might be different groups of entities within a typology of transportation.

Uncertainty Branch of political analysis which argues that leadership and influence within organizations tends to be enjoyed by those perceived as dealing with the sources of greatest ambiguity.

Unitary Form of management in which the views of top management are assumed to be shared by everyone. Conflict is treated as **pathological** rather than a reflection of different interpretations and interests.

Utilitarian Useful, especially in a practical way, but also refers to utilitarianism, which is a doctrine that judges actions on their outcomes in terms of overall increases in 'good' or happiness, for example.

Value free That which is seen to be objective – i.e., detached from particular personal values. Critical theory questions its existence.

Values Has a variety of meanings in organization studies, but in the specific sense intended by Schein it encompasses his 'middle level' of organizational culture, located between basic assumptions and cultural artefacts. Values derive from basic assumptions and inform cultural artefacts. They involve shared organizational responses to questions such as 'What are we doing?' and 'Why are we doing it?', and might include a commitment to profit maximization or a focus on equal opportunities.

Vignettes Brief excerpts from a larger story that may help us to understand what happens to people in everyday life.

Whistle-blowing When an organizational member tells the organizational hierarchy, and subsequently the wider world, of unethical or illegal practices being conducted inside their organization.

Work group A small number of people working in a collaborative style with individual input and accountability. An example can be your discussions in small seminar group.

Work intensification Working conditions in which workers are subject to constant pressures to increase output and productivity levels.

Working to rule The way employees, when in dispute with employers, may revert to formally prescribed ways of working that disrupt efficiency and effectiveness by replacing informal practices with rigid and often time-consuming procedural requirements.

Work–life balance General term to refer to how far work dominates people's lives over and above any other considerations.

Index

abattoir work 397–9, 406–7
Ackroyd and Crowdy's study 397–9, 406–7
action-based organizations 358
actions 206
actor-network theory (ANT) 448,
    475–80, 488
administration 250
affirmative action 167
'Against Learning' (Contu et al.) 230
age 174, 192
agency 280–1
airlines 382–3, 392–3
Alcohol With Out Liquid™ (AWOL™)
    473, 478
alienation 59, 60–2, 64
American Express 185
AML 118–20, 141
ANT (actor-network theory) 448,
    475–80, 488
anticipatory socialization 207
anxiety 98, 103, 105
apples 521
ascribed behaviour 5
Australia 541
authoritarian groups 126–8
authoritarian personality 104
authority 351, 379
authority-compliance management 313
autocracy 356, 363
automation 315
autonomous responsibility 126
avatars 101
AWOL™ (Alcohol With Out Liquid™)
    473, 478

Bandura, Albert 53, 75
banking 16, 175–6, 185–6, 335, 567–8
bar-bistros 245–9
barriers to entry 262
Bartlett and Ghoshal's model 506–8
basic assumptions 381
behaviour 4–5
bet-your-company culture 391
bicycles 470–1
binary logic 559
black boxes 9
Boeing 583
Bond, James 488
bonus schemes 341–2
bounded rationality 365–6
bourgeois thinking 280
BPR (business process re-engineering)
    266–7, 421
brainstorming 206, 207

Braverman, Harry 64–5, 229–30, 281–4
Briggs, Katherine C. 80, 89–92
British Airways 382–3, 392–3
Bullshit Bingo 328
Burawoy, Michael 65, 285–7
bureaucracy 363, 412, 535–60
bureaucratic formalized control 508
Burnham, David 46–7
Burns and Stalker's case study 353–7, 364
business ethics 32, 566 see also ethics
business process re-engineering (BPR)
    266–7, 421

call centres 567
capital 370
capitalism 60–2, 305–6, 527
capitalist societies 580
car manufacture 125, 315–16, 529–30
Casey, Catherine 71
chains of command 247, 251–2
change 411–41
    resistance to 425–7, 437–40
change tolerance 133
Churchill, Winston 322
classification of knowledge 202
cliques 366
cluster culture 385–6
clustering of firms 422
coalitions 366–7
coal mining 126
co-determination 363
codified knowledge 203
coffee 520–1
cognitive knowledge 205
cognitivism 206
collective unconscious 87
collectivism 512
Collinson's study 405–6
colonization 30
commitment 52
committee systems 357
commodities 203
commoditized knowledge 220–3
common sense 8–9, 32
communities of practice (COPs) 128,
    200–1, 208
CompCo 541
competitive advantage 200
computers 501
conception 59
conceptual framework 596–7
concept view of organizations 27–8
conflict 329, 359–60, 362, 434–7
conscience 67–8, 569, 572

consent 145, 146
constitutive approach to leadership 333
constructivists 474
content theories of motivation 41, 74
contestability 216
contextual embeddedness 31
contingency approach to organizations 548
contingency theory 255–6
    of leadership 323–6, 332–3
continuous improvement 124, 126–8
control 52, 71, 75, 144–6
control by culture and networks 509
Cooperative Bank 567–8, 583–4
COPs (communities of practice) 128,
    200–1, 208
corporate heroes 88
corporate social responsibility (CSR) 565–6
counselling 101
country club management 313
creativity 3
criminality 96
critical, meaning of 33
critical diversity 185–6
critical HRM 179–84
critical reflection 338
critical structuralism 369
CRM (customer relationship management)
    201–2, 217, 226
cross-functional teams 136
CSR (corporate social responsibility) 565–6
CTMs (cultural transmission mechanisms)
    387–8
cultural artefacts 380
cultural awareness 514
cultural barriers 203
cultural differentiation 386
cultural engineering 381–3, 392–3
cultural tactics 384
cultural transmission mechanisms (CTMs)
    387–8
cultural values 133–4, 384
culture 377–407
    bet-your-company culture 391
    contingency argument 385–9
    empirical studies 390–4
    'has' theory 300, 381–96, 403–5
    'horses for courses' argument 385–9
    institutional approach 225
    'is' theory 399–407
    Japanese corporations 314
    national 509–15
    'one best culture' argument 384–5
    person/cluster culture 385–6
    power culture 385

process culture 391
role culture 385
synthetic 105
task culture 385–6
tough-guy culture 390–1
work hard/play hard culture 391
custom and practice 241
customer relationship management (CRM)
    201–2, 217, 226
cynicism 105

data 203
DC (direct control) 412, 428–9, 435
death of distance 450
decision-making 352, 357–73
decision objectives 361
decision premises 361
decision processes 361
definitions, universal 27
dehumanization 580
de-layering 244
delegated responsibility 241
democracy 363
democratic groups 126–8
depersonalization 246–7
deregulation of markets 565
de-skilling 229–30
determinism 134, 559–60
    technological 447, 453–80
Deutsche Bank 185–6
dialectic of control 285
digital divide 458
direct (management) control (DC) 412,
    428–9, 435
direct democracy 363
dirty jobs 396–9, 406–7
disability 186–9
disciplinary power 58, 69–70
discourses 231
discrimination 166–8
disembodied managers 372–3
disembodied relations 32, 192
disintermediation 264
dispositional factors 133
distributed leadership 314–15
diversity 169–76, 185–6, 189–90
diversity management 165–6
division of labour 355
DLL (double-loop learning') 206
'Do Free Market Governments Create
    Crisis-Ridden Societies?' (Richard-
    son and Curwen) 576–7, 581
double-loop learning' (DLL) 206
du Gay, Paul 555–6
dysfunctions of conflict 367

eclectic theory 504–5
economic gloom 18
economic power of multinationals 519–21
economics 7
Edison, Thomas 466
education 16, 24–5
educational organizations 24

efficiency 550
electronics industry 353–7
elites 357
emancipation 216
emergent sectors 364–5
employee psychology 309–10
empowerment 140–1, 254
entity view of organizations 25–6
environments 252
equity theory 47
Ernst & Young 185
esprit de corps 242
essence 90
essentialist leadership 331–2
ethics 32, 334–5, 564–92
ethnography 549
eugenics 95
excellence movement 431
executive pay 62
existential anxiety 103
expectancy 50–1
experience 2, 5–7, 50
experiential learning cycle 214
experiential knowledge 232
experiential study of personality 80
expert power 140–1
explicit knowledge 210–11
exploitation 279–80, 581
exports 499
externalization 59
extroversion 96
extroverts 88–9
Eysenck, Hans J. 94–5
Eysenck, Michael W. 94–5

factor analysis 94–5
factory system 280–1, 487
factory workers 405–6
fads 215
fairness 132–4
fashions 215
Fayol, Henri 250, 307–8
FDI (foreign direct investment) 519
femininity 512
feminism 579
The Feminist Case Against Bureaucracy
    (Ferguson) 557
feminization 169–70
financial flexibility 422
financial incentives 62
financial services 171–3, 175–5, 340–1
Fleming, Ian 488
flexibility 419
flexible firms 421–4
flexible specialization 547–8
Follett, Mary Parker 246, 307–8
football 29
Fordism 311, 315, 418, 424–8
foreign direct investment (FDI) 519
formalization 257–8
Foucault, Michel 69–70, 187–9, 182
four temperaments 85–6
Foxconn 501

franchising 500
fraudulent behaviour 17, 335
freedom 3, 35–6, 216, 596
free will 134
Fromm, Erich 104
functional flexibility 422
functionalism 383

game-playing 30–1
gender diversity 133
Giggs, Ryan 352, 355
Glazier, Malcolm 29
global financial crisis 16, 18, 62
global firms 50
globalization 378, 490–530
global markets 520–1
goal displacement 545
greedy institutions 404
group dynamics 102
group norms 125
group phenomena 116
groups 114–15 *see also* teams
groupthink 117, 394

Hackman, J. Richard 49–50, 74
Harzing's control focus 508–9
'has' theory of culture 300, 381–96, 403–5
Hawthorne effect 125
headcounts 283
hegemonic control 229
Herald of Free Enterprise 576, 581
Hertzberg, Frederick 48, 74
hierarchical levels 4–5
hierarchy of needs 42–5, 55, 98–101
Hitler, Adolph 322
Hofstede, Geert 510–13
Holocaust 554–5
homosexuality 96
'horses for courses' argument 385–9
hotels 459–60
HP 137
HRM (human resource management) 70,
    160–4, 169–76, 176–84
human capital 131
human dignity 144
human dimension of work 309–17
human relations thinking 310–11
human resource management (HRM) 70,
    160–4, 169–76, 176–84
hybrids 253

ICTs (information and communication
    technologies) 266–7, 364–5
idealized picture of teamwork 142
ideal types of organization 356
identity 13, 19, 20, 34, 79, 81, 103, 596
ideology 228
ideology of a privileged male elite 219
idiographic approach to personality 80,
    84–5, 97
impersonal relations 32
'the individual,' end of 102–4
individualism 378, 512

individualizing process 223–4
inequality 35, 596–7
informality 125, 257
information 203
information and communication
    technologies (ICTs) 266–7, 364–5
information flows 372
inhibition 98
innovation 126–8, 202, 213, 411–41
insecurity 13–14, 33, 75, 596
institutional approach 230
institutional economics 259–60
institutionalization 22–3
institutional theory 224, 260–1
instrumentality 50, 51
instrumental rationality 3, 28–32
intangibles 212
integral learning 207
intellectual property rights (IPR) 214
internalized behaviour 205
internal motivation 49–50
international firms 507
internationalization 504
intersectionality 189–90
interstices of organizations 351
intersubjectivity 396
introverts 88–9
investor confidence 17–18
invisible power 522–4
invoked purposes 5
IPR (intellectual property rights) 214
isolated individuals 61
isomorphic organizations 224

James Bond 488
Japan 51, 314, 378, 510, 515
Japanization 184, 431–3
JIT (just-in-time) 418–19
job enrichment 420
Jung, Carl 86–8
just-in-time (JIT) 418–19

kaizen 122
key concepts 33–7
King's Cross underground fire 576, 581
KM (knowledge management) 200, 202,
    219–23
knowing 204–5
knowledge 198–201, 203–5, 596
    classification 202
    commoditized 220–3
    critical view of 231–2
    and power 35
    progressive theories 218
    studies 214–15
    transferability 213–14
knowledge construction 206
knowledge diffusion 224
knowledge domains 136
knowledge-economies 200
knowledge management 200, 202,
    219–23
knowledge production 276

knowledge transformation 214
Kolb's experiential learning cycle 214

Labor and Monopoly Capital (Braverman)
    64–5, 229–30, 281–4
labour 64–5, 370
labour adjustment 519–20
labourist views 223
Laing, Ronald 103–4
Latham, Gary P. 54
leadership 134–6, 319–26
    alternative conception of 336
    constitutive approach 333
    contingency theories 323–6, 332–3
    critical approach 327–34, 340–4
    distributed 314–15
    essentialist 331–2
    and ethics 334–5
    limitations of the mainstream
        approaches 326–7
    and management 297–300, 330
    and management development 336–8
    and masculinity 335
    and personality 92–3
    and sexuality 335
league tables 15
leakage 200
lean production 121–3, 143–4, 413–17,
    418–19, 420
learning 2, 205–8, 209
    critical view of 231–2
    experiential cycle 214
    progressive theories 218
    studies 214–15
learning organizations 218–19
learning styles 205
legacy systems 265
legitimacy 360
leisure 19
Levinson, Harry 52–3
licensing 500
*Life on the Line in Contemporary Manufac-
    turing* (Delbridge) 558
Locke, Edwin A. 54
long-term orientation 512
Luddites 460–1, 487
Luthans, Fred 55, 75

McClelland, David 46–7, 74
McDonaldization of education 16
The McDonaldization of Society (Ritzer) 556
McDonalds 500, 506
McGregor, Douglas 45–6, 55, 63, 74, 311
machine tools 464–5
male elite, ideology of 219
management
    as an ideology 228
    behavioural approach 317–19
    and capitalism 305–6
    classical thinking 306–8
    as commoditized knowledge 220–3
    critical approach 327–30, 340–4
    as a discipline 304–6

disembodied 372–3
    of diversity 165–68
    divine right 578
    as a dominant discourse 220
    ethics 582
    as a function 304–5
    Guillen's models 230
    and leadership 297–300, 330
    limitations of the mainstream
        approaches 326–7
    of people 158–90
    politics of 338–9
    principles of 306–7
    roles 317–19
    as a social group 304–5
management by example (MBE) 388
management by objectives (MBO) 312
management cadres 514–15
management grid 312
management ideas 210–11, 227–8
management knowledge 198–9, 209–12,
    225–7
managerialism 15–16, 158–9
managerial prerogative 338–9
managing people 3, 23
Manchester United 29
Manufacturing Consent (Burawoy) 65,
    285–7
marketing personality 104
Marxism 58–62, 278–9, 370, 579
masculine discourses 372
masculinity 335, 512
Maslow, Abraham 42–5, 55, 63, 74, 98–101
mass production 412
matrix structures 251–2
Mayo, Elton 310
MBE (management by example) 388
MBO (management by objectives) 312
MBTI (Myers-Briggs type indicator) test 80,
    89–92, 93–4
Mead, George Herbert 66, 67
mean production 143–4
mechanistic organizations 355
Men and Women of the Corporation
    (Kanter) 549
mentors 222–3
Men Who Manage (Dalton) 549
messengers 91–2
micro-politics 361
Milgram experiments 586–9
mining 126
Mintzberg, Henry 317–18
MNCs (multinational companies) 502–30,
    575–6
mobile phones 450, 476–7, 478
mobilization of bias 361, 362
*Models of Management: Work, Authority
    and Organisation in a Comparative
    Perspective* (Guillen) 230
modernism 222
monitoring and control
    248–9
monopoly capital 64–5

motivation
  and alienation 64
  content theories 41
  critical approaches 57–72
  and economic inequality 63–4
  internal 49–50
  Japanese employees 510
  and leadership 307
  mainstream approaches 55–7
  of managers 46–7, 48
  Marxist analyses 58–62
  process theories 41
  self-motivation 52–5
  study of 40
motivation theory as ideology 63
multiculturalism 389
multidisciplinary teams 136
multimembership 128
multinational companies (MNCs) 502–30,
  575–6
multiskilling 419
multitasking 419
Myers-Briggs type indicator (MBTI) test 80,
  89–92, 93–4

Nagashino, battle of 487
narcissism 98
national culture 509–15
National Health Service (NHS) 434–7
negotiated orders 362, 367
Neimark, Marilyn 585–6
neoclassical economics 278
neo-imperialism 220
network organizations 548
networks 224
network society 548
network theory 263–4
neurosis 98, 101
neutering of ideas 229
New Right 378
NHS (National Health Service) 434–7
Nike 497–8, 516–19
nomothetic approach to personality 80, 84–5
non-rigorous knowledge management 202
normalization 280
normative control 275, 554
normative orientation 317
numerical flexibility 422
numerically controlled machine tools 464–5
NUMMI 121–3, 124

OB (organizational behaviour) 5, 7, 14, 18,
  452
obedience 580–1, 584–5
objectification 59
objective knowledge 205
OBM (original brand manufacturing) 501
occupational identity 434
OEM (original equipment manufacturers) 501
Oldham, Greg R. 49–50
oligopolistic markets 260
OLPC (One Laptop Per Child) initiative
  458–9

On Being at Work (Harding) 558
'one best culture' argument 384–5
one best way 242
One Laptop Per Child (OLPC) initiative
  458–9
ontology 395
open systems thinking 253–5, 308–9
organic organizations 355
organizational behaviour (OB) 5, 7, 14,
  18, 452
organizational charts 357
organizational culture *see* culture
organizational forms 417, 420–1,
  421–4, 436–7
organizational need 140–1
organizational operations 378
organizational values 314
organization men 404
organizations
  characteristics of 10
  competing logics of 14–15
  and contemporary society 18
  definition 4
  and technology 269–71
  unnaturalness 18
organization structure and design 240–89
  classical theories 249–52
  critical approach to 273–8
  and technology 268–9
orientation 134
original brand manufacturing (OBM) 501
original equipment manufacturers (OEM)
  501
orthodoxy 33
Ouchi, William 314
output control 508–9
outsourcing 260
overseas production 501–2

PA (professional autonomy) 435
panaceas 139
panopticon 287–8
participation 126–8
passive learning 10
pathologized stress 231
people management 158–90
performance measurement 15
personal centralized control 508
personality
  authoritarian 104
  classification of 80, 82
  criminal 96
  definition 83
  dimensions 96
  experiential study of 80
  genetic causation 96
  idiographic approach 80, 84–5, 97
  and job performance 96–7
  and leadership 92–3
  marketing 104
  nomothetic approach 80, 84–5
  proactive 96
  psychodynamic approach 97–9

  and science 79–80
  of science 95–7
  science of 93–5
  social construction 80
  social determination 95
  split personalities 103–4
  tests 93–5 *see also* Myers-Briggs type
    indicator test
personality theory 86–8
person culture 385–6
personnel management 158–90
piecework 285
pluralism 160–1, 358–60, 367–8
plurality of power 362
political activity in organizations 351–73
political power of multinationals 521–4
political rule systems 358–9, 363
political structures 354
political systems 357
politics 7
pollution 569
population ecology theory 263
positivism 80–1
post-bureaucracy 535–60
post-Fordism 418, 424–8
post-modernism 579
post-modernity 229
poverty 58
power
  invisible 522–4
  and knowledge 35
  and management knowledge 222–3
  plurality of 362
  productive 34
  relational 351, 366–7, 596
  and roles 26
  and the self 66
  visible 521–2
power culture 385
power distance 134, 511–12
power relations 140–1, 379
practical hermeneutics 396
principles of administration 250
principles of management 306–7
prisons 288–9
private–public partnerships 16–17
private sector companies 16
privatization 15, 275
proactive personality 96
procedural justice 47
process culture 391
process theories of motivation 41, 74, 75
processual knowledge 205, 232
process view of organizations 26–7
Procrustes 229
product differentiation 315, 497
productivity targets 341–2
product life cycles 503–4
professional autonomy (PA) 435
Programmable Subcutaneous Visible
  Implant (PSVI) 461
projects 116
project teams 208, 209

prostitution 398
PSVI (Programmable Subcutaneous Visible Implant) 461
psychodynamics 97–9, 223–32
psychological contracts 379
psychology 7
psychometric tests 82–3
psychosis 98
public goods 15
public sector organizations 15–18, 421
publishing 221
purposeful actors 358
purposes 4, 5–6

quality circles 123
quality of working life movements 123–4
quotas 286

RA (responsible autonomy) 429, 435–6
radioactive waste 472, 488
rational choice 261–2
rational everyday 87
rationality 537
  bounded 365–6
  instrumental 3, 28–32
  substantive 551–2
rationalizing work practices 244
rational processes 360
real teams 117–18
red tape 537
regression 98
reification 59, 60
relations of production 285–6
relative power 366–7
relevant social groups (RSGs) 472, 488
religious belief 378
religious conversion 220
representative democracy 363
resistance to change 425–7, 437–40
resource dependency 262–3
responsible autonomy (RA) 429, 435–6
rhetoric 199–200
rhetorical perspective 226–7
robots 459–60
role culture 385
role formalization 364–5
roles 26
routines 22–3
Rover Cars 529–30
RSGs (relevant social groups) 472, 488
rule systems 358–9, 363

sabotage 30–1
satisficing 212
schizophrenic self 103–4
science 79–81, 95–7
scientific management 41–2, 49, 55–7, 74, 250–1, 309–10, 378, 424–8
scientism 230
SCOT (social construction of technology) 448, 468–74
Scotland 353–7
sedimented power relations 141

self 58, 61–2, 66–9, 103–4
self-actualization 99–100
self-discipline 146–8, 287–8
self-esteem 215–16
self-leadership 135–6
self-managing teams 125
self-motivation 52–5, 75
'The Selling of Ethics: The Ethics of Business Meets the Business of Ethics' (Neimark) 585–6
Senge, Peter 127
service industries 378
7-S framework 316
Sewell, Graham 71
sexual deviance 96
sexuality and leadership 335
shadow world 87
shop floors 4–5
shyness 95
skill profiles 8, 9–10
social capital 131
social construction of personality 80
social construction of technology (SCOT) 448, 468–74
social loafing 116
social needs 125
social shaping of technology 448, 463–7
social systems 124
sociology 7
socio-technical systems 126
Space 17 541
span of control 241–2, 247, 255
split personalities 103–4
sponsor-protégé relationships 366
SST (social shaping of technology) 448, 463–7
stakeholder theory 570
standardization 124
standard-setting bodies 224
start-ups 539
static knowledge 205
statistical probability 544
statistical process control 268
stickiness 213
stirrups 456–7
strategic contingency 164
structuralist approaches 370
structural knowledge 205
students 11–13
subcontracting 500–1
subcontractors 575
subcultures 386
subjectivity of labour 282
subordination 279
substantive rationality 551–2
subsystems 256
SuperLeadership 134–5
supply chains 262, 422
surveillance 146–8
sustainable development 525
sweatshop labour 583
'Sweatshops and Respect for Persons' (Arnold and Bowie) 575–6

symbolic violence 13
synthetic cultures 105
System 4 management 313
systems thinking 252–6

tacit knowledge 60, 270–1
tacit skills 257–8
task culture 385–6
taxation 520
Taylor, Frederick 41–2, 49, 55–7, 74, 75, 250–1, 309
TD (technological determinism) 447, 453–80, 487
team-based projects 116
teambuilding 115–16
team design 130–1
team development 130
team discipline 118
team effectiveness 129, 131
team human capital 131
team learning 127
team management 313
teams 114–24, 136–7, 138–50 see also teamwork
team social capital 131
teamwork 146–50, 419
  fairness 132–4
  idealized picture 142
  resistance to 131–2, 148–9
  trust 132–4
technical knowledge 383
technical work 378
technocracy 363
technological determinism 447, 453–80, 487
technological frames (TF) 488
technology 268–71, 447–80
temperaments 85–6
TF (technological frames) 488
theory–practice gap 31–2
Theory X 45, 163, 311–12, 314, 316, 378
Theory Y 45, 163, 311–12, 313, 314, 316
Theory Z 314–15, 316, 384–5
therapy 101
'third-age' workers 170–1, 174
Thomas, Kenneth W. 54
timekeeping 339–40
total quality management (TQM) 267–8
tough-guy culture 390–1
Townley, Barbara 70
TQM (total quality management) 267–8
training 303
trait theory 94
transcendence 100
transferability of knowledge 213–14
transferable skills 275
translated knowledge 206
transnational firms 507–8
transnationality 502
trust 132–4
truth 216–17, 230
typologies 358

uncertainty 362
uncertainty avoidance 512
understanding 206
unitary management 160
Universal 539–40
universal definitions 352
universalist solutions 509–15
unskilled work 5
user involvement 270–1
utilitarianism 230, 573
The Utopia of Rules (Graeber) 557

valence 50, 51
value-free organizational aims 231
values 380–1

varieties of capitalism approach 527
Velthouse, Betty A. 54
vignettes 13
violence 13
virtual organizations 264–6
virtual teams 136–7
visibility 69–71
visible power 521–2
Volvo 125
Vroom, Victor 50–1, 74

watches 461
Weber, Max 370, 537–8, 551
Welch, Jack 298
whistle-blowing 589–91

Wilkinson, Barry 71
women managers 515
women workers 174–5
Work and the Corrosion of Character
    (Sennett) 557
work groups 115
work hard/play hard culture 391
working to rule 257–8
work intensification 412
work-life balance 271–2
work organization 278–9
workplace culture 180–1

ZTC Ryland 105–6

Credit Lines

Credit Lines